D0831173

VOLUME EIGHT
PAPYRUS—REGENSBURG

THE BRITISH ENCYCLOPEDIA

IN TEN VOLUMES
ILLUSTRATED

THE BRITISH ENCYCLOPEDIA

ILLUSTRATED

With an Introduction by
CYRIL NORWOOD, M.A., D. Litt.,
Headmaster of Harrow

Prepared under the general editorship of J. M. Parrish, M.A. (Oxon.), John R. Crossland, F.R.G.S., and Angelo S. Rappoport, Ph.D., B. ès L., with the specialist assistance and contributions of over 100 experts

VOLUME
EIGHT

ODHAMS PRESS LIMITED
LONDON, W.C. 2

Printed in Great Britain

KEY TO PRONUNCIATION

The method of marking pronunciations here employed is either (1) by marking the syllable on which the accent falls, or (2) by a simple system of transliteration, to which the following is the Key :

VOWELS

ā, as in *fate*, or in *bare*.

ä, as in *alms*, Fr. *âme*, Ger. B*ah*n = á of Indian names.

ȧ, the same sound short or medium, as in Fr. b*a*l, Ger. M*a*nn.

a, as in f*a*t.

ạ, as in f*a*ll.

a, obscure, as in rur*a*l, similar to *u* in b*u*t, ė in h*e*r : common in Indian names.

ē, as in m*e* = *i* in mach*i*ne.

e, as in m*e*t.

ė, as in h*e*r.

ī, as in p*i*ne, or as *ei* in Ger. m*ei*n.

i, as in p*i*n, also used for the short sound corresponding to ē, as in French and Italian words.

eu, a long sound as in Fr. j*eû*ne = Ger. long *ö*, as in S*ö*hne, G*ö*the (Goethe).

eu, corresponding sound short or medium, as in Fr. p*eu* = Ger. *ö* short.

ō, as in n*o*te, m*oa*n.

o, as in n*o*t, s*o*ft—that is, short or medium.

ö, as in m*o*ve, tw*o*.

ū, as in t*u*be.

u, as in t*u*b : similar to ė and also to *a*.

ụ, as in b*u*ll.

ü, as in Sc. ab*u*ne = Fr. *û* as in d*û*, Ger. *ü* long as in gr*ü*n, B*ü*hne.

u̇, the corresponding short or medium sound, as in Fr. b*u*t, Ger. M*ü*ller.

oi, as in *oi*l.

ou, as in p*ou*nd ; or as *au* in Ger. H*au*s.

1*

CONSONANTS

Of the *consonants*, **b, d, f, h, j, k, l, m, n, ng, p, sh, t, v, z,** always have their common English sounds, when used to transliterate foreign words. The letter **c** is not used by itself in re-writing for pronunciation, s or k being used instead. The only consonantal symbols, therefore, that require explanation are the following:

ch is always as in ri*ch*.

d, nearly as *th* in *th*is = Sp. *d* in Ma*d*ri*d*, etc.

g is always hard, as in *g*o.

h represents the guttural in Scotch lo*ch*, Ger. na*ch*, also other similar gutturals.

ṇ, Fr. nasal *n* as in bo*n*.

r represents both English *r*, and *r* in foreign words, which is generally much more strongly trilled.

s, always as in *s*o.

th, as *th* in *th*in.

th, as *th* in *th*is.

w always consonantal, as in *w*e.

x = ks, which are used instead.

y always consonantal, as in *y*ea (Fr. *ligne* would be re-written lēny).

zh, as *s* in plea*s*ure = Fr. *j*.

THE BRITISH ENCYCLOPEDIA

VOLUME VIII

PAPY'RUS (*Papўrus Antiquōrum*, or *Cypĕrus papўrus*). An aquatic plant belonging to the nat. ord. Cyperaceæ or sedges. It has acquired celebrity from furnishing the paper of the ancient Egyptians. The rhizome is very large, hard, and creeping; the aerial stem is several

Papyrus

inches thick, naked, except at the base, 8 to 15 or more feet high, triangular above, and terminated by a compound, wide-spreading, and beautiful umbel, which is surrounded with an involucre composed of eight large sword-shaped leaves. The little scaly spikelets of inconspicuous flowers are placed at the extremity of the rays of this umbel.

Formerly it was extensively cultivated in Lower Egypt, but is now rare there. It is abundant in the equatorial regions of Africa in many places, and is found also in Western Africa and in Southern Italy. The inhabitants of some countries where it grows manufacture it into various articles, including sail-cloth, cordage, and even wearing-apparel and boats.

Among the ancient Egyptians its uses were equally numerous, but it is best known as furnishing a sort of paper. This consisted of thin strips carefully separated from the stem longitudinally, laid side by side, and then covered transversely by shorter strips, the whole being caused to adhere together by the use of water and probably some gummy matter. A sheet of this kind formed really a sort of mat. In extensive writings a number of these sheets were united into one long roll, the writing materials being a reed pen and ink made of animal charcoal and oil.

Many papyrus manuscripts still extant are of little value, but others discovered in Egypt have given us valuable Greek works, such as the *Orations* of Hyperides, Aristotle's *On the Constitution of Athens*, poems of Bacchylides, etc.—Cf. Sir F. G. Kenyon, *The Palæography of Greek Papyri*.

PAR. A term used in commerce and banking. When stocks, shares, etc., stand at their face value they are said to be *at par*. When lower they are described as *below par*, and when purchase price rises beyond face value *above par*.—e.g.
£100 stock quoted at £100 is at par.
£100 stock quoted at £85 is below par.
£100 stock quoted at £115 is above par.

PARA. A small Levantine coin, of copper or copper and silver alloy, representing the fortieth part of a Turkish piastre (gurush). In Turkey pieces of 40, 20, 10, and 5 paras are minted.

PARÁ. State of Brazil, one of the largest and commercially the most important: the most northerly of the republic. It occupies both sides of the Lower Amazon, and consists chiefly of vast alluvial plains connected with this river and its tributaries. These latter comprise the Tapajos and the Xingu, besides many others, the Tocantins being another great stream from the south. The province possesses immense forests, and is extremely fertile, but there is little cultivation, the inhabitants being generally fewer than one to the square mile. The trade centres in the capital, and is facilitated by steamboats navigating the Amazon and Tocantins. Much rubber is produced. Area, 443,789 sq. miles; pop. (1929), 1,432,401.

PARÁ, or BELEM DO PARÁ. A city and seaport of Brazil, the capital of the state of Pará, on the estuary of the Pará or Tocantins. The principal buildings are the Governor's palace, the cathedral, and the churches of Santa Anna and São João Baptista. It is the seat of the Legislative Assembly of the state. The port, defended by forts, is capable of admitting vessels of large size. The principal exports are rubber, cacao, Brazil-nuts, rice, piassava, annatto, and cotton. Pop. 279,491.

PARABLE. A fable or allegorical representation of something real in nature or life, from which a moral is drawn for instruction. The word is derived from the Greek *parabolē*, which literally signifies "a throwing beside", and hence a comparison or illustration. By the Hellenistic writers the word is used almost invariably as the equivalent of the Hebrew *mashal*, meaning similitude, and applied alike to short proverbs, dark prophetic utterances, and tales illustrative of moral truths.

All the evangelists, except John, who employs the term *paroimia*, use the word to designate the parables of Christ. The parable is a mode of teaching peculiarly adapted to the Eastern mind, and was common among the Jews before the appearance of Christ. It is exemplified in the Old Testament in the parable addressed by Nathan to David (2 Sam. xii.), and there are frequent examples of it in the *Talmud*.—Cf. G. Murray, *Jesus and His Parables*.

PARAB'OLA. One of the curves known as conic sections. The method of obtaining a parabola from a right cone is explained at CONIC SECTIONS. It may also be defined as the curve traced out by a point which moves in such a way that its distance from a fixed point, called the "focus", is always equal to its perpendicular distance from a fixed straight line, called the "directrix". The path of a projectile in vacuo, when not a vertical straight line, is a parabola.

PARACEL'SUS (Philippus Aureolus Theophrastus Bombastus von Hohenheim). Born at Einsiedeln, in the canton of Schwyz, in Switzerland, in 1493, died in 1541. Dissatisfied with the means of acquiring knowledge in his native country, he travelled over the greater part of Europe, everywhere seeking to add to his knowledge.

In the course of his travels he became acquainted with remedies not in common use among physicians (probably preparations of mercury), by means of which he performed extraordinary cures, and obtained a great reputation. In 1526 he accepted the chair of medicine offered him by the magistrates of Basel, and lectured there till the spring of 1528.

The failure of a lawsuit, and the consequent quarrel with the judges, led him to resume his wandering life, at first accompanied by his pupil Oporinus, who, however, disgusted with his violence and intemperance, at length left him. He died at the hospital of St. Sebastian at Salzburg. For a long time he was regarded as little better than a charlatan, but he enriched science, particularly chemistry and medicine, with some valuable discoveries, and, indeed, is sometimes looked upon as the founder of modern therapeutics.—Cf. A. M. Stoddart, *Life of Paracelsus*.

PARACHUTES. A parachute consists of a circular piece of fabric, usually silk, 28 feet in diameter with cords, attached at intervals round the periphery, leading to a suspension rope to which the harness worn by the parachutist is attached. A small circular hole, or "vent", is cut in the centre to allow air to escape in order to avoid excessive oscillation. This and the "fluting" round the edges resulting from the pull of the cords reduces the effective diameter to about 20 feet.

Hence, with an 11-stone man the surface is loaded to about ½ lb. per square foot, which will reduce the rate of descent of a man of the above weight to 16 feet per second (approximately 11 miles per hour). This produces a shock on landing equivalent to jumping off a wall 4 feet high. A parachute will open to its full extent in about five or six seconds, or after a drop of about 100 feet. A parachutist has jumped without harm from the top of the Tower Bridge in London—a height of 153 feet.

An aircraft parachute is packed in

the following manner: The centre of the parachute is attached by a loop of light cord to the top of the inside of the case, and the parachute is then laid in folds in the case with the cords put in last. A light canvas cover, with a hole in the centre for the main suspension rope, is then attached to the bottom of the case by four loops of light cord. The case is then firmly attached by its top to the aircraft, and the suspension rope attached by a spring hook to the harness worn by the parachutist.

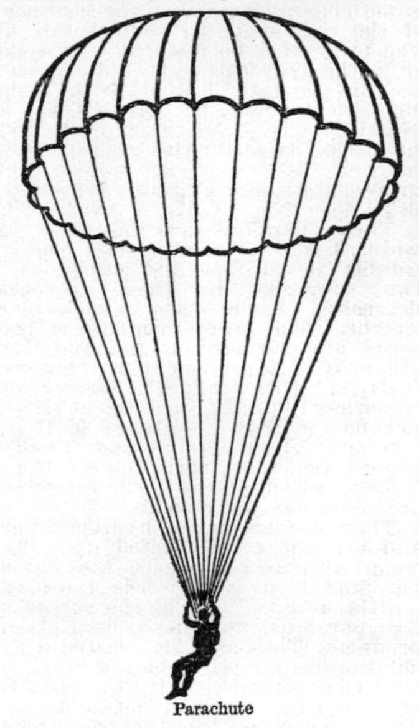
Parachute

On jumping, the weight of the parachutist coming on the suspension rope breaks away the canvas cover of the case, and the cords and folds of the parachute drop down out of the case. When these are all clear the weight comes on the light cord loop attaching the centre of the parachute to the top of the case and on this breaking, the parachute falls clear and gradually opens as the air gets inside the folds.

There are other types of parachute fitted with various mechanical devices to ensure rapid opening, but the type described is the oldest, simplest, and on the whole, most reliable if carefully packed in such a way that there is no fear of the cords being entangled. Parachutes which are contained in a case worn on an aeroplane pilot's back are known as "pack-type" parachutes.

The invention of the parachute is attributable to Leonardo da Vinci (A.D. 1500), the famous Italian artist and scientist; while the first parachute descent was made from a balloon in 1797 by a Frenchman named Garnerin.

PARADISE. A name introduced into modern languages for the Garden of Eden, and hence used to indicate any abode of happiness. The word is derived from the Persian *pairidaeza,* signifying a garden or deer park of the Persian kings, and was introduced into the Greek language in the form of *paradeisos* by Xenophon, who became acquainted with it probably during the expedition of the Ten Thousand. In his *Divina Commedia* Dante gives a description of Paradise as conceived in mediæval times.

The place between Paradise and Purgatory, where sinners who have sinned unconsciously and without intention are awaiting the Day of Judgment, is termed the **Paradise of Fools.**

PAR'ADOX. A statement or proposition which seems to be absurd, or at variance with common sense, or to contradict some previously ascertained truth, though, when duly investigated, it may prove to be well founded. Among modern writers who are masters of paradox may be mentioned G. B. Shaw, G. K. Chesterton, and Oscar Wilde.

PARADOX'URE (*Paradoxūrus niger*). An animal of the civet family (Viverridæ), common in India, and known also as the palm-cat from its habit of climbing palm trees to eat their fruit. It can curl its tail into a tight spiral.

PARAFFIN. The name given to the members of a series of chemical compounds containing hydrogen and carbon (*see* PARAFFIN SERIES). In the popular sense, paraffin includes paraffin-oil used for burning, liquid paraffin used medicinally, and paraffin-wax. These are all obtained from sources of mineral origin, namely, from oil-shale, natural petroleum (q.v.), brown coal-tar, and ozokerite.

Dr. James Young founded the oil-shale or paraffin industry in Scotland in 1850, and it is still very largely confined to that country.

The shale is distilled in long, upright retorts, whereby an impure and tarry-looking oil is collected. One ton of shale yields from 22 to 38 gallons of crude oil. This crude or mixed oil is then purified by further distillation to remove fractions of lower boiling-point. The remaining oil is cleansed by treatment, first with strong sulphuric acid, and, after being allowed to settle, with a solution of caustic soda. It is then distilled fractionally, and yields products in the following order: naphtha or petrol up to 150° C., paraffin-oil from 150° C. to 300° C., and above 300° C., a small quantity of lubricating oil.

The heavy residue which does not distil over is frozen to a solid mass of impure wax known as scale. This crude wax is purified in several stages. First it is melted and treated with a small proportion of naphtha then resolidified or caked and placed in a hydraulic press to remove oil and greasy hydrocarbons. This treatment is repeated till all such impurities have been removed.

The next step is to remove all traces of the odour of naphtha. This is done by treating the melted wax with high-pressure steam in iron vessels. Finally the wax is decolorised by being mixed, while still liquid, with animal charcoal or other decolorising substances. After standing for some time it is filtered to remove particles of charcoal. The resulting liquid is quite clear and colourless, and when solidified is ready for making into candles, etc. Paraffin-oil and wax are obtained from petroleum and coal-tar by methods of fractional distillation similar to that already described.

Ozokerite (q.v.) is the only naturally occurring form of paraffin-wax. It is a fairly pure wax, melting at from 60° to 80° C., and miners' candles have long been made from it in the districts where it is found. A substance called ceresin, closely resembling bees'-wax, is prepared from ozokerite. Pure paraffin-wax is a white, semi-transparent solid which melts between 40° C. and 65° C.

It is lighter than water, having a specific gravity of about ·9. It is used chiefly for making candles, which consist of about 90 per cent of wax and 10 per cent stearic acid. These candles are superior in illuminating power to those made from spermaceti and bees'-wax. Its other uses are for soaking match-flints, rendering paper transparent, dressing cloth, and making materials waterproof.

Paraffin-oil is a colourless liquid of high boiling-point and specific gravity about ·85. It is used for burning, and can serve as a lubricant.

Pure liquid paraffin is tasteless and odourless, the disagreeable smell of ordinary paraffin being due to a small quantity of impurity. Pure refined liquid paraffin is used medicinally.

PARAFFIN SERIES. A homologous series of hydrocarbons of general formula C_nH_{2n+2} (where n = number of carbon atoms). The simplest of these hydrocarbons is *methane* or marsh gas (CH_4). It is a colourless gas and is the product of decay or breakdown of many carbonaceous substances.

The members of the paraffin series may all be prepared by the same general methods; for instance, if the corresponding sodium salt of the fatty acid be distilled with soda lime, the hydrocarbon is obtained, e.g. sodium acetate heated with soda lime yields methane, $CH_3COONa + NaOH = CH_4 + Na_2CO_3$; or, if alkyl halide be treated with sodium, the halogen is removed, two alkyl groups unite, and a paraffin is formed, $2C_2H_5I + 2Na = C_4H_{10} + 2NaI$.

These paraffins are insoluble in water, the lower members are readily soluble in alcohol and ether, and the solubility in these solvents decreases with increase in molecular weight. The lower members of the series are gaseous: methane (CH_4), ethane (C_2H_6), propane (C_3H_8), butane (C_4H_{10}); then follow a series of colourless liquids: pentane (C_5H_{12}), hexane (C_6H_{14}), heptane (C_7H_{16}), octane (C_8H_{18}), etc.; and finally those members with more than sixteen carbon atoms in the molecule are colourless waxy solids.

They are saturated hydrocarbons and are not readily acted upon by chemical reagents, hence the name *paraffins* from two words meaning "little affinity". Chlorine attacks the paraffins, forming substitution products. Thus methane treated with chlorine forms methyl chloride (CH_3Cl) methylene chloride (CH_2Cl_2), chloroform ($CHCl_3$), carbon tetrachloride (CCl_4), depending on the conditions and the amount of chlorine used.

Numerous cases of isomerism occur in the series; there are two hydrocarbons of formula C_4H_{10}, three of formula C_5H_{12}, five of formula C_6H_{14}, etc. The boiling-points of the normal paraffins steadily rise as the molecular weight increases, the specific gravity increases, and the solubility decreases.

Industrially the paraffins are important; the are obtained by the destructive distillation of wood and coal, and from oil deposits in various parts of the world. Petroleum, earth oil, rock oil, or mineral oil contains paraffins in varying proportion. How these hydrocarbons have been formed is not known; according to some theories, petroleum has been produced by heat and pressure on the fatty remains of fish. Moissan suggested that they have been produced by the action of water on metallic carbides in the interior of the earth.

American petroleum consists almost entirely of normal paraffins, with small quantities of other hydrocarbons. The paraffins are applied in quantity for illuminating and heating purposes, also as solvents for oils and resins. Paraffin-wax is a mixture of higher solid hydrocarbons of the series, and about 350,000 tons of the material are produced annually from petroleum and shale-oil.

PA'RAGUAY. An inland republic of South America, extending between the Rivers Paraná (east) and Pilcomayo (west), and bisected by the Paraguay, the eastern region being known as the "Oriental", and the region west of the river as the "Occidental". **Paraguay Oriental** may be described as Paraguay Proper. It is the more populous region, and has been divided by

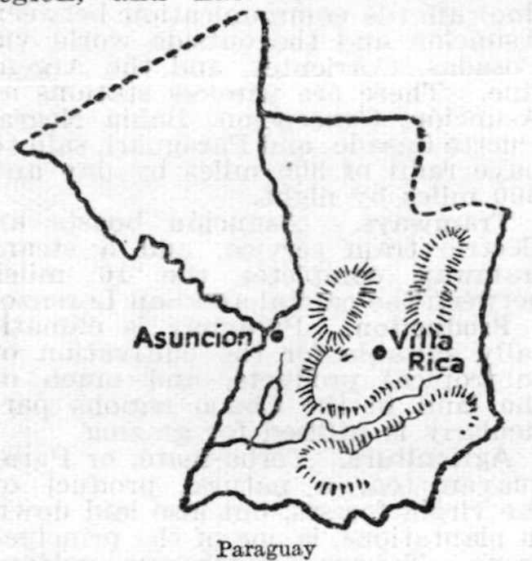

Paraguay

nature into two fairly well-defined zones: west and south, large open plains with patches of forest, drained by numerous streams; east and north, high, rolling country, covered with immense forests, relieved, here and there, by scanty patches of grazing-land. It is divided into twelve departments, subdivided into ninety-three *partidos*. Area, 61,647 sq. miles.

The **Chaco Territory (Paraguay Occidental)** has roughly the shape of an inverted triangle, with an arbitrary northern base to Chuquisaca Province, Bolivia, the enclosing sides (Rivers Paraguay and Pilcomayo) meeting as an apex at their confluence below Asunción.

By the Buenos Aires Treaty (1876), when the respective frontiers of Argentina and Paraguay were fixed, the President of the United States, in arbitration, awarded to Paraguay all that portion of the Gran Chaco between the Rio Verde and the Pilcomayo (1878). It consists mainly of grassy plains, palm groves, and great forests of valuable timbers, and although largely unexplored, it is gradually being opened up to civilisation.

Paraguayan sovereign rights in this region are disputed by Bolivia, and serious trouble occurred in 1928, resulting in the severance of diplomatic relations between the two countries.

In Aug. 1932 the dispute with Bolivia over the frontier territory broke out anew, and some fighting took place along the Paraguay River. In 1933 the question was submitted to the League of Nations.

The area of the country is approximately 100,000 sq. miles. The capital of Paraguay is Asunción (pop. 90,003.

Climate. The climate of Paraguay is temperate, and the year has two seasons, summer (October to March) and winter (April to September). The temperature varies between 81° F. in summer and 71° F. in winter, with a mean of 75° or 76° F.

Social Conditions: the People. In Paraguay Proper the inhabitants comprise Guaraní Indian people, Europeans, and some negro blood, but the Guaraní element predominates. The total population (1930) is about 851,564, exclusive of the Chaco Indians, approximately 67,000 to 68,000 in number. The foreign (European) populations received a large increase at the close of the European War by the immigration of Germano-Austrian citizens numbering upwards of 1000, but the bulk of the non-Paraguayan people are either Argentinian or Italian, with small numbers of Brazilians, French, English, and about 7000 Spanish.

Language. The official language of the state is Spanish, but Guaraní is universally spoken, and in places Tupi is understood.

Currency. Paper pesos (240 = £1 sterling British) and nickel coins are in circulation. No gold or silver is current, but the gold dollar ($5·33 gold to £1 sterling British) is the basis.

Weights, etc. In 1901 the metric system was adopted, but the native arroba = 25·35 lb., and quintal = 101·4 lb., etc., are still in use.

Religion. The established State religion is Roman Catholicism, but freedom and toleration are granted to all creeds, even to the Mennonites, who are obnoxious to America in general. Asunción is suffragan to Buenos Aires, and is the only bishopric.

Education. By law education is free and compulsory, but in many cases it cannot be enforced, as there are no schools. The system is generally at a low ebb, but there are national colleges (secondary schools) at Asunción, Villa Rica, and Pilar, and a university at Asunción, granting degrees in law and medicine, and certificates in accountancy, pharmacy, and obstetrics. There are also six normal schools, a national library, and a botanic-zoological garden under the department of Public Instruction.

Defence. A small standing army on the Prussian model is maintained, comprising about 100 officers and 2800 men. Military service is general and compulsory for two years. All Paraguay is divided, for defence purposes, into five military zones. There is a river flotilla of three gunboats, the largest being about 200 tons.

Economic—Communications. Paraguay suffers greatly from the inadequacy of her inland transport systems, and, although provided with splendid and extensively used natural waterways, these require cleaning, and in some parts dredging, to be efficient.

Railways. The Paraguay Central Railway [1] runs from Asunción to Encarnacion on the Rio Alto Paraná (232 miles), where it is linked up with the system of Argentina at Posadas by means of a train-ferry. The gauge is standard (4 feet 8½ inches). A metre-gauge railway (El Ferrocarril del Norte) runs from Concepcion to Horqueta (33 miles). The Azucarera Paraguaya at Tebicuari, in the department of Ibytimi, and several of the Chaco tannin factors, own industrial lines of metre gauge and 10 to 50 miles in length for the transport of their own raw materials.

From Posadas there is a large tourist traffic to the famous Iguazú Falls, situated 20 miles from the mouth of the Rio Iguazú, a tributary of the Paraná. They are nearly 3 miles wide, and are broken up by rocks and islets into a score of falls, the highest of which is 215 feet (cf. *Niagara*, which are much smaller in every way).

Light-draught steamers leave Posadas, and steam up the Paraná to the mouth of the Iguazú, where passengers are transferred to canoes. Canoes are the only means of reaching the falls, and for journeys beyond it a portage of nearly 40 miles is necessary.

Telephones and Telegraphs. There are wireless stations at Asunción, Concepcion, and Paraguari. A line of telegraph extends alongside the railway; the national telegraph (1440 miles of wire and 915 miles of line) affords communication between Asunción and the outside world via Posadas, Corrientes, and the Argentine. There are wireless stations at Asunción, Concepcion, Bahia Negra, Puerto Casado, and Paraguari, said to have radii of 300 miles by day and 600 miles by night.

Tramways. Asunción boasts an electric tram service, and a steam tramway completes the 10 miles between the capital and San Lorenzo.

Production. Paraguay is climatically suitable for the cultivation of subtropical products, and much of the land in the Chaco regions particularly is utilised for grazing.

Agriculture. Yerba-maté, or Paraguayan tea, a natural product of the virgin forests, but also laid down in plantations, is one of the principal crops. Tobacco, sugar-cane, cotton, rice, ground-nuts (used locally for food, the oil being utilised for soap-making), and fruit (grape-fruit, mangoes, and alligator pears for Buenos Aires markets) are the chief agricultural products. Orange trees are found in enormous quantities all over the country, but, through lack of transport, the bulk of the crop (including tangerines) is sold in Argentina, 30 per cent being lost through damage in transit. In 1932, 62,410,000 oranges and 11,738,000 tangerines were exported.

Forestry. Timber is available in practically unlimited quantities, and thousands of miles of virgin forest are untrod and untapped. Many rare and valuable woods are found but are uncut, the cheaper timbers finding a readier market. In the Chaco,

[1] The Company have a concession permitting them to extend their line to Bella Vista, on the Brazilian frontier, Dr. Cincinnato Braga, a Brazilian engineer and agriculturist, has obtained from Brazil a concession for the construction of a railway running due west from Porto União, on the line connecting São Paolo with the Uruguayan border, to Villa Rica on the Central Paraguay line. This line will cross the Paraná River *en route*, and will skirt the northern edge of Misiones (North Argentina). A branch line already runs east to the Brazilian coast at São Francisco, and this link would offer for the first time to North Paraguay a quick, direct route to the sea. A second concession permits the construction of an extension of the existing South Brazilian Railway system from the Rio Paraná opposite Tibiriça to Porto Alegro, where the track will bifurcate, one branch extending to Ponte Poro on the Brazilio-Paraguayan frontier, whence a line will be projected from Asunción. River-steamers from the Paraguayan capital will also serve Porto Murtinho (on Paraguay River), another proposed railhead. The vast importance of such and other systems cannot be overestimated, for, when completed, they will enable Paraguay to compete on an equal basis with the other great South American powers for a place in the world's markets that is at present denied her.

quebracho is the only timber cut for commercial purposes (*see* MANUFACTURES).

Minerals. Mineral resources are unexplored, but workable deposits of rich iron ore exist in many parts, and there are several deserted mines that were used by Lopez in wartime. Rich deposits of magnetic iron, hydric oxides, and brown hematite exist in the vicinity of Ibicui, Quiquyo, and Caapucú; copper pyrites and peroxide of manganese are also abundant, as are limestone (much worked), marble, granite and porphyry, serpentine, kaolin, and large beds of lithographic stone. Natural deposits of salt exist at Lambaré. Oil exists (but is not yet exploited), but there is no coal.

Manufactures. Petit-grain oil is obtained from the leaves of the bitter orange tree, and is a staple article of export. There are two breweries (Asunción), some soap-factories, tanneries, lime- and cement-factories, a large flour-mill (Asunción) grinding wheat from Argentina, and a biscuit-factory. There are seven sugar-factories but no refinery, and only ordinary unrefined sugar is produced. During the European War cattle-raising progressed rapidly, and there was a boom in meat-packing, but all the canneries have now closed down.

The quebracho industry is confined to the Chaco, and the logs are absorbed by the tannin-factories, which exported 35,834 tons of extract of quebracho or tannin in 1931.

There is some shipbuilding of flat-bottomed barges (20 to 100 tons), and at Asunción, Concepcion, Encarnacion, and Pilar there are saw-mills. Wooden articles are also made in the capital.

Imports and Exports. The largest imports are from Argentina and the United Kingdom, with the United States a bad third. The imports from and exports to the United Kingdom in 1932 were £84,703, and £12,007 respectively. Exports are chiefly to Argentina, but it must be recollected that all imports and exports pass through Argentina, and statistics of goods in transit naturally inflate those of that country.

History. Sebastian Cabot discovered modern Paraguay in 1527. Asunción was established as a port by Juan de Ayolas in 1535, and from it the Spanish *conquistadores* reduced La Guayra and the Gran Chaco. All the Spanish territories were known as Paraguay, which at that time included large slices of Brazil, Argentina, and Uruguay. The Franciscans and Jesuits followed each other as missionaries, and in 1776 Paraguay, which had been erected into a separate government in 1620, became subordinate to the vice-royalty of Buenos Aires.

Paraguayan independence of Spain was declared in 1811. The administration passed (1815) into the hands of Dr. J. G. R. Francia, who, as dictator, exercised absolute power until his death (1840), when, after a short interregnum, Carlos Antonio Lopez, his nephew, was appointed joint consul (1842). In 1844 a National Congress elected Lopez to the presidency, and on his death (1862) he was succeeded by his son Francisco Solano Lopez (q.v.), who promptly (1864) quarrelled with the Brazilian Government, marched his armies through Argentina to the invasion of Brazil, and fought for five years the Argentina-Brazil-Uruguayan coalition, who invaded Paraguay.

At the close of the war Lopez was killed in the battle of Aquidaban, or Cerro Corá (1st March, 1870), but by that time nine-tenths of the male population of Paraguay had been exterminated. The Brazilian army of occupation was evacuated in 1876, and only the whole-hearted efforts of Argentina, with one eye fixed on the balance of Latin American power, prevented the annexation of Paraguay by her conqueror.

Government. The present Constitution was adopted on 25th Nov., 1870. The executive is in the hands of a President (elected for five years) and five ministers; the legislative authority is vested in a Senate (one paid member to 12,000 inhabitants) and a Chamber of Deputies (one paid member to 6000 inhabitants), both Houses being chosen by universal suffrage. The electoral law of 1916 provides for 20 Senators and 40 Deputies. The Vice-President of the republic is President of the Senate.

BIBLIOGRAPHY: W. Parker, *Paraguayans of To-day*; A. E. Elliot, *Paraguay, its Cultural Heritage, Social Conditions, and Educational Problems*; Annual Message of President of the Republic upon opening of Congress on 1st April; F. A. Bordon, *Paraguay*; *Guia Geografica de Turismo*; J. W. Hills and I. Dunbar, *The Golden River*; *Sport and Travel in Paraguay*; C. Baez, *Le Paraguay*.

PARAGUAY. A river of South America, which rises in the Brazilian state of Matto Grosso, takes a course generally southwards, and joins the Paraná at the south-west angle of the state of Paraguay after a course of some 1800 miles. It receives the Pilcomayo, Vermejo, and other large rivers, and is a valuable highway of trade to Paraguay and Brazil.

PARAHYBA (pȧ-rȧ-ē'bȧ). A maritime state of Brazil, between Rio-Grande-do-Norte on the north and Pernambuco on the south. Cotton and cassava are raised. There is a wet season from March to June. Area, 28,846 sq. miles; pop. 1,322,069. The River Parahyba traverses the state. It rises in the Pernambuco borderland, and falls into the Atlantic after a course of 270 miles. The state capital is Parahyba, on the river estuary, with an outport at Cabedello farther down. Pop. 74,104.

PARAKEETS, or **PARROQUETS.** A sub-family or group of the Parrots, characterised by their generally small size and their long tail-feathers. The islands of the Eastern Archipelago form the chief habitat of these birds, but species also occur in India and Australia.

Amongst the most familiar forms are the rose-ringed and Alexandrine parakeets. The former (*Palæornis*

Parakeet

torquāta), found in India and on the eastern coasts of Africa, has a bright-green body and a pink circle round the neck. The Alexandrine parakeet (*P. alexandri*) of India is a nearly allied species. These birds may be taught to speak with distinctness.

The ground parakeets of Australia live amongst the reeds and grass of swamps, generally in solitary pairs. The common ground parakeet of Australia (*Pezopŏrus formōsus*) possesses a green and black plumage, the tail being similarly coloured, and the body-feathers having each a band of dark-brown hue.

The grass parakeets of Australia, of which the small warbling parakeet (*Melopsittăcus undulātus*) is a good example, inhabit the central flat lands of Australia, and feed on the seeds of the grasses covering the plains. They perch on the eucalypti or gum trees during the day, and the nests are situated in the hollows of these trees.

PAR'ALLAX. The apparent change of place which bodies undergo by being viewed from different points.

In astronomy, the parallax of the sun, moon, a planet, or comet means the difference in its apparent position when viewed from the surface and (hypothetically) from the centre of the earth. This difference vanishes when the object is overhead, and is greater when it appears on the horizon. In the latter instance it is called the *horizontal parallax*, often, however, simply the parallax.

For distinction, in other cases the expression *parallax in altitude* is used. In the case of a star (or a nebula), parallax means the angle subtended by the radius of the earth's orbit at the star's distance. It is thus the maximum distance to which the star appears displaced from its mean, or heliocentric position, on account of our revolution round the sun. For the star supposed to be nearest to us it amounts to only 0.76 seconds.

PARALLEL MOTION. A mechanism for constraining a point to move in a straight line. More accurately, but less commonly, this device is termed a *straight-line motion*. The motion produced is proportionate to that given to the mechanism. In the indicator (q.v.) the motions of the piston, which depend upon the steam or gas pressures, are multiplied by such a mechanism. James Watt invented a motion of this type for use in his beam engines. Many of these mechanisms are only straight-line motions within the limited range of their use. Peaucellier's cell or parallel motion consists of seven links, and is one of the few which could be used for extreme travels, as it is a true straight-line motion.

PARALLELOGRAM OF FORCES. An important dynamical principle, deduced by Newton, which may be stated thus: If two forces acting in different directions on a particle at the same time be represented in magnitude and direction by two straight lines meeting at the particle, their resultant effect in giving motion to the particle is that of a force represented in magnitude and direction by the diagonal (terminating in the particle) of the parallelogram, of which the two former lines are two sides.

PARAL'YSIS. Loss of the power of movement, which is caused by injury or disease of the brain, spinal cord, or nerves, or to an affection of the muscular substance itself. When the paralysis is limited to one side of the body, and the voluntary power of moving the muscles is lost, this is usually due to disease of the brain, and receives the specific name of **hemiplegia.** It is generally caused by the bursting of a blood-vessel in the brain; it may also be due to a blood-vessel being blocked by a clot of blood.

The paralysis may be sudden and without unconsciousness, or it may be gradual and attended with sickness, faintness, and confusion of mind. In ordinary cases it will be found that one side of the body is powerless, the face twisted, the speech thick and indistinct. Recovery may be complete, or partial, or the attack may prove fatal. In any case the condition is liable to recur after partial or complete recovery.

When one side of the body and the opposite side of the face is affected, the disease, which has its seat in the region of the medulla oblongata, receives the name of **crossed paralysis,** and is considered more dangerous than ordinary hemiplegia.

When, again, the disease is situated in the spinal cord, the paralysis, which receives the name of **paraplegia,** may affect either the upper or lower part of the body, or motion may be lost on one side and sensation on the other.

Local paralysis is the term used when disease or injury affects a specific nerve-trunk, and has no connection with disease of the brain or spinal cord. The effect of this local paralysis is to deprive the muscles of their nerve-supply, in which case they lose their power, becoming weak and faint.

PARALYSIS IN CATTLE. Cattle at all ages are liable to spinal trouble, resulting in paralysis, temporary or permanent. It most commonly arises in young stock, sometimes in adults, from the presence of bladder worms, such as cause the gid in sheep. The pressure of the growing bladder in the brain may cause fits, sidelong walking, or inability to use one side or one half of the body, the hind extremities being more often affected than the fore-limbs. There is also a dropsical condition of the spinal cord, which causes more or less paralysis, according to the degree of pressure. This overtakes weaklings, and others that have been exposed to hardships of travel by land or sea, and exposure to chilling winds, without exercise.

Where the trouble is due to hydatids or bladder worms, no direct remedies can be applied, but animals often outgrow it if carefully fed, and the bowels kept lax. The bladders attain maximum size, and then gradually shrink if the patient lives long enough. Unsteady gait and difficulty of progression indicate more a hydatid pressure than spinal meningitis.

Treatment of paralysis in adults is not likely to be of much avail, unless some brain disturbance is dependent on digestive troubles. For spinal meningitis the whole length of the spine is rubbed with a strong liniment at intervals of two or three days by way of counter-irritation. Turpentine 1 part, ammonia 1 part, and linseed oil 3 parts is suggested. Besides a preliminary purge, a daily dose for a yearling or calf over six months old of 1 drachm of iodide of potassium, 1 drachm of nitrate of potassium, and 20 grains each of powdered nux vomica and sulphate of iron may be given after the first few days. Good, regular feeding and careful management succeed in the majority of cases; and many a staggering calf by this means grows into a good bullock.—Cf. *Standard Cyclopædia of Modern Agriculture* (Gresham Publishing Company).

PARAMAR'IBO. Capital of Guiana or Surinam, situated at the junction of the Surinam and Commewine Rivers about 10 miles from the sea. It has a commodious fortified harbour, and is the centre of the Dutch West Indian trade, and exports sugar, coffee, cacao, rum, and annatto seeds. Pop 47,318.

PARAMAT'TA, or PARRAMATTA. A light twilled fabric with a weft of combed merino wool and a cotton warp. It probably takes its name from Paramatta, a town in New South Wales; Paramatta cloths or tweeds made from Australian wools were first made. Fine cloths are now made from Botany and cross-bred wools at Bradford, in Yorkshire, where they are still largely manufactured.

PARANÁ. The second largest river of South America, draining a larger basin than any other river in the New World except the Amazon and the Mississippi. It is formed by the junction of two streams, the Rio Grande and the Paranahyba, which meet in Brazil, and it discharges itself into the estuary of the La Plata, the latter part of its course being through the Argentine.

Its principal tributaries are the Paraguay and the Salado, both from the right. All the tributaries on its left are comparatively short. Its total length is about 2500 miles. In breadth, current, and volume of water the Paraná has ten times the magnitude of the Paraguay, which is itself superior to the greatest European rivers. It is an important water-way to the interior of the country, though with obstructions at certain points. The river was first ascended in 1526 by Sebastian Cabot.

PARANÁ. A state of Southern Brazil, bounded on the north by the state of São Paulo, on the east by the Atlantic Ocean, on the south by the state of Santa Catharina, and on the west by Paraguay and the province of Matto Grosso. Cotton, rice, yerba-maté, and coffee are cultivated, and lumbering is carried on to some extent. There are numerous German and Polish colonies in the state. Chief town, Curytiba. Area, 93,269 sq. miles ; pop. 974,273 (est.).

PARASELENE. Also called a mock moon, a luminous appearance at a distance from the moon's position in the sky, produced by refractive effects acting upon the moon's rays, in precisely the same manner as parhelia are produced from the solar beams. *See* PARHELION ; HALO.

PAR'ASITES. The name applied to animals which attach themselves to the exterior (ectoparasites), or inhabit various situations in the interior (endoparasites), of the bodies of other animals, living at their expense. They include such forms as round worms, tape-worms, flukes, fish-lice, bird-lice, and common lice. Plants are also attached by animal parasites, such as eel-worms. *See* COMMENSALISM.

PARASITIC DISEASES. Are those produced by the action of any animal or plant on the human body, and thus include all diseases due to germs, but the term is more generally confined to diseases produced by parasites visible to the naked eye. Examples of these are tape-worm, trichina, guinea-worm, louse, acarus, producing scabies and many others.

PARASITIC PLANTS. Such plants as grow on others, from which they receive their nourishment. In this class are many Fungi, such as the rusts, smuts, and mildews. Among larger parasites are the mistletoe; and the genus Rafflesia, belonging to Sumatra and Java. Parasites are distinguished from *epiphytes*, inasmuch as the latter, though they grow upon other plants, are not nourished by them. *See* EPIPHYTE.

PARAVANE. A naval device used during the European War, which secured the immunity of ships steaming at sea from anchored mines. The "Otter" device was used by over 2700 vessels of the mercantile marine, and a similar system was introduced into the Grand Fleet during 1916.

The paravane consisted of a torpedo-shaped body fitted with hydrovanes, at one end of which was a float, and at the other end a weight. There was also a rudder, regulating depth of flotation by means of a hydrostatic valve.

A pair of paravanes was towed, one on either beam, by each ship entering a mine-field. On the mooring-chain of a mine coming in contact with the tow-rope, the mine was deflected from the ship, and had naturally to pass the paravane to escape. The nose of the paravane was fitted with a heavy cutter-bracket and serrated knife-blade that, on contact, snapped the mooring-chain, and, by releasing the sinker, allowed the mine to rise to certain destruction by gun-fire.

The destructive paravane, of similar construction, was towed in a similar way ; but the cylinders were filled with 300 lb. of T.N.T., and were aligned at a depth of 35 fathoms or thereabouts. On encountering a submarine, the charge was exploded by electricity operated from the ship. The device generally proved effective enough, although less so than the depth-charge.

PARAY LE MONIAL. A town of France, department of Saône-et-Loire, on the Paris-Lyons Railway. It is a place of pilgrimage, as the holy nun Marie Alacoque (died 1690) is said to have had visions of the Saviour there. Pop. 5000.

PARCHIM (par'*h*ēm). A town of Germany, in Mecklenburg-Schwerin, on the Elde. It has manufactures of woollen cloth, flour, oil, paper, and sawmills. It was the birth-place of Count von Moltke. Pop. 11,857,

PARCHMENT (Fr. *parchemin* ; Lat. *pergamina*), the skins of sheep, she-goats, and several other animals, so dressed or prepared as to be rendered fit for writing on. This is done by stretching the skin on a frame, separating all the flesh and hair from the skin, reducing its thickness with a sharp instrument, and smoothing the surface with pumice-stone covered with pulverised chalk or slaked lime. After it is reduced to something less than half its original thickness, it is smoothed and slowly dried for use.

The name parchment signifies literally paper of Pergamum (Asia Minor), where parchment was first extensively brought into use about 200 B.C., when Eumenes, King of Pergamum, decided to found a library in that city which should rival the famous Alexandrian library. The Jews, however, had books written on the skins of animals in David's time; and according to Herodotus the Ionians wrote upon goats' and sheep skins. *Vellum* is a finer kind prepared from the skins of calves or kids. Parchment is now chiefly used for writing important legal documents on.

PARDON. In England, in nearly all cases of crimes except where there is an impeachment, a pardon from the Crown may be granted before a trial as well as after; and it stops further progress in the inquiry and prosecution at whatever time it is granted.

In cases of impeachment no pardon can now be granted by the Crown while the prosecution is pending; but after conviction of the offender it may be granted, as in other cases. Pardon was formerly granted by the Crown under the great seal, but by 7 and 8 Geo. IV. cap. xxviii s. 13 it was made sufficient for the sovereign to issue a warrant for the purpose under his sign-manual, and countersigned by a Secretary of State. The sovereign acts upon the representation of the Home Secretary.

In America the Constitution provides that the President "shall have power to grant reprieves and pardons for offences against the United States, except in cases of impeachment." The Senate has the whole power of trying impeachments.

PAR'DUBICE. A town of Czechoslovakia, in Bohemia, at the junction of the Chrudimka with the Elbe. Pop. 28,841.

PARÉ (pärā), **Ambroise.** French surgeon, born early in the sixteenth century at Laval, died in 1590. He studied in Paris, and for a time acted as an army-surgeon. In 1552 he became surgeon to Henry II., under whose successors (Francis II., Charles IX., and Henry III.) he held the same post.

PAREIASAURUS. A fossil reptile of primitive type, from Permian strata in South Africa and North Russia. It is one of the Theromorpha (q.v.).

PARENT AND CHILD. Besides being a natural relationship, it has its legal aspects, in which legitimacy and illegitimacy form a clear distinction. All children born in lawful wedlock, or within a satisfactory time afterwards, are considered legitimate; but the common law of England and Ireland does not compel parents to maintain their children. If the parents fail to do so, however, in the case of a child unable to earn its own living, the poor-law authority performs this duty, and by so doing can obtain the power, under an order from a justice of the peace, to compel the parents or other relatives to make a contribution for that purpose.

Beyond this there is no legal provision for the maintenance of children by their parents; yet where the child contracts a debt, as for necessary food, clothes, etc., the parents will usually be found liable. Similarly the law does not compel children to maintain their parents, unless the latter become chargeable to the parish. Formerly a parent was not called upon to educate his children, but the elementary education Acts have changed this.

When the children are legitimate, the common law provides that the father shall be their guardian until their majority; but various statutes have suspended the common law on the subject, and the matter is now governed by the Guardianship of Infants Act, 1925, the object of which is to give both parents equal rights over their children. On the death of the father the mother is now guardian alone, or jointly with any guardian appointed by the father or the court. In case of divorce the court may make regulations as to maintenance, custody, etc.

At death parents may, under a will duly executed, disinherit their children; but in the event of intestacy if there is no surviving parent the children share the whole estate, real and personal, in equal shares. (*See* DESCENT.)

In the case of an illegitimate child the mother may summon the putative father to appear before a magistrate. When the affiliation charge is proved, the magistrates can order him to pay the lying-in expenses, and a weekly sum not exceeding twenty shillings until the child's sixteenth year. He is not, however, in law regarded as the father of the child, and hence neither can such a child inherit any of his property, nor is he entitled to the custody of the child.

In Scotland the law upon this question differs in many points from the law in England and Ireland. Thus in Scotland parent and child are legally bound at common law to maintain each other, and this liability may descend after death to the representatives who are *lucrati* (or benefited) by the succession.

It has always been the law in Scotland that an illegitimate child becomes legitimate on the subsequent marriage of his parents, but by the Legitimation Act of 1926 this is now the law in England and Wales also. A distinction in Scotland is that the father cannot disinherit his child, children being entitled to a share of his personal estate known as *legitim*.

In the question of custody the father has the preference, but the interests of the child is the paramount consideration, and upon his decease the law transfers authority to the mother. By the Guardianship of Infants (Scotland) Act (1886), it is provided that the court in pronouncing decree for judicial separation or divorce may declare the offending parent to be a person unfit to have charge of the children of the marriage, even after the death of the other parent. *See* ILLEGITIMACY; LEGITIMATION.

PARGETTING, or PARGE-WORK. A term used for plaster-work of various kinds, but commonly applied to a particular sort of ornamental plaster, with patterns and ornaments raised or indented upon it, much used in the interior and often on the exterior of houses of the Tudor period. Numbers of wooden houses so ornamented on the outside, and belonging to the time of Queen Elizabeth, are still to be met with.

PARHE'LION, or mock sun, an effect produced, but comparatively rarely in our latitudes, from the refraction of the sun's light by minute ice-crystals floating in the higher atmosphere. The halo of 22° radius is much less rare. Sometimes a circle of light is seen passing horizontally through the sun, and right round the sky at the same altitude. Upon this circle, and near to where it intersects the halo, there may appear intensified portions which give practically the appearance of additional suns.

These are parhelia or mock suns. Under certain conditions they may also appear in other situations relative to the sun. Instead of sun-like images, there may be patches with prismatic tints—coloured parhelia. In the polar regions especially, circles and bright patches of various positions and sizes may at times be seen simultaneously. These can be explained as due to rays which have entered and traversed the minute hexagonal ice-prisms in different ways, and undergone diverse processes of refraction or reflection.

PA'RIAH. A term loosely applied to any of the lowest class of people in Hindustan, who have, properly speaking, no caste. Properly, however, Pariah (a Tamil name) is applied to the members of a somewhat widely spread race in Southern India, generally of the Hindu religion, and though regarded by the Hindus as of the lowest grade, yet superior to some ten other castes in their own country. They are frequently serfs to the agricultural class, or servants to Europeans. The term is figuratively applied to any social outcast.—Cf. H. H. Risley, *The Tribes and Castes of Bengal*.

PARI'NI, Giuseppe. Italian poet and satirist, born in 1729, died in 1799. He studied at Milan, published some youthful poetry, and wrote a brilliant satire on the Milanese aristocracy entitled *Il Giorno* (The Day). From 1733 on he was professor of rhetoric at the Brera, Milan.

PARIS. In Greek mythology, also called Alexander, the second son of Priam, King of Troy, by Hecuba. His mother dreamed before his birth that she had brought forth a firebrand, which was interpreted to mean that he would cause the destruction of Troy. To prevent this their child was exposed on Mount Ida, where he was discovered by a shepherd, who brought him up as his own son. Here his grace and courage commended him to the favour of Œnone, a nymph of Ida, whom he married.

At the marriage of Peleus and Thetis a dispute arose whether Hera, Athena, or Aphroditē was the most beautiful, and as such entitled to the golden apple. Paris was chosen judge, and decided in favour of Aphroditē, who had promised him the fairest woman in the world for his wife. Subsequently he visited Sparta, the residence of Menelaus, who had married Helena (or Helen) the fairest woman of the age, whom he persuaded to elope with him. This led to the siege of Troy, at the capture of which he was killed by an arrow.

PARIS, Louis Albert Philippe d'Orleans, Comte de. Son of the duc d'Orleans, and grandson of Louis-Philippe, born 1838, died in 1894. After the Revolution of 1848 he resided chiefly in Claremont, England, where he was educated by his mother. He took part in the American Civil War, and on his return to Europe he married his cousin the Princess Marie-Isabelle, eldest daughter of the duc de Montpensier. After the Franco-German War he was admitted a member of the first National Assembly.

On the death of the comte de Chambord, the comte de Paris was recognised as head of the Royal House of France, but under the Expulsion Bill of 1886 he was forbidden to enter France. He wrote a *History* of the Civil War in America, and a work on *English Trade Unions*.

PARIS, Matthew. An English historian, born about 1195, died 1259.

He entered the Benedictine monastery of St. Albans, and in 1235 succeeded Roger of Wendover as chronicler to the monastery. He was very intimate with Henry III., and had a large number of influential friends besides. In 1248 he went on an ecclesiastical mission to Norway.

He is characterised as at once a mathematician, poet, orator, theologian, painter, and architect. His principal works are his *Historia Major* (or *Chronica Majora*), written in Latin, and comprising a sketch of the history of the world down to his own times, the latter portion (1235-59) being, however, the only part exclusively his; the *Historia Anglorum*, called also *Historia Minor*, a sort of abridgment of the former; and also lives of the Abbots of St. Albans and of the Kings of Mercia.

PARIS (ancient **Lutetia**). The capital of France and of the department of Seine, lies in the Seine Valley ("Paris Basin"), surrounded by Jurassic heights. Through the valley the river runs from east to west, enclosing two islands, upon which part of the city is built. It is navigable by small steamers. The river, which sweeps through the city in a great curve, is crossed by thirty bridges, the more important being Pont Neuf, Pont de la Concorde, Pont Alexandre III., Pont de l'Alma, and Pont d'Iéna.

Until after the European War the city was surrounded by a line of fortifications 25 miles long, but they are now being demolished. It is also encircled by the Ceinture Railway.

The climate of Paris is temperate and agreeable. The rainiest month is June; the driest, February.

The city is divided into twenty numbered arrondissements, at the head of each of which is a *maire* (mayor). Each arrondissement is divided into four quarters, each of which sends a member to the municipal council. At the head are the Prefect of the Seine and the Prefect of the Police. The former is chief of public services; the latter attends chiefly to public safety, traffic, aliens, public morals, law courts, prison services, and the Garde Républicaine.

The water-supply of the city is partly derived from the Seine, the Marne, the Vannes, artesian wells, etc.; partly from the Vigne and Aire, by a great aqueduct 63 miles long.

One of the most striking features of Paris is the street-plan, which, as even Paris of to-day, was originated by Napoleon III. during the Second Empire, and planned by Baron Haussmann, Prefect of the Seine, the emperors' ablest coadjutor. The broad boulevards are as useful as traffic arteries as they are unique. From south to north the Boulevard St. Michel runs over the Cité and joins the Boulevard de Sébastopol with its extension the Boulevard de Strasbourg.

Upon the Place de l'Étoile (Arc de Triomphe) twelve magnificent avenues converge. On the south side is the Boulevard Raspail, joining, towards the riverside, the Boulevard Saint Germain, which curves away to the Pont Sully and merges on the other side with the Boulevard Henri IV. The Grands Boulevards extend, under varying names, from the Madeleine to the Place de la Bastille. Many other streets and avenues are household words throughout Europe.

Squares, Parks, etc. Among the most notable public squares or *places* is the Place de la Concorde, one of the largest and most beautiful squares in Europe, adorned by fountains and statues, and occupied by the obelisk of Luxor. This obelisk is a monolith of reddish granite from the quarries of *Syene* (Aswan), 76 feet in height and 240 tons in weight. It was erected by Rameses II. (Sesostris the Great), King of Egypt, before the temple of Amenhotep III. at Thebes (modern *Luxor*), and was intended to honour Ammon Ra, the chief Egyptian deity. In 1830 it was presented to Louis Philippe by Mahomet Ali, Pasha of Egypt, and was placed in position by Lebas in 1836. The Place de la Concorde was so named in 1799; in 1814 it became the Place de Louis XV., and in 1826 Place de Louis XVI. After 1830 it reverted to the old name, and the obelisk was installed there because of a decision to decorate the square with monuments of a non-political nature only.

Others are the Place Vendôme, with column to Napoleon I.; Place des Victoires, with equestrian statue of Louis XIV.; Place de la Bastille, with the column of July; Place de la République, with colossal statue of the Republic; and the Place de l'Étoile, with the Arc de Triomphe, the most imposing triumphal arch in existence. The square is named from the star formed by the twelve radiating boulevards. Napoleon I. conceived the project (1806) of erecting four such arches, and completed one in the Place du Carrousel. The Arc de l'Étoile was erected by Louis Philippe (1836).

Within the city are situated the gardens of the Tuileries, which are adorned with numerous statues and fountains; the gardens of the Luxembourg, in which are fine conservatories of rare plants; the Jardin des Plantes, in which are the botanical and zoological gardens, hothouses, museums, etc., which have made this scientific institution famous; the Buttes-Chaumont Gardens, in which an extensive old quarry has been turned to good account in enhancing the beauty of the situation; the Parc Monceau; and the Champs Élysées, the last-named being a favourite promenade of all classes. But the most extensive parks are outside the city, such as the Bois de Boulogne and the Bois de Vincennes.

The most celebrated and extensive cemetery in Paris is Père la Chaise (106½ acres), named after the Jesuit confessor of Louis XIV., whose country seat occupied the site. It was laid out in 1804, and contains the graves of Sièyes (died 1836), member of the Directory; Laffitte (died (1840), the banker; Macdonald (died 1840), duc de Tarente and Maréchal de France; Kellermann (died 1820), duc de Valmy and Maréchal de France; the Queen of Oude (died 1858); Chopin (died 1849), the pianist and composer; Barras (died 1829), of the Directory; Marshal Ney (shot 1815); Marshal Masséna (died 1817); Marshal Grouchy (died 1847); Alfred de Musset (died 1857); and Rossini (died 1868), the composer; and a host of others whose memories are yet green.

The Catacombs are ancient quarries which extend under a portion of the southern part of the city, and in them are deposited the bones removed from old cemeteries now built over.

Churches. Of the churches of Paris the most celebrated is the cathedral of Notre Dame, situated on the Ile de la Cité. The present edifice was begun in 1163 on the site of a fourth-century foundation, and was consecrated in 1182, although unfinished until the thirteenth century. It contains many valuable treasures, including a fragment and a nail of the original "true" cross. The church of La Madeleine (or church of St. Mary Magdalene) is an imposing church in the square of the same name. The foundation was laid by Louis XV. in 1764.

The church of Ste. Geneviève, built about the close of the eighteenth century, was after its completion set apart, under the title of the Panthéon, as the burying-place of illustrious Frenchmen. Ste. Geneviève was buried on the site in A.D. 512, and a church was erected over her tomb. This gave place to a church which was in turn replaced by the present structure. The title Panthéon was originally instituted by decree of the Convention in 1791.

Others are: St. Gervais, bombarded by the German long-range gun "Big Bertha" on Good Friday, 1918; St. Roch; St. Sulpice; Notre Dame de Lorette; St. Vincent de Paul; and St. Germain l'Auxerrois, founded before the time of Charlemagne, the present edifice dating from the fifteenth century. On the very summit of Montmartre is the church of the Sacred Heart, founded in 1874.

Palaces and Public Buildings. Notable among the public buildings of Paris are its palaces. The Louvre is one of the most important public buildings of Paris, and derives its name from its location on the site of an ancient shooting-box in an afforested region frequented by wolves, and called the *Lupara* or *Louverie.* The modern buildings were founded in 1541 by Francis I., and building was continued by Henri II., Catherine de' Médicis (Francis II. and Henri III.), and by Henri IV. Louis XIII. and Louis XIV. both extended the original plans, but their successors (Louis XV. and Louis XVI.) preferred the Tuileries and Versailles to the Louvre, and abandoned the work.

Napoleon conceived the plan of joining the Louvre and the Tuileries by means of a gallery which was completed as far as the pavilion de Rohan before his downfall, and the grand project was accomplished by Visconti and Lefuel under the guidance of Napoleon III. The combined buildings cover an area of 48 acres, and since 1793 the old Louvre has been used as a museum. The North Palace of the New Louvre is occupied by the Ministry of Finance. In 1871 the Communists burned down that part of the connecting wing nearest the Tuileries, and few architectural details have been preserved.

The Palais du Luxembourg, on the south side of the river, has very extensive gardens attached to it, and contains the Musée du Luxembourg, appropriated to the works of modern French artists, with an annexe in the Palais du Jeu de Paume in the Tuileries Gardens. The Palais du Luxembourg originated in the mansion and garden of the duc de Piney-Luxembourg, whose grounds were purchased by Maria de' Médicis, widow of Henri IV., in 1612, and who built the present palace (which is the meeting-place of the Senate).

The Palais Royal is a famed resort. The Palais de l'Élysée, situated in the Rue St. Honoré, with a large garden, is now the residence of the President of the Republic. The Chambre des Députés—known under the Empire as the Palais du Corps Législatif—is the building in which the Deputies meet.

The *salons* are held in the Grand

Palais des Beaux-Arts, erected for the exhibition of 1900. The Hôtel de Ville is situated in the Place de l'Hôtel de Ville, formerly Place de Grève, on the right bank of the river. Destroyed by the Communists in 1871, it has been re-erected on the same site with even greater magnificence, in the Renaissance style. The Hôtel des Invalides, built in 1670, is used as a retreat for disabled soldiers. The church attached contains the burial-place of the first Napoleon.

The Palais de Justice is an irregular mass of buildings occupying the greater part of the western extremity of the Ile de la Cité. Opposite the Palais de Justice is the Tribunal de Commerce. The Exchange (La Bourse) was completed in 1826; it is in the form of a parallelogram, 212 feet by 126 feet, surrounded by a range of sixty-six columns. The extensive markets form a striking feature of Paris, the most important being the Halles Centrales, where fish, poultry, butcher-meat, and garden produce are sold. A notable and unique structure is the Eiffel Tower, built in connection with the exhibition of 1889, on the Champ de Mars, a structure of iron lattice-work 985 feet high, which is used for broadcasting by wireless, and fulfils the function of a gigantic aerial. There are seven other broadcasting stations.

Education, Libraries, etc. The chief institution of higher education is the University of Paris, connected with the Sorbonne. Among Parisian schools the most important are: Descartes (formerly Louis le Grand): St. Louis; Corneille (formerly Collège Henri IV.); Charlemagne; Fontanes (formerly Condorcet); de Vanves; the École Polytechnique, for military and civil engineers, etc.; École des Beaux Arts; School of Oriental Languages; Conservatoire des Arts et Métiers; and the Conservatoire de Musique.

Of the libraries the most important is the Bibliothèque Nationale, others being those of the Arsenal, Ste. Geneviève, Mazarin, de la Ville, de l'Insitut, and de l'Université (the Sorbonne). There are also libraries subsidised by the municipality in all the arrondissements.

Among museums, besides the Louvre and the Luxembourg, there may be noted the Musée d'Artillerie, in the Hôtel des Invalides, containing suits of ancient armour, arms, etc.; the Conservatoire des Arts et Métiers; the city historical museum or Musée Carnavalet; the Petit Palais des Beaux-Arts, containing the Dutuit and other collections left to the City of Paris; the Trocadéro Palace, containing ethnographical curiosities, casts of sculpture, etc.; and the Cluny Museum, containing an extensive collection of the products of the art and artistic handicrafts of the Middle Ages.

Theatres. The theatres of Paris are more numerous than those of any other city in the world. The most important are the Opera House, a gorgeous edifice of great size, built between 1861-75; the Théâtre Français; the Odéon; the Théâtre de la Gaîté, for vaudevilles and melodramas; Théâtre des Folies Dramatiques; Théâtre du Châtelet; Théâtre du Vaudeville; Théâtre des Variétés; Théâtre de la Porte St. Martin; and the Théâtre de l'Ambigu Comique.

Industries and Trade. The most important manufactures are articles of jewellery and the precious metals, trinkets of various kinds, fine hardware, paper-hangings, saddlery and other articles in leather, cabinet-work, carriages, various articles of dress, silk and woollen tissues (particularly shawls and carpets), Gobelin tapestry, lace, embroidery, artificial flowers, combs, machines, scientific instruments, types, books, engravings, refined sugar, tobacco (a Government monopoly), chemical products, etc.

That which is distinctively Parisian is the making of all kinds of small ornamental articles, which are called, *articles de Paris*. A large trade is carried on by the Seine both above and below Paris as well as by canals.

Population. According to approximate estimates the population of Paris was, in 1474, 150,000; under Henri II. (1547-59), 210,000; in 1590, 200,000; under Louis XIV. (1643-1715), 492,600; in 1856 (before the annexation of the parts beyond the old *mur d'octroi*), 1,174,346; 1861 (after the annexation), 1,667,841; in 1901, 2,714,068; in 1911, 2,888,110; in 1926, 2,871,429. It is now estimated at 2,891,020.

History. The first appearance of Paris in history is on the occasion of Caesar's conquest of Gaul, when the small tribe of the Parisii were found inhabiting the banks of the *Sequana* or Seine, and whose chief town was *Lutetia*, on the modern isle of La Cité. St Denis suffered martyrdom on Montmartre in or about the year A.D. 250, and Julian resided at Lutetia in 360. The name was then changed to *Parisii*, and the political franchise bestowed upon it. Gratian was defeated and slain at Parisii by Maximus in 383.

In the beginning of the fifth century it suffered much from the northern hordes, and ultimately fell into the hands of the Franks, headed by Clovis (son of Childeric, the King of Tournay), who founded the Merovingian dynasty. Pepin became king in 752, and founded the Carlovingian dynasty. In 987 the Capetian dynasty was established in the person of Hugh Capet, from whose reign downwards Paris long continued to be the residence of the Kings of France, and obtained (under St. Louis) many municipal privileges. In 1250 Robert Sorbon, the king's confessor, founded the University of the Sorbonne.

In 1483, under Charles VIII., Paris was ravaged by pestilence and famine, and such was the desolation that wolves appeared in herds and prowled about the streets. In the reign of Louis XIV. the Paris walls were levelled to the ground after having stood for about 300 years, and what are now the principal boulevards were formed on their site (1670). Only the Bastille was left (till 1789), and in place of the four principal gates of the old walls, four triumphal arches were erected, two of which, the Porte St. Denis and Porte St. Martin, still stand.

Many of the finest edifices of Paris were destroyed during the Revolution, but the work of embellishment was resumed by the Directory, and continued by all subsequent Governments. The reign of Napoleon III. is specially noteworthy in this respect. Under the emperor's instructions Baron Haussmann opened up new and spacious streets and beautified the city to a great extent.

Among modern events in the history of Paris are the siege of the city by the Germans in the war of 1870-1, and the subsequent siege by the French National Government in order to wrest the city from the hands of the Commune.

Paris was the scene of international exhibitions in 1855, 1867, 1878, and 1889, but the greatest was that of 1900, which presented an epitome of the progress of the nineteenth century. It was visited by 47,000,000 persons, or about two-thirds more than the number who visited that of 1889.

During the European War Paris suffered severely from air-raids, and from 23rd March to 5th Aug., 1918, it was bombarded by long-range guns. The Peace Conferences of 1919 and 1920 were held in Paris.

BIBLIOGRAPHY: E. V. Lucas, *A Wanderer in Paris*; H. Belloc, *Paris*; P. G. Hamerton, *Paris in Old and Present Times*; W. Walton, *Paris from the Earliest Period to the Present Day*; T. Okey, *The Story of Paris*; R. H. Sherard, *Modern Paris*; see also *Histoire générale de la ville de Paris* (published by the municipality).

PARIS. A city of Texas, United States, the county seat of Lamar county; served by the Texas and Pacific, the St. Louis and San Francisco, and other railways. It is a cotton-trading and manufacturing centre, and has also brick-, furniture-, and woodworking-factories. Paris was founded in 1841, and became a city in 1905. Pop. 15,649.

PARIS. A city of Illinois, United States, the county seat of Edgar county; served by the Vandalia and the New York Central Railways, on the latter of which it is an important junction. There is a large trade in agricultural produce. Paris was founded in 1825, and became a city in 1873. Pop. (1930), 8,781.

PARIS. A genus of plants of the nat. ord. Trilliaceæ. *P. quadrifolia* (herb-paris, true-love, or one-berry) is not uncommon in Britain, being

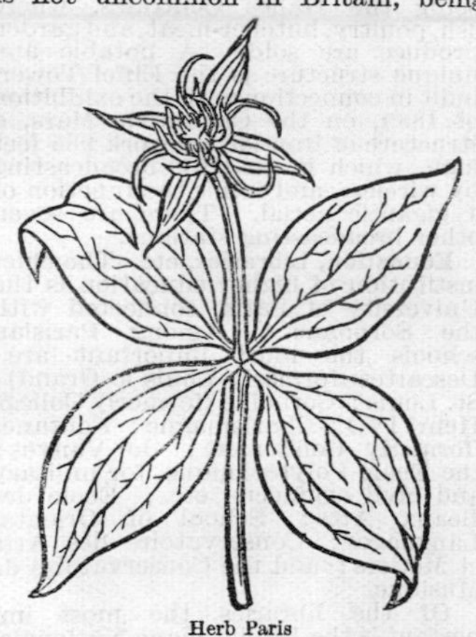

Herb Paris

found in moist, shady woods. It has a simple stem bearing a whorl of four ovate leaves near the summit, and a solitary greenish flower. The fruit is a purplish-black berry and the roots are purgative.

PARIS, TREATIES OF. Of the numerous treaties bearing this designation a few only of the most important can be mentioned here. On 10th Feb., 1763, a treaty of peace was signed between France, Spain, Portugal, and England, in which Canada was ceded to Great Britain. On 6th Feb., 1778, was signed that between France and the United States, in which the independence of the latter country was recognised.

A treaty was signed between Napoleon I. and the Allies, ratified 11th April, 1814, by which Napoleon was deposed and banished to Elba. The treaty for the conclusion of peace between Russia on the one hand, and France, Sardinia, Austria, Turkey, and Great Britain on the other, at the end of the Crimean War, was ratified 30th March, 1856.

The treaty concluded between Germany and the Allies at the end of the European War is officially styled the Treaty of Versailles. It was signed at Versailles, near Paris, on 28th June, 1919.

PARIS, UNIVERSITY OF. One of the oldest and largest universities in the world. It came into existence in the beginning of the thirteenth century, and was long the most famous centre of learning in Europe. It was suppressed in 1793 along with the other French universities, a new system being then introduced. It was reorganised by Napoleon in 1808, and was known as the Facultés de Paris until 1896, when it was differently constituted by the law of 10th July. *See* FRANCE (EDUCATION).

PARIS BASIN. In geology, the great area of Tertiary strata on which Paris is situated. Besides a rich fossil fauna of marine and freshwater mollusca, the remains of mammals are abundant and interesting.

PARISH (Gr. *paroikia*, neighbourhood). A district originally marked out as that belonging to one church, and having its spiritual wants under the particular charge of its own minister.

Parishes have existed in England for more than a thousand years. According to Camden, England was divided into parishes by Archbishop Honorius about the year 630. But the more probable view is that they were gradually formed at various dates between the seventh and the eleventh centuries. They were originally ecclesiastical divisions, but in England especially, the parish became an important subdivision of the country for purposes of local self-government, most of the local rates and taxes being confined within that area, and to a certain extent self-imposed.

The importance of the parish has increased since 1894, when an Act was passed by which a *parish council* was established in all rural parishes having a population of 300 or more; the council—a body of from five to fifteen persons elected by popular vote—having various powers, such as the provision of allotments where demanded, the acquisition of land for recreation purposes, the provision of a public water-supply, rights of way, etc. The term of office of a parish councillor is now three years.

In all rural parishes there also is a *parish meeting* consisting of registered parochial electors, and the meeting exercises a general control over the parish council and its expenditure, and decides whether certain acts regarding public improvements, lighting and watching, burials, etc., are to be adopted.

In Scotland the division into parishes was complete about the beginning of the thirteenth century, and the parish was recognised for certain civil purposes as well as for purposes purely ecclesiastical. Formerly each parish in Scotland had a parish school, and the parochial board managed the poor relief.

By the Local Government (Scotland) Act, 1929, the powers and duties of the parish council were transferred in large burghs to the town council, and in landward areas and small burghs (with the exception of certain functions transferred to district councils) to the reconstituted county councils.

Mungo Park

PARK, Mungo. British explorer, born near Selkirk, in Scotland, 1771, died 1806. Educated at Edinburgh for the medical profession, he received an appointment as assistant-surgeon on board an East Indiaman and made a voyage to India. Returning to England in 1793, he was engaged by the African Society to trace the course of the Niger. He reached the Gambia at the end of 1795, and, advancing north-eastward, arrived at the Niger near Segu. After exploring part of the course of the river he returned home, and published his *Travels in the Interior of Africa* in 1799.

He settled at Peebles as a country doctor, but in 1805 accepted command of a Government expedition to the Niger. Having advanced from Pisania on the Gambia to Sansanding on the Niger, he built a boat at the latter place, with the intention of following the Niger to the sea. It was afterwards ascertained that the expedition advanced down the river as far as Boussa, where it was attacked by the natives. It is supposed that Mungo Park was drowned in his efforts to escape. *The Journal* of his second expedition as far as the Niger was published in 1815.

PARK. In a legal sense, a large piece of ground enclosed and privileged for wild beasts of chase, by the monarch's grant, or by prescription. The only distinction between a *chace* and a *park* was, that the latter was enclosed, whereas a chace was always open. The term now commonly means a considerable piece of ornamental ground connected with a gentleman's residence; or an enclosed piece of public ground devoted to recreation, often in or near a large town.

PARKER, Sir Gilbert. British novelist, born in Canada, 23rd Nov., 1862; he was educated at Trinity College, Toronto. After travelling extensively he organised the first Imperial Universities Conference in London, 1903. He was M.P. for Gravesend from 1900-18, was knighted in 1902, and created a baronet in 1915. He was Chairman of S. African Association for nine years, and took charge of American Publicity in the Great War. His writings include poems, plays, and novels, the last-named dealing largely with French-Canadian life. He also wrote a *History of Old Quebec* in 1903. A recent publication is *The Promised Land* (1928). He died 6th Sept., 1932.

PARKER, Sir Hyde. British sailor, born in 1714; entered the navy about 1738, fought against the French and Spaniards, and became vice-admiral. In 1781 he engaged a Dutch fleet off the Dogger Bank without definite result. In 1782 he was lost on his way to take command in the East Indies.

PARKER, Sir Hyde. British sailor, son of the preceding, born 1739, died 1807; distinguished himself in the American and the French War, and in 1801 commanded the fleet which was sent to the Baltic to break up the northern coalition, when Nelson so distinguished himself.

PARKER, Joseph. Nonconformist preacher and author, born at Hexham-on-Tyne in 1830, and died in 1902. In 1853 he became minister of an Independent or Congregational church at Banbury, and five years later removed to Manchester as pastor of Cavendish Chapel. This post he held till his appointment in 1869 to the Poultry Chapel in Holborn, London, which was replaced in 1874 by the City Temple.

He was for many years one of the most popular of metropolitan preachers, and was the author of various religious works. His most important literary undertaking was his *People's Bible*, a series of discourses forming a pastoral commentary (25 vols., 1885-95). In 1899 he issued his autobiography, under the title *A Preacher's Life*.

PARKER, Matthew. Archbishop of Canterbury, born at Norwich 1504, died 1575. He was the son of a cloth-presser, was educated at Corpus Christi College, Cambridge, and ordained in 1527. In 1535 he became chaplain to Anne Boleyn, in 1537 to Henry VIII., and in 1544 he was appointed master of Corpus Christi College, Cambridge, and elected vice-chancellor of that university the following year. When Queen Mary succeeded to the throne, Parker was deprived of his offices, and remained in concealment until the accession of Elizabeth in 1558.

By royal command he was summoned to Lambeth, and appointed Archbishop of Canterbury. It was while he held this office that he had what is known as the Bishops' Bible translated from the text of Cranmer, and published at his own expense. He was the founder of the Antiquarian Society, a collector of manuscripts, which he presented to his college, and editor of the *Chronicles* of Walsingham, Matthew Paris, and Roger of Wendover.

PARKER, Theodore. American divine, son of a Massachusetts farmer, born at Lexington 1810, died at Florence 1860. He studied at Harvard University, and in 1837 was settled as a Unitarian preacher at West Roxbury. Although his doctrine was accounted heterodox, yet such was his eloquence and ability that he soon became famous over New England as a preacher and lecturer.

In 1843 he visited England, France, Italy, and Germany, and settled as a preacher in Boston on his return. He was a prominent advocate of the abolition of slavery. The principal of his published works are: *Occasional Sermons and Speeches* and *Sermons on Theism, Atheism, and the Popular Theology.*

PARKERSBURG. A city of West Virginia, United States, the county seat of Wood county, on the Ohio; and served by the Baltimore & Ohio, the Baltimore & Ohio South-Western, and the Little Kanawha Railways; by electric traction to Marietta, Ohio; and by steamboats to river-ports. It is the seat of an Anglican bishop. There are large deposits of oil, coal, natural gas, and fireclay in the vicinity, and Parkersburg is generally an oil-refining and pottery-manufacturing centre. It was settled in 1789, and became a city in 1903. Pop. 29,623.

PARKES, Sir Henry. Australian statesman, born at Stoneleigh, in Warwickshire, 27th May, 1815; he emigrated at the age of 24 and engaged in journalism at Sydney. His able discussion of public questions led to his being elected in 1854 a member of the Legislative Council. In 1866 he became a member of the ministry in which he subsequently held several offices, becoming Premier of New South Wales in 1872. He was premier five times, and was a warm supporter of Free Trade. He died 27th April, 1896.

PARLIAMENT. Strictly speaking, composed of the Sovereign and the three Estates of the Realm, viz. the Lords Spiritual, the Lords Temporal, and the Commons; but inasmuch as the Sovereign acts only on the advice of the ministers, Parliament, for all practical purposes, is the legislature composed of the House of Lords and the House of Commons. The House of Lords is the more ancient of the two, but the House of Commons, has, by steady evolution, become by far the more important, and has complete control of the nation's purse and power of raising money.

Early History. The germ of the British Parliament is to be traced to the Witenagemot, the general council or assembly of wise men, of early Saxon times. The name of Parliament was first applied to this council in the time of Edward the Confessor, although it was not a representative body.

After the Norman Conquest the Great Council of the Realm, first summoned in 1070, replaced the Witenagemot; it was attended by twelve landed representatives from each county. At first its authority and functions were limited, and in fact became almost nominal. During the reign of Henry II., the first Plantagenet king (1154-89), it was summoned regularly, and in the inclusion of the knights of the shires among the nobles is to be discerned the germ of the Lower House, the Commons.

The year 1215 marks a great step. By Magna Charta the Constitution of the Council was more clearly defined, and its powers over taxation were formally recognised for the first time.

A distinction was also made between the greater and the lesser barons; while the former were to be summoned personally by special writ, the latter were to be called by a general writ addressed to the sheriffs, a system which may be regarded as the beginnings of popular representation. During the eighty years' conflict over the Charter which followed, Simon de Montfort, by summoning to the Parliament of 1265 two citizens from each town, in addition to the nobles and the knights of the shires, laid the actual foundation of the House of Commons.

The term Parliament first appeared in the Statutes of Westminster in 1272. Welsh representatives were added in 1322, and some twenty years later the division took place which developed into the two-chamber system. The official and hereditary elements, i.e. the clergy and the baronage, became an Upper Assembly, while the knights and the burgesses, who met in the old chapel of St. Stephens and elected their first Speaker, Peter de la Mare, in 1377, became known as the Commons. The journals of the two Houses began to be kept and Acts of Parliament printed in 1509.

A long struggle between the Sovereign and Parliament began with the Stewart period; it ended in the Revolution of 1688, which drove James II. into exile and definitely transferred the principal authority from the monarch to the representatives of the people.

Before the end of the seventeenth century, government by party had been introduced by William III. choosing his ministers from that section which was stronger in the Commons, and owing to George I. being ignorant of English and George II. having but an imperfect command of the language, and to the fact, also, that both these kings had little interest in British politics, the Cabinet system, with one of the ministers presiding, became established in the eighteenth century.

Modern Development. The Parliament of Scotland was merged with that of England in 1707, and in 1801 the union with Ireland led to a further enlargement. The House of Commons, however, was a very undemocratic body. Its representation was most unequal; towns like Birmingham and Manchester had no members, and large landowners, members of the House of Lords, owned "pocket boroughs" for which they nominated representatives.

Pitt brought forward a motion for electoral reform in 1785, but it was not until the great Reform Act of 1832 that a change was made. It was rendered imperative by the transformation in English life due to the great growth of industrialism and of the large towns, and to the increase and importance of the middle-classes. The Act of 1832 broke the monopoly of power possessed by the land-owning aristocracy, and altered the centre of gravity in politics by giving the vote to the middle-class. The Reform Act of 1867 extended the franchise, making the town artisan the arbiter, and in 1884 a further Act gave the vote to the unskilled and agricultural labourers.

By this time the power of the Commons had become supreme, but serious differences of opinion arose with the House of Lords, mainly over the question of Home Rule for Ireland (q.v.). This eventually led to the passing, in 1911, of the Parliament Act, which completely changed the relations of the two Houses.

The Act, which the Lords only accepted with the utmost reluctance on the threat of the creation of a large number of Liberal peers to ensure its passing, deprives the House of Lords of its former power of rejecting a Money Bill, and completely ignores the veto of the Upper House by providing that when a Bill is passed in three successive sessions by the Commons and is rejected by the Lords, it nevertheless becomes law.

A further striking advance in democratic government was the passing of the Representation of the People Acts of 1918, which, by granting the franchise to women over the age of thirty, raised the number of electors to more than twenty millions, or nearly half the population, and gave the right to women to sit in the Commons. It also increased the number of members to 707.

Houses of Parliament

House of Lords Reform. At present peeresses in their own right are not entitled to sit in the House of Lords, but all parties are committed to a reform of the Upper House, and a more representative Second Chamber, partly elected or nominated, appears to be in sight. At present membership is confined to a certain number of bishops (including the three archbishops), hereditary and new peers, whose number may be unlimited, and to the Law Lords, who are life peers, and are appointed for the purpose of exercising the judicial functions still held by the House of Lords as the final Court of Appeal. A struggle is certain on the question of the powers of the Second Chamber.

A feature of the House of Commons to-day is the multiplication of parties and the growth of the Labour Party. The Labour Party came into power for the first time in 1924 and held office from January to November of that year. Again in 1929 a Labour Ministry was formed. The result of the 1931 election, however, was an overwhelming majority for the National party, an alliance of Conservatives with a small section of the Labour Party under Ramsay Macdonald.

The first woman to be elected member of Parliament was Countess Markiewicz, and the first to sit in the House of Commons was Lady Astor, who was first elected in 1919. In the Labour Government of 1929 for the first time women held ministerial office. Since 1911 members of the House of Commons have received an annual salary of £400.—BIBLIOGRAPHY: G. B. Smith, *History of the English Parliament*; M. White, *Inner Life of the House of Commons*; J. H. B. Masterman, *The House of Commons: its Place in National History*; A. F. Pollard, *The Evolution of Parliament*; G. L. Dickinson, *The Development of Parliament in the Nineteenth Century*.

PARMA. A province of Emilia, North Italy, drained by affluents of the Po, which forms its northernmost boundary. Area, 1334 sq. miles; pop. 373,695.

PARMA. A city of Emilia, North Italy, capital of the province of Parma and on the river of that name. It is surrounded in part by a line of ramparts and bastions, and though an old town has quite a modern aspect. Among buildings are the cathedral, built between 1058 and 1106; the baptistery, a structure of marble in the Lombard-Romanesque style (1196-1270); the church of La Steccata; the church of San Giovanni which, with the cathedral and other churches and buildings, contains paintings by Correggio and Mazzuoli, who were born here; the ducal palace, now the prefecture; the Palazzo dello Pilotta, comprising the museum of antiquities, picture gallery, and library (containing over 300,000 volumes and 5000 manuscripts); and the university, founded in 1482. Parma was originally an Etruscan town, and became a Roman colony in 183 B.C. The manufactures are of silk, cottons, woollens, felt hats, etc. Pop. 71,271.

PARMA, DUCHY OF. Formerly an independent state of Upper Italy, but since 1860 incorporated in the Kingdom of Italy, and divided into the provinces of Parma and Piacenza. It comprehended the three duchies of Parma proper, Placentia or Piacenza, and Guastalla, and had an area of about 2266 sq. miles. Parma anciently formed part of Gallia, Cispadana, and Liguria. Charlemagne made a present of it to the Pope; but it subsequently became an independent republic, and in the sixteenth century was erected into a duchy which was long ruled by the Farnese dukes.

The victories of the French in Italy in the beginning of last century enabled Napoleon to seize the duchy and attach it to his Kingdom of Italy. After Napoleon's downfall it fell to his widow, the Archduchess Marie Louise, for life, and on her death in 1847 to the Duke of Lucca. The last duke, Robert, was deposed in 1860, and the duchy became part of the Kingdom of Italy.

PARMEN'IDES (-dēz). Greek philosopher, head of the Eleatic school, native of Elea, in Italy, and flourished about the middle of the fifth century B.C. In 450 he went to Athens, accompanied by his pupil Zeno, and there became acquainted, according to Plato, with Socrates. Like Xenophanes he developed his philosophy in a didactic poem *On Nature*, of which about 160 lines are still extant. One part of this poem dealt with what *is* or "Truth," and the second part with what only *appears* or "Opinion."

PARMOOR, Baron. English politician. Charles Alfred Cripps was born 3rd Oct., 1852, and educated at Winchester and New College, Oxford. Called to the Bar in 1877, he became a Q.C. in 1890, and made a great reputation as an ecclesiastical lawyer. He was elected M.P. for the Stroud Division of Gloucestershire in 1895, representing that constituency until 1900. Later he represented Stretford, Lancs., and Wycombe Division of Bucks. He was made a K.C.V.O. in 1908 and elevated to the peerage in 1914. Specially appointed a judicial member of the Privy Council in 1914, he became Lord President of the Council in the Socialist Ministry of 1924, and held this post again from 1929-31. He has written on *Principles of Compensation* and *The Laws of Church and Clergy*.

PARNAHYBA (pár-nà-ē'bà). A town and river of Brazil. The river rises in the north-east of the province of Bahia, flows north-east, forms the boundary between the provinces of Piauhy and Maranhão, and falls into the Atlantic below Parnahyba; total course, about 750 miles. The port of Parnahyba admits only small vessels, but has an enormous export of hides, tobacco, cotton, and other produce of Piauhy state. Pop. of town, 15,000.

PARNASSIANS. A school of French poets, deriving its name from the *Parnasse Contemporain*, a collection of poems published in 1866. Another collection appeared in 1869 and in 1876. The ideal of the Parnassians was "L'Art pour l'art" (Art for Art's sake), a poetic dogma formulated by Théophile Gautier, to which his friend Baudelaire (1821-67) adhered. In 1866 a group of poets in favour of this doctrine foregathered in the house of Leconte de Lisle and composed verses, wherein art was supposed to be cultivated for art's sake, and where personal feeling and anything of a didactic nature was avoided.

An offshoot of the Romantic school, the Parnassians aimed at the achievement of perfection in form and thought. To the Parnassians belonged Catulle Mendès, Armand Silvestre, François Coppée, and Sully Prudhomme.

PARNAS'SUS, or LIAKU'RA. A mountain of Greece, situated in Phocis, 65 miles north-west of Athens. It has two prominent peaks, one of which was dedicated to the worship of Bacchus, and the other to Apollo and the Muses, while on its southern slope was situated Delphi and the Castalian fount. Its height is 8068 feet, and a magnificent view is obtained from its top.

PARNELL, Charles Stewart. Irish Nationalist, born at his father's estate of Avondale, County Wicklow, Ireland, in 1846, died 6th Oct., 1891. He was connected on his father's side with a family that originally belonged to Congleton, Cheshire, and whose members included Parnell the poet, and Sir John Parnell, Chancellor of the Exchequer in Grattan's Parliament; while his mother was the daughter of Commodore Stewart of the United States navy.

He was educated at Magdalene College, Cambridge; became member of Parliament for Meath in 1875; organised the "active" Home Rule party, and developed its obstruction tactics; and in 1879 formally adopted the policy of the newly formed Land League, was an active member of it, and was chosen president of the organisation. In 1880 he was returned for the City of Cork, and was chosen as leader of the Irish party. In the session of 1881 he opposed the Crimes Act and the Land Act; was arrested (13th Oct.) under the terms of the former, along with other members of his party; and was lodged in Kilmainham Jail, from whence he was not released until the following May.

In 1883 he was the recipient of a large money testimonial (chiefly collected in America), and in this year was active in organising the newly formed National League. At the general election of 1885 he was re-elected for Cork, and next year he and his followers supported the Home Rule proposals introduced by Gladstone, while he also brought in a Bill for the relief of Irish tenants that was rejected.

In 1887 he and other members of his party were accused by *The Times* newspaper of complicity with

Charles Parnell

the crimes and outrages committed in Ireland. To investigate this charge a Commission of three judges was appointed by the Government in 1888, with the result that Parnell was acquitted of all the graver charges.

Soon afterwards, however, Parnell was implicated in a divorce scandal. He figured as the co-respondent in an action for divorce brought by Captain O'Shea. In Nov., 1890, the divorce was granted, and Parnell condemned to pay the costs. Gladstone now demanded his retirement from the leadership, and he was denounced by the Irish priesthood. Parnell struggled desperately for his position, but his health broke down, and he died suddenly a year later.—BIBLIOGRAPHY: R. B. O'Brien, *Life of Charles Stewart Parnell*; Viscount Bryce, *Studies in Contemporary Biography*; K. O'Shea, *Charles Stewart*

Parnell: his Love Story and Political Life.

PARODY. An imitation of a work more or less closely modelled on the original, but so turned as to produce a ridiculous effect. According to the statement of Aristotle in his *Poetics*, the inventor of the parody was one Hegemon of Thasos, who wrote a burlesque *War of the Giants*. Parody, however, is probably far older than this; it is as old as art itself. Hipponax (q.v.) was one of the earliest parodists, and the *Batrachomyomachia*, or Battle of the Frogs and Mice, which dates back to the fifth century B.C., is an amusing though scarcely a brilliant parody of Homer.

The parodies written by Aristophanes are unsurpassable. In the *Acharnians*, the *Thesmophoriazusæ*, and the *Frogs* he has parodied Euripides with unerring skill; nor does the last-mentioned play spare Æschylus, though it treats him rather less irreverently. In the hands of Aristophanes the parody becomes not merely an amusing thing, but a vehicle for criticism of the wisest and wittiest kind.

Among later Greek writers, Herodas in the second of his *Mimes* caught the exact style of some of the Attic orators, especially that of Hyperides. The heavier-handed Romans did not excel in parody; but there is some to be found in the *Satires* of Persius, and we possess a somewhat puerile parody of Catullus's poem on his yacht, said to be the work of Virgil.

The earliest of great English poets is also the earliest English parodist. Chaucer's *Tale of Sir Thopas* is a first-rate parody of the early metrical romance, and is, in fact, a penetrating criticism upon the literary value of such compositions. Shakespeare did not think parody beneath his notice; witness the First Player's speech in *Hamlet*, ii. 2, which parodies the older school of tragedy. Ben Jonson delighted in the parody, and travestied Daniel and Marston with much success. His parody of Wither's well-known poem *Shall I wasting in despair* is too much a mere verbal echo.

Parody took a new lease of life on the appearance of John Philips's *The Splendid Shilling* (1701), which applied the grandeur of Miltonic diction to a ludicrously mean subject. I. H. Browne's *A Pipe of Tobacco* (1736) contained clever parodies of Young, Thomson, Cibber, and others.

John Hookham Frere and George Canning contributed many singularly happy parodies to the *Anti-Jacobin* (1797). Southey was often the object of their attentions; but *The Loves of the Triangles* is a faithful parody of Erasmus Darwin's *Loves of the Plants*. The *Rejected Addresses* (1812) of the brothers Horace and James Smith contains many brilliant parodies. Scott, on reading the parody of himself, exclaimed, "I certainly must have written this myself, although I forget upon what occasion."

"Lewis Carroll" wrote parodies so good as to eclipse entirely the originals. Many who are familiar with Alice's version of *You are old, Father William*, have never heard of Southey's poem *The Old Man's Comforts and how he gained them*. Dr. Watts is treated with equal lack of respect. To parody a bombastic or even a dignified poem is comparatively easy; it is a much harder task to parody a piece of light or comic verse. This has been done with great cleverness by A. C. Hilton, whose *The Vulture and the Husbandman* is as good as *The Walrus and the Carpenter*, and whose *Heathen Pass-ee* is if anything better than Bret Harte's *Heathen Chinee*.

The king of modern parodists is C. S. Calverley. His profound classical scholarship helped him to perfection in his art. His translations into Greek and Latin verse may with all possible respect be called parodies of the Greek and Latin poets. His *Carmen Sæculare*, an astounding piece of Latinity, is a more self-conscious parody of the ancients. His parodies of Martin Tupper and Jean Ingelow and, above all, of Browning can be equalled only by the Euripidean parodies in Aristophanes. J. K. Stephen, an acknowledged follower of Calverley, is sometimes almost as good. His sonnet to Wordsworth contains a just criticism on the dual nature of the work of that poet, and his parodies of Browning and Walt Whitman are felicitous. Tennyson laid himself open to the attacks of parodists, which he did not relish; Calverley travestied him, and Swinburne too was wicked enough to write a poem entitled *The Higher Pantheism in a Nutshell*, which ended with the line:

> Fiddle, we know, is diddle; and diddle, we take it, is dee.

W. S. Gilbert in his *Princess Ida* made a "respectful operatic perversion" of *The Princess*. Swinburne excelled as a parodist, and did not spare even himself. His *Nephelidia* is a merciless piece of self-criticism. Among more recent parodists the outstanding names are those of Sir Owen Seaman, J. C. Squire, and E. V. Knox. Seaman's

works include *Cap and Bells*, *A Harvest of Chaff*, and *Interludes of an Editor* (1929), besides many more in which his skill as a parodist is displayed. J. C. Squire published *Collected Parodies* in 1921, and in 1928 *Apes and Parrots*. E. V. Knox's *Parodies Regained* and *Fiction As She Is Wrote* are examples of this form of humour.

The art of the parodist is not an easy one. Parodies of tedious authors tend to be as tedious as the original, and sometimes the unconscious humour of the original is greater than the conscious fun of the parody. Wordsworth's *Peter Bell* is more amusing than the parodies of Reynolds and Shelley, who had not "a kind of miraculous gift to make it absurder than it was." The quality which chiefly renders a poem liable to parody is insincerity. A good parody is not a mere verbal echo; it is a form of criticism, and a means of exposing falsities in art.—BIBLIOGRAPHY: W. Jerrold and R. M. Leonard, *A Century of Parody and Imitation*; W. Hamilton, *Parodies of the Works of English and American Authors*; A. Symons, *A Book of Parodies*.

PA'ROS. A mountainous island in the Ægean Sea, belonging to Greece. It is one of the Cyclades, 4½ miles west of Naxos; length, 13 miles; breadth, 10 miles. Its marble has been famous from ancient times, and is the material of which some of the most celebrated pieces of statuary are composed. The Arundel marbles, now in the British Museum, were brought to England from Paros in 1667. Paros was the birthplace of the poet Archilochus and the painter Polygnotus. Parikia, a seaport on the north-west coast, is the chief village; pop. 2500. Area, 96 sq. miles; pop. of island, 7800.

PARO'TID GLAND. In anatomy, one of the salivary glands, there being two parotids, one on either side of the face, immediately in front of the external ear, and communicating with the mouth by a duct.

PAROTI'TIS. Inflammation of the parotid gland, situated at the back of the cheek between the angle of the jaw and the ear. On account of the tightness of the structures around, any inflammation of the gland is especially painful, owing to the tension produced. Epidemic parotitis is mumps (q.v.).

PARR, Samuel. English scholar, born 1747, died 1825. He was educated at Harrow and Cambridge; taught successively in the grammar schools of Stanhope, Colchester, and Norwich; and in 1783 became perpetual curate of Hatton, in Warwickshire. Here he engaged in literature, and became noted among his contemporaries as a classic purist and bitter polemic.

His writings are quite impossible to read nowadays. He was a good though somewhat narrow scholar of the old school; but his reputation was largely due to the Whig party, which set him up as a rival to the Tory Dr. Johnson, a man of much greater gifts.

PARR, Thomas. Better known as *Old Parr*. He was born, it is said, in 1483 at Winnington, Shropshire, and died in 1635, he being then in his 152nd year. A metrical account of his career was published in 1635 by John Taylor the "water poet," and he was buried in Westminster Abbey, where a monument records his longevity. His age, however, has been disputed, and doubtless he was not nearly so old as represented.

PARR. A small fish common in the rivers of England and Scotland, at one time believed to be a distinct species of the genus Salmo, but now

Parr (*Salmo salar*)

almost universally regarded as the young of the salmon for the first two years of life, during which they live and feed in fresh water. The term is also applied to the young of any of the Salmonidæ.

PARROT. A name common to birds of the family Psittacidæ, of the order Cuculiformes, which also includes cuckoos and plantain-eaters. The bill is hooked and rounded on all sides, and is much used in climbing. The tarsi are generally short and strong, the toes being arranged two forwards and two backwards. The tongue, unlike that of most other birds, is soft and fleshy throughout its whole extent. The wings are of moderate size, but the tail is often elongated, and in some cases assists in climbing. The plumage is generally brilliant.

Parrots breed in hollow trees, and subsist on fruits and seeds. Several species can not only imitate the various tones of the human voice, but also exercise in some cases actual conversational powers. Some live to a great age, instances being known of these birds reaching seventy and even ninety years.

The species are numerous, and are

known under the various names of parrots, parakeets, macaws, lorikeets, lories, and cockatoos (see these articles), the name parrot, when used distinctively, being generally applied to species of some size, that have a strongly hooked upper mandible and a tail short or of medium length.

They are natives of both tropical and subtropical regions, and even extend northwards into the United States, and south to the Straits of

Parrots

1, Grey parrot (*Psittăcus erythăcus*). 2, Lorikeet (*Trichoglossus Novæ-Hollandiæ*). 3, Great black cockatoo (*Microglossus aterrimus*). 4, Grass-parakeet (*Neophema pulchella*).

Magellan, New Zealand, and Tasmania. The best-known species is the Grey Parrot (*Psittăcus erythăcus*) of Western Africa, which can be most easily trained to talk. The Green Parrots (Chrysōtis) are also common as domestic pets, being brought from the tropical regions of South America. The Carolina parrot (*Conūrus carolinensis*) is found in the United States, and is gregarious in its habits.

PARROT-FISH. The popular name of spiny-finned fishes included in Scarus and allied genera, family Scaridæ, remarkable for the beak-like plates into which the teeth of either jaw are united, and for their brilliancy of colour, from one or other of which circumstances they have received their popular name. They feed on vegetable matter, corals, and molluscs. Most of the species are tropical, abounding in the neighbourhood of coral-reefs, but one, *S. cretensis*, the *scarus* of the ancients, and esteemed by them the most delicate of all fishes, is found in the Mediterranean.

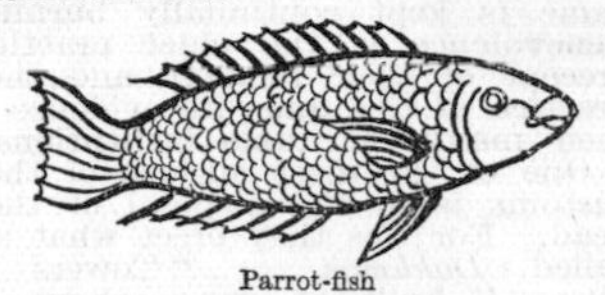

Parrot-fish

PARRY, Sir Charles Hubert. English composer, born at Bournemouth, 27th Feb., 1848; he was educated at Eton and Exeter College, Oxford. He obtained his Mus.Bac. at age of 18, Mus.D., Cambridge 1883, Oxford 1884, Dublin 1891, and was knighted 1898. He became first professor and later principal of the Royal College of Music, Choragus of Oxford University 1883, and Professor of Music in 1900. His works include concertos, symphonies, and other compositions. He also wrote on music in *Grove's Dictionary*, and his *Studies of Great Composers* and *The Evolution of the Art of Music* are recognised classics of musical literature. He died 7th Oct., 1918.

PARRY, Sir William Edward. British explorer, born at Bath 1790, died 1855. He joined the navy in 1803, became lieutenant in 1810, took part in the successful expedition up the Connecticut River in 1813, and continued on the North American station till 1817.

In the following year he was appointed commander of the *Alexander* in an expedition to the Arctic regions under Sir John Ross, and during the succeeding nine years he commanded various expeditions on his own account in efforts to find a north-west passage and to reach the north pole. He afterwards filled various Government situations, became Rear-admiral of the White, lieutenant-governor of Greenwich Hospital, and received the honour of knighthood. His works include: *Voyages for the North-West Passage* and *Narrative of an Attempt to reach the North Pole in Boats.*

PARSIS, or PARSEES'. The name given in India to the fire-worshipping followers of Zoroaster, chiefly settled in Bombay, Surat, etc., where they are amongst the most successful merchants. After the conquest of Persia by Islam in the eight century, many Zoroastrians left the country to gain greater religious liberty, and settled in India.

They have a great reverence for fire in all its forms, since they find in it the symbol of the good deity Ahurâ-Mazda (Ormuzd). To this divinity they dedicated "fire-temples," on whose altar the sacred flame is kept continually burning. Benevolence is the chief practical precept of their religion, and their practice of this finds its evidence in their many charitable institutions.

One of the most curious of their customs is in the disposal of their dead. For this they erect what are called *Dakhmas*, or "Towers of Silence," built of stone, about 25 feet high, and with a small door to admit the corpse. Inside is a large pit with a raised circular platform round it on which the body is exposed that it may be denuded of flesh by vultures, after which the bones drop through an iron grating into the pit below. In this observance they strictly adhere to the precepts of the *Avesta*. The number of Parsees in India in 1921 was over 100,000.—Cf. J. J. Modi, *The Religious System of the Parsis*.

PARSLEY. A plant of the nat. ord. Umbelliferæ, one species of which, the common parsley (*Petroselīnum satīvum*), is a well-known garden vegetable, used for communicating an aromatic and agreeable flavour to soups and other dishes. It is a native of Sardinia, introduced into Britain about the middle of the sixteenth century. A variety with curled leaflets is generally preferred to that with plain leaflets, as being finer flavoured. Hamburg parsley is a variety with a large white root shaped like a carrot, for which it is cultivated.

PARSNIP. A plant of the genus Pastinăca, nat. ord. Umbelliferæ, the *P. satīva* (common or garden parsnip), of which there are many varieties. It is a tall, erect plant, with pinnate leaves and bright-yellow flowers, common throughout England and in most parts of Europe, and much cultivated for its roots, which have been used as an esculent from a very early period. The plants are usually sown in the spring, and the roots, which are at their best in September, are of a sweetish, slightly aromatic taste. They are also cultivated as food for the use of cattle.

PARSON. In English ecclesiastical law, the rector or incumbent of a parish; also, in a wider sense, any one that has a parochial charge or cure of souls. Four requisites are necessary to constitute a parson, viz. holy orders, presentation, institution, and induction. His duties consist chiefly of performing divine service and administering the sacraments.

PARSONS, Sir Charles Algernon. British engineer and inventor of the steam turbine, born 13th June, 1854, the fourth son of the third Earl of Rosse; he was educated privately and at St. John's College, Cambridge. He founded the firm of C. A. Parsons & Co., Engineers, Heaton, Newcastle-on-Tyne, and was also chairman of the Parsons Marine Steam Turbine Co., Ltd., and chairman of Rosse, Ltd., Optical Works, Clapham Common. He was created K.C.B. 1911, and given the O.M. 1927. He was president of the Institute of Physics, British Association, and North-East Coast Institution of Engineers and Shipbuilders. He died 12th Feb., 1931.

PARTABGARH. A native state of Rájputána, India. The inhabitants are mainly Bhils. Partabgarh, which is connected with Mandasor (20 miles) on the Rájputána Railway, is the capital. State area, 886 sq. miles; pop. (state), 76,539; (town), 9819.—Partabgarh is also a district in the Fyzabad division of the United Provinces; served by a branch of the Oudh & Rohilkand Railway. Bela is the capital. Area, 1442 sq. miles; pop. (district), 900,000.

PARTHENOGEN'ESIS. In botany, an aberrant mode of reproduction, in which an ovum gives rise to an embryo without previous fertilisation; it occurs in dandelion, hawkweeds, lady's mantles, in some ferns, and in *Chara crinita*, but is somewhat rare in the vegetable kingdom. It is a special form of the more general phenomenon of *apogamy*, which includes all cases of aberrant propagation involving the absence of sexual fusion where this should normally occur.

PARTHENOGEN'ESIS (Gr. *parthenos*, a virgin; *genesis*, birth). In zoology, a term applied to the production of new individuals from virgin females by means of unfertilised ova. We find several examples of this peculiar phenomenon among insects.

The most notable are the aphides or plant-lice, whose fertilised ova, deposited in the autumn, lie without apparent development throughout the winter, and in the following spring produce modified females only. These females, without sexual connection, give birth to a second generation like to themselves, and this form of reproduction is indefinitely repeated. In the succeeding autumn, however, male insects appear in the brood, and the ova are again fertilised. The phenomenon is known as *heterogamy*.

Another case of parthenogenesis is found in the queen-bee. The eggs which produce neuters or females are impregnated in the usual way, but the eggs which produce the males are not fertilised. Further examples are afforded by flukes, and some of the smaller Crustacea.

PAR'THENON (Gr., from *parthenos*, a virgin, i.e. Athena). A celebrated Grecian temple of Athena, on the Acropolis of Athens, one of the finest monuments of ancient architecture. It is built of marble, in the Doric style, and had originally 8 columns on each of the two fronts, with 17 columns on the sides, or 46 in all, of which 32 are still standing; length, 228 feet; breadth, 101 feet; and height to the apex of the pediments, 64 feet; height of columns, 34 feet 3 inches. The pediments were filled with large statues, the metopes adorned with sculptures in relief.

After serving as a Christian church and as a mosque, it was rendered useless for any such purpose in 1687 by the explosion of a quantity of gunpowder which the Turks had placed in it during the siege of Athens by the Venetians. Though the more precious pieces of sculpture have been dispersed among various European collections (*see* ELGIN MARBLES), the Parthenon still bears an imposing aspect.—Cf. A. S. Murray, *The Sculptures of the Parthenon*.

PARTHENOPE'AN REPUBLIC. The name given to the state into which the Kingdom of Naples was transformed by the French Republicans. After the flight of Ferdinand IV., King of the Two Sicilies, the republic was proclaimed on 23rd Jan., 1799, by orders of the Directory. The name was chosen because in the earliest times the city of Naples was called Parthenope. The republic existed only for five months, for on the 13th June of the same year Cardinal Ruffo, at the head of a mixed body of troops, took possession of Naples, and the republic terminated.

PARTHIA. In the widest sense, Parthia was the Parthian Empire, lying between the Euphrates, the Oxus, the Caspian Sea, and the Arabian Sea. In the narrowest sense, Parthia was the small country formerly inhabited by the Parthians, and situated in the north-western part of the modern Persian province of Khorasan.

The Parthians were of Scythian origin, fought only on horseback, and were celebrated for their skill in archery. They were subject successively to Persians, Macedonians, and Syrians, and they resisted the Romans with various fortune. The Parthian dynasty, founded by Arsaces (256 B.C.), was succeeded by the Sassanidæ, the latter being founded by Artaxerxes (A.D. 214), a Persian, who conquered all Central Asia. These again were followed by the conquering Mahommedans. *See* PERSIA.

PARTICK (ancient **Perdyc**). A district of Glasgow, Scotland, but formerly a separate municipal and police burgh of the parish of Govan, Lanarkshire, separated from Glasgow by the Kelvin. It is an industrial region, and was absorbed by Glasgow in 1912. The flour-mills (the Bunhouse Mills) are supposed to have been presented to the bakers of Glasgow by the Regent Murray as a reward for supplying him with bread at the battle of Langside (1568). Partick is of great antiquity, and had a bishop's palace. Pop. (1931), 52,271.

PARTNERSHIP. The association of two or more persons for the purpose of undertaking and prosecuting conjointly any business, occupation, or calling; or a voluntary contract, by words or writing, between two or more persons, for joining together their money, goods, labour, skill, or all or any of them, upon an agreement that the gain or loss shall be divided in certain proportions amongst them, depending upon the amount of money, capital, stock, etc., furnished by each partner.

Partnership may be constituted by certain acts connected with the undertaking apart from any deed or oral contract. The duration of the partnership may be limited by the contract or agreement, or it may be left indefinite, subject to dissolution by mutual consent.

The members of a partnership are called *nominal* when they have not any actual interest in the trade or business, or its profits; but, by allowing their names to be used, hold themselves out to the world as apparently having an interest; *dormant* or *sleeping* when they are merely passive in the firm, in contradistinction to those who are active and conduct the business as principals, and are known as *ostensible* partners. There are now also limited partners.

A partnership may be engaged in a particular branch of business, apart from business in which any one partner may embark, but such reservation must be specified in the deed of contract. Each member of a partnership is liable, jointly with the other members, for the debts of the firm contracted during his partnership. A nominal partner may also be liable to anyone who contracts with the partnership on the faith of his name. Each partner is the agent of the partnership, and must account to it for any benefit derived from the use of its property or business connection without the consent of his partners. When the partners in a firm exceed ten where the partnership is for banking purposes, and twenty in other cases, the partnership must be registered as a joint-stock company—with or without limited liability.

The law of partnership in England, Scotland, and Ireland was consolidated by an Act of 1890, which did not include joint-stock companies. In Scots law, the partnership is treated as a distinct person. Each partner may sue the firm, and the firm may be made bankrupt without any of the partners being sequestrated. The partners are, however, liable jointly and severally to creditors in payment of its debts. *See* LIMITED LIABILITY COMPANIES.

PARTRIDGE, Sir Bernard. English artist, born in London 11th Oct., 1861, son of Professor Richard Partridge, F.R.S., president of Royal College of Surgeons. He was educated at Stonyhurst College, and worked from 1880-84 in stained glass designing and decorative painting, subsequently in book and press illustration. He joined the staff of *Punch* in 1891, later becoming its chief cartoonist, and was knighted in 1925.

Partridge

PARTRIDGE. A well-known game-bird of the pheasant family (Phasianidæ). The common partridge (*Perdix cinerea*) is the most plentiful of all game-birds in Britain, and occurs in nearly all parts of Europe, in North Africa, and in some parts of Western Asia. The wings and tail are short, the tarsi as well as the toes naked, and the tarsi not spurred. The greater part of the plumage is ash-grey finely varied with brown and black. They feed on grain and other seeds, insects and their larvæ and pupæ, and are chiefly found in cultivated grounds.

Besides this species there are the red-legged French, or Guernsey, partridge (*Caccabis rufa*), which may now be found in considerable numbers in different parts of England; the Greek partridge (*C. saxatilis*), the African partridge, the Arabian partridge, the Indian partridge. The name partridge is loosely applied in the United States to several North American species of the genus Ortyx or quails, and to some other birds.

PARTRIDGE-BERRY. A North American plant of the heath family, *Gaultheria procumbens*, also called winter-green. It and *G. shallon*, both with edible berries, are hardy in Britain. Also a North American shrub, *Mitchella repens*, a pretty little trailing plant, with white fragrant flowers and scarlet berries, nat. ord. Rubiaceæ.

PARTRIDGE-WOOD. A very pretty hardwood obtained from the West Indies and Brazil, and much esteemed for cabinet-work. It is generally of a reddish colour, in various shades from light to dark, the shades being mingled in thin streaks. It is said to be yielded by a leguminous tree, *Andira inermis*, and other South American and West Indian trees.

PARTY-WALL. The wall that separates two houses from one another. *Prima facie* such a wall, together with the land upon which it stands, belongs equally to the landlords of the two tenements, who are tenants in common, and are both liable to maintain it.

PASCAL, Blaise. French philosopher, mathematician, and theologian, born at Clermont, in Auvergne, 1623, died 1662. In early youth he showed a decided inclination for geometry, and so rapid was his advance that while yet in his sixteenth year he wrote a treatise on conic sections, which received the astonished commendation of Descartes. His studies in languages, logic, physics, and philosophy were pursued with such assiduity that his health was irrecoverably gone in his eighteenth year. In 1647 he invented a calculating machine, and about the same time he made several discoveries concerning the equilibrium of fluids, the weight of the atmosphere, etc.

He now came under the influence of the Jansenists—Arnauld and others—and from 1654 he lived much at the monastery of Port Royal, and partly accepted its rigorous rule, though he never actually became a solitaire. He afterwards retired to a country estate, and finally returned to Paris, where he closed a life of almost unbroken ill-health.

About 1655 he wrote, in defence of his Jansenist friend Arnauld, his famous *Provincial Letters* (*Lettres écrites par Louis de Montalte à un provincial de ses amis*). Pascal's *Provinciales,* or *Lettres,* are rightly considered a model of the didactic epistolary style in French literature. They are a bitter satire upon the lax morality of the Jesuits, and were immensely popular, but brought down censures, both civil and ecclesiastical, upon the author.

His second great work, *Pensées sur la religion et sur quelques autres sujets,* was published posthumously in 1670. It consists of fragments of an unfinished work entitled *Apologie de la religion chrétienne,* and has exercised a considerable influence upon theology.—BIBLIOGRAPHY: J. L. Bertrand, *Blaise Pascal*; H. R. Jordan, *Blaise Pascal: a Study in Religious Psychology*; E. Boutroux, *Pascal*; E. Strowski, *Pascal et son temps.*

PAS-DE-CALAIS. A maritime department of Northern France, forming the principal part of pre-Revolutionary Artois, and embracing also a part of Picardy; area, 2606 sq. miles. Its coast, extending about 80 miles, presents a long tract of low sand-hills, but near Boulogne forms a lofty crumbling cliff. The interior is generally flat; the chief rivers are the Scarpe and the Lys; there is a network of canals tapping the coal-fields.

Arras is the capital; the principal harbours are Boulogne and Calais; other towns are Wimereux, Agincourt, Lens, and St. Omer. The chief mineral is coal. There are numerous iron-foundries, glass-works, potteries, tanneries, bleach-works, mills, and factories of all kinds. It was invaded by the Germans during the European War, and part of it remained in the enemy's possession until the end of 1918. Pop. 1,205,191.

PASHA, or **PACHA** (from the Pers. *pad,* protecting, and *shah,* sovereign). In Turkey, an honorary title once bestowed on princes of the blood, but now conferred upon military commanders of high rank and the governors of provinces. It is superior to that of *bey.* There are three grades, and they used to be distinguished by horse-tails waving from a lance as a distinctive badge. Three horse-tails were allotted to the highest dignitaries; the pashas of two tails were generally the governors of the more important provinces; and the lowest rank, of one tail, was held by minor provincial governors.

PASHT. In Egyptian mythology, a goddess chiefly worshipped in Bubastus, in Lower Egypt, whence her alternative name of *Bubastes.* She was the daughter of the great goddess Isis. She was represented with the head of a cat, the animal sacred to her.

PASQUE FLOWER. The name given to *Anemōne Pulsatilla,* nat. ord. Ranunculaceæ, a plant with purplish flowers found on the continent of Europe, and so named because its petals are frequently used to dye Easter or *pasque* eggs. The flower blossoms in spring, and its leaves when crushed emit an acrid poisonous juice.

PAS'QUINADE. A lampoon, "squib," or piece of satire, usually, but not invariably, affixed to some public place. The term is derived from a statue at Rome named *Pasquino* or *Pasquillus.* Pasquino was a cobbler or schoolmaster of a sarcastic nature who lived in the fifteenth century. When excavating the site of his shop, near the Palace Braschi, a statue of a gladiator was found in 1501, and erected by Cardinal Caraffa. It was named after the sardonic schoolmaster. Poems were attached to it, most of them attacking the Pope and high dignitaries of the Church.

A companion statue, *Marforio,* was found in the forum on the Campus Martius; hence the name. Marforio usually asked the questions and Pasquino gave the answers. Both statues are mentioned by Rabelais (book ii., chap. 7) in a part of his book written about 1532. A collection of pasquinades was published in 1544. The practice of writing pasquinades became less common, but there was a great revival of it about 1590. Thomas Nash (q.v.), writing about 1589, first made Pasquin a favourite pseudonym in England.

PASSAROWITZ. A town of Yugoslavia, in Serbia, near the Morava River, 37 miles E.S.E. of Belgrade. The Treaty of Passarowitz was concluded on 21st July, 1718, by Venice and the Emperor Charles VI. with the Porte. It terminated the war begun in 1714 by the Porte, and in which the Turks gained the Morea in 1715.

PASSAU (ancient **Castra Batava**). A town of Bavaria, at the junction of the Inn and Danube. The principal building is the cathedral of St. Stephen (1665-80). There is an important trade in timber. The ancient fortress of Oberhaus crowns a precipitous wooded height (426 feet) on the left bank of the Danube opposite Passau. Pop. 24,428.

Passau, The Treaty of, was signed in 1552, when Charles V., intimidated by the victories of Maurice of Saxony, was compelled to do justice to the Protestants, and to grant them full toleration for their religion.

PASSCHENDÆLE. A ridge and village in Belgium, province of West Flanders, the scene of severe fighting during the European War. Both ridge and village were captured by the Germans in Oct., 1914, and were ultimately regained by the Belgians four years later. *See* EUROPEAN WAR.

PASSENGER PIGEON. A bird of the Pigeon family, which abounds in America. It is the *Ectopistes migratorius,* and is distinguished from the common pigeon chiefly by its long graduated tail. It is about 15 inches

Passenger Pigeon

in length, with finely tinted plumage, small head, and long wings. The multiplication of these pigeons is so rapid, and their destructive power so great, that they are obliged to migrate from place to place in vast flocks to obtain their food. The larger breeding-places are said to cover a forest area of about 40 sq. miles.

PASSENGERS. In law the railway and other public carriers contract to carry passengers without any negligence on their (the carriers') part. In case of accident it lies on the carrier to show that it was from no fault or negligence on his part, or on the part of his servants, that the accident occurred. Hence all passengers injured (or in case of death their nearest relatives) have a claim for compensation, unless it can be proved that the accident was due to the fault of the passenger, or of someone over whom the carrier had no control, or to inevitable accident.

Passengers by sea are carried subject to the same general law as those by land: the carriers are bound to observe all due precautions to prevent accident or delay. No imigrant ship having more than 50 steerage passengers or more than 300 persons in all on board, and no other foreign-going ship having more than 100 persons on board, can proceed on its voyage without a duly qualified medical practitioner. In the case of imminent danger from tempest or enemies passengers may be called upon by the master or commander of the ship to lend their assistance for the general safety.

PASSFIELD, Baron. Sidney James Webb, born 13th July, 1859. At one time he was a clerk in the lower division of the War Office. A noted economist, he became, in 1912, professor at the London School of Economics. In 1922 he entered Parliament for the Seaham division, Co. Durham. He has been a member of several royal commissions and numerous departmental committees. In the Socialist Ministry of 1924 he was president of the Board of Trade, and in 1929 he became Secretary of State for the Colonies. He is the author of many works on economic and social subjects.

PASSFIELD, Lady. Better known as Beatrice Webb, the daughter of Richard Potter, at one time chairman of the G.W. Railway. She is keenly interested in social and industrial questions, and was a member of the Royal Commission on Poor Law and Unemployment, 1905-9. She is the author of *The Co-operative Movement in Great Britain* and, with her husband, whom she married in 1892, of the *History of Trade Unionism* and other works.

PASSIFLORACEÆ. A natural order of polypetalous dicotyledons, comprising some 300 species, natives of warm countries, mostly tendril-climbers. The principal genus is Passiflōra. *See* PASSION-FLOWER.

PASSING-BELL. The bell that was rung in former times at the hour of a person's death, from the belief that devils lay in wait to afflict the soul the moment when it escaped from the body, and that bells had the power to terrify evil spirits. In the proper sense of the term it has now ceased to be heard, but the tolling of bells at deaths or funerals is still a usage, more particularly as a mark of respect.

PASSION-FLOWER (Passiflōra). A large genus of climbing plants belonging to the nat. ord. Passifloraceæ. They are all tendril-climbers, often scrambling over trees to a considerable length, and in many cases are most beautiful objects, on account of their large, rich, or gaily coloured flowers, which are often succeeded by orange-coloured edible fruits, for

Passion-flower

which indeed they are chiefly valued in the countries where they grow wild.

Passiflōra laurifolia produces the water-lemon of the West Indies, and *P. maliformis* bears the sweet calabash. The name is applied more especially to *P. cœrulĕa,* which is commonly cultivated in England out of doors, and is the one to which the genus owes its name.

PASSIVE RESISTERS. A term applied to those Nonconformists in England and Wales who, being opposed to the Education Acts of 1902 and 1903, refused to pay the education rate, preferring distraint upon their goods to voluntary payment. The movement became widespread, the chief grounds of opposition being the granting of rate-aid to schools giving denominational instruction, and the insufficient representation of the taxpayers in the management of voluntary schools supported out of the rates.

Passive resisters have been prominent on various other occasions in English history, examples being the Nonconformist clergymen at the time of the Restoration, and the Nonjurors. The term passive resistance was also applied to the resistance of the Belgians to the German system of government during the European War.

PAS'SOVER. A feast of the Jews, instituted to commemorate the providential escape of the Hebrews in Egypt, when God, smiting the first-born of the Egyptians, *passed over* the houses of the Israelites, which were marked with the blood of the paschal lamb. It was celebrated on the first full moon of the spring, from the 14th to the 21st of the month Nisan, which was the first month of the sacred year. During the eight days of the feast the Israelites were permitted to eat only unleavened bread, hence the Passover was also called the "feast of unleavened bread." Every householder with his family ate on the first evening a lamb killed by the priest, which was served up without breaking the bones.

The Passover was the principal Jewish festival. Modern critics regard this festival as having originally no connection with Egypt. It was the feast of spring, and had naturally arisen among a pastoral people. The lamb was an offering of thanksgiving for increase of flocks. Passover was observed by Christ on the night before His crucifixion, when He instituted the Eucharist.

PASSPORT. A warrant of protection and authority to travel, granted to persons moving from place to place, by a competent authority. In most states no foreigner is allowed to travel without a passport from his Government, and in all cases the visitor to the continent of Europe is wiser to provide himself with one, if only as a means of identification.

Passports to British subjects are granted at the Passport branch of the Foreign Office, London. The commonest procedure is to apply to a good travel bureau for an application form, fill in the particulars required, sign the form, and have it verified by a justice of the peace, minister of religion, banker, or other qualified person named on the form. Unmounted photographs (2½ by 1½ inches or thereabouts) are required in triplicate, and should be attached to the form.

The completed document should be returned to the travel bureau, accompanied by the necessary fee (5*s.*), and the application will be put through under their guidance. From four to five clear days' notice should be given. A birth-certificate may be required on occasion, and *visas* are required by the consuls of the countries to which it is proposed to proceed. A fee is usually demanded for a *visa.*

PASSY. A western suburb of Paris, in the sixteenth arrondissement and in the neighbourhood of the Bois de Boulogne.

PASTA, Giuditta. Operatic singer, born at Como, near Milan, in 1798, of Jewish parents, died 1865. She appeared at first without success, but in 1819-22 her reputation steadily increased, and up till 1833 she held one of the foremost places on the lyric stage, which she then quitted. She was specially distinguished in the tragic opera; Bellini wrote for her his *Norma* and *Sonnambula*, and she made the rôles of Medea, Desdemona, and Semiramide her own.

PASTE. A composition in which there is just sufficient moisture to soften without liquefying the mass, as the paste made of flour used in cookery. The term is also applied to a highly refractive variety of glass, a composition of pounded rock-crystal melted with alkaline salts, and coloured with metallic oxides: used for making imitation gems. One variety of it is called *Strass*.

PASTEUR (pas-*teur*), **Louis.** French biological chemist and bacteriologist, born at Dôle, Jura, 27th Dec., 1822, died in Paris 28th Sept., 1895. He was educated chiefly at the École Normale, Paris, where in 1847 he took his degree as doctor. The following year he was appointed professor of physics in Strasbourg, where he devoted much research to the subject of fermentation; in 1857 he received the appointment of dean in the Faculty of Sciences, Lille; in 1863 he became professor of geology, chemistry, and physics at the Ecole des Beaux Arts, Paris; and in 1867 professor of chemistry at the Sorbonne. He became a member of the French Academy in 1882.

Louis Pasteur

He was especially successful in proving the part played by microbes in fermentation and decomposition, in introducing a successful treatment of disease in silkworms and cattle, and achieved great success in his efforts to check hydrophobia by means of inoculation. To enable him to deal with this disease under the best conditions a **Pasteur Institute** was opened in Paris on 14th Nov., 1888, where patients are received from all parts of Europe. Pasteur Institutes now exist throughout Europe and in the United States.—Cf. René Valery-Radot, *Life of Pasteur*.

PASTEURISATION. A process named after Pasteur, the eminent French scientist, whereby the temperature of a liquid is raised sufficiently high to kill off susceptible forms of germ-life. The process may be applied to almost any liquid, but is peculiarly adaptable to cow's milk used for human consumption, and about 80 per cent of all milk consumed in the large cities of Great Britain is pasteurised. Milk may not be "sterilised" by pasteurising, and the two terms should not be confused.

Bacteria. One great advantage of pasteurisation lies in the fact that the *tubercle bacilli* it may contain are eliminated. Dr. W. E. Carnegie-Dickson says: "What is known as 'surgical tuberculosis,' i.e. tuberculosis of bones and joints and glands, is mostly due to tubercle bacilli derived from milk. . . . In the Royal Hospital for Sick Children, Edinburgh, operations for tuberculosis constitute some 50 per cent of all operations done, . . . and in the post-mortem room, in 30 per cent of a consecutive series of over 600 autopsies, . . . death was directly due to the tubercle bacillus."

Important experimental work proves that 60 to 90 per cent of all cases of surgical tuberculosis in children treated are due to infection with the bovine bacillus derived from milk or its products, such as butter, cream, and cheese, which have been manufactured from tuberculous milk. Treated in a careless manner, and exposed to infection at every step from the cow to the consumer, milk will undoubtedly become one of the most dangerous food-stuffs known to mankind. Properly pasteurised and cleanly treated, it may be comparatively pure.

Method. There are two systems of pasteurisation: (*a*) *holding* and (*b*) *flash*; and different modifications of these are adopted to fall into line with local requirements and the purpose for which the "milk" or cream is required. Where pasteurised milk is required for human consumption, the object is to eliminate non-sporing[1] organisms without effecting any radical changes in its chemical composition.

a. Holding.—This method is especially favoured by experts for milk or cream intended for sale. Professor Leitch (Glasgow) favours an exposure to 140° F. for thirty minutes, with a reduction of one minute in the time of exposure for every degree above 140° F. In no case, however, should exposure be for less than ten minutes. Jensen and Plattner do not favour temperatures higher than 140° F. but, generally speaking, a temperature of 158° to 160° F., maintained for half an hour, will eliminate most harmful organisms which exist in milk of average purity.

b. Flash.—Where low pasteurising temperatures are adopted, the process is naturally much longer than where temperatures are high, and at between 160° to 180° F. the exposure is only momentary. This method is very suitable for pasteurising cream for butter-making. In Denmark, pasteurisation to a temperature of 80° C. (176° F.) is compulsory in the case of cream for butter-making, and, as at all temperatures over 160° F., a distinctly cooked flavour is imparted to both cream and fresh butter, although in the latter case the flavour disappears after a few days' storage.

During both processes the milk or cream must be agitated continuously, for, when milk is heated, a film of a protective nature is derived from the milk proteids (especially casein) and surrounds the bacteria, retarding, if not entirely preventing, the destruction of non-sporing forms. Thorough agitation is essential to break the film.

Immediately after pasteurisation the milk should be cooled to a reasonably low temperature, preferably under 50° F., and should be kept at that temperature. Cooling as much as heating is an essential part of the process of pasteurisation. Many kinds of machinery are used, but a simple pasteuriser is an ordinary enamelled pail fitted with a lid and agitator, and held in a boiler or pot of water until the exposure to heat shall have been complete.

[1] Certain germs have the power of forming spores, a dormant or resting form which enables a germ to endure adverse conditions without being "killed". In forming spore the protoplasm contracts, and assumes a thick membrane, a spherical or oval body being formed. When the spore-wall is complete the germ-cell or outer membrane is disrupted, and the germ remains in a highly resistant form, ready to resume its functions of fission (multiplication and reproduction) on the return of normal conditions. Under these circumstances the dangers of drinking old pasteurised milk cannot be over-emphasised. When pasteurised, the milk loses the normal lactic microbes (*Streptococcus lacticus*), and only spores will remain to develop into their full normal lives without such warnings as sourness of smell or taste.

Points in Pasteurisation : *Advantages.*—(*a*) Enhanced keeping quality of milk or butter made from pasteurised cream. (*b*) The most harmful non-sporing germs eliminated. (*c*) Food and undesirable taints (including garlic flavour) eliminated. (*d*) Pronounced uniformity both in butter and in milk. (*e*) Pasteurised milk more easily separated by cream separator than raw milk.

Disadvantages.—(*a*) The cream layer is only one-half that of raw milk. (*b*) At high temperatures (much over 160° F.) certain chemical changes occur, i.e. sugar ($C_{12}H_{22}O_{11}$) may be caramelised; viscosity diminished; enzymes weakened and destroyed above 170° F.; digestibility of proteids impaired by partial decomposition; milk appears thin, necessitating thickening with gum-tragacanth or some gelatinous compound; calcium salts and albumen may be precipitated; boiled taste; vitamines entirely destroyed; coagulation if temperature is high enough (i.e. perfectly fresh milk heated at 100° C. for twelve hours, 130° C. for one hour, or 150° C. for three minutes, will coagulate).

BIBLIOGRAPHY: R. H. Leitch, *Butter-making on the Farm* (West of Scotland Agricultural College); Muir and Ritchie, *Bacteriology*; W. E. Carnegie-Dickson, *Bacteriology*; Janet E. Lane-Claypon, *Milk and its Hygienic Relations*.

PASTO. A city of Colombia, South America, capital of the province of Nariño, on an elevated plain (8347 feet altitude) overshadowed by the volcano of Pasto (13,900 feet altitude). It is a bishopric, has a university, and is on the frequented trade routes near the Ecuadorian frontier. There are woollen-factories. Pasto was founded by Pizarro in 1539. Pop. 40,000.

PASTON LETTERS. The correspondence of the Pastons, a family of Norfolk squires, has been, since its first (though incomplete) publication in 1787-9, a most valuable source of English history, and especially of social history, in the fifteenth century. The earliest of the letters was written in 1422 and the latest in 1509, and they relate both to public affairs and to the domestic and business concerns of the Pastons and their patrons, friends, and dependents.

Paston is a village about 20 miles from Norwich, and William Paston (1378-1444), a native of the district, who made money as a lawyer in

London and became a judge, bought land in Paston and in the neighbourhood. He married an heiress, and his son, John Paston (1421-66), was a considerable landowner. He was also a lawyer, and many of the most interesting letters were addressed to him by his wife, who reported the progress of family affairs and the gossip of the time.

The Wars of the Roses imperilled the safety of the Paston property, and in 1459 John Paston was left a large amount of land, including the castle of Caister, by Sir John Fastolf. The will was disputed, not only by legal means, and a petty civil war was waged between the Pastons and the Dukes of Norfolk.

The struggle continued through the lifetime of John Paston and his eldest son, Sir John Paston (1442-79), until in 1474 a compromise was arranged. In the course of these years the castle was taken and re-taken several times. The letters throw a vivid light upon the lawless condition of England in the end of the reign of Henry VI. and the beginning of that of Edward IV.

Sir John Paston was succeeded by his brother, also called John, who died in 1503, shortly before the series of letters closes. The correspondence is most important for about thirty years after 1445, not only for public events, but also for manners and customs.

By some fortunate accident the letters were preserved, and the last descendant of the family, William Paston, second Earl of Yarmouth, sold most of them to Le Neve, an antiquary of the early eighteenth century. After the publication of four volumes in 1787-9 by John Fenn, and a fifth in 1823, the originals were lost, and their authenticity was questioned, but a large number of the originals have been recovered, together with manuscripts not included in the Yarmouth sale. A complete edition was published by the late James Gairdner in 1904.

PASTOR. A genus of birds belonging to the starling family, found in the north of Africa, Syria, and India. The rose-coloured pastor (*P. roseus*) is the only European specimen, and, being a good singer, is a favourite cage-bird.

PASTORAL. A branch of literature which deals, in a more or less direct form, with rustic life. The pastoral is a striking example of how the genius of one man influenced literature for over two thousand years.

Classical. Theocritus, a native of Syracuse, was the originator of pastoral poetry. His poems, which are for the most part very beautiful, have a certain amount of realism in them, and describe something not very different from the life of Sicilian shepherds in the third century B.C. His two successors, Bion and Moschus, are celebrated chiefly for their laments; Bion wrote a *Lament for Adonis* and Moschus a *Lament for Bion.*

Theocritus was imitated and transplanted to Italy by Virgil, a much greater poet and artist, who nevertheless failed to retain some of the charm of the Greek. Virgil's *Eclogues* are the least mature of his poems, but they show many examples of the consummate finish which he could give to his lines. They had great influence upon pastoral poetry, as had his much more mature *Georgics,* which, though not strictly speaking pastorals, are a glorification of rustic life. Calpurnius Siculus and Nemesianus were direct followers of Virgil, and minor poets of some charm, but the influence of the *Eclogues* is seen in the works of many writers of poetry of all kinds.

Renaissance. After the revival of learning the pastoral became an important branch of literature, and it would not be possible to mention all the poets who attempted to write it. In Italy Petrarch and Boccaccio both wrote pastorals; Sannazaro's *Arcadia,* Tasso's *Aminta,* and Guarini's *Pastor Fido* were immensely admired and frequently imitated. Baptista Spagnuoli Mantuanus (mentioned by Shakespeare in *Love's Labour's Lost*) wrote twelve frigid eclogues which won great renown mainly owing to their excellent moral tone.

In France Marot was the chief exponent of the new fashion. The late Greek novelist Longus, who wrote *Daphnis and Chloe,* made the pastoral romance fashionable, and so was responsible indirectly for Sidney's *Arcadia.* In Spain Montemayor and Cervantes both wrote pastorals, though the latter made fun of the whole bucolic convention in *Don Quixote.*

Pastoral poetry in England owed much of its vogue to Spenser, whose *Shepheard's Calender* is one of the greatest English pastorals. The popularity of the pastoral was also due not a little to the book which sixteenth and seventeenth century Englishmen knew and reverenced above all others. The Bible, with its idyllic representation of pastoral life in the Old Testament, and its description of Christ as the Good Shepherd in the New Testament, made the pastoral a more serious form of writing than it would otherwise have been. Moreover, the easy identification of pastor, a shepherd, with pastor in its ecclesiastical sense made the pastoral a convenient form for covert satire upon the Church.

In English Drama. The pastoral invaded English drama at its greatest period. Some foreshadowing of this may be seen in the miracle-play known as the *Wakefield Second Shepherd's Play* (one of the Towneley plays), where the Biblical shepherds have come alive in a pleasing and unexpected fashion. Fletcher's *Faithful Shepherdess* is an imitation of Guarini's masterpiece, and a delightful play.

Ben Jonson's beautiful un-Jonsonian fragment *The Sad Shepherd* is a wonderfully fresh and captivating play, which introduces Robin Hood and his merry men in Sherwood. Randolph's *Amyntas* is a play of some charm, and proves the versatility of its author.

Shakespeare has set the stamp of his genius upon the pastoral in *As You Like It,* and in his final period, when he was "On the Heights" as Dowden so aptly expressed it, he returned to the pastoral in *The Winter's Tale.* In the shepherd scenes of this play the pastoral reaches its greatest height.

In English Poetry. Among writers of pastoral poetry, as distinct from pastoral drama, may be mentioned Drayton, Browne, Wither, Herrick, and Milton. During the Great Rebellion and after the Restoration pastoral poetry became extinct, but it enjoyed a kind of revival in the early eighteenth century. Pope and Ambrose Philips produced highly artificial eclogues, and the former wrote a paper to *The Guardian* (No. 40) in which he expounded, more or less ironically, his views upon pastoral poetry.

Gay's *Shepherd's Week* was originally intended to pour ridicule upon the pastoral, but the author's real poetical gifts were too strong for him, and forced him to write a series of realistic and genuine poems. Ramsay's *Gentle Shepherd* (1725) was the last bucolic drama produced in Britain. The dirge-element, which was so strong a feature in the poems of Bion and Moschus, was anglicised by Milton in *Lycidas,* and has influenced such poems as Shelley's *Adonais* and Arnold's *Thyrsis.*

Except in such poems as these, the pastoral has not survived, save as an element in burlesque. Swift had suggested to Gay that he should write a Newgate pastoral, but Gay wrote instead *The Beggar's Opera.* Samuel Butler the Second wrote a stock-exchange oratorio buffo called *Narcissus,* which is a kind of pastoral. Gilbert's *Iolanthe* introduces Strephon, an Arcadian shepherd, who is a fairy down to the waist, and Phyllis, an Arcadian shepherdess and ward in Chancery.

Except in the hands of the greatest masters, the pastoral has been an artificial and conventional species of literature. It has as a rule been written by town-dwellers for town-dwellers. It is sometimes ridiculous; the pastoral convention was seen at its most absurd when Marie Antoinette played at being a shepherdess in the gardens of Trianon, while outside the French Revolution was coming to a head.

At its worst, however, the pastoral has given us some silly but innocuous verse; at its best it has given us Theocritus, Virgil, *The Winter's Tale,* and *Lycidas.*—BIBLIOGRAPHY: W. W. Greg, *Pastoral Poetry and Pastoral Drama*; E. K. Chambers, *English Pastorals.*

PATA'GIUM. The name applied to the expansion of the skin by means of which bats fly, and such forms as flying squirrels, flying lizards, etc., support themselves in the air, as by a parachute.

PATAGO'NIA. A name which has no political significance, and is applied to the region lying east of the Andes and south of the Rio Negro. Formerly it was applied to the whole portion of South America extending north from the Straits of Magellan. It is divided between Chile and Argentina. The Straits of Magellan separate the mainland from the innumerable islands of Tierra del Fuego. On the straits is the Chilian seaport of Punta Arenas, one of the most southerly towns in the world.

Patagonia east of the Andes consists mainly of vast undulating plains, frequently covered with shingle and broken up by ridges of rock. The vegetation is scanty, except in the region adjoining the Andes, and in many places there are shallow salt-lakes and lagoons. The chief rivers are the Rio Negro, the Chupat, the Rio Desire, and the Rio Chico, all of which have their sources in the Andes and run eastward. There are few, if any, good seaports.

The native Patagonians are nearly extinct. They are a tall, muscular race averaging never less than 6 feet in height, with black hair, thick lips, and skin of a dark-brown colour. They are a nomad race, whose chief occupation is in hunting and cattle-breeding, and are remarkable swimmers. In various parts white settlers have taken up land, and many sheep and cattle are reared even far south. The country was discovered by Magellan in 1520.

PATALIPUTRA. An ancient city

of India, the *Palibothra* of Megasthenes, the Greek historian, Strabo, Pliny, and others. It was the capital of the Nanda dynasty and of the Maurya dynasty, which was founded by Chandragupta, and which succeeded the Nanda as rulers of Magadha.

It was to the court of Chandragupta (Sandracottus) that Megasthenes was accredited as ambassador from Seleucus Nicator about the year 300 B.C. Megasthenes, whose account is preserved by Arrian, says: "The capital city of India is Palibothra, in the confines of the Prasii, near the confluence of the two great rivers Erannoboas and Ganges. Erannoboas is reckoned the third river throughout all India, and is inferior to none but the Indus and the Ganges, into the last of which it discharges its waters."

According to the Vayu-Purana, the city of Kusu-Mapura or Pataliputra was founded by Raja Udayaswa, the grandson of Ajatasatru, the contemporary of Buddha. According to Buddhist tradition, where Buddha crossed the Ganges on his last journey from Rajagriha to Vaisalis, the two ministers of Ajatasatru, King of Magadha, were engaged in building a fort at the village of Patali, as a check upon the Wajji or people of Vriji. Buddha then predicted it would become a great city.

Diodorus attributes the foundation of the city to Heracles, meaning Bala-Rama, the brother of Krishna. Probably, then, the building of the city had been completed by 450 B.C. Eventually it was deserted for Rajagriha or Bihar, and a Chinese missionary who visited the place in A.D. 640 states that Pataliputra was a mass of ruins when he saw it. Dowson was the first to expound the theory of Pataliputra and modern Patna being coextensive. *See* PATNA.

PATCHOU'LI. A perfume obtained from the dried leaves and branches of the *Pogostēmon patchouli*.

PATENT. A privilege from the Crown granted by "letters patent" conveying to the individual or individuals specified therein the sole right to make, use or dispose of some new invention or discovery for a certain limited period, which in the United Kingdom may run to sixteen (formerly fourteen) years or even longer; that is, for a further five, or in exceptional cases ten years more, should the inventor be able to prove that the invention, though of public utility, has been up till that time inadequately remunerative to him.

The Statute of Monopolies, 1623, required that an applicant for a patent should be the first and true inventor of a new manufacture which was not prejudicial to the State or unlawful, e.g. something which might raise prices. The law is now governed by the Patents and Designs Acts, 1907-19, as amended by the Patents and Designs (Convention) Act, 1928, and the Patent Rules, 1920.

Procedure. Patents are obtained directly from the Comptroller General of Patents at the Patent Office, London. The person applying must furnish a provisional specification giving a general account of the nature of the article or invention which he wishes to be patented, and within nine months (which on payment of a fee may be extended by one month), thereafter a complete specification, particularly describing the nature and working of the invention, and containing a statement of claim.

The application and specification are submitted to an examiner connected with the Patent Office, and if he reports that everything is satisfactory and done in due form, the invention properly described, etc., the application is accepted. Otherwise the party may have to make amendments in his application and specification.

Appeal may be made from the Comptroller to a Law Officer of the Crown (the Solicitor-General) who decides the matter. If approved, the specification is printed and published, but the patent is not granted till after two months, within which time any person may oppose the grant on sufficient grounds, e.g. that the invention is not new, that it does not belong to the applicant, etc. Here again, the Law Officer may have to give his decision.

When a complete specification has been presented there is an official investigation of the specifications for British patents for not more than fifty years back to discover whether the invention claim has been anticipated either wholly or in part, which thus serves as a guide to would-be patentees. If such anticipation is proved the applicant has the opportunity to amend his specification within such time as may be prescribed, and failing such amendment, reference to prior specification may be made by the Comptroller in the specification in question by way of notice to the public.

Restriction. In order to prevent the almost entire manufacture abroad of articles patented in the United Kingdom, any person may, not less than three years (1928 Act) after the date of the patent, apply for its revocation on the ground that the patented article or process is manufactured or carried on exclusively or mainly outside the United Kingdom without satisfactory reasons. A person interested may also at any time apply on the ground that the monopoly rights under the patent have been abused.

Fees. The fees for procuring a patent and keeping it in force are spread over the full period of sixteen years. The fees for sealing the patent amount to £1 and at the end of four years renewal fees must be paid every year, such fees amounting to £5 for the fifth year, £6 for the sixth year, and so on, until the sixteenth year when the fee is £16. In default of such payment the patent will lapse. Patents are usually taken out through professional patent agents who have to be registered by the Board of Trade.

Infringement of Rights. When the rights of a patentee are being infringed he can protect them by an action at law, and his suit will be upheld if he can prove that the main elements of his invention have been infringed, but he cannot recover damages from an innocent infringer reasonably unaware of the patent, but the person injured may get an injunction. A patent once granted can be revoked if it can be shown that the patentee is not the inventor.

The patent laws vary considerably in foreign countries, and the British Dominions. Arrangements may be made with the governments of foreign states and British possessions for the mutual protection of inventions. An applicant, his agent, or assignee in such foreign state or British possession is entitled to a patent in the United Kingdom if applied for within twelve months of his application in his own country.

An illustrated official journal of patented inventions, reports of patent cases, decided by courts of law, and printed specifications of all patents are issued by the Patent Office in London, from which the current Rules, Regulations, etc., may be obtained. There is also an extensive patent library and museum open to the public. A patentee may assign his monopoly by deed, in which case the assignee stands in the place of the original patentee or he may grant a licence to make the patented article under the patent for a specified time and on certain conditions.—Cf. Terrell, *Letters Patent for Inventions* (7th edition, 1927).

PATENT MEDICINES. Medicinal preparations made by various individuals, companies, and corporations, and sold by them under distinctive names. The term is nowadays practically synonymous with *proprietary medicines*, for the true patent medicines, whose composition and modes of preparation are described when a patent is being obtained, are for the most part definite chemical substances for use in medicine. Aspirin and antipyrine were at one time patent medicines in this sense.

In the majority of cases the proprietor or inventor of a medicinal preparation does not apply for protection under the patent laws, but registers the name thereof under the trade-mark Acts, for he depends chiefly on advertisements in the press or otherwise to bring his preparation into common use.

As the element of ownership is the chief factor in these cases, they are known as proprietary medicines. These are divisible into two groups, viz. (1) those in which the composition is stated on the package, wrapper, or container, or a reference given to a well-known book of "known, admitted, and approved remedies" recognised by the Board of Customs and Excise; (2) those in which the composition is not stated.

The first group contains a large number of preparations in demand by the public and the medical profession, being in fact ready-made prescriptions, and have only one objection against them, i.e. the "art of prescribing" is apt to suffer by their use. The second group also contains a number of preparations, as purgative pills, in great public demand, to which no serious objection is taken by medical practitioners; but just because they are "secret remedies" serious abuses have crept in.

Medicine stamp duty is payable on all patent or proprietary medicines belonging to group (2) of the foregoing classification. It varies with the selling price, being threepence when that is one shilling or under, sixpence when half a crown or under, and so on, being twice the pre-war duty. In virtue of this duty a licence for the sale of those medicines must be obtained from the Board of Customs and Excise.

PATER, Walter. British essayist and critic, born in London in 1839, died at Oxford in 1894. Educated at King's School, Canterbury, and Queen's College, Oxford, he was elected to a fellowship at Brasenose College, and his life was chiefly spent in retirement at Oxford.

His works are not numerous, but they are all characterised by careful construction, accurate and wide knowledge, and a fastidiously exact, though at times over-elaborated style. They comprise: *The Renais-*

sance: Studies in Art and Literature (1873), a series of detached essays; *Marius the Epicurean: his Sensations and Ideas* (1885); *Imaginary Portraits* (1887); *Appreciations* (1889) (of Wordsworth, Coleridge, Lamb, Sir Thomas Browne, Rossetti, etc.), with an *Essay on Style*; and *Plato and Platonism*, a series of lectures (1893).

Walter Pater

Besides these there were published posthumously *Greek Studies* (1895); *Miscellaneous Studies* (1895); and *Gaston de Latour*, an unfinished romance (1896).

PAT'ERA. A shallow, circular, saucer-like vessel used by the Greeks and Romans in their sacrifices and libations. The name is applied in

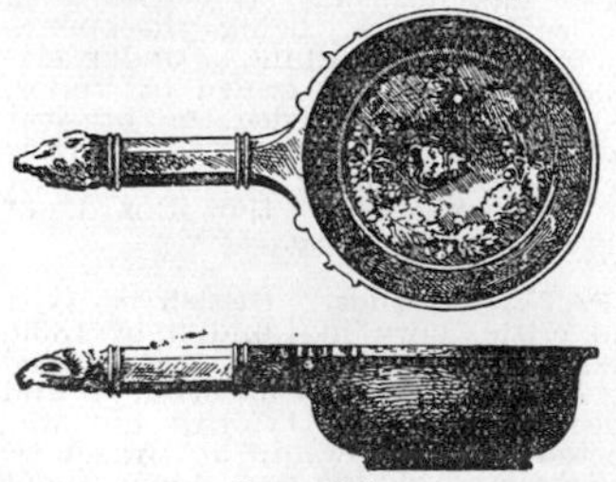

Roman Patera

architecture to the representation of a flat, round dish in bas-relief, used as an ornament in friezes, etc., but many flat ornaments are now called pateras which have no resemblance to dishes. The term is also inappropriately applied to the variously shaped flat ornaments frequently used in the perpendicular style of Gothic.

PATER'CULUS, Gaius Velleius. An ancient Roman historian, born about 19 B.C., died about A.D. 31. He served under Tiberius in Germany as commander of the cavalry, and in the first year of that emperor's reign was nominated prætor. Nothing further is known of him except that he composed a compendium of Roman history to the year A.D. 30 in two books, of which the beginning and a portion following the eighth chapter of the first book are wanting.

PATER'NIANS. A heretical sect of the fifth century, followers of *Paternus*, who are said to have held that God made the nobler parts of man and Satan the lower. Hence they served God with the former parts and the devil with the latter.

PATERNO (ancient **Hybla Galeatis,** or **Hybla Minor**). A town of Sicily, in the province of Catania, at the foot of Mount Etna. In the vicinity are mineral-springs and the remains of baths and ancient bridges. Pop. 34,000.

PATERSON, William. Financier and founder of the Bank of England. He was born in Dumfriesshire 1665, died in London 1719. He went through England as a pedlar, settled for a time at Bristol, and subsequently resided in the Bahama Islands. In 1694 he founded the Bank of England, being one of its first directors. Before this time he had conceived the project of founding a free emporium of trade in Darien, and in 1695 he obtained the sanction of a Scottish Act of Parliament constituting the Darien Company. After the failure of this great scheme he returned to England, broken in health and fortune.

When the Treaty of Union between England and Scotland was concluded in 1707, Paterson, who was one of its warmest advocates, after much difficulty received an indemnity (of £18,000) for the losses he had sustained. He was a great financial genius, but most of his views (such as his advocacy of free-trade) were far in advance of his time.—Cf. Bannister, *Life of W. Paterson*.

PATERSON. A city of New Jersey, United States, the county seat of Passaic county, on the Passaic River; served by the Delaware, Lackawanna, & Western, the Erie, and the New York, Susquehanna, & Western Railways, and by electric traction lines. It is a great manufacturing centre, and the home of the silk industry of the United States. Hydro-electric power is provided by the river, which falls 70 feet (50 feet perpendicularly) at this point. Paterson was founded in 1791, and became a city in 1851. Pop. 138,513.

PATHANS (patăn). The generic name by which the Mahommedan people living on and beyond the north-west frontier of India are known. As used now, the name Pathan is made to include all Pushtu-speaking tribes, and thus takes in the Afghan; but the real Pathan is probably an aborigine, whose ancestors were settled in the same inhospitable tracts of country the tribes now occupy, centuries before the arrival of the people whom we know as Afghans.

The Pathans proper are divided into large tribes, each of which in its turn is again split up into clans or khels. Its principal big tribes are the Yusufzais (Yusuf = Joseph), Khattaks, Mohmands, Afridis, Wazirs, and Mahsuds. The first two of these tribes live mainly in the British administrative territory, while the other four have their being beyond the border, and are independent.

Each tribe differs from the others in many respects, each having its own peculiar customs and dialect of Pushtu. But there is one point in which all are alike: they are all truculent to a degree, and are continually fighting among themselves. Fighting is their very existence, the be-all and end-all of their life.

To a certain extent the nature of this country, composed as it is of barren, inhospitable hills, is partly responsible for this, for, seeing that the country can produce next to nothing, the Pathan has to rely for his sustenance on what he can take from others. Consequently, raids into the settled and cultivated country over the border are the natural results. But the orthodox Pathan does not confine his activities to robbing and murdering sleek Hindu traders in the bazaars of Peshawur. The blood-lust will out, and when a commercial raid is out of the question, our Pathan will turn to his friends and relations in order to find a target for his gun or meat for his knife.

Two men from different clans were once discussing the respective heights of two hills, one being in A territory and one in B. Each claimed the honours for the hill in his own territory, and, being unable to agree and not knowing, of course, how to measure the heights, drew their knives and set upon each other. The fight resulted in the death of one man, *and* a blood-feud between the two clans, which exists to the present day, though the episode took place an unknown number of years ago. Some ten years ago, one man snatched the cap off the head of another, and, in the words of the Pathan who told the writer the story, "the result was terrible, six murders on the spot, besides a few wounded, and all in fifteen minutes."

The "offensive spirit" is inculcated into Pathan youths by pitting them against inferior foes selected from the animal kingdom, in order to fit them by a system of graduated steps to take on one of their friends or near relations. A boy of eight, armed with a stick, has to defeat and kill an infuriated snake or a mongoose (a large, ferret-like animal). In due course he deals with a porcupine, and finally with a specially trained fighting ram, and, after a successful interview with this, is permitted to carry a knife, and murder his own kind.

This sort of training, combined with the hard life that is a necessary corollary to the nature of this country, makes the Pathan a hardy and fearless soldier. They are also much addicted to sports of all kinds, especially hunting, tent-pegging, archery, and cock-, bull-, dog-, and ram-fighting. Small-bore rifles are worth their weight in silver across the border, so that regiments on the frontier have to keep a particularly sharp look-out against rifle thieves.

Pathans are enlisted in considerable numbers into the frontier force regiments of the Indian army. They fight loyally for us when in the army, and with just as much gusto against us when they return to "civil" life after their period of service has expired. The frontier militias and khassadars (levies) are entirely composed of local Pathans.

PATHOL'OGY deals with departures from the normal state of the body and the causes underlying such changes. Therefore the foundations of the science of pathology are physiology and anatomy. Owing to its structure the body does work, which may be mechanical, e.g. muscular contraction, or chemical, e.g. secretion of saliva or gastric juice. Further, the wear and tear of the tissues is repaired, and at certain periods growth of the whole body or of certain organs occurs.

Accordingly, pathology is concerned with alterations in structure or function. Structural changes are comprised in *pathological anatomy*; such alterations may be relatively gross and readily recognisable by the unaided eye, or they may require high magnifications of the microscope for their detection. A true understanding of structural changes was first rendered possible by the discovery that cells constitute the essential elements of which the bodies of higher animals are composed, and the doctrine enunciated by Virchow that every cell is derived from a pre-existing cell ("omnis cellula e cellula") has been universally accepted.

Chemical pathology deals with aberrations in the composition of the cells and their products. Closely related to this department is the investigation of physical or physico-chemical changes; since living protoplasm consists of materials in the colloid state, such alterations are likely to have far-reaching consequences. Knowledge of these branches of pathology is of more recent growth than that of pathological anatomy, and great advances may be expected along these lines. A striking instance of disease with a physico-chemical basis is hæmophilia; in this condition slight injuries lead to severe and long-continued loss of blood, yet no anatomical abnormality can be found in the blood-vessels or other tissues. In diabetes, also, a disease in which the body fails to utilise sugar, no anatomical lesion is constantly found.

External Causes of Disease. *Etiology* is the branch of pathology which is concerned with the causes of disease. These most frequently are *external*; thus it is a general principle that the body from the fœtal stage until adult life exhibits structures and functions which, in the absence of external disturbance, are extremely constant, and which, therefore, are defined as constituting the physiological or healthy state.

The normal body has great capacity for adapting itself to external conditions; in fact, the manifestations of life consist mainly in responses to external stimuli. This is well seen in the case of individual cells, which in the living state possess a highly selective behaviour towards substances with which they come into contact, e.g. salts or dyestuffs; many such substances are strictly excluded from entrance into a cell so long as the latter is alive, although after death they quickly diffuse through its substance.

But when external agencies are excessive or of particular kinds, they tend to be pathogenic, i.e. to produce disease. Thus mechanical violence (trauma) or excessive heat and cold are pathogenic agencies; more subtle forms of injury result from X-rays and other radiations. Injury of various kinds may be inflicted by chemical agents, e.g. strong acids and alkalis, and alkaloids.

Bacteria are an important group of pathogenic agents, and they lead to a great variety of pathological effects. Certain bacteria can enter and flourish in the living tissues; these acts are summed up in the term *infection*. In virtue of being endowed with life and the capacity for multiplication, it follows that the entrance of minute numbers of bacteria may suffice to set up disease.

Some organisms, such as the bacilli of diphtheria or tetanus, settle at the point of entry into the body, and produce harmful effects by secreting powerful poisons (toxins), which act on the nervous system; again, others enter the blood-stream and proliferate actively there, causing septicæmia. Very important are the pyogenic bacteria, which cause suppuration and wound-infections. In addition to bacteria, unicellular microscopic animals (protozoa) are the cause of malaria, sleeping sickness, amœbic dysentery, etc.

There are a number of important infections in which the causal agent has not yet been identified, e.g. scarlet fever, measles, smallpox; the reason for such failure probably is the minute size of the organisms, which consequently are termed "invisible viruses". Higher animal forms, especially species of worms, cause important diseases, e.g. bilharziosis and ankylostomiasis.

Internal Causes of Disease. Certain glands produce internal secretions which are poured into the blood-stream. In the case of the thyroid gland, absence of the secretion causes myxœdema; excessive or perverted secretion causes exophthalmic goitre. In most cases the basis of the disturbed function of such glands is obscure.

In old age the tissues commonly show changes which are regarded as pathological if they occur earlier in life; hence it is a debatable point how far old age is a disease. Pathological changes may be classified as degenerative or reactive, according as they exhibit evidence of damage or of reaction to the pathogenic agent.

Necrosis or death of tissue, e.g. produced by cutting off the blood-supply, is an example of the former; the latter is illustrated by hypertrophy or increase in the essential tissue of an organ, e.g. of the heart muscle in valvular disease of the heart.

In general, the most specialised tissues show least reparative power; when there is loss of substance, as in a wound, repair is mainly effected by the connective tissue, which proliferates to form granulation tissue; the latter finally becomes mature connective tissue.

The term *inflammation* is applied to a series of changes, partly degenerative, partly reparative, which occur when an injurious agent, often micro-organisms, damages tissues without immediately killing the part. Reactive processes may lead to recovery; in the case of infections, cure is frequently accompanied by insusceptibility to a second attack, which is called *acquired immunity*.

Tumours are pathological conditions, which cannot be classed either as degenerative or reparative. They are new growths of tissue which do not serve any purpose of the body in which they arise. Some tumours grow slowly and remain localised (simple tumours). Others (carcinoma, sarcoma) spread through the body owing to their constituent cells being carried by the blood- and lymph-streams to distant organs, where they settle and grow; such malignant tumours destroy the tissues.

So far their cause in unknown; but they have been produced experimentally by certain forms of chronic irritation, e.g. in rats round parasitic worms (gonglyonema neoplastica of Fibiger) and on the skin of mice by application of tar.

PATIA'LA. Indian native state and town in the Punjab, the largest of the three Sikh Phulkian states, Patiala, Natha, and Jind; area, 5932 sq. miles. Besides the usual agricultural products, the state has slate-, lead-, marble-, and copper-mines. Pop. of the state, 1,625,520. The capital is Patiala, on the Rajpura-Bhatinda branch of the North-Western Railway. It was founded in 1752 by Sardar Ala Singh, and has a pop. of 47,531.

PAT'INA. In the fine arts, the fine green rust with which ancient bronzes and copper coins and medals become covered by lying in particular soils, which, like varnish, is at once preservative and ornamental. An artificial patina is produced by the forgers of antiquities by acting on them with acetic acid, but it is not durable.

PATMORE, Coventry Kearsey Deighton. English poet, born in 1823, died in 1896. He published his first volume of poems in 1844, became assistant librarian at the British Museum, and associated himself with the Pre-Raphaelite movement. His reputation as a poet was established by the publication of the four parts of *The Angel in the House* (1854-63), which he revised in successive editions. Besides this he published *The Unknown Eros and other Odes*, a poetical anthology called the *Children's Garland*; and a *Memoir of B. W. Procter* (Barry Cornwall).

PATMOS. An island of Asia Minor, in the Archipelago, about 28 miles S.S.W. of Samos; greatest length, 12 miles; breadth, nearly 6 miles. It became Italian by the Treaty of Lausanne (1923). The island is an irregular mass of barren rock, and the population (mostly Greeks) find their chief occupation in fishing. Near the excellent natural harbour of La Scala is the small town of Patmos, overlooked by the old monastery of St. John, in a grotto of which, it is said, the Apostle John saw his apocalyptic visions. Pop. (1927), 2500.

PATNA. A native state of Bihar and Orissa, India, tributary to Orissa, in the basin of the Mahanadi River. The people are Oriyās. Patna was included in the Central Provinces until 1905. Bolangir is the capital. Area, 2399 sq. miles; pop. 494,456.

PATNA. A district, division, and city of Bihar and Orissa, India. The district lies south of the Ganges and east of the Son, and is devoted to agriculture. Area, 2075 sq. miles; pop. 1,610,000. The division comprises the districts of Patna, Gaya, and Shahabad. Area, 11,150 sq. miles; pop. 5,635,000. The city of Patna is in Bihar and Orissa, and is second only to Calcutta as the Bengalese metropolis. It lies on the Ganges, and is served by the East Indian Railway from Calcutta. Patna is the ancient *Pataliputra* (q.v.), and as *Palibothra* it was once capital of India. Pop. 158,230.

PATON, Sir Joseph Noel. Historical painter. Born at Dunfermline in 1821, died in 1901. He studied for some time at the Royal Academy; attracted attention by his outline etchings illustrative of Shakespeare and Shelley; exhibited his first picture of *Ruth Gleaning* at Edinburgh in 1844; gained one of three premiums at the Westminster competition by his fresco of the *Spirit of Religion*, and a prize of £300 by his paintings *Christ Bearing the Cross* and *The Reconciliation of Oberon and Titania*.

During subsequent years he produced many pictures, some well known by engravings, such as *The Pursuit of Pleasure*; *Home*, a soldier's return from the Crimea; *In Memoriam*, a scene from the relief of Lucknow; *Mors Janua Vitæ*; *Faith and Reason*; *Lux in Tenebris*; and *The Man with the Muck-rake*.

PATRAS (ancient **Patræ**). A seaport of Greece, in the north-west of the Morea, on the gulf of the same name. It was one of the twelve cities of the Achæan Confederacy of ancient Greece, and is the only survivor. Pop. 61,278.—The Gulf of Patras lies between the north-west part of the Morea and Northern Greece, and communicates on the east with the Gulf of Lepanto.

PATRIARCHS (from the Gr. *patria*, tribe, *archein*, to rule). Heads of families or tribes, and specifically the three Fathers of the Hebrew race, Abraham, Isaac, and Jacob. The term at a later period became the title of the presidents of the Sanhedrin, which exercised a general authority over the Jews of Syria and Persia after the destruction of

Patriarch

Jerusalem. From them the title was adopted by the Christians, who applied it, from the beginning of the fifth century, to the Bishops of Rome, Constantinople, Alexandria, Antioch, and Jerusalem.

The Patriarch of Rome became the supreme pontiff of the West, the four heads of the Eastern Church preserving the title of patriarch. The Patriarch of Constantinople is the primate of the Greek Church in the Ottoman Empire, and bears the title of *œcumenical*.

PATRICIANS (Lat. *patricius*, from *pater*, father). The name given by the Romans to the members and descendants by blood or adoption of the original *gentes*, houses or clans who, after the plebeians became a distinct order, constituted the aristocracy of the city and territory.

PATRICK (Patricius), **ST.** Patron saint of Ireland. He was born about A.D. 396, probably, as suggested by Rhys, somewhere in the valley of the modern Severn, but claimed by Scots tradition as Old Kilpatrick, near Dumbarton, on the River Clyde. His father, a decurion in the Roman army, retired to a farm on the Solway, whence, at the age of sixteen, Patrick was carried off by a band of marauders and sold as a slave to the Irish of Dalaradia.

After six years he made his escape, and, resolving to devote himself to the conversion of Ireland, prepared himself for the priesthood, probably at the monastic institution founded by St. Ninian at Candida Casa (Whithorn), in Galloway.

Having been ordained a bishop and received the Papal benediction from Celestine I., he went over to Ireland about the year 432. Here he is said to have founded over 360 churches, baptised with his own hand more than 12,000 persons, and ordained a great number of priests. The date of his death is probably 469; it took place at a place called Saul, near Downpatrick, and his relics were preserved at Downpatrick till the time of the Reformation.

His authentic literary remains consist of his *Confessions* and a letter addressed to Coroticus, a Brythonic king of Strathclyde. Many points connected with the life of St. Patrick are doubtful, and regarding his position in the history of Irish Christianity different views are held. Some authorities identify him with Palladius.—Cf. E. J. Newell, *St. Patrick: his Life and Teaching*.

PATRICK, ST., ORDER OF. An Irish order of knighthood, instituted in 1783 by George III., originally consisting of the sovereign, the Lord-Lieutenant of Ireland for the time being (who is the Grand Master of the order), and fifteen knights; but by a statute in 1833 the order was enlarged and the number of knights raised to twenty-two.

The badge of the order is of gold, oval in shape, with the cross of St. Patrick surmounted by a shamrock in the centre, and round this is a blue enamelled band bearing the motto "Quis separabit." The badge is suspended to a collar of roses and harps by means of an imperial crown and gold harp. The mantle and hood are of sky-blue tabinet, lined with white silk.

PATROC'LUS. In Greek story, the friend of Achilles, whom he accompanied to the Trojan War. His success was at first brilliant; but, Apollo having stunned him and rendered him defenceless, he was slain by Euphorbus and Hector.

PA'TRON. In the Roman Republic, a patrician who had plebeians, called *clients*, under his immediate protection, and whose interests he supported by his authority and influence. In later times the term patron was applied to every protector or influential promoter of the interests of others; hence the saints who were believed to watch over the interests of particular persons, places, or trades were called *patron saints*.

PAT'RONAGE, ECCLESIASTICAL. The right of presenting a fit person to a vacant benefice. In the earlier ages the bishops appointed the holders of all benefices, but subsequently when proprietors of lands began to erect and endow churches they obtained the privilege of nominating the clergyman. For a considerable time not only the nomination but also the investiture of the clergy was in the hands of laymen; but the hierarchy began to consider this an infringement of its prerogatives, and several successive Popes and Councils declared that the investiture was not valid unless it had also received the sanction of the ecclesiastical authority.

Ecclesiastical patronage thus came to reside mainly in the Pope, and the principal benefices in Europe were filled by Italian ecclesiastics, who were often ignorant of the language of their flocks. In England this led to the Statutes of Provisors (1350-1415), by which persons who should attempt to enforce such appointments were subjected to severe penalties.

In England the sovereign is the patron paramount of all benefices which do not belong to other patrons; but a vast number of livings are in the gift of private persons, who possess the *advowson* as attached to their property.

In Scotland the statute which abolished Popery and recognised the reformed religion reserved the right of presentation to lay patrons (1567), and a subsequent statute (1592) asserted the rights of the Crown and lay patrons in still stronger terms. On the establishment of Episcopacy the same principle was adopted in the Act of 1612, by which presentations were appointed to be directed to the bishop.

After the re-establishment of presbytery patronage was abolished (1649). It was again restored, however; again abolished; and again restored, in the last instance by the Act 10 Anne, cap. xii.; and this rule remained with slight modification till 1874, when an Act was passed by which the right of choosing their own minister devolved upon the congregation, the former patron to receive as compensation a sum equal to one year's stipend.

PATTI, Adelina Maria Clorinda. Famous operatic singer, born at Madrid in 1843, died 27th Sept., 1919. She received her musical training from her brother-in-law, Maurice Strakosch; made her début

Adelina Patti

in New York in 1859 as Lucia; and in 1861 appeared at Covent Garden, London, in the parts of Amina, Violetta, Zerlina, and Martha. In 1868 she married the Marquis de Caux, but got a divorce in 1883. In 1886 she married Signor Nicolini, and in 1899 Baron Cederström. Her remains were interred in Père Lachaise, Paris.

PATTISON, Mark. English writer, born in 1813, died in 1884. Educated at Oriel College, Oxford, he became a Fellow of Lincoln College in 1839; studied theology, was ordained, and won the Denyer theological prize. In

1853 he was appointed tutor of his college, and in 1861 became rector (or head) of Lincoln College. He devoted himself to university reform, for this purpose made many journeys to Germany, and was assistant-commissioner on the Educational Commission of the Duke of Newcastle.

He was a contributor to the famous *Essays and Reviews*, and published an edition of Pope's *Epistles and Satires* (1869), a work on *Isaac Casaubon* (1875), a memoir of *Milton* in the English Men of Letters Series (1879), the *Sonnets of Milton* (1883), and numerous articles in reviews.

PAU (pō). A town of France, capital of the department of Basses-Pyrénées (formerly of Béarn), on a height above the Gave-du-Pau, and on the southern railway to Toulouse. Among its chief buildings are two Gothic churches, a palace of justice, and a winter palace built in 1896. The town is dominated by the castle in which Henry IV. was born. The oldest part is supposed to date from 1363, and the whole is well preserved. Pau is a favourite winter-resort, enjoying a mild dry climate, with no sudden variations of temperature. Pop. 38,962.

PAUL. The name of five Popes. **Paul I.,** Pope from 757-767, brother of Stephen II., stood on good terms with Pepin and Charlemagne.—**Paul II.,** Pope from 1464-71, a native of Venice, originally called Pietro Barbo, caused a crusade to be preached against the Hussites.—**Paul III.,** Pope from 1534-49, formerly Alessandro Farnese, excommunicated Henry VIII. (1535), concurred in the foundation of the Order of Jesuits, opened the Council of Trent, defended himself by his legates in the conferences between Catholics and Protestants at the Diets of Worms and Ratisbon, and established a general Inquisition for the suppression of Protestantism.—**Paul IV.,** Pope from 1555-9, formerly John Peter Caraffa, energetically directed the power of the Inquisition against everything tending to favour Protestantism, and established an *Index Librorum Prohibitorum*.—**Paul V.,** Pope from 1605-21, formerly Camillo Borghese, succeeded Leo XI.

PAUL I. Tsar of Russia, son of Peter III. and Catherine II. Born in 1754, died 24th March, 1801. On the death of Catherine in 1796 he succeeded to the throne, and began his reign with acts of generosity. He put an end to the war with Persia, and liberated the Poles who were in confinement in Russia. He joined the coalition against France, and sent 100,000 men, under Suwarov and Korsakov, to Italy and Switzerland, and some to Holland, but he afterwards favoured the cause of Napoleon.

Paul caused himself to be declared Grand Master of the Knights of Malta (1798), but Britain, having conquered the island in 1800, refused to surrender it to the Russian emperor. He therefore laid an embargo on all British ships in the Russian ports, and prevailed upon the Swedish, Danish, and Prussian courts to enter into a convention against Great Britain. At length (1801) the internal administration and his increasing acts of tyranny gave rise to a strong popular discontent, and he was assassinated in his bed.

PAUL, ST. A few years after the birth of Jesus, another Jewish child was born who was to play a part in the interpretation and extension of the religion of Jesus, second to none but the founder. This Jew was born not in Palestine but in Tarsus, the famous capital of the Roman province of Cilicia, in Asia Minor. His parents were both Jews, and from his father the lad inherited the coveted privilege of being a Roman citizen.

Early Years. Tarsus was a well-known centre of education and culture. But this young Jew was sent by his parents to be trained, at any rate after his childhood, in the rabbinic school at Jerusalem, where he had the good fortune to be a pupil of Gamaliel I. He may have been studying there when Jesus was arrested and executed at Jerusalem, but he was not an adherent of the Galilean prophet. During this early period of his life he was an ardent Jew, passionately keen upon the faith of his race, a member of the Pharisaic party which represented the zeal and orthodoxy of Judaism.

This youth was called Saul, after the first King of Israel, to whose clan of Benjamin he belonged. He had a second name, Paul or Paulus, like many Jews who were in touch with the outside world, where a double name was normal. Whether "Paul" was the name given to him at birth by his parents, or whether he assumed it afterwards, is indeed a disputed point.

His first relations with Christianity were hostile. The synagogue of the Cilicians, to which he would naturally be attached in Jerusalem, was involved in the bitter controversy over Stephen, who relentlessly expounded the issue between Judaism and Christianity. This was shortly after the crucifixion. Paul assisted those who murdered Stephen, although his assistance was passive.

But his energy soon carried him into active measures against what he regarded as a pestilent heresy; he was commissioned by the authorities at Jerusalem to travel north to Damascus and stamp out a local growth of Christianity which had appeared in the ghetto. Evidently Paul was regarded as one of the most promising young leaders of Judaism in its militant Pharisaic form.

Conversion. It was on this tour that he suddenly became a Christian. As he reached Damascus he had a vision of Jesus, accompanied by some physical crisis. The next news that reached the capital was that Paul had gone over to the new faith. The Christians were as astounded as the Jews; they heard that "he who persecuted us in times past now preacheth the faith which once he destroyed."

The inwardness of Paul's conversion may be made out in part from autobiographical hints in his later letters. Evidently he had been secretly dissatisfied with Judaism, and his very effect to suppress Christianity may have been whetted by a desire to stifle his doubts by means of action. In any case, he proved a redoubtable accession to the Christian religion. His powers of thought and organisation were now flung into the task of consolidating and expanding Christianity with the same zeal with which he had once attacked it.

His restatement of Christianity involved a severe criticism of the Pharisaic Judaism from which he had broken away. This is sometimes viewed as unfair. But Paul estimated Judaism as Luther estimated mediæval Romanism, not as a cold historical critic, but as one who had suffered from its religious aberrations.

He realised, more thoroughly than even Stephen had, the freedom from the law which was involved in the principles of Jesus. Wellhausen is right in declaring that "Paul was really the man who best understood the Master and carried on His work," for, although his methods of argument are often tinged with rabbinic dialectic, and although his theological speculations are fresh, his redemptive interpretation of Christianity is essentially true to the implication of the original faith. He was not the first to preach the freedom of the Gospel for people of non-Jewish birth. But he was the first to carry out this tenet logically, in thought and practice.

All this, however, was in the future. For a time Paul was left in obscurity. After his conversion, followed by a brief period of retirement, he did some effective preaching at Damascus and at Jerusalem, but his life was in danger from the irate Jews. He then retired to his own country. In Cilicia and Syria he spent from ten to fourteen years, evangelising, no doubt, but apparently ignored by the main body of the Church in Palestine. During this period his mind improved. But one result of the long interval is that Paul, like Knox, was a middle-aged man before he was summoned to his life-work.

The first Christian who recollected him was Barnabas. The growth of the Christian mission at Antioch necessitated help from the outside; Barnabas bethought him of Paul, who was summoned from Cilicia and associated for a whole year with him at Antioch.

First Foreign Mission. From this time forward he is in the main current of Christianity. Even before the Council at Jerusalem, which permitted the mission to non-Jews, Paul was dispatched along with Barnabas by the Church of Antioch as the first foreign mission. This occupied them for not less than three years. It embraced Cyprus and some districts in Pisidia and Pamphylia on the mainland, to the south of Asia Minor.

The success of this mission startled the conservative Jewish Christians at Jerusalem, who were opposed to anyone entering the Christian Church except by accepting the Jewish law. The controversy was decided in favour of Paul and his party, thanks largely to the good sense of Peter. Whereupon Paul set out on a fresh tour, first in Asia Minor, and then in Europe, which he reached by sailing across the Ægean from Tarsus. He and his colleagues founded a line of Churches from Macedonia right down to Corinth, the one city in which little success was won being Athens. This fruitful and difficult mission must have occupied nearly three years. Paul then made Ephesus his head-quarters, from which he could keep in touch with the European Churches and also organise a Christian propaganda in Asia itself. This mission lasted for two years, at the end of which a local riot obliged him to withdraw.

Captivity and Death. He then left for Jerusalem, never to return. In the capital he was arrested at the instigation of some Asiatic Jews, and spent the rest of his life as a prisoner, first in Jerusalem, then at Cæsarea, and finally in Rome.

He must have spent from six to ten years in captivity; the chronological data are uncertain, however, and the one point which emerges with undisputed clearness is that he shifted the venue of his trial from Palestine to Rome by appealing to the emperor. This was because he exercised one of the rights which he enjoyed as a Roman citizen.

What happened to him in the end we do not know. That he was put to death is certain. But why and when we cannot tell. Later traditions fix his martyrdom in the latter years of Nero's reign, and it must have occurred before the burning of Rome in A.D. 67. When he died he would be about or slightly over sixty years of age. His main work for Christianity had been done since he was forty.

Work. How important that work was, history can now appreciate. In his day Paul was thwarted and suspected by many men within the Church. He was followed by conservative Jewish Christians, who maligned his character and unsettled his Churches. He was also in repeated danger, owing to the deadly hatred of the Jews, who realised his worth perhaps more keenly than most of his fellow-Christians did. When he died it seemed as if his work was threatened with an eclipse, and his particular theology was soon misunderstood or ignored by the Church.

Other influences came to the front. But Paul had finally won the battle of Christianity against Jewish conservatism within as well as without the Church. After him, the law no longer oppressed converts from paganism. He had also given an impetus to the interpretation of Christianity which was of vital importance; he had drawn probably upon contemporary speculations in hellenistic religion, and his views of Christianity may have been indebted here and there to the mystery-religions, but his theology was his own, and it was dominated by a sense of the supreme position of Jesus as Lord.

Furthermore, as an organiser and a propagandist—for Paul was both, in addition to being a thinker—he had broken new territory for the faith. He had not only shown how Christianity could not remain a plant in Jewish soil if it was to survive and thrive, but had proved that it could be transplanted to the outside provinces of the empire. "The future history of Europe and America for two thousand years," as Dean Inge observes, "perhaps for all time, was determined by his missionary journeys and hurried writings. It is impossible to guess what would have become of Christianity if he had never lived; we cannot even be sure that the name of Jesus would still be honoured amongst men."

Writings. These "hurried writings" are his letters, composed during the afternoon of his life, to meet exigences of his mission. They are all written to Churches which he had founded, with the exception of two, viz. Romans and Colossians. One is a semi-private note (Philemon). Another, the so-called epistle to The Ephesians, was addressed to a wider circle of Churches, and may have been written by one of his disciples.

These epistles, two to Timothy and one to Titus, may contain fragments from his pen, but in their present form are the work of a later writer belonging to his school. It is from these letters, and from the story in the book of Acts, written by his medical friend Luke, that the biographical outline of Paul's life can be recovered.

BIBLIOGRAPHY: From the vast bibliography, these items may be selected. (*a*) Biographical sketches by Conybeare and Howson, *Life and Epistles of St. Paul* (1877); W. M. Ramsay, *St. Paul the Traveller and the Roman Citizen* (1895); A. Sabatier, *The Apostle Paul* (1906); and G. A. Deissmann, *St. Paul* (1912). (*b*) Studies of his letters and theology by B. Jowett, *Epistles of St. Paul* (3rd edition, 1894); A. B. Bruce, *St. Paul's Conception of Christianity* (1894); Kirsopp Lake, *The Earlier Epistles of St. Paul* (1911); P. Gardner, *The Religious Experience of St. Paul* (1911); H. A. A. Kennedy, *St. Paul and the Mystery-Religions* (1913); W. Morgan, *The Religion and Theology of Paul* (1917); B. W. Bacon, *Jesus and Paul* (1921); and J. G. Machen, *The Origin of Paul's Religion* (1921). (*c*) General estimates by E. Renan, *Saint Paul* (1869); C. G. Montefiore, *Judaism and St. Paul* (1914); and Dean Inge, in *Outspoken Essays*.

PAUL, ST. VINCENT DE. Roman Catholic philanthropist, born of poor parents in Southern France in 1576, died in 1660. Educated at Dax and Toulouse, he was ordained a priest in 1600; in 1605 he was captured by pirates; remained in slavery in Tunis for two years, and finally escaped to France. He afterwards visited Rome, from whence he was sent on a mission to Paris, where he became almoner to Queen Margaret of Valois.

In 1616 he began the labours which occupied so large a portion of his life, and which included the foundation of the institution called the Priests of the Mission or Lazarists, the reformation of the hospitals, the institution of the Sisterhood of Charity, and the instruction of idiots at his priory of St. Lazare. Among the last acts of his life was the foundation of an asylum for aged working-people of both sexes, and a hospital for all the poor of Paris, which was opened in 1657. He was canonised in 1737.

PAUL-BONCOUR, Joseph. French politician. He was born at St. Aignan, 4th Aug., 1873. As an independent Socialist he was elected to the Chamber and became Labour Minister (1911) in the Cabinet. After the War, in which he served, he took an important part in the work of the League of Nations, as a French representative. In 1932 he became Minister for War in the Cabinet headed by Edouard Herriot (q.v.).

PAULICIANS. An Oriental anti-Catholic sect founded in the seventh century (possibly earlier) in Armenia. Gibbon (*Decline and Fall of the Roman Empire*, chap. liv.) says of the Paulicians that "they gloried in their affinity to the Apostle of the Gentiles."

The invincible spirit which they had kindled continued to live and breathe in the Western World, and they may be considered as the precursors of Protestantism. They rejected the adoration of the Virgin and the saints; refused homage to the cross; denied the validity of the sacraments; interpreted spiritually baptism and the Lord's Supper; would not recognise any priestly dignity; and their public wor hip was altogether free from ritual. They suffered severe persecution at the hands of the Byzantine emperors, but as late as the sixteenth century remnants of the sect were found in Bulgaria.

PAULSEN, Friedrich. German philosopher of the Neo-Kantian school, born 16th July, 1846, died 14th Aug., 1908. He studied at Erlangen and Berlin, where he became professor of philosophy in 1878. A disciple of Fechner, he adopted the latter's theory of the parallelism of the mental and the physical. His works include: *Kant, der Philosoph des Protestantismus*; *Schopenhauer, Hamlet und Mephistopheles*; *Ethik*; and *Einleitung in die Philosophie*.

PAULUS ÆGINE'TA. Greek physician, born, it is supposed, in the seventh century in the Island of Ægina, and connected with the medical school at Alexandria. He abridged the works of Galen, and was deeply read in those of Hippocrates and others. His *Synopsis of the Medical Art* has been translated into English.

PAULUS DIAC'ONUS. Italian ecclesiastic and mediæval historian, born about A.D. 730, died about 800. He was educated in the court of the Lombard kings at Pavia. In 781 he was called to the court of Charlemagne, and was one of the principal instruments of the intellectual reforms effected by the emperor in the countries of Western Europe. Paulus drew up a book of homilies from the Fathers, wrote a history of the Bishops of Metz, and a history of the Lombards.

PAUSA'NIAS. A Spartan general, nephew of Leonidas. He commanded the allied Greeks against the Persians at the battle of Platæa in 479 B.C. To himself alone he ascribed the victory, and his pretensions became insupportable when he afterwards, with a combined Greek fleet, delivered Greece, Cyprus, and finally Byzantium from the Persian rule. At length he entered into secret negotiations with Xerxes, and conceived the design of making himself master of Greece. To escape arrest he sought shelter in the temple of Athene at Sparta, where he was shut in by the enraged people and starved to death (467 B.C.).

PAUSANIAS. A Greek traveller and geographer who lived in the second century after Christ, and of whose personal history nothing is known. His *Hellados Periēgēsis* (Peregrination of Hellas) is an itinerary in ten books of his travels, which were extensive. He appears to have visited the whole of the Peloponnesus, Rome, Syria, and Palestine. He describes temples, theatres, tombs, statues, pictures, and monuments of every sort. He also mentions mountains, rivers, and fountains, and the mythological stories connected with them. His observation is accurate, and his descriptions simple and reliable. His work also contains a great deal of matter relating to history, mythology, and art. The principal English edition is that by Sir J. G. Frazer, with translation and commentary.

PA'VIA. A province of Lombardy, North Italy, extending between the Ligurian Apennines and the valley of the Po. Area, 1144 sq. miles; pop. 481,884.

PAVIA (ancient **TICINUM**). A city of Lombardy, Italy, the capital of the province of Pavia, on the Ticino, near its junction with the Po. The city is still partly surrounded by old walls and fortifications, and is connected with the Adriatic by the Po and Ticino, and with Milan by a canal. The principal buildings are the cathedral (founded 1487), containing the tomb of St. Augustine; the church of San Michele, dating from the eleventh century; and the university, founded in 1361 by Galeazzo II. on the site of an establishment founded by Lanfranc (died 1088).

The manufactures are unimportant, and the trade almost entirely local. About 4 miles to the north is the Certosa di Pavia, an old Carthusian monastery.

Pavia was a place of importance in the time of Augustus. It was afterwards the capital of the Lombard kings. Near it in 1525 the Imperialists defeated the French and took prisoner their king, Francis I. Pop. 50,419.

PAVLOVA, Anna. Russian dancer, born at Leningrad, 31st Jan., 1885, she entered the Imperial Ballet School at the age of 10. Attached to, and later *prima ballerina* of, the Marianski Theatre, Leningrad, she subsequently appeared at the Imperial Opera House, and first visited London, with Michael Mordkin, in 1910. In 1923-4-5 she appeared with her own company at the Covent Garden Opera House, always meeting with enthusiastic reception. She died 22nd Jan., 1931.

PAVLOGRAD. A town of Southern Russia, on the Voltcha, and in the government of Yekaterinoslav; served by the Sevastopol-Kursk Railway. Pop. 42,043.

PAWL. *See* RATCHET.

PAWNBROKERS. Persons who lend money on goods *pledged* or deposited with them at a legally fixed rate of interest, and under the restriction of a Government licence. Although this mode of borrowing is occasionally taken advantage of by all classes, and bankers, when they accept security for their advances act on the same principle as the pawnbroker, the business, as a special one, originates chiefly in the necessities of the poor.

In the Middle Ages lending upon pledges was a trade almost exclusively pursued by Jews and Lombards. On the European continent this form of borrowing is partly conducted by charitable institutions called Monts de Piété. In England pawnbrokers were recognised by statute in the reign of James I., and in 1872 an Act was passed to consolidate all the Acts relating to pawnbrokers in Great Britain; but it does not extend to Ireland.

Every person who keeps a shop for the sale of goods, and pays or advances any sum of money upon such goods not exceeding £10, on an agreement, express or implied, that these goods or chattels may afterwards be repurchased or redeemed, shall be deemed a pawnbroker. They are required to take out a licence (£7, 10*s*. per annum). Pawn-tickets are given for goods taken in pledge, and the interest charged is fixed by law. By the Act of 1872, on a loan under 40*s*., ½*d*. may be charged on every 2*s*. for a period not exceeding one month, and so on at the same rate per calendar month; and when the sum is above 40*s*., ½*d*. may similarly be charged on every 2*s*. 6*d*. An Act of 1922 authorises an additional charge of ½*d*. on each 5*s*. advanced in the case of loans not exceeding 40*s*.

When the pawn-ticket has been lost, a printed form of declaration may be got and filled up in place of it. Goods pledged and not redeemed may be sold after twelve months and seven days from the date of pledge. At the end of that time pledges pawned for 10*s*. or under become the property of the pawnbroker. Pledges for more than 10*s*. must be disposed of by public auction, subject to certain regulations, and they continue redeemable until so disposed of.

The entry of sale may be inspected within three years by the pledger in the broker's books, and in the catalogue of sale certified by the auctioneer, and he may claim any surplus above loan and profit with the necessary charges. When the loan exceeds 40*s*., the pawnbroker is at liberty to make a special contract with the pawner, but the Moneylenders Act, 1927, gives the court power to reopen the transaction.

PAWTUCK'ET. A city of Rhode Island, United States, in Providence county, on the Blackstone River; served by the New York, New Haven, & Hartford Railroad, and by the river, which is navigable below the falls. Samuel Slater established at Pawtucket the first of the United States cotton-mills (1790), and the city is now a great manufacturing centre. It was founded about 1670, and became a city in 1885 after the absorption of townships on both sides of the river. Pop. 77,149.

PAX. An ecclesiastical utensil in the Roman Catholic Church, formed usually of a plate of metal, chased, engraved, or inlaid with figures representing the Virgin and Child, the crucifixion, etc., which, having been kissed by the priest during the *Agnus Dei* of the High Mass, is handed to the acolyte, who presents it to be kissed by each of the ecclesiastics officiating, saying to them *Pax tecum* (peace to thee). The decorations of the pax are frequently very rich.

PAXOS, or PAXO. One of the Ionian Islands, belonging to Greece, 8 miles south of Corfu. It is nearly 5 miles long and 2 miles broad, and consists of a mass of limestone rock. Principal product, olive-oil of the finest quality. Pop. 4000.

PAXTON, Sir Joseph. British gardener and architect, born in Bedfordshire 1801, died 1865. He was educated at the free school of Woburn; became gardener, and in 1826 estate manager to the Duke of Devonshire at Chatsworth, in Derbyshire. In 1851 he designed the Crystal Palace for the great International Exhibition (London), and soon after was knighted. He edited *The Horticultural Register*, *The Magazine of Botany*, *The Cottage Calendar*; and was the author (with Lindley) of a *Botanical Dictionary* and of *Paxton's Flower Garden*. From 1854 until his death he was member of Parliament for Coventry.

PAYMASTER. An officer in the British army and navy, through whom the officers and men receive their pay. The Army Pay Department comprises chief-paymasters, staff-paymasters, and paymasters, all with the rank of officers, while there is a corps of clerks, and a corps of accountants for costing purposes. Naval paymasters are administrative officers with a multiplicity of duties. They are responsible chiefly for pay and messing, but also deal with matters such as clothing and the victualling and fitting out of ships. In battle paymasters and their staffs are attached to the surgeons, and act as stretcher-bearers, etc. *See under* OFFICERS.

PAYMASTER-GENERAL. A British Government officer whose duties were formerly limited to the army, but who now acts as paymaster-general of all the services. Formerly it was a lucrative, but is now an unpaid office. The assistant paymaster-general, however, is a paid official, with a staff under him.

PAYN, James. British novelist, born at Cheltenham in 1830, died in 1898. Educated at Eton, Woolwich Academy, and Trinity College, Cambridge, he published poems and contributed to periodicals. He became editor of *Chambers's Journal* in 1858, and of the *Cornhill Magazine* in 1883; wrote many novels, including *Lost Sir Massingberd*, *Found Dead*, *By Proxy*, *The Talk of the Town*, *The Luck of the Darrels*, *The Heir of the Ages*; besides *Literary Recollections* and *Gleams of Memory*.

PAYSANDÚ. A department of Western Uruguay, South America, on the Rio Uruguay, which separates it from the Entre Rios province of Argentina. It is entirely devoted to stock-raising, and is of great importance as a beef-producer. Capital, Paysandú. Area, 5115 sq. miles; pop. (1931), 70,091.

PAYSANDÚ. A city of Uruguay, South America, capital of the department of Paysandú, on the Rio Uruguay, and one of the principal seaports of the Uruguayan Republic. It is served by railway to Montevideo and Buenos Aires in the south, and to the Brazilian frontier in the north. There are extensive abattoirs, and a large trade in live-stock is carried on through the port, which is at the head of low-water navigation on the river. Paysandú was founded in 1772, and is named in honour of Father (Pai) Sandú, who settled there in that year. Pop. (1931), 26,000.

PAYTA. A seaport of Northern Peru, in the department of Piura, and connected by railway with Piura, the capital of the department. Cotton is exported. The port is equipped for oil traffic. Pop. 4000.

PEA. A well-known leguminous plant of the genus Pisum, the *P. sativum*, of many varieties. It is a climbing annual plant, a native of the south of Europe, and has been cultivated from remote antiquity. It forms one of the most valuable of culinary vegetables; contains much farinaceous and saccharine matter, and is therefore highly nutritious.

It is cultivated in the garden and in the field. Its seed-vessel is a pod containing one row of round seeds, which are at first soft and juicy, in which state they are used for the table under the name of *green peas*. They afterwards harden and become farinaceous. A whitish sort, which readily splits when subjected to the action of millstones, is used in considerable quantities for soups, and especially for sea-stores. There is a blue sort which answers the same purpose.

PEA-BEETLE. A coleopterous insect (*Bruchus pisi*) about ¼ inch long, black, with white spots and dots on the wing-cases, very destructive to crops of pease in the south of Europe and in North America. Called also *Pea-bug, Pea-chafer,* and *Pea-weevil.*

PEABODY, George. American philanthropist, born at Danvers, Massachusetts, 1795, died 1869. In 1843 he came to London and established the firm of George Peabody & Co., exchange brokers and money-lenders. Having acquired a large fortune, he gave £100,000 to establish a free library in his native town; presented £200,000 to found a free library and institute of art and science at Baltimore; and in 1862 placed £150,000 in the hands of trustees for the benefit of the poor of London, to be employed in building model dwelling-houses. He afterwards added £350,000 to this benefaction.

PEACE CONFERENCE. A term applied to a meeting of representatives of different nations to settle important questions, territorial and otherwise. A peace conference usually takes place after hostilities, as the peace conference of the Allies in 1919 after the European War. The term is, however, also applied to the international conferences held at The Hague in 1899 and 1907. (*See* PEACE MOVEMENT.) Several other peace conferences have been convened since 1919, at Cannes, Hythe, Boulogne, Spa, Genoa, and The Hague.

PEACE MOVEMENT. The modern peace movement may be said to have originated in 1462, when Georg Podiebrad, King of Bohemia (1420-71), proposed a plan for a federation of Christian nations. Towards the end of the sixteenth century Henri IV. of France advanced a similar plan. Numerous schemes for the purpose of assuring a permanent world peace followed during the seventeenth and eighteenth centuries, such as those of Emeric Cruce (1590-1648), the Abbé St. Pierre (1658-1743), and others. Grotius wrote his famous work *De jure belli et pacis* (1625). Leibnitz and the Encyclopædists, and Joseph Priestley, in England, were in favour of peace, whilst Jeremy Bentham (1748-1832) elaborated a plan for a universal and permanent peace. In Germany, too, Lessing and Herder raised their voices in favour of peace, and in 1793 Kant wrote a plea for eternal peace.

After the Napoleonic wars pacifism gained ground and peace organisations were founded. The first peace society was organised in London in 1816, and another was founded at Geneva in 1830. In 1889 the first World's Peace Congress was held in Paris, and in 1898 Ivan de Block published his monumental work on war, a work which is said to have suggested to Nicholas II., Tsar of Russia, the idea of inviting the Powers to meet in conference at The Hague. Peace organisations have since multiplied, and Nobel peace prizes have been distributed, but no peace propaganda could prevent the European War.

After the War came the establishment of the League of Nations, and the inauguration of the greatest peace movement of modern times. By substituting arbitration and an international code of laws for the argument of force, the League aimed to eliminate the possibility of war. In several cases it was conspicuously successful, notably in settling the dispute between Greece and Bulgaria in 1925.

From 1920 all disputes calling for judicial settlement were referred to an international law-court or tribunal established in that year at the Hague.

In 1928 the Paris Peace Pact, signed by 59 nations, condemned recourse to war for the solution of international controversies. It strongly imposes the obligation to seek settlement in every case by pacific means.

Since then most countries of the world have agreed in declaring war illegal, unless undertaken in self-defence, or in defence of the community of nations.

See LEAGUE OF NATIONS.—BIBLIOGRAPHY: Norman Angell (R. N. A. Lane), *The Great Illusion*; E. B. Krehbiel, *Nationalism, War, and Peace*; C. C. Morrison, *The Outlawry of War* (1927); J. S. Bassett, *The League of Nations* (1928); J. T. Shotwell, *The Pact of Paris* (1928).

PEACE RIVER. A river of Canada, which rises in the Rockies of British Columbia, flows north-eastwards, receives the drainage of Lake Athabasca, and finally enters the Great Slave Lake under the name of the Slave River. It is 1054 miles in length, and is navigable for a large part of its course.

PEACH. A tree and its fruit, of the almond genus (ord. Rosaceæ), the *Prunus persica,* of many varieties. This is a delicious fruit, the produce of warm or temperate climates. The tree is of moderate stature, but varies in this respect according to soil and climate. The varieties of the fruit, which is a large downy drupe containing a stone, are very numerous, differing in size, flavour, and time of ripening, but they are principally of two sorts, the *free-stones* and the *cling-stones,* so called according as the stone separates readily or adheres to the flesh. The peach tree is supposed to have been introduced into Europe from Persia. In the southern parts of England it is grown out of doors, and in the United States it is extensively cultivated, great quantities being canned for export. The ripe fruit is distilled and made into peach brandy. The nectarine is a smooth variety of the peach.

PEACOCK, Thomas Love. English novelist and poet, was born in 1785, and died in 1866. His father, a wealthy glass-merchant, died when Peacock was three. He was educated at a private school at Englefield Green, but was mainly a self-taught scholar, acquiring a wide knowledge of classical literature, especially Greek poetry. He became an intimate friend of Shelley, whom he met in 1812. His enthusiasm for Greek literature was infectious, and immensely beneficial to the work of Shelley. Peacock, after a more or less desultory career, entered the employment of the East India Company in 1819, and served it faithfully until 1856. He played an important part in promoting the construction of iron steamships for Eastern waters.

Peacock's poems, with the exception of *Rhododaphne* and the lyrics embedded in the novels, are not of much account. His reputation rests upon his seven novels, which are *Headlong Hall* (1816), *Melincourt* (1817), *Nightmare Abbey* (1818), *Maid Marian* (1822), *The Misfortunes of Elphin* (1829), *Crotchet Castle* (1831), and, after a long silence, *Gryll Grange* (1860). Of these *Nightmare Abbey* and *Crotchet Castle* are perhaps the most brilliant.

Maid Marian and *The Misfortunes of Elphin* are somewhat different from the others, as they use the form of a romantic tale as a stalking-horse, from behind which they shoot at contemporary follies. *Melincourt*, which has for its hero an almost human orang-utan, is the only failure of the series. *Gryll Grange* is almost as fresh and humorous as the earlier novels, and is a wonderful piece of work for a man of seventy-five.

Peacock's novels have a charm and fascination that is all their own. They appeal to the head rather than to the heart, but have always found "fit audience though few." They are practically without plot, and their characters are not men, but personified "humours" like those of Ben Jonson. Their virtue lies in their grace of style, accuracy of natural description, and sound common sense, and also depends not a little upon the charming lyrics they contain. In this last respect they resemble the ancient Menippean satire, and the *Satiricon* of Petronius (q.v.). They have already outlived, and will doubtless continue to outlive, many novels that were not "caviare to the general."—Cf. A. M. Freeman, *Thomas Love Peacock*.

PEACOCK, called also **PEAFOWL.** A large and beautiful bird of the pheasant family (Phasianidæ), genus Pavo. The common peacock, *P. cristātus*, is a native of India and South-Eastern Asia. This bird is characterised by a crest of peculiar form, and by the tail-coverts of the male extending far beyond the quills, and being capable of erection into a broad and gorgeous disc. The shining, lax, and silky barbs of

Peacock

these feathers, and the eye-like spots which decorate their extremities, are known to every one.

The colours and plumage are said to be more brilliant in the wild than in the domesticated state. The wild peahen lays from twenty-five to thirty eggs, and produces only a single brood in each year. The young birds of both sexes are feathered alike for the first two years; and in the third year the tail-coverts of the male begin to be developed and to assume their lustrous appearance. The black-shouldered or Japan peacock (*P. nigripennis*) is regarded as a variety of the common species; the Javan peacock (*P. muticus*) is a distinct form.

PEACOCK-BUTTERFLY. A name given by collectors of insects to butterflies of the species *Vanessa io*, from the eyes on their wings resembling the eyes on peacocks' feathers.

PEACOCK-FISH. A fish of the Mediterranean and Indian Seas (*Crenilabrus pavo*), characterised by the brilliancy of its hues—green, yellow, and red.

PEA-CRAB. A small brachyurous

crustacean of the genus Pinnothēres, which lives in the shells of oysters, mussels, and other bivalves. Two or three species are met with in Britain.

PEAK, or HIGH PEAK. A district of England, forming the north-west angle of Derbyshire and the southern end of the Pennine Chain, and consisting of a wild and romantic tract, full of hills, valleys, and moors, and celebrated for its limestone caverns and grottoes. The famous Peak Cavern at Castleton, the capital of the Peak District, is a spacious limestone cavern, entered by a natural arch 40 feet high and more than 100 feet wide. Near Castleton is Peveril Castle, which figures in Scott's *Peveril of the Peak*.

PEA-MAGGOT. The caterpillar of the pea-moth (*Grapholitha pisana*), which lays its eggs in peas, to which the larva is very destructive. It is common in Britain, and especially mischievous in wet seasons.

PEA-ORE. The name given to granular argilaceous oxide of iron, from its occurring in small masses or grains, nearly or quite spherical, and of the size of a pea.

PEAR. A tree of the genus Pyrus, ord. Rosaceæ, *P. commūnis*, which grows wild in many parts of Europe and Asia, and from which the numerous cultivated varieties have originated. The fruit is characterised by a saccharine aromatic juice, a soft and pearly liquid pulp, melting in the mouth, as in the butter-pear; or by a firm and crisp consistence, as in the winter bergamots.

The pear is chiefly propagated by grafting or budding on the wild pear stock, or on stocks raised from the seeds of cultivated pears, called free stocks. It is also grafted on the quince, the medlar, and the white thorn. At the present day more than 200 varieties are enumerated, and constant accessions are made every year.

France and the north of Italy are celebrated for the perfection to which they have carried the culture of this fruit. Numerous varieties are cultivated solely for the purpose of making perry, a liquor analogous to cider, and prepared nearly in the same manner. The wood is fine-grained, of a yellowish colour, and susceptible of a brilliant polish. In the early ages of Greece it was employed in statuary; now it is used for musical instruments, the handles of carpenters' tools, in wood-engraving, etc.

PEARL. The name applied to a concretion produced within the shells of certain species of molluscs, mostly bivalves, as the result of some abnormal secretory process. These concretions are highly valued, and are classed among the gems.

Production of Pearls. The production of a pearl is generally begun by the introduction of some foreign body, such as a grain of sand or a parasite, within the mantle-lobes. The presence of this body has the effect of setting up an irritant action, resulting in the deposition by the mantle of a quantity of nacreous material over the offending particle.

This material, in certain species of molluscs, is of such a texture and character, and is so deposited in regular laminæ or layers, that in due time the structure known as a "pearl," varying in worth and brilliancy, is formed. It has been

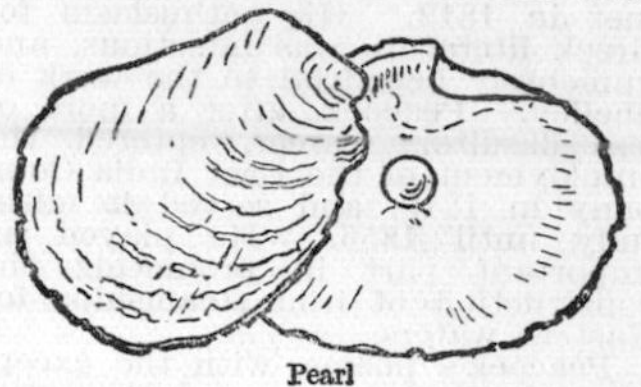

Pearl

demonstrated in the case of the "orient" pearls from the Gulf of Manaar that their formation is caused by the dead embryos of a kind of tape-worm, which passes through the other stages of its existence in the file-fish and a kind of ray.

Chief amongst pearl-forming molluscs are the pearl-oyster (*Meleagrīna margaritifĕra*), the pearl-mussel (*Avicŭla margaritifĕra*), and the fresh-water mussels (genus Unio) of British rivers. Pink pearls are chiefly obtained from the giant conch shell (*Strombus gigas*) of the West Indies.

Pearl-Oyster Fisheries. The chief pearl-oyster fisheries are those of Ceylon, which, together with the fisheries in the Persian Gulf, were known to the ancients. The chief seat of the Ceylon fishery is in the Gulf of Manaar, on the north-east of the island. It begins in February or March, and extends over a period of about a month, a large fleet of boats being usually engaged in it.

The average depth at which the oysters are found varies from 60 to 70 feet, and the divers are let down by a stout rope weighted by a heavy stone. Having gathered a number of the oysters into a net, at the end of half a minute or so the diver is pulled up. The oysters being carried to shore, and laid in piles, in about ten days become thoroughly decomposed. They are then thrown into sea-water, and carefully examined for pearls; whilst the shells, after being cleaned, are split into layers for the sake of the mother-of-pearl.

The pearl-fisheries of Ceylon are a Government monopoly, but the revenue derived from them is not a regular one, the fishery sometimes failing for years in succession. There was no fishery, for example, between 1837 and 1854, or between 1891 and 1902. The best pearls are found about Ceylon, Persia, and other Eastern coasts, and inferior ones on the tropical coasts of America.

The pearl-oyster occurs throughout the Pacific. Very fine pearls are obtained from the Sulu Archipelago in the north-east of Borneo. For some time pearl-fishing has been practised with success in Australian seas, the diving-dress being used. It is carried on also in the Gulf of Mexico, upon the coast of California, and in the vicinity of Panamá.

Pearls have also been obtained from the fresh-water mussels of British streams, and Scottish pearls were famed even in the Middle Ages. The Scottish pearl-fishery, after being abandoned for years, was revived in 1860, and in 1865 the produce of the season's fishing in the Scottish rivers was worth at least £12,000. The yield, however, has not been maintained.

Many rivers of Ireland and Wales furnish pearls. The pearl-fisheries of Britain are now, however, practically neglected, but river-pearls are systematically sought for in Germany, in the United States, and especially in China.

Decoration and Ornament. Pearls have formed valued articles of decoration and ornament from the earliest times. They were first sought for superstitious reasons, in the belief that they averted misfortune and brought luck. Julius Cæsar presented Servilia, the mother of Marcus Brutus, with a pearl valued in modern computation at £48,000; while Cleopatra was said to have swallowed one gem valued at £60,000 or £80,000. A pearl purchased by the traveller Tavernier is alleged to have been sold by him to the Shah of Persia for £180,000. The "Pilgrim" pearl of Moscow is diaphanous in character, and weighs 24 carats.

Artificial pearls are largely made in France, Germany, and Italy. They are very well imitated by the scales of certain fishes, such as the bleak. A substitute for black pearls is found in close-grained hæmatite, not too highly polished, and pink pearls are imitated by turning small spheres out of the rosy part of the conch-shell.

PEARL ISLANDS (Sp. *Arch. de las Perlas*). A Pacific archipelago, in the Gulf of Panamá, belonging to the Republic of Panamá. The principal islands are: Del Rey, San José, and Pedro Gonzales, but there are many others. The name is derived from the actively worked pearl-fisheries in surrounding waters.

PEARL LORE. It is uncertain at what period pearls first came into use as ornaments and charms. The ancient Egyptians collected in pre-Dynastic times freshwater pearl mussels from the Nile, and utilised their valves as receptacles for face-paint, etc. The Nile oyster (Ætheria) has been found in tombs of the Empire period. Pearls and pearl-shell were obtained from the Red Sea also. There is evidence to show that the Egyptians used pearl-shell for ornaments as early as the Sixth Dynasty.

Petrie in his *Amulets* (London, 1914, p. 27) refers to Red Sea pearl-shells found in graves of the Twelfth Dynasty, and engraved with the name of Senusert I. Pearls were given a religious value and associated with the mother goddess. During the Empire period (*c.* 1500 B.C.) pearls were worn by Egyptian women with shells, coral, precious stones, gold, etc. Neck ornaments adorned with pearls were worn by both sexes.

The extensive use of pearls in Egypt, however; dates from the Persian conquest. No doubt pearls were very expensive. They were obtained not only from the Red Sea but from East Africa. It is believed that King Solomon imported pearls from the north-east coast of Portuguese East Africa. At an early period pearls were obtained in the Persian Gulf. Pearls were used in Persia in the seventh century B.C. Assyrian monarchs depicted on bas-reliefs are seen to be adorned with them. Nose-rings with pearls were worn by Sassanian ladies.

The Greeks and Romans attached a religious value to pearls. Homer's Juno wears "earrings of three drops" (*Iliad*, xiv., 183) which may have been pearls; the Persian women wore pearls in threes, and the Grecian men of rank wore, as did Persian noblemen, a pearl earring in the right ear. According to Pliny, pearls became very fashionable in Rome after the surrender of Alexandria.

Pearls were used to decorate Roman temple altars. Julius Cæsar presented a breastplate adorned with British pearls to Venus. This goddess, the Greek Aphrodite, personified a pearl in one of her phases, and was shown in human form sitting on a shell and being raised by sea-gods above the waves. Pearls were appreciated in ancient Britain. Fragments of pearl-shell have been found in the hand-made pottery of the early Britons. In Gaelic manuscript stories regarding Cuchullin that hero wears pearls in his hair. Freshwater pearls were searched for and used by Scandinavians and the peoples of Central Europe.

Pearls are referred to in ancient Hindu literature. Gods and human beings wore pearls and pearl-shell. According to the Sanskrit work *Atharvaveda* (*c.* 500 B.C.), pearls and pearl-shell ensured long life. Buddhists added to their stock of religious merit and power by accumulating pearls and precious stones. The pearl-fisheries of Ceylon, Madras, etc., are of considerable antiquity. Pearls were placed in the mouths of the dead in India when Marco Polo visited that country six centuries ago. The same custom obtained in China. Both in China and India ground pearls were used as medicine; it was believed that the " life-giving pearl " would prolong life.

In Old Persian the pearl was called *margan*, which signifies " life-giver." Pearls have long been fished for in Malaysia, Indonesia, and Polynesia. In these countries, as in China, pearls are connected with " wonder beasts " of the dragon order. The Chinese dragon is closely associated with pearls. Like the Indian nagas (serpent deities), the Chinese dragons spit out pearls. " Thunder pearls " are " dropped from dragons' mouths." Like jade, the pearl is supposed to be impregnated with *yang* (life-giving) substance, and there are Chinese literary references to " pearls of jade."

The pearl was connected with the moon, and was supposed to shine in darkness. There are Chinese references to " the pearl of the moon," and to the moon as a " night-shining pearl." This connection between the pearl and heaven is found in Gaelic, *neamh* being the sky and *neamhnuid* the pearl. Both names are derived from the root *nem.* In Dante's *Paradiso* the moon is referred to as " the eternal pearl." The pearl was likewise connected with the moon by the pre-Columbian Americans.

In India and Japan there are Buddhist legends about the " precious pearl which grants all desires." This pearl was obtained from a sea-dragon. Two magic jewels that caused the sea to flow and ebb were pearls. Pearls have been found in pre-Columbian graves in North America. The Mexicans, when first visited by the Spaniards, were found to be admirers of pearls, which they used to decorate their gods and temples, as did the Hindus, Romans, and others.

In Peru the Incas used pearls as artificial eyes for their mummies, as the Egyptians formerly used pearl-shell. Many ancient peoples believed that pearls were congealed dewdrops, or that they were formed by drops of rain. The belief among early Christians that pearls originated from " angels' tears " was evidently of pagan origin. In Scandinavia pearls, amber, precious stones, etc., were supposed to have originated from the tears of the goddess Freyja. The dragons of China which spat pearls were rain-producers.

It was apparently because pearls were supposed to originate in life-giving water, or from tears of deities, that they were regarded as elixirs and used as medicine, and also as charms. When placed in the mouth of the dead, pearls were believed to facilitate their resurrection. The pearls worn by warriors were supposed to protect them. As the pearls radiated sacred influence, being of divine origin, the Buddhist habit of accumulating them, and the Roman habit of presenting them to deities, can be understood.

De Groot, in his *The Religious System of China* (p. 136), states that pearls, jade, gold, etc., were supposed by the ancient Chinese to be " imbued with influences emitted from the heavens." The modern belief that pearls " sicken " when the wearer falls into bad health is probably a survival from the time when pearls were regarded as " life-givers."

PEARL STONE. A glassy rhyolite with perlitic structure that is, with minute curving cracks developed during cooling, which divide it into little globular bodies with a pearly lustre.

PEARSON, John. English divine, born at Snoring, Norfolk, about 1613, died 1688. Educated at Eton and Cambridge, he took orders in 1639, and held successively the livings of Torrington in Suffolk, and of St. Clement Eastcheap, London. He became professor of divinity at Cambridge in 1661, and Bishop of Chester in 1672, and was considered one of the most learned Englishmen of his time. His chief work is an *Exposition of the Creed* (1659).

PEARY, Robert Edwin. American Arctic explorer, born in 1856, died in 1920. He entered the United States navy in 1881, and after serving for a time as assistant engineer in connection with the surveys for the Nicaragua Ship Canal, made a voyage to Greenland and penetrated some distance inland. In 1891-2 he demonstrated that Greenland was an island. His second expedition to the north of that country took place in 1893-5, and he made other Arctic voyages in 1896 and 1897.

In 1898 he set out on a fresh voyage of exploration in Greenland and the Polar seas, from which he returned in Sept., 1902, having reached 84° 17′ N.

Robert Peary

lat. He again set out in 1905, and in Nov., 1906, word was received from him that he had reached lat. 87° 6′, or within 203 miles of the North Pole, the highest latitude ever attained. On his next expedition he appears to have reached the Pole, or a point close to it, early in 1909. He published *Northward over the Great Ice*, a record of his Arctic work (2 vols., 1898); *Nearest the Pole* (1907); and *The North Pole* (1910).

PEASANTS' REVOLT. The most notable social or class war in English history is the Peasants' Revolt of 1381. Its real cause was an attempt by landlords to solve the labour problem of this time by reimposing obligations of serfdom or villeinage, which was becoming obsolete, but the occasion was a poll-tax or Government impost per head of the population. Many parishes gave fraudulent returns of the numbers of inhabitants, so as to diminish the total assessment on the parish, and, consequently, the amount of each individual's payment.

The frauds were discovered, and the tax was exacted with such severity that the peasants of Essex, Kent, Norfolk, Suffolk, and Cambridgeshire broke into rebellion, and marched to London in June, 1381. The young king, Richard II., agreed at Mile End to accede to their demands and to abolish serfdom, but the rebels were not satisfied, and there was a great riot in London, in which many houses were pillaged and burned, and the Archbishop of Canterbury and the Lord Treasurer were murdered.

On the following day (14th June) there was another conference at Smithfield, in the course of which the rebel leader, Wat Tyler, was killed, and the boy-king declared that he himself would be their leader. While the conference was in progress, the Mayor of London brought troops and the rebels were surrounded. In spite of the royal promises, the rebellion was followed by very severe measures, and Parliament refused to abolish serfdom. Economic conditions continued to lead to its disappearance, but the revolt rather hindered than helped the process.—BIBLIOGRAPHY: Sir C. W. C. Oman, *The Great Revolt of 1831*; G. M. Trevelyan, *England in the Age of Wycliffe*.

PEASANTS' WAR. An insurrectionary movement among the German peasantry, which took place in 1522-5. The immediate cause of this movement was religious fanaticism, but the pent-up forces by which it was impelled grew out of the long course of oppression to which feudal customs and priestly tyranny had subjected the people. As in France before the Revolution, so in Germany at the time of the Reformation the double yoke of civil and ecclesiastic bondage had been growing heavier until it had become intolerable.

The insurrection broke out in the Black Forest area, and soon spread over Franconia and Thuringia. The mobs destroyed convents and castles, pillaged and murdered, and were guilty of fearful and atrocious cruelties. Luther denounced the excesses of the peasants, and their army, under the command of Münzer, was overwhelmed at Frankenhausen (15th May, 1525) by the Landgrave Philip the Magnanimous of Hesse and dispersed. It is estimated that over 100,000 persons lost their lives in these risings, which for the time gave a severe blow to the Reformation. *See* JACQUERIE.—Cf. E. B. Bax, *The Peasants' War in Germany* (*The Social Side of the Reformation*).

PEAT. A kind of turfy substance consisting of vegetable matter which has accumulated by constant growth and decay in hollows or moist situations on land not in a state of cultivation, always more or less saturated with water, and consisting of the remains, more or less decomposed, of the mosses Sphagnum and Hypnum and other marsh plants.

Peat is generally of a black or dark-brown colour, or when recently formed, of a yellowish-brown; it is soft and of a viscid consistence, but it becomes hard and darker by exposure to the air. When thoroughly dried it burns, giving out a gentle heat without much smoke; it is much used as fuel in those countries where it abounds, as in Scotland and Ireland. It often covers large areas, forming what are called peat-bogs, and in these the accumulation of solid peat may reach a great depth, sometimes 50 feet or more. When prepared for fuel in the ordinary way, it is dug from the bog in rectangular brick-like masses, which are set up to dry on the spot, and when sufficiently dried are carried away and stacked.

Peat, as it is cut from the bog, contains from 80 to 90 per cent of water, and when air-dried the water still forms 15 to 25 per cent of its weight. To increase its value as fuel several methods for drying and condensing it have been employed. It is used as litter; as an absorbent and packing, fruits and vegetables being kept fresh by it; as a source of gas and paraffin; a material for woven fabrics, etc. *See* FUEL.

PEAUCELLIER'S CELL. *See* PARALLEL MOTION.

PEBA. A species of the armadillo (*Tatusia novemcincta*) found in various parts of South America. Its flesh is much valued by the natives.

PÉBRINE. A French name for a destructive epizootic disease among silk-worms due to protozoan parasites, which swarm in the blood and all the tissues of the body, passing into the undeveloped eggs of the females, so that it is hereditary, but only on the side of the mother. It is contagious and infectious, the parasites passing from the bodies of the diseased caterpillars into the alimentary canal of healthy silk-worms in their neighbourhood.

PEC. A town of Montenegro, Yugoslavia, 75 miles E.N.E. of Cetinje. Pop. 14,000.

PECAN′, or PECAN-NUT. A species of hickory (*Carya olivæformis*) and its fruit, growing in North America. It is a large tree, with hard, very tough wood, pinnate leaves, and catkins of small flowers. The nuts are occasionally to be met with in British fruit-shops.

PEC′CARY (Dicotyles). A genus of hoofed mammals, included in the Artiodactyle ("eventoed") section of that order, and constituting a distinct family (Dicotylidæ) closely allied to swine. These animals are exclusively confined to America, in which continent they represent the true swine of the Old World. In general form the peccaries resemble small pigs. The best-known species are the collared peccary (*Dicotyles torquātus*) and the white-lipped peccary (*D. labiatus*). The former occurs abundantly in South America, and also extends into North America, living generally in small flocks,

Peccary

which do not hesitate to attack with their tusks anyone who meddles with them.

Their food consists of maize, potatoes, sugar-canes, and similar materials; and cultivated fields suffer much from their raids. This species of peccary is readily domesticated. The flesh is savoury, and less fat than pork. The peccary possesses a glandular sac or pouch, situated in the loins, which secretes a strongly smelling fluid of fœtid nature. This must be cut away immediately on killing a peccary, to avoid contaminating the flesh.

PECOP′TERIS. A genus of fossil ferns occurring from the Carboniferous to the Jurassic systems, named from the comb-like arrangement of the leaflets.

PECOS RIVER. A river of the United States. It rises in New Mexico, flows through Texas, and enters the Rio Grande; course, 750 miles.

PECS. Formerly Funfkirchen (q.v.).

PECTEN. A genus of bivalve molluscs, the type of a special family (Pectinidæ) allied to oysters, and popularly designated under the name of "scallop-shells." Numerous species of pecten—180 or more—are known. The common pecten (*P. operculāris*) and the frill or great scallop (*P. maximus*) are the most common forms. The latter form is esteemed a delicacy, and as such is sold in the London markets.

The shell of this species was borne in the Middle Ages by pilgrims in their hats, as a sign that they had visited the Holy Land. The shell is somewhat rounded, and terminates superiorly in a triangular "ear," in which the hinge exists. The name "pecten" (Lat. for "comb") is derived from the indentation of the edges and surfaces of the shell.

PECTINIBRANCHIATA. Those sea-snails having comb-like branchiæ or gills, as the purple shells (Murex), whelk (Buccinum), cowries (Cypræa), etc.

PEC'TOLITE. A mineral consisting of hydrous calcium sodium silicate. It is a tough greyish or whitish mineral occurring in basic lavas, in aggregated crystals of a silky lustre, commonly arranged in radiated forms.

PECULIAR. In canon law, a particular parish or church which has jurisdiction within itself, and exemption from that of the ordinary or bishop's court. The *Court of Peculiars*, in England, is a branch of the Court of Arches which has jurisdiction over all the parishes in the province of Canterbury which are exempt from the ordinary jurisdiction, and subject to the metropolitan only.

PECULIAR PEOPLE, or PLUMSTEAD PECULIARS. A Protestant sect founded in 1838 by John Banyard, and found chiefly in Kent, England. They believe in the efficiency of prayer without the use of any efforts on their own part. In sickness they reject the aid of physicians, accepting James, v., 14, 15 in a strictly literal sense. They have also certain peculiarities of dress, etc. *See* FAITH-HEALING.

PEDEE', GREAT and LITTLE. Two rivers in the United States. The former rises in North Carolina, enters South Carolina, and falls into the Atlantic: total course, 360 miles, of which 200 miles are navigable for boats of 60 or 70 tons. Little Pedee rises in North Carolina, and enters the Great Pedee 32 miles above its embouchure.

PEDE'TES (Gr. *pēdētēs*, a leaper). A genus of rodent mammals, of which the only species is *P. capensis* (the jumping-hare of South Africa). This constitutes a distinct family (Pedetidæ) related to the jerboas.

PED'ICEL. In botany, the stalk that supports one flower only when there are several on a peduncle.

PEDICELLA'RIÆ. Specialised spines attached to the skin or outer surface of star-fishes, sea-urchins, and other Echinodermata. Each pedicellaria consists essentially of a stalk attached to the organism, and bearing at its free extremity two or more movable blades or jaws, which open and close on foreign particles so as to retain them.

PEDICULA'RIS. An extensive genus of herbaceous perennials, chiefly European, of the nat. ord. Scrophulariaceæ. Two British species are common, *P. palustris* and *P. sylvatica*; they are herbs of brownish hue, with deeply divided leaves and showy pink flowers, growing in moist pastures, and commonly known as Lousewort.

PEDILAN'THUS. A genus of South American plants belonging to the nat. ord. Euphorbiaceæ, of which one species (*P. tithymaloides*), used medicinally in the West Indies, is known under the name of ipecacuanha, and is employed for the same purpose as that drug.

PED'IMENT. In classic architecture, the triangular mass resembling a gable, above the entablature at the end of buildings or over porticoes. The pediment is surrounded by a cornice, and is often ornamented with sculpture. The triangular finishings over doors and windows are also called pediments. In the debased Roman style the same name is given to these same parts, though not triangular in their form. In the architecture of the Middle Ages small gables and triangular decorations over openings, niches, etc., are called pediments.

PEDIPALPI. An order of arachnidans, comprising the whip-scorpions, and other unfamiliar forms.

PEDLARS and HAWKERS. Itinerant dealers who carry their goods from place to place for sale. The Hawkers' Act (1888) defines a hawker as one who travels with a horse or other beast bearing or drawing a burden; the Pedlars' Act (1871) describes a pedlar as one travelling without a horse, etc. Certificates for the latter (5*s*. annually) are given by the chief officer of police of the district for which they are asked, to persons of good character, who must satisfy the officer they are seventeen years of age, have resided for one month in the district, and intend to carry on the business of a pedlar in good faith. These certificates may be extended to other police districts by endorsement of the chief of police, at a charge not exceeding sixpence for each endorsement. Hawkers' licenses are granted by the excise, and cost £2 annually.

PEDOM'ETER. An instrument made in the form of a watch and carried in a pocket by a pedestrian, to enable him to know what distance he has walked. The mechanism consists of a heavy pendulum which receives an impulse every time a step is made, a spring to bring back the pendulum to its normal position, and a ratchet which is operated from

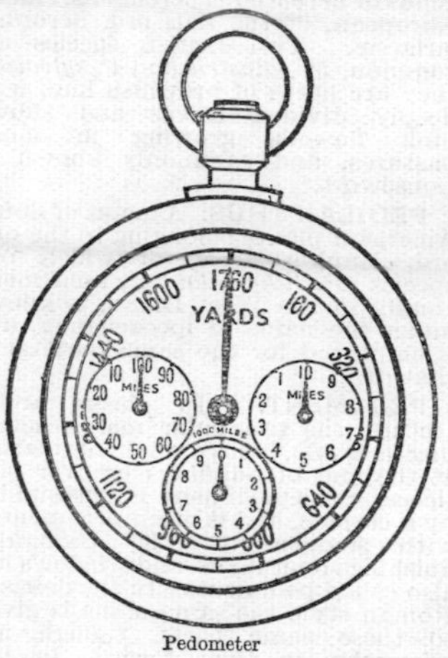

Pedometer

the pendulum and gives motion to a train of wheels. The dial is graduated in miles and yards. The instrument should be tested by walking known distances and checking the readings. Adjustments of the length of the pendulum change the readings, and may be required before the instrument can be relied upon by the user.

PEDRO II, Emperor of Brazil. Born at Rio de Janeiro 1825, died in 1891. He succeeded to the throne on the abdication of his father, Dom Pedro I., in 1831, and married the Princess Theresa Christina Maria (died 1890), sister of Francis I., King of Naples, in 1843. Brazil prospered greatly under the rule of Pedro II., who did much to develop its resources in every direction. In 1871 he issued an imperial decree for the gradual abolition of slavery, which totally ceased in Brazil in May, 1888. He was deposed by the Revolution of Nov., 1889, and died at Paris.

PEEBLES. A royal and municipal burgh of Scotland, the county town of Peeblesshire, on the Tweed; served by the L.N.E. and L.M.S. Railways. It is an angling resort; tweeds and other cloth are manufactured.

The name is derived from the *pebylls* (tents) of the Gadeni which occupied the site in Roman times, and the town was long a favourite haunt of the Scottish kings, who hunted periodically in Ettrick Forest. It became a royal burgh in 1367 by charter of Alexander III. A notable building is the Chambers Institution, presented to the town in 1859 by William Chambers, the Edinburgh publisher. This building was originally the Queensberry Lodging, town house of the Earls of March, and was restored and enlarged by Andrew Carnegie during 1912. Pop. (1931), 5853.

PEEBLESSHIRE, or TWEEDDALE. An inland county of Scotland; area, 222,240 acres. The greater part of the surface consists of mountain, moor, and bog, and the main industry is sheep-farming. Highest summit, Broad Law, 2734 feet, near the south border. White and red freestone are common in the northern part of the county, and both coal and limestone have been wrought at various points. Peeblesshire is a great sheep-raising county. The Tweed is the only notable river, but its affluents include the Manor, Lyne, and Biggar. The L.N.E. and L.M.S. Railways provide communications. With Midlothian Peeblesshire returns two members to Parliament. Pop. (1931), 15,050.—Cf. Sir H. Maxwell, *The Story of the Tweed.*

PEEKSKILL. An industrial town of Westchester county, New York, United States, on Hudson River; served by the New York Central and Hudson River Railway, and by river-steamers. It was founded in 1764, and was incorporated in 1816. Pop. 17,125.

PEEL, Arthur Wellesley. Viscount, youngest son of Sir Robert Peel, born 1829, died in 1912. He was educated at Eton and Oxford; was member for Warwick (1865-95); parliamentary secretary to Poor-law Board (1868-71); secretary to Board of Trade (1871-3); patronage secretary to Treasury (1873-4); under secretary for Home Department (1880); succeeded Sir Henry Brand in 1884 as Speaker of the House of Commons, retiring in 1895; was chairman of the Licensing Commission of 1896-1900, and drafted the minority report.

PEEL, Sir Robert. British statesman, born 5th Feb., 1788, near Bury, in Lancashire, died 2nd July, 1850. His father, who had raised himself from a comparatively humble station to be the largest cotton-manufacturer in the world, was created a baronet in 1800, and left behind him a fortune of nearly £2,000,000, of which the largest share was inherited by his eldest son Robert. Young Peel was sent to Harrow and Oxford, where he took his bachelor's degree in 1808, with double first-class honours.

Immediately on attaining his majority he was elected member of Parliament for Cashel; in 1810 he became Under Secretary of State for the Colonies; and from 1812 to 1818 he was Chief Secretary for Ireland. In 1817 he was elected as member for the University of Oxford. The following year he resigned his office in the ministry, of which he still continued to be a supporter, and began to take a leading part in the discussion of the difficult financial questions then pending. In 1822, under the Liverpool ministry, he became Home Secretary, and continued in this office till the dissolution. Refusing to take office under Canning, he joined the ministry of the Duke of Wellington in 1828 as Home Secretary.

The principal act of this ministry was the passing of the Roman Catholic Relief Bill, which cost Peel his seat for Oxford. Peel also passed the New Metropolitan Police Act, which gave rise to the new nicknames Bobbies and Peelers for the London police. In 1830 he succeeded his father as baronet. At the close of this year the ministry resigned in consequence of the increasing agitation for parliamentary reform, and was succeeded by the reform ministry of Earl Grey.

Peel strenuously opposed the Bill, but after it became law he declared his intention frankly to accept it, and began vigorously to prepare his party for the change in its circumstances. In the election of 1832 he was returned for Tamworth, for which he continued to sit during the remainder of his life.

On the dismissal of the Whig Government in 1834 Peel undertook the government, but his party in the House being in a minority, the task was hopeless. After a brief struggle the ministry resigned, and was succeeded by the Whig ministry of Lord Melbourne, which lasted from 1835 to 1841. The general election of 1841 gave a large majority to Sir Robert Peel, and the formation of a Conservative ministry could no longer be delayed.

There was a strong agitation for the repeal of the corn-laws, but Peel himself was in favour of a modification of the sliding scale of duty which had existed since 1828. Other measures of the session of 1842 were the imposition of an income-tax for three years, and a revision of the tariff. In 1844 and 1845 he passed his celebrated English and Scotch Banking Acts. During the recess in 1845 the potato-rot and famine in Ireland brought the question of the corn-laws to a crisis, and Peel declared in favour of their total repeal. The Act repealing the corn-laws (after a modified duty for three years) was passed on 26th June, 1846. On the same day the ministry was defeated in the House of Commons on the Irish Coercion Bill, and on the 29th of June Sir Robert Peel resigned.

On 29th June, 1850, he was thrown from his horse, and received injuries of which he died three days later. By his will he renounced a peerage for his family, as he had before declined the Garter for himself. In his private capacity Sir Robert Peel was a generous patron of literature and art, and his collections of pictures were somewhat celebrated.—BIBLIOGRAPHY: T. Doubleday, *The Political Life of Sir R. Peel*; J. R. Thursfield, *Peel* (in Twelve English Statesmen Series); F. P. G. Guizot, *Sir Robert Peel: étude d'histoire contemporaine.*

PEEL. An ancient seaport, town, and watering-place on the west coast of the Isle of Man; served by railway from Douglas and by road. There is an extensive fishing industry. On St. Patrick's Isle, joined to the mainland by a causeway, stands the ruin of Peel Castle, and the roofless remains of the cathedral of St. German's. The castle is mentioned by Sir Walter Scott (Fenella's Tower, etc.) in *Peveril of the Peak.* Among notable prisoners of Peel were the Earl of Warwick (1397) and the Duchess of Gloucester, (1444). The name is of Keltic origin meaning "fort," e.g. "peel-towers" (q.v.) of the Scottish borderland derive their name from the same source. Pop. (1931), 2476.

PEELE, George. English dramatist and poet, born in London in 1558, and died in or before 1598. His father was clerk of Christ's Hospital, and an able man with original views about book-keeping. Peele was educated at Christ's Hospital and at Broadgates Hall (now Pembroke College), Oxford; he migrated, however, to Christ Church, whence he graduated B.A. in 1577 and M.A. in 1579. After leaving Oxford he led a Bohemian life in London, and was a friend of Greene, Nash, and Marlowe.

He married, in 1583, a lady of property, but did not become any more sober in his mode of living.

Little more is known of his life, but he died before Sept., 1598, when Francis Meres, in his *Palladis Tamia*, wrote, "As Anacreon died by the pot, so George Peele by the pox." Some nine years after his death there appeared a collection of *facetiæ* entitled *Merrie conceited Jests of George Peele.* Some of these jests are much older than Peele, but some passages are biographical. Upon one of these stories is based *The Puritan, or the Widow of Watling Street*, a play sometimes misattributed to Shakespeare. Its hero, George Pyeboard, is Peele himself ("peel" is a baker's board for shoving pies in and out of the oven).

His Plays. Peele's pastoral comedy *The Araygnement of Paris* appeared about 1581. It is a graceful play, full of skilful flattery of Queen Elizabeth. *King Edward I.* (to reduce its lengthy title to a reasonable compass) is a chronicle-history which misrepresents Queen Elinor because she was a Spaniard. It probably appeared soon after the defeat of the Armada. *The Battell of Alcazar* is a vigorous play which is probably by Peele. *The Old Wives' Tale* is one of the most amusing of Peele's plays. It is usually considered to be a skit upon romantic drama, and so a forerunner of *The Knight of the Burning Pestle*; but some critics consider that it exemplifies rather than satirises a certain kind of folly.

The Love of King David and Fair Bethsabe (1588) owes its plot entirely to the Old Testament, and was probably written as a counterblast to those who charged the drama with lack of respectability. Fleay credits (or perhaps it would be more correct to say discredits) Peele with the authorship of *The Wisdom of Doctor Doddipoll, Wily Beguiled,* and *The Life and Death of Jack Straw.*

Peele had not the natural gifts that a dramatist should have; his very considerable gifts were purely poetical. He wrote plays simply to make a livelihood; he had no literary conscience, and something of the university man's contempt for his uneducated audience. *The Old Wives' Tale* probably gives his views upon contemporary drama. He could not handle a plot, or a dramatic situation. His work, however, is full of variety and interest, and he has a real gift for musical effect. His poems contain some beautiful passages, of which the best known is:

His helmet now shall make a hive for bees,
  And lovers' songs be turned to holy psalms;
A man at arms must now serve on his knees.
  And feed on prayers, which are old age's alms.

—BIBLIOGRAPHY: G. C. Odell, *Peele as a Dramatist* (*The Bibliographer*, vol. ii., 1903); Sir A. W. Ward, *English Dramatic Literature*; J. A. Symonds, *Shakspere's Predecessors.*

PEEL-TOWER, or simply **PEEL.** The name given on the Scottish borders to small residential towers erected for defence against predatory excursions. They were usually square

Peel Tower

buildings with turrets at the angles. The lower part was vaulted, and served for the accommodation of horses and cattle. *See* PEEL.

PEEP-O'-DAY BOYS. An organisation of Protestant Ulstermen formed in Ireland in 1784, shortly after the volunteer movement. They were so named from visiting the houses of the "defenders," their antagonists, at daybreak in search of arms.

PEEPUL, PIPUL, or **SACRED FIG** (*Ficus religiosa*). A species of fig tree common in India, and held sacred by the Hindus and Buddhists. Its leaves are heart-shaped on long stalks. It attains a great age, and is usually planted near temples, where it affords shelter to the devotees. Vishnu is said to have been born under a peeulp tree. Its fruits are edible, but not much esteemed.

PEER (Fr. *pair*, from Lat. *par*, equal). Literally an equal, one of the same rank and station. In this sense it is used by the common law of England, which declares that every person is to be tried by his peers. Peer also signifies in Britain a member of one of the five degrees of nobility that constitute the *peerage* (duke, marquess, earl, viscount, baron). The dignity and privileges of peers originated with the growth of the feudal system, the peers being originally the chief vassals holding fiefs directly from the Crown, and having, in virtue of their position, the hereditary right of acting as royal counsellors. Subsequently not all the Crown vassals appeared at court as advisers of the king, but only those who were summoned to appear by writ.

This custom grew at length into a rule, and these summonses were considered proofs of hereditary peerage. Peers are now created by letters patent. The British peerage collectively consists of peers of England, of Scotland, of Great Britain, of Ireland, and of the United Kingdom, but only a portion of the Scottish and Irish peers are peers of Parliament. A peerage may be limited to sons and their descendants, or extended by special remainder to daughters or a brother. Women can be peeresses in their own right, but in 1922 failed to establish their right to sit in the House of Lords. *See* BRITAIN; NOBILITY; PARLIAMENT.

PEG'ASUS. In Greek mythology, a winged horse, said to have sprung from the trunk of Medusa. Bellerophon made use of Pegasus in his fight with the Chimæra. With the stroke

Pegasus

of his hoof Pegasus called forth the sacred well Hippocrene, on Mount Helicon, from which he was in later times called the horse of the muses.

PEGASUS. In zoology, a genus of small spiny-finned fishes inhabiting the Indian Ocean and Western Pacific.

PEG'MATITE. A coarse granite rock occurring as veins, composed mainly of potassium felspar and quartz, typically intergrown with each other. It is used in the manufacture of porcelain.

PEGU. A division, district, and town of Burma. The division of Pegu comprises the districts of Rangoon (city), Hanthawadi, Pegu, Prome, and Tharrawadi, east of the Irrawaddy River. Area, 13,707 sq. miles; pop. about 2,030,044.—The district of Pegu was formed in 1883, and extends between the Sittang River (west side) and the Pegu Yoma range. Rice is produced in large quantities, and is the only agricultural product. Area, 4275 sq. miles; pop. 429,000.—The town of Pegu stands on Pegu River, and is a junction for Moulmein and Mandalay on the railway from Rangoon. It was formerly the capital of Lower Burma, and is supposed to have been founded in A.D. 573 as first capital of the Talings. During both first and second Burmese Wars it was the scene of considerable fighting. Pop. 19,000. The Pegu River rises in the Pegu Yoma range, and joins the Rangoon River below Rangoon City after a course of 180 miles. The Pegu Yoma range extends roughly north and south for some 200 miles between Sittang and the Irrawaddy. The maximum elevation is about 2000 feet. In the afforested slopes and valleys teak and other valuable timbers are found.

PEI-HO (pe-i-hō'). A river of Northern China, rises near the Great Wall, and flows south-east to the Gulf of Chih-li, which it enters after a course of about 350 miles. The Pei-ho system has a drainage area of over 50,000 sq. miles. At its mouth is the small town of Taku, with several forts, which were captured by an Anglo-French force on 20th May, 1858, and again on 21st Aug., 1860, and were finally stormed by European and Japanese troops on 17th June, 1900.

PEINE FORTE ET DURE (pen fort e dür). A punishment formerly inflicted upon a prisoner who refused to plead guilty or not guilty when put on trial for felony. He was put into a low dark chamber, and laid on his back naked, on the floor. As great a weight of iron as he could bear was then laid upon him until he died or answered.

PEIPING, or **PEKING** ("northern capital" as opposed to Nanking). Capital of China till 1928, in the province of Chih-li, about 35 miles from the Great Wall, and 90 miles from the Gulf of Chih-li; served by the Peiping-Mukden Railway. The entire circuit of the walls and suburbs of Peiping is reckoned at 30 miles. There are in all sixteen gates leading into the city, each protected by a semicircular enceinte, and a higher tower built in galleries. The city consists of two portions, the north or Tartar city, and the south or Chinese city. The former is built in the shape of a parallelogram, and consists of three enclosures, one within the other, each surrounded by its own wall.

The Government offices are situated in the Tartar city, which also contains the foreign legations. The Tartar city really consists of a number of cities, with the former Forbidden City in the centre, which is surrounded by the Hwang, or Imperial City. In the Chinese city broad straight streets run from gate to gate, intersecting each other at right angles, but they are unpaved, and in rainy weather impassable from mud. Amongst the principal public buildings of Peiping are the Temple of Eternal Peace, belonging to the lamas; the Mahommedan mosque; the observatory; the Temple of Agriculture; the Temple of Heaven (1421); the National University founded in 1898, and a branch of the Chiaotung University founded in 1921. Peiping has little or no trade except that which is produced by the wants of its population.

Temple of Heaven at Peiping

For nearly 1000 years Peiping has existed as an important city under different names and in various hands. It became capital of the Chinese Empire in 1403, and has been the capital city of all China, Imperial and Republican, since that time. During the Boxer risings and the siege of the legations (1900) Peiping suffered severely, and politically the city passed through anxious days in course of the 1911 Revolution and the subsequent accession of Yuan-Shih-Kai to supreme presidential power.

In May, 1922, the disruption of China seemed assured, and Canton, governed by Dr. Sun Yat Sen, threatened to supplant Peiping as the Chinese capital. Under Wu-Pei-fu the armies of Chih-li entirely defeated the pro-Japanese forces of Marshal Chang-Tso-lin, and compelled his retirement from the capital to Manchuria, where he set up an opposition government, but left unshaken the power of Peiping as capital city and the key to China. Pop. 1,297,718 (including 2000 foreigners).—Cf. Juliet Bredon, *Peking*.

PEIPUS (pe'i-pųs), or **CHUDSKOE OZERO.** A lake of Russia, between Russia, Estonia, and Livonia, comprising three distinct basins (Peipus Proper, Pskov, and the Warm Lake), with a total length of 70 miles and an area of 1356 sq. miles. It discharges by the Narova into the Gulf of Finland. The fisheries are valuable.

PEKAN'. A species of marten (*Mustēla pennanti*) nearly allied to the sable, found in woody regions of North America from lat. 35° to 65°. It attains a length of from 3 to 4 feet; feeds on mice, frogs, fish, etc., and is valued for its fur.

PEKIN. A city of Illinois, United States, the county seat of Tazewell county, on the Illinois River; served by the Atchison, Topeka, & Santa Fé, the Illinois Central, and by six other railways. It is an agricultural centre, a shipping point within the Illinois coal-fields, and an industrial, transport, and trading city in general. Pekin was settled in 1830, and was incorporated in 1839 and 1874. Pop. 16,129.

PELA'GIUS. British theologian, author and systematiser of the doctrine known as Pelagianism. His name is supposed to be a Græcised form of the Cymric Morgan (sea-begotten). He was not a monk, but he adhered to monastic discipline, and distinguished himself by his sanctity and purity of life. He came to Rome in the beginning of the fifth century, and is there said to have learned the opinions afterwards identified with his name from a monk Ruffinus, whose teaching was founded on that of Origen. In A.D. 410, during Alaric's third siege of the city, he escaped with his convert and pupil, Cœlestius, to Northern Africa, and had gone from there to Palestine before the meeting of the Council of Carthage (411-12) which condemned Cœlestius.

In Palestine he lived unmolested and revered until 415, when Orosius, a Spanish priest, came from Augustine to warn Jerome against him. The result was that he was prosecuted for heresy, but two councils (at Jerusalem, and at Diospolis, the ancient Lydda) pronounced him orthodox. He was subsequently expelled from Jerusalem, however, in consequence of condemnations by the Council of Carthage in A.D. 417 and 418, and by a synod held at Antioch in A.D. 421. Nothing is known of his subsequent career.

His doctrine, known as Pelagianism, included a denial of original sin or the taint of Adam; the maintenance of the doctrine of free-will and the merit of good works; and of the power in man to receive or reject the gospel.

The promulgation of his views by Pelagius was nearly simultaneous with that of the orthodox theory of original sin, etc., by Augustine, and in the development of his doctrine Augustine was influenced by his opposition to Pelagianism.

A doctrine subsequently distinguished as *semi-Pelagianism* was taught by John Cassian, a monk of Constantinople, ordained a deacon by Chrysostom in 403. Semi-Pelagianism was also condemned. The term "Pelagianism" has been continued to modern times to denote views which minimise the effects of the fall and unduly exalt man's natural ability.—Cf. R. G. Parsons, article in Hastings's *Encyclopædia of Religion and Ethics*.

PELAS'GIANS. A prehistoric race widely spread over the whole of Greece, the coasts and islands of the Ægean, and also in Asia Minor and Italy. The Pelasgians are mentioned by Homer, who speaks of them as dwelling in Argos and in Epirus. Hesiod mentions Dodona as their seat, whilst Strabo speaks of them as an ancient tribe spread over the whole of Hellas. Some writers regarded them as a great and widely spread people, inhabiting all the countries from the Po to the Bosporus, and supplying a common foundation to the Greek and Latin peoples and languages.

Other writers, however, receive the entire tradition of the Pelasgians with scepticism. One view is that they were the earliest Hellenic inhabitants of Greece. Another is that they belong to the Mediterranean or Brown race, who preceded the Hellenes or Greeks in Greece, and attained an advanced civilisation. Various monuments and remains found in Italy, Greece, and Asia Minor have been attributed to them. The monumental remains belong to the style of architecture called Cyclopean.

PELEUS (pē'lūs). In Greek mythology, son of Æăcus, King of Ægina. After many adventures he became master of a part of Thessaly, and married the nymph Thetis, by whom he became the father of Achilles. The nuptials were celebrated on Mount Pelion, and honoured with the presence of all the gods except Eris, the goddess of discord.

PELEW', or PALAU ISLANDS. A group belonging to the Caroline Archipelago, in the North Pacific Ocean. They are twenty-six in number, and lie within a coral barrier reef. The southern islands are of coralline formation; the northern are volcanic. They are healthy climatically, but many are uninhabited. Babeltop is the largest island. The inhabitants are of Micronesian origin. Phosphates, copra, bêche-de-mer, and tropical fruits are produced.

The Pelew Islands were sighted by Villalobos (1543) and named the Arrecifos. Prior to the European War they belonged to Germany, who had acquired the group from Spain in 1899, but during the war they were occupied by the Allies. By the Treaty of Versailles the islands are now administered by Japan as mandatory power. Area 200 sq. miles; pop 7257 (including 1 European, 206 Japanese and 4598 natives). *See* YAP.

PEL'ICAN. The name of several web-footed birds of the genus Pelecānus, constituting a distinct family (Pelicanidæ). They are larger than the swan, have a great extent of wing, and are excellent swimmers. Pelicans are gregarious, and frequent the neighbourhood of rivers, lakes, and the sea-coast, feeding chiefly on fish,

Pelicans
1, White pelican. 2, Australian pelican
3, Saw-billed pelican

which they capture with great adroitness. They have a large flattened bill, the upper mandible terminated by a strong hook, which curves over the tip of the lower one; beneath the lower mandible, which is composed of two flexible, bony branches meeting at the tip, a great pouch of naked skin is appended, capable of holding a considerable number of fish, and thus enabling the bird to dispose of the superfluous quantity which may be taken during fishing expeditions, either for its own consumption or for the nourishment of its young.

The species are found in Europe, Asia, Africa, and America. They sometimes perch upon trees; the nest is of rough construction usually placed close to the water. The common or white pelican (*P. onocrotălus*) is coloured a delicate white, tinged with rose or pink. The young birds are fed by the parents with fishes from the pouch, and the males are said to feed the incubating females in a similar manner.

The common pelican inhabits Europe, Asia, and Africa. About the middle of September flocks repair to Egypt. During the summer months they take up their abode on the borders of the Black Sea and the shores of Greece. They are rare in France and unknown in Britain. The pelican is not only susceptible of domestication, but may even be trained to fish for its master.

PE'LION. A mountain of ancient Greece, in Thessaly, near the sea, 5308 feet high. In the war of the Titans with the gods the former, say the poets, piled Pelion upon Ossa to aid them in climbing to Olympus.

PÉLISSIER (pā-lēs-yā), **Jean Jacques Aimable, Duc de Malakoff.** Marshall of France, born in 1794, died in Algeria 1864. Educated at La Flèche and St. Cyr, he served in Spain (1823), in the Morea (1828-9), and in Algeria (1830-55). In 1855 he succeeded Canrobert as commander-in-chief of the French army in the Crimea, and took part in the siege of Sebastopol. He received the marshal's baton, and an annual pension of 100,000 francs. Ambassador to England (1858), he was appointed Governor-General of Algeria (1860).

PELLA. Ancient capital of Macedonia, and the birth-place of Alexander the Great. It surrendered to Paulus Æmilius 168 B.C., and from a large and magnificent city it sunk, under the Romans, to a mere station.

PELLAG'RA. A chronic endemic disease, the true cause of which is not yet definitely ascertained. The symptoms, which are referred chiefly to the skin, the intestinal tract, and the nervous system, are always most marked in the spring and autumn months, and are in abeyance during the winter months. It is widespread in Southern Europe and North Africa, and affects mostly agricultural workers of a poor class, whose dietary is limited. It does not appear to be communicable from man to man.

The theory of its cause which has had most support is that it is due to the consumption of diseased maize, but recently the food-deficiency theory has been put forward, and it has been demonstrated that there is a deficiency of certain elements of diet in many pellagrins. The facts that it occurs commonly in an impoverished population and is increased by war conditions support this view. The prognosis is always serious, and it is estimated that the death-rate from the initial attack is about 15 per cent. The duration of the disease is very protracted, and though obstinate cases may recover, relapses are common.

PELLIA. A genus of Liverworts, belonging to the group Jungermanniales, but having a flat lobed thallus instead of the leafy shoot which is more typical of that section. *P. epiphylla* is very common on wet banks, walls, etc.

PEL'LICO, Silvio. Italian poet and patriot, born 1788 at Saluzzo, in Piedmont, died in 1854. By his tragedies of *Laodamia* and *Francesca da Rimini* (represented in 1818) he earned an honourable place among Italian poets. In the same year, with Manzoni and others, he established the periodical *Il Conciliatore*.

In consequence of the liberal spirit displayed in his productions he was in 1820, along with several of his friends, arrested on the charge of belonging to the Carbonari, and in 1822 was condemned to death, but the sentence was commuted to imprisonment in the Austrian prison of the Spielberg for fifteen years. In 1830 he was set at liberty. Pellico has given a most interesting account of his ten years' sufferings in *Le Mie Prigioni* (My Prisons), which has been translated into many languages. His tragedy *Francesca da Rimini* (1818) was greatly admired by Lord Byron, whose *Manfred* Silvio Pellico translated into Italian.

PEL'LITORY, or SPANISH CHAMOMILE (*Anacyclus Pyrethrum*). A plant nearly resembling chamomile, of the same order and belonging to an allied genus, a native of the Levant and of Southern Europe. It was introduced into England in 1750, and is chewed to relieve toothache and rheumatism of the gums. A genus of plants (Parietaria) of the nettle order is also known as pellitory, or wall-pellitory. The common wall-pellitory (*P. officinālis*) is a herbaceous perennial, with prostrate or erect branched stems, ovate leaves, and small flowers. It contains nitre, and was formerly used as a diuretic.

PELOP'IDAS. In ancient Greek history, a Theban general and statesman who lived in intimate friendship with Epaminondas. The supremacy of the Spartan faction in Thebes forced Pelopidas, with other exiles, to take refuge in Athens, but he returned in 379 B.C., and succeeded in overthrowing the Spartan party and recovering the citadel of Thebes. In the war which followed with Sparta Pelopidas distinguished himself in the battle of Tegyra (375) and of Leuctra (371), by which Thebes became for a time the leading power of Greece. In 364 he was sent against Alexander of Pheræ, tyrant of Thessaly, whom he defeated in the battle of Cynoscephalæ, though he himself was slain.

PELOPONNE'SUS (Gr. "Island of Pelops"). The peninsula which comprehends the most southern part of Greece, generally called the Morea. The Peloponnesus was conquered some time after the Trojan War by the Heraclidæ, or descendants of Hercules. Peloponnesus was anciently divided into six states: Messenia, Laconia (Sparta), Elis, Arcadia, Achaia, and Argolis, to which some add Sicyon. *See* GREECE.

PE'LOPS. In Greek mythology, son of Tantalus, King of Lydia. He married Hippodamia, a daughter of King Œnomaus of Elis, and succeeded his father-in-law in that kingdom. Peloponnesus received its name from him. Of his sons, Atreus and Thyestes are most celebrated.

PELO'RIA (Gr. *pelōr*, a monster). In botany, the appearance of regularity of structure in the flowers of plants which normally bear irregular flowers, instances of which occur in the snap-dragon and the toad-flax, which being normally irregular, assume a symmetrical form.

PELU'SIUM (the "Sin" of the Scriptures). A city of ancient Egypt, situated on the eastern arm of the Nile delta, about 2½ miles from the sea, near the modern Damietta. It was called by the Egyptians Peremoun, which signifies mud-city. Manetho mentions its original name as *Abaris*, or *Anaris*.

PELVETIA. A genus of Brown Algæ, family Fucaceæ. *P. canaliculata* is a small wrack abundant about high-water mark on rocky coasts.

PELVIS (Lat. *pelvis*, a basin). The bony basin formed by the "haunch-bones" and sacrum of Vertebrata, which constitutes the girdle or arch giving support to the lower or hinder limbs. The pelvis thus corresponds to the shoulder-girdle of the upper- or fore-limbs; and forms a cavity or basin in which several of the abdominal viscera, and organs relating to reproduction and the urinary functions are protected and contained.

The pelvis consists of four bones, the front and sides being formed by the two *ossa innominata* or innominate bones, and the circle being completed behind by the *sacrum* and the *coccyx*. Each innominate bone consists in early life of three pieces termed *ilium*, *ischium*, and *pubis*, and they meet in front at the *symphysis pubis*. The pelvis of man differs materially from that of woman, the differences having chiefly reference to the greater capacity required for the womb during pregnancy, and for the expulsion of the child at birth. It also varies somewhat in the different races of men.

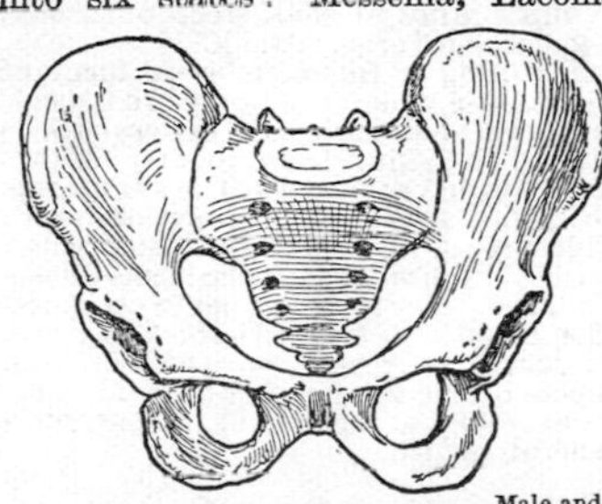
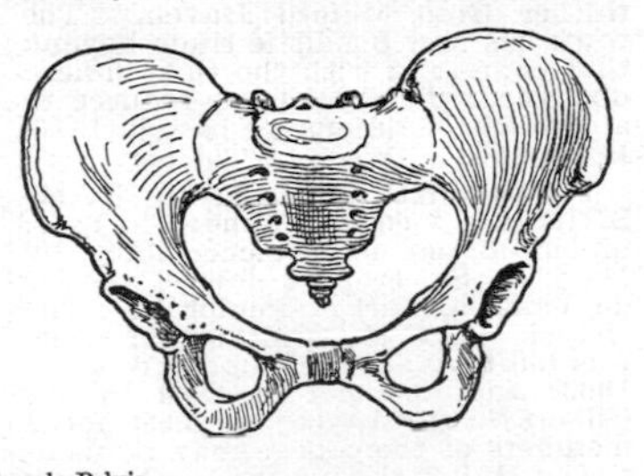

Male and Female Pelvis
The male pelvis (*left*) is stronger, deeper, and narrower than the female (*right*)
The latter has the wider opening necessary for child-birth

PEMBA. An island of the Indian Ocean, off the Tanganyika coast, forming part of the Sultanate of Zanzibar, from which it lies 30 miles to the north-east, in 5° S. lat. It is 40 miles long by 10 miles broad, and has an area of 380 sq. miles. Pop. 87,650. *See* ZANZIBAR.

PEM'BERTON. A district of Wigan, Lancashire; served by the L.M.S. Railway. From 1894 it was a separate urban district, but became a part of the county borough of Wigan in 1904.

PEM'BREY. A seaport of Carmarthenshire, South Wales, on the Burry inlet, 5 miles west of Llanelly; served by the Great Western Railway. There are dock and harbour accommodation, tin- and copper-works, and a large transit trade in coal. A complete mobilisation of industry was effected for the manufacture of munitions during the European War.

PEM'BROKE. A municipal borough and seaport of South Wales, capital of the county of the same name, on a creek on the southern side of Milford Haven; served by the Great Western Railway. On the west side are the ruins of the mediæval castle of Pembroke, the remains of which give evidence of its former magnificence. On the north-west side is Pembroke Dock, otherwise called Pater, a small village until 1814, when the royal dockyard for the construction of ships of war was removed thither from Milford Haven. The town has now but little trade beyond that connected with the Government dockyard. Pembroke was reduced to a care and maintenance base in 1926. Pop. (1931), 12,008.

PEMBROKE COLLEGE, CAMBRIDGE. A college founded in 1347, under the name of Valence-Mary, by Mary de St. Paul, widow of Aymer de Valence, Earl of Pembroke. The chapel, which is Corinthian in style, was built by Sir Christopher Wren in 1663, and enlarged in 1880 by Sir Gilbert Scott. Among the most noted members of the college may be mentioned Ridley the martyr, Archbishop Whitgift, Spenser and Gray the poets.

PEMBROKE COLLEGE, OXFORD. Originally Broadgates Hall, it was founded in the year 1624 by James I., and obtained its name from William Herbert, Earl of Pembroke. Shenstone, Blackstone, and Dr. Johnson were Pembroke men.

PEMBROKESHIRE. A maritime county of Wales; area, 393,003 acres. Its coast-line is deeply indented, and in the south is the harbour of Milford Haven. The surface is generally undulating, and greatly diversified with hills and dales. Lead, iron, slate, and coal are worked. In the south part the limestone and Old Red Sandstone formation afford soils of excellent quality, but in the coal and slate districts the land is very inferior. Chief towns: Haverfordwest, Pembroke, and Tenby. Pop. (1931), 87,179.

PEM'MICAN. Originally a Cree (North American) Indian preparation consisting of the lean portions of meat dried by the sun or wind, and then pounded into a paste and tightly pressed into cakes. It is extensively used in Polar expeditions on account of its smallness of bulk and good keeping properties.

PEM'PHIGUS. The name given to a group of skin diseases, all characterised by the formation of bullæ (blisters), but varying considerably in their course and result. Acute malignant pemphigus is an acute infectious disease, usually following a septic wound in the hand, and its onset is marked by rigors, high temperature, sickness and diarrhœa, and a widespread bullous eruption. It has a high mortality.

Chronic pemphigus is characterised by the formation of blisters upon healthy skin. It is slowly progressive, and often ends fatally. The blisters at first contain clear fluid, but may suppurate, and the surrounding skin then shows a red halo. Along with the skin eruption there is wasting and debility, and, at each fresh outbreak, a general feverish attack.

Pemphigus foliaceus is a form of the disease where the bullæ are flaccid, and in which there is a general shedding of the skin. It frequently follows the chronic variety, but the symptoms are more severe, the eruption more widespread, and the fatal result much earlier. Pemphigus pruriginosus differs from the other forms in being attended with intense itching. It shows a great tendency to recur, but beyond the effects of the intense itching and pain, there is no disturbance of the patient's general health.

PEN (Lat. *penna*, pen, feather). An instrument for writing with a fluid ink. Pens of some sort have been in use from very early times, adapted to the material on which the characters were to be inscribed.

Earliest Writing Implements. The metallic stilus for the production of incised letters was probably the earliest writing implement. It was used by the Romans for writing on tablets coated with wax; but both they and the Greeks also used what is the true ancient representative of the modern pen, namely, a hollow reed, as is yet common in Eastern countries.

It has been asserted that quills were used for writing as early as the fifth century A.D. In Europe they were long the only writing implement, the sorts generally used being those of the goose and swan. Up till the end of the first quarter of the nineteenth century these formed the principal materials from which pens were made. In 1803 Wise produced steel pens of a barrel form, mounted in a bone case for carrying in the pocket. They were of indifferent make, and, being expensive, were very little used.

Joseph Gillott commenced the manufacture about 1820, and succeeded in making the pen of thinner and more elastic steel, giving it a higher temper and finish. Shortly afterwards Josiah Mason approached James Perry, a London stationer and pen-maker, and offered to manufacture steel pens for him which would be stamped with the seller's, not the manufacturer's, name. Perry accepted this offer, and Mason started his works and was able to produce better pens than other makers, through devising improvements in machinery and processes until the excellent pen-nibs we know to-day were the standard article of manufacture.

Modern Processes. In the modern process cast steel is rolled to the requisite width, and the blanks are stamped out and names embossed upon them. The blanks are then heated again and formed to their curved shape. The nibs are tempered by heating and afterwards quenching in oil. The slit in the pen is cut with very sharp-edged tools. The pens are then scoured, polished, and packed ready for the market. The century from the introduction of Gillott's first pen witnessed the reduction to a thousandth part of the original price of steel pens. Birmingham is the principal centre of the steel-pen industry, and the university of that city stands as a memorial to the successful life of Sir Josiah Mason.

Gold pen-nibs tipped with iridium or its alloy with platinum are in extensive use in fountain-pens. Joseph Bramah (q.v.) invented this type of pen. Ink is contained in a reservoir in the barrel of the pen, and passes to the nib through a capillary tube, the space it previously occupied being filled with incoming air. The size of the tube and the form of the "feed" are the most important features in a fountain-pen.

Self filling pens have rubber tubes which can be emptied of air by operating a device which compresses the tube, and then filled with ink by placing the end of the pen into an ink-pot and relieving the pressure on the tube. Another form makes use of a small piston which is operated to draw in a barrelful of ink. Stylograph pens have a wire passing through a hole in the pen-point. The hole is bushed with a thin metallic tube, and the wire has at the end a piece of iridium or platinum-iridium wire. The wire inside the barrel has the form of a spiral spring.

PENAL SERVITUDE. In Britain, a punishment for criminal offences, ranging from five years up to the life of the convict. It was substituted for transportation when that punishment was abolished (1857).

PENANCE (Lat. *pœnitentia*, repentance). In theology, a self-imposed or accepted punishment, by which a repentant sinner expresses his sorrow for sin and seeks to atone for it. The idea of penance was already familiar to heathen nations, and the unnatural austerities of the Hindus may be said to furnish a striking example of penance. In the early Christian Church penances were of three kinds —secret, public, and solemn.

The first consisted of such actions as are commonly imposed by confessors at the present day, as the repetition of certain prayers, etc. Public penance was in use from the earliest days of the Church. It was often very severe, and the penitents had to make a public confession of their sins in the Church. It became gradually the custom of the bishops to commute the canonical penances for pious works, such as pilgrimages, alms-deeds, and other works of charity —and these again were exchanged for indulgences.

In the Roman Catholic Church penance is one of the seven sacraments. The matter of it consists of the three acts of the penitent: (1) contrition, or heartfelt sorrow for sin as being an offence against God; (2) confession to an authorised priest; and (3) satisfaction, or the acceptance and performance of certain penitential works in atonement of the sin; and the form of the sacrament is the sentence of absolution from sin pronounced by the priest who received the confession, and has been satisfied of the earnest repentance of the sinner. According to the doctrine of the Protestants there is no such sacrament; they consider repentance and faith as the only requisites for forgiveness.

PENANG'. The most northerly division of the British Crown colony of the Straits Settlements. It consists of Penang Island, Province Wellesley on the mainland, and the Dindings. Penang is situated at the north entrance of the Straits of Malacca, off the west coast of the Malay Peninsula. Area of Penang, 108 sq. miles; total area, 282 sq. miles. Two-fifths of Penang is plain, and the rest hills—for the most part wooded—which rise to a height of 2734 feet in the peak now used as a sanatorium.

The climate is hot, but very healthy. The island produces coco-nuts and areca-nuts, nutmegs and cloves, rice, sugar, coffee, and pepper. Georgetown, or Penang, is the capital and port of the settlement. The harbour is the strait between island and mainland.

Penang was made over by treaty to the East India Company in 1785 by the Raja of Kedah, and with Province Wellesley, a long strip of the Malay Peninsula opposite, it now forms one of the Straits Settlements, having a resident Councillor to control administration. Pop. of Penang, Wellesley, and the Dindings, 357,875.

PENARTH'. An urban district and seaport of Glamorganshire, South Wales, on the Ely, opposite Cardiff; served by the Great Western Railway. Penarth was an obscure village until the extension of its tidal harbour (1884), which has made it an important shipping-port for the minerals of South Wales. It is frequented in summer as a bathing-place and seaside-resort. Pop. (1931), 17,710.

PENA'TES. Roman gods of the store-room and kitchen. The images of these gods were kept in the penetralia, or central part of every house, each family having its own Penates and the state its public Penates. The Lares were included among the Penates, but were not the only Penates; for each family had generally but one Lar, whereas the Penates are usually spoken of in the plural. Their worship was closely connected with that of Vesta.

PENCIL. An instrument used for painting, drawing, and writing. The first pencils used by artists were probably pieces of coloured earth or chalk cut into a form convenient for holding in the hand. On the introduction of moist colours, however, delicate brushes of fine hairs were used. Pencils of this kind, and of various degrees of fineness, are now almost solely used by painters for laying on their colours; but in China and Japan they are generally employed, instead of pens, for writing.

The hairs used for these pencils are obtained from the camel, badger, squirrel, sable, goat, etc. The hairs, being selected, are bound in a little roll by a string tied tightly round their root ends. The roll is then fixed into the end of a quill tube. For larger pencils a socket of tin-plate is used instead of the quill.

Black-lead pencils, for writing or drawing, are made of slips of graphite or plumbago (otherwise known as black-lead), generally cased in cedar wood. The finest qualities of graphite used to be obtained only from the Borrowdale mines in Cumberland. Blocks of graphite, however, are now rarely found of such size and purity that they can be sawn up into the small square slices of ordinary pencil length; but a method has been devised of purifying the inferior varieties, which are ground to a fine powder, levigated or washed until pure, intimately mixed with clay in various proportions, and afterwards solidified by pressure.

The comparative hardness and blackness of pencils are attained by the degree of heat to which they are subjected and the proportion of graphite and clay in the leads. Nürnberg is the great centre of the lead-pencil trade.

Coloured pencils are prepared from various chalks, such as are used for crayons, instead of from graphite. Pencils for writing on slate are made by cutting slate into small square pieces and rounding them, or into narrow slips and encasing them in wood.

PENDANT. In architecture, a hanging ornament used in the vaults and timber roofs of Gothic buildings, more particularly in late Gothic work. In vaulted roofs pendants are of stone, and generally richly carved; in timber roofs they are of wood variously decorated. Fine examples of stone pendants are to be seen in the chapel of Henry VII. at Westminster Abbey.

PENDEN'TIVE. In architecture, the portion of a dome-shaped vault which descends into a corner of a quadrangular opening when a ceiling of this kind is placed over a straight-sided area; in Gothic architecture, the portion of a groined ceiling springing from one pillar or impost, and bounded by the ridges or apices of the longitudinal and transverse vaults.

PENDULUM. In the widest sense, a heavy body suspended so that it is free to turn or swing upon an axis which does not pass through its centre of gravity. Its only position of stable equilibrium is one in which its centre of gravity is in the same vertical plane with the axis. If the body is displaced from this position, it will tend to return to it, and it will oscillate or swing from one side of that position to the other until its energy is destroyed by friction, and it at length comes to rest.

A small, heavy body suspended from a fixed point by a string, and caused to vibrate without much friction, is called a "simple pendulum." When the swings of a simple pendulum are not too great—that is, when they are never more than about 3° on each side of the position of rest—the pendulum is isochronous, that is, each swing occupies the same time, and its period is given by the equation

$$T = 2\pi\sqrt{l \div g};$$

where T is the period of a complete vibration, π is the well-known mathematical number 3·1416, l the length of the pendulum in feet, and g the acceleration due to gravity, or 32·19 feet per second per second at London. The "seconds" pendulum has for its time of vibration (half its complete period) one second. In the above equation, putting for T two seconds, and for g 32·19, we find the length of the seconds pendulum at London to be 3·26 feet, or 39·1 inches.

A true simple pendulum is a mathematical abstraction : a heavy particle, an inextensible and inflexible weightless string, and no friction ; these conditions are only approximated to in nature. The ordinary pendulum is what is properly a "compound pendulum."

A compound pendulum, as seen in clocks, is usually a rigid, heavy, pendulous body, varying in size according to the size of the clock, but the "seconds" pendulum may be considered the standard. The pendulum is connected with the clockwork by means of the escapement, and is what renders the going of the clock uniform. (*See* CLOCK.)

In a clock it is necessary that the period of vibration of the pendulum should be constant. As all substances expand and contract with heat and cold, the dimensions of a swinging body, and consequently its period of vibration, are subject to continual change.

But *compensation pendulums* can be constructed, the period of which is independent of temperature. These are given particular names, according to their forms and materials, as the *gridiron pendulum*, the *mercurial pendulum*, etc. The former is composed of a number of rods so connected that the expansion or contraction of certain of them is counteracted by that of the others.

The *mercurial pendulum* consists of one rod with a vessel containing mercury at the lower end, so adjusted in quantity that whatever alterations take place in the length of the pendulum, the centre of oscillation remains the same, the mercury ascending when the rod descends, and vice versa. For the use of the pendulum in determinations of the value of the acceleration g, *see* GRAVITY.

PENEL'OPĒ. In Greek legend, the wife of Odysseus (Ulysses) and mother of Telemachus. During the protracted absence of Odysseus, Penelopē was surrounded by a host of suitors, whom she put off on the pretext that before she could make up her mind she must first finish a winding-sheet which she was weaving for her father-in-law Laërtes. To gain time she undid by night the work she had done by day. Odysseus returned in time to protect his spouse and slay the obnoxious wooers who had been living in riot and wasting his property.

PENEPLAIN. A term meaning "almost a plane," invented by the geographer W. M. Davis for the nearly even surface produced across a country of uniform or very mixed types of rock by prolonged processes of subaerial denudation. Peneplains may be uplifted after being worked down to the base-level of the district, and may be warped in the process ; but they will long preserve their characters, while they are being slowly eroded and dissected into less regular and often mountainous forms. An alternative spelling of the word is peneplane.

PENGUIN. The name given to swimming birds adapted for living almost entirely in the water, and constituting a distinct order (Sphenisciformes) including a single family (Spheniscidæ). They possess only

Penguin

rudimentary wings, destitute of quill-feathers, and covered with a scaly integument or skin.

Although useless as organs of flight, the wings are very effective aids in diving, and on land they may be used after the fashion of fore-limbs. The legs are placed at the hinder extremity of the body, and the birds assume an erect attitude when on land. The toes are completely webbed.

They inhabit chiefly the high southern latitudes, congregating sometimes in colonies of from 30,000 to 40,000.

There are three different types of penguins, represented by the king penguin, the jackass penguin, and the rockhopper, constituting respectively the generic groups Aptenodȳtes, Spheniscus, and Eudyptes. The jackass penguin and the rockhopper are about 2 feet 3 inches in height, and the king penguin somewhat larger, while the emperor penguin (*Apteno-*

dÿtes forsteri) attains 3 feet; but a fossil penguin of the Upper Eocene stood from 6 to 7 feet high.

PENICILLIUM. A genus of Ascomycetous Fungi, group Plectascineæ. *P. crustaceum* is the common blue mould, a saprophyte of universal occurrence on stale bread, jam, damp leather, and paper, in fact on any moist substance containing even a trace of nutrient material.

PENICU'IK. A police burgh of Midlothian, Scotland, on the North Esk; served by the London & North-Eastern Railway. It has paper-mills, and coal-, shale-, and ironstone-mines. Objects of interest include the tower of the ancient church of St. Kentigern. Pop. (1931), 2750.

PENIN'SULA (Lat. *pene*, almost, and *insula*, an island). A portion of land almost surrounded by water, and connected with the mainland by a narrow neck or isthmus, e.g. the Iberian Peninsula (Spain and Portugal), the Scandinavian Peninsula (Norway and Sweden), Corea, Italy, and Malaya.

PENINSULAR WAR. The war in the Spanish Peninsula (1808-14) was a direct result of the "Continental System" by which Napoleon I. forbade commercial intercourse with Great Britain, for it was the hesitation of Portugal to obey the Berlin and Milan Decrees that led the French to invade the country and depose the House of Braganza. Immediately afterwards Napoleon forced his ally, Charles IV. of Spain, to give up his crown, and placed his own brother Joseph on the throne.

Insurrections against French military occupation broke out both in Portugal and in Spain, and in the summer of 1808 the British Government sent Sir Arthur Wellesley with 10,000 men to aid the Portuguese and co-operate with the Spanish Nationalists. He landed at Oporto, and, on his way to relieve Lisbon, won at Vimiero (21st Aug.) the first land-battle won by the British on European soil since the outbreak of war in 1793.

Unfortunately, two senior officers arrived on the day of the battle, and they prevented Wellesley from pursuing his advantage, and made the Convention of Cintra, by which the French army was allowed to evacuate Portugal.

All three generals were recalled, and Sir John Moore took command. He marched into Spain, but the defeat of the Spaniards by Napoleon forced him to retreat upon Corunna, in the north of Spain, where he had arranged for British transports to receive his troops. In the battle which he was compelled to fight before the embarkation, Moore was killed (16th Jan., 1809), but Marshal Soult was defeated, and Moore had saved the south of Spain and given the Spaniards a chance of recovery.

Wellesley was sent back in April, 1809, and in July he won, on Spanish soil, the victory of Talavera, for which he was raised to the peerage as Viscount Wellington. But in the autumn his position was threatened by the movement of French armies, and he had to retreat to the Portuguese border. Early in 1810 he crossed into Portugal and slowly retired towards Torres Vedras, where he had constructed great entrenched lines from the River Tagus to the sea. The British army spent the winter of 1810-11 at Torres Vedras, which the French vainly besieged.

When they withdrew in the spring of 1811, Wellington attacked them and won some victories, but considerable time was spent in the long-continued sieges of two fortresses, Badajos and Ciudad Rodrigo. Both fell early in 1812, and in July of the same year Wellington gained a crushing victory at Salamanca and entered Madrid.

He had now driven the French from Galicia and a large part of Castile, but a fresh concentration of French armies under Soult compelled him, by the end of the year, to abandon Madrid and retire again to the borders of Portugal. The French armies separated to find winter quarters, and Wellington designed the campaign of 1813 to prevent their concentrating again.

He had himself received reinforcements, and by a sudden movement in the early summer he attacked a French army under Joseph Bonaparte, who was awaiting the arrival of troops from Aragon and Catalonia. The battle of Vittoria (21st June) was another crushing victory, and the "King of Spain" fled into France, while the British besieged fortresses on the frontier. Soult attempted to raise the sieges and to retrieve the fortunes of the French arms in the Peninsula, but Wellington defeated him at the battle of the Pyrenees, and drove him across the frontier in the beginning of August.

He then invaded France, and in November won another victory on the River Nivelle. In the spring of 1814 he completed his task by continuing his invasion of France, beating Soult at Orthes (27th Feb.), and gaining his last victory at Toulouse on 10th April, four days after the first abdication of Napoleon. For his services in the Peninsula Wellington was raised, by successive steps, from a viscounty to a dukedom, and was given the rank of field-marshal.

The six years' campaign had an important influence upon the fortunes of Napoleon, though it was not until Waterloo that he personally met Wellington in the field. He himself described the campaigns in the Peninsula as "a running sore," and the demands made by his commanders in Spain for man-power and supplies constituted a constant and severe drain upon the resources at his disposal.

At the end of his struggle with the Central Powers of Europe, Napoleon found himself dependent upon an army of raw recruits because large forces of experienced troops had been wasted in the Peninsular fighting. The steadfastness of the British Government and the combination of patient waiting with swift action which marked Wellington's conduct of operations had their reward in sapping the strength of Napoleon's military empire. — BIBLIOGRAPHY: Sir W. Napier, *History of the War in the Peninsula and South of France*; Sir C. W. C. Oman, *History of the Peninsular War*; *Wellington's Army*.

PEN'ISTONE. A market town of Yorkshire (West Riding), England, on the Don; served by the London & North-Eastern and the London, Midland & Scottish Railways. The Grammar School was founded in 1392. The town gives name to a parliamentary division, returning one member to Parliament. Pop. (1931), 3264.

PENITENTIAL PSALMS. The seven psalms vi., xxxii., xxxviii., li., cii., cxxx., cxliii. of the Authorised Version, so termed as being specially expressive of contrition. Reference is made to them by Origen. They have a special place in the breviary of the Roman Church. The psalm most frequently repeated as being the most penitential is the *Miserere*, Psalm li. of the Authorised Version.

PENITENTIARY. At the court of Rome, an office in which the secret bulls, graces, or dispensations relating to cases of conscience, confession, etc., are examined and dispatched; also an officer in some Roman Catholic cathedrals, vested with power from the bishop to absolve in cases referred to him. The Pope has a grand penitentiary, who is a cardinal and is chief of the other penitentiaries. The word is also used to denote a form of prison in the United States.

PENN, William. The founder of the state of Pennsylvania, was born in London in 1644, died at Ruscombe, Berks, 30th July, 1718. He was the only son of Admiral Sir William Penn. In his fifteenth year he was entered as a gentleman commoner at Christ Church, Oxford, where he imbibed Quaker views, and was expelled from the university. His father sent him on travels in France and Holland and in 1666 committed to him the management of a considerable estate in Ireland. At Cork he was committed to prison for attending Quaker meetings, and although he was very soon liberated he had to leave Ireland.

In 1668 Penn appeared as a preacher and an author, and on account of an essay, entitled *The Sandy Foundation*

William Penn

Shaken, he was imprisoned in the Tower, where he remained seven months. During this time he wrote his most celebrated works, *No Cross, no Crown*, and *Innocency with her Open Face*. In 1670 Sir William died, fully reconciled to his son, to whom he left his estates and all his property.

Penn preached his message in England, Holland, and Germany, but as the persecutions of Dissenters continued to rage, he turned his thoughts towards the New World. From his father he had inherited a claim upon the Government of £16,000, and in settlement of his claim the Government in 1681 granted him large territories in North America, the present state of Pennsylvania, with right to found a colony or society with such laws and institutions as expressed his views and principles.

The following year Penn went over to America and laid the foundations of his colony on a democratical basis, and with a greater degree of religious liberty than had at that time been allowed in the world. A great number of settlers, not only Quakers, but members of all denominations, Englishmen, Germans, Swedes, gathered together; the city of Philadelphia was laid out upon the banks of the Delaware, and the colony soon came into a most flourishing condition. He remained in the province about two years, adjusting its concerns, and establishing a friendly intercourse with his colonial neighbours.

Soon after Penn returned to England King Charles died (1685); and the respect which James II. bore to the late admiral, who had recommended his son to his favour, procured to him free access at court. He made use of this advantage to solicit the discharge of his persecuted brethren, 1500 of whom remained in prison at the decease of the late king; and his influence is thought to have hastened, if it did not occasion, the proclamation for a general pardon, and the repeal of religious tests and penalties.

At the Revolution in 1688 Penn's intimacy with the abdicated monarch created suspicions, in consequence of which he was accused of treason, and withdrew from public notice till 1693. In 1699 he again sailed for Pennsylvania, intending to make it the place of his future residence; but he returned to England again in 1701.—Cf. Mrs. Colquhoun Grant, *Quaker and Courtier: the Life and Work of William Penn.*

PENNANT, Thomas. English naturalist and antiquary, born at Downing, in Flintshire, in 1726, died in 1798. He studied at Oxford, and early devoted himself to natural history and archæology. His chief works are: *British Zoology* (1761-9), *Synopsis of Quadrupeds* (1771), *Genera of Birds* (1773), *Arctic Zoology* (3 vols., 1784-7), *Tours in Scotland* (3 vols., 1790), *Tour in Wales* (2 vols., 1778-81), and *Account of London* (1790).

PENNAT'ULA. A genus of Cœlenterate animals (populary known by the name of "sea-pens" or "cockscombs"), class Anthozoa, sub-class Alcyonaria. The sea-pens consist each of a compound organism, which may be described as consisting of a main stem or *cœnosarc*, with lateral pinnæ or branches. These branches are crowded on their upper margins with the little polyps or individual animals that make up the compound mass, and which are connected together through the fleshy medium or cœnosarc. The lower end of the stem is fleshy, destitute of polyps, and contains an internal coral-rod. By this fleshy root the sea-pens attach themselves loosely to the mud of the sea-bed.

The British species (*P. phosphorĕa*), averaging about 3 or 4 inches in length, derives its scientific name from its property of emitting a phosphorescent light.

PENNISETUM. A genus of tropical and subtropical grasses. *P. typhoideum* is the pearl-millet, a grass of some economic importance in India.

PENNSYLVANIA. A state in the Middle Atlantic division of the United States. Three divisions of the Appalachians traverse the state from north-east to south-west; in the south-east it occupies a part of the coastal plain, and a small portion of the Erie Plain is also included in the north-western corner. The state is drained mainly by the Susquehanna (drainage area, 21,000 sq. miles), the Delaware (6440 sq. miles), and the combined Monongahela-Ohio-Alleghany system (14,000 sq. miles).

Towns. Harrisburg (pop. 1931, 80,339) is the state capital, but Philadelphia (pop. 1,950,961) is the largest city; others are Pittsburgh (669,817), Scranton (143,433), Reading (111,171), and Erie (115,967), but there are many cities of over 30,000 inhabitants. There were (1930) 12,749 miles of steam and 3621 miles of electric railway track, including the systems of the Pennsylvania, the Lehigh Valley, the Erie, Baltimore, & Ohio, the Delaware, Lackawanna, & Western, and the Buffalo, Rochester, & Pittsburgh. There is an extensive canal system.

Population, etc. The population includes Asiatics and negroes, but is mainly of English stock, although there are also large numbers of Germans, Austrians, Irish, and Italian. Of religions, Roman Catholicism predominates. Agriculture, market-gardening, horticulture, and forestry are widely practised, the products including wheat (1931, 19,756,000 bushels), oats (28,143,000 bushels), tobacco (58,487,000 lb.), maize, rye buckwheat, potatoes, and hay.,

Productions. Pennsylvania is the leading United States producer of coal, both anthracite and bituminous; petroleum, natural gas, iron (magnetite and hematite) ores, and stone are also worked. In leather production the state also leads, as in iron-working around Pittsburgh as a consequence of the contiguous coal-fields. Other important manufactures are in textiles, and include woollens, carpets, hosiery, and silk and cotton goods.

Education. Education is compulsory between the ages of eight and fourteen years; there are a State college, normal schools, a subsidised (Federal) Agricultural Experiment Station, and three non-sectarian and four sectarian (Lutheran, Roman Catholic, Presbyterian, and Baptist) universities. Area, 45,126 sq. miles (294 sq. miles being water). An additional 891 sq. miles of Lake Erie is nominally included within the state sovereignty. Pop. (1931), 9,631,350. *See* PENN, WILLIAM.

Government. Pennsylvania was one of the original thirteen states. It was settled between 1650 and 1660 by the Society of Friends (Quakers), but before that time there had been Scandinavian and Flemish settlements on the Lower Delaware. There are 67 counties. Modern government consists of a Governor and a Legislature, comprising a Senate (50 members, elected for four years, 25 seeking biennial re-election) and a House of Representatives (207 members, elected for two years). Two Senators and 34 Representatives are sent to Congress.—BIBLIOGRAPHY: G. P. Donehoo, *Pennsylvania*; A. E. Martin and H. H. Shenk, *Pennsylvania History: Told by Contemporaries.*

PENNY. A British coin (formerly of copper, since 1860 of bronze) and money of account, the twelfth part of a shilling. It was at first a silver coin weighing about 22½ grains troy, or the two-hundred-and-fortieth part of a Saxon pound.

Till the time of Edward I. it was so deeply indented by a cross mark that it could be broken into halves (thence

Silver Penny of time of William the First

called **halfpenny**) or quarters (fourthings or **farthings**). Its weight was steadily decreased till at last, in the reign of Elizabeth, it was fixed at $7\frac{23}{31}$ grains, or the sixty-second part of an ounce of silver. Copper pennies were first coined in 1797, but copper halfpennies and farthings had been in use from 1672. The old Scots penny was only $\frac{1}{12}$*d.* sterling in value, the pound being equal to 20*d.* sterling.

PENNYROYAL. A species of mint (*Mentha Pulegium*) formerly in considerable repute as a medicine, but now almost totally neglected. *See* MINT.

PENNYWORT. A name given to several plants with round or peltate leaves, such as the *Cotylēdon umbilīcus* also known as *navelwort*, and the *Hydrocotȳle vulgāris*, or *marsh pennywort*, a small umbelliferous plant growing in marshy places.

PENOB'SCOT. The largest river of Maine, United States. It rises near the Canadian border, and flows 350 miles south by west to Penobscot Bay. It is navigable for ships to Bangor, 60 miles, where the tide rises 17 feet.

PENOLOGY. Deals with the punishment and the prevention of crime. No organised society can exist if its members do not obey its laws, and every community has to face the problem of dealing with its law-breakers. The penalties attached to transgressions are said to be based either on the principle of (*a*) retribution—the exaction from the offender of something equivalent to the loss or damage he has caused by his offence; (*b*) deterrence—the reaction on others from a knowledge of the consequences his act has brought on the offender; (*c*) reformation—the conversion of the offender to a better sense of his duties as a citizen, and his education and training as a means to the proper discharge of these duties; or on some combination of these.

The principle of retribution is now little supported. A life for a life is sometimes exacted, but it is mainly on the ground of deterrence. There is wide divergence of opinion as to the deterrent effect on others of capital punishment; the only certainty is that it is effective in the case of the person who suffers it.

Physical Punishment. In more primitive communities, and in Great Britain until comparatively recent times, the penalties of crime were mainly physical. It was only in the nineteenth century that the death penalty was abolished for many crimes that are now visited with short periods of imprisonment, or even with an admonition. Our forefathers had not the same estimate as we have of the value of life. They may not have considered their own lives of less importance, but they had less regard for the lives of those who committed crime.

If the crime were a serious one, the culprit was hanged; if it were less serious, he might be whipped. In certain cases he was banished, on pain of death if he returned. There was no pretence at reform. It was presumed that he could behave if he chose to do so, and if he broke the law he had to take the consequence.

It would be rash to assume that the laws then were any more unsuited to existing conditions than ours are. They were harsh, but they were not always harshly applied save to the stranger; for generally we tolerate more from those we know than from those we do not know.

The death penalty is now seldom exacted save for murder, and many homicides escape it. Flogging can only be inflicted in England and Ireland for certain serious crimes, and in Scotland it is abolished save in the convict prison. Fine or imprisonment has taken the place of these penalties in most cases; and public opinion seems to be moving in the direction of their abolition, not because the arguments in favour of that course are altogether convincing, but because of the growth of a sentiment against the employment of methods that seem brutal.

Any reasonable objection to physical penalties applies in degree to imprisonment, and the justification for employing one or another must be founded on evidence that, in the public interest, nothing better can be done.

Banishment from the realm, or from a part of it, for crime, has ceased. In the nineteenth century many were transported to the antipodes and put to work there, but the horrors to which they were subjected, and the objection of the colonies to receive them, caused the practice to be stopped. Penal servitude is now undergone in British prisons, though the convict is still liable to serve his sentence in any part of the king's dominions.

The deterrent effect of any penalty depends mainly on the certainty that it will be inflicted. Outside influences have always been in operation to interfere with the application of laws. The character of the person injured may prevent the culprit from getting his due, and the character of the offender and his connections may deflect the sword of justice. There is nothing like absolute certainty as to what will happen to the criminal who is caught; and the "sporting chance" tends in many cases to neutralise the deterrent effect of punishment. It is far from uncommon for men to believe that though others have failed in an undertaking they will succeed; and this frame of mind is not peculiar to good citizens.

Objections to Punishment. The objection to all punishments is that the result cannot be estimated. Whether a man is flogged, or imprisoned for a determinate period, if he is set free he may revert to the course of conduct that brought punishment on him. He has paid the penalty of his crime. He has done an injury and submitted to one, and the account is square. That is not only his view, but it is the view that the law takes. If he does well, so much the better; and if he does ill, the process can be repeated.

This must be poor consolation to the people he may injure and the taxpayers who have to support him; but the punishment of crime and the prevention of crime are not merely different, but opposite things. The factors that make for the committing of crime are many and varied, and some of them are social conditions that tend to produce other ills in the community; but in any individual case the causes of criminality might be sought with some hope of success if cure rather than punishment were the primary object.

It is by no means certain that all who commit crime wish to do otherwise, but it is probable that if they knew they were to be prevented from following their inclinations, and were only allowed a conditional liberty until they had learned the need for behaving as good citizens, they would curb their vicious propensities.

Necessity for Individual Treatment. Wholesale schemes of reform have been projected and tried and changed; but the product of reformatories is disappointing, and the association of social defectives with one another is not to their advantage nor to that of the community. It is becoming recognised that making the punishment fit the crime only results in evil. The personality of the criminal has to be taken into consideration even though all that is sought is his punishment, for it cannot be assumed that if the criminal is punished the community is made safe.

The mental condition of the criminal is always in question. We have long ceased to send lunatics to prison, and now the mentally defective are excluded also; but mental defect only accounts for the conduct of a small number of criminals and in their cases if it furnishes a reason for keeping them out of prison, it equally makes it necessary to place them under restraint. It is unsafe to form an opinion on a person's character from consideration of any isolated act on his part; and the fact that a man has broken the law does not in itself enable anyone to say how he can best be treated in the interests of the community.

In consequence of his offence his liberty is forfeited; but it is only possible to prescribe rationally for his treatment in detail on a knowledge of his history and of his qualities much more extensive than, and different in character from, that placed before the courts—which are only concerned with the question of his guilt or innocence of the charge before them.

If he is found guilty, he is sentenced to the penalty the law prescribes for the crime he has committed; and that penalty takes small account of the peculiarities of the person to whom it is applied. It is nobody's business to seek to find the causes of his conduct; though it seems reasonable to suppose that unless he is brought to see that it is not worth his while to persist in law-breaking, there is little hope of his doing well.

The penalties prescribed by the law may have a good effect on some; but the fact that so many repeat their offence shows that in their cases the desired result has not been obtained. It has been argued that the penalties themselves are accountable for the continuance in crime of those who suffer them; but there is no more reason to blame them for causing criminals to continue in crime than to credit them with the changed conduct of those who cease from it.

Men are so unlike, and the motives that appeal to one are so different from those that influence another, that all systems for dealing with criminals in the mass are sure to fail with many, as they always have done; and opinion is steadily advancing in favour of the individual treatment of the offender. His liberty being forfeited, what is to be done with him? The answer must depend on who and what he is. The safety of the community must be the first consideration, and security must be taken against injury at his hands. He must be taught that his restoration to liberty will depend on his own conduct.

All efforts at improving his efficiency as a worker and cultivating his intellect, if not based on this, are likely to result in making him a greater nuisance. He should not be turned loose on society to do what he likes; but he should be caused to undergo a period of probation under guardianship and supervision, during which his will and his power to conform to the law would be demonstrated in conditions that would continue after he had full liberty. His sentence would be determined as its conditions would be modified, not by the lapse of any period of time fixed beforehand, but by his own continued good conduct.

PENRHYN, or TONGAREVA. A coral atoll of Oceania, a dependency of the Dominion of New Zealand, 720 miles north of Rarotonga (Cook Islands). The enclosed lagoon has a large area, and is rich in pearl-shell, which provides a large pearling industry. Penrhyn was discovered in 1788, and annexed to New Zealand in June, 1901. Pop. (1925), 395.

PENRITH. An urban district and town of Cumberland, England, on the Eamont; served by the L.M.S. and L.N.E. Railways. There are a fourteenth-century grammar school and the ruins of a castle. It is an ancient town of Keltic foundation, and had a fair and market granted by Henry III. (1222). The parish church of St. Andrew was founded before 1223, from which date the list of vicars is complete. Pop. (1931), 9065.

PENRYN. A municipal borough and port of Cornwall, England, at the head of the estuary of the Penryn River; served by a branch of the Great Western Railway. Chemicals, bone-manure, paper, liquors, and leather are manufactured, and granite from local quarries is dressed. It is of ancient foundation, and stood within the domains of the Bishops of Exeter, which are mentioned in *Domesday Book*. Pop. (1931), 3414.

PENSACOLA. A city and port of entry of Florida, United States, the county seat of Escambia county, on Pensacola Bay; served by the Louisville & Nashville, and the Pensacola, Alabama, & Tennessee Railways, and by ocean-going steamships to European and American ports. The extensive land-locked harbour is defended by three forts, which also protect the United States navy-yard.

Coal, timber, phosphates, naval stores, fish, cotton and cotton-seed oil, and feeding-stuffs make up the bulk of the transit trade, and Pensacola is generally a great depot of naval stores. Manufactures include wooden articles, manures, and drugs. The site was settled by the Spanish in 1696, and the settlement was captured twice in 1719 by the Sieur de Bienville, French Governor of Louisiana, who razed it to the ground. In 1763 the Floridas were ceded to Great Britain, and in 1821 passed finally to the United States. Pensacola became a city in 1895. Pop. 31,579.

PENSIONS (Lat. *pensio*, payment). Annual grants of money, usually in consideration of services rendered. In Britain, besides Old Age Pensions (q.v.) and pensions paid to judges, civil servants, employees of local authorities, teachers, and others on retirement and properly known as superannuation allowances, there are pensions payable to certain retired ministers of the Crown who have served a specified number of years in office, to persons distinguished in art, science, and literature, or their dependents (Civil List pensions), and to the Crown forces.

Until 1916 the administration of pensions to the forces was controlled by the Admiralty, the War Office, the Chelsea Commissioners, and the Royal Patriotic Fund; and it was not until that year that there was any system of unified control. In that year the Ministry of Pensions was formed to take over the entire administration of wound and disability pensions, service pensions continuing in the hands of the Admiralty and War Office. Improvements were effected. Thus disabilities were classified and facial disfigurement made pensionable; the alternative pension was introduced; earning capacity was excluded from consideration in standard pension claims; and pensioners' widows were given the right to one-half of their late husbands' pensions during widowhood. Every man suffering from a disability due to or aggravated by service in the European War, and not attributable to his fault or neglect, is entitled to a pension. The standard pensions for army privates, seamen, marines, or airmen are as follows:

	Pension p. c.	Weekly
1. Loss of two or more limbs; arm and eye; leg and eye; both hands; both feet; hand and foot; or both eyes. Complete disablement. Incurable disease; etc. ..	100	40*s*.
2. Loss of right arm from shoulder	90	36*s*.
3. Loss of leg, right arm below shoulder; left arm from shoulder; severe facial disfigurement; loss of speech	80	32*s*.
4. Less severe specified amputations; total deafness	70	28*s*.
5. Still less severe specified amputations	60	24*s*.
6. Leg amputated below knee; left arm below elbow; loss of eye	50	20*s*.
7. Loss of thumb; four fingers of right hand; etc.	40	16*s*.
8. Similar injuries to left hand	30	12*s*.
9. Loss of two fingers of either hand; etc.	20	8*s*.

In 1928 the Government decided that the above rates should not be reduced according to the cost of living. These rates are based on the cost of living in 1919, and are subject to increase should the cost of living ever rise above that of 1919. For cases above the rank of private there is a similar scale, the full pension for a warrant officer, Class I., being 60*s*. per week.

A wife's allowance not exceeding 10*s*. per week, and graduated according to the scale of the man's own pension, is given to a married warrant officer, non-commissioned officer, or man, unless the marriage took place after discharge, after the war, or after the disablement. If the spouses are separated, the allowance may be paid to the wife.

The maximum children allowances (which are also graduated) are 10*s*. and 7*s*. 6*d*. per week for the first two children and 6*s*. for each other child when no wife allowance is paid, and 7*s*. 6*d*. for the first and 6*s*. for each other child when there is a wife allowance. A childless widow under forty years of age receives 20*s*. to 30*s*., and a widow over forty or with pensioned children 26*s*. 8*d*. to 40*s*. per week, according to the husband's rank. The children are pensioned on the highest children scale.

Parents and other dependents of deceased fighting-men are pensioned if dependent on the deceased, or in pecuniary need and incapable of self-support (maximum pension, 20*s*. weekly).

The alternative pension is a substitute for the standard pension and wives' and children's allowances. It is the difference between pre-war and present earning capacity (60 per cent being added to pre-war earnings), but pension and earnings together must not exceed £5 per week. In 1932 there were 904,240 pensioners. The Veterans' Bureau, the Bureau of Pensions, and the National Home for Disabled Volunteer Soldiers were combined in 1930 under the name of Veterans' Administration.

The state schemes include the Old Age Pensions (q.v.) introduced in 1908, and the pensions granted under National Health Insurance Acts (1925–9), namely the Widows' and Orphans' and Old Age (contributory) Pensions. The latter scheme provides a pension of 10*s*. per week each for the insured worker and his wife at the age of 65; (*See* NATIONAL HEALTH INSURANCE). The workers make weekly payments in contribution by means of stamps affixed to a card. The Health Insurance scheme also provides a pension of 10*s*. for the widow of the worker, receiving 5*s*. for the first and 3*s*. for other children. Orphaned children of an insured worker receive 7*s*. 6*d*. each. The same acts provide for a blind person receiving a pension of 10*s*. per week at the age of 50. With regard to the unemployed, medical benefit will be continued till the end of 1933, and pension rights till 1935.

What are termed civil list pensions are granted by the crown to necessitous persons who have attained distinction in art, literature or science, or to their dependents.

PEN'TACLE. A figure consisting of five straight lines crossing and joined so as to form a five-pointed star. It was a symbol among the Gnostics,

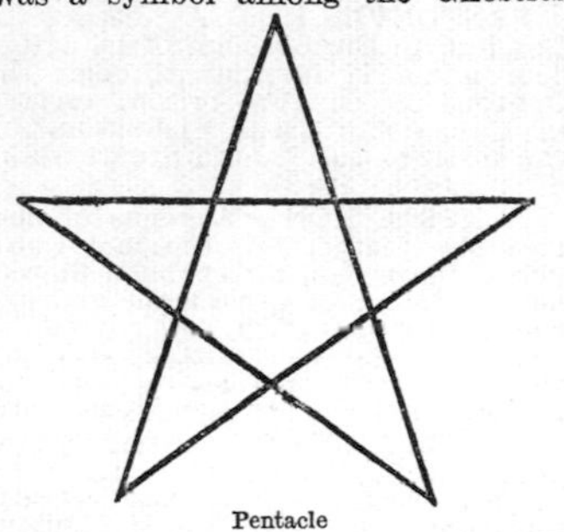

Pentacle

and was employed with superstitious import by the astrologers and mystics of the Middle Ages.

PENTAC'RINUS. A genus of graceful encrinites or stone-lilies, most of the species of which are extinct. Fossil pentacrinites abound in all strata from the Lias onwards, while some species still exist in the deep sea, with others belonging to the closely allied genus Metacrinus.

PENTAM'ERA. One of the primary sections into which beetles are divided, including those which have five joints on the tarsus of each leg.

PENTAM'ETER (Gr. *pente*, five, and *metron*, measure). In prosody, a verse consisting of five feet. The verse consists of two parts, called penthemimers, which are kept distinct. The first penthemimer contains two feet (dactyls or spondees) and a long syllable. The second contains also two feet (both dactyls) and a long syllable. The pentameter, when wedded to its heroic consort the hexameter, forms the elegiac couplet. It never is used alone. There were many writers of elegiacs among the ancient Greeks, but the couplet enjoyed an even greater vogue among the Romans. Catullus, Tibullus, and Propertius all wrote elegiacs, and Ovid brought this form of composition to an almost monotonous perfection.

PEN'TATEUCH. A collective term for the first five books in the Old Testament. It is derived from a Greek adjective which means five-volumed (*penta* = five, *teuchos* = volume); "the five-volumed book was the title of Genesis, Exodus, Leviticus, Numbers, Deuteronomy. It was simply a literary term. The Jews used "Torah" ("instruction," "injunction") as their religious description, for which the word "Law" is not an exact equivalent. "Law" calls up associations in a modern mind which "Torah" did not for a Jew; besides, these five books contain much more than legal injunctions or codes for the regulation of social and civil life.

Still, it was these five books which contained the commands, promises, and revelations of God by means of which the community of Israel had been formed and organised; and while "Torah" might be applied to the whole of the Old Testament or employed in a general sense, it came to be attached specifically to what was known later as the *Pentateuch*, i.e. to the first of the three divisions of the Old Testament, the other two being "The Prophets" (i.e. the books of Joshua, Judges, Samuel, and Kings, with the three major and the twelve minor prophets) and "The Writings" (including Daniel and the rest of the Old Testament.)

The *Pentateuch* is not a legal code, but a continuous history which runs from the creation of the world to the settlement of Israel in Canaan. The five volumes of which it is composed were not canonised until after the exile, in the fifth century B.C., and they did not assume their final form until the third century B.C., when they were translated into Greek. But they contain some early material, which can be disentangled from the subsequent traditions and legal collections.

The books of the *Pentateuch* are books made out of books; at least three or four documents can be detected running through them, and indeed, through the book of Joshua as well. The age, origin, and relations of these documents form the problem of the literary study of the *Pentateuch*, or, as scholars now prefer to say, the *Hexateuch* (the six volumes, i.e. including Joshua).

It is possible that some of the early traditions may go back to Moses, but the final editing of the books did not take place until long after the death of Moses, and none of the independent narratives which underlie the *Pentateuch* can be connected with him as author.

It was the veneration of later-Jews for Moses, and the belief that the beginnings of their community-life were connected with his legislation that led to the conviction that he had written the five books in which the origins of the nation were described, the theory being "that every Jewish leader of Israel wrote down by divine authority the events of his own time, so that the sacred history is like a daybook constantly written up to date. No part of the Bible corresponds to this description, and the *Pentateuch* as little as any" (W. Robertson Smith). Even the authors of the sources lived later than Moses, and the watermarks of the five books show that they presuppose the period of the kings and a prolonged residence in Canaan. But in these old uncritical days it was not difficult to believe that because the law of Moses (i.e. the legislation enacted by Moses) had been vital to Israel, therefore he must have written all the books in which that law was enshrined.

Hence the five books came to be known as "the Law of Moses." Authority carried with it authorship according to this view. For the history of Judaism the belief was of enormous importance; it explains the tenacity and self-confidence of the religion; it helped to consolidate the nation, although it now turns out to be unfounded.—BIBLIOGRAPHY: W. Robertson Smith, *The Old Testament in the Jewish Church* (1881, 1892); D. C. Simpson, *Pentateuchal Criticism* (1914); A. T. Chapman, *Introduction to the Pentateuch* (1911), with the section in S. R. Driver's *Introduction to the Literature of the Old Testament.*

PEN'TECOST (Gr. *pentekoste*, the fiftieth). A Jewish festival, held on the fiftieth day after the Passover, in celebration of the ingathering and thanksgiving for the harvest. It was also called the *Feast of Weeks*, because it was celebrated seven weeks after the Passover. Tradition connects this festival with the giving of the law on Sinai, and considers it as the birthday of Judaism. It is also a festival of the Christian Church, occurring fifty days after Easter, in commemoration of the descent of the Holy Ghost on the disciples, called in England *Whitsuntide.*

PENTLAND FIRTH. A channel separating the mainland of Scotland from the Orkney Islands, and connecting the North Sea with the Atlantic Ocean. It is about 14 miles long east to west, and 6 to 8 miles broad. A current, setting from east to west, flows through it with a velocity of 3 to 9 miles an hour, causing many eddies and rendering its navigation difficult and dangerous. The Pentland Skerries include two islets and several rocks.

PENTLAND HILLS. A range of Scotland, in the counties of Edinburgh, Peebles, and Lanark, commencing 4½ miles south by west of Edinburgh, and extending southwest for about 16 miles. The highest summit, Scald Law, is 1898 feet above sea-level. The water-supply of Edinburgh comes from springs in the Pentlands.

PENTONVILLE. A district of London, in the borough of Islington. The name is familiar through the Pentonville convict prison, erected in Caledonian Road, Islington, by the birth-place of John Stuart Mill. Sir J. Jebb (1842).

PENTSTE'MON. A genus of herbaceous plants, of the nat. ord. Scrophulariaceæ, with tubular flowers having four perfect stamens and one rudimentary. They are natives of America, and are distinguished by their showy flowers of various colours—red, purple, blue, white, etc.

PENUM'BRA. The partial shadow between the full light and the total shadow caused by an opaque body, intercepting the light from a luminous body, the penumbra being the result of rays emitted by part of the luminous body. An eye placed in the penumbra would see part of the luminous body, part being eclipsed by the opaque body; an eye placed in the umbra, or place of total shadow, would receive no rays from the luminous body. Thus in an eclipse of the sun, an observer situated in the penumbra sees a partial eclipse; one in the umbra, a total eclipse. The latter phenomenon, of course, can be seen only if the moon's umbra reaches the earth.

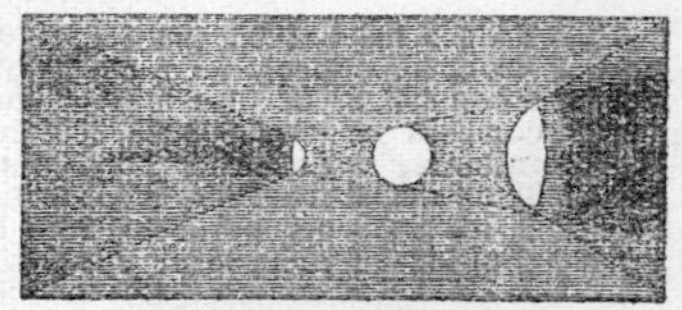

Umbra and Penumbra

The cut shows the phenomena of the umbra and penumbra in the case of a luminous body between two opaque bodies, the one larger, the other smaller than itself. Since the earth and moon, and indeed all the other bodies of the solar system, are much smaller than the sun, in all their cases the umbra is a cone tapering to a point, as shown on the left-hand side of the cut. *See* ECLIPSE.

PENZA. A former government of Russia, bounded by Nijni-Novgorod, Tambov, Saratov, and Simbirsk; area, 14,996 sq. miles; pop. 2,207,000. The forests are extensive. The chief exports are corn, spirits, timber, metals, and oils.

PENZA. The capital of the government of same name, stands at the junction of the Penza and Sura, on the Morshansk-Syzran Railway. It was founded in 1666 as a defence against Tartar incursions; has a cathedral, and several other churches. Pop. 91,924.

PENZANCE'. A municipal borough and seaport of Cornwall, England, on Mount's Bay; a terminal station of the Great Western Railway, and the most westerly town of England. The climate is so mild that Penzance has found favour as a health-resort. The harbour, formed by two piers, is commodious, and has dry-docking accommodation. It is a centre for the pilchard and mackerel fisheries, the former fish being largely exported to Italy. Tin and china clay are also shipped, and early vegetables are sent to London. There are no buildings of antiquarian interest.

As a fishing-village Penzance existed from the fourteenth century, and was the property of the manor of Alverton. The Spanish devastated Penzance in 1595, and as a consequence the rebuilt town was incorporated in 1614. It was made a stannary town in 1663 (Charles II.). Pop. (1931), 11,342.

PE'ONY (Pæonia). A genus of plants belonging to the nat. ord. Ranunculaceæ, and very generally cultivated in gardens for the sake of their large showy flowers. The species are mostly herbaceous, having perennial tuberous roots and large deeply lobed leaves. The flowers are solitary, and of a variety of colours, crimson, purplish, pink, yellow, and white. The flowers, however, have no smell, or not an agreeable one, except in the case of a shrubby species, *P. Moutan*, a native of China, of which several varieties, with beautiful whitish flowers stained with pink, are cultivated in gardens. The roots and seeds of all the species are emetic and cathartic in moderate doses. *P. officinālis* or *festīva*, the common peony of cottage gardens, was formerly in great repute as a medicine.

PEOPLE'S PALACE. A building at 309 Mile End Road, East End of London, opened by Queen Victoria in May, 1887. The nucleus of the palace was the Beaumont Institute, founded by J. T. B. Beaumont (died 1840), who left £12,500 to establish an institution for the moral and intellectual improvement of the working-classes in the East End of London. A movement set on foot by a novel by Sir Walter Besant—*All Sorts and Conditions of Men* (1882)—resulted in raising the fund to £75,000. The foundation includes a technical school (East London College) affiliated to London University and the Queen's Hall, for exhibitions and amusements.

PEO'RIA. A city and port of entry of Illinois, United States, the county seat of Peoria county, on Lake Peoria (Illinois River); served by the Chicago, Rock Island, & Pacific, the Chicago & Alton, Illinois Central, and ten other railways. There is a Roman Catholic cathedral (St. Mary's). From Peoria the Illinois River is navigable to its mouth (St. Louis), and the steamer traffic in grain, etc., ex Peoria is enormous. The Michigan Canal runs to Chicago. Manufactures include automobiles, agricultural machinery, canned-meats, and glucose. Peoria originated in a village established on the present site in 1778. It became a town in 1835, and a city in 1845. Pop. 104,969.

PEPERI'NO. The Italian name for a volcanic tuff composed of sand, scoriæ, etc., cemented together. It is so named from the small peppercorn-like fragments of which it is composed. The Tarpeian Rock in Rome is composed of red peperino, and the catacombs are the hollows of old quarries dug in it.

PEPEROMIA. A large tropical genus of Piperaceæ, mostly small herbs, many epiphytic, with fleshy leaves. Some are grown in hot-houses for their ornamental foliage.

PEPIN. The name of three Frankish rulers under the last kings of the Merovingian dynasty. Pepin I., or Pepin of Landen (died A.D. 639), was major-domo of King Dagobert I. His son, Pepin II., or Pepin of Heristal, major-domo at the court of Dagobert II., was, after the death of the king, appointed Duke of the Franks, and under a feeble regency ruled the kingdom with almost despotic sway. Charles Martel was his natural son.

Pepin le Bref, son of Charles Martel, and grandson of Pepin of Heristal, was, by agreement with the Pope, proclaimed King of the Franks in 752, after the deposition of Childeric III. He defeated the Langobardi in Italy, and made the Holy See a present of the lands which he conquered from them—the origin of the temporal power of the Popes. He became the founder of the Carlovingian dynasty, being succeeded at his death in 768 by his son, Charles the Great, usually called Charlemagne.

PEPPER (Piper). A genus of plants, the type of the nat. ord. Piperaceæ. The *Piper nigrum*, which furnishes the black pepper of commerce is a native of the East

Indies, where it is cultivated on an extensive scale. It is a climbing plant with broad, ovate, acuminate leaves, and little globular berries, which, when ripe, are of a bright-red colour. The pepper of Malacca, Java, and especially of Sumatra, is the most esteemed. Its culture has been introduced into various other tropical countries.

White pepper is the best and soundest of the berries, gathered

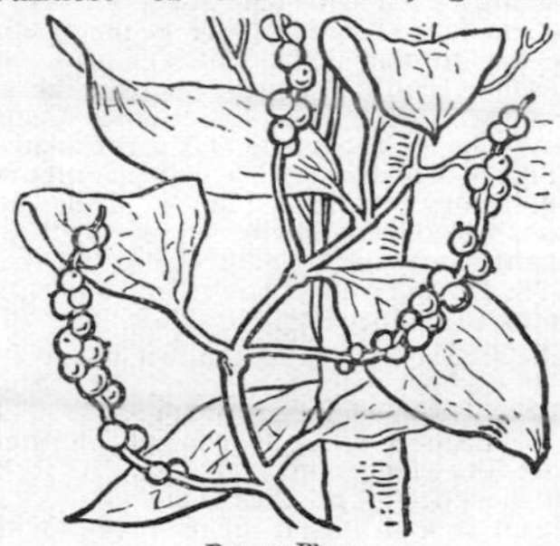

Pepper Plant

when fully ripe, and deprived of their external skin. The betel (*P. Betle*), belongs to the same genus. Cayenne pepper, Guinea pepper, bird pepper, etc., are the produce of species of Capsicum, nat. ord. Solanaceæ. Jamaica pepper is pimento or allspice.

PEPPERWORT. A plant of the genus Lepidium, one species of which (*L. sativum*), the common-garden cress, is cultivated for the table.

PEP'SIN. A ferment found in the gastric juice, and which, along with hydrochloric acid, is the chief factor in the digestion of proteins in the stomach. It differs from nearly all other enzymes (ferments) in the body in that it requires an acid medium in order that it may act. Pepsin, prepared from the lining membrane of the stomach of the pig or sheep, is used medicinally in cases of impaired digestion.

PEPYS, Samuel. English diarist and naval official, born in 1633, and died in 1703. His father was a London tailor, so his unfailing interest in clothes, especially his own, was probably hereditary. He was educated at St. Paul's School and at Magdalene College, Cambridge. He became clerk of the king's ships and clerk of the Privy Seal in 1660, Surveyor-General of the Victualling Office in 1665, and Secretary of the Admiralty in 1684. He was deprived of his office at the Revolution, and lived in retirement until his death.

As a naval official Pepys showed himself both brilliant and reliable. The Restoration was a time of great difficulty for the Admiralty officials, and it is not too much to say that Pepys did more than any of his contemporaries to make the navy efficient. Pepys lived a very full life and had many interests. He was devoted to music and the drama. He was elected an F.R.S. in 1665, and was president of the Royal Society from 1684 to 1686.

Pepys left his books, some 3000 in number, as well as manuscripts

Samuel Pepys

and papers, to Magdalene College, Cambridge. Among these books was his diary, written in the system of shorthand which had been expounded in Thomas Shelton's *Tachygraphy* (1641). The manuscript was in six quarto volumes, and extended to 3012 pages. It was not deciphered until 1819, when the Hon. George Neville, master of Magdalene, urged on by the success of Evelyn's *Diary* (published 1818), got John Smith, then an undergraduate of St. John's College, to decipher it. It was first published in 1825, under the editorship of Lord Braybrooke. It at once became famous.

The *Diary* begins on 1st Jan., 1660, and ends on 31st May, 1669, when Pepys believed he was going blind. The author was therefore twenty-seven years of age when he began to write his *Diary*, and thirty-six when he ended it.

It is a unique work. It is not merely that it gives a graphic picture of social life at the time of the Restoration, that it gives invaluable accounts of men in high places, and important information about the stage and indeed about countless interesting subjects. It is an unequalled piece of self-revelation. Lovers of Pepys may be said to know him better than they know themselves, because he has recorded not only those things which men do not tell to other men, but also those things which men do not acknowledge even to themselves. It is thus one of the most curious and interesting books in the world.

An edition, much more complete than the 1825 one, appeared between 1875 and 1879, Mynors Bright being the editor. An even fuller edition by H. B. Wheatley, containing all of the *Diary* that is fit for publication, appeared between 1893 and 1899.—BIBLIOGRAPHY: E. H. Moorhouse, *Samuel Pepys: Administrator, Observer, Gossip*; H. B. Wheatley, *Samuel Pepys and the World he lived in.*

PERA. *See* CONSTANTINOPLE.

PERAK. One of the Federated Malay States, British Malaya, with a long seaboard to the Straits of Malacca; traversed by two mountain chains and drained mainly by the Perak, the largest river. Tin, rubber, sugar, and coco-nuts are the staple exports, but rice (padi) is largely cultivated for export, the Krian irrigation works watering over 70,000 acres and forming also a reserve of drinking-water.

The main irrigation canal is 21 miles in length, and has about 200 miles of distributory channels. The eastern trunk line of the Federation Railways traverses the state, with branches to Port Weld, Tronoh, and Telok Anson. Taiping is the chief town.

Perak came under British influence in 1826, and in 1874 a British Resident was appointed (Treaty of Pangkor). On the murder of the Resident (1875) order was restored by British troops, and in July, 1896, the four Protected States (Perak, Pahang, Selangor, and Negri Sembilan) made a treaty with the British Government providing for an administrative federation under a Chief Secretary. Area, 7800 sq. miles; pop. (1931), 765,989. *See* MALAYA.

PERCEPTION. A term used in psychology and epistemology, and denoting a sensory experience involving meaning. It is the faculty or peculiar part of man's constitution by which he acquires knowledge through the medium or instrumentality of the bodily organs; the act of apprehending material objects or qualities through the senses. The perceptive faculty is exercised through the instrumentality of the senses; thus we see by means of the eye and hear by means of the ear. A person in whom these organs are wanting or defective will not perceive at all, or perceive imperfectly.

The impression made on the organs of sense affects the nerves, and by them is conveyed to the brain. The necessity of this communication may be ascertained by experiment: if the nerve appropriated to any organ be cut or tied, there is no perception; and the same result is observed in certain disordered conditions of the brain, even though the organs of sense and the nerves duly perform their special functions.

Although philosophers in all ages have endeavoured to explain the functions of the brain and nerves in connection with perception, all that can be affirmed with certainty respecting the means of perception is that when an impression is made on the physical organs and conveyed by the nerves to the brain, perception takes place. The impressions so communicated are the occasions of the mind perceiving, but we can assign no reason why it should do so invariably under such circumstances and not under any other, further than that such is the constitution of our nature.

Perception is to be distinguished both from *sensation*, which is the result of a *stimulation* of the senses, and does not imply recognition of the object, and also from *ideas*, which are experiences in the absence of the object. Whilst ideas consist only in memory elements, perceptions imply both memory experiences and sensory elements.

Two great disputes are connected with perception, both brought into full prominence by Bishop Berkeley. The first is the origin of our judgments of the distances and real magnitudes of visible bodies. Berkeley maintained, in opposition to the common notions on this subject, that these were learned by experience and not by the mere act of vision.

The second question has reference to the grounds we have for asserting the existence of an external material world, which, according to Berkeley, was connected with the other. Seeing that perception is a mental act, and knowledge is something contained in a mind, what reason have we for believing in the existence of objects apart from our minds? or what is the mode of existence of the so-called external world?—BIBLIOGRAPHY: G. T. Ladd, *Philosophy of Knowledge*; W. Hamilton, *Discussions on Philosophy*; R. Adamson, *The Development of Modern Philosophy*.

PER'CEVAL, Spencer. British statesman, son of John Perceval, Earl of Egmont, born 1762, died in 1812. Educated at Harrow and Trinity College, Cambridge, he practised at the Bar, and entered Parliament in 1796. In 1801 he became Solicitor-General, and in 1802 Attorney-General. In 1807 he was appointed Chancellor of the Exchequer, and on the death of the Duke of Portland, in 1809, he became Premier. In this post he continued till 11th May, 1812, when a madman named Bellingham shot him dead with a pistol in the lobby of the House of Commons.

Perceval was a keen debater and a fluent and graceful speaker, but was shallow and intolerant, and unequal to the task of leading the councils of a great nation.

PERCH. A genus of spiny-finned fishes, forming the type of the perch family (Percidæ). The common perch (*Perca fluviatilis*) is a common tenant of freshwater lakes and rivers. The body is broad, and somewhat flattened laterally. There are two dorsal fins, the anterior supported by very strong

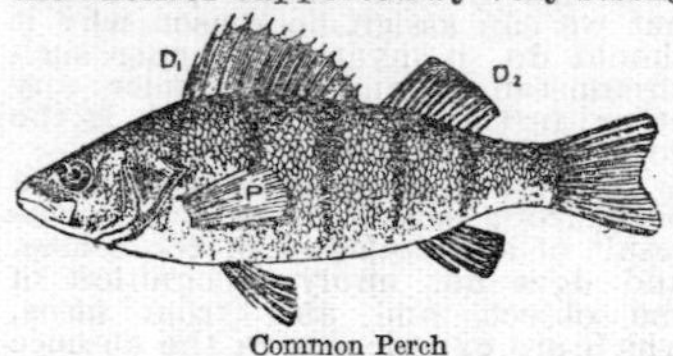

Common Perch

P, Pectoral fin. D_1 and D_2, Dorsal fins

spines. It is coloured a greenish-brown on the upper parts, the belly being of a yellowish or golden white. The sides are marked with from five to seven blackish bands. The average weight is from 2 to 3 lb. The perch is a voracious feeder, devouring smaller fishes, worms, crustaceans, etc.

A closely allied family (Serranidæ) includes the sea-perch or bass (*Labrax lupus*), which is plentiful on the southern coasts of Britain and in the Mediterranean; and also the numerous species of Serranus, which range through tropical and temperate seas. For the climbing-perch of India, *see* CLIMBING-PERCH.

PERCHLORATES AND PERCHLORIC ACID. Perchloric acid ($HClO_4$) is prepared by the action of concentrated sulphuric acid on potassium perchlorate. It is a colourless, syrupy liquid, which has strong oxidising properties, and when brought in contact with organic matter is decomposed immediately.

The acid is unstable, but it forms a series of stable salts which are soluble in water. The least soluble of the salts are the potassium salt, $KClO_4$, and the rubidium salt, $RbClO_4$; the former is used for estimating the potassium in soils. The salts are also oxidising agents, and are sometimes employed in the preparation of certain explosives, e.g. *permonit*, a mixture of ammonium nitrate, potassium perchlorate, and T.N.T.

PERCUSSION. In medicine, that method of diagnosis which consists in striking gently on the surface of one of the cavities of the body, and then endeavouring to ascertain from the sound produced the condition of the organ lying beneath. Percussion is most frequently used on the chest, but it is also occasionally applied to the cavity of the abdomen, the head, etc.

PERCY. The name of a noble family who came to England with William the Conqueror, and whose head, William de Percy, obtained thirty knights' fees in the north of England. A descendant, also named William, who lived in the early part of the twelfth century, left behind him two daughters, the elder of whom died childless, and the younger, Agnes, married Josceline of Lorain, brother-in-law of Henry I., who assumed the surname of his bride.

His son, Richard de Percy, was one of the twenty-five barons who extorted Magna Charta from King John. His great grandson, Henry, Lord Percy, was created Earl of Northumberland in 1337. He was Marshal of England at the coronation of Richard II., against whom, however, he took up arms, and succeeded in placing the crown on the head of the Lancastrian aspirant, Henry IV. He took up arms against this king also, but his forces were beaten at Shrewsbury (1403), where his son, Henry Percy (Hotspur), fell; and again at Barnham Moor (1407-8), where he himself fell.

His titles were forfeited, but were revived in favour of his grandson Henry, who was appointed Lord High Constable of England, and who fell fighting in the Lancastrian cause at St. Albans (1453). For the same cause his son and successor shared the same fate at Towton (1461).

The fourth earl was murdered during a popular rising, caused by his enforcing a subsidy ordered by the avaricious Henry VII. The sixth and seventh earls fell by the hands of the executioner in the reigns of Edward VI. and Elizabeth respectively. The eighth died a violent death in the Tower, where he was confined on a charge of taking part in a plot in favour of Mary of Scotland. Algernon, the tenth earl, took part in the Civil War against Charles I., and afterwards used all his influence to bring about the Restoration.

Josceline, the eleventh earl, died without male issue ; his only daughter married Charles, Duke of Somerset, and became the mother of Algernon, Duke of Somerset, who was created Earl of Northumberland, with remainder to his son-in-law, Sir Hugh Smithson, a Yorkshire baronet of good family.

The latter succeeded to the earldom in 1750, assuming the name of Percy, and in 1766 received the ducal title. The present duke (who succeeded in 1930) thus represents the female line of the ancient historical House.—Cf. G. Brenan, *History of the House of Percy*.

PERCY, Thomas. Bishop of Dromore, born at Bridgenorth in 1728, and died at Dromore in 1811. He graduated M.A. at Christ Church, Oxford, in 1753. He was then presented to the living of Easton Maudit, and in 1756 to Wilby, in Northamptonshire, and in 1766 he became domestic chaplain to the Duke of Northumberland. In 1769 he was appointed chaplain to the king, and in 1778 raised to the deanery of Carlisle, which he resigned four years after for the Irish bishopric of Dromore.

The most popular of his works is his *Reliques of Ancient English Poetry*, based on an old manuscript collection of poetry, but much modernised in style. The work was published in 1765, and materially helped to give a more natural and vigorous tone to English literature, then deeply tainted with conventionalism.—Cf. A. C. C. Gaussen, *Percy : Prelate and Poet*.

PEREKOP′ (ancient **Taphros**). A town of South Russia, on the Isthmus of Perekop, and in the government of Taurida, formerly a place of some military importance. Fighting took place at Perekop in 1919-20 between the Soviet troops and the counter-revolutionaries. Pop. 6000.

PEREKOP. An isthmus, about 20 miles long, by 4 miles wide where narrowest, connecting the peninsula of the Crimea with the mainland, and separating the Sea of Azov from the Black Sea.

PÈRE-LA-CHAISE(pār-lȧ-shāz). A cemetery of Paris, opened in 1804. It occupies ground a part of which was granted to Père de la Chaise, or Chaize, confessor of Louis XIV. *See* PARIS.

PERENNIAL. In botany, a term applied to those plants whose roots subsist for a number of years, whether they retain their leaves in winter or not. Those which retain their leaves are called *evergreens*, such as cast their leaves are called *deciduous*. Perennial herbaceous plants, like trees and shrubs, produce flowers and fruit year after year.

PERENNIBRANCHIATA. A section of the amphibian order Urodela, in which the branchiæ or gills of early life persist throughout the entire existence of the animal, instead of disappearing when the lungs are developed. Examples are seen in the Proteus, Siren, and Axolotl. *See* AMPHIBIA.

PEREYASLAVL. An old town of Southern Russia, in the government of Poltava. It was founded in A.D. 993 by Vladimir of Muscovy, and was the seat of a principality from 1054. It fell to the Mongols in 1239. Pop. 18,000.

PEREYASLAVL-ZALYESSKII. An old town of Central Russia, in the government of Vladimir. It was founded in 1152 by the Prince of Suzdal, and was the seat of a principality from 1195 to 1302. Pop. 9000.

PERFECTIONISTS, or **BIBLE COMMUNISTS,** popularly named **FREE-LOVERS.** An American sect founded in 1838 by John Humphrey Noyes (1811-86). Noyes was employed as a law-clerk at Putney, in Vermont, when the fierce religious revival of 1831 spread over the New England states, but he abandoned law for religion, and took upon himself the restoration of the primitive Christian ideal.

His distinctive doctrines were : (1) reconciliation to God and salvation from sin—purely matters of faith ; (2) recognition of the brotherhood and the equality of man and woman ; and (3) community of labour and its fruits.

In 1838 he succeeded in organising a society giving expression to his views at Putney. The society practised community of goods and community of wives. A system of complex marriage was established, by which each man became the husband and brother of every woman, and every woman the wife and sister of every man. They rejected all laws and rules of conduct, except those which each believer formulated for himself, maintaining that true believers were free to follow the indications of the Holy Spirit in all things, nothing being good or bad in itself.

To prevent the disastrous result naturally arising from the ignorant exercise of individual liberty, the Perfectionists introduced the "principle of sympathy," or free public opinion.

In 1847 about fifty members of the family bought a piece of forest-land at Oneida Creek, New York State, and there established a communistic society. At one time this society numbered over 300 members, with a branch community of 50 or 60 members at Wallingford, Connecticut.

So things went on for thirty years; but the public opinion of the neighbourhood began to demand that the social practices of the society should be abandoned; and this was done in 1879 under the counsel of Noyes himself. Marriage and family life were introduced; and in 1880 communism of property gave way to joint-stock, and the society was legally incorporated as the Oneida Community, Limited. Some communistic features, however, were preserved, such as common dwellings, a common laundry, library, reading-room, etc.

PERFUMES. These are obtained from both natural and artificial sources. Natural perfumes are preparations of the pleasant-smelling essential oils chiefly obtained from plants. Several are obtained from animals. Artificial perfumes are chemicals, many of which actually occur in essential oils. The chief distinction between essential and common oils, apart from their odour, lies in the much greater volatility of the former. If a drop of each is placed on paper, the grease-spot produced by the common oil will remain long after all trace of the other has disappeared. Further, common oils are not soluble in water; essential oils are slightly soluble, e.g. rose-water.

Natural Perfumes: Distillation. The extraction of the oils from plants forms a large industry, notably in France, Australia, and the United States, and it is effected by five different methods. In extraction by *distillation*, the method generally adopted, the part of the plant containing the perfume (petal, leaf, root, etc.) is, if necessary, cut into small pieces and placed in a still. Steam is blown in, and carries over with it the oil into the condenser. The oil is then run from the surface of the condensed water on which it floats. In the case of the valuable otto of rose, the condensed water, which contains small quantities of the perfume, is used again for generating steam.

The method of **maceration** is used when distillation would injure the delicacy of the perfume. Violets are macerated by hand in hot lard, in which the perfume is absorbed, and from which it is afterwards extracted by shaking with alcohol. Another method is by *direct extraction*, the usual solvent being light petroleum. After extraction, the solvent is removed by distillation, leaving behind the essential oil.

The method of **enfleurage** is used for plants, such as jasmine, which continue to form and emit the perfume after they have been gathered. The flowers are placed at the bottom of a vertical chamber, and a slow stream of moist air is passed upwards through the chamber, carrying the perfume, as long as it is emitted, over a number of glass shelves spread with lard. The oil is extracted from the lard with alcohol.

Finally, **expression** is used in rare cases, e.g. orange, lemon, bergamot, where the oil can actually be squeezed from the rind of the fruit. The yield of oil is usually small and varies with the plant, e.g. 1 cwt. lavender flowers yields about 32 oz., and 1 cwt. rose blossoms ½ oz.

The chief perfumes obtained from animals are musk, civet, and ambergris. These animal perfumes are overpowering, and need to be diluted very considerably to render them pleasant.

Liquid perfumes are prepared by dissolving a relatively small quantity of the essential oil, or a mixture of oils, in pure alcohol. So-called *fixateurs* are used, e.g. benzyl salicylate, and it is claimed that they assist in the retention of the perfume.

Besides the use of essential oils in all branches of perfumery, some of them have a wider application as flavouring essences in confectionery and cookery, also in liqueurs, in non-alcoholic drinks, and in pharmaceutical preparations.

Artificial Perfumes. The artificial perfume industry is one of recent but rapid development, and now produces large quantities of perfumes and flavouring essences. Successful substitutes for the perfumes of the rose, lily-of-the-valley, lilac, violet, etc., are now being sold. The first notable step was made by Perkin in 1868, when he prepared coumarin, a chemical substance to which the perfume of the tonquin bean is due. In many cases the substance to which the perfume of the natural oil is due is manufactured chemically and used as a substitute for the natural perfume, e.g. benzaldehyde is used instead of oil of bitter almonds. In other cases substances not occurring in the natural oil but possessing a similar perfume are used as substitutes; nitro-benzene, e.g. which smells like bitter almonds, is used for scenting cheap soap. In otto of rose the principal ingredient is geraniol. Wintergreen owes its scent to the presence of methyl salicylate, and pineapple its fragrance to ethyl butyrate.

PER'GAMUS, or **PERGAMUM.** An ancient city of Mysia, in Asia Minor, north of Smyrna, represented by the modern Bergama. Pergamus was famous for its manufacture of parchment, which derives its name (*Pergamena charta*) from this place. Many fine remains testify to the ancient splendours of the city, and extensive excavations have been carried out since 1878 with excellent results. The remains of the great altar of Zeus, erected during the reign of Eumenes II. (197-159 B.C.), and the ruins of a Roman theatre and circus have been found.

Pergamus was founded by Pergamus, son of Andromachus, and was conquered by Alexander, becoming then the property of Lysimachus. For many years an independent monarchy, it ultimately fell to the Romans, and then to the Arabs in 1336. Pergamus was one of the first towns to embrace Christianity, and was one of the seven churches of Asia addressed by St. John in his apocalyptic epistles (Rev. ii. 12-17).

PERGOLE'SI, Giovanni Battista. Italian musical composer, born in 1710, died in 1736. He studied at the conservatory of music at Naples, produced his first oratorio and his first opera in 1731, and was appointed chapel-master at Loretto in 1734. His sacred compositions and his chamber music rank high in the history of music. Among Italian composers Pergolesi is noted for the purity of his style.

PE'RIANTH. In botany, the floral envelope, the calyx and corolla, or either. This term is applied when the calyx and corolla are combined so that they cannot be satisfactorily distinguished from each other, as in many monocotyledonous plants, the tulip, orchis, etc. The perianth is called *single* when it consists of one verticil, and *double* when it consists of both calyx and corolla.

PERICARDI'TIS. Inflammation of the membranous sac (pericardium, q.v.) containing the heart. In the acute stage of the disease there is exudation of lymph or serum; at a later stage false membranes are formed; and at a still later stage the two sides become glued together, forming adherent pericardium. This is generally followed by changes in the substance of the heart, or in its internal surface, orifices, or valves, and a fatal termination is rarely long delayed. The symptoms of pericarditis are: pain, more or less acute, in the situation of the heart; fever is present, with loss of appetite and dry tongue. An anxious respiration and a feeling of overwhelming oppression are also present, with frequent sighing, which gives momentary relief. Most of the symptoms are aggravated by motion or a high temperature.

For the diagnosis of pericarditis we must rely mainly on the physical signs, but it is only when the effusion is considerable that investigation by percussion is of much use. In ordinary cases, where adhesion takes place, there may be an apparently complete recovery at the end of three weeks or less; but adhesion frequently gives rise to other structural changes of the heart, and then fatal disease of that organ almost always follows. In slight cases a real cure without adhesion may be effected.

PERICAR'DIUM. The investing fibro-serous sac or bag of the heart in man and other animals. In man it contains the heart and origin of the great vessels. It consists of two layers, an outer or *fibrous* and an inner or *serous* layer. The inner surface of the membrane secretes a serous fluid, which in health is present only in sufficient quantity to lubricate the heart, and so to facilitate its movements within the sac.

PER'ICARP. In botany, the seed-vessel of a plant, or the whole case or covering in which the seed is enclosed. The pericarp often consists of very distinct layers, as in the plum and other drupes, in which the external skin forms the *epicarp*, the pulp or flesh the *mesocarp*, and the stone which encases the seed the *endocarp*. Pericarps receive such names as capsule, silique, legume, drupe, berry, nut, etc.

PER'ICLES (-klēz). Athenian statesman, the greatest of ancient Greece, born about 490 B.C., died 429. He was the son of Xanthippus, a celebrated general who won a victory over the Persians at Mycale, and his instructors were Anaxagoras and Zeno of Elea. He was connected by family relations with the aristocracy, but as Cimon was already at its head he endeavoured to gain the favour of the popular party. In this he fully succeeded by his eloquence, abilities, and political tactics, so that on the death of Cimon, in 449

B.C., Pericles became virtual ruler of Athens.

By his great public works he flattered the vanity of the Athenians, while he beautified the city and employed many labourers and artists. His chief aim was to make Athens undoubtedly the first power in Greece, as well as the chief centre of art and literature, and this position she attained and held for a number of years. At the commencement of the Peloponnesian War (431 B.C.), in which Athens had to contend against Sparta and other states, Pericles was made commander - in - chief. The Spartans advanced into Attica, but Pericles had made the rural population take refuge in Athens and refused battle. After they retired he led an army into Megaris, and next year he commanded a powerful fleet sent against the Peloponnesus.

In 430 B.C. a plague broke out at Athens, and for a brief period Pericles lost his popularity and was deprived of the command. The people, however, soon recalled him to the head of the state, but amid his numerous civil cares he was afflicted by domestic calamities. Many of his friends, and his two sons, Xanthippus and Paralus, were carried off by the plague; and to console him for this loss the Athenians allowed him to legitimise his son by Aspasia.

He now sank into a lingering sickness, and died 429 B.C., in the third year of the Peloponnesian War. By the death of Pericles Athens lost her most distinguished citizen, a man whose intellectual breadth, elevated moral tone, and superiority to the prejudices of the age had placed him above his compatriots. His name is connected with the highest glory of art, science, and power in Athens. The golden age of Grecian art ceased with Pericles.—BIBLIOGRAPHY: Thucydides, *History* (Book i. and Book ii. 1-65); W. W. Lloyd, *The Age of Pericles.*

PERIDINEÆ. A group of minute unicellular plants, with brown chromatophores. They form a large proportion of the ocean plankton, and play an important part as food for various marine animals.

PER'IDOT. A name given by jewellers to the green transparent varieties of olivine. It is usually some shade of olive-green or leek-green. Peridot is found in Brazil, Arizona, New Mexico, and Egypt. It is softer than most gem-stones, is difficult to polish, and liable to lose its lustre. *See* CHRYSOLITE.

PERIDOTITE. Any igneous rock specially rich in olivine, and entirely or almost devoid of felspar.

PERIGEE (-jē). That point in the orbit of the moon which is at the least distance from the earth. *See* APOGEE.

PÉRIGORD (pā-ri-gōr), A pre-Revolutionary province of France. It formed part of the military government of Guienne and Gascony, and is now represented by Dordogne and part of Lot-et-Garonne.

PÉRIGUEUX (pā-ri-*geu*; the *Vesunna* mentioned by Cæsar). A town of France, formerly capital of Périgord, now chief town of the department of Dordogne, on the Isle; a junction on the Orléans Railway. The cathedral of S. Front, built between 984 and 1047 (according to some authorities at the beginning of the twelfth century), was restored in the latter half of the nineteenth century. There are bombazine- and serge-factories, iron- and copper-foundries, and a large trade in flour, wine, brandy, and the famous *pâtés de Périgord.* Pop. 33,988.

PERIGYNOUS FLOWERS. Those in which the receptacle forms a cup, with the sepals, petals, and stamens

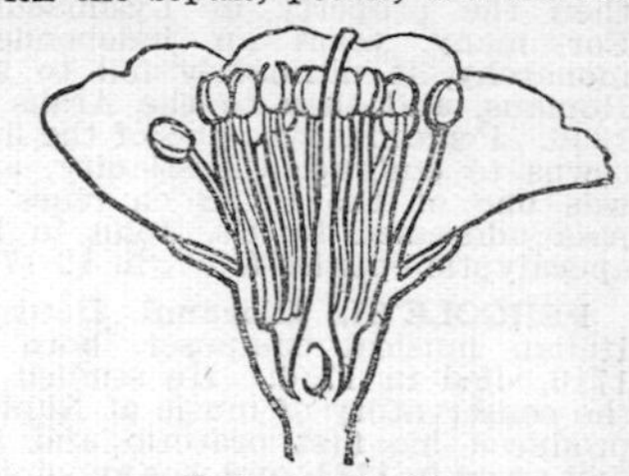

Perigynous Flowers

inserted on its margin, the gynœcium being enclosed in the cup but not fused with it; the rose is a good example.

PERIHE'LION (Gr. *peri*, near, and *hēlios*, the sun). That point in the orbit of the earth or any other planet which is at the least distance from the sun. The "perihelion distance" of a heavenly body is its distance from the sun at its nearest approach.

PERILLA. A genus of Labiatæ *P. nankinensis*, an annual herb with deep purple leaves, is a favourite bedding plant.

PERIM. A British island in the Strait of Bab-el-Mandeb, at the entrance to the Red Sea, about 10 miles from the Abyssinian and 1½ miles from the Arabian shore. It has been held by Great Britain since 1857, and is under the Residency of Aden. It is of consequence from its commanding position, which renders it the key of the Red Sea. On its south-west side is a well-sheltered harbour. Communications are maintained by submarine cable with Aden, Egypt, and Zanzibar. Area, 7 sq. miles; pop. (including garrison), 200.

PERIODICALS. These are publications which appear at regular intervals. They range from newspapers other than the dailies to reviews and magazines published quarterly, or even half-yearly, and embrace every conceivable interest from the popular and the flippant to the abstruse and the learned.

Evolution of Periodicals. In recent years they have been affected by the amazing development of the daily newspaper, and their evolution is still proceeding. The whole gamut of their activity now comes within the scope of the daily paper.

From the extremes of the absurdly comic to the profoundly serious, the dailies have made remarkable inroads into their once special preserves, and the periodicals have had to condition themselves accordingly. One great advantage the periodicals possess over the newspaper—time for consideration of subjects and for printing.

This affords scope for more reasoned treatment in the monthly reviews and for a better and more artistic style of printing, a matter of importance with regard to illustrations. Yet, in dealing with general topics and particularly politics, the periodicals are frequently at a disadvantage as compared with the dailies. The latter by going to press several times daily are regularly more up-to-date, owing to the fact that the weeklies and the monthlies are compelled to print a day or even a week in advance of publication. This is a factor which is bound to militate against the general periodical more and more as the technical facilities for rapid treatment of news are improved.

The weekly newspaper has already suffered. Once it was the indispensable adjunct of every home; now its special features are incorporated in the daily press, and its need is passing. To a lesser extent the same law applies to the weekly and monthly reviews and even the magazines. Special and expert articles appear in the dailies, in instalments when they are of great length; short stories and serials are now established features of the daily paper, and no longer stamp the periodicals with a character once their own.

Trade Periodicals and Propaganda. In some degree, also, the same is to be noted of trade periodicals and publications of a propagandist character. Many newspapers have regular columns dealing with scientific and trade subjects, and, moreover, they cater for the advertisers interested in those matters. They have thus invaded the peculiar province for which class periodicals have been established—a means of inter-communication in the particular sphere. An instance of this is the theatrical page every Thursday in *The Daily Telegraph*, with its columns of advertisements preferred by many actors and actresses to those of the theatrical journals.

As for propaganda organisations, a notice in the columns of the dailies with their huge circulations is obviously of greater value than the distribution of a periodical with a limited issue which probably reaches the converted only. Women and even children are increasingly catered for in the dailies, and with everything regarded from the point of "news" calculated to interest some section of the vast daily newspaper clientele, the need of the periodical becomes steadily lessened.

Nevertheless, the periodicals have still a considerable future. Many of them, local, religious, and trade journals, for instance, deal intensively with subjects which always will appeal to certain classes; highly technical and scientific matters cannot be treated exhaustively in the general press, which must inevitably aim at the "popular" view.

The size of the average periodical is an important item in its favour. Not only is it more convenient to read, but it is easier to keep and file for reference. Even to the great mass of readers of ephemeral matter the periodical offers attractions. Since education became compulsory and general, the reading public has grown to enormous proportions, and publications of the *Tit-Bits* variety will always be popular.

It was a stroke of genius on the part of the late Sir George Newnes, who founded that paper, to realise the desire for that kind of reading. Much of the *Tit-Bits* matter finds its way into the daily press, but masses of people love to take up a paper devoted to light literature only. Conversely, there are serious-minded people of every gradation, from the perfectly normal to the extreme crank, who prefer to devote time to concentrated study of special subjects in periodicals.

Fiction. Fiction and picture magazines have their particular public, and the artistic excellence of the illustrations is not only a delight to the readers, but a circumstance which advertisers take into calculation in their anxiety to catch the eye of the people. Colour printing is in the experimental stage as regards newspaper work, but it is an increasingly important feature of trade journals and other periodicals.

A class of periodicals still in its infancy and likely to expand is that issued by large firms for their own workers. This is a development of the club and society magazine, to which the employees and clients of the firms are encouraged to contribute. To some of these periodicals famous writers are already contributing. Periodical publications which are quite frankly of an advertising character are also issued by some large business houses, with features devised to meet popular tastes.

Theatrical programmes are also developing on these lines, and some football-match programmes partake of the nature of popular publications. The *cacoethes scribendi* will ever be a human impulse, and wherever men, women or children congregate for a common object, be it in school, or in camp, or in workshop, sooner or later, if the association be in any way keen, the desire will express itself to secure a printed record. Some of the most interesting periodicals the world has known have been the outcome of such efforts.—BIBLIOGRAPHY: J. B. Williams, *History of English Journalism to the Foundation of the Gazette*; Street's *Newspaper Directory*.

PERIODIC TABLE, THE. The accompanying table shows the Periodic System (*see* CHEMISTRY) in a form well adapted for the study of the elements in their chemical relationships. Above the symbols of the elements are the atomic numbers, below them are the atomic weights. Apart from hydrogen, the table comprises two short periods of eight elements each; two long periods, each of eighteen elements, complete except for an element following Mo; and three partial long periods, the gap between Ce and Ta being filled by the rare-earth metals.

Notwithstanding the spaces that appear vacant in the lower part of the table, the sequence of atomic numbers indicates that only five elements remain undiscovered: two members of the manganese family (43 and 75), one rare-earth metal (61), a halogen (75), and an alkali metal masurium (43), illinium (61), and rhenium (75), have been detected by their spectra.

In the short periods transition is from strongly metallic alkali metal to strongly non-metallic halogen. In the long periods there are A and B sub-periods coupled by triads of the eighth group, e.g. K to Mn and Cu to Br, coupled by Fe, Co, Ni. The members of these sub-periods in vertical columns constitute respectively the A and B sub-groups, e.g. K, Rb, Cs are sub-group 1A, and Cu, Ag, Au sub-group 1B.

The elements of the B sub-groups are always on a lower level of metallic power than the corresponding elements of the A sub-groups, e.g. Cu is less metallic than K, Zn than Ca, Br than Mn; consequently they form volatile hydrides and alkyl-compounds, which are not formed by the A sub-group elements, and their oxides are more acidic than the corresponding oxides of the latter elements.

Further, except in group 8 and sub-groups 1B and 2B, there is increase of metallic or decrease of non-metallic properties, with rise of atomic weight, i.e. from Li to Cs, and from F to I, but not from Ni to Pt, nor from Zn to Hg. So the strongest non-metals are found in the upper right-hand region of the table, and the strongest metals in the lower left-hand region. This is exemplified by F and Cs, the most intense non-metal and metal respectively.

The elements of the short periods are related to those of the long periods in the following way. In group 1 the alkali metals Li and Na belong to the remaining alkali metals K, Rb, Cs in group 1A. In group 2 Be and Mg are followed by Zn, Cd, and Hg in the B sub-group rather than by the alkaline earth metals of the A sub-group; and in all the succeeding groups the elements of the short periods are related to the corresponding elements of the B rather than of the A sub-groups.

In the long periods the relationships of the elements of the A sub-groups to the corresponding elements of the B sub-groups are noteworthy; for the greatest contrasts are found in the extreme groups, and the least in the more central groups. Thus the contrasts between the alkali metals and Cu, Ag, and Au, and between Mn and the halogens, are greatest, whilst the contrast between the elements of group 4A and those of group 4B is least. *See* CHEMISTRY; ISOTOPES; MATTER.

PERIOS'TEUM. The fibrous membrane investing the bones, and which serves as a medium for the transmission of the nutritive blood-vessels of the bone. The periosteum firmly

PERIODIC TABLE

							1 **H** 1·008	
2 **He** 4·00	3 **Li** 6·94	4 **Be** 9·1	5 **B** 10·9	6 **C** 12·005	7 **N** 14·008	8 **O** 16·00	9 **F** 19·0	SHORT PERIODS
10 **Ne** 20·2	11 **Na** 23·00	12 **Mg** 24·32	13 **Al** 27·1	14 **Si** 28·3	15 **P** 31·04	16 **S** 32·06	17 **Cl** 35·46	

0	1	2	3	4	5	6	7	GROUP 8			1	2	3	4	5	6	7
18 **A** 39·9	19 **K** 39·10	20 **Ca** 40·07	21 **Sc** 45·1	22 **Ti** 48·1	23 **V** 51·0	24 **Cr** 52·0	25 **Mn** 54·93	26 **Fe** 55·84	27 **Co** 58·97	28 **Ni** 58·68	29 **Cu** 63·57	30 **Zn** 65·37	31 **Ga** 70·1	32 **Ge** 72·5	33 **As** 74·96	34 **Se** 79·2	35 **Er** 79·92
36 **Kr** 82·92	37 **Rb** 85·45	38 **Sr** 87·63	39 **Y** 89·33	40 **Zr** 90·6	41 **Nb** 93·1	42 **Mo** 96·0	43	44 **Ru** 101·7	45 **Rh** 102·9	46 **Pd** 106·7	47 **Ag** 107·88	48 **Cd** 112·40	49 **In** 114·8	50 **Sn** 118·7	51 **Sb** 120·2	52 **Te** 127·5	53 **I** 126·92
54 **Xe** 130·2	55 **Cs** 132·81	56 **Ba** 137·37	57 **La** 139·0	58 **Ce** 140·25		(61 missing)											
		Rare Earth Metals			73 **Ta** 181·5	74 **W** 184·0	75	76 **Os** 190·9	77 **Ir** 193·1	78 **Pt** 195·2	79 **Au** 197·2	80 **Hg** 200·6	81 **Tl** 204·0	82 **Pb** 207·20	83 **Bi** 208·0	84 **Po**	85
86 **Nt** 222·4	87	88 **Ra** 226·0	89 **Ac**	90 **Th** 232·15	91 **Bv**	92 **U** 238·2											

A SUB GROUPS (0–7) B SUB GROUPS (1–7)

LONG PERIODS

adheres to the surface of bones (including the inside of the long bones), save at their gristly or cartilaginous extremities, and it becomes continuous with the tendons or ligaments inserted into bones. When the periosteum, through disease or injury, becomes affected, the blood-supply and nutrition of the bone suffer, and in consequence the bone-tissue dies or becomes *necrosed*, and is exfoliated or thrown off. When a bone is fractured, the periosteum plays an important part in the repair of the injury, new osseous material being deposited by the membrane.

PERIPATETIC PHILOSOPHY. A name applied to the philosophy of the school of Aristotle, derived either from the shady walk (*peripatos*) of the Lyceum, where the master lectured, or from the fact that he was accustomed to walk up and down with his disciples whilst he expounded to them his doctrines (Gr. *peri*, about; *patein*, to walk).

Generally speaking, Aristotle's philosophy is an empirical realism, i.e. particulars exist, but genera and species are only abstractions. Knowledge, however, is impossible through sense alone. Although the concrete particular claims reality, it is the universal alone that is the object of knowledge. The laws and causes of the world, Aristotle maintained, must be sought for not in the facts themselves but behind them, and motion necessarily presupposes a prime mover and a transcendent Deity.

The philosophy of Aristotle starts from his criticism of the Platonic doctrine of ideas, in combating which he is led to the fundamental antithesis of his philosophy, that between matter and form. The notion or idea of a thing is not, according to Aristotle, a separate existence different from the thing itself, but is related to the thing only as form to matter. Every sensible thing is a compound of matter and form, the matter being the substance of which the thing consists, while the form is that which makes it a particular thing (a stone, for example, and not a tree), and therefore the same as its notion or idea.

The form is the true nature of a thing. Origination is merely matter acquiring form; it is merely a transition from potential to actual existence. Everything that actually exists previously existed potentially in the matter of which it is composed. Matter is thus related to form as potentiality to actuality.

And as there is, on the one hand, formless matter, which is mere potentiality without actuality, on the other hand there is pure form, which is pure actuality without potentiality. This pure form is the eternal Being, styled by Aristotle the first or prime mover. The whole of nature forms a scale rising from the lower to the higher of these extremes, from pure matter to pure form, and the whole of nature is an endeavour of all matter to become pure form.

Motion is the transition from the potential to the actual. Space is the possibility of motion. Time is the measure of motion. The universe is a vast sphere in constant motion, in the centre of which is our earth. On this earth, as in all nature, there is a regular scale of beings, the highest of which is man, possessed of reason.

The soul, which is merely the animating principle of the body, and stands to the body in the relation of a form to matter, cannot be thought of as separated from the body; but the reason is something higher than that, and as a pure intellectual principle exists apart from the body, and does not share in its mortality.

Practical philosophy Aristotle divided into ethics, economics, and politics. According to his ethical system, the highest good is happiness, which depends upon the rational or virtuous activity of the soul throughout life. Virtue is proficiency in willing what is conformed to reason.

The Peripatetic school continued at Athens uninterruptedly till the time of Augustus. Among the philosophers who proceeded from it, after the death of the master, were: Theophrastus, author of several works on natural history; Eudemus, the author or editor of the *Eudemian Ethics*, which are probably a recension of Aristotle's lectures; Critolaus, Diodorus, and Cratippus.

These philosophers abandoned for the most part the metaphysical side of Aristotle's teaching, and chiefly developed his ethical doctrines. Strato of Lampsacus earned the title of "the Physicist" by rejecting the principle of the *nous* or reason of Aristotle's system, and upholding nature as the source of all existence, even of thought.

Later Peripatetics returned again to the metaphysical speculations of their master, and many of them distinguished themselves as commentators upon his works. Of these may be mentioned: Andronicus of Rhodes (58 B.C.); Nicolaus Damascenus (in the beginning of the Christian era); Aspasius (A.D. 80); Alexander of Aphrodisias (A.D. 200), the most celebrated of them all; and Boëthius, who translated the works of Aristotle into Latin. No one of the philosophical schools of antiquity maintained its influence so long as the Peripatetic.

The philosophy of the Arabians was exclusively Aristotelian. We find the Peripatetic philosophy in the Christian Church as early as the time of the Arian controversy, and a Peripatetic sect, differing from the Scholastics, arose in the fifteenth and sixteenth centuries. Even in modern times the principles of Peripatetic philosophy have served as the rule in philosophical inquiries.—BIBLIOGRAPHY: Sir H. Jones, *The Schools of Philosophy*; E. Zeller, *Die Philosophie der Griechen*.

PERIP'ATUS. A genus of primitive worm-like arthropods remarkable alike for their peculiar geographical distribution and their anatomical characters. They have soft, caterpillar-like bodies bearing from seven to twenty pairs of legs, each leg ending in a pair of claws. There are two jaws, each armed with a pair of cutting blades. They have antennæ and two simple eyes, and their respiratory system consists of tracheæ as in insects, but it is of a more rudimentary character. They live under stones and in rotting wood, defending themselves when molested by ejecting slime from two papillæ near the mouth.

All species are viviparous. This genus probably represents an archaic type which connects together annelids and air-breathing arthropods. The first-known species came from St. Vincent, in the West Indies, but subsequent species have been found in Cape Colony, New Zealand, South America, and Australia. Some authorities group these animals in three or four different genera. They constitute a distinct class (Prototracheata) of air-breathing arthropods.

PERISCOPE. A device used in submarines to observe the position of craft on the surface when the submarine is submerged. The periscope is enclosed in a long tube which projects through the roof of the submarine. It consists of a combination of lenses and prisms, arranged in such relationship as to provide a reflected image of whatever is in front of the lens and prism at the top of the periscope tube.

Eyepieces at the foot of the tube are used for observation. Vertical and horizontal scales marked on a glass in the eyepiece fitment are useful in sighting the enemy craft before firing a torpedo. The periscope tube can be raised and lowered by gearing, can be turned round to get views of all the surrounding sea, and is provided with a valve which can be closed if the top part is destroyed by gun-fire or other cause.

The combination of two simple mirrors on a collapsible frame to

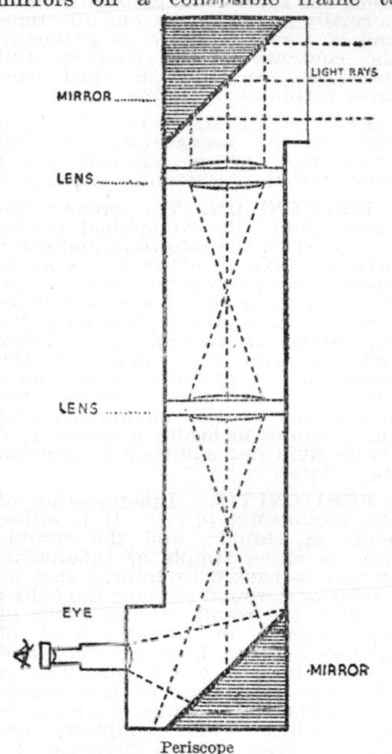

Periscope

obtain the view of objects over obstructions has also been given this name. Such appliances were in use in the European War for observation from the comparative security of the trenches.

PERISPERM. In botany, nutritive tissue in the ripe seed derived from the nucellus of the ovule; it is seen in seeds of pepper and water-lily.

PERISSODAC'TYLA (Gr. *perissos*, odd, uneven; *daktylos*, finger or toe), one of the two great divisions of the order of Ungulata or hoofed mammals, the animals included in which are distinguished by the fact that the toes, numbering one or three, are odd or uneven in number. This term is opposed to the Artiodactyla or "Even-toed" Ungulata. The horse, tapir, and rhinoceros comprise the three existing types.

PERISTALTIC MOTION, or **PERISTALSIS.** The name given to the motion arising from stimulation of involuntary muscles, and is seen in the intestines, when a ring-like contraction is produced at the point of stimulation and slowly passes along the tube. This peristaltic wave normally passes in only one direction, and so serves to drive on gradually the contents of the stomach and intestines, the lining of which contains involuntary muscle fibres.

PERITHECIUM. In Fungi, a flask-shaped ascus-fruit, opening when ripe by a terminal pore; characteristic of Pyrenomycetes (q.v.).

PERITONE'UM. The serous membrane lining the abdominal cavity and covering the intestines and other organs. Like all other serous membranes, the peritoneum presents the structure of a closed sac, one layer (*parietal*) lining the abdominal walls, the other or *visceral* layer being reflected over the organs of the abdomen. A cavity—the *peritoneal cavity*—is thus enclosed between the two layers of the membrane, and this contains in health a quantity of serous fluid just sufficient to moisten its surfaces.

PERITONI'TIS. Inflammation of the peritoneum (q.v.). It is either acute or chronic, and the chronic form is either simple or tubercular. It may be caused by injuries such as a blow or a wound piercing the belly; is often the result of ulcerations of the stomach or bowels; and of diseases of liver, kidneys, etc.; and is sometimes a grave complication of septic conditions of the womb. The commonest cause perhaps is appendicitis. The symptoms are chiefly severe pain, increased by pressure, and fever. The only rational treatment of this grave condition is to remove the cause, usually by a surgical operation.

PERIWINKLE (Vinca). A genus of herbaceous or suffruticose plants of the nat. ord. Apocynaceæ or Dogbane family. The greater and lesser periwinkle (*Vinca major* and *Vinca minor*) are hardy plants, which blossom in early spring, and are pretty common in woods, hedges, and thickets in many parts of Europe and in the south of England. Their flowers are of a fine blue colour, but when cultivated in gardens they may be made to yield purple and variegated flowers, both single and double.

PERIWINKLE (Littorina). A genus of marine snails, common on the British coasts. The shell is spiral, has few whorls, and is without a nacreous lining; the aperture is rounded and entire or unnotched (holostomatous). The common periwinkle (*L. littorea*) occupies the zone between high- and low-water marks, and is gathered and eaten in immense quantities. It is called the *wilk* in Scotland, in some parts simply the *buckie,* but is quite different from the mollusc called *whelk* (Buccinum) in England.

PERJURY. The act or crime of wilfully giving false testimony in judicial proceedings in a matter material to the issue or cause in question. The penalties of perjury attach to wilful falsehood in an affirmation made by a Quaker or other witness where such affirmation is received in lieu of an oath. By the law of Moses (Deut. xix. 16), "If a false witness rise up against any man . . . then shall ye do unto him as he had thought to have done unto his brother."

Gellius mentions that persons who had perjured themselves were thrown from the Tarpeian Rock. Perjury is a misdemeanour punishable by fine, imprisonment, or penal servitude. One who incites another to commit perjury (subornation of perjury) is liable to similar penalties. Popularly, the mere act of making a false oath, or of violating an oath, provided it be lawful, is considered perjury.

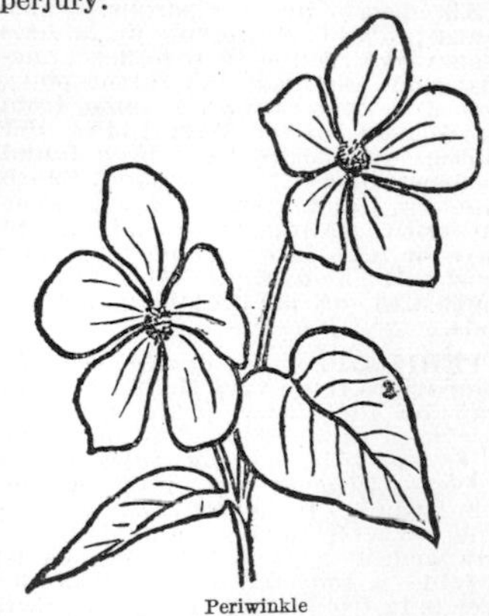

Periwinkle

PERKIN, Sir William Henry. English chemist, born at Shadwell in 1838, died 1907. He was educated privately and at the City of London School. After studying chemistry under Hofmann in the Royal College of Chemistry, London, he was appointed an honorary assistant to the professor. In a laboratory which he fitted up at home he conducted much of his early research work. During the Easter vacation of 1856, with the idea of synthesising quinine, Perkin tried with a negative result the experiment of oxidising a salt of allyltoluidine with potassium-dichromate.

On repeating the experiment with aniline, however, he obtained a dark-coloured precipitate which proved to be a colouring-matter possessed of dyeing properties, and was the first aniline dye to be discovered. He resigned his college post, and with his father and brother started a chemical factory at Greenford Green. The new dye was patented in 1856 (Eng. Pat. 1984), and was manufactured under the name of aniline purple or tyrian purple; the name mauve, by which it was generally known later, was given to it in France.

To Perkin's discovery of the first of the aniline dyes was ultimately due the supersession of vegetable by chemical dye-stuffs. Perkins continued his experimental work in pure and applied chemistry, and made many discoveries in the field of synthetic dye-stuffs. He was honoured by British, American, French, and German universities and learned societies.

His three sons, William Henry Perkin, Ph.D., D.Sc., F.R.S., professor of organic chemistry in the Victoria University of Manchester; Arthur George Perkin, F.R.S., professor of colour chemistry and dyeing, University of Leeds; and Frederick Mollwo Perkin, Ph.D., have all distinguished themselves in the same department of science as their father.

PERLIS. The most northerly unfederated state of British Malaya, on the west coast, with a seaboard of 28 miles. It lies on the Siamese frontier, and is traversed by the western trunk line of the Malayan Singapore-Siam Railway (*see* MALAYA). There are 36½ miles of metalled and about 26½ miles of other roadways. Kangar, on the River Perlis, is the capital.

Tin and guano deposits are extensive throughout the state; rice is cultivated, with some rubber and coco-nuts. Area, 316 sq. miles (including the Island of Langkawi); population, 49,297 (seven-eighths Malay; the remainder Chinese and Siamese). Siam surrendered her sovereign rights in Perlis to the British Empire (1909), and the Sultan now rules under the advice of a British Resident.

PERM. A former government of Russia, partly in Europe and partly in Asia; area, 127,502 sq. miles. It is traversed by the Ural mountains. The government is rich in minerals, comprising iron, silver, copper, platinum, nickel, lead, and gold. Pop. 4,000,000.

PERM. The capital of the Russian government of Perm, situated on the Kama. It has flourishing industries in iron, steel, leather, and furs. The copper-mines, to which the town owes its existence, were discovered in the seventeenth century. In Dec., 1918, the town was captured by General Koltshak. Pop. 84,815.

PERMAN'GANATE. Any salt of the unstable acid permanganic acid ($HMnO_4$). Potassium permanganate ($KMnO_4$) crystallises in blackish lustrous needles, soluble in water, giving a deep purple solution. It is usually prepared by heating together caustic potash, potassium chlorate, and manganese dioxide, extracting with water and passing CO_2 through the liquid. The solution acts as a disinfectant and oxidiser. *Condy's fluid* is essentially a solution of sodium and potassium permanganates.

PERMIAN. In geology, a system of rocks which received its name from covering an extensive area in the government of Perm in Russia. The system is poorly represented in Britain, but marine deposits of some importance occur in North America and India. The system succeeds the Carboniferous often without unconformity, and contains a Palæozoic flora and a notable development of primitive reptiles. The Permian period is also remarkable for the occurrence of an ice-age affecting lands now within or near the tropics.

PERMISSIVE BILL. A Bill which has been repeatedly brought before the British Parliament, and whose object is to empower a majority in any locality to veto, if so pleased, the issue of all licences for the sale of liquor in that locality. The principle of the Bill is known as *Local Option* (q.v.).

PERMUTATIONS AND COMBINATIONS. A section of algebra concerned with problems of arrangement and selection. The letters *a*, *b*, *c* can be arranged in 6 ays, viz. *abc, acb, bac, bca, cab, cba*. In other words, the number of permutations (or arrangements) of 3 things taken all together is 6. An arrangement may possibly not contain all the letters which appear in the question, e.g. we may wish to find the number of arrangements of 3 letters taken from the 5 letters *a*, *b*, *c*, *d*, *e*.

To solve this problem, imagine a row of 3 boxes, into which the 3 letters are to be put. The first box

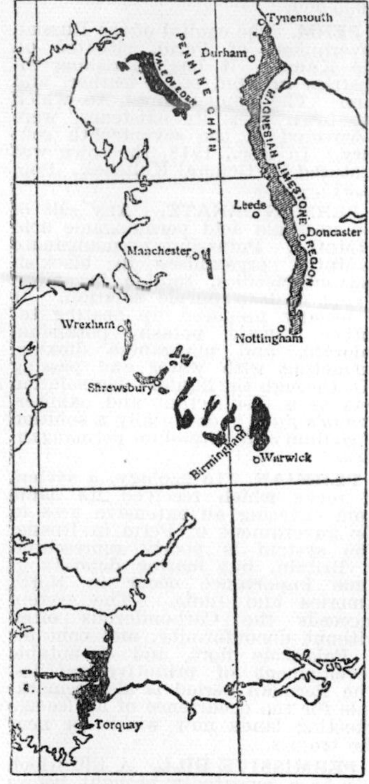

Map showing distribution of Permian Strata in Britain

Ordinary types (conglomerates, sandstones, and shales) shown black; magnesian-limestone (dolomite) type shaded.

may be filled in 5 ways, and after it has been filled there are 4 letters from which to choose 1 to fill the second box. There are therefore 5 × 4 or 20 ways of filling the first two boxes, as may easily be verified by writing down all the possible ways, viz. *ab*, *ac*, *ad*, *ae*, *ba*, etc.

In the same way it may be shown that there are 5 × 4 × 3 or 60 ways of filling the 3 boxes, so that the number of permutations of 5 things taken 3 at a time is 5 × 4 × 3. Similarly, the number of permutations of n things taken r at a time is $n(n - 1)(n - 2) \ldots$ to r factors, the last factor being $n - r + 1$. As a special case, the number of permutations of n letters taken all together is the product of all the integers from n down to 1, or from 1 up to n.

This product is an important number in many branches of mathematics; it is called *factorial n*, and is written $n!$. We can now easily deduce the number of ways of *selecting* r things out of n, the order of arrangement being a matter of indifference. For the r letters in any one selection can, as we have just seen, be permuted among themselves in $r!$ ways. Hence the number of permutations of n things taken r at a time is $r!$ times the number of selections.

The number of selections (or combinations) of n things r at a time is therefore $\{n(n - 1)(n - 2) \ldots (n - r + 1)\} \div r!$. As an example, the number of ways of selecting 4 cards out of 52 is $(52 \cdot 51 \cdot 50 \cdot 49) \div (1 \cdot 2 \cdot 3 \cdot 4)$. The chance of the 4 selected cards being 4 specified cards, say the 4 aces, is the ratio of the number of favourable cases (which here is 1) to the total number of cases, i.e. the chance is $(1 \cdot 2 \cdot 3 \cdot 4) \div (52 \cdot 51 \cdot 50 \cdot 49)$, or 1 in 270,725. *See* PROBABILITY.

PERNAMBU'CO. A north-eastern maritime state of Brazil. It is divided physically into three regions, viz. a coastal plain, low and wooded, but hot and humid; a high inland plateau, stony and dry, with hot days and cool nights; and an intermediate region of slopes and terraces, with light vegetation and a dry, bearable climate.

The Rio de San Francisco traverses for a distance the southern boundary and, with its affluents, drains the inland plateau. Coastal streams include the Goyanna, Una, Ipojuca, and the Jacuhipe, a tributary of the Una, which on the south forms a part of the boundary with Alagôas state.

Pernambuco is mainly devoted to agriculture, and produces sugar, coffee (in places), and fruit in the lowlands, cotton in the highlands, which are also devoted to stock-raising, and tobacco, maize, coconuts, bananas, and tropical produce in the intervening slopes. Cigar-making and cotton-weaving are the staple manufacturing industries. Railways are, the Sul de Pernambuco, Recife & São Francisco, Central de Pernambuco, and the line between

Pernambuco and Timbauba, with branches—in all about 1300 miles, all of which have termini at Pernambuco.

Pernambuco or Recife is the capital; other towns are Bezerros, Limoeiro, Bom Jardim, and Gloria de Goytá, averaging 20,000 inhabitants. Area of state, 49,560 sq. miles; pop. (est.), 2,869,814, or 57·9 persons to the square mile. Pernambuco is thus, after the Federal district and Rio de Janeiro, the most densely peopled state of the republic.

PERNAMBUCO, or RECIFE. A seaport-city of Brazil, capital of the state of Pernambuco, the point upon which all the State railways converge, and the third city of Brazil. Ocean-going liners use the harbour, and there is also cable and wireless (from Olinda) communication. Coffee, rum, sugar, molasses, hides, rubber, and dye-woods are exported. Recife (Port. *Cidade do Recife*, the city of the reef), the alternative name for Pernambuco, is the name of an adjacent city now swallowed up by its larger neighbour. Pop. (1930), 340,543.

PERNAU, or PÄRNU. A port of Estonia, at the mouth of the River Parnova, half a mile above the Bay of Pernau, a northerly arm of the Gulf of Riga. It was founded by a bishop of Oesel (1255), and was finally taken by the Russians in 1710. Pernau is a railway centre connecting with Riga, Leningrad, and Pskov, and the harbour is ice-free as a general rule between 23rd April and 9th Dec., or for about 230 days. Pop. 21,000.

PÉRONNE. A town of France, in the department of Somme, on the Somme. It is of great historical interest, and was the scene of the starvation of Charles the Simple by the Count of Vermandois, by whom he was incarcerated about A.D. 928. It passed to Burgundy in 1435 by the Treaty of Arras, but was repurchased by Louis XI., and eventually capitulated to Charles the Bold (1465).

Scott (*Quentin Durward*) describes Péronne and the castle in which Charles detained Louis XI. During the Franco-Prussian War it was bombarded from 27th Dec., 1870, to 9th Jan., 1871, when it capitulated because of an outbreak of smallpox. As a crowning misfortune Péronne was almost entirely devastated during the European War (1914-8).

During their "race to the sea" the Germans occupied the town (Sept., 1914), and held it until the Allied advance to the Hindenburg Line (March, 1917). During Ludendorff's supreme effort of 1918 (24th March) it was again lost to the Allies, but fell to the Australians, who stormed the protecting heights (Mont St. Quentin) in Sept., 1918. Péronne and Maricourt were "adopted" by Blackburn. Pop. 4700.

PERONOSPORACEÆ. The principal family of Oomycetes, including many important parasites, e.g. *Phytophthora infestans* (potato-blight), *Plasmopara viticola* (false mildew of vine), *Bremia lactucæ* (lettuce mildew), and species of Peronospora, attacking maize, beet, onion, tobacco, etc.

PEROXIDES. A general name applied to oxides containing more oxygen than the ordinary oxide. A part of the oxygen is loosely combined and easily liberated, hence the peroxides are oxidising agents. Examples are: barium peroxide (BaO_2), lead peroxide (PbO_2), and hydrogen peroxide (H_2O_2).

PERPENDICULAR STYLE. In architecture, a variety of the pointed Gothic, the latest variety to be introduced, sometimes called the *florid* or *Tudor* style of *Gothic*. It prevailed in England from about the

Perpendicular Style, Abbey Church, Bath

end of the fourteenth to the middle of the sixteenth century.

It is chiefly characterised by the predominance of straight lines in the design, and especially in its tracery. Another feature is the lofty square towers of its churches, divided into stages by bands, and each stage filled with windows. The mullions of the windows are vertical, generally rise to the main arches, and are often crossed by horizontal bars or transoms. Large windows are a distinctive feature of this style. The tracery of the doors is similar to that of the windows.

There are two kinds of roof peculiar to the style—the vaulted roof, with fan-tracery, and the open timber-roof. Nearly all the colleges of Oxford and Cambridge are specimens of it, and it is also exemplified more or less in many of the English cathedrals; while the majority of the old parish churches of England are also in this style.

PERPETUAL MOTION. That motion is perpetual is obvious; in fact it would be impossible to point to a visible object which is absolutely at rest, to say nothing of the molecules of which every material object is composed, which we know to be continually in a state of violent motion. Even the solid earth on which we stand is subject to continual tremors, which are rendered visible by the seismograph.

But the "perpetuum mobile," the search for which has fascinated the minds of countless inventors throughout the centuries, just as the quest of "the philosopher's stone" and "the elixir of life" captivated the imagination of the alchemists, is a different problem from that of merely constructing something which will always be in motion. The problem is: to construct some mechanism or machine which will give out more energy than is put into it, and will continue to do so for an indefinite period.

Modern science has decided that "the perpetual motion" in this sense is an impossibility, since it is absolutely inconsistent with the well-established physical generalisation which is called the Law of the Conservation of Energy.

The impossibility of "the perpetual motion" was recognised by the Academy of Sciences of Paris as long ago as 1775, when it decided that no communication would be considered by it which claimed to solve the problem in question, classing it along with "the squaring of the circle" and other mathematical impossibilities.

But this decision has by no means suppressed the race of enthusiastic perpetuum mobilists, each continually hoping by modifications of design to overcome the remaining obstacles that prevent his machine from running of itself.

PERPETUITIES. A perpetuity has been defined as "such a limitation of property as renders it inalienable beyond the period allowed by law." The power of disposing of one's own property involves a right to fix successive periods during which different persons shall enjoy the property.

Thus a man with a wife and two unmarried children may leave his estate to his wife for her life, and then to his children in equal shares. But he may fear that his children will dispose of the property to the detriment of possible unborn grandchildren. Therefore he will wish to give his children only a life interest.

It is, however, manifest that this tying up of the property can be extended indefinitely, and that a dead man will in this way control numerous descendants living many hundred years after his death. Therefore, as a matter of public policy, it became necessary for our courts to fix a maximum time within which a person can prevent the disposal of property with which he has parted. The period so fixed is a life or lives in being (at the time when the document affecting the property takes effect) and a period of 21 years. This is known as the *Rule against Perpetuities.*

Just as the rule against perpetuities applies to restraints on land, goods or capital, so it has been necessary to provide against the accumulation of income. This has been done by the Accumulations Act of 1800 and 1892, now embodied in the Law of Property Act, 1925, which provides that income shall not be accumulated for longer than either (*a*) the life of the disposer of the property, or (*b*) 21 years from his death, or (*c*) during the minority of any person living at his death, or (*d*) during the minority of any person interested in the property.

The Act of 1800 was passed owing to the eccentric will of a French refugee named Peter Thellusson, who left all his property upon trust to be accumulated until all his sons' descendants living at his death had died, the funds so accumulated then to be divided between his sons' eldest male descendants, and in default of heirs the money was to be used towards the reduction of the National Debt.

It was estimated that none of the property could be touched for nearly 80 years, when its value would not be less than £19,000,000. The House of Lords upheld the validity of the will, but owing to the expense involved in the litigation there was no fabulous fortune when the trust came to an end some 60 years later.

The Superannuation and other Trusts (Validation) Act, 1927, passed in consequence of the offer to the Treasury of a large sum to be held in trust for the reduction of the National Debt 50 years later, has altered the law by permitting income to be accumulated for that purpose.

PERPIGNAN (per-pēn-yäṇ). A town of Southern France, capital of the department Pyrénées-Orientales, on the Têt. Guarding the entrance from Spain into France by the East Pyrenees, it is strongly fortified, has a citadel and other works, and ranks as a fortress of the first class.

The city has much of the Spanish character. The principal building is the cathedral of S. Jean, founded in 1324 by Sancho II., King of Majorca. Perpignan was formerly the capital of the county of Roussillon, was long under Spanish rule, and was not united to France till the Treaty of the Pyrenees in 1659. Pop. 73,962.

PERRAULT (pā-rō), **Charles.** French author, born 1628, died 1703; superintendent of royal buildings under Colbert. His highly mediocre poem *Le Siècle de Louis le Grand* (1687) gave rise to the famous controversy on the comparative merits of the ancients and moderns, and the author was violently attacked by Boileau.

He is best known by his *Contes de ma Mère l'Oye* (Tales of Mother Goose), the classic nursery tales of France, which have procured for him the title of "inventor of the French Fairy Tales." The first conte, *Grisélidis*, appeared in 1691, and among the others are: *Little Red Riding Hood, Bluebeard, Puss-in-Boots, Cinderella, Tom Thumb*, etc. He also wrote *Les Hommes illustres qui ont paru en France pendant ce siècle.* A monument was erected to his memory in the Jardin des Tuileries, Paris, in 1910.

PERRY. A fermented liquor made from the juice of pears. It is analogous to cider, and is prepared much in the same way. Best perry contains about 9 per cent of absolute alcohol, ordinary from 5 per cent to 7 per cent.

PERSECUTIONS. The name usually applied to periods during which the early Christians were subjected to cruel treatment on account of their religion. Ten of these are usually counted. The *first persecution* (64-68) was carried on under Nero. The Apostles Peter and Paul suffered in this persecution. The *second persecution* (95-96) was raised by the Emperor Domitian. It is generally held that St. John was exiled to Patmos at this time. The *third persecution* began in the third year of Trajan (100).

This persecution continued for several years in many parts of the empire, and the severity of it appears from the great number of martyrs mentioned in the old martyrologies. The *fourth persecution*, under Marcus Aurelius (161-180), raged with particular fury in Smyrna and Lyons, and Vienne in Gaul. Polycarp and Justin Martyr are famous victims of this period. The *fifth* began in 197 under Severus. During the *sixth persecution*, under Maximian (235-238), only Christian teachers and ministers were persecuted.

Decius began his reign (249) with a persecution of the Christians (the *seventh*) throughout his dominions. This was the first really general persecution. Valerian in 257 put to death few but the clergy (*eighth persecution*); and the execution of the edict of Aurelian against the Christians (274)—the *ninth persecution*, as it was called—was prevented by his violent death.

A severe persecution of the Christians (the *tenth*) took place under the Emperor Diocletian (303). Throughout the Roman Empire their churches were destroyed, their sacred books burned, and all imaginable means of inhuman violence employed to induce them to renounce their faith.

Persecutions, principally directed against the clergy, continued with more or less vigour until Constantine the Great (312 and 313) restored to the Christians full liberty and the use of their churches and goods; and his conversion to Christianity made it the established religion in the Roman Empire.—BIBLIOGRAPHY: E. Gibbon, *Decline and Fall of the Roman Empire*; E. G. Hardy, *Christianity and the Roman Government.*

PERSEIDS. A stream of meteors the maximum of whose period of activity occurs about 9th to 11th Aug. They are so called because they seem to radiate from the constellation Perseus.

PERSEPH'ONĒ (Lat. *Proserpĭna*, anglicised *Proserpine*). In Greek mythology, the daughter of Zeus and Dēmētēr (Ceres). While she was gathering flowers near Enna, in Sicily, she was carried off by Pluto, who made her his wife. In answer to the prayers of Dēmētēr she was permitted to spend the spring and summer of each year in the upper world. In Homer she bears the name of Persephoneia. The chief seats of the worship of Persephonē were Attica and Sicily.

In the festivals held in her honour in autumn the celebrants were dressed in mourning in token of lamentation for her being carried off by Pluto, while at the spring festivals they were clad in gay attire in token of joy at her return. The story of Persephonē is universally held to be a mythical account of the changes of the seasons, and the ancients themselves saw in the abduction of Persephonē a symbol of autumn, when the fruits of nature disappear, and in her return a symbol of spring.

PERSEP'OLIS. A Persian city of great antiquity, famous for its magnificent ruins. It is situated in a fertile valley of the present province of Farsistan. Its foundation is generally ascribed to Cyrus, although some credit Cambyses, but its history is involved in much doubt. It was one of Persia's capitals, and the place of burial for many of its monarchs; and it was the residence of Darius III. when it was taken in 331 B.C. by Alexander the Great, who gave it up to pillage and destruction. The remains of large marble columns, vast portals, walls, huge figures, and bas-reliefs amply prove the former magnificence of its royal palace and temples.

PERSEUS (per'sūs). In Greek mythology, son of Danaë and Zeus. He was set adrift in the sea on his birth, in a chest along with his mother. But the chest reached the Island of Seriphos, and Perseus was brought up by the king of the island, who exacted a promise from him to fetch the head of the Gorgon Medusa. This he accomplished under the guidance of Hermes and Athena, and with the assistance of the nymphs.

He also delivered Andromeda from a sea-monster, an exploit which is frequently figured in ancient art. He was King of Tiryns and founder of Mycenæ. After his death Perseus was worshipped as a hero, and placed among the stars.

PERSEUS. The last king of the Macedonians, and an illegitimate son of Philip V.; succeeded his father 178 B.C., and entered keenly into the hostilities which had previously broken out against Rome. The Romans sent an army against him and gained a signal victory at Pydna 168 B.C. Perseus fled to Samothrace, but was given up to the Romans, and some years after died in captivity at Alba, near Rome.

PERSEUS. A northern constellation surrounded by Andromeda, Aries, Taurus, Auriga, Camelopardus, and Cassiopeia. It is traversed by the Milky Way, and contains a magnificent double cluster of stars. A brilliant "Nova" appeared in Perseus in 1901.

PERSHING, John Joseph. American soldier, born in Linn county, Missouri, on 13th Sept., 1860. He graduated from West Point, joined the 6th Cavalry (1886), was employed against the Apache (1886) and Sioux (1890) Indians, and was distinguished for gallantry during the Spanish-American War (1898).

After being instructor at West Point, he was successively organiser of the bureau of insular affairs under the War Department (1899), general of the army operating against Mindanao in the Philippines (1902), and military attaché at Tokyo (1905-6), accompanying Kuroki's army in Manchuria during the Russo-Japanese War of 1905. From 1909 to 1913 he was Military Governor of the Moro Province, in the Philippines, and became brigadier-general of the 8th Brigade in California, where his wife and three daughters perished in the burning of the Presidio (1915).

In 1916 he led the American punitive expedition against General Villa (Mexico), and in May, 1917, commanded the United States Expeditionary Forces destined for Europe, and had a division in France during June of that year. He organised the Meuse offensive of the United States armies during 1918. In that year also he received the G.C.B., and in 1919 he was made a freeman of the City of London. He was Chief of Staff from 1921 to 1924 with the rank of general. In 1931 he published *My Experiences in the World War*.

PERSIA, or IRAN. A kingdom of Asia, occupying the western portion of the Plateau of Iran. The modern kingdom is not co-extensive with that of the Medes and Persians of remote history, but is to some extent of territorial dimensions equal to those of Persia Proper of scriptural and ancient history. The capital is Tehran.

Physiography. Modern Persia has been described as "a sandy plain surrounded by mountains," and as such it is treated in some geographies. Although the general disposition of the interior mountain ranges is disputed, the Iran Plateau is believed to have an area of 628,000 sq. miles. It consists of a central area of plateau, rimmed by high mountains and two outlying lowlands.

The central plateau is divided by a ridge of higher land into the *Dasht-i-Kavir* or Great Salt Desert in the north, and the *Dasht-i-Lut* or Great Sand Desert in the south. Both these zones are devoid of vegetation, and form one of the most desolate regions in the world. In the *Dasht-i-Kavir* are wide stretches of solid rock-salt.[1] The Elburz and Khorassan mountains mark the northern edge of the plateau, the Elburz forming a single range falling precipitously to the outlying lowland along the Caspian Sea, and reaching its culminating point in Mount Demavend (18,600 feet altitude).

The Khorassan Mountains consist of two lower chains separated by a long valley running east and west. The Caspian littoral is long and narrow, but fertile. Serried ranks of limestone ridges, generally grouped as the Zagros Mountains, mark the western border of the plateau. They stretch from the region of Lake Van to the Persian Gulf, with an average width of 200 miles, the culminating point being Mount Kuh-i-Rang (12,800 feet altitude).

In the south-west the Karun River basin forms a second area of outlying lowland. Along the eastern frontier the western mountains curve eastward to the mountains of Baluchistan, and the central deserts and depressions are carried eastward by the Seistan depression.

Climate. Broadly, there are three climatic divisions. In the central plateau there are extremes of summer heat and winter cold, combined with a low rainfall and wide diurnal changes in temperature. The Caspian littoral, partly afforested, ranges as the altitude from sub-tropical to temperate conditions, with humidity and general conditions provocative of malaria and intermittent fevers. The lowlands of the Persian Gulf are exceedingly sun-scorched and unhealthy, with long spells of damp, enervating heat, and little or no rainfall.

Communications and Towns. In any country that is almost entirely devoid of railways and water-ways, and where a subsidiary system of passable roads is non-existent, mankind invariably seeks the "line of least resistance," and commerce tends to resolve itself largely into a question of trade routes (see map). The total railway mileage of Persia is only 350, but a new railway line (910 miles) is under construction which will join up Khormusa on the Persian Gulf and Randar Shah on the Caspian Sea.

At the head of the Persian Gulf the River Karun is open to navigation as far as Ahwaz. The Karun River joins the Tigris at Mohammerah, a river-port accessible to all ocean-going steamships that can cross the "bar," and the 180 kilometres to Ahwaz can be accomplished by flat-bottomed boats at all seasons. A British company runs a weekly steamer service. From Ahwaz, Isfahān may be reached in from twenty to thirty days, according to season, and Shustar by two steamers navigating the Upper Karun River.

Basra is reached in three hours by motor, and Susa by like means in six hours. The principal ports in the Persian Gulf are Bushire, Lingeh, Bandar 'Abbās, Chahbar, Jask, Mohammerah, and Abadan. Customs-houses for overland trade exist also at Ahwaz, Tehrān (pop. 350,000), Sehneh, Quasr-i-Shirin, Kermanshah (pop. 40,000), Luzdab, Nussrat Abad, Meshed (pop. 85,000), Kariz, Bunder Gaz, Meshedi Sar, Enzeli, Astara, Urmia, Tabriz (pop. 180,000), Khoi, Suj Bulag (Azerbaijan), and Julfa. Other towns are Isfahān (100,000), Kerman (40,000), Yezd (30,000), Barfrush (30,000), Shiraz (35,000), Hamadan, Kazvin, Kum, Kashan (each with between 15,000 and 30,000 inhabitants), and Resht (80,000).

The spelling of place names adopted here is that published by the Permanent Committee on Geographical Names, of the Royal Geographical Society.

Production and Commerce. Silk, wheat, barley, rice, fruits, gums (especially tragacanth), wool, cotton, opium, and carpets are produced. Mineral wealth is comparatively unexploited, but the Anglo-Persian Oil Company produces enormous quantities of petroleum from the Karun Valley (near Ahwaz mainly), and there are indications of oil all over Persia, but especially in the hinterland of Bushire, the Caspian littoral, and the Island of Kishm.

There are important oil-refineries at Abadan. Turquoises are mined at Nishapur, and copper, coal, and salt exist throughout Khorassan generally. Along the Persian Gulf naphtha and rock-salt are the chief minerals. Kerman in the south produces copper, lead, manganese, borax, turquoise, iron, and mercury. Lingeh is a pearling centre.

Exports. The major portion of Persian exports have ordinarily consisted of commodities produced in the northern and central provinces, and exported across the northern frontiers to Russian and other markets. During the Russian Revolution and the subsequently unsettled period these goods could not be exported, and, on account of long and costly inland

[1] The plateaux of Iran (Persia) and of Seistan (Afghanistan) are both areas of internal drainage. They are enclosed between the Elburz-Hindu-Kush on the north and the mountain loop of Persia and Baluchistan on the south. The rivers of these basins have no outlet to the sea, and, as is usual under such conditions, their floors are largely desert, the sheets of salt being deposited by the evaporation of the flood-waters.

transport, their dispatch to any other frontier of Persia would not have been within the bounds of economic possibility.

The exceptions are carpets, silks, and opium, which command monopolist prices, and would therefore show a profit in any case. Persia has ironically been described as "an estate of the Anglo-Persian Oil Company," and this is substantially true, for much of the national revenue is derived from royalties on Anglo-Persian oil production, and from Anglo-Persian expenditure on local supplies and services. Petroleum is the largest export, and the annual value is by far in excess of all the other exports combined.

Imports. Imports are mainly of sugar, cotton, tissues, and tea, with rice, live-stock, and cotton threads in the second division of importance. The third class comprises iron and steel goods, pure-wool tissues, mercery and smallwares, machinery, and matches.

Great Britain. During 1929-30 British commercial interests in Persia were predominant, and exceeded those of all other foreign countries combined, 55 per cent of trade passing through British hands. Next in importance are Russia, Egypt, Belgium, and the Netherlands. As in the case of Paraguay, a considerable amount of trade goes to swell the statistics of other countries. The Anglo-Persian Oil Company makes large exports of oil and oil products to Egyptian ports for retransmission to final destinations. 'Iraq is also a Persian transit country. *See* PERSIAN GULF.

Currency, Weights, and Measures. There is a silver monetary standard, the unit being the *rial* (4·14 grammes). It is equivalent to the *kran* which is now obsolete, but is still in circulation. The gold standard has not been in force since 1932. 20 *shâhîs* make 1 *kran.* Copper coins are the *pûl*; 2 *pûl* = 1 *shâhî*, 4 *shâhîs* = 1 *abbâsî*, and 10 *pûl* or 5 *shâhîs* = ¼ *kran.* Gold coins are of 2, 5, 10, ¼, ½, 1 *tomans*, but are not in circulation. 1 gold *toman* = 22 *kran.* The unit of weight is the *man* or *batman*, which is variable. The Tabriz *man* (*man-i-Tabriz*) is recognised everywhere.

A *man* is made up of 40 *sîr* or 640 *misgâls*, 16 *misgâls* being equal to 1 *sîr.* 5 *sîr* make an *abbâsî*, 8 of which are equal to 1 *man-i-Tabriz.* Roughly, a Tabriz *man* equals 7·27 Russian pounds, or 2·970 French kilogrammes, or 6 lb. 9 oz. English, in European terms of weight, but 6½ lb. is generally reckoned to the *man.* The *zar* or *gaz* is the unit of measure. A *farsakh* = 6000 *zar* of 44·09 inches = 4·17 miles. By a Government Decree the metric system was introduced in 1929.

Social Conditions. The people of Persia are mainly Iranians, or pure Persians and Turanians. About three million nomadic Arabs, Turks, Kurds, Gipsies, and Baluchis are also indigenous. The European population does not exceed 1500 on any but the most extraordinary occasions. Three-quarters of the people embrace Shiite Mahommedanism, to which sect the Shah must belong, this being one of the essentials to succession.

Of the remaining religions Sunnite Mahommedanism is pre-eminent, the others including Parsîs, Armenians, Nestorians, and the inevitable Jews. The Persian priesthood is very powerful, but anyone who can read, understand, and interpret the *Koran* may become a mullah. Kerbela or Najaf is the principal seat of the priesthood. The Gregorian Armenians have two bishoprics, one seated at Tabriz, and the other at Isfahān.

A bishop of the Roman Catholic Armenians resides at Isfahān, and another of the Latin rite at Urmia. Education is progressive, and is mainly developed on European principles. There is a polytechnic school at Tehrān with European professors. Military schools (at Tabriz and Tehrān), a political school, and a French school are all open.

Area and Population. The area of Persia is about 628,000 sq. miles, divided into thirty-three provinces, and containing a population variously estimated at from 8 to 10 millions.

Government. In Persia the Shah is virtually an absolute ruler. Officially he is called the *Shâhînshâh*, or King of Kings, which merely reflects the custom of most Mussulman countries, as, for instance, Abyssinia or Morocco, in flattering the ruler. By the Constitution of 1906 there is an elected National Assembly or *Majlis.* The government is now in the hands of a Cabinet. The governors-general of provinces, who are called *Wâli* or *Hâkim*, are assisted by governors of their own choosing, and are directly responsible to the Cabinet and Majlis. All towns have mayors.

Defence. The army has a total strength of 46,000 all ranks. There are five divisions, one of which possesses a few tanks, armoured cars, and caterpillars. There is a small air force, and a navy of three gunboats. Military service has been compulsory since 1926.

History. The original country of the Persians occupied a small portion of modern Persia on the north of the Persian Gulf. After being under the Assyrians, and next under the Medes, Cyrus (559-529 B.C.). by conquering and uniting Media, Babylonia, Lydia, and all Asia Minor, became the founder of the Persian Empire. The empire was further extended by his son and successor Cambyses (529-522 B.C.), who conquered Tyre, Cyprus, and Egypt; and by Darius I., who subdued Thrace and Macedonia, and a small part of India. His son Xerxes (486-465 B.C.) reduced Egypt, which had revolted under his father, and also continued the war against the European Greeks, but was defeated on the field of Marathon and at Salamis (480 B.C.), and obliged to defend himself against their attacks in a disastrous war. Artaxerxes I. (465-425 B.C.) had a long and comparatively peaceful reign.

Artaxerxes was followed by Darius II. or Darius Nothus, Artaxerxes II. (Mnemon), Artaxerxes III. (Ochus), and Darius III. (Codomannus, 338-330 B.C.), the last of this dynasty, known as the Achæmenian dynasty. He was defeated by Alexander the Great in three battles, lost his life, and the empire passed into the hands of his conqueror.

On the dissolution of the Macedonian Empire, after the death of Alexander (323), Persia ultimately fell to his general Seleucus and his successors the Seleucidæ (312). They reigned over it till 236 B.C., when the last Seleucus was defeated and taken prisoner by Arsaces I., the founder of the dynasty of the Arsacidæ and of the Parthian Empire, of which Persia formed a portion, and which lasted till A.D. 226.

The supremacy was then recovered by Persia in the person of Ardishír Babigán (Artaxerxes), who obtained the sovereignty of all Central Asia, and left it to his descendants, the Sassanidæ, so called from Sassan,

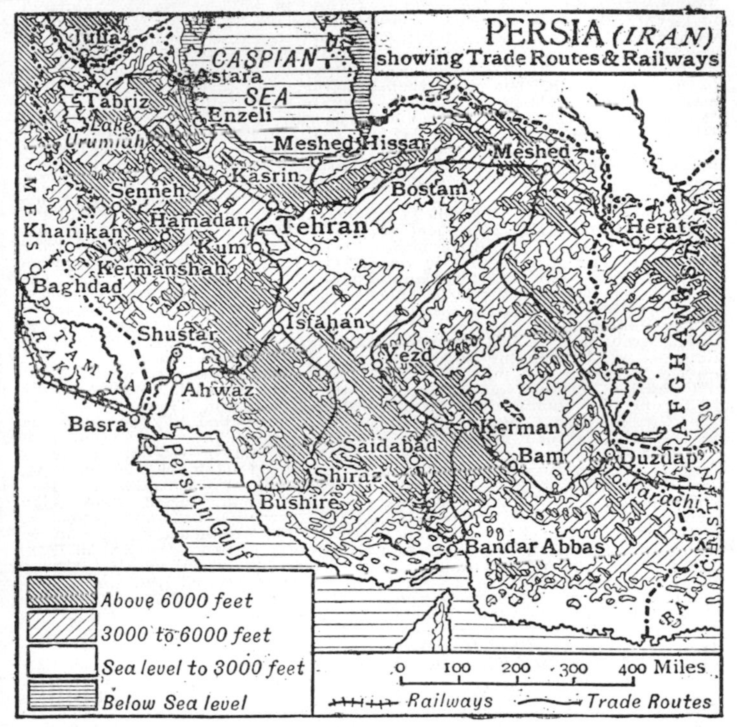

the grandfather of Ardishír. This dynasty continued to reign for about 417 years, under twenty-six sovereigns.

The reign of Sapor II., called the Great (310-381), and that of Chosroes I. (Khosru, 531-579), were perhaps the most notable of the whole dynasty. The latter extended the Persian Empire from the Mediterranean to the Indus, from the Jaxartes to Arabia and the confines of Egypt. He waged successful wars with the Indians, Turks, Romans, and Arabs.

Chosroes II. (591-628) made extensive conquests, but lost them again in the middle of the reign of the Byzantine Emperor Heraclius. His son Ardishír (Artaxerxes) III., but seven years old, succeeded him, but was murdered a few days after his accession. He was the last descendant of the Sassanidæ in the male line. Numerous revolutions now followed, until Yezdigerd III., a nephew of Chosroes II., ascended the throne in 632 at the age of sixteen. He was attacked and defeated by Caliph Omar in 633-639, and Persia became for more than 150 years a province of the Mahommedan Empire.

The Arab conquest had a profound influence on Persian life as well as on the language and religion. The old Persian religion was given up in favour of Mahommedanism, only the Guebres (q.v.) remaining true to the faith of their fathers.

About the beginning of the ninth century the Persian territories began to be broken up into numerous petty states. The Seljuks, a Turkish dynasty, who first became powerful about 1037, extended their dominion over several Persian provinces, and Malek-Shah, the most powerful of them, conquered also Georgia, Syria, and Asia Minor. Through Genghis Khan the Tartars and Mongols became dominant in Persia about 1220, and they preserved this ascendancy till the beginning of the fifteenth century.

Then appeared (1387) Timour the Lame (Tamerlane) at the head of a new horde of Mongols, who conquered Persia and filled the world from Hindustan to the extremities of Asia Minor with terror. But the death of this famous conqueror in 1405 was followed not long after by the downfall of the Mongol dominion in Persia, where the Turkomans thenceforward remained masters for 100 years.

The Turkomans were succeeded by the Sufi dynasty (1501-1736). The first sovereign of this dynasty, Ismail Sufi, pretended to be descended from Ali, the son-in-law of Mahomet. He assumed the title of Shah, and introduced the sect of Ali (the Shiite or Shiah sect). The great Shah Abbas (1587-1628) introduced absolute power, and made Isfahan his capital.

Under Shah Soliman (1666-94) the empire declined, and entirely sunk under his son Hussein. A period of revolts and anarchy followed until Kuli Khan ascended the throne in 1736 as Nadir Shah, and restored Persia to her former importance by successful wars and a strong government. In 1747 Nadir was murdered by the commanders of his guards, and his death threw the empire again into confusion.

Kerim Khan, who had served under Nadir, succeeded, after a long period of anarchy, in making himself master of whole of the Western Iran or modern Persia. He died in 1779. New disturbances arose after his death, and continued till a eunuch, Aga Mahomet, a Turkoman belonging to the noblest family of the tribe of the Kajars, and man of uncommon qualities, seated himself on the throne, which he left to his nephew Baba Khan. The latter began to reign in 1796 under the name of Futteh Ali Shah, and fixed his residence at Tehrān.

This monarch's reign was in great part taken up with disastrous wars with Russia and Turkey. In 1813 he was compelled to cede to Russia all his possessions to the north of Armenia, and in 1828 his share of Armenia. Futteh Ali died in 1834, leaving the crown to his grandson Mahomet Shah, during whose reign Persia became constantly weaker, and Russian influence in the country constantly greater. He died in 1848, and was succeeded on the throne by his son Nassr-ed-Din, born 1829.

This ruler had to suppress a number of insurrections, and in 1851 a serious rebellion of the Pure Persian party in Khorassan, who refused obedience to the Kajar dynasty on religious grounds. In May, 1852, he annexed the Sultanate of Herat, but was compelled to relinquish it by the British, and a second occupation in 1855 resulted in the landing of a British force on the Persian Gulf, the capture of Bushire, and the Peace of Paris (3rd March, 1857).

Persia has since come into the possession of portions of territory formerly belonging to Omân, Afghanistan, and Baluchistan. On the north-east the boundary between Persia and the Russian territory beyond the Caspian, after remaining long uncertain, was settled in the end of 1881. The Shah was assassinated in 1896, and his son and successor, Muzaffar-ed-Din, abdicated in 1906 in favour of his son, Mahomet Ali. The Constitution of 1906 (see above) was bitterly opposed by the Shah, and the mullahs or priests who favoured the old absolutism.

The Shah was deposed in 1909, and his son, Ahmed Mirza, a child of eleven, was placed on the throne. In 1924 a determined attempt to introduce a republican government met with failure, but in 1925 Ahmed Mirza, who had been absent from the country for over two years, was deposed and the government was handed over to Reza Khan, the Premier.

In Dec., 1925, Reza Khan **was** made Shah, and in 1926 his son became Crown Prince. In 1907 a convention was signed between Great Britain and Russia in reference to Persia, and fixing the respective spheres of influence of the two countries. This convention was recognised by Persia in 1912. In 1921 Persia entered into a full and binding treaty with Soviet Russia. Though neutral during the European War, Persia suffered much, being constantly fought over. — BIBLIOGRAPHY: Sir P. M. Sykes, *A History of Persia*; G. H. Ebtehaj, *Guide Book on Persia*; I. K. Sadiq, *Modern Persia and her Educational System*; and A. C. Edwards, *A Persian Caravan*.

Language and Literature. The oldest form of the language is called Old Bactrian or Zend. It is that in which the *Zendavesta* (or sacred Zoroastrian writings) was originally composed, and is very closely allied to the Old Sanskrit of the *Vedas*. The next development of the Iranian language is the Old Persian of the cuneiform inscriptions of the Achæmenian dynasty. We then lose sight of the Iranian language, and in the inscriptions and coins of the Sassanian kings, and in the translation of the *Zendavesta* made during the period of their sway in Persia, we find a language called Pehlevi or Pehlvi, which is strictly merely a mode of writing Persian, in which the words are partly represented by their Semitic equivalents.

This curious disguised language is also known as *Middle Persian*, *New Persian* was the next development, and is represented in its oldest form in the *Shanameh* of Firdusi (about A.D. 1000). In its later form it is largely mingled with Arab words and phrases, introduced with Mahommedanism after the Arab conquest. The written character is the Arabic, but with four additional letters with three points.

The Persians possess rich literary treasures in poetry, history, and geography, but principally in the former. Among the most brilliant of Persian poets are: Rudagi, a lyric and didactic poet (about 952), regarded as the father of modern Persian poetry; the epic poet Firdusi (beginning of eleventh century), whose most celebrated work is the poetical history the *Shanameh* (Book of Kings) in 6000 couplets. Omar Khayyám (died 1123), the author of celebrated *Quatrains*; Nisâmi (twelfth century), a didactic poet; Sadi (thirteenth century), a lyric and moral poet, author of the *Gulistan* (Rose Garden), a collection of stories; Rumi, his contemporary, a great mystic and didactic writer; Hafiz (born about the beginning of the fourteenth century), the most celebrated writer of odes; and Jami (fifteenth century), one of the most productive and most captivating of Persian poets. In the sixteenth century literary production almost ceased.

The Persians are remarkable as being the only Mahommedan nation which has cultivated the drama. Their productions in this province of literature closely resemble the mysteries of the Middle Ages, and abound in natural and affecting lyrical passages. Not less numerous are the prose fables, tales, and narratives, many of which have been translated into English, French, German, and other European languages. It was also through the Persian that much of the Indian literature in fables and tales was transmitted to the Arabs, and thence to Europe.

In the departments of history, geography, and statistics the Persians have some large and valuable works. Tabari is the earliest historian (died A.D. 922). Mirkhond, who flourished in the fifteenth century, wrote a voluminous work on the *History of Persia* down to 1471. Geometry and astronomy were also cultivated with ardour by the Persians, but their knowledge of these subjects is in a great measure borrowed from the Arabians. Religious works are also numerous; besides those treating of Mahomet and Mahommedan religion, they have translations of the *Pentateuch* and the *Gospels*, as well as translations of recent scientific and educational works. —BIBLIOGRAPHY: E. G. Browne, *Literary History of Persia*; C. H. A. Field, *Persian Literature*; J. Darmesteter, *Les Origines de la poésie persane*.

PERSIAN GULF (ancient **Persicus Sinus**). A gulf separating Persia from Arabia, and communicating with the Indian Ocean, by the Strait of Ormuz, 35 miles wide; greatest length, 520 miles; breadth, 150 to 200 miles. It receives the waters of the united Euphrates and Tigris, and of a number of small streams. There are many islands in the gulf; the largest are: Kishim, Ormuz, and the Bahrein Isles; in the neighbourhood of the latter there are lucrative pearl-fisheries. The principal port is Bushire; others are; Lingeh, Bandar 'Abbās, Chahbar, Jask, Mohammerah, and Abadan.

Of the steamers entering the Persian Gulf, about 96 per cent are British, therefore it "seems but in accordance with the fitness of things that Great Britain, which for many years has policed and protected the Gulf, rid it of pirates, purged it of the illicit arms traffic, freed it from the slave trade, surveyed and charted it, buoyed and lighted it, and developed as far as practicable its ports, should now round off this long record of arduous service by performing the bulk of the commercial shipping movements" (Major Temple).

Conditions in the Persian Gulf are favourable to the growth of the pearl oyster. The water is shallow and free from silt; the temperature is suitable for diving purposes from three to four months in the year. About 75,000 persons are engaged in the industry.—Cf. Major B. Temple, I.A.R.O., *Persia: Trade and Transport Conditions* (H.M. Stationery Office).

PERSIAN POWDER. An efficacious insecticide introduced from the East, and prepared from the flowers of the *Chrysanthemum carneum* or *roseum*, nat. ord. Compositæ, a native of the Caucasus and Persia.

PERSIAN WHEEL, or NORIA. A machine for raising water to irrigate meadows, etc., employed from time immemorial in Asia and Africa, and introduced by the Saracens into Spain and other European countries. It consists of a double water-wheel, with float-boards on one side and a series of buckets on the other, which are movable about an axis above their centre of gravity. The wheel is placed in a stream, the water turns it, and the filled buckets ascend; when they reach the highest point, their lower ends strike against a fixed obstacle, and the water is discharged into a reservoir.

In Portugal, Spain, south of France, and Italy this contrivance is extensively used; and has been modified to enable it to draw water also from ponds and wells, animals supplying the motive power, and pots, leather or other bags taking the place of buckets.

PERSIM'MON. The fruit of the *Diospy̆ros virginiānā*, a tree (a species of ebony) inhabiting the United States of America, more especially the southern states, where it attains the height of 60 feet or more. The fruit is succulent, reddish, and about the size of a small plum, containing a few oval stones. It is powerfully astringent when green, but when fully ripe the pulp becomes soft, palatable, and very sweet.

PER'SIUS (Aulus Persius Flaccus). Roman satirist, born A.D. 34, and died A.D. 62. Little is known of his life, but it would seem to have been uneventful. He was well-born and rich, and lived the retired life of a student, surrounded by devoted female relatives.

He was an intimate friend and pupil of the Stoic philosopher Cornutus, and was profoundly influenced in his life and thought by Stoicism. He died of some disease of the stomach at the age of twenty-eight, leaving the reputation of having been a retiring, modest, and lovable man.

His small book of six satires was posthumously published by his friends Cornutus and Bassus. It at once became popular. Owing to his earnestness and high moral tone Persius became a favourite author with the early Christian Fathers.

He owes a considerable amount of his fame to the difficulty of his style. He has always been a happy hunting-ground for scholiasts of all ages and countries. His difficulty lies in obscure allusions as well as in recondite words. He was a student above everything else; and, unlike Shakespeare, he needed the spectacles of books to read nature.

He derived most of his knowledge of life from Horace, and seemed more familiar with the Rome of Horace's *Satires* and *Epistles* than with the actual Rome of his own day. "Probably no writer ever borrowed so much and yet left on the mind so decided an impression of originality" (Conington). His opening satire on the literary taste of the day is perhaps the best of the six; but his most pleasing passages are those in which he speaks of himself and his gentle, studious life.—Cf. J. Conington and H. Nettleship, *Persius' Satires* (text, translation, and commentary).

PERSONAL ACTIONS. In law, actions brought for the specific recovery of goods and chattels, or for the redress of breaches of contract or other injuries, in contradistinction to *real actions*, brought for the recovery of lands, tenements, and other heritable property.

PERSONALTY, or **PERSONAL PROPERTY.** Movables; chattels; things belonging to the person, as money, jewels, furniture, etc., as distinguished from *real* estate in lands and houses. In the law of England the distinction between *real* and *personal* property is very nearly the same as the distinction between *heritable* and *moveable* property in the law of Scotland.

PERSPECTIVE. The application of the rules of geometry, and in particular of projection, to representing solid objects on a plane surface, so that they appear to the eye as does the object itself. From every visible point on an object in space, rays of light pass to the eye of a spectator. The points in which these rays cut any vertical plane between the spectator and the object are the *projection* on that plane of the visible parts of the object; and together they make up on the plane an image which gives the same impression to the eye as the object itself.

For example, if an object is placed behind an upright sheet of glass, on which with a brush and ink the outlines of the object as seen through the glass are traced, this tracing will give a representation of the object. As, however, the light reflected to the eye from different parts varies in colour and intensity, to obtain a complete representation these variations should be recorded on the plane. Thus perspective is classed as *linear*, which is concerned with representing the shapes of objects and their position by means of lines; and *aerial*, which attains the same ends by means of variations in colour and in light and shade.

In actual working, the plane on which the objects are to be represented is known as the *picture plane*, and is always regarded as vertical. The spectator is assumed to be standing on a horizontal plane extending an infinite distance; and the line in which this is cut by the picture plane is called the *ground line.* If there is a series of parallel lines passing through the picture plane and receding indefinitely, they appear to meet at the point on the picture plane where a line drawn from the eye parallel to the given lines cuts the picture plane. This is called their *vanishing point.*

Similarly, a system of parallel planes cutting the picture plane and receding to infinity appears to meet on the line in which a plane parallel to the others and passing through the eye cuts the picture plane. This is known as their *vanishing line.* The line in which any plane cuts the picture plane is called its *near edge*; and that in which it cuts the ground plane, its *trace.* The vanishing line of all horizontal planes is, of course, a horizontal line on a level with the spectator's eye, and is called the *horizon*; and the point on it directly opposite the eye is the *point of sight.*

It should be noted that, owing to the curvature of the earth's surface, the horizon in nature (where sea and sky appear to meet) is always slightly below the horizon in perspective. Since all lines on horizontal planes are themselves horizontal, their vanishing points always lie on the horizon; and parallel lines on a horizontal plane appear to meet in the same point thereon. Also, since all lines perpendicular to the picture plane are parallel to the line passing through the eye and the point of sight, all

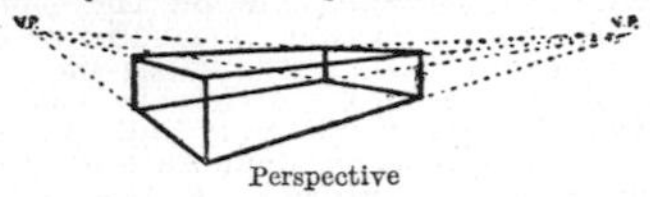

Perspective

such lines vanish to the point of sight.

These are the main conceptions, which, with their developments and applications, are fundamental in perspective. By their aid, any plane or straight line in space can be represented; and by means of *measuring points* and other devices, the exact size they appear to the eye can be represented.

For representing recurring geometrical patterns, or rows of objects at equal intervals, perspective is especially valuable. By its means, also, the appearance of all the simpler geometrical forms, both plane and solid, can be given; and from this help obtained in dealing with more complicated and irregular forms. In practice, artists have sometimes used the *camera lucida* (q.v.) or *camera obscura* (q.v.) to assist them in dealing with complicated problems in working from nature.

Historically, the theory and use of perspective is comparatively modern. It is doubtful whether it was known among the Greeks; and in Eastern art it has played no part. In the West, it first becomes important in fifteenth-century Italy, where its study proved peculiarly congenial to the restless scientific temperament of the Florentines, typified by Paolo Uccello. In the work of the Paduan school it played a prominent part, and soon became a regular element in artistic training.

Scientific knowledge and artistic use, however, have not always moved together, and certain painters (for example, Canaletto) who relied much on perspective sometimes show a curious failure to grasp its principles, which results in surprising errors.—BIBLIOGRAPHY: G. A. Storey, *Perspective*; R. Vicat Cole, *Perspective as applied to Pictures*; Lewes R. Crosskey, *Elementary Perspective*.

PERSPIRATION, or **SWEAT.** The secretion from the sweat-glands, which are found in the skin; in man they are most abundant on the palms and soles. Different animals vary much as to the amount of sweat they secrete, and the part of the body where it is most abundant. Thus the ox perspires much less than the horse or sheep, while perspiration is absent in the rat, rabbit, or goat. Pigs perspire mostly on the snout; dogs and cats on the feet. When the secretion is small, it is evaporated from the surface of the skin at once, and this is called insensible perspiration; but when it is increased or evaporation prevented, drops appear on the skin, and this is known as sensible perspiration.

The drier and hotter the air the greater is the proportion of insensible to sensible perspiration. It is estimated that a man secretes 2 lb. of sweat in the twenty-four hours. The secretion of sweat is controlled by special nerve fibres, and varies with their stimulation, while certain drugs by paralysing these fibres diminish perspiration. Sweat secretion is also affected by changes in the circulation.

Sweat, usually acid in reaction, becomes alkaline when profuse. It has a characteristic odour, saltish taste, and a specific gravity of 1·005. It is largely made up of water, with various salts, fats, epithelial debris, and a trace of urea. It is an excretion whereby the body gets rid of waste products, and also in civilised conditions of life a factor affecting the heat regulation of the body.

PERTH. A royal and municipal burgh, the county town of Perthshire, Scotland, on the Tay; served by the L.M.S. and L.N.E. Railways, which connect Aberdeen, Dundee, Glasgow, Edinburgh, and Inverness to a common station. The river and fine surrounding scenery give this city a most attractive appearance. The North and South Inches, two fine public parks, extend along the river bank, and a stone bridge, a girder bridge, and a railway bridge span the river.

Among interesting buildings is St. John's Church, a thirteenth-century foundation which gave to Perth its early name of St. Johnstoun or St. John's Town, and in which John Knox preached his famous sermon against idolatry in 1559. The episcopal cathedral (St. Ninian's) is modern (1850-90), and there is a general convict prison. There are also infantry barracks. Perth is famous for dye-works, but has some manufactures, including ink, linen, brewing, iron-founding, and chemicals. It is a seaport, and has a traffic with Dundee and points along the coast. Perth has also some claims to be regarded as a Scottish holiday-resort. Pop. (1931), 34,807.

Perth was founded by Agricola in A.D. 69, and was known to the Romans as *Victoria*, remaining in their possession for over 300 years. It was a favourite seat of the Scottish kings, who held many Parliaments there. A charter was granted in 1106, but Perth was raised to the dignity of a royal burgh by William the Lyon (1210), and was the Scottish capital until 1482, when Parliament was transferred to Edinburgh.

James I. was assassinated by Walter, Earl of Atholl, at Blackfriars monastery (1437). Scott (*Fair Maid of Perth*) has described the combat between the Clan Chattan and the Clan Quhele which took place on North Inch in the presence of the king (Robert III.) and his consort. During both '15 and '45 the magistrates remained loyal, although both Pretenders visited the town and the Old Pretender was actually proclaimed king at the Mercat Cross.—Cf. S. Cowen, *The Ancient Capital of Scotland*.

PERTH. A city, the capital of West Australia, on the Swan River. There are Protestant and Roman Catholic cathedrals, a museum and art gallery, zoological park, and the University of West Australia. The city is served by electric tramways, and has several race-courses. With the Swan River Settlements, Perth was founded in 1829, and became a city in 1880. It became of importance on the local discovery of gold during 1890. Pop. (1931), 209,729.

PERTH, THE FIVE ARTICLES OF. A measure passed in a General Assembly of the Church of Scotland, convened in 1618 at Perth by the order of James VI., in his attempt to crush Scottish Presbyterianism. The first of these articles required communicants to receive the elements kneeling; the second permitted the dispensation of the communion privately in case of sickness; the third allowed private baptism on sufficient cause being shown; the fourth required that children of eight years should be confirmed by the bishop; and the fifth enjoined the observance of Christmas, Good Friday, Easter, Ascension, and Whitsunday. These articles were ratified by the Estates in 1621, but in the Assembly held at Glasgow in 1638 the Assembly of Perth was declared to be unlawful and null, and the Five Articles were formally condemned.

PERTHSHIRE. A county of Scotland, has an extreme length, east to west, of 63 miles; breadth, north to south, 60 miles; area, 1,664,690 acres, of which 32,000 are water. This county offers some of the finest and most diversified scenery in Scotland, some of the most fertile land in Britain, and agriculture may be seen here in a high state of perfection.

The Grampians, which occupy the north and north-west of the county, culminate in several high peaks, including Ben Lawers (3984 feet), and the Ochil and Sidlaw ranges occupy the south-east. The principal rivers are the Tay, the basin of which comprises nearly the whole county; the Forth, Earn, Teith, Lyon, Garry, and Tummel.

The chief lakes are Loch Tay, Loch Ericht, Loch Rannoch, and Loch Katrine. The chief agricultural district is the Carse of Gowrie, on the north bank of the Tay estuary. The salmon-fisheries on the Tay are very valuable. Principal towns: Perth, Blairgowrie, Crieff, and Dunblane. Pop. (1931), 120,772.—Cf. *Perthshire* (in Cambridge County Geographies).

PER'TINAX, Publius Helvius. A Roman emperor, born in A.D. 120, the son of a freedman. He distinguished himself in the army, and attracted the attention of Marcus Aurelius, who elevated him to the consulate in 179. During the reign of Commodus, Pertinax was employed in Britain and Africa, and finally made prefect of Rome. After the murder of Commodus he was proclaimed emperor in 193, but in three months was murdered by the prætorian guards.

PERTURBATIONS. The orbital irregularities or deviations of the planets from their regular elliptic orbits. These deviations arise, in the case of the primary planets, from the mutual gravitations of these planets towards each other, which derange their elliptic motions round the sun; and in that of the secondaries, partly from the mutual gravitation of the secondaries of the same system, similarly deranging their elliptic motions round their respective primaries, and partly from the unequal attraction of the sun on them and on their primaries.

The perturbations of the moon are particularly large and difficult of computation, on account of the very large proportion which the influence of the chief perturbing body, the sun, bears to that of the earth.

PERU'. A republic of the west coast of South America, with a seaboard of 1240 miles on the Pacific Ocean. It is divided into twenty departments and three provinces as follows:

Division	Area, English Sq. Miles	Capital
Department:		
Amazonas ..	13,943	Chachapoyas.
Ancachs ..	14,700	Huaraz.
Apurimac ..	8,187	Abancay.
Arequipa ..	21,947	Arequipa.
Ayacucho ..	18,185	Ayacucho.
Cajamarca ..	12,538	Cajamarca.
Cuzco	55,716	Cuzco.
Huancavelica ..	8,297	Huancavelica.
Huanuco ..	15,425	Huanuco.
Ica	8,596	Ica.
Junin	22,814	Huancayo.
Lambayeque ..	4,614	Chiclayo.
Liberdad ..	10,206	Trujillo.
Lima	15,048	Lima.
Loreto	163,240	Iquitos.
Madre de Dios ..	58,827	Maldonado.
Piura	15,190	Piura.
Puno	26,133	Puno.
San Martin ..	17,448	—
Tacna ..	12,590	Tacna.
Provinces:		
Callao	14	Callao.
Moquegua ..	5,549	Moquegua.
Tumbes ..	1,590	Tumbes.
Total ..	530,797	

These are divided into 113 provinces, subdivided into 930 districts.

Physiography. Like Ecuador and Colombia, Peru is divided longitudinally into three clearly defined regions. (1) The coast, extending between the Pacific and the foothills of the Andes; an arid desert 20 miles in width, broken very occasionally by Andean streams. (2) The mountains (running from south-east to north-west), comprising the three chains into which the Andes are subdivided, viz. the Western Maritime Cordillera, the Cordillera Central, and the Cordillera Oriental, a region about 250 miles broad, divided into *sierras* or mountain slopes and valleys, and the *puna* or elevated wildernesses.

The Maritime and Central Cordilleras are roughly parallel, and run at no great distance from each other. They are of different structures and ages, and contain many volcanoes, semi-active and quiescent. Peruvian geographers confine the term *Andes* to the Cordillera Oriental, which rises from the basin of the Amazon and forms the inner wall of the system.

It is composed of very ancient rocks which are not volcanic, beds of limestone, probably deposited during the same period as the English chalk, resting upon the eastern flanks. As already noted, the main structural lines of the Cordilleras trend from south-east to north-west, though they may be deflected, as in Peru, by the influence of the older mountain system which has produced the sharp bending of the coast-line in the southern region of that country.

The Cordillera Oriental rises in the south to Illampu and Illimani (more than 21,000 feet altitude), and is cut by six rivers, the Marañon, Huallaga, Perene, Mantaro, Apurimac, and Paucartambo. Numerous streams rise on the slopes of the Cordillera Central, which forms the true water-parting of the Peruvian-Andean system, and break through the Western Cordillera to the sea. Only one stream, the Marañon, pierces the Cordillera Central, which is connected with the Eastern Andes by the transverse mountain knot of Vilcañota.

The Maritime Cordillera has no connection with the Chilian coastal range. It comprises a series of volcanic peaks overlooking the coast and rising to Lirima (19,000 feet) and Tocora (20,000 feet). North of the equator it bifurcates, the eastern area being the Cordillera Nevada, and the western the Cordillera Negra. (3) The third region is the tropical lowlands, the *Montaña*, lying in the basin of the Amazon, and skirting the eastern foothills of the Andes. It is traversed by great navigable rivers, including the Marañon, which is joined by the Huallaga and by the mighty Ucayali. In the south the component streams of the Beni form the drainage system.

Lakes. Lake Titicaca (q.v.) forms by far the largest body of fresh water in South America. Half of it is in Peru. Lake Junin, or *Chinchaycocha* is drained by the Mantaro, one of the head-streams of the Ucayali. It is 36 miles long by 7 miles broad, and stands at an altitude of 13,415 feet.

Climate. The climate depends upon the altitude. Just as in Mexico, there are the hot zone, the temperate zone, and the cool zone, but the great height of the Andes adds another belt, the Paramos or cold zone, which begins above the tree-line at an altitude of about 10,000 feet. The winds, mostly from the east, which blow over the eastern ridges of the Andes, deposit most of their moisture on the eastern slopes of these giant mountains, blow over the plateau, and over the Pacific slope generally, as cool dry winds, without yielding a drop of moisture.

Dense fogs, however, the result of the meeting of the cold current that flows along the South American coasts with the warmer equatorial water, help to nourish the scanty vegetation of the coastal region during the winter season, and the

Map of Peru

temperature of the coast-lands is moderated by the sea breezes and by the cold ocean current along the coast. At Lima the temperature is moderate (about 68° F.), but, notwithstanding, the low coastal regions are anything but healthy.

Social Conditions: *The People.* The inhabitants of Peru comprise pure whites, Asiatics (mainly Chinese), Africans, Indians, and mixed breeds, but the dominant race is mainly of Spanish-Indian extraction. The civilised Indians are represented by the *Quichua-Aymara* group of the *sierras* and the *Yuncas* of the Pacific slopes. In addition there are the savage Indian tribes of the Montaña, divided into *Cholos* (upland group) and *Zambos, Chunchos* or barbaros of the eastern forests.

There has been no census since 1876, when the population was returned as 2,660,881, and all estimates (1927, 6,147,000) are pure guess-work. By an Act of Congress dated 30th Oct., 1920, a census was authorised.

Religion. Political and religious liberty is absolute under the terms of the Constitution (18th Jan., 1920), but the Roman Catholic religion is the faith of the State. The archbishopric of Lima dates from 1545, and there are thirteen bishoprics, two apostolic vicarages, and two apostolic prefectures. All property of the Church is the property of the State.

Education. Elementary education is nominally free and compulsory between the ages of seven and fourteen years, but the regulations are not enforced. A central university is located at Lima (founded 1551), and there are also universities at Arequipa, Cuzco, and Trujillo, and schools of mines, civil engineering, agriculture, and arts and trades established at the capital (Lima). Salt is a Government monopoly, which was created in 1896 to raise money for the ransoming of Peru's "lost provinces," Tacna-Arica (q.v.). It produces about a quarter of a million pounds sterling per annum.

Currency. Gold became the standard in 1901. The *libra* is equivalent in standard and weight to the pound sterling, which is also accepted. 10 *soles* = £1. Notes of 10*s*., £1, £5. and £10 gold value are in circulation, and there are also 50-cent nickel coins. Bronze coins are 1 and 2 *centavo* pieces (100 *centavos* = 1 *sol*).

Weights and Measures. The French system was established in 1869, and is in general use.

Towns. The capital is Lima (pop. 316,000); Callao, the port of Lima, is also one of the best on the coast, and through it 70 per cent of Peruvian imports and 30 per cent of the exports are passed (pop. 77,000); others are Mollendo, Cuzco (pop. 40,000); Arequipa (65,000); Iquitos (10,000); Ayacucho (20,000), Huaráz (20,000), and Huacho (20,000).

Transport and Communications. In 1929 there were 11,202 miles of road suitable for motor traffic, and 20,174 miles in all (including projected roads). 90 per cent of the railways in active operation belong to the Peruvian Corporation, Ltd., a British syndicate. In 1930 there was a total working length of 2810 miles, including 2168 miles privately owned and 642 retained by the State.

Principal Lines.—1. Mollendo-Arequipa: 172 kilometres of standard gauge Branches: (*a*) Ensenada Station to Pampa Blanco sugar estate; 2-feet narrow-gauge line. (*b*) Ramal Station to Sotillo; standard gauge. The ultimate destination is Moges Valley, 130 kilometres from Ramal.

2. Arequipa-Puno: 351 kilometres; standard gauge, 4 feet 8½ inches.
3. Juliaca-Cuzco: 338 kilometres; standard gauge; a branch of the Arequipa-Puno trunk line.
4. Cuzco-Santa Ana: 175 kilometres: 3-feet narrow gauge.
5. Puno-Guaqui: steamer across Lake Titicaca; 120 miles.
6. Guaqui-La Paz: 67 kilometres; 1-metre gauge; 87 miles are steam and 10 miles electric traction.
7. Ilo-Moquegua: 98 kilometres; standard gauge.
   1-6 belong to the Peruvian Corporation, excepting the branch from Ensenada. 7 belongs to the State, but is managed by the Corporation.
8. Paita-Piura: 60 miles; standard gauge.
9. Pacasmayo-Guadalupe: 63 miles; standard gauge.
10. Pisco-Ica: 46 miles; standard gauge.
11. Lima-Lurin: 28·5 miles; narrow gauge.

It will be noted that there is a trunk line from Arequipa to La Paz (Bolivia) via Puno and Lake Titicaca. In 1928 an air mail service was introduced between Lima and different points in the Republic.

Shipping. There are regular coasting services, and British, Dutch, American, Chinese, Chilian, Italian, French, Japanese, and German companies maintain trans-oceanic services at regular intervals—the majority sailing via Panamá if approaching from the Atlantic.

Wireless, etc. In 1927 there were twenty-seven wireless stations; three submarine cables connect Peru and Chile, and one connects Peru with the northern republics. The Marconi Company administers all posts, telegraphs, and wireless services for a period of twenty-five years commencing 1st May, 1921.

Production: *Agriculture.* The principal products in order of importance are sugar, cotton, wool, hides and skins. The castor-oil plant is indigenous. Rice, wheat, barley, potatoes, coca (from which cocaine is made), a little wild rubber, and some wild sisal-hemp are also produced.

Minerals. Oil (petroleum), copper, silver, gold, vanadium ore, tungsten ore, salt, lead, molybdenum ore, antimony ore, bismuth, zinc, and borates are all worked. A little coal is worked, and there are some known fields of anthracite.

Commerce. Peru is primarily an exporter of raw materials and an importer of manufactured goods, but there are more or less feeble manufacturing industries in brewing, tanning, iron-founding, flour-milling (one mill), match-making (one factory), cotton-seed oil, boots and shoes (one factory), hats (one factory), and mineral-waters.

Exports. The principal are sugar, copper, cotton, petroleum, and wool.

Imports. These are mainly textiles, machinery, foodstuffs, coal, and industrial oils.

Defence: *Army.* Military service is universal and compulsory, and comprises two years active, five years in first reserve, five in the second, and twenty years in the national guard. There are five divisions, supplied respectively by the five military districts into which the country is divided. There are two battalions to a regiment, and each division comprises two or three regiments, one machine-gun company being allotted to each regiment, a regiment of mountain artillery, a cavalry regiment (two squadrons), a railway company, a labour company, a geographical section, and medical and commissariat services.

Peace establishment is about 7500 of all ranks, and there are 8000 police and gendarmerie. Armament comprises the 1912 Mauser rifle (Peruvian model), cavalry Mauser carbine, and Schneider Canet gun (artillery). There is a system of rifle-clubs, having an aggregate membership of 16,000 marksmen from 176 State-aided clubs.

Navy. There is a river flotilla on the Amazon comprising two gunboats. Two cruisers (3200 tons displacement, 24 knots speed), one destroyer, four submarines, and one submarine tender complete the equipment for defence.

Government, etc. The government is based on a Constitution adopted on 18th Jan., 1920. The legislative power is in the hands of a Senate of 35 members and a House of Representatives of 110 members, both elected by direct vote and totally renewed every five years. The President, elected for five years, is the head of the executive, and is assisted by two Vice-Presidents, both elected for five years also, but they take the place of the President only in case of his death or incapacity.

The Presidents are also elected by direct vote, but the Vice-Presidents are not paid as such. Each department is governed by a Prefect, and each province by a Sub-Prefect, and there are also three regional Congresses, North, South, and Central. The Constitution was amended slightly in 1927.

History. Of the early history of Peru we are almost ignorant, but existing ruins, spoils secured by the Spaniards, and the descriptions left us by the historians of the Spanish conquest, sufficiently prove that the ancient Peruvians had no mean knowledge of architecture, sculpture, metal-work, etc. They also had made considerable progress in astronomical science.

The early religion of the Peruvians is bound up in the god Viracocha, the creator of the sun and the stars, and from him the Incas or emperors claimed descent as the sons of the sun. Under the Incas the empire was divided into four parts, corresponding to the four cardinal points; each division had a separate government, presided over by a viceroy of royal blood. All the land belonged to the Inca; and trade was carried on by barter, money being unknown.

The thirteenth monarch of the Incas was reigning when the Spanish adventurer Pizarro disembarked in Peru in 1531. The Inca was taken prisoner (1532), numbers of his subjects were massacred, and the whole country fell in a short time into the hands of the invaders. It was then formed into a Spanish viceroyalty; subsequently part of it was incorporated in New Granada, and the viceroyalty of Buenos Aires was constructed out of some of the provinces. In 1821 the country proclaimed its independence, but did not obtain actual freedom from Spanish rule until 1824, after a prolonged war.

Since then Peru, like the rest of the South American republics, has suffered much from dissensions and revolutions. In the spring of 1879 Peru joined Bolivia in a war against Chile, which resulted in the complete defeat of both the former. Peru ceded the province of Tarapacá absolutely to Chile, who also obtained provisional possession of the provinces of Tacna and Arica, the Alsace-Lorraine of Latin-America (Treaty of Ancon, 8th March, 1884). A plebiscite to determine the ownership of these "lost provinces" should have been taken in 1894 after ten years' occupation, but Chile ignored this provision.

The dispute regarding Tacna and Arica (see *Tacna-Arica*) was finally settled after much disputing in 1929, Tacna going to Peru, and Arica to Chile. The boundary dispute with Bolivia was settled in 1927-8, that with Colombia was settled in 1928, and that with Brazil was settled in 1927. Peru favoured the Allied cause during the European War. See articles on departments, towns, etc.

BIBLIOGRAPHY: A. Dell, *Llama Land*; G. R. Johnson and Raye R. Platt, *Peru from the Air*; W. M. McGovern, *Jungle Paths and Inca Ruins*; A. H. Verrill, *Under Peruvian Skies*; Department of Overseas Trade Reports; J. Ritchie, *Peru*; G. H. Stuart, *The Governmental System of Peru*; Statistical Abstract of Peru.

PERU. A city of Indiana, United States, the county seat of Miami county, on the Wabash River;

served by the Wabash, the Lake Erie & Western, and the Chicago, Cincinnati & Louisville Railways, and by electric-traction lines to Warsaw and Indianapolis. There are large railway shops, and Peru is an important produce-marketing centre. It was settled in 1834, and became a city in 1867. Pop. 12,730.

PERU BALSAM. A resinous product obtained from certain species of Myroxylon, ord. Leguminosæ, natives of tropical America, used in medicine and perfumery. The *white Peru balsam*, a pale-yellow, transparent, and syrupy liquid, is produced from the inner coating and seed of the fruit; it hardens and becomes reddish on exposure to air, and is then called *dry*, *brown*, or *red Peru balsam*. By boiling the bark and twigs of the tree a dark-brown syrup, of vanilla-like odour, sharp and bitter taste, is obtained, the *black Peru balsam* of commerce.

PERUGIA (pe-rö'jià). A province of Umbria, Central Italy, with which it is coextensive. It is traversed by the Apennines, watered by the Tiber, and contains the Lago Trasimeno (ancient *Trasimenŭs Lacus*), which is 9 miles west of the city of Perugia. Minerals, including coal and iron, are worked in the mountains, and the valleys are rich producers of cereals, olive-oil, and wines. Area, 2455 sq. miles; pop. (1931), 514,946.

PERUGIA (ancient **Perusia**). A town of Central Italy, capital of the province of the same name, on the Tiber. It is surrounded by old walls, and is rich in art and literary treasures, and has many remarkable buildings, including a Gothic cathedral of the fifteenth century (still unfinished), a number of churches and monasteries, a town hall (Italian-Gothic, begun 1281), and a university (founded in 1307). The manufactures are not of much consequence. Perugia was an old Etruscan city, and was conquered by Rome in 310 B.C. It was incorporated in the Papal States in the middle of the sixteenth century, and in 1860 passed to the Sardinians and became part of the new Kingdom of Italy. Pop. (1931), 79,447.

PERUGINO (per-u-jē'nō), properly **Pietro Vannucci.** One of the chief painters of the Umbrian school, born at Citta della Pieve in 1446, died at Fontignano in 1523. He spent his youth in Perugia, whence he derived his nickname, and there studied under Florenzo di Lorenzo. Later he worked in Florence, and in 1480 went to Rome to assist in decorating the Sixtine Chapel with the frescoes commissioned by Sixtus IV. His art shows the mysticism and lyrical character of the Umbrians, and their fondness for spacious landscape settings. His earlier paintings are mainly in tempera, and show his qualities at their best. His later work in oil tends towards mannerism and repetition. Among his most characteristic and remarkable works is the fresco of the *Crucifixion* in the Church of Sta. Maria Maddelena dei Pazzi, Florence. He is represented in the National Gallery by a *Virgin and Child with St. John* and a *Virgin and Child with St. Francis and St. Jerome*, both typical works. His influence on subsequent painting was considerable. His most celebrated pupil was Raphael, whose earlier work especially owes much to his master.

PERUZZI (pā-rųt'sē), **Baldassari.** Architect and painter of the Roman school, born at Sienna 1481, died at Rome 1537. He designed the Farnesina Villa on the banks of the Tiber, and he succeeded Raphael as architect of St. Peter's. His best existing works in fresco are at Sienna.

PES'ARO (ancient **Pisaurum**). A city and seaport of Italy, capital of the province of Pesaro-e-Urbino, near the mouth of the Foglia, on the Adriatic. It is the seat of a bishop. The fortress of the Sforzas, dating from 1474, still remains. The trade in the wine, fruit (particularly figs), oil, silk, and other products of the district is considerable. The composer Rossini was born here in 1792, and founded a conservatoire in the town. Pop. 34,881.

PESARO-E-URBINO. A department of North Italy, in the Marches compartimento, lying between the Adriatic and the Apennines. Iron is worked in the mountains, and the rich valleys produce olive-oil, wine, cereals, and fruit. Sericulture is practised. Area, 1118 sq. miles; pop. (1931), 294,360.

PESCADORES. A group of Japanese islands in Formosa Strait. The total area is 49 sq. miles; and the population is 50,000. They were ceded by China in 1895. The official Japanese name is *Hoko To*.

PESHAWAR. A district and town of the North-West Frontier Province of India. The district is a mountain-girt depression peopled by Pathans and some commercial Hindus. The Indus traverses the south-east, and the district is irrigated by the Swat River Canal. Cereals, cotton, and some sugar-cane are produced. From Attock to Peshawar the North-Western Railway traverses the district. In 1930 there was fighting between the Afridi and British. Area, 2607 sq. miles; pop. (estimated), 800,000. The city of Peshawar is the capital and lies on the Bara, 10½ miles from the eastern entrance to the Khyber Pass. There are cantonments 2 miles outside the native city, which makes Peshawar the chief garrison town on the frontier. Pop. 121,966.

PESSIMISM. The antithesis of optimism; a term applied to the attitude of those who, either in consequence of the keen sense of evil and misery in the world, or as the result of a philosophical analysis of life, regard the universe, especially in its relation to man, as radically bad. Pessimism is thus either temperamental or philosophical.

From time to time a note of pessimism is sounded among every nation, just as almost every individual may sometimes be on the verge of despair. As long, however, as nations or individuals are reacting against such a feeling of melancholy, their attitude cannot yet be termed pessimism. The real pessimist is he who always and persistently looks upon the dark side of things, and who maintains that existence is fundamentally bad and could not be worse.

Just, however, as there are *meliorists*, i.e. those who admit that although the world is good it could be made better, so also there are *pejorists*, i.e. people who maintain that the world is evil but could have been worse. The Old Testament is generally optimistic, but here and there a cry of despair is uttered, as in Job and Ecclesiastes, i. 2-18 ("Vanity of vanities, all is vanity").

In the New Testament the pessimistic note is much stronger. A semi-philosophical pessimism runs through the whole doctrine of the ancient Brahmanical teachers of India, but it is in Buddhism that pessimism received its most definite formulation. The keynote of Buddhism is the idea that life is perfect misery. Neo-Platonism had a distinctly pessimistic character, and influenced many Christian mystics, who expressed opinions regarding the worthlessness of life and the evil of the world.

As for literature, there is hardly a great poet who was not pessimistic at times. Homer and Hesiod, Theognis and Sophocles often utter a cry of despair, and the last maintained that "it were better for man not to have been born" (*Œdipus Coloneus*, line 1225). After the French Revolution, when a general disappointment had taken hold of humanity, when a feeling of *malaise* and unrest was noticeable everywhere, and a wave of pessimism swept over Europe, poets gave expression to this pessimistic feeling, and philosophers elaborated systems.

Byron in England, Baudelaire and De Musset in France, Heine in Germany, Pushkin in Russia, and Leopardi in Italy uttered cries of despair and were pessimistically inclined. The two modern philosophers who propounded pessimisic systems were Schopenhauer (q.v.) and von Hartmann. The former, who based his theories upon the pessimistic side of Hegel's doctrine, came to the conclusion that death, being the negation of individuality, is the one good in life.—BIBLIOGRAPHY: J. Sully, *Pessimism*; R. M. Wenley, *Aspects of Pessimism*; A. Kowalevski, *Studien zur Psychologie des Pessimismus*.

PESTALOZZI, Johann Heinrich. Swiss educationalist, and principal founder of modern pedagogy, born 1746, died 1827. He first studied theology, then law; and subsequently became concerned in a calico manufactory. Afterwards he devoted his time and substance to the children of paupers, whom he collected in large numbers in his own house, and this good work he carried on for over twenty years without outside aid or even sympathy. The want of means at last compelled him to abandon his gratuitous institution, and to seek pupils who could pay for their maintenance and instruction.

After a few years' successful teaching in various places he opened a school in the Castle of Yverdon (canton Vaud), which the Government had placed at his disposal. His novel *Lienhardt und Gertrud* (Leonard and Gertrude, 1781-9, 4 vols.) exerted a powerful moral influence, while his educational treatises have laid the foundation for the more rational system of elementary instruction which now obtains in Europe.

The grand principle that lay at the basis of Pestalozzi's method was that of communicating all instruction by direct appeal to the senses and the understanding, and forming the child by constantly calling all his powers into exercise, instead of making him a mere passive recipient, selecting the subjects of study in such a way that each step should best aid the further progress of the pupil.—Cf. J. A. Green, *Life and Work of Pestalozzi*.

PESTALOZZIA. A genus of Fungi Imperfecti, section Melanconiales. *P. Guepini* is a dangerous pest (grey blight) of the tea-plant in Assam.

Collecting and burning of infected leaves is suggested as a remedy. *P. Hartigii* kills seedling Conifers.

PÉTAIN, Henri Philippe. French soldier, born at Cauchy-la-Tour, Pas-de-Calais, on 24th April, 1856. Educated at St. Cyr, he joined the infantry, and became a colonel in 1910. At the outbreak of the European War he was in command of the 4th Brigade, and gained military acclamation by his work in Artois during 1915.

In September of that year he succeeded Castelnau in command of the Second Army, and took part in the Champagne offensive. In Feb., 1916, he assumed command of the troops before Verdun, and his brilliant defence of the fortress-city is one of the epics of the war. Subsequently he commanded the Armies of the Centre and, in May, 1917, he succeeded Nivelle as Commander-in-Chief in the north and north-east, retaining his command on the appointment of Foch as Generalissimo (March, 1918). He led the French into Metz on 19th Nov., 1918, and was made a Marshal of France. In 1925 he supervised reinforcements sent against rebels in Morocco. From 1922 to 1931 he was Inspector-General of the French Army.

PET'ALITE. A rare mineral, a silicate of aluminium and lithium, containing about 4 per cent of lithia and as much as 78 per cent of silica. Its specific gravity is unusually low, only 2·4. It occurs in masses of foliated structure; colour white, occasionally tinged with red, green, or blue.

PETCHO'RA. A river of Russia; it rises in the north of the government of Perm, on the western slope of the Ural Mountains, and after a course of about 990 miles falls into a bay of the Arctic Ocean by a number of mouths.

PETER, the Apostle. Commonly called Saint Peter, one of the twelve Apostles of Jesus Christ. He was a Galilean fisherman from Bethsaida, originally named *Simeon*, or *Shim'ōn*, the son of Jona, and brother of St. Andrew, who conducted him to Christ. Jesus greeted Simon with the significant words, "Thou art Simon the son of Jona; thou shalt be called Cephas" (in Gr. *Petros*, a stone, whence the name Peter). After the miraculous draught of fishes Peter became a regular and intimate disciple of our Lord.

The impetuosity of his character led Peter, especially in the early days of his apostleship, to commit many faults which drew upon him the rebuke of his divine Master. His zeal and eloquence made him often the speaker on behalf of his fellow Apostles on important occasions, and his opinions had great influence in the Christian churches.

On one memorable occasion he incurred the rebuke of the Apostle Paul in consequence of his behaviour towards the Gentile Christians in regard to social intercourse. Nothing certain is known of his subsequent life, but it is almost beyond doubt that he was a joint-founder of the Church at Rome, and that he suffered martyrdom there, most likely under Nero, about A.D. 64.

The only written documents left by Peter are his two *Epistles*. The genuineness of the *First Epistle*, the authenticity of which has been denied by Rationalist critics, Harnack, and the Tübingen school, is placed beyond all reasonable doubt, both the external and internal evidence being of the strongest description.

The authenticity of the *Second Epistle* has been disputed by numerous critics on what appears to be plausible grounds. Doubts of its genuineness already existed in the time of Eusebius, and it was not admitted into the New Testament canon till A.D. 393.—Cf. Taylor, *Peter the Apostle*.

PETER, the Cruel. King of Castile and Leon, born 1334, succeeded his father Alfonso XI. 1350, and died 1369. His reign was one long series of cruelties and despotic acts. The year following his coronation he put to death Eleanora de Guzman, his father's mistress. In 1353 he married, though contrary to his will, Blanche of Bourbon, whom, however, he abandoned two days after his marriage in order to rejoin his mistress Maria Padilla. The queen was imprisoned and divorced, and his mistress's relations appointed to the highest offices. He then married the beautiful Juana de Castro, but only to abandon her after a few months.

Dethroned in 1366, he was reinstated the following year by an army lent by Edward the Black Prince. Executions and confiscations naturally followed, but these fresh cruelties only helped to swell the ranks of his opponents, of whom the chief was his half-brother Henry of Transtamara. In 1369 Henry gained a signal victory over Peter at Montiel, and the latter was slain in a sword combat with his brother.

PETER, the Hermit. A monk of Amiens, whose preaching, after a pilgrimage to Jerusalem (end of the eleventh century), gave rise to the first Crusade. Peter led the way through Hungary at the head of an undisciplined multitude of more than 30,000 men, a comparatively small number of whom survived to reach their destination, and distinguished himself by his personal courage at the storming of the holy city. On his return to his native country he founded the abbey of Noirmoutier, and died its first superior in 1115.

PETER I. (the Great), Alexeievitsh. Emperor of Russia, born 1672, died 28th Jan., 1725. He was the eldest son by his second wife of the Tsar Alexis Mikhailovitsh. Peter's half-brother Feodor, who succeeded his father in 1676, died in 1682. Peter then succeeded to the Tsardom jointly with his brother Ivan, a feeble-

Peter the Great

minded prince, whilst his sister Sophia was appointed regent. In 1689, however, Peter wrested the power from his sister, confined her in a convent, and was virtually sole emperor, though, till the death of his brother in 1697, he associated his name with his own in the ukases of the empire.

He now determined to do what he could to raise his country out of its barbarism, and to place its people in the ranks of civilised nations. His journey to Holland and England (1697-8), when he practically worked in shipyards, is familiar; and the knowledge he there gained was amply profited by on his return. He not only created a navy, but gave Russia a seaboard and seaports by wresting the Baltic provinces from Charles XII. of Sweden. Young Russian nobles were obliged to travel; schools of navigation and mathematics were founded; agriculture was improved by the introduction of implements, seeds, and superior breeds of cattle.

Peter imported foreign artisans of all kinds, established manufactories of arms, tools, and fabrics, and distributed metallurgists through the mining districts of Russia; roads and canals were made to foster internal commerce and to extend trade with Asia. In 1703 he laid the foundation of St. Petersburg (now Leningrad), and twenty years later of its Academy of Sciences.

Laws and institutions which in any way interfered with his projects he either abolished or altered. In his zeal to do good he was too frequently injudicious in choosing times and seasons, and the least show of opposition irritated him into ferocity. He repudiated his wife a few years after marriage for her reactionary leanings; for the same reason his son Alexis was ill-treated, compelled to renounce the succession, and condemned to death, but died suddenly before sentence could be carried out.

In 1707 Peter married his mistress Catherine; this marriage was publicly celebrated in 1712; Catherine was crowned in 1724, and succeeded the Tsar after his death.—Cf. K. Waliszewski, *Peter the Great.*

PETER II., Alexeievitsh. Tsar of Russia, grandson of Peter the Great and son of Alexis; ascended the throne in consequence of the will of Catherine I., in 1727, when but thirteen years old. He died in 1730 of the smallpox, and was succeeded by Anna Ivanovna.

PETER III., Feodorovitsh. Tsar of Russia, born 1728, the son of Anna Petrovna, daughter of Peter the Great and the Duke of Holstein. Peter III. ascended the throne in 1762, but on account of his German proclivities and other causes a conspiracy broke out on 8th July, 1762; he abdicated on the 10th, and was murdered on the 17th of the same month.

PETER I., Karageorgevitsh. King of the triune Kingdom of Yugo-Slavia (Serbs, Croats, and Slovenes), was born in 1844, the son of Alexander Karageorgevitsh and the grandson of Karageorge. He was educated at St. Cyr while an exile, and married Princess Zorka, the daughter of Nicholas of Montenegro, in 1883.

In the early hours of the morning of the 11th June, 1903, King Alexander (Obrenovitsh) and Queen Draga of Serbia were brutally murdered in the royal palace at Belgrade, and the regicides, headed by Colonel Mashin, a brother-in-law of the murdered queen, formed a Provisional Government and proclaimed Prince Peter Karageorgevitsh King of Serbia.

All the European Powers were represented at his coronation in Sept., 1904, excepting Great Britain, who did not resume diplomatic relations with the new monarchy until 1906. King Peter committed the regency of the kingdom to Prince Alexander, his second son, in June, 1914, but he remained with his armies during the European War, retiring to Greece, an exile, in 1916. On the formation of the triune kingdom he returned to Belgrade, and died there on 16th Aug., 1921.—Cf. R. Chambry, *Pierre I., Roi de Serbie.*

PETERBOROUGH, Charles Mordaunt, Earl of. Born about 1658, died in 1735. He succeeded his father, Lord Mordaunt, 1675, and his uncle in the earldom of Peterborough (1697). William of Orange created him Earl of Monmouth and appointed him First Commissioner of the Treasury for his services in connection with the dethronement of James II. He eminently distinguished himself in Spain as a commander in the Spanish Succession War (1705), especially by the capture of Barcelona, and received the thanks of the British Parliament. He also held several diplomatic posts; was created a Knight of the Garter (1713), and general of the British marine forces (1722).

PETERBOROUGH. An episcopal city and municipal borough of England, the latter partly in Huntingdonshire, the former in county Northampton, on the Nene. The principal building is its cathedral (S. Peter), originally founded in 655, destroyed by the Danes in 870; rebuilt in 966, and again partly destroyed by fire in 1116. It has had its present form since early in the sixteenth century. The bishopric was founded by Henry VIII. (1541), and his wife, Catharine of Aragon, was interred in the cathedral. Peterborough received a municipal charter in 1874. Pop. (1931), 43,558.

PETERBOROUGH. A city of Ontario, Canada, the county town of Peterborough county, on the Otonabee; served by the Canadian Pacific and by National (Grand Trunk) lines. There is also a local electric-traction system, hydro-electric power being derived from the five falls of the Otonabee, which have a total perpendicular drop of 50 feet. The Trent Canal gives entry to Lake Ontario. Machinery of all kinds is manufactured. Pop. 22,327.

PETERBOROUGH, SOKE OF. A district around the city of Peterborough, England. It is a separate administrative county; area, 53,760 acres; pop. 51,845.

PETERHEAD'. A parliamentary burgh and seaport of Aberdeenshire, Scotland, on Peterhead Bay; served by the L.N.E. Railway. The town is built of red granite, obtained from quarries in the neighbourhood, and has a statue of Field-Marshal James Keith, presented by William I., Emperor of Germany. The town has a good trade, and is an important centre of the herring-fishery. Peterhead belongs to the Elgin group of parliamentary burghs. A national harbour of refuge was constructed between 1886 and 1921, mainly by convict labour. Pop. 13,126.

PETERHOF. A town of Russia, 15 miles south-west of Leningrad, founded by Peter the Great in 1711. It is celebrated for its summer palace, in Versailles style, a favourite residence of the former Tsars of Russia. Pop. 16,000.

PETERHOUSE, or ST. PETER'S COLLEGE (Cambridge). Founded in 1257 (charter 1284) by Hugh de Balsham, Bishop of Ely. Isaac Barrow, Archbishop Whitgift, Thomas Gray, and Lord Kelvin were members of the college, which is the oldest college in the university.

PETERLOO' MASSACRE. The name popularly given to the dispersal of an open-air meeting of about 60,000 people, held on 16th July, 1819, in St. Peter's Field, Manchester, in favour of parliamentary reform. A number of persons were injured and eight killed. The word Peterloo is a burlesque of Waterloo.

PETERSBURG. A city and port of entry of Virginia, United States, at the head of navigation on the Appomattox River; served by the Seaboard Air-line; Norfolk & Western, and the Atlantic Coast-line Railways. Hydro-electric power is provided by falls above the city. Petersburg was originally built as Fort Henry, on the site of an Indian village (1645), and the town was founded in 1733 as Peter's Point. It became a city in 1850, and was besieged by the Federals under Grant (1864-5) as the "last citadel of the Confederacy." Pop. (1930), 28,564.

PETERSFIELD. An urban district of Hampshire, England, with a fine Norman church of the twelfth century. It was a parliamentary borough from 1553 to 1885, returning two and afterwards one member to Parliament. Pop. 4386.

PETER'S PENCE. A papal tribute collected in several of the western countries of Europe. The idea of an annual tribute seems to have originated in England before the Norman Conquest, and was exacted from every householder of a certain standing about St. Peter's Day, originally for the support of an English college or hospice in Rome. Withheld by England in 1316, the tribute was finally abolished by Henry VIII. This contribution was sometimes also called *Rome-scot.* A free-will contribution called Peter's Pence is still collected among Roman Catholics, especially since the abolition of the Pope's temporal power.

PETERWARDEIN, or **PETERVARAD.** A town of Yugoslavia, on the Danube, opposite Neusatz (Novisad), 45 miles north-west of Belgrade. Pop. (1931), 4386.

PET'IOLE. In botany, a leaf-stalk; the stalk of a leaf, which connects the blade with the branch or stem. When the petiole is wanting, the leaf is said to be sessile. In general, however, it is distinctly marked, and is usually either round, or half-cylindrical and channelled on the upper side.

PETITION (Lat. *petere*, to seek). A representation of grievances with an appeal for redress. The most important are petitions to Parliament. Since the Revolution of 1688 the subject's right to petition has been freely admitted. By the forms of the Houses of Parliament certain regulations must be complied with by petitioners, or their petitions will be rejected.

A petition to the House of Lords must be addressed "To the Lords Spiritual and Temporal in Parliament assembled;" the form of address to the House of Commons is, "To the Honourable the Commons of the United Kingdom in Parliament assembled." The petition must begin, "The Humble Petition of . . . showeth;" if from an individual, it must state his name, address, and occupation. Immediately before the signatures the petition must close with the words "And your petitioners, as in duty bound, will ever pray."

One signature at least must be on the same sheet or parchment as the petition. The signatures or marks of the petitioners must be made by themselves, not by agents, however deputed. A chairman cannot sign for a public meeting, but the common seal of the corporation is received for a corporate body. Petitions for the remission of customs or duties can only be presented with the consent of the Crown. The mode of obtaining redress for the improper election of a member of Parliament is by petition to two judges of the King's Bench Division of the High Court.

PETITION OF RIGHT. In English history, a parliamentary declaration of the rights and liberties of the people, assented to by Charles I. in the beginning of his reign (1628), and considered a constitutional document second in importance only to Magna Charta. The petition demanded: (1) that no freeman should be forced to pay any tax, loan, or benevolence, unless in accordance with an Act of Parliament; (2) that no freeman should be imprisoned contrary to the laws of the land; (3) that soldiers and sailors should not be billeted on private persons; (4) commissions to punish soldiers and sailors by martial law should be abolished.

PETÖFI (pe-*teu'*fē), **Sandor.** Hungarian poet, born in 1823, died in 1849. In his youth he was for some time a common soldier and then a strolling player; in 1843 he contributed to the journals several poems which attracted instant attention; he also wrote several dramas and novels; his lyric of *Most vagy sohā* (Now or Never) became the war-song (1848) of the Revolution. In the Revolutionary War he was appointed an adjutant under Bem, and was killed in the battle of Schässburg. Petöfi was certainly the greatest literary genius of Hungary, and he may be considered as one of the greatest lyric poets of the nineteenth century. An English version of his poems was published in London in 1866 by Sir John Bowring.

PETRA (Gr. *petra*, rock). The name of several ancient towns, the most important of which are as follows:

Europe. (1) A city of Sicily, mentioned by Pliny and Ptolemy, which may be represented by the modern Petralia. (2) A fortress of Macedonia, which commanded a pass leading to Pythium, in Thessaly, by the back of Olympus.

Asia. (1) A town in the land of the Lazi, in Colchis, founded by one of Justinian's generals to dominate the Lazi. It was destroyed by the Romans in A.D. 551, and the extant ruins are now called Oudjenar. (2) A mighty fortress of Sogdiana, attacked by Alexander and held by Arimazes. It is probably the modern Kohiten.

(3) The most important Petra was the chief town of Arabia Petræa. It was the capital of the Idumæans and subsequently of the Nabatæi. The modern name is Wadi-Musa. Petra was situated in the eastern part of Arabia Petræa, in the district called, under the Christian emperors of Rome, Palæstina Tertia. Ancient

geographers placed it in the northern district; modern ones place it in the southern portion, *Esh-Sherrah*, the Seir, or mountain land of the Old Testament (Gen. xxxvi. 8).

The site is a wilderness overtopped by Mount Hor, and diversified by cliffs, ravines, plains, and watered valleys. The valley of Wadi-Musa was formerly the only roadway to Petra, and even now it is the principal one.

Among the objects of interest, all hewn out of the living rock, are the amphitheatre of thirty-three tiers with accommodation for 3000 spectators, which is strangely surrounded by tombs; the rose-coloured *Khuzneh* with two rows of six columns over one another, with statues between, and with capitals and sculptured pediments, the upper one of which is divided by a little round temple surmounted by an urn. The Arabs believe that the urn contains a treasure, *Al-Khuzneh*, whence the name. There are also the remains of a *Deir* or cloister, and of thousands of rock-tombs.

Petra was successively in the hands of the Judæans, Nabatæans, and Macedonians. In A.D. 105 A. Cornelius Palma subdued the city for Trajan, and under Roman rule many of the finest tombs, etc., were erected. Frequently prophesied in Scripture, the destruction of Petra was accomplished by the Mahommedans (seventh century A.D.), and the site was for long unknown. It was discovered by Burckhardt.

PETRARCH (pet′rärk), **Francesco Petrarca.** An Italian poet and humanist, born at Arezzo 20th July, 1304, died 18th July, 1374. His father being an exile from Florence, his earliest years were spent at Incisa, in the vale of Arno, and afterwards with his father at Carpentras, near Avignon, where he began his education. He afterwards studied law at Montpellier and Bologna, but his own inclinations led him to devote his time to Latin and the Provençal poets.

It was at Avignon in 1327 that he first saw, in the church of St. Claire, the Laura who exercised so great an influence on his life and lyrics. It is supposed that her name was Laura de Noves, that she had become the wife of Hughes de Sade two years before she was seen by Petrarch, and that she died in 1348 a virtuous wife and the mother of a large family. After this first meeting Petrarch remained at Avignon three years, singing his purely Platonic love, and haunting Laura at church and in her walks. He then left Avignon for Lombez (French department of Gers), where he held a canonry gifted by Pope Benedict XII., and afterwards visited Paris, Brabant, Ghent, the Rhine, etc. In 1337 he returned to Avignon, bought a small estate at Vaucluse, in order to be near Laura, and here for three years wrote numerous sonnets in her praise.

It was upon his Latin scholarship, however, that he rested his hopes of fame. His Latin works were highly esteemed, and in 1341 he was called to Rome to receive the laureate crown awarded for his Latin poem of *Africa*, an epic on the Punic wars.

In his travels Petrarch made valuable discoveries, which have placed him high among the restorers of

Petrarch

letters. He had advanced views for his age on history and science, despising legends and astrology, and recommending true research. In politics his views were equally advanced, and while he severely criticised the vices of the clergy, he had no sympathy with the scepticism which was common among the scholars of the day.

At Parma he learned the death of Laura, which he recorded on his copy of Virgil, and celebrated in his *Trionfi*. A large part of his time was employed in various diplomatic missions, and in 1370 he took up his residence at Arqua, near Padua, where he passed his remaining years in religious exercises.

Works. Among his Latin works are three books of letters (*Epistolæ Familiares*) and twelve *Eclogues*, his poem *Africa*, and various philosophical, religious, political, and historical treatises. Petrarch's fame, however, is based upon his Italian verse, which consists chiefly of the

Trionfi and the *Canzoniere.* The first is allegorical and moral in its nature, whilst in the latter the love motive is paramount, although many of the sonnets are pervaded by moral and patriotic feelings. The majority of the sonnets are in praise of golden-haired Laura, living or dead, but numerous sonnets breathe the passion of patriotism.

Lamartine and other critics looked upon Petrarch as "the most accomplished of the poets of sentiment," whilst Renan styled him "le premier homme moderne." Educated in the school of the ancients, he declared war on the scholasticism of his age. The spiritual and intellectual descendant of Greece, be became the father of the new learning of the Renaissance.

He was the pioneer of humanism (q.v.), and the first of modern poets who refined and dignified the language of love. He was at once a pagan filled with the sense of beauty, and a Christian imbued with the ideals of asceticism and mysticism.—BIBLIOGRAPHY: H. C. Hollway-Calthrop, *Petrarch: his Life and Times*; M. F. Jerrold, *Francesco Petrarca, Poet and Humanist*; P. Borghesi, *Petrarch and his Influence on English Literature*; P. de Nolhac, *Pétrarque et l'Humanisme*; A. J. F. Mézières, *Pétrarque: étude d'après de nouveaux documents.*

PETREL. The common name of web-footed oceanic birds of the family Procellariidæ. The petrels are nocturnal in their habits, breed in holes in the rocks, lay but one egg, and are almost all of small size and more or less sombre plumage. The smaller

Stormy Petrel (*Procellaria pelagica*)

species are well known to sailors under the name of "Mother Carey's chickens," and their appearance is supposed to presage a storm.

The term stormy petrel is more exclusively applied to the *Procellaria pelagica*, a bird which seems to run in a remarkable manner along the surface of the sea, where it picks up its food.

PETRIE, Sir Flinders. British Egyptologist, born in 1853, and educated privately. During the five years 1875-80 he carried out investigations in British archæology, the results being published in the works *Inductive Metrology* (1877) and *Stonehenge: Plans, Description, and Theories* (1880). Proceeding to Egypt, he made a careful survey in 1881-2 of the Pyramids of Gizeh, and in 1884-6 continued his work under the auspices of the Egyptian Exploration Fund Committee. He excavated the site of Tanis, and discovered and excavated Naukratis, Am, and Daphnæ. Among his publications are: *A Season in Egypt* (1888), *Historical Scarabs* (1889), *Ten Years' Digging in Egypt* (1893), *History of Egypt* (1894-1905), *Egyptian Tales, Decorative Art* (1895), *Religion and Conscience in Ancient Egypt* (1898), *Syria and Egypt* (1898), *Methods and Aims in Archæology* (1904), *Revolutions of Civilisation* (1911), *Eastern Exploration* (1919), *Religious Life in Ancient Egypt* (1924), and *Seventy Years in Archæology* (1931).

PETROBRU'SIANS. The followers of *Peter* (Pierre) de *Bruys*, a Provençal, who in the beginning of the twelfth century preached against the doctrine of baptismal regeneration, the use of churches, altars, crucifixes, relics, etc., prayers for the dead, and the doctrine of the real presence.

PETROL. *See* PETROLEUM.

PETRO'LEUM, or MINERAL OIL. A natural oil consisting almost entirely of hydrocarbons. It is obtained from the earth's crust in two ways, namely by means of oil-borings or oil-wells, and by the distillation of oil-bearing rocks or oil-shale (*see* PARAFFIN). Although the fire-worshippers, as early as 600 B.C., were attracted by the "eternal fires" to Baku, on the Caspian Sea, where inflammable gases issued from the ground, the idea of utilising the oil to any extent for practical purposes is little more than a century old.

The oil industry can be said to have started in Russia in 1813, in the United States in 1859, and in Galicia and Rumania modern methods of boring were introduced in 1881. The oil-shale industry began in Scotland in 1850. Geologically the world's oil-fields may be divided into two groups, namely those occurring in Palæozoic strata, as in Pennsylvania, and those occurring in Upper Cretaceous and Tertiary strata, as in California, the Caucasus, Galicia, Rumania, Burma, and the Dutch East Indies.

The oil usually occurs in beds of a sandy or porous nature which are overlain by clay or impervious beds. It is perhaps surprising that oil is very rarely found to occur in conjunction with coal. The oil-shales of Scotland belong to the Lower Carboniferous series, and those found in the United States to the Devonian series. In prospecting for oil the most important considerations, apart from knowledge given by the geological survey, are surface indications, such as oil-springs and emanations of natural gas.

Boring for oil is carried out either by the percussion method or the

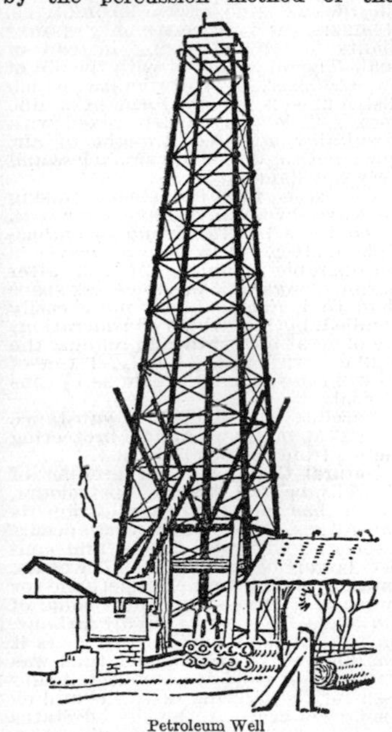

Petroleum Well

rotary method. In the former a steel boring-tool is alternately raised and allowed to fall, and before each fall it is turned through a small angle. In this way a circular hole is gradually chipped out. The fragments of rock are removed from the hole from time to time by means of a pump.

The rotary method makes use of a hollow, cylindrical tool, the lower edge of which is provided with teeth like a saw or with diamonds. It is kept cool by a stream of water. By this means a core of rock is cut out. The diameter of the hole made by either method is about 18 inches at the surface, and is gradually decreased the greater the depth.

Many difficulties are encountered, such as the falling in of the sides in soft strata, and the occurrence of water under great pressure at various depths. These difficulties are overcome by lining the hole with steel tubes. It often occurs when the oil-bearing rock is first pierced that the oil rushes up the bore-hole with great violence, producing a fountain of oil. The classical example of this is the great Droojba Well in the Baku district, which in 1883 spouted for four months to a height of from 100 to 300 feet, and as a result about 100 million gallons of oil ran to waste.

Even if spouting occurs it does not usually last long, and then recourse is made to forcing the oil up by compressed air. In some cases the difficulty of this operation is increased by the viscosity of the petroleum, as in the Burma oil-fields. The oil is conveyed to the refineries, which are usually many miles distant, by means of tank railway cars, oil barges, or pipe lines. Pipe lines sometimes run several hundred miles, and are divided into sections of 40 or 50 miles. At the end of each section the oil is delivered into tanks and then pumped along the next section, as it is not possible to force the oil farther than this.

The output of crude petroleum from the chief oil-fields in 1927, expressed in thousands of barrels of 42 gallons, was as follows: United States, 905,800; Mexico, 64,200; Russia, 72,400; Dutch East Indies, 21,400; Persia, 36,800; India, 8200; Rumania, 26,100; Venezuela, 64,400. The output from oil-shales is relatively insignificant. The output of Scottish oil-shale is approximately 3,000,000 tons per annum.

Crude petroleum is a dark-brown liquid possessing a disagreeable smell. It is slightly lighter than water, its specific gravity usually being between 0·94 and 0·98. Crude petroleum is a mixture of a large number of substances, mostly compounds of carbon and hydrogen. It consists chiefly of hydrocarbons of the paraffin series (*see* PARAFFIN).

Russian petroleum contains a large proportion of another series of hydrocarbons called naphthenes, which are very similar in their properties to the paraffins. The composition of the petroleum found in Borneo is unusual, as it includes a large quantity of hydrocarbons of the benzene series, such as benzene, toluene, and xylene.

Burma petroleum contains a large proportion of the higher members of the paraffin series; hence its greater viscosity. In addition to these important constituents, petroleum contains minute quantities of compounds containing nitrogen and sulphur.

Refining. Crude petroleum is not very suitable for direct practical application, and it is therefore refined or separated into a number of different fractions, each fraction consisting of a limited number of hydrocarbons and having its special commercial use. The crude oil is distilled from vessels holding about 50,000 gallons, and the distillate is collected in several different fractions. These fractions are then further subdivided by fractional distillation into products ready for commercial use.

The first fraction collected is the oil, which distils over up to a temperature of about 80° C., and it consists chiefly of the fifth and sixth members of the paraffin series, namely pentane and hexane. The fraction yields light and easily volatile oils, which on account of their volatility catch fire very readily, and are therefore to be used with considerable caution. They are known commercially by names such as gasoline, rhigolene, and petroleum ether, and they find application in industry as solvents for oils, fats, resins, and rubber; in surgery for producing local insensibility by freezing; and to produce air-gas for lighting country houses.

The second fraction is collected up to about 150° C., and yields principally petrol or motor spirit, which is sometimes called benzine. This latter is a confusing term, as petrol is quite different from coal-tar benzene, and rarely contains hydrocarbons of the benzene series. It consists principally of heptane, octane, and nonane.

The chief use of petrol is as a source of power in internal-combustion engines. Used in this way, 1 lb. of petrol will generate as much mechanical energy as every 3½ lb. of coal used in a good steam plant. Petrol is therefore a more economical source of energy than coal.

The engine trouble of "knocking" or detonation which arises when a car is accelerating or climbing with open throttle on top gear is greatly mitigated by the addition of 6 c.c. of "ethyl" fluid to the gallon of petrol. The percentage composition of ethyl is, approximately: lead-tetra-ethyl, 54·5; ethylene dibromide, 36·5; monochlor-naphthalene, 9. Suspicions of danger to health in its use were allayed, and by 1928 the use of ethyl had become general. Another use of petrol is for carburetting coal-gas. A third use of petrol is for dry-cleaning purposes.

The third fraction is collected between 150° C. and 300° C., and consists of a mixture of all the members of the paraffin series from decane to octadecane. It furnishes oils used for illuminating purposes, known as paraffin oil, mineral colza, and kerosene.

The fourth part or fraction is the residue left in the still after the boiling temperature has reached 300° C. This fraction consists of the higher members of the paraffin series, and furnishes such products as lubricating oil, other heavy oils used as fuels, vaseline, and solid paraffin or paraffin-wax (*see* PARAFFIN).

The heavy fuel oils are used in internal-combustion engines, such as the Diesel engine, also in locomotives, steamers, and in stationary power plants for steam raising instead of coal. The oil is burned with the aid of an atomiser, a contrivance which distributes it in the form of a fine spray. This spray, when mixed with a suitably adjusted draught of air, burns with a practically smokeless and very hot flame.

Oil as a fuel for steam raising possesses several advantages over coal. It contains practically no incombustible matter, whereas coal leaves a considerable quantity of ash after burning. Again, it occupies less space than coal, and is much more easily handled, both of which considerations are of great importance in refilling the bunkers with fuel. Lastly, 1 ton of oil will raise as much steam as 1½ tons of coal.

Vaseline is a semi-solid substance used as an ointment and for protecting metals from corrosion or rust.

Natural Gas. Another product of oil-wells, besides the crude petroleum, which has practical application is natural gas. This almost always occurs associated with oil-borings, and consists largely of the first member of the paraffin series, namely methane or marsh gas. It also contains some of the olefine series of hydrocarbons, such as ethylene. For many years it was allowed to escape and thus was wasted, but now it is collected and used for the lighting of towns and as a source of heat. In the United States in 1919, 735,000 million cubic feet were consumed.

Origin of Petroleum. Various theories have been put forward to account for the formation of petroleum. Some of these assert that the oil is of inorganic origin, attributing its formation to purely chemical processes taking place within the earth; whilst others favour the idea of an organic origin, which undoubtedly applies to the formation of coal.

The chief supporter of the inorganic theory was Mendeléev. He assumed that in regions of high temperature at a considerable distance below the surface of the earth large quantities of carbides of heavy metals, such as iron and manganese, occur. During times of considerable upheaval in the history of the earth cracks may have formed in its crust, allowing the surface waters to descend and come in contact with the carbides.

The action of water on metallic carbides is to form hydrocarbons and oxides of the metals. The hydrocarbons formed will be driven by the intense heat into cooler regions, where they will condense and collect. The fact that large supplies of oil are derived from Palæozoic strata which contain organic or fossil remains in insignificant quantities is in support of the inorganic theory.

An alternative inorganic theory has been proposed by Sabatier. He assumes the presence of the alkali metals, sodium and potassium, in addition to the carbides of the heavy metals. The action of water on the alkali metals produces hydrogen, and on the carbides produces hydrocarbons, such as acetylene. The hydrogen and acetylene then combine, under the catalytic influence of the metals, nickel, iron, and others, to form a mixture of hydrocarbons.

The organic theory suggests that oil is the product of accumulations of decaying organic matter, both vegetable and animal, which have subsequently been overlain and subjected to heating. That oils similar to natural petroleum are produced by heating organic matter is proved by the distillation of coal.

Neither of these theories is wholly satisfactory, and it is possible that petroleum arises from both organic and inorganic sources. On the other hand, there is little doubt that the oil of oil-shales is, like coal, of organic origin.

Petroleum as a Source of Energy. Next to coal, petroleum is the greatest natural source of energy at present available. A number of estimates have been made of the duration of the world's supply, which vary from 100 to 1000 years.

The output of oil has increased in greater proportion than the number of wells; but the oil-shales form a more permanent supply, those of Scotland and Australia yielding an oil which even now competes in price with petroleum from wells.

The Devonian shales of the United States are much poorer in oil, but a considerable rise in the price of oil from other sources would enable them to be worked economically, and they extend over many thousands of square miles. It is probable, however, that the supply of oil will be exhausted before the supply of coal.

Flash-point. The flash-point of an oil is the lowest temperature at which the vapour which it gives off forms an inflammable mixture with the air immediately above the oil.

Very volatile oils, such as the motor spirits, petrol, benzol, and alcohol, possess a high vapour pressure, and flash at temperatures well below the freezing-point of water. They must therefore be handled at a safe distance from a flame and stored under special conditions. Light oils which have a closed flash-point of less than 73° F. are also subject to special restrictions as regards handling and transport in Great Britain.

The flash-point throws no light on the quality of an oil either for fuel or for lubrication, though it does give some idea of its composition. It can be stated, however, that a light oil cannot be successfully used as a motor spirit in the ordinary way unless its flash-point is very low.

To obtain comparable and concordant results it is necessary to carry out the test under specified conditions with regard to size of vessel, quantity of oil, speed of heating, size of ignition flame, frequency of injection of flame, and rate of stirring, and standard apparatus must be used.

Another point to be carefully distinguished from the flash-point is the *ignition temperature*, that is, the temperature at which the oil will spontaneously ignite without flame contact. This test is generally carried out in a platinum crucible placed in a block of steel heated by a Bunsen burner. When the ignition-point is reached, a drop of the oil allowed to fall into the crucible will inflame, causing a mild explosion.

The following is a list of flash-points of petroleum and other oils.

Motor spirit	below 30° F.
Crude petroleum	30° to 300° F.
Paraffin-oil	100° to 200° F.
Crude coal-tar	100° to 190° F.
Fuel oils	140° F. upwards.
Spindle oils	320° to 390° F.
Cylinder oils	360° to 540° F.
Castor-oil	527° F.
Linseed-oil	545° F.
Rape-oil (refined)	580° F.

See FUEL; THERMAL VALUE OF FUELS.

BIBLIOGRAPHY: J. A. Greene, *A Treatise on British Mineral Oil*; Sir Boverton Redwood, *A Treatise on Petroleum*; H. Moore, *Liquid Fuels for Internal Combustion Engines*; J. S. S. Brame, *Fuel: Solid, Liquid, and Gaseous*; V. B. Lewes, *Liquid and Gaseous Fuels*.

PETROL'OGY. The science dealing with rocks, formerly regarded as a branch of mineralogy, but now fundamental among the studies required of the trained geologist. The principles and the growth of petrology are treated in the article on *Geology*. *Petrography* is strictly the description of rocks; but the term is often used as synonymous with petrology, since all description must be founded on systematic studies.

PETRONIUS, Gaius (usually surnamed **Arbiter**). Latin novelist, author of the *Satiricon*. Most competent authorities agree in identifying the author of the earliest novel with the Petronius who lived in the reign of Nero, and who is described by Tacitus in the sixteenth book of the *Annals*. Tacitus tells us that Petronius passed his days in sleep and his nights in business and pleasure; he was an epicure, not a prodigal; he was a refined and cultivated voluptuary. He won the title of *elegantiæ arbiter* at Nero's court, and was "the glass of fashion and the mould of form." He incurred the jealousy of Tigellinus, and was compelled to commit suicide, which he did in characteristic fashion by having his veins opened and tied up, while he listened to the recitation of light verse. Finally he sent to Nero a list of the emperor's abominations and the names of his partners in vice.

The theory that in the *Satiricon* we have Petronius's dying message to Nero is German in its origin, and has absolutely nothing to recommend it. It is impossible to believe that a dying man could write a novel as long as *Tom Jones*, for the very considerable fragments of the work which we possess are merely excerpts from the fifteenth and sixteenth books, and the whole novel must have been extremely long.

This theory has misled some scholars into identifying some of the characters with real persons. Another theory is that the *Satiricon* is a kind of comic epic, a burlesque on Homer, the wrath of Priapus, on account of Encolpius, the hero, killing the sacred goose, taking the place of the wrath of Achilles. This theory is not at all probable; nor is any theory tenable which attributes a purpose or a definite plan to this remarkable novel. Petronius followed his own whim, though in describing the vices of low life he may have desired to glorify the more refined vices of the court.

In form the *Satiricon* is a Menippean satire, that is to say, a mixture of prose and verse. It deals with the adventures of two Greek rogues, Encolpius and Ascyltos, and their boy Giton. Eumolpus, an old inveterate poet, is another principal character. The scene of the novel is varied; the main incidents seem to have taken place at Cumæ, other incidents took place on board ship, and others at Croton. Some of the lost books seem to have had their scene laid at Marseilles.

By far the longest as well as the most interesting fragment which we possess is the famous Dinner of Trimalchio. This fragment was only found in its entirety in 1663. It is of the utmost importance, both for the subtlety of its character delineation and for the light it throws on manners and customs. Trimalchio, the self-made man, is faithfully depicted, as are the freedmen with their commonplace and tedious table-talk. Interesting stories of were-wolves and witches are told.

Other noteworthy passages in the novel are those which deal with the decadence of art and letters, with education, and with the legacy-hunters of Croton. Two long poems are embedded in the novel, one apparently a sort of skit on Nero's poem on the fall of Troy, and the other an attempt to show how Lucan should have written the *Pharsalia*.

Petronius was a great stylist and critic; his Latin, when not purposely debased (as it is in the talk of some of the uneducated characters), is the best Latin of the Silver Age, and his remarks on art and literature are penetrating and illuminating. But it is as the earliest novelist that he is chiefly remembered. His novel is original and unique. In the vitality of his characters and in subtle humour it is not too much to say that he is almost Shakespearean.—BIBLIOGRAPHY: W. D. Lowe, *Cena Trimalchionis* (text, notes, and translation); Michael Heseltine, *Petronius* (text and translation, Loeb Library); Collignon, *Étude sur Pétrone*; Sir Samuel Dill, *Roman Society from Nero to Marcus Aurelius*.

PETROPAVLOVSK'. A town of the government of Akmolinsk, Asiatic Russia, on the Ishim; served by the Siberian Railway. It has soap and leather manufactures, and trades in cereals, wool, and cloth. Pop. 43,000.

PETROP'OLIS. A town and health-resort of Brazil, in the state of Rio de Janeiro. It was founded in 1845 by German colonists, and was state capital from 1893 until 1903. Pop. 30,000-40,000.

PETROVSK'. A town of Russia, in the government of Saratov; served by the Atkarsk-Volsk Railway. It was founded in 1698 by Peter the Great. Pop. 19,208.

PETROZAVODSK'. A town in Russia, capital of the Karelian A.S.S.R., on Lake Onega, Leningrad. It has an iron-foundry, founded by

Peter the Great in 1703, and a cannon-foundry, established in 1774. Pop. 18,800.

PETTICHAPS, or **PETTYCHAPS.** A casual name for the garden warbler (*Sylvia horticola*).

PETTIE, John. Scottish painter, born at Edinburgh in 1839, died in 1893. He studied at the Royal Scottish Academy; exhibited *The Prison Pet* (1859) at Edinburgh, and began in the following year to exhibit in London. Remarkable alike for vigorous conception and technical dexterity, his historical and genre paintings have been numerous. Of these may be mentioned: *What d'ye lack, Madam* (1861); *The Drum-head Court Martial* (1864); *Arrest for Witchcraft* (1866); *Disgrace of Wolsey* (1869); *Scene in the Temple Gardens* (1871); *Juliet and Friar Laurence* (1874); *Sword and Dagger Fight* (1877); *Challenged* (1885); *The Chieftain's Candlesticks* (1886); *Two Strings to her Bow* (1887); and *The Traitor* (1888).

PETTY, Sir William. English statistician and economist, born at Romsey, Hampshire, 1623, died 1687. He was educated in his native town and in Normandy; served for a time in the navy; studied medicine at Utrecht, Leyden, and Paris; came to Oxford, and was (1649) elected a Fellow of Brasenose; became professor of anatomy (1651); and in the following year joined the army in Ireland as a physician. Here he was appointed surveyor of the forfeited Irish estates (1654), and produced the Down Survey of Irish Lands. He became secretary to Henry Cromwell, the Lord-Lieutenant; and in 1658 entered Parliament. He wrote a *Treatise of Taxes and Contributions*.

PETTY OFFICER. A rating in the Royal Navy, equivalent in rank to a sergeant or staff-sergeant of the Royal Army or Royal Marines, according to seniority. The distinguishing badge of a petty officer is the crossed hooks surmounted by a crown, worn in red or gold, according to dress, on the left arm. All petty officers are now ranked as "first-class," but formerly there were two divisions, a "first-class" and a "second-class." The second of these was distinguished by a single hook identical with that worn by a leading seaman, but surmounted by a crown, and the rating was equivalent to that of lance- or full sergeant in the Royal Army or Royal Marines. A few such "second-class rates" existed in the early days of the European War, but are now extinct.

As in the case of officers, there are two branches, administrative and executive, the latter (seamen and stokers) being distinguished from clerks, etc., by the form of dress, which, but for the badges, is identical with that of the ordinary seaman. Chief petty officers, equivalent to company sergeant-majors in the Royal Army, wear "square-rig," i.e. collar and tie, qualification badges (seaman-gunner, etc.) being worn on the jacket lapel. In the case of stokers there are chief stokers and mechanicians, the latter being senior. Chief writers, chief cooks, and chief signalmen (or yeomen of signals), etc., all wear square rig, and are distinguished by their collar badges.

PETU'NIA. A genus of American herbaceous plants, nat. ord. Solanaceæ, nearly allied to tobacco. They are much prized by horticulturists for the beauty of their flowers.

PETWORTH-MARBLE. Also called *Sussex-marble*, from being worked at Petworth, in Sussex, a variously coloured limestone occurring in the Weald clay, and composed of the remains of freshwater shells.

PEUTINGERIAN TABLE. A table of the roads of the ancient Roman world, written on parchment, and found in 1507 by Conrad Celtes in the library of the Benedictine monastery at Tegernsee, in Bavaria. The document was so named from Conrad *Peutinger*, a native of Augsburg, who was the first to make it generally known. The document traces roads through India to numerous trade-places as far as the mouth of the Ganges. It is supposed to have been constructed about A.D. 226.

PEWTER. An alloy of tin and lead, or of tin with proportions of lead, zinc, bismuth, antimony, or copper, and used for domestic utensils. One of the finest sorts of pewter is composed of 100 parts of tin to 17 parts of antimony, while the common pewter of which beer-mugs and other vessels are made consists of 4 parts of tin and 1 of lead. The kind of pewter of which tea-pots are made (called Britannia-metal) is an alloy of tin, brass, antimony, and bismuth.

PEYER'S GLANDS. In anatomy, the clustered masses of lymphoid tissue in the walls of the ileum (small intestine), first discovered by a Swiss anatomist named Peyer. *See* INTESTINE.

PÉZENAS (pā-zē-näs, Gallic *Piscennæ*). A town of France, in the department of Hérault, on the left bank of the Hérault, at the confluence of the Peine, 25 miles W.S.W. of Montpellier. It has a trade in spirits and wine. At Pézenas Molière wrote his comedy *Les Précieuses ridicules*. Pop. 7000.

PEZIZA. An extensive genus of Ascomycetous Fungi, group Discomycetes, saprophytes growing on soil, dead twigs, etc. Most have large, fleshy, often brightly coloured apothecia, *P. aurantia*, of a brilliant orange colour, and *P. (sarcoscypha) coccinea*, with cups of a deep crimson hue, being particularly handsome species.

PFENNIG. A small copper or rather bronze coin current in Germany, of which 100 = 1 mark; so that 10 pfennige were worth before the European War a little over an English penny. After 1915 iron, aluminium, and zinc pieces were coined.

PFORZHEIM (pforts'hīm). A town and railway junction of Baden, Germany, on the northern edge of the Black Forest, at the junction of the Nagold with the Enz. The chief industries are in the making of gold and silver trinkets, machinery, castings, tools, chemicals, leather, paper, cloth, and beer. Pforzheim was settled by the Romans. Pop. 78,973.

PHACOCHERE (fā'ko-kēr), or **PHACOCHŒRE.** The wart-hog of Africa, genus Phacochœrus, akin to the swine, characterised by a large wart-like excrescence on each side of the face. The tusks of the male project 8 or 9 inches beyond the lips, and form terrible weapons. There are two species, *P. æthiopicus* and *P. africanus*.

PHA'COPS. *See* TRILOBITES.

PHÆDO. A Greek philosopher. Born in Elis, he came to Athens about 400 B.C., where he became acquainted with Socrates and one of his most devoted disciples. After the death of his master he returned to his native town and founded a Socratic school of philosophy. Plato's dialogue on the immortality of the soul bears the name of *Phædo*.

PHÆDRA. In Greek legend, daughter of Minos, King of Crete, and of Pasiphaë, sister of Ariadne and wife of Theseus. She falsely accused her stepson, Hippolytus, of attempting to seduce her, an injustice of which she afterwards repented, and was either killed by her husband or committed suicide. Sophocles wrote a *Phædra* which is lost; and the story is the subject of Euripides's extant play the *Hippolytus*. The Euripidean tragedy was imitated by Seneca in his *Phædra*, and by Racine in his masterpiece *Phèdre*.

PHÆDRUS. A Latin fabulist of the Augustan age, who translated and imitated the fables of Æsop. He was a Thracian slave brought to Rome, and manumitted by Augustus. Some authorities have doubted the genuineness of the fables ascribed to Phædrus, but their style is favourable to the supposition of their genuineness. There are five books containing ninety-seven fables attributed to him, besides certain others. In the prologue to the first book Phædrus declares his work to be a free translation of Æsop, but in subsequent books he hints at having taken greater liberties with his subject, and introduced fables of his own under the name of Æsop.

PHÆOPHYCEÆ. *See* BROWN ALGÆ.

PHA'ĔTHŌN. In Greek mythology, the son of Helios (the sun). One day he obtained leave from his father to drive the chariot of the sun, but being unable to restrain the horses Zeus struck him with a thunderbolt and hurled him headlong into the River Po. His sisters found him there, and lamented for him. They were changed into poplars, and their tears into amber.

PHAGEDENA. A form of spreading sloughing ulceration, usually seen in assocation with venereal disease, and occurring in unhealthy people. Unless treated, it spreads extensively, and causes much loss of tissue.

PHAGOCYTES. Those cells of the body, chiefly the white blood corpuscles (leucocytes), capable of absorbing bacteria—a process known as phagocytosis, first brought forward by Metshnikov to explain the facts of immunity. After observation he came to the conclusion that successful resistance of an animal (or man) to disease depended on the activity of certain cells, called phagocytes; and insusceptibility to a disease was indicated by rapid action on the part of the phagocytes in destroying the bacteria and preventing even local damage. In moderately susceptible cases there occurs a local inflammation, due to the increase of blood-cells (phagocytes) brought to envelop and finally destroy the invading organisms, and, on the other hand, in highly susceptible cases phagocytosis did not occur or was only imperfect. His theory is now largely accepted as a rational explanation of the action of blood-cells on bacteria.

PHAL'ANGER. The name given to the members of a family of marsupial mammals inhabiting Australasia. They are generally of the size of a cat, are nocturnal in their habits, and live in trees, feeding on insects, fruits, and leaves. The vulpine phalanger or vulpine opossum is a common type. *See also* FLYING PHALANGER.

PHALAN'GES (-jēz). The name applied to the separate bones of which the digits (or fingers and toes) of vertebrates are composed. Each digit or finger of the human hand consists of three phalanges, with the exception of the pollex or thumb, which is composed of two only.

PHAL'ANX. A name given generally by the Greeks to the whole of the heavy-armed infantry of an army, but more specifically to each of the grand divisions of that class of troops when formed in ranks and files close and deep, with their shields joined and their pikes crossing each other. The Spartan phalanx was commonly eight men deep, while the Theban phalanx was much deeper.

PHAL'ARIS. A tyrant of Agrigentum, in Sicily (probably between 571 and 549 B.C.), chiefly celebrated in tradition for his cruelty. He is said to have burned his victims in a brazen bull, within which a slow fire was kindled. By means of pipes fitted in its nostrils the shrieks of the tyrant's victims became like the bellowing of the animal. He was represented in later times as a patron of literature and quite a humane man. The letters of Phalaris, of which an English edition was published in 1695, were shown to be spurious by Richard Bentley in his *Dissertation on Phalaris* (1699).

PHAL'ARIS. A small genus of grasses, of which the seed of one of the species, *P. canariensis*, or canary-grass, is extensively employed as food for birds, and commonly known as canary-seed.

Phalangers
Left, Squirrel Flying Phalanger
Right, Vulpine Phalanger

PHALAROPE (fal'a-rōp). The common name of several grallatorial birds forming the genus Phalarŏpus. The grey phalarope (*P. lobătus*), frequently seen in Britain in the course of its migration from its arctic breeding-place to its southern winter quarters, is a beautiful bird, rather over 8 inches long, with a short tall and slender, straight bill. The red-

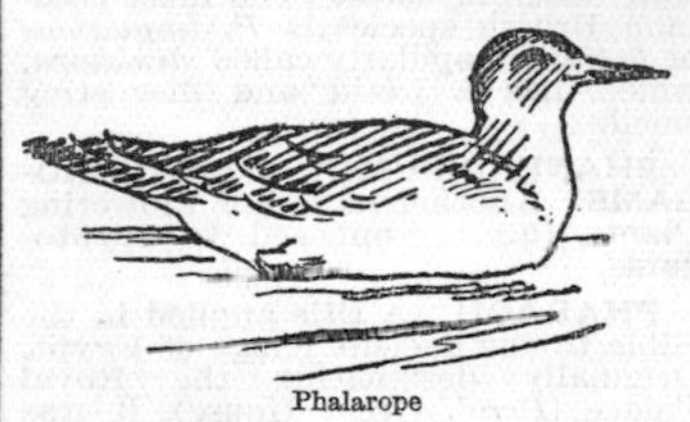

Phalarope

necked phalarope (*P. hyperborĕus*), which breeds in some of the most northern Scottish islands, is rather smaller than the grey phalarope.

PHALLISM. Adoration of the generative organs as symbols of the creative powers of nature, or worship of the reproductive powers of nature as symbolised by the organs of sex. These symbols were almost in universal use in ancient religions, and phallic worship was both religious and magical. Religion has become more and more refined even among primitive and savage races, and phallic worship as a religious cult is quite a rare occurrence now. In spite, however, of the advance of civilisation, phallism is still prominent in magic, which retains the baser elements of religion, and ministers to all sexual impulses, prescribing philtres and spells, and making use of amulets.

Originally phallic worship had an allegorical meaning. It was the result of gratitude and veneration for the bounties of nature, expressed in actions of sacrifice and supplication.

In Egypt the symbolism of phallic worship was associated with the worship of the bull Apis, and with the feasts of Osiris, the solar divinity. The same symbolism is found among the Phœnicians and Babylonians, and was adopted by the Jews from their idolatrous neighbours.

In Greece these symbols did not appear in the primitive mythology of the Hellenic race. They were introduced with the worship of Dionysus, and afterwards applied to that of other divinities, particularly Demeter, Aphrodite, and Apollo. Everywhere phallic worship sooner or later became associated with obscenities and licentious rites. Such was the case especially in Rome during the latter half of her history, where the offences produced by these rites were so great that they had to be forbidden by law.—BIBLIOGRAPHY: J. G. R. Forlong, *Rivers of Life*; C. Howard, *Sex Worship*.

PHALLUS, or ITHYPHALLUS. In botany, a genus of Fungi of the division Gastromycetes. The most common British species is *P. impudīcus* or *fœtidus*, popularly called *stinkhorn*, which has a fœtid and disgusting smell.

PHANEROGA'MIA, or PHANEROGAMS. Another name for Flowering Plants (q.v.): opposed to cryptogams.

PHARAOH. A title applied in the Bible to the ancient Kings of Egypt. Originally designating the Royal Palace (*Pero'*, Great House), it was applied to the Government and to the ruler himself, as in modern times the Sublime Porte is used for the Turkish

Pharaoh

Government, the Vatican for the Papal see, Downing Street or Quay d'Orsay for the British or French Government. With the beginning of the 25th dynasty (tenth to eighth century B.C.) Pharaoh is added to the other titles before the king's name, whilst in the 25th dynasty it was the only title prefixed to the king's personal name. The first king mentioned by name in the Bible is Shishak I., a contemporary of Jeroboam.

The Pharaoh under whom Joseph held office was, as is generally admitted, one of the Hyksos or shepherd kings, whilst the Pharaohs of the Hebrew oppression and Exodus were Rameses II., the Sesostris of the Greeks, and his son Meneptah II. The exodus took place under the reign of the latter, or under that of his successor, Seti II.

PHARISEES. A religious party among the Jews which had risen into great influence at the time of Christ, and played a prominent part in the events recorded in the New Testament. They became a definite party during the Maccabæan revolt, and especially when John Hyrcanus began to reign as a secular prince and made alliances with other powers. At the time of Christ the Pharisees stood as the national party in politics and religion—the opponents of the Sadducees.

The fundamental principle of the Pharisees was that of the existence of an oral law to complete and explain the written law. This oral law declared the continuance of life after the death of the body, and the resurrection of the dead. This authoritative tradition received in process of time additions which were not pretended to be derived directly from Moses, but to which the Pharisees often attached more weight than to the law itself. They also practised a rigid separation from all intercourse with the mass of the people, whom they called *am-hā-ārez* (people of the land). This was one of the reasons why they were such bitter opponents of Jesus, in spite of the fact that they were cherishing Messianic hopes. Jesus was mingling freely with publicans and sinners, *am-hā-ārez* (Mark, ii. 15-17).

The Pharisees were a body of pious and learned men, patriots and nationalists, but their views, as testified by the Apostle Paul, were narrow, bigoted, ignorant, and intolerant. Among the charges which Jesus brought against them was that of misunderstanding and misinterpreting their own prophets.

PHARMACOPŒ'IA (Gr. *pharmakon*, a drug; *poiein*, to make). The name applied to a book containing descriptions of the various substances and drugs used in medicine, with formulæ showing the composition of the derivatives thereof with directions for their preparation. Such books have been issued by many hospital authorities for use in their own institutions, and for the guidance of medical practitioners and pharmacists interested in the work done therein; as an example that of the Westminster Ophthalmic Hospital may be given.

Previous to 1864 the Colleges of Physicians of London, Edinburgh, and Dublin each issued a pharmacopœia to cover medical practice in England, Scotland, and Ireland respectively, but in that year *The British Pharmacopœia* was published under the direction of the General Council of Medical Education and Registration of the United Kingdom, pursuant to the Medical Acts of 1858 and 1862, and immediately replaced these three authorities. *The British Pharmacopœia* has been republished many times. In 1914 its scope was extended to cover the requirements of the British Dominions. At the same time, to promote uniformity in the pharmacopœial usage of different countries, certain changes were made in the preparation, composition and strength of important galenical compounds containing potent ingredients, so that the 1914 edition was national in the broadest sense of the term, and also to a certain extent international in its scope. A new edition, embodying many changes, was published in 1932.

The preparation of *The British Pharmacopœia* takes many years, and entails the co-operation of medical, pharmaceutical, chemical, and botanical authorities throughout the empire. As a result of this, it represents the position of our medical and scientific knowledge at the date of its publication. The chemical tests for purity, as one might expect in such a medical production, are of the highest degree of accuracy, and apply to definite chemical substances like potassium bromide as well as to such natural mixtures as cod liver oil. Its standards are recognised commercially, and to say that a substance is " B.P." is to assert that it will pass all the tests of *The British Pharmacopœia* and is therefore above suspicion, while in courts of law it is accepted as a standard for the substances and mixtures which it defines.

In accordance with modern scientific practice the centigrade thermometric scale and the metric system of weights and measures are used for all pharmaceutical and analytical computations ; doses, however, are given both in the metric and imperial systems.

Other nationalities have their own pharmacopœias, though not always bearing this name, as, for example, those of France, Italy, Japan, and the United States.

PHAR'MACY (Gr. *pharmakon*, a drug). The science and art of the preparation and combination of drugs so as to render them fit for administration or for external application to the human frame. Pharmacy is coeval with human needs, for accident and disease have always been the lot of man. From the earliest times pharmacy has been the hand-maiden of medicine and surgery, and the medicine-man who discovered that spider's webs and certain down-covered leaves could arrest capillary hæmorrhages practised pharmacy by modifying these simple natural methods of treatment.

Many names of rulers, physicians, and philosophers have been handed down to us from dates antecedent to and at the beginning of the Christian era as associated with pharmacy, but it is difficult in the majority of cases to identify with accuracy the substances and drugs to which they refer. For example, the " hemlock " which Socrates was obliged to drink may or may not have been the hemlock of our day, *Conium maculatum*, though on physiological grounds there is reason for believing they were identical. In the sixteenth century and later there were pharmaceutical preparations in frequent use, such as mithridatum and diascordium, complex mixtures of forty ingredients, associated with the ancient names of Mithridates and Dioscorides.

Historical Survey. The progress of pharmacy in Great Britain is known with accuracy from about 1511, in which year the first Medical Act of Parliament was passed, whereby the faculty of medicine was vested in one body of practitioners who practised medicine, surgery, and pharmacy. The physicians allied themselves with pharmacy, and their assistants, who prepared the medicaments for use, were known as apothecaries. Gradually the latter acquired a working knowledge of the art of the treatment of diseases, and soon began to treat patients on their own account, as well as to act as preparers of medicine.

In 1540 physicians were empowered by Act of Parliament to enter the houses of apothecaries in London " to search, view, and see the apothecaries' wares, drugs, and stuffs, and to destroy such as they found corrupt or unfit for use." In 1553 this right of search and destruction was extended to " druggists, distillers, sellers of waters and oils, and preparers of chemical medicine." In 1617 the apothecaries obtained a charter entitling them " to sell drugs and prepare and compound medicines according to the physicians' orders and direction," the latter still possessing the right of search ; in 1623 the Society of Apothecaries established a dispensary for the purpose of making the most important preparations for the use of their own members, and in 1671 made an addition of a chemical laboratory for their own members primarily, but subsequently for the public at large. It is from this period that the name " Apothecaries' Hall " dates, a name which carries with it still a certain amount of dignity.

The apothecaries became so prosperous by virtue of their ability to practice medicine and pharmacy that in 1694 the physicians, who suffered materially from this encroachment on their domain of medicine, established dispensaries of their own, which prospered and enjoyed the patronage of the public. We have reason to believe that the assistants employed and instructed by the physicians at these institutions became dispensing chemists on their own account, and from these the origin of chemists and druggists of the present day may be dated.

In 1793 the chemists and druggists had become such rivals to the apothecaries that the latter endeavoured by Act of Parliament to retain for themselves the practice of pharmacy, but this was unavailing. In 1841 the chemists and druggists founded a society under the name of The Pharmaceutical Society of Great Britain, which has existed to the present day, with the laudable objects of "benefiting the public, elevating the profession of pharmacy by furnishing the means of proper instruction, protecting the collective and individual interests and privileges of all its members, and establishing a club for the relief of decayed and distressed members."

The Pharmaceutical Society of Great Britain early in its career established a School of Pharmacy for the education of its members, and in 1852 obtained its first Pharmacy Act, whereby the titles "Pharmaceutical Chemist" and "Chemist and Druggist" were confined to its members.

In 1864 a second Pharmacy Act was obtained, whereby, for the protection of the public, the retail sale of poisons was made the peculiar province of members of the Pharmaceutical Society and of those who had been registered by the registrar of the society, with an exception in favour of medical practitioners who wished to do likewise. It is on this account that the dispensing of medicines is confined to chemists and druggists and pharmaceutical chemists to-day.

Of recent years the term "chemist," though belonging legally to those registered under the Pharmacy Acts, has come into common use as signifying those who deal in pure chemistry, as teachers, analysts, manufacturers, etc., and to avoid confusion, the term "pharmacist" is now legally confined to registered "chemists and druggists," and will in course of time be the common appellation of members of the craft.

The Dangerous Drugs Act of 1920 has further strengthened the position of the pharmacists by a process of authorisation confined to registered chemists and druggists and pharmaceutical chemists, but the authorisation may be withdrawn under certain conditions, with the result that the person concerned can sell and dispense certain poisonous substances, but not such as are specifically detailed in the Dangerous Drugs Act, viz. cocaine, opium, etc. In order that the wholesale and export trade in these drugs may not be unnecessarily curtailed, licences are issued to those engaged in these businesses, under certain conditions.

The practice of pharmacy is based on chemistry, physics, botany, and zoology, and has become, in recent years, so intricate that a given individual can only cultivate a small portion of the craft. In the sphere of crude drugs the pharmacist was dependent on the liberality of Nature, and attempted to gain a sufficiency of them by widespread searching and collection wherever the particular plants in which he was interested were known to occur. This practice has given place to large farms, where important medicinal plants, such as belladonna, henbane, and digitalis (foxglove), and such aromatic herbs as fennel and anise are cultivated on a very large scale with great advantage as to quality and quantity.

In the same way plants which cannot be raised in the British Isles are cultivated abroad, two of the most important being the opium poppy (*Papaver somniferum*) and cinchona trees (*Cinchona succirubra*), the bark of which yields the valuable drug quinine, and for which immense tracts of land are under cultivation in the temperate regions of India, Java, and South America.

Manufacture. From the farm to the factory is but a step, and pharmacy on a manufacturing scale is the result. This includes drying-presses, where the plants are slowly dried to preserve the colour and to retain their properties unchanged; storing for a variable time, reaching to three years in the case of cascara sagrada before it is fit for medicinal use; grinding- and cutting-machines to reduce the drugs to suitable degrees of fineness for extraction of the soluble active principles by means of alcohol, ether, or water; percolators of immense size to enable this extraction to be performed efficiently; open and vacuum pans for the concentration of the percolates; and lastly, chemical testing to adjust the strength in active principles of the various preparations.

Extracts may be liquid and solid; the liquids are usually made of such a strength that one ounce of drug is represented by one fluid ounce of extract; this simple rule is varied in the case of powerful remedies, as nux vomica, ipecacuanha, and aconite, where an elaborate chemical process is undertaken to determine the amount of important alkaloidal matter in the preparation, which is thereafter diluted with the appropriate solvent, so that it contains a definite percentage of pure or mixed alkaloids.

In many instances, as in the cases of ergot and digitalis, it is not possible in the present state of our chemical knowledge to value a preparation by analysis, and recourse is therefore made to physiological testing, i.e. by experimentation upon the lower animals, as the guinea-pig and the barn-door cock. This method is not recognised by *The British Pharmacopœia*, but nevertheless is commonly accepted as a proof of quality.

Aromatic waters, such as dill and peppermint, are made by distillation with water of the drug or the volatile oil; while certain "spirits," especially "spirits of sal volatile," are prepared by the same process. Ointments, which were formerly made by stirring the medicament into the melted ointment-basis, are now made by a cold process, the active ingredient, as zinci oxidum or acidum boricum, being mixed with the ointment-basis in a special mill, giving a product so free from gritty particles that one is often in doubt as to the presence or absence of the active ingredient.

Pills, also, have shared in the pharmaceutical progress; at one time made laboriously by hand, they are now made by elaborate machinery capable of turning out thousands of pills per hour, perfectly rounded, and only requiring a sugar coating to render them suitable for the market. They have a great rival in "compressed drugs," in which the drug, in a pure state or in combination with others, is mixed with a suitable binding material, and delivered in definite quantities to a stamping-machine, which compresses the whole into a solid tablet form having the excellent property of disintegrating rapidly in presence of moisture. "Compressed drugs" have also largely replaced the mixed powders of the last generation, especially those in common use, such as grey powder.

Dispensing. In dispensing, the pharmacist practises these and other operations on a small scale, weighing, measuring, and mixing the various preparations prescribed by the medical practitioner, always endeavouring to present a finished article to the patient which will produce the expected results. This is the "art of dispensing," to acquire proficiency in which demands much experience, for physical and chemical incompatibility has to be overcome somehow in order that therapeutical compatibility may remain. Further, when an unusually large dose of any therapeutic agent is prescribed, "it is the duty of the pharmacist or dispenser to satisfy himself that the prescriber's intentions have been correctly interpreted."

It is curious to note in this connection that while all quantities for the preparation of pharmacopœial articles are now given in the metric system, and though it is permissible for medical practitioners to use this system in their prescribing, they prefer to use the apothecaries' measure and the symbols hallowed by centuries of usage. It is not mere prejudice, for it does not seem reasonable to make a change as long as medicines are taken by the tea, dessert, or table-spoonful instead of cubic centimetres.

The following abbreviations are used by medical practitioners in writing their prescriptions:

Gr. = grain.
℈ = scruple (20 grains).
ʒ = drachm (60 grains).
℥ = ounce apothecaries' (480 grains).

The fluid ounce is the volume of 1 ounce avoirdupois (43·75 grains) of water measured at 16·7° C.; the eighth part of a fluid ounce is a fluid drachm. The symbols given above for drachm and apothecaries' ounce are also used for fluid drachm and fluid ounce. In dispensing, the rule is "solids by weight, liquids by measure;" hence the exact meaning of the symbol used is given by the physical conditions of the substance to the name of which it is attached.

♏ = minim, the sixtieth part of a fluid drachm.
Gtt. = (gutta), drop.
Cochl. = (cochleāre), spoonful.
Cochl. mag. = (cochleāre magnum), tablespoonful.
Cochl. parv. = (cochleāre parvum), teaspoonful.
i̇, j̇ = one (in writing quantities, Latin numerals are used).
ss. = (semisse) half (an ounce or whatever symbol or quantity it follows).
āā or ana = of each.
q. s. = quantum sufficiat (as much as may be necessary).

PHAROS. ISLAND OF. Close to and now part of Alexandria, which protected the port of that city. On the eastern promontory of the island stood the lighthouse of Alexandria, so famous in antiquity, and considered one of the wonders of the world, built 300 years B.C.

PHARSA'LUS. A town of ancient Thessaly, near which Cæsar defeated Pompey 48 B.C. It is now represented by the small town Phersala, seat of a Greek archbishop. Pop. 1363.

PHARYNGOBRANCHII (fa-rin-go-brang'ki-ī; "pharynx-gilled"). The name sometimes applied to the Cephalochorda, a sub-phylum of vertebrate animals, represented solely by the lancelet (q.v.).

PHARYNGOGNATHI (fa-rin-gog'-na-thi). A group of spiny-finned fishes, which includes the wrasses, the parrot-fishes, the garfish, saury-pikes, and flying-fish.

PHARYNX (fa'ringks). The term applied to the muscular sac which intervenes between the cavity of the mouth and the narrow œsophagus, with which it is continuous. It is of a funnel shape, and about 4 inches in

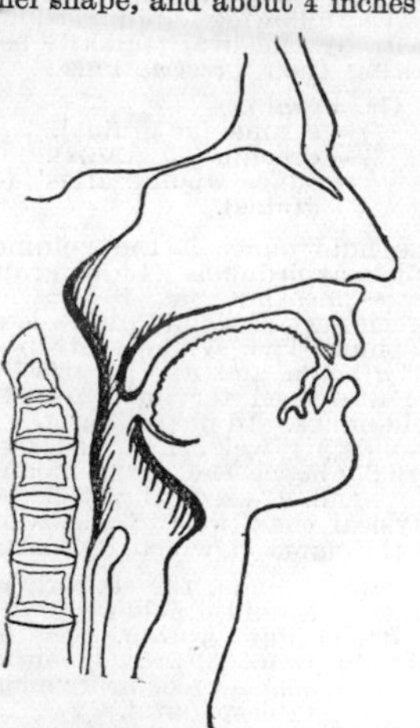

Diagram showing the Pharynx

length; the posterior nostrils open into it above the soft palate, while the larynx, with its lid, the epiglottis, is in front and below. The contraction of the pharynx transmits the food from the mouth to the œsophagus. From it proceed the eustachian tubes to the ears.

PHASCOLOG'ALE. A genus of small marsupials, closely allied to the dasyures, found throughout Australia, New Guinea, etc.

PHASE'OLUS. The genus of leguminous plants to which belong the kidney-bean and scarlet-runner. *See* FRENCH BEANS.

PHASE RULE. *See* SOLUTION.

PHAS'MIDÆ. Stick and leaf insects, a family of orthopterous insects allied to the Mantidæ, restricted to warm countries, and remarkable for their very close resemblance to the objects in the midst of which they live, this peculiarity being their only protection against their enemies.

The family includes the genera Phasma, Phyllium, Cladomorphus, etc. Some of them are destitute of wings, and have the appearance of dead twigs, while the absence of motion in the insects adds to the deception. In others, as the genus Phyllium, the wings have the appearance of withered leaves, while the brighter hue of the wing-covers of a few of larger size give to the animal the appearance of a fresher leaf.

PHEASANT. The general name given to many of the game-birds included in a sub-family (Phasianinæ) of the pheasant family (Phasianidæ), which comprises several genera besides that of the pheasants proper, Phasiānus. There are usually naked spaces of skin on the head or cheeks,

Silver Pheasant

and often combs or wattles. The plumage of the males is brilliant, that of the females more sober, and the males carry spurs on the tarso-metatarsus. The wings are short, the tail long, the three front toes are united by a membrane up to the first joint, and the hinder toe is articulated to the tarsus. The food consists of grain, soft herbage, roots, and insects. They are chiefly terrestrial in habits, taking short rapid flights when alarmed. The pheasants are polygamous, the males and females consorting together during the breeding-time, which occurs in spring.

The common pheasant (*Phasiănus colchicus*), now fully domesticated in Britain, but originally said to be a native of the banks of the Phasis in Western Asia, and to have been introduced by the Romans, is the familiar species. It extends in its distribution from the Caspian over South-East Europe. These birds breed freely in a domesticated state. The pheasant will interbreed with the common fowl, the Guinea fowl, and even with the black grouse; and there are white and pied varieties of the common species. The hybrid pro-

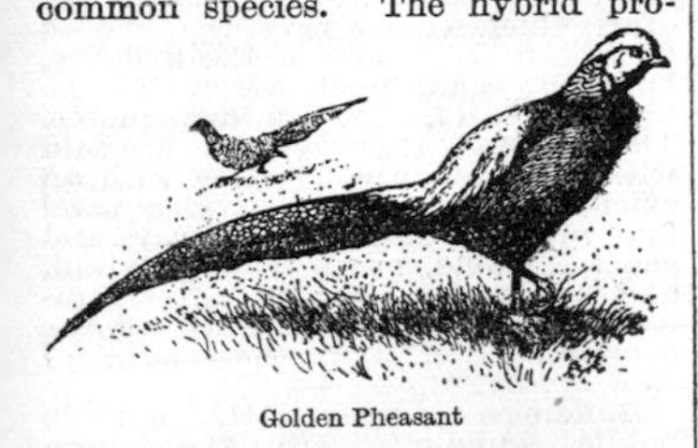

Golden Pheasant

duced by the union of a cock-pheasant with the common hen is termed a *pero*.

Other species inhabiting Southern Asia and the Eastern Archipelago are the Diard's pheasant of Japan (*P. versicolor*); Reeve's pheasant (*P. reevesi*) of China; and Soemmering's pheasant (*P. soemmeringii*), found in Japan. There are various others often put in different genera, as the silver pheasants (genus Gennæus) of China, Burmah, and various parts of India, with a generally white plumage, the feathers marked with fine black lines; and the golden pheasant of Tibet and China, the type of the genus Chrysolophus. It is noted for its brilliant colours and magnificent crest. *See also* ARGUS PHEASANT; TRAGOPAN.

PHEASANT SHELL (Phasianella). A genus of sea-snails, found in South America, India, Australia, the Mediterranean, etc. The shell is spiral and obovate, the outside polished and richly coloured.

PHEI'DIAS. A celebrated Athenian sculptor, born about 490 B.C., died about 435 B.C. Among his works were three statues of Athena in the Acropolis of Athens mentioned by Pausanias, but of which nothing now remains. One, of colossal size, was in bronze, and represented the goddess in the attitude of battle. The second, which measured with its pedestal about 41½ feet in height, stood in the Parthenon, was made of ivory and gold, and represented Athena standing with a spear in one hand and an image of Victory in the other. The third, in bronze, of smaller size, was called the *beautiful*, on account of its exquisite proportions. Another colossal statue in ivory and gold, that of Zeus at Olympia, was ranked among the wonders of the world. It was removed to Constantinople by Theodosius I., and was destroyed by fire in A.D. 475.

Pheidias superintended the erection of many of the finest buildings of Athens while Pericles was in power; and the sculpture of the Parthenon was probably in part by him, and as a whole reflects his spirit and influence. The bulk of the surviving pieces (known as the Elgin Marbles) are now in the British Museum, and show the nobility of conception and monumental treatment for which Pheidias is famous. Accused falsely of peculation and impiety, Pheidias is said to have died in prison.

PHELLOGEN. In botany, the actively dividing layer (meristem) in woody stems and roots which gives rise to the protective cork and bark; also called cork-cambium.

PHELPS, Samuel. British actor, born in Devonport 1806, died 1878. He was apprenticed to a printer, but took to the stage in 1827, and ten years later was appearing in London in leading Shakespearean characters, and was one of the leading performers under Macready at Covent Garden. From 1844 to 1862 he was joint manager of Sadler's Wells Theatre, where he produced thirty-four of Shakespeare's plays. He was regarded as the most accomplished Shakespearean actor of his day, excelling more especially in comedy parts such as Bottom, Justice Shallow, etc. He published an edition of Shakespeare in 1853.

PHENACETIN, or PHENACITINE. A white crystalline substance with the composition $C_{10}H_{13}O_2N$, which is an acetyl derivative of para-phenetidine. It is used in medicine as an antipyretic. The physiological action consists of a sedative action on the sensory tracts of the spinal cord, and a depressant action on the heart.

PHENOL. *See* CARBOLIC ACID.

PHENOM'ENALISM. A philosophical term designating any system of thought concerned with appearances.

It is applied to the following two theories. (1) We only know phenomena, i.e. our knowledge is limited and our consciousness cannot penetrate to reality itself, although the thing in itself exists. This view, whilst admitting the reality of the thing in itself, denies our capacity of knowing it. It is a theory related to Agnosticism and Empiricism. (2) All our knowledge is only phenomenal, i.e. the world we experience is only a world of mind and not a world of things, as things in themselves do not exist at the back of phenomena. Reality is directly present to consciousness. Among the philosophers who have elaborated systems of phenomenalism are Hume, Berkeley, Locke, F. A. Lange, and others.—Cf. F. H. Bradley, *Appearance and Reality*.

PHERÆ. An ancient city of Thessaly, which under the rule of tyrants of its own became a controlling power of the whole of Thessaly, and for long made its influence felt in the affairs of Greece. In 352 B.C. it became subject, with the rest of Thessaly, to Philip of Macedon.

PHERECYDES (fer-i-sī'dēz). A Greek philosopher of the sixth century B.C., a native of the Island of Syros, and a contemporary of Thales. He is said to have taught the doctrine of metempsychosis, or of the immortality of the soul, and to have been the instructor of Pythagoras. Some fragments of his work are extant.

PHIGALI'A (modern **PAVLITZA**, in the province of Messenia). A city of Arcadia, ancient Greece. On one of the mountains, Mount Cotylium, to the north-east of the site of Phigalia, is situated the temple of Apollo Epicurius, built in the time of the Peloponnesian War by Ictinus, the architect of the Parthenon at Athens, and still one of the best-preserved temples in Greece. The frieze, which was usually on the exterior of the temple, was here in the interior, and with the metopes was of Parian marble. The friezes, which were the glory of the temple, were purchased by the British Government in 1814 for £15,000, and are now in the British Museum. The subjects are the battle of the Lapithæ and the Centaurs, and that between the Amazons and the Greeks, the school being that of Pheidias.

PHILADELPHIA. (1) An ancient city of Palestine, east of the Jordan, originally Rabbath-Ammon, the ancient capital of the Ammonites.

(2) An important city in the east of Lydia.

PHILADELPHIA. A city and port of entry of Pennsylvania, United States, on the Delaware River; served by the Baltimore & Ohio, and by ramifications of the Pennsylvania Railways, and also by inter-urban electric-traction services, and elevated and subway lines. Philadelphia has a population three times greater than that of any other city in the state. The site is nearly flat, but slopes gently both towards the Delaware and the Schuylkill.

Streets, Squares, etc. It is laid out on the usual transatlantic chess-board pattern (*see* NEW YORK CITY). Market Street, the great central street running east and west, and continuously built upon for over 4 miles, has a width of 100 feet; Broad Street, the principal central street running north and south, is built upon to about the same length, and is 113 feet in width. Most of the other chief streets vary from 50 to 66 feet broad, some of the avenues, however, being much wider. At the intersection of some are fine squares. The principal thoroughfares are laid with the lines in connection with an efficient system of tramways. Several fine bridges, both for railway and general traffic, span the Schuylkill, and a regular service of steam-ferries across the Delaware affords communication with the shores of New Jersey.

Buildings. Among the notable public buildings are the State House, containing a large room called Independence Hall, from the circumstance that the Declaration of Independence was signed here (4th July, 1776); the custom-house, a white marble edifice; the United States mint, a marble-fronted building; the new post office, a large and handsome granite structure with a dome; the new city hall, a splendid building of granite and marble, completed in 1889, with a tower 450 feet high, surmounted by a statue of William Penn; Girard College, a fine example of the Corinthian style; the buildings of Pennsylvania University; the permanent exhibition buildings (erected for the Centennial Exhibition of 1876), with the annexed Memorial and Horticultural Halls; and the splendid building accommodating the Academy of Fine Arts.

Education. The educational establishments include the Pennsylvania University; the Jefferson Medical College; University Medical College; the Women's Medical College; the Academy of Fine Arts; the School of Design for Women; the Academy of Natural Sciences; the Franklin Institute; numerous colleges, academies, and other educational institutions, supported by the various

NATIONAL BANK AND U.S. MINT, PHILADELPHIA

religious denominations; the Girard College, devoted to the secular education of orphan boys; and the public schools. Many of the above institutions possess extensive and valuable libraries, in addition to which are the large collections belonging to the Library Company, and to the Mercantile Library; and Philadelphia is one of the recognised centres of literary, dramatic, and artistic culture.

In addition to the public squares the chief place of outdoor recreation is Fairmount Park, with an area of 2740 acres, possessing much natural beauty, being well-wooded and having a great variety of surface.

Trade. Philadelphia ranks high as a centre of foreign, inland, and coasting trade. The leading exports are grain, provisions, petroleum, anthracite and gas-coal, iron and ironwares, lumber, tobacco, and cotton (raw and manufactured). The principal imports consist of cotton, woollen, and flax goods, tinplate, iron and iron ore, chemicals, etc. Philadelphia is a great industrial centre, the first in the United States for shipbuilding, locomotives, and carpets. The other leading manufactures include iron and steel, machinery and tools, refined sugar, leather, woollens and cottons, clothing, boots and shoes, beer, and household furniture. It has two broadcasting stations.

History. Philadelphia was founded and named by William Penn in 1682 as the capital of his colony of Pennsylvania. For a long time it was almost exclusively occupied and controlled by Quakers. Many of its most important improvements were due to Benjamin Franklin, and it played a most prominent part during the Revolutionary War. In 1876 (a hundred years after the Declaration of Independence) a Centennial Exhibition was held there. Pop. 1,950,961.

PHILÆ. A small island of the Nile, in Upper Egypt, just above the first cataract, 5 miles south of Aswan. It contains some remarkable ruins, among which are temples, obelisks, etc. The most ancient of the temples was erected by Nectanebus I., the last of the native Pharaohs, about 378-360 B.C. There is also a great temple to Isis, built between 247 and 222 B.C.

PHILANTHROPINISM, or **PHILANTHROPY** (Gr. *philanthropos*, loving humanity). A term applied to the system of education established by Basedow (q.v.). The theories of Basedow are based upon the ideas and teaching of Rousseau, and he introduced a method of instruction which was attractive and pleasant for the pupils. They were not only trained in a gentle manner (hence *philanthropinism*), but were made to study such subjects as were useful and practical.

PHILATELY. The science of collecting postage stamps. The word is derived from the Greek *philos*, loving, and *ateleia*, which means exemption from payment, i.e. stamps took the place of a cash payment at the moment of posting. The hobby sprang into favour within a few years of the issue of the first postage label, which was on 1st May, 1840. On that day the famous "Penny Black" of Great Britain came into existence, its issue being necessitated by the introduction of penny postage on 10th Jan., 1840.

Philatelists are divided into two main groups. The first and larger group comprises those who collect any and every stamp, as long as it is entitled to consideration; whilst the second is composed of enthusiasts who limit their sphere of operations to one definite country, area, or type of stamp.

General collecting is particularly suited to the needs of the young, in so much as it fosters an interest in world-wide matters of history, geography, politics, currency, etc. But the drawback to general collecting lies in the fact that so many stamps have been issued—there are now some 20,000 distinct varieties—that

The Temple on Island of Philae

no one, however enthusiastic he may be, can hope to see more than a small percentage of this huge total represented in his albums.

Specialised collecting, on the other hand, is more likely to find favour with the adult philatelist. As a rule a particular country is chosen, and not only are the regular varieties sought for, but search is made for minute shades of colour, eccentricities of printing, differences of perforation, varying kinds of paper, etc. The skill and perseverance required to bring such a collection to anything approaching finality is, of course, considerable.

One of the most noted collectors of postage stamps of all nations and ages is His Majesty King George V. whose magnificent collection is worth thousands of pounds.

Specialised collections, as we have indicated, are usually concerned with a definite country, but some philatelists select a group that does not depend on any territorial considerations, so that we find albums devoted to stamps used in various wars, stamps printed only by the line-engraving process, stamps bearing the head of one particular monarch, and so on.

Whether the philatelist be a general collector or one who specialises, he needs to exercise great discrimination when gathering together the items for his albums. No stamp which is torn, discoloured, heavily obliterated, or mutilated in the smallest degree should be deemed worthy of a place in the collection. A sharp watch must also be kept for forgeries, of which there are thousands of specimens awaiting the credulous. The expert can identify a forgery by some mysterious intuition; the novice will be seldom misled if he compares each doubtful label with the particulars set out in whichever catalogue he chooses to follow.

But torn specimens and forgeries are not the only items which should be shunned by the discriminating collector. Many genuine stamps are not worth the slightest consideration. We have in mind the issues which certain countries print not so much for postal purposes as to please the eye of the unsuspecting novice. Such speculative issues emanate largely from South and Central America as well as New Europe, and are sold in greater quantities to collectors than to people who wish to frank their letters. As a rule these issues are made to celebrate some event, important or otherwise, and are designed and produced in lavish style.

Among the stamps which will always be prized are the early issues and especially the high values of Great Britain. The embossed adhesives of 1847-54, the first surface-printed issue of 1855, and the series which followed in 1862 increase in value each year. Some of these stamps, it is true, are worth only a few shillings, but others sell for many pounds, while one at least, the 10*d.* red-brown of 1865, changed hands a few years ago for £240. The early issues of Australia, chiefly those printed by Messrs. Perkins, Bacon & Co., are also much sought after, and the same can be said of the first sets of the various Canadian provinces. The original issues of the United States, of France, and of the Italian states are also among the most valuable stamps. All these stamps are gilt-edge investments.

Of one rare and attractive stamp only twenty-six copies are known, but others are probably still awaiting to be unearthed. This is the "Post Office" 2*d.* deep-blue Mauritius, issued in 1847. In Paris, a single copy, nicely post-marked and well preserved, was sold for the fabulous sum of £4670. Some years ago the price was less than £10!

As rare specimens of various issues are being periodically brought to light, those who are lucky enough to chance upon such finds cannot be too strongly urged to dispose of their discoveries with caution. The first offer may be absurdly small, and in the long run the best price is gained at auction. Whilst awaiting a sale, stamps should be most carefully handled, blocks and panes should not be split into small sections, and used specimens must not be torn from their original envelopes.

PHILE'MON. A Greek dramatist of the fourth century B.C. Fragments of his comedies still exist, and are usually printed in editions of Menander, who was his contemporary and rival. He resided for some time at the court of Ptolemy, and is said to have died after laughing too heartily at the success of one of his plays. He was an admirer of Euripides, and said that if he were quite sure that the dead had perception he would hang himself to see Euripides. He was imitated by Plautus in his *Mercator* and *Trinummus.* We have the titles of fifty-seven of his plays, but no complete play.

PHILE'MON, EPISTLE OF PAUL TO. One of the books of the New Testament. This epistle, according to the prevalent opinion, was, together with the epistles to the Ephesians, Colossians, and Philippians, written from Rome during St. Paul's first imprisonment in that city. In this letter Paul appeals to his friend on behalf of one Onesimus, a runaway slave, who had become a convert to Christianity. Paul pleads for the culprit, and even hints at emancipation. The epistle throws light upon the Apostle's attitude towards slavery, and although he does not recommend abolition, he pleads for a humane and brotherly treatment, based on Christian principles.—Cf. J. Moffat, *Introduction to the Literature of the New Testament*.

PHILE'TAS OF COS. Greek grammarian and poet, flourished between 350 and 290 B.C. He wrote elegies, epigrams, and prose grammatical works. He was preceptor to Ptolemy Philadelphus, and a favourite model of Theocritus. Fragments of his poems are extant.

PHIL'IDOR, François André Danican. French musical composer and celebrated chess-player, born 1726, died 1795. He travelled in Holland, Germany, and England, and in 1753 he set Dryden's *Ode for St. Cecilia's Day* to music. He produced about twenty operas at the Opéra Comique, and set to music Horace's *Carmen Seculare*, his best work. The chess opening known as Phillidor's Defence consists in Black replying to White's second move of Kt to KB3 by playing P to Q3.

PHILIP. One of the twelve Apostles, according to John's gospel "of Bethsaida, the city of Andrew and Peter," who was called to follow Jesus at Bethany. In the Western Church he is commemorated on 1st May.

PHILIP. The Evangelist, often confounded with Philip the Apostle, first mentioned in Acts, vi. 5, preached at Smyrna, where Simon Magus was one of his converts; baptised the Ethiopian eunuch; entertained Paul and his companion on their way to Jerusalem, and "had four daughters which did prophesy."

PHILIP II. King of Macedonia, the most famous of the five Macedonian kings of this name, was a son of Amyntas II., born 382 B.C. He passed a portion of his early years in Thebes, where he became well acquainted with Greek literature and politics, and succeeded his elder brother Perdiccas in 360. His position at first was not very secure, but as he had few scruples and was a man of the highest talents both for war and diplomacy, in a short time he had firmly established himself, had reorganised the Macedonian army, and proceeded to extend his sway beyond his own kingdom. His ambition was to make himself, in the first place, supreme in Greece, and to accomplish this he began by seizing the Greek towns on his borders: Amphipolis, which gave him access to the gold-mines of Mount Pangæus, Potidæa, Olynthus, etc.

The "sacred war" carried on by the Amphictyonic Council against the Phocians gave Philip his first opportunity for interfering directly in the affairs of Greece. (*See* GREECE.) After the capture of Methone, between 354 and 352, Philip made himself master of Thessaly, and endeavoured to force the pass of Thermopylæ, but was repulsed by the Athenians; Philip, however, compensated himself by equipping a navy to harass the Athenian commerce. The terror of his name now provoked the *Philippics* of Demosthenes, who endeavoured to rouse the people of Athens to form a general league of the Greeks against him; but by 346 he was master of the Phocian cities and of the pass of Thermopylæ, and as general to the

Philip II of Macedonia

Amphictyon Council he was the crowned protector of the Grecian faith. In the spirit proper to his office he marched into Greece to punish the Locrians for an act of profanity; but instead he seized the city of Elatea, and began to fortify it.

Demosthenes now exerted all his eloquence and statesmanship to raise the ancient spirit of Grecian independence, and a powerful army was soon in the field, but being without able or patriotic commanders, it was defeated at the decisive battle of Chæroneia in Aug., 338 B.C. After this last struggle for freedom Philip was acknowledged chief of the whole Hellenic world, and at a congress held at Corinth he was appointed commander of the Greek forces, and was to organise an expedition against Persia. While preparing for this enterprise he was murdered in 336 B.C., some say at the instigation of his wife Olympias. —Cf. D. G. Hogarth, *Philip and Alexander of Macedon*.

PHILIP I. King of France, son of Henry I., born 1052, died in 1108. He succeeded to the throne under the guardianship of Baldwin V., Count of Flanders, in 1060. The Norman Conquest of England took place in his reign, and he supported Prince Robert, son of the Conqueror, in his revolt against his father. He was a worthless debauchee, and was detested by his subjects.

PHILIP II. Augustus, King of France, born 1165, died in 1223. He was crowned as successor during the lifetime of his father Louis VII. whom he succeeded in 1180. One of his first measures was the banishment of the Jews from the kingdom, and the confiscation of their property. Philip next endeavoured to repress the tryanny and rapacity of the nobles, which he effected partly by art and partly by force.

In 1190 he embarked at Genoa on a crusade to the Holy Land, where he met Richard Cœur de Lion, who was engaged in the same cause in Sicily. The jealousies and disputes which divided the two kings induced Philip to return home the next year. He invaded Normandy during Richard's captivity (1193), confiscated the possessions of King John in France after the death of Prince Arthur (1203), prepared to invade England at the instance of the Pope (1213), turned his arms against Flanders, and gained the celebrated battle of Bouvines (1214).

Philip III of France

PHILIP III. King of France (called the *Hardy*), the son of Louis IX. and Margaret of Provence, born 1245, and died in 1285. He succeeded his father in 1270. In 1271 he possessed himself of Toulouse on the death of his uncle Alphonso; in 1272 he repressed the revolt of Roger, Count of Foix; and in 1276 sustained a war against Alphonso X., King of Castile. The invasion of Sicily by Peter of Aragon, and the massacre of the French, known as "the Sicilian vespers," caused him to make war against that prince.

PHILIP IV. (*Le Bel*). King of France, born in 1268, and died in 1314. He married Joanna, Queen of Navarre, in 1284, and succeeded his father in 1285. He attempted to take Guienne from Edward I. of England, but afterwards entered into an alliance with that monarch, and gave him his daughter in marriage (1299), from which originated the claim of Edward III. to the crown of France.

He was long engaged in war with Flanders, and treated the country as a French dependency, but was defeated at Courtrai in 1302. Philip had been engaged at the same time in a violent dispute with Pope Boniface VIII., and he publicly burned the Pope's Bull excommunicating him. On the death of Boniface and of Benedict XI., Clement V., who succeeded the latter, was elected by the influence of Philip, and fixed his residence at Avignon.

The result of the king's alliance with the new Pope was the destruction of the order of the Templars (1307-12), and the seizure by the king of their goods and estates was one of its fruits. Philip left numerous ordinances for the administration of the kingdom, which mark the decline of feudalism and the growth of the royal power. He also convoked and consulted the States General for the first time.—Cf. E. Boutaric, *La France sous Philippe le Bel.*

PHILIP VI. (of Valois). King of France, first of the Valois line, born in 1293, died in 1350. He was the nephew of Philip IV., to whose last son, Charles IV., he succeeded in virtue of the Salique law. In his reign occurred the wars with Edward III. of England, who claimed the French crown as grandson, by his mother, of Philip IV. His reign was unfortunate for France on account of the beginning of the Hundred Years' War; and he has left an evil memory by his persecutions of Jews and heretics, his confiscations and exactions.

PHILIP II. (of Spain). The son of Charles V. and Isabella of Portugal, was born at Valladolid in 1527, died in 1598. He was married in succession to the Princess Mary of Portugal (1543), and to Mary of England in 1554, the same year in which he became King of Naples and Sicily by the abdication of his father. In 1555 his father resolved to abdicate the sovereignty of the Netherlands in Philip's favour. This was done in public assembly at Brussels on 25th Oct., 1555; and on 16th Jan., 1556, in the same hall he received, in presence of the Spanish grandees then in the Netherlands, the crown of Spain, with its possessions in Asia, Africa, and America. His first act was to propose a truce with France, which was broken almost as soon as concluded. On the death of Mary in 1558 Philip made proposals of marriage to her sister and successor, Elizabeth, but was refused. In 1559 the French War was concluded by the Peace of Câteau-Cambrésis and the marriage of Philip to Elizabeth of France, daughter of Henri II.

The king then returned to Spain, resolved upon checking the progress which the Reformation had made there. On his arrival in his native country he had the satisfaction of being present at an *auto-de-fé*; and a few years' perseverance in similar measures extinguished the light of the Reformation, together with the spirit of freedom and enterprise in Spain.

In Naples, as in Spain, his zeal led him to persecute the Protestants; but it was in the Netherlands that his bigotry and obstinacy had their most disastrous, though ultimately fortunate results. In 1566 the revolt of the Netherlands commenced, which ended in the separation of the seven northern provinces from the crown of Spain, and their formation into the Dutch Republic. This struggle lasted about thirty years, till the close of Philip's reign. The rebellion ruined the prosperity of Philip's dominions, whilst Spain's naval supremacy was shattered by the defeat of the Armada which Philip sent against England in 1588.

Few kings have been the subjects of so much historical controversy or so diversely judged as Philip of Spain. Execrated by not a few, he was worshipped by others. He was the "prudent king" of the Spaniards, and the "demon of the south" of the Protestants. Impartial modern historians, however, agree that although full of faults, he was not without virtues. "He had devoted his life to the task of establishing the universal supremacy of Catholicism." He looked upon himself as a sort of junior partner of Providence, and he did not scruple to encourage cruelty and assassination if they furthered his purpose. Even Catholics admit that "imbued with ideas of absolutism, he was led into acts disapproved by the moral law." On the other hand, he was industrious, pious, and to some extent conscientious, and he was also a patron of arts.—BIBLIOGRAPHY: M. A. S. Hume, *Spain: its Greatness and Decay*; *Philip II.*; W. H. Prescott, *History of the Reign of Philip II.*; H. Forneron, *Histoire de Philippe II.*

PHILIP V. (of Spain). The first Spanish king of the Bourbon dynasty, was born at Versailles 1683, died 1746. He was the grandson of Louis XIV. of France, and succeeded to the crown of Spain by the will of Charles II., who died without direct heirs, as the grandson of Charles's elder sister. On the death of Charles in Nov., 1700, he was immediately proclaimed king, and the result was the War of the Spanish Succession, which began in 1702. By the Treaty of Utrecht (1713) he was recognised as King of Spain, but Gibraltar was lost to Spain, Minorca was also ceded to England, Sicily to Savoy, the Netherlands, Naples, and the Milanese to Austria. He married Elizabeth Farnese, niece of the Duke of Parma, in 1714, and Alberoni, the minister of the Duke of Parma in Spain, became Prime-Minister. The king was, however, compelled to dismiss him in 1719, on account of the hostility aroused among Powers against Alberoni, who wished to regain the lost Spanish possessions in Italy.

In 1724 Philip resigned the crown of Spain in favour of his son Don Louis, but the death of Louis a few months later induced him to resume the royal power. Philip was constantly governed by favourites, and his constitutional melancholy at last completely incapacitated him for business.

PHILIP (*the Bold*). Duke of Burgundy, son of John II., King of France, born in 1342, died in 1404. He fought at Poitiers (1356), where, according to Froissart, he acquired the surname of the Bold. He shared his father's captivity in England, and on his return his father, whose favourite he was, made him Duke of Touraine, gave him the Duchy of Burgundy, and made him premier peer of France. Philip was one of the most powerful French princes during the minority of Charles VI., during whose insanity he acted as regent, retaining the regency till his death.

PHILIPHAUGH. A locality in Scotland 1 mile S.W. of Selkirk, the scene of Sir David Leslie's victory over the Marquess of Montrose, 13th Sept., 1645. A monument marks the field.

PHILIPPEVILLE (ancient **RUSI-**

CADA). A city and port of Algeria, the chief town of an arrondissement in the department of Constantine, on the Bay of Stora; served by railway connecting with Constantine, Batna, and Biskra, for which it is the seaward terminus. It was founded by the French in 1837, but occupies the site of successive Phœnician and Roman settlements, and the Roman reservoirs, largely restored and fed by canal from the Wadi Beni Meleh, are still the source of Philippeville's water-supply. There are remains also of a Roman amphitheatre. In 1914 the city was bombarded by the cruisers *Goeben* and *Breslau*. Pop. 47,750.

PHILIP'PI. A city of Macedonia, now in ruins, founded by Philip of Macedon about 356 B.C. The two battles fought in 42 B.C., which resulted in the overthrow of Brutus and Cassius by Antony and Octavius, were fought here. Philippi was visited on several occasions by the Apostle Paul, who addressed to the Church there one of his epistles.

PHILIP'PIANS, Epistle to the. One of St. Paul's epistles. The keynote of the letter is an expression of the sentiments of joy and gratitude which the Apostle cherishes in regard to the Philippians. The epistle is supposed to have been written from Rome towards the close of his first imprisonment there, about A.D. 63. Some authorities suppose it to have been written in Cæsarea. The genuineness of this epistle has been little questioned. It is referred to, though not quoted, in the epistle of Polycarp and by Tertullian and other early Fathers. Epaphroditus, who conveyed it, was the messenger of the Philippians to Paul, and had been ill at Rome, which had been a cause of anxiety to the Philippians. Paul, therefore, hastened his return, and sent this epistle by him.

PHILIPPINE ISLANDS. The largest island group of the Malay Archipelago, extending between Taiwan in the north and Borneo and the Moluccas in the south, and embracing in its 2441 named islands (another 4642 are unnamed) an area of 114,400 sq. miles. The population (1930 estimate) is 12,604,100, the indigenous population being of Malay extraction, and 91·5 per cent of Christian faith, mainly Roman Catholic.[1] Manila (q.v.) is the capital and administrative centre.

The eleven principal islands are: Luzon (area, 40,814 sq. miles); Mindanao (36,906 sq. miles); Samar (5124 sq. miles); Negros (4903 sq. miles); Palawan (4500 sq. miles); Panay (4448 sq. miles); Mindoro (3794 sq. miles); Leyte (2799 sq. miles); Cebú (1695 sq. miles); Bohol (1534 sq. miles); and Masbate (1255 sq. miles). Iloilo on Panay (pop.) 67,143, Cebú on Cebú (86,152), Zamboanga on Mindanao (47,302), and Laoag (40,879), Legaspi or Albay (33,000), Vigan (19,939), and Naga (9468) on Luzon are the principal towns. As in India, there is a summer capital, Baguio, in the Mountain Province, the Philippine Simla.

Climate. The average temperatures are high, with excessive humidity,

A scene in the Phillipines

a heavy rainfall, and occasional typhoons of exceptional violence which usually cause much loss of life.

Communications. Manila is the great centre of both *Thalassic* and *Oceanic* inter-communication and trade, the other principal ports being Iloilo (Panay) and Cebú (Cebú). There are 837 miles of railway (1931), 705 miles being Government controlled, and inland water-ways are navigable for many miles by small craft and by bamboo rafts.

Production. The staple products are manila hemp (abacá), rice, sugar-cane, coco-nuts, tobacco, maguey, and corn, rice being the most important crop and the staple native food. Agriculture is the principal industry, but is very primitive. Coco-nut oil is manufactured in nine large factories. Over 70,000 sq. miles of the Philippines are afforested, and produce gums and resins, bamboo, rattan, and dye-woods. Gold, iron, silver, manganese, and copper are among metallic minerals. Natural mineral-waters, salt, gems, gypsum, natural gas, petroleum, asbestos,

[1] There is an independent Filipino Church, founded in 1901, but their religious dogmas are practically identical with those of the Roman Catholic Church.

lime, clay, stone, and coal are also worked. Hats made from pandan, bamboo, etc., form an important article of manufacture and export to Great Britain and other European countries, and to the United States.

Commerce. The great bulk of trade is with the United States, Japan, and China, but exports to Great Britain and the Netherlands are large and steady.

Education. Education is free and undenominational, English being the recognised language. There is a State University of the Philippines, and a Roman Catholic university (San Tomas) controlled by the Dominican order. Public newspapers and periodicals include English, Spanish, bi-lingual (English-Spanish), Chinese, and many others in miscellaneous dialects and tongues; the total being 195.

Government. The Philippines are administered by a Governor-General representing the United States. He is appointed by the President of the United States in consultation with the Senate of that Power. In the same manner, a Vice-Governor is appointed to fill the office of Secretary of Public Instruction. The Governor-General is the chief executive, and under him are the six executive departments of the Interior, Public Instruction, Agriculture, Commerce and Communications, Finance, and Justice. There is a legislature comprising a Senate (24 members, 22 elected and 2 appointed) and a House of Representatives (96 members, all elected by popular vote).

The Council of State connects the legislative and executive bodies, and comprises the Governor-General (President), the respective Presidents of the Senate and House of Representatives, and the departmental secretaries, who are all Filipinos. There are 36 provinces and 12 "special" provinces, the latter being managed by a Bureau of non-Christian Tribes, and the former individually by officials elected on a popular vote.

History. Magellan discovered the Philippines in March, 1521, and was killed on the Island of Mactan. He named the archipelago San Lazarus. Villabos named some of the islands the "Islas Filipinas," and, in an expedition fitted out by Philip II. of Spain (1561), the sailing directions make use of the new title as covering the entire archipelago. San Miguel was founded by Miguel Lopez de Degaspi in 1565, and was the first permanent Spanish settlement. Under Spanish rule missionaries were imported, and the Roman Catholic faith was preached throughout the islands.

In 1762 Manila was taken and held until 1764 by a British fleet of thirteen ships under Admiral Cornish, and the Americans seized it in 1898 (Spanish-American War). By a treaty signed at Paris on 10th Dec., 1898, the islands passed from Spain to the United States, under whose government economic development has been steady and political stability assured.—BIBLIOGRAPHY: L. H. Fernandez, *The Philippine Republic*; W. C. Forbes, *The Philippine Islands*; D. R. Williams, *The United States and the Philippines*; K. Mayo, *The Isles of Fear*; Dean C. Worcester, *The Philippines, Past and Present.*

PHILIPPOP'OLIS, or PLOVDIV. A city of Bulgaria, on the Maritsa; served by the Sofia-Istanbul trunk line of the transcontinental railway from Vienna, via Belgrade. The city is built mainly on a hill which overlooks the river, and is the centre of a large trade, its manufactures being silk, cotton, and leather. Philippopolis is so named from Philip of Macedon, who captured the Thracian town of Eumolpia, which he made a frontier post. As a Roman city (*Trimontium*) it was the capital of Thracia. Pop. (1926), 84,655.

PHILIPPSBURG. A town of Baden on the Rhine; served by the Bruchsal-Germersheim Railway. It was formerly a celebrated imperial fortress. In 1734 it was captured by the French under the Duke of Berwick (who lost his life here), and its fortifications were razed in 1800. Pop. about 4000.

PHILIPS, Ambrose. English poetaster, born of a Leicester family in 1671, died 1749. He was educated at St. John's College, Cambridge, and subsequently became one of the wits who frequented "Button's coffee-house" in London. As a Whig politician he obtained various lucrative posts from the House of Hanover, while as a poet he was ridiculed by Swift and Pope, receiving the nickname of "Namby Pamby." He wrote six pastorals and three tragedies: *The Distrest Mother* (1712), taken from Racine; *The Briton* (1722); and *Humphrey, Duke of Gloucester* (1723).

PHILIPS, John. An English poet, born in Oxfordshire 1676, died at Hereford 1708. He was educated at Christ Church, Oxford, where he produced *The Splendid Shilling*, a burlesque poem in Miltonic blank verse. He subsequently wrote *Blenheim*, a poem in celebration of the Duke of Marlborough's victory;

and *Cyder*, a work in imitation of Virgil's *Georgics*.

PHILIS'TINES. The name of a people or race who lived south-west of Judæa, on the coast of the Mediterranean Sea. They came from Caphtor (Egy. *Kptar*), now identified with Crete (*Amos*, ix., 7), and permanently settled in Canaan during the reign of Rameses III. (about 1200-1169 B.C.). They occupied five cities, Ashdod, Gaza, Gath, Ashkelon, and Ekron, which formed a kind of confederacy under five lords or chiefs.

They then established themselves all over the land, which has been named Palestine after them. During the reigns of Saul and David they had attained their highest power, but being constantly at war with the Hebrews, they were several times defeated by the latter. The country of the Philistines was subdued by Tiglath-Pileser (734 B.C.) and their independence entirely crushed by Sennacherib, and Zidka of Ashkelon, who ruled also over Joppa, was carried off to Assyria.

Racially there is much similarity between the Philistines and other Mediterranean peoples. They were to a certain extent advanced in civilisation when they came to Syria, had a knowledge of metals, were the inventors of the art of the smith, had iron tools and weapons, and most probably a system of writing.

It was, above all, their political organisation which distinguished the Philistines from their Semitic neighbours. They seem to have possessed a deeper sense of individual liberty, and to have enjoyed more freedom than the Semites. Nothing is known of their original speech. In Syria they adopted the language of Canaan, and in the time of Nehemiah the speech of Ashdod still differed from that of Jerusalem. Their principal god was Dagon, who had temples at Gaza and Ashdod. They also worshipped Astarte and Baal.—Cf. R. A. S. Macalister, *The Philistines: their History and Civilisation*.

PHILLIP, John. British painter, one of the greatest colourists of the British school, born at Aberdeen 1817, died 1867. He came to London in 1836 and studied at the schools of the Royal Academy. From 1838 to 1851 his pictures consisted mainly of portraits and subjects from Scottish life, such as *The Catechism* (1847), *The Baptism* (1850), and *The Scotch Washing* (1851). In 1852 and 1856 he visited Spain, and he again returned to that country in 1860. While resident there he was greatly influenced by the works of the Spanish masters, and especially by those of Velasquez. His style completely changed, his subjects became Spanish, and his grasp of colour, composition, and character vastly improved. It is his pictures of Spanish life that have made him famous.

PHILLIPS, Stephen. British dramatist and poet, born in 1868, and died in 1915. He was educated at Stratford and Peterborough, and was for a short time at Queens' College, Cambridge. For six years he was a member of Sir F. R. Benson's dramatic company, and, after being an army tutor, he adopted literature as a profession. His principal volumes of poetry are *Marpessa* (1890), *Eremus* (1894), and *Christ in Hades* (1896).

In response to a certain demand for a literary drama, Phillips wrote *Paolo and Francesca* (1900), which was produced at the St. James's Theatre in 1901. It was extremely successful, owing its success, however, not so much to its literary merits as to the total absence of such merits in contemporary dramas. His other plays include: *Herod* (1900), *Ulysses* (1902), *The Sin of David* (1904) and *Nero* (1906). None of these was so popular as *Paolo and Francesca*. They are all somewhat florid and declamatory, but have some value as stage-plays owing to their author's practical knowledge of the stage. Phillips to some extent outlived his reputation.

PHILLIPS, Wendell. American abolitionist, born at Boston, United States, 1811, died 1884. He was educated at Harvard University, studied law, and was called to the Bar (1834); joined the movement for the abolition of slavery in 1837 and gave it the aid of his oratorical gifts and unremitting advocacy until in 1865 the negroes of the United States were made free citizens. His *Speeches, Letters, and Lectures* were published in 1863.

PHILLPOTTS, Eden. British novelist and dramatist. Born in India, 4th Nov., 1862, and educated at Plymouth, he published a series of novels with a Devonshire and especially a Dartmoor setting. These include *Children of the Mist* (1898), *The American Prisoner* (1904), *The Mother* (1908), and *Widecombe Fair* (1913). Of his plays, *The Farmer's Wife* (1917) and *Yellow Sands* (1926) were outstanding successes, also *Buy a Broom* (1929), *Jane's Legacy* (1931). He also published in 1931 a book of essays, *A Point of View*.

PHILO (often called *Philo Judæus*). Jewish philosopher and theologian, born at Alexandria about 20 B.C.

He belonged to a wealthy family and received a liberal education, being brought up in the Alexandrian school of hellenised Judaism. The Hebrew Scriptures he knew only through the *Septuagint*. In A.D. 40 he was sent as one of a deputation from the Jews of Alexandria to the Emperor Caligula, to persuade him to revoke the decree by which he compelled the Jews to pay divine honours to his statue.

Philosophy. Philo's philosophy was strictly theosophical, resting on the Scriptures, as an inspired revelation, and those systems of Greek philosophy which best harmonised with the Scriptures, such as the philosophy of the Stoics and of Plato. He conceived the Deity as transcendent, most universal of beings, higher than knowledge, goodness, or beauty *per se*, and manifesting Himself in the material universe by His creative activity or operations, nowhere in His essence. Between God and the world he places the Logos, which he calls the Son of God, the Paraclete, and Mediator between God and man. It contains in itself the powers or spiritual forms which pervade the universe, and which are creative. Out of unqualified matter, passive and lifeless, destitute of form and quality, God created the world by means of the Logos, or the agencies and potencies residing in it. The law, Philo maintained, was an emanation from Him who was both the creator and the father of the universe, and in harmony with nature.—BIBLIOGRAPHY: J. Drummond, *Philo Judæus*; Schürer, *The Jewish People in the Time of Jesus Christ*.

PHILOLOGY AND LINGUISTICS. The term *philology* originally meant the study, both literary and linguistic, of the writings of a people, especially of the Greeks and the Romans. It was an historical science, concerned with the critical study of literature from the archæological, artistic, and mythological points of view. It included, in addition to the study of national cultural values—for it investigated writings of a people for the purpose of learning its thoughts, culture, and art—also a linguistic side. On the Continent the term is still used in this sense, whilst the science of language itself is termed *linguistique* in France, or *Sprachwissenschaft* in Germany.

Indeed there is a vast difference between philology and the science of language, the former being an historical, the latter a natural science which studies the constituent elements of a language, and the various forms and changes which these elements undergo, or are capable of undergoing. It treats of sounds and word formation, syntax (correct use), and developments of meanings. It is therefore divided into *phonetics*, or *phonology*, *morphology* (Gr. *morphē*, shape), *comparative syntax*, and *semasiology* (Gr. *semasia*, meaning). Schleicher (1821-68) rightly pointed out that the student of language resembles the botanist, who studies plants and the laws of their structure, whilst the philologist is more like a horticulturist, who cares more for the beauty of form, for colour and perfume.

In England, however, the term philology, in its modern usage, is applied to the science of language, and when we speak of philologists we mean the students of language and of its principles in general. When, for purposes of comparison, this science, instead of limiting itself to *one* language, includes several languages of a kindred group, it becomes comparative, and is termed *comparative philology*. The reason of this shifting of the term and its application to linguistics is due to the fact that the first scholars who inaugurated the science of language were philologists, or students of national culture and of the criticism of ancient literature.

The Origin of Language. Of the origin of speech we know little. From very early times speech has been recognised as the chief criterion whereby to distinguish man from the brutes. Yet, as elsewhere in nature, the hard-and-fast line is drawn only by man to suit the systems which he constructs; in nature itself clearly marked divisions are not conspicuous.

Darwin observed in the case of the dog that the species which had associated with man, and had, so to speak, shared in his civilisation, had developed several notes which are entirely wanting in the cry of the wild dog. It may be plausibly argued that the same is true of man; that he, possessing at first but a few incoherent and inarticulate cries to indicate pleasure or pain, amazement or fear, developed in process of time, as his needs and his skill in supplying them increased, a system of sounds which conveyed those impressions with more precision to his associates. Most animals, at any rate probably all gregarious animals, are able to impart to their comrades warning of impending danger, or to indicate the proximity of food. But, so far as we can tell, man is the only animal which can communicate information to his fellows regarding the nature of the impending danger, or the kind of food which he has discovered. Man has therefore rightly been defined as "a speaking animal."

Besides the cries of pain, pleasure, and other feelings to which the first elements of language have been attributed, a considerable number of sounds arose from imitation of animals' cries. Imitation may arise from two causes, from delight in mimicry, or from the inspiration of necessity as an aid in the arts of hunting. It is no doubt true that many of the imitative (onomatopoeic) forms of modern languages are of comparatively recent origin; but we have no reason to believe that forces operating in recent times in language have not operated throughout the history of the race, while the necessity for these imitative sounds was, in primitive times, certainly more pressing. Moreover, whatever the natural gifts of the human being for the art of mimicry, it is certain that in the early years of childhood, after the first months of infancy are passed, imitation is the method by which most things are learnt. The theories which attribute the origin of language to imitation and exclamation are known respectively as the *bow-wow* and *pooh-pooh* theories.

A third possible source of language ought also to be mentioned. Children have often been observed in their play to invent a vocabulary for themselves, a great deal of which was composed of babbling sounds, without reference to the words of the language that they knew. Often words of this sort, or others which have been manufactured out of ordinary words metamorphosed beyond recognition by infantile talk, remain a part of the nursery vocabulary long after the speakers are perfectly competent to talk the language of their parents. The nursery language is not permanent, because of the overpowering influence of the language current in the larger world outside; it would not, however, be unreasonable to assume that primitive man, who was more like the infant in his development, and was not exposed to similar external influences, may have manufactured no small part of his vocabulary on the same principles.

It is this side of language which most closely approaches to singing. Some authorities, indeed, contend, and not without plausibility, that man might with equal propriety be defined as a singing animal. The difference between speech and song consists in the greater variety of pitch which prevails in the latter, and in the more rhythmic intervals between the sounds.

It has been observed that the higher the civilisation of a people the more monotonous is the pitch of its language. All languages, however even though, like English, they may carry this monotony very far, nevertheless vary the pitch of individual words and syllables in the sentence. Some of the languages belonging to the same family as English, such as Swedish and Norwegian, retain a large number of tones, which literary English has lost, though tones of the same sort may be heard in various English dialects.

Another problem connected with the origin of language is that of the relation between speech and thought. Professor Max Müller held very emphatically that thought was impossible without speech, and conversely that speech was impossible without thought, the two being facets, as it were, of the same diamond. The first part of the theory was held strongly also by the German philosopher Noiré. Professor Max Müller's theories and views have been contradicted by W. D. Whitney (1827-94) in his famous work *Life and Growth of Language*.

Change in Language. Language is ever in a state of flux. Even when to some extent stereotyped by the existence of a literature, it is continually changing. We have only to think of the tremendous changes which have taken place within the last thousand years in English—the tongue of a community with a continuous literature and uninterrupted political development—to realise how great in a short time the changes might easily be in a small community loosely held together and without either literature or stable political institutions. Nor is the possibility of change confined to vocabulary. The pronunciation of language is continually changing. In Queen Anne's time *tea* was pronounced, as it still is dialectically in Scotland and Ireland, *tae* or *tay*.

Here thou great Anna whom three realms obey,
Dost sometimes counsel take and sometimes tea.

Since the time of the poet Cowper *balcony* has followed the analogy of the majority of English words, and has transferred its accent from the second syllable to the first. Even in the present day, when communication between all parts of the world is so easy, the pronunciation of an American is easily distinguishable from that of an Englishman, even if there be no difference in vocabulary. Another type of English bids fair to develop in Australia. And here it is of importance to note that there is no necessary connection between race and language, although it is a frequent and widespread error to assume that different portions of the same race will talk the same language, or at any rate languages closely akin. Yet instances within the period covered by historical records will illustrate the fallacy. The people of Cornwall and of Wales are of the same origin; but while in Wales the language is still spoken which was spoken at the time of the Saxon invasion, in Cornwall it has been replaced by English. Similarly, the Roman conquest of ancient France (Gaul) caused the inhabitants to resign their earlier language in favour of a dialectic form of Latin, the language of their conquerors from Italy.

The alterations and changes of a language are due to various causes. They are either connected with the mechanism of speech, and are called phonetic change (*see* PHONETICS), or are due to assimilation. The greatest change-effecting cause in language is, however, analogy. Language consists in the communication, by means of sounds, of one's ideas; it is an improvement upon gesture and is less laborious. Now this tendency of labour-saving always continues, and the human mind is always ready to simplify and to systematise. All the phenomena of formation or change in language due to that instinct of simplifying are classed under analogy. The notion of a plural, for instance, was commonly associated with the sign *s*, and people consequently said *eyes* and *heads*, instead of *eyn* and *head*, just as children will say *foots* and *mans*. The evolution of language has therefore always been in the direction of the least effort, not only to the speaker, but also to the hearer.

The history of the vocabulary of a language—of its words as distinct from its sounds—is no less complicated than that of the sounds themselves. In any language the part that consists of original creations is comparatively small. A large proportion of the words are formations derived, as we have just seen, by additions and modifications of various kinds from words already existing. A third series of words, which in most languages form an important part of the whole vocabulary, consists of words taken over either from other dialects of the same language or from other languages. No language is so remarkable in this respect as English, the vocabulary of which includes words borrowed from almost every language under the sun.

With regard to words borrowed from other dialects of the language itself, this may be exemplified by the fact that in English the southern *vat* has replaced the older *fat* still found in the Bible (twice in *Joel*), while *fox* has displaced the older *vox*, which still survives in its feminine *vixen*. From northern dialects the borrowings have been more numerous. The same influences affect the syntax of a language. Languages of kindred formation probably affect one another most readily. On the other hand, the syntax of English has to some extent been modified by French influences.

Morphology. According to the structure of the words (*morphology*), philologists have classified the languages of the world into three great divisions, including within them various families of languages which are similar in formation but are not necessarily directly related.

1. **Isolating Languages.** Of these Chinese is the most typical. Here there is no difference distinguishable between the parts of speech. Each symbol of the extremely complicated system of writing represents a monosyllabic word which expresses a general idea without regard to the nature of that idea, or to whether it has the value of a verb or of a substantive. The meaning of the passage has to be gathered (*a*) from the order of the words, (*b*) from the intonation. In Chinese, and also in the other monosyllabic languages, though to a less extent, there are a number of tones which distinguish words containing the same articulated sounds one from another.

2. **Agglutinative Languages.** Here suffixes are added to roots to indicate various relations. The same suffixes appear in the verb and in the substantive in different relations. Thus in Hungarian, which is one of these languages, we find:

ház-unk, our house.	***var-unk***, we sow.
háza-tok, your (plural) house.	***var-tok***, you sow.
ház-ok, their house.	***var-n-ak***, they sow.

Owing to the possibility of adding together a great number of suffixes in the agglutinative languages, there is no difficulty in expressing a statement of considerable length by one word. The boundary-line between agglutinative and inflectional languages is not always easy to draw. Thus Finnish, the most highly developed of these languages, appears, as far as its substantive is concerned, to be an inflectional language of a very elaborate kind, there being at least fifteen cases. Contrary to the practice of inflectional languages like Latin or Greek, the same suffix is applied to the same case in both singular and plural.

3. **Inflectional Languages.** These

are represented by the two groups of the Semitic and Indo-European languages. It is from the speakers of languages of these two groups that almost everything most beneficial to the development of the human race has sprung.

The Semitic languages are: (*a*) Hebrew, closely akin to which were the other ancient dialects of Canaan, Moabite, Phœnician, etc.; (*b*) Arabic, widely spread as the result of Mahommedan conquests; (*c*) Aramaic, the language of ancient Syria, which in Palestine also had taken the place of Hebrew as a spoken language before the Christian era; and (*d*) Assyrian, which has been recovered from countless inscriptions upon clay tablets found on the sites of ancient cities like Nineveh and Babylon. The different Semitic languages do not differ more from one another than do Romance languages like French, Italian, and Spanish. The most characteristic feature of the Semitic language is that, with rare exceptions, all roots have three consonants or semi-consonants, which, in combination with vowels, form series of words. The verb system is much less perfectly developed than that of the Indo-Germanic languages.

Indo-European Languages. To the Indo-European system belong a number of languages and dialects which fall easily into nine groups. These languages are widely spread, extending from India to Iceland in the Old World, and since the end of the fifteenth century having been disseminated over the whole of America, Australia, New Zealand, and the East Indies as the language of European conquerors or colonisers of those lands.

The system has been called by other names, as Aryan, which is, however, more appropriately applied to the most easterly group of the languages. The name Indo-European is commonly used, but seems to imply that the languages are spoken only in India and Europe, which is inaccurate, as is also the notion that all Indian and European languages belong to this system. In Southern India the Dravidian languages, of which the chief representatives are Tamil and Telugu, are agglutinative languages, and therefore of a different type, while in Europe, Turkish, Hungarian, Finnish, and Lapp belong to an agglutinative system.

Parent-speech. The languages belonging to this system are descended from an original language long since lost. Where this language was spoken it is difficult definitely to decide. The best authorities incline to the view that it was in the great plain between the Baltic and the Black Sea. The language was highly developed before the Indo-Germanic community broke up. Before the languages separated one from another this original speech had at least seven cases in the noun declension besides the vocative, which is the bare stem. In the verb there was a very elaborate distinction of two voices—active and middle, of three moods—indicative, subjunctive, and optative. The imperative was to the verb what the vocative was to the noun, simply the bare stem, while the infinitive is in all the languages only stereotyped case forms from various noun stems.

The Nine Groups of the Indo-European System. 1. The first member of the nine groups into which this family of languages is divided is the *Indian*. The earliest representative of this is Sanskrit. The earliest literature belonging to the Indo-European family is contained in the hymns of the *Rig Veda*, some of which go back to 1500 or 2000 years B.C., while some authorities would put them much earlier. A further stage in the breakdown of the form system is seen in Prakrit, and later in Pâli, which stands in the same relation to Sanskrit as Italian does to Latin. Pâli was the language of the great Buddhist revival, which had spread over a large part of India by 270 B.C. The modern dialects of Northern India, Hindi, Bengali, etc., and the language of the Gipsies are still more decadent descendants of Sanskrit.

2. *Iranian*, including Zend (Old Bactrian), was the language spoken in ancient times in the eastern part of the Persian Empire. It is the language of the religion of Zoroaster, which still survives among the fire-worshippers of Eastern Persia and the Parsis of Bombay. Within Zend there is noticeable a difference of dialect between the hymns (*Gatha*) and the rest of the Zoroastrian literature, the hymns being more archaic than the rest, and standing in the same relation to the later Avesta that the *Veda* does to classical Sanskrit.

The Old Persian of the cuneiform inscriptions (see *Cuneiform Writing*) begins with the inscriptions of Darius Hystaspes (about 520 B.C.). These, and above all the great Behistun inscription engraved on the face of a precipitous cliff 300 feet from the ground, are the most important, but others of various dates exist down to about 350 B.C.

3. Proceeding westwards, the next member of the stock which we find is the *Armenian*. This language,

which possesses a literature going back to the fifth century A.D., is so full of Iranian words that till 1875 it was looked upon as a branch of Iranian. It differs, however, from Iranian in preserving the original sounds.

4. More important in the history of the world is the next group—*Greek.* The earliest Greek writings preserved to us are the Homeric poems. The language of these poems, however, is clearly a literary language—Epic—and not the spoken dialect of a particular place. Owing to the geographical formation of Greece, the language was broken up into a multitude of dialects.

5. Next in order comes *Albanian,* the modern representative of the ancient Illyrian. This has only recently been recognised as a separate member of the system, its vocabulary being even more packed with foreign words than is Armenian. Latin, Slavonic, Greek, and Turkish have all contributed some elements. Its literature does not extend farther back than the seventeenth century.

6. *Italic,* or the dialects of Italy. These fall, on the one hand, into Latin and the little-known dialects of Falerii and Præneste; on the other hand, into Oscan, the language of the ancient Samnites and of Campania; the dialects of various smaller tribes, including the Sabines, Pelignians, etc.; and the dialect of Umbria, in North-Eastern Italy. Vulgar Latin was the parent of the Romance languages, which are: French, Italian Spanish, Portuguese, Rhæto-Romanic or Roumansch (spoken in East Switzerland), Rumanian, and Provençal. The earliest inscriptions (one of a brooch found at Præneste in 1886, another on a broken pyramidal pillar discovered during excavations in the Roman Forum in 1899) do not go farther back than the sixth century B.C. The classical period of the literature is comprised within the century preceding and the century following the birth of Christ. The later literature, however, is of great interest to the student of language.

7. *Celtic.* Here the ancient language of Gaul, of which some fragments remain. Welsh, Cornish, and Breton—the language of settlers from Cornwall in the ancient Armorica—form one group, while Irish, Scottish Gaelic, and Manx form the other. The oldest Runic, or Ogham, inscriptions go back probably to A.D. 500 or 600. In Irish and Welsh there is a large literature, beginning with the eleventh or twelfth century.

8. The *Germanic* or *Teutonic* dialects. The oldest literature in these is the fragmentary Gothic translation of the Bible made by Bishop Wulfila (Ulfilas) in the fourth century. The Norse, the earliest remains of which are the Runic inscriptions from Jutland and Schleswig, which date probably as early as the third or fourth century A.D., splits after the age of the Vikings into four dialects—Icelandic, Norwegian, Swedish and Danish. Icelandic possesses the best early literature in any Germanic language. A third group of these dialects is the West Germanic, comprising Old English (Anglo-Saxon), Frisian, Low German, Low Franconian (whence Dutch and Flemish), and High German. The English settlers in Britain came from Friesland and the neighbouring coasts as far as Jutland, and in the fifth century A.D. ousted the Britons from the eastern side of England and drove them into the mountainous districts of the west.

9. The *Slavonic* group. This group falls into two sections: (*a*) the Baltic or Lettic, including Lithuanian and Lettish, which are still living languages, and Old Prussian; (*b*) Slavonic proper, which includes a great variety of dialects, the oldest literature existing in the Old Bulgarian or Old Church Slavonic.

Comparative Philology. The evidence that all these languages are closely akin is to be found in the great number of words that they possess in common, in the similarity of their structure, their inflections, their manner of compounding words—in short, in their family likeness. This likeness can only be accounted for by supposing that these languages are all descended from one common language, the primitive Teutonic, which must have been spoken at a remote period by the ancestors of the present Teutonic peoples, there being then only one Teutonic people as well as one Teutonic tongue. In their earliest form, therefore, and when they began to be differentiated, these languages must have had the character of mere dialects, and it is only in so far as each has had a history and literature of its own that they have attained the rank of independent languages.

How remote the period may have been when the ancestors of the Teutons, the Celts, the Slavs, the Greeks, Romans, Persians, and Hindus were living together and speaking a common language is uncertain. Yet the general character of their language is approximately known, and philologists tell us with some confidence what consonant and what vowel sounds the Aryan parent-speech must have possessed, which were the forms of its inflections, and what, at the least, must have been the extent of its vocabulary, judging from the words that can still be traced as forming a common possession of the sister tongues of the family.

Grimm's Law. In order to understand how it is that many words in the different Aryan tongues have the same origin, though superficially they may appear very different, it is necessary to know something of Grimm's Law. This law, which, like a natural law, is simply a statement of observed facts, is so named from the great philologist who first definitely laid it down as the result of observation and comparison of the relative linguistic phenomena. It concerns the so-called "mute" consonants (*t, d, th*; *k, g, h, (ch)*; *p, b, f*), and takes effect more especially when these are initial.

According to it, in words and roots that form a common possession of the Aryan tongues, being inherited by them from the parent-speech, where in English (more especially Anglo-Saxon) and in most of the Teutonic tongues we find *t, d,* or *th,* we find in Latin, Greek, and Sanskrit not these letters, but respectively *d* instead of *t,* an aspirated sound instead of *d,* and *t* instead of *th.* That is, an English *t* corresponds to a Latin, Greek, and Sanskrit *d,* as is seen in *tame,* compared with Lat. *domare,* Gr. *damaein,* Skt. *dam,* to tame; and English *d* corresponds to Latin *f,* Greek *th,* Sanskrit *dh,* as in Eng. *door,* Lat. *fores,* Gr. *thyra,* Skt. *dvara* (for original *dhvara*), a door; an English *th* corresponds to Latin, Greek, and Sanskrit *t,* as in *thin,* compared with Lat. *tenuis,* Gr. *tanaos,* Skt. *tanu,* from root *tan,* to stretch.

If we next take the gutturals, we find that English *k* (or *c* hard), *g, h* correspond respectively in the above languages to *g, h (ch, gh), k,* as is seen in Eng. *kin,* Lat. *genus,* Gr. *genos,* Skt. *janas* (where *j* is for original *g*); Eng. *goose* (modified from original *gans*), compared with Lat. *anser* (for older *hanser*), Gr. *chēn,* Skt. *hansa*; Eng. *head* (A.-Sax. *heafod*), Lat. *caput,* Gr. *kephalē,* Skt. *kapala.* Similarly, *b* in English corresponds to *f* in Latin, *ph* in Greek, and *bh* in Sanskrit, as in *brother* = Lat. *frater,* Gr. *phratēr,* Skt. *bhratri,* Russ. *brat,* a brother; *f* in English to *p* in Latin, Greek, and Sanskrit, as in *father* = Lat. *pater,* Gr. *patēr,* Skt. *pitri,* father. Certain exceptions to the law are accounted for by a subsidiary law of more recent discovery than Grimm's Law, known as *Verner's Law,* and formulating certain facts connected with the original accentuation of Aryan words.

The Science of Comparative Philology. The science of philology is of quite modern origin, being hardly, if at all, older than the nineteenth century. Speculations on language and its nature were indulged in by the ancient Greeks; but as the Greeks knew little or nothing of any language but their own, they had not sufficient materials wherewith to construct a science of language. In later times materials became more abundant, as scholars studied Hebrew, Greek, Latin, Arabic, etc.; but it was the introduction of Sanskrit to the Western world, and its observed similarity in many respects to Greek, that led to the establishment of comparative philology on a true scientific basis, an achievement which was largely due to the labours of Bopp, Pott, Schleicher, and other scholars.

Yet though most valuable results have been attained and many languages have been studied and classified, much remains to be done, much remains uncertain and must always remain so. One great difficulty that the philologist has to grapple with is the want of historical documents to throw light on the history of the great majority of languages, as only a very few possess a literature dating from before the Christian era, and far the greater number have no literature at all.

A new school of philology arose between 1870 and 1880, and Osthoff and Brugman, Grassmann and Delbrück did valuable work, and discovered new laws, especially with regard to the original vowel system. It was proved that the three simple vowels in the Sanskrit and Gothic were not the only vowels in the original language. Whilst the old school of philologists in studying language had begun with the dead languages, the new school started with the study of living languages, and worked backwards to the dead languages. This school also introduced the study of *semantics* or *semasiology,* or the development of the meaning of words, the foundations of which were laid by Michel Bréal.

BIBLIOGRAPHY: J. Peile, *Primer of Philology*; A. H. Sayce, *Introduction to the Science of Language*; W. D. Whitney, *The Life and Growth of Language*; H. Paul, *Principles of the History of Language*; J. M. Edmonds, *An Introduction to Comparative Philology*; T. G. Tucker, *Introduction to the Natural History of Language*; L. Bloomfield, *An Introduction to the Study of Lan-*

guage ; A. Hovelacque, *La Linguistique*.

PHILOME'LA. In Greek mythology, a daughter of Pandion, King of Athens, who being violated and deprived of her tongue by Tereus, the husband of her sister Procne, made known her wrong to the latter by embroidering it in tapestry. In revenge the sisters murdered Itys, the son of Procne by Tereus, and served him up to his father. Tereus pursued them, but they were changed by the gods into birds, Philomela and Procne into a nightingale and a swallow, and Tereus into a hoopoe.

PHILOPŒ'MEN. Ancient Greek statesman and general, born at Megalopolis, in Arcadia, about 252 B.C., died about 183. Having distinguished himself in war against the Spartans, he was, in 208 B.C., appointed commander-in-chief of the forces of the Achæan League. He organised the Achæan army, defeated and slew with his own hand Machanidas, tyrant of Sparta, and subsequently defeated Nabis, the successor of Machanidas. He induced the Spartans to join the Achæan League ; but, soon becoming dissatisfied, they separated from the confederacy, and called in the Romans to their assistance.

Philopœmen, as commander of the Achæans, declared war against Sparta, and, having taken the city, treated it with the greatest severity. The Romans, however, interfered, and Sparta was again admitted into the confederacy as an independent state. Messene now revolted, and Philopœmen, though broken by infirmity and disease, drove back the insurgents but was afterwards taken prisoner, carried in chains to Messene, and compelled to drink poison.

PHILOS'OPHY, as the term implies, means love of wisdom, the yearning and striving after knowledge. We are informed by Herodotus that Crœsus said to Solon: "I have heard that thou hast travelled over many countries philosophising," by which he meant that he tried to acquire knowledge. The word thus owes its origin to both an admission of ignorance and a desire for knowledge. Socrates called himself a philosopher in contradistinction to the Sophists, although he did not exactly mean that he was ignorant of the facts explained by them. What he really meant was that they pretended to know more than they really did, and that their knowledge had to be criticised.

Scope and Meaning of Philosophy. Broadly speaking, philosophy is thought applied to the nature of the real world around us and to all its manifestations, both to the life in the vast universe of which we are a part and to the life within us. It differs, however, from pure science in many ways. In the first place, science deals with details, and is, so to say, departmental. Every science and every art is concerned with certain conceptions and assumptions ; their sphere is limited by the boundary-line of the finite, and their data are taken from experience. Philosophy, on the contrary, inquires into the very essence of things, criticises the very conceptions and assumptions of science, investigates the principles which lie behind the data of each science, and upon which the sciences establish themselves unquestionably. We thus speak of a philosophy of mathematics and of a philosophy of art, of a philosophy of religion and of a philosophy of history.

The business of philosophy is thus both to reflect and to criticise. Whilst each science is concerned only with its own branch of knowledge, philosophy deals with things as a whole, embracing the macrocosm and the microcosm. It endeavours to find answers to the questions: What exists ? How did it come into existence ? Why do we act thus and not otherwise ? In what relation does an idea or an object stand to other ideas or objects ?

It is, however, a mistake to imagine that philosophy is something apart from real life, or that it only deals with the pale ghosts of conceptions, belonging rather to heaven than to earth. On the contrary, whilst it endeavours to *know*, independently of practical use or utility, to discover the reason and connection of things, the aim of philosophy is to find truth, expose error, shatter old creeds and ideals, and set up new ones to which humanity can cling. Philosophy is therefore not only critical, but also constructive. It explains the world and the meaning of life, and shapes human actions and human conduct. Its school is the world, its subject-matter is the phenomena of the universe, and its textbook is human reason.

The term philosophy has, however, not always been understood and defined in the same way by all philosophers. Originally it indicated simply the spirit of inquiry, and the early thinkers applied the term to the whole range of human knowledge of their period. It was the aggregate of all the sciences. Plato defined it as the acquisition of true knowledge, whilst Epicurus and the Stoics gave it a more practical turn. In the Middle Ages philosophy became an attempt to reconcile faith and reason. Bacon and Descartes looked upon it as the universal science, whilst for Locke it was an analysis of the human understanding. Kant, opposing both empiricism and dogmaticism, looked upon philosophy as "the legislation of human reason," or critical analysis.

The Problems of Philosophy. The problems of philosophy, which thinkers of all ages have endeavoured to solve, have been numerous, but not always the same. This they could not have been. Human thought bears the impress of progress and evolution, and constantly old problems disappear, new ones taking their place. Scarcely has an answer been found to an old perplexing question when a new question arises. Mighty revolutions in the domain of human thought have solved old riddles, but new ones continually emerge on the horizon of human thought.

The problems of philosophy are psychological, ethical, metaphysical, epistemological, and theological. In other words, they deal (1) with the science of mind, and with the phenomena of consciousness, with sensations, emotions and thoughts—reason and memory, association of ideas and language. (2) With the origin and source of our sense of morality, the end and purpose of human moral conduct, and the moral standard by which our actions are regulated. (3) With being *per se*, with appearance and reality, matter, and spirit. (4) With the question of the nature of knowledge, its origin, its validity, and its limits. (5) With the questions relating to the transcendent power behind the phenomena of nature, or the existence and attributes of God. According to the manner and method in which philosophers have endeavoured to solve these problems, numerous philosophical systems and schools have arisen, which will be referred to in the following section.

History of Philosophy. The history of philosophy is the sum total of the fundamental conceptions, theories, and doctrines of the great philosophers of all ages, giving in chronological order their views of the world and their judgments of life. Without entering into the details of the philosophical problems discussed and investigated by philosophic thinkers, from Thales to Bergson, and from Anaximander to James, we will give in the following pages a brief historical outline of the principal features characterising the various epochs of philosophic development. The history of philosophy can be divided into the following periods, each stamped with its own characteristic feature:

1. The philosophy of the Greeks.
2. Hellenistic-Roman philosophy.
3. Mediæval philosophy.
4. Modern philosophy.

(1) Although Greek thought had been influenced by the civilisation of the East, and especially of Egypt, the origin of philosophy is a result of the Greek spirit. Whilst the Orientals collected a mass of information, they, as a rule, sought that information merely for the purpose of practical needs. The Greeks, however, were the first to develop the scientific and independent work of intelligence, and to seek knowledge for its own sake. "Supported on the shoulders of Egypt and Babylon," writes Gomperz (*Greek Thinkers*), "the genius of Greece could take wing without check or restraint, and venture a flight that was to lead it to the highest attainable goals." Theirs is the merit of the scientific development of philosophy, their characteristic trait being, according to Plato, investigation.

The three periods of Greek philosophy are: the cosmological, the anthropological, and the systematic. The first Greek philosophers were physicists, and their interests were centred in astronomical, geographical, and physical questions. They at first tried to find formulæ for the universal mutability of things, and their theories were an attempt to solve the question of change in the universe. They formulated an answer to the question: "What is the original cause of things which outlasts all temporal change, and what is the nature of this cause, or of this cosmic matter?"

From nature-knowledge Greek philosophers then turned their gaze and investigations to human activities, man's ideation and will, and the manner in which ideas and volitions arise. They also investigated the question whether there is anything universally valid, true and right and good in itself, independently of individual opinions. According to Aristotle, the philosophers had sought to find the material and the formal principles of all things. Whilst, however, the cosmological and anthropological philosophers had only tried to find a solution to a limited number of questions, the systematic philosophers, like Plato and Aristotle, investigated the entire compass of scientific problems, and gave the world all-embracing systems, and a crystallisation of the entire content of Greek thought. Thus the first problem of Greek philosophy was to explain the enigma of external nature, to solve the problem not of the soul but of the world.

Thales (about 600 B.C.) stands at the head of the Ionian school, which, with the Eleatic school, was the chief representative of speculative thought in pre-Socratic times. The material principle sought by the Ionian school was assumed to be water by Thales, a primitive infinite but undetermined matter by Anaximander, and air by Anaximenes. The Pythagoreans substituted a symbolic principle—number—for the sensuous principle ; but the Eleatics, transcending alike the sensuous principle of the Ionians and the quantitative principle of the Pythagoreans, conceived of pure being as the one sole substance, the phenomenal world being viewed as unreal. The three great philosophers of this school are its founder Xenophanes, Parmenides, and Zeno.

The transition from abstract to concrete being, from the Eleatic principle of unity to the world of phenomena, was attempted by Heraclitus (about 520 B.C.), who asserted for an absolute principle the unity of being and non-being, or becoming. Empedocles (440 B.C.) advanced the theory that matter was the principle of permanent being, while force was the principle of movement. The two moving forces in his system were love and hate. According to the Atomists, on the other hand, who are represented by Leucippus and Democritus (450 B.C.), the moving forces became an unintelligible necessity giving form to the world.

Anaxagoras (born about 500 B.C.) asserted that reason was the principle, and his mere expression of a spiritual principle is sufficient to mark an era in philosophy. In the hands of the Sophists this principle, in the sense of individual reason, became the occasion of their denial of all objective reality. In Socrates (470-399 B.C.), who united scientific method and a high ethical and religious spirit, the destructive teaching of the Sophists found its keenest opponent.

The Cynics, Cyrenaics, and Megarians severally professed to regard Socrates as their founder, the Cynics, however, defining the end of action as self-sufficiency, the Cyrenaics as pleasure, and the Megarians as reason. With Plato (427-347) philosophy lost its one-sided character. He was professedly a disciple of Socrates, but his system of idealism is his own.

Plato's ideal theory is criticised by Aristotle for giving no real explanation of the connection between the phenomenal and the ideal. In Aristotle's own system, instead of beginning with the general and the absolute, as Plato had done, he begins with the particular and individual. His whole philosophy is a description of the given and empirical, and his method is induction. The three schools of Greek philosophy which followed the systems of Plato and Aristotle, and which mark the declining days of Greece, are those of the Stoics, Epicureans, and Sceptics.

(2) The fundamental character of the Hellenistic-Roman period is erudition rather than speculation. It was a new departure, due to the state of general culture and to the new turn Greek political and social life had taken. Coming under the Roman sway, Greek thought underwent a complete change, and national religion and customary morality were shaken to their foundations. Philosophy assumed a practical aspect, and " men sought " as Windelband says, " to find in philosophy a compensation for religious faith ". The Romans, too, being a practical people, were not greatly interested in purely theoretical problems, and it was a complete art of living, a guide for life that they sought in philosophy.

Such were the tendencies of the Stoic and Epicurean schools. Hellenistic-Roman philosophy had therefore an ethical stamp.

On the other hand, the civilisation of the Roman Empire, as time went on, exhibited extreme contrasts in daily life, and a sense of injustice and feeling of revolt took hold of many millions. Luxury and misery, abundance and starvation were witnessed side by side, and the feeling of discontent and dissatisfaction stimulated a craving and a hope for some future compensation. Salvation was sought in a world beyond the senses. Political questions were relegated to the background, and philosophy was permeated by a religious spirit ; it became mystical and theosophical. The systems of stoicism, epicureanism, and scepticism were followed by those of Neo-Platonism, gnosticism, and Judæo-Hellenic philosophy.

(3) The chief aim of Christian philosophy was, broadly speaking, the definition and justification of Christian doctrines. Its task was to show how the truths of Christianity were acceptable to reason. The whole course of Christian philosophy may be divided into two great periods. The first, the Patristic period, began with the opening of the Christian era and

lasted until the age of Augustine (354-430), whilst the other extended from the ninth to the fifteenth century. The latter period is termed the Scholastic.

"Scholasticism," wrote Hegel, "is not a fixed doctrine, like Platonism or scepticism, but an endeavour to propound theology scientifically." It was an attempt to reconcile the spheres of reason and faith. Whilst Patristic philosophy is the outcome of classical antiquity only, Scholastic philosophy may be said to be the result of a new civilisation, that of the Germanic and Neo-Latin worlds.

(4) The fourth period, that of modern philosophy, begins with the Renaissance and continues to the present time. The dawn of modern philosophy was brought about by two great historical movements—the Renaissance, or the Revival of Learning and of classical antiquity, and the Reformation. On the one hand, the mediæval mind, weary of dry scholasticism, turned to Greek culture and Greek thought, whilst, on the other, the Reformation had stimulated a revolt against the authority of the Church and fostered the development of individual judgment.

Hegel

Modern philosophy, therefore, is distinguished by a spirit of individualism and independence. It is a transition from faith to reason. It has been rightly defined as "Protestantism in the sphere of the thinking spirit." It was both naturalistic and individualistic in its tendencies. First appealing to individual reason, setting it up as the final court of judgment, and submitting everything to the test of reason, it gradually began to call reason itself into question. It evolved from rationalism to empiricism, criticism, scepticism, positivism, and pragmatism.

Bacon and Locke on the one hand, and Descartes on the other, stand respectively at the head of the two systems—empiricism and idealism—which begin modern philosophy. Bacon created no definite system of philosophy, but gave a new direction to thought, the empiricism which he founded finally developing into scepticism. The system of Descartes was opposed by Gassendi, and received modifications at the hands of others, especially Malebranche. The most important successor, however, of Descartes was Spinoza, who reduced the three Cartesian substances, the ground of all things, that excludes from itself all negation or determination, and is named God or Nature.

Locke (1632-1704) is regarded as the father of modern materialism and empiricism. As occupying the general position of Locke, mention may be made of Isaac Newton, Samuel Clarke, William Wollaston, the Earl of Shaftesbury, and Francis Hutcheson. The philosophy of Locke received a further development in France, where Condillac sought to explain the development of humanity by the simple development of the sensations. Then followed the materialism of Helvetius, d'Holbach, La Mettrie, and others, including several of the Encyclopedists.

In opposition to this materialistic tendency arose the idealism of Leibnitz and Berkeley. The theories of Leibnitz were systematised by Wolff, and from his time to Kant German philosophy assumed no new standpoint. Berkeley (1684-1753), founding on Locke's principle that we are percipient of nothing but our own perceptions and ideas, argued that the existence of bodies out of a mind perceiving them is impossible, and a contradiction in terms.

Granting the premises of Berkeley, his conclusions could not be refuted; but it was reserved for Hume to trace out the ultimate consequences of the Cartesian and Lockian philosophy, and thus, though unintentionally, by a sort of *reductio ad absurdum*, to produce the great metaphysical revolution of which Reid and Kant were the first movers. The Scottish or "common-sense" school of philosophy, with Reid (1710-96) at its head, has the merit of having first strongly inculcated the necessity of admitting certain principles independent of experience as the indispensable conditions of thought itself. Dugald Stewart, with some deviations, followed in the track of his master; but Thomas Brown departed on many points of fundamental importance from Reid's philosophy.

The same occasion that gave rise to the Scottish school also produced the philosophy of Immanuel Kant. Kant (1724-1804), who may be justly regarded as the father of the philosophy of the nineteenth century, sought to bring together into unity the one-sided endeavours of his predecessors in the Realistic and Idealistic schools. He took up a critical standpoint, and from it instituted an inquiry into the origin of our experience or cognition. One of the ablest opponents of the Kantian Philosophy, Jacobi, took the standpoint of faith in opposition to that of criticism, in order to give theoretic certainty to the postulates of the practical reason.

In the hands of Fichte the critical idealism of Kant becomes absolutely subjective idealism. "All that is, is ego;" this is the principle of the Fichtian system: the world is merely phenomenal, consciousness is a phenomenon, perception is a dream. Fichte's subjective idealism found its continuation in the objective idealism of Schelling and the absolute idealism of Hegel. Schelling (1775-1854) started from the ego of Fichte, and by a combination of the doctrine of the ego with Spinozism transformed it into the system of identity.

Hegel (1770-1831), developing this principle of identity, created the system of absolute idealism. In his philosophy he aims at elevating consciousness to the standpoint of absolute knowledge, and systematically developing the entire contents of this knowledge by means of the dialectical method. Schleiermacher (1768-1834) promulgated an eclecticism to which Plato, Spinoza, Kant, and Schelling were the chief contributors. Schopenhauer (1788-1860) developed a doctrine which may be described as a transitional form from the idealism of Kant to realism.

In opposition to Fichte's subjective idealism, and to Schelling's renewed Spinozism, Herbart (1776-1841) developed a philosophic scheme on the basis of the realistic elements in the Kantian philosophy, as also of Eleatic, Platonic, and Leibnitzian doctrines. After the death of Hegel, Feuerbach, Richter, Strauss, Arnold Ruge, and others developed, in an extreme manner, Hegelian thought. Beneke (1798-1854), in opposition to Hegel and to Herbart, developed, on the basis of certain doctrines of English and Scottish philosophers, a psychologico-philosophical doctrine, resting exclusively on internal experience.

During recent years in Germany Hegelianism has counted more adherents than any other system. Next to it has stood the Herbartian school; and more recently the modification of systems through a return to Aristotle or Kant, and the study of philosophy upon its historic side, have occupied the larger number of minds. The teachings of Schopenhauer and Beneke, as also of Krause, Baader, Günther, and others, have been reproduced and modified by individual disciples.

Materialism is represented by Vogt, Moleschott, and Büchner, and sensualism in Czolbe and others. While resting in part upon the basis of the doctrines of earlier thinkers, Trendelenburg, Fechner, Lotze, and others have advanced in new and peculiar paths. The doctrines of H. Ritter, Carus, Weisse, Friedrich Nietzsche, and other also merit attention. Though philosophy of late years has nowhere been cultivated to such an extent as in Germany, other countries have made no inconsiderable contributions to philosophical science. In France two philosophical tendencies opposed the sensualism and materialism so universal at the beginning of the nineteenth century. Of these one was theosophical, and the other found expression in the Eclectic and Spiritualistic school which was founded by Royer-Collard as the disciple of Reid, which was further built up by Cousin, who incorporated into its body of doctrines a number of German philosophies, and in which the Cartesian tradition was renewed.

Less brilliant than Cousin, but possessing no small merit as a thinker, Jouffroy attempted to unite the philosophy of his predecessor, Maine de Biran, to that of the Scottish school, and became associated with the Spiritualistic school, to which also belong the names of Garnier, Janet, Rémusat, Franck, Jules Simon, and others. This school has contended valiantly against the pantheistic tendencies of the age. Independent systems are those of Pierre Leroux, Lamennais, Jean Reynaud, and Buchez. Materialism has its supporters in Cabanis, who sees in thought only a secretion of the brain, Broussais, Gall, and others. Positivism, founded by Auguste Comte, numbers not a few followers on the Continent and in England.

In Great Britain the Scottish school had later exponents in Sir James Mackintosh (1765-1832) and Sir William Hamilton (1788-1856), the last-named being, moreover, largely influenced in some points of his psychology by Kant. Our knowledge, according to Hamilton, is conditioned by our faculties; we have no faculty for comprehending the infinite and absolute; and all human philosophy, therefore, treats only of the relative and phenomenal. The absolute, as unknowable, is transferred from the province of philosophy to that of religion, from reason to faith. Mansel and McCosh may be mentioned as disciples of Hamilton.

Ferrier (1808-64) assumed a polemical attitude towards the common-sense school in respect of its fundamental peculiarity, as he viewed it, of absorbing philosophy into psychology, as well as on minor details of the system. The associational psychology of Hartley, Priestley, and Darwin has its representatives in the nineteenth century in James Mill (1773-1836) and his son John Stuart Mill (1806-73), who make the principle of association the sole explanation of psychical phenomena. Bain, Grote, and Lewes follow more or less in the same track.

Herbert Spencer attempted to widen the psychological principles of the associational psychology into a universal doctrine of evolution, which should not only provide for the evolution of all forms of being, but also of the fundamental principles of philosophy itself. T. H. Green, J. and E. Caird, and W. Wallace have been exponents of the Hegelian philosophy. In America, as in England, philosophy has been prosecuted more as an applied science, and in its special relations to morals, politics, and theology. Speculation there has been widely influenced by Scottish philosophy.

The philosophy of the last fifty years is characterised by a growing demand for a scientific world-theory. Criticism has become a vital factor, and the problem of the ability of the human intellect to construct a world-theory has again been raised. There is a reaction against idealism and rationalism, and a shifting of the interest from universals to particulars, from logic to intuition, from intellect to the will.

Some modern philosophers maintain that the human intellect is unable to solve the world-riddle, that metaphysics is impossible, and that knowledge is limited to the study of facts of experience, or is only an instrument in the service of the will to live. Others think that the source of knowledge lies not in the intellect but in feeling, belief, or intuition.

A prominent place in the philosophy of the present day is also occupied by the problem of values, and some philosophers are becoming convinced that the value of existence cannot be established purely theoretically.

Among recent philosophers of note we may mention: Andrew Seth, D. G. Ritchie, A. J. Balfour, W. S. Jevons, Leslie Stephen, James Sully, and H. Sidgwick in Britain; Paul Janet, E. Boutroux, A. Fouillée, and Henri Bergson in France; and F. Paulsen, Kuno Fischer, Herman Cohen, and R. Eucken in Germany.

BIBLIOGRAPHY: W. Turner, *History of Philosophy*; H. Höffding, *A Brief History of Modern Philosophy*; R. Falckenberg, *History of Modern Philosophy*. W. T. Marvin, *The History of European Philosophy*; F. Thilly, *History of Philosophy*; A. Schwegler, *Handbook of Philosophy*; A Windelband, *A History of Philosophy*; P. Janet and G. Séailles, *Histoire de la philosophie*; B. A. W. Russell, *The Problems of Philosophy*; A. S. Rappoport, *A Primer of Philosophy*.

PHILOS'TRATUS, Flavius. Greek sophist, born at Lemnos about the middle of the second century of our era. He taught rhetoric at Athens and subsequently at Rome, where he obtained the favour of the Emperor Septimius Severus, and he accompanied the Empress Julia Domna in her travels. His principal work is his *Life of Apollonius of Tyana*, supposed by some critics to be written as a counterblast to the Gospels. His other works are the *Heroica*, a history in dialogue of the heroes of the Trojan War; *Lives of the Sophists*; and *Letters*.

PHLEBI'TIS. Inflammation of the walls of a vein, and since such inflammation almost always leads to clotting of the blood inside the vein (venous thrombosis), the two conditions should be considered together. The chief causes that bring about these conditions are injury to a part, after-effects of an operation, infection spread from some other region of the body, severe debility and cachexia, and certain infectious fevers.

Various veins of the body may be affected, and when superficial, can be felt as a firm cord under the skin. When deep, the thrombosed vein cannot be palpated, but there is much tenderness and pain in the region. The most frequently affected veins are those of the thigh, and a form of venous obstruction in the thigh due to thrombosis, known as phlegmasia alba dolens (white leg), occurs in women during the puerperium, and causes much swelling of the limb. Recovery usually follows in simple cases, but great care should be taken on account of the risk of a portion of the clot becoming detached and carried in the circulation to the lungs, where it causes an embolism.

Rest in bed for three to six weeks until all pain over the course of the vein has disappeared is imperative, and all sudden movements and exertion should be avoided.

PHLEBOT'OMY, or **VENESECTION.** The opening of a vein to let a certain amount of blood out. As a method of treating various diseases it has been used by the medical profession from earliest times, and was so widely practised in the eighteenth century and the beginning of the nineteenth that it has to-day fallen into almost complete disuse as a reaction to the former abuse. There are certain conditions when it can be employed with benefit, as when there is engorgement of the veins as a result of failure of the heart, especially in plethoric subjects, also in cases of high blood-pressure, Bright's disease, and in toxæmic states like uræmia, eclampsia, and diabetic coma. The method of cupping (q.v.) and the application of leeches produce similar, but slower, effects in these conditions.

PHLEG'MASIA. A diffuse inflammation of the tissues. Plegmasia alba dolens (milk leg) is an inflammation of the leg in women during the puerperium, due to phlebitis (q.v.).

PHLŒM, or **BAST.** In botany, that part of the conducting or vascular tissue which serves for the transmission of proteins, sugars, etc., i.e. of the "plastic" materials manufactured principally in the leaves. Its most important constituents are the sieve-tubes (q.v.); fibrous elements (bast fibres) are also frequently present, e.g. in the lime.

PHLOGIS'TON. An element or principle supposed by Stahl (1697) to exist in all inflammable substances, and to be separated from them by the process of combustion. The phlogiston theory held the field for nearly a hundred years. The very ablest investigators, such as Cavendish, Black, Scheele, and Priestley, were firm believers in the doctrine. Priestley, when he discovered oxygen, called it dephlogisticated air. Nitrogen he called phlogisticated air. When an ore was smelted it was supposed to absorb the phlogiston evolved during the combustion of the fuel in the furnace, and so to be converted into the metal. The metal itself, again, when heated, was dephlogisticated and converted into a "calx." The difficulty about the calx—the oxide, as we should now say—being heavier than the original metal was either ignored or explained by regarding phlogiston as a "principle of levity." Phlogiston was, in fact, a sort of negative oxygen, oxygen and phlogiston being related in much the same way as positive and negative electricity.

The death-blow to the theory was given by Lavoisier (1775), who was the first to propose what everybody nowadays believes to be the correct description of combustion. Priestley held to the old doctrine to the last. *See* CHEMISTRY.

PHLOX. A genus of perennial herbaceous plants of the nat. ord. Polemoniaceæ, natives for the most part of North America, though some of the species are to be met with in Asia. The flowers, which are favourites in

Phlox

gardens, are of a purple or violet colour, more rarely white or red, with a salver-shaped corolla, and a narrow sub-cylindrical tube longer than the calyx. The trailing kinds are excellent for rock-work.

PHO'CION. Athenian general and statesman, supposed to have been born about 402 B.C. According to Plutarch, he was nominated commander forty-five times without once applying for the office. He always led a simple life, and cultivated his small farm with his own hands. As the leader of the conservative or aristocratic party he opposed Demosthenes on the question of war with Philip of Macedon. He subsequently condemned the confederacy against Alexander the Great, and, after Alexander's death (323 B.C.), the war with Antipater. On each occasion Phocion was employed to make terms with the victorious Macedonians. In 318 Phocion was accused of treason for allowing Polysperchon to occupy the Piræus, and condemned to drink the hemlock. His remains, however, were shortly afterwards buried at public expense and his accusers punished.

PHOCIS (Gr. *Phōkis*). A division of ancient Greece, on the north side of the Gulf of Corinth, between Bœotia on the east and Doris and the *Locri Ozolæ* on the west. The principal rivers were the Cephissus and Plistus, and the principal mountain Parnassus, on which was situated Delphi with its celebrated oracle. The country is mountainous and unproductive, the valley of the Cephissus being almost the only fertile tract in it.

The Phocians were an industrious people, and subsisted chiefly by agriculture. They were distinguished for their bravery, of which they gave signal proof in the war with the Thessalians, and in the Persian and Peloponnesian Wars. The Phocians were the cause of the *Sacred War*, so destructive to Greece, and shared the fate of their countrymen after the battle of Chæronea (338 B.C.).

PHŒNICIA. A country on the coast of Syria, bounded on the east by Mount Lebanon. The Greeks and Romans knew it as the Region of Palms, or "the country where the palm grew." Phœnicia proper was a tract of country stretching along the eastern shore of the Mediterranean, not much more than 28 miles in length, and little more than 1 mile in average breadth, Sidon being situated near its northern, and Tyre not far from its southern boundary. In its widest sense Phœnicia seems to have meant the whole seaboard from the Gulf of Issus to the southern desert, but generally it was regarded as beginning at the north with the Island of Aradus, and extending south to the town of Dora, below the promontory of Carmel.

The country is watered by several streams flowing from Lebanon to the sea, and is fertile in timber, corn, and fruits. Besides the cities of Sidon and Tyre, Phœnicia was anciently studded with numerous smaller towns, forming almost an unbroken line along the coast. Among these towns were Arvad, Arka, Tripolis, Berytus, and Sarepta.

The Phœnicians, like the Jews, were Semites, being derived from the Aramæan wave of immigration, which formed permanent settlements in Northern Syria. Their immigration to the coast of the Mediterranean must have taken place about 2500 B.C. or earlier. The settlement of Israel in Canaan did not produce any great or permanent change on Phœnicia. The tribes of Naphtali, Asher, and Dan, to which it was assigned, did not conquer Phœnicia, but occupied only a small portion of it; and the subsequent relations of Israel and Phœnicia were for the most part those of amity, intercourse, and reciprocal advantage.

The wealth and power of the Phœnicians arose from their command of the sea, and it was their policy not to provoke any of the nations to the east of them, and not to quarrel unnecessarily with Israel,

Phœnician Merchants

which was their granary. The relation between Hiram and David was probably but a sample of such international treaties and intercourse. After the division of the Hebrew kingdom Phœnicia would naturally cultivate alliance with the Ten Tribes nearest to it, and Ahab married a Phœnician princess.

The wealth and commerce of the country had brought art and refinement, but effeminacy and licentiousness sapped the power of self-defence. A rich and unwarlike people could not but lure the conquerors to an easy prey, and the country was thus successively incorporated in the Assyrian, Babylonian, and Persian Empires, although the cities retained more or less their independence. It was next conquered by Alexander the Great, and henceforth simply formed part of Syria.

Constitution and Government. As was the case in Canaan at the invasion, each Phœnician city was governed by a king or petty chief. A powerful aristocracy existed in the chief towns, and there were also elective magistrates, called by the Romans *suffĕtes*, a disguised form of the Hebrew *soffet*. Sidon, and afterwards Tyre, exercised a hegemony over the other states. The relation of Phœnicia to her colonies does not seem to have been very close. Their religion, however, bound the mother country and the colonies in a common worship. Carthage often sent presents to the chief Phœnician god; so did Gades and other settlements.

Commerce. From a very early period the Phœnicians occupied themselves in distant voyages, and they must speedily have acquired a style of substantial shipbuilding. The "ships of Tarshish" became famous and Xenophon passes a high eulogy on a Phœnician ship. They were skilled in navigation and the nautical applications of astronomy. Lebanon supplied them with abundance of timber, and Cyprus gave them all necessary naval equipments, from the keel to the top-sails. In the reign of Pharaoh-Necho these daring navigators even circumnavigated Africa, and the Phœnicians furnished Xerxes with 300 ships, which took part in the battle of Salamis.

The commerce of Tyre reached through the world. It traded in the produce of the whole known world, the spices and stones of Arabia, the myrrh and frankincense of Sabæa, the linen and corn of Egypt, the ivory and "bright iron" and ebony and cotton fabrics of India, and the tin from Cornwall and Devonshire. Fishing was also an important industry, and the Tyrians sold fish in Jerusalem. The Phœnicians excelled in the manufacture of the purple dye from the shell-fish *murex* abundant on its coasts. The glass of Sidon was no less famous than the Tyrian dye. Phœnicia produced also articles of silver and gold as well as of brass, and Homer describes Sidon as abounding in works of brass; its inhabitants were also skilled in architecture and in mining. The *Maabed* of Amrit, or Marathus, and two other similar shrines were discovered by Renan. The two famous pillars of the temple of Jersualem, Jachin and Boaz, and the altar of gold were works of Phœnician artists.

Colonies. The maritime knowledge and experience of Phœnicia led to the plantation of numerous colonies in Cyprus, Rhodes, and the islands of the Ægean—the Cyclades and Sporades—in Sicily, in Sardinia, the Balearic Islands, and in Spain. The most celebrated of the Phœnician colonies, however, was Carthage, in Northern Africa, which extended its sway over the Spanish peninsula and disputed with Rome the supremacy of the Mediterranean. They purchased slaves from the northern shores of the Black Sea, and they also kidnapped and sold the children of Israel—a practice which brought upon them the denunciations of the prophets, and a just retaliation was predicted to fall upon them.

Religion. The religion of the Phœnicians was a species of nature-worship, the objects of adoration being the sun, moon, and five planets; or in another form it was the worship of male and female reproductive powers—the former represented as Baal and the latter as Baalith, Ashtoreth, or Astarte. The god called El, a sort of Phœnician Cronos or Saturn, resembling the Moloch or Milcom of the Ammonites, had human sacrifices offered to him. Marine deities must have held a prominent place in their pantheon—deities corresponding to the Greek Nereus and Poseidon, which last was worshipped at Berytus. In the oldest temples there were no images, but there were rude fetishes—conical or oblong stones, possibly aerolites "fallen from heaven," and fossil belemnites.

Language. The language of Phœnicia belonged to the Hebrew-Phœnician division of the Semitic languages, representing in general an archaic stage of Hebrew and Moabitic. As Phœnician spread over the Punic colonies, the diffusion gave rise to variations both of dialect and script. The Phœnician alphabet derived from the South-Arabian, is the ancestor of the Græco-Roman alphabets. The names of the so-called Cadmæan letters of the Greek alphabet have no meaning in Greek, but have each a significance in Hebrew and Phœnician. Thus *aleph* means an ox, *beth*, a house, *gimel* or *gamal*, a camel, etc.

The sources of our knowledge of Phœnician are the transliteration of Phœnician phrases in the *Pœnulus* of Plautus, proper names and words found in the Old Testament, and the numerous inscriptions on tombs, votive tablets, and coins found in many places in Cyprus, Malta, Sidon, Sicily, Sardinia, and Africa. The longest of the inscriptions are those found upon the sarcophagus of King Eshmunazar, King of Sidon, discovered in 1855, and now in the

Louvre; on a tablet discovered at Marseilles in 1845; and another found at Larnaka in 1879.

BIBLIOGRAPHY: G. Rawlinson, *History of Phœnicia*; N. Davis, *Carthage and her Remains*; Renan, *Mission de Phénicie*; Movers, *Die Phœnizier*; Schroeder, *Die phœnizische Sprache*; G. A. Cooke, *Text-book of North-Semitic Inscriptions*.

PHŒNIX (Gr. *phoinix*). A fabulous Egyptian bird, about the size of an eagle, with plumage partly red and partly golden. Of the various stories told of it by Herodotus and others the most popular is to the effect that the bird, at an age of

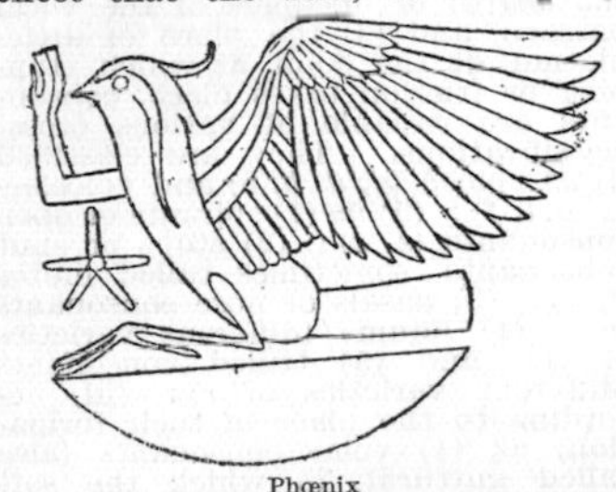

Phœnix

From an Egyptian wall painting (after Wilkinson)

500 years, conscious of its approaching death, built a funeral pile of wood and aromatic gums, which it lighted with the fanning of its wings, and rose from the flames with a new life. It symbolised the morning sun rising out of the glow of dawn, and was looked upon by the Egyptians as the sacred bird of the sun-god Ra.

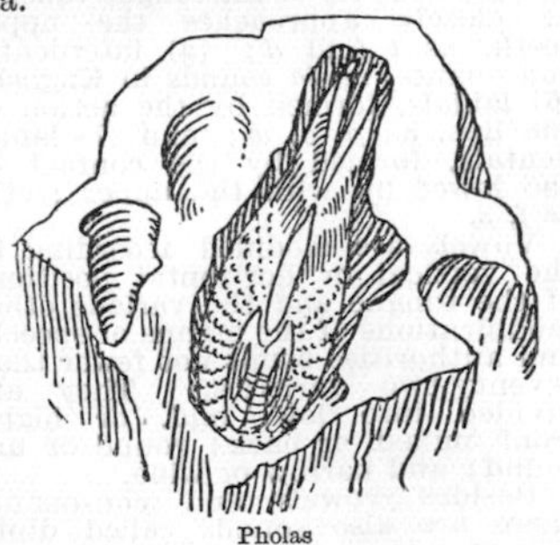

Pholas

PHOLAS. A genus of marine bivalve molluscs, forming the type of the family Pholadidæ, in which the shell gapes at both ends. The shell, which is of thin white texture, is studded over on its outer surface with numerous rasp-like prominences, by means of which the animal excavates burrows in wood, rocks, indurated clay, etc., maintaining communication with the outer world by means of long breathing-tubes or siphons with fringed edges. They are popularly known as "piddocks," and are eaten on many parts of the British coasts. The common species is the *Pholas dactylus*; and the *P. candida*, *P. parva*, and *P. crispata* are also found in Britain. These molluscs appear to possess the power of emitting a phosphorescent light, *P. dactylus* being specially noted on this account.

PHOMA. A genus of Fungi Imperfecti, section Sphæropsidiaceæ, including several parasitic species, the best-known being *P. sanguinolenta*, which attacks the carrot, damaging the shoots and destroying the bloom, so that infected plants set no seed.

PHONET'ICS (Gr. *phonē*, voice). The science of speech sounds and art of pronunciation, is that part of language study which deals with articulate sounds uttered by the human voice or used in a particular language. It not only ascertains the mechanism of voice production, investigates the structure of the various organs both producing and perceiving sounds, but also deals with the representation by alphabetical characters of the vocal sounds employed in a language. It is thus a science related to physics, as it is concerned with the acoustic analysis of sound, to physiology, as it investigates the functions of the organs producing sounds, and to philology or linguistics, as it deals with the elements of language.

Phonetics deals not only with the mechanism of speech and the classification of sounds, but also with accent, stress or emphasis, tone of voice, and the quantity or duration of a sound. The science of phonetics is important, nay necessary, for the theoretical understanding and practical acquisition of a foreign language, and also for the study and correct pronunciation of one's own mother tongue.

The Mechanism of Speech. Speech is the result of breath expelled by the lungs and modified in the throat and the mouth, and in the production of speech sounds machinery of a somewhat complicated kind is employed. The lips, the teeth, the tongue, the gums, and the palate (both hard and soft) take part in the operation of producing speech sounds. Most important of all are the vocal chords, pieces of membrane attached to each side of a cartilaginous box (the larynx) in the throat. The vibration of the edges of these chords when stretched tight, so as to leave only a narrow slit between them, is produced by the expiration of the breath.

The sounds called vowels are produced by the vibration of the vocal chords, and are distinguished one from another by the position of the tongue and the shape of the mouth cavity. Thus, for the production of *a* (pronounced as *ah!*) the tongue lies in the mouth, but rises somewhat at the back; for *o* the lips are rounded; for *i* (pronounced as *ee* in *seen*) the upper surface of the tongue is approached to the roof of the mouth behind the teeth, while the jaws are not so wide apart as for *a*. For *u* the lips are protruded as well as rounded; *e* (pronounced as in *red*) occupies a position between *a* and *i*.

For the pronunciation of *p*, *t*, *k* (pronounced as *ip*, *it*, *ik*) it will be found that the mouth passage is entirely closed for a brief space by the lips for *p*, by the tongue against (in English behind) the teeth for *t*, against the palate for *k*, while in their production the vocal chords do not vibrate. The sounds *b*, *d*, *g* (in *gig*) differ only from *p*, *t*, *k* in being produced with vibration of the vocal chords. In producing all these sounds the breath is kept from passing through the nose. If the nose passage is left open we produce, instead of *b*, *d*, *g*, the sounds *m*, *n*, *ng* (in *sing*). These last, as the nose is open, are called *nasal*, and are continuous sounds, that is, can be prolonged till the breath is exhausted.

Sonants and Consonants, Vowels and Semi-vowels. Old phoneticians divided the alphabet into *vowels*, meaning sounds capable of being produced alone, and *consonants*, or sounds incapable of being so produced. This classification, however, has been found to be scientifically inexact. In words like *bosom*, *arbre*, *Handel*, the liquids *m*, *r*, and *l* form syllables in themselves, and we thus see that some consonants are capable of syllabic value. The modern classification, therefore, is into *sonants* and *consonants*, the first including all those sounds which are not serving in consonantal function, whether vowels or not. In other words, sonants are "accent-bearing sounds or syllable-forming, including both vowels and consonants."

The distinction between vowels and consonants proper lies in the fact that the former consist of a vibration of the vocal chords, modified in the pharynx by the tongue and the soft palate without audible friction, whilst the latter are the result either of audible friction (*s*), or of the stopping of breath in some parts of the mouth or throat (*t*). "In the vowels the primary element is the action of the glottis, whilst the configuration of the throat or the mouth is of secondary importance; in consonants the reverse is the case" (J. M. Edmonds, *An Introduction to Comparative Philology*, p. 20).

According to the various principles of (1) their kind of articulation, (2) the degree of openness of the vocal passage, and (3) the place of articulation, or the point at which stopping or friction takes place, consonants are capable of various cross-classifications. They are classified (i) as voiced (*g*, *d*, *b*, *v*) and voiceless (*k*, *p*, *t*, *f*): (ii) as (1) spirants or open consonants (*s*, *z*); (2) stops or shut consonants, sometimes called mutes (*t*, *d*); (3) nasals or nose consonants (*n*); (4) liquids (different varieties of *l*); and (5) trilled consonants (different varieties of *r*): (iii) according to the place of their formation, as (1) velar consonants (also called guttural, in which the soft palate and back of the tongue are mainly concerned), as *c* in *cat*, *ch* in *loch*; (2) palatal or front consonants, formed by a narrowing between the tongue and the hard palate, as *k* in *kit*, *king*, *give*; (3) cerebral consonants or sibilants, formed by the blade of the tongue and the front of the hard palate, as *s* in *pleasure*, *sh* in *ship*; (4) dental consonants or teeth-roof consonants, in which the tip of the tongue touches or closely approaches the upper teeth, as *t* and *d*; (5) interdental consonants, as *th* sounds in English; (6) labials, formed by the action of the lips, as *p*, *b*, *w*; and (7) labiodentals, formed by the contact of the lower lip with the upper teeth, as *f*, *v*.

Vowels are modified according to the vertical or horizontal positions of the tongue and the various other modifications of the organs of speech, and authorities count not fewer than seventy-two varieties. They are divided into low, mid, or high; front, mixed, or back; round or unround; and narrow or wide.

Besides vowels and consonants there are also sounds called diphthongs, or combinations of two sonants, glides, or transitions of sounds, and aspirates. Different languages sometimes make finer distinctions between the sounds, such as the dentals, produced against the sockets (*alveoli*) of the teeth, and called *alveolar*, and the genuine dentals. In the original language from which English is descended we distinguish the palatals, produced farther forward in the mouth as compared with other gutturals, which, being supposed to be produced against the *velum*, or soft palate, are called velar. It is the task of philology to ascertain for the earlier forms of language what were the exact sounds then existing, the written forms of any language giving but the most imperfect clue to the actual sounds.—BIBLIOGRAPHY: H. Sweet, *A Primer of Phonetics*; J. M. Edmonds, *An Introduction to Comparative Philology*; L. Soames, *Introduction to English, French, and German Phonetics*; T. G. Tucker, *Introduction to the Natural History of Language*; E. Sievers, *Grundzüge der Phonetik* (full bibliography).

PHO'NOGRAPH. *See* GRAMOPHONE.

PHO'NOLITE. A translation into a Greek form of the quarryman's term "clink-stone," given to certain compact fissile trachytic lavas that rang, as slates do, when struck with the pick. Microscopic research shows that these compact rocks form a special class of trachyte, characterised by the presence of nepheline, leucite, haüyne, nosean, or of all of these, in addition to alkali felspars. Phonolite often forms dome-like masses where it has been protruded in volcanic necks, as in the north of Bohemia.

PHOSPHATE. In Chemistry, the generic term for the salts of phosphoric acid (q.v.). They play a leading part in the chemistry of animal and plant life, the most important being the phosphates of sodium, of calcium, and of magnesium. In agriculture the adequate supply of phosphates to plants in the form of manures becomes a matter of necessity in all deplenished soils. These phosphatic manures consist for the most part of bones, ground bones, mineral phosphates (apatite, phosphorite, coprolites), basic slag, superphosphates and reduced superphosphates (both prepared by treating broken-up bones with sulphuric acid), bone-ash, and phosphatic guano. *See* SOILS AND MANURES; BONE MANURE; PHOSPHORUS.

PHOSPHATIC DIATHESIS. A constitutional predisposition of the body tissues to the formation of the phosphates of magnesium, ammonia, and calcium, seen by their being deposited in the urine.

PHOSPHORES'CENCE. A term commonly applied to the emission of light by bodies which are not obviously undergoing combustion. The effect is now included under the more general name "luminescence." When the emission of light is accompanied by chemical action, it is termed *chemiluminescence*, as when phosphorus oxidises slowly in moist air. Light of this nature is emitted by glow-worms and fire-flies, by those marine organisms which cause phosphorescence in the sea, by certain deep-sea fishes, and by decaying fish and rotten wood.

When a body becomes self-luminous as the result of being exposed to light, the effect is called *photoluminescence*. If the body is self-luminous only while receiving the light rays, the effect is termed *fluorescence* (q.v.); if the luminosity persists after the exciting radiation has been withdrawn, the luminosity is called *phosphorescence*, and the effects may last, in different substances, from a fraction of a second to several weeks. This property is possessed by the sulphides of calcium, strontium, and barium, especially when prepared with a small addition of bismuth, copper, or manganese. The well-known Balmain's luminous paint consists chiefly of calcium sulphide with a small addition of bismuth. Such material is used on the dials of watches and magnetic compasses to make them visible in the dark. Phosphorescent bodies become less luminous when cooled; but some substances, such as ivory, paper, and feathers, only become phosphorescent when cooled to the temperature of liquid air (−190° C.).

Thermoluminescence is the name given to the luminous glow observed, for example, in fluorspar when gently heated in the dark. *Triboluminescence* is that variety of light emission which is caused by mechanical action, and which is seen when a lump of sugar is crushed in the dark, or when two pieces of quartz are rubbed together.

Electroluminescence is sometimes seen as a glow in a gas through which an electric discharge has passed, or in the glow of a diamond or ruby after being subjected to the action of kathode rays. *Crystalloluminescence* may be observed in arsenious acid as the substance crystallises from a solution in hydrochloric acid.

PHOSPHORIC ACID, or ORTHOPHOSPHORIC ACID, (H_3PO_4). A tribasic acid obtained by oxidising red phosphorus with nitric acid, or on the large scale by decomposition of *bone ash* (mainly calcium phosphate, $Ca_3(PO_4)_2$) with sulphuric acid. By evaporation of a solution of ortho-phosphoric acid in vacuo over sulphuric acid, it may be obtained in colourless crystals of melting-point 38·6° C., but usually it is a thick, syrupy liquid. If heated for some time above 215° C., ortho-phosphoric acid loses water, and is transformed into meta-phosphoric acid or glacial phosphoric acid, (HPO_3), a deliquescent vitreous solid. A dilute solution of phosphoric acid is used in medicine, chiefly as a gastric stimulant and to quench thirst. The acid is comparatively inactive, and can be given internally in fairly large doses.

PHOS'PHORITE. A name for massive calcium phosphate, which may be apatite from veins, or concretionary, as in Southern Russia, or a replacement of extensive beds of limestone, as in Northern Africa. Phosphorite with more than 23 per cent of phosphorus pentoxide is valuable as an agricultural fertiliser.

PHOSPHOROSCOPE. An instrument designed by Becquerel to test bodies which are phosphorescent only for a very short period after exposure to light, such as Iceland spar and uranium compounds. By its means many substances hitherto unsuspected of phosphorescence have been proved capable of remaining luminous for very short periods. The name is also given to a philosophical toy for showing phosphorescent substances in the dark.

PHOSPHOROUS ACID, (H_3PO_3). An acid produced by exposing sticks of phosphorus to moist air, and in several other ways. Phosphorous acid exists usually in the form of a thick uncrystallisable syrup, but it may also be obtained crystallised. It is a powerful reducing agent, and precipitates gold and silver from solutions of their salts.

PHOS'PHORUS (symbol, P; atomic weight, 31·04). One of the non-metallic elements. It does not occur free in nature, as it very readily combines with oxygen and other substances; in the combined state, however, it is fairly plentiful and very widely distributed. Its most important derivative is *calcium phosphate* or *phosphate of lime*, $Ca_3(PO_4)_2$; this occurs as the minerals *apatite*, *phosphorite*, *coprolite*; also in bones of animals and in soils and plants. It is manufactured from bone or from native mineral phosphate of lime by heating a mixture of the phosphate with silica and carbon in an electric furnace, when phosphorus vapour is liberated and condensed under water.

Yellow phosphorus is a translucent solid, and when pure is almost colourless; it is slightly soluble in water, soluble in ether and carbon disulphide; is easily cut with a knife, and melts at 44·1° C. It is exceedingly inflammable, and oxidises so readily that it cannot be kept exposed to air but must be preserved under water. If exposed to moist air, it undergoes oxidation and emits a white vapour of alliaceous odour, which appears luminous in the dark. Owing to the inflammability of the substance, it must not be handled or cut in the dry state, as even the heat of the hand may cause it to inflame, and it causes painful burns.

When phosphorus burns in oxygen or rapidly in air, it gives out a bright white light and is transformed into phosphorus pentoxide, (P_2O_5), a white flocculent powder which dissolves in water, yielding phosphoric acid. Phosphorus is chemically very reactive, and combines with most of the elements; with the metals it forms the *phosphides*, e.g. calcium phosphide, (Ca_3P_2).

Yellow phosphorus was chiefly used for the preparation of lucifer matches, but, owing to the dangerous nature of the element and its harmful effect on the workers, its use was discontinued, and where lucifer matches are manufactured the sulphide of phosphorus, P_4S_3, is used. *See* MATCHES.

Phosphorus presents a good example of an allotropic element; the second modification is known as *red phosphorus* or *amorphous phosphorus*. Red phosphorus is made from the yellow variety by keeping the element heated for a considerable time to a temperature of 200° to 300° C. out of contact with air. The yellow waxy solid is slowly changed into a red powder. This red modification has properties very different from the yellow variety; thus it is insoluble in carbon disulphide, it may be left exposed to air, and it does not catch fire. Yellow phosphorus is exceedingly poisonous, red phosphorus is non-poisonous. The red variety is used for the preparation of safety matches—phosphorus being one of the ingredients of the striking surface. If kept heated to its boiling-point, it changes back to the yellow modification.

PHO'TIUS. Byzantine theologian and scholar, born at Constantinople (about 820) of patrician parents. He became Secretary of State under the Emperor Michael III., and was intimate with the minister Bardas, uncle of the emperor. On the deposition of the patriarch Ignatius, the emperor raised Photius to the patriarchal dignity. This was opposed by Pope Nicholas I., whom Photius excommunicated, thereby laying the foundation of the schism between the Eastern and Western Churches. But the Emperor Michael having been murdered in 867 by Basil, who was raised to the throne, that prince immediately replaced Ignatius, and banished Photius, who, however, resumed his dignity on the death of Ignatius in 878.

On the accession of Leo, son of Basil, to the imperial throne in 886, Photius was again deposed, and banished to a monastery in Armenia, where he died in 891. Photius was an able ecclesiastical statesman, and a man of great intellect, erudition, and literary power. His chief work is the *Myriobiblon*, a sort of review of 280 works which he had read, and most of which are now lost. He also wrote a theological work, *Amphilochia*, and compiled a lexicon of the words occurring in the Greek orators and historians.

PHOTO-CHEMISTRY. That branch of general chemistry which deals with the relations of chemical action and of chemical constitution to light, or, more generally, to all electromagnetic radiation, including ultraviolet rays and X-rays. The effects of chemical constitution on optical phenomena are discussed in the articles *Colour*, *Dispersion*, *Fluorescence*, *Light*, *Phosphorescence*, *Polarisation of Light*, *Refraction*, *Saccharimeter*, *Spectrum*, and *Spectroscopy*.

There are many well-known examples of the influence of light on chemical action, such as the combination of hydrogen and chlorine to form hydrochloric acid when exposed to sunlight. But the most important instances of photo-chemical action occur in the processes of photography (q.v.) and in photo-synthesis, the process by which plants use the energy of sunlight to assimilate carbon from the atmosphere. *See* CARBON ASSIMILATION; PHOTOGRAPHY; PHYSICAL CHEMISTRY.

PHOTO-ELECTRIC EFFECT. An electrical action produced by light. The term is sometimes applied to each of the following actions, but is more often confined to the first: (1) an emission of electrons from solids; (2) an increase in the electrical conductivity of certain badly conducting solids; (3) an E.M.F. between an illuminated and a non-illuminated electrode immersed in certain liquids.

(1) This action, first clearly described by Hallwachs (1888), is of great theoretical importance (*see* QUANTUM THEORY); it is now known to be essentially similar to the emission of secondary β-radiation under the action of X-rays. It occurs in all substances illuminated by light of suitable frequency, but is most easily studied in metals. The electrons emerge in all directions from the illuminated surface with all velocities up to a certain maximum. If V is the potential difference through which an electron bearing a charge e has to fall in order to acquire this maximum velocity, then V is given by Einstein's equation $e(V+V_0)=h\nu$, where ν is the frequency of the incident light, h is Planck's constant (*see* QUANTUM THEORY), and V_0 a constant characteristic of the illuminated surface. V_0 is less for the more electropositive metal, and the difference between V_0 for any two metals is equal to the contact potential or Volta effect (q.v.) between them; but V_0 is greatly affected (usually increased) by the presence of gas films and other impurities on the surface. If $h\nu$ is less than eV_0, no electrons are emitted; consequently there is a minimum frequency for each metal below which light will not cause this photo-electric effect. The alkali metals (except lithium) respond to visible light; the common metals only to ultra-violet light.

The conditions determining the number of electrons emitted (and thus the current flowing) are more complex. The number is proportional, *ceteris paribus*, to the light absorbed at the surface; its ratio to the light energy absorbed increases in general with ν and decreases as V_0 increases. But the alkali metals show a selective effect, in addition to this normal effect, which rises to a sharp maximum for a particular value of ν. The selective effect is produced only by the component of the light polarised with the electric vector in the plane of incidence; the normal effect is independent of polarization.

Both effects can be greatly increased in the alkali metals by converting the surface into a colloidal modification by making it the cathode of a discharge through hydrogen at a low pressure. *Photo-electric cells*, consisting of gas-filled or vacuum tubes, in which the cathode is a thin film of potassium on copper, are useful in photometry. When light falls on the cathode a minute electric current is produced, proportional to the amount of light. The current is amplified by thermionic valves. The process has important applications to picture telegraphy, talking films, and television, the problem in these cases being similar to that of amplification in wireless reception.—BIBLIOGRAPHY: A. L. Hughes, *Photo-electricity*; H. S. Allen, *Photo-electricity*.

PHOTO-ENGRAVING. Printing term. Exposure of a prepared plate under the negative of a line drawing renders the lines insoluble while the balance may be removed, enabling reproductions to be printed. Pictures must first be photographed through a "screen," breaking the image into dots. Exposure and development of a prepared copper plate under the negative permits the copper plate subsequently to be etched into similar dots from which reproductions may be printed.

PHOTOGRAMMETRY. A method of surveying by means of photography. The angular distance subtended by any two objects which appear upon a photograph, at the position occupied by the optical centre of the lens (*see* OPTICS; LENS) during exposure, can be calculated. Thus, if we consider the photographic plate to be held vertical, and the optical axis of the camera lens to be horizontal, we may consider the plate as a tangent to a horizontal arc whose radius is the focal length and whose centre is the optical centre of the lens. The camera becomes in this way a substitute for theodolites or plane tables, and rays may be drawn from the known position of the camera to all points whose images appear on the plate. If two known positions are occupied by the camera, then the positions of any point or feature which appears on both photographs may be fixed by the intersection of rays, providing that the orientation of the camera is known in each case.

It is easy to ascertain the positions of a few clearly defined objects in this way and with sufficient accuracy for medium and small scale surveys, but it is very difficult to ensure that the whole area to be mapped is included upon at least two plates, and it is equally difficult to recognise badly defined points from their images on different plates. Photogrammetric surveys on vertical plates are generally confined, therefore, to areas such as the Alps, the Rockies, and the Himálaya, where the outline is sharp and distinctive.

The camera need not, theoretically, be held vertical, for, so long as the position of the camera, its orientation, and the angle of inclination are known, plotting may be carried out, but with so much added difficulty that in practice all surveying cameras or "photo-theodolites" for use from ground stations are intended to be carefully levelled.

Aerial Photogrammetry. Since the development of dirigible aircraft, photogrammetry has been applied to photographs taken from the air. In its most favourable case, where the plane of the plate is parallel to the plane of the map, and the ground itself is flat, the resulting photograph becomes a plan, whose scale is governed by the height of exposure and the principal distance of the camera. Such photographs are rarely obtainable in practice, for lack of any means of maintaining the camera in a fixed position relative to the earth, and because the earth is not generally flat.

Providing, however, the pilot is trained to fly straight and level, that there are numerous control-points whose images can be seen on the photographs, and that the ground is not markedly hilly, fairly good small-scale maps may be made on the assumption that the planes are parallel.

For more accurate mapping from air photographs each point must be plotted separately. This can be done from individual photographs, providing that the ground is flat, or by the intersection of rays from two or more photographs if the ground be markedly uneven, but in either case the position of four control-points must appear on each photograph.

Photogrammetry on vertical, horizontal, or inclined plates has had little commercial development, but may be of value to large national surveys for use in conjunction with other methods.

Stereophotogrammetry. A remarkable development of photographic surveying is stereophotogrammetry. The human power of judging distance is principally due to the divergence of rays from an object to the pupils of the eye, or, in other words, to the angle subtended at the object by the eyebase. This stereoscopic effect can be magnified optically both by enlarging the eyebase and by magnifying the object. In stereophotogrammetry distance is judged not on the ground, but on two photographic plates taken in the same vertical plane at the ends of a short measured base.

Several types of stereoscopic microscope or comparator have been made, but the Zeiss comparator, designed by Professor Pulfrich of Jena, is the best and most complete. By its aid the bearing, distance, and height of all objects common to both photographs may be measured relatively to one end of the base.

At this stage of its development stereophotogrammetry has this great advantage over simple photogrammetry: that the difficulties of the identification of points on two separate plates are eliminated, and even flattish country can be mapped without difficulty.

The Stereoautograph. A further development, the stereoautograph, invented by Captain von Orel, makes it possible to plot automatically and without calculation from the comparator. Thus, contours may be traced direct in addition to detail which can be actually seen. Were it not for the difficulty and expense of procuring these instruments, stereophotogrammetry would already have gone far to replace other methods of surveying at medium scales and for engineering purposes. *See* SURVEYING; PHOTOGRAPHY.

PHOTOGRAPHY. The word *photography* was first used by Sir John Herschel in 1840. It signifies a drawing made by light (Gr. *phos*, light, and *grapho*, I write). There are two main functions of photography: (1) the production of an image by the camera; (2) the fixation of that image by chemical means. Then there is the reproduction of any number of positives from the negative image obtained in the camera.

Early History. The camera was invented 350 years before photography, and it was, as its name implies, a chamber or room. This dark room was called a *camera obscura,* and there was practically no invention required, as any dark room with a small hole in the window-shutter would produce an inverted image of the sun-lit scene outside. Later there was invented the *camera lucida* (q.v.), the principle of which is shown in fig. 1. To the observer the image appears to be on the paper placed on the table, and he is able to make a drawing by tracing round it. It was the beauty of these camera images which suggested to several men that light itself might produce a permanent picture.

A German physician, Johann Heinrich Schulze, discovered that a mixture of chalk with a solution of silver nitrate became blackened by sunlight. He cut out stencils of letters and words, and, placing these over the mixture, he succeeded in getting a black image of them. This was undoubtedly a case of writing or drawing by light.

Dr. William Lewis, of Kingston-on-Thames, repeated Schulze's experiments in 1763, and made notes concerning them. On the death of Lewis in 1781 his notebooks were purchased by Josiah Wedgwood, the potter, who also took Lewis's assistant—Chisholm—into his employment, making him tutor to his son Tom. In 1790 we find young Tom Wedgwood making experiments with pieces of white paper and leather treated with silver nitrate, and with the agency of light he made faithful copies of transparent drawings.

In 1802 Tom Wedgwood and Humphry Davy sent a paper to the Royal Institution (London) describing experiments with silver nitrate on paper, but with no means of fixing the image permanently. Wedgwood and Davy attempted to entrap the image of the camera obscura, but without success, although they succeeded with the more concentrated image of a solar microscope, which was practically a daylight magic lantern.

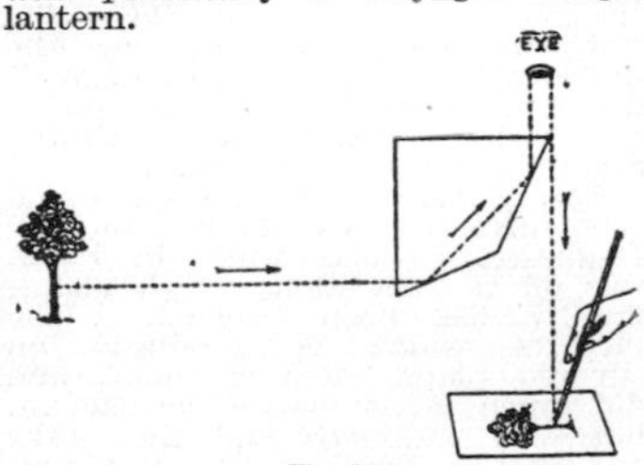

Fig. 1

New Processes. Then followed William Henry Fox Talbot, a grandson of the Earl of Ilchester, who succeeded in obtaining a paper negative of Lacock Abbey, his country home, in 1835. He was led to this through failing to trace the images of the camera lucida. Talbot's experiments were undoubtedly an extension of the experiments which Wedgwood and Davy had made some thirty years earlier.

In 1841 Talbot patented a new process, which he named *calotype* (signifying beautiful pictures), but the public christened it *talbotype* after its inventor. In this process he treated the paper with iodide of silver, and, immediately before exposing it in the camera, he washed it over with a mixture of aceto-nitrate and gallo-nitrate of silver.

A great advance had been made in 1841 by the introduction of a portrait lens invented by Joseph Petzval, who was professor of mathematics in the University of Vienna. By using a larger aperture he was able to increase the illumination and consequently to reduce the time of exposure; the principle which he introduced is the same as used to-day.

In 1840 Sir John Herschel introduced glass plates in place of paper negatives, but these had no supporting film. As already stated, it was Herschel who first used the word *photography*, the art having been known previously as *photogenic drawing*. It was not until 1848 that a supporting film was suggested by Niepce de St. Victor, who was a nephew of Joseph Nicephore Niepce. The first supporting film was the white of an egg, this albumen being spread over the glass, and the silver salts being contained in it.

In 1851 Frederick Scott Archer invented the wet collodion plate, and he introduced a method of converting the negatives into positives. The *tintype* photographs still taken at some English watering-places and at country fairs are descendants of the Scott Archer process. After the wet collodion plate there came the dry gelatine plate of Dr. R. L. Maddox in 1871, and by 1880 dry plates were being marketed in the United States by George Eastman.

The *daguerreotype* process, which was invented by Louis Jacques Daguerre, a scene-painter in Paris, was off the line along which photography has been evolved. The pictures which he produced on silvered plates were excellent, and did much to popularise the camera, but only indirectly did they take any part in the evolution of photography. Daguerreotype portraits were often tinted by hand, and the colour effects produced were sometimes very pleasing; but so early as 1861 there was established a *three-colour process* of photography by the distinguished physicist Clerk Maxwell, and this was modified by F. E. Ives in 1888.

With the exception of two experimental methods, all colour photography is based upon Clerk Maxwell's three-colour process. Three negatives are taken through red, green, and blue screens respectively, as in the Ives and Sanger-Shepherd processes; or all may be combined in one negative by taking the picture through a glass screen covered with coloured lines, red, green, and blue successively, as is done in the Joly process; or the negative itself may contain very fine starch grains dyed these three colours, through which the negative is taken and converted by chemical means into a transparent positive, so that it is viewed through the coloured starch grains as in the Lumière process.

In modern photographic processes we have to deal with the exposure of the sensitised surface, the production of the negative, and the preparation of positive prints. The time of exposure of the sensitised film or plate is dependent not only upon the amount of light available at the time of exposure, but also upon the particular kind of lens used; further, upon the amount of stopping down of the lens, and also upon the sensitivity of the chemically prepared surface.

Focus. There is great variety in the construction of photographic lenses, the production of which demands considerable mathematical knowledge. The simple uncorrected lens is still used by some photographers who do not care for definition, but the construction of modern lenses takes into account the fact that the focus of the chemical rays differs from that of the visual rays; the modern lens is *achromatic*.

Many small hand cameras are made with a fixed focus. A lens is generally described as being of a certain focus, working at a certain aperture, and covering a certain size of plate. The *focus* (strictly *focal length*) of a lens (q.v.) is the distance from the plate or ground-glass screen to the lens, when it is focused on an object at such a distance that everything beyond it is also in focus. We may focus some object so that its image on the screen is exactly the same size as the object; the lens will then be found to be the same distance from the image as it is from the object. If this distance measures 16 inches, the focus of the lens would be known as 8-inch. Then the desired aperture is obtained by stopping down the lens.

The stops are never described by the diameter of the aperture, but by the relationship between that diameter and the focus of the lens. Therefore, when the stop has a diameter of 1 inch, and it is used with a lens having a focus of 8 inches, the stop would be called F/8, because the diameter of the stop would be one-eighth of the focus of the lens. This is a common relationship in modern lenses, the largest stop employed having a diameter one-eight of the focus of the lens. The next size smaller is F/11·3 stop, which only admits one-half of the light of F/8 stop, so that it requires twice the time of exposure. The smaller stops are F/16, F/22·6, F/32, F/45, and F/64, but few lenses now go to a stop of F/64, though this was common for very fine definition with the old rapid rectilinear lenses. The general principle of an R.R. (rapid rectilinear) lens is shown in fig. 2.

An R.R. lens is a good all round one, but there are more modern lenses which cost more money, such as an *anastigmat*, which soon shows its superiority if employed at large apertures on subjects with fine details, and especially if used for copying flat objects.

All Kodak cameras have the stops marked on the U.S., or " uniform system ", which states F/4 as 1, and follows with F/5·6 as 2 (*requiring twice the exposure of F/4*); F/8 is marked 4 (*four times the exposure of F/4*), and so on, until F/64 is marked U.S. 256, with which stop 256 times the exposure of F/4 must be given. In both systems each succeeding stop requires twice the exposure of the preceding one. It is obvious that the object of the lens is to admit as much light as possible, and at the same time to focus the rays correctly.

In pinhole photography, which dispenses with the lens, there is,

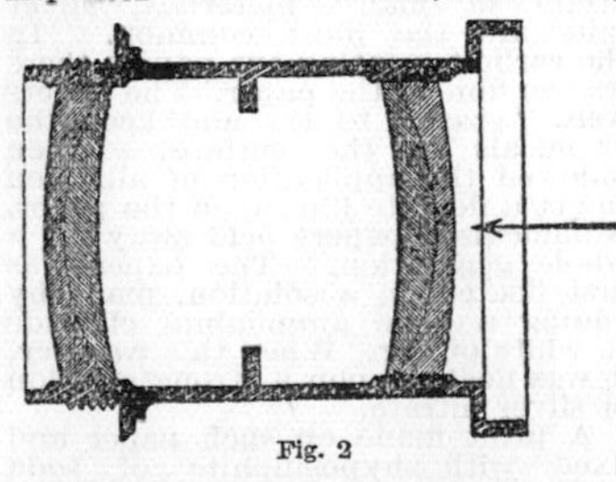

Fig. 2

of course, no particular focal length. If an object is desired to cover the greater part of the plate, the camera bellows may be extended, making the image larger and larger until the desired size is obtained, but the pinhole must be very small if the picture is to be sharp. It is usual to have a very small round hole drilled in a sheet of metal. The hole required for good work may measure from one fiftieth to one seventy-fifth of an inch. But for the fact that the pinhole admits so little light, necessitating a very long exposure, it would be used more often.

The sensitive coating which is to be affected by the light may be supported on glass or celluloid. Both of these are very much superior to the paper negatives of Fox Talbot, as paper is not easily made translucent, which is necessary to obtain the reproductions of positives through the negatives. The glass negative has the advantage of rigidity, but the disadvantage of weight, which disadvantage, however, is discounted for some purposes by the fact that it costs very much less than celluloid; the roll-film on celluloid may cost three times as much as glass.

The reason why the roll-film is so popular is the convenience of daylight loading of the camera and daylight development of the negative. These advantages, added to its light weight and small bulk, are a great asset, though it is possible to make more rapid glass plates than roll-films, and celluloid films will not keep as well as glass plates. Very rapid plates should not be used excepting where their speed is a necessity. Slower plates have a more opaque film, and they possess a greater range of exposure. Correct exposure is the key to successful photography. It used to be thought possible to remedy an incorrectly exposed plate in the process of development by compensating for over or under exposure, but this has been found to be a fallacy.

Exposure. A great deal of useful research on the subject of exposure was made by Dr. Hurter, an eminent chemist, and Mr. V. C. Driffield, an engineer, who collaborated with him. They found that most sensitised plates possessed a great deal of latitude as to correct exposure. For instance, when the time necessary for a perfect negative was obtained, it was found that an equally perfect negative might be obtained with twice, four, eight, or it might on occasion even be thirty-two, times as long.

This latitude is dependent upon three factors: (1) the subject, (2) the nature of the sensitised film, and (3) the thickness of the coating. The thicker the plate is coated (up to a certain point) the greater is the latitude. Generally speaking, the slower the response of the chemically prepared surface the greater is the latitude in exposure. It will be clear that exposure is influenced by the following factors: (i) the rapidity of movement of the object, or of the camera itself if it is travelling; (ii) the amount of light available; (iii) the focus of the lens and its stopping down; (iv) the sensitiveness of the plate; (v) the nature of the subject itself.

It is a difficult task to determine all these factors at the time of exposure. Tables for correct exposure have been published, but these were never of much value, and have been superseded by the researches of Hurter and Driffield. These investigations showed that the influence of the height of the sun was a perfectly definite one, and they obtained time curves of the changes in the power of daylight due to the height of the sun. These curves led to the invention of the *actinograph*, by which exposures may be estimated. The height of the sun is not the only factor, for the dust in the atmosphere plays an important part; this is very noticeable in the red sunset.

The results of the researches of Hurter and Driffield are embodied in the H. & D. numbers. Plates marked H. & D. 100 require only half of the exposure of these marked H. & D. 50. The only point which is really left to the judgment of the photographer is the nature of the subject itself. Yellow and red objects may require as much as twice the average exposure, and so on. We must, of course, take into account the distance of the most important part of the subject; the nearer it is to the camera the longer exposure will it require.

Developing. The sensitised coating of the photographic plate is of great interest and considerable mystery. We do not understand the nature of the latent image which we know is produced in the plate, and which is invisible until development. The sensitive surface of the plate or film consists of gelatine, throughout which there are distributed small particles of bromide of silver. The particle of silver bromide is composed of the two elementary substances — bromine and silver — in combination with each other. The compound substance has properties entirely different from the elements of which it is composed.

The action of light falling upon this compound is to make it less stable. One cannot note any difference in its appearance, nor can one detect any chemical alteration, but there is no doubt that in some mysterious way the bombardment of the light has left the substance in a less stable condition, but a further bombardment of light renders it stable again; a still further attack of light renders it so unstable that the bromide and the silver part company.

The developing solution takes away the bromine from the silver bromide particles which have been exposed to light, leaving the silver coating, but those particles which were sheltered by some dark part of the image remain unaffected. These unaffected salts must be removed by the fixing-bath, or they would still be susceptible to any further exposure to light.

The developer consists of three reagents: (1) a developing agent, (2) an accelerator, (3) a retarder. These two additional reagents are to balance the action of the developing agent, just as in the case of the sails and ballast of a ship. There is a fourth constituent added to the developer, to prevent staining by the new compound formed by the bromine combining with the developer. The fourth constituent keeps the developer clear.

The developing agent may be pyrogallic acid. The accelerator is an alkali, because the developing agents are more ready to take up bromine in the presence of an alkali. Without this alkali, the plate would require a very prolonged treatment in the developer. Acetone or formic aldehyde may be used as accelerators. The retarder is generally potassium bromide, and the stain preventer is usually sodium sulphite.

Printing. In the photographic print we have a reversal of the lights and shades of the negative. Although it is possible to get photographic prints in many materials, silver salts are the most common. In the earliest printing-out papers there was no film on the paper. The papers were "sized" to try and keep the chemicals to the surface. Then followed the application of albumen to get a definite film upon the paper. Albumenised papers held sway for a whole generation. The paper was first floated on a solution, made by adding a little ammonium chloride to white of egg. When this was dry, it was floated upon a strong solution of silver nitrate.

A print made on such paper and fixed with hyposulphite of soda would have a rather disagreeable red colour, and to rectify this and produce a print with a more agreeable purple, or a brown colour approaching black, the print was "toned" in a solution containing gold or platinum. Then followed other forms of printing-out papers, among which were self-toning papers, which had the necessary gold salt added to the emulsion.

In contradistinction to printing-out papers, there are "bromide papers", in which a latent image is formed and developed as in the case of a negative. Bromide paper is paper prepared with a suitable surface and then coated with a bromide of silver gelatine emulsion, but the emulsion is made less sensitive than for negative work. These papers are known as "gas-light papers", because they are exposed under the negative for a few seconds to the light from a gas-flame or other artificial light. The fixing-bath for a printed positive serves the same purpose as for a glass or film negative: to remove the unaffected chemicals, and thus prevent further action under the influence of light. There are other papers, giving a platinum and a carbon image, which give fine permanent results.

For a cheap method of printing engineers' drawings, etc., a paper is coated with iron salt, and after exposure under a negative it is plunged into a solution of potassium ferricyanide. The salt that has been acted upon by light will give a dark-blue insoluble deposit with the ferricyanide, while the unaffected salt will be soluble, and can be washed away with water. The ferricyanide may be mixed with the iron salt and the paper coated with the mixture, then after exposure the print print needs only to be washed in water (*see* CYANIDES).

Practical Applications. The application of photography to the production of moving pictures has been

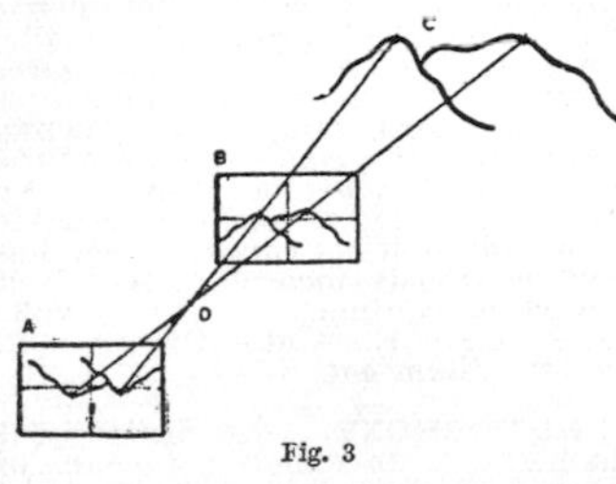

Fig. 3

dealt with under CINEMATOGRAPH. It plays an important part in the making of book illustrations. Its application in X-ray work is well known, as also its aid to the astronomer in recording the spectra of the different stars and in making a detailed survey of the heavens. It is a convenient adjunct to microscopy in all its branches, one of which is in connection with metallurgy, enabling the student and the manufacturer to study the construction of the metals. In aviation it gives the aeronaut a means of recording a bird's-eye view of the country over which he passes. It also supplies the civil engineer with a quick method of surveying, one principle being as indicated in the illustration (fig. 3).

A is a negative of the landscape C, while B is a print of the negative. The lines joining similar points in A and B will produce the same angles as those joining the same points in A and C; therefore the angles for the distant landscape may be reproduced at any time by placing the point B the same distance from the optical axis D as A is from it.

The advantage in photogrammetry (q.v.), or photographic surveying, is that the field work may be done in a very short time, a permanent record being obtained immediately, but the work is not so accurate as with a plane table. There is a special camera or *phototheodolite* with the necessary scales; to be quite accurate, the camera would require to have a pinhole in place of a lens.

By means of *telephoto lenses* photographs may be taken of very distant objects. Again, photographs may be taken by means of *ultra-violet light*, which has no effect upon our sense of vision; and the ether-waves beyond the red end of the spectrum, the *infra-red*, may also produce images on the photographic plate, although these rays cannot be detected by the eye.—BIBLIOGRAPHY: *Photography as a Scientific Implement*; Alfred Watkins, *Photography*; Chapman Jones, *Photography of To-day*; C. R. Gibson, *Romance of Modern Photography*.

PHOTOM'ETER. An apparatus used for comparing the luminous intensities of different sources of light. Let L be the light emitted per second by a small source of light; then the light which passes per second through unit area of a sphere of radius r with its centre at the source is $L/4\pi r^2$. This is a measure of the intensity of illumination I of a screen at the distance r, and for normal rays I varies directly as the intensity of the source, and inversely as the square of its distance. Thus, if two sources of luminosities L_1 and L_2 produce equal illumination at distances r_1 and r_2, $L_1/r_1^2 = L_2/r_2^2$, or $L_1/L_2 = r_1^2/r_2^2$, an equation which forms the basis of photometric calculations.

In Bouguer's photometer (1729) the two lights are set in front of a thin sheet of translucent paper divided by an opaque partition placed in front so that each source illuminates one-half of the screen only. By varying the distances of the lamps from the screen, equality of illumination is obtained, and a measurement of the distance of each source from the middle of the screen gives, by the above equation, the ratio of the luminosities. With other photometers a similar procedure is followed.

Rumford (1794) placed the sources on two tables set at about 60°. The screen was placed at the junction of the tables, and two vertical cylinders cast on the screen shadows which touched but did not overlap. The lamps were moved until the shadows were equally dark. In the common use of this photometer only one rod is employed to cast the shadows.

In Ritchie's photometer (1826) a white isosceles wedge is placed between the two illuminants with its edges vertical, and each of two sides receives light from one source. Viewing the wedge from the side, its position on the line joining the two

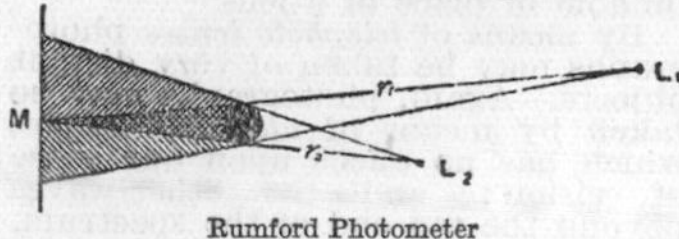

Rumford Photometer

lamps is adjusted until the two faces appear equally bright.

In Joly's photometer (1888) the wedge is replaced by two rectangular blocks of paraffin separated by tinfoil.

The modern form of Bunsen's photometer (1841) uses a sheet of paper, with a grease spot in the middle, placed between the two

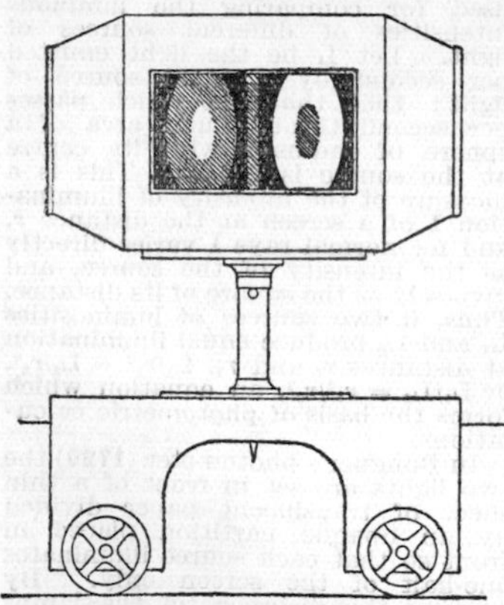
Bunsen Photometer

lights. The paper is moved between the sources until the appearance of the grease spot is the same as seen from either side. The comparison is rendered easier by setting two plane mirrors so that both sides of the grease spot can be seen simultaneously.

Lummer and Brodhun's photometer (1889) is a modification of an older form used by Swan (1849). The light from each source is reflected by different paths to the adjacent faces of a cube formed from a pair of right-angled prisms, the hypotenuse sides of which are cemented by a central transparent patch of Canada balsam. The rays from one source pass straight through both prisms by way of the balsam, whilst the light from the other source enters the second prism and is totally reflected at the surface surrounding the balsam, and continues, parallel to the central beam, into a low-power microscope, by means of which the comparison is made.

The Flicker photometer was designed by Whitman (1896) to compare the luminosities of lights of different colours. By using a rotating sector, or a rotating wheel with a rim suitably bevelled or provided with a series of mirrors, the light is directed to the eye alternately from each source. A flickering effect is produced, which disappears when proper adjustment is made.

In order to reduce the photometric comparison to terms of candle-power, the luminosity of one source requires to be known. If one source is a standard lamp (*see* CANDLE STANDARD), the candle-power of the second lamp may be found. An electric glow-lamp forms a reliable sub-standard if its candle-power has been previously measured, and if it is used in conjunction with a voltmeter and rheostat.—Cf. A. P. Trotter, *Illumination*.

PHO'TOPHONE. An instrument which transmits sounds by means of a beam of light. It was invented in 1878 by Bell and Tainter, and utilised the Bell telephone in conjunction with a selenium "cell", the properties of which had been discovered by May five years previously.

When light falls on a selenium cell or bridge, the electrical resistance of the cell diminishes, and a stronger current is enabled to pass from a battery round a circuit which includes the cell. In the silenium cell used by Bell and Tainter, the resistance changed from about 1200 ohms in the dark to 600 ohms in the light. In the photophone as used by these experimenters, sunlight was reflected from a mirror to a flexible reflecting membrane which directed the rays to a large parabolic mirror at the receiving-station. The rays were focused by the mirror on a selenium cell connected in series with a battery and telephone. When the voice of the speaker was directed on to the transmitting membrane, the latter vibrated in resonance, and, becoming alternately concave and convex, caused the reflected rays to become alternately convergent and divergent.

The intensity of the light concentrated on the selenium cell thus varied with the same frequency as that of the sound-wave which actuated the membrane, and corresponding variations were impressed on the electric current through the telephone, which reproduced the sounds spoken into the distant membrane.

Other forms of transmitter have been designed; in the most successful of these, the beam from an electric arc search-light was employed. The sound-waves actuated a microphone placed in a branch circuit of the arc, and variations of the current in the arc were caused, which gave rise to variations in the intensity of the transmitting beam of light. The speaking range has a limit of about 20 miles.—Cf. Ruhmer, *Wireless Telephony* (translated by J. E. Murray, 1908).

PHO'TOSPHERE. Literally "sphere of light;" the shell of incandescent matter which forms the luminous surface of the sun, and from which we chiefly receive its light. The photosphere is overlaid by the reversing layer, in which occurs the absorption producing the Fraunhofer lines, by the chromosphere, and the corona.

PHOTOSYNTHESIS. *See* CARBON ASSIMILATION.

PHRAGMITES (frag-mī'tēz). A genus of large grasses widely spread, and usually known as reeds. *P. commūnis*, the only British species, is the largest grass in the British Islands.

PHRENOL'OGY (Gr. *phrēn*, mind, *logos*, discourse). The term applied to the wild speculations of Gall and Spurzheim, founded upon (1) the claim that the brain, as the organ of the mind, is not so much a single organ as a complex congeries of organs; and (2) the supposed existence of a certain correspondence between the aptitudes of the individual and the configuration of his skull. The development of physiology has shown that while there is some slight justification for the underlying principle, the scheme elaborated by Gall and Spurzheim is wholly fantastic and false.

PHRYGIA. In ancient geography, a region comprising the western-central part of Asia Minor, containing the cities Apamea, Laodicea, and Colossæ. The inhabitants were early civilised, and paid much attention to grazing and tillage. The early history of Phrygia is mythological. Several of its kings of the names of Gordius and Midas are mentioned. On the death of Adrastus (560 B.C.) the royal family of Phrygia became extinct, and the kingdom became a province of Lydia. It afterwards formed a part of the Persian, and still later of the Roman Empire.

PHRY'NICHUS. Greek comic poet, a contemporary and rival of Aristophanes, who accused him of vulgarity and plagiarism. His plays are all lost, only a few fragments surviving. Aristophanes beat Phrynichus's *Solitary* with the *Birds*, and his *Muses* with the *Frogs*.

PHTHISIS (thī'sis). Greek word, "wasting," formerly applied—like consumption—specifically to the wasting lung-disease now called tuberculosis (q.v.). It should be distinguished from chronic interstitial pneumonia.

PHYCOMYCETES, or **LOWER FUNGI.** A common name for the lower and more primitive families of the Fungi (q.v.).

PHYLAC'TERY (Gr. *phylacterion*, safeguard). Among the Jews, strips of parchment inscribed with certain texts from the Old Testament, and enclosed within a small leathern case, which is fastened with straps on the forehead just above and between the eyes, and on the left arm near the region of the heart. The four passages inscribed upon the phylactery are Ex. xiii. 1-10, 11-16; Deut. vi, 4-9; xi. 13-21.

The custom was founded on a literal interpretation of Ex. xiii. 16; Deut. vi. 8; xi. 18. The word occurs only once in the New Testament (Matt. xxiii. 5), in the discourse of the Saviour against the Pharisees. The Jews call the phylacteries *tephillin*, plural of *tephillah*, a prayer.

The orthodox Jews still consider it a sacred religious duty to wear the phylacteries during morning prayer every day except on Saturdays and high festivals. In their origin they were regarded as amulets, which protected the wearer from the power of demons, and hence their name.

PHYLLODE. In botany, the name given to a leaf-stalk when it becomes developed into a flattened expansion like a leaf, as in some Australian species of accacia and certain other plants.

PHYLLOP'ODA (" leaf-footed "). A sub-order of Crustacea, possessing numerous feet, numbering eight pairs at least, the first pair being natatory in character. The feet are of foliaceous or leaf-like structure, and are provided with branchial appendages, adapted to subserve the breathing or respiratory function. The carapace, or shelly covering protecting the head and chest, may be well developed or the body may be destitute of a covering.

In their development the Phyllopoda pass through a metamorphosis; and in their earliest state the embryos appear as in the "nauplius" form (*see* NAUPLIUS). All the Phyllopoda are of small size. The order is represented by the familiar "fairy shrimps" (Chirocephalus), met with in freshwater ponds, and the curious "brine shrimps" (Artemia), found in the brine-pans of salt-works and in the salt lakes of both the Old and New Worlds.

PHYLLOSTOMATIDÆ. The vampire bats, an American family of bats, including the true blood-sucking vampire (*Desmodus rufus*). *See* VAMPIRE-BAT.

PHYLLOTAXIS. In botany, the mode of insertion of leaves on the axis. Many ingenious theories have been advanced to account for the almost mathematical exactness of phyllotaxis, but the problem is still unsolved.

PHYLLOXE'RA. A genus of plant-lice, family Aphidæ, ord. Hemiptera. The type of the genus is *Phylloxera quercus*, a species which lives upon oak trees; but the *Phylloxera vastatrix*, or grape Phylloxera, a species which injuriously affects the vine, has attracted so much attention by its ravages that it has come to be known as *the* Phylloxera. It presents itself in two types, the one gall-inhabiting (*gallicola*), and the other root-inhabiting (*radicola*).

Its proper home is North America, where it was known early in the history of grape-culture, and where it doubtless existed on wild vines from time immemorial. It was discovered in England in 1863, and about the same time it made its appearance in France, where it committed great ravages, inflicting immense loss upon the owners of vineyards.

Widening its area not only by natural means, but also by commerce in vines and cuttings, it was carried from infected to non-infected districts, and spread to Spain, Portugal, Switzerland, Austria, Prussia, and to all the grape-growing countries of Europe. Only where the soil was of a sandy nature did the vineyards escape.

In 1885 its presence was discovered in Australia, at the Cape of Good Hope, and in Algeria; and, generally speaking, it has now obtained a foothold, at least in restricted localities, in every country where the grapevine is cultivated.

Vines attacked by Phylloxera generally show external signs the second year of attack in a sickly yellowish appearance of the foliage and in stunted growth, and the third year they frequently perish, all the finer roots having decayed. Grafting European on American vines has proved the best means of checking this pest.

PHYLOGENESIS, or **PHYLOGENY.** In biology, the race-history of an animal or vegetable type, a term much used by evolutionary biologists and philosophers. It has been shown that ontogenesis, or the life-history of an individual, is a more or less imperfect recapitulation of its phylogenesis (Law of Recapitulation).

PHYSA'LIA. A genus of marine animals of the class Hydrozoa, of the sub-class Siphonophora. The *P. atlantica* is known by the name of the *Portuguese man-of-war*. These hydrozoa are characterised by the presence of one or more large air-sacs, by which they float on the surface of the ocean. Numerous tentacles depend from the under side, one class short and the other long. The shorter are the nutritive individuals of the colony; the longer, which in a Physalia 5 or 6 inches long are capable of being extended to 12 or 18 feet, possess a remarkable stinging power, and are probably used to stun their prey.

PHYSICAL CHEMISTRY. This may be defined as the science which deals with the *mechanism* of chemical phenomena. It attempts to find an "explanation" of the observational facts of inorganic chemistry, organic chemistry, colloid chemistry, bio-chemistry, and chemical technology. By the term "explanation" is meant the restatement of the chemical phenomenon in terms of purely physical (i.e. mechanical) concepts, that is, the demonstration that the chemical phenomenon is precisely what is to be expected, provided certain mechanical theorems or principals are applicable to the behaviour of those excessively minute material units in terms of which chemical change takes place. These material units are the molecules of which matter in bulk is composed, molecules themselves possessing an atomic and ultimately an electronic structure (*see* MATTER; RAYS, ELECTRIC; RADIO-ACTIVITY; ELECTRON; IONISATION).

The development of physical chemistry has been rendered possible by the application of two, or possibly three, different modes of treatment. The first consists in the application of the kinetic molecular theory. The second mode, namely the thermodynamical, was first applied by Horstmann (1869), whilst the third mode, namely the application of statistical mechanics together with its modification known as the Quantum Theory (q.v.), has only recently begun to play a part in the development of chemical theory.

Kinetic Molecular Theory. Examining a chemical phenomenon from the point of view of elementary kinetic molecular theory, we attempt to visualise the occurrence in terms of the molecules, atoms or electrons taking part, attributing to these natural units purely mechanical properties, such as mass, velocity, momentum, forces of attraction and of repulsion (*see* DYNAMICS; KINETICS).

The word elementary is used here to indicate that we artificially simplify the actual mechanism by attributing *average* values to molecular properties. On this basis, the reaction between two molecules in a gaseous mixture, for example, is regarded as due primarily to collisions. The more frequent the collitions, i.e. the more highly concentrated the gas mixture, and the higher the temperature, the more rapidly does the chemical change take place (*see* KINETIC THEORY OF GASES).

Recent investigation has indeed shown that other considerations enter, notably that the molecules must be in a certain state or condition in respect of internal energy before a collision will be chemically effective. Apart from this, however, it has been found possible to express chemical reactivity in terms of a law, the Law of Mass Action (*see* MASS ACTION), according to which the rate of chemical change between two different molecules is proportional to the product of the concentrations of the two gases in the mixture. Applying this idea to two opposing reactions, we arrive at the concept of *chemical equilibrium*, essentially dynamic, due to the existence of equal and opposite rates of chemical change.

Thermodynamic Treatment. In the thermodynamic treatment of chemical processes we set aside completely all molecular considerations (*see* THERMODYNAMICS). Thermodynamical reasoning is based entirely on the concept that all material changes are accompanied by energy changes, and from the thermodynamic point of view the latter alone are considered. This mode of treatment is characterised by its generalised nature, as distinct from the specialised concepts involved in the kinetic molecular theory. There are two classical principles or laws upon which thermodynamical considerations rest, and the introduction of these into chemistry has led to conclusions, e.g. the colligative properties of solutions (*see* SOLUTION), which could not have been obtained on any other basis. The very generality of treatment which characterises thermodynamics makes it difficult to apply, but once it is applied the conclusion is unassailable.

Since the concept of time is absent from thermodynamical reasoning, we cannot, by this method, deal with a phenomenon such as chemical rate or velocity. We can deal, however, with chemical equilibrium, and it is possible, for example, to calculate with precision the effect of an alteration in temperature upon the position of the equilibrium finally attained in a chemical process, in terms of the heat of the reaction, chemical reactions being accompanied in general by an evolution or an absorption of heat.

As a further example of its utility it may be mentioned that thermodynamical reasoning has to a large extent solved the problem of determining quantitatively what is meant by the term *chemical affinity*, a term the very familiarity of which has somewhat obscured its indefiniteness. This problem has, in fact, within recent years involved a considerable extension of the fundamental concepts of thermodynamics themselves by indicating the existence of a new principle, the so-called Third Law of Thermodynamics.

Statistical Mechanics. The introduction of statistical mechanics into chemical processes is in a sense a return to the kinetic molecular theory, but on an altogether wider basis. We no longer regard every molecule in a material system as identical in all respects with every other molecule. We recognise that there are individual physical differences which must be allowed for.

Since, however, there are vast numbers of molecules in any system, even the most dilute, with which we usually deal, it is obviously impossible to consider each molecule by itself, more especially as every molecule is changing in various ways with the time. Instead, we make allowance for individual characteristics by introducing *probability considerations* into the purely mechanical theory adopted.

On this basis we know, with regard to the speed of molecules for example, that in a system consisting of many molecules a large proportion possesses speed which lies very near to a "most probable speed," whilst only a very small proportion possesses either very large or very small speeds relative to the most probable value.

It is almost certain that the internal energy in the molecules is distributed in a similar manner, and the conclusion has now been reached that it is only that very small fraction of the total molecules, which possesses excessively great internal energy, which is really concerned in chemical changes. On the basis of what is now known as classical statistical mechanics, the variation of, say, internal energy amongst molecules is regarded as continuous, that is, the internal energy of any individual molecule might differ by an *infinitely* small amount from the energy of another molecule.

The Quantum Theory. The most recent development of statistical mechanics, known as the *Quantum Theory*, virtually denies this, and replaces it by the concept of discrete alterations in energy content in *finite* (though still very small) amounts. Each of these minimum amounts is known as a quantum. This is only a crude way of expressing the idea, but it is sufficient to indicate the essential characteristic of quantum treatment. The introduction of such ideas into chemical theory has only taken place within the last few years, but it has already become evident that the ultimately satisfactory theory of chemical processes will be attained on this basis. For bibliography see CHEMISTRY.

PHYSICIANS, ROYAL COLLEGE OF (LONDON). A body which owes its origin to the exertions of Thomas Linacre, one of the physicians of Henry VIII., who, through the influence of Cardinal Wolsey, obtained in 1518 from that monarch letters patent incorporating himself with certain other physicians named, and all other men of the same faculty in London, as one body. Various privileges were accorded to them, the chief of which was that of prohibiting anyone from practising as a physician in London, or within a circuit of 7 miles round it, unless he had first obtained a licence from this corporation.

A charter granted four years later confirmed the privileges of the body, except that graduates of Oxford and Cambridge were permitted to practise within the jurisdiction of the college without previously being examined by it. Various charters have been granted to the body subsequently, but since the passing of the Medical Act of 1858, by which any duly qualified practitioner is entitled to practise according to his qualifications in any part of His Majesty's dominions, the licence of the college is not necessary to those practising in London or within 7 miles round.

The Royal College of Physicians of London is represented by one member in the General Medical Council established by the Medical Act of 1858. The college consists of fellows, licentiates, and members, the first being elected from among the members, whilst the others are admitted by examination. The building of the college, formerly in Warwick Lane, is now situated in Pall Mall East, London.

The Royal College of Physicians, Edinburgh, was incorporated by royal charter dated the 26th of Nov., 1681, and empowered to make laws for promoting the art of physic, and to regulate the practice thereof in Edinburgh and Leith. Its fellows and licentiates are entitled to be registered as qualified medical practitioners. The Royal Faculty of Physicians and Surgeons, Glasgow, has a like status, and combines with the Royal College of Physicians, Edinburgh, and the Royal College of Surgeons, Edinburgh, to grant a triple qualification, after a joint examination.

PHYSIC-NUT. The seed of the *Jatrŏpha curcas*, or the plant itself, a shrub belonging to the nat. ord. Euphorbiaceæ, a native of intertropical countries, principally the East and West Indies. The seeds have strong emetic and purgative properties, due to a fixed oil used in medicine, under the name of *Jatropha-oil*, for the same purposes as croton-oil, although it is less powerful. French or Spanish physic-nuts are the seeds of *J. multifida*, and yield Oil of Pinhoen, similar in its properties to Jatropha-oil.

PHYSICS. A general term signifying the aggregate of the sciences dealing with such natural phenomena as motion, force, heat, light, sound, electricity, magnetism, elasticity, capillarity, osmose, diffusion, solution, and change of state. Its scope extends over all properties of matter which are not specifically biological or chemical. Aristotle's treatise τὰ φυσικά, from which the word physics is derived, embraced nature-knowledge of all kinds, but chemistry and biology are not now reckoned to belong to the realm of physics, though biological facts and processes have their physical aspect, and the dividing line between physics and chemistry is hard to draw. In biology, for example, the methods of physics apply to such subjects as measurement of sap- and blood-pressure, and the mechanics of the skeleton and muscles, but physics takes no account of the special character of living matter: thus the physical theory of *sound* deals with the mechanics of wave-motion and the mechanism of the ear, but stops short at the threshold of sensation of sound.

It may be taken that physics attempts to classify and explain natural phenomena in terms of certain special concepts, such as attraction and repulsion, cohesion, temperature, state of aggregation, as well as motion, mass, force, stress, strain, and energy. Chemistry and astronomy are really departments of physics, to which independent status has been given, the former dealing with a very special type of physical event, called chemical action, while the latter is simply the physics (including the dynamics) of the celestial bodies. In Britain there has been a tendency to restrict the signification of *physics* by excluding dynamics, "natural philosophy" being used to denote physics in the wider sense.

Such sciences as geology and mineralogy, which lean towards description and history rather than towards causal analysis, are not usually classed under physics, but rather as branches of natural science, along with such biological sciences as botany, zoology, etc.

Among the physical sciences, dynamics has premier place, as its fundamental concepts—matter and motion—are pre-eminently simple and precise. In the development of physics there has been a continual effort to explain all physical phenomena in terms of the dynamics of matter and ether. Great advances in this direction were made in the nineteenth century, with the result that the most important chapters in the textbooks of physics have now an essentially dynamical character. The names of Laplace, Poisson, Fourier, Fresnel, Young, Faraday, Thomson, Joule, Maxwell, Gauss, Helmholtz, Hertz, and others will always be associated with these great advances.

The twentieth century has already witnessed a rejuvenation of the whole of physical science through the remarkable achievements in divining and observing not merely the atomic constitution of matter, but even the structure of the atoms, and in detecting the motions and mutual actions of the electrons and nuclei which compose them. Radioactivity, electron, quantum, these are the magic words of the new century which are expected to give the clue to many a hitherto hidden secret of nature.

The change of outlook which has come about since the discovery, near the end of the last century, of X-rays, radioactivity and the ionisation of gases, has been stupendous. The younger generation of physicists, naturally enough, take little interest in the well-worn fields in which their predecessors won their triumphs. To the research student and the accomplished physicist alike, the properties of the atom and the whole domain of high-vacuum technique are incomparably more attractive, offering as they do an almost certain prospect of rich reward for their assiduous cultivator. Recent textbooks are: *A Textbook of Physics*, by E. Grimsehl (elementary); *The Student's Physics* (advanced).

PHYSIOCRATIC SYSTEM (Gr. *physis*, nature; *kratein*, to rule). A system of political economy. It was advocated by a French school which flourished in the second half of the eighteenth century, and the members of which wrote against the abuses of the mercantile system. It was a system of government based on nature, and was supposed to lead to justice and order. The watchword of the Physiocrats, who were known to their contemporaries as *les économistes*, was *laissez faire, laissez passer*, and they advocated industrial freedom, natural liberty, and the advancement of agriculture.

The term *physiocratic* was first used in 1799 by Du Pont de Nemours. The head of the school and the founder of the system was Francis Quesnay (1694-1774), physician to Louis XV., who was a follower of Descartes and in favour of the reign of natural law (hence *physiocracy*). Quesnay observed the very depressed state of agriculture in France whilst travelling with the king, and ascribed it to the mercantile system under Colbert, which favoured the industry of the cities. He published his *Tableau économique avec son explication* (1758), and developed his system in his *La Physiocratie, ou constitution naturelle du gouvernement le plus avantageux au genre humain* (Paris, 1767).

A whole school, called the Physiocratic, soon sprang up. It was not, however, until the reign of Louis XVI., under the minister Turgot, that the followers of the system came into office. Their authority again sank, but in the Revolution they had for several years a decided preponderance in the Convention. Joseph II. of Austria, and Leopold of Tuscany, his brother, were friendly to the system, but did not allow the perfect freedom of trade which it recommended.

Principles. The principles of the physiocratic system are: (1) The earth is the only source of all national wealth; and only those who use or increase the natural powers operating in the vegetable and animal kingdoms, as farmers, fishermen, herdsmen, or miners, add to the amount of national wealth. All other workers, such as mechanics, manufacturers, or merchants, produce nothing which can increase the public wealth; they only change the form of the articles produced by the former classes, and their wages will always be paid by the surplus of raw products which the farmer saves from his own consumption. The merchant only promotes the exchange of goods. Still less is it in the power of public officers and men in similar employments to increase the elements of wealth.

(2) All members of the community, therefore, are divided into productive and unproductive. To the latter class belong scholars, artists, mechanics, merchants, etc., because all of them are to be supported by the productions of the earth, without having assisted directly in producing them. What they save from the wages received from the mass of the natural products, in various forms, contributes, indeed, to national wealth, and they become thereby a useful class of citizens, indirectly increasing wealth. It is only by their means, moreover, that the agriculturist is enabled to devote himself exclusively to the tillage of the soil.

(3) From this it follows that the unrestricted exercise of all honest occupations is necessary to the wealth of both classes. The physiocratic system inculcates freedom in regard to foreign commerce, as well as to the mechanic arts, considering it a matter of indifference whether the products of a country are consumed by natives or by foreigners.

(4) As according to this system all wealth is derived from the soil, the only subject taxed should be the net produce of the soil.

Without criticising this system in detail, it may be pointed out that it is based upon a misconception of nature and its products. The fire of the steam-engine is as much a productive natural power as that producing grain, and the plough as much a machine as the steam-engine. Besides, if wages are regulated by the "iron law," both in commerce and manufactures as well as in agriculture, then the "net product" is made up of wealth created by the three classes, agricultural, manufacturing, and commercial. — BIBLIOGRAPHY: H. Higgs, *The Physiocrats*; Yves Guyot, *Quesnay et la physiocratie*; R. Sabatier, *La Théorie du commerce chez les physiocrates.*

PHYSIOG'NOMY. The subject which treats of the means of judging character from the countenance. Aristotle is the first who is known to have made any attempts in physiognomy. He observed that each animal has a special predominant instinct, as the fox cunning, the wolf ferocity, and so forth, and from this he concluded that men whose features resemble those of certain animals will have similar qualities to those animals.

Baptista della Porta, in his work *De Humana Physiognomia* (1586), revived this theory and carried it farther. The theory was adopted and illustrated by the French painter Lebrun, in the next century, and by Tischbein, a German painter of the eighteenth century. The anatomist Camper sought new data in a comparison of the heads of different types of the human family, and in attempting to deduce the degree of intelligence belonging to each type from the size of the facial angle.

Lavater was the first to develop an elaborate system of physiognomy, the scope of which he enlarged so as to include all the relations between the physical and moral nature of man. *See* LAVATER.

PHYSIOGRAPHY, or PHYSICAL GEOGRAPHY. One of the great divisions of general geography which treats of the natural features of the earth's surface and their distribution, and of the general relationship of the lithosphere (earth's crust) to the hydrosphere (watery envelope) and atmosphere (gaseous envelope), and, in a lesser degree, considers the interrelationship of the two latter forms with reference to the biosphere, or organic life upon the earth. There is no clearly defined line of demarcation between physical geography and physiography. Some authorities indeed, such as Linnæus and Huxley, give the term physiography a narrower meaning, but it will be used here as comprehending the whole subject of physical geography.

Definition. Physiography is defined by Herbertson (*Guide to Geographical Books*) as "the systematic study of the forces of nature, and their effects in their local and general aspects." Dynamical geography (*geodynamics*) is directly concerned with the distribution of forces, the study of the distribution of forms being covered by morphological geography (*geomorphology*). Geomorphology, however, is not only concerned with the distribution of forms on the lithosphere, it also seeks to describe their structure. In its broadest definition it is concerned with the shape of the earth as a whole, and with the forms and subdivisions of the lithosphere, hydrosphere, atmosphere, and biosphere, but it is usually restricted in meaning to the consideration of land or crust forms only.

Overlapping Sciences. Physiography is in no small degree dependent upon the results of three other sciences, although it has no interest whatever in the processes by which these results are obtained. A study of land forms would be very unsatisfactory without a corresponding consideration of their origin, and in this phase geology and physiography overlap and are mutually indispensable. Meteorology is applied to the study of physiography through climatology; sunshine, temperature, and moisture being the principal subjects considered. Oceanography and hydrography perform for the oceans the functions exercised by meteorology in relation to the atmosphere, but with certain modifications. As in the case of geology, so much overlapping occurs between physiography and the two latter sciences that it would be difficult if not impossible to define their respective limits.

Physical conditions exert an enormous influence on the organic life of the lithosphere, and determine, in a greater or less degree, the kind of people who shall live on a particular part of the earth's surface, their mode of life, manner of dress, state of comfort, wealth, and health. Vegetable life is also dependent upon favourable physical conditions, and to man, as other mammals, vegetation is as imperative a necessity as water. From these considerations it follows that no study of physiography could be complete without a passing note of how uncontrollable physical conditions have affected organic life.

Outlines. In the physiographical review of any region a close investigation of the following features will provide a handy skeleton of the complete structure.

1. *Land.*—Shape and Size; orography, i.e. highlands, mountains, plateaux, etc.; watersheds; plains and peneplains; valleys and passes; coastal features, i.e. gulfs, bays, etc.; vegetation; geological structure and nature of rocks, folds, faults, rift valleys, etc.

2. *Water.*—Bathymetrical study of ocean; currents; lakes; river systems; coastal features (including estuaries, bays, and gulfs, etc.); submarine land forms, i.e. depressions, basins, troughs, trenches, deeps, rises, ridges, plateaux, etc.

3. *Air.*—Climate, including temperature, rainfall, sunshine, prevailing winds, etc.

It is important to consult such articles as *Earth*; *Hydrography*; *Oceanography*; *Meteorology*; *Geography*; *Geology*; *Earthquake*; *Climate*; etc.; and physiographical notes on various countries.

BIBLIOGRAPHY: J. W. Gregory, *Geography: Structural, Physical, and Comparative*; R. D. Salisbury, *Physiography*; N. S. Shaler, *Aspects of the Earth*; E. Suess, *Das Antliz der Erde* (4 vols. and index; English translation by Hertha Sollas, *The Face of the Earth*)—this is the classical work on the subject; A. J. Herbertson, *Outlines of Physiography* and *A Handbook of Geography* (2 vols.); Marie C. Stopes, *The Study of Plant Life* (chap. xxxiv. *Physical Geography and Plants*, and chap xxxv. *Plant Maps*, both written up in a popular form); E. H. L. Schwarz, *Causal Geology*; A. E. M. Geddes, *Meteorology*.

PHYSIOLOGICAL CHEMISTRY. The living cell consists of a mixture of organic and inorganic substances dissolved or suspended in water, the water constituting about three-fourths of the total mass of the cell. Of the organic substances, *proteins*, *carbohydrates*, and *fats* are the most important. The simpler organic materials are mostly stages either in the synthesis or decomposition of these substances.

The Proteins. Of the three groups, proteins, carbohydrates, and fats, the proteins alone contain nitrogen in their molecule. On decomposition the proteins yield various *amino-acids* (fatty or dibasic acids in which one or more of the hydrogen atoms has been replaced by an NH_2 group), according to the type of protein decomposed. This fact, coupled with the well-known work of Emil Fischer, who showed that amino-acids could be linked together in acid-amide chains, i.e. the COOH group of one combining with the NH_2 group of the next, ($CH_2(NH_2)CO[OHH]HNCH_2COOH$), thus forming a peptide, and that, if the chains so formed included sufficient and the proper type of amino-acids, many of the characteristic reactions of proteins could be obtained, has proved that the various proteins consist of unions of various amino-acids.

Amino-acids may have one amino-group in their molecule, as in *glycine*, $(CH_2(NH_2)COOH)$, or two, as in *ornithine*, $(CH_2(NH_2)CH_2CH_2CHNH_2COOH)$. Amino-derivatives of di-carboxylic acids are also found, e.g. *aspartic acid*, $(HOOCCH_2CH(NH_2)COOH)$, as also similar derivatives of sulphur-containing acids, e.g. *cysteine*, $(CH_2SHCH(NH_2)COOH)$. Again, the amino-acid may be linked to a cyclic compound, as in *phenylalanine*,

```
        H
        C
     //   \
   HC      CH
    |      ||
   HC      CH
     \\   /
        C
        |
        CH2CH(NH2)COOH,
```

where the amino-propionic acid is combined with a benzene ring; or to an heterocyclic compound, as in *histidine*,

```
      CH
    /    \\
  HN      N
   |      |
  HC======C—CH2CH(NH2)COOH,
```

where amino-propionic acid is combined with the iminazole ring.

Of the amino-acids, *tyrosine* and *tryptophane* deserve special mention. Tyrosine, a compound of amino-propionic acid with hydroxybenzene, and present in may proteins, is of importance as a source of the organic or ethereal sulphates of the urine. By bacterial action in the intestine, the amino-acid is separated and the remaining phenol is absorbed, then combined with acid potassium sulphate to render it non-toxic, and excreted in this form in the urine. Tryptophane, a compound of amino-propionic acid with the heterocyclic indol ring, under bacterial influence in the intestine, forms *indol* and *methylindol* or *scatol*, and these substances similarly form the *indoxyl* and *scatoxyl sulphates* of the urine.

Other Nitrogenous Substances of Physiological Importance.—Urea,

```
        NH2
       /
  O=C
       \
        NH2,
```

regarded as the diamide of carbonic acid, is formed in the body by the dehydration of the ammonium carbonate, which results from a combination with carbonic acid of the ammonia produced from the NH_2 groups of waste amino-acids. *Guanidine*,

```
         NH2
        /
  HN=C
        \
         NH2,
```

a substance, as the formula shows, intimately related to urea, has been found in the human subject in the form of methyl- and dimethyl-guanidine in the urine, blood, and certain tissue extracts. It is also a constituent of most proteins in the form of *arginine*, a compound of guanidine and amino-valerianic acid. Guanidine, chemically, and possibly metabolically, is also related to *creatine* (methyl - guanidine - acetic acid). This substance is a constant constituent of muscular tissue, and its anhydride, *creatinine*, is a normal constituent of all mammalian urines.

Of derivatives of the *pyrimidine* structure,

```
   N=CH
   |   |
  HC   CH
  ||   ||
   N—CH,
```

three substances, *uracil* or dioxypyrimidine, *thymine* or methyldioxypyrimidine, and *cytosine* or aminooxypyrimidine, occur as components of *nucleic acids*.

From the substance *purine*, of structural formula,

```
   N=CH
   |   |
  HC   C—NH
  ||   ||     \
  ||   ||      CH,
  ||   ||     //
   N—C—N
```

which, it will be noticed, is a combination of the pyrimidine and iminazole nuclei, several substances, the interrelation of which is shown in the following formulæ, purine, $C_5H_4N_4$; hypoxanthine, $C_5H_4N_4O$; xanthine, $C_5H_4N_4O_2$; uric acid, $C_5H_4N_4O_3$; adenine, $C_5H_3(NH_2)N_4$; guanine, $C_5H_3(NH_2)N_4O$, are derived. Hypoxanthine and xanthine are found widely distributed in the tissues of both animals and plants, as also adenine and guanine, which in addition, are constituents of the nucleic acids. In the human organism all are ultimately changed into the most highly oxidised form, viz. uric acid.

The *nucleic acids*, united with proteins, form the nucleoproteins of the nuclei. They consist of phosphoric acid, a carbohydrate, two purine bases, and two pyrimidine bases, the exact way in which these components are combined being unknown. The carbohydrate of the animal nucleic acids is a hexose (see below), that of plants a pentose, the pyrimidine bases of the animal type being cytosine and thymine, those of the vegetable world cytosine and uracil.

Of the metabolism of the *sulphur* of the protein molecule little is known, but cysteine, already mentioned, is probably an intermediate product. An oxidation product of cysteine, viz. *taurine*, is found in combination with a complex acid, *cholalic acid*, in the bile. A similar compound of this acid with glycine, *glycocholic acid*, is also a constituent of bile.

The Carbohydrates. These are so called because of their empirical formula, $(CH_2O)n$, representing a combination of carbon and water. There may be any number of carbon atoms from two to nine in their molecule, those of most physiological importance having five or six. The *hexoses*, or 6-carbon atom type, are often called sugars. They may exist as single molecules, the *monosaccharides*, or two molecules may combine together with loss of water, giving the formula $C_{12}H_{22}O_{11}$, forming the *disaccharides*. Further combination of more molecules with loss of water gives rise to *tetra-* and *polysaccharides*. Similar combinations may occur among numbers of the *pentose* or 5-carbon atom group.

The pentoses are widely distributed in plants as a component of their nucleic acids.

Hexoses.—Monosaccharides. The most important are *glucose, lævulose,* and *galactose.* Glucose occurs in sweet fruits, honey, etc., and is an aldehyde, i.e. it possesses a CHO grouping, its formula being $CH_2OH{\cdot}CHOH{\cdot}CHOH{\cdot}CHOH{\cdot}CHOH{\cdot}CHO$. Lævulose is also found in fruits; it is an example of a ketone sugar, possessing a CO grouping, $CH_2OH{\cdot}CHOH{\cdot}CHOH{\cdot}CHOH{\cdot}CO{\cdot}CH_2OH$. Galactose is found mainly in combination with glucose in milk-sugar (lactose).

Disaccharides. Of these there are many, the most important being *cane-sugar*, a combination of glucose and lævulose; *lactose*, consisting of glucose and galactose; and *maltose*, made up of two glucose molecules.

Polysaccharides. The most important are those composed of glucose units. To this group belong *vegetable starch*, the *dextrins*, *glycogen* or *animal starch*, the form in which the carbohydrate excess of the animal body is stored, and *cellulose*, which forms the basis of the cell-walls of plants.

Along with the carbohydrates must be mentioned two acids which are probably products of their metabolism. *Lactic acid* or hydroxy-propionic acid, $(CH_3{\cdot}CHOH{\cdot}COOH)$ plays an important rôle in muscular contraction; and *pyruvic acid* $(CH_3{\cdot}CO{\cdot}COOH)$, is of importance because, since its formation from aminopropionic acid and its synthesis to higher fatty acids have been shown to be possible, it may represent the turning-point in the interchange, one into another, of proteins, carbohydrates, and fats.

The Fats. Fats and oils are combinations of the higher fatty acids, mainly *stearic, palmitic*, and *oleic*, with the trihydric alcohol *glycerol*. Palmitic and stearic acids are saturated acids, i.e. each valency of every carbon atom is satisfied. Oleic is an unsaturated acid, there being a double linking in the middle of the chain $(—CH_2—CH{=}CH—CH_2—)$. The position of such double linkages probably determines the point of rupture of the molecule in its biological oxidation. The lower fatty acids occur to a small extent in many fats and fatty secretions like milk. Higher alcohols, such as *cholesterol*, are also found, particularly in nervous tissue, bile, and red blood-corpuscles, and also united to higher fatty acids forming waxes.

The decomposition of fat is believed to take place by the introduction of double bonds (desaturation) and by a series of oxidations at the penultimate CH_2 grouping (the β position). The ultimate result of these processes would be the formation of *β-hydroxybutyric acid*. Normally this is completely oxidised to carbonic acid and water, but in defective fat metabolism β-hydroxybutyric acid, along with its oxidation products *diacetic acid* and *acetone*, may appear in blood and urine.

Along with the fats may be mentioned somewhat similar compounds which contain phosphorus and nitrogen in their molecule, the *phosphatides* or *lipins*, e.g. *lecithin*, where two of the replaceable hydrogen atoms of glycerol are replaced by palmitic acid, and the third by phosphoric acid and a nitrogenous base, *choline*.

BIBLIOGRAPHY: R. H. A. Plimmer, *Practical Organic and Biochemistry*; H. E. Roaf, *Biological Chemistry*; *Monographs on Biochemistry*, edited by R. H. A. Plimmer and F. G. Hopkins; E. V. M'Collum, *The Newer Knowledge of Nutrition*; W. M. Bayliss, *The Nature of Enzyme Action*.

PHYSIOLOGY. The study of the phenomena presented by *living* organisms whether animal or vegetable. Vegetable physiology, however, belongs rather to the province of botany, and the study of animal physiology has been directed mainly to the higher animals and particularly to man. Hence the following brief outline is largely that of human physiology. It is a consideration of how the mechanism of the body works.

In early and in mediæval times philosophers employed their energies in speculations as to the functions of the various organs and parts of the body with which the study of anatomy had made them familiar. These speculations were limited only by the imagination of the theorist, and, as they were wholly unsupported by observation or experiment, they not only failed to advance knowledge, but even acted as a barrier to real progress.

With the advent of the Baconian philosophy, which demanded not theories but facts derived from observation and experiment, physiology freed itself from the trammels imposed by the schoolmen and rapidly attained the dignity of an experimental science. Since then progress has been slow but sure: slow, because of all experimental sciences physiology presents probably the greatest difficulties; sure, because the advances has been based on gradually accumulated facts.

The methods employed in the investigation of the body processes are those of the chemist and the physicist. We are learning more and more to apply such methods to physiological problems, and with advances in the fundamental sciences of chemistry and physics new methods become available to the physiologist. No person can hope to understand the problems of physiology who has not a competent knowledge of chemistry and physics.

Since physiology is concerned with the phenomena of life, we must first endeavour to explain what constitutes life. The main characteristics of a living organism are that it is capable of (1) taking in and utilising food, (2) reacting to changes in its surroundings, (3) growing, (4) reproducing itself. Some organisms consist of a single cell, but all the higher forms of life are aggregations of vast multitudes of cells. Every cell, however, is composed of a living material called *protoplasm*, and it is this which exhibits the properties just mentioned.

Structure of the Body. It is obvious that different parts of the body are composed of very different materials, e.g. we have bone, muscle, fat, etc. This difference in structure is associated with a difference in function or division of labour. Certain cells are grouped together and specialised to perform one particular process.

Thus we have bone—forming a rigid support for the soft tissues; muscle—capable of contracting; skin—forming a covering for the body; mucous membranes—lining the hollow internal organs; glands—aggregations of cells which secrete fluids; nervous tissue—for conducting nervous impulses.

These specialised cells are grouped into organs and systems. Each system subserves certain requirements and contributes its quota to the needs of the body, but it is essential to regard the different systems as interdependent. No one system can function abnormally or cease to function without seriously interfering with the others.

Metabolism. Protoplasm exists in a state of incessant change. It is being continuously built up and broken down. The sum total of these changes is termed *metabolism*. Such a process necessarily involves the expenditure and the storing up of energy. Now one of the greatest general laws of the physical world is that of conservation of energy, which affirms that energy cannot be created, although it may be transformed and appear as work or as heat.

The body is no exception to this law. It cannot manufacture energy, but must receive it in the form of food. Food contains large stores of potential energy which the body has the power of liberating. In the tissues of the body there is a considerable reserve of potential energy which can be drawn on if necessary, as in complete or partial starvation. This device can be resorted to only for a limited time, and during that time the body steadily wastes away. If, on the other hand, more energy (i.e. food) than is necessary is supplied, the surplus is got rid of in the form of heat. For the most part heat derived from food is not wasted, as a certain temperature is required for the survival of warm-blooded animals.

Food. Food is to the body what fuel is to the engine. Neither can continue to function unless it is fed. Any food, no matter of what form, can be shown to belong to one of three great classes, viz. *proteins*, *carbohydrates*, and *fats*. All these contain the elements carbon, hydrogen, and oxygen, but the proteins contain in addition nitrogen and sulphur. Food-stuffs, as a rule, are not composed entirely of one class, but have greater or less quantities of the others admixed. For example, meat is chiefly protein, bread is chiefly carbohydrate, and butter is almost all fat. *See* PHYSIOLOGICAL CHEMISTRY; FOODS AND FOOD VALUES.

Foods as ingested are inert, but the large amount of carbon they contain can be oxidised, i.e. it can form a chemical compound with oxygen, and in so doing can liberate a large quantity of energy, just as coal does when it is burnt. The body has the power of carrying out this oxidation process gradually and quietly, and it does so by producing certain substances called *enzymes* or *ferments*.

Enzymes.—Our knowledge of enzymes is confined almost entirely to a recognition of their action. They act powerfully in minute quantities. They are not used up in the process. A given enzyme acts only on one particular substance, or perhaps on a small group of similar substances. The action may be to break down a complex substance into simpler ones, or from simple substances to build up a complex one.

Digestive System. The digestive system or alimentary tract is a long tube beginning at the mouth. From here the masticated food passes down the œsophagus or gullet into the stomach, where it remains for some time subjected to the digestive action of the gastric juice. It then enters the small intestine, in which the digestive process is completed; the resulting products are absorbed into the blood, and the useless residue passes on into the large intestine, finally leaving the body by the rectum. The passage of food along the tube is effected by the rhythmic contraction and relaxation of the muscular fibres in its wall.

The digestive juices are formed in small glands in the mucous membranes lining the tract, but important aids are afforded by the *liver* and the *pancreas*, two glands which pour their secretions into the commencement of the small intestine.

Excretory System. The breaking down processes of metabolism result in the production of various waste products, just as a fire produces ashes. These waste products must be removed because they tend to clog the mechanism, and many of them, besides, are injurious to the body. The process of disposal is called *excretion*. The chief channels by which they leave the body are (1) the kidneys, which form the urine; (2) the intestine, which gets rid of waste matters in the fæces; (3) the lungs, which give off carbon dioxide; (4) the skin, which forms the sweat.

Circulatory System. The products of digestion are distributed to all parts of the body by the *circulatory system*. This consists of a central pump, the *heart*, with muscular walls which contract rhythmically. It is divided into two halves, a left and a right. The left heart forces the blood through a series of branching channels, the *arteries*, which form a network all over the body. Other channels, the *veins*, carry the blood to the right heart. The blood on its return is pumped through the lungs, to be aerated before passing to the left heart and being again distributed to the body.

Respiratory System. The lungs are contained in the chest, and air is forced in and out by the action of special muscles. The air comes into intimate contact with the blood circulating through the lungs, and oxygen is taken up and carried to the tissues. The great waste product of metabolism, carbon dioxide, is carried by the blood to the lungs, and there it passes out into the air. Thus the blood arrives at the lungs charged with carbon dioxide, and leaves them charged with oxygen.

Blood. The blood, therefore, supplies the whole body with food and with oxygen. Its oxygen-carrying power is due to a pigment called *hæmoglobin*, contained in myriads of tiny cells floating in the fluid part of the blood. There are also cells which act as scavengers. They play an important rôle in maintaining health by attacking and eating up the organisms which produce disease.

Receptors. It is essential for an organism that, in order to survive, it should be capable of adapting itself to changes in its surroundings. The range of adaptation depends partly on the capacity to receive impressions from external changes. Such changes are called *stimuli*, and in the higher animals special organs are set aside for their reception. These organs may be designated in the most general terms as *receptors*, but the most important are commonly known as the special sense organs. Thus we have the eye responding to light, the ear to sound, etc.

Effectors. The animal provided with the most elaborate receptor organs for appreciating changes in its environment would derive little benefit if it was unable to respond to those changes. Consequently the development of the receptor system has been accompanied by that of mechanisms for reacting to external changes. This *effector system*, as we may call it, consists of the muscles. Skeletal muscle is attached to the bones, and enables the animal to perform movements. Visceral muscle is found in the internal organs, and controls their action.

Nervous System. With advances in the development of receptors and effectors, it becomes necessary to avoid the conflict of dissimilar reactions to different stimuli, and desirable that reactions should be carried out speedily. This leads to the formation of connecting-links between receptors and effectors, which, increasing in complexity, come to constitute the *nervous system* and to dominate all the other systems in the body. These links consist of specialised cells with long branching processes. The whole cell forms a *neuron,* and the nervous system is built up of vast numbers of these units. The separate neurons are brought into functional continuity by the close approximation of their processes, but there is no structural continuity. This conception forms the basis of modern views regarding the action of the nervous system.

In the higher animals the nervous system may be divided into two parts: a central part, consisting of the *brain* and *spinal cord*; and a peripheral part, consisting of the *nerves* linking the various organs to the central part. Impulses travelling along the nervous system are divided into *afferent,* or those passing towards the centre, and *efferent,* or those passing towards the periphery.

The spinal cord acts as a central exchange, sorting out the incoming messages from the receptors and the outgoing messages to the effectors, and carrying them to their various destinations. In the spinal cord impulses from receptors may be directed along outgoing channels to effectors, and give rise to what are known as *reflex actions,* i.e. actions in which consciousness is not involved.

The spinal cord expands at the head end into the brain. At its base are various sub-stations concerned with the control of such vital processes as circulation and respiration. The *cerebellum* or lesser brain controls muscular co-ordination and equilibrium. But the height of nervous development is reached in the brain proper or *cerebrum.* Here we have the seat of consciousness, of willed actions, of memory and intellectual processes. In man the cerebrum surpasses in development that of any other animal. Apart from its relatively enormous size, its outer layer or *cortex,* consisting of innumerable nerve-cells, is very thick, and is thrown into folds or convolutions which greatly increase its area. This elaborate convolution is a distinctive feature of the human brain, and the advance in complexity from savage to civilised man is readily perceptible.

Endocrinetes. There is a small group of glands which pour their secretions directly into the blood, and are therefore called the ductless glands or *endocrinetes.* Although many of them are of minute size, their action is of such importance in regulating the general metabolism that any departure from normal function produces serious and often fatal results.

Reproduction. In order to provide for the continuation of the species, certain cells are grouped to form reproductive organs.

The foregoing description gives, however imperfectly, some idea of the multifarious processes at work in the human body. Physiology, regarded purely as a science, is concerned with nothing else, but the physiologist's studies correlate the normal with the abnormal. Hence physiology is also the foundation of medicine. To understand the departures from the normal which constitute disease, the physician must be acquainted with the normal. He is constantly employing his knowledge of physiology, and every advance therein furnishes him with additions to that knowledge and with new weapons for his struggle with disease.

PHYTOLAC'CA. A genus of tropical or sub-tropical herbaceous plants, type of the nat. ord. Phytolaccaceæ. One species is the American pokeweed.

PHYTOPHTHORA. A genus of Fungi, family Peronosporaceæ. *P. infestans* is the potato-blight, one of the worst diseases of the potato, though not so deadly now as during the first decade of its ravages in Europe (1840-50). The disease shows itself first in the form of brown patches on the leaves; these spread, the leaves curl and decay, and in severe cases the entire haulm may blacken and rot in a few days.

The mycelium of the fungus lives in the intercellular spaces of the shoot, but sends forth fertile branches through the stomata into the air, bearing numerous little oval conidia that spread the infection, especially in warm, damp weather, since each conidium produces a number of actively swimming zoospores if it falls into a drop of water. The mycelium finally spreads to the tubers, which may also, when young, be directly infected by zoospores, and either causes them to rot or more often hibernates in them and starts the disease afresh if infected tubers are planted as "seed."

The best preventive remedies are destruction of infected plants and planting of "seed" from a non-infected crop of one of the varieties least susceptible to the disease; an attack that has started may be checked by spraying the foliage with Bordeaux mixture.

PIACENZA (pyȧ-chen'tsȧ). A province of Emilia, North Italy, belonging to the basin of the Po. Area,

994 sq. miles; pop. (1931), 290,387.

PIACENZA (ancient **PLACENTIA**). A city of North Italy, capital of the province of Piacenza, at the confluence of the Trebbia with the Po. Being a place of strategic importance, it has long been fortified, and is still surrounded by walls with bastions and fosse, outside which is a series of detached forts.

The principal edifices are the cathedral, in the Lombard-Romanesque style (mostly built between 1122 and 1233), and other churches; the town house (Palazzo Communale), of the thirteenth century, one of the finest structures of its kind, and the Palazzo Farnese (now used as barracks). Piacenza is an important railway centre. The manufactures consist of cotton goods, woollens, stockings, hats, and leather, and there are also several silk-spinning and paper-mills. Pop. 65,712.

Piacenza was originally a Roman colony, founded in 219 B.C. Between 997 and 1035 it was governed by its bishops. In 1447 it was captured and sacked by Francesco Sforza; and in 1545 it was united with Parma to form an hereditary duchy for Pier-luigi Farnese, son of Pope Paul III.

PIANA DEI GRECI (pyä'nȧ de-i-grā'chē). A town of Sicily, in the province and 10 miles S.S.W. of the city of Palermo. Silks and woollens are manufactured. Pop. 8500.

PIANOFORTE. Musical instruments in general may from one point of view be divided into two classes: those which have come down to us from early times with little or no alteration of their original form, and those which in their present shape are the result of a gradual evolution. Of the former the trombone is the outstanding example, while among the more numerous members of the second class the organ and the pianoforte take a prominent place. The reason for this will be apparent when it is remembered that these two instruments are dependent for their perfection on a highly elaborate mechanism, and their rate of progress has therefore inevitably been conditioned by the rate of advance in mechanical ingenuity. It would be unwise to say that either the organ or pianoforte is now in its final state. Indeed, the pianoforte has quite recently (1922) taken a new and very important step onward, as will be shown later in this article.

Early History. The pianoforte is the latest and most popular representative of a large class of stringed instruments which derive their tone from a momentary excitation of the strings, in contrast to those of the violin class, in which the making of sound by means of the bow is a continuing process. The ultimate ancestor of the pianoforte is the psaltery. This ancient instrument was in its essentials merely a simple form of the dulcimer, being held in the hand or hung round the neck, while the strings were sounded by the fingers or by a plectrum instead of by hammers, as in the case of the true dulcimer. There are many highly appreciative references to it in early writings, and Chaucer, in the *Miller's Tale*, makes mention of it in the familiar lines:

> And all above ther lay a gay sautrie
> On which he made on nightes melodie,
> So swetely, that all the chambre rong,
> And *Angelus ad virginem* he song.

The spinet and harpsichord are a direct development from the psaltery, and, with the clavichord, are the prototypes of the pianoforte. The

Pianoforte

spinet, which is really only the oblong form of the harpsichord, was, like the latter, a very favourite instrument in its day, particularly in England, where it was more commonly called the virginal or virginals. Some lexicographers have derived this alternative name from the fact that "maids and virgins do most commonly play on them", but it is much more probable that the instrument was so named because of its use in accompanying the *Angelus ad Virginem*; for, as it is interesting to note, it followed its parent, the psaltery, in the performance of this worthy office.

The Harpsichord. The harpsichord, which, it should be remembered, includes the spinet and virginal, was during the sixteenth, seventeenth, and eighteenth centuries as universally popular as the pianoforte is to-day. It was the instrument that Bach and Handel played and wrote for, and they preferred it to the newer pianoforte, which was just becoming known in the days of their prime, and was still largely in the experimental stage.

The tone production in the harpsichord was effected by means of *jacks,* little wooden uprights placed on the end of the keys opposite to that touched by the performer. At the top of the jacks was fixed a point or plectrum made of crow quill or hard leather, which was forced past the wire by the descent of the key, and in its passage plucked or twanged the wire into sound. The mechanism was therefore no more than an elaborated application of the plectrum principle, and sound gradations were entirely beyond the immediate control of the player. The tone was brilliant but lacking in delicacy, and so short-lived that all kinds of embellishments were in use in harpsichord music to give a semblance of rhythmic vitality and continuity of sound. The instrument was generally made with two keyboards, and provided with stops, by means of which changes from loud to soft could be made and even a limited amount of tone contrast introduced.

The case of a harpsichord was very often embellished with fine paintings done by contemporary masters, and with appropriate mottoes, such as *Sic transit gloria mundi,* in which an obvious reference is made to the short-lived nature of music in general and of harpsichord tone in particular.

The Clavichord. The clavichord, the other immediate predecessor of the pianoforte, differed from the harpsichord in one or two important details. In its mechanism the plectrum-like quill or piece of hard leather was replaced by a small wedge or tangent of brass about an eighth of an inch broad at the top. When the key was put down, this tangent rose to meet the string and, pressing against it, set it in vibration. Further, by remaining in contact with the wire it fixed the vibrating length of the latter, and so decided the pitch of the resulting sound. The method of tone-production in the clavichord was therefore based on that of the monochord with movable bridge, from which, indeed, it was directly derived.

The instrument also differed from the harpsichord in its tonal results. They were delicate and charming, suggesting a kind of diffidence which sensitive musicians found very agreeable. By means of the tangent the player could feel himself in much more intimate association with the string than was ever possible while playing the harpsichord, and a good performer on a good instrument could even secure variations of tone-amount, and had the high pleasure of controlling these variations directly through his manner of using the key.

It was also possible to repeat a note several times without quitting the key, with a charming effect which was not possible on the harpsichord and cannot be obtained from the pianoforte. It was indicated by the German word *bebung,* and Beethoven has introduced an imitation of it in one of his latest sonatas, Op. 110 in A flat. He had a great admiration for the clavichord, because of its powers of tone-control and expressive interpretation. Mozart also played the instrument, and it was a favourite with the great Bach and his son Emanuel. If we regard the harpsichord and the clavichord as the parents of the pianoforte, then they might be said to stand in the relation of father and mother respectively.

Invention of the Pianoforte. The aim of the first makers of pianofortes was to combine the good features of the harpsichord and the clavichord. The former could give brilliance and speed of execution, but could only vary the tone-amount by artificial means, which included the use of swell shutters on the organ principle. The latter could give great sweetness of tone and delicate variations of tone-amount, but could only be heard in a small space, and was therefore quite useless for public performance. It was also seriously lacking when sparkling *staccato* effects were required.

In connection with the actual invention of the pianoforte, the usual conflicting claims are met with. France, Germany, and Italy are competitors for the honour, but the fullest investigation has clearly established the right of Italy to the distinction. She therefore provides in this matter one more example in music of her power to originate and her inability to bring to perfection, for Italy at the present time does not harbour any of the great centres of pianoforte-making.

Bartolommeo Cristofori (1651-1731) was the name of the inventor of the pianoforte. He was a harpsichord-maker of Padua, who removed about 1687 to Florence, where, in 1711, he produced the first of the new instruments. It is significant that during the eighteenth century the new invention was as often called fortepiano as pianoforte. This indicates clearly that the name was given to distinguish it from all other instruments of its class by means of its special feature the power to give soft or loud tones at the will of the performer; and it was this power which Cristofori had decided to make the goal of his endeavours.

The Hopper. His first step was to replace the tangent of the clavichord with the hammer, the idea for which he took from the dulcimer. But a serious difficulty at once confronted him. It will be remembered that the tangent of the clavichord remained in contact with the string as long as the key was held down; and while this was an essential part of the instrument's mechanism, it had a damping effect upon the tone, which has been well described as a "blocking" of the sound.

Cristofori saw that it would be necessary in his new instrument to provide some means whereby the hammer, after setting the wire in vibration, could fall back, even though the key were still depressed, and leave the wire in perfect freedom to continue sounding. There is no means of knowing how long it took him to solve this problem, but in devising the contrivance called the "hopper" he provided a complete solution; in a greatly improved form it is still one of the main features of the pianoforte mechanism.

The hopper is actuated by the key, and rises as the latter is put down, in the manner of the jack in a harpsichord. At its upper end it is in contact with the under surface of the hammer-shaft, which therefore rises with it and moves the hammer-head towards the wire. Before this journey to the wire is completed, the hopper, owing to the construction of the mechanism, slips out of contact with the hammer-shaft and returns to its first position, leaving the hammer free to fall back into its original place as soon as its act of tone-making is finished. (It should be understood that the details of the above description are only applicable to the actions of grand pianos; but the main principle is the same in all classes of instruments.)

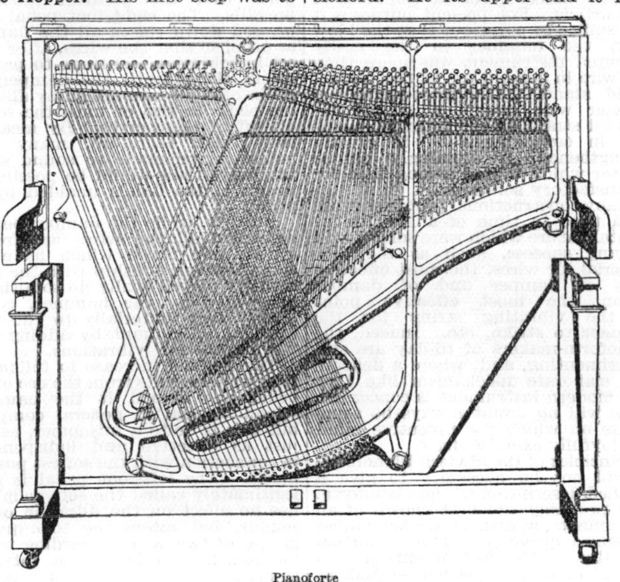

Pianoforte

A view of the interior—keyboard and hammers removed. By permission of Messrs. John Broadwood & Sons, Ltd.

Constructional Problems. It is not too much to say that, in solving this initial difficulty, Cristofori had made the pianoforte possible.

There were still many other serious problems to be solved, but they only arose after Cristofori had so cleverly devised the hopper. He is entitled to much honour in this connection.

Any readers who desire to follow the development of the pianoforte through all its stages may be recommended to read the standard works on the subject given at the close of this article. For present purposes it will suffice to point out that the blow from the hammer in the newly invented instrument was more than the wire in general use at that period could stand. The introduction of heavier wire caused a greatly increased strain on the framing, which had in consequence to be greatly strengthened, a seemingly simple matter which waited a long time for a satisfactory solution.

Many constructional problems arose from time to time of a less fundamental nature which were solved with varying success, such as the best material for wires, the most effective form of damper and of damper action, the most effective point on the vibrating string for the hammer to strike, etc. Indeed, the pianoforte-makers of to-day are still experimenting, and, where a delicate and elaborate mechanism like that of a modern instrument is concerned, there will no doubt always be some points on which the inventive mind will joyfully exercise itself.

Principles of the Modern Pianoforte. It will not be necessary to give a detailed description of the pianoforte. It is probably the best-known of all instruments, and there are few homes without a specimen. The proportion of really worthy instruments in this host of pianofortes is not so high as could be wished, and there are many households in which this most willing and serviceable of music-makers is less looked after than any other piece of domestic furniture. Perhaps a wider knowledge of its qualities and merits will lead in time to a more sympathetic understanding of its very modest needs; it will then be more difficult than it is now to find a piano that is hopelessly out of tune, or has some notes which do not sound or some keys which will not rise after they are played, or pedals which do not act.

The great value of the instrument for music and musicians lies in its sensitive response to the touch of the player and its power to render complete harmony. Through the wonderfully delicate action the pianist while playing is in the most intimate connection with the wires, and the expressive quality of his performance, supposing he has a good instrument, is entirely his own. Any defects in the instrument mean a loss of sensitiveness, and the player is immediately handicapped.

On the harmonic side the pedals play a vital part; indeed, without them the piano would not have established itself as a serious musical instrument. Yet it is perhaps on this point that the greatest ignorance prevails. The right-foot pedal when pressed down raises all the dampers at once, so that the wires, after being set in vibration, continue to produce sound either until the dampers are again brought into action by allowing the pedal to rise or until the sounds die off of themselves. By means of this pedal, therefore, many more notes can be made to sound simultaneously than would be possible by means of the hands unaided by the pedal.

Further, while the damper-pedal is depressed *all* the wires are free to sound, and those which have any acoustical relationship with the notes actually played really do so although untouched by the hammer, contributing very materially to the tonal quality and amount by adding their "sympathetic" vibrations.

The marked increase in fullness of tone which results from the use of this pedal has earned it the name of "loud" pedal in general company, but this is quite a misnomer, as it is just as effective and indispensable in connection with the softest possible music. The left-foot pedal is more legitimately called the soft pedal. It has no effect on the duration of the sounds, but alters the tone-quality in one of two ways according to the mechanism adopted. The intended result is only secured by a side-long movement of the entire action, whereby the hammers can only engage with one or two strings of the three which go to each note. The untouched string or strings then sound sympathetically, since all three are tuned in unison, and impart a veiled quality to the soft tone which makes it quite distinctive.

In the second and less legitimate form of soft-pedal mechanism the hammers are moved nearer to the wires, which lessens the striking distance and consequently the amount of tone available, or a piece of felt or cloth is brought into position between the wires and the hammers, which again softens the tone, though sometimes with disastrous effects on the quality.

Recent Improvements. A new piano, the invention of Mr. Emmanuel

Moor, the composer, will probably in course of time revolutionise not only the playing of the instrument, but also the manner of writing music for it. It has two keyboards, the lower of which is exactly as in the ordinary piano, excepting that there is attached to the back end of each white key a raised portion which brings it to the level of the black keys. By this means easy access may be had to the upper keyboard, which is tuned throughout an octave higher than the lower one. The keyboards may be used separately or coupled together. There is also a contrivance for converting the instrument into a very fair representation of the harpsichord. It is called the "Duplex-coupler" piano.—BIBLIOGRAPHY: E. F. Rimbault, *The Pianoforte* (1860); A. J. Hipkins, *History of the Pianoforte* (1897); Grove's *Dictionary of Music and Musicians* (vol. iii., 1907), articles *Pianoforte* and *Pianoforte-playing*; *Music and Letters* for Jan., 1922. *The Pianoforte of Emmanuel Moor*, by Donald Tovey.

PIASSA'BA, or **PIASSA'VA.** A strong vegetable fibre imported from Brazil, and largely used for making brooms. It is chiefly obtained from palms such as *Attalĕa funifĕra* and *Leopoldinia piassăba*. The fibre proceeds from the decaying leaves, the petioles of which separate at the base into long, coarse, pendulous fringes. It was first utilised in England, and the consumption is now large. Other European countries also consume considerable quantities.

PIASTRE (pi-às'tr; It. *piastra*). A name first applied to a Spanish coin which, about the middle of the sixteenth century, obtained almost universal currency. It is now the name of a Turkish and an Egyptian coin. The Turks mint coins ½, 1, 5, 10, and 20 silver piastre pieces, and gold pieces of 25, 50, 100, 250, and 500 piastres. The nominal value of a piastre is 2½*d.*, and the 100-piastre piece is called a *mejideh*, or Turkish pound (£T1). The Egyptian piastre is worth a little more than the Turkish. The piastre is divided into 40 *paras*.

PIAT'RA. A town of Rumania, on the Bistritsa, 53 miles south-west of Jassy. It carries on a large trade in grain and timber. Pop. 30,211.

PIAUHY (pi-ou-ē'), or **PIAUHI.** A state of Northern Brazil, bounded by the Atlantic and the states of Ceará, Pernambuco, Bahia, and Maranhão, from which latter it is separated by the Parnahyba; area, 116,494 sq. miles. Its coast-line is not above 10 miles in length. The rearing of cattle, esteemed the best in Brazil constitutes the principal source of wealth. Capital, Therezina; port, Parnahyba. Pop. (1929), 809,508.

PIAVE. A river of North Italy, rising in the Carnic Alps, and flowing in a south-easterly direction to Porto di Cortellazo, where it enters the Adriatic. During the European War the Piave formed a line of Italian defence, and gave its name to three of the bloodiest battles of the Austro-Italian campaign.

The first followed closely upon the Italian disaster at Caporetto. At Caporetto the Austro-German armies under General Otto von Below (Fourteenth Army) were divided into four "groups," and successfully attacked the left wing and centre of the Italian Second Army (24th Oct., 1917, a.m.). Although only a local victory, the crisis came when the troops driven out of the Caporetto-Tolmino sector got out of control and, in their disordered retreat, carried back the concentrating detachments of reserves. On 25th Oct. (p.m.) General Capello proposed to General Cadorna an immediate retreat to the line of the Tagliamento.

The Second Army had now completely crumbled, and the breach was widening dangerously when Cadorna gave the order for a general retreat to the Piave in order to shorten his line (26th Oct., p.m.). Five of the eight army corps which composed the Second Army had already been almost completely disintegrated, and it was obvious that the Tagliamento was no longer a suitable line on which to make a stand. By Saturday, 27th Oct., the whole Italian line was in full retreat. In May, 1916, Cadorna had given orders for the construction of suitable defences on the mountain ridges between the Brenta and Piave, and to the north-east of Asiago. To this line the Italians retreated in hopeless confusion.

First Battle. General Cadorna was superseded by General Diaz and a new Italian High Command, and an Allied mission (Mr. Ll. George, MM. Painlevé and Barthou, and Generals Smuts, Foch, Henry Wilson, and Robertson) hastened to Italy. Affairs had become serious. On 10th Nov., 1917, the enemy engaged the Italian Fourth Army on the Middle Piave. It was a feeler, and a general battle immediately developed. The Italian positions were maintained.

Second Battle. In March, 1918, four French and two British divisions were rushed from Italy to reinforce the Allied armies in France, on account of the collapse of the British Fifth Army during the German offensive. The Italian 2nd Corps was also drafted and Diaz then commanded 50 Italian and 5 Allied Divisions, as against 60 Austrian divisions which had been completely reorganised while in winter quarters.

On 15th June the Austrians advanced to exterminate the Allied army, and concentrated mainly astride the Oderzo-Tréviso Railway. Although immediately held up, they succeeded in establishing three bridge-heads across the Piave, and made some local gains, to which the closely knit defensive system of the Italian army held them as in a vice. The Piave rose in flood, and after a week of terrible battling the Austrians were compelled to withdraw.

armies (8th Aug., 1918). The Italians had now 51 Italian, 3 British, 2 French, 1 Czechoslovak divisions, and 1 United States Infantry regiment—827 battalions, supported by 7000 guns and trench mortars.

At three o'clock on the morning of 24th Oct. (anniversary of Caporetto disaster) the battle commenced between the Brenta and the Piave; at 7.15 a.m. the infantry advanced, and the battle raged until the 27th, when the Italians succeeded in establishing three bridge-heads on the Piave. On the 30th the Austrian line crumbled, and by 1st Nov. the Italians had reoccupied the line of the Tagliamento.

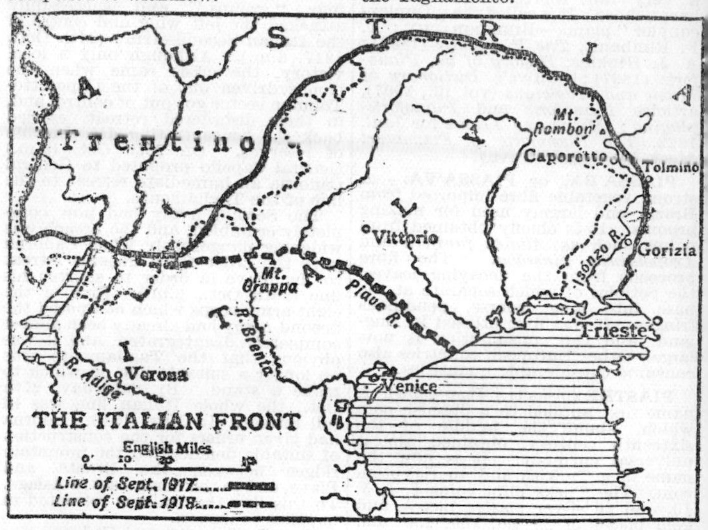

THE ITALIAN FRONT

Third Battle. Their failure in June, 1918, killed the last vestige of Austrian hopes for "peace by victory." Their enormous losses had shaken their *moral*, and the Italian High Command immediately grasped their advantage. But their own losses and the fact that the reinforcements were already tired precluded the idea of an immediate Italian advance. "The planned offensive had to aim at assisting the general effort of the Allies . . . to drive the attack home with all available forces . . . to obtain a real superiority of forces . . . and to gain a decision at one blow" (Diaz).

In the west the successful advances of the French were followed by the savage onslaught of the British

PIAZ'ZA. Italian word for a square or open space. The most famous is the piazza of St. Mark in Venice. They are found in other Italian cities.

PIAZZA-ARMERI'NA. A city of Sicily, in the province of Caltanisetta and 16½ miles E.S.E. of the town of Caltanisetta. Wines, oil, and nuts are traded. Pop. 25,000.

PIBROCH (pē'bro*h* ; Gael, *piobaireachd*, art of playing the bagpipe). A wild, irregular species of music peculiar to the Highlands of Scotland. It is performed on a bagpipe, and adapted to excite or assuage passion, and particularly to rouse a martial spirit among troops going to battle. The pibroch produces by imitative sounds the different phases of a battle

—the march, the conflict, the flight, the pursuit, and the lament for the fallen.

PIC'ARDY. One of the pre-Revolutionary provinces of France, in the northern part of the country, lying between the English Channel, Normandy, and Artois, now divided among the departments of Pas-de-Calais, Somme, Aisne, Oise, and Nord. The capital was Amiens.

PICARESQUE NOVEL, THE. A type of fiction dealing with the adventures of rogues (Sp. *picaron*, a rogue). The prototype of this kind of novel is the *Satiricon* of Petronius Arbiter, which describes the disreputable adventures of Encolpius, Ascyltos, and Giton in Cumæ and neighbouring towns. There is a certain picaresque element in the *Golden Ass* of Apuleius, where, in addition to stories of witches and magic, there are also tales of brigands and rascals. Some passages of Lucian describe the adventures of some quite pronounced rogues.

But as a definite branch of literature the picaresque novel originated in Spain with the publication of *Lazarillo de Tormes* in 1554. This novel may be said to mark an epoch in literature, as it dealt with everyday life as opposed to chivalry and romance.

For some while Spain was the home of the rogue-novel, some of the most remarkable being Mateo Aleman's *Guzman de Alfarache* (1599); *La Picara Justina* (1605), which recounts the adventures of a female rogue, and which may have suggested Moll Flanders to Defoe; *Marcos de Obregon* (1618); and Quevedo's *Vida del Buscon* (1626). Two of the *Novelas Ejemplares* of Cervantes (published 1613) also treat of roguery.

The picaresque novel soon made its way to England. The credit of writing the earliest one in English belongs to Thomas Nash, who published *The Unfortunate Traveller: or The Life of Jack Wilton* in 1594. Some of Defoe's work must be classed as picaresque, especially *Moll Flanders* and *Colonel Jack* (both published 1722.)

To France, however, belongs the crowning glory of the picaresque novel. Scarron's *Roman comique* (1651) and Furetière's *Roman bourgeois* (1666) show picaresque tendencies; but in *Gil Blas de Santillane* (1715) Le Sage crystallised and intensified all the most attractive features of the rogue-novel. Le Sage's originality has been attacked, and it is true that he drew much of his material from Spanish sources, but in the proper sense of the word he is as original as most great writers. His influence is plainly to be seen in the work of several great English novelists.

Fielding seems to have followed Cervantes rather than Le Sage, but his *History of Mr. Jonathan Wild the Great* (1743) is a picaroon novel. Smollett wrote several books which may fairly be classed as picaresque novels, especially noteworthy being *Ferdinand Count Fathom* (1753). Dickens carried on some features of the Smollettian tradition, especially in his early work; *Pickwick* (1837) and *Oliver Twist* (1838) are perhaps better classed as peripatetic novels, but the latter devotes a considerable amount of space to thieves and roguery. Thackeray's *Barry Lyndon* (1844) portrays a fairly complete rogue.

The Adventures of Hajji Baba of Ispahan, published by James Justinian Morier in 1824, is a very amusing and clever example of a rogue novel. Sir Walter Scott reviewed it for the *Quarterly*, and referred to the hero as the Oriental Gil Blas, thus showing that he did not shrink from comparing it with the greatest of all picaresque novels.—BIBLIOGRAPHY: F. W. Chandler, *Romances of Roguery*; F. M. Warren, *History of the Novel previous to the Seventeenth Century*; Sir Walter Raleigh, *The English Novel*.

PICAS'SO. Name taken by Pablo Ruiz, Spanish painter. Born at Malaga, on Oct. 23, 1881, he came to Paris and was associated with Braque (1906-12) becoming known for his Cubist works. He was influenced by Cézanne and El Greco. Later he reverted to the manner of Ingres, turning out pictures in a less challenging style. In 1931 an exhibition of his works was held in London.

PIC'CADILLY. London thoroughfare. It runs from Hyde Park corner to Piccadilly Circus. Here are a number of the principal clubs, several hotels, and Burlington House, occupied by the Royal Academy, the Royal Society of Arts, etc. Regent St. crosses Piccadilly Circus, and Coventry St., Shaftesbury Ave., and Glasshouse St. lead out of it.

PICCINI (pit-chē'nē), **Niccolo.** Italian musical composer, born in 1728, died in 1800. He composed comic and serious operas, chiefly for the stages of Rome and Naples, with such success that for many years he was without a rival in Italy. In 1776 he accepted an invitation, on very favourable terms, from the French court, and went to Paris, where he engaged in the famous musical contest with Gluck. In his later years he fell into misfortunes. He wrote over 150 operas, besides numerous oratorios and cantatas.

PIC'COLO. An instrument of the flute family, used in orchestras and military bands. The name is the Italian word for "little," and the full name of the instrument is *flauto piccolo* or little flute. It is half the length of the flute, and therefore sounds an octave higher than the latter, and its fingering and technique are exactly the same. It has a working compass of two octaves and a sixth, with D for the lowest note and B flat for the highest in the case of the orchestral piccolo. Two more semitones are possible at the top of the compass, but are too little under control and too unpleasant in effect to be of any practical value.

Owing to its high pitch and somewhat colourless quality of tone, it is not so generally useful as the flute, but for its own special effects no other instrument could take its place. It is a favourite with most composers, and they gladly avail themselves of its services on appropriate occasions.

PICCOLOM'INI. A noble Siennese family, still flourishing in Italy in two branches. The two most celebrated members are: (1) Æneas Sylvius Bartholomæus, afterwards Pope Pius (Pio) II. (q.v.). (2) Octavio, a grand-nephew of the first, born in 1599, died in Vienna in 1656. He was one of the distinguished generals of the Thirty Years' War, was a favourite of Wallenstein, and fought at Lutzen (1632). He participated in the plot which resulted in Wallenstein's assassination. He took part in the battle of Nördlingen, and was then sent to the Netherlands, where he remained till 1648. In 1650 he was created a prince and duke of Amalfi.

Octavio Piccolomini

PIC DU MIDI. A name given to more than one summit of the Pyrenees, as the Pic du Midi de Bigorre, or Bagnères (9440 feet), and the Pic du Midi d'Ossau (9465 feet).

PICE (pīs). A small Indian copper coin, value about one farthing sterling. It is subdivided into three *pies*.

PICEA. *See* NORWAY SPRUCE.

PICHEGRU (pēsh-gru), **Charles.** French general, born at Arbois, department of Jura, 1761, died in 1804. For some time a tutor at the College of Brienne, he soon exchanged this profession for that of a soldier. Commander-in-Chief of the army of the Rhine in 1793, and of the army of the north in 1794, he subjugated Holland, and entered Amsterdam in Jan., 1795. Disgusted with the anarchical state of affairs then prevailing in the capital, he entered into negotiations with the Bourbons, and became the soul of the party hostile to the Revolution. Transported to Cayenne in 1797, he escaped to England, where he entered into a conspiracy with George Cadoudal to assassinate Napoleon. Having gone to Paris for this purpose, he was captured by the police, and committed to the Temple prison, where he was found strangled.

PICHINCH'A. A volcano of Ecuador, in the Western Cordillera, north-west of Quito; height, 15,900 feet.

PICHINCHA. A province of Ecuador. Quito is the capital. This province, with a pop. of 240,000, is the most densely peopled area of the Republic.

PI'CIDÆ. The woodpecker and wryneck family, so named from the chief genus, Picus. *See* WOODPECKER.

PICK'EREL. The American name for some of the smaller kinds of pike.

PICKERING. An urban district and town of England, in North Riding of Yorkshire; a railway junction on the L.N.E. Railway. It is a town of great antiquity. Its castle was the prison of Richard II. in 1399. Pop. (1931), 3668.

PICK'ETING. Term denoting the posting of persons about a works, during a strike, to dissuade the employees from working. Made illegal in 1875 (so far as any compulsion was brought to bear by the pickets), what is termed peaceful picketing was legalised by an Act of 1906. An enactment of 1927, following on the general strike of 1926, made picketing illegal, if committed in respect of a strike declared unlawful. *See* TRADE UNION.

PICK'FORD, Mary (*née* **SMITH**). American cinema actress, born in Toronto, 8th April, 1893; she married Douglas Fairbanks, 28th March, 1920. Appearing on the stage in 1898, she afterwards acted in New York, and began screen work under D. W. Griffith. The Mary Pickford Film Corporation was formed in 1916 and gave her the highest salary in the profession. She appeared in many films, including *Rebecca of Sunnybrook Farm*, *Daddy Long-Legs*, and *Coquette*. In 1919 she became an independent producer.

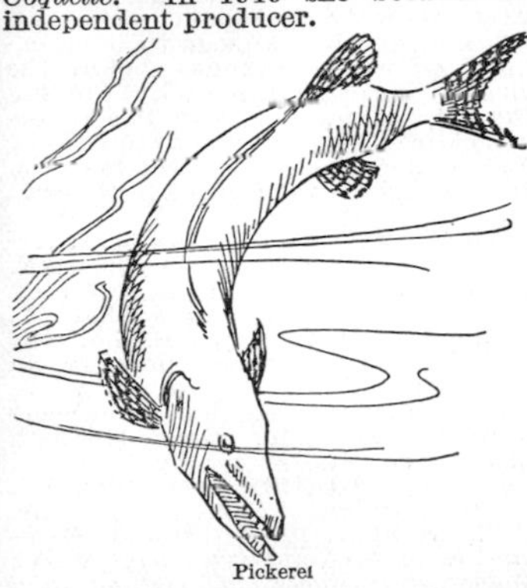

Pickerel

PICKLES. Food-stuffs preserved in vinegar or brine. In early times in agricultural countries the farmers killed at Michaelmas the cattle which were to be used as food during the winter, and preserved the flesh by the use of this process. In those days winter vegetables were few and pickled vegetables were in extensive use.

The processes of pickling are different, to some extent, for each type of food-stuff. Olives, capers, walnuts, and similar articles are preserved for use as appetisers in a simple solution of salt or brine. Cucumbers, green tomatoes, onions, cauliflowers, and other vegetables are cleaned, cut to size, and subjected to boiling vinegar, with which they are allowed to simmer for some time. After the process is completed the pickles are bottled. Sauerkraut is cabbage cut fine and allowed to ferment in its own juice and salt.

There is a considerable trade in pickled fish, especially herrings, for the German, Scandinavian, and Russian markets. Pickled mackerel is a popular dish with the poorer part of the population of America. Meat is pickled with solutions of mixtures of common or rock-salt, more or less sugar, some saltpetre, and such things as coriander seeds, dried bay leaves, garlic, etc. To ensure effective pickling, some of the solution is filtered or siphoned, so that it is quite clear, and is then injected into the meat by the use of a hand-pump and a sharp-pointed nozzle.

PICO. A Portuguese island in the Atlantic, forming one of the Azores group. It consists of a single volcanic mountain, which terminates in a peak (El Pico) 7613 feet high. Wine and oranges are produced. Area, 175 sq. miles; pop. 25,000.

PICRIC ACID. A yellow crystalline substance, $C_6H_2(NO_2)_3OH$, obtained by the action of nitric acid upon phenol and its allied compounds. It is of a very poisonous nature. Its salts, the picrates, explode when struck or heated, and are used as explosives. Other uses to which this substance is put are small in extent compared with its use as an explosive, but it is also used as a dye and in relieving the pain of burns in industrial works.

PICTOG'RAPHY, or PICTURE WRITING. Use of pictorial symbols to denote facts, events, or ideas. Derived from the primeval arts of design, it was man's earliest method of making a more or less self-explanatory record. In the early metal ages of the Old World it was destined to pass into alphabetic writing. Carried during the pre-metallic age into America, it developed local systems of picture-writing among the N. American plains Indians, and a more complex symbolism among the pre-Columbian Maya and Aztec peoples.

PICTON, Sir Thomas. British soldier, born in Pembrokeshire 1758;

Sir T. Picton

entered the army in 1771, and, after serving in the West Indies, rose to the rank of colonel, and became Governor of Trinidad in 1797. His next service was the capture of Flushing, of which he was appointed Governor in 1809. He afterwards distinguished himself in the Peninsular War at Badajoz, Vittoria, Ciudad Rodrigo, etc. He was killed at Waterloo in 1815.

PICTOU. A seaport and port of entry of Nova Scotia, Canada, on the C.N.R. Coal is mined and largely exported, and there are other industries. Pop. 3152.

PICTS. When Agricola invaded Scotland, the chief native tribe was known as the Caledonians. In the fourth century the Caledonians had become a division of the Picts. The tribal name of the Caledonians afterwards dropped out of use. The first Roman reference to the Picts dates from A.D. 297. By the fourth century Scotland, formerly called Caledonia, was known as Pictland, Pictavia. Evidently the Picts had become the dominant people, and the overlords of the aboriginal Britons of the north, who were called in Gaelic the Cruithne the Q-Celtic rendering of the P-Celtic Prydein (Britons).

There were Cruithne in Ireland also. Cruithne should not be translated "Picts" but "Britons." In Old Welsh the Picts were called Peithwyr (Pictmen), a name derived from Pect, the Old Scots form of which is Pecht (or Peght, as used by Sir Walter Scott in *The Pirate*). Celtic scholars reject the derivation of the tribal name from the Latin *pictus*. "Pecti," writes Professor W. J. Watson, "cannot be separated etymologically from Pictones, the name of a Gaulish tribe on the Bay of Biscay. . . . Their name shows the same variation between Pict-ones and Pect-ones. We may therefore claim Pecti as a genuine Celtic word."

Apparently the Pictones colonised Orkney and Shetland. The Gaelic evidence shows that the Picts were divided into two sections called the Orcs (young boars) and the Cats. Orkney was known as Inse Orcc ("Isles of Boars") and Shetland as Inse Catt ("Isles of Cats"). The people of Caithness (Catness) and of Sutherland are still known in Gaelic as the "Catach," and the Duke of Sutherland is "Diuc Chat" ("Duke of the Cats"). The Norsemen called the sea between the islands and the mainland *Pettaland-fjordhr*, i.e. Pictland Firth, now Pentland Firth. In the Irish *Book of Ballymote* it is stated that "Cairneach was for seven years in the sovereignty of Britons and Cats and Orcs and Saxons."

The Picts are associated in tradition with the brochs which so closely resemble the *nuraghi* of Sardinia. These brochs are most numerous in the north. On the west they are distributed as far south as Wigtownshire, and on the east as far south as Berwickshire.

The Pictish skiffs were large, open boats with twenty oars a side, painted a neutral tint, the sails being dyed in the same colour. It is believed that the Picts turned Hadrian's Wall from the sea. Their allies on the west were the Dalriadic Scots, and on the east they appear to have co-operated with "Saxons" before the close of the Roman period. Claudian (fourth century) refers to Theodosius attacking Picts and Saxons in Orkney and Thule (Shetland), and Scots in Ireland (*De Quarto Consulatu Honorii*, line 31).

The Pictish capital was at Inverness in the middle of the sixth century, and it was in his palace on the banks of Loch Ness that St. Columba found King Brude, the Pictish king, and was successful in converting him to Christianity. In the ninth century the Picts and Scots were united under King Kenneth macAlpin, whose mother was a Pict. *See* SCOTLAND; STRATHCLYDE.—BIBLIOGRAPHY: W. F. Skene, *Celtic Scotland* (vol. i.) and *Highlanders of Scotland* (vol. i.); W. C. Mackenzie, *Races of Ireland and Scotland* (with a bibliography).

PICUS. An old sylvan deity in Italy, who was represented with the head of a woodpecker (Lat. *picus*), and presided over divination.

PIDGIN-ENGLISH (Chinese corruption of "business English"). A language used in the ports of China and elsewhere in the East, as also on the coast of West Africa, as a medium of communication between natives and foreigners. Occasionally it is used as a lingua franca by the natives themselves hailing from different districts and speaking various dialects. Pidgin-English consists of monosyllabic English words and an admixture of Malay, Portuguese, Chinese, and miscellaneous words of many languages.

PIEDMONT (It. *Piemonte*). A department of Italy, between Switzerland, Lombardy, Liguria, and France, and divided into the provinces of Alessandria, Aosta, Cuneo, Novara, Torino, and Vercelli. Area, 11,331 sq. miles; pop. 3,497,799. It forms the upper valley of the River Po, and derives its name, signifying "foot of the mountain," from its situation at the base of the loftiest ranges of the Alps, by which it is enclosed on all sides except towards the Lombard plain. Maize, rice, wine, olives, oil, nuts, hemp, and silk are produced. Minerals include salt, coal, copper, lead, and silver. The chief town is Turin. *See* SARDINIA; SAVOY, HOUSE OF; ITALY.

PIEPOWDER COURT, or **PIEPOUDRE COURT** (O.F. *piepoudreux*, pedlar, dusty foot). A court formerly set up at fairs and markets in England for the summary administration of justice in cases arising there. It is also called the Court of Dusty Foot, which has the same meaning as piepowder. It was the lowest court of justice, and was so called from the circumstance that the litigants were usually tradesmen who travelled from one fair or market to another.

PIER. *See* JETTY.

PIETA. Term in art used for a representation of the Virgin embracing the dead body of Jesus, or of similar scenes at the deposition from the Cross. La Pieta, a group of sculpture of this type executed in St. Peter's, Rome, was one of the early masterpieces of Michelangelo, and this subject also has been the theme of many paintings.

PIETERMARITZBURG. A city of the Union of South Africa, capital of the province of Natal; served by railway from Durban. It was founded in 1843, and named after the Boer leaders Pieter Retief and Gert Maritz. It has wide streets planted with trees, and contains the Governor's residence, Government buildings, fine town hall (1901) with large organ, two cathedrals, and a college. Pop. (1921), 31,893 (17,998 white); white pop. (1931), 21,566.

PI'ETISM. A term often applied in derision to ill-regulated religious excitement and mysticism, or to a devotional attitude. Like "Methodist," the term Pietist was originally bestowed in contempt. More strictly, however, it was the name given to the religious views of a group of Lutheran reformers in Leipzig, who began in 1689 to deliver ascetic lectures on the New Testament to the students and citizens.

The idea of imparting theological instruction in a popular way came from their friend and teacher Spener (the German Fénelon), who had held religious meetings in Frankfort from the year 1670, at which the laity prayed and were allowed to ask questions. The Leipzig lectures were put a stop to as being hostile to good government, but the influence of the Pietists led to the foundation (1695) of the University of Halle, which became the centre of evangelical religion in Germany. The leading adherents of Spener were appointed its first professors, among them Francke, the founder of the celebrated Waisenhaus or orphanage at Halle.

The Pietists were noted for their preference for practical as opposed to doctrinal religion, but they never formed a separate sect. The Jansenism and Quietism of France, and the Methodism of England, sprang from sources similar to those of the German pietism.—Cf. A. Ritschl, *Geschichte des Pietismus*.

PIEZOM'ETER (Gr. *piezo*, I compress). An instrument used by Oersted for measuring the compressibility of liquids. A tall, thick-walled glass vessel with a layer of mercury at the bottom is filled up with water. The vessel is closed by a strong brass cap bored centrally, and fitted with a water-tight screw piston, by means of which pressure is applied to the water. The liquid to be compressed is contained within a glass bulb provided with a long capillary neck, and the bulb is immersed in the water of the vessel with the mouth of the capillary tube opening under the mercury. A tube containing air also opens under the mercury and acts as a pressure gauge. On screwing down the piston the rise of the mercury in the capillary indicates the compression of the liquid, and if the volumes of the bulb and tube are known, the compressibility of the liquid can be determined.

For water and mercury, within certain limits, the decrease of volume is proportional to the increase of pressure; also, liquids regain their original volume on removal of the pressure, liquids being in this respect perfectly elastic. The compressibility of water is 1 part in 22,000 per atmosphere of pressure, that of mercury 1 part in 270,000.

PIG, or **HOG.** When used in the broadest sense, the name of omnivorous animals belonging to the swine family (Suidæ) of even-toed, non-ruminating hoofed mammals. They are small or of moderate size, and possess a flexible snout, used for rooting in the ground, and ending in a bare disc perforated by the nostrils. The feet are four-toed, though the small outer toes do not reach the ground, except in swampy places, where they serve as "stops" to check sinking-in.

Swine are widely distributed through most parts of the Old World, but are replaced in America by the peccaries, which belong to a distinct family (Dicotylidæ). The type genus is Sus, and of this the most familiar species is the wild boar (*S. scrofa*), abundant in many parts of Europe and Asia, and formerly native to Britain. The closely allied Indian wild boar (*S. cristatus*) is the one that figures in "pig-sticking" exploits. A small species of pig (*S. andamanensis*) is native to the Andaman

Common British Pig

Islands, and the pygmy hog (*S. salvaniana*) lives in the forest regions on the south of the Himálaya.

Other species range through Malaya as far east as Celebes, and still others are found in New Guinea and Japan. The Senaar pig (*S. senaarensis*) is native to North-Eastern Africa. Other African swine are the red river hogs (species of Potamochœrus) and the wart hogs (species of Phacochœrus), the latter possessing enormous tusks and curious knobs on the face. The Babyroussa (Babirusa) is peculiar to Celebes, and is distinguished by the scantiness of its hair and extremely long, upwardly curved tusks in both jaws.—BIBLIOGRAPHY: R. Lydekker, *Royal Natural History*; F. E. Beddard, *Mammalia* (Cambridge Natural History Series); Sanders Spencer, *Pigs: Breeds and Management*; *British Breeds of Live-stock* (Ministry of Agriculture); W. Fream, *Elements of Agriculture*; articles in *Standard Cyclopedia of Modern Agriculture*.

PIGEON. The common name for many members of a family of birds (Columbidæ) also including the doves. The upper mandible is arched towards its apex, and of horny consistence; a second curve exists at its base, where there is a cartilaginous plate or piece through which the nostrils pass. The crop is of large size. Pigeons are generally strong on the wing. They are mostly arboreal in habits, perching upon trees, and building their nests in elevated situations. Both sexes incubate; and these birds generally pair for life, the loss or death of a mate being in many cases apparently mourned and grieved over, and the survivor frequently refusing to be consoled by another mate. The song consists of the well-known plaintive *cooing*.

The pigeons are distributed in every quarter of the globe, but attain the greatest luxuriance of plumage in warm and tropical regions. The pigeon family is divided into various groups. The true pigeons or Columbinæ are represented by the stock-dove (*Columba œnas*) of the southern English counties, which has been credited with being the progenitor of the domestic pigeon. The ring-dove or cushat (*C. palumbus*) is the largest British species, and has a wide distribution.

The rock-dove (*C. livia*) forms the species from which the various domestic varieties have sprung. The house-pigeons, tumblers, fantails, pouters, carriers, and jacobins are the chief varieties of the rock-pigeon, and have been employed by Darwin (*Origin of Species* and *Animals under Domestication*) to illustrate many of the points involved in his theory of "descent by natural selection."

The turtle-dove (*Turtur communis*), found in Britain in summer, is also

Pigeons

1, Stock-dove. 2, Homing or Racing Pigeon (Blue Chequer). 3, Victoria Crowned Pigeon. 4, Pouter. 5, White Fantail.

a representative species. Other forms are the Treroninæ or fruit-pigeons of India, the Eastern Archipelago, and Australia; and the Gourinæ or ground-pigeons, the largest of the group, including the crowned pigeon (*Goura coronāta*) of the Eastern

Archipelago. See CARRIER PIGEON; PASSENGER PIGEON; TURTLE-DOVE; etc.

PIGEON-PEA. The fruit of the leguminous shrub *Cajanus indicus*, a native of India, but now cultivated in tropical Africa and America. In India the pigeon-pea forms a pulse of general use. Called also *Angola Pea* and *Congo Pea*.

PIG-FARMING. The commonest British pigs and their characteristics are as follows:

Large White.—White in colour; long and deep carcass; ears long and inclined forward. *Objections.*—Blue spots on skin; coarse, pendulous ears; heavy jowls; coarse skin and hair; black hairs.

Middle Whites.—Same as Large White excepting ears, which should be erect and smaller.

Berkshires.—Black in colour, with white blaze on face, white tip to the tail, and white feet; ears erect. *Objections.*—Narrow forehead; short snout; heavy jowls; thick, coarse, or much inclined (forward) ears; white or rusty patches of hair.

Large Blacks.—Black in colour, with long, thin ears covering the eyes and snout.

Tamworths.—Golden-red in colour; long snout; pricked ears. *Objections.*—Black hairs; black spots on skin; drooping ears; upturned snout.

Lincolnshire Curly-coated.—White in colour; curly hair; long, thin ears covering eyes and snout.

The commercial pig of to-day, wherever bred, is a descendant of the wild hog, which at one time was common in Britain. As definite breeds, the English pigs have been evolved within the last seventy years, chiefly by a judicious crossing with Neapolitan and Chinese varieties, and at the present day all, without exception, of the improved pigs in the world owe both their increased size and their quality to one or more of the above varieties.

There are now no known varieties in any country which can compete with British native breeds, even including those American pigs which practically owe their existence to them. Ireland, although a great pig-breeding country, has no breed of her own; in Scotland pigs are not generally popular, and no effort is made to popularise them, so that English breeds dominate the world, and nowhere is it possible to find pigs that are able to bear comparison with such standard breeds as the Large White, which is not only most popular in Britain, but has been used more extensively than any other variety for the improvement of pigs abroad. It possesses, when at its best, all the qualities which are calculated to produce an abundance of fine meat and to repay the breeder and feeder for his pains. It was freely used by the Danes in building their great bacon industry, as well as by the Germans, French, and Americans.

The Large White is a prolific, hardy pig of good constitution and even temper, of a shape adapted to the production of the most useful sides of bacon, and such as can be modified to meet the requirements of the curer or pork-butcher. The sows are good dams, producing large litters of strong pigs which grow with great rapidity. At all ages they are good growers and good feeders, making the most of their food, and producing soon after weaning 1 lb. of live weight for 4 lb. of good meal. Any of the Whites, Large, Middle, or Small are good for the breeder, and as such can be recommended.

Management.—Of all domesticated animals the pig has the least care and attention bestowed upon it, and it seems to be a commonly accepted opinion that any inexperienced person may keep and breed good pigs. Pig-feeding and management is a difficult art, of which the mastery can only be obtained by a long, practical apprenticeship, combined with a certain amount of theoretical study.

The domestic pig is by nature as cleanly an animal as the ewe or the mare, and it is mainly due to misconception and carelessness that "pig" has become synonymous with "filth," in which all pigs are absurdly supposed to benefit by wallowing. Certain factors have contributed greatly to the neglect of the pig, but one of them is markedly outstanding, namely, that the pig appears to possess the power of making great progress under conditions of gross neglect, and this progress is not infrequently so great as considerably to benefit the neglectful owner.

Again, a pig matures within a much shorter period than any other domestic animal, the average being only seven months. The sow also possesses remarkable powers of multiplication and reproduction, as many as thirteen piglings being bred in one year by a sow, as compared with the single annual calf of the cow, or foal of the brood mare.

Mating.—Care must be taken in the choice of a sow for breeding purposes, and also in the boar for mating, as the male tends to impart a large proportion of his character to the offspring, particularly when a pure-bred boar is mated with a mongrel. The age prescribed for a female pig to be mated with the boar varies between six and twelve months, but if she has been fairly well reared and the probable time of year of her farrowing will prove suitable, she may be served when eight months old.

A young sow should farrow in the early part of March, as the young pigs will naturally thrive better in spring than at any other season, and the sow will regain her strength and complete her growth better in the summer than during the winter months. There is a marked difference in the prolificacy of sows, as there is also in their capacity to produce a quantity of rich milk extending over a period of at least eight weeks.

It is not always advisable to leave on the sow the whole of a large litter which she may produce, and although a matured and judiciously fed sow will have no trouble in rearing as many as twelve pigs, the exact number allowed to remain has never been authoritatively fixed. Two of the principal drawbacks to allowing a young sow to rear a large litter of pigs are the loss of flesh and the check to the growth and development of the dam that invariably ensue.

Feeding.—Opinions differ as to the best method of feeding pigs at varying ages, but the following is recommended by Sanders Spencer, the well-known pig-breeding expert. "The sow pigs intended for breeding purposes are usually weaned when about six weeks old. The best single food for sows suckling their litter, and also for the latter when weaned, is the offal from the grinding of wheat, known variously as 'sharps,' 'middlings,' or 'thirds,' etc., according to district, whilst the best addition to this is skimmed milk, where procurable, then separated milk, buttermilk, and whey, all in comparatively small quantities, fed at first through the sow, but subsequently, when the pigs are a few weeks old, mixed with their food. Indigestion and constipation attack the youngsters where much separated milk is fed, and this can only be remedied by the addition of some oil or fat, which unfortunately proves on occasion too rich for the immature digestive organs of the little pigs. When they are from three to four months old, barley-, oat-, pea-, or wheat-meal may generally be added to the sharps fed, until at five months of age the meal automatically becomes the staple food, with an occasional dose of milk in small quantity. During spring and summer, tares, clover, lucerne, and cabbages, or other greenstuffs, materially assist the fattening process; and in winter, mangold, turnips, swedes, and kohlrabi, etc., take their place. Save for potatoes, cooked vegetable food is neither economical nor beneficial."

The weight at which pigs should be sold depends solely upon the demands of the market they are reared to supply.—Cf. *Live-stock of the Farm* (vol. v.), editor, Professor C. Byrner Jones.

PIG'IRON. Crude iron, the product of the blast-furnace, containing about 3 per cent of carbon and small quantities of silicon, manganese, sulphur, and phosphorus. It is hard, brittle, and moderately fusible, and is cast in U-shaped moulds called "pigs."

PIGMENTS. *See* PAINTS AND PIGMENTS.

PIG-STICKING. Sport of hunting the wild boar, popular in India. Huntsmen in parties of three or four pursue the animal, when beaten out of cover, and endeavour to ride it down and spear it.

PIKA. The calling-hare (*Lagōmys*), an animal nearly allied to the hares, and forming the family Lagomyidæ. It is found in Russia, Siberia, and North America, and is remarkable for the manner in which it stores up its winter provision, and also for its voice, the tone of which so much resembles that of a quail as to be often mistaken for it.

PIKE. A genus of fishes belonging to the ord. Teleostei, and included in the soft-finned division of the order. The pikes form the types of the family Esocidæ, in which group the body is lengthened, flattened on

Pike (*Esox lucius*)

the back, and tapering abruptly towards the tail. One dorsal fin exists, this structure being placed far back on the body, and opposite the anal fin. The lower jaw projects. Teeth are present in plentiful array, and are borne by almost every bone entering into the composition of the mouth.

The common pike (*Esox lucius*) occurs in the rivers of Europe and North America. It is fished chiefly for the sake of its flesh, which is accounted exceedingly wholesome. The pikes are very long-lived, and form the tyrants of their sphere, being the most voracious of freshwater fishes. When fully grown, the pike may attain a length of 5 or 6 feet, and there are numerous instances on record in which these fishes have greatly exceeded that length.

The sea pikes (Belone), also known as gar-pikes (*see* GAR-FISH), and the saury pike (*Scomberesox saurus*) belong to a different family (Scomberesocidæ). The bony pike (Lepidosteus) of North American lakes and rivers belongs to a widely different order. *See* BONY PIKE.

PIKE. A sort of lance, a weapon much used in the Middle Ages as an arm for infantry. It was from 16 to 18 feet long, and consisted of a pole with an iron point. For some time every company in the armies of Europe consisted of at least two-thirds pike-men and one-third harquebusiers. Gustavus Adolphus omitted the pike-men in some regiments entirely. The invention of the bayonet about 1690 drove the pike out of use.

PIKE-PERCH (Lucioperca). A genus of fishes closely allied to the perch, but showing a resemblance to the pike in its elongated body and head. Like the pike, it is a dangerous enemy to other freshwater fishes, but the flavour of its flesh is excellent. In Europe it occurs in two species. It also occurs in the fresh waters of North America, such as the Great Lakes, the Upper Mississippi, and the Ohio.

PIKE'S PEAK. A peak of the Rocky Mountains, in the centre of the state of Colorado, United States. It was discovered by Lieutenant Z. M. Pike in 1806, and was first ascended by a party under Major S. H. Long (1819). A rack-rail line of railway, 9 miles long, runs to the top of the mountain, upon which a powerful search-light is stationed.

PILAS'TER. A square pillar projecting from a pier or a wall to the extent of from one-fourth to one-third of its breadth. Pilasters originated in Grecian architecture. In Roman they were sometimes tapered like columns, and finished with capitals modelled after the order with which they were used. *See* COLUMN.

PILATE, Pontius. Roman procurator of Judæa (A.D. 26-36). Nothing is known of his early history. He was a narrow-minded and impolitic governor, and at the very beginning of his term of office commotions arose among the Jews at Jerusalem. When Christ had been condemned to death by the Jewish priests, who had no power of inflicting capital punishments, He was carried by them to Pilate to be executed. Yielding to the clamours of the Jews, the Roman governor ordered Jesus to be executed, but permitted Joseph of Arimathea to take His body and bury it.

Philo speaks of Pilate as an obstinate and merciless man, but from the Canonical Gospels he appears to have been possessed of a sense of justice, and stress is laid upon the fact that he made a serious effort to acquit Christ. Pilate was afterwards removed from his office by Vitellius, prefect of Syria (A.D. 36), and, according to tradition, was banished by Caligula to Vienna (Vienne), in Gaul, where he is said to have died or committed suicide some years after.—Cf. Matt. xxvii. 2, 11-27; Luke iii. 1; xxiii. 1-25, 50-52.

PILA'TUS. A mountain mass of Switzerland, on the borders of the cantons of Lucerne and Unterwalden Its loftiest peak, the Tomlishorn, attains a height of 7116 feet. It is

Mt. Pilatus

almost as great a favourite with mountain climbers as the Rigi, on account of the imposing views of the Bernese mountain scenery obtained from various points. A railway to the summit was opened in 1889.

PIL'CHARD (*Clupea pilchardus*). A species of fishes included in the family and genus of the herrings (Clupeidæ), which they much resemble though rather smaller. They frequent the coasts of Britain all the year round. The usual spawning time is October. They are found in greatest plenty on the southern coasts of England, the Cornwall pilchard fisheries being those best known and most celebrated. Pilchards are chiefly consumed in Spain, Italy, and France during Lent and other fasting seasons. Many of the commercial "sardines" are in reality young pilchards. *See* SARDINE.

PILCOMA'YO. A river of South America, which rises in Bolivia, on the eastern declivities of the Andes, and falls into the Paraguay, near Asunción, after forming the boundary between Paraguay and the Argentine Republic. Its entire length is between 1500 and 1600 miles. The Pilaya and the Paspaya are the principal affluents.

PILE-DWELLING. Primitive habitation built on piles. This constructional method arose in neolithic

Europe, especially on shallow lake-margins, and continued through the early metal ages. It still occurs in aboriginal Africa, pile-granaries for protection from animal depredation being also used, as formerly by the Maori. Borneo raises piles 40 ft. high. In New Guinea and neighbouring islands pile-villages resembling those of neolithic Europe often extend far out to sea. They occur also in the Burmese Shan States and the Nicobars. *See* LAKE-DWELLING.

PILES, or **HÆMORRHOIDS.** Dilated condition of the veins at the lower end of the rectum, sometimes protruding through the anus and accompanied by bleeding. Since they are usually caused by constipation or some internal disorder, strict attention should be paid to the diet and general health. Diet should be simple and contain plenty of fruit and vegetables ; alcohol is prohibited; drastic purges should be avoided, but the bowels can be regulated with liquid paraffin. Scrupulous cleanliness of the parts is essential, and the application of vaseline will aid in defecation. If the condition is severe a doctor should be consulted.

PILE'WORT, or **LESSER CELANDINE.** Perennial herb of the buttercup family (*Ranunculus ficaria*). The fibrous roots develop annually several small stout cylindrical tubers, used by herbalists for curing piles, and when boiled an agreeable pot-herb. The shining stalked, heart-shaped leaves contrast with the starry, single bright-yellow 1 in. flowers. *See* CELANDINE.

PILGRIMAGE OF GRACE. An insurrectionary movement in 1536-7, consequent upon the proceedings of Henry VIII. in regard to the Church. The movement arose in Lincolnshire, and then spread to Yorkshire. The insurgents demanded the fall of Cromwell, redress to the Church, and reunion with Rome. Mustering to the number of 30,000, the rebels, under Robert Aske, Lord Darcey, and Sir Robert Constable, marched upon York, and within a few days were masters of England north of the Humber. Henry temporised, promising a free Parliament at York ; but when the insurgents returned home all concessions were revoked, and a renewal of the revolt was suppressed with great rigour. Many perished by the block, the gibbet, and the stake.

PILGRIM FATHERS. The foundation of the first British Empire (i.e. of the empire as it existed before 1783) was closely connected with religious divisions in England and the refusal of toleration to Nonconformists by James I. Elizabethan efforts to found colonies on the eastern coast of North America had been unsuccessful, but a settlement was made in Virginia in 1609, and it attracted the attention of a body of Puritans, belonging to Scrooby and Gainsborough, who had fled from England to Holland. They entered into negotiations with a London Company to which the Virginia Company had ceded some of its rights, and obtained permission to found a colony near the mouth of the Hudson River. The English Government put no obstacles in the way, and the exiles sailed from Delftshaven in July, 1620.

They called at Southampton, from which, on 5th Aug., 120 of their number sailed for America in the *Mayflower* and the *Speedwell*. The last-named vessel was compelled to return as unseaworthy, but about 100 left Plymouth on 6th Sept. in the *Mayflower*. They reached the coast of North America in December, but stress of weather prevented their making for their intended destination at the mouth of the Hudson, and they landed in the region of Cape Cod, where they founded the colony of New Plymouth, as " loyal subjects of our dread sovereign, King James " (21st Dec., 1620).

Before landing they had drawn up a written constitution for the new colony, agreeing to form themselves into a " body politic," and promising due obedience to laws which they were to draw up. They suffered many hardships on their arrival, and about half their number died in the first winter.

The dangers by which they were surrounded led them to try a short-lived system of having all things in common. The London Company, which had permitted their settlement near the Hudson, made difficulties about the position of the new colony, and the colonists were unable to bring their democratic constitution—government by the whole body of freemen—into operation until 1627. By that date they had received small accessions to their numbers, which were greatly increased after the grant of a charter to the Massachusetts Company in 1629.

The name " Pilgrim Fathers " is sometimes loosely used for all the settlers up to 1629 and even later, but it properly belongs to the emigrants in the *Mayflower*.—BIBLIOGRAPHY : A. Ames, *The Mayflower and her Log* ; B. M'Manus, *The Voyage of the Mayflower*.

PILGRIMS (O.Fr. *pelegrin* ; Fr.

pélerin; Lat. *peregrinus*, foreigner). Persons who visit distant places, considered sacred, for religious purposes. The practice of making pilgrimages to places of peculiar sanctity is as ancient as it is widespread. The ancient Egyptians and Syrians had privileged temples, to which worshippers came from distant parts. The chief temples of Greece and Asia Minor swarmed with strangers.

Christian Pilgrimage. But it is in Christianity and Mahommedanism that the practice has attained its greatest development. The first Christian pilgrimages were made to the graves of the martyrs. By the end of the fourth and the beginning of the fifth century the custom had become so general as to lead to abuses. Throughout the Middle Ages, and especially about the year 1000, the religious fervour of the people manifested itself in numerous pilgrimages, especially to Jerusalem.

The outrages inflicted on the Christian pilgrims by the Saracens led to the Crusades, which were themselves nothing else than gigantic armed pilgrimages. The shrine of Our Lady of Loretto, near Rome, that of St. James of Compostella in Spain, of St. Martin of Tours in France, were all sacred spots to which, from the tenth to the thirteenth century, and even much later, pilgrims resorted in innumerable crowds; and from the end of the twelfth century the shrine of St. Thomas à Becket at Canterbury had the same honour in England. Other places of pilgrimage in England were St. Albans, Walsingham, Lichfield, Bury St. Edmunds, and Peterborough.

The pilgrims usually wore a broad hat, grey or black cloak, and carried a long staff. A bottle or bell was the badge of pilgrims from Canterbury, whilst a string of scallop shells was that of pilgrims from Compostella. Palmers were pilgrims who had completed a pilgrimage to the Holy Land and had carried away a palm leaf.

After the Reformation the practice of making pilgrimages fell more and more into abeyance, and the spirit which led to it seems almost to have become extinct among Christians, although there are still occasional outbursts of it among the Roman Catholics, as in the modern pilgrimages to Paray-le-Monial, Lourdes, Iona, and Holy Island. In the Greek Church, Mount Athos is the chief shrine of pilgrimage.

Mahommedan and Hindu Pilgrimages. For Mahommedans the great place of pilgrimage is Mecca, which was the resort of Arabian pilgrims long before the time of Mahomet. Every year just before the feast of Bairam large caravans arrive at Mecca from all quarters. The pilgrims who join these caravans have in view not only the performance of a religious duty, but also the object of doing some business.

Among the Hindus and the Buddhists also the practice of performing pilgrimages largely prevails. The principal resorts of pilgrims in India are the sacred city of Benares, the rock-cut temples of the Island of Elephanta, the pagoda of Juggernaut, and the temples of Ellora.—BIBLIOGRAPHY: J. Jusserand, *English Wayfaring Life in the Middle Ages*; J. C. Wall, *Shrines of British Saints*.

PIL'GRIM'S WAY. Road used by pilgrims through Winchester to the shrine of St. Thomas à Becket at Canterbury, following, in part, a more ancient track. It is about 120 miles long and goes *via* Alresford, Farnham, Albury Pk., Burford Bridge, Merstham, Chevening, Mosham, West Malling, Hollingbourne and Charing.

PILGRIM TRUST. Fund founded in 1930 by an American, Edward Stephen Harkness. He set aside a sum of £2,000,000, the interest of which is devoted to assisting charitable causes in Great Britain, in recognition of the way the country had discharged its obligations since the war. A trust was formally instituted with Mr. Stanley Baldwin, M.P., as president and Mr. Thomas Jones as secretary.

PILIBHIT. A district and town in the Bareilly division of the United Provinces, India. The district lies close to the Himálaya, and is a plain watered by the Sarda River and by the Rohilkhand canals. The Oudh-Rohilkhand Railway (Lucknow-Bareilly section) traverses the district. Area, 1350 sq. miles; pop. about 480,000. The town of Pilibhit stands on the Desha River. In 1740 it was seized by the Rohilla leader Háfiz Rahmat Khán, who made it his capital. In the western outskirts stand his cathedral-mosque and the remains of his palace. Pop. 32,344.

PILLAU (pil'ou). A seaport of Germany in East Prussia, at the entrance of the Frisches Haff. Large vessels for Königsberg may be partially unloaded at Pillau, which is connected with Königsberg by the Königsberg Ship Canal, dredged to a depth of 21 feet. The railway from Lyck through Königsberg has its seaward terminus at Pillau, which is thus connected direct with Bialystock, on the Warsaw-Moscow line. After the opening of the ship canal Pillau lost much of its importance, but has still two docks and can accommodate vessels of 1500 tons. The Pillau Deep is a fortified channel protected by moles, and forms an entrance 328 yards wide and 27 feet deep (minimum) to the Frisches Haff. It is kept open in winter by ice-breakers. Pop. 8000.

PIL'LORY. A frame of wood erected on posts, with movable boards, and holes through which were put the head and hands of a criminal for punishment. In this

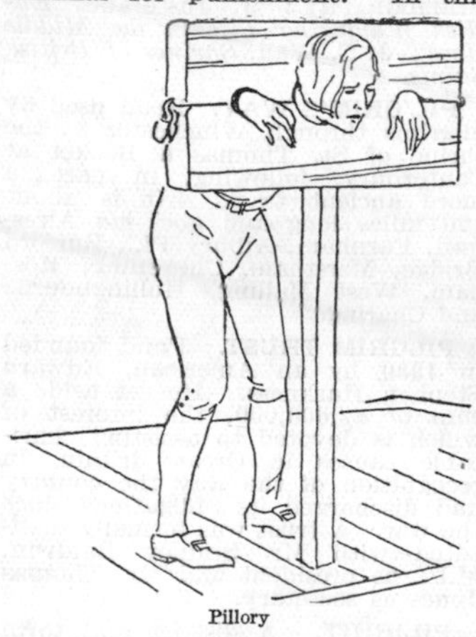

Pillory

manner persons were formerly exposed to public view, and generally to public insult. It was a common punishment in Britain for forestallers, users of false weights, those guilty of perjury, forgery, and libel. After 1637 restrictions were put upon the press, and the pillory became the punishment of all those who had printed books without licence or published seditious writings. The punishment was abolished in 1816 in all cases except that of perjury, and it was abolished altogether in 1837. The pillory was used in Germany and France, and was in use in the United States till 1839.

PILOBOLUS. A remarkable genus of Zygomycetous Fungi, allied to Mucor. *Pilobolus crystallinus* regularly appears on horse-dung. Each sporangium is borne on a stout, erect hypha (sporangiophore), 1 to 1½ inches high, which swells up into a club-shaped bulb at its upper end. The osmotic pressure inside this bulb is very great, and when the sporangium is ripe, it is thrown bodily to a considerable distance by the sudden bursting of the bulb. The mass of spores is sticky, and adheres to any object it may strike, normally a blade of grass or other herbage; if it is swallowed by a horse, the spores pass unharmed through the alimentary tract and germinate in the dung.

The sporangiophore is very sensitive to light (positively heliotropic; *see* HELIOTROPISM), and Buller has shown that the bulb, besides serving to disperse the spores explosively, also acts as a light-perceiving sense-organ. This curious fungus is readily obtained for observation by keeping some fresh horse-dung under a bell-jar for about a week.

PILOCARPIDINE. An alkaloid ($C_{10}H_{14}N_2O_2$), occurring along with pilocarpine (q.v.) and isopilocarpine in jaborandi.

PILOCARPINE. An alkaloid obtained from the dried leaves of *Pilocarpus pinnatifolius*, a South American plant of the ord. Rutaceæ (rue). It is a very powerful drug, and acts as an antidote in cases of poisoning by belladonna. *See* JABORANDI.

PILOT. A person qualified to navigate a vessel within a particular district. The pilots of the United Kingdom are formed into associations at different places by ancient charters of incorporation, or by particular statutes. The principal of these associations are the Brotherhood of Trinity House of Deptford Strond; the Fellowship of the Pilots of Dover, Deal, and the Isle of Thanet, or the Cinque Port Pilots; and the Trinity Houses of Hull and Newcastle. The Trinity House of Deptford Strond regulates the pilotage of the Thames and Medway, and of the coast from Orfordness to the Isle of Wight; besides which it is entrusted with the general regulation and superintendence of pilotage for the United Kingdom. (*See* TRINITY HOUSE.)

The law relating to British pilots and pilotage is contained in various Acts. By the existing law, oversea vessels must employ a pilot in those parts of the voyage where a pilot is employed by regulation or usage. A master refusing to take a pilot vitiates the insurance on the vessel; while a pilot refusing to perform the duty for which he is licensed renders himself liable to penalties. The master or owner of a vessel is not responsible for damage caused by the fault or incapacity of any qualified pilot, where the employment of such pilot is compulsory; but the pilot must not be interfered with in the discharge of his duties.

Pilotage fees depend on the distance and the draught of water of the vessel piloted. Masters and mates passing the requisite examination are entitled to pilotage certificates to conduct their own vessels.

PILOT-FISH (*Naucrătes ductor*). A genus of Teleostean fishes included in the Carangidæ or horse-mackerel family. The pilot-fish was formerly supposed to act as a pilot to the mariner, and is still supposed to act as such to sharks. It often follows in the wake of ships for long distances, associating with sharks and devouring the refuse thrown overboard. The average length is about 12 inches. In general form it resembles the mackerel.

PILSEN, or PLZEN. A town and railway junction of Western Bohemia, Czechoslovakia, at the confluence of the Mies and Radbusa. It consists of the town proper, with promenades on the site of the old ramparts, and of three suburbs. The principal buildings are the church (1292) and town house. The chief article of manufacture and commerce is beer. The second town of Bohemia, Pilsen dates from 1272, but is mentioned as early as 976 as the scene of a battle between Boleslas and the Emperor Otto II. During the Thirty Years' War it was for a time the head-quarters of Wallenstein. Pop. (1930), 114,150.

PILSUDSKI, Joseph. Polish soldier and statesman. He was born at Zulov,

Joseph Pilsudski

in the province of Vilna, in 1867. His intense patriotism early found him disfavour in Russian eyes, and he was exiled and imprisoned on various occasions prior to the European War. On the outbreak of war he invaded Russia at the head of a Polish legion (6th Aug., 1914), and became a member of the Polish Council of State when the Austro-German conquest was complete. When the State of Poland was recreated, he became head of the Provisional Government, and became President on 20th Feb., 1919, by popular election. He led the Poles to the invasion of the Ukraine in July, 1920. In 1926 he headed a revolt which brought about the fall of the government, himself becoming Premier and Minister of War. Resigning the major office, 1928, he became virtual dictator. Pilsudski again became Prime Minister in 1930, but in March, 1932, he was appointed Minister of Military Affairs, and Alexander Prystor took office as Premier. He has written many historical works dealing mainly with Poland's struggles for independence, including *Historical Corrections* (1931). *See* POLAND.

PILT'DOWN SKULL. Fossil human bones discovered at Pilt Down, Sussex, 1911-15. Quaternary gravels yielded fragments of a skull, partly mineralised, the right half of a lower jaw and some teeth. Subsequently an implement hewn from an elephant's thigh-bone emerged close by. Named *Eoanthropus*, "dawn-man", the remains represent the oldest known human race in Europe.

PIMELO'DUS. A genus of catfishes (Siluridæ), found in South America, and supposed to abound in subterranean lakes, as one species (*P. cyclōpum*).

PIMEN'TO, or JAMAICA PEPPER. Dried fruit of a W. Indian evergreen tree of the myrtle order (*Pimenta officinalis*), widely grown in Jamaica and Central America. Also called allspice, because its flavour supposedly combines those of cinnamon, nutmeg and cloves. Its essential oil, largely eugenol, is used in pharmacy like oil of cloves and for perfuming soaps.

PIM'LICO. District of London between Chelsea and Westminster, in the city of Westminster. It is bounded by the Thames on the S. and E., Chelsea on the W., and Belgravia and Victoria St., Westminster, on the N. Pimlico Road connects Royal Hospital Road and Buckingham Palace Road.

PIM'PERNEL (Anagallis). A genus of plants belonging to the nat. ord. Primulaceæ. The *Anagallis arvensis* or field pimpernel, a beautiful annual, is commonly known in England (where the scarlet-flowered variety is by far the most common) as the "shepherd's or poor man's weather-glass", from the fact that its flowers do not open in rainy weather. The bog pimpernel (*A. tenella*) grows in the drier parts of marches in England. The blue and lilac varieties of the *A. collīna*, originally a native of South Africa, have been introduced into

Scarlet Pimpernel

gardens in Great Britain, where they have a fine effect. The water pimpernel is the *Veronica Anagallis*; the yellow pimpernel, *Lysimachia nemŏrum*.

PIN AND PIN MANUFACTURE. The domestic pin was introduced during the fifteenth century. Prior to that time fastenings of a very primitive type were used, but even during the Bronze Age the pins of brooches were carefully made and finished. A statute of 1483 prohibited the importation of pins from the Continent, and sixty years later an Act prohibited the sale of pins unless made "double-headed", or with heads "fast soldered to the shank".

The industry was mainly developed in France, and despite all regulations and enactments French pins were sold in the British markets. They were expensive, which made "pin-money" a serious consideration for the ladies. Tilsby introduced pin-making into Gloucestershire in 1626, but little progress was made in this industry during the next two centuries.

In 1817 Seth Hunt patented a machine for the manufacture of pins in which head, shaft, and point were fashioned from the one piece, but little use was made of this invention. Wright designed a machine in 1824 which was later developed by Shuttleworth and Tyler, who made improvements in pin-making quite comparable with those Mason made in pen-making. The old processes of manufacture, which Adam Smith described as an example of the division of labour, have been entirely superseded by the use of machinery, not only to make the pins, but also to stick them in rows in the paper in which they are sold.

In the modern pin-making machine the wire from a coil is first straightened by being drawn through a series of steel pins or stops. The end is passed through a hole in a small steel anvil, and is then hammered until the head is formed. A tool then parts the pin-blank from the rest of the wire, and the operation is repeated. The blanks, with the heads uppermost, fall into slanting grooves, and are guided between revolving files, which shape the points. The pins fall into a box, and are finished by tinning.

The paper on which the pins are to be mounted is passed between corrugated wheels to form the waves in it. The pins are brushed into a number of grooves and fall forward. At the end of the journey through the grooves, a steel plate is made to come down over the pin-heads and force the pins into the paper, which is fed forward to a suitable position for the purpose. A movable steel arm prevents any but the first row of pins from being pressed into the paper until the proper time.

Hair-pins are made by first cutting the suitable lengths of wire, which pieces are fed forward in guides, and later caught between a pair of movable steel jaws which move downwards. During this action the wire is pressed inwards from each side by means of wheels, whose distance apart can be regulated to suit the dimensions required. When the wire has to be waved, the wheels are made with suitable corrugations on their edges.

PINA CLOTH, or PINA MUSLIN. A costly fabric made in Manila from the unspun fibres of the leaves of the cultivated pineapple plant (*Ananas sativus*). Its colour is almost white, but has a slight tinge of yellow in it. In spite of the delicacy of its texture it is remarkably strong. Its chief use is for making ladies' pocket handkerchiefs, light dresses, and similar articles. It is frequently adorned with exquisite embroidery.

PINAR' DEL RIO. A town and province of Cuba. The town is situated 90 miles by railway from Havana, in the famous Vuelta de Abajo, where the best tobacco grows. Pop. 17,506.—The province has an area of 5206 sq. miles; pop. 324,066. It raises some of the world's finest tobacco; sugar, coffee and fruits; timber, and cattle are also produced.

PINCHBECK. An alloy containing about 80 per cent of copper and 20 per cent of zinc, used as a substitute for bronze and for making cheap watch-cases and imitation jewellery. By association the word is used to indicate anything spurious, counterfeit, or cheap. It is named after the inventor, a London watchmaker of the eighteenth century.

PINDAR (Pindaros). The greatest lyric poet of Greece, was born about 522 B.C. and died 443 B.C. He belonged to a noble Theban family, which liked to trace its descent back to Cadmus. He is said to have studied at Athens under Apollodorus and Lasus of Hermione, and he was always a lover of the Athenians, who eventually made him honorary consul, and presented him with a large sum of money. Pindar began to write poetry when young; the technique of his branch of poetry was difficult to master, and he served a long apprenticeship.

Little is known of the events of his life, but it is made clear not only by tradition but by his writings that he was a deeply religious man. His reputation was very great both during his life and after his death. There is a well-attested story that when Alexander the Great sacked Thebes in 335 B.C. he ordered it all to be destroyed save the citadel, the temples and Pindar's house. This story is alluded to in Milton's well-known sonnet *When the Assault was intended to the City*.

Pindar wrote lyric poetry of all kinds—hymns, pæans, dithyrambs, processional songs, choral songs for maidens, dance-songs, encomia, drinking-songs, dirges, and odes of victory. With the exception of the last class, all these poems are lost or are only represented by inconsiderable fragments.

The Pindaric Odes. The *Epinicia* (Odes of Victory) consist of forty-four odes arranged in four books: (1) Olympian odes, fourteen odes for the winners of the wild olive wreath in the Olympian games, held at Olympia in honour of Zeus once in four years; (2) Pythian odes, twelve odes for winners of the laurel wreath in the Pythian games, held at Delphi in honour of Apollo once in four years; (3) Nemean odes, eleven odes for winners of the pine wreath in the Nemean games, held at Nemea in honour of Zeus once in two years; and (4) Isthmian odes, seven odes for winners of the parsley wreath in the Isthmian games, held in the Isthmus of Corinth once in two years.

Pindar's odes are distinguished by their great boldness of diction, their daring use of simile and metaphor, their poetical inversion of the natural order of words, and their audacious coining of new words. The main portion of each ode consists of a myth more or less closely connected with the victor's city or family; the ode closes by alluding to the victor's good luck or good guidance. The religious element is very prominent, as is the poet's elevated and austere morality, which had as its central idea the theory that acquired excellences were of no importance in comparison with native temperament.

Pindar is a magnificent poet, and serves to link the Homeric epos to the Athenian drama. He is the most Homeric of all the lyric poets known to us, and yet has some of the qualities that go to make a great dramatist. — BIBLIOGRAPHY: (Editions) B. L. Gildersleeve, *Olympian and Pythian Odes*; J. B. Bury, *Nemean and Isthmian Odes*; (Translations) E. Myers, *Extant Odes of Pindar*; C. Mayne, *Olympian Odes*; (Criticism) F. D. Morice, *Pindar* (Ancient Classics for English Readers Series); A. Croiset, *La poésie de Pindare, et les lois du lyrisme grec.*

PIN'DARIS (that is, *freebooters*). A name given to the marauding companies of mounted robbers which remained in force after the fall of the Mogul Empire. They were descended mostly from the caste of Mahommedan warriors, which formerly received high pay from the Indian princes, and they were secretly excited by the Indian tributaries to attack the Company. Between 1804 and 1816 they became not only dangerous to English rule, but were also the terror of the native population. In 1817 Hastings, the British Governor-General, determined on the destruction of these robbers, whose force was estimated at 40,000 horse. Attacked on all sides, they were conquered and dispersed. Garrisons were placed in some fortresses, and the native states of the infested district were formally taken under British protection.

PIND DADAN KHAN. A town in the Jhelum district of the Punjab, India. It stands on the Jhelum River, and is served by the Sind-Sāgah branch of the North-Western Railway. There is a trade in salt. Pop. 11,000.

PINDUS. The ancient name of the principal mountain range of Northern Greece, forming the watershed of the country and the boundary between Thessaly and Epirus. It was, like Helicon and Parnassus, a seat of Apollo and the Muses.

PINE. The popular name of trees of the Coniferous genus Pinus, family Pinaceæ, which is divided into two sections, namely, (1) Abietineæ, the fir tribe; and (2) Cupressineæ, the cypress tribe. The pines belong to the former section, and are distinguished from the spruce, larch, fir, cedar, etc., chiefly by having persistent leaves in clusters of two to five on short shoots borne in the axils of membranous scales. All the European species, except *P. Cembra*, have only two leaves in a sheath; most of the Asiatic and American kinds have three or five leaves. The cones also afford an important ready means of distinction and classification.

The Scots pine or fir (*P. sylvestris*) is a tall, straight, hardy tree, from 60 to 100 feet high; a native of most parts of Europe, flowering in May and June, and having many varieties. The leaves are rigid, in pairs, somewhat waved and twisted; the lower branches are somewhat pendant; the bark is of a reddish tinge, sometimes rough and furrowed. The leaves are distinguishable from those of all other pines in which they occur in pairs by their glaucous hue, especially when young.

The Scots pine almost always occurs in masses; it is considered full grown and fit to be cut down for timber in fifty or sixty years; but in the north of Scotland, where pine forests grew to perfection in former times, the tree continued to increase in bulk for three or four centuries. The tree is most abundant in the north of Europe, between lat. 52° and 65°. There are extensive forests of it in Russia, Poland, Sweden, Norway, Germany, the Alps, the Pyrenees, and the Vosges. In Scotland it grows at the height of 2700 feet on the Grampians.

The Corsican pine (*P. Laricio*) grows to a height of from 80 to 100 feet, and in the Island of Corsica it is said to reach an altitude of 140 to 150 feet. The pinaster, or cluster pine (*P. pinaster*), is indigenous to the south of Europe, to the west of Asia, the Himálaya, and, it seems, even to China. It is a large, handsome, pyramidal tree, varying from 40 to 60 feet in height. Its cones point upwards, in star-like clusters, whence the name pinaster or star pine. In France, especially between Bayonne and Bordeaux, it covers immense tracts of barren sand, in which it has been planted to prevent the sand from drifting.

The stone pine (*P. pinĕa*) is a lofty tree in the south of Europe, where it is a native; its spreading head forms a kind of parasol; the trunk is 50 or 60 feet high, and clear of branches. In Britain the stone pine seldom exceeds the size of a large bush, although specimens have reached a height of 30 and 40 feet. Sabine's pine (*P. Sabiniāna*) was discovered in California in 1826. The leaves are in threes, rarely in fours, from 11 to 14 inches long; the trees are of a tapering form, straight, and from 40 to 120 feet high, with trunks from 3 to 12 feet in diameter. The Arolla pine (*P. Cembra*) is a native of Switzerland and Siberia.

The red Canadian pine (*P. resinōsa*), or yellow pine, inhabits the whole of Canada from the Atlantic to the Pacific, and is also found in the northern and eastern parts of the

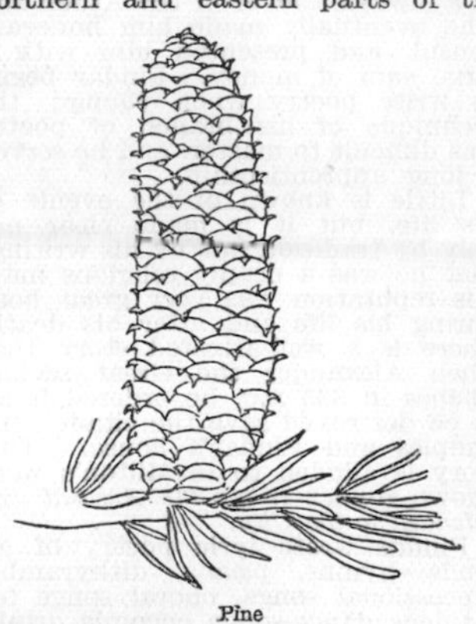

Pine

United States. The trunk rises to the height of 70 or 80 feet, by about 2 feet in diameter at the base, and is chiefly remarkable for its uniform size for two-thirds of its length. The wood is yellowish, compact, fine-grained, resinous, and durable. The true yellow pine (*P. variabĭlis*) rises to the height of 50 or 60 feet, by 15 or 18 inches in diameter at base. The cones are small, oval, and armed with fine spines. The timber is largely used in shipbuilding and for house timber.

The Labrador or Banks's pine (*P. Banksiāna*) is usually a low straggling tree, growing among barren rocks to a height of from 5 to 8 feet, but may attain three times that height. The cones are recurved and twisted; and the leaves are regularly distributed over the branches. In Nova Scotia and the state of Maine it is known as the scrub pine, and in Canada as the grey pine.

The other American pines are the Jersey pine (*P. inops*), the trunk of which is too small to be of any utility in the arts; the pitch pine (*P. rigida*), which is most abundant along the Atlantic coast, and the wood of which, when the tree grows in a dry, gravelly soil, is compact, heavy, and contains a large proportion of resin; the loblolly pine (*P. tæda*), the timber of which decays speedily on being exposed to the air; the long-leaved pine (*P. palustris*), also called yellow pine and pitch pine, which abounds in the lower parts of the Carolinas, Georgia, and Florida, furnishing resin, tar, pitch, and turpentine, and most excellent timber; the Weymouth pine (*P. strobus*), the timber of which, though not without essential defects, is consumed in much greater quantities, and for a far greater variety of purposes, than almost any other; and Lambert's pine (*P. Lambertiana*), which grows between the fortieth and forty-third parallels of latitude, and about 100 miles from the Pacific. It is of gigantic size, the trunk rising from 150 to upwards of 200 feet, and being from 7 to nearly 20 feet in diameter.

PINE'AL BODY. In anatomy, a body, about the size and shape of a cherry-stone, attached to the roof of the brain-stem. It represents the remains of a median eye found in certain reptiles and lowlier vertebrates. It was considered by the ancients to be the seat of the soul.

PINEAPPLE (*Ananas sativus*). A plant belonging to the nat. ord. Bromeliaceæ, much esteemed for its richly flavoured fruit, which somewhat resembles a pine-cone. A native of tropical America, it is now naturalised in many hot countries, is also cultivated in hot-houses, and is imported in quantities into Britain, the United States, etc. The plant yields the fibre of which pina cloth (q.v.) is made. The fibre is used for textile purposes in China, and to some extent in India, and it is believed that in the latter country the fibre might easily come to be of commercial importance.

PINE-CHAFER, or **PINE BEETLE** (*Hylesinus piniperda*). A species of beetle which infests Scots pines. It feeds on the young shoots of these trees and eats its way into the heart, thus converting the shoot into a tube.

PINE-FINCH, or **PINE-GROSBEAK** (*Pyrrhŭla enucleātor*). A perching bird belonging to the finch family (Fringillidæ). It is of larger size than its near relative the common bullfinch, and measures from 8 to 9 inches in length. It occurs in the Arctic and northern regions of both Old and New Worlds. It is more rarely found in the temperate portions of Europe.

PINEL', Philippe. French physician, born in 1745 at St. André, died in Paris, 1826. He studied at Toulouse and Montpellier, and in 1791 came into notice by his treatise *Sur l'aliénation mentale*. In the following year he was made directing physician at the Bicêtre, and in 1794 at Salpêtrière. By his writings and by his management of these two asylums, in which he introduced the humane treatment of the insane, Pinel laid the foundations of the great reform that has been effected in treating mental diseases.

PINERO, Sir Arthur Wing. English dramatist. Born in 1855. His father was a Jewish solicitor of Portuguese extraction. He was educated at private schools, and became an actor in 1874, remaining on the stage until 1881. He commenced his career as a dramatist by writing *£200 a Year* (1877). His earlier plays were for the most part farces, *The Magistrate* (1885), *The Schoolmistress*, and *Dandy Dick*. These farces, while sufficiently amusing, were nevertheless a trifle out of date even when they first appeared; like Falstaff, they were born with a white head.

The Magistrate had a second avatar as *The Boy*. Pinero's early serious plays were *The Squire* (1881) and *The Profligate* (1889). The former owed its popularity in part to its rural setting, and the latter secured a masterly third act by means of sacrificing probability and abusing coincidence. *Sweet Lavender*, a sentimental comedy, was extremely successful, and has been frequently revived.

The Second Mrs. Tanqueray (1893) is Pinero's masterpiece, and brought him into the front rank of living dramatists. It was written under the influence of Ibsen, but is a powerful and highly original piece of work. Some of its popularity was due to Mrs. Patrick Campbell, but the main part was due to its intrinsic merits.

Among Pinero's later plays are *The Notorious Mrs. Ebbsmith* (1895), *The Gay Lord Quex* (1899), *His House in Order* (1906), *The Mind the Paint Girl* (1912), *A Seat in the Park* (1922), and *The Enchanted Cottage* (1922). Pinero was knighted in 1909. He is a master of dramatic situation, and has a good practical knowledge of the needs and limitations of the stage.

PINERO'LO (Fr. *Pignerol*). An ancient city of Italy, province of Turin, at the mouth of the Val Clusone. The manufactures are chiefly cotton, woollen, and silk goods. It belonged to Savoy from 1042, but the French held it for a series of years on several occasions; and its citadel was the prison of Fouquet and of the Man in the Iron Mask. Pop. 18,200.

PINES, ISLE OF. *See* NEW CALEDONIA.

PINE WOOL. The short, fine fibres of the leaf needles of the pine tree. The preparation of this material is chiefly carried on in Germany and Sweden. It is used for making wadding, a coarse kind of blanket, stuffing cushions, mattresses, etc., and mixed with other fibres of a longer staple.

PINEY TALLOW, called also **MALABAR TALLOW.** A fatty substance resembling wax, obtained by boiling with water the fruit of the *Vateria Indica,* a tree common on the Malabar coast. It forms excellent candles.

PINEY VARNISH. A resin used as a varnish, obtained from two trees of Southern India and Ceylon, *Vateria indica* and *V. acuminata.* It is known also as piney resin, white dammer, and Indian copal, and is got by making incisions in the bark of the tree or into its substance. It is soluble in turpentine and drying oils.

PING-PONG, or **TABLE-TENNIS.** The game, generally considered, consists in knocking a little celluloid ball over a low net by means of a small racket.

Play.—Twenty points up is the usual game, one point being lost by the striker for each fault, or for volleying, hitting a ball so that it does not bounce on the table on the opposite side of the net, or failure to knock a ball in play over the net after the first but before the second bounce. No player may serve more than five times successively, and the service changes with each five points scored. Not infrequently ends are changed when 5, 15, 25, and 35 points are called.

Apparatus.—The regulation size for a ping-pong table is 9 by 5 feet; the net, 6¾ inches in height, but lowered by ⅛ inch for each foot of shortage in the length of the table. The height of the table should be 2 feet 6 inches. Rackets may be of any type or of any material, but generally they should not exceed 7 by 6 inches in playing surface.

PINGUIC'ULA. A genus of plants of the nat. ord. Lentibulariaceæ, with rosettes of fleshy radical leaves, and solitary purple, violet, or yellow flowers. *See* BUTTERWORT.

PINION. A toothed wheel of small diameter, used in association with a larger gear-wheel or with a rack. Pinions are frequently simple rings of cast iron or steel, with the teeth cut on the outer edge, and with an internal diameter suitable to the shaft. In some cases the pinion and shaft are solid, cut from the same billet. Pinions with helical teeth are used in marine propulsion. *See* GEARING.

Noiseless pinions built up of layers of paper, cloth, raw hide, and vulcanised fibre have been introduced for machine drives from high-speed electric motors. The comparative lack of strength of such wheels is compensated for by the use of greater widths of wheels and tooth dimensions than those suitable for iron or steel pinions.

PINK (Dianthus). A genus of plants belonging to the nat. ord. Caryophyllaceæ. More than 200 species are known, many of which are natives of the northern and temperate parts of the European continent. Their roots are annual or perennial; the stems herbaceous and jointed; the leaves opposite and entire; and the flowers terminal, aggregate, or solitary, and always beautiful. The clove pink or carnation, and the garden pink, of which there are many varieties, are familiar species.

PINKERTON, John. A Scottish savant, born at Edinburgh in 1758, died in 1826. He was trained for the law, but in 1780 went to London to devote himself to literature, and by his *Letters on Literature* obtained the acquaintance of Horace Walpole. His more valuable publications are: *Ancient Scottish Poems,* from the Manuscript Collection of Sir Richard Maitland of Lethington, with *Notes and a Glossary* (1786); *Inquiry into the History of Scotland preceding the Reign of Malcolm III.* (1790); *The Medallic History of England till the Revolution* (1790); *History of Scotland from the Accession of the House of Stuart to that of Mary* (1797); *Iconographia scotica* (1797); a *General Collection of Voyages and Travels* in 17 large volumes (1807-14); *Petralogy* (1811); *A Modern Atlas* (1819).

PINK' EYE. Contagious and infectious disease of horses (equine influenza). The membranes of the eye become red and swollen, so that the eye takes on a deep red tinge. The name is also applied to an infective conjunctivitis in human beings.

PINKIE', BATTLE OF. Fought 10th Sept., 1547, near Musselburgh, between an English army of 16,000, led by the Protector, Somerset, and the Scots, 23,000 strong. The purpose of the invasion was the enforcement of a treaty of marriage between Edward VI. and Mary, Queen of Scots. The Scots were completely defeated.

PINNA. A genus of bivalve molluscs included in the family of wing-shells (Aviculidæ). The genus is represented by the *Pinna pectināta* of the British coasts, by the *P. nobilis* of the Mediterranean Sea, by the *P. bullāta, P. rudis, P. nigrīna,* and by other species. Some species attain large dimensions, being as much as

2 feet long. The "byssus," by which they adhere to rocks, is remarkably long, and of strong silky texture, and is capable of being woven into cloth upon which a very high value is set. This manufacture was known to the ancients, and is still practised in Italy to some extent.

PINNACE. One of the boats of a man-of-war, used to carry the officers to and from the shore. It is usually rowed with eight oars, or is fitted for steam or petrol propulsion. A pinnace is also a small vessel used at sea, having sails and oars, and two or three masts schooner-rigged.

PINNACLE. In architecture, any lesser structure that rises above the roof of a building, or that capes and terminates the higher parts of angles or of buttresses. The application of the term is now generally limited to an ornamental pointed mass rising

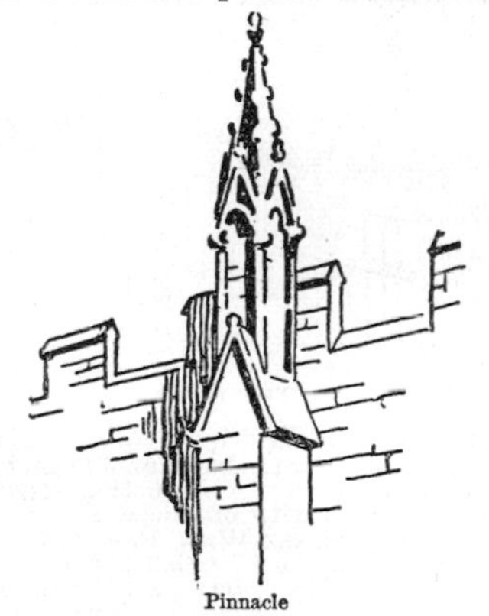

Pinnacle

from angles, buttresses, or parapets, and usually adorned with rich and varied devices. They are usually square in plan, but are sometimes octagonal, and in a few instances hexagonal and pentagonal. The tops are generally crocketed, and have finials on the points.

PINNATE. In botany, formed like a feather. A pinnate leaf is a species of compound leaf wherein a single petiole has several leaflets or pinnæ attached to each side of it.

PIN'NER. District of Middlesex, 2¾ miles from Harrow-on-the-Hill and 12½ miles N.W. of London, on the Pin (Metro., L.M.S. and L.N.E. Rlys.). The flint stone church of St. John the Baptist dates from the fourteenth century, and contains a mural monument to H. J. Pye, the poet laureate.

PINNIPEDIA. A section of the carnivorous order of mammals, in which the fore- and hind-limbs are short, and are expanded into broad webbed swimming paddles. The section comprises the sea-lions, seals, and walruses.

PINSK. A town of Poland, in the province of Polesie, on the Pina; served by the Brest-Bryansk railway. In 1132 it was in the government of Minsk. It stands among marshes, and is built of wood. During the European War Pinsk was occupied by the Germans under Mackensen (Sept., 1915). In 1920, during the Russo-Polish campaign, it was occupied by the Poles, but was subsequently retaken by the Bolshevist troops. Pop. 40,000.

PINT. *See* WEIGHTS AND MEASURES.

PINTAIL DUCK, or **SEA PHEASANT.** A genus of ducks, so named from the elongated form of the tail-feathers. In size the common pintail duck (*Dafīla acūta*) is equal to the mallard. These birds are found on

Pintail Duck

the British coasts in summer, but migrate southwards in winter. They are common in the Mississippi Valley, and they occur on the Mediterranean coasts, in the Gulf of Mexico, in the West Indian Islands, and in Africa. They breed in confinement, and the flesh is savoury.

PINTURICCHIO (pin-tų-rik'yō); "the little painter"). Italian painter of the Umbrian school, whose real name was *Bernardino di Betti*, was born at Perugia in 1454, and died at Siena in 1513. He lived for a time at Rome, and while there was engaged on the frescoes of the Sistine Chapel, being at this time under the influence of Perugino. His chief work was a series of mural paintings illustrating the life of Pope Pius II. (Æneas Silvius), in the cathedral library at Siena. There are also fine frescoes by him in the Buffalini Chapel of the church St. Maria in Araceli, Rome.

PINWELL, George John. British artist. Born in London in 1842, and died in 1875. In 1863 he began drawing on wood for the brothers Dalziel and others, and illustrated several works, including *The Vicar of Wakefield*. He was also employed on several periodicals. He began water-colour painting, in which he was very successful, in 1865, his pictures including two subjects from Browning's *Pied Piper of Hamelin* (1869), *The Elixir of Love* (1870), *Away from Town* (1871), *Gilbert à Becket's Troth* (1872), *The Great Lady* (1873), and *We fell out, my Wife and I* (1875). He was elected an Associate of the Society of Painters in Water-colours in 1869, and full member in 1870.

PINX'TON. Market town of Derbyshire, 6 miles from Mansfield, by L.M.S. and L.N.E. Railways. Extensive coal mines are near, and lace is made. Pop. 5348.

PINZON'. A family of Spanish navigators, natives of Palos, who were associated with Columbus in the discovery of America.—Martin Alfonso, the eldest, was of great assistance to Columbus in fitting out his fleet, and in the voyage commanded the *Pinta*.—Vicente Yañez, his brother, commanded the *Niña* in the first voyage of Columbus.—Francisco Martin, the third brother, was pilot of the *Pinta* in the first voyage of Columbus. From him descended the noble Spanish family of Pinzon.

PIOMBI'NO. Formerly an independent principality of Italy, now part of the province of Pisa. From 1233 to 1399 it belonged to Pisa, and was afterwards ruled by independent princes until 1801, when it was incorporated with France. A principality under Elise Bacciochi, a sister of Napoleon, from 1805 to 1814, it was united with the Duchy of Tuscany in 1815.

PIOMBINO. A town of Italy, province of Pisa, on the sea-coast opposite the Island of Elba. It has old fortifications, a good harbour, and manufactures of Bessemer steel and military projectiles. Pop. 8000.

PIOMBO, Sebastiano Luciani del. Italian painter, born at Venice in 1485, died in 1547. He studied under Giovanni Bellini and Giorgione, whose fine colouring he imitated. Coming to Rome about 1512, he was induced by Michelangelo to enter into rivalry with Raphael. When Raphael painted his celebrated *Transfiguration*, Sebastiano attempted to surpass it by painting *The Raising of Lazarus*, which is considered his greatest work, and is now in the National Gallery, London. Other important works are *The Scourging of Our Lord* and *A Holy Family*. His chief merit, however, lay in single figures and portraits, such as his *Clement VII*.

PIONEERS AND PIONEER BATTALIONS. Pioneers are military artificers, and pioneer battalions are units which are trained for the purpose of performing the ordinary duties of infantry, and, at the same time, the more elementary of those which would normally come into the province of the Royal Engineers. In a battalion of infantry the pioneer-sergeant and his assistants include men trained in the trades of carpenter, blacksmith, and so on, and in the exercise of these trades they are very useful members of the battalion.

In former days pioneers, in order to distinguish them from the other rank and file of the unit, were permitted to wear beards, and on a march moved at the head of the battalion, carrying the tools of their trade, to enable them to clear away any obstructions that might be met with on the road.

Pioneer

In the European War. Pioneer battalions are in the British service of very modern date, having only come into existence during the European War. Then, among the New Army units raised in districts where the available personnel consisted largely of miners, a considerable number of pioneer battalions were formed, with the idea of using them on service in such a way that their peculiar technical knowledge should be used to the best advantage. These were the pioneer battalions which gave such a good account of themselves in the war, either as fighters or as miners. Now that the New Army and its service battalions have ceased to exist, there are no longer any pioneer battalions in the British service.

In India. Though, as we have seen, pioneer battalions do not form parts of the regular British Army, yet in India they have existed as units of the infantry of the Indian army for many years. In that army some ten or twelve infantry regiments are known as pioneers, and the name has a definite significance, for these regiments are trained in peace-time and made available in war-time for the execution of many kinds of military works, such as road- and railway-making, or for purely infantry work as required. Their work can, in fact, be considered complementary to that of the Indian sappers and miners officered by Royal Engineer officers. British officers of Indian pioneers are, on the contrary, infantry officers who undergo a special course of instruction in pioneer work.

PIOTRKÓW. A town of Poland, capital of the district of the same name. It is on the River Strada, and is served by the Warsaw-Vienna Railway. It was at one time the seat of the Polish Diet, and the kings were elected there. Pop. (1931), 51,281.—The district has an area of 4729 sq. miles. It is one of the industrial areas of Poland, Lodz, an important textile centre, being the largest town. Pop. 2,000,000. *See* POLAND.

PIOZZI, Hester Lynch Salusbury. British authoress, the daughter of John Salusbury of Bodvel, Carnarvonshire, born in 1741, died at Clifton 1821. In 1763 she was married to Henry Thrale, a wealthy brewer of Southwark, London, which borough he then represented in Parliament. Soon after her marriage she gathered round her a brilliant circle, including above all Dr. Johnson, who lived with the Thrales several days in each week for sixteen years.

Mr. Thrale dying in 1781, his widow, who was the mother of four daughters, married in 1784 Piozzi, a Florentine music-master, then resident in Bath. This alliance was keenly resented by all her friends, and Johnson entirely gave up her society. She wrote a few poems and an autobiography, but she is chiefly known by her *Anecdotes of the late Samuel Johnson, during the last Twenty Years of his Life* (1786), and *Letters to and from the late Samuel Johnson, LL.D.* (1788).

PIPA. A genus of toads, of which the best-known species is the *Pipa americana* of Surinam and Brazil, popularly designated the Surinam toad. The tongue and teeth are wanting in this family. The pipa is one of the most repulsive looking of the toads, and is noted as exemplifying, in the case of the female animals, an anomalous mode of developing the eggs and young. A number of pits or depressions termed " dorsal cells " appear to be formed on the back of the female pipas at the breeding season. In each cell an egg is deposited, the eggs being first deposited by the female in water after the usual method, and being impregnated by the male, who then collects the eggs and places them in the female's back. Each cell appears to be closed by a lid-like fold, and within the cells the eggs are hatched and the young pass their tadpole state.

Pipa Toad

PIPE. A tube, usually circular in cross-section, which is used for the distribution of such fluids as water, steam, coal-gas, and compressed air.

The material of which the pipe is made is determined after consideration of the properties of the substance to be conveyed and its condition of pressure and temperature. Cast-iron steam-pipes are still used for low pressures, but they are heavy, liable to fracture if struck, and very rigid at bends. Cast iron is never used for pipes which are to convey superheated steam, because of the peculiar breakdown of structure which takes place in cast iron when it is subjected to high temperatures. Important steam-pipes are usually made of mild steel, solid drawn or welded, and with the flanges screwed on or welded.

Steam-pipes. Steam-pipes are subjected to considerable temperature changes, and they expand and contract by amounts which must be allowed for in designing a pipe range. To permit this expansion to take place, expansion joints or bends are introduced into the system. The joints are made with pieces of copper pipe provided with flanges, or with pipes one of which is inside the other and thus free to expand. Bends, if of large radius, may introduce sufficient flexibility into a pipe range to permit all the possible expansion to take place.

Steam-pipes are supported on rollers to permit the pipes to expand towards the bends and expansion joints. At all joints in a steam-pipe system rings of packing material are used to ensure steam tightness. If expansion can take place freely, these joints will remain intact. Steam leaks at the joints will be early seen in a system where the expansion has not been completely allowed for. Steam-pipes are subject to water-hammer, due to the acceleration of water which remains in pockets or low parts of the pipe range, and is set in motion by the condensation of entrapped steam.

Gas-pipes, etc. Wrought-iron welded tubes have come into very extensive use for the distribution of gas. Solid-drawn weldless tubes are used for boiler-tubes, hydraulic pipes, and such purposes as shafting and boring-rods. Cast-iron pipes used for water-mains are usually cast vertically to ensure soundness of the metal throughout its structure. Remelted cast iron is used for hydraulic power-mains, the pipes of which are tested under considerable pressures before being put into actual use. If the pressure in use is 700 to 900 lb. per square inch, a test pressure of 2500 lb. per square inch is used, and this value is increased for higher service pressures.

PIPE CLAY. Fine white plastic clay containing a higher percentage of silica than kaolin or china clay, and used for making pipes, tiles, and as cleaning material for leather.

PIPE LINE. Continuous line of pipes for carrying water from a reservoir, or for the transport of petroleum, from the oil well to the refinery or port. Oil can thus be brought over great distances, as in the United States where there are over 90,000 miles of underground pipes of 4 to 12 inch in diameter, also in Persia where oil is carried for 150 miles across deserts and over mountains.

PIPE, TOBACCO. A bowl and connecting tube, made of baked clay, wood, stone, or other material, and used in smoking tobacco. The cheap clay pipes, which were once in universal use in Great Britain and are still much used, are made of a fine-grained white, plastic clay, found chiefly in the Isle of Purbeck in Dorsetshire, and at Newton Abbot in Devonshire. The chief processes in the manufacture of clay pipes are moulding and baking.

Finer and more expensive pipes are made of meerschaum, a somewhat plastic magnesian stone of a soft, greasy feel. Sometimes the bowl alone (which is frequently artistically carved) is of meerschaum, the stem being of wood, the best sorts of which are got from the young stems of the Mahaleb cherry, grown near Vienna, the mock orange of Hungary, and the jessamine sticks of Turkey. The stem, whether of the same material as the bowl or of wood, is usually provided with a mouthpiece of ivory, silver, or amber, the last being preferred. Briar-root pipes, with the bowl and stem of one piece of wood, and provided with amber, ivory, or bone mouthpieces, are made of the roots of a large variety of heath (Fr. *bruyère*).

The Persian *hookah* is a pipe of great size, the bowl of which is set upon an airtight vessel partially filled with water, and has a small tube which passes down into the water; the long flexible smoking-tube is inserted in the side of the vessel, and the smoke is made to pass through the water, being thus cooled and deprived of some noxious properties.

Upon the American continent pipes have been in use from a very remote period. Indian pipes, with elaborately carved soapstone bowls and ornamented wooden stems, or entirely of baked clay, have been found in the ancient mounds of the West, together with other relics of an unknown race. *See* CALUMET.

PIPE-FISHES (Syngnathus). Fishes nearly allied to the curious little forms popularly known as "sea-horses" (*see* HIPPOCAMPUS), and included with them in the same family (Syngnathidæ). They are distinguished by a

Pipe-fish

long and tapering body, and by jaws united to form a tube or pipe, bearing the mouth at the tip. The *Syngnathus acus* is the most familiar British species. It averages 20 inches in length. The largest of the British species is said to attain a length of 3 feet.

A very remarkable circumstance in connection with the pipe-fishes consists in the males of some species possessing a pouch-like fold, situated at the base of the tail, in which the eggs are contained after being extruded from the body of the females, and in which the young, after hatching, continue to reside for a time.

The name pipe-fish is also applied to the members of the genus Fistularia, belonging to a different family (Fistulariidæ), and also known as flute-mouths. The bones of the face are prolonged to form a tubular structure, at the extremity of which the mouth opens. The *Fistularia tabaccaria* of the Antilles, averaging about 3 feet in length, represents this genus.

PIPERA'CEÆ. The peppers, a natural order of shrubby or herbaceous apetalous dicotyledons, inhabiting the hottest parts of the globe, particularly India and South America. The general properties of the order are aromatic, pungent, and stimulant. The dried unripe fruits of *Piper nigrum* constitute black pepper (*see* PEPPER). The fruit of *Piper* (*Cubeba*) *officinālis*, a climbing plant of Java and other Indian islands, is the Cubeb pepper (*see* CUBEBS). The leaves and unripe fruit of *P. angustifolium* constitute the aromatic, fragrant, and astringent substance called *matico* or *matica*, which has been recommended for checking hæmorrhage.

The leaves of *P. Betle* (*Chavica Betle*) are chewed in the East as a means of intoxication (*see Betel*). The root of *Macropiper methysticum* is the *kava* of the South Sea Islanders, and is used in the preparation of a stimulating beverage.

PIPE ROLL. A term applied to the Annual or Great Rolls of the English Exchequer, preserved in the Record Office, London. They are so called on account of their being rolled into the shape of pipes, or because they were sent to the Crown Office in cylinders. The Rolls relate to all matters connected with the revenues of the Crown, and extend from the reign of Henry II. (1156) to 1833. In 1883 a society (The Pipe Roll Society) was formed with the intention of publishing all the Pipe Rolls.

PIPING-CROW. A bird of New South Wales, remarkable for its power of mimicking the voices of other birds.

Piping Crow

It is the *Gymnorhina tibicen* and related species. It belongs to the shrike family.

PIPISTRELLE (*Vesperugo pipistrellus*). The familiar little bat which occurs throughout Britain, and flits about during twilight. It is of small size, and possesses a mouse-like body covered with hair, from which resemblance its popular name of Flittermouse has been derived. It passes the winter, like most other bats, in a state of torpidity; but appears to hibernate for a shorter period than other and larger species.

PIPIT, or **TITLARK** (Anthus). A genus of perching birds possessing striking affinities with the larks, which they resemble in the large size of the hinder claw, but commonly classed with the wagtails (Motacillidæ), which they closely resemble in their habit of running swiftly on the ground. The meadow pipit or titlark (*Anthus pratensis*) is the commonest British species. The shore pipit or rock lark (*A. obscurus*) frequents the sea-beach, and feeds on molluscs and crustacea. The tree pipit (*A. trivialis*) is a summer visitant only in the British Isles. All the pipits build their nests on the ground. The song in all consists of a clear simple note, that of the tree pipit being imitated by the words *pit-pit*.

PIPPIN. The name given to a certain class of dessert apples, probably because the trees were raised from the pips or seeds, and bore the apples which gave them celebrity without grafting. They seem to have been introduced into Great Britain from France, and were little known there until about the end of the sixteenth century. The Ribston, Golden, Cox's Orange, and Newton Pippin are favourite varieties.

PIPRA. A genus of perching birds which inhabit South America. *See* MANAKIN.

PIPSISSEWA. Also known as *chimaphila* and *prince's pine*, a North American evergreen plant (*Chimaphila umbellata*) of the heath order (Ericaceæ). From its leaves are made a powder and a fluid extract, used in America in kidney complaints, scrofula, rheumatism, etc.

PIQUA. A city of Ohio, United States, in Miami county, on the Miami River; served by the Cincinnati, Hamilton, & Dayton, and the Pittsburgh, Cincinnati, Chicago, & St. Louis Railways, and by the Miami & Erie Canal. There are some manufactures. Piqua, originally a settlement of a division of the Shawnee Indians, was founded in 1809 as Washington, the present name being adopted in 1823, and the town became a city in 1846. Pop. 16,009.

PIQUET'. A game at cards played between two persons with thirty-two cards, all the plain cards below seven being thrown aside. In playing, the cards rank in order as follows: the ace (which counts eleven), the king, queen, and knave (each of which counts ten), and the plain cards (each of which counts according to the number of its pips). The player who first reaches 100 has the game.

The score is made up by reckoning in the following manner: carte blanche, the point, the sequence, the quatorze, the cards, and the capot. Carte blanche is a hand of twelve plain cards, and counts ten for the player who holds it. The point is the suit of highest value, the value being determined by the number it makes up when the cards held are added together. The sequence is composed of a regular succession of cards in one suit. The quatorze is composed of four aces, four kings, four queens, four knaves, or four tens, and counts fourteen.

The winner of the greatest number of tricks counts ten in addition (the "cards"); if he holds all the tricks, he counts forty in addition (the "capot"). If a player scores twenty-nine in hand and one for the card he leads, before his opponent counts anything, he at once adds thirty to his score; this is called "pique." Should a player score thirty by the cards in his hand, by scores that reckon in order before his adversary can count, he obtains the "repique," which enables him to add sixty to his score. The scores are recorded according to the following table of precedence: (1) carte blanche, (2) point, (3) sequences, (4) quatorzes and trios, (5) points made in play, and (6) the cards. If one player scores a hundred before the other obtains fifty, he wins a double.

PI'RACY. The crime of robbery and depredation committed upon the high seas. It is an offence against the universal law of society, a pirate being, according to Sir Edward Coke, *hostis humani generis*. In England the offence was formerly cognisable only by the Admiralty courts, which proceeded without a jury, in a method founded upon the civil law; but now any justices of assize, or oyer and terminer, or jail delivery, may try persons accused of piracy.

Piracy, in the common sense of the word, is distinguished from privateering by the fact that the pirate sails without any commission, and under no national flag, and attacks the subjects of all nations alike; the privateer acts under a commission from a belligerent power, which authorises him to attack, plunder, and destroy the vessels which he may encounter belonging to the hostile state.

PIRÆ'US (Gr. *Peiraieus*). One of the chief seaports of ancient Greece. It was situated about 5 miles from Athens, with which it was connected by rail and by the two "Long Walls," and the whole Peninsula of Peiraieus was surrounded by a wall 60 stadia in circumference, about 60 feet (40 cubits) in height, and probably 14 or 15 feet thick. The Peiraieus was fortified by the architect Hippodamus of Miletus to the order of Themistocles, and the town proper was laid out for Pericles by the same architect.

The modern Piræus has three harbours: two on the east side, anciently named Zea (now Stratiotiki) and Munychia (now Phanari), and one (the largest) on the west side, called simply Piræus, or the Harbour. When Greece was liberated from Turkish rule, the Piræus was merely a scene of ruins. Pop. 251,330. *See* ATHENS (latter portion of article).

PIRANHA, or CARIBA (Serrasalmo). A voracious freshwater fish of tropical America. It is 3 or 4 feet in length, and its jaws are armed with sharp lancet-shaped teeth, from which cattle when fording rivers sometimes suffer terribly.

PIRATES. Pirates have existed as such from the earliest times, and although the act of piracy is now universally regarded as a ghastly crime against all mankind, yet there have been many occasions upon which the depredations of a pirate have not only been helpful to his nation as a body, but have also been officially encouraged and more or less legalised. Naval warfare is a vastly different proposition to warfare by land, and naval tactics, as exemplified in the "head," "prize," "blood-money," and prize courts of the twentieth century, may be summed up as involving the seizure of as much enemy property as possible, and the subsequent distribution of the booty by a gradation according to rank.

Privateers and Pirates. This was the policy of the ancient Greeks, of the Romans and Carthaginians, of the Vikings, of the Moors after the disruption of the Caliphate of Cordoba, of the privateers fitted out privately during the reign of "good Queen Bess," and furnished with letters of marque authorising them to prey upon the shipping of that most obnoxious enemy of England, Philip of Spain; and within the last few years the same policy directed German activity at sea when she turned loose upon the international maritime highways such ships as the *Moewe* and *Emden* and her commerce-destroying submarines.

Commerce-destroyers, however, are not technically considered as "pirates," although Lord Nelson once ventured the opinion that they were "little better." Piracy, then, until within comparatively recent times, was synonymous with and was the direct accompaniment of naval warfare, in which every stranger was a prospective enemy, and every enemy meant more plunder. This was ultimately reflected more in the spending and drinking capacity of the individual seaman than in the pride and glory of conquest, and honour and prestige in the profession of arms.

The Tuatha de Danaan. In remote ages pirates were of a quite different type to their more modern descendants, for not only did they raid and plunder by land—a proceeding which may be accounted for by the smallness of the ships of the time, their small carrying capacity offering little or no booty—but they also infested whole countries, suppressed nationalities, and even established permanent colonies. An instance of this is afforded by one of the primitive peoples of Ireland—the *Tuatha de Danaan*, who came probably from Mediterranean lands and settled in that country. In the preface to M'Firbis's *Book of Genealogies* we read:

> ". . . Every one who is fair-haired, vengeful, large, and every plunderer . . . who are adepts in all Druidical and magical arts,—they are the descendants of the Tuatha de Danaan in Erin."

The Tuatha de Danaan, then, were a tall, fair race, with a propensity alike for magic and piracy.

The Norse Pirates. When Haco of Norway sailed to the invasion of Scotland (Alexander III.) in 1263, he had with him one Roderic, a pirate chief, who claimed Bute as his inheritance, but who had been opposed by the islanders and outlawed by Alexander. Haco was little better than a pirate himself, and while his fleet of 160 galleys was anchored in Kilbrannan Sound, between the mainland of Scotland and the Island of Arran, he dispatched 60 ships up Loch Long under the command of Magnus, King of Man (modern Isle of Man), four Hebridean chiefs, and two Norse captains.

This fleet ravaged and pillaged to the head of the loch, and drew its galleys across the narrow isthmus of Arrochar-Tarbet which separates Loch Long from Loch Lomond. The Scots of Lennox and Loch Lomondside in general had found a safehold in the islands of the inland loch, little anticipating the stratagem which the inherent boldness of the Norsemen and the lightness of their craft enabled them to conceive, and they were all put to the sword and their houses and goods burnt and plundered by the conquerors, who even penetrated to the wealthy inland town of Stirling, looting and burning the adjacent countryside on their way.

On their return they dragged their boats back from Tarbet to Arrochar and set sail; but a terrific storm arose, and ten galleys were completely wrecked. The remaining vessels did not rejoin Haco in the Firth of Clyde until three days after the Scottish victory at Largs.

Drake and Hawkins. Piracy at this time was obviously an organised division of legitimate warfare. The post-Elizabethan buccaneer, engaged in offensive operations for his own benefit, was non-existent, and cannot be said to have become common among Englishmen until the time of Hawkins and Francis Drake.

The early career of Francis Drake provides an index to the misfortunes and bitterness that accompanied the transition period from honest seamanship to piracy, its more glamorous counterpart. Drake was early apprenticed to the sea, and eventually became owner-master of his own vessel. He invested his savings in a trading expedition to San Juan de Ulloa, but was treacherously attacked by a Spanish admiral, his companions being murdered and his ships burnt and pillaged, and Drake returned to England, ruined and dispirited, nursing in his heart an unquenchable thirst for vengeance against Spain, and considering from that time that all Spanish merchantmen were a fair prey.

For four years he worked to re-establish himself, and eventually, keeping his own counsel, he commissioned at Plymouth a sloop (the *Dragon*) and two small pinnaces, in which he set sail in the autumn of 1572. At this time Spanish gold was brought across Panamá by pack-mule train from the Peruvian mines, and was reshipped at the mouth of the Chagres River. Drake was always silent regarding his exploit at Panamá, and the customary wild rumours advertised his success in glowing terms, making many others wish to share in his exploits and, incidentally, to get rich quickly and easily.

Briefly, Drake surprised the mule-train and possessed himself of an enormous plunder in precious metals and stones. He sailed down the Atlantic coast of South America into the Pacific, capturing and plundering everything Spanish by sea, and within a reasonable distance by land, rounded the Cape of Good Hope, touched at Sierra Leone, and swept triumphantly into Plymouth Harbour, having circumnavigated the globe.

Drake and his kinsman Hawkins were undoubtedly corsairs of the same stuff as Odysseus or the Vikings, but their patriotic efforts to support their queen and their nation have raised them to a place in history which, although they may be sneered at privately as pirates, is publicly sanctioned by their feats as empire-builders.

Bartholomew Roberts. The pirate of the romantic novel has never existed outside the imagination of the novelist, but in Bartholomew Roberts some critics have identified the Cleveland of Sir Walter Scott's *Pirate*. While this may be so, it is an undoubted fact that the names of Cleveland's associates are identical with those of Roberts's henchmen. Bartholomew Roberts was a native of Pembrokeshire, where he was born in 1682. He was mate of a vessel captured and plundered by Howel Davis at Anamaboe, in the Guineas, and was retained by that worthy, who was killed six weeks later in a fray at Prince's Island, Roberts becoming captain in his place. Roberts was the last of the great pirates, and was said to be comparatively a humane person.

The following are extracts from Pyle's version of the articles drawn up by Bartholomew Roberts and subscribed to on oath by his satellites:

1. Every man has a vote in affairs of moment, and is entitled to equal provision in the matter of provisions and strong liquors. . . .

2. Every man to be called fairly in turn by list on board of prizes . . . and to be allowed a shift of clothes . . . over and above his proper share. Marooning the punishment for defrauding the ship's company in any way or for deserting ship or quarters in battle. Desertion might also be punishable with death.

3. No dicing or gaming with cards for money.

4. All lights to be doused by eight in the evening, and drinking after that hour to be on the open deck. (Roberts was only a moderate drinker, and is supposed to have framed this article in an ineffectual attempt to suppress orgies of drinking.)

5. Piece, pistols, and cutlass to be kept clean and fit. (Pistols were slung by a cord over the shoulders, and arms generally were scrupulously cleaned and delighted in.)

6. No boy or woman allowed on board. (To carry one of the opposite sex to sea in disguise was punishable with death.)

7. Differences of opinion to be discussed with arms and ashore, not on board ship.

8. £1000 per man to have been shared before a disruption is proposed. Men losing limbs to receive 800 dollars from the "pool," lesser wounds being remunerated in proportion. (The captain and quartermaster each received two shares in a prize, the master, boatswain, and gunner receiving one share and a half respectively. Other officers were paid one share and a quarter.)

Pirate Coasts. It remains to be noted that archipelagos and deeply indented coast-lines are peculiarly suitable as lurking-places for pirates. This accounts for regular gangs frequenting definite zones, their marauding expeditions outside of their specific "preserves" partaking of the same nature as naval raids on definite objectives, too frequently dictated and carried on under the pressure of a dire necessity. Such places as the Norwegian fiords, the Ægean Archipelago, the Indian Ocean, the West Indies, Nancowry, and the Cicilian and Dalmatian coasts were therefore eminently suitable, and were much used by pirate gangs.

Modern navies, the paid servants of the states to which they belong, have now an iron-handed control of the recognised international maritime highways, and their abolition or partial disablement as a preventive force would herald the return of the pirate, just as the disbandment of police forces or gendarmerie by land would expose all honest people to the rapacity of marauding freebooters and would even threaten the perversion of the law-abiding citizen. *See* DRAKE; HAWKINS; KIDD; NANCOWRY; PRIVATEER; ROBERTS, BARTHOLOMEW; ROGERS; VIKINGS.—BIBLIOGRAPHY: Howard Pyle (editor), *The Buccaneers and Marooners of America*; J. A. Froude, *English Seamen in the Sixteenth Century*.

PIRNA. A town of Saxony, on the Elbe. It originated in a Slavonic settlement which became united with Meissen, and passed to Saxony about 1405. Dominating the town is the Sonnenstein, erected by Augustus I., Elector of Saxony, and once the most important fortress on the Elbe. Glass and pottery are manufactured in the town. Pop. (1925), 31,215.

PIRON (pē-rōṇ), **Alexis.** French wit, poet, and dramatist, born at Dijon in 1689, died in 1773. He studied law at Besançon; but having gone to Paris, he wrote for the Theatre of the Opéra-Comique, and his first piece, *Arléquin Deucalion*, was composed in two days. In 1738 he produced his *chef-d'œuvre*, *Métromanie*, a comedy excelling in plot, style, humour, and vivacity almost every other composition of the kind. His attempts to gain admission to the Académie Française failed. Piron revenged himself by calling the Academy *Les invalides du bel esprit*, and by composing the humorous epitaph:

> Ci-gît Piron, qui ne fut rien,
> Pas même Académicien.

PIROT. A town of Serbia, Yugoslavia, on the Nishava; served by the Nish-Sofia-Istanbul trunk line. It is the capital of the department of Pirot. Carpets and cloth are manufactured. Pirot was occupied and held by Bulgar troops during the Serbo-Bulgarian War of 1885, and was again taken by the Bulgarian armies on 26th Oct., 1915. A Serbo-French detachment re-entered the town on 14th Oct. 1918. Pop. 11,000.—The department has an area of 900 sq. miles, and a pop. of about 114,000.

PISA. A maritime province of Tuscany, North Italy, on the Ligurian Sea, drained in the north by the Arno. Marble, copper, and coal are among the minerals produced. Oil, wine, and cereals are also produced, and cottons, soap, and glass are among the manufactures. Area, 943 sq. miles; pop. (1931), 335,187.

PISA (ancient **Pisæ**). A city of Tuscany, North Italy, capital of the province of Pisa, on the Arno, 6 miles from the Ligurian Sea, connected by rail with Florence, etc. Pisa is of immense historical interest in view of her former hegemony in art and letters, and it was the foundation of the cathedral of Pisa that ushered in the splendour and glory of Italian mediæval art. This cathedral, constructed entirely of white marble, was consecrated by Pope Gelasius II. in 1118, and was restored between 1597 and 1604; the baptistery, also in white marble, was begun by Diotisalvi in 1153, but was not completed until about 1278.

A world-famous Pisan sight is the Campanile, or "leaning tower," a clock-tower begun by the architects Bonnanus of Pisa and William of Innsbruck in 1174. It was completed by Tommaso Pisano in 1350, and is eight stories (179 feet) high. The cause of its remarkable oblique position (16½ feet off the perpendicular) is not known. Within the tower are six bells, one 6 tons in weight. (See illustration on p. 224.)

The Campo Santo (burial-ground) is peculiarly sacred. It was founded between 1188 and 1200 by Archbishop Ubaldo, who sanctified the ground by depositing thereon fifty-three shiploads of earth from Calvary.

One of the Pisan institutions that has lost little of its former importance is the university, a twelfth-century foundation, accommodated in a building of 1493, extended by Cosimo I. in 1542-3. Galilei was professor of mathematics at Pisa in 1589. There is a university library of about a quarter of a million volumes.

The leading manufacture is of cottons. Near by there are a royal stud-farm (horses and dromedaries) and mineral-springs. Pop. 73,041.

History. All authors agree in representing *Pisæ* as a very ancient city, but accounts of its early history are confused and unreliable. There is reason to believe, however, that it was one of the early Pelasgic settlements on the coasts of Etruria, which subsequently fell under the domination of the Etruscans. There are no extant remains of the Etruscan occupation, and practically nothing is known of the city as an Etruscan possession.

In 180 B.C. it became a Roman colony, and was named by Augustus *Colonia Julia Pisana*. About the beginning of the Christian era it was a flourishing city. On the fall of the Roman Empire it was pillaged by the Goths, and afterwards subjected by the Longobards. In the tenth century it had succeeded in taking a lead among the Italian states; but, after protracted and unsuccessful wars with Genoa at the end of the thirteenth, and with Florence at the end of the fifteenth century, it was finally compelled by famine to submit to the Florentines (8th June, 1509), and thus ceased for ever to be independent. On the ruins of Pisa was founded the power of the Grand-Duchy of Tuscany.

PISA, COUNCIL OF. A general Council of the Roman Catholic Church, held to consider the pretensions of the rival Popes of Avignon and of Rome, opened 25th March, 1409. The rival Popes, Benedict XIII. (of Avignon) and Gregory XII. (of Rome), were summoned to appear within a stated period, but refused to comply. After mature deliberation both Popes were formally deposed, and Cardinal Pietro Philargi, Archbishop of Milan, was elected Pope (Alexander V.). The authority of the Council was not, however, generally recognised, and it was not until 1417 that the schism can be said to have terminated. There were two other Councils at Pisa, one in 1133, and another in 1511.

PISAGUA. A seaport of the province of Tarapacá, Chile; served by railway from Iquique. It is a great transport centre for nitrate of soda. On 19th Nov., 1879, the allied (Peruvian and Bolivian) armies were defeated by the Chilians at Pisagua. Pop. about 3000.

PISANO (pi-sä′no), **Andrea.** Italian sculptor and architect, born at Pontedera *c.* 1270. He decorated, in relief, a set of bronze doors for the baptistery at Florence. He died *c.* 1349.

PISANO, Niccola. Born *c.* 1206; produced the sculptured pulpit in the baptistery of Pisa, his birthplace, and also that of the cathedral at Siena. He died in 1278.

PISANO, Giovanni. Son of the above. Born *c.* 1250; built the tomb of Benedict XI. at Perugia. He died *c.* 1330.

PISANO, or PISANELLO, Vittore.

PISA: LEANING TOWER

An artist and medallist. Born at San Vigilio *c.* 1380; he was responsible for portrait medals of many of the contemporary princes. He died in 1456.

PISCES (The Fishes). The twelfth and last of the signs of the zodiac, which the sun enters about 19th Feb. The constellation of the name does not now correspond with the sign, but contains the vernal point, or First Point of Aries. *See* PRECESSION OF THE EQUINOXES.

PISCICUL'TURE. The art of pisciculture has been practised from very early times. It is known that in 1000 B.C. the Chinese reared fish both for ornament and for the table by procuring fish eggs and caring for them in specially constructed ponds. The Greeks and Romans stocked ponds (vivaria) and lakes, by throwing in spawn. With the spread of Christianity and periodic abstention from meat, fish culture spread all over Europe; every large establishment and monastery had its fish-ponds, stocked with carp, eels, etc.

Modern Methods. At the present time the term pisciculture is used for various operations, including (*a*) the artificial fecundation of ova and care of the larvæ, for the purpose of restocking depleted waters, or for the introduction of species into countries to which they are not indigenous; (*b*) the acclimatisation of fish by use of such larvæ or of adults; (*c*) fish-farming and allied activities.

(*a*) **Hatching and Rearing.** The first recorded experiments in artificial fertilisation were carried out by Ludwig Jacobi in Westphalia in 1747. He mingled the milt of the male with ova from the female trout, and raised the fry to the age of six months. Karl Lund in Sweden soon followed him, and by 1845 experimental fertilisation and study of the fry had been extended to salmon and various other fishes. Ripe or mature fish are selected from fish penned in enclosures; the signs of ripeness are readily evident to the expert. The female is induced to extrude the ova into trays by gentle pressure, the male is similarly treated, and fertilisation is thus effected. In the "dry" method no water is added until milt and ova have been mingled together by gentle stirring. The "dry" has superseded the "wet" method, in which water was added before the milt, as it has been found that in the old method a certain proportion of ova remained sterile. Subsequent treatment depends on the character of the eggs.

(1) *Heavy non-adhesive eggs* (trout, salmon) are washed and placed on perforated tin trays (zinc has been found to be injurious). The eggs require much oxygen, which is supplied by a continuous stream of pure water. When the eggs hatch, the larvæ live for some time by the absorption of food from the yolk sac, which lies beneath the body. If intended for transportation, the fry are usually sent at this stage; in other cases they are kept in rearing-ponds until over a year old, the trays used being kept in constant motion. When the sac has been absorbed, the fry are fed at frequent intervals on finely ground fish or liver, or a commercial food prepared for the purpose. After attaining a certain size they can be turned into the rearing-ponds and fed on liver and the larvæ of insects.

(2) *Heavy adhesive eggs* (herring, smelt, perch) have been dealt with on an experimental scale.

(3) *Semi-buoyant eggs.* White fish (*Coregonus albula*) is hatched on a commercial scale in the United States.

(4) *Buoyant eggs* (cod, plaice, soles, turbot, etc.) are kept in continuous motion. The fry are fed on plankton (q.v.).

Freshwater Hatcheries. The most extensive are in the United States and in Canada. France and Germany have State-aided hatcheries, and Great Britain has many commercial hatcheries.

Marine Hatcheries. Millions of cod and plaice eggs are hatched annually for the Norwegian Government. The larvæ are liberated when able to search for their own food. The Fishery Board for Scotland has since 1894 been concerned in hatching sea fish (cod, etc.), first at Dunbar, afterwards at Nigg. A considerable number of plaice and other flat fish are hatched at Port Erin, the hatchery being supported by the Manx Government, and at Piel.

(*b*) **Acclimatisation.** By the transportation of fry across the continent the shad has been placed on the Pacific seaboard of the United States. The introduction of adult fish into a country has been particularly successful in the case of German carp in America, this fish being set out in waters unsuitable for salmon. Trout and salmon have been introduced into New Zealand and Australia.

(*c*) **Fish-farming, Eel Farms.** Elvers coming up from the sea are caught in tidal waters by means of partially open boxes filled with weed. Great numbers are taken in this way by the Ministry of Agriculture and Fisheries at Epney, on the Severn, and are traded within the kingdom, and also exported. In Denmark elvers are taken in the same way, and are fed with unmarketable fish in lagoons close to the coast.

Plaice. Plaice are transplanted from the open sea to the protected waters of the Lim Fjord in Denmark, and from the crowded coastal grounds to the Dogger Bank.

BIBLIOGRAPHY: Bulletins of the Bureau of Fisheries, Washington, United States; contributions to Canadian Biology, Ottawa; Annual Reports of the Fishery Board for Scotland, the Lancashire and Western Sea Fisheries Committee, and the Danish Marine Biological Station; International North Sea Fishery Investigations, Southern Area, 1904-9.

PISCID'IA. A genus of plants, nat. ord. Leguminosæ, the species being West Indian trees. The bark of the root of *P. Erythrina* (dog-wood tree) is a powerful narcotic, and is used as a substitute for opium, and also for poisoning fish. The timber makes excellent piles for docks and wharves, being heavy, resinous, and almost imperishable.

PISCI'NA. In ecclesiastical usage, a small basin supplied with water, set in a niche or recess on the south side of the altar in churches. It is used to hold the water in which the priest washes his hands, and for rinsing the chalice.

PISÉ (pē'sā). Material for forming the walls of cottages, agricultural buildings, etc., consisting of stiff clayey materials usually mixed with gravel well rammed into a frame, and when dry forming a good strong wall. These walls are thicker at bottom than at top. They must not be built too rapidly.

PISHIN. A district of British India, in Baluchistan; traversed by the Quetta-Kandahar Railway. It consists of a plain surrounded on three sides by hills rising to the height of about 11,000 feet, while the general height of the plain is 5000 feet. The people live mostly by pasturage or agriculture. It was occupied by the British in 1878, and assigned to them (from Afghanistan) by the Treaty of Gandamak in 1879. Area, 2720 sq. miles; pop. about 60,000.

PISID'IA. In ancient geography, a province of Asia Minor, situated between Phrygia, Cilicia, Pamphylia, Lycia, and Caria. The inhabitants were warlike mountaineers, and were never really subdued by the Romans.

PISIS'TRATUS (Gr. *Peisistratos*). "Tyrant" of Athens, descended from Codrus, the last King of Athens, born not later than 612 B.C., and died in 527 B.C. He was rich, handsome, and eloquent, and, being by nature ambitious, he soon placed himself at the head of one of the three parties into which Attica was then divided.

By putting himself forward as the patron and benefactor of the poor, and by advocating civil equality and a democratic constitution, he was able (notwithstanding the opposition of Solon) to seize upon the acropolis (citadel) in 560 B.C., and thus to make himself master, or, as the Greeks termed it, "tyrant" of the city. But though a tyrant in the Greek sense, his use of power was by no means tyrannical. He made no attempt to abolish the wise laws of Solon, but confirmed and extended their authority. He was, however, twice driven from Athens; but in the eleventh year of his second banishment succeeded in making himself master of the sovereignty for the third time.

Pisistratus erected splendid public buildings at Athens, established a public library, and collected and arranged the poems of Homer, and conducted himself with so much prudence and clemency that his country scarcely ever enjoyed a longer term of peace and prosperity. He left two sons, Hippias and Hipparchus, to inherit his power, who were not, however, able to preserve it.

PI'SOLITE. A rock composed of globules about the size of a pea, usually formed round a minute grain of sand or other foreign body, and joined with a cement. The material is commonly calcite or aragonite, but iron ores are often pisolitic. *See* OÖLITE.

PISTACHIO (pis-tā'shi-o). A tree of several species, of the genus Pistacia, nat. ord Anacardiaceæ, growing to the height of 15 to 20 feet. *P. vera* yields the well-known pistachio-nut, which contains a kernel of a pleasant taste, resembling that of the almond, wholesome and nutritive, yielding a pleasant oil. It is a native of Western Asia, but is much cultivated in the south of Europe. The gum named mastic is obtained from *P. lentiscus*, as well as from *P. atlantica*. *See* MASTIC.

PISTIL. In botany, the female or central seed-bearing organ of a phanerogamous flower, consisting of one or more *carpels* or modified leaves. There may be only a single pistil or several in the same flower. It consists essentially of two parts, the *ovary*, containing the ovules or young seeds, and the *stigma*, a cellular secreting body, which is either seated immediately on the ovary (as in the tulip and poppy), and is then called *sessile*, or is borne on a stalk called a *style* interposed between the ovary and stigma. It is on the stigma that the pollen falls, this pollination being followed by *fertilisation*, as a result of which the ovule develops into the seed. *See* BOTANY; FLOWER; PLACENTA.

PISTOIA (pis-tō'yȧ; ancient **Pistoriæ**). A walled city of Tuscany, North Italy, in the province of Florence, on the Ombrone. The Romanesque cathedral of S. Jacopo dates from the twelfth to thirteenth century, and the thirteenth-century campanile, originally a fortified tower called the Torre del Podestà, bears the arms of governors of the town. There are manufactures of iron and steel goods, fire-arms, and linen. Pistols were first made here, and received their name from the town. Pistoia is mentioned in ancient history as the scene of the defeat and death of Catiline in 62 B.C., and it was the focus of the mediæval struggles of the Guelphs and Ghibellines. In the history of art Pistoia ranks in importance between Florence and Pisa. Pop. 70,397.

PISTOL. A fire-arm designed to be used and fired by one hand only, though some of the modern varieties of automatic pistols can be fitted to a temporary stock (formed of the wooden holster or pistol-case) and fired from the shoulder, thus giving a greater degree of steadiness. The name is generally accepted (cf. Grose, *Military Antiquities*, 1786) to have been derived from the town of Pistoia, in Tuscany, where the original weapon of this class was invented in the fifteenth century. This early pistol was known as a "dag," and was fired by means of a "match" held by a curved arm of iron, which, being pivoted in the middle, was brought down on to the priming by pressure on the lower end as on a trigger.

Wheel-lock. Although this appears to have been the earliest method of ignition, it was very quickly superseded by the "wheel-lock," combined with the flint-and-steel method of ignition. This wheel-lock, according to an ancient manuscript quoted by Grose (vol. i), consisted of a small wheel attached to the right side of the pistol, and connecting inside the weapon with a spring operating the hammer. The wheel, on being rotated by means of a key, compressed the spring, and at the same time uncovered the priming-powder in the pan; all that then remained to be done was to press the trigger, when the hammer holding a flint fell on the steel of the priming-pan, and the resulting spark ignited the powder.

As the knowledge of the science of gun-making increased, improvements were made in pistols, which, in a general way, followed much on the same lines of development as the musket, though the actual method of ignition by means of flint and steel remained in favour for very many years. The wheel-lock mechanism, however, was discarded in favour of a simpler contrivance of springs contained entirely in the inside of the pistol.

Flint-lock. As fire-arms began to be adopted—possibly somewhat diffidently—by soldiers, so the pistol, as being not entirely unsuitable for use on horseback, became the arm of cavalry, the German Reiters (mercenary troops) being credited with its use as early as 1544. In any case, it was in full use as a cavalry weapon in the seventeenth century, and Grose gives a selection of woodcuts depicting the use of the weapon by a mounted dragoon in the first half of the century. The weapon then in use was a clumsy flint-lock contrivance, with a barrel 1 foot long and a probable over all length of some 20 inches.

This weapon was carried in a holster on the off side of the pommel of the saddle, and all operations necessary for loading and firing were carried out when mounted. A rather later variety of the pistol, marked "Tower," was fitted on the left side with a spring clip, by means of which it could be carried on the belt or sash. To such an extent was the pistol relied on that, on the Continent at least, it became the chief arm of the greater part of the cavalry, to the entire exclusion of the *arme blanche*.

Duelling Pistols. It is, however, in connection with the practice of duelling that the pistol is best known, and was brought to a high degree of accuracy by the skilled gun-makers of the eighteenth century; in fact, the eighteenth and early nineteenth centuries may be considered the age in which the pistol —in its muzzle-loading form—has its greatest vogue. Duelling, the direct descendant of the ancient trial by battle, became in its later years (the last duel in England took place in the 'forties of last century) an undoubted scandal; but the fact remains that it was a custom, and the gun-makers were quick to take advantage of it and improve the make of pistols in accordance with the extent of knowledge then possessed by them.

Horse-Pistols. Pistols were also required by travellers for their personal protection on a journey, there being at that time no civil police, although there was no lack of desperadoes throughout the country. Consequently gun-makers, in addition to perfecting the duelling pistol—a heavy but well-balanced and elaborately got up weapon with a hair trigger—produced other varieties for more everyday use, i.e. horse-pistols, meant to be carried in holsters attached to the saddle; sash or belt pistols, to be worn on a waist-belt; and pocket pistols of a smaller and lighter make, to be carried in the large pockets of the coat of the period. In due course the percussion principle—invented by Forsyth early in the nineteenth century—was adopted by most makers of pistols, and gave a considerable fillip to their development.

Repeating Pistols. For very many years—in fact from soon after pistols were first invented—attempts had been made to contrive a weapon which would lessen one of the chief disadvantages under which the single-barrel pistol necessarily laboured. This disadvantage, which was more obvious in the pistol than in the musket—the pistol being essentially an arm of opportunity and only used at close quarters—consisted in the absolute impossibility of reloading in a hurry; thus, should the first and important shot prove a failure, the pistol was useless except as a missile weapon.

Attempts to remedy this state of affairs, by the invention of a repeating pistol, were many and various, ranging from the fixed barrel, with a cylinder revolved by hand, of the sixteenth-century match-lock pistols, through the multi-barrelled pistols or "pepper-pots" of flint-lock and percussion days, down to the fixed barrel and mechanically revolving cylinder of the modern revolver. Blanch, in his *Century of Guns*, gives, among others, a representation of a flint-lock revolver made by Collier in 1818, with one barrel and a revolving cylinder, and another of an earlier type of pepper-pot, so arranged that at the first discharge two barrels were fired, still leaving four more for eventualities.

The Colt. But in course of time, and as normal conditions of life became rather more settled, the development of the pistol into the modern revolver was transferred to the less settled parts of the world, and it probably received more attention in America, and more especially in the Western States. There, in 1835, Colonel Colt patented his fixed-barrel revolver provided with a cylinder, which was loaded as a muzzle-loader from the front of the cylinder, each compartment of which had a nipple requiring to be capped; the action of cocking the hammer revolved the cylinder.

Although this was the first of the modern revolvers, Adams of London improved on this, and invented a revolver having what is known as a double-action, by which is meant that the revolution of the cylinder is effected either by pulling the trigger or cocking the hammer. This method, which is practically universal in modern revolvers, makes, of course, for rapidity of fire. A still more modern development of the arm is the automatic pistol, in which the force of the recoil is made use of in much the same manner as in machine-guns.

The Webley. The revolver in use in the British service at the present time is the "Webley," of which the length of the barrel is 4 inches and length over all 10½ inches, with a calibre of ·441 inches. The cylinder holds six cartridges, and the weight of the pistol is 2 lb. 8 oz. This is the service pattern, though others with longer barrels are made for the more accurate purposes of match-shooting. Among other revolvers and automatic pistols are the Smith & Wesson revolver, and the Webley, Colt, and Browning automatic pistols, besides many of German manufacture.

PISTOLE (pis-tōl'). The French name for the Spanish gold unit, a double *escudo* worth 16*s.* 11½*d.* English. It was in use from 1537, and is now obsolete. Coins of similar value, such as the *Louis d'or,* also received this name.

PISTON. In engineering, a movable flat or dished plate or cylinder which is used for the purpose of transmitting the pressures of some medium, such as water, steam, or gases, to the mechanism of an engine. The term is also used for the same device when used to transmit the pressure component of available power to a medium the pressure on which is to be raised.

The piston has a reciprocating motion, under the action of the varying pressure upon it. The form it takes is varied to suit the individual requirements of each case. In an engine the piston must be free to move to and fro with little frictional resistance, but at the same time must be so constructed as to prevent leakage taking place between it and the cylinder or liner.

Piston-rings are introduced into grooves cut in the cylindrical face of the piston of a steam- or gas-engine piston to prevent this leakage. These piston-rings are commonly made of cast iron and of a diameter slightly greater than that of the engine cylinder. A portion of each ring is cut out. The ring can then be inserted in its groove in the piston, and the gap in the ring closed up by compression to allow the piston to be passed into the cylinder. The ring

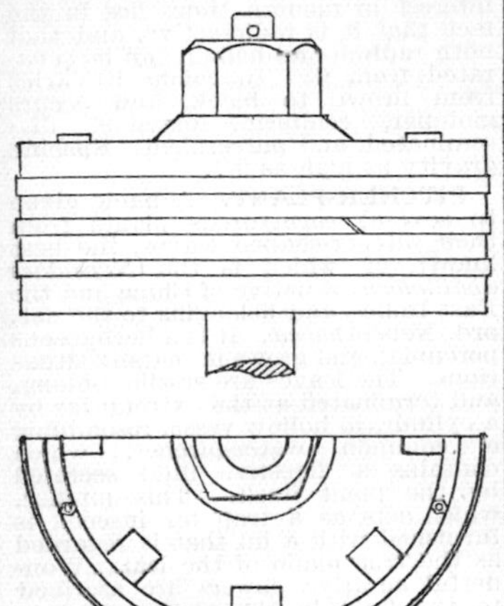

Steam-engine Piston

always presses against the cylinder-wall, in consequence of the forces which tend to restore it to its original form. Two or three rings are used on each piston, with their ring-gaps arranged at such intervals as to make the possibility of leakage very small. Rings, in some designs, are pressed outwards by small steel springs inserted in recesses in the piston. The variety of patent piston-ring arrangements is almost limitless.

Gas-engine pistons usually have quite distinctive forms. In a single-acting gas-engine the piston is made in the form of a long cylindrical cup, in which fits the gudgeon-pin, which is used to connect the piston to the connecting-rod. In engines of this type working on the two-stroke cycle, a shaped projection on the top of the piston acts as a gas-deflector (*see* MOTOR-CAR ENGINES). More rings are used on a gas-engine piston than on a steam-engine piston, because the pressures in use are greater. The piston of a double-acting gas-engine is usually made hollow, and provided with cooling water. Where pistons are to be used with hydraulic plant, packing materials, such as leather, tallowed rope, and many trade preparations, are used instead of rings.

PITCAIRN ISLAND. An island in the South Pacific, 100 miles south of the Tuamotu (Low Archipelago); length, 2¼ miles; breadth, about 1 mile. It was discovered by Carteret in 1767, and named after the midshipman who first sighted it. Since 1839 it has been a British possession. Its coast is almost perpendicular throughout its whole extent, fringed with formidable rocks and reefs, accessible only at two points, and not at all in stormy weather.

Pitcairn Island is chiefly remarkable as the home of the descendants of the *Bounty* mutineers, nine of whom, together with six men and twelve women, natives of Tahiti, landed here in 1790. Violent dissensions soon arose, and at the end of ten years the only survivors were John Adams, an Englishman (whose real name was said to have been Alexander Smith), the females, and nineteen children.

They were found in 1808 by the American, Captain Folger, who reported the discovery to the British Government. The interest thus aroused soon brought other visitors to the island, all of whom dilated with enthusiasm on the virtuous, sober, and industrious life led by the inhabitants. They became, however, too numerous to subsist comfortably on this small island, and they were transferred, to the number of 194, to Norfolk Island in 1856, but about 40 soon returned.

In 1881 the inhabitants numbered 96; in 1901, 126; and in 1914, 140 (35 being adult males, 39 adult females, and 66 children). Pop. (1921), 174. By religion they are Seventh Day Adventists. Taro, sugar-cane, yams, sweet potatoes, melons, oranges, pumpkins, bananas, pineapples, and arrowroot are products, with some coffee.

PITCH. There are three principal kinds of pitch, namely, coal-pitch, wood-pitch, and the naturally occurring mineral-pitch, usually called asphalt.

Coal-pitch is obtained from coal-tar, being the residue left in the still when the distillation of coal-tar is completed (*see* COAL-TAR). According as the distillation is interrupted earlier or later, soft or hard pitch is produced. One ton of coal-tar produces on the average ·54 ton of pitch. It consists chiefly of a mixture of hydrocarbons.

Pitch is a black, lustrous substance which breaks with a conchoidal fracture. Although it can be broken and is hard and apparently solid, it is in reality a very viscous fluid, for it will flow extremely slowly under the influence of its own weight. Soft pitch begins to melt at about 40° C., and hard pitch at about 100° C. If pitch is distilled, heavy oils are collected, and coke remains in the still as the final product. It is used for making briquettes, asphalt, asphalt paper, roofing felt, for tarring the surfaces of roads, and for the preparation of black varnishes and lacquer.

Briquettes contain from 5 to 10 per cent of pitch as a binding material for coal-dust. In making asphalt, pitch is used in conjunction with natural pitch, and is mixed with about three times its weight of stony material, such as sand and gravel, before being laid down. Varnishes are made from pitch by mixing it with creosote oil or coal-tar naphtha. Such varnishes are very effective in protecting wood-, iron-, or stone-work from corrosion and rendering materials waterproof.

Natural asphalt or mineral pitch is found in Trinidad and Syria (*see* ASPHALT). Wood-pitch is the product left behind in the still after the distillation of wood-tar (*see* WOOD-TAR). It is a dark, resinous substance, and is used for caulking ships, and for making waterproof cements, cobbler's wax, etc.

PITCH, in music, may be defined as the position of any particular note in the great ascending scale of sounds extending from the lowest or "gravest" to the highest or most "acute." It may be exactly indicated by giving the number of double vibrations per second which will produce it. The higher this number is the higher in pitch is the resulting sound.

The lack of a universally accepted standard of pitch in the past has been the source of much inconvenience in connection with musical performances, but at the close of the nineteenth century the French *diapason normal* was generally adopted. This gives A on the second space of the treble stave as = 439 double vibrations per second, and is generally referred to in this country as the "new" philharmonic pitch. The corresponding number for C on the third space of the treble stave is $\frac{6}{5} \times 439 = 527$; for C an octave lower (i.e. the middle C of the piano) the number is $\frac{3}{5} \times 439 = 263$ (*see* ACOUSTICS).

Unfortunately our military bands are still at the old, higher pitch. For theoretical purposes the number for the middle C of the piano is often taken to be 256. This is thought to correspond closely to the "classical" pitch, used, e.g., by Bach, Handel, and Beethoven.

PITCHBLENDE. A mineral chiefly found in Saxony and Cornwall in association with lead, copper, or tin ores, and composed of uranium oxides with some lead. Its special interest in modern times lies in the fact that it is radio-active, and that both radium and helium can be separated from it. In colour it varies from brown to black, and occurs globular, reniform, massive, disseminated, and pulverulent. Specific gravity as high as 9·7.

PITCHER-PLANT. A name given to several carnivorous plants from their pitcher-shaped leaves, the best known of which is the *Nepenthes distillatoria*, a native of China and the East Indies, and belonging to the nat. ord. Nepenthaceæ. It is a herbaceous perennial, and grows in marshy situations. The leaves are sessile, oblong, and terminated at the extremities by a cylindrical hollow vessel resembling a common water-pitcher, which contains a digestive fluid secreted by the plant itself. This pitcher, which acts as a trap for insects, is furnished with a lid that is regarded as the true blade of the leaf. Wonderful curative powers are ascribed to the fluid in the pitcher and to the leaf and the root of this plant by the natives of the East Indies and Madagascar. *See* CARNIVOROUS PLANTS.

PITCH LAKE. Name given to a lake of asphalt at La Brea, in the extreme S.W. of the Island of Trinidad. Its area is about 100 acres, and while the asphalt is firm and solid near the shore it is soft and boiling at the centre.

PITCHSTONE. A volcanic glassy rock with a pitchy look, not so highly vitreous as obsidian. It occurs commonly as dykes, where rapid cooling of a lava with a high percentage of silica has taken place. *Tachylyte* is, however, a pitchstone of basaltic composition.

PITCH'URIM-BEANS. The name given to the lobes of the drupe of *Nectandra puchury*, a South American species of laurel, used by chocolate-makers as a substitute for vanilla.

PITH. The cylindrical or angular column of parenchyma at or near the centre of the stem of a plant, also called the *medulla*. It is not usually continued into the root, but is always directly connected with the terminal bud of the stem, and also by means of the medullary rays with the cortex. The pith is at first succulent and of a greenish colour, afterwards it becomes dry, and in many plants its cells are broken up, leaving large cavities. It serves chiefly for storage.

PITHECANTHROPUS ERECTUS. The name given by E. Dubois (afterwards professor of geology in the University of Amsterdam) to a very primitive extinct member of the human family, the fossilised remains of which were found by him in 1891 and 1892 near Trinil, on the bank of the Solo River in Central Java. The parts recovered were a skull-cap, two teeth, and a thigh bone in a bed that contained the fossilised remains of many extinct mammals, the Indian analogies of which led Dubois to believe that in Pithecanthropus he had discovered a so-called "missing link" of Pliocene age; but subsequent investigations, and especially those carried out by the Selenka Expedition, have discredited the belief in the Pliocene date assigned to the beds, and have strengthened the evidence in favour of referring them to the Early Pleistocene age.

The discovery of these fossils aroused widespread controversy when Dubois' account of them was first published in 1894; and the disputes which then began have not yet been settled. Apart from the question of age, to which reference has already been made, there are two other categories of controversial issues. In the first place, many competent biologists refuse to admit that the skull-cap, teeth, and femur are parts of one individual or even of the same genus of living creatures; but Dubois replies to this criticism by the statement that all the fragments were found in the same geological horizon and probably represent parts of one individual, whose straight thigh is regarded as evidence for the invention of the specific name *erectus* given by Dubois to Pithecanthropus.

Then there is the further problem as to the rank of Pithecanthropus. Dubois claimed that it was a "missing link" intermediate between men and apes. Many German and some French authorities contend that the skull-cap is that of a gigantic ape akin to the gibbon. But the anatomical characters of the brain (as revealed by the mould of the inside of the skull) make it quite certain that neither of these pretended explanations is justifiable. Pithecanthropus is certainly a member of the human family, and far and away the earliest and most primitive human genus of which we have any exact knowledge concerning the form of the head.

A fossil tooth found in America early in 1922 suggests the former existence of an even more primitive member of the human family, who lived in what is now Nebraska in Pliocene times; but until we know something of the form of the head of this creature, which Professor Osborn has named Hesperopithecus, we cannot be certain of its right to be included within our family, although

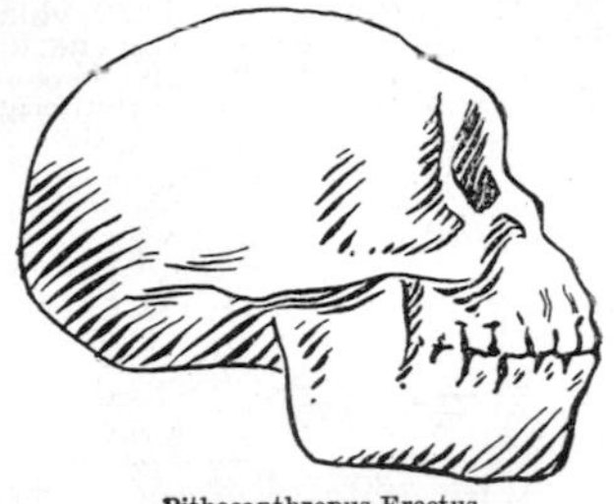

Pithecanthropus Erectus

the resemblance of its tooth to that of Pithecanthropus suggests a close kinship to the latter.

PITLOCHRY. A village and tourist centre of Perthshire, Scotland, on the Tummel, and served by the L.M.S. Railway. There is a large hydropathic establishment. Tweed is woven and whisky distilled. Near by are the Pass of Killiecrankie, Loch Tummel, and the Falls of Tummel. Pop. 1714.

PITMAN, Sir Isaac. The inventor of a system of shorthand. Born at Trowbridge, Wiltshire, in 1813, and died in 1897. In 1832 he became a schoolmaster, and published his *Stenographic Sound-Hand* in 1837. From this time he devoted himself to perfecting his shorthand system and to spelling reform. His *Phonetic Journal* was founded at Bath in 1842, and was the beginning of the publishing house of Isaac Pitman & Sons. Sir Isaac was knighted in 1894. —Cf. A. Baker, *Life of Sir Isaac Pitman.*

PITT, William. British statesman, younger son of the Earl of Chatham, born at Hayes, Kent, 28th May, 1759, died 23rd Jan., 1806. He possessed a remarkably precocious intellect, but as his physical powers were weak, he was educated privately till his fourteenth year, when he entered Pembroke College, Cambridge. He was called to the Bar in 1780, and entered Parliament the following year as member for Appleby.

His success in the House was of unparalleled rapidity. He supported Burke's Financial Reform Bill, and spoke in favour of parliamentary reform; became Chancellor of the Exchequer at twenty-three, under the Earl of Shelburne, and in the following year attained the position of Prime Minister. Although strongly supported by the sovereign, he stood opposed to a large majority of the House of Commons, and a dissolution took place in March, 1786.

At the general election which followed, the voice of the nation appeared decidedly in his favour, and some of the strongest aristocratical interests in the country were defeated, Pitt himself being returned by the University of Cambridge. His first measure was the passing of his India Bill, establishing the board of control, which was followed by much of that fiscal and financial regulation that gave so much *éclat* to the early period of his administration. The establishment of the delusive scheme of a sinking fund followed in 1786, and his Regency Bill in 1788.

Pitt the Younger

The French Revolution now broke out, and in 1793 war arose between Great Britain and France, a conflict which brought a heavy responsibility on Pitt, and immense sacrifices and burdens on his country. In 1800 the Irish union was accomplished. In 1801 the opposition to the Irish Catholics caused Pitt to resign his post. The new minister, who had renewed the war, unable to maintain his ground, resigned; and in 1804 Pitt resumed his post at the Treasury.

Returning to power, he exerted all the energy of his character to render the contest successful, and found means to engage the two great military powers of Russia and Austria in a new coalition, which was dissolved by the battle of Austerlitz. This event he did not survive long; his constitution, weakened by hereditary gout, rapidly yielded to the joint attack of disease and anxiety. Parliament decreed a public funeral to his honour, and a grant of £40,000 to pay his debts.

Pitt was more a man of expedients than of principles. A warm advocate of parliamentary reform in the outset of his career, he soon abandoned the cause. He spoke and voted in favour of the abolition of the slave-trade, but did not make a ministerial measure of it. As a financier he was an expert in practice rather than scientifically grounded, while the waste of his war-time expenditure was extreme. Neither can it be said that any decided social amelioration was due to his influence. His ruling passion was love of power, but he was above the meanness of avarice, and his personal disinterestedness was extreme.

As an orator he was, on the whole, more impressive than his father or even Burke, the indignant severity and keenness of his sarcasm being unequalled.—BIBLIOGRAPHY: Lord Rosebery, *William Pitt* (Twelve English Statesmen Series); Charles Whibley, *Political Portraits*; D. O. Madden, *The Age of Pitt and Fox*; J. H. Rose, *Life of Pitt*.

PIT'TACUS. One of the seven wise men of Greece, born about 652 B.C., died 569 at Mitylene, on the Island of Lesbos. He was highly celebrated as a warrior, a statesman, a philosopher, and a poet. In 589 the citizens raised him to the dictatorship, an office which he filled for ten years, when he voluntarily resigned it.

PITTENWEEM. A royal and municipal burgh and seaport town of Fifeshire, Scotland, on the Firth of Forth; served by the London and North-Eastern Railway. There is a fishing and curing industry. Pittenweem became a royal burgh in 1542. Pop. (1931), 1619.

PITTSBURGH. A city and port of entry of Pennsylvania, United States, the county seat of Allegheny county, on the Ohio, formed at this point by the combination of the Allegheny and Monongahela Rivers; served by the Baltimore and Ohio lines of the Pennsylvania, the Pittsburgh, & Lake Erie, the Buffalo, Rochester, & Pittsburgh, and half a dozen other railways. It is admirably situated for trade, having ample river and railway connection with the great commercial emporiums of the east, west, and south, while in the immediate neighbourhood there are immense coal deposits.

These exceptional advantages have made Pittsburgh the chief centre of the American iron and steel industry. The glass manufactures of Pittsburgh also rank first in importance in the United States; cotton goods, leather, earthenware, white lead, soda, tobacco, and spirits are largely produced; but the chief exports are iron and steel, hardware and machinery, glass, coal, and coke.

Pittsburgh consists of the town proper and of several large suburbs, and with those that are on the opposite side of the rivers the connection is kept up by many bridges. Of the adjacent places, some, though separately incorporated, are really suburbs of Pittsburgh; the most important, Allegheny, on the right bank of the Allegheny River, a favourite residence with the wealthier classes, was united with Pittsburgh in 1908.

The city possesses many fine public buildings and institutions. Among these are Pittsburgh University with many departments, and the Carnegie Institute, including library, art, musical, and technical departments, and museum. There are three broadcasting stations. Pop. 669,817.

Pittsburgh occupies the site of a fort called Du Quesne, built by the French in 1754, captured by the British in 1758, and named after William Pitt, Earl of Chatham. It was chartered in 1816.

PITTSFIELD. A city of Massachusetts, United States, the county seat of Berkshire county, on the Housatonic; served by the New York, New Haven, & Hartford, and the Boston & Albany Railways. It has manufactures of cotton and woollen goods, silk, castings, machinery, tools, paper, boots and shoes, and malt products. Pittsfield was settled in 1743 and 1749, and became a city in 1891. Pop. 49,677.

PITTSTON. A city of Pennsylvania, United States, in Luzerne county, on the Susquehanna River; served by the Erie, the Lehigh Valley, the Central of New Jersey, the Delaware, Lackawanna, & Western, and the Lackawanna & Wyoming Valley Railways, and by electric railways to Scranton, Plymouth, etc. It lies in the chief anthracite coal area of the United States. Pittston was settled in 1770, and became a city in 1894. The name commemorates William Pitt (Earl of Chatham). Pop. 18,246.

PITUITARY BODY, or PITUITARY GLAND. A small body situated towards the base of the brain. The name, derived from the Lat. *pituita*, phlegm, was given to it because it was supposed to discharge phlegm or mucus down the nostrils.

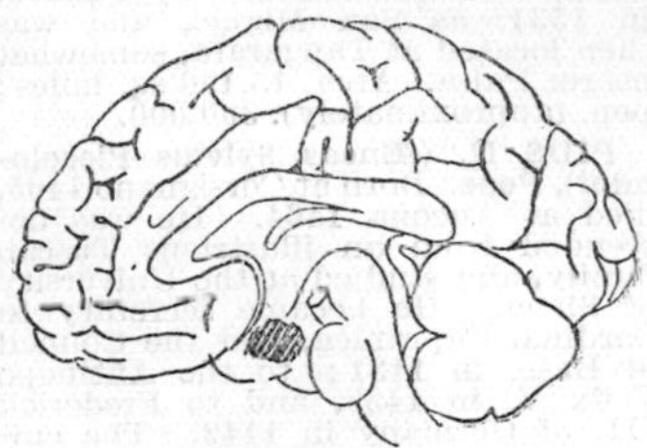

Pituitary Gland

PITYRI'ASIS. A chronic skin affection characterised by scaling of small portions of the skin. The disease is very common, and may affect the scalp and later the body. In the scalp it is known as pityriasis capitis or dandruff, and shows easily detached scales, leading to atrophy of the hair. It appears in childhood between the ages of six and ten, and many members of the same family may be affected. It may persist for years, and if untreated lead to a gradual loss of hair, leaving a smooth, shining baldness (alopecia).

In the body the condition is known as pityriasis circinata, and affects at first chiefly the upper part of the chest in front and behind. Later the eruption spreads to other parts. It begins as a small spot, pink in colour, and covered with a greasy scale. This spreads and forms a ring, and when the disease is well established the ring-like grouping is typical.

Treatment of the scalp is essential, as it is the origin of the trouble, and this is done by suitable lotions, used as a shampoo, or by antiseptic ointment. Pityriasis of the body is best treated with sulphur ointment. If the condition were satisfactorily treated in childhood, there would be few eruptions among adults.

PIU'RA. The northernmost maritime department of Peru, partly belonging to the torrid coastal plain, and partly within the broken mountainous region of the Western Cordillera. Petroleum, sulphur, and salt are produced; the making of panama hats is a universal cottage industry; sheep, cattle, goats, and mules are raised in the hinterland, and some rough cotton and tobacco are produced in the uplands of the interior and in the valleys of the Chira,

Piura, and Tumbes, which traverse the coastal plain. The two former valleys are irrigated and densely peopled. Piura is the capital, and is connected by railway with Paita, on the coast (Paita-Piura Railway, 61 miles). It was founded by Pizarro, in 1531, as San Miguel, and was then located at Tangarara, somewhat nearer Paita. Area, 15,190 sq. miles; pop. (approximately), 300,000.

PIUS II. (Æneas Sylvius Piccolomini), Pope. Born at Corsignano 1405, died at Ancona 1464. He was descended from an illustrious Tuscan family, and studied at the University of Siena. He became secretary to Cardinal Capranica, and the Council of Basel in 1431; to the Antipope Felix V. in 1439, and to Frederick III. of Germany in 1442. The emperor sent him as Imperial Ambassador to a Diet at Ratisbon, and in 1446 to Pope Eugenius IV. to negotiate the submission of Germany. He gained the favour of Eugenius, whom he had formerly opposed, and by his successor was created Bishop of Trieste in 1447, and cardinal in 1456.

He succeeded Calixtus III. as pontiff in 1458. In 1460 he published a Bull condemning the doctrine he had in former years so vigorously defended: the superiority of a general council to the Pope. He roused Christendom against the Turks, and planned a crusade against Islam, but died before he had time to carry it into effect.

Pius II. was one of the most learned men of his age, and the literary fame of Æneas Sylvius has somewhat eclipsed his historical importance as Pope.—Cf. C. M. Ady, *Pius II., the Humanist Pope.*

PIUS V. (Michele Ghislieri), Pope. Born in 1504, died 1572. He was raised to the cardinalate by Paul IV. in 1557, appointed inquisitor in Lombardy, then inquisitor-general, and chosen Pope in 1565. Pius V. chiefly distinguished himself by his cruel persecutions of Protestants and Jews; the Bull *In Cœna Domini* was renewed by him, and the authority of the *Index Expurgatorius* enforced. In 1570 he excommunicated Elizabeth of England. He lent his influence and assistance to Charles IX. of France against his Protestant subjects, and to the Venetians and Spaniards in their war against the Turks. He was canonised by Clement XI. in 1712, and his festival is held on 11th May.

PIUS VI. (Giovanni Angelo Braschi), Pope. Born at Cesena 1717, died at Valence 1799. He held important offices under several pontiffs, was raised to the cardinalate by Clement XIV., and succeeded him in 1775. Several beneficent reforms were introduced by him in the finance department; he also improved the Vatican museum, drained the Pontine Marshes, reconstructed the port of Ancona, and embellished Rome. The French Revolution, however, hastened the decay of the temporal power of the holy see. In 1791 Avignon and the county of Venaissin were reunited to France, and by the Treaty of Tolentino (1797) he lost the Romagna, Bologna, and Ferrara. In 1798 General Berthier established the Roman Republic, and the Pope, having refused to renounce his temporal sovereignty, was carried off a prisoner to France, where he died.

PIUS VII. (Gregorio Barnaba Chiaramonti), Pope. Born at Cesena in 1742, died 1823. A Benedictine monk for several years, he became Bishop of Imola and cardinal in 1785. His friendly attitude towards the Cisalpine Republic secured him the favour of France, and the election to the Papal chair in 1800. He concluded a concordat with Napoleon in 1801, but aroused the open enmity of the emperor by refusing to recognise his brother Joseph as King of Naples.

The results were the incorporation of the Papal cities, and shortly after of Rome itself, with the Kingdom of Italy, and the arrest of the Pope (6th July, 1809) and his confinement in Savona and afterwards at Fontainebleau. He was released in 1814, and restored to the possession of all the Papal territory except Avignon and Venaissin in France, and a narrow strip of land beyond the Po. His subsequent government was politically and ecclesiastically of a reactionary character.

PIUS IX. (Giovanni Maria Mastai-Ferretti), Pope. Born 13th May, 1792, died 7th Feb., 1878. Ordained in 1819, he was appointed Archbishop of Spoleto in 1827, and raised to the cardinalate in 1840. Elected Pope in 1846, on the death of Gregory XVI., his accession was signalised by the release of 2000 political prisoners, followed by a complete amnesty.

Inspired by the dream of a free Italy, Pius IX. was anxious to realise the ideal of a federated Italy under the supremacy of the Popes. Having declared himself against war with Austria, he was compelled in consequence of a series of riots to flee. A Roman Republic was proclaimed (Feb., 1849), with Mazzini at its head. Restored by French troops, he returned in 1850. In 1870 the dogma of Papal infallibility was established by the Ecumenical Council.

By this time the Pope's dominions had been greatly reduced, and what remained of the temporal power was secured by the presence of French troops at Rome. But the downfall of Napoleon III. caused their withdrawal; the Italian troops took possession, and the political rule of the holy see was at an end.—Cf. Raffaele de Cesare, *Last Days of Papal Rome, 1850-1870*.

PIUS X. (Giuseppe Sarto), Bishop of Rome and Supreme Pontiff of the Roman Catholic Church. Born of humble parents at Riete, in the province of Tréviso, Italy, in 1835, and died in 1914. He was ordained in 1858, and was appointed canon of the cathedral and superior of the seminary at Tréviso in 1875. In 1880 he refused the bishopric of Tréviso, but four years later he was compelled by Leo XIII. to accept that of Mantua, and became (12th June, 1893) Cardinal and Patriarch of Venice.

He succeeded Leo XIII. on 4th Aug., 1903, and occupied the Papal chair for eleven years, during which he enforced a vigorous policy of reform and reconstruction within the Church. On the outbreak of the European War he refused to comply with the Austrian emperor's request for his blessing, saying, "I bless peace, not war," and there can be no doubt that the European War materially hastened his end.

PIUS XI. (Achille Ratti), Bishop of Rome and Supreme Pontiff of the Roman Catholic Church. Born on 31st March, 1857, at Desio, near Milan, where his parents were engaged in the manufacture of silk, and was ordained in 1879. In 1900 he visited England to carry out research work in the Bodleian Library at Oxford, and also visited Manchester as the guest of his friend the Bishop of Salford. Pius X. appointed him prefect of the Ambrosian Library in 1906, and ten years later he was also called to the prefecture of the Vatican Library, where he speedily became distinguished for his great learning and piety and for his affability of manner, all of which qualities endeared him to those cardinals with whom he came frequently in contact. He is a keen student of history and philology, and is said to have an almost perfect knowledge of twenty-seven languages, ancient and modern.

Benedict XV. appointed him Apostolic Nuncio, and entrusted him with a mission of great delicacy in Poland (1918), on the successful accomplishment of which Benedict speedily demonstrated his appreciation by nominating him simultaneously to the Roman Purple and to the archbishopric of Milan (13th June, 1921), recently vacated by the death of Cardinal Ferrari. On 6th June, 1919, he had been made an archbishop of the Curia, with the titular see of Lepanto, and in April, 1921, he became titular Archbishop of Adana.

On the death of Benedict XV., Cardinal Ratti became Pope as Pius XI., and his appointment was acclaimed by the multitude. The notable achievement of his pontificate was the ending of the anomalous condition between state and church existing since 1870, and the re-establishment of the temporal power of the papacy in 1929, which involved the creation of the Vatican City as a state ruled by the pontiff. This was brought about by the Lateran Treaty between Italy and the Holy See, duly ratified at the Vatican in 1929. An enthusiastic mountaineer in earlier years, Pope Pius published his *Climbs on Alpine Peaks* in 1923.

PIZAR'RO, Francisco. Spanish adventurer and conqueror of Peru, born at Trujillo in 1478. He was the illegitimate son of an hidalgo, Gonzalo Pizarro, and was first a swineherd and then a soldier. The spirit of adventure which at that time pervaded Spain prompted him to seek fortune in the newly found continent of America, where he participated in various military and trading expeditions.

While resident near Panamá he became associated with two other adventurers, Hernando Lugue, or de Luguos, and Diego de Almagro. In 1524 they jointly fitted out an expedition with a view to exploration and conquest, and on their second voyage discovered Peru, but finding their force inadequate for conquering the country, Pizarro returned to Spain for assistance.

He arrived in Seville in 1528, was granted the necessary powers and a small force, and recrossed the Atlantic in 1531. The following year he arrived in Peru during a civil war, treacherously seized the person of the reigning Inca at a friendly banquet, and, after extorting an immense ransom, put him to death.

The whole empire was gradually conquered without much opposition, but its settlement was long in abeyance owing to a feud between Pizarro and Almagro. Hernando Pizarro, a brother of the general, strangled Almagro in 1537. This act was avenged in 1541 when a son of Almagro murdered Francisco Pizarro in his palace at Lima. Lima was founded by Pizarro in 1535, and his remains are interred in the cathedral of that city, also founded by him.—Cf. F. A. Ober, *Pizarro and the Conquest of Peru.*

PLACEN'TA. The structure attached to the lining of the womb, which provides the means whereby the fœtus, or unborn embryo, obtains from the mother's blood the nutriment needed for its growth. In its most typical form it is met with in the higher Mammalia, which used to be called *placental* mammals, under the belief that lower Mammalia, the two orders Monotremata and Marsupialia, did not develop a placenta; but in 1895 J. P. Hill showed that in some of the marsupials (more especially *Perameles*) a true placenta was found. Certain analogous structures also exist in connection with the development of the young of some species of sharks and dog-fishes.

By the end of pregnancy the human placenta forms a disc-like mass, measuring 7½ inches across, ¾ inch thick, and about 20 ounces in weight. Connected with it near the middle is the umbilical cord, by means of which the growing embryo is attached to the placenta. By means of blood-vessels in the umbilical cord the blood of the embryo is carried to the placenta, where it circulates in minute branching processes that are exposed to the blood of the mother, by means of which its supply of oxygen and food material is replenished, and the waste materials brought from the embryo are got rid of. At the end of pregnancy the placenta is thrown off as the after-birth, after the child itself has been expelled.

PLACENTA. In botany, a ridge of cellular tissue at the inner or ventral suture of a carpel, to which the ovules or seeds are attached either immediately or by stalks (funicles), as in the pod of the pea. The placenta is formed on each margin of the carpel, and is therefore essentially double. When the pistil is formed by one carpel, the inner margins unite in the axis, and usually form a common placenta. When the pistil is composed of several carpels, there are generally separate placentas at each of their margins. The term *parietal placenta* is applied to one not projecting far inwards, or one essentially constituted of the wall of the seed-vessel. The form of placentation forms an important distinction between the various orders of plants.

PLACENTI'TIS. Inflammation of the placenta, and may be acute or chronic. The acute form frequently arises as a result of infection spreading from the membranes which cover the fœtus in utero. If severe, this will cause the death of the fœtus, and probably result in abortion. The chronic form may be due to tuberculosis or syphilis.

PLAC'ER. Term used in mining for alluvial deposits containing gold and tin ores, as well as rarer metals, and consisting of sands, grits, and fine to coarse gravels. They represent generally river and lake deposits of recent geological formation, but in Australia and California the placers or "deep leads" are ancient river beds buried beneath basalt.

PLACOID. A term used to designate a variety of scales covering the bodies of the Elasmobranchii (sharks, skates, rays, etc.), the Placoidei of Agassiz. These structures consist of detached bony grains, tubercles, or plates, of which the latter are not uncommonly armed with spines. They resemble teeth in structure, and the smaller ones are often termed "dermal denticles."

PLA'GIOCLASE. A name for all the felspars that crystallise in the triclinic system, and thus have their two cleavages oblique (Gr. *plagios*) to one another. Repeated lamellar twinning is characteristic.

PLAGIOS'TOMI (Gr. *plagios*, oblique, *stoma*, mouth). An order of fishes of the sub-class Elasmobranchii. The skeleton is cartilaginous; the mouth a transverse slit, situated on the under surface of the head; and the teeth numerous. The Plagiostomi include sharks, dog-fishes, rays, saw-fishes, etc.

PLAGUE. An acute infectious disease caused by the bacillus pestis, and occurring in two chief forms, the bubonic and the pneumonic. It is a disease of great antiquity, and was apparently present in ancient Egypt, also probably in the empires of Asia Minor, and there are records of the plague of Athens and of an outbreak in the reign of Marcus Aurelius.

From the great plague in the days of Justinian in the sixth century down to the middle of the seventeenth century epidemics of varying severity occurred throughout Europe. The most disastrous of these was the famous "Black Death" of the fourteenth century, which spread over Europe and destroyed one-fourth of the population. In the seventeenth century the Great Plague of London caused the death of 70,000 people within the city.

During the eighteenth and nineteenth centuries it gradually became much rarer, till it had all but disappeared, except for some parts of China and North-West India, when again in 1894 there was a fresh outbreak at Hong-Kong, from which seaport it was spread to Japan, Australia, South and North America, Egypt, South Africa, West Indies, and to some European ports, where there were slight outbreaks. It is now definitely established that the disease is spread to man by the bite of the rat-flea which has been previously living on an infected rat. Rats are very susceptible to plague, and the wide distribution of the last outbreak was due to infected rats being carried by shipping practically all over the world.

In any outbreak, or as a prevention to an outbreak, the most important factor is the destruction of rats, and especially those infected or liable to be so. The disease will never make serious headway in countries where rats and human beings do not occupy the same house, but in the East, where there are still devastating outbreaks, this condition widely exists. Of the two types, the more common is the bubonic, and the outstanding feature is a bubo or inflamed lymphatic gland. This may form an abscess and the condition remain local, in which case the patient probably recovers, or a general septicæmia may result and the patient dies.

The pneumonic type is a very acute plague pneumonia, and as the lungs are affected, with each cough the patient spreads millions of bacilli into the atmosphere, hence its extreme infectivity. It is probably the most infectious condition known. The virulence of this type is very high, as nearly every case dies. Various curative serums have been tried, but none has given favourable results; but prophylactic vaccine is used on a very large scale in the East, and is thoroughly established as a preventive agent. When an epidemic threatens, the whole population should be inoculated.

PLAICE (*Pleuronectes platessa*). A common flat-fish, largely used as food, which attains an average length of 12 or 18 inches. The dark or upper side is coloured brown, spotted with red or orange; the body is comparatively smooth; the ventral fins are situated on the throat, and are thus jugular in position; the mouth is of small size, and provided with minute teeth. These fishes are all "ground-fishes," that is, feed and swim near the bottom of the sea. They are caught chiefly by means of trawl-nets.

PLAIN. One of the positive land forms. Plains receive a variety of names in different countries, as *steppes* in Russia and Asia; *savannas, prairies, pampas,* etc., in America. *See* GEOGRAPHY, under *Land Forms,* sect. i. (*a*).

PLAINFIELD. A city of New Jersey and residential suburb of New York City, United States, in Union county; served by the Central of New Jersey and electric railways. There are varied manufactures. Plainfield district was settled in 1684, but the township was only founded in 1847, and it became a city in 1867. Pop. 34,422.

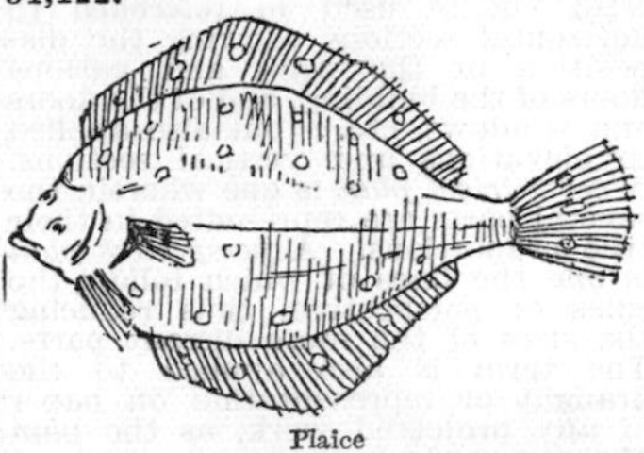
Plaice

PLAIN-SONG. The earliest form of art-music, and at its zenith in the fifth and sixth centuries. It was inevitably purely melodic in its nature, since harmonic treatment in music had still to be thought of and slowly elaborated, but with the simple means at its command it reached in a comparatively short time a very high degree of artistic excellence, and when properly rendered has great powers of eloquence even at the present day. It is further distinguished from the music of today by its freedom from the rhythmic control of the bar-line and the cadence, both of which exercise a somewhat despotic influence in harmonic music.

This *unmeasured* character constitutes a real difficulty for the modern musician who would render plain-song as it should be sung, since the "tyranny of the bar-line" is all-pervading; but the present tendency in music is markedly towards a greater rhythmic freedom, and the near future may bring to harmonic music that plasticity which is one of the most expressive elements in true plain-song. Then plain-song itself may come into that wider favour to which it is entitled by its beauty and expressive power.

At present its true value is known and appreciated by comparatively few. All early melody music which is unmeasured is plain-song, but the term is more particularly associated in the minds of musicians with the music of the early Roman Catholic Church. It was, naturally, written in the old modes or early forms of the scale.

PLAIS'TOW. District of London, between Canning Town and West Ham, 4 miles from London (Fenchurch Street), on the L.N.E. and L.M.S. Railways; it houses a number of factories, chemical works, and engineering establishments. Pop. 35,900.

PLAN. In architecture, a drawing showing the design of a building, a term chiefly used in reference to horizontal sections showing the disposition of the walls and various floors of the building, and of the doors and windows, etc.; but also applied to elevations and vertical sections. A *geometrical plan* is one wherein the several parts are represented in their true proportions. A *perspective plan* is one the lines of which follow the rules of perspective, thus reducing the sizes of the more distant parts. The term is also applied to the draught or representation on paper of any projected work, as the *plan* of a city or of a harbour.

PLANARIANS. A group of soft-bodied flat-worms, of the class Turbellaria, mostly oval or elliptical in shape, and not unlike the foot of a gasteropodous mollusc. Some are aquatic in their habits, occurring in fresh water or on the sea-shore, but land planarians abound in the warmer parts of the globe, some being of large size (6 to 9 inches long). The male and female organs are united in the same individual, and the process of reproduction may be either sexual, by means of true ova, or non-sexual, by internal gemmation or transverse fission.

PLANCHETTE. A thin heart-shaped piece of wood supported on two castors at the ends of the base, and on an ordinary pencil at the apex. If the finger-tips be placed upon the instrument, the pencil may readily be made to trace characters even without conscious movement on the part of the operator. When used by some persons, it seems to begin to move of its own accord after a little while, and if the person wishes, for instance, to have an answer to a certain question, writing may be formed on the sheet of paper on which the instrument is placed, containing something more or less pertinent to the matter, but probably never anything that is not more or less consciously in the operator's mind. It has figured much in spiritualistic séances, where it has afforded disembodied spirits an opportunity for exercising their literary talent, and it has enjoyed some popularity as a drawing-room entertainer.

PLANE. *See* TOOLS.

PLANET. A celestial body which revolves about the sun as its centre (*primary planets*), or a body revolving about another planet as its centre (*secondary planets*, *satellites*, or *moons*). The known *major* planets are, in the order of their proximity to the sun, Mercury, Venus, the Earth, Mars, Jupiter, Saturn, Uranus, Neptune, and Pluto. They shine by reflected sunlight. Mercury, Venus, Mars, Jupiter, and Saturn were known to the ancients. Uranus was discovered through observation by Herschel in 1781, while the discovery of Neptune was the result of pure intellectual work, the calculating of Leverrier and Adams (1845).

	Mean Distance from the Sun	Distance from the Earth		Time of Revolution round the Sun	Time of Rotation on Axis		
		Greatest	Least				
	Miles	Miles	Miles	Mean Solar Days	h.	m.	s.
Mercury	36,000,000	134,800,000	50,900,000	87·9692		?	
Venus	67,200,000	161,200,000	24,500,000	224·7007		?	
The Earth ..	92,900,000	— —	— —	365·2563	23	56	4
Mars	141,500,000	248,600,000	34,500,000	686·9794	24	37	23
Jupiter	483,300,000	599,500,000	367,200,000	4332·5848	9	55	
Saturn	886,100,000	1,027,200,000	745,100,000	10759·2197	10	30	
Uranus	1,782,000,000	1,956,900,000	1,607,300,000	30688·3900	10	45	
Neptune	2,792,000,000	2,909,100,000	2,675,000,000	60181·1132		?	
Pluto	3,700,000,000	4,640,000,000	2,750,000,000	90500 (app.)		?	

The planetoids or asteroids are small bodies discovered since the beginning of the nineteenth century, mainly between the orbits of Mars and Jupiter. The number of these asteroids is annually increased by fresh discoveries; over 1000 are now known.

Mercury, Venus, the Earth, and Mars closely resemble one another in many respects. They are all of moderate size, with great densities, the earth weighing as much as five and a half times an equal bulk of water. Jupiter, Saturn, Uranus, and Neptune, on the other hand, are of enormous size, of small densities, Saturn weighing less than an equal bulk of water, and probably possess a high temperature. The most colossal of the planets is Jupiter; its volume exceeds that of the earth about 1300 times. Saturn is next in size.

Mars, Jupiter, Saturn, Uranus, and Neptune, being outside the earth's orbit, are sometimes called the *superior planets*; Venus and Mercury, being within the earth's orbit, are called *inferior planets*. The family of major planets has also been subdivided into *intra-asteroidal* planets—Mercury, Venus, the Earth, Mars; and *extra-asteroidal* planets—Jupiter, Saturn, Uranus, and Neptune, the character of the two being very different, as above described. The major planet which approaches nearest to the earth is Venus, the least distance in round numbers being 25 millions of miles; the most distant is Pluto, a small planet discovered in 1930. We give here a comparative table of the planets; *See* also the separate articles.

PLANE TREE (Platănus). A genus of trees, nat. ord. Platanaceæ. *P. occidentālis*, the American plane tree or button wood (the *sycāmore* or *cotton tree* of the West), abounds in

Western Plane

American forests, and on the banks of the Ohio attains sometimes a diameter of from 10 to 14 feet, rising 60 or 70 feet without a branch. The bark is pale-green and smooth, and its epidermis detaches in portions; the fresh roots are a beautiful red; the leaves are alternate, palmated, or lobed; and the flowers are united in little globular, pendent balls. The wood in seasoning takes a dull red colour, is fine-grained, and susceptible of a good polish, but speedily decays on exposure to the weather.

The Oriental plane (*P. orientālis*) resembles the preceding, and is plentiful in the forests of Western Asia. The *P. orientālis* and *P. acerifolia*, from being able to withstand the deleterious influences of a smoky atmosphere, are among the trees most suitable for planting in towns. The *Acer pseudo-platănus*, the common sycamore or greater maple, is called in Scotland the plane tree.

PLANIM'ETER. An instrument for measuring areas, no matter how irregular, which is used extensively in engineering calculations. The determination of the mean pressure on an engine piston from the indicator-diagram may be cited as an example of its use. These diagrams are not of any regular form, but the area can readily be obtained by the use of the planimeter, and the mean height deduced by dividing the area by the measured length.

Amsler's planimeter has two arms, one of which is held in a carriage which is hinged to the other. At the extreme end of the one arm a needle-point is provided as a centre about which the instrument can be moved when in use, and at the extreme end of the other arm the tracing-point is fixed.

The area to be measured is traced out in a clockwise direction. A graduated revolving wheel records the area of the figure in units, which depend upon the position of the carriage. Marked positions on the tracer-arm of the planimeter indicate where the carriage must be fixed to work with particular units. For the theory of the instrument *see* B. Williamson, INTEGRAL CALCULUS.

PLANING-MACHINE. *See* MACHINE TOOLS.

PLANKTON and **NEKTON.** Collective terms applied to assemblages of certain aquatic organisms. Plants and animals that float or drift at or near the surface of the sea or of fresh water, are known as *Plankton,* while the actively swimming and usually predacious animals that do not descend to great depths make up the *nekton*. It may be added that deep-water forms are collectively called *benthos*.

Plankton. The plants of this assemblage include not only large forms, such as the gulf-weed of the Sargasso Sea, but vast numbers of microscopic species, of which the most interesting are the flinty-shelled diatoms, which serve as food to the shoals of minute crustacea that constitute the aliment of many fishes, and are the ultimate source of the mysterious vitamines that give one of its valuable properties to cod-liver oil.

Plankton animals are usually transparent or translucent, and many of them are buoyed up by bubbles of gas or by oil globules. Among them are many Protozoa, including various Foraminifera, and when these die their calcareous shells settle down on large areas of the sea-floor to make up calcareous "ooze," which when consolidated and raised above the surface becomes chalk. The phosphorescence of the sea is largely due to the night-light animalcule (Noctiluca), and other floating Protozoa are the ray animalcules (Radiolaria) with flinty skeletons.

Plankton also includes many of the jelly-fishes, some annelids, echinoderm larvæ, and shoals of Crustacea, especially the fork-footed forms (Copepoda), that constitute the staple diet of the herring and some other valuable food-fishes. Mollusca are also present, especially the wing-footed snails (Pteropoda), of which vast shoals are swallowed wholesale by the whalebone whale. Among the primitive vertebrates we find various ascidians, such as the salps (Salpa) and the phosphorescent fire-cylinders (Pyrosoma), while the floating eggs of most marine fishes belong to the plankton, as do the transparent larvæ that hatch out from them.

Many elaborate investigations have been and are being made on plankton, and these are of great importance with regard to fisheries. Quantitative methods, first devised by Hensen, but now much improved, have given remarkable results. It has been calculated, for example, that the plankton of the 16 square miles of the Eckernförde (in the Baltic) contains something like 15,600 billion Copepoda, enough to feed 534 million of herrings for a year.

Nekton. The most important animals of this assemblage are squids and cuttle-fishes; a great many fishes; some of the aquatic birds, of which penguins are the most remarkable; and various aquatic mammals, including seals and sea-lions (Pinnipedia), Sirenia, and Cetacea. The birds and Pinnipedia, of course, only partly belong to the nekton, as they spend part of their time on land, while birds are largely creatures of the air.

PLANTAGENET. A surname first adopted by Geoffrey, Comte d'Anjou, and said to have originated from his wearing a sprig of broom (*plante de genêt*) in his cap. This name was borne by the fourteen kings (from Henry II. to Richard III.) who occupied the English throne from 1154-1485. In 1400 the family was divided into the branches of Lancaster (Red Rose) and York (White Rose), and from their reunion in 1485 sprang the House of Tudor. *See* ENGLAND.

PLANTAGIN'EÆ, or PLANTAGINA'CEÆ. The plantains, a small natural order of gamopetalous dicotyledons. It consists of herbaceous, rarely suffrutescent, plants, with alternate or radical, rarely opposite, leaves, and inconspicuous flowers on scapes arising from the lower leaves. The rib-grass or rib-wort (*Plantāgo lanceolāta*), the root and leaves of which were formerly used in medicine as astringents, is a common type found all over Europe.

PLANTAIN (*Plantāgo major*), or **GREAT PLANTAIN.** A common weed, the leaves of which are all radical, oval, and petiolate, and have rising from amongst them several long cylindrical spikes of greenish

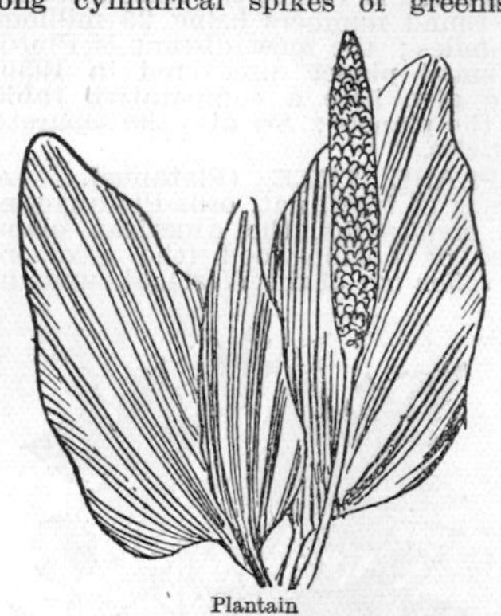

Plantain

inconspicuous flowers. The root and seed are still occasionally employed in the treatment of diarrhœa, dysentery, and external sores; the seeds are also collected for the food of birds.

PLAN'TAIN LILY. Genus of perennial herbs of the lily order (*Funkia*), of Japanese origin. The roots form a bundle of tubers from which emerge large oval or heart-shaped leaves, parallel-veined, sometimes white-striped. The flower-stems bear spikes of white or lilac bell-shaped flowers.

PLANTAIN, or PLANTAIN TREE. The type of the nat. ord. Musaceæ.

Musa paradisiăca, a native of the East Indies, is cultivated in almost all tropical countries. The stem is soft, herbaceous, 15 to 20 feet high, with leaves often more than 6 feet long and nearly 2 feet broad. The fruit grows in clusters, is about 1 inch in diameter, and 8 or 9 inches long. The stem dies down after fruiting; but the root-stock is perennial, and sends up numerous fresh shoots annually. It is easily propagated by suckers.

The banana (q.v.) is a closely allied variety or species. Their fruits are among the most useful in the vegetable kingdom, and form the entire sustenance of many of the inhabitants of tropical climates. A dwarf variety, *M. chinensis*, produces a fruit in European hot-houses. The fibres of the leaf-stalks of *M. textilis* of the Philippine Islands supplies Manila hemp or abaca, from which cordage of the strongest character is made, the finer fibres being used in making cloth.

PLANTAIN-EATERS. A group of perching birds, family Musophagidæ. The genus *Musophăga* of tropical Africa includes the most typical forms. These birds chiefly feed upon the fruit of the banana and plantain trees. The base of the bill appears as a broad plate covering the forehead. The plumage exhibits brilliant coloration. The members of the genus *Corythaix* or *Turacus* possess a bill of ordinary size and conformation, and feed on insects in addition to fruits.

PLANT-ANATOMY. The investigation of the internal structure of plants, carried out mainly by the microscopic examination of very thin sections cut in various planes across the organ it is desired to study. As a rule the material has to be previously hardened by preservation in alcohol, and the sections "stained" with aniline or other dyes in order to bring out the structure more clearly.

The facts discovered by the anatomical method are of the greatest interest both to the plant-physiologist and to the student of evolution; they have also a practical bearing on the identification of drugs, timbers, adulterations in food-stuffs, etc. *See* BOTANY.—BIBLIOGRAPHY: G. F. Scott Elliot, *First Lessons in Practical Botany*; F. O. Bower and D. T. Gwynne Vaughan, *Practical Botany for Beginners*; G. Haberlandt, *Physiological Plant-anatomy*.

PLANTATION. A term formerly used to designate a colony. The term was applied to an estate or tract of land in the Southern States of America, the West Indies, etc., cultivated chiefly by negroes or other non-European labourers, and the general term *plantation* is used throughout Malaya, Oceania, India, and Africa, etc., to cultivated areas, confined principally to tea, palm, rubber, cotton, sugar, tobacco, and rice.

PLANT-BREEDING, as a science, is a comparatively recent development, though agriculturists, seedsmen, and gardeners have from the earliest times endeavoured to improve useful and ornamental plants by selecting the most promising varieties and strains. Institutes for scientific research in this branch of applied botany were established as long ago as 1886 in Sweden and Denmark, where their work has effected a remarkable improvement in the principal crops. England, Scotland, and Wales now each possess a recognised plant-breeding station, and similar institutions are to be found in many of our dominions and colonies, in most European countries, and in the United States.

PLANT ENZYMES. The nature and classification of enzymes in general have been dealt with under *Fermentation*. A few examples of their occurrence in plants may be given here. *Cytases* transform the hemi-celluloses of seeds into sugar. *Lipases* act on fatty oils, with formation of glycerine (a good food-material) and fatty acids; they are found especially in germinating oily seeds, such as castor-oil bean. *Proteases* decompose proteins into simpler compounds; an interesting occurrence of these is in carnivorous plants, such as Nepenthes and Drosera.

Among *glucoside-splitting enzymes* is the *emulsin* of bitter almonds, which breaks up amygdaline into glucose, prussic acid, and benzaldehyde. The above are all *hydrolysing* enzymes, which break down complex substances by introducing molecules of water, and play an essential part in the activities of every living cell. *Zymase* of yeast, which effects the alcoholic fermentation of sugar, is an example of a *fermenting* enzyme. *Oxidising* enzymes are widely distributed in plants, the browning of a cut apple being a familiar example of their action.

PLANTIGRA'DA, or **PLANTIGRADES.** Carnivorous animals in which the whole or nearly the whole sole of the foot is applied to the ground in walking. This section includes the bears, raccoons, coatis, and badgers. Carnivora which, like the weasels and civets, use only part of the sole in walking, are termed *semi-plantigrada.*

PLANT-PATHOLOGY. The study of disease in plants, one of the most important of the practical aspects of botanical science. All civilised countries now maintain large staffs of experts and elaborately equipped stations for research on diseases of economic plants, especially on those due to fungoid and bacterial parasites, which cause enormous material loss, largely preventable by the application of appropriate remedial measures.—BIBLIOGRAPHY: Marshall Ward, *Diseases of Plants*; G. Massee, *Textbook of Plant-diseases.*

PLANT-PHYSIOLOGY. The branch of botany which deals with the vital activity of plants, i.e. with the structure and properties of their living substance or protoplasm, and with the various "functions," such as the intake and output of water, carbon assimilation and nutrition generally, respiration, growth, movement, etc. *See* BOTANY.—BIBLIOGRAPHY: Reynolds Green, *Vegetable Physiology*; L. Jost, *Lectures on the Physiology of Plants.*

PLANT-SYMBOLISM. In ancient Egypt certain marsh plants and other curative herbs were supposed to have had origin from the tears of beneficent deities, and certain poisonous plants from the tears of evil demons. It was thus believed that the active principle of the curative or poisonous herb was the "life substance" of a supernatural being.

Celtic curative herbs were originally connected with deities. The dandelion is still "the plant of Bride" (Brigit). Some plants, like "St. John's Wort" (St. Columba's herb), were taken over by early missionaries, while the metrical plant-charms were given a Christian significance, and plants were blessed "in the name of the Father, Son, and Holy Ghost." Herbs were gathered with ceremony. When the wild hyacinth, called in Gaelic *lus an tàlaidh* ("the enticing plant," i.e. love-causing plant), was sought for, one had to face the south and draw the plant out of the ground immediately before sunrise. The mugwort (a species of Artemisia) was a plant which "Christ had among strangers;" it protected and strengthened travellers and cured women's diseases. Other plants protected individuals and houses against witchcraft, the evil eye, etc.

There are many links between the herb-lore of Britain and that of the Continent. In Greece the mug-wort was connected with the goddess Artemis. Dr. Rendel Harris, in his *Ascent of Olympus*, has shown that the goddess was not only the giver of the plant but a personification, in one of her aspects, of the plant itself.

Mistletoe was regarded as an "all heal." It was used in religious ceremonies in Europe, and across Asia as far as east Kamchatka. In Gaelic lore the parasitic plant is regarded as the "king," because it "holds captive . . . all tough trees." Ivy, which was sacred, had a similar reputation, and was carved on aniconic pillars in Europe and Asia, while witch doctors made use of it for medicinal purposes. Ivy-clad pillars were gods in Siberia, as in Greece.

The mandrake was a love-plant, and one used to cure women's diseases in Asia and Europe. In China it is called *ginseng*, and the Chinese import it from Korea. The Greeks connected it with their love-goddess Aphrodite. It was supposed that the mandrake shrieked when pulled out of the ground. A dog was prompted to pull it, and the animal died immediately afterwards. The Homeric "moly," the "charmed herb" given by the god Hermes to Odysseus to protect him against the spells of Circe, is believed to be the mandrake.

In Northern Europe the place of the mandrake was taken by the apple, which was also a love-enticer and a fruit of longevity. Mandrake lore was attached likewise to rowan berries, which "make evil charms of no avail," as does the Homeric moly.

> Rowan, ash and red thread (thread)
> Gar the witches tyne their speed.

The custom of adorning walls with holly, ivy, and mistletoe at Christmas survives from the time when houses were charmed against attack by supernatural beings and witches.

PLASEN'CIA. A walled city in Spain, Estremadura, almost surrounded by the River Yerte, 120 miles W.S.W. of Madrid. Its cathedral, episcopal palace, and ruined towers are the chief objects of interest. Pop. 9500.

PLASMA. A green variety of chalcedony, which, especially in ancient times, was used for ornamental purposes.

PLASMODIOPHORA. *See* FINGERS-AND-TOES.

PLASSEY. A village in Bengal, on the Bhagirathi. Here, on 23rd June, 1757, Colonel, afterwards Lord Clive, with 900 Europeans and 2100 sepoys, defeated Suraj-ud-Dowlah with an army consisting of 50,000 foot and 18,000 horse, and laid the foundation of the British Empire in India.

PLASTERING. The art of covering the surface of masonry or woodwork with a plastic material in order to give it a smooth and uniform surface, and generally in interiors to fit it for painting or decoration.

In plastering the interior of houses the first coat is generally of lime, thoroughly slacked, so as to be free from any tendency to absorb moisture, and mixed with sand and cow's hair. For the purpose of receiving this coat the wall is generally first covered with laths or thin strips of wood, with narrow interstices between.

The face of the first coat, which should be of considerable thickness, is trowelled, or indented with cross-lines by the trowel, to form a key for the finishing coats. The second coat is applied to this when it is thoroughly dried. It is rubbed in with a flat board so as thoroughly to fill the indentations and cover the unequal surface of the first coat with a smooth and even one. In plastering walls great care must be taken to have the surface perfectly vertical. The setting coat, which is of pure lime, or for mouldings or finer work of plaster of Paris or stucco, is applied to the second coat before it is quite dry. A thin coating of plaster of Paris is frequently applied to ceilings after the setting coat.

PLASTER OF PARIS. The name given to gypsum (q.v.) when calcined at about 400° F. and ground. It is used for taking casts, for decorative mouldings, and in some parts of the European continent for flooring, where it is treated after laying with zinc and iron sulphates. If one part of powdered gypsum be mixed with two and a half parts of water, a thin pulp is formed, which after a time sets to a hard, compact mass. By adding a small quantity of lime to the moistened gypsum, a very hard marble-like substance is obtained on setting.

PLASTERS. Sticky, adhesive applications which are chiefly used to give mechanical support, to protect cuts and abrasions, or to fix dressings, but which may be impregnated with some medicinal substance to produce a local reaction on the skin, e.g. belladonna, cantharides, etc. The basis of most plasters is lead, isinglass, or resin, and plasters of the latter two stick more firmly than the older lead plaster. Plasters are always applied spread on a cloth.

PLASTIC CLAY. In geology, a name given to one of the lower beds of the Eocene system in France and England, from its being used in the manufacture of pottery. It is a marine deposit.

PLATA, RIO DE LA (River of Silver), or **RIVER PLATE.** Runs for more than 200 miles between the Argentine Republic and Uruguay, and is not, strictly speaking, a river, but rather an estuary, formed by the junction of the Rivers Paraná and Uruguay. It flows into the Atlantic between Cape St. Antonio and Cape St. Mary, at which point it is 170 miles wide. On its banks are the cities and ports of Montevideo and Buenos Aires. Navigation is hampered in some parts of the river by shallow water and sandbanks. It was discovered in 1515 by Juan Diaz de Solis, and called Rio de Solis; it owes its present name to the navigator Cabot.

PLATÆ'A. A city of ancient Greece, in Bœotia, now wholly in ruins. It has a permanent place in history on account of the great battle which was fought in its vicinity in Sept., 479 B.C., when 100,000 Greeks under Pausanias of Sparta defeated about thrice that number of Persians under Mardonius.

PLATANIS'TA. A freshwater dolphin, differing chiefly from the true Delphinidæ in its blow-hole being a longitudinal instead of transverse fissure. It is represented by a single species (*P. gangetica*), which inhabits the estuary of the Ganges. An allied form (*Inia geoffrensis*) inhabits the Amazon.

PLAT'ANUS. *See* PLANE TREE.

PLATE. The term generally applied to products of the gold- and silversmith's art other than coins or articles of personal ornament. That the art of working in gold was early known is proved by the discovery at Stonehenge of a sword of the Bronze Age (now in the Devizes Museum), in which the hilt is adorned with marvellously minute and elaborate work in that metal. Gold was, in early times, more generally in use than silver, the latter metal being less often found in a pure state, and also being more difficult to work.

The Biblical account of the construction and adornment of Solomon's temple furnishes details of elaborate sacred plate, and the Homeric heroes carried shields and armour made of gold and richly worked. Greek knowledge of the goldsmith's art, as also the supply of precious metal, was drawn from the East. Phidias and the somewhat later craftsman

Mentor may be named as prominent Greek artists of this class.

The Romans, though not themselves excelling as artists, had the power and wealth to command the services of Grecian workers. In 1868 a quantity of splendid Roman plate, dating from the first to the fourth centuries of our era, and including silver dishes, stew-pans, cups, vases, etc., was discovered at Hildesheim, in Hanover; while under the imperial rule articles of household luxury were often of great size and value, silver centre-dishes weighing 500 lb. being seen upon the tables of the rich.

Byzantine art of this class was in a flourishing condition from the fourth to the eleventh centuries. About the latter date a great revival in metal-working swept over Western Europe, including Britain. Such abbeys as those of Tours, in France, and Ely, in England, became centres of plate-production, the workers being at once artists and craftsmen. Monastic and church architecture suggested many favourite designs, diversified by the introduction of monstrous and supernatural figures. Of monastic production was probably the beautiful twelfth-century candlestick of silver alloy made in Gloucester and now at South Kensington.

By the thirteenth century goldsmiths' guilds began to appear, plate became secular rather than religious in its origin, as well as in its character and use, and it assumed a prominent place upon the tables of the wealthy and noble. The salt-cellar, forming a dividing-point between the family and guests above, and the menials and dependents below, offered a field for decoration, as did the central *nef*, a model ship on wheels, laden with spices or comfits.

In the fourteenth and fifteenth centuries connoisseurs secured possession of the productions of the della Robbia and of the Arditi of Florence; still later of that unsurpassed blend of artist and scoundrel, Benvenuto Cellini. To vie with these masters of the south, Northern Europe offered the work of Augsburg and Nürnberg. Henry VIII. possessed a fine display of plate, nor did Holbein disdain to design gold cups.

In Britain, during recent times, the artist rarely executes his own conceptions, leaving the actual craftsmanship to a merely faithful mechanic; perhaps as a consequence of this division of the art, the nineteenth century can show but little better plate than that seen in race-cups and similar trophies.

Among the truest taste surviving is that found in the East, where Kashmir and Benares, with other Indian cities, still produce some really high-class work. For *Hall-marks* on plate, see separate heading. — BIBLIOGRAPHY: Benvenuto Cellini, *Treatises on Goldsmithing and Sculpture* (Ashbee's translation, 1898); J. H. Pollen, *Gold and Silversmith's Work* (1875); Henry Wilson, *Silver Work and Jewellery* (1903); also works by J. W. Caldecott and W. J. Cripps.

PLATEAU. In physical geography, one of the positive land forms. *See* GEOGRAPHY.

PLATE RIVER. *See* PLATA.

PLATING. This consists of covering the surface of one metal with another metal, generally with the object of affording greater protection from attack by noxious gases or other corroding agencies. The process was formerly largely used to supply a surface of precious metal, such as silver or gold, on to a base of an inferior metal, such as copper or German silver. The process consisted in fusing a slab of silver on to one or both sides of the base metal, and afterwards rolling down the compound slab into sheets of suitable thickness. Since the introduction of electro-plating methods, this process has largely fallen into disuse, although it is still used to some extent for covering steel with copper and for similar purposes. *See* ELECTRO-PLATING; GALVANISED IRON.

PLAT'INUM. One of the metals occurring in the mineral *native platinum.* This occurs mostly in small irregular grains, generally contains a little iron, and in addition iridium, osmium, rhodium, palladium, ruthenium (hence called the "platinum metals"), and also sometimes copper, chromium, and titanium. It was first obtained in Peru, and has since been found in various other localities, such as Canada, Oregon, the West Indies, Brazil, Colombia, Borneo, etc., but the chief supply of platinum comes from the Ural Mountains. Platinum was there discovered in beds of auriferous sands in 1823, and has been worked by the Russian Government since 1828.

Properties. Pure platinum is almost as white as silver, takes a brilliant polish, and is highly ductile and malleable. It is the heaviest of the ordinary metals, and the least expansive when heated; specific gravity, 21·53 rolled, 21·15 cast. It undergoes no change from the combined agency of air and moisture, and it may be exposed to the strongest heat of a smith's forge without suffering either oxidation or fusion. It fuses in the flame of the oxyhydrogen blowpipe at a temperature of 1710° C., and may readily be welded at a red heat. Platinum is not attacked by any of the pure acids. Its only solvents are chlorine and nitro-hydrochloric acid (*aqua regia*), which act upon it with greater difficulty than on gold.

In a finely divided state (spongy platinum and platinum black) it has the power of absorbing and condensing large quantities of gases, and in this form is also largely used as a catalytic agent, causing certain chemical reactions to take place without apparently taking part in them. On account of its great infusibility, and its power generally of withstanding the action of chemical reagents, platinum is much used as a material for making vessels to be used in the chemical laboratory. Crucibles, evaporating dishes, etc., are very often made of platinum. The salts of readily reducible metals, such as silver, lead, tin, etc.; solid alkalis, especially baryta; or oxidising agents such as nitre, should not be fused in platinum vessels. It is also used to a certain extent as a setting for jewels.

Alloys. The useful alloys of platinum are not numerous. With silver it forms a tolerably fusible white alloy, malleable and brilliant when polished, used by dentists and commonly known as dental alloy. Gold, at a forge heat, alloys with platinum in all proportions. Alloyed with iridium (a rare metal of the same group) it possesses an excellent and unalterable surface for fine engraving, as in the scales of astronomical instruments, etc. This alloy has also been adopted for the construction of international standards of length and weight. Mercury, by trituration with spongy platinum, forms an amalgam at first soft, but it soon becomes firm, and has been much used in obtaining malleable platinum.

A coating of platinum can be given to copper and other metals by applying to them an amalgam of spongy platinum and 5 parts of mercury; the latter metal is then volatilised by heat. Lead combines with platinum readily; and iron and copper in like manner. The last-mentioned, when added in the proportion of 7 parts to 16 parts of platinum and 1 part of zinc, and fused in a crucible under charcoal powder, forms the alloy called artificial gold. An alloy of platinum, iridium, and rhodium is used for making crucibles, etc. It is harder than pure platinum, is less easily attacked by chemical reagents, and not so readily fusible. Platinum wires, in conjunction with wires of platinum alloy containing 10 per cent of rhodium or iridium, are largely used for the hot junctions of thermo-electric pyrometers.

PLATO. Ancient Greek philosopher, and the founder of one of the great schools of Greek philosophy, born at Athens, or near it on the Island of Ægina, in 429 B.C. (87th Olympiad, on the seventh day of the month Thargelion), and died in 347. He belonged to an aristocratic family, and hence, perhaps, his contempt for democracy. His father, Ariston, is said to have been a descendant of Codrus, and his mother, Perictione, a relation of Solon.

He received a liberal education, obtained prizes at the Olympic and Isthmian games, and studied philosophy under Cratylus, a disciple of

Plato

Heraclitus, who had maintained that all things are in a state of flux, a teaching which he never forgot. He also studied music, painting, and poetry, and was preparing a tetralogy for the theatre when, about his twentieth year, he came under the influence of Socrates.

The result was that he threw his dramatic manuscripts into the fire and henceforth devoted himself to philosophy. His own name was Aristocles, and it was Socrates who called him Plato on account of his wide forehead and broad shoulders. For ten years, until the death of Socrates (399 B.C.), he was a constant and favourite pupil of the latter.

After the death of Socrates, Plato is supposed to have left Athens with a view to improving his mind by travel. He is said to have retired first to Megara, in company with Euclid and the majority of the Socratic philosophers, and then to have visited Cyrene, where he studied under Theodorus, the mathematician. He visited the courts of Dionysius the Elder and of Dionysius the Younger in Sicily, and is also said to have travelled in Egypt. About 389 or 388 B.C. he returned to Athens, and began to teach his philosophical system in a gymnasium known as the Academy. He had a patrimony sufficient for his wants, and taught without remuneration.

Works. The reputed works of Plato consist of dialogues and letters, but the latter are now regarded as spurious. The genuineness of most of the dialogues is generally admitted, although their chronology is a matter of uncertainty. The first attempt at a critical classification was made by Schleiermacher, who adopted an arrangement into three divisions, according to the leading doctrines he believed they were intended to teach.

The chief works in the first section are: *Phædrus, Protagoras, Parmenides, Lysis, Laches, Charmides,* and *Euthyphron*; in the second, *Theætetus, Sophistes, Politicus, Phædo, Philebus, Gorgias, Meno, Euthydemus, Cratylus,* and *Symposium*; in the third, the *Republic, Timæus, Critias,* and the *Leges* or *Laws.* Hermann attempted to make out a chronological arrangement, and other scholars, especially Lutoslawski, have attempted various theories of constructive arrangement. These schemes in general proceed on the assumption that each dialogue, being an artistic whole, forms a link in a chain. Grote and others, however, do not admit that Plato followed any plan, either artistic or didactic.

Apart from their philosophical teaching, the dialogues of Plato are admirable as works of literature, especially for their dramatic truthfulness, and exhibit Greek prose in its highest perfection. In all of them Socrates (idealised) appears as one of the speakers. They contain also lively and accurate accounts of previous systems of Greek philosophy and their teachers, introduced not merely for historical purpose, but incidentally to the analysis of their opinions.

Plato's Philosophy. The philosophy of Plato is one of the grandest efforts ever made by the human mind to compass the problem of life. The great aim of philosophical teaching was, according to Plato, that of leading the mind of the inquirer to the discovery of truth rather than that of imparting it dogmatically. Oral teaching was therefore superior to writing. This accounts for the conversational form given to most of Plato's works. He originated the division of philosophy into the three branches of ethics, physics, and dialectics, though these names were first applied by his disciple Xenocrates.

We have said that Plato had never forgotten the teaching of Heraclitus, that everything is in a state of flux. From Socrates, however, he had learned the importance of universals, and he came to the conclusion that existence supposes superior principles of unity and perfection. Above eternally changing, imperfect sensible things there must be a stable reality. In the eternal reality of things there must be a principle which contains in a superior form all the perfections which are so imperfectly realised in man or animal.

Like Socrates, Plato employed the dialectical method, and by means of dialectics he rose to first principles, exact definitions, essentials, and universals, from which he judged particular cases. Like Socrates, he attached importance to the study of the inner man, and endeavoured to form general ideas under the form of definitions.

The Theory of Ideas. The cardinal principle of Plato's dialectical system is the doctrine of ideas, but his method of developing his principles has left some room for doubt or misunderstanding as to what this doctrine really was. Differences upon the subject began early, and different opinions are still expressed by critics. This doctrine, however, so pervades the entire system of Platonic dialectics, ethics, and physics, of all of which it is the fertilising or creative principle, that if we give a due attention to its place in each, we can hardly miss a substantially accurate conception of it. From a comparison of various statements which Plato has made respecting ideas, a theory of them may be traced in relation to the various parts of his system.

Respecting the historical origin of the doctrine of ideas, Aristotle has left an interesting statement, which renders it probable that it was during the lifetime of Socrates that it was first conceived. Plato, he says, derived from Cratylus, the Heraclitean, the doctrine that the sensuous is subject to perpetual change. This he ever afterwards maintained, and when he learned from Socrates of conceptions, which, when once rightly defined, remain for ever invariable, he believed that their counterparts must not be sought in the sensuous world, but that there must be other existences, which were the objects of conceptual cognition, and these objects he named *ideas.* Euclid of Megara has also been credited with exercising a considerable influence on the development of his views.

The philosophical genesis of the doctrine of ideas is not uncertain. It was in the human mind and in the analysis of its conceptions that Plato found it. The word had been used before his time, and has been used since, to signify the mental image by which an object of sense is reproduced in the mind. This is not Plato's idea. Such an image is merely the concrete conception. Plato's idea is derived from an analysis of conception. It represents, as indicated in the passage in Aristotle above referred to, the immutable element in conception.

Here, however, a misunderstanding is apt to arise from the terms employed in modern philosophy. It is common now to analyse conception or cognition into two elements, the universal or invariable, and the particular or variable; the former is the ego, or subject considered apart from the matter or object of cognition. This distinction is not that of the Platonic analysis.

It is not the relation of the mind to the conception, but the particular conception itself, whether in or out of the mind, that is the subject of it. In this conception, in each such conception, Plato finds an immutable element which he calls its idea. This he illustrates in many ways, and in regard to a great variety of subjects. That which forms, perhaps, the basis on which the Platonic structure has been reared, and which best serves to illustrate its distinctive principle, is the case of opposite or contrasted conceptions. In the statement that Simmias is large in comparison with Socrates, but small in comparison with Phædo, we appear to view largeness and smallness as purely relative conceptions, since in the one case we predicate the one, and in the other case the other of the same individual.

But when we subject these conceptions to the scrutiny of reason, we find that they cannot be wholly relative. The comparative implies the positive, for unless there were something absolute and immutable in the conception of largeness, it could not be compared with smallness or anything else. If the conception were transient in the individual mind, the comparison would be transient also, and an object which was conceived of at one time as relatively large in comparison with another, might be conceived of at another as relatively small in comparison with the same object; or if the conception varied in different minds, the ground of the comparison would vary in like manner.

But largeness is always conceived of as bearing the same relation to smallness, and we mean the same thing in the above comparison when we say that Simmias is larger than Socrates, as when we say that Phædo is larger than Simmias. There must therefore be something positive in the conceptions both of largeness and smallness to allow of their being thus constantly opposed; but this cannot be the particular amount of largeness contained in Simmias, seeing he is large in the one case and small in the other. Hence Plato distinguishes between the concrete quality as conceived to exist in an object, and the *idea* of the quality. The former is *mutable*, the latter *immutable*; but the quality always partakes of the idea, otherwise it would cease to exist.

Plato is thus the founder of objective idealism, i.e. of that system and conception of life which seeks the highest values not in sensible empirical reality, but in the ideals, the prototypes of perfect forms of imperfect and eternally changing reality. Whilst agreeing with the Eleatics that reality does not change (for ideas are immutable), he admits with Heraclitus that there is change in the world of experience or of phenomena. Such is the basis of the Platonic sphere of ideas.

True science, according to Plato, has to do with those material forms and imperfect intelligences which we encounter in our daily intercourse with men; but it investigates the nature of those purer and more perfect patterns which were the models after which all created beings were formed. These perfect types he supposes to have existed from all eternity, and he calls them the *ideas* of the great original Intelligence. As these cannot be perceived by the human senses, whatever knowledge we derive from that source is unsatisfactory and uncertain. Plato, therefore, maintains that degree of scepticism which denies all permanent authority to the evidence of sense.

Having discovered or created the realm of ideas, he surveyed it throughout. He defined its most excellent forms as beauty, justice, and virtue, and having done so, he determined what was the supreme and dominant principle of the whole. It is the idea of the Good. The harmony of intelligence throughout its entire extent with goodness is, perhaps, the highest attainment of Plato's philosophy. His objective idealism differs to this extent from the theories of modern idealists, Kant, for instance, in so far as he allegorises his ideas, gives them life and creative power, and seats them on thrones in places beyond the vault of heaven.

Ethics. The ethical system of Plato was in direct dependence upon his dialectics, and will require little illustration. He believed that the ideas of all existing things were originally contained in God. These ideas were each the perfection of its kind, and as such were viewed by God with approval and love. God, Himself being infinitely good, was the object of all imitation to intelligent beings, hence the ethics of Plato had a double foundation, the imitation of God and the realisation of ideas, which were in each particular the models of perfection.

Cosmogony. Plato's cosmical theories stood professedly on a different foundation from his dialectics and ethics. Matter did not come within the scope of his dialectical analysis. He had accepted a preconceived view of it which excluded it from dialectical treatment; consequently it had no place in his world of ideas and no relation with God, upon whom they depended. He consequently gave it an existence independent of God as a formless, passive, inert mass without qualities or conditions. To his cosmical theories he attributed only probability, holding that the dialectical method, by which alone truth could be discovered, was applicable only to ideas and the discovery of moral principles.

The most valuable part of Plato's cosmogony is its first principle, that God, who is without envy, planned all things that they should be as nearly as possible like Himself. He first made the soul of the world, which, being intermediate between the sensible and the intellectual, forms a connecting-link between them. It is formed of two opposite principles, the one indivisible and immutable, the other mutable and divisible, and these are combined by an intermediate principle. To this soul He joined the material body. All things were created according to ideas, which were the perfection of each kind. Thus every individual in a species, for example, partakes of the idea of the species, but the individual is always inferior to the ideal.

The soul of man, like the soul of the world, consists of three parts or elements. Plato attributes to it not only immortality but pre-existence. Sometimes this is predicated of the whole, sometimes only of the superior part. To the highest part of the soul, which has the head as its seat, he gives the cogitative powers and the desires appropriate to them; the intermediate part of the soul, having its seat in the heart, is distinguished by active impulses; the third part, with its seat in the bowels, by animal affections.

Virtue, which is essentially one, has three distinct phases, corresponding to the threefold division of the soul. The virtue of the highest is wisdom, of the second courage, of the third temperance. The emotional part of the soul should govern the sensual, and be under the government of the intellectual. Sexual love, separated from concupiscence, he regarded as a link between the sensual and the intellectual, and as consisting in an aspiration and perpetual striving after the immortal and eternal.

Politics. Plato's political treatises are the application of his ethical principles to social organisation. In his *Republic* he does this without any regard to the practical, his object apparently being to sketch the ideal of a state which should serve as an abstract model of the things to be aimed at in social organisation rather than to show how any particular object can be practically accomplished. The book of *Laws* is a sort of compromise between the speculative ideas of Plato and the actual state of society.

He bases his *Republic* on the principle that the constitution of the state should correspond with that of the individual in order to allow the moral nature of the individual due scope for development. As he makes three parts of the soul, so he divides the state into three classes, the magisterial, the military, and the working, the last of which, like the sensuous part of the soul is to be in complete subordination to the other two. The magisterial class is selected from among the middle-class, the youth of which are to be carefully trained in science and virtue.

The details are worked out into a multitude of arrangements, many of which are arbitrary, tyrannical, or impracticable. All art is excluded which does not consist in the imitation of the Good. Women receive the same education as men, and partake in their gymnastic exercises. Marriage and the intercourse of the sexes are the subject of very arbitrary and curious regulations.

Of the three forms of government, monarchical, aristocratic, and democratic, he classes the first as best, the last as worst. The true king will always govern better than the law, for he will take account of particular cases and circumstances. As his knowledge of these is limited, the law is good as supplying particular principles, but it should depend ultimately on the king. Laws consecrated by custom should be considered inviolable.

But space will not permit us to give any adequate account of Plato's political theories, which are a mixture of things, good, bad, and indifferent, borrowed from all the various forms of government and social organisation, from theocracy to democracy, with original speculations, excellent in intention, but often arbitrary and chimerical, which have nevertheless been the fruitful source of subsequent speculations.

Plato was of an idealistic and even religious nature. He constantly rose above experience, and yearned for the realm of ideals, that world of light where "pure forms dwell." It is the realm of the True, the Good, and the Beautiful. A Rationalist in his theory of knowledge, maintaining that truth can only be obtained by reason and intelligence, he was a dualist in psychology and eudemonistic, or rather hedonistic, in his ethics. His doctrines exercised a considerable influence on Aristotle and the Stoics, on Cicero, and on Plutarch, and prepared the way for Neo-Platonism. The influence of Platonism made itself again felt during the Renaissance, and it may be said to be increasing to-day.

A Latin translation of Plato's works was made by Marsilius Ficinus in 1483-4, and the first edition of the text by Aldus appeared in 1513. Modern editions are those of Immanuel Bekker (1816-23) and J. Burnett (1902). Complete English translations are those of Sydenham and Taylor (1804) and Jowett (1871-92).—BIBLIOGRAPHY: Th. Gomperz, *Greek Thinkers*; G. Grote, *Plato and the other Companions of Socrates*; Walter Pater, *Plato and Platonism*; A. E. Taylor, *Plato*; J. A. Stewart, *Plato's Doctrine of Ideas*; W. Lutoslawski, *Origin and Growth of Plato's Logic*; D. G. Ritchie, *Plato*; A. Fouillée, *La Philosophie de Platon.*

PLATOON. From the French *peloton*, a group or detachment of soldiers. The word was formerly in use in the British army to describe a sub-division of a company, and was then for a long period supplanted by the word section, meaning the fourth part of an infantry company consisting of 100 men. Early in 1914, when the British infantry organisation was altered to provide battalions of four large (or double) companies, the word was reintroduced to describe the main divisions of these companies.

Thus "platoon" in these days means the fourth part of a company. Each platoon is commanded by a junior officer, and has a sergeant as second in command, with the title of platoon sergeant; it is again subdivided into four sections, commanded by junior non-commissioned officers; the normal strength of a section for administrative purposes is ten, of whom no more than six will be taken into action on any given occasion.

The platoon is an important link in the chain of responsibility, and the "platoon spirit" is encouraged by every possible means. The platoon commander is responsible to his immediate superior—the company commander—for the entire training and well-being of his command, and the men of his platoon are encouraged to look to him for help and assistance, both in military and personal matters. *See* ARMY; FIRE-TACTICS; INFANTRY.

PLATTE (plat), or **NEBRASKA.** A river of Nebraska, United States, formed by the union of the North and South Forks of the Platte, which rise in the Rockies, in the state of Colorado. The united stream falls into the Missouri after a course of about 210 miles. The North Platte has a length of 650 miles, and the South Platte 500 miles, prior to their union. All are entirely unnavigable.

PLATTSBURG. A city of New York, United States, the county seat of Clinton county, on Lake Champlain at the mouth of the Saranac River; served by the Delaware & Hudson Railway, and by lake-steamers. It has a harbour, and is a port of entry for the Champlain district. The town was founded in 1784, and became a city in 1902. Pop. 13,349.

PLATYCERIUM. A genus of tropical ferns, growing as epiphytes or on steep rock-faces. They have leaves of two kinds, viz., erect "mantle" or "bracket" leaves, which cling closely to the supporting surface and thus form humus-collecting niches, and pendulous structures, which bear the sporangia, besides performing the ordinary functions of leaves; the latter are forked and bear some resemblance to the antlers of a stag, hence the popular name stag-horn ferns. *P. alcicorne* and *P. grande* are commonly grown in hot-houses.

PLATYHELMIA ("flat-worms"). A phylum of unsegmented flattened worms, comprising Turbellaria, Trematoda (flukes), and Cestoda (tapeworms).

PLATYPUS. *See* DUCK-BILLED PLATYPUS.

PLAUEN. A manufacturing town and railway junction of Saxony, on the Elster. It is a great centre of the German cotton manufacture (Plauen goods), and also produces machinery, paper, leather, and all kinds of embroidered goods. Plauen is first mentioned in history in 1122. Pop. (1925), 111,436.

PLAUTUS, Titus Maccius. Roman comic dramatist. Born at the

Umbrian village of Sarsina about 254 B.C., and died in 184 B.C. He probably came to Rome at an early age, though it is doubtful whether he ever became a full Roman citizen. He first of all obtained some kind of work in a theatre, though it is not clear whether he was a dresser, a scene-shifter, or a stage-carpenter. Whatever was the nature of his employment, it gave him a great insight into stage devices, and was of the greatest value to him when he commenced dramatist. With his earnings from the theatre Plautus went into some business, but lost all his money, and was forced to enter the service of a baker, who employed him in grinding with a hand-mill.

While thus engaged he wrote three plays, the sale of which enabled him to leave the baker and devote himself to writing comedies. He was then probably about thirty years of age, and continued to write until his death at the age of seventy. In the time of Varro (116-28 B.C.) one hundred and thirty plays were attributed to Plautus. Varro went carefully into the authenticity of these plays, and decided that only twenty-one were really by Plautus. All of these twenty-one plays, except the *Vidularia*, have been preserved.

The names of the extant comedies of Plautus are : *Amphitruo*, *Asinaria*, *Aulularia*, *Captivi*, *Curculio*, *Casina*, *Cistellaria*, *Epidicus*, *Bacchides*, *Mostellaria*, *Menæchmi*, *Miles Gloriosus*, *Mercator*, *Pseudolus*, *Pœnulus*, *Persa*, *Rudens*, *Stichus*, *Trinummus*, and *Truculentus*. These comedies are all adaptations from Greek originals, but Plautus has adapted so skilfully that most of his plays read like original works. On closer examination, however, there appears a curious blending of Greek and Roman customs in his plays, which makes them hardly less unreal than Addison's Romans with wigs and swords.

In spite of this and of their stock characters and conventional situations, almost all of the plays of Plautus are excellent, while some are superlatively good. The *Amphitruo* is a mythological burlesque of the best quality, and introduces the beautifully drawn character of Alcmena. The nemesis of the jester has overtaken some of the work of Plautus, and when he is serious he is sometimes not taken seriously by his commentators. This play has been imitated but not bettered by Molière, as has the *Aulularia*, which suggested *L'Avare* to the later and greater poet.

The *Captivi* is the noblest of all the plays. Lessing, with Teutonic thoroughness, "repeatedly read it with the view of discovering some fault in it," but was obliged to confess it was perfect. The *Trinummus* is also a fine play, and the *Menæchmi* is a roaring farce, which Shakespeare imitated in *The Comedy of Errors*. Shakespeare did not improve the play by duplicating the pairs of twins.

The *Rudens* stands alone as a romantic comedy ; it breathes something of the spirit of *The Tempest* or *The Winter's Tale*, and is a most attractive play. The *Bacchides*, *Mostellaria*, *Pseudolus*, and *Miles Gloriosus* are all good plays ; the last-named gave to the stage one of its favourite stock characters, seen to perfection in Shakespeare's Parolles and Jonson's Bobadil. The remaining plays, with the exception of the *Stichus*, are not so interesting, and depend too much upon a series of highly complicated intrigues.

Plautus enjoyed a great reputation during his lifetime, and for many years after his death. Ælius Stilo said that if the Muses wished to speak in Latin they would speak with the language of Plautus (Quintilian, x., i., 99). After the Revival of Learning, Plautus took rank as one of the greatest dramatists of antiquity. His reputation was greater than it would have been had Aristophanes been better known. His influence on comedy was immense, and is noticeable in the works of Shakespeare and Jonson, as well as in the efforts of the youngest tyro who wrote a play to be acted in his college. His influence extended throughout all Europe ; it was quite as strong as the influence of Seneca upon tragedy, and was very much more wholesome.

Plautus is indeed a great laughter-maker ; he employs every device for amusing his audience—farcical situations, caricature, repartee, caustic humour, and puns of the basest kind. In his opulence of humour, his never-failing animal spirits, and his laugh "broad as ten thousand beeves at pasture" Plautus resembles Shakespeare. In their lives they were not dissimilar. They were both wise rather than learned, both educated by life itself, not by books or universities. They both had a connection with the stage before they began to write for it. Julius Cæsar once deviated into verse and called Terence "a halved Menander." It is at least equally true to say that Plautus is a halved Shakespeare. He is that half of Shakespeare which is of the earth, earthy.—BIBLIOGRAPHY : W. Y. Sellar, *Roman Poets of the Republic* ; W. M. Lindsay, *Plautus* (Oxford Texts) ; J. W. Duff, *Literary History of Rome* ; W. L. Collins, *Plautus and Terence*.

PLAYER-PIANO. Inventors gave their attention in early days to the

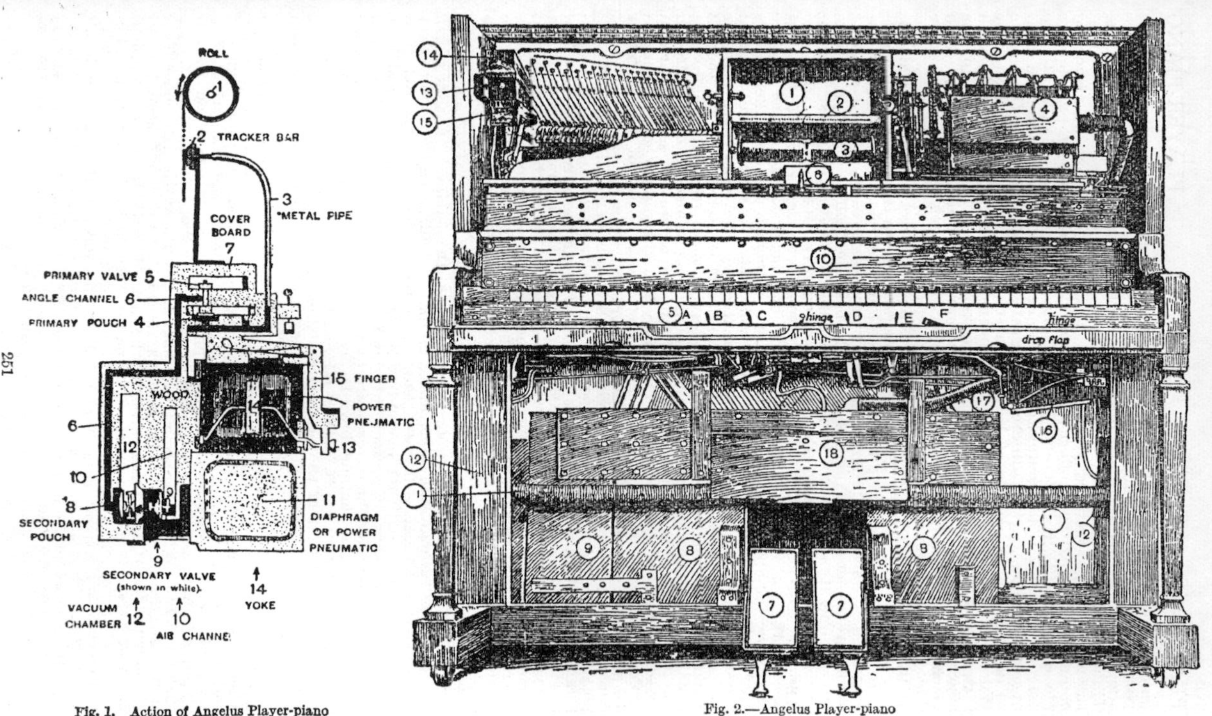

Fig. 1. Action of Angelus Player-piano

Fig. 2.—Angelus Player-piano

perfecting of mechanical means of playing musical instruments, and about a century ago the Paris firm of Thibouville, Lamy et Cie, produced the mechanically operated piano as a commercial article. The modern piano-player is essentially different, however, in that it is a pneumatically operated mechanism. It is interesting to note that E. H. White of Messrs. Wilcox & White of Connecticut, the inventor of both the built-in type and also the form having the operating mechanism in a separate case, produced his first combined instrument in 1895, and the first separate-player two years later.

In the early years of the twentieth century considerable progress was made in the design of pianos with internal operating gear, and this type seems now to be decidedly the more popular. The gear which is used to operate the notes is called the action. By its use the air-pressure allowed to operate through the perforations on the music-roll actuates the striking mechanism. The gear is held from striking by a vacuum created by the pedal-operated bellows. The instant the vacuum is broken the note in question is struck.

Construction. The details of such an action are shown in fig. 1, which depicts the mechanism of the Angelus player-piano. The music-roll (1), perforated in positions corresponding to the notes to be struck, passes over the tracker-bar (2), which is provided with a series of holes, one for each note of the piano. A metal pipe connects each of these openings to what is termed a primary pouch (4). If there is a hole over the opening on the tracker-bar corresponding to this note, the air will pass through the pipe, and, inflating this pouch, will raise the primary valve (5). This operation allows the atmospheric pressure, always operative under the cover-board (7), to act within the channel down to the secondary pouch (8), where a similar action to that of the primary valve takes place.

This secondary valve (9), when thrust forward by the action of the air-pouch (8), cuts off the normal air which is always present in the channel (10) and the diaphragm or power pneumatic (11), thus compelling the diaphragm to exhaust into the vacuum chambers (12). When this occurs, the diaphragm draws with it the lever or action wire (13), which passes through the yoke (14), and thus raises the finger (15), which throws up the ordinary piano-action from underneath, compelling the hammer to hit the wire. To make the diagram clear, the valves are only shown in a single row. In an actual player the valves are in two or more rows, and staggered to get them within the required space to coincide with each note of the piano.

The relationship of the associated mechanisms can be seen by reference to fig. 2. The pedals (7) operate two bellows or exhausters (8), and thus create a partial vacuum in the reserve chest (18). The chest is connected by means of the two tubes (11) with choker-valves (12), and so to the pneumatic actions behind (10), which have been previously described in reference to fig. 1.

The bass section of the piano is operated separately from the treble section, and this necessitates the use of two choker-valves. By separating the bass and treble sections, it is made possible to soften either section independently of the other. The two buttons, one for each of the two sections, below the keyboard (5A) are used to operate valves in the chokers which act to reduce the vacuum created by the exhauster. An air motor (4) is used to operate the roll receiving-spool through chain-drive and gearing. The air is drawn through the motor by way of a governor and tube into the main chest of the exhauster. The use of the governor ensures an even speed of the motor at all speeds of pedalling.

The bellows (14 and 15) are operated through the valve-box (13). The purpose of the bellows (14) is to raise the dampers of the piano-action, and thus give a sustaining effect; it is operated by means of a tube from the tracker-bar supplied with air through perforations in the roll. The other bellows (15) acts to raise the hammers towards the strings of the piano, giving an additional softening effect when required; it is operated from the lever (5B). The next lever fitment in front of the keyboard is the re-roll lever (5C), which when placed in the re-roll position causes the winding-gear to be reversed, so that the motor rewinds the roll on its spool. By means of this lever the operator can delete any part of a composition.

The tempo-lever (5D) works the pointer (6), which moves over a scale. It can be set to suit the statements of the tempo on the roll at any time. The phrasing-lever (5F) gives an instantaneous control of the tempo. A slight pressure on the left end effects a retard, a momentary hesitation in the act of striking, or a complete pause, just as the player thinks the music demands; whilst an equally slight pressure on the right end will accelerate the time to any degree required. Immediately the key is released the normal or basic time is resumed.

The melodant-lever controls the operation of a device for the purpose of giving expression. By its use the solo or theme is emphasised, while the accompaniment is kept soft and subdued. The single long holes at each end of the tracker-bar are used to operate this action, and the pipes from these holes are connected to the bass and treble chokers. The sustaining-pedal lever (5E) lifts the piano-action dampers off the strings to create sustained or singing tones.

The music-rolls are marked to show the principal changes required, the pianist being expected to make the many lesser ones as his feelings prompt him. The Artistyle rolls have all the changes concentrated into a single expression- and tempo-line. These rolls are edited by prominent musicians, and contain markings for all those subtle changes that make for artistic interpretation.

The Reproducing Player-piano. The most recent development in the player-piano, and one which will undoubtedly have considerable effect in the future, is the Reproducing Player-piano. This instrument, in addition to acting as the ordinary player-piano, is so constructed that when using the specially recorded music-rolls it gives a faithfully exact interpretation of the playing of the pianist who has actually recorded the roll. In the Artrio Angelus Reproducing Player-piano, an electric motor is usually incorporated, operating the exhausters by suitable connections, and so eliminating the use of the foot-pedals in the ordinary player.

We are indebted to Messrs. Sir Herbert Marshall & Sons, Ltd., of London, for information for the preparation of our description and illustrations.

PLAYFAIR, John. Scottish natural philosopher, geologist, and mathematician, born in Forfarshire 1748, died at Edinburgh 1819. Entering the University of St. Andrews at fourteen, he soon displayed a special talent for mathematics and natural philosophy. In 1785 he was chosen assistant professor of mathematics in the University of Edinburgh. In 1802 appeared his *Illustrations of the Huttonian Theory of the Earth*, and in the following year a *Biographical Account of Dr. James Hutton*. In 1805 he obtained the chair of natural philosophy in Edinburgh University. The Royal Society of London elected him a Fellow in 1807. He published *Elements of Geometry* and *Outlines of Natural Philosophy*, and contributed many valuable papers to the *Transactions* of the Royal Societies of Edinburgh and London, and to the *Edinburgh Review*.

Playfair's Axiom, which states that "two intersecting straight lines cannot both be parallel to a third straight line," is adopted in many modern editions of Euclid in place of the difficult twelfth axiom.

PLAYFAIR, Lyon, Baron. British scientist and politician. Born at Meerut, Bengal, in 1819, and died in 1898. He was educated at St. Andrews and Edinburgh Universities, and studied chemistry under Graham in Glasgow and London, and under Liebig at Giessen. His able reports on the sanitary condition of the large towns of Britain, and his valuable services as special commissioner at the London Exhibition of 1851, first brought him prominently before the public.

Baron Playfair

He became connected with the science and art department at its establishment in 1853, inspector-general of Government museums and schools of science in 1856, and was professor of chemistry at Edinburgh University from 1858 to 1869. He held several important offices under Liberal Governments, and was created a K.C.B. in 1883, and raised to the peerage in 1892.

Besides scientific memoirs, he published numerous papers on political, social, and educational subjects. Most of his economical essays were collected and published under the title *Subjects of Social Welfare*.

PLEADING. In law, the statement of a case, whether embodied in a written document (statement of claim or of defence) or maintained orally in debate. A plaintiff or pursuer must put in a written statement of the alleged facts on which he bases his claim. These allegations are then admitted or denied by the defendant either categorically or with qualifications, and he also sets forth the facts which he alleges in defence. The purpose of these proceedings is to bring the points at issue clearly before the parties and the court.

PLEASLEY. Village of Derbyshire and Nottinghamshire, 3 miles from Mansfield, on the River Meden. It is served by the L.M.S. and L.N.E. Railways. There are silk and cotton mills and coal mines in the vicinity. Pop. 2510.

PLEBEIANS (ple-bē'anz), or **PLEBS.** The whole government of ancient Rome, with the enjoyment of all its offices, belonged exclusively to the patricians, with whom the plebeians could not even intermarry. The civil history of Rome is to a great extent composed of the struggles of the plebeians to assert their claim to the place in the commonwealth to which their numbers and social importance entitled them.

The struggle lasted for more than 200 years. The establishment of the tribunes (494 B.C.), the law of the twelve tables (451-450 B.C.), the Lex Canuleia (445 B.C.), permitting intermarriages, the admission to the censorship (351 B.C.), to the prætorship (336 B.C.), and to the offices of pontifex and augur (300 B.C.), were the leading steps in a succession of victories which culminated (286 B.C.) in the Lex Hortensia, which gave the *plebescīta* of the people the force of law. From this time the privileges of the two classes may be said to have been equal.

PLEB'ISCITE (Lat. *plebs*, people, *scitum*, decree, from *scire*, to know). A term applied in the Roman Republic to the resolutions proposed by the tribunes of the people, and then adopted by the plebeians in the *comitia tributa*, i.e. assemblies by tribes. These laws were at first subject to the consent of the Senate, but after the expulsion of the decemvirs, by the laws Horatio et Valeria and Hortensia, plebiscites had at once force of law, and became binding on both plebeians and patricians.

In modern Europe a plebiscite is a vote of the electors of a state expressed on a question of public importance. In France the idea of plebiscites was revived during the Revolution of 1793. It was by plebiscite that Louis Napoleon was elected Prince-President of France in 1848, and emperor in 1852. Another example was the revision of the Constitution in May, 1870. After the European War the ownership of certain districts was decided by a plebiscite, the inhabitants indicating by a direct vote the nation by whom they would prefer to be governed. Examples are afforded by the Flensborg (Slesvig-Holstein), Vilna, and Upper Silesian plebiscites. *See* REFERENDUM, SAAR.

PLECTASCINEÆ. A group of Ascomycetous Fungi comprising several families, in particular the Aspergillaceæ, to which belong the common green (*Aspergillus* or *Eurotium*) and blue (*Penicillium*) moulds. *Onygena* and the stag-truffles (*Elaphomyces*) also belong to this section. The distinctive feature of the group is the closed ascus-fruit (cleistocarp), in which the numerous asci are distributed irregularly among sterile hyphæ.

PLECTOG'NATHI. A sub-order of Teleostean fishes, distinguished by the maxillary and intermaxillary bones on each side of the jaw being firmly united together by bony union. The head is large, and the union of its bones firmer than in any other Teleostei; the body generally short, skin horny, fins small and soft. As examples of the chief fishes included in this group may be mentioned trunk-fishes, file-fishes, globe-fishes, sun-fishes, etc.

PLEIADES (plī'a-dēz). The so-called "seven stars" in the neck of the constellation Taurus. Six stars are discernible by anyone of normal vision, and those of specially acute vision can detect a few more. Ancient Greek legends associate the Pleiades with the seven daughters of Atlas and the nymph Pleione, fabled to have been placed as stars in the sky. The fading of the seventh was variously explained. In powerful telescopes the cluster displays hundreds of stars, and photography has shown that they are all involved in a faint nebula.

PLEISTOCENE (plīs'to-sēn; Gr. *pleistos*, most, and *kainos*, recent). In geology, the highest division of the Cainozoic group, before the Recent series of deposits. The fossil remains belong almost wholly to existing species. The Pleistocene mammals include a few extinct forms. It includes the last Glacial epoch, and the deposits of this epoch have yielded the Heidelberg jaw and other traces of man.

PLEOCHROISM. The property whereby many translucent coloured minerals appear of different tints when light is transmitted through them in different directions. *See* DICHROIC CRYSTALS.

PLE'ONASTE. Variety of the gemstone, spinel. It is an aluminate of magnesia, and contains iron in addition. It occurs as dark-green or black octahedral crystals of a higher specific gravity than typical spinel and as a constituent of garnet-bearing gneisses and other metamorphic rocks. It is also called ceylonite.

PLESIOSAU'RUS. A genus of extinct amphibious reptiles, nearly allied to Ichthyosaurus. The remains of this curious genus were first brought to light in the Lias of Lyme Regis in 1821, but over twenty British species are now known, and they have formed the subject of important memoirs by Owen and other palæontologists.

Its neck was of great length, exceeding that of its body; it possessed a trunk and tail of the proportions of an ordinary quadruped; to these were added the paddles of a whale. The neck vertebræ numbered twenty-four to forty-one. From twenty to twenty-five dorsal segments existed; and two sacral vertebræ and from thirty to forty caudal segments completed the spine. No distinct breast-bone was developed. The head was not more than $\frac{1}{12}$th or $\frac{1}{13}$th of the length of the body; the snout of a tapering form; the orbits were large and wide. The teeth were conical, slender, curved inwards, finely striated on the enamelled surface, and hollow throughout the interior.

These animals appear to have lived in shallow seas and estuaries, and, in the opinion of some, they swam upon or near the surface, having the somewhat stiff neck arched, and darting it down at the fish within reach. Some of the Plesiosauri were upwards of 20 feet long. Their remains occur from the Lias to the Upper Cretaceous rocks inclusive, the genus being thus exclusively of Mesozoic age.

PLETH'ORA. A term sometimes used for the condition known as *full-blooded*, at one time supposed to be due to an excess of blood in the human system. A florid face, rose-coloured skin, swollen blood-vessels, frequent nose-bleeding, drowsiness and heavy feeling in the limbs, and a hard and full pulse are symptoms of this condition, which is habitual in many persons, and if not actually a disease, yet predisposes to inflammations, congestions, and hæmorrhages.

Plethora may, however, develop in persons of all conditions and ages as the result of too much stimulating food (as an excessive meat-diet), overeating, large consumption of malt and spirituous liquors, residence in northern and elevated regions with sharp, dry air, want of exercise, too much sleep, amputation of a limb—in short, of any action tending unduly to increase the volume of blood. Plethora of a mild form may be reduced by copious draughts of diluents, a vegetable diet, and plenty of exercise; but in cases requiring prompt relief leeches or bleeding must be resorted to.

PLEURA. The serous membrane enveloping each lung. One layer of pleura adheres closely to the surface of the lung and provides it with its smooth and slippery covering, and this is called the visceral layer, while the other layer, which adheres to the inner surface of the chest-wall, is called the parietal layer. These layers, in health, are everywhere in contact,

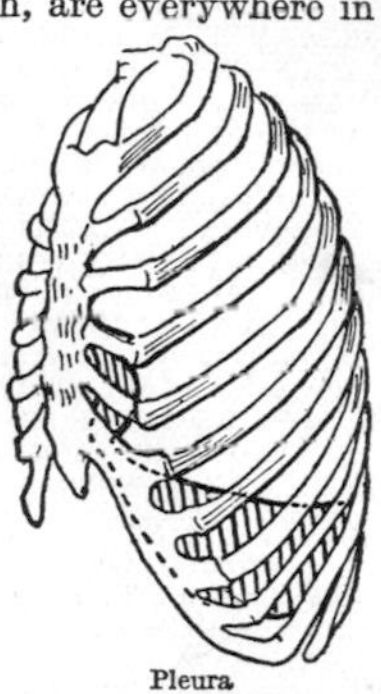

Pleura

with only as much fluid between them as will ensure the lungs gliding easily in expansion and contraction. The pleura is frequently the seat of inflammation, known as pleurisy (q.v.).

PLEURISY. Inflammation of the pleural membrane of the lungs (*see* PLEURA), usually accompanied by some effusion of fluid, and most frequently occurring in an acute form. Probably all cases of pleural inflammation are due to bacterial infection, but many different microbes give rise to purulent inflammation, while by far the commonest cause of simple non-purulent pleurisy is the tubercle bacillus. Along with the pleural inflammation there is an effusion of sero-fibrinous fluid of varying amount, sometimes so slight that it is absorbed immediately (*dry pleurisy*). In more severe cases the effusion is poured out more quickly and abundantly, with the result that it accumulates and a corresponding area of lung becomes collapsed, leading to the heart being displaced toward the healthy lung.

The onset is usually sudden, with shivering and a rapid rise of temperature, but it may be insidious, with indefinite pain and slight general disturbance. When the condition is established, there is general *malaise*, with loss of appetite and digestive disturbances; but the most important local symptom is pain—very sharp and severe when drawing in the breath or coughing. The pain generally subsides in three to four days, after the effusion has become abundant, and later, shortness of breath may develop as a result of the large accumulation of fluid. The patient tends to lie on the affected side in order to give the sound lung as much freedom as possible.

Pleurisy is most common between the ages of twenty and forty, but may occur at any age, and it is sometimes seen as the terminal state in elderly people with Bright's disease. Adhesions of the pleura and the changes in the collapsed portion of the lung may lead to imperfect expansion of the lung for all time; but the most important result is the fact that an attack of pleurisy is presumptive evidence of tubercle, and the future development of tuberculosis of the lung must always be considered. The patient should avoid unfavourable conditions, and as much as possible lead an out-of-door life as an attempt to counteract this danger.

PLEURONECTIDÆ. A family of Teleostei, including the flat-fishes, such as soles, flounders, brill, turbot, halibut, plaice, dab, etc. They swim vertically when young, but subsequently tilt over to one side; that which faces upwards (right or left) becomes dark, while that turned towards the sea-bottom (left or right) assumes a pale tint. The eye of the latter side migrates to that which faces upwards.

PLEURO-PNEUMONIA. In cattle, lung disease which is distinguished from inflammation of the lungs and their covering membranes mainly by its greater period of latency in the system. Accidental or sporadic pleuro-pneumonia invades the chest in a few hours, or days at most, in the usual way, while the specific infectious disease may be a month or six weeks in developing definite symptoms. It is not rare for two or three months to intervene between the time of infection and the presence of positive diagnostic symptoms.

The first sign is that of fever, increased temperature, coat standing up along the back, some shivering and tenderness, and crouching when pinched over the spine. Cough and accelerated breath follow, constipation, loss of appetite, horns and muzzle hot and cold alternately, and loss of milk in cows. The cough increases, and the symptoms generally become aggravated in the suffering beast, which separates itself from the herd in a field. Such a train of symptoms, coming at a time when infectious pleuro-pneumonia is known to be prevalent in a district or country, should be sufficient to warn the owner to seek official inspection and expert opinion as provided by the local authority at the public expense.

PLEVNA, or PLEVEN. A town of Bulgaria, near the River Vid, a tributary of the Danube; served by the Sofia-Varna Railway, with a line to Nikopolis (on the Danube). It is famous for the resistance of its garrison under Osman Nuri Pasha when besieged during the Russo-Turkish War (1877-8), and has also been the scene of great battles. Wine is produced in the adjacent countryside, and leather in the town, and there is a large cattle trade. Pop. 28,775.

PLEYEL, Ignaz Josef. Austrian composer, born at Ruppertsthal (Austria) 1757, died at Paris 1831. He studied under Haydn, and rapidly created a reputation in Italy, France, and England. He founded a piano business at Paris, which became one of the most important in Europe, and edited the *Bibliothèque Musicale*, in which he inserted the best works of the Italian, German, and French composers. His own works, chiefly instrumental pieces, are light, pleasing, and expressive.

PLICA POLONICA. The name given to the mass of matted hair and crusts found in pustular dermatitis of the scalp, produced by the irritation of long-standing and neglected infection by pediculi. The name was first used about Polish Jews, among whom this condition was at one time not infrequent.

PLIMSOLL, Samuel, "the sailors' friend." British politician, born at Bristol in 1824, died in 1898. He became clerk and later manager in a

Samuel Plimsoll

brewery, and in 1853 set up in business in London as a coal merchant. He began to take an active interest in the condition of sailors in the mercantile marine, agitating against the practice of putting to sea "coffin-ships," which were unseaworthy, over-insured, and in many cases never meant to survive the journey. He entered Parliament as a Liberal for Derby in 1868, and made repeated efforts to get a Bill passed putting his views into effect. In 1873 he published *Our Seamen*. In 1876 the Merchant Shipping Act was passed, which imposed penalties on unseaworthy vessels, and provided for a compulsory fixed load-line (commonly known as the Plimsoll mark). In 1880 Plimsoll gave up his seat at Derby to Sir William Harcourt, and did not again enter Parliament. *See* SHIPPING.

PLINTH. Architectural term for the projecting base of a wall, or the square base of a column. In mediæval buildings the plinth may be simply chamfered or in others richly moulded, and in buildings of the perpendicular style in England it is panelled to give verticality. In later architecture it is usually plain.

PLINY THE ELDER. Gaius Plinius Secundus, known as "the Elder" to distinguish him from his nephew, was born at Comum A.D. 23, and died at

Pliny the Elder

Stabiæ A.D. 79. He came to Rome while still young, and at the age of twenty-three he went to Germany with L. Pomponius Secundus (of whom he wrote a biography in two books), and was appointed to command a troop of cavalry.

With characteristic diligence he wrote *A Manual of Spear-throwing for Cavalry*. He also wrote a *History of the German Wars*. He returned to Rome in A.D. 52, studied for the Bar, and practised as a pleader for some time. About this time he wrote *Studiosus*, a work dealing with the education of an orator, and a grammatical treatise entitled *Dubius Sermo*. After being procurator in Spain, he returned to Rome in the reign of Vespasian, and wrote a continuation, in thirty-one books, of the history of Aufidius Bassus.

Pliny was a most indefatigable student. He was always either reading or being read to, and he made notes of everything and had an amanuensis at hand to make excerpts. At his death he left behind 160 volumes of notes, written in very small writing on both sides of the paper. In A.D. 79 Pliny was commanding the fleet at Misenum, and was suffocated by sulphurous vapours during the celebrated eruption of Vesuvius which overwhelmed Herculaneum and Pompeii.

The only work of Pliny which has been preserved is his *Natural History* in thirty-seven books. This work is a kind of encyclopedia, and deals with astronomy, geography, zoology, botany (sixteen books), and mineralogy. It is an ill-balanced and unequal work. Its geography and zoology are especially unsound. Some parts of the latter are better described as unnatural than as natural history, and some of the wonderful animals described reappear in *The Travels of Sir John Mandeville*, in the mediæval *Bestiaries*, and in some of the writings of the Euphuistic school.

Pliny devoured too many books, and reproduced them in an undigested state, but we owe to him much curious information that is not preserved elsewhere.—BIBLIOGRAPHY: K. Jex Blake, *The Elder Pliny's Chapters on the History of Art*; J. Bostock and H. J. Riley, *Pliny's Natural History* (translation).

PLINY THE YOUNGER. Publius Cæcilius Secundus, later known as Gaius Plinius Cæcilius Secundus, nephew of Pliny the Elder, was born at Comum about A.D. 61, and died A.D. 113. His father died when he was quite young, and he was adopted by his uncle. He was elaborately educated at Rome, and was eventually called to the Bar, where he acquired a reputation for eloquence.

He inherited his uncle's fortune when seventeen years old, and seems also to have inherited some of his learning and a little of his diligence. He held in turn all the usual public appointments, being prætor in A.D. 93 and consul in A.D. 100. In the latter year he published his *Panegyric on Trajan*, a speech delivered in the emperor's presence but refurbished before publication. It is still extant, but is somewhat too fulsome in its eulogy to be quite pleasant reading. In about A.D. 111 he was sent to Bithynia as proprætor, and remained there some fifteen months. Besides the *Panegyric on Trajan*, we possess nine books of *Letters*, and one book of *Letters to Trajan*.

Pliny's *Letters*, though bearing obvious signs of having been written with a view to subsequent publication, are extremely interesting, and give us a vivid picture of the life of a gentleman and a man of letters in the first century A.D. Pliny knew all the most interesting men of his day; Tacitus and Suetonius were among his friends, and Martial and Silius Italicus among his acquaintances. His relations with the Emperor Trajan were very cordial, and the collection of *Letters to Trajan*, which includes Trajan's answers, is a most valuable addition to our knowledge of Roman provincial government. Letter XCVI., and the reply to it, XCVII., provide us with a picture of the early Christians and the Roman policy towards them.

Pliny was a munificent benefactor of his native town; and in a somewhat corrupt age he was a thoroughly good man, though his life was somewhat "faultily faultless, icily regular."—BIBLIOGRAPHY: J. D. Lewis, *Pliny's Letters* (translation); A. Church and W. J. Brodribb, *Pliny's Letters* (Ancient Classics for English Readers Series).

PLI'OCENE (Gr. *pleion*, more, *kainos*, recent). The name given by Lyell to the latest system of the Tertiary or Cainozoic group of strata.

Map showing Area of Pliocene Strata in Eastern England

Lyell's Newer Pliocene included beds, such as those covering a large area in Sicily, which contained a marine molluscan fauna almost identical with that of modern seas; in some beds only 5 per cent of the species are extinct. His Older Pliocene included the Sub-Apennine beds, with 50 per cent of molluscan species still living, and yet folded on the flanks of the Apennines, showing the recent uplift of the Italian area.

The European Pliocene consists of the following stages in ascending order, Sarmatian, Pontian, Placentian, Astian, and Sicilian, and the marine beds are best studied in Northern Italy. The modern continents were gradually being evolved throughout the period, and the Lower Pliocene beds of Provence, Attica, and the Himálayan foothills have furnished remarkable evidence of the terrestrial mammalian life of the period. The Pliocene mammals often link existing genera, and the elephant and the horse appear side by side with ancestral types. The erect "ape-man," Pithecanthropus, of Java is probably of Upper Pliocene age.

In Britain the Pliocene beds are poorly developed, occurring mostly in the east of the counties of Norfolk, Suffolk, and Essex. In ascending order, the series are the Coralline Crag, the Red Crag, the Norwich Crag and Chillesford Beds, and the Forest Bed of Cromer. Molluscan remains are abundant, and it is claimed that flint implements worked by man occur on some horizons. The marine Lenham Beds on the chalk downs of Kent attest the earth-movements that have taken place since early Pliocene times.

PLOCK (plotsk). A district of Poland, traversed by the Vistula and the Narev. The area is flat, marshy, and largely afforested. Corn, potatoes, sugar-beet, and rye are the principal agricultural products. Area, 3641 sq. miles; pop. about 800,000.

PLOCK, or PLOTZK. A town of Poland, capital of the district of Plock, on the Vistula. There are river-steamer connections with Warsaw. Plock was formerly capital of the Principality of Masovia. There is an extensive transit trade. In Nov., 1914 (European War), Plock was taken by the Germans. The cathedral dates from the tenth century. Pop. 35,200.

PLOEGSTEERT. A village and wood of Belgium, known to the British forces during the European War as "Plug Street." The village is some 8 miles south of Ypres, and about 3½ miles north of Armentières. It was in the "Ypres salient."

PLOËSTI. A town of Rumania, capital of the department of Prahova. It fell to the Austro-German armies on 6th Dec., 1916, and is, by virtue of its position as the outlet for the valleys of the Prahova and Teleajenu, a great railway junction and road-converging centre, and the capital of the Rumanian oil industry. Pop. 77,325.

PLOTI'NUS. The systematic founder of Neo-Platonism, born about A.D. 203 or 204 at Lycopolis, in Egypt, died between A.D. 262 and 270. It is conjectured that he was of Roman descent, probably a freed-man. It was in his twenty-eighth year that the desire to study philosophy awoke in him. As his first teacher, Alexandriens, gave him no satisfaction, he fell into great despondency, and was brought by a friend to Ammonius Saccas, a philosopher who was brought up a Christian and wrote some works on Christian theology, but who, according to Porphyry (controverted by Eusebius and Jerome), reverted to paganism. He remained with him till his thirty-ninth year.

In 242 he joined the expedition of the Emperor Gordian to the East, in order to learn the philosophy of the Persians and Indians. After the death of Gordian he reached Antioch with great difficulty, and arrived at Rome in his fortieth year. It was here he subsequently lived and taught. About 254 his friends induced him to put his doctrines in writing. From this time till he was joined by Porphyry (about 262-264) he composed twenty-one books, which were only put into the hands of the initiated. During Porphyry's stay in Rome Plotinus composed twenty-four books, and after Porphyry had left for Sicily (267-268) nine others.

Plotinus's discourse, as well as his writing, was marked by energy and enthusiasm. His teaching secured him great respect and popularity among those who did not receive Christianity. He enjoyed the favour of the Emperor Gallienus, who gave him permission to rebuild two destroyed towns in Campania, with a view to their being governed according to the laws of Plato. He retired to Campania, living in the country house of a deceased friend named Zethus, and died there.

Philosophy derived from Plato. Plotinus was one of the great masters of philosophy. The value of his system depends less upon the intrinsic truth it contains than upon its historical importance and its adaptation to a certain class of human sympathies.

It was to Plato that Plotinus looked as his great authority. He believed himself a strict follower of Plato, and his own system a legitimate development of the principles of that great philosopher. He used Plato's term, the *Good*, for his highest generalisation; but he uses it in a wholly different, and even opposite, sense from Plato.

The Good with Plato was a synthesis of all that is highest and most excellent in intelligence; with Plotinus it is an abstraction from which every determinate quality is removed; and there is a corresponding difference in the ethical developments of their systems. With Plato the highest attainment of human morality is the imitation of God through the ideas discoverable by human reason, which he has placed in created things; Plotinus despises all imitations, as well as the ideal qualities which are to be imitated, and finds the practical aim of his philosophy in the direct union of the human spirit with the deity.

Philosophic System. The highest generalisation of Plotinus, which he calls the Good, is a pure undetermined abstraction. Out of the indetermination springs a trinity which is the source of all subsequent being. The original unity, by the excess of its energy, sends forth an image of itself, as the sun emits rays. This image, which is the beginning of plurality, and the source of all determinations, also exists absolutely, and is the immediate productive power of the indeterminate unity. Turning with an involuntary movement towards its original in order to behold it, it generates spirit, which is the source of intelligence or thought.

Every act of thought directed to the unconditioned produces a real existence, an idea; all these ideas differ in form, but are one in substance. The soul is developed out of the spirit as the idea contained in it; being the immediate product of the spirit, it has a share in all ideas, of which it is itself one. It has, in contradistinction to the spirit, the power of looking out from itself, and thus in imagining the world unites the sensuous with the intelligent. The sensuous is the image of the soul, as the soul is of the spirit. Matter is the lowest boundary of being, the necessary contrast of the good, and in so far negative and evil; but in its susceptibility of form it partakes of the positive and the good.

This extraordinary system is the result of a severe system of dialectic. Plotinus believed that he followed Plato in making error and imperfection consist in multiplicity and division, and truth in simplicity and unity. Consequently the higher he could go in generalisation, the nearer he approached to the source of truth, the primary form of being. Now he found that the conception of being itself was complex, and above that conception stood the conception of unity; but even to name unity was to dissolve it, hence his highest generalisation was the unnameable.

But the aim of Plotinus was not

merely to know but to reach this undefined source of being, of which even being itself could not be predicated. Thinking or meditation, which is the mere act of intelligence, Plotinus held to be incompetent to reach unconditioned being, which is grasped only by intuition. Truth accordingly, he held, stands in no need of demonstration. It is comprehended immediately when the spirit sees only itself. In this pure state, to which he gave the name of *ecstasy*, the Absolute Being gazes upon itself through the medium of our spirits. Porphyry records that Plotinus had succeeded in raising himself to this state four times, while he himself had done so only once.

Mysticism. In virtue of this superrational method the Neo-Platonic philosophy became the system of mysticism. The mysticism of Plotinus has a certain analogy with the leading doctrines of Christianity, since both affirm the possibility of a direct communion between God and man. Christianity, however, recognises this possibility only through the condescension of God in coming down to man, a condescension independent of human efforts, whilst Plotinus establishes this communion through the power inherent in man to rise by abstraction to God.—BIBLIOGRAPHY: A. W. Benn, *The Greek Philosophers*; E. Caird, *Evolution of Theology in the Greek Philosophers*; B. A. G. Fuller, *The Problem of Evil in Plotinus*; W. R. Inge, *The Religious Philosophy of Plotinus and some Modern Philosophies of Religion*; also article in Hastings's *Encyclopedia of Religion and Ethics*.

PLOUGH. Since prehistoric times the plough has been the most useful and universally adopted agricultural implement. Although the early Egyptian plough merely consisted of a piece of wood to which an iron point was attached, and that of the eighteenth century was unwieldy with its wooden mould-board, whilst the modern one can be worked with much ease, the object of all has been to incorporate in the soil the surface vegetation and bring up fresh soil to receive seed.

At the present time there are many different types, but the wheeled single furrow is probably the most common, other forms differing only slightly in construction. Its component parts are the beam, wheels, skim coulter, coulter, frame and its fittings, and the handles.

Beam. The beam is a strong iron bar to which all other parts are attached. At its front end it carries the "tee-head", a T-shaped piece of iron with a curved crosspiece, perforated to receive in any position the locking-pin of the "hake head." This is provided with vertical notches into which fits the draft chain for hauling the plough. The depth of ploughing is somewhat governed by raising or lowering the position of the draft chain, but the width is controlled by the position of the locking-pin in the tee-head. Sometimes the draft is taken from a rod attached to the beam in front of the mould-board.

Wheels. Although occasionally absent, two wheels are usually fitted by means of standards to a crossbar, which is clamped to the beam behind the tee-head. The smaller one, moving on the unploughed land and regulating the depth of the ploughing by means of the variable length of its standard, is called the "land wheel". The larger "furrow wheel", carried on the right of the beam, runs along the furrow, controlling the width of slice cut. In wheelless ploughs, the depth and width are controlled by the ploughman from the handles.

Skim coulter. Situated on the beam behind the wheels and in front of the coulter is the "skim coulter", a miniature plough, which, whilst not strictly essential, is useful for paring off surface-matted grass, weeds, and manure, which it throws into the bottom of the furrow, ensuring their rotting.

Coulter. The coulter is passed through a socket in the beam and held in position by means of a clamp. Since its object is to make the vertical cut, it is so set that it projects forwards, making an angle of about 60° with the horizontal. It has a fairly sharp edge and pointed lower extremity which is situated about 3 inches above the point of the share. Such a coulter is sometimes replaced by a disc one on light land free from stones, where earth pushed before the ordinary one blocks the plough.

Frame. The frame, made of cast iron, cast steel, or wrought iron, has attached to its under side a smooth flat bar, termed the "slade", on which the plough moves easily. The share is fitted to the front end of the slade and makes the horizontal cut by means of its fairly broad sharp point and acute edge, set at about 60° to the slade. Shares of chilled cast iron keep their edge best, but they may be made of steel or ordinary cast iron. Above the slade is fitted the "land-cap" which, pressing against the side of the unploughed land, keeps the earth from falling into the furrow. The "mould-board" or "breast", fitted on the right side of the frame and kept rigid by couplings and the breast stay, is made of steel, cast iron, or chilled cast iron. It is fairly long and so shaped that it causes the furrow slice to move through a spiral curve over its convex surface, thereby inverting the cut slice.

Handles. Handles are bolted to the beam. Held together by iron rods, they are relatively long and give the ploughman control of the implement.

Other types of plough include: (*a*) The *Scotch swing* plough, which has a shorter beam, longer handles, and no wheels. (*b*) The *digging* plough with a "shin piece" forming the front of the breast and taking the place of the coulter. On account of its short concave mould-board tending to push over the earth into a fine friable state and its light draft, it is becoming very popular. (*c*) *Double-furrow* plough, of the digging or common type, and constructed to turn two furrows at a time. (*d*) *Multiple* or *gang* plough, popular in the colonies, and suited for turning many furrows. (*e*) *Tractor* plough, of two or more furrows, fitted with a special device for raising the mould-boards at the end of the furrow. (*f*) *Turn-wrest* plough, fitted with a reversible mould-board so that the furrows are all laid in the same direction, commonly used in hilly land. (*g*) *Subsoil* plough, fitted with a device for stirring up the subsoil without bringing it to the surface. (*h*) *Ridging* plough, fitted with two adjustable mould-boards for making drills suitable for green crops. (*i*) Special purpose ploughs such as *potato raising* plough, *draining* plough, and *gripping* plough.

Ploughing is an art which requires much skill and experience. To do good work, the ploughman should be capable of directing his horses by speech with only a very occasional use of reins; he must have a properly "set" plough with a correctly regulated draft; and, whilst keeping the plough moving along a straight path steadily, he must not bring undue pressure on the handles. If the turf is well buried, land well consolidated in straight laid furrows, finishes shallow and a good seed bed left, the soil has been well ploughed. The depth of ploughing, which averages from 5 to 8 inches, varies with the nature of the soil and crop.

PLOUGH-MONDAY. In England, the first Monday after Twelfth Day. On Plough-Monday the ploughmen in the northern part of England used to draw a plough from door to door, and beg money (plough money) for drink.

PLOVDIV. *See* PHILIPPOPOLIS.

PLOVER. The common name of a number of cosmopolitan birds belonging to Charadrius and allied genera. They are gregarious, and most of them are partial to the muddy borders of rivers and marshy situations, subsisting on worms and various aquatic insects; but some of them affect dry, sandy shores.

Their general features are: bill long, slender, straight, compressed; nostrils basal and longitudinal; legs long and slender, with three toes before, the outer connected to the middle one by a short web; wings

Golden Plover

middle-sized. Most of them moult twice a year, and the males and females are seldom very dissimilar in appearance. All lay their eggs on the ground, but do not construct a nest. They run much on the soil, patting it with their feet to bring out the worms, etc. The golden plover (*Charadrius pluvialis*), also called yellow and whistling plover, is the best known. Another familiar species is the green plover, peewit, or lapwing (*Vanellus cristatus*), of which the olive-green dark-spotted eggs are considered a delicacy by epicures.

PLÜCKER, Julius. German mathematician and physicist. Born in 1801, died 1868. He studied at Bonn, Heidelberg, Berlin, and Paris. He was appointed ordinary professor of mathematics at Halle in 1834, and at Bonn in 1836. At Halle he published *System der analytischen Geometrie*, and at Bonn *Theorie der algebraischen Curven*. He was the first to use the method of abridged notation in co-ordinate geometry. The six important equations connecting the number of singularities of various kinds in an algebraic curve are still known as Plücker's equations.

In 1847 Plücker was made professor of physics at Bonn. He did some notable work in magnetism, and was the orginator of the idea of spectrum analysis. In 1865 he returned to mathematics, and invented the system of line geometry. His work on this subject was left unfinished, but was completed and published by his assistant and pupil Felix Klein, afterwards professor at Göttingen, and one of the most distinguished mathematicians of the end of the nineteenth and beginning of the twentieth centuries.

PLUM (Prunus). A genus of plants belonging to the nat. ord. Rosaceæ, sub-ord. Amygdaleæ. About a dozen species are known, all inhabiting the north temperate regions of the globe. They are small trees or shrubs, with alternate leaves and white flowers, either solitary or disposed in fascicles in the axils of the leaves. The common garden plum (*P. domestica*), introduced from Asia Minor, is the most extensively cultivated, and its fruit is one of the most familiar of the stone-fruits.

The varieties are very numerous, differing in size, form, colour, and taste. Some are mostly eaten fresh, some are dried and sold as prunes, others again are preserved in sugar, alcohol, syrup, or vinegar. They make also excellent jams and jellies, and the syrup from stewed plums forms a refreshing drink for invalids, and a mild aperient for children. Perhaps the most popular of all is the greengage. A very easily grown sort is the *P. damascēna* or damson. The wood of the plum tree is hard, compact, traversed with reddish veins, susceptible of a fine polish, and is frequently employed by turners and cabinet-makers.

The sloe or black-thorn (*P. spinōsa*) is a species of wild plum bearing a small, round, blue-black, and extremely sour fruit, which is made into sloe-gin and prune-wine, the latter being chiefly employed by distillers, wine and spirit merchants, etc., for fining, colouring, purifying, and mellowing spirits.

PLUMBAGINA'CEÆ, or **PLUMBAGIN'EÆ.** A natural order of gamopetalous dicotyledons, consisting of (chiefly maritime) herbs, somewhat shrubby below, with alternate leaves, and regular pentamerous, often blue or pink flowers. As garden plants nearly the whole of the order is much prized for beauty, particularly the Statices. The common thrift or sea-pink (*Armeria maritima*), with grass-like leaves and heads of bright-pink flowers, is a familiar example. The type of this order is the genus Plumbāgo. It consists of perennial herbs or undershrubs, with pretty blue, white, or rose-coloured flowers in spikes at the ends of the branches.

P. europœa is employed by beggars to raise ulcers upon their bodies to excite pity. Its root contains a peculiar crystallisable substance which gives to the skin a lead-grey colour, whence the plant has been called *leadwort*.

PLUMBING. During more recent times the work of the plumber has changed, and instead of being merely a worker with lead, as the name implies, he has developed into a domestic engineer. His work chiefly consists of laying or fixing piping, outside or inside buildings, for distributing either hot or cold water to the various points required; of taking the cold-water supplies from street mains, or from wells, streams, or other available source; of erecting the various sanitary fixtures in buildings; of conveying waste discharges from sanitary fixtures to the drainage system; of executing drainage work, and observing that all liquid waste discharges are effectively disposed of, either by being discharged into a sewer, or into a private sewage-purification system; of taking precautions to prevent the contamination of the water-supply after it has left the street mains, or wells, or streams; of preventing sewage gases or drain air gaining access to habitable buildings, and all enclosures where the presence of these gases would be detrimental to health; of rendering roofs watertight, and of conducting the rain-water intercepted by roofs into the drainage system; of executing gas-fitting work for either lighting, heating, cooking, or for power purposes; and of erecting centralised systems for the warming of buildings.

Cold-water Supply. When water is obtained from a Local Authority or Water Board it is supplied on either the "constant" or intermittent principle. More commonly the supply is constant, and this minimises the risks of pollution, as the water is fresh and there is no need to store it in cisterns. In high-lying districts an intermittent, or partially intermittent, supply of water may be the only one obtainable. Under these conditions cisterns require to be fixed at high levels in buildings, in order that water may be stored ready for use. In these cases water is more liable to pollution, owing to dirt or foreign matter gaining access to the cisterns, or a storage receptacle itself may be the cause of water pollution.

Domestic Hot-water Supplies. Water for domestic purposes may be heated by a boiler behind a fire, either in a sitting-room or in a kitchen range. A gas-heater may take the place of a coal fire, or an independent class of boiler may be used. The principle is the same in either case, and a complete system consists of a heater or boiler, hot-water storage-tank, circulating pipes between the boiler and hot-water storage-tank, an overhead cold-water supply-cistern, and piping for the distribution of the hot water. At the outset the heat from the fire is conducted through the metal of which the boiler is made, and the water inside the boiler has its temperature raised by coming into contact with the heated surfaces. The water in the hot storage-tank is heated by convection, owing to its circulating between the boiler and the tank. The outflow of water through any draw-off tap is directly due to the water-pressure in the overhead cistern, and the outflow is not influenced by the temperature of the water itself.

Drainage Work. Drain pipes may be either of iron or of earthenware, the former material being the more suitable where drains require to be laid through buildings, or where work of a high-class character is required. The principal points requiring attention are: drains should be laid in straight lines on firm beds between changes of direction, be suitably jointed, made readily accessible, be well ventilated throughout their entire length, be laid with gradients that yield a self-cleansing velocity, be as simple and short as practicable, whilst all gully traps should be avoided that are not absolutely necessary.

Soil, Waste, and Rain-water Pipes. The pipes for carrying off the waste matter from sanitary fixtures, and those for conducting the rain-water from roofs, are usually of cast iron. Soil pipes are sometimes made of lead, but this material is unsuitable for long waste pipes through which hot and cold water alternately flow. The usual method is to discharge the waste matter from water-closets through pipes quite distinct from those that convey the waste water from sinks, baths, and lavatories. There is, however, a movement to simplify the present practice, and to make use of fewer pipes. The details of construction of all sanitary work are regulated by by-laws that are put into operation by Local Authorities through sanitary inspectors, health officers, or other officials.

Sanitary Fixtures. The features that should be incorporated in all these fixtures are simplicity of construction and cleanliness. For general buildings water-closets take two principal forms, the "wash-down" and "siphonic" types. In the former the pans are cleansed by the force and body of flushing water that carry the waste matter forward and through the trap. In the siphonic form the contents of the basin are removed by siphonage, instead of depending upon the impact of the flushing water. Lavatories, baths, and sinks should be provided with large accessible overflows and waste outlets, and be free from inaccessible parts in which filth may accumulate.

External Roof Work. In order to render roofs watertight where two or more intersect, or where chimneys or other forms of construction pass through them, or where the roof comes in contact with walls, or where large flat surfaces interpose, lead work is usually carried out. Sheet lead has the advantages that it can be simply worked into various shapes and readily applied. Lead work is also durable, and can be executed at reasonable cost. Sheet copper or zinc is occasionally substituted for lead where a lighter material is desirable or necessary. Copper is a very serviceable material but more costly to apply, whilst zinc is unsuitable in towns and manufacturing districts on account of its tendency to corrode. Zinc may, however, be used in country districts where sulphurous fumes are absent.

Lead Burning. A method of jointing lead work. It is displacing soldering in many cases, owing to its lower cost. A blow-pipe is used for lead burning, and the gases employed are usually hydrogen and atmospheric air, or coal-gas and oxygen. Each combination of gases, when ignited and in the right proportions, produces a hot clean flame. There are different ways in which burnt joints are made, but, speaking briefly, they are formed either by overlapping the edges of the lead and fusing the one into the other by the blow-pipe flame, or by fusing the edges to be joined with an additional body of material that is supplied by a thin bar or strip of lead, as the joint is being made.

PLUME-BIRD. The *Epimăchus magnus*, or long-tailed bird of paradise, with plumage showing the most brilliant hues of scarlet, emerald, violet, and ultramarine. It is a native of New Guinea. See illus. p. 264.

PLUME - MOTHS (Pterophoridæ). A small family of moths remarkable for having their wings split up into a number of plumes, usually the fore-wings into two and the hind-wings into three. The white plume-moth (*Pterophŏrus pentadactўlus*) is a pretty insect with snowy white wings, and is common in gardens.

PLUMER, Herbert Charles Onslow, First Viscount. British soldier. He was born 13th March, 1857, and joined the Royal Army (Yorkshire and Lancashire Regiment) in 1876. He served in the Sudan (1884), commanded a mounted force during the Matabele Rising in South Africa (1896), and raised the Rhodesia Field Force which he commanded during the South African War (1899-1902). During the latter campaign he was made a C.B. and aide-de-camp to the queen, and at its close he became major-general.

Until the outbreak of the European War he successively held the posts of brigade-commander (1902-4), quarter-master-general (1905), Fifth Divisional commander (1905), and Commander-in-Chief, Northern Command (1911-14). He was knighted in 1906, and promoted lieutenant-general in 1908.

In May, 1915, General Plumer was appointed to command the Second Army on the Western front (European War), and was practically inactive

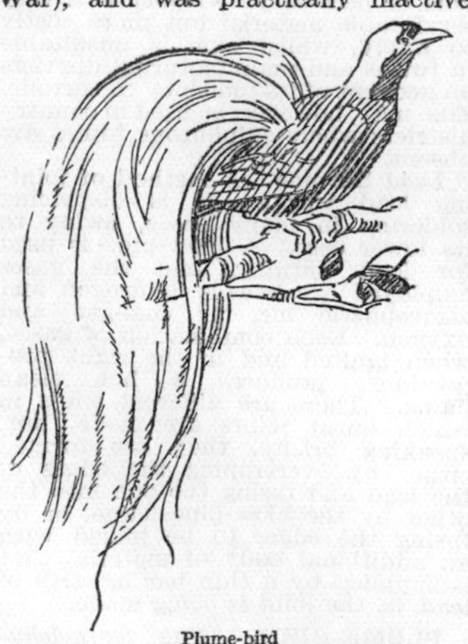

Plume-bird

during the years 1915 and 1916. On 7th June, 1917, he gained a decisive victory at Messines, and was subsequently employed in consolidating the Allied positions in the Ypres salient.

After the Italian disaster at Caporetto, Plumer was dispatched with Allied reinforcements to the basin of the Po (Nov., 1917), but was urgently recalled in March, 1918, to command the Second Army prior to the great German offensive. During the British advance which

Viscount Plumer

commenced in Aug., 1918, General Plumer was distinguished for his strategy, foresight, and complete command of affairs, and was largely instrumental in driving the Germans out of Belgian Flanders. In 1919 he was made Field-Marshal and was raised to the peerage as Baron Plumer of Messines and Bilton, receiving also a grant of £30,000. He was Governor and Commander-in-Chief of Malta, 1919-24, and High Commissioner for Palestine, 1925-28. He was made a Viscount in 1929, and died in 1932.

PLUMSTEAD. A district of London forming part of the metropolitan borough of Woolwich. It is in Kent, 11½ miles from Charing Cross, and is served by the Southern Railway, and by tramways and omnibuses.

King Edgar gave Plumstead Manor to the Augustinian foundation at Canterbury (A.D. 960), and it passed in the eighteenth century to Queen's College, Oxford. Plumstead Marshes (2000 acres) were walled in by the monks of the twelfth-century Augustinian foundation, Lesnes Abbey, but were submerged between 1527 and 1563, when the work of reclamation was begun.

PLU'MULE. In botany, that part of the seed which grows into the shoot of the future plant. In the seeds of the bean, horse-chestnut, etc., the plumule is distinctly visible, but in plants generally it is scarcely perceptible without the aid of a magnifying glass, and in many it does not appear till the seed begins to germinate.

PLUNKETT, Sir Horace Curzon. Irish statesman, youngest son of sixteenth Baron Dunsany; he was born 24th Oct., 1864. He represented Co. Dublin S. in Parliament, 1892-1900, founded the Irish Agricultural Organisation Society and established the Agricultural Co-operative Movement. From 1899-1907 he was Vice-President of the Department of Agriculture for Ireland. In 1917 he was chosen President of the Irish Convention. He died 26th March, 1932.

PLURALISM, in metaphysics, is the doctrine which maintains that being and reality can be reduced to a multiplicity of relatively independent, single elements. It is thus the antithesis of singularism (monism), which teaches that multiplicity is appearance and not reality. Pluralists are: Democritus, Leibnitz, Lotze, Haeckel, and others.

Some of the pluralists taught a materialistic pluralism (atomic theory), others a spiritualistic pluralism (monads). None of these pluralists, however, denied the absolute unity of the universe. Modern pluralism, on the contrary, denies the fundamental completeness of the universe, and conceives reality as in a state of becoming. The unity of the universe is not to be sought in the past and retrospectively, but in the future and its possibilities. The new pluralism has been championed in recent times by W. James. *See* PRAGMATISM.

PLURALITY, in ecclesiastical law, signifies the holding by the same person of two or more benefices. Pluralities were forbidden by the canon law, but the bishops and the Pope assumed the right of granting dispensations to hold them. They were prohibited by the Councils of Chalcedon (451), Nicæa (787), and Lateran (1215). In England pluralities in the Church are forbidden excepting in particular cases, such as where two livings are within 3 miles of each other, and the value and population small.

PLURAL VOTING. System allowing a person to cast more than one vote in an election, e.g. in virtue of different qualifications, residential and business. For parliamentary elections in Great Britain a person may not have more than two votes, and these must be given in two constituencies.

PLUSH. A fabric similar to velvet, from which it differs only in having a longer and denser pile. The pile is formed from cotton, silk, or other warp yarns; thus imitation sealskins have a pile which when dyed resembles the real article. During the operation of weaving, wires are inserted under the warp yarns, and the upper bends of the loops thus formed are cut by a knife edge on the end of the wire as the latter is withdrawn mechanically. The pile threads are naturally bound securely to the foundation of the fabric, in the formation of which yarns spun from other fibres are used. Several wires are used, and they are drawn out one by one.

Two fabrics are often woven face to face, and the pile threads which bridge the gap between the two cloths are cut in the loom as the two cloths are being woven, or else cut after the fabrics leave the loom. This method of weaving is termed "double-plush" weaving, and its chief advantage is that no wires are required for the operation. In some looms for double-plush weaving, however, another advantage obtains in that two shuttles are sent across simultaneously, one for each cloth. Such cloth is manufactured in several countries, e.g. Great Britain, America, France, Germany, and the products used for curtains, upholstery, and the like.

PLUTARCH. Greek biographer and miscellaneous writer, born about A.D. 46, and died about A.D. 120. His native town was Chæronea, in Bœotia, where he spent much of his life and where he died. He was educated at Athens, and spent some years at Rome, where he lectured on philosophy and (according to a mediæval authority) acted as tutor to the future Emperor Hadrian. This is almost all that is known about the life of Plutarch.

Plutarch's reputation rests upon his *Parallel Lives*, a collection of forty-six biographies arranged in pairs, each pair consisting of a Greek and a Roman whose careers or characters were more or less alike. This book had an influence upon the Revival of Learning greater, perhaps, than that of any other book, and it did more to interpret ancient Greece and Rome to modern Europe than many works of greater creative genius. Plutarch did not intend to write history but biography; he rightly argued that a man's character was shown not so much by his behaviour in the crises of his life as by his ordinary conversation, and by his jests and apophthegms. His biographies, accordingly, are admirable specimens of portrait-drawing; though he has done much research and consulted many authorities, his work is alive, not "made tongue-tied by authorities."

Plutarch is one of the few authors who lose little by being read in a translation. Amyot's famous translation into French is more accurate but hardly less renowned than the English version of it by Sir Thomas North. Shakespeare used North's translation when writing *Julius Cæsar, Coriolanus,* and *Antony and Cleopatra.* Plutarch's other writings, above sixty in number, are grouped under the general title of *Moralia.*

Plutarch

These works vary greatly in value, some of them being highly entertaining, some preserving important information, and some being devoid of interest. A few of the last class at any rate are not genuine. These treatises deal with such subjects as *The Cessation of Oracles, The Education of Children,* and *The Ill-nature of Herodotus.*—BIBLIOGRAPHY: R. C. Trench, *A Popular Introduction to Plutarch*; J. Oakesmith, *The Religion of Plutarch as expounded in his Ethics*; Sir J. P. Mahaffy, *Silver Age of the Greek World.*

PLUTO. In classical mythology, the god of the infernal regions, the ruler of the dead. He was a son of Cronus and Rhea, a brother of Zeus (Jupiter) and Poseidon (Neptune), and to him, on the partition of the world, fell the kingdom of the shades. He married Persephŏnē. By the Greeks he was generally called Hades, and by the Romans Orcus, Tartarus, and Dis Pater.

The worship of Pluto was extensively spread among the Greeks and Romans. The cypress, the box, the narcissus, and the plant adiantum (maiden-hair) were sacred to him; oxen and goats were sacrificed to him in the shades of night, and his priests were crowned with cypress. He is represented in gloomy majesty, his forehead shaded by his hair, and with a thick beard. In his hand he holds a two-forked sceptre, a staff, or a key; by his side is Cerberus. (For the planet, *see* PLANET.)

PLUTONIC ROCKS. Crystalline rocks, such as granites, greenstones, and others, of igneous origin, which have consolidated at great depths below the surface of the earth. They are distinguished from those called volcanic rocks, although both series are igneous, the volcanic rocks having solidified at or near the surface.

PLUTUS. In Greek mythology, the god of riches, to be distinguished from Pluto (q.v.). Zeus struck him blind because he confined his gifts to the good; and he thenceforth conferred them equally on the good and the bad. His residence was under the earth. Plutus is the subject of the last, the most freely annotated, and the least amusing of the eleven extant comedies of Aristophanes.

PLUVIOSE. The month of rain, the fifth month of the French Republican calendar, beginning on 20th, 21st, or 22nd Jan., and ending 19th, 20th, or 21st Feb.

PLYMOUTH (plim'uth). A city seaport, municipal, parliamentary, and county borough of England, in Devonshire, at the head of Plymouth Sound, between the estuaries of the Plym and Tamar; served by the Southern and Great Western Railways. Taken in its largest sense, Plymouth comprehends what are called the "Three Towns," or Devonport on the west, Stonehouse in the centre, and Plymouth proper on the east.

Plymouth proper covers an area of about 1 sq. mile, the site being uneven and somewhat rugged, consisting of a central hollow and two considerable eminences, one on the north, forming the suburbs, and the other, called the Hoe, on the south, laid out as a promenade and recreation ground. The old Eddystone Lighthouse has been re-erected in Hoe Park, which also contains a statue of Sir Francis Drake by Boehm. The top of the Hoe offers magnificent land and sea views.

The guild-hall, a Gothic building, is the finest modern edifice (1870-4), and has a tower nearly 200 feet high; among other buildings are St. Andrew's Church and the Athenæum. The citadel, an obsolete fortification built by Charles II., is another object of interest.

The manufactures are not very extensive, and chiefly connected with ships' stores for the naval depôt at Devonport; but the fisheries are valuable, and Plymouth has a large export and coasting trade. Its chief importance lies in its position as a naval station.

Thanks to extensive and sheltered harbours, Plymouth rose from a mere fishing-village to the rank of foremost port of England under Elizabeth, and is now as a naval port second only to Portsmouth. The Western Harbour, or the Hamoaze (mouth of the Tamar), is specially devoted to the Royal Navy, and here (in Devonport, q.v.) are the dockyard, and Keyham steamyard; the victualling yard, marine barracks, and naval hospital being in Stonehouse. The harbour accommodation of Plymouth proper consists of Sutton Pool and the Great Western Railway Docks in Mill Bay, with the Catwater, or estuary of the Plym. It is supplied with water from Dartmoor by a *leat* or channel constructed by Sir Francis Drake. Subsequent to the European War, Plymouth "adopted" the town of Estaires. Pop. (1931), 208,166.

PLYMOUTH. A town of Massachusetts, United States, the county seat of Plymouth county, on the Plymouth Harbour arm of Cape Cod Bay; served by the New York, New Haven, & Hartford Railway, by electric-traction lines, and by steamers (in season) to Boston. There are many interesting landmarks and curiosities. Plymouth was the scene of the landing of the Pilgrim Fathers in 1620, and the exact spot is marked by a granite boulder known as Plymouth Rock. Pop. 13,042.

PLYMOUTH. The capital of the Island of Montserrat (q.v.), Leeward Islands, West Indies. Pop. (1931), 1700.

PLYMOUTH BRETHREN. A Protestant sect which first appeared at Plymouth in 1830, and has since considerably extended over Great Britain, the United States, and among the Protestants of France, Switzerland, and Italy. They object to national Churches as being too lax, and to dissenting Churches as too sectarian, recognising all as brethren who believe in Christ and the Holy Spirit as his Vicar. They acknowledge no form of Church government nor any office of the ministry, all males being regarded by them as equally entitled to "prophesy" or preach.

At first they were also called Darbyites, after John Nelson Darby, originally a barrister, subsequently a clergyman of the Church of England, to whose efforts their origin and the diffusion of their principles are mainly to be ascribed.

They entertain millenarian hopes, baptise adults, and administer the sacrament, which each takes for himself, each Sunday. At their meetings a pause of unbroken silence ensues when no one is moved to speak. They hold both civil governments and ecclesiastical organisations to be under divine reprobation, the former as atheistic, the latter as in a state of apostasy.

PLYMOUTH SOUND. An arm of the sea, on the south-west coast of England, between the counties of Devon and Cornwall. It is about 3 miles wide at its entrance, bounded by elevated land, which descends abruptly to the sea. It contains Drake Island, which is fortified, and is protected by the Plymouth Breakwater, 1 mile long.

PLYMPTON. Market town of Devon. It is 5 miles from Plymouth, on the G.W. Rly. and stands on the River Plym. Sir Joshua Reynolds was born here.

PLYNLYMMON. Welsh mountain. It is 10 miles W. of Llanidloes, on the borders of Montgomeryshire and Cardiganshire, and is 2468 feet in height. Here are the sources of the Wye and Severn, and of the Llyfnant and the Rheidol.

PLYWOOD. Name given to thin boards made of layers of wood, usually three in number, and cemented or glued together under pressure, the grain of the middle layer being placed at right angles to that of the outer layers. Plywood is light and has the advantage of being less liable to warp or split than ordinary boards. It is used in aeroplane construction and box manufacture, also for furniture and as panels for walls and ceilings.

PLZEN. *See* PILSEN.

PNEUMATIC DISPATCH. A system of transmitting papers, money, and other small articles in hollow carriers forced or drawn through tubes. This is the method used by the British post office for the conveyance of telegraph forms from the post offices in the central districts of large towns to the general post offices. The "carriers" are forced or drawn through tubes passing underground. Compressed air, usually at 10 lb. per square inch, or a vacuum of generally 6½ lb. per square inch provides the propelling force. The tubes in this case are made of lead and 3, 2¼, or 1½ inches diameter, the medium size being generally used. When manufactured, the tubes are in 28-feet lengths, and are laid in wooden troughs for protection during handling. Every care is taken to ensure that the tubes are circular, of uniform diameter, and smooth.

The tubes are joined up in position, the joint being made while a steel mandril occupies the tubes at the butted ends to ensure smoothness and correct diameter. Iron pipes are passed over the lead ones for protection before the earth is replaced and the road made up. The carriers are cylindrical tubes of gutta-percha covered with felt, and a little over 6 inches long. A " skirt " projects beyond the open end of the carrier, and is useful in preventing leaks. The speed of the carrier is roughly stated as from 20 to 30 miles an hour in tubes not exceeding 1 mile in length.

The tubes used in installations inside offices and warehouses are generally made of brass or copper. The circuit in this case is provided with loop connections to the various departments.

PNEUMATIC POWER TRANSMISSION. Compressed air is a very serviceable and effective medium for the transmission of power. In large engineering works and shipbuilding yards it is customary to have a central air-compressor station from which pipes convey compressed air to pneumatic tools of all characters. In the installation at the Armstrong Naval Shipbuilding Yard at High Walker on Tyne there are eight electric-driven air-compressors, capable of raising the pressure of a total of 13,600 cubic feet of free air per minute to 100 lb. per square inch. The total horse-power is 2500. The compressed air is stored in a cylindrical steel tank 30 feet high and 8 feet diameter. From the store the air is conveyed through mains, 14 inches diameter, to the various sections of the works, and smaller pipes within the departments are tapped at various points to provide air-supply for the tools.

Air-compressors of this character have a form somewhat resembling that of a steam-engine, but their internal construction is different in many respects. The cycle is commonly performed on both sides of the piston, but sometimes the cylinder to one side of the piston is used for the first stage in the compression, and to the other side for the high-pressure operations. As air is compressed some part of the energy expended is used in raising the temperature. This loss is reduced by the use of an efficient cooling system, comprising water-jackets and injection-jets. When two-stage compression is used, the air is passed from the low-pressure cylinder to an intercooler, where its temperature is reduced before it passes into the high-pressure cylinder. These intercoolers consist of simple cast-iron vessels, through which the air is made to take a circuitous path between tubes or metal faces kept cool by running water.

Small portable air-compressors driven by petrol- or paraffin-engines have been introduced into engineering. Pneumatic hammers, chipping-tools, and grinding-machines are very useful in welding work where repairs have to be made without removing the parts of the broken structure to an engineering works. In such cases they receive their air-supply from these small units.

In Britain it is common for public authorities or limited companies to supply electricity, gas, and water under pressure to power users, but the supply of compressed air for some reason or another has received little, if any, attention. Compressed air provides a means of economical power transmission which has many advantages. In Paris compressed air is supplied by a public company from two central stations through many miles of piping, the most distant point of delivery being about 5 miles from the station. Small tradesmen use air-motors, frequently old steam-engines, to drive their machines. The air-supply is usually passed through pipes placed in the stove, so that a certain amount of pre-heating can be obtained. The actual amount of work obtained from each pound of air used is proportional to the absolute temperature of the air at entry.

An attempt was made in 1887 to prevent the formation of ice and snow in the ports of an air-motor by the simple expedient of pre-heating the air, and it is said that it was during these tests that the great gain in economy produced was first noticed. A system of power transmission which permits the consumer to increase the efficiency of his power plant by using a small amount of the waste heat from his stove has much to recommend it. Compressed air is used to a large extent in coal-mines for the operation of coal-cutters. Other uses are referred to in the article COMPRESSED AIR.

PNEUMATICS. That branch of physics which treats of the mechanical properties of elastic fluids, and particularly of atmospheric air. The chemical properties of elastic fluids (air and gases) belong to chemistry. Pneumatics treats of the weight, pressure, equilibrium, elasticity, density, condensation, rarefaction, resistance, motion, etc., of air; it treats also of air considered as the medium of sound (acoustics), and as the vehicle of heat, moisture, etc. It also includes the description of those machines which depend chiefly for their action on the pressure and elasticity of air, as the various kinds of pumps, artificial fountains, etc. The weight of the air, and its pressure on all bodies on the earth's surface, were quite unknown to the ancients. Their discovery is due to Torricelli, who gave the correct explanation of the failure of a suction-pump to raise water beyond a certain height, a fact which had been observed by Galilei. *See* AERONAUTICS; AIR-PUMP; ATMOSPHERE; BAROMETER; DIVING-BELL; GASES, PROPERTIES OF; HYDROSTATICS; MANOMETER; PUMPS.

PNEUMONIA. Several diseases are caused by the germ known as the *pneumococcus*, of which lobar and lobular pneumonia are the most important.

Lobar Pneumonia. Lobar pneumonia is an acute infection characterised by inflammation of the lungs, with severe toxæmia and fever, and usually ending by crisis. The disease was known to Hippocrates and the old Greek physicians, and since then has apparently been well known to each successive generation of medical practitioners. It is one of the most widespread and fatal of all acute diseases, and is world-wide in its distribution. It is common in Great Britain, and even more common in the United States of America. It attacks all ages, but in young children the pneumonia is much more likely to be of the lobular type (broncho-pneumonia), while lobar pneumonia is found frequently in adolescence, young adults, middle life, and the elderly.

Causes. Males are more frequently affected than females, because of their greater liability to exposure to cold and hardship, which are, along with alcoholism, the most prominent predisposing causes. Any debilitating cause, however, renders a person more susceptible, and in no other acute disease are recurrences so frequent. Climate does not appear to have much influence, as it prevails equally in hot and cold countries, but the dry, overheated air of the houses in America, with the contrasting cold out of doors, favours catarrhal infections in the air-passages, and explains in part the high incidence of the disease there. Almost all the statistics show that the disease is most frequent in the late winter and early spring months. In considering the conditions that favour infection, it has to be remembered that the majority of people harbour the germ of pneumonia in the mouth or nose or throat, and that the virulence of the germ varies at different periods. It thus becomes a contest between the degree of resistance and the virulence of the germ, and such factors as catarrh of the upper air-passages, exposure to cold, alcoholism, etc., lower the resistance and give the germ, till then held in check, a chance to establish itself and produce the acute infection.

Symptoms. Probably the incubation period is very short, and, as a rule, the disease starts abruptly with a severe, well-marked chill. This may be so sudden that a rigor sets in when a person is at work or going about. There is a rapid rise of temperature, with headache and general pains, and in a short time there follows definite and very severe pain in the affected side of the chest. After two or three days the typical pneumonia picture is seen. The patient lies flat in bed, usually on the affected side, with flushed face and giving short rapid breaths, accompanied by an expiratory grunt. The alæ of the nose dilate with each breath: the eyes are bright, often with unequal pupils; herpes appear on the lips. The patient has an anxious expression, giving frequent short coughs, which cause marked pain, and there is a tough, blood-stained spit. This state continues, or may become worse, and death occurs, either from early heart failure, or more frequently from the action of the poison on the vasomotor centres, causing a progressive lowering of the blood-pressure.

On the other hand, after about a week the crisis may take place and the patient recover. The crisis, which may appear as early as the third day and as late as the twelfth, is usually seen about the seventh day, and with it there is a very rapid fall of temperature, with a marked abatement of the symptoms. Usually there is abundant perspiration, and the patient falls into a comfortable sleep. There is always a certain degree of pleurisy (q.v.) present whenever the inflammation reaches the pleural membrane, and this is the cause of the very severe local pain. The most common complications are pericarditis, endocarditis, and meningitis. Relapses are rare, but recurrences after a period of time are common, and a person may have several attacks of pneumonia. Convalescence is rapid, and it is uncommon to have sequelæ. The mortality varies according to the age of the patient. Between the ages of twenty and thirty it is about 20 per cent, between thirty and forty about 30 per cent, after that with each decade it rises till above the age of sixty over one-half of those attacked die.

Lobular Pneumonia. Lobular pneumonia, or broncho-pneumonia, is an acute infection of the smaller air-passages and the related lobules. The disease may be either primary,

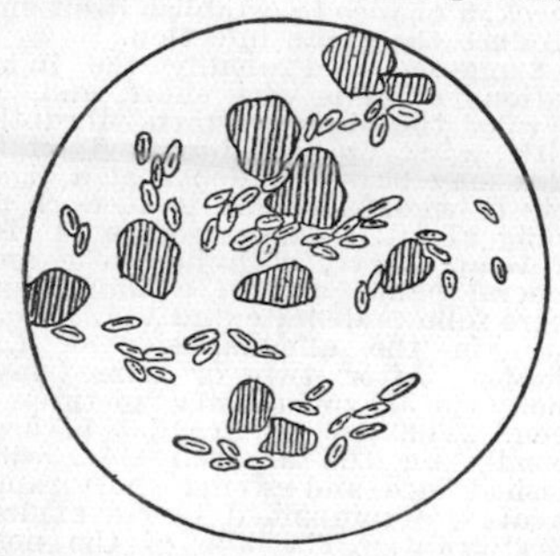

Pneumococci germs of pneumonia under microscope

and set in without any previous bronchitis, or it may be secondary to bronchitis in measles, whooping-cough, diphtheria, influenza, scarlet fever, and other infectious diseases. The primary form usually attacks children under two years, while the secondary type, more frequently seen, follows the infectious diseases, and causes more deaths than are due directly to the fevers themselves. Secondary broncho-pneumonia may further arise when some foreign body gets into the smaller bronchial tubes, and occurs in cases of loss of sensation of the larynx, as in coma, after operations about the mouth or nose, in tracheotomy, and in cancer of the larynx. It is known as aspiration pneumonia.

Most cases of broncho-pneumonia are in children under five years, and it has been found that rickets and diarrhœa are marked predisposing causes. It is widespread, but prevails most extensively among the poorer classes. The primary form sets in abruptly, and runs a somewhat similar course to lobar pneumonia, but does not terminate with such a definite crisis, while the secondary form does not terminate by crisis at all, but by a gradual fall of temperature, called lysis. It begins as a bronchitis, and usually follows measles or one of the infectious diseases, when, after a diminution of the original fever symptoms, there is an accession of fever with cough, rapid breathing, and increased pulse, and the child becomes very ill.

The primary form is not nearly so serious or fatal, as when in its secondary form broncho-pneumonia attacks a child already weakened and debilitated by some other disease.

The death-rate in children is between 30 and 40 per cent, and it has been observed that thin, wiry children stand the attack better than the fat, flabby ones.

Aspiration pneumonia, which usually occurs in adults, is a very fatal disease. Care of a child during measles, whooping-cough, and similar diseases can do much to prevent the onset of broncho-pneumonia, and for this purpose the most important measures are avoidance of chill and attention to catarrh of the nose and throat.

In all forms of pneumonia careful nursing and constant watch over the patient's condition are essential, and many cases which are dangerously ill for several days may be brought over the critical period by these steps.

PNÔM-PENH. The capital of Cambodia, French Indo-China. It lies at the head of ocean-going navigation on the Mekong River, and has good quays and embankments. There is a large trade, and there is a cotton-ginning mill at Khsach-Kandal, an adjacent hamlet. Cattle-breeding is a native industry in the district between Pnôm-penh and Manila. Good roads lead from the town (1) to the Gulf of Siam, and (2) to the district south-west of the lakes. Pnôm-penh has been almost entirely rebuilt by the French, and is traversed by boulevards. The principal buildings are of an ecclesiastical nature, and include the palaces of the Buddhist priests and the pagoda. Pop. (1931), 96,000.

PO (ancient **Padus** or **Eridănus**). The largest river of Italy. It rises on the confines of France and Piedmont in Monte Viso, one of the Cottian Alps, and flows through Piedmont, Lombardy, and Venetia to the Adriatic (about 450 miles). It divides the great plain of Lombardy into two nearly equal parts, receives many streams flowing south from the Alps, and others that flow north from a part of the Apennine range, and serves as an inland waterway for over three-quarters of its course. The total catchment area is about 28,000 sq. miles. Its principal affluents are: on the left, the Baltea, Sesia, Ticino, Adda, and Mincio; on the right, the Tanaro, Trebbia, and Panaro.

The Po, in spite of embankments, etc., is the cause of frequent inundations, especially near its mouth. The Adriatic Sea is a foundered area like the western basin of the Mediterranean, and it has probably sunk in times so geologically recent that the ancestors of the jackals, that lived till lately on the Island of Pacman, off Dalmatia, may have walked there overland. The basin of the Po (or Plain of Lombardy) occupies a depression (part of the foundered area) between the Alps and the Northern Apennines, and is a landward continuation of the depression, the lower part of which is occupied by the Adriatic.

POA. A large genus of grasses, natives of temperate countries. Many are useful pasture grasses, e.g. *P. pratensis* (smooth stalked meadow-grass) and *P. trivialis* (rough-stalked meadow-grass); *P. nemoralis* is valuable for lawns. *P. annua* is one of the commonest of weeds.

POACHING. In English law, a term applied to the act of unlawfully trespassing on another's property for the purpose of stealing or killing game, or of catching fish. For the law relating to game, *see* GAME LAWS.

In England, when a person's land adjoins a stream where there is no ebb and flow, that person is assumed to have an exclusive right to fish in the stream as far as his land extends, and up to the middle of the stream; and so also when a person's land encloses a pond, the fish in that pond belong to him.

Where several properties are contiguous to the same lake, the right of fishing belongs to the proprietors, in proportions to the value of their respective titles. Generally the public have the right of fishing in a public river, that is, one in which there is ebb and flow; but an exclusive right is held by some proprietors by virtue of royal franchises or otherwise.

Persons who in the daytime angle for fish in waters where they have no right or leave are liable to have their tackle seized by the owner of the land or fishery, or his servant, and if they submit they are liable to no other penalty. The owner or his servant may deprive the angler of his fishing-gear. Angling by night in private waters entails a penalty of £2, and if done in water adjoining or belonging to a dwelling-house, of £5.

Any person, not an angler, found fish-poaching on private property is liable to a fine of £5, in addition to forfeiture of the fish. If the act is committed on land belonging to the dwelling-house of the owner, it becomes a misdemeanour, and such a fish-poacher, when caught in the act, may be arrested by anybody. Anglers cannot be arrested, even in the latter case.

A number of laws have been passed in regard to fishing for salmon and other freshwater fish, and a close time has been established varying somewhat for different localities, as well for rod-fishing as for net-fishing. In England a licence is generally necessary to fish for salmon, trout, or char (but the salmon licence includes the latter), but not in Scotland. In Scotland the punishment for poaching salmon is a fine not less than 10*s.* nor more than £5, together with the forfeiture of the fish taken, and the boat, tackle, etc., employed by the poacher, if the sheriff or justice think fit.

Anyone not an angler poaching trout or any other freshwater fish renders himself liable to a penalty of £5, besides forfeiting the fish caught. A person who merely angles for trout in places where he has no leave to fish is only liable to an action at law.

POCAHONTAS. A celebrated North American Indian princess, daughter of Powhatan, a warrior of Virginia, born in 1595. She is said to have shown a great friendship for the English who colonised Virginia, and to have prevailed on her father to spare the life of Captain John Smith, his prisoner. After Captain Smith had left the colony she was kept for some time as a hostage by the English (1612). During this detention she was converted to Christianity and christened Rebecca, and in 1613 was married to John Rolfe, an Englishman, who in 1616 took her on a visit to England. She died the following year, and left one son, who was educated in London, and had many descendants in Virginia.—Cf. E. D. Neill, *Pocahontas and her Companions.*

POCHARD (Nyroca). A name of ducks inhabiting the Arctic regions, but migrating southwards in winter. They are marine in habits, and feed upon crustaceans, worms, molluscs, and aquatic plants. The flesh of several is much prized as food. A typical form and one of the best known is the *N. ferīna*, the common pochard, called also dunbird, red-headed poker, red-headed widgeon or duck. The head

Pochard

and neck are bright chestnut; eyes red; bill long; a broad, transverse, and dark-blue band on the upper mandible; length, 16 to 17 inches; weight, 1 to 2 lb. Other species are the scaup pochard (*N. marīla*); the tufted pochard (*N. cristāta*); and the canvas-back duck of North America (*N. vallisneria*), so highly esteemed by epicures.

POCKLINGTON. An urban district and market town of Yorkshire (East Riding), England; served by the London & North-Eastern Railway, and by canal to the Derwent. The parish church (All Saints') is mainly in the Early English style. The grammar school was founded in 1515. Pop. (1931), 2640.

POCOCK, Edward. An English Oriental scholar, born at Oxford 1604, where he died 1691. He graduated at Oxford, was ordained priest in 1628, and became chaplain to the English factory at Aleppo (1629-36). Laud engaged him to collect manuscripts and coins for the University of Oxford, and in 1636 chose him to fill the newly founded Arabic professorship at that university. He was appointed to the Hebrew chair at Oxford in 1648, together with the rich canonry of Christ Church; but from 1650 to 1660 he was deprived of his church preferment. His works are of great value to Oriental and Biblical students.

POD. In botany, a general term applied to various forms of seed-vessels of plants, such as the legume, the loment, the siliqua, the silicle, the follicle, the capsule, etc.

PODAG′RA. The form of gout which recurs at regular intervals, generally in the spring and autumn, and attacks the joints of the foot, and especially that of the great toe. It causes a sharp, burning pain, aggravated by movement or pressure on the part. The term podagra is not now used much.

PODAR′GUS. A genus of Australasian nocturnal birds of the goatsucker family. Like the goatsuckers, their mouths have a very wide gape. By day they are exces-

Podargus

sively drowsy. There are several species, one of which, Cuvier's podargus (*P. cuvieri*), is known among the Australians by the name of "more pork" from its strange cry.

PODESTÀ. An Italian word derived from the Lat. *potestas*, power, equivalent in its original meaning to a holder of power or authority. In the Middle Ages the podestà wielded almost dictatorial power in many of the Italian cities. In the modern Kingdom of Italy he is the chief official of a commune, corresponding to the French *maire*.

PODGORI′CA. Formerly a Turkish stronghold against Montenegro, but incorporated with that principality (1880), and now a part of Yugoslavia. It lies about 35 miles north of Scutari, at the foot of a range of mountains, and is the largest town of Montenegro. In the European War it was invested by the Austrians in 1916, and fell to the Allies in Nov., 1918. Pop. 15,000.

PODIEBRAD (pod′ye-bråd), **George.** King of Bohemia, born 1420 of a noble family, died 1471. When a mere youth he entered into the Hussite movement against Austria. In 1453 he was acknowledged Regent of Bohemia during the minority of the young King Ladislas, and on the death of the latter in 1457 became King of Bohemia. He strove to bring about a peaceful settlement of religious discussions, but failed in his endeavours, and was excommunicated by Pope Paul II. in 1465. At the instigation of the Pope, Matthias Corvinus, King of Hungary and son-in-law of Podiebrad, invaded Bohemia, but was defeated and sued for peace.

PODO'LIA. A government of South-Western Russia; area, 16,224 sq. miles. The country is mostly flat, but a low branch of the Carpathians extends through it in an easterly direction. The principal rivers are the Dniester and the Bug. Podolia forms one of the most valuable agricultural possessions of Russia. Manufactures include beet-sugar, spirits, flour, and tobacco. Pop. 4,000,000. Capital, Kamenetz-Podolsk.

PODOPHTHAL'MATA ("stalk-eyed"). A division of the higher Crustacea, primarily distinguished by compound eyes supported upon movable stalks termed *peduncles*. This division includes the orders Stomapoda and Decapoda, the former of which is represented by the "locust" shrimps, whilst the latter includes the familiar crabs, lobsters, common shrimps, hermit crabs, and their allies. *See* CRUSTACEA; SHRIMP.

PODOPH'YLLIN. A resin obtained from the root-stock of the may-apple (*Podophyllum peltatum*; *see* MAY-APPLE). It is of a brownish-yellow colour, dissolves readily in alcohol, and has been admitted to the pharmacopœias of many countries as a purgative; it is particularly beneficial in cases of sluggish liver, having much the same effect as mercury, but in some constitutions produces severe griping.

PODOSTEMACEÆ. A small but remarkable natural order of Polypetalous dicotyledons, allied to Saxifragaceæ. The species are found on rocks in swiftly flowing water, and are the only Flowering Plants capable of growing under these conditions. They consist of little but submerged flattened green roots, which perform all the vegetative functions, and in due course bear short-lived aerial flowering shoots.

PODU'RIDÆ. A family of apterous (wingless) insects, belonging to the sub-ord. Collembola, distinguished by the possession of an elastic forked caudal appendage, which is folded under the body when at rest, and by the sudden extension of which they are enabled to effect considerable leaps; hence their popular name of spring-tails. Their scales are favourite test objects for microscopes.

POE, Edgar Allan. American poet and romantic writer, born at Boston 1809, died at Baltimore 1849. His father and mother were actors, and being left an orphan when a mere child, he was adopted by Mr. Allan, a wealthy Richmond merchant, who resided in England from 1815 to 1820, and sent young Poe to school at Stoke-Newington. On his return to America he attended a school at Richmond, Virginia, and finally entered the University of Virginia (1826). Here he displayed great talents, but also contracted a taste for fast living which occasioned

Edgar Allan Poe

quarrels with his benefactor, and caused him to run away to Boston, where he published a booklet containing *Tamerlane* and other poems. He was next a private soldier for over a year. In 1829 a reconciliation with Mr. Allan took place, and he was sent as cadet to the military academy at West Point. Further irregularities brought about his expulsion, and also a complete rupture with Mr. Allan.

His literary career may be said to have begun in 1833, when he gained the prize offered by the *Baltimore Saturday Visitor* for a tale. He then became successively editor of the newly founded *Southern Literary Messenger* at Richmond, contributor to the *New York Review*, and editor of Burton's *Gentleman's Magazine* and *Graham's Magazine* at Philadelphia. For these periodicals he wrote a number of tales, exhibiting a weird yet fascinating imagination. While at Richmond, in 1836, he married his cousin, Virginia Clemm.

The great event in Poe's life was the publication at New York in 1845 of his poem *The Raven*, which spread his fame to the whole English-speaking world. He was subsequently connected with *The Home Journal* and *The Broadway Journal* (at New York). Other poems of this or a later period were *The Bells, Ulalume, Annabel Lee,* and *To Annie.* In 1847 his wife died. Passing through Baltimore in 1849, on his way to New York to make preparations for a second marriage, he was led to excessive drinking, and died from its effects at the hospital.

Among his most noteworthy tales are: *The Gold Bug, The Fall of the House of Usher, The Murders in the Rue Morgue,* and *The Descent into the Maelstrom.* Poe's career is sad enough, and his faults were sufficiently numerous, but the public were led to believe by Rufus Griswold, his first biographer, that his character was blacker than it really seems to have been.—BIBLIOGRAPHY: J. H. Ingram, *Edgar Allan Poe: his Life, Letters, and Opinions*; G. E. Woodberry, *Life of E. A. Poe*; L. N. Chase, *Poe and his Poetry.*

POET LAUREATE. Office of crowned poet, or poet at the Court. The Greeks and Romans used to crown poets with laurel, and Petrarch was thus crowned at Rome in 1341. Though Chaucer and later Skelton styled themselves poet laureate the office really commenced with the giving of a pension of 100 marks to Ben Jonson by James I. Charles I. made the pension £100 and added a tierce of Canary. When Southey was made laureate a money payment was made in lieu of the wine. In modern times the laureateship has been held by Wordsworth, Tennyson, Robert Bridges, and John Masefield (1930).

POE'RIO, Carlo. Italian statesman, born at Naples 1803, died at Florence 1867. Like his father Giuseppe Poerio, he often opposed the actions of the Bourbon kings of Naples, and frequently devoted his talents as an advocate to the cause of political offenders. He thus became a suspect, and from 1837 to 1848 suffered varous terms of imprisonment. The Revolution of the latter year released him from prison and placed him at the head of the Neapolitan police and of the Ministry of Public Instruction, but finding it impossible to get the Bourbons to fulfil their promises, he resigned. He sat in the new Parliament, and acted with the Opposition.

In July, 1849, he was arrested and condemned without defence to twenty-four years' imprisonment. The barbarous treatment he received in prison gave occasion to Gladstone's famous *Two Letters to Lord Aberdeen,* written in 1851 from Naples. In 1859 his sentence was commuted to transportation to South America; but he and his companions in misfortune effected a landing at Cork, in Ireland, and thence proceeded to London. In 1861 he was elected vice-president of the Italian Chamber of Deputies, and remained till his death one of the chiefs of the constitutional liberal party.

POETRY. It is notoriously difficult to define poetry. Many attempts at so doing have been made with very little success. Matthew Arnold called it "a criticism of life." Carlyle said that "all poetry, if we go to that with it, is but a giving of names;" in which case Adam must have been the earliest and greatest poet. Watts-Dunton gave a carefully thought-out definition: "Absolute poetry is the concrete and artistic expression of the human mind in emotional and rhythmical language." St. Augustine called poetry "devils' wine," and Wordsworth called it "the breath and finer spirit of all knowledge." Dr. Johnson defined poetry as "the art of uniting pleasure with truth, by calling imagination to the help of reason." "What is poetry," wrote Mill, "but the thought and words in which emotion spontaneously embodies itself." According to Coleridge, poetry is "a species of composition opposed to science, as having intellectual pleasure for its object and as attaining its end by means of language natural to us in a state of excitement." "True poetry," wrote Goethe, "is an earthly gospel setting us free, by an inner serenity and outward soothing effect from the burdens of life." Hazlitt defined poetry, in its matter and form, as "natural imagery or feeling combined with passion and fancy. It is the universal language which the heart holds with nature itself." For Shelley poetry is "that which lifts the veil from the hidden beauty of the world," whilst Poe called it "a rhythmical creation of beauty." *The New English Dictionary* defines it as "The expression or embodiment of beautiful or elevated thought, imagination, or feeling, in language adapted to stir the imagination and emotions, both immediately and also through the harmonic suggestions latent in or implied by the words and connections of words actually used, such language containing a rhythmical element, and having usually a metrical form."

Although it is so hard to give a definition of poetry, most men have little difficulty in recognising it when they see it. It is, however, customary to apply the term "poetry" only to the loftier and more successful specimens of the poetic art. Poetry which is of a less elevated kind, or which is full of errors in technique, is usually known as verse.

Poetry as Imitation. Aristotle has said that all poetry, of whatever kind it may be, is a mode of imitation. Man is the most imitative of living creatures, and takes pleasure in seeing things imitated. Imitation is one instinct of our nature; another deeply rooted instinct is love of rhythm and harmony. Poetry has sprung from these two instincts.

Poetry as Interpretation. Broadly speaking, poetry is the emotional and imaginative interpretation of life, just as literature is an interpretation of life. The poet goes to the essence of life, penetrates reality, apprehends facts emotionally, and communicates the feelings aroused in him to his listeners. In his interpretation of life emotion and imagination predominate, and he appeals to our feelings and passions through the medium of rhythmical language, the natural speech of excitement.

When man is excited, swayed by feeling or passion, his language—the vehicle by which he expresses his thoughts and communicates them to others—becomes rhythmical, for exalted moods and a state of ecstasy stimulate such language, as in the case of orators. Thus one of the chief traits of poetry is that it peculiarly affects the imagination and the feelings. When we speak of actions or the creations of genius as poetical, the term implies that they had their origin in conceptions in which imagination and the feelings were chief agents. Hence the universality of poetry, hence the preponderance of the poetical in the language of early nations, when man for the first time began to express vivid emotions and daring conceptions in words.

A common idea, the result of experience and reasoning, may be conceived by the poet in such a way as to strike our feelings with peculiar force; or ideas which, though elevated in themselves are familiar to all, may receive new impressiveness from a new and striking way of expressing them. It is gratifying to find a new conception of a familiar idea presenting the subject in a light in which we had never viewed it. "Poets," wrote Shelley, "make things familiar look unfamiliar." They "see the world in a grain of sand, and a heaven in a wild flower."

Grasping the mystery and beauty of things, the poet interprets them in his own individual way, but always stimulated by emotions and aided by imagination. He becomes not only "a dreamer after dark," but "a speaker of essential truth." He speaks in rhythm, because, as Browning once said, "his brain beats in rhythm."

But mere rhythmical language does not yet constitute poetry, for impassioned prose is also rhythmical. Poetry is more than rhythmical language, it is, to borrow Professor Mackail's expression, "rhythm in verses." Just, however, as impassioned language, coloured words, and the "purple patches" against which Horace warned poets do not constitute poetry, so is a treatise on agriculture in verse not a poetical creation. It is the union between imagination and emotion on the one hand, and rhythm in verse on the other, which constitutes poetry.

Although, as an art, the chief function of poetry is to give æsthetic pleasure, and, like music, it addresses itself to the ear, true poetry appeals not only to our feelings and senses, but also to our intellect. It creates beauty, but it also stimulates thought.

Divisions. According to its subjects, and the relation which the poet holds to his productions, poetry is divided into the poetry of subjective feeling, or lyrical poetry; narrative poetry, including the ballad and the epic; dramatic poetry; didactic poetry, presenting science or art under their beautiful and generally attractive aspects; and satirical poetry.

Poetics. The theory of poetry, or its philosophy, is called *poetics*. It is one of the theories earliest developed, and æsthetics grew out of it. Among the Greeks Aristotle treated it in his *Peri poiētikēs*; among the Romans, Horace, in his *Ars Poetica*, or *Letter to the Pisos*, deals with the subject more briefly. In modern times it has been treated by Vida, Torquato Tasso, and many other Italians; by Boileau, Scaliger, Racine, D'Alembert, Marmontel, Baumgarten (the founder of æsthetics), Lessing, Klopstock, W. von Humboldt, Herder, Schiller, Goethe, the Schlegels, Hegel, and others; in English by Blair, Wordsworth, Campbell, Hazlitt, and others.

History. We may divide the history of poetry into two periods: the one before the birth of Christ, the other since.

Hebrew. The Hebrews are the first people from whom poetical productions have descended to our times. Only obscure traces remain of any earlier poetry of the Indians, Persians, Syrians, and Arabians. The religious poetry of the Hebrews is of very ancient date, and possesses a solemn character, distinct from that of the other nations of antiquity. It begins with cosmogony, becomes at a later period of a warlike character, then assumes the form of sacred songs in the time of David, and attains under Solomon (from 1044 to 975) its greatest elevation, after which it assumes a prophetical character. The fragments which have come down to us from the flourishing period of Indian poetry, some centuries before Christ, are of an original character and peculiar delicacy.

Greek. We next come to classic antiquity, and become acquainted with poetry in the plastic character which it assumed in Asia Minor and Greece, under the influence of the prevailing paganism, which received such rich and various hues from the glowing imagination of the people. Greek poetry may again be divided into three periods: the first of these extends from the earliest times of Greece to the Persian wars. The poetry of the Greeks begins in Thrace and Asia Minor, and the great national epics of Homer, or the Homeridæ, the rhapsodists, the cyclic and gnomic poets, indicate a wide diffusion of poetry at that time. Lyric poetry soon attained a peculiar eminence. The second period extends from the Persian wars to the time of Alexander the Great. It is the flourishing period of the dramatic art, and of cultivated Greek poetry in general. The third period shows the decline of Greek poetry under the successors of Alexander, and the revival of the same in Alexandria.

Roman. The language of the Romans was not employed in poetry till a late period, and until the Second Punic War, or until the time in which they became closely connected with the Greeks, the Romans made only rude essays in poetry. The era of Augustus was the golden age of their poetry, and it thereafter declined steadily until the introduction of the Christian religion and the irruption of the barbarians. When the Christian religion became prevalent, we find the Latin language applied in Christian worship to a mystic religious poetry; and later, in the ninth, tenth, and succeeding centuries, employed by learned men in imitations of the old Roman poetry. Contemporary with these we witness the rise of Arabian poetry.

French. A peculiar poetry sprang up among the French, in the time of the Provençals or Troubadours of the south, and the Trouvères of the north, in the eleventh century. In its devotion, valour, and love the spirit of chivalry is apparent. This romantic poetry of the Franks declined into mere artificial rhyming after the end of the twelfth century. Under the dominion of Francis I. poetry somewhat revived; but the age of Louis XIV. was the golden era of French poetry, although it often, but in its own manner, imitated the ancients and modernised ancient materials. Rhetorical elegance and easy wit were its chief aim.

Italian. Modern Italian poetry sprang from the Provençal. But a poetry of a natural character began in Sicily after the thirteenth century, and flourished, particularly from the time of Dante and Petrarch to that of Ariosto and Tasso, in the thirteenth fourteenth, and fifteenth centuries, and thence declined into bombast and imitation.

Spanish. Spanish poetry was originally a branch of Provençal; and the earliest Castilian poetry, properly so called, belongs to the thirteenth century; but it began to flourish under the administration of Charles I., and declined under Philip IV. Simultaneous with it, and in connection with it, flourished Portuguese poetry.

German. German poetry, which is closely connected with the northern, and has its own epic cycle, flourished at various times, and with much variety of character, but most vigorously when free from the influence of foreign models.

English. The origin of English and Scottish poetry is lost, like that of the German, in the distant period of the bards; it was refined by the Norman-French poetry. But the flourishing period of English poetry is placed in the times of Queen Elizabeth, although Chaucer is considered the father of modern English poetry.

Scandinavian. The Scandinavian poetry presents chivalry peculiarly coloured by the northern character, since the thirteenth century, when the German *Heldenbuch* (Book of Heroes) was introduced into Norway, and foreign tales became blended with native ones.—BIBLIOGRAPHY: Matthew Arnold, *Essays in Criticism*; Bliss Perry, *A Study of Poetry*; J. C. Shairp, *Aspects of Poetry*; A. S. Cook, *The Art of Poetry*; W. H. Hudson, *An Introduction to the Study of Literature*; Sir Philip Sidney, *The Defense of Poesie*; Gayley and Scott, *Introduction to the Methods and Materials of Literary Criticism*; G. Saintsbury, *History of Criticism*.

POGGIO BRACCIOLINI (pod'jō brât-chō-lē'ni). Italian scholar and author, born 1380, died 1459. He came early under the influence of the revival of literature kindled in Italy by Petrarch and Boccaccio.

About 1402 he became writer of the apostolic letters under Boniface IX., and for fifty years remained connected with the Papal curia in posts of confidence and dignity. He was a great enthusiast for literature, and unearthed a mass of valuable works which hitherto had been unknown. His own writings embrace a variety of subjects, ranging from moral essays on the miseries of human life and the vicissitudes of fortune, to improper *fabliaux* in Latin, and he excelled as a polemical writer.

POGROMS. A term applied to anti-Jewish riots and massacres taking place in Russia from time to time. Although the Jews have suffered in that country at various times, pogroms may be said to have become a regular feature since 1881, after the assassination of Alexander II. Anxious to turn the public discontent into another channel, and to divert the thoughts of the people from revolutionary propaganda to race-hatred, the Government frequently arranged pogroms, and made the Jews the scapegoats of a reactionary policy. Terrible pogroms took place at Kishinev, in Bessarabia, in 1903, and again in 1905, after the October Manifesto, when Tsar Nicholas II. had promised his country a Constitution. Pogroms have unfortunately not ceased even after the Revolution of 1917, and have been of frequent occurrence under the Soviet régime and the rule of the Bolsheviks.

POILU (pwȧ'lü'). Name given to a French private soldier. The word means "hairy" and, originally applied to a recruit, was used commonly during the Great War for soldiers in the trenches, when many were obliged to let their beards grow. The term thus came into general use to denote a common soldier in the French army.

POINCARÉ, Jules Henri. French mathematician, born at Nancy in 1854, and died in 1912. After passing through the Polytechnic School and the School of Mines, he was engaged for a year or two as a mining-engineer at Versoul. Having obtained his doctorate in mathematical science, he became a lecturer at the Polytechnic School in 1883, and remained there till 1897. In 1886 he was appointed to the professorship of mathematical physics at the Sorbonne, and in 1896 to that of celestial mechanics. He was elected to the Academy in 1887.

In 1889 he carried off the great prize offered by the King of Sweden for competition among the mathematicians of Europe, with a memoir on the problem of three bodies. The award was made by an international jury, who were guided by a report drawn up by Weierstrass. From that time Poincaré was regarded by general consent as the ablest mathematician of his day. His researches cover nearly the whole range of mathematics and mathematical physics. He also earned high distinction as a philosopher, being one of a small band of mathematicians whose work forms perhaps the most notable recent contribution to philosophy.

He had a happy knack of popular writing, and his expositions of recent advances in physical science have had a wide circulation. Poincaré's most important work is scattered over innumerable mathematical journals. Among his books are: *Théorie des fonctions fuchsiennes, Cours de physique mathématique* (13 vols.), *Méthodes nouvelles de la mécanique céleste, Oscillations électriques, Théorie de Maxwell et les oscillations hertziennes, Théorie du potentiel newtonien, Calcul des probabilités, Science et hypothèse, La Valeur de la science.*

POINCARÉ, Raymond. Ninth President of the French Republic, born at Bar-le-Duc, in Lorraine, on 20th Aug., 1860, the son of a civil engineer. He is a member of a family of distinguished scholars, lawyers, and scientists; his brother Lucien was an eminent physicist, and Jules Henri Poincaré, the mathematician, was his cousin. Educated at Bar-le-Duc and at the Lycée Henri IV. in Paris, he studied law, a profession chosen for him by his mother. At the boarding-house in the Latin Quarter where he lived he met Gabriel Hanotaux and Alexandre Millerand, with whom he formed a strong friendship.

He practised the legal profession for some time, contributing at the same time articles and poems to the *Echo de l'Est,* the *Voltaire* (under the pseudonym of Jacques Aubertin), and to the *République Française.* A brilliant orator, noted for style and perfect form of his speeches, he soon gained distinction in his career. His future, however, lay neither in the legal profession nor in literature, but in politics.

Elected to the Chamber of Deputies in 1887, he made his first speech in defence of the Budget presented by Rouvier. He refused the portfolio of Minister of Finance offered to him by Méline in 1893, but accepted that of Minister of Public Instruction in the Dupuy Cabinet in April of the same year. In 1894 he was Minister of Finance, an office in which he greatly distinguished himself. In 1903 he was elected to the Senate, and in 1912 he succeeded M. Caillaux as Premier, Bourgeois, Briand, Millerand, and Barthou consenting to collaborate with him, Poincaré himself assuming the portfolio of Foreign Affairs. Whilst vigorously supporting the French Alliance with Russia and the *entente cordiale* with England, he advocated the necessity for keeping the military and naval forces of France in a state of efficiency. In Jan., 1913, he was elected President of the French Republic, and the election was hailed with enthusiasm not only by the Nationalist party, but by the country in general.

Ominous signs were already appearing on the political horizon of Europe, and a conflagration in the East seemed inevitable. It was therefore of paramount importance for France to have at the Elysée a man who was not a mere figure-head, but a statesman whose characteristics were a clear conception of government, a high intelligence, and energy and will-power in cases of emergency. The country was not deceived. The President's personal influence made itself felt in various important measures, and particularly in foreign affairs. Poincaré was indeed the first President of the third Republic to exercise considerable political influence. During the European War he was indefatigable. By his brilliant speeches he fanned the flame of patriotism of his countrymen, and by his optimism he inspired hope in those pessimists who frequently were on the verge of despair.

When he thought that the hour of Clemenceau had arrived, and that no one else was capable of carrying the war to a successful issue, he did not hesitate to call to power his former political opponent. He had the supreme satisfaction of seeing Alsace-Lorraine restored to France during his presidency. When his term of office expired in 1920, Poincaré did not retire from public life, but returned to the Senate as member for the Meuse. He was elected to the Académie Française in 1909, and in 1914 the honour of being made Rector of the University of Glasgow was conferred upon him. A clever lawyer, a brilliant orator, a distinguished writer, and a skilful politician, Poincaré was one of France's greatest Presidents. On the 10th Feb., 1920, the Chamber of Deputies paid him the homage of deciding to inscribe his name among those Frenchmen "who had deserved well of their country."

During 1920-1 Poincaré's vast influence in French politics was exemplified in the "campaign of hate" against Germany, which he personally fomented, and which eventually narrowed down to a criticism of the policy of Lloyd George and his alleged leniency towards Germany, particularly in the matter of reparations. Poincaré was all for the aggrandisement of France and the humiliation of Germany, anxious to take a terrible revenge for the bitter cup of sorrow the German War Lords had forced France to drink to the dregs, in the closing days of the tottering empire of the last Napoleon. As a result, during the Cannes Conference of 1922, Briand was compelled to return to Paris to give an account of his premiership and to explain away, if he could, the proposed Anglo-French Treaty of Defence. On 13th Jan., Briand resigned, and Poincaré was asked by President Millerand to form a new Cabinet. He held office as Prime Minister and Minister for Foreign Affairs till 1924, and in 1926 he became Prime Minister and Minister of Finance. He relinquished the Finance Ministry in 1928, and resigned from the Premiership in 1929. His works include: *Idées contemporaines* (1906), *Questions et figures politiques* (1907), and *Comment la France est gouvernée*.—Cf. Henri Girard, *Raymond Poincaré*.

POINSETTIA. The *Euphorbia pulcherrima*, a Mexican plant in general cultivation in greenhouses, conspicuous for the large and brilliant red floral leaves (flower-like leafy bracts) surrounding its small yellow flowers.

POINT. In mediæval music, a dot affecting note-duration. Known as points of augmentation, division, perfection, and alteration, points fulfilled the functions of modern dots and barlines. Point also denoted a mediæval note, and also a place of dramatic, or contrapuntal interest in a composition.

An **organ-point** is succession of harmonies progressing over a pedal bass-note; also the chord introducing a concerto's *cadenza*.

POINTE-À-PITRE (pwânt-à-pē-tr). The principal port of the French West Indian island Guadeloupe, on the south-west coast of Grande-Terre, and one of the most important commercial towns of the Antilles. There is a fine harbour, and sugar, cacao, and vanilla are traded. The town, mostly built of wood, was destroyed by fire in 1780, by an earthquake in 1843, and again by fire in 1871. Pop. (1932), 30,465.

POINTE-DES-GALETS. The chief port of the French island of Réunion.

POINTER. A breed of sporting dogs, nearly allied to the true hounds. The original breed is Spanish, but a cross with the fox-hound is now generally used. It is smooth, short-haired, generally marked black and white like the fox-hound, but occasionally a uniform black. It derives its name from its habit of stopping and pointing with the head in the direction of game, discovered by a very acute sense of smell. The dog once having pointed remains perfectly quiet. This faculty in the pointer is hereditary, but is better developed by training.

POINT-TO-POINT. Type of steeplechase for hunters, usually over a course of three or four miles. Originally these races were run over a straight course, i.e. from one point to another across country.

POISON. *See* TOXICOLOGY.

POISON-GAS WARFARE. Poison gases have introduced great problems in warfare, because they can be made secretly in large quantities at short notice by modifying the chemical processes essential in industry, especially those used in dye manufacture. A nation like Germany, with almost a monopoly to-day in the making of dyes, would have an enormous and perhaps a decisive advantage in making war; therefore, whatever the economic sacrifice entailed, it is essential for the safety of ourselves and the other nations to build up strong dye industries.

The Germans first employed poison-gas clouds against the French on 22nd April, 1915 (on a 4-mile front north of the Ypres salient); two days later they attacked the Canadians in the same manner. This use of poisons was a direct violation of the Conventions signed by Germany at The Hague. Fortunately for the British and the Entente, although there is evidence that the Germans had made considerable preparations for chemical warfare, they had not evolved a suitable technique, for had they then understood the possibilities of this new weapon, they might well have obtained a decision by their treachery.

The Germans generated their cloud by means of cylinders emplaced in the front-line trenches, and discharged through pipes pushed through the parapet. The cylinders had a siphon tube going to the bottom, and the chlorine was expelled by its own vapour pressure, just as soda-water is expelled by the carbonic acid gas in the siphon.

As the opposing trench lines were by no means regular, but consisted of a series of salients and re-entrants, the possible wind directions which would carry gas from one small part of the German (or Allied) front line to the opposing front line were extremely circumscribed, and were unsuitable on the next small section of front; therefore it was impossible to make a gas-attack by means of cylinders so emplaced on a sufficiently long front to enable the attacking troops to break through and win a decisive battle. As the use of poisons was contrary to Article 23 (*a* and *e*) of The Hague Conventions, and the International Declaration of 29th July, 1899, forbidding the use of projectiles having for their "sole object" the spreading of "deleterious and asphyxiating gases," neither the English nor the French had made preparation for nor considered the use of anything beyond lachrymators or tear gases (which would put men temporarily out of action without causing them permanent injury). The Germans first used chlorine, an exceedingly cruel poison, but effective only against men devoid of any form of protection.

In Germany chlorine was one of the chemicals required for the dye industries, but in England and France only very small quantities were manufactured in peace time, and the Allies were forced to build special factories immediately in order to retaliate. In retaliating, the Allied staffs decided to copy the German methods and the gas used, chlorine, and the first British gas-attack took place on 25th Sept., 1915, as part of the preparation for the Loos offensive. During 1916 phosgene (carbonyl chloride), which is far more toxic, was used in the same manner as chlorine, but owing to the low vapour pressure of phosgene at ordinary temperatures, it was necessary to dilute the phosgene with 50 per cent of chlorine in order to expel it from the cylinders and to atomise it at the nozzle.

Apart from using gas in the form of wind-borne clouds produced by cylinders, in 1915 the Germans commenced to fill shells with lethal gases, and the tactical advantages of gas-shell proved so great for blanketing enemy batteries during an attack, harrying reliefs, disorganising rail-heads and transport, as well as in battle, that its employment increased enormously as the war progressed, and led in turn to the production of special gases for each particular purpose, such as the celebrated ypérite or "mustard gas" (dichlordiethyl sulphide), a liquid which remained a long while on the ground evaporating slowly, and had a most insidious action on the eyes and lungs, causing temporary or permanent blindness after exposure to a very low concentration, and blisters on the skin which, though they did not appear at once, were most painful, disabling, and slow to heal.

The nature of gas-clouds showed that, while the use of cylinders from trenches was a poor method of producing them, it was impossible, by means of artillery shell, to generate clouds which would not only be lethal on the area of initiation, but which would travel long distances and remain lethal. The failure was due to the small capacity of the shell. The stresses on a shell fired from a gun being very great, the walls of the shell have to be thick. Hence the volume available for gas is small, so that the weight of gas thrown is insignificant in comparison with the weight of the shell, and the cost is high in proportion to the result. There is a further difficulty. The thick walls of the shell necessitate powerful bursting charges, which dissipate the gas. For these reasons ypérite was by far the most successful gas-shell filling, and ypérite was not a gas at all, but a liquid of high boiling-point (217° C.) which vaporised very slowly. Only 3 per cent of the casualties due to ypérite died, but the casualties caused were far more numerous, proportionately, than those from shells with more lethal fillings, because even with the most deadly of gases it was never possible to concentrate sufficient guns on an area to produce a cloud which would travel and kill.

For gas-cloud attacks the cylinder method, therefore, held the field for some time. General wind forecasts were given by the meteorologists during the war with astonishing accuracy, but to forecast with certainty the precise wind-direction in a given locality days ahead was impossible. Consequently, apart from the objections already enumerated, the tactical value of this method was much diminished, owing to the uncertainty whether the operation would be carried through at a given time. It was plain, therefore, that if the advantage of large lethal clouds travelling several miles over the enemy position were to be obtained with reasonable certainty at a given time, so that they would be of tactical use, the cloud must be developed on the enemy's position and not just in front of the attacking troops.

The Livens Projector (invented by Captain W. H. Livens, R.E., first used in 1916) was the means by which an entirely new form of bombardment and cloud-gas technique became possible. Projectors were very light muzzle-loading mortars electrically fired, so designed that they could be manufactured cheaply and rapidly in enormous numbers. The gas was contained in a light steel drum or bomb weighing only 65 lb., which was easily carried by one man, and yet was strong enough for ranges of over a mile. The projectors were emplaced touching each other in long, shallow trenches in rows, small steel base-plates preventing the recoil burying the mortar-tube too deeply. They were fired in salvos, the maximum salvo recorded being over 6000 drums, which would generate a cloud containing nearly 100 tons weight of gas. Captured German orders showed that the danger-zone from these clouds extended for over 10 kilometres (or 7 miles from the area of origin), and such concentrations of gas were produced by these salvos that the Germans were killed in many cases before they could put on their gas-masks, or in spite of such protection as their gas-masks afforded them. The Allies manufactured more than 200,000 Livens Projectors during the war, and, in spite of the German advantage in gas-manufacturing capacity, this invention gave the Allies the initiative in cloud-gas warfare.

The gases used during the war may be divided into three classes.

(a) *Non-lethal irritants*, the first gases considered by the English and French. The chief of these were *lachrymators*, remaining a long while on the ground and evaporating slowly, acting on the eyes, and usually persistent. They had an iodine or bromine base, the best known being *ethyl iodoacetate*, *benzyl* and *xylyl bromide*, and *brominated ketones*, the last three chiefly used by the Germans.

(b) *Lethal irritants*, acting on the mucous membranes, eyes, and skin. The chief examples used by the Germans, and the date from which they were used, are as follows:

Persistent: "mustard oil" (*dichlordiethyl sulphide*), boiling-point 217° C. (July, 1917).

Non-persistent: phenylcarbylamine chloride, boiling-point, 209° C. (Sept., 1917); *dichlorethylarsine*, boiling-point, 156° C.; *diphenylchlorarsine*, solid, melting point, 46° C., in German "Blue Cross" shell; *diphenylcyanoarsine*, melting-point, 23° C., in German "Blue Cross" shell; *chloropicrin* (usually mixed with phosgene or stannic chloride); *chlorine* (the first cloud-gas used).

(c) *Lethal and non-persistent: phosgene* (*carbonyl chloride*), used much in cloud form as well as for filling trench-mortar bombs and shells, very lethal, with a curious delayed action; *trichlormethyl chloroformate* and *chlormethyl chloroformate*, German "Green Cross" shell fillings similar to phosgene in effect; *cyanogen compounds*, immediately fatal in concentrations of 1 : 1000 air, but unstable and not dense enough for the cloud to travel.

Protection against Gas. The first gas-masks (improvised by Sir William Ramsay the day of the original German attack) were bands or mouth-pads of flannel or wool, worn across the face and tied behind the head; these were soaked in hyposulphite of soda, to which a little glycerine was added so that they would keep moist; these masks gave very fair protection against low concentrations of chlorine.

There is a cast of a dead body in the museum at Pompeii showing a similar type of improvised gas-mask, which brought home to the writer the fact, not generally realised, that the great death-roll in that catastrophe of ancient times was not due to the lava stream, or even the shower of ashes, but to the vast discharges of sulphur gases carried by the wind from the mountain over the doomed cities.

All the gas-masks used during the war were really filters, which removed the poisons from the air breathed by the man, but did not supply him with air to breathe (as oxygen apparatus does), and the list of gases which were used will make clear the difficulties in devising a mask which would give

Mask used as a protection against Poison Gas

perfect protection against them all, remain efficient under active-service conditions, and be neither heavy nor bulky. The English respirator adopted finally consisted of a cylindrical container filled with vegetable charcoal, made from the hardest and densest nut-shells or fruit-stones available, and soda-lime-permanganate granules, with other chemicals introduced into the granules as required to absorb the various new gases as they were brought out. This cylinder was connected by a tube with a face-piece or mask fitting tightly over the face. Rubber inlet and outlet valves prevented air reaching the lungs without passing through the filter on inspiration, and prevented the moist air, expelled by the lungs on expiration, from traversing the filter and lowering its efficiency.

This mask, which was more efficient and more adaptable than the German device, the Allies owed to the work of Major Bertram Lambert at Oxford, in devising the granules; to the organising genius of the late Colonel E. F. Harrison; and to the vision and foresight of General H. F. Thuillier (then Director of Gas Services in France, and later Controller of the Chemical Warfare Department of the Ministry of Munitions, England). General Hartley's method of protecting dug-outs and gun-positions by a simple and efficient form of blanket-screen also proved valuable.

If there is a future war, it may be necessary to protect not only the fighting forces against gas, but the civilian population also. There are many grave difficulties which must be overcome if such protection is to be efficient, for developments during the last years of the past war showed that, in spite of the fact that more casualties were then due to gas than to any other weapon, the possible horrors of future gas-warfare have only been foreshadowed. In framing international regulations against gas-warfare the difficulty will always remain that, like Germany, any dishonest nation with a chemical industry can secretly prepare an overwhelming chemical offensive against unprotected peoples.

BIBLIOGRAPHY: For further information see *Chemical Warfare* (a paper read by Brigadier-General H. Hartley, C.B.E., M.C., before the British Association, 1919); *Journal of Industrial and Engineering Chemistry*, published by the American Chemical Society (various papers, 1919-20); *The Riddle of the Rhine*, by Major V. Lefebure, O.B.E., a book discussing the menace of the German chemical factories (Collins, 1921); *America's Munitions, 1917-1919*, by the Hon. Benedict Crowell, United States Assistant Secretary of State for War and Director of Munitions Supply.

POISON IVY, or **POISON OAK** (*Rhus toxicodendron*). A trailing or climbing shrub of the ord. Terebinthaceæ, found in Canada and the United States.

POISON-NUT. A name for *Strychnos nux-vomica*, an evergreen tree of the nat. ord. Loganiaceæ, the seeds of which yield strychnine. (*See* NUX-VOMICA.) Also a name for the *Tanghinia venenifera*, of the nat. ord. Apocynaceæ, the fruit of which is a drupe enclosing a kernel extremely poisonous. It used to be employed in Madagascar as an ordeal-test of guilt or innocence, the result generally being the death of the suspected person.

POISONOUS PLANTS. The chief British narcotic vegetable poisons are those derived from the plants Monk's-hood or Wolf's-bane, Deadly Nightshade, Belladonna or Dwale, Henbane, and Thorn-apple. The first of these (*Aconītum napellus*) is intensely poisonous, owing to the presence of an alkaloid known as *aconitin*; the chief antidotes are atropine, belladonna, and digitalis. The Deadly Nightshade (*Atropa belladonna*) owes its poisonous properties to the active principle *atropine*. An antidote is tannic acid, 20 grains in water; the stomach should be emptied, and brandy and water given as stimulants. Similar treatment is prescribed in the case of poisoning from the Thorn-apple (*Datūra stramonium*). Henbane (*Hyoscyămus niger*) has properties similar to those of belladonna.

A considerable number of common British plants contain irritant or narcotico-irritant poisons. Among these is the Cuckoo-pint or Wake-robin (*Arum maculātum*), the remedy for which is castor-oil, hot coffee, stimulants, and warm poulticing.

Several well-known members of the ord. Umbelliferæ contain a poison whose action starts in the lower limbs; these include the Common or Spotted Hemlock (*Conium maculātum*), the Water Hemlock (*Cicūta virōsa*), the Hemlock Water Dropwort (*Œnanthe crocāta*), and the Fool's Parsley (*Æthūsa cynapium*). Among their antidotes are oak bark decoction, tannic and gallic acids, hot tea or other similar substances; stimulants should be given.

The antidote which is given in the case of Meadow Saffron (*Colchicum autumnāle*) is atropine, the stomach having first of all been emptied. For the Woody Nightshade or Bittersweet (*Solānum dulcamāra*), castor-oil, stimulants, etc., are prescribed, in addition to the emetics to be employed in all cases. The berries of the Common Privet have also proved fatal.

The well-known Foxglove (*Digitālis purpurea*) owes its poisonous character to a powerful principle *digitalin*; the administration of atropine is, as a general rule, all that is needed, and a recumbent position should be maintained. Other poisonous plants are the Cypress Spurge (*Euphorbia cyparissias*), the Pasque-flower (*Anemōne pulsatilla*), the Mezereon (*Daphne mezereum*), the Herb Paris (*Paris quadrifolia*), and Laburnum (*Cytisus laburnum*).

Mistakes are often made in distinguishing edible from poisonous Fungi. The edible kinds mostly grow solitarily in dry, airy places, while poisonous varieties grow in clusters in woods and damp, dark places. Bright-coloured species should generally be avoided.

POISSON, Siméon Denis. French mathematician, born in 1781, died 1840. In 1798 he entered the Ecole Polytechnique, where his talent soon showed itself, and Lacroix, Legendre, Lagrange, and Laplace all befriended him. He succeeded Fourier as professor at the Ecole Polytechnique in 1808, and in 1809 was appointed first professor of mechanics at the Sorbonne. Poisson published more than three hundred works, some of them elaborate treatises, mostly on mathematical physics.—*Poisson's equation* is an extension of Laplace's equation (q.v.). It is $d^2V/dx^2 + d^2V/dy^2 + d^2V/dz^2 + 4\pi\rho = 0$, where V is the potential (q.v.) at (x, y, z) due to a distribution of electricity of volume density ρ.

POITIERS (pwȧ-tyā), or **POICTIERS.** A city of France, capital of the department of Vienne, on the Clain. The principal edifice is the cathedral (St. Pierre), founded by Henry II. of England about 1162.

Poitiers is one of the most ancient towns of France, and the vestiges of

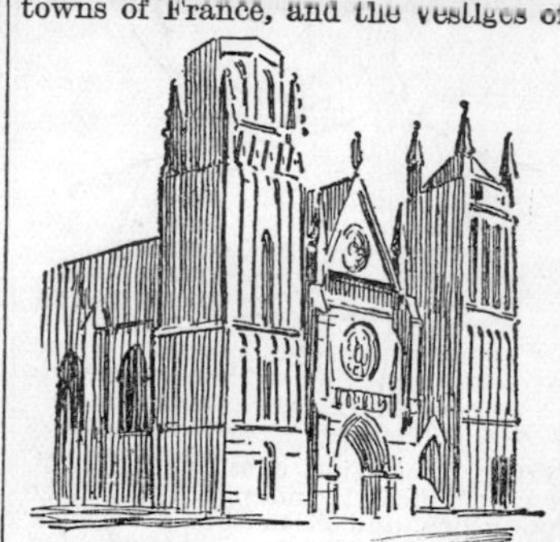

Poitiers: Cathedral of St. Pierre

a Roman palace, of Roman baths, of an aqueduct, and an amphitheatre still remain. It is named after the Gallic tribe of the *Pictones*. Two famous battles were fought in its vicinity, that in which Charles Martel defeated the Saracen army in 732, and that between the French under their king, John II., and the English under Edward the Black Prince in 1356. Poitiers was capital of the pre-Revolutionary province of Poitou. The manufactures are unimportant, but there is a large trade. Pop. 41,000.

POITOU (pwȧ-tö). One of the pre-Revolutionary provinces of France, between Brittany and Anjou on the north, Berry on the east, the Atlantic on the west, and Angoumois and Saintonge on the south. It was divided into Lower Poitou and Upper

POISONOUS PLANTS
1, Meadow Saffron. 2, Cuckoo-pint. 3, Bittersweet.

Poitou, now co-extensive with the provinces of La Vendée and Upper Poitou and with Deux-Sèvres and Vienne respectively. Poitiers was the capital. Henry II. of England acquired possession of Poitou by his marriage with Eleanor, heiress of the last Duke of Aquitaine (*see* AQUITANIA).

POKER. A card game played with a full pack of ordinary playing-cards, generally including the joker, in which the winner is determined by the value of the combinations of cards he holds. The origin of the game is obscure, but it has been more played by Americans than any other people. It is played by two to six people, each receiving five cards from the one whose turn it is to deal. The scale of values of hands runs: *a pair*, e.g. two threes or two jacks; *three of a kind*; *a straight*, five cards in order of value but of various suits; *a flush*, any five cards of the same suit; *a full house*, three of a kind and a pair; *four of a kind*; *a straight flush*, five cards in order of value and of the same suit. If the joker is used, the additional combination *five of a kind* ranks highest of all.

The play varies considerably. After the deal a start is made with small bets, usually to a prescribed limited value. Any player is at liberty to drop out, but if he continues to play he must bring up the value of his stake to the common level. Those still in the game then discard some or all of their five cards, and have others dealt to them to make up their hands. Betting then starts in earnest, each being allowed to raise the bet to any extent up to a certain limit. One after another the players fall out until the betting has reached a satisfying value, when one of the players calls the hands to be shown, and puts in the amount of the last "raise." The holder of the best hand takes all stakes, including those forfeited by players falling out. If all but one fall out, the stakes go to the one still in.

The game has considerable possibilities of bluffing in it. Stakes can be put up in amounts of such a character as to convince the other players that one's hand is very different from what it is. The game is a dangerous one to play with strangers, as it is one of the most popular with card-markers, card-manipulators, and other American tricksters.—Cf. *The Handbook of Games*, vol. ii. (Bohn's Libraries).

POKER-WORK. Form of decorative art, effected by burning a design on wood, leather, velvet, and other materials with a heated metallic point. First accomplished with a red-hot "poker," e.g. the pyrographic drawings on lime-trees and other woods by John Cranch (1751-1823), it is now done with hollow needles heated in spirit lamps.

POKEWEED. The *Phytolacca decandra*, a North American branching herbaceous plant, ord. Phytolaccaceæ, which is naturalised in some parts of Europe and Asia. Its root acts as a powerful emetic and cathartic, but its use is attended with narcotic effects. Its berries are said to possess the same quality; they are employed as a remedy for chronic and syphilitic rheumatism, and for allaying syphiloid pains. The leaves are extremely acrid, but the young shoots, which lose this quality by boiling in water, are eaten in the United States.

POLA. A town of Italy, in Istria, on the Adriatic, formerly the principal naval base of Austria-Hungary. It is an ancient place whose authentic history dates back to its capture by the Romans in 179 B.C., and it was for a long time the principal town of Istria. Its former importance is well attested by architectural remains, chief among which are a colossal and well-preserved amphitheatre and two temples.

Pola had sunk to the level of a mere fishing-place with some 800 or 900 inhabitants, when, in 1848, the Austrian Government, tempted by excellent harbour accommodation, selected it as their chief naval station, and by the erection of dockyards, of an arsenal, barracks, and other Government establishments, infused new life into it. There are two harbours (naval and mercantile), extensive fortifications, and barracks.

During the European War the Italian fleet blockaded an enemy squadron in Pola harbour, and made several raids, in course of one of which an Austrian capital ship was torpedoed. Croatian seamen boarded the surrendered vessels in Oct., 1918, when the Italians raided the harbour again, and precipitated an Italian-Yugoslav crisis by destroying the *Viribus Unitis*. By the Treaty of St. Germain (1919) Pola passed definitely to Italy. Pop. (1931), 55,559.

POLACCA. A three-masted vessel used in the Mediterranean. The fore- and main-masts are usually of one piece, so that they have neither tops, caps, nor cross-trees. It carries a fore-and-aft sail on the mizzen-mast, and square sails on the main-mast and fore-mast.

POLAND. A republic of Europe, lying approximately between 48° and 55° N. lat., and between 16° and 28° E. long. It spans the great North

European Plain from the Baltic seaboard to the Carpathians, and is broadly a transition area between the German plain in the west and the vast plain of Russia in the east. In the south the frontier follows the crests of the Carpathians, and includes most of the former Austrian province of Galicia; to the east, the frontier marches with that of Russia and the Ukraine via the Pripet marshes; north is the Baltic. From the Carpathians the boundary follows the water-parting between the Oder and Warthe, crosses the Warthe between Landsberg and Posen, and then curves north east across the plain to the coast, a little west of Danzig.

Area and Population. Poland is the sixth state of Europe in size and population, and is divided into 16 counties and 264 districts as follows:

County	No. of Districts	Population, 1931 Census
1. Warsaw ..	23	2,532,528
2. Lodz	13	2,632,434
3. Kielce ..	16	2,935,680
4. Lublin ..	19	2,468,391
5. Bialystok ..	14	1,640,374
6. Nowogródek ..	11	1,054,846
7. Wolyn ..	9	2,081,501
8. Polesia ..	9	1,133,398
9. Poznan ..	36	2,112,871
10. Pomorze ..	18	1,086,144
11. Kraków ..	23	2,297,027
12. Lwów ..	27	3,127,138
13. Stanislawów ..	16	1,475,954
14. Tarnopol ..	17	1,599,574
15. Silesia ..	6	1,298,851
16. Vilna * ..	—	1,272,851
Military ..	—	205,163
Total		30,954,725
City of Warsaw ..		1,178,211
Grand total population		32,132,936

* The Vilna territory (area 10,814 sq. miles) is included here, but it is important to see page 288.

The approximate total area of Poland is 149,960 sq. miles.

Towns. Warsaw is the capital and the principal town; others are: Lodz (pop. 1931, 605,287), Lwów (Lemberg; 316,177), Kraków (Cracow; 221,260), Wilno (194,049), and Katawice (127,841).

Physiography. Poland may be divided into five distinct areas. (1) The mountain area, which falls through forested slopes and upland pastures to (2) the southern plateau, having an average altitude of 900 feet, and bisected by the Vistula.

(3) The basin of the Middle Vistula, a low, wooded plain from 300 to 400 feet in altitude, was the cradle of the Polish race. It rises northward to the lake-studded Baltic Plateau, and forms the grain-producing area of Poland. Within recent geological times the whole lowland area was a vast glacial lake, or a series of glacial lakes, and it is to the silt deposits of these lakes that the district owes its modern prosperity. The complicated river-system is also attributed to this geological fact.

(4) Separating the Central Plain from the coastal belt rise the Northern Uplands, rounded hills of some 700 feet in height, interspersed with peatbogs, marshes, sandy areas, and many lakes and ponds, and traversed by slow-flowing rivers.

(5) The coastal belt is sandy and shallow, frequently ice-bound in winter. Linking up the first four physical conditions is the Vistula, falling into the sea at Danzig which,

Polacca

nominally a free and independent port, forms the natural outlet northward for the whole of the Polish plain.

Climate. Climatically Poland is also a transition area between the continental climate of Eastern Europe and the more oceanic climate of the West.

Social Conditions: Religion. There is no national Church, and all denominations are tolerated, but by Article 117 of the Polish Constitution, Roman Catholicism is stated to be the dominant religion, and to that faith 74·9 (1932) per cent of the population belong. Others are Russian Orthodox (12·5 per cent), Jews (about 9·6 per cent), and Protestants.

Education. Elementary education is free and compulsory. There are five universities (Cracow, Posen, Lublin, Warsaw, Wilno, and Lwów), the Free University in Lodz, polytechnics at Warsaw and Lwów, an academy of fine arts, two agricultural colleges, one forestry school, a mining college, two veterinary colleges, and the Academy of Science (Cracow), the principal scientific institution of Poland.

Money. The monetary unit is the zloty of 100 grosz (normally 43·38 zlotys = £1 sterling).

Weights and Measures. The metric system is officially compulsory.

Production : Agriculture. Poland is essentially an agricultural country, and many of her industries, such as sugar - refining, distilling, and starch-making are directly dependent upon other agricultural productivity. Wheat, rye, barley, oats, and potatoes, sugar-beet, hemp, hops, tobacco, and chicory are important.

Forestry. 20,563,853 acres of the productive area of the state is forested, and of this 7,494,973 acres belong to the state. A bill passed by the *Sejm* (Diet) in 1920 limited the size of estates near large towns.

Minerals. There are coal-fields, in the Cracow basin, capable of considerable development, but Polish coal-production is more or less dependent upon the more rich fields of Upper Silesia in the area allotted to Poland by the League of Nations (i.e. around Königshütte). Small quantities of other minerals are found, especially salt from Wieliczka (near Cracow, in Galicia). Before the European War Galicia produced about 5 per cent of the world's total petroleum output.

Manufactures. There are three main groups of industrial centres, and all the industries of Poland are represented in Warsaw, half-way between Cracow and Danzig. These are principally manufactures of textiles and of paper, and paper-bags of various kinds.

Commerce. The absence of good strategic frontiers east and west, i.e. at the points of greatest danger, has repeatedly proved a disastrous disadvantage to Poland in her twofold military capacity of (1) buffer between Slav and Teuton, and (2) frontier guard of Europe against Asiatic invaders. But the trade relations of the area in peace are exceptionally good. The most valuable exports (total value in 1932 about £42,900,456) are timber, coal, pigs, zinc, textiles, dairy produce, and petroleum. Imports (total value in 1932 about £38,286,748) include machinery, cotton, chemicals, metals, corn, leather, and wool.

Communications. There are over 12,417 miles of State-owned railways (Dec., 1932), and 28,582 miles of roads. 1701 miles of navigable waterways are accessible by vessels of over 400 tons for a distance of 298 miles. By Act of the *Sejm* (Diet), Poland is engaged in the foundation of a national mercantile marine. In 1932 she had 33 vessels of 67,834 tons gross, while Danzig had 51 vessels of 212,890 tons gross.

Defence. The army is organised on a conscription basis, service being universal and compulsory, and there are ten military districts. The strength of the army in 1932 was 17,905 officers and 265,871 other ranks. The fortresses of Poland are: Thorn, Posen, Cracow, Przemysl, Brest-Litowsk, Grodno, Osowiec, Warsaw, Modlin, and Deblin. There is a river fleet of twelve gunboats on the Vistula.

History. The Poles, like the Russians, are a Slavonic race, and are first spoken of as the Polani, a tribe or people between the Vistula and Oder. The country was divided into small communities until the reign of Mieczyslaw I. (962-992) of the Piast dynasty, who renounced paganism in favour of Christianity, and was a vassal of the German Emperor. He was succeeded by Boleslaw the Great (992-1025), who raised Poland into an independent

Poland: Belvedere Palace, Warsaw

kingdom and increased its territories. In succeeding reigns the country was involved in war with Germany, the heathen Prussians, the Teutonic knights, and with Russia. The last of the Piast dynasty was Casimir the Great (1364-70), during whose reign the material prosperity of Poland greatly increased.

He was succeeded by his nephew, Louis of Anjou, King of Hungary, whose daughter Hedwig was recognised as queen in 1384, and having married Yagello, Prince of Lithuania, thus established the dynasty of the Yagellons, which lasted from 1386 to 1572. During this period Poland attained its most powerful and flourishing condition. In 1572 the Yagellon dynasty became extinct in the male line, and the monarchy, hitherto elective in theory, now became so in fact.

The more important of the elective kings were Sigismund III. (1587-1637), Wladislaw or Ladislaus IV. (1632-48), John Casimir (1648-69), and the Polish general Sobieski, who became king under the title of John III. (1674-96). He was succeeded by Augustus II., Elector of Saxony, who got entangled in the war of Russia with Charles XII., and had as a rival in the kingdom Stanislaus Lesczynski.

Augustus III. (1733-63) followed, and by the end of his reign internal dissensions and other causes had brought the country into a state of helplessness.

In 1772, under the last feeble king, Stanislaus Augustus (1764-95), the first actual partition of Poland took place, when about a third of her territories were seized by Prussia, Austria, and Russia, the respective shares of the spoil being Prussia 13,415 sq. miles, Austria 27,000 sq. miles, and Russia 42,000 sq. miles. What remained to Poland was completely under Russian influence.

Another partition in 1793 gave Russia nearly 97,000 sq. miles and

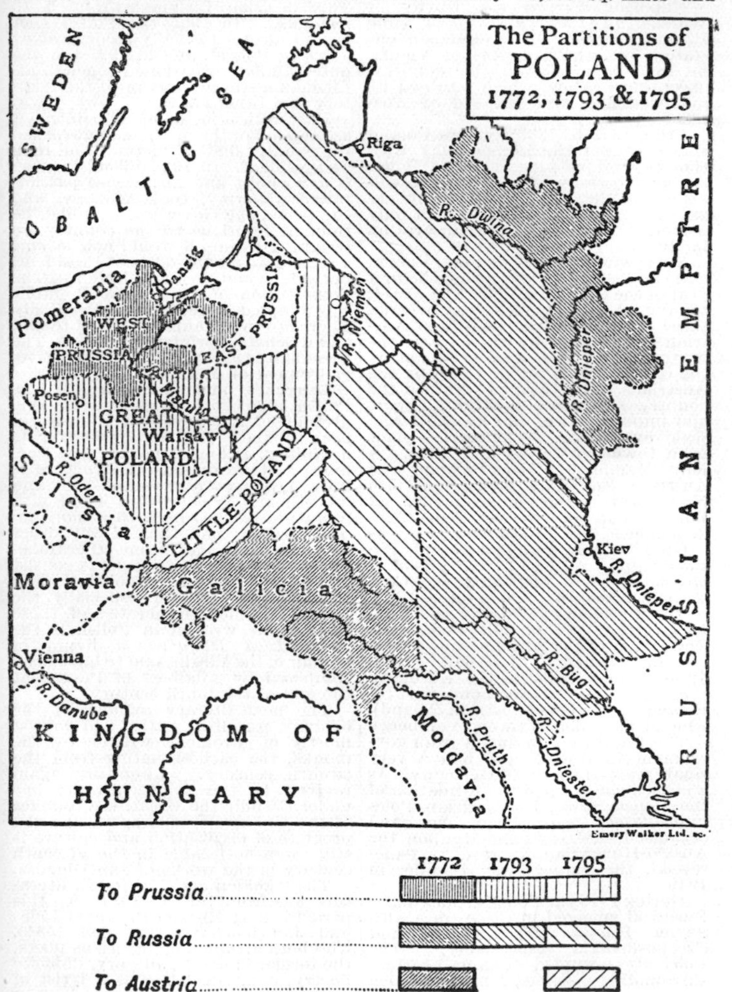

Prussia 22,500 sq. miles. A third partition took place in 1795 after the heroic attempt of Kosciusko to save his country, and the last King of Poland became a pensionary of the Russian court. The successive partitions gave Russia upwards of 180,000 sq. miles, Austria about 45,000 sq. miles, and Prussia 57,000 sq. miles.

Napoleon formed the Duchy of Warsaw in 1807, and for a time Poland became a semi-independent state; but the Congress of Vienna in 1815 repartitioned the country, excepting Cracow, which retained its independence until annexed by Austria in 1835.

From 1815 to 1830 Russian Poland was a constitutional monarchy with the emperor as king, but the Poles, taking occasion of the French Revolution, at the latter date rashly engaged in an insurrection, which only hastened their complete absorption in Russia.

European War. Congress Poland was the theatre of war during the first year of the European War (Aug., 1914, to Aug., 1915): Galicia was overrun three times by the Russian and Austrian armies, and for three years the northern provinces were occupied by the Germans and the southern by the Austrians. The Germans drained the country by heavy taxation, export and import duties, and by the large-scale evacuation of industrial plant from towns, factories, and mills. A joint Manifesto of the German and Austrian Emperors proclaimed (5th Nov., 1916) the independence of Poland, and on 9th Nov., 1918, independence was proclaimed.

On 14th Nov. Marshal Joseph Pilsudski (q.v.) returned from prison in Magdeburg and convoked the Constituent Assembly, which elected him to the presidency. He was re-elected for a further term on 20th Feb., 1919. The Treaty of Versailles acknowledged the independence of Poland (28th June, 1919). Prior to the European War the only autonomous part of Poland was Galicia (Austrian Poland), which had a Diet at Lwów (Lemberg).

The Poles were excluded from government in Russia, and had a very small representation in Germany. As a consequence, upon the formation of the Polish State, the Galician Poles immediately went into office and organised the Government upon the Austro-Hungarian pattern. Paderewski, the pianist, was Premier in 1919.

During 1919 the Polish armies under Pilsudski engaged in three wars with Soviet Russia, the Ukraine, and Czechoslovakia respectively. The Poles also occupied Vilna and certain surrounding districts, a matter which caused much trouble with Lithuania. The Poles claimed the city on account of the language and population, and the Lithuanians claimed it on the grounds of history and tradition. The League of Nations made unsuccessful attempts to settle the dispute, and in 1923 the Conference of Ambassadors definitely assigned Vilna to Poland. This decision Lithuania refused to recognise. In 1925 the Polish Diet passed an Act formally incorporating Vilna in Poland, and in 1927 the dispute almost occasioned open war. Lithuania still lays claim to the territory (*see* LITHUANIA).

Pilsudski, prior to his appointment as marshal of the army, had governed the country first as Dictator and then as President. In 1926 Pilsudski, who is a Socialist and an intense patriot, raised an army, took Warsaw, and compelled the Government, which he thought injurious to the country, to resign. He himself would not become a candidate for the office of President, but his nominee was elected. The Constitution of the Polish Republic was adopted in 1921 (amended 1926). There are two chambers, a Diet (*Sejm*) and a Senate, both being elected. The President is assisted by an Executive, or Council of Ministers.

Language and Literature. The Polish language belongs to the Slavic division of the Aryan or Indo-European tongues. It is remarkable for its flexibility, richness, power, and harmony; its grammatical structure is fully developed and established, and its orthography is precise. The Polish literature reaches back to a more remote period than that of any other Slavonic language except the Bohemian. The oldest monuments consist of warlike, historical, political, and religious poems, more especially the last. The most celebrated of these monuments written in Polish is the *Bogarodzica Dziewica,* a hymn in honour of the Virgin, said to have been composed by Adalbert of Prague at the end of the tenth century.

The next literary remains of the country are all in Latin, and consist mostly of chronicles written by the monks, the earliest dating from the twelfth century. Literature again revived in the fourteenth century under Casimir the Great, the founder of the University of Cracow, and the progress of civilisation and culture is still more noticeable in the fifteenth century in the works of Jan Dlugosz.

The "golden age" of Polish literature was from 1521 to 1621. To this period belong Nicolas Rej (died 1568) and Jan Kochanowski (died 1584), who both attained eminence as poets, the former in satire, allegory, didactic poetry, etc., the latter as a lyrist of the highest rank. Among the other poets of the century were Szarzynski (died 1581) and Szymonowicz (Simonides), author of *Polish Idylls*. It was in the sixteenth century also that the first histories in the language of the people were written.

This flourishing period of Polish literature was followed by a period of Jesuit supremacy and literary decline, which lasted till about the middle of the eighteenth century. About that time the influence of the French civilisation was widely felt in Poland, and prepared the way for the revival of letters. The most distinguished authors of the latter part of the eighteenth century are Naruszewicz, who wrote odes, idylls, satires, etc., and Krasicki (1734-1801), who also distinguished himself in various fields.

The literary activity of Poland did not cease after the overthrow of the political independence of the country. It is indeed only after its loss of independence that Poland's literature acquired a European importance. After the year 1815 Vilna became the literary centre of Poland, and here a number of the most enthusiastic spirits of the country associated together and endeavoured to propagate the influence of English and German literature, in opposition to the prevailing French tendencies.

Among Polish poets of the nineteenth century may be noted Mickiewicz (1789-1855), Krasinski (1812-59), Slowacki (1809-49), and Zaleski (1802-86). Kraszewski (1812-87), novelist and political and historical writer, was one of the most prolific of Polish authors. In recent times the Polish novel is more representative of the epoch than are Polish drama and poetry. Among the best-known writers are Henryk Sienkiewicz, Eliza Orzeszkowa, and the leader of Young Poland, Stanislaw Pszybiszewski, whose works, *The Children of Satan* and *Homo Sapiens*, met with considerable success.

BIBLIOGRAPHY: Concise Statistical Year Book of Poland; R. Dyboski, *Poland, Old and New*; Dr. W. K. Korostowetz, *The Re-birth of Poland*; R. Machray, *Poland, 1914-1931*; F. W. von Oertzen, *So This is Poland*; Dr. M. Orlowiez, *Poland and its Curiosities*; I. Triebe, *Zehn Jahre polnische Waehrung*; F. Bujak, *Poland's Economic Development* (translated from the Polish).

POLAR EXPLORATION. *See* NORTH POLAR EXPEDITIONS; SOUTH POLAR EXPEDITIONS.

POLARISATION OF LIGHT. An alteration in the properties of light, produced by reflection, or by refraction through certain bodies; the alteration is not visible to the naked eye. When a beam of light falls obliquely on a plane glass surface, part of the light is reflected and part is refracted. Each of the two beams has now different properties from the incident beam; the reflected beam is not reflected from a second surface with equal facility in every direction, but appears bright and dim alternately as the second reflector turns round while keeping the angle of incidence constant. The light is now partially polarised, and polarisation attains a maximum for a glass reflector when the angle of incidence is 57½°; this is called the polarising angle, and Brewster showed that the tangent of the polarising angle is equal to the refractive index of the reflecting medium. The refracted ray is also partially polarised, and a simple polariser may be constructed by placing a number of microscope cover glasses in a perforated pill-box, the glasses being set at about 33° to the incident light. The emergent light can thus be examined by a similar "pile of plates" used as an analyser.

Polarisation also takes place when light is refracted through certain crystals, or through transparent isotropic substances, such as glass or celluloid, when in a state of strain. Crystals, except those which belong to the regular or isometric system, appear to possess the property of double refraction in some measure, and all rays which are doubly refracted are at the same time polarised. On looking through a rhomb of Iceland spar at a black dot on a white paper, two dots are seen, and on turning the rhomb on the paper, one dot is seen to revolve round the other. One ray obeys the ordinary laws of refraction, and the other does not; hence one is called the ordinary ray, and the other the extraordinary ray. The optical distinction between these two rays is the following. In a ray of common light the ether vibrations are transverse or across the path of the ray, and in every direction, whether in straight, elliptical, or other paths. When a ray of light enters a crystal, the latter constrains the heterogeneous vibrations of the incident light which are resolved into vibrations in two directions only, and rays of plane polarised light emerge. The vibrations in the ordinary ray are perpendicular to the plane of incidence, whilst those of the extraordinary ray take place in this plane and at right angles to those of the ordinary ray. In polarisation by reflection the vibrations of the reflected ray are perpendicular to the plane of incidence and parallel to the reflecting surface; the refracted ray is constituted by vibrations perpendicular to this direction in the plane of incidence.

In general, a doubly refracting crystal gives rise to two rays, but all such substances possess one or two directions along which a ray may pass without being broken into two. These directions are called optic axes, and a crystal is said to be uniaxial or biaxial according as it possesses one or two optic axes; Iceland spar and quartz are uniaxial, and nitre and cerussite are examples of biaxial crystals. The optic axis is merely a direction and not a particular path

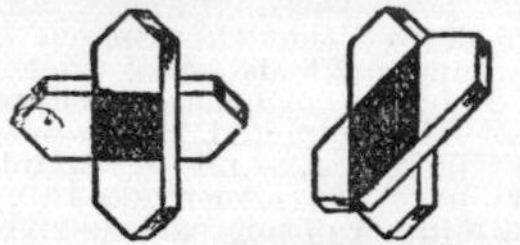

Polarisation of Light

in the crystal. In quartz the axis is perpendicular to the hexagonal section of the crystal; and in Iceland spar or calcite it is equally inclined to the three faces forming the obtuse angle of the rhombic crystal.

Tourmaline is a crystal which possesses a remarkable property; it occurs as green, pink, and brown crystals, of which the brown variety is best suited for polarisation experiments. Plates of tourmaline cut parallel to the axis and about $\frac{1}{10}$ inch thick can completely absorb the ordinary ray, and two tourmalines made up in the form of "tongs" form a convenient small polariscope, giving a dark field when the tourmalines are crossed (see fig.). Another crystal polariser is made from Iceland spar. The Nicol prism is made from a long rhomb of spar, the end faces of which are cut to make angles of 68° with the two nearest long edges; the rhomb is then cut in halves by a plane perpendicular to the newly cut faces and to the plane containing the two long edges mentioned. The two halves are cemented together again with Canada balsam, which has a refractive index less than Iceland spar for the ordinary ray, but greater than that for the extraordinary ray. The effect is such that when rays parallel to the long edges pass into the prism by an end face, they are doubly refracted, and the ordinary rays are totally reflected at the balsam and are absorbed at the side, whilst the extraordinary rays pass through the prism. Two Nicol prisms give, when "crossed," a dark field, which becomes bright on interposing a doubly refracting crystal. Many beautiful colours may be obtained in this way with thin plates of mica and selenite. A Nicol prism is part of the equipment of the polariscope, saccharimeter, and geologist's microscope.

The optical behaviour of Iceland spar and quartz differs in one important particular. As seen in the Nicol prism, the ordinary ray is refracted more than the extraordinary; but in quartz the opposite is the case. For this reason quartz, ice, and other crystals are termed positive, while Iceland spar, tourmaline, ruby, and others are called negative crystals.

If a plate of quartz or Iceland spar is cut parallel to the axis, and rays fall normally on it, the two polarised rays are not separated in direction, but one travels more slowly than the other, and, their vibrations being at right angles, the resultant motion on emergence is, in general, elliptical, and the emergent light is said to be elliptically polarised. If the difference of phase in the two rays is 90°, and the amplitudes are equal, the emergent ray will be circularly polarised.

Another optical property may be exhibited by means of a plate of quartz cut perpendicular to the axis. When the plate is put between crossed Nicol prisms used with monochromatic light, the light passes through the analyser; it is plane polarised, but its plane of polarisation has been rotated on passing through the quartz. Different specimens of quartz are found in which the directions of rotation of the plane of polarisation are opposite to one another; these are distinguished as right-handed and left-handed quartz, according as, on looking in the direction in which the ray is travelling, the turning is clockwise or the reverse. A solution of cane-sugar is dextro-rotatory, whilst one of fruit-sugar is lævo-rotatory. Rotatory substances are examined by means of a saccharimeter (q.v.), by which are determined the direction and amount of the rotation; from the observations the amount of active material present may be calculated.

Professor Coker has applied the properties of polarised light as a means of investigating, for engineering purposes, the variations of stress in plates and springs made of xylonite.—

BIBLIOGRAPHY: R. T. Glazebrook, *Physical Optics*; E. Edser, *Light for Students*.

POLARISCOPE. An instrument for exhibiting polarised light, and for examining transparent substances with regard to their polarising properties. It contains a polariser A (see fig.), an analyser B, and a platform CC to hold the specimen, and provided with a scale in degrees.

The polariser and analyser are

similar in construction, and consist in the simplest form of two glass plates, or, better, two piles of thin glass plates. These plates are set to reflect light at the polarising angle, viz. 57½° for glass; and light reflected from A is directed to B. On examining the light reflected from B, as this plate

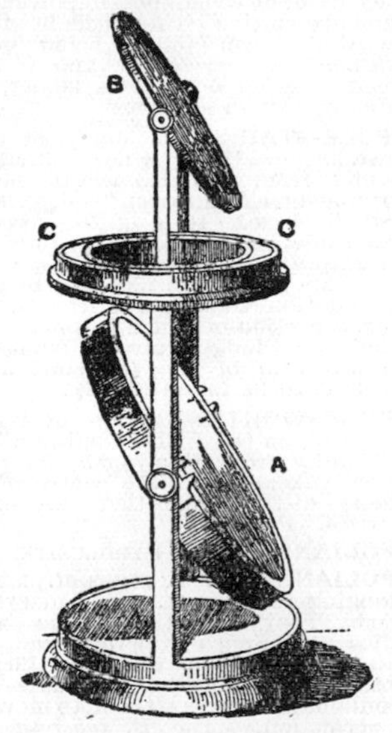

Malus' Polariscope

is rotated round a vertical axis, it is found to be almost extinguished for a given position of B, in which the principal planes (which contain the incident and reflected rays) of the two mirrors are at right angles to each other.

On interposing a piece of mica, quartz, or Iceland spar, and rotating the specimen on the platform, the light appears again by reflection from B, and is now coloured. No effect is obtained with unstrained glass or with crystals belonging to the cubical system, such as diamond, and the polariscope may be used to discriminate between "pebble" and glass lenses, and between real and artificial gems, with the exception mentioned.

In another form of polariscope the principle of refraction is employed, and both polariser and analyser are formed of Nicol prisms. *See* POLARISATION OF LIGHT.

POLAR REGIONS. Term applied to those regions which surround the geographical poles and lie within the Arctic and Antarctic circles, 23½° from the poles. In these areas sunlight or darkness extend over 24 hours at a time. They are characterised by extreme cold and the prevalence of ice over both sea and land. The northern ice cap forms a plain at sea level over the Arctic Ocean except over the land surface. The southern ice cap covers an elevated land area. *See* ANTARCTIC; ARCTIC.

POLDER. The name given in the Netherlands to an area of land reclaimed from the sea, a marsh, or a lake by artificial drainage, protected by dikes, and brought under cultivation. There are good examples in the four polders of the Zuider Zee littoral. The polders were for the most part formerly permanently submerged areas. The usual method of procedure in the formation of a polder is to enclose the portion to be reclaimed by an embankment, and construct a channel having its bed sufficiently high to cause a current towards the sea or river. The water is then pumped into this canal by means of pumping apparatus driven by steam or otherwise. *See* NETHERLANDS; ZUIDER ZEE.

POLE, Reginald. English cardinal and statesman, born in Staffordshire 1500, died 1558. He was the son of Sir Richard Pole, Lord Montacute, cousin to Henry VII., by Margaret, daughter of the Duke of Clarence, brother to Edward IV. Educated at Oxford, he had several benefices conferred on him by Henry VIII., with whom he was a great favourite. In 1519 he visited Italy, and fixed his residence at Padua. He returned to England in 1525, but about 1531 lost the favour of Henry by his opposition to the divorce of Queen Catherine. He retired to the Continent for safety, was attainted, and his mother and brother were executed. On the accession of Mary (1553) he returned to England as Papal legate, and on the death of Cranmer became Archbishop of Canterbury, being at the same time elected chancellor of the Universities of Oxford and Cambridge. He died in Lambeth Palace the day after Mary's death. He seems to have been noted for his mildness, generosity, and comparative moderation, in an age when persecution was deemed lawful on all sides.

POLE. The name given to either extremity of the axis round which the earth revolves. The northern one is called the *north pole*, and the southern the *south pole*. Each of these poles is 90° distant from every part of the equator. *See* GEOGRAPHY.

In astronomy, the name is given to each of the two points in which the axis of the earth is supposed to meet the sphere of the heavens. The stars appear to revolve round the elevated or visible pole.

In a wider sense a pole is a point on the surface of any sphere equally distant from every point of the circumference of a great circle of the sphere; or a point 90° distant from the plane of a great circle, and in a line passing perpendicularly through the centre, called the axis. Thus the zenith and nadir are the *poles* of the horizon. So the *poles* of the ecliptic are two points of the sphere whose distance from the poles of the earth's equator is equal to the obliquity of the ecliptic; they are 90° distant from every part of the ecliptic.

Pole, in physics, denotes the points of a body at which electric or magnetic forces of opposite qualities are centred, as the poles of a magnet, the north pole of a needle, the poles of a battery.

POLECAT. A name common to several species of digitigrade carnivora of the weasel family (Mustelidæ). The common polecat (*Putorius fœtidus*) is found in most parts of Europe. Its body is about 17 inches long, and the tail 6 inches. The colour is dark-brown.

Polecat (*Putorius fœtidus*)

It is a nocturnal animal, sleeping during the day and searching for its prey at night. It is especially destructive to poultry, rabbits, and game, as pheasants, so that in Britain it is being rapidly exterminated by gamekeepers, farmers, and others. Frogs, toads, newts, and fish are often stored as food by this voracious animal. It has glands secreting a fetid liquor, somewhat like that of the American skunk, which it ejects when irritated or alarmed.

The name of "Foumart" is also applied to the polecat; and its fur, which is imported in large quantities from Northern Europe, is known as that of the "Fitch." Its hairs are used in the making of a superior kind of artists' brush.

POLEMONIA'CEÆ. A natural order of gamopetalous dicotyledons with a trifid stigma, three-celled fruit, and seeds attached to an axile placenta, the embryo lying in the midst of albumen. They consist for the most part of gay-flowered herbaceous plants, natives of temperate countries, and particularly abundant in the north-western parts of America. They are of no economical importance. Some are cultivated for their beauty, the well-known phlox being one. *Polemonium cœruleum,* known as Greek valerian or Jacob's ladder, is the only British species.

POLE-STAR. The star α of the constellation Ursa Minor, situated about 1° from the north celestial pole, round which it apparently describes a small circle. It is of the second magnitude, and is of great use to navigators in the northern hemisphere. Two stars called the pointers, in the constellation Ursa Major (the Great Bear, a portion of which is commonly called the Plough), always point in the direction of the pole-star, and enable it to be found readily.

POLESWORTH. Village of Warwickshire, on the L.M.S. Railway. It is 4 miles from Tamworth, on the River Anker. It is the centre of a colliery district, and there are also quarries. Pop. 6280.

POLIANITE. *See* PYROLUSITE.

POLIAN'THES. A genus of plants belonging to the nat. ord. Amaryllidaceæ. They are natives of the East Indies and South America, and in Britain require the aid of artificial heat, and the shelter of frame or greenhouse, to bring them to flower in perfection. The *P. tuberosa* or tuberose is well known for its delicious fragrance. *See* TUBEROSE.

POLICE (po-lēs'). The system instituted by a community to maintain public order, liberty, and the security of life and property. In its most popular acceptation the *police* signifies the administration of the municipal laws and regulations of a city or incorporated town or borough. The primary object of the police system is the prevention of crime and the pursuit of offenders; but it is also subservient to other purposes, such as the suppression of mendicancy, the preservation of order, the removal of obstructions and nuisances, and the enforcing of those local and general laws which relate to the public health, order, safety, and comfort. The term is also applied to the body of men by which the laws and regulations are enforced. A police force is usually made up partly of men in uniform, and known to everybody, and partly of men in plain clothes, who are known as detectives.

The police system in England, as at present organised, dates from 1829, when the remodelling of the police system of the metropolis led the way to the adoption of a uniform system for the whole country. In 1829 Sir Robert Peel got an Act passed "for improving the police in and near the Metropolis." Several modifications were introduced by subsequent Acts of Parliament, especially by 2 and 3 Vict. caps. xlvii. and xciv. (1839); and other cities and boroughs from this time forward successively acquired by separate Acts of Parliament, the necessary powers to enable them to institute and maintain a police force on the model of the metropolitan force.

In 1839 and 1840 Acts were passed providing for the appointment of a county constabulary, organised and maintained in accordance with rules prescribed by the Secretary of State for the Home Department. The county magistrates, however, were left the option of taking advantage of these Acts, and accordingly many counties took no steps in the matter. But by 19 and 20 Vict. cap. lxix. (1856) it was made compulsory, and there is now a county constabulary force in every county (as well as a borough police), which reports annually to the Secretary of State, the force being under the periodical inspection of officers appointed by the Crown. By the Local Government Act of 1888 the management of the county police is put under the county council and justices jointly, the police of boroughs having a population of less than 20,000 being also put under the county council.

The total number of the police in England and Wales on September 29, 1932, was 58,529. Of these the metropolitan police numbered 20,073, forming a distinct body directly under the Home Secretary. The police are supported partly by local assessment, partly by the general revenue of the country. They are not allowed to be members of a trade union, but those below the rank of superintendent may join the Police Federation. The employment of women police was commenced in 1920. There are over 6500 police in Scotland.

POLICE COURT. Court of summary jurisdiction. In London they are presided over by a stipendiary (paid) magistrate, as in certain other towns. Generally, however, it is Justices of the Peace (unpaid) who act as judges. Justices are appointed by the crown on the advice of the Lord Chancellor, stipendiaries on the petition of a municipal borough council to the Home Secretary.

POLISHING. The process by which the surface of a material is made to assume a perfectly smooth and glossy appearance, usually by friction. The article to be polished must first be made smooth and even. In the case of wood, one of the most common processes is known as French polish (q.v.). With metals, the processes are varied to suit the character of the material and the purpose the polishing is to serve. A process known as "lapping" is used in polishing cutting implements, such as razors. This is performed with a revolving wheel made up of segments of wood, with the fibres arranged approximately in radial lines. The wood is covered with an alloy of tin and lead. Other polishing work is performed with leather-covered wheels and fine emery powder. Metal-working of this character is usually finished with crocus. Jewellery is polished with rouge, either on a buff (a revolving pad made up of circular sheets of cloth), or by hand with the use of a rag.

In metallography great care must be taken in the preparation of the specimens cut from the billets. The first process consists of grinding with emery on a revolving wooden wheel. Finer and finer grades of emery are used towards the end, and before using the papers for the last stages they are rubbed against a hard steel surface to remove any coarse particles. The process is completed by rubbing with wet cloths or parchment, covered with jewellers' rouge. Tin-putty, lead siftings, and tripoli are common materials used in the polishing of glass, marble, granite, and other ornamental stones. Furniture-polishes are made of shellac, gums, and a solvent such as spirits of wine, or are water solutions of bees'-wax, white wax, and soap.

POLISHING-SLATE. A grey or yellowish deposit, composed of the siliceous remains of microscopic organisms, found in Bohemia and in Auvergne, and used for polishing glass, marble, and metals.

POLITIAN, or POLIZIANO (po-let-se-a'no), **Angelo** (Latinised form, *Politianus*). Italian scholar and poet, born 1454, died 1494. The first production which brought him into notice was a Latin poem on the tournament of Giulio de' Medici. He became an ecclesiastic, and acquired the favour of Lorenzo de' Medici, who made him tutor to his children, and presented him with a canonry in the Cathedral of Florence. In 1484 he visited Rome, and after his return to Florence he lectured with distinguished success on the Latin and Greek languages, and likewise on philosophy. He wrote an *Account of the Conspiracy of the Pizza,* a Latin translation of Herodian, and a collection of Greek epigrams, besides Latin odes and epigrams, and a Latin poem entitled *Rusticus.* He also contributed greatly to the correction and illustration of the *Pandects.*

POLITICAL ECONOMY. *See* ECONOMICS.

POLITICS. Since its origination by the Greeks the term has become expanded in its meaning. To-day it connotes two things: (1) the science and art of government, i.e. the conduct of man to State, State to man, or State to State; (2) the organisation of the people, and the art of influencing public opinion with the view of serving or controlling the State. The second is the more generally accepted interpretation in modern times, with a tendency towards the cynical view, implying that politics are becoming more and more professional and even sinister. This, however, may be but a phase, inevitable in the development of the distribution of power. Greek philosophers noted three forms of government, or social organisation—monarchy, oligarchy, and democracy. The Romans added nothing to these theories, and later, feudalism and the Roman Church were dominant.

With the Renaissance new theories began to be evolved, with steady advancement from the obnoxious principles of Machiavelli, through Grotius and Hobbes to Rousseau. But before then the doctrine of the divine right of kings had been assailed both by the nobles and the people, that is, by the aristocracy and by the democracy, who each, and sometimes in unison—as in the action which led to the foundation of Parliament—made demands for a voice in government. This conflict became continuous, with periods of revolution, civil war, and curtailment of the power of the Church. Every movement saw a deeper significance attached to the ethics of government. It was not merely that power passed little by little from the few to the many, but that the few were made to realise their responsibilities and the necessity of surrendering their privileges, whilst the majority gradually accepted the theories of their advanced advocates that the science of government embraced the whole welfare of the peoples.

Royal prerogative gave way to popular liberty with the utmost reluctance. The struggle towards democracy was fitful; the nobles yielded with bad grace; the privileges which appertained to the possession of land are still jealously regarded by the aristocracy; and it cannot be said that all that has been gained by the masses is deemed wise or useful by those who maintain that society falls into two classes, roughly, the rulers and the workers.

Party Government. With the growth of parliamentary institutions as the instrument to secure the power of the people, parties became defined in politics. In England there were the Tories, more generally known as the Conservatives, who were comprised of the "upper" classes and their adherents; and the Whigs, who later developed into Liberals, with an advanced element known as the Radicals. The Tory view may be defined as postulating the duty of the class to govern the people (for their good), a version of benevolent despotism; the Whig conception was that the elected representatives were trustees of the nation, with the right to rule according to their discretion; the Radical idea, now fairly generally accepted, was that the people should govern themselves through the House of Commons. The opinion is still held by some that whilst Radicals might originate theories, Tories and Whigs must administer.

In this way parties became organised with the object of controlling Parliament from without, through the electors and the constituents. Politics resolved themselves into party government. The party in the majority became the party in power, forming the Cabinet, and devising and carrying out the programme of legislation; whilst the minority constitutes the Opposition, whose function is to criticise, and resist as well as assist.

Periodically, a coalition is formed by two parties, but there is usually a reversion to party, despite the criticism that the sharp cut leads to abuses in the struggle of the "outs" to become the "ins." Party, however, means organisation and discipline; it tends to stabilise opinion and to minimise the evil of the group system, which is irritating and makes for insecurity. With the increase in the number of electors another party arose, the Labour Party, which, in Parliament, and in the country, has made extraordinary progress in a comparatively short time. (*See*

LABOUR PARTY.) It contains advanced elements imbued with some of the modern ideas of politics and theories of the State and Government — socialism, syndicalism, and communism. The struggle against the old forms of authority, as, for instance, the continuance of the House of Lords on the hereditary principle, is growing to such an extent that many Tories admit the need for the reconstitution of the Second Chamber on a more democratic basis.

Politics are thus in a continual state of flux, and with the recognised aim of Parliament being the welfare of the nation, morality now plays an important part in political theory. Politics embrace the whole field of sociology. Woman now has the vote, and the life of the people is controlled and directed from the cradle to the grave, and before and after, for antenatal care of the child by attention to the expectant mother is a part of political science, and duties exacted from the estates of the dead are an integral part of national finance, contributing no small share to the revenue. The control of Parliament, legislation, and local administration from without is increasing. Party organisations and non-party associations, formed to promote and protect specific interests, exert influence and pressure on members of the House of Commons and local councillors, who are continually reminded that they are representatives of those who possess the votes which elect them. Virtually the whole country is organised, and politics have become, often willy-nilly, the daily concern of the whole nation. There are those who hold that members of Parliament are thus tending to become delegates rather than representatives. These criticisms or fears may, however, be said to emanate from reactionaries, who regard parliamentary institutions with suspicion and democracy as an evil. Democracy, realising this, continues to push forward to assert the sovereign rights of the people.

The argument is, that all matters are the care of the State, that legislation can and must adjust every anomaly and remove all evils, and that in this way the nation benefits. This all-embracing view has given rise to a growing counter-opinion that too much legislation is an evil, subversive of individual effort and private initiative, and, furthermore, that it encourages abuse of the privileges and benefits promoted by the State. The European War not only overthrew monarchies, but brought new ideas into politics. National effort secured unity and a breakdown of social barriers, but this gave way to other class distinctions and bitterness, due to profiteering, the wide distribution of honours —always a subject of political criticism—leading to the formation of a new plutocracy, rousing the enmity of the old aristocracy as well as the scorn of the democracy. The power of wealth being intensified, the resentment of the masses was accentuated into a demand for a new relation between master and man, so that the latter should have a greater share in the product and a voice also in the control of industry. Even before the war the desire for closer international relations was manifest. International Socialist and Labour conferences were held, and out of the peace conferences there grew the League of Nations, the political possibilities of which are illimitable, but as yet problematic.

POLK (pōk), **James Knox.** President of the United States between the years 1845 and 1849; born in 1795 in North Carolina, died at Nashville 1849. He studied law, entered Congress as representative of Tennessee in 1825, and was Speaker of the House of Representatives from 1835 to 1838. His advocacy of the annexation of Texas led to his election as President in 1844. The annexation of Texas, the Mexican War, the acquisition of Upper California and New Mexico, and the settlement of the Oregon boundary were the chief events of his term of office.

POLKA A round dance which originated in Bohemia about 1830. The music to it is in $\frac{2}{4}$ time, with the third quaver accented. There are three steps in each bar, the fourth beat being always a rest. Introduced into Western Europe about 1840, the dance soon became very popular.

POLL. Term denoting the voting or taking of votes at an election. It is applied also to the register of those entitled to vote. The place where the votes are recorded is called a polling booth. At company meetings (e.g. for the election of directors) a poll is taken, the shareholders having votes proportional to the number of shares held. The word is old English for head. *See* POLL TAX.

POLLACK (*Gadus pollachius*). A fish of the cod family. The pollack belongs to the same genus as the whiting (*G. merlangus*) and cod (*G. morrhua*); the members of this genus possessing three dorsal fins and two anals. The lower jaw is longer than the upper jaw, and the tail is forked, but not very deeply. It inhabits the

Atlantic Ocean, and is common on all the British coasts, as well as on the shores of Norway. The northern coasts of Britain appear to be those on which these fishes are most abundant. The pollacks are gregarious in habits, and swim in shoals. They

Pollack

bite keenly at either bait or fly, and afford good eating. They are called *Lythe* in Scotland.

POLLAN. The "freshwater herring" (*Coregŏnus pollan*), a species of fishes belonging to the Salmonidæ. It is an Irish species found in Lough Neagh, and is generally about 9 or 10 inches in length. Related species are found in Lough Erne and the Shannon lakes. There is also a Scottish species (*C. clupeoïdes*) in Loch Lomond, known as the Powan. *See* VENDACE.

POLLANARRUA. The former name of an ancient capital of Ceylon, now called Topare (q.v).

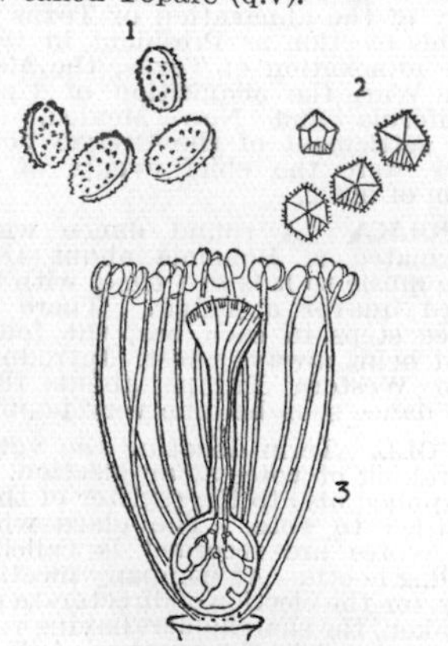

Pollen and Pollination

1 and 2. Pollen grains seen under microscope. 1, Water-lily. 2, Dandelion. 3, Flower of Rock Rose, stripped of petals and sepals and showing stigma, style and ovary in longitudinal section (magnified).

POLLEN. The powdery substance produced in the anthers of Flowering Plants. It consists of numerous minute rounded or ellipsoidal cells (pollen-grains), with fairly thick walls, which are usually ornamented with ridges, spines, or other markings. The contents are dense cytoplasm with reserve-material (oil, starch, etc.) suspended in it, a rounded *vegetative* or *tube nucleus*, and a spindle-shaped *generative nucleus*.

Pollen is dispersed either by wind, in which case it is dry and dusty, or by animals (usually insects), when it is moist and sticky. When deposited on the stigma (or placed in a suitable nutrient solution, e.g. 8 to 10 per cent cane-sugar for pollen of wild hyacinth), a pollen-grain germinates by emitting a *pollen-tube*, which grows down through the style into the ovary, and finally through the micropyle of an ovule to the ovum. The tube nucleus controls the growth of this pollen-tube; the generative nucleus also passes into the tube and divides into two *male nuclei*, which are the male gametes. Pollen-grains correspond to microspores, being formed in fours from the pollen mother-cells of the anther by a reduction division. *See* HETEROSPORY.

POLLEN-PROTECTION. A feature in the structure of many flowers, especially in moist climates, where protection of pollen against wetting by rain or dew is secured by a variety of devices, such as infolding of the petals, curving of the flower-stalk, etc. There is a detailed account, with figs., in Kerner and Oliver, *Natural History of Plants*.

POLLINATION. In Flowering Plants, the transference of pollen from the stamens to the stigma of the same (self-pollination) or of another (cross-pollination) flower of the same species; a necessary preliminary to fertilisation.

POLLIO, Gaius Asinius. A Roman of plebeian family, born 76 B.C., died A.D. 4. He took a prominent part in the Civil War, and accompanied Julius Cæsar to Pharsalia, and then to the African and Spanish Wars. After obtaining the consulship he commanded in Illyria and Dalmatia, and for his victories was honoured with a triumph (39 B.C.), He afterwards devoted most of his time to literary pursuits, but acted both as a Senator and an advocate. His works, consisting of speeches, tragedies, and a history of the Civil War in seventeen books, have all been lost. He was the friend of Virgil, who dedicated to him his fourth *Eclogue*, and of Horace, and founded the first public library in Rome.

POLLOCK, Sir Frederick. British jurist, born in London in 1845, and educated at Eton and at Trinity College, Cambridge, of which he became Fellow in 1868. He was called to the Bar at Lincoln's Inn in 1871, and in 1882-3 he was professor of jurisprudence in University College, London. From 1883 to 1903 he occupied the chair of jurisprudence at Oxford, and from 1884 to 1890 he was professor of common law in the Inns of Court.

Among his published works are: *Digest of the Law of Partnership*, *Introduction to the History of the Science of Politics*, and *A First Book of Jurisprudence* (6th ed., 1930). With F. W. Maitland he wrote a *History of English Law before Edward I.*

POLLOK, Robert. A Scottish poet, born at Muirhouse, in the parish of Eaglesham, Renfrewshire, 1799, died at Southampton 1827. He is the author of a series of *Tales of the Covenanters*, and a blank verse poem, *The Course of Time*, which in spite of many faults enjoyed a wonderful popularity both in Britain and America.

POLLOKSHAWS. District of Glasgow with which it was incorporated in 1912. It is an industrial district with iron-foundries, cotton mills, etc.

POLL-TAX. A tax levied per head in proportion to the rank or fortune of the individual; a capitation tax. This tax was first levied in England in 1377 and 1380, to defray the expenses of the French War; its collection in 1381 led to the insurrection of Wat Tyler. The hearth-money of the reign of King William III. was virtually a poll-tax, and was equally unpopular, though it led to no outbreak.

POLLUX. *See* CASTOR AND POLLUX.

POLLUX, Julius. A Greek sophist and grammarian, born at Naucratis, Egypt, about A.D. 135. He went to Rome during the reign of Marcus Aurelius, who appointed him one of the preceptors of his son Commodus. He wrote several works, all of which have perished except his *Onomasticon*, dedicated to Commodus, and therefore published before 177. This work is of great value in the study of Greek antiquity.

POLO, Gaspar Gil. A Spanish poet, born at Valencia about 1517, died 1572. His reputation was established by his *Diana Enamorada*, a pastoral romance, partly in prose and partly in verse, a continuation of Montemayor's *Diana*, from which Shakespeare took the plot of *The Two Gentlemen of Verona*. Cervantes excepts the *Diana* of Polo from his list (in *Don Quixote*) of works condemned to be burned. It has been translated into French, English, and Latin.

POLO, Marco. Venetian traveller, born about the year 1254, died probably in Jan., 1324. His father Nicolo was the son of Andrea Polo, a patrician of Venice. In 1271 he accompanied his father and his uncle Matteo on an expedition to China, which the latter had already visited in 1269. After reaching the court of Kûblai, the Great Khan of the Mongols, Marco rapidly learned the language and customs of the Mongols, and became a favourite with the khan, who employed him on various missions to the neighbouring princes. Soon afterwards he was made Governor of Yangtchou, in Eastern China, an appointment he held for three years. In 1292 the three Polos accompanied an escort of a Mongolian princess to Persia. After arriving at Tehrān they heard of Kûblai's death, and resolved to return home. They reached Venice in 1295.

In the following year Marco Polo took part in the naval battle of Curzola, in which he was taken prisoner. During his captivity he dictated to a fellow-prisoner, Rustichello or Rusticiano of Pisa, an account of all his travels, which was finished in 1298. His book—known as the *Book of Marco Polo*—has gone through numerous editions in the various European languages, but the best is that of Colonel (Sir Henry) Yule, accompanied with a great amount of learned elucidation and illustration. It was originally written in French, but Latin and Italian manuscripts of it are more common.

POLO. A game which has been described as a sort of hockey on horseback, the essential feature being to drive a ball through a goal, the players being mounted on "polo-ponies." The term appears to be derived from *pulu*, which is Tibetan for "a ball," the game being of Oriental origin, probably from Persia, whence it extended into India. It was introduced into this country in 1869 by the 10th Hussars and rapidly became popular, although owing to the expense, principally the maintenance of a number of highly skilled and necessarily expensive ponies, it is restricted to the wealthy classes, chiefly members of the aristocracy and crack cavalry regiments, although abroad, e.g. at Gibraltar, Malta, and in India, it is more within the means of the less affluent.

In this country the clubs of Ranelagh, Roehampton, and Hurlingham (the last named being the principal authority for the game and arbiter of the rules) in London are the chief venues. The most important contests are the Ranelagh Open Cup, the Hurlingham Challenge Cup, the Inter-Regimental Cup, the Oxford and Cambridge match, and an international match between England and America. The first of these international contests was played in New York in 1886; since then there have been seven other contests, the honours having been equally divided.

The rules have been modified from time to time, and even to this day there is no uniformity. The size of the ponies is limited to 14 hands 2 inches. The size of the ground is

Polo-player

variable within certain limits, although usually 300 yards long and 200 yards wide. Its boundaries are marked by white boards raised 10 inches from the ground. The goals at the extremities are 8 yards wide. The teams, originally eight a side, are now restricted to four a side. The ball is of willow or alder, painted white, and 3 inches in diameter. The sticks are approximately 4 feet 6 inches in length, with a cross-piece at one end for striking the ball.

The players are usually described as Nos. 1, 2, 3, and 4. No. 1 devotes himself to the back player of the opposing side, and is in the most difficult position of all. No. 2 plays right forward, and is selected for his hitting-power. No 3 occupies an intermediate position. No. 4, or back, is usually taken by the captain to direct players in front.

The play consists of six periods or *chukkas* (so spelt by the Hurlingham Club) of eight minutes' duration, with three-minute intervals between each, during which ponies are changed. Both player and pony are essential factors in skilful play, and a great deal depends upon the quickness of a pony to answer his rider's command. Roughly speaking, the principles underlying hockey govern the rules of the game; there is no off-side rule, but there are rules providing precautions to avoid dangerous collisions so far as possible. No player may hit the ball when he is dismounted, and in the event of his stick breaking he must gallop to the boundary-line to obtain a fresh one.

Nobody interested in polo should omit to read Rudyard Kipling's short story *The Maltese Cat* (in the volume entitled *The Day's Work*), which is an enthralling and technically accurate description of a match. *See* POLO PONY.

POLONAISE (It. *Polacca*). A Polish national dance, which has been imitated, but with much variation, by other nations. The *Polonaise*, in music, is a movement of three crotchets in a bar, characterised by a seeming irregularity of rhythm, produced by the syncopation of the last note in a bar with the first note of the bar following, in the upper part of melody, while the normal time is preserved in the bass.

POLONIUM. The name given by Mme Curie to the first radio-active substance which she succeeded in separating in her celebrated experiments on uranium minerals in 1898. Its atomic weight is 210, and atomic number 84. Its activity, as measured by the α-rays, is 5000 times that of radium. The activity decays to half its original value in 136 days. In the series of transformations undergone by radium, polonium is the last product but one, being identical with radium F. There are strong reasons for believing that the final product is one of the isotopes of lead, but definite experimental verification that polonium becomes transformed into lead is still wanting. *See* ISOTOPES; RADIO-ACTIVITY; RADIUM.

POLO-PONY. The ideal polo-pony stands 14 hands 2 inches high, "Hurlingham measurement," i.e. a little over the strict measurement of the show-yard. As the thoroughbred is the best exponent of pace, the breeder must ensure that his ponies are as nearly thoroughbred as possible on the sire's side, with sufficient good conformation, pluck, and stamina on the dam's side to ensure worth. In polo, pace naturally enough is indispensable, but the pony must also be broken to stick and ball and to bending, and such training demands good horsemanship, good hands, a little patience, and an infinite amount of perseverance. The value of any polo-pony is dependent solely upon his training and his aptitude for the game, although looks may also be taken into consideration.—Cf. article in *Live Stock of the Farm* (Professor C. Bryner Jones, M.Sc., editor), vol. iii.

PO'LOTSK. An ancient town of Russia, in the former government of Vitebsk, at the confluence of the Polotka and Dvina; connected by rail with Vitebsk. The dilapidated castle (Kremlin) was built by Stephen Bathory, King of Poland, in the sixteenth century. There were an upper castle and a lower castle, connected by a bridge. In the remains of the former stands the Greek Catholic cathedral of St. Sophia, built in the eighteenth century on the site of a fifteenth-century foundation. Pop. 32,000.

Polotsk is mentioned in A.D. 862. From 980 it was an independent principality, but fell to the Lithuanians in 1320, and was finally subjugated by them in 1385. Stephen Bathory took Polotsk from the Russians, who, under Ivan the Terrible, had captured it in 1563, and it became definitely Polish in 1582. During the partitions of Poland the town was frequently burned and plundered, and was finally annexed to Russia in 1772. In March, 1918 (European War), it was invested by the Germans.

POLPERRO. Village of Cornwall, on the south coast, 13 miles from Bodmin. It is a centre of the pilchard fishery.

POLTA'VA, or **PULTAWA.** A former government of Russia, in the Ukraine; area, about 19,265 sq. miles. It consists of an extensive and somewhat monotonous flat, watered by several tributaries of the Dnieper. It was one of the most fertile and best cultivated portions of the Russian Empire. Live-stock and bee-rearing are important branches of the rural economy. Both manufactures and trade are of limited extent. Pop. about 3,900,000. *See* UKRAINE.

POLTAVA. A town of Russia, capital of the government of Poltava, on the Poltavka and Vorskla Rivers at their confluence; served by the Kiev-Kharkov Railway, of which it is a junction. Wool is the great staple of trade. Horses, cattle, and sheep are sold. Poltava contains a monument to Peter the Great, who here defeated Charles XII. in 1709. The town fell to the Germans in March, 1918 (European War), and was taken by Denikin during the "White" campaign of 1919. Pop. (1926), 89,391.

POLTERGEIST. German word, "racketing spirit," denoting the supposed agent of inexplicable noises in or about a house, e.g. movement of furniture and breakages of crockery. Widely distributed in time and space, often attributed to spiritistic agency, such phenomena are sometimes due to obvious trickery, sometimes elude all intelligible explanation. The lack of adequate motive, and the frequent association with the occurrences of a person of abnormal mental powers, puzzle inquirers.

POLYAN'DRY (Gr. *polys*, many, and *aner, andros*, a man). A form of marriage in which one woman has more than one husband at a time. There are two types of polyandry, the fraternal form (in which the husbands are brothers), existing among the Tibetans, and the non-fraternal, among the Nayars of India. Polyandry prevailed among the Celts of Britain in Cæsar's time, and occurs yet among the Eskimo, the Aleutians, some tribes of American Indians, and in the South Seas. The practice is believed to have had its origin in unfertile regions in an endeavour to check the undue pressure of population on the means of subsistence. The antithesis of polyandry is polygyny, or plurality of wives.

POLYANTHUS. A beautiful and favourite variety of the common

Polyanthus

cowslip (*Primŭla veris*), a native of most parts of Europe. The leaves are obovate, oblong, toothed, rugose, and villous beneath. The flowers are in umbels on a scape of flower-stalk 3 to 6 inches or more in length.

Plants may be propagated from seeds, but they may also be readily increased by division.

POLYB'IUS. Greek historian, born about 204 B.C., and died 122 B.C. His father, Lycortas, was one of the leaders of the Achæan League, and an intimate friend of Philopœmen. At the age of twenty-four he entered into the military and political service of the League. After the subjugation of Perseus, King of Macedonia, by the Romans (168 B.C.) Polybius found himself among the thousand Achæans summoned to Rome to explain before the Senate why the League had not aided the Roman army in Macedonia. While in Italy he formed an intimate friendship with L. Æmilius Paullus and his two sons Scipio and Fabius. He accompanied Scipio (P. Cornelius Scipio Africanus the Younger) on his African campaign, and was an eye-witness of the destruction of Carthage. He returned to Greece in 146, just after the fall of Corinth, and exerted himself successfully to obtain moderate terms from the Romans for his countrymen.

His principal work is his history of Rome, from 220 to 140 B.C. It was written in forty books, but only the first five and fairly considerable fragments of the others are extant.

Polybius has almost all the qualities which go to make a good historian, except brilliance and an attractive style. He spared no trouble in making his researches. Not only did he ransack the public archives in many places for documentary records, but he undertook many journeys solely with the view of making himself acquainted with the terrain of the battles he was describing. He was studiously impartial, and was skilful in weighing contradictory evidence. Many of the events he related took place in his own lifetime, and some in his own presence. In spite of all these advantages he is little read; indeed it is hardly too much to say he is never read for pleasure, but purely on account of the invaluable information which he conveys. He is a classic illustration of the rule that literary style cannot be neglected with impunity.—BIBLIOGRAPHY: W. W. Capes, *The History of the Achæan League*; J. B. Bury, *Ancient Greek Historians.*

POL'YCARP. Apostolic Father and one of the early Christian martyrs. According to Irenæus, he was a disciple of the Apostle John, and was born probably in Smyrna about A.D. 69 or 70; martyred 155 or 156. According to a legendary fragment ascribed to a writer named Pionius, he was consecrated bishop of his native city by St. John. During the persecution under Marcus Aurelius, Polycarp was seized and brought before the Roman proconsul at Smyrna. Having refused to renounce his faith, he was condemned to the flames. He wrote several letters, which were current in the early Church, but have all perished except one addressed to the Philippians, which appears to have been written about 115, and is valuable for its quotations from the apostolic writings.

POLYCLI'TUS OF SICYON. Greek sculptor and architect, who flourished about 452-412 B.C., and stood at the head of the Argive school. He excelled in the representation of athletic types, and reduced the proportions of the male human form to a rule or canon, exemplified in his *Doryphorus* (Spear-bearer), of which a copy is at Naples. Other important works were: *Diadumenos* (copy in British Museum), *An Amazon* (copy in Berlin), and a great chryselephantine (gold and ivory) statue of Hera. He also distinguished himself as an architect.

POLYC'RATÊS. Tyrant of Samos during the time of the elder Syrus. He made himself master of the island by violence, and, having secured absolute sway, seized upon several of the neighbouring islands and some towns upon the mainland. The story of his friendship with Amasis, King of Egypt, and the latter's alarm at Polycratês' good fortune, is told by Herodotus. At the advice of Amasis, the tyrant cast his signet-ring, the possession which he valued most, into the sea, but the next day it was found in the inside of a big fish which a fisherman had brought to Polycratês as a gift. In 522 B.C. the Persian satrap Oroetes treacherously invited Polycratês to his palace, and there crucified him. Polycratês seems to have had much taste for learning and the arts, and greatly promoted the refinement of the samians.

POLYEM'BRYONY. In botany, a phenomenon occurring, sometimes regularly and sometimes abnormally, in the development of the ovules of Flowering Plants, consisting in the existence of two or more embryos in the same seed; frequent in the orange.

POLYG'ALA. A genus of plants of the nat. ord. Polygalaceæ. The species abound in milky juice, and are found in most parts of the world. The root of *P. senĕga* (senega or seneca root or

Virginian snake-root) is a stimulating diuretic, useful in pneumonia, asthma, and rheumatism. *P. vulgāris*, or milk-wort, is a British plant, common in dry pastures.

POLYGALA'CEÆ. A natural order of herbs or shrubs, with alternate, exstipulate, simple leaves; irregular hermaphrodite flowers; diadelphous or monadelphous stamens; anthers opening at the apex by a pore or chink. Nearly half the species are comprised in the genus Polygala, and are very generally distributed. The plants of this order are mostly bitter, and acrid or astringent.

POLYG'AMY (Gr. *polys*, many, *gamos*, marriage). A term usually applied to that form of marriage in which a man has more than one wife. The term, however, includes as well the custom of one woman having several husbands, its antithesis being *monogamy*. In ancient times polygamy was practised by all the Eastern nations, and was sanctioned or at least tolerated by their religions. It was permitted to some extent among the Greeks, but entirely disappeared with the later development of Greek civilisation. To the ancient Romans and Germanic races it was unknown. It prevailed among the Jewish patriarchs both before and under the Mosaic law, but in the New Testament we meet with no trace of it. Polygamy has never been tolerated among Christians, although the New Testament contains no injunction against it. It is, however, practised by the Mahommedans. A statute of Edward I. treated polygamy as a capital crime.

POL'YGLOT (Gr. *polys*, many, and *glōtta*, language) is more particularly used to denote a copy of the Holy Scriptures in which two, three, or more translations are given, with or without the original. The first great work of the sort is the *Complutensian Polyglot*, prepared under the direction of Cardinal Ximenes, and splendidly printed (1514-7), in six folio volumes, at Alcala de Henares, called in Latin *Complutum*, whence the name of the work. It contains the Hebrew text of the Old Testament, with the *Vulgate*, the *Septuagint*, with an interlinear Latin version, and a Chaldee paraphrase (which is also accompanied by a Latin translation).

Another celebrated *Polyglot* is that of Antwerp, called the *Royal Bible* because Philip II. of Spain bore part of the cost of publication. It was conducted by the learned Spanish theologian Benedict Arias Montanus, assisted by other scholars. It appeared at Antwerp in eight folio volumes (1569-72).

The *Paris Polyglot* appeared in 1645, ten folio volumes. The *London* or *Walton's Polyglot*, in ten languages, appeared in six folio volumes, with two supplementary volumes (London, 1654-7). It was conducted under the care of Bryan Walton, afterwards Bishop of Chester, and contains all that is in the *Paris Polyglot*, but with many additions and improvements. It contains the original text according to several copies, with an Ethiopic and a Persian translation, and the Latin versions of each.

Bagster's Polyglot (folio, London, 1831) contains the entire Bible in Hebrew, Greek, English, Latin, French, Italian, Spanish, and German, with a Syriac version of the New Testament in addition.

POLYGNO'TUS. Greek painter, flourished from 450 to 410 B.C. He was a native of the Island of Thasos, and was instructed in his art by his father Aglaophon. Cimon, the rival of Pericles, brought him to Athens and employed him to decorate the Stoa Pœcilē, or painted portico at Athens. His works were probably on wood. Polygnotus is represented as being the first who made painting independent of sculpture.

POL'YGON. Term used in plane geometry for a plane figure having more than four sides. A polygon is termed regular when it is both equiangular and equilateral. Regular polygons are named according to the number of sides, from five to twelve, as follows: pentagon, hexagon, heptagon, octagon, nonagon, decagon, undecagon, and duodecagon.

POLYGONA'CEÆ. A natural order of apetalous dicotyledons, with trigonal fruit, and usually with stipules united into a tube or ocrea, through which the stem passes. They have astringent and acid properties; some are purgative, and a few are acrid. Among the best-known species are rhubarb, the docks, and the sorrels. *See* POLYGONUM.

POLYG'ONUM. A genus of plants, nat. ord. Polygonaceæ. They are found in the temperate regions of Europe, Africa, North America, and Asia. They are herbaceous, rarely shrubby plants, with alternate stipulate or exstipulate leaves, and spikes of small pink flowers. Several British species are known by the name of persicarias. *See* BISTORT; BUCKWHEAT; KNOT-GRASS.

POLYGYN'IA. One of the orders

in the fifth, sixth, twelfth, and thirteenth classes of the Linnæan system, comprehending those plants which have flowers with many pistils, or in which the pistils or styles are more than twelve in number.

POLYHE'DRON. A solid figure contained by plane faces. It is said to be convex if it lies entirely on one side of its face. In a *regular* convex polyhedron, sometimes called a Platonic solid, the faces are equal regular polygons, and the solid angles are equal. The last proposition of the thirteenth book of Euclid's *Elements* shows that there cannot be more than five of these regular polyhedra. The five are: (1) the tetrahedron, formed by 4 equilateral triangles; (2) the cube, by 6 squares; (3) the octahedron, by 8 equilateral triangles; (4) the dodecahedron, by 12 pentagons; (5) the icosahedron, by 20 equilateral triangles.

It may easily be verified from the figures that in each case the sum of the number of faces and the number of vertices is greater by two than the number of edges, a theorem usually ascribed to Euler.

POLYM'ERISM, or POLYMERISATION. In chemistry, the formation of new molecules by union of several into one. Thus acetylene, if heated in a sealed tube, may be polymerised to benzene,

$$3C_2H_2 = C_6H_6.$$

(3 molecules acetylene = 1 molecule benzene.)

Acetaldehyde may be polymerised to paraldehyde,

$$3CH_3CHO = C_6H_{12}O_3.$$

(3 molecules acetaldehyde = 1 molecule paraldehyde.)

The sugar-like body *formose* may be formed by the polymerisation of formaldehyde,

$$6HCHO = C_6H_{12}O_6.$$

(6 molecules formaldehyde = 1 molecule formose.)

Many substances polymerise spontaneously, others are polymerised by heat, or the change may be brought about by the addition of a chemical reagent.

Polymerisation entirely changes the chemical properties of the substance, the atoms in the molecule becoming rearranged. Thus benzene has properties totally different from acetylene; paraldehyde has none of the properties of acetaldehyde nor of the aldehydes generally.

POLYMOR'PHISM. The property possessed by certain bodies of crystallising in two or more forms not derivable one from the other in accordance with the Law of Rationality that governs natural crystal forms. Thus mercuric iodide separates from a solution in tables belonging to the tetragonal system; if these crystals are heated, they sublime and condense in forms belonging to the orthorhombic system. The aluminium silicate Al_2SiO_5 crystallises in three distinct series of crystallographic forms, thus furnishing three mineral species, andalusite, sillimanite, and kyanite. *See* CRYSTAL.

POLYNE'SIA (Gr. *polys*, many, *nēsos*, island). A great division of Oceania, lying east of Melanesia and Micronesia. The principal island-groups are: Hawaii, the Phœnix, Marquesas, Paumotu, Society, Ellice, Samoa, Union, Manihiki, and Tonga groups. See under OCEANIA; and articles on separate island-groups.

Polynesian People. The name given to the native populations (and their speech) of New Zealand (Maori), Tonga, Samoa, Tahiti, Marquesas, Hawaii, and the eastern parts of the Fiji group; in other words, the earliest inhabitants of those islands in the Pacific Ocean lying east of a line drawn through the Fiji Islands from Hawaii to New Zealand. The islands to the west of this line belong mainly to the Melanesian or to the Papuan peoples, or a mixture of these, the one with the other or with Polynesians, Indonesians, or Malays.

The Polynesians are a mixed population, the chief racial ingredients of which consist of an admixture of peoples akin to the so-called Mediterranean or Brown race of Western Asia and Europe, and the southern branch of the Armenoid or Alpine race, who more than fifty centuries ago had already made their way to the shores of the Eastern Mediterranean and the Persian Gulf. These littoral populations acquired from the Egyptians the art of boatbuilding and the practical knowledge of navigation, and several millennia ago made their way by sea to India, where they were the means of communicating to their kinsmen of the Brown race in Southern India the germs of Western culture.

In course of time these ancient mariners pushed farther east to Burma and Malaya, to Indonesia and Melanesia, thence to the more easterly islands of the Pacific Ocean, to which they gave their earliest human inhabitants, with their language and culture. In every successive stage of their wanderings new racial ingredients were added to the original Brown-Alpine mixture, in India, Indonesia, and Melanesia, so that the Polynesian, in spite of certain obvious European resemblances, reveals very definite traits of Malay and Melanesian influence. In some of the Polynesian islands, in fact, the Melanesian strain may be most obtrusive, as in Easter Island, even though the language and culture are unmistakably Polynesian.

From their history it is not surprising to find that the Polynesians were the most expert mariners of all primitive peoples, skilfully navigating large double canoes hundreds or even thousands of miles. They served as the bond of union and the means of maintaining a remarkably uniform culture and speech throughout the far-flung islands of their vast domain. By means of these ships and sailors, not only were Western culture and the essentially Egyptian art of navigation originally introduced into Polynesia, but also for many centuries afterwards the influence of later developments in the art and practice of civilisation continued to be introduced into Polynesia, and in fact to be transmitted right across the Pacific Ocean to Central America and Peru, where the germs of Old World culture were planted, probably from about 300 B.C. to A.D. 1200, but mainly between A.D. 300 and A.D. 700.

Scene in Polynesia

Polynesian Language. One of the many elements that establish the proof of the origin of the Polynesian people and their culture is afforded by their language. The remarkable uniformity of the spoken tongue, and the traditions which are preserved by its means throughout the vast expanse of the Pacific, is a striking testimony of the perfection of the process of linking up all these scattered islands by sea-going ships. In spite of the marked contrast between the European-like people of Polynesia and the negro-like inhabitants of Malanesia, there is a great deal in common between their languages, not only in vocabulary, but also in the more fundamental features of grammatical structure and phonetic character; and when we go farther west to Indonesia, we find still more interesting linguistic resemblances, which enable us to visualise the geographical route taken by the ancestral Polynesian wanderers.

The brilliant researches of the Austrian philologist Father Schmidt (see especially *Bull. de l'école française d'extrême orient,* 1907, page 213) have revealed a definite kinship between the languages spoken in Polynesia, Melanesia, and Indonesia (which he groups together as the Austronesian tongue), and those of the people of South-Eastern Asia known as the Mon-Khmer languages, and of certain peoples of Assam and India, such as the Mundas and Santhals, which Schmidt calls the Austro-Asiatic tongues. This affords the most definite evidence of the derivation of the Polynesian language from Southern India via Indonesia and Melanesia. But ethnological research, and especially the investigations carried out by the late Dr. Rivers and W. J. Perry, have revealed in the social organisation, the customs and beliefs, very definite corroboration of this general conclusion, as well as more precise information as to a series of waves of Western culture that passed into Polynesia and carried there such distinctively Egyptian practices as mummification, megalithic building, sun-worship, the dual organisation of society, and a variety of other equally characteristic elements of the most primitive form of civilisation known to us.

The researches of W. J. Perry have demonstrated conclusively that the chief factor in determining the movements of the original Polynesians toward the islands after which they are named was the search for pearls and pearl-shell. Wherever such shells were abundant the wandering sailors settled down to exploit the beds, and incidentally they planted their characteristic social customs and religious beliefs, arts and crafts, which have survived until the present day to reveal the places of the longest sojourn of the culture-bearers who also transmitted the civilisation of the Old World to America.

For fuller information concerning the people, their customs, beliefs and history, the reader should consult such works as those enumerated below.—BIBLIOGRAPHY: W. H. R. Rivers, *The History of Melanesian Society*; G. Elliot Smith, *The Migration of Early Culture*; S. Percy Smith, *Hawaiki: the Original Home of the Maori*; W. Churchill, *The Polynesian Wanderings*; A. Krämer, *Die Samoa-Inseln*; G. Brown, *Melanesians and Polynesians*; H. Mager, *Le Monde polynésien*; A. H. Keane, *Man, Past and Present*; Sir G. Grey, *Polynesian Mythology*.

POLYP, or POLYPE. A term which has been very variously and indiscriminately applied to different animals. It has thus been used to designate any animal of low organisation, such as the sea-anemones, corals, and their allies; or it has been employed to indicate animals which, like the cœlenterate zoophytes or Hydrozoa, and the Polyzoa, bear a close resemblance to plants. It is now generally applied to any single member of the class Anthozoa, represented by the sea-anemones, corals, and the like: or any member (or zooid) of a compound organism belonging to that class.

The term *polypide* is employed to designate each member or zooid of the compound forms included in the Polyzoa. The name *polypidom* applies to the entire outer framework or skeleton of a compound form such as a hydrozoan zoophyte. The word *polypite* refers to each separate zooid

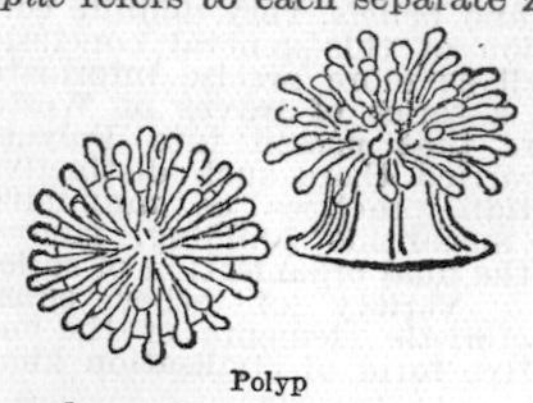

Polyp

or member of a compound zoophyte or hydrozoon. The *polypary* of a hydrozoon specially refers to the horny or chitinous covering secreted by the Hydrozoa.

POLYPETALOUS FLOWERS. Those in which the petals are quite separate from one another, a condition characteristic of a large section of dicotyledons, including the Ranunculaceæ, Cruciferæ, Caryophyllaceæ, Rosaceæ, Leguminosæ, Umbelliferæ, etc. Opposed to gamopetalous flowers, in which the petals are more or less coherent.

POLYPHE'MUS. In Greek mythology, the most famous of the Cyclops, who is described as a cannibal giant with one eye in his forehead, living alone in a cave of Mount Ætna and feeding his flocks on that mountain. Odysseus and his companions having been driven upon the shore by a storm, unwarily took refuge in his cave, and Polyphemus killed and ate four of the strangers. Odysseus, however, intoxicated the monster with wine, and as soon as he fell asleep bored out his one eye with the blazing end of a stake. He then

Polyphemus

escaped from the cave with his companions. Polyphemus was the despised lover of the nymph Galatea.

POLYPH'ONY. Musical combination of various strands of melody, each individually interesting. The polyphonic school of music reached its climax in the 16th century music of Palestrina and his contemporaries, of whom William Byrd was the chief exponent in England.

POLYPODIACEÆ. The largest family of Leptosporangiate Ferns, probably not a natural group, but composed of the most advanced members of several series derived from the more primitive families. Most of the species are herbaceous ferns with relatively small creeping stems and large pinnately branched leaves, but many depart from this type in various ways. The family includes most of the more familiar ferns, such as bracken, male-fern, hart's-tongue, hard-fern, maiden-hair, polypody, etc.

POLYP'ORUS. A genus of Basidiomycetous Fungi, type of the family Polyporineæ (shelf- or bracket-fungi). The *P. destructor* is one of the pests of wooden constructions, producing what is sometimes termed *dry-rot*, although the true dry-rot is a different plant (*Merulius lacrymans*). *P. squamosus* kills a variety of trees, and *P. betulinus* is a common parasite on the birch.

POLYP'TERUS (Bichir). A genus of fishes inhabiting the Nile, and also the rivers of tropical Africa that flow into the Atlantic. Except the *reed-fish* (q.v.), they are the only surviving members of the Crossopterygii, a very ancient order of fishes dating from the Devonian, and the type of a special family, the Polypteridæ. Their most singular characteristic is the structure of the dorsal fin, which instead of being continuous is separated into twelve or sixteen strong spines distributed along the back, each bordered behind by a small soft fin. In the young there is an external gill. The *Polypterus bichir* attains to a length of 4 foot.

POLYPUS, or POLYP. In medicine, a pedunculated tumour found in various parts of the body, especially in the nose, ear, rectum, and uterus. Nasal polypi are frequent, and their effect varies from a slight difficulty in breathing to complete obstruction of the affected nostril. Polypi of the uterine wall are also common, and may be either hard or soft. They may attain to a considerable size, and should be dealt with surgically, as they may slough or become malignant.

POLYSIPHONIA. A large genus of Red Algæ, with numerous British species, one of the most abundant being *P. fastigiala*, which always grows epiphytically on the large wrack *Ascophyllum nodosum*. The life-history of *P. violacea* has been fully worked out; there are three sets of individuals, viz. male, bearing antheridia; female, bearing carpogonia; and neuter, bearing asexual spores (tetraspores). The fertilised ovum of a carpogonium gives rise, by a complex series of divisions, to carpospores, which on germination grow into neuter plants; whereas the tetraspores give rise to male and female individuals. There is therefore here an alternation of generations, comparable to that of a fern, except that the gametophyte (male and female plants) and sporophyte (neuter plants) generations are identical in form. The nuclear cycle is normal, duplications of chromosomes taking place at the fertilisation of the ovum, reduction of chromosomes at the formation of tetraspores. *See* GENERATIONS, ALTERNATION OF.

POLYTECHNIC INSTITUTIONS. The first institution of this character was founded by John Anderson, professor of natural philosophy in Glasgow, who left the whole of his personal property with some trifling exceptions "to the public for the good of mankind and the improvement of science, in an institution to be denominated Anderson's University." James Watt owed much to the inspiration of John Anderson, the repair of whose model of a Newcomen engine was the engineer's introduction to the steam-engine.

The college was established in 1796 with a charter from the magistrates of the city, and was subsequently incorporated as Anderson's College under an Act of Parliament of 1877, and with other similar institutions in later years became the Royal Technical College.

Dr. George Birkbeck was appointed to the chair of natural philosophy and chemistry in 1799, and Mechanics' Institutions owe their origin to the successful classes which he started in the following year. He gave up this post in 1804, and started practice as a physician in London. In 1823, when the classes in Glasgow had grown to such dimensions as to warrant the establishment of the Glasgow Mechanics' Institution, an article in *The Mechanics' Magazine* suggested a similar foundation in London. Dr. Birkbeck took up the suggestion, provided money to build a lecture-room, and carried the scheme to success in spite of the ridicule of critics and the many quarrels of the governing body.

Besides the institution bearing Dr. Birkbeck's name, there were one or two early ventures in London, notably The Adelaide Gallery, called after the queen of William IV., and the institution known to-day as Regent Street Polytechnic. These were little more than museums of scientific instruments where occasionally lectures were given. The second named is popularly associated with "Professor" Pepper, the author of *The Boys' Playbook of Science* and "Pepper's Ghost" (*see* OPTICAL ILLUSIONS). Both these institutions failed, and the Regent Street building was for long disused, until Quintin Hogg purchased it in 1880 and started an evangelistic institute, at which classes of various kinds were held, which gradually developed into the Polytechnic of to-day.

The People's Palace owes its origin to the suggestions for improved facilities for education and social intercourse among working-men contained in Sir Walter Besant's novel *All Sorts and Conditions of Men*.

The London polytechnics have been largely supported by the wealthy city guilds, and many of them have successful technical and science classes for day students, and some are "schools" of the London University.

POLYTHALA'MIA. A group of Foraminifera occupying compound chambered cells of minute size. In some instances each cell of the common shell presents only one external opening, but more commonly it is punctured with numerous minute pores or foramina, through which the animal can protrude filaments. Their remains constitute the bulk of the chalk and tertiary limestone. *See* FORAMINIFERA.

POLYTHE'ISM (Gr. *polys*, many, *theos*, god). The belief in, and worship of, a plurality of gods; opposed to monotheism, the belief in, and worship of, one god. It is still a matter of debate whether polytheism is a primary form of human belief or a degeneration from an original monotheistic idea. It is argued, on the one hand, that the sense of personal dependence, the feeling that there was an undefined power, a mysterious *something* around and above him, did not primarily present itself to the mind of man except under a form of unity. His earliest religion would therefore be of a monotheistic character.

Those who affirm that polytheism was a primary form of religious belief argue that man, ignorant of the nature of his own life, and of the nature, origin, and properties of other objects, could at first only attribute vaguely to all visible things the same kind of conscious existence as that which belonged to himself. Thus the sun, moon, and stars would all be living beings; and as affecting the conditions of men they would be loved or feared. Polytheism existed among the ancient Hebrews, and in the religions of Assyria and Babylonia, Egypt, Greece, and Rome.—Cf. G. F. Moore, *History of Religions*.

POLYTRICHUM. A genus of Mosses, with several British species, of which *P. commune* is abundant in woods and on moors. The plants are large, and have a relatively complicated internal structure, with rudimentary vascular bundles, etc.; the leaves roll up in dry air, like those of many grasses.

POLYZO'A, or **BRYOZOA** (Gr. *polys*, many, *zōon*, animal). A phylum of invertebrate animals, generally known by the popular names of "sea-mosses" and "sea-mats." They are usually compound, forming associated growths or colonies of animals produced by gemmation from a single original individual, and inhabit a *polyzoarium* or aggregate of cells, corresponding to the polypidom of the composite hydroids.

The polypide, or individual polyzoon, lives in a separate cell or chamber, has a distinct alimentary canal suspended freely in a body cavity, and the reproductive organs contained within the body. The body is enclosed in a double-walled sac, the outer layer (*ectocyst*) of which is chitinous or calcareous, and the inner (*endocyst*) a delicate membranous layer. On the ectocyst are seen certain peculiar processes called "bird's-head processes," or *avicularia*, from their shape, the use of which is unknown.

The mouth-opening at the upper part of each cell is surrounded by a circlet of hollow ciliated tentacles, which perform the function of respiration, and are supported on the *lophophore*; and the mouth may be overhung by a sort of valve called the *epistome*. All the Polyzoa are hermaphrodite. In many cases there are *ovicells* or sacs into which the fertilised ova pass. From these proceed free-swimming ciliated embryos which develop into polypides. Continuous gemmation exists in all.

The Polyzoa are classed into two groups: Ectoprocta and Entoprocta. The Ectoprocta are divided into two orders of Phylactolæmata, with a crescentic lophophore and an epistome; and Gymnolæmata, with a circular lophophore and no epistome. One of the Entoprocta, *Loxosoma*, is the only non-colonial member of the phylum. They are all aquatic in their habits, the marine Polyzoa being common to all seas, but the freshwater genera are mostly confined to the north temperate zone. They are sometimes confounded with the hydroid zoophytes (*see* HYDROZOA), but are much higher in the scale. An old name for them is *corallines*, and their fossil remains largely make up the Coralline Crag, a subdivision of the Pliocene strata.

POMA'CEÆ, or **PO'MEÆ.** A division of the nat. ord. Rosaceæ, to which the apple, pear, quince, and medlar belong. It differs from Rosaceæ proper in having an inferior ovary. The fruit is always a *pome*, with a crustaceous core or bony stones.

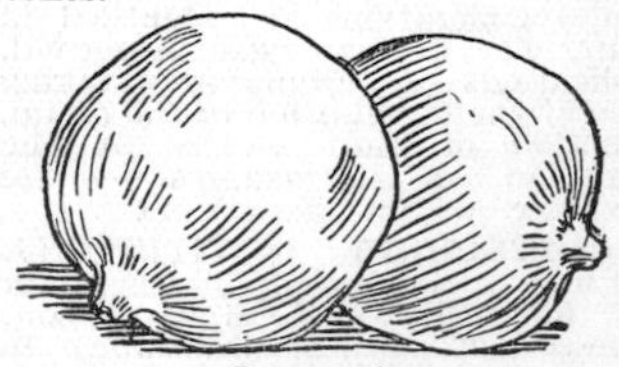

Pomegranates

POMEGRANATE (pom'gra-nāt; *Punica granătum*, allied to Myrtaceæ). A dense shrub, from 8 to 20 feet high, supposed to have belonged originally to the north of Africa, and subsequently introduced into Italy. It was called by the Romans *malum Punicum*, or Carthaginian apple. The leaves are opposite, lanceolate, entire, and smooth; the flowers are large and of a brilliant red; the fruit is as large as an orange, having a hard rind filled with a soft pulp and numerous red seeds. The pulp is more or less acid and slightly astringent. The pomegranate is extensively cultivated throughout Southern Europe, and sometimes attains a great size. Another species (*P. nana*) inhabits the West Indies and Guiana.

POM'ELO (*Citrus Pompelmoos*). Also known as *Pompelo* and *Pompelmoose*, a plant closely allied to and resembling the orange and shaddock, and sometimes regarded as merely a variety of the latter. Its fruit is sometimes called the *forbidden fruit*. *See* GRAPE-FRUIT.

POMERA'NIA (Ger. *Pommern*). A maritime district of Prussia, bounded by the Baltic, Mecklenburg, Brandenburg, and Poland; area, 11,663 sq. miles. The coast is low and sandy and lined by numerous lagoons. The chief islands along the coast are Rügen, Usedom, and Wollin. The interior is flat and in parts marshy, and is remarkable for the number of its lakes. The principal rivers are the Oder, Persante, and Stolpe. Flax, hemp, tobacco, and cereals are raised, and some sheep are bred. Herring-, eel-, and lamprey-fisheries are extensive. A considerable general and transit trade is carried on. The centre of trade is Stettin, which ranks as one of the chief commercial cities of Prussia. Pomerania is divided into the districts of Stralsund, Stettin, and Köslin.

Pomerania appears to have been originally inhabited by Goths, Vandals, and Slavs. The first mention of it in history is in 1140. It long remained an independent duchy, and in 1637, on the extinction of the ducal family, it was annexed to Sweden. On the death of Charles XII. it was ceded to the electoral House of Brandenburg, with the exception of a part which subsequently was also obtained by Prussia. Pop. (1910), 1,718,860; (1919), 1,787,193; (1925), 1,878,781.

POMERA'NIAN DOG. Breed of dog, called in Germany the Spitz, akin to the Eskimo and other Arctic breeds. It is strongly built, scaling 20 lb. and more, long-haired, with sharply-pointed muzzle, upright and pointed ears and thick, bushy, back-curled tail. In Britain it usually occurs in a dwarfed form as the "pom," weighing approximately 5 lb.

POMO'NA. In Roman mythology, the goddess of fruit, and wife of Vertumnus. At Rome she was usually represented with a basket of fruit, or with fruit in her bosom.

POMO'NA, or MAINLAND. The central and largest of the Orkney Islands, Scotland; area, 150 sq. miles; pop. (1931), 13,406. It is extremely irregular in shape, but is roughly divided into two unequal portions by Kirkwall Bay and Scapa Flow (q.v.). On the western side the coast is practically unbroken, but on the east and south it is deeply indented and provides several good harbours. The surface is covered in great part by moor and heath, but good pasture is also to be found, and in the valleys peat-mosses intermingle with stretches of productive soil. The principal towns are Kirkwall (the Orcadian capital) and Stromness. *See* ORKNEY ISLANDS.

POMPADOUR (poṇp-å-dör), **Jeanne Antoinette Poisson, Marquise de.** Mistress of Louis XV.; born in 1721, and died at Versailles in the

Marquise de Pompadour

year 1764. She was of obscure parents bearing the name of Poisson, but Lenormant de Tournehem, a rich farmer-general, was supposed to have been her father. In 1741 she married her cousin, Lenormant d'Etioles. A few years later she succeeded in attracting the attention of the king, and soon entirely engrossed his favour. In 1745 she appeared at court as the Marquise de Pompadour. Here she at first posed as the patroness of learning and the arts, but with the decay of her charms she devoted her attention to politics. For almost twenty years she played a predominant part in all State affairs. Her favourites filled the most important offices, and it was through her influence that France ranged herself on the side of her hereditary enemy, Austria, in the Seven Years' War.—Cf. P. de Nolhac, *Louis XV. et Mme de Pompadour.*

POMPEII (pom-pā'yē). An ancient town of Italy, in Campania, near the Bay of Naples, about 12 miles south-east of the city of that name, and at the base of Mount Vesuvius on its southern side. Before the close of the Republic, and under the early emperors, Pompeii became a favourite retreat of wealthy Romans. In A.D. 63 a fearful earthquake occurred, which destroyed a great part of the town. The work of rebuilding was soon commenced, and the new town had a population of some 30,000 when it was overtaken by another catastrophe on 24th Aug., A.D. 79. This consisted in an eruption of Mount Vesuvius, which suddenly belched forth tremendous showers of ashes, and white-hot lava, etc., so as to overwhelm the city for a considerable depth. The present superincumbent mass is about 20 feet in thickness. A portion of this was formed by subsequent eruptions, but the town had been buried by the first catastrophe and entirely lost to view.

Pompeii was consigned to oblivion during the Middle Ages, and it was not until 1748, when a peasant in sinking a well discovered a painted chamber with statues and other objects of antiquity, that anything like a real interest in the locality was excited. Excavations were now prosecuted, and in 1755 the amphitheatre, theatre, and other parts were cleared out. Under the Bourbons the excavations were carried out on a very unsatisfactory plan. Statues and articles of value alone were extricated, whilst the buildings were suffered to fall into decay or covered up again. To the short reign of Murat (1808-15) we are indebted for the excavation of the Forum, the town walls, the Street of Tombs, and many private houses. Subsequently the Government of Victor Emmanuel assigned £2500 annually for the prosecution of the excavations, and a regular plan has been adopted, according to which the ruins are systematically explored and carefully preserved.

The town is built in the form of an irregular oval extending from east to west. The circumference of the walls amounts to 2925 yards. The area within the walls is estimated at 160 acres; greatest length, ¾ mile; greatest breadth, ½ mile. There are eight gates. The streets are straight and narrow and paved with large polygonal blocks of lava. The houses are usually constructed of concrete; occasionally they are brick.

Numerous staircases prove that the houses were of two or three stories. The ground floor of the larger houses was generally occupied by shops. Most of the larger houses are entered from the street by a narrow passage (*vestibulum*) leading to an internal hall (*atrium*), which provided the surrounding chambers with light and was the medium of communication; beyond the latter is another large public apartment termed the *tabulinum.* The other portion of the house comprised the private rooms of the family. All the apartments are small. The shops were small and all of one character, having the business part in front and one or two small chambers behind, with a single large opening serving for both door and window.

The chief public buildings are the so-called Temple of Jupiter, the Temple of Venus, the Basilica, the Temple of Mercury, the Curia, and the Pantheon or Temple of Augustus. There are several interesting private buildings scattered through the town, including the villa of Diomedes, the house of Sallust, and the house of Marcus Lucretius. The Museum of Naples owes many of its most interesting features to the antiquities excavated in Pompeii.—Cf. J. F. Horne, *Buried Cities of Vesuvius: Herculaneum and Pompeii.*

POMPEY. In full **Gnæus Pompeius Magnus.** Roman general and triumvir, born 106 B.C., the son of Gnæus Pompeius Strabo, an able general. In 89 B.C. he served with distinction under his father in the war against the Italian allies. In the struggle between Marius and Sulla, Pompey raised three legions to aid the latter, and regained all the territories of Africa which had forsaken the interest of Sulla. This success excited the jealousy of Sulla, who recalled him to Rome. On his return Sulla greeted him with the surname of Magnus (Great). Pompey demanded a triumph, to which Sulla reluctantly consented. He entered Rome in triumph in Sept., 81, and was the first Roman permitted to do so without possessing a higher dignity than that of equestrian rank.

After the death of Sulla, Pompey put an end to the war which the revolt of Sertorius in Spain had

POMPEII

occasioned, and in 71 obtained a second triumph. In this year, although not of legal age and without official experience, he was elected consul with Crassus. In 67 he cleared the Mediterranean of pirates, and destroyed their strongholds on the coast of Cilicia. In the four years 65-62 he conquered Mithridates, Tigranes, and Antiochus, King of Syria. At the same time he subdued the Jews and took Jerusalem by storm. He returned to Italy in 62 and disbanded his army, but did not enter Rome until the following year, when he was honoured with a third triumph.

Pompey, in order to strengthen his position, united his interest with that of Cæsar and Crassus and thus formed the first triumvirate. This agreement was concluded by the marriage of Pompey with Cæsar's daughter Julia; but the powerful confederacy was soon broken. During Cæsar's absence in Gaul, Pompey ingratiated himself with the Senate, was appointed sole consul, and the most important State offices were filled with Cæsar's enemies. Through his influence Cæsar was proclaimed an enemy to the State, and his rival was appointed general of the army of the republic. Cæsar crossed the Rubicon in 49 (*see* CÆSAR), and in sixty days was master of Italy without striking a blow. Pompey crossed over to Greece, and in this country, on the plains of Pharsalia, occurred the decisive battle which made Cæsar master of the Roman world. The defeated triumvir fled to Egypt, where he hoped to find a safe asylum. The ministers of Ptolemy betrayed him, and he was stabbed on landing by one of his former centurions (48 B.C.)—Cf. Sir C. W. C. Oman, *Seven Roman Statesmen of the Later Republic.*

POMPEY'S PILLAR. An ancient monument in Alexandria, Egypt. It consists of a Corinthian capital, shaft, base, and pedestal. The total height of the column is 98 feet 9 inches; the shaft, a monolith of red granite from Aswan, is 67 feet long, and 9 feet in diameter below and not quite 8 feet at top. It was erected in A.D. 302 by a Roman prefect named Posidius, and was dedicated to the Emperor Diocletian. The name arose from an erroneous statement that the pillar marked the burial-place of Pompey.

PONAPE. Chief of the Caroline Islands (q.v.); area, 340 sq. miles; pop. (1930), 8910.

PONCE DE LEON (pon'the de le-on'), **Juan.** Spanish explorer, born about 1460, died at Cuba 1521. He accompanied Columbus on his second expedition in 1493, was sent by Ovando to conquer the Island of Porto Rico, and in 1513, during a voyage to the north, discovered Florida. He returned to Spain, and was appointed by Ferdinand Governor of the Island of Florida, as he called it, on condition that he should colonise it. Ponce de Leon was killed by the natives whilst attempting to take possession of his colony in 1521.

PONCE DE LEON, Luis. Spanish lyric poet, born in 1527, died 1591. He entered the order of St. Augustine at the age of sixteen, and became professor of sacred literature at Salamanca. He translated the *Song of Solomon* into Castilian, for which he was brought before the Inquisition at Valladolid (1572) and thrown into prison. At the end of five years he was liberated and reinstated in all his offices, and was elected head of his order.

Ponce de Leon

PONDICHERRY (Fr. *Pondichéry*). A town, capital of the French East Indian settlement of the same name, on the east or Coromandel coast, 85 miles south by west of Madras. Its territory is surrounded on the land side by the British district of South Arcot, and has an area of 115 sq. miles; pop. 46,849. The town stands on a sandy beach, and consists of two divisions separated by a canal. The "White Town," or European quarter, on the east, facing the sea, is very regularly laid out, with well-built houses. The "Black Town," or native quarter, on the west, consists of houses or huts of brick or earth, and a few pagodas. There is an iron pier, and railway communication with the South Indian system was opened in 1879. The settlement was purchased by the French from the Bejapoor rajah in 1672, and has been repeatedly in the hands of the British.

PONDOLAND. A north-eastern maritime territory of Cape Province, South Africa, abutting on Natal, 90 miles from N.E. to S.W., and about 50 miles from N.W. to S.E. It was the last remnant of independent Kaffraria, became a British protectorate in 1884, and was annexed to the Cape in 1894. The native Pondos are of Zulu stock. Area, 3906 sq. miles ; pop. 264,827 (263,392 being Pondos of Zulu stock).

POND'WEED (*Potamogeton*). Genus of waterweeds of the grasswrack order. They are aquatic herbs with leaves submerged and translucent or floating and opaque. Of the numerous British species some have leaves 10 in. across, others are threadlike. The allied sweet-scented Cape pondweed, *Oponogeton,* flowers freely during the winter in Great Britain.

PONIATOWSKI. The name of an illustrious Polish family. Stanislas, Count Poniatowski, born 1678, died 1762, is known for his connection with Charles XII., whom he followed into Turkey. He wrote *Remarques d'un Seigneur Polonais sur l'histoire de Charles XII. par Voltaire* (Hague, 1741).

His eldest son, Stanislas Augustus, born 1732, the favourite of Catherine II., was elected King of Poland in 1764.

Jozef, the nephew of King Stanislas, born in 1762, served against the Russians in 1792, and in 1794 joined the Poles in their attempt to drive the Russians out of the country, and commanded a division at the sieges of Warsaw. In 1809 he commanded the Polish army against the superior Austrian force which was sent to occupy the Duchy of Warsaw, and compelled it to retire. In 1812 he led the Polish forces against Russia. During the battle of Leipzig, Napoleon created him a marshal.

PONSARD (poŋ-sär), **François.** French dramatist, born at Vienne, in Dauphiné, 1814, died 1867. His first success was his *Lucrèce*, produced in 1843, and welcomed as a return to classicism. Among his other pieces are: *Agnès de Méranie*; *Charlotte Corday*; and *L'Honneur et l'argent*, a fine comedy of manners. He became a member of the Academy in 1855.

PONTA DELGA'DA. A seaport and the capital of the administrative district of St. Michael's (with St. Mary) in the Azores. It is located on the south side of the Island of St. Michael's, and has a good harbour protected by a breakwater over 2500 feet in length. Ponta-Delgada combines its functions as capital with those of a health-resort, and it is also the commercial centre of the archipelago. The chief exports are wheat, maize, and oranges. There is a cathedral, and a monastery of some note. Pop. 16,179.

PONT-À-MOUSSON. A town of France, department of Meurthe-et-Moselle, on the canalised River Moselle, and connected by rail with Nancy (17 miles). There is a large church dedicated to St. Martin, and a modern seminary is located within the buildings of the ancient Abbey of St. Mary. Pont-à-Mousson was the seat of a university from 1571 to 1763. The town originated in the ninth century, and was a lordship which became a marquessate about 1354. Pop. 14,009.

PONTEFRACT (colloquially **POMFRET**). A municipal borough and market town of Yorkshire (West Riding), England, on an eminence near the confluence of the Aire and Calder; served by the London, Midland, and Scottish, and London & North-Eastern Railways.

Chief Buildings. The chief antiquity of the town is the castle, which originally covered 8 acres. It is now partly a museum, and the lands are used as a public park. Other objects of interest are an ancient hermitage hewn out in solid rock and dating from 1396. On St. Thomas's Hill, Thomas, Earl of Lancaster, was beheaded in 1322, the place being indicated by a windmill. The grammar school, now occupying modern buildings, was founded in the pre-Elizabethan period, and the town hall stands on the site of the old Saxon Moot-Hall, which was superseded by another structure in 1656.

Manufactures and Industries. Pontefract is noted for the preparation from liquorice of small lozenges, known for centuries as "Pomfret cakes." Tanning, brewing, corn-milling, and brick-making are representative industries. Pop. (1931), 19,053.

History. Pontefract originated in Kirkby, which, in the time of the *Domesday Book*, was a member of the manor of Tateshall (which is now called Tanshelf, and is a suburb of modern Pontefract). Richard II. was imprisoned and murdered in the castle in 1399. During the Wars of the Roses, Pontefract espoused the Lancastrian cause and was loyal to Henry VI. Pontefract Castle was the last garrison to hold out for Charles I., and was dismantled in 1649.—

BIBLIOGRAPHY: G. Fox, *The History of Pontefract*; B. Boothroyd, *The*

History of the Ancient Borough of Pontefract; A. H. Norway, *Highways and Byways in Yorkshire*; T. Paulden, *Pontefract Castle: an account of how it was taken, and how General Rainsborough was surprised at Doncaster, anno 1648* (4to, London, 1702); and *An account of the Taking and Surrender of Pontefract Castle* (4to, Oxford, 1747).

PONTEVEDRA. A maritime province of North-Western Spain, on the Atlantic. All the rivers flow to the Atlantic, the Minho forming the southern boundary; others are the Ulla, Lerez, and Umia. The climate is mild and the rainfall heavy, with heavy fogs in summer and violent storms in winter. Pontevedra (capital) Vigo (seaport), La Estrada, Tuy, and Redondela are important towns. At Tuy the Spanish and Portuguese railways meet and the line bifurcates, one branch following the coast via Redondela (branch to Vigo), and the other traversing the Minho Valley. Cattle are raised, and hams, eggs, wines, and leather are exported. Area, 1695 sq. miles; pop. (1931), 570,988 (or 336·8 per square mile).

PONTEVEDRA (Roman **DUO PONTES** or **PONS VETUS**). A city and the capital of the province of Pontevedra, Spain, on the Bay of Pontevedra, near the mouth of the Lerez; served by the Corunna-Santiago-Tuy line of the Spanish railways. Pontevedra is mainly granite-built, and is partly enclosed by mediæval walls, and spanning the Lerez there is an ancient Roman bridge (*Pons Vetus*) of twelve arches, from which the town derives its name. There is an extensive sardine-fishery in the Bay of Pontevedra. Pop. about 25,000.

PON'TIFEX. The title borne by the members of the most important of the priestly colleges among the Romans. Their institution was ascribed to Numa, and their number varied at different periods from four to sixteen. The *pontifex maximus*, or chief pontiff, held his office for life, and could not leave Italy. In the time of the Empire the office was held by the emperor himself, until the times of Theodosius. The title was subsequently assumed by the Popes.

PONTINE MARSHES. An extensive, malarious tract of marshy land in Italy, in the southern part of the Roman Campagna, extending along the Mediterranean seaboard for about 27 miles, with a mean breadth of 8½ miles. In ancient times it was well drained, but on the subjugation of the Volscii by the Romans the drainage system became ineffective, and the land assumed practically its present form. By the construction of the Appian Way, Appius Claudius endeavoured to drain it (312 B.C.), and several Popes subsequently made attempts at reclamation. The Italian Government voted a large sum for drainage, but this has been found possible only in parts.

PONTOISE (pon-twäz; ancient **BRIVA ISARÆ**). A town of France, in the department of Seine-et-Oise, at the confluence of the Viosne with the Oise. It has manufactures of chemical products and hosiery, and a trade in grain. Pop. about 9000.

Pontoise existed in the time of the Gauls as *Briva Isaræ*, which means Bridge of the Oise, and became the capital of French Vexin. It was a meeting-place on several occasions of the Parlement of Paris, and offered a refuge to Louis XIV. and Mazarin during the Fronde.

PONTOON'. A flat-bottomed, wooden boat used as a support for the roadway of a floating bridge (from the Lat. *pons*, a bridge). The pontoon in use in the British service is 21 feet long, and is made in two sections, coupled together and known as the bow section and the stern section; of these the bow section is the longer by 2 feet; the beam or width is 5 feet 3 inches, tapering at the bow to 2 feet 6 inches; depth, 2 feet 5 inches. The weight of each section is 5 cwt. The super-structure necessary to complete the bridge consists of a "saddle beam" fixed on the thwarts of the pontoon, on which are laid the "baulks" or road-bearers; these in their turn support the "chesses" or planks which form the roadway, and which are kept in place by "ribands;" for the shore end other baulks are required.

Special wagons are provided for the carriage of pontoons and superstructure, one wagon being arranged to carry the two sections of a pontoon and sufficient superstructure for a "bay" of 15 feet. Trestles of heavy baulks bolted together are often used in combination with pontoons, and both pontoons and trestles form part of the equipment of a field company Royal Engineers, two trestles being carried on a special wagon.

With pontoons three types of bridge, capable of carrying the heaviest loads other than railway trains, can be constructed. These are known as light, medium, and heavy.

Light Bridges. The floating piers consist of a single pontoon, and a roadway of 9 feet width is provided.

Medium Bridge. In this type six *sections* of pontoons are formed into a raft to form each pier, and a roadway of about 9½ feet is provided. Chesses are laid double.

Heavy Bridge. Nine sections are used for each pier, the width of roadway being the same as in a medium bridge. Chesses are laid treble.

Pontoons lend themselves very conveniently to the construction of rafts for various purposes, a four-pontoon raft being capable of carrying 100 infantry soldiers, or 12 horses and their riders, or 1 gun and limber with a proportion of personnel. With three heavy pontoons (length, 41

Pontoon Bridge

feet) and special super-structure, a raft to carry up to 35 tons can be made.

Pontoon bridges are normally formed in one of four ways: (*a*) By connecting the pontoons at the head of the bridge. (*b*) By making rafts, floating them into position, and then connecting them. (*c*) By making the bridge alongside the bank, and then allowing it to be swung to the opposite side by the force of the current. (*d*) By pushing out the head of the bridge and connecting other pontoons successively from the shore, until the original head reaches the other side. This is known as "booming out."

PONTUS. A kingdom in Asia Minor (so called from the Pontus Euxinus, on which it lay), which extended from Halys on the west to Colchis on the east, and was bounded on the north by the Euxine Sea, and on the south by Galatia, Cappadocia, and Armenia Minor. The first king was Artabazes, son of Darius. The kingdom was in its most flourishing state under Mithridates the Great. But soon after his death (63 B.C.) it was conquered by Pompey, and made tributary to the Roman Empire.

PONTYPOOL. An urban district and market town of Monmouthshire, England, on an acclivity above the Afon Lywd (affluent of the Usk); served by the London, Midland & Scottish and Great Western Railways, and by the Monmouthshire Canal, which connects it with Newport. Its existence is due to its proximity to the great South Wales coal-fields. Industries are connected more or less with mining, and with the manufacture of iron and steel and tin-plates. Pop. (1931), 6788.

PONTYPRIDD. An urban district and market town of Glamorganshire, Wales, at the confluence of the Rhondda and the Taff; served by the Great Western Railway, and by the Glamorganshire Canal. Pontypridd came into prominence and rapidly progressed when the Taff Vale lines were pushed through in 1840. The name (New Bridge) is derived from the wonderful old one-arch bridge spanning the Taff, which was designed and erected in 1755 by a self-taught mason named Edwards. Pontypridd is the metropolis of the Rhondda Valley, and is dependent on the coal-fields there for existence. There are iron- and brass-foundries, and anchor-, chain-, and chemical-works. Pop. (1931), 42,757.

PONY. The oldest known breed and the smallest variety of the domesticated horse, ranging in height between 8 or 9 and 14 hands. Of the many varieties of ponies the following are typical British breeds:

Connemara. At one time flourished on the mountains of Ireland. It is similar to the Highland pony, has good riding shoulders, and jumps well. In the Irish islands they average 12 hands 2 inches, but may attain 14 hands 1 inch on the mainland, as a result of better food and more suitable climate. The prevailing colour is dun.

Dartmoor. A small and blood-like pony with capital shoulders. Stallions attain 14 hands; mares average 13 hands 2 inches. The prevailing colours are brown, black, or bay; grey is allowable, but other colours are objected to.

Exmoor. A very hardy, untiring pony, capable of carrying enormous loads on little food. It is a handsome animal averaging 12 hands, but should never exceed 13 hands. The prevailing colours are dark-bay or brown, with short black legs.

Highland. The breed that carried the Highlanders of the hills on many a long journey before roads existed in the mountainous regions of North and North-Western Scotland. There are many subdivisions, but the original type cannot be obliterated by crossing. The Barra ponies are of 11 hands 2 inches upwards; Skye, about 13 hands 3 inches; and Mainland breeds vary between 14 hands and 14 hands 2 inches. The Highland is a good saddle pony, capable of wonderful feats of endurance.

New Forest. A good pony of from 12 to 13 hands high; short on the leg, with capital pasterns. All colours are allowable, but dun is not often seen. Greys, however, are frequently met with, and flea-bitten greys are said to be descended from an Arab sent to the Forest by the Prince Consort of Queen Victoria. They are very handsome animals, and possess a striking Arab character.

In the breeding of ponies the fundamental considerations are smallness, beauty, and compactness, combined with practical utility. *See* HORSE; POLO-PONY; SHETLAND PONY.

POODLE. A small variety of dog covered with long, curling hair, and remarkable for its great intelligence

Poodle

and affection. The usual colour is white, but black and blue are also bred.

POOL. *See* BILLIARDS.

POOLE. An ancient municipal borough and seaport, a county of a town, in Dorsetshire, England, on a peninsula on the north part of Poole Harbour; served by the Southern Railway. Cordage, sailcloth, pottery, flour, and agricultural tools are made. Poole Harbour is an arm of the English Channel extending inland to a depth of about 7 miles, with an average breadth of 5 miles. In the harbour there are several low islands, the largest, Branksea, containing a sixteenth-century castle. From Branksea also potters' clay is sent to the Staffordshire potteries. Pop. (1931), 57,258.

In mediæval times Poole was a flourishing seaport, which was incorporated and erected into a county by Elizabeth (1569). Charles II. gave it a charter in 1667, and it was separately represented in Parliament from 1362 until 1885.

POONA, or **PUNA.** A city and district of India, in the Presidency of Bombay, and at the confluence of the Mula and Mutha Rivers; served by the Great Indian Peninsular Railway from Bombay. The Deccan college for classics, mathematics, and philosophy, and a college of science with special training in civil engineering, also training college, female normal school, and other schools, public library, hospital, arsenal, and barracks are established at Poona. It is a health-resort, and from July to November is the seat of the Bombay Government.

Manufactures include gold and silver jewellery, small ornaments in brass, copper, and ivory, and silk and cotton fabrics. It is an important military station and road junction.

Until 1817 Poona was the capital of the Peshwa rulers of the Marathi Confederacy. A battle was fought there on 16th Nov., 1817, between the British and the Peshwa, and the city fell to the British on 19th Nov. Pop. 214,796.

The district has an area of 5348 sq. miles, and a pop. of 1,100,000. It is an elevated tableland, watered by the Bhima and its tributaries, and abounding in isolated heights, formerly crowned with strong fortresses. Inhabitants chiefly Marathis.

POON (or **POONA**) **WOOD.** The wood of the poon tree (*Calophyllum inophyllum* and *Calophyllum angustifolium*), a native of India. It is of a light, porous texture, and is much used in the East Indies in shipbuilding for planks and spar. The Calcutta poon is preferred to that of other districts. Poon seed yields an oil called *dilo,* poon-seed oil, etc.

POOR AND POOR LAWS. A full history of the poor, in the widest sense in which the term is used, would be a history of the bulk of mankind, since the standard of living varies in different countries and at different times, and the majority of human beings are always in danger of

TYPES OF PONY

1, Dartmoor Pony. 2, Connemara Pony. 3, New Forest Pony and Foal.
4, Highland Pony. 5, Exmoor Pony.

sinking below the current standard. Here, however, it will be possible only to give some account of the legal poor; of the provision which has been made from time to time by the State for the relief of destitution in Great Britain.

The origins of the poor law are derived from feudalism. The obligation of the serf to work on the manor carried with it a certain right to maintenance. When this condition of "status" gradually changed to a system of contract, the duty of maintaining the destitute labourer was transferred from the manor to the parish. According to a passage quoted from Horne's *Mirror* in *Coke's Institutes,* it was ordained by kings before the Conquest that the poor should be sustained by parsons, rectors, and parishioners, "so that no one should die from lack of sustenance."

The Poor Relief Act, 1601 (43 Elizabeth c. 2), which closed a series of experimental laws passed in the Tudor period for the relief of the impotent poor and the regulation of begging, is generally treated as the first English poor law. This measure was passed for a limited period only, but it was renewed at the beginning of the reign of James I., and made perpetual in 1641. Its chief purposes were:

(*a*) "For setting to work the Children of all such whose Parents shall not by the said Church-wardens and Overseers . . . be thought able to keep and maintain their children;

(*b*) "And also for setting to work all such persons, married or unmarried as having no Means to maintain them, use no ordinary or daily Trade of Life to get their Living by;

(*c*) "And also to raise weekly or otherwise (by taxation of every Inhabitant . . .) a convenient Stock of Flax, Hemp, Wool, Thread, Iron, and other Ware and Stuff, to set the Poor on Work;

(*d*) "And also competent Sums of Money for and towards the necessary Relief of the Lame, Impotent, Old, Blind, and such other among them being Poor and not able to work;

(*e*) "And also for the putting out of such Children to be Apprentices . . ."

In the reign of Charles II. an Act was passed, which is usually called the "Settlement Act," the effect of which was to prevent labourers from moving freely from one parish into another. This Act was denounced by Adam Smith as "an evident violation of natural liberty and justice," and was modified in 1795.

The period between 1793 and 1815 was one of almost continuous war; prices rushed up, harvests were exceptionally bad, the population increased with a rapidity hitherto unknown, and food was at famine prices. In May, 1795, the magistrates of Berkshire met at Speenhamland and decided to supplement wages out of the parish rates. They drew up and published a scale, by which every poor and industrious person should receive from the parish enough to make up his wages to 3*s.* a week for himself and 1*s.* 6*d.* a week for each member of his family, when the loaf cost a shilling. If the price of bread rose, the dole was to be increased proportionately. The magistrates in many other counties adopted the same scale, and the result was that agricultural wages remained unduly low, pauperism became general, and the poor rate rose rapidly.

In 1832 a Commission was appointed "to make diligent and full inquiry into the practical operation of the laws for the relief of the poor in England and Wales, and into the manner in which those laws were administered, and to report their opinion as to what beneficial alterations could be made." The Commissioners reported that "the great source of abuse was the outdoor relief afforded to the able-bodied on their own account or on that of their families, given either in kind or in money," and that "great maladministration existed in the workhouses." They proposed considerable alterations in the law, and most of their suggestions were carried out in the Poor Law Amendment Act, 1834.

The intention of this Act was to restore the original provision of the Statute of Elizabeth by which relief to able-bodied persons or their families was to be given in workhouses, while outdoor relief was confined to the impotent. A beneficial alteration which had occurred in the meantime—the gradual grouping of parishes into unions—was maintained and extended to the whole of England.

The administration of the poor law is controlled by the Ministry of Health (the local Government Board until 1919). Until 1930 it issued orders to local boards of guardians who were elected by the ratepayers. These guardians could, within the discretion allowed to them by statutes and orders, vary the procedure very considerably between one parish and another; with the result that a class of applicants who had no chance of receiving outdoor relief in one union might get it easily in another. To check the resultant extravagance an Act was passed in 1926 authorising the Minister of Health to supersede any board of guardians who fail to perform their duty and to appoint in their place other persons for a period not exceeding twelve months. This Act, with various other provisions, was consolidated in the Poor Law Act, 1927.

That the English poor law was unsatisfactory in many respects had long been generally admitted. As the position then stood the union as the unit of poor law administration had become too small to bear equably the present burden, and the difficulty was stated in a memorandum issued in July, 1928, by the Ministry of Health, in which it was stated that "one union may be weighed down by an excessive burden, while its neighbour may escape with a comparatively light load though parts of both areas may be much alike." To remedy this, in 1930 boards of guardians were abolished and their functions taken over by the county and county burgh councils. *See* SETTLEMENT; VAGRANTS.—BIBLIOGRAPHY: Nicholls, *History of the English Poor Law*; B. Webb, *The Prevention of Destitution.*

POPAYÁN. A city of Colombia, capital of the department of Cauca, on a plain between the Purace Volcano (15,420 feet altitude) and one of the tributaries of the headwaters of the Cauca. It is the seat of a Roman Catholic archbishopric, and of the departmental University of Popayán, once of considerable reputation. The bishopric dates from 1547. Pop. 32,000.

Popayán was founded in 1538, and the name is eponymous, commemorating Payan, an Indian chief, upon the site of whose settlement the town was founded. It was for long of commercial importance, but the manufactures are now negligible.

POPE (Lat. *papa*; Gr. *papas*, father). The title at present given solely to the Bishop of Rome, who is the head of the Roman Catholic Church. Besides the bishopric of the Roman diocese, the Pope also holds certain other dignities. His full title is as follows: Bishop of Rome, Vicar of Jesus Christ, Successor of St. Peter, Supreme Pontiff of the Universal Church, Patriarch of the West, Primate of Italy, and Sovereign of the Temporal Dominions of the Holy Roman Church. The title seems to have been used at first in the early Church as a title of reverence given to ecclesiastics generally, and at the present time it is applied in the Greek Church to all priests.

In the early Western Church the title of Pope was ultimately bestowed upon the metropolitan bishops, but in the struggle for pre-eminence the claim to be recognised as the only Pope was enforced by the Bishop of Rome. This claim of pre-eminence was founded on the belief, supported by the early traditions of the Church, that the Apostle Peter planted a Church in Rome, and that he died there as a martyr. This tradition, taken in connection with the alleged pre-eminence of Peter among Christ's disciples, came to be regarded as sufficient reason for the primacy of the Bishop of Rome in the Church. Consequently from the end of the fourth century the Bishop of Rome was the first among the five patriarchs or superior bishops of Christendom. A decree of the Emperor Valentian III. (445) acknowledged the Bishop of Rome as Primate, but until the eighth century many measures of the Popes met with violent opposition. Leo the Great (440-461) was the first to base his claims to the primacy on divine authority by appealing to Matt. xvi. 18; and he did much to establish the theory that bishops in disputes with their metropolitans had a right of appeal to Rome. The Eastern Church always resisted the see of Rome, and this mainly occasioned the schism that in 1054 divided Christendom into the Greek and Roman Churches.

The temporal power of the Pope was restored by the Italian Government in 1929, and the Vatican City is now an independent state. (It is most important to consult the article PAPACY.) For Roman Catholics the Pope is still the supreme authority in all matters of faith. He has supreme powers in all matters of discipline and faith over all and each of the pastors and of the faithful. The special prerogatives of the Pope were clearly defined by the Decrees of the Vatican Council of 1870. This Council also taught that when the pontiff speaks *ex cathedra*, that is, when he, in virtue of his apostolic office, defines a doctrine of faith and morals to be held by the whole Church, he possesses infallibility by divine assistance. The Pope cannot annul the constitution of the Church as ordained by Christ. He may condemn or prohibit books, alter the rites of the Church, and reserve to himself the canonisation of saints.

A Pope has no power to nominate his successor, election being entirely in the hands of the cardinals, who are not bound to choose one of their own body. The Pope's dress consists of a white silk robe and a scarlet mantle. The Pope ranks as the first of Christian Princes, and in Catholic countries his ambassadors have precedence over other members of the diplomatic corps. The Papal insignia are the tiara or triple crown, the straight crosier, and the pallium. He is addressed as " Your Holiness," and refers to himself as *Servus Servorum Dei*, servant of the servants of God. For a history of the papacy *see* PAPACY.—BIBLIOGRAPHY: H. K. Mann, *Lives of the Popes in the Early Middle Ages*; L. Pastor, *History of the Popes from the Close of the Middle Ages.*

Subjoined is a table of the Popes, according to the Roman Notizie, with the dates of the commencement of their pontificates. The names printed in italics are those of Antipopes:

St. Peter	A.D. 42
St. Linus	66
St. Anacletus	78
St. Clement I	91
St. Evaristus	100
St. Alexander I	108
St. Sixtus I	119
St. Telesphorus	127
St. Hyginus	139
St. Pius I	142
St. Anicetus	157
St. Soterus	168
St. Eleutherius	177
St. Victor I	193
St. Zephirinus	202
St. Callixtus I	217
St. Urban I	223
St. Pontianus	230
St. Anterus	235
St. Fabian	236
St. Cornelius	250
St. Lucius I—*Novatianus*	252
St. Stephen I	253
St. Sixtus II	257
St. Dionysius	259
St. Felix I	269
St. Eutychianus	275
St. Caius	283
St. Marcellinus	296
(See vacant 3 years and 6 months.)	
St. Marcellus I	308
St. Eusebius	310
St. Melchiades or Miltiades	311
St. Sylvester I	314
St. Marcus	336
St. Julius I	337
Liberius	352
St. Felix II (sometimes reckoned an Antipope)	355
St. Damasus I	366
St. Siricius	384
St. Anastasius I	398
St. Innocent I	402
St. Zosimus	417
St. Boniface I—*Eulalius*	418
St. Celestine I	422
St. Sixtus III	432
St. Leo I (the Great)	440
St. Hilary	461
St. Simplicius	468
St. Felix III	483
St. Gelasius I	492
St. Anastasius II	496
St. Symmachus	498
St. Hormisdas—*Lawrence*	514
St. John I	523
St. Felix IV	526
Boniface II—*Dioscorus*	530
John II	533
St. Agapetus I	535
St. Sylverius	536
Vigilius	537
Pelagius I	555
John III	560
Benedict (I) Bonosus	574
Pelagius II	578
St. Gregory I (the Great)	590
Sabinianus	604
Boniface III	607
St. Boniface IV	608
St. Deusdedit	615
Boniface V	619
Honorius I	625
(See vacant 1 year and 7 months.)	
Severinus	640
John IV	640
Theodorus I	642
St. Martin I	649
St. Eugenius I	654
St. Vitalianus	657
Adeodatus	672
Donus or Domnus I	676
St. Agathon	678
St. Leo II	682
St. Benedict II	684
John V	685
Conon—*Theodorus; Paschal*	686
St. Sergius I	687
John VI	701
John VII	705
Sisinnius	708
Constantine	708
St. Gregory II	715
St. Gregory III	731
St. Zachary	741
Stephen II (died before consecration)	752
Stephen III	752
St. Paul I—*Constantine; Theophylactus; Philip*	757
Stephen IV	768
Adrian I	772
St. Leo III	795
Stephen V	816
St. Paschal I	817
Eugenius II	824
Valentinus	827
Gregory IV	827
Sergius II	844
St. Leo IV	847
Benedict III—*Anastasius*	855
St. Nicholas I	858
Adrian II	867
John VIII	872
Marinus I, or Martin II	882
Adrian III	884
Stephen VI	885
Formosus	891
Boniface VI (reigned only 18 days)	896
Stephen VII	896
Romanus	897
Theodorus II—*Sergius III*	898
John IX	898
Benedict IV	900
Leo V	903
Christopher	903
Sergius III	904
Anastasius III	911
Lando	913
John X	914
Leo VI	928
Stephen VIII	929
John XI	931
Leo VII	936
Stephen IX	939
Marinus II, or Martin III	943
Agapetus II	946
John XII—*Leo VIII*	956
Benedict V	964
John XIII	965
Benedict VI	972
Donus or Domnus II	974
Benedict VII	975
John XIV—*Boniface VII*	983
John XV	985
Gregory V—*John XVI*	996
Sylvester II	999
John XVI or XVII	1003
John XVII or XVIII	1003
Sergius IV	1009
Benedict VIII—*Gregory VI*	1012
John XVIII or XIX	1024
Benedict IX (deposed)—*John XX*	1033
Gregory VI—*Sylvester III*	1045
Clement II	1046
Damasus II—*Benedict IX* attempts to resume the throne	1048
St. Leo IX	1049
Victor II	1055
Stephen X	1057
Benedict X	1058
Nicholas II	1058
Alexander II—*Honorius II*	1061
Gregory VII (Hildebrand)—*Clement III*	1073
(See vacant 1 year.)	
Victor III	1086
Urban II	1088
Paschal II	1099
Gelasius II—*Gregory VIII*	1118
Callixtus II	1119
Honorius II—*Celestine II*	1124
Innocent II—*Anacletus II; Victor IV*	1130
Celestinus II	1143
Lucius II	1144
Eugenius III	1145
Anastasius IV	1153
Adrian IV (Nicholas Breakspear, an Englishman)	1154
Alexander III—*Victor V; Paschal III; Calixtus III; Innocent III*	1159
Lucius III	1181
Urban III	1185
Gregory VIII	1187
Clement III	1187
Celestinus III	1191
Innocent III	1198
Honorius III	1216
Gregory IX	1227
Celestinus IV	1241
(See vacant 1 year and 7 months.)	
Innocent IV	1243
Alexander IV	1254
Urban IV	1261
Clement IV	1265
(See vacant 2 years and 9 months.)	
Gregory X	1271
Innocent V	1276
Adrian V	1276
John XIX or XX or XXI	1276
Nicholas III	1277
Martin IV	1281
Honorius IV	1285
Nicholas IV	1288

Pope	Year
(See vacant 2 years and 3 months.)	
St. Celestinus V	A.D. 1294
Boniface VIII	1294
Benedict XI	1303
Clement V (papacy removed to Avignon)	1305
(See vacant 2 years and 3 months.)	
John XXII	1316
Benedict XII—*Nicholas V at Rome*	1334
Clement VI	1342
Innocent VI	1352
Urban V—*Clement VII*	1362
Gregory XI (throne restored to Rome)	1370
Urban VI	1378
Boniface IX—*Benedict XIII at Avignon*	1389
Innocent VII	1404
Gregory XII	1406
Alexander V	1409
John XXIII	1410
Martin V—*Clement VIII*	1417
Eugenius IV—*Felix V*	1431
Nicholas V	1447
Callixtus III	1455
Pius II	1458
Paul II	1464
Sixtus IV	1471
Innocent VIII	1484
Alexander VI	1492
Pius III	1503
Julius II	1503
Leo X	1513
Adrian VI	1522
Clement VII	1523
Paul III	1534
Julius III	1550
Marcellus II	1555
Paul IV	1555
Pius IV	1559
St. Pius V	1566
Gregory XIII	1572
Sixtus V	1585
Urban VII	1590
Gregory XIV	1590
Innocent IX	1591
Clement VIII	1592
Leo XI	1605
Paul V	1605
Gregory XV	1621
Urban VIII	1623
Innocent X	1644
Alexander VII	1655
Clement IX	1667
Clement X	1670
Innocent XI	1676
Alexander VIII	1689
Innocent XII	1691
Clement XI	1700
Innocent XIII	1721
Benedict XIII	1724
Clement XII	1730
Benedict XIV	1740
Clement XIII	1758
Clement XIV	1769
Pius VI	1775
Pius VII	1800
Leo XII	1823
Pius VIII	1829
Gregory XVI	1831
Pius IX	1846
Leo XIII	1878
Pius X	1903
Benedict XV	1914
Pius XI	1922

POPE, Alexander. English poet, born on 21st May, 1688, died on 30th May, 1744. His father was a Roman Catholic linen-draper of Lombard Street; his mother's maiden name was Edith Turner, and she was of a good middle-class family. He was the only child of the marriage, and both his parents were nearly fifty years of age when he was born. He inherited a tendency to nervous headaches from his mother, and a feeble frame from his father. His delicacy of health was greatly increased by his precocious application to study. Owing to his health or his religion or both he did not attend any good school or college, but was sent to one or two small Catholic schools, and received private tuition from one or two incompetent Catholic priests. He was thus largely self-taught, and, although he assimilated much knowledge of various kinds and was indefatigable in his devotion to his books, he was never a scholar. His religion closed the learned professions to him, and his physique rendered him unfit for commercial life, so he early decided to devote himself to literature, after a brief attempt to become efficient as a painter. His father adopted a wise policy of non-interference, being always ready to help his brilliant son, but never anxious to dictate to him.

While still at school he wrote a play based on Ogilby's translation of the *Iliad*, and an epic called *Alcander, Prince of Rhodes*. Both these compositions are lost. He made the acquaintance of the dramatist Wycherley, who encouraged him to write pastorals, and of the critic Walsh, who recommended him to write "correctly," a piece of advice which he never forgot. Long afterwards Pope published his correspondence with Wycherley, after emending it so as to make his own conduct appear in a favourable light.

Pope apprenticed himself to the art of poetry with the greatest ardour. He studied widely, and experimented in translating and adapting. Dryden was his model, and in imitation of him he "translated" some Chaucer, *The Merchant's Tale*, *The Wife of Bath's Prologue*, and *The House of Fame*, and made a version of the first book of the *Thebais* of Statius to set against Dryden's *Æneid*. It is typical of his not impeccable taste that he ranked Statius as the equal of Virgil. Work of this kind increased his powers, and developed his great natural gifts as a metrist. His *Pastorals* were published in 1709 in a miscellany which included similar work by Ambrose Philips, whom Pope afterwards held up to ridicule in *The Guardian*, and immortalised as "Namby-pamby" in *The Dunciad*.

The *Essay on Criticism* appeared in 1711; it is an astonishingly mature poem, full of sound precepts, and brilliantly written. It was not intended, as some critics seem to suppose, to supersede Aristotle and Horace; it was intended to express in the choicest language some of the commonplaces of contemporary criticism, and could not have attained its object more fully than it has done. *The Messiah*, a sacred eclogue, which was No. 378 of *The Spectator*, was in its time a much-admired poem, but it reads to-day somewhat like a copy of verses sent in for the Seatonian Prize.

The Rape of the Lock appeared in its original form in 1712; in 1714 it appeared in its final and greatly improved form, with the "machinery" of sylphs and gnomes added. Robert, seventh Baron Petre, had cut off a lock of Miss Arabella Fermor's hair, and the poem was intended to heal the breach in friendship caused by this action. *The Rape of the Lock*, which was written in imitation of Boileau's *Lutrin*, far surpassed its model, and remains the greatest of mock-heroic poems. It was the first poem to impress upon the French the fact that they had not the entire monopoly of exquisitely finished and dainty workmanship. It is perhaps for this reason that the French critic Taine has done such signal injustice to this poem. *Windsor Forest*, an artificial poem of no great merit, appeared in 1713. About this time Pope commenced his life-long friendship with Swift.

In 1713 Pope definitely embarked upon the enterprise of translating Homer. This work was to be published by subscription, and most of the eminent men of the day gave their support to the undertaking. The *Iliad* was published between 1715 and 1720, and the *Odyssey* was completed by 1725. The translation of the *Iliad* was entirely the work of Pope, though the notes were by different hands; Elijah Fenton translated four books of the *Odyssey*, and William Broome eight. Pope's treatment of his collaborators was unjust and far from generous; though it was entirely to his name that the enterprise owed its success. He cleared over £8000 by his *Homer*; this being the first instance in English literature of a substantial fortune made by a man of letters. He invested his money securely, and lived in comfort for the rest of his life. Opinions will always differ as to the merits of Pope's translation; most critics will agree with Bentley, who said, "A fine poem, Mr. Pope, but you must not call it Homer." Sir Leslie Stephen said that Pope's ignorance of Greek was "an awkward qualification for a translator of Homer," but the ignorance of poetry displayed by most other Homeric translators is a qualification hardly less awkward. Other translations cannot be called Homer either, and few of them can be called fine poems. Whatever benefit Pope corferred upon literature by translating Homer, the effect of his translation upon his own work was entirely salutary. From his labours he gained something of that solidarity and complete mastery of his materials that Shakespeare gained by writing his English historical plays.

In 1725 Pope published an edition of Shakespeare's plays in six volumes. He was in many ways singularly ill-fitted for this task, being without many of the qualities required by a Shakespearean editor. He was especially lacking in patience. Still, he made many improvements in the text, and many acute suggestions in his notes. Shakespeare never again had the advantage of being edited by a man of genius and a poet, since Johnson was no poet, and many of the later editors were undistinguished by the slightest talent, and unacquainted with the rudiments of poetry. Pope's Shakespeare had the effect of embroiling him in a quarrel with Lewis Theobald the critic, who became the hero of *The Dunciad*, which first appeared in 1728. In a later edition Theobald was dethroned, and Colley Cibber, poet-laureate and poetaster, reigned in his stead. *The Dunciad* is a masterly satire upon pedants and dunces; it is not malignant, as it has sometimes been represented as being, but is rather inspired by a love of mischief and malice. Pope could not say with Swift, "I am misanthropos, and hate mankind;" he hated his critics and enemies only, and contrived to settle many old scores in this remarkable poem.

Pope's *Essay on Man* (1733) was largely an exposition of the clear but shallow philosophy of Lord Bolingbroke, which was called by the irreverent "The New Gospel according to St. John." It is brilliantly written, and full of phrases which have become part of the language. Its orthodoxy was ably defended by Warburton, who became the accepted commentator upon the works of Pope. The *Moral Essays* and *Imitations of Horace* contain much of Pope's best work, though they are marred to some extent by too much bitterness. No poems in all English literature are more vigorous and terse.

The transactions which led up to the publication of Pope's letters in a "genuine" edition of 1737 are tortuous and complicated beyond unravelling here. The facts were investigated by C. W. Dilke with exemplary patience. The letters themselves are not interesting, having been in some cases written with a view to publication, and in many cases too carefully edited by their author.

In making an estimate of Pope as a man and as an author it is necessary always to bear in mind his physical infirmities. It was his deformed body which made him super-sensitive, and it was his super-sensitiveness which made him so unforgiving an enemy. His good qualities were numerous and vital; he was a devoted son to both father and mother, a faithful friend to those who were faithful to him, and honourably independent as a literary man. The worst of his faults was vanity, which made him conceal the amount of sheer hard work some of his poems cost him, and caused him to attribute to his extreme youth work done or at any rate revised at a later date. Honourable in his private life, when it came to literary transactions Pope adopted a tortuous policy of a kind usually associated in the English mind with the followers of Ignatius Loyola. Pope lived in an age of venom, when party feeling ran higher than it had done before or has done since. He was a bitter controversialist because all his contemporaries were equally bitter, though less able. He would have been a better artist had he remembered Bentley's dictum that no man was ever written out of reputation but by himself.

As a poet Pope was long immoderately praised, and then the tide turned and he was unduly depreciated. He has been attacked as a corrupter of taste and the founder of a school of machine-made poetry. The truth is that he was the chief ornament and culminating point of a school rather than its tyrannical head or founder. He was not a literary dictator like Ben Jonson or his namesake Samuel; he did not wield the bludgeon, but the rapier, though like that of Laertes it was "unbated and envenomed." Pope simply brought to completion the poetical methods of Dryden, Waller, and others. As regards metre, his services to the heroic couplet were like those of Ovid to the elegiac couplet. He brought it to an almost monotonous perfection. He was a scupulous reviser of his work, as careful as Tennyson, and a better self-critic. His work could hardly be bettered; he has provided us with a multitude of quotations, as apt as those of his favourite Horace. In an artificial age, somewhat given to foppery, he had the good taste to translate the world's greatest epic poet and to edit the world's greatest dramatic poet. True, he performed neither task well, but his attempt shows the natural vigour of his mind. His keen, incisive lines will live when much so-called "natural" poetry has been forgotten.—BIBLIOGRAPHY: Sir L. Stephen, *Pope* (English Men of Letters Series); C. W. Dilke, *The Papers of a Critic*; W. J. Courthope, *The Life of Alexander Pope*; O. Elton, *The Augustan Ages*; J. Dennis, *The Age of Pope*; S. T. Coleridge, *Biographia Literaria*; W. Wordsworth, *Preface* to *Lyrical Ballads*.

POPERINGHE. A town of West Flanders, Belgium, on the Vleirbeck, a tributary of the Yser. It is a centre of the hop-growing industry, and trades in pottery, lace goods, and locally raised tobacco. There are also tanneries. Pop. 11,554.

Poperinghe was reduced to insignificance by its larger and more powerful neighbour Ypres in the fourteenth century. During the European War it was invested by the Germans, but was retaken (Oct., 1914). In April, 1918, during Ludendorff's great drive, it was fiercely bombarded by the Germans.

POPISH PLOT. The name given to an imaginary conspiracy which Titus Oates (q.v.) pretended to have discovered in 1678, and by which he succeeded in deluding the mind of the nation over a space of two years, and causing the death of many innocent Catholics. Oates alleged that the plot was formed by the Jesuits and Roman Catholics for the purpose of murdering the king, Charles II., and subverting the Protestant religion. Godfrey, a justice of the peace to whom Oates gave evidence, was found dead in a ditch (17th Oct.), and the Papists were accused of his murder, though nothing transpired to substantiate the charge. Parliament met soon afterwards, and the Commons passed a Bill to exclude Catholics from both Houses. Oates received a pension, and this encouraged Bedloe, a noted thief and impostor, to come forward and confirm Oates's statements. In 1680 Viscount Stafford was impeached by the Commons, condemned by the Lords, and executed (29th Dec.) as an accomplice of the plot, on the evidence of Oates and two of his associates. Soon after the accession of James II. (1685) Oates was convicted of perjury and other crimes.

POPLAR (Popŭlus). A well-known genus of hardy deciduous trees, nat. ord. Salicaceæ, with both barren and fertile flowers in catkins, stamens four to thirty, leaves alternate, broad, with long and slender footstalks flattened vertically, the leaves having generally more or less of a tremulous motion. About eighteen species have been observed, natives of Europe, Central and Northern Asia, and North America. Some of the poplars are the most rapid growers of all hardy forest trees. They thrive under a variety of conditions as regards soil, etc., but do best in damp situations. The timber of the poplar is light and soft, and not very valuable.

P. fastigiāta, the common Lombardy poplar, is well known as a

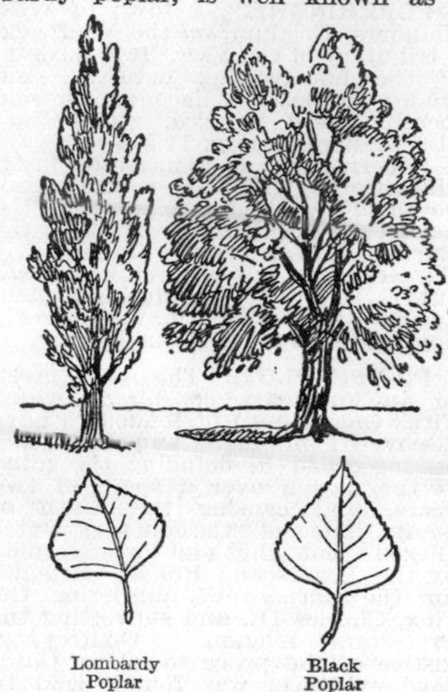

Lombardy Poplar Black Poplar

tall tree with slender branches almost upright; it reaches a height of 100 to 150 feet. *P. nigra* is the common black poplar. *P. tremŭla* is the aspen. *P. alba*, the white poplar, often attains a height of 100 feet. *P. balsamifĕra* is the balsam-poplar or tacamahac of the United States; *P. monilifĕra*, the cotton-wood of America; *P. candicans*, the Ontario poplar.

POPLAR. An eastern metropolitan borough of London. It is part of the densely populated and dingy area of London known as the East End, and includes the parishes of Bow, Poplar, and Bromley, with the East and West India Docks, Millwall Docks, Blackwall, and the Isle of Dogs. Blackwall has been a commercial shipping-centre from remote times, and Sir Walter Raleigh and Sebastian Cabot are said to have lived there. Two tunnels connect Poplar with the southern side of the Thames. The first was constructed in 1902 for foot passengers, and runs from Cubitt Town (Isle of Dogs) to Greenwich. The other lies lower down the river and is known as the Blackwall Tunnel, and was completed in 1897. Poplar Hospital dates from 1855, and treats about 100,000 patients annually. Pop. (1931), 155,083.

POPLIN. A fabric with a maximum number of fine warp threads and a minimum number of thick weft threads, the structure forming the well-known ribbed effect termed repp. In the best poplins the warp is of silk and the weft of woollen or worsted, the weft being entirely hidden. In the cheaper makes worsted yarns are used for warp, and cheap woollen yarns for weft. Figured poplins are very common, but the above general structure is maintained. The manufacture of poplin was introduced into Ireland from France in 1775 by Protestant refugees, and Ireland is still famous for its production.

POPOCATEPETL (Aztec, *popoca*, to smoke, and *tepetl*, a mountain). An active volcano in Mexico, in the province of Puebla; lat. 18° 59′ 47″ N.; long. 98° 33′ 1″ W.; altitude, 17,884 feet. The crater is 3 miles in circumference and 1000 feet deep, and provides pure sulphur, which is secured by the Indians and sent down by chute. To an altitude of 13,000 feet the mountain slopes are afforested. Diego de Ordez, sent by Cortés, was the first European to ascend the mountain (1519). Although the last eruption was in 1802, the snow-cap disappeared prior to the great Mexican earthquakes of 1909, and from this it may be inferred that there is still some volcanic activity present.

POPPY. The common name for plants of the genus Papāver, type

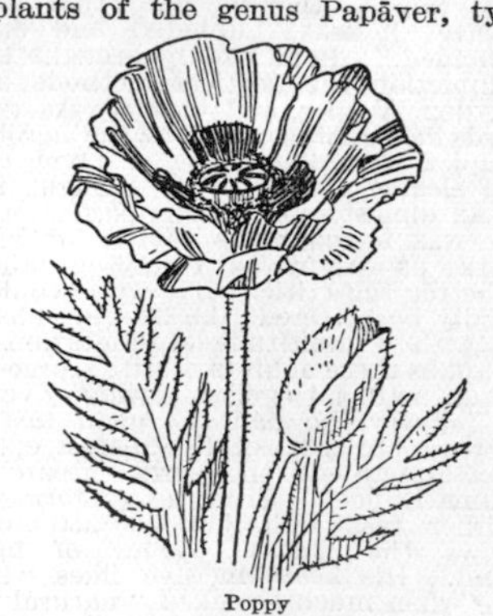

Poppy

of the ord. Papaveraceæ. The species of poppy are herbaceous plants, all bearing large, brilliant, but fugacious flowers. The white poppy (*P. somniferum*) yields the well-known opium of commerce. (*See* OPIUM.)

Most of the species are natives of Europe, and four are truly natives of Britain. They often occur as weeds in fields and waste places, and are frequently also cultivated in gardens for ornament. The seeds of the white poppy yield a fixed harmless oil employed for culinary purposes; and the oil-cake is used for feeding cattle.

The roots of the poppy are annual or perennial; the calyx is composed of two leaves, and the corolla of four petals; the stamens are numerous, and the capsule is one-celled, with several longitudinal partitions, and contains a multitude of seeds.

POPULATION. By the population of a country is meant the total number of human beings living within its frontiers; and the economic theory of population is concerned with the causes which bring about changes in that number. The population of this country is ascertained by a *census*, taken every ten years, and there are similar provisions for the periodic enumeration of the people in all civilised countries. The most notable feature of the returns for the last quarter of a century has been the decline in Western Europe of both the birth-rate and the death-rate. The lower birth-rate is attributed mainly to the deliberate limitation of families; the lower death-rate to better methods of combating disease, especially among infants. The principal figures are given in the *Statesman's Year Book*.

Economic Theory. Most animals and plants have a reproductive power far in excess of the space and nourishment available upon the earth to enable their offspring to grow to maturity. Their numbers are held in check mainly by the simple process of starvation. Mankind alone has learned how, through co-operation, to exercise a vast control over his environment, and to make the soil yield far more human food than it would yield unaided. Nevertheless, even human beings are ultimately restricted in number by their pressure upon the means of subsistence. In favourable circumstances, such as, for instance, those of North America during the eighteenth century, the population has been known to double itself every twenty or twenty-five years, apart from any increase due to immigration. What prevents the population of the whole world from increasing at the same rate? The answer to this question was given by Thomas Robert Malthus in his *Essay on the Principle of Population*, first published in 1798. The ultimate check to population, he said, appears to be a want of food; but this ultimate check is never the immediate check, except in cases of actual famine. The immediate check consists in "all those customs, and all those diseases, which seem to be generated by a scarcity of the means of subsistence; and all those causes, independent of this scarcity, whether of a moral or physical nature, which tend prematurely to weaken and destroy the human frame." These checks to population, which are constantly operating with more or less force in every society, are all resolvable, according to Malthus, into "moral restraint, vice, and misery."

Malthus's *Essay* is the classic exposition of the economic theory of population, but it does not clearly explain why the supply of human food should not increase as rapidly as the population. "For every mouth God sends a pair of hands." Why, therefore, should not the soil be made to yield subsistence for any number of human beings, however great? It remained for Ricardo and John Stuart Mill to formulate the law, or tendency, of diminishing returns in agriculture, which answers this question.

Land differs from the other agents of production, labour and capital, in that its supply is, broadly speaking, fixed and unalterable. An increase in population implies an increase in the supply of labour. The supply of capital will probably expand at least proportionately to the increase in population. But the supply of land remains unchanged. Nevertheless, as the population increases, the demand for land increases, and, the supply being fixed, men are obliged to study the means by which they can bring new and presumably inferior land into cultivation, or get an ever-increasing quantity of produce from the same quantity of land. There are two ways in which this can be done. The first is by discovering and applying improved methods of production. The second is by using increasing quantities of the other agents of production—capital and labour. Turgot said: "Seed thrown on a soil naturally fertile but totally unprepared would be expenditure almost entirely wasted. If the ground were once tilled the produce would be greater; tilling it a second and third time might not merely double and triple, but quadruple or decuple the produce,

sometimes wrongly called Licinio. His family name was Sacchi, and he usually called himself Pordenone, from his native town in Friuli. He executed many works for his native place; some also for Mantua, Vicenza, and Genoa; but his greatest works were for Venice. Specimens of his works are to be found in many of the principal galleries of Europe.

PORGIE (*Pagrus vulgaris*). A fish of the family Sparidæ, with an oblong body, scaly cheeks, and one dorsal fin, found off the coasts of the United States. It is one of the most important food fishes, and attains a length of 18 inches and a weight of 4 lb. The name is also given to the Menhaden (q.v.).

PORISM. A kind of geometrical proposition with which Greek geometers took a good deal to do, but the nature of which is not known for certain, no books of porisms having come down to us. The generally accepted explanation of the word is that given by Playfair, viz. "a proposition affirming the possibility of finding such conditions as will render a certain problem indeterminate, or capable of innumerable solutions." A simple example would be the problem of drawing a plane triangle with angles of m, n, and p degrees. Unless $m + n + p = 180$, there is no solution; but if this condition is fulfilled, there is an infinite number. Again, given two circles of radii R and r, R the greater, with their centres at distance d, it may be proposed to draw a triangle inscribed in the one and escribed to the other. If $d^2 = R^2 - 2Rr$, there is an infinite number of solutions; if d^2 and $R^2 - 2Rr$ are not equal, the problem is impossible.

PORK. The flesh of swine; it is one of the most important and widely used species of animal food. Pork is coarser and ranker than beef or mutton, but when of good quality and well cured, it develops a richness and delicacy of flavour in marked contrast with the dryness and insipidity of other salted meat. The abundance and digestive quality of its fat renders it a suitable diet for cold climates. The swine was forbidden to be eaten by the Mosaic law, and is regarded by the Jews as especially typical of the unclean animals. Other Eastern nations had similar opinions as to the use of pork. Pork contains less fibrine, albuminous and gelatinous matter than beef or mutton.

PORLOCK. Village of Somerset, 6 miles from Minehead. It was once an important seaport, though the sea has since receded and the coast is now a mile or so away.

Porlock Hill, nearby, is a noted test hill for motorists. Pop. 970.

POROGAMY. In Flowering Plants, the normal type of fertilisation, in which the pollen-tube penetrates to the ovum through the micropyle: opposed to *chalazogamy* (q.v.). *See* OVULE.

PORPHYR'IO. A genus of birds of the rail family, including the *P. hyacinthinus* (purple or hyacinthine gallinule), a bird found in Europe, Asia, and Africa, and remarkable for the structure of its beak and the length of its legs. It feeds on seeds

Porphyrio

and other hard substances, and lives in the neighbourhood of water, its long toes enabling it to run over the aquatic plants with great facility. It is about 18 inches long, of a beautiful blue colour, the bill and feet red.

PORPHYRY (**Porphyrios**). Neo-Platonist philosopher, born at Batanea, in Syria, in 233, died in 304. His original name was Malchus (king). He studied under Longinus at Athens, and at the age of thirty placed himself under the teaching of Plotinus at Rome. About 268 he went to Sicily, where he is said to have written his treatise against the Christians, which was publicly burned by the Emperor Theodosius, and is only known from fragments in the authors who have refuted him.

Porphyry recognised Christ as an eminent philosopher, but he charged the Christians with corrupting his doctrines. In some of his works he dealt with speculative philosophy, but the majority were devoted to the history of philosophy. The most important of those extant are his *Life of Plotinus* and *Life of Pythagoras*.

PORPHYRY (Gr. *porphyreos*, purple). An igneous rock with a compact ground through which crystals of another tint are scattered, so as to give it a speckled aspect. The original type was the purple-red *antique porphyry* (the *porfido rosso* *antico* of the Italians), quarried by the Romans, but not by the Egyptians, at Jebel Dukhan, in the eastern desert of Egypt. It is an altered andesitic lava, with small white, yellowish, or pinkish felspars in a deep pink ground, the colour being due to manganese silicates. The name porphyry became transferred to rocks of other colours with a similar structure, and geologists now apply the term *porphyritic* to any igneous rock in which larger crystals are set in a ground of smaller ones or even in a glass.

The green porphyry of Greece, coloured by epidote, was used by the Romans; but polished columns, vases, and slabs of the "imperial" red porphyry found especial favour. The sarcophagi of Nero and Hadrian were made of this very handsome rock. A porphyry with large grey-green labradorite felspars in a dark-green ground forms a considerable part of Lambay Island, off the Dublin coast.

PORPOISE. A genus of cetacean mammals, belonging to the family Delphinidæ (dolphins, etc.). The

Porpoises (*Phocœna communis*)

common porpoise (*Phocœna commūnis*) is the smallest and most familiar of all Cetacea, and occurs plentifully off the British coasts and in the North Sea. It attains an average length of 5 feet. The front of the head is convex in form, and has the spiracle or blow-hole in the middle line. The eyes and ears are small. The caudal fin is horizontal and flattened. The neck is very short. The fore-limbs project from the body. No hind-limbs are developed. The teeth are small with blunted crowns. The stomach is in three portions.

The porpoise feeds almost entirely on herrings and other fish, and herds or "schools" of porpoises follow the herring-shoals, amongst which they prove very destructive.

An allied species is the round-headed porpoise, or "caaing whale" of the Shetlanders. These latter measure from 20 to 24 feet in length, and are hunted for the sake of the oil. *See* CAAING WHALE.

POR'PORA, Niccolo Antonio. Italian composer; born at Naples about 1685, died there in 1767. His first opera, *Ariana e Teseo*, was produced at Vienna in 1717. In 1725 he went to Vienna, and subsequently paid professional visits to Rome, Venice, and Dresden. In 1729 a party in London, which was discontented with Handel, opened a second opera-house, and called Porpora to take the direction of it. Porpora was successful, and Handel after a heavy pecuniary loss gave up the theatre, and devoted himself to oratorio. Porpora afterwards returned to the Continent, and died in great poverty at Naples.

PORSEN'NA, or POR'SENA, Lars. The king of the Etrurian city Clusium, according to the legend narrated by Livy, who received the Tarquins when they were expelled from Rome, and after in vain endeavouring to effect their restoration by negotiation, advanced with an army to Rome. He was checked by Horatius Cocles, who defended the bridge over the Tiber leading to Rome.

PORSON, Richard. English classical scholar. He was born in 1759, and died in 1808. His father was parish clerk at East Ruston, in Norfolk, and the curate of the parish made himself responsible for Porson's early education, having perceived in him signs of unusual ability. A neighbouring squire of the name of Norris (founder of the Norrisian professorship of divinity at Cambridge) took an interest in the boy, and, finding he was too old to be entered at the Charterhouse, sent him to Eton, where he remained from 1774 to 1778. He went up to Trinity College, Cambridge, in 1778, became a scholar of the college in 1780, and Craven scholar in 1781. In 1782 he graduated B.A., being third in the second class (senior optimes) of the mathematical tripos. In the same year he was awarded the first chancellor's medal, and was elected a Fellow of Trinity.

His reputation became European after his publication of *Short Notes upon Toup's Emendations of Suidas* (1790). In 1787 he wrote a series of three sarcastic letters to *The Gentleman's Magazine*, ironically eulogising and at the same time parodying Hawkins's pompous *Life of Dr. Johnson*; and in the next year he contributed to the same periodical his *Letters to Archdeacon Travis*, in which he finally disposed of all claims of 1st John, v. 7 (the three heavenly witnesses) to be authentic.

In 1792 he vacated his fellowship (which was only tenable by a layman for seven years after taking the M.A. degree) rather than take holy orders, as he was not prepared to subscribe the Thirty-nine Articles. In the same year he was elected regius professor of Greek at Cambridge, with a salary of £40 a year. He only accepted the post when he found that ordination was not required. In 1795 he edited the plays of Æschylus for the Foulis press at Glasgow, and between 1797 and 1801 he edited four plays of Euripides—*Hecuba*, *Orestes*, *Phœnissæ*, and *Medea*.

He married in 1796, but his wife died of a decline five months later. His health began to fail about 1804; in 1806 he was appointed librarian to the London Institution. He was struck down with apoplexy in the Strand on 19th Sept., 1808, and died six days later. Towards the end of his life he had become a heavy drinker, and there is no doubt that his habits shortened his life and decreased his powers of working.

Porson was not merely one of the greatest, if not the greatest, of English classical scholars; he was a man of wide general reading, and was richly endowed with dry humour and caustic wit. His adaptation of an epigram of Phocylides still gives an unholy joy to those who do not admire Teutonic scholarship:

> The Germans in Greek
> Are sadly to seek;
> Not five in five score,
> But ninety-five more;
> All, save only Hermann,
> And—Hermann's a German.

This is his neat rhymed Latin epigram upon four prolific poetasters of his day:

> Poetis nos laetamur tribus,
> Pye, Petro Pindar, Parvo Pybus.
> Si ulterius ire pergis,
> Adde his Sir James Bland Burges.

Among his favourite English authors were Shakespeare, Milton, Dryden, Pope, Richardson, Smollet, and Swift. He had not a little of Swift's cutting humour; for example, he wrote to the master of Trinity about the Greek professorship that "if the place remains a sinecure, the number of qualified persons will be greatly increased." As a scholar Porson was chiefly celebrated for his textual criticism. His emendations were numerous, brilliant, and convincing. His services to Æschylus, Aristophanes, Euripides, and Athenæus were especially conspicuous. His mathematical training helped him to attain clearness and accuracy in his scholarship. He had an invincible love for the truth, and his chief objection to entering the Church was that he found he would require about fifty years' reading to satisfy his mind on all points.

The Porsonian tradition dominated classical scholarship at Cambridge for more than half a century after Porson's death; even still there are traces of it to be found. Porson's methods, in the hands of men who had none of his genius, and less than none of his humour, were apt to become somewhat dry and stereotyped. Scholarship of this kind became too narrow to be of educational value to the ordinary man; professional scholars before long evolved different methods of work, based upon a deeper knowledge of the comparative values of manuscripts. There is nothing discreditable to Porson in these facts, however; he was a great pioneer, and added greatly to scholarship by clearing up many points of Greek idiom, by inaugurating the methodical study of Greek metres, and by making brilliant emendations.

No account of Porson, however brief, would be complete without some reference to his wonderful hand-writing, which was, unlike that of most men of genius, almost perfect. It was small, in some cases almost microscopic, but exquisitely neat. The Greek type which is commonly in use in Great Britain was originally based upon Porson's hand-writing.

PORT ADELAIDE. The chief seaport of South Australia, the port of the city of Adelaide, with which it is connected by rail ($7\frac{1}{2}$ miles). It is on the estuary of the Torrens, which enters the Gulf of St. Vincent. The harbour accommodates all ocean-going steamers, and is a port of call for all mail steamers. Cereals are exported. Pop. 30,116.

PORTADOWN′. A market town and river port of County Armagh, Northern Ireland, on the Bann (navigable to vessels of 90 tons); served by the Great Northern Railway, and the junction of the lines to Clones, Dublin, and Omagh. It has manufactures of linen and cambric, and a brisk trade in agricultural produce. Pop. (1926), 11,991.

PORTAGE LA PRAIRIE. A town of Manitoba, Canada, on the Assiniboine; served by the transcontinental railways. It is the centre of an opulent wheat-producing area, and has a large trade in cereals. Pop. 6597.

PORTAL CIRCULATION. A subordinate part of the venous circulation. The venus blood from the intestines and some of the abdominal organs is carried into the portal vein, and carried by that vessel to the liver, where it is distributed. It is then gathered again into the hepatic veins and passes into the general venous circulation.

PORT ALFRED. A seaside resort of Cape Province, South Africa, between Port Elizabeth and East London. Pop. 2173 (873 white).

PORTAR'LINGTON. Town of the Irish Free State. It is on the River Barrow, 42 miles from Dublin, on the G. S. Rlys. The town gives its name to an earldom, created in 1785. Since 1900 it has been held by Lionel A. H. S. Dawson-Damer (b. 1883). The title of the eldest son is Viscount Carlow.

PORT ARTHUR. A city, lake-port, and railway centre of Ontario, Canada, on Thunder Bay, Lake Superior; served by the Canadian Pacific and National Railways. It is a lake terminus of the Canadian National Railway, and is also on the Canadian Pacific. Mining and lumbering are carried on. There are huge grain-elevators, and a large trade. Pop. 15,000.

PORT ARTHUR. A fortified seaport of Manchuria, at the southernmost extremity of the Liao-tung Peninsula. Port Arthur is an outstation of the Chinese customs district, which has its headquarters at Dairen. The port is ice-free throughout the year, and is protected by a breakwater 1000 yards long. The South Manchuria Railway Company controls the sheds and warehouses. This railway connects Port Arthur and Dairen with Mukden, Kharbin, and the Chinese Eastern Railway system. Pop. 14-15,000.

Originally a Chinese fortress and arsenal, Port Arthur was captured by the Japanese under Oyama in 1894, but was restored to China under pressure by the Great Powers. By an agreement dated 27th March, 1898, the fortress and the adjacent port of Talien-wan (Dalny or Dairen) were leased to Russia, and Port Arthur was fortified by that country as the eastern base for her naval forces. During the Russo-Japanese War (1904-5) Port Arthur was invested by the Japanese by land and by sea, and was surrendered by General Stoessel on 2nd Jan., 1905. Japan gained the town by the Treaty of Portsmouth (New Hampshire), and a further lease of ninety-nine years was granted by China in 1915. *See* JAPAN.

PORT AUGUSTA. A seaport of South Australia, at the head of Spencer Gulf. It is the headquarters and the southern terminal of the transcontinental lines to Oodnadatta and Kalgoorlie. There is a cathedral, and Port Augusta is the see of a Roman Catholic archbishop. Ostrich-farming is carried on in the neighbourhood, and the port is the natural outlet for the vast wool-producing pasture-lands of the South Australian hinterland, and for mine products of gold, silver, copper, coal, and iron. Pop. about 1500.

PORT-AU-PRINCE. The capital and seaport of the Republic of Haiti, West Indies. There is an excellent harbour, which maintains a large transit trade in hides, coffee, and other national products. There is a cathedral. The town was first laid out in 1749, and has twice been destroyed by earthquakes. Pop. 79,797.

PORT BLAIR. A penal settlement in the Andaman Islands, Bay of Bengal, consisting of the South Andaman and adjacent islands; area, 473 sq. miles. Port Blair, on the east coast of South Andaman Island, is the capital and chief seaport, the administrative centre of the penal settlement being on Ross Island, which lies across the entrance to the magnificent harbour. On Ross Island there is a lighthouse with a visibility of 19 miles. Wireless telegraphy between Port Blair and Diamond Island, off the coast of Burma, has been worked successfully since 1905. The town is garrisoned by British and native (Indian) infantry. Since 1921 the sending of convicts has ceased. In 1932 there were 7672 convicts at Port Blair.

PORT CHALMERS. *See* DUNEDIN.

PORTCUL'LIS. Stout grating made of heavy crossed timbers with the lower projecting points tipped with iron. A portcullis was suspended over the gateway of a castle as a means of defence and made to slide up and down in grooves at the side of the entrance.

PORTE, OTTOMAN, or **SUBLIME PORTE.** The common term for the Turkish Government. The chief office of the Ottoman Empire is styled *Babi-'ali,* literally the High Gate, from the gate (*bab*) of the palace at which justice was administered. The French translation of this term is *Sublime Porte,* and has been adopted in the English language.

PORT EDGAR. A harbour of West Falkland, Falkland Islands.

PORT ELIZABETH. A seaport of Cape Province, South Africa, on Algoa Bay, the fifth South African city in point of size, and a great emporium of trade for the eastern section of the colony. The port is owned and administered by the State, and is sometimes known as "the Liverpool of South Africa." Pop. (1921), 45,927, 25,940 being white. White pop. (1931), 43,835.

Bartholomew Diaz discovered Algoa Bay in 1488, and named it Bahia de Roca. During the sixteenth century it became known as the Bahia de Lagoa, from which the present name is derived. In 1799 Colonel Vandeleur built a fort, which he called Fort Frederick, in honour of the Duke of York, and round this fort the settlement of Port Elizabeth had its beginning.

PORT ELLEN. A harbour in the Island of Islay, Scotland.

PORTEOUS RIOT. An incident in Scottish history, originating in the fact that in 1736 Captain John Porteous, a commander of the Edinburgh City Guard, fired on a mob, killing and wounding a number. For this he was tried and condemned to death, but was subsequently reprieved. On the night of 7th Sept., however, a number of persons dragged him from the Tolbooth, where he was confined, to the Grassmarket, and hanged him there. None of those concerned were ever brought to justice. The incident is dealt with in Scott's *Heart of Midlothian*.

PORTER, Jane. Novelist, born at Durham in 1776; died in 1850. Educated at Edinburgh, she spent most of her life with her mother and sister in or near London. Her first work (1803) was *Thaddeus of Warsaw*, a highly popular historical romance, and a still greater success attended *The Scottish Chiefs* (1809). She also wrote *The Pastor's Fireside*, and *Sir Edward Seaward's Narrative of his Shipwreck*, a piece of fiction which she claimed to have edited.

PORT ERIN. A watering-place of the Isle of Man, on Port Erin Bay; served by rail from Douglas (15 miles). The massive breakwater of the harbour is in ruins. There is a piscicultural station and a marine biological station. Golf-links and sea-bathing provide attraction for tourists.

PORT FUAD. A town of Egypt, on the Asiatic bank of the Suez Canal opposite Port Said. It was opened in 1926, contains the Canal Company's works, and is largely residential. It may in time become the rail-head for Palestine. Pop. 30,000.

PORT GLASGOW. A municipal and police burgh and seaport of Renfrewshire, Scotland, on the Firth of Clyde; served by the Glasgow-Gourock branch of the L.M.S. Railway. The town nestles at the foot of a massive slope 700 feet in height. There are several fine buildings, but the principal features of the town are the shipyards and their coadjutors in iron-founding and engineering, and the extensive port which was originally what the name implies, the port of Glasgow. Near by are the ruins of Newark Castle, a sixteenth-century keep that was once a stronghold of the Dennistouns.

In 1668, when the Clyde was easily fordable where it now gives passage to transatlantic liners, a piece of land was purchased from the Maxwells by the magistrates of Glasgow, and a harbour was constructed, the resulting settlement being erected into a separate parish in 1695 as New Port Glasgow. Port Glasgow became a burgh of barony in 1775, but, with the erection of Glasgow into a first-class seaport, its maritime trade vanished. Pop. (1931), 19,580.

PORT HARCOURT. A seaport of Nigeria, on a creek of the Bonny and New Calabar Rivers; the seaward terminal of the eastern railway system of Nigeria. A cliff rises to a height of over 40 feet, and alongside this there is a water-depth of over 50 feet. The port is named after Lewis Harcourt (Viscount Harcourt), who was Colonial Secretary when it was discovered.

PORTHCAWL. Seaport and urban district of Glamorganshire, Wales. It is 6 miles W.S.W. from Bridgend and 30 miles from Cardiff, on the G.W. Railway. Pop. 6642.

PORT HERALD. A town in Nyasaland, on the Shiré River, 50 miles below Blantyre.

PORT HOPE. Port and town of Ontario, Canada. It is the principal town of Durham Co., on the north shore of Lake Ontario, 63 miles from Toronto. There is a good harbour, and the town is served by three railways, besides its connection with the principal lake ports by steamer services. In addition to manufacturing industries, the town has an extensive distributing trade in local produce. Pop. 62,500.

PORT HURON. A city and port of entry of Michigan, United States, the county seat of St. Clair county, on the St. Clair River where it leaves Lake Huron; served by the Grand Trunk and other railways, and by inter-port steamboats to Chicago, etc. The railway passes by a tunnel (6000 feet) under the St. Clair to Sarnia, in Canada. It has an extensive lumber trade, railway workshops, shipyards, saw-, flour-, and planing-mills.

Port Huron originated in Fort St. Joseph, established by the French in 1686. As a village it was laid out in 1790, and was called La

Rivière de Lude. In 1828 it became Desmond, and was incorporated as a city under its present name in 1857. Pop. (1930), 31,361.

PORTICI (por'ti-chē). A town of Campania, Southern Italy, in the province of Naples, on the Gulf of Naples at the base of Vesuvius. It is about 5 miles east of the city of Naples, but is connected with it by the long village of S. Giovanni a Teduccio. An active fishery is carried on. Pop. 14,400.

PORTISHEAD. Familiarly *Posset*, a watering-place of England, in Somersetshire, on the Severn estuary; served by the Great Western Railway. The dock covers 12 acres, and belongs to the Port of Bristol. Pop. (1931), 3908.

PORT JACKSON. An extensive inlet on the coast of New South Wales, forming a well-sheltered harbour. Sydney lies along the southern shore. The inlet is island-studded, has a good depth of water in every part, and is the fortified base of the Australasian naval forces. Port Jackson was discovered by Captain Philip in 1788, but was named by Captain Cook in 1770, who had passed the towering North and South Heads without noticing the vastness of the harbour to which they act as sentinels and shelters. *See* SYDNEY.

PORTLAND. A city and port of entry of Maine, United States, the county seat of Cumberland county, on a peninsula at the western extremity of Casco Bay; served by the Maine Central, Boston & Maine, and Grand Trunk Railways, and by transatlantic steamers and coasting vessels (to New York, St. John, N.B., and Boston, etc.). Locomotives, cars, etc., are made; there are also shipbuilding yards, glassworks, potteries, and rope-walks; and the refining of petroleum and sugar is extensively carried on.

Portland is the largest city of Maine, and is connected by ferry with South Portland. The harbour is fortified, and is easy of access, capacious, safe, deep enough for the largest vessels, and rarely obstructed with ice; hence it is a convenient winter port for traffic between Britain and Canada. The principal exports are timber, fish, beef, and butter.

Portland originated in the settlement of Falmouth (1718), which became a town in 1786. In 1832 it became a city, having been state capital until that time (1820-32). Pop. (1930), 70,810.

PORTLAND. A city and port of entry of Oregon, United States, the county seat of Multnomah county, on the left bank of Willamette River; served by the Canadian Pacific, Northern Pacific, Southern Pacific, and Great Northern Railways, and by transpacific steamers from China and Japan, etc., and coastwise to San Francisco and British Columbian ports. Portland is the largest town in Oregon, and has a Protestant Episcopal cathedral, Columbia University (Roman Catholic), law and medical faculties of the University of Oregon, and a military academy.

The harbour is extensive, and handles fish (salmon especially) and the timber, cereals, and fruit of the Willamette and Columbia Valleys. As a manufacturing centre Portland is the metropolis of the state, lumber and timber products, flour, tinned salmon, and cordage being among the principal items. Railway rolling-stock is also repaired. Portland was founded in 1845, and became a city in 1851. Pop. (1930), 301,815.

PORTLAND, DUKE OF. English title created in 1716. An earldom of Portland, held by the Weston family, 1633-88, became extinct, and was revived by William III. for Hans William Bentinck in 1689. His son Henry became first duke. **William Henry Cavendish Bentinck** (1738-1809) assumed the additional surname Cavendish in 1801, having married, in 1766, the daughter of the Duke of Devonshire. Lord-Lieutenant of Ireland, 1782, and Prime Minister, 1783, he was Home Secretary in Pitt's Government, 1794-1801, and again Prime Minister, 1807-09. William John, fifth Duke (1800-79) was an eccentric who led the life of a recluse. His nephew, William John Arthur (born 1857), the sixth duke, was Master of the Horse, 1886-92, and again in 1895-1905. He is Lord-Lieutenant of Nottinghamshire. The eldest son is entitled Marquess of Titchfield. The chief family seat is Welbeck Abbey, Notts.

PORTLAND, ISLE OF. A peninsula, supposed to have been formerly an island, in the county of Dorset, 50 miles W.S.W. of Southampton, in the English Channel. It is attached to the mainland by a long ridge of shingle called the Chesil Bank, and it consists mainly of the well-known Portland stone, which was chiefly worked by convicts from the convict prison (since 1921 a borstal institution). Farming, sheep-rearing, fishing, etc., are carried on. The south extremity of the island is called the *Bill of Portland*, and between it and a bank called the Shambles is a dangerous current called the *Race of Port-*

land. Pop. (1931), 12,018. *See* PORTLAND BREAKWATER.

PORTLAND BEDS. In geology, a division of the Upper Jurassic series occurring between the Purbeck Beds and the Kimmeridge Clay, consisting of beds of hard oolitic limestone and freestone interstratified with clays and resting on light-coloured sands which contain fossils, chiefly mollusca and fish, with a few reptiles. They are named from the rocks of the series forming the Isle of *Portland*, in Dorsetshire, whence they may be traced through Wiltshire as far as Oxfordshire. The continental Portlandian stage is on the same horizon.

PORTLAND BREAKWATER. The greatest work of the kind in Britain, runs from the north-east shoulder of the Isle of Portland in a north-east direction, with a bend towards the English Channel, and is continued by two new breakwaters extending towards Weymouth, complete protection thus being given to a large expanse of water, and a great harbour of refuge being provided. The original work consists of a sea-wall 100 feet high, 300 feet thick at the base, and narrowing to the summit, and has a length of 1⅝ miles, consisting of two portions, one connected with the shore, 1900 feet in length, and another of 6200 feet in length, separated from the former by an opening 400 feet wide, through which ships can pass straight to sea. It is protected by two circular forts, the principal at the north end of the longer portion.

The work, which was carried out by Government, occupied a period of nearly twenty-five years, ending with 1872, and cost £1,033,600, exclusive of convict labour. The new breakwater, which is in two sections each about 4500 feet long, extends from the shore near Weymouth to a point about 700 feet from the older structure. The whole work encloses an area of over 2000 acres of water, three-quarters of it over 30 feet deep at low water.

PORTLAND CEMENT. *See* HYDRAULIC CEMENT.

PORTLAND STONE. An oolitic limestone occurring in great abundance in the Isle of Portland, England. It is one of the members of the Portland Beds, and is much used in building, being soft when quarried, but hardening on exposure to the atmosphere. St. Paul's Cathedral, London, is built of it.

PORTLAND (or BARBERINI) VASE. A celebrated ancient cinerary urn or vase, of the third century after Christ, found in the tomb of the Emperor Alexander Severus. It is of transparent dark-blue glass, coated with opaque white glass, which has been cut down in the manner of a cameo, so as to give on each side groups of figures delicately executed in relief, representing the marriage of Peleus and Thetis. In 1810 the Duke of Portland, its owner, allowed it to be placed in the British Museum, where it remained intact till the year 1845, when it was broken by a madman. The pieces were carefully collected and very successfully re-united, and in this state it still remains in the museum, and is exhibited to visitors. The vase was frequently copied by Wedgwood.—Cf. J. Wedgwood, *The Portland Vase.*

The Portland Vase

PORT - LOUIS, or ISLE DE FRANCE. The capital of the Island of Mauritius, on the north-west coast, beautifully situated in a cove formed by a series of basaltic hills, partially wooded, varying in height from 1058 to 2639 feet. The site is rather unhealthy. A mountain stream traverses the town, and an open space like a racecourse lies behind it. There are barracks, theatre, public library, two observatories (astronomical and meteorological), botanic garden, hospital, and Anglican and Roman Catholic cathedrals.

The town and harbour are highly fortified. Exports are principally sugar, coco-nut oil, and fibre. In recent years the greater part of Port-Louis has passed from European to Indian and Chinese hands. Pop. (1931), with suburbs, 54,290.

PORT LYTTELTON. Same as Lyttelton (q.v.).

PORTMADOC. Urban district, seaport and market town of Caernarvonshire, on Tremadoc Bay, 16 miles from Caernarvon, on the G.W. Railway. It is the port for the slate quarries of Blaenan Festiniog. Pop. (1931), 3986.

PORT-MAHON (Roman *Portus Magonis*). A Spanish naval station and seaport, the capital of the Island of Minorca, situated on a narrow inlet in the south-east of the island. The harbour is one of the finest in the Mediterranean, and an important trade is carried on.

Under James Stanhope (later Earl Stanhope) the island was seized in 1708 by the British, and Port-Mahon became a flourishing city. In 1718 it became a free port, but fell to the French in 1756 through Admiral Byng's failure to raise the siege of San Felipe. In 1802 it was ceded to Spain (Treaty of Amiens). Pop. 18,000.

PORT MELBOURNE. A seaside suburb of Melbourne, Australia, with large docks.

PORT MORESBY. The capital and chief seaport of the Australian dependency of Papua, on the south coast of the Island of New Guinea. There is a wireless station, and communication with Sydney is maintained by steamer. Near Port Moresby a large mineral-field of promising copper deposits is being vigorously developed, and a railway connects it with the coast. It is the seat of the supreme court. Pop. 3000.

PORT NELSON. A port on Hudson Bay.

PORT NOLLOTH. A port of Little Namaqualand, South-West Africa. It is the seaward terminus of a light railway running through the hills for about 50 miles to Steinkopf, where it turns south to O'okiep, a copper-mining centre. It is served by steamer from Cape Town. The climate is exceedingly dry, and water has to be transported in tank-cars by the railway from holes some 5 miles distant in the hinterland.

Port Nolloth was the scene of the opening of General Botha's campaign during the European War, when, in Sept., 1914, the first of the Union forces arrived from Cape Town. The hinterland is very hilly and rough, and almost wholly waterless. Pop. about 1600.

PORTO ALEGRE. A city and seaport of Brazil, capital of the state of Rio Grande do Sul. There is a commodious harbour. Porto Alegre is the seat of a Roman Catholic bishop, and, as a consequence, there is a cathedral. There are many educational establishments. An extensive transit trade is carried on, and Porto Alegre is considered the chief manufacturing town of the state, producing macaroni, preserves, soap, candles, leather goods, iron goods, cotton fabrics, dairy produce, and furniture. There are also shipyards, used for the construction of lake and river vessels. Population, (1930), 273,376.

PORTOBELLO. A watering-place, Firth of Forth, Scotland, part of Edinburgh.

PORT OF SPAIN. The chief town and seaport of the Island of Trinidad, West Indies, on the east coast. It is a wireless station, and is a port of call for ocean-going steamers and many coasting lines. There are Anglican and Roman Catholic cathedrals. Cocoa and sugar are the chief exports. Pop. (1931), 70,641.

PORTO MAURIZIO, now **IMPERIA.** A maritime frontier department of Liguria, Italy, traversed by spurs of the Alps. All the chief towns of the Italian Riviera are in Porto Maurizio. The coastal railway from Nice to Genoa and the line from Ventimiglia to Cuneo serve the province. Olives and oil, fruits and flowers are the principal products. Porto Maurizio is the capital. Area, 456 sq. miles; pop. (1931), 162,383.

PORTO MAURIZIO. A seaport-city of Italy, capital of the province of Porto Maurizio; served by the railway from Nice (46 miles) to Genoa (70 miles). The city is united with Oneglia as a commune, and both are famed for their olives and the quality of the oil they produce. They are much frequented for sea bathing. Pop. (commune), 28,727.

PORTO NOVO. A town and port of India, in the South Arcot district of Madras, at the mouth of the Vellar River. The English settlement was established in 1683, but the Portuguese had founded here, in the latter part of the sixteenth century, the first European settlement on the Coromandel coast. Pop. about 6000.

PORTO NOVO. The capital and port of Dahomey, French West Africa. Pop. 23,614.

PORTO PRAIA. The capital of Santiago, Cape Verde Islands. Pop. 21,000.

PORTO RICO. One of the larger West Indian Islands, the smallest but most densely peopled of the Greater Antilles. It lies to the east of Santo Domingo (Haiti), from which it is separated by the Mona Passage. By an Act of Congress, 1932, the name was changed to Puerto Rico.

Physiography. The interior of the

island is an elevated plateau, traversed from west to east by several low, wooded ranges which culminate in the Peak of El Yunque (4985 feet altitude). This range descends abruptly to the sea on all sides, but there are coastal plains of limited extent on the northern and southern seaboards. There are few indentations that provide safe harbourage, and all rivers are rapid and practically unnavigable.

Climate. The climate is fairly healthy, for the island lies in the region of the "north-east trades." The average annual temperature varies between 78° and 82° F., falling to 56° in winter, and rising to 100° F. in summer. Hurricanes and cyclones are prevalent. Area, 3435 sq. miles.

People. The inhabitants are decidedly mixed, varying in colour from pure white, through all the shades of yellow and brown, to jet black. In 1930 the total pop. was returned as 1,543,913 (449·5 per square mile). According to colour, this was distributed as follows: white, 1,141,111; coloured, 397,156; foreign-born white, 5605; others, 38. During the inter-censal period (1920-30) the white population increased by 20.9 per cent, and the coloured by 13·1 per cent.

Education. School attendance has been compulsory since 1899. The University of Porto Rico is located at Rio Piedras, near San Juan, and accepts students of both sexes.

Production and Commerce. 63 per cent of the people of Porto Rico are engaged in agriculture, fisheries, and mining; 21 per cent in domestic and personal services; 8 per cent in manufacturing industries; and 8 per cent in trade and transport services. The higher slopes of the hills are still covered with the remains of the primeval forests with which the island was once entirely covered, but the forests have in great part given place to coffee-bushes, sugar-cane, tobacco, and other plants of economic value. The mineral resources are negligible, but heavy deposits of phosphates exist on the north coast, and guano is found on Mona Island.

Among the principal island products are: tobacco, sugar, coffee, fruits (pine-apples, coco-nuts, grape-fruit, and oranges), sea-island cotton, sisal and other textile fibres, guano, phosphate, and vegetables. Manufactures consist chiefly of cigars, cigarettes, hats, and embroideries. Nine-tenths of the exports go to the United States, and roughly eleven-twelfths of the imports are received from or via that country.

Communications. There are over 1080 miles of road in Porto Rico, and some 310 miles of railway, which encircles the coasts and also taps the hinterland from Rio Piedras to Caguas.

Towns. San Juan is the chief port and naval station, and has an entrance 600 yards wide and 30 feet deep. Pop. (1930), 114,715. Other towns are Ponce (87,604) and Mayaguez (58,270).

Government. Columbus discovered Porto Rico in 1493, and it was conquered by Ponce de Leon in 1508, but received little attention from Spain until the rebellion of the native Indians in 1811, when they were practically extirpated by the conquerors. In April, 1898, war broke out between the United States and Spain, and the Americans took the island, which was ceded to them by the treaty of 10th Dec., 1898. The "Organic Act" of Congress (Jones Act), passed in 1917, granted rights of American citizenship to the Porto Ricans.

The Government is representative, the executive power being in the hands of a Governor appointed by the President of the United States, and the legislative power is vested in a legislature of two elective Houses. These are the Senate (19 members, 2 elected from each of the 7 senatorial districts and 5 Senators at large) and the House of Representatives (39 members, 1 from each of the 35 representative districts and 4 elected at large). A Resident Commissioner to the United States is elected by the people for a term of four years, and represents them in Congress. Seven heads of departments form an advisory council (Executive Council) to the Governor. Dependent islands are Vieques (pop. 10,582) and Culebra.—BIBLIOGRAPHY: F. A. Ober, *Puerto Rico and its Resources*; R. T. Hill, *Cuba and Porto Rico*.

PORT-PATRICK. A seaport of Wigtownshire, Scotland, on the Irish Sea, the nearest port in Britain to Ireland, the distance being only 21 miles. The town is connected with Stranraer (7 miles) by the Portpatrick and Wigtownshire Light Railway. Pop. (1931), 1109.

PORT PHILLIP. A bay of Victoria, Australia, on which stands Melbourne.

PORT PIRIE. A seaport of South Australia, on Spencer Gulf. It has silver-smelting works (for Broken Hill Mines) and exports wheat. Pop. 9446.

PORTREE. The chief town in the island of Skye, Scotland. Pop. (1931), 2008.

PORT-ROYAL. A fortified port and naval station on the south-east coast of Jamaica, on a tongue of land forming the south side of the harbour of Kingston. Its harbour is the headquarters in the West Indies for British ships of war, and it contains a naval dockyard, barracks, arsenal, and hospital. It has been often damaged by earthquakes. Pop. 1200.

PORT-ROYAL. The name of a convent of the Cistercian or Bernardine nuns, and also of a school of theological thought. It became famous in the seventeenth century as the centre of the Jansenist controversy. It was situated near Chevreuse (department of Seine-et-Oise), about 15 miles S.W. of Paris, and was founded in 1204 by Matthieu de Montmorency, under the rule of St. Bernard.

Port-Royal, like many other religious houses, had fallen into degenerate habits, when in 1609 the abbess Jacqueline-Marie-Angélique-Arnauld undertook its reform. The number of nuns increased considerably under her rule, and in 1625 they amounted to eighty. The building thus became too small, and the insalubrity of the situation induced them to seek another site. The mother of the abbess purchased the house of Cluny, in the Faubourg Saint-Jacques, Paris, to which a body of the nuns removed. The two sections of the convent were now distinguished as Port-Royal des Champs and Port-Royal de Paris.

About 1636 a group of eminent literary men of decided religious tendencies took up their residence at Les Granges, near Port-Royal des Champs, where they devoted themselves to religious exercises and the education of youth. These were regarded as forming a joint community with the nuns of Port-Royal, among whom most of them had relatives. Among the number were Antoine Arnauld, Arnauld d'Antilly, Lemaistre de Sacy and his two brothers, all relatives of the abbess; Nicole, and subsequently Pascal, whose sister Jacqueline was at Port-Royal.

The educational institution, thus founded, which flourished till 1660, became a powerful rival to the institution of the Jesuits, and as the founders adopted the views of Jansenius, subsequently condemned by the Pope, a formidable quarrel ensued, in which the Port-Royalist nuns, siding with their male friends, became subject to the relentless persecution of the Jesuits, which culminated in the complete subversion of their institution. Port-Royal des Champs was finally suppressed by a Bull of Pope Clement II. (1709), and its property given to Port-Royal de Paris. The latter continued its existence to the Revolution, when its house was converted into a prison, and subsequently (1814) into a maternity hospital.—BIBLIOGRAPHY: Sainte-Beuve, *Port-Royal*; E. Romanes, *Story of Port-Royal*; M. E. Lowndes, *The Nuns of Port-Royal as seen in their own Narratives*; L. Rea, *Enthusiasts of Port-Royal*.

PORTRUSH'. The chief watering-place of Northern Ireland, in County Antrim; served by the Midland (Northern Counties) Railway, and by steamboats to English, Scottish, and Irish ports. It is connected with the Giant's Causeway (q.v.) by an electric tramway (7 miles). Near by are the ruins of Dunluce Castle, originally in possession of the M'Quillan family, but taken from them by the M'Donnells of the Isles in the sixteenth century. Randal, the son of Sorley Boyc, was made Viscount Dunluce by James I. Pop. (1926), 2952.

PORT SAID. A town of Egypt, on the Mediterranean, at the northern entrance of the Suez Canal. It was begun simultaneously with the canal in 1859, being designed for its terminal port. There is an outer harbour formed by two piers jutting out into the sea, each terminated by a small lighthouse. This admits large ocean steamers, which thus sail into the inner harbour and from it into the canal. Near the entrance to the inner harbour is a lofty lighthouse with a powerful light. Pop. including Ismailia (1927), 104,603.

PORTSEA. An island of Hampshire, England, about 5 miles long (north to south) by about 3 miles broad. It is connected with the mainland by a bridge. *See* PORTSMOUTH.

PORTSLADE. A watering-place of Sussex, England, near Brighton.

PORTSMOUTH. A municipal, county, and parliamentary borough, city, seaport and naval base of England, in Hampshire, on the Island of Portsea, which is separated from the mainland on the north by Portsbridge Canal, is bounded on the east by Langston Harbour, on the west by Portsmouth Harbour, and on the south by Spithead roadstead. It consists of the five chief districts—Portsmouth proper, Portsea, Landport, Southsea, and Cosham. Portsmouth and Portsea are the seat of the naval dockyard; Landport is mostly an artisan quarter; and Southsea is a favourite seaside resort. The church of St. Thomas became pro-cathedral in 1924 when the town was made the seat of a new diocese of Portsmouth and the Isle of Wight. Southsea Castle with its adjacent earthworks, the batteries of the Gosport side, and the circular forts built out in the roadstead command the entrance to Portsmouth Harbour. The northern,

Cosham, area is mainly agricultural.

The royal dockyard covers an area of about 500 acres, and is considered the largest and most magnificent establishment of the kind in the world. In connection with it there are hospitals, a naval college, torpedo range, and barracks. About 15,000 men are employed in the repair and refitting of naval vessels. The navy gunnery school and ranges are in Whale Island, within the harbour. Portsmouth dockyard existed as such in the fifteenth century, was definitely adopted as a base about 1540, and has been increasing both in size and importance from that date.

Portsmouth has no manufactures of consequence, except those immediately connected with its naval establishments, and a few large breweries. Its coasting trade is of great extent.

An extensive and systematic series of fortifications ensure the complete defence of the harbour works. They extend along a curve of about 1½ miles at the north side of Portsea Island. A series of hills, 4 miles to the north of Portsmouth, and commanding its front to the sea, is well fortified with strong forts. On the Gosport side a line of forts extends for 4 miles. The county and parliamentary borough includes nearly the whole of the Island of Portsea. Pop. (1931), 249,288.

PORTSMOUTH. A city and port of entry of New Hampshire, United States, one of the county seats of Rockingham county, on the Piscataqua; served by the Boston & Maine and electric traction railways. A Government navy yard is located on Shoal Island, within the harbour. It is officially called the Portsmouth Navy Yard, but is not included within the township. It is in Kittery, Maine, but Portsmouth is its port of entry.

Portsmouth was founded in 1623, and (with Dover) is the oldest settlement in the state. It became a city in 1849, and was state capital from the constitution of New Hampshire as a province until 1775. Portsmouth is the only seaport in the state. The peace treaty between Japan and Russia was concluded there in 1905. Pop. (1930), 14,495.

PORTSMOUTH. A city of Ohio, United States, the county seat of Scioto county, at the confluence of the Scioto and Ohio Rivers; served by the Baltimore & Ohio South-Western, the Chesapeake & Ohio, and the Norfolk & Western Railways, and by the Ohio & Erie (Portsmouth to Cleveland) Canal. Portsmouth is the metropolis of an agricultural, mining, and quarrying region. It was settled in 1803, and became a city in 1851. Pop. (1930), 42,560.

PORTSMOUTH. A city of Virginia, United States, in Norfolk county, on the Elizabeth River directly opposite Norfolk; served by the Chesapeake & Ohio Railway, the Atlantic Coast Line, Seaboard Air Line, and electric traction lines. It is the seat of a United States navy yard (Norfolk Yard), one of the largest in the country, covering 450 acres. There are few manufactures, but the city is the centre of the Virginian oyster-fishery. In 1858 it became a city. Pop. (1930), 45,704.

PORT STANLEY. The capital and chief seaport of the Falkland Islands. Pop. 890.

PORT SUDAN. The principal seaport of the Anglo-Egyptian Sudan, on the Red Sea; served by a branch of the riverain railway from Atbara, which bifurcates at Hanbûk for Port Sudan and Suâkin. Gum, ivory, cotton, sesame, and much coal are among the goods handled at the port, which is also the headquarters of the Sudanese customs administration.

PORT SUNLIGHT. *See* GARDEN CITIES.

PORT SWETTENHAM. Seaport of Selangor, Federated Malay States, the port of Kuala Lumpur.

PORT TALBOT. A seaport of Glamorgan, Wales, on Swansea Bay, formed by the amalgamation of Aberavon and Margam. Pop. (1931), 40,672.

POR'TUGAL. A republic in the south-west of Europe, forming the west part of the Iberian Peninsula; bounded east and north by Spain, and west and south by the Atlantic; greatest length, north to south, 345 miles; greatest breadth, 140 miles.

Extent. The seven old provinces, Entre Minho - e - Douro, Tras - os - Montes, Beiras (Upper and Lower), Estremadura, Alemtejo, and Algarve, now form seventeen districts, as shown in the table on p. 337. The Azores are divided into three districts, and Madeira forms one district. These islands are regarded as an integral part of the Republic.

Chief Towns (q.v.).

Town	Pop.	Town	Pop.
Lisbon ..	594,390	Covilhã ..	15,640
Oporto ..	232,380	Faro ..	12,925
Setubal ..	37,074	Tavira ..	11,043
Funchal ..	25,000	Portalegre	11,171
Braga ..	21,970	Aveiro ..	10,357
Coimbra ..	27,333	Elvas ..	11,747
Evora ..	22,061	Castello	9,820
Ponta Delgada (Azores) ..	17,000	Beja ..	10,521

Physiography. The coast-line runs from the north in a south-south-westerly direction till it reaches Cape St. Vincent, where it suddenly turns east. It is occasionally bold, and rises to a great height; but the greater part is low and marshy, and not infrequently lined by dangerous sands and reefs. The interior is generally mountainous, a number of ranges stretching across the country, forming a succession of independent river basins, while their ramifications form the watersheds of numerous subsidiary streams, and enclose many beautiful valleys. The loftiest range is the Serra d'Estrella, a continuation of the central chain stretching across Spain. The greater part of Portugal is occupied by ancient rocks of Archæan and Palæozoic age, and by eruptive masses which probably date from varying periods.

Rivers. No important rivers rise within the country. The principal rivers are the Douro, Tagus, and Guadiana, which are described separately. The Minho is the most northerly river, and is inferior in size only to those mentioned.

Climate. The climate is greatly modified by the proximity of the sea and the height of the mountains. In general the winter is short and mild, and in some places never completely interrupts the course of vegetation. Early in February vegetation is in full vigour; during the month of July the heat is often extreme, and the country assumes, particularly in its lower levels, a very parched appearance. The drought generally continues into September; then the rains begin, and a second spring unfolds. Winter begins at the end of November. In the mountainous districts the loftier summits obtain a covering of snow, which they retain for months; but south of the Douro, and at a moderate elevation, snow does not lie long. The

Home

Districts and Provinces[1]	Area in sq. Miles	Population (1930)
Viana do Castelo ..	857	223,142
Braga	1,040	399,342
Porto	893	796,188
Entre Minho-e-Douro	2,790	1,418,672
Vila Real	1,650	253,959
Bragança	2,513	191,179
Tras-os-Montes ..	4,163	435,138
Aveiro	1,065	365,073
Viseu	1,937	415,063
Coimbra	1,508	387,808
Guarda	2,116	256,425
Castello Branco ..	2,582	265,573
Beira	9,208	1,689,942
Leiria	1,317	314,540
Santarem	2,555	368,610
Lisbon	1,062	906,582
Setubal	2,003	229,028
Estremadura	6,937	1,818,760
Portalegre	2,405	162,588
Evora	2,856	180,852
Beja	3,958	235,943
Alemtejo	9,219	579,383
Algarve (Faro) ..	1,937	292,634
Total Continental ..	34,254	6,234,529
Islands:		
Azores	922	253,596
Madeira	314	210,220
Total Insular ..	1,236	463,816

Dependencies

	Area in sq. Miles	Population
India—Goa	1,300	569,187
Damã	140	
Diu	20	
Timor	7,330	451,604
China: Macao, etc.	4	157,175
Total Asia	8,794	1,177,966
Africa—Cape Verde Islands ..	1,511	153,700
Guinea	13,944	364,929
Principe and São Thomé	315	59,055
Angola	486,079	4,181,730
Mozambique	297,657	3,995,831
Total Africa	799,506	8,755,245
Total Colonies	808,300	9,933,211

Summary	Sq. Miles	Population
Continent	34,254	6,234,529
Islands[2]	1,236	463,816
Colonies	808,300	9,933,211
Grand Total	843,790	16,631,556

[2] Madeira and the Azores are not considered as dependencies or colonies but as provinces of Portugal proper.

[1] The provinces are described under separate articles throughout this work.

mean annual temperature of Lisbon is about 56°.

Social Conditions: *People.* The people are of very mixed blood—Basque, Celtic, Roman, Arabic, and even African. As is often typical of seafaring people, the women distinctly outnumber the men — by 111 to 100.

Religion.—Roman Catholicism is the predominant religious faith, but all denominations are tolerated, and there is absolute freedom. There are three archiepiscopal sees, Lisbon (seven suffragans), Braga (five suffragans), and Evora (two).

Defence.—Military service is compulsory. The army peace strength (1931) was 4901 officers and 50,475 other ranks. There is also a Republican Guard (215 officers, 5412 other ranks), and a Fiscal Guard (total strength, 5285). The navy has four cruisers and various small craft.

Education.—Elementary education is free and compulsory, and secondary and higher instruction are also provided. There are three universities, located at Lisbon, Oporto, and Coimbra respectively. A technical school (Lisbon) instructs in engineering, etc., and there are also commercial academies, a military academy (Lisbon), a naval college, and art and music institutions at Lisbon and Oporto.

Money, etc.—By a decree of the Provisional Government (22nd May, 1911, altered 1931) the unit is the gold *escudo* of 100 *centavos*. There are gold coins of 250, 100, and 50 *escudos*, silver pieces value 10, 5, and 2½ *escudos*, Alpaca coins value 1 and ½ *escudo*, and bronze coins of 20, 10, and 5 *centavos* respectively. The sovereign and half-sovereign (British) are accepted by law, and are respectively equivalent to 110 and 55 gold *escudos*. Legal time is based on the meridian of Greenwich. The metric system of weights and measures is the legal standard.

Communications. The Lisbon-Badajoz Railway, opened in 1853, was the first railway in Portugal, and, prior to 1851, there was not a carriage road in the state that was worthy of the name. Nowadays there are two State railways of 824 miles in length, and five private lines of 1177 miles. The total mileage was (1931) 2125. The standard gauge is 5 feet 5¾ inches, but two lines have 3-feet-3⅜-inch and 2-feet-11½-inch gauges respectively. There are post office, telegraph, radiograph and telephone, inland and international services.

Production. 25 per cent of all land is uncultivated; 37·4 per cent is cultivated for cereals, etc.; 5·4 per cent is under vineyards; 6·2 per cent under fruit trees; and 26 per cent is afforested. For production, the country may be divided into four regions; *north*—producing maize and cattle; *south*—producing wheat and pigs; *central*—producing wheat and maize; *mountain*—producing rye, sheep, and goats. All these regions have vineyards and produce wine, the vintage amounting to 162,350,000 gallons in 1931. In addition, figs, tomatoes, oranges, onions, and potatoes are widely raised, and olive-oil to the extent of 15,741,600 gallons was produced in 1931. Roughly 800,000 acres are covered by olive trees.

Cork is a great source of Portuguese wealth, 84,283 tons being produced in 1930. About 1,382,373 acres are laid down to cork trees. Others are pine (2,795,020 acres), oak (1,205,148 acres), chestnut (210,513 acres), Pyrenean oak, etc. (165,532 acres).

Minerals.—Wolfram is the chief mineral; iron, manganese, copper, lead, tin, antimony, and gold are found. Coal is scarce, and transport conditions do not encourage the exploitation of known deposits.

Fisheries.—53,999 of the people of Portugal are engaged in the fisheries, about 14,153 vessels being employed. Sardines and tunny are exported. The sardine industry is centred around Setubal.

Manufactures.—*Azulejos* or porcelain tiles are still actively manufactured. There are large textile factories. Some chinaware, lace, and embroidery are also made.

Government, etc. Till 1910 Portugal was a kingdom, the crown being hereditary both in the male and female line. The Constitution recognised four powers in the state—the legislative, executive, judicial, and moderating, the last vested in the sovereign. There were two Chambers, the Chamber of Peers and the Chamber of Deputies. On 20th Aug., 1911, a new Constitution was adopted, and provides for two Chambers. The first is called the National Council (164 members, elected by direct suffrage for three years), and the Upper or Second Chamber has 71 members, elected by all municipal councils, one-half retiring every three years. The President of the Republic is elected by both Chambers for a period of four years, and he cannot seek re-election.

History. The Phœnicians, Carthaginians, and Greeks early traded to this part of the peninsula, the original inhabitants of which are spoken of as Lusitanians, the country being called Lusitania. It was afterwards conquered by the Romans, who introduced into it their own civilisation. The country was afterwards overrun by Alani, Suevi, Goths, and Vandals, and in the eighth century (712) was conquered by the Saracens. When the Spaniards finally wrested the country between the Minho and the Douro from Moorish hands, they placed counts or governors over this region.

Henry the Younger of Burgundy, grandson of Hugh Capet, came into Spain about 1090, to seek his fortune in the wars against the Moors. Alphonso VI. gave him the hand of his daughter, and appointed him (1095) count and governor of the provinces Entre Douro-e-Minho, Traz-os-Montes, part of Beira, etc. The count, who owed feudal services to the Castilian kings, was permitted to hold in his own right whatever conquests he should make from the Moors beyond the Tagus (1112).

Henry's son, Alphonso I., defeated Alphonso, King of Castile, in 1137, and made himself independent. In 1139 he gained the brilliant victory of Ourique over the Moors, and was saluted on the field King of Portugal. The Cortes convened by Alphonso in 1143 at Lamego confirmed him in the royal title, and in 1181 gave to the kingdom a code of laws and a Constitution. Alphonso extended his dominions to the borders of Algarve, and took Santarem in 1143. The capture of Lisbon (1147), which was effected by the aid of some English Crusaders and others, was one of the most brilliant events of his warlike life.

The succeeding reigns from Alphonso I. to Dionysius (1279) are noteworthy chiefly for the conquest of Algarve (1251) and a conflict with the Pope, who several times put the kingdom under interdict. Dionysius's wise encouragement of commerce, agriculture, manufactures, and navigation laid the foundation of the future greatness of Portugal. He liberally patronised learning, and founded a university at Lisbon, transferred in 1308 to Coimbra. By these and other acts of a wise and beneficent administration he earned the title of *father of his country*. He was succeeded by Alphonso IV., who, in conjunction with Alphonso II. of Castile, defeated the Moors at Salado in 1340. Alphonso's son Pedro (1357-76) was succeeded by his son Ferdinand (1367-83), the last male of the legitimate line.

John I., a natural son of Pedro, Grand Master of the Order of Avis, was recognised king by the Cortes, and reigned from 1385-1433. In 1415 he took Ceuta, on the African coast, the first of a series of enterprises which resulted in those great expeditions of discovery on which the renown of Portugal rests. In this reign were founded the first Portuguese colonies, Porto Santo (1418), Madeira (1420), the Azores (1433), and those on the Gold Coast.

The reigns of his son Edward (1433-8) and his grandson Alphonso V. were less brilliant than that of John I.; but the latter was surpassed by that of John II. (1481-95), perhaps the ablest of Portuguese rulers. In his reign began a violent struggle with the nobility, whose power had become very great under his indulgent predecessors. The expeditions of discovery were continued with ardour and scientific method. Bartolommeo Diaz doubled the Cape of Good Hope in 1487, and Vasco da Gama reached India in 1498. In 1500 Cabral took possession of Brazil. While these great events were still in progress John II. was succeeded by his cousin Emanuel (1495-1521). The conquests of Albuquerque and Almeida made him master of numerous possessions in the islands and mainland of India, and in 1518 Lope de Soares opened a commerce with China. Emanuel ruled from Bab-al-mandeb to the Straits of Malacca, and the power of Portugal had now reached its height.

In the reign of John III., son of Emanuel (1521-57), Indian discoveries and commerce were still farther extended; but the rapid accumulation of wealth through the importation of the precious metals, and the monopoly of the commerce between Europe and India, proved disadvantageous to home industry. The wisdom which had hitherto so largely guided the counsels of the Kings of Portugal now seemed to forsake them. The Inquisition was introduced (1536), and the Jesuits were admitted (1540). Sebastian, the grandson of John III., who had introduced the Jesuits, having had his mind inflamed by them against the Moors of Africa, lost his life in the battle against these infidels (1578).

In 1580 the direct male line of the Kings of Portugal came to an end, and Philip II. of Spain obtained possession of the throne and annexed the country. Although the Spanish yoke was grievous to the Portuguese, and many efforts were made to break it, the power of Philip was too great to be shaken. Portugal thus continued under the dominion of Spain till 1640, and her vast colonial possessions were united to the already splendid acquisitions of her rival. But these now began to fall into the hands of the Dutch, who, being provoked by hostile measures of Philip, attacked the Portuguese as well as the Spanish possessions both in India and America. They deprived the Portuguese of the Moluccas, of their settlements in Guinea, of Malacca, and of Ceylon. They also acquired about half of Brazil, which, after the re-establishment of Portuguese independence, they restored for a pecuniary compensation.

In 1640, by a successful revolt of the nobles, Portugal recovered her independence, and John IV., Duke of Braganza, reigned till 1656, when he was succeeded by Alphonso VI. In 1661 Charles II., King of England, married Catherine of Braganza, and a permanent alliance between Great Britain and Portugal was thus established. Pedro II., who deposed Alphonso VI., concluded a treaty with Spain (1668), by which the independence of the country was acknowledged. During the long reign of John V. (1706-50) some vigour was exerted in regard to foreign relations, while under his son and successor Joseph I. (1750-77), the Marquis of Pombal, a vigorous reformer such as Portugal required, administered the government.

On the accession of Maria Francisca Isabella, eldest daughter of Joseph, in 1777, the power was in the hands of an ignorant nobility and a not less ignorant clergy. In 1792, on account of the sickness of the queen, Juan Maria José, Prince of Brazil (the title of the Prince-Royal until 1816), was declared regent. Portugal's connections with England then involved the country in war with Napoleon, and when the latter made an attempt to seize the kingdom, the royal family fled to Brazil.

Queen Maria died in 1816, and John VI. ascended the throne of Portugal and Brazil, but continued to reside in the latter country, leaving Portugal in the hands of the British. But absence of the court was viewed with dislike by the nation, and the general feeling required some fundamental changes in the government. A revolution in favour of constitutional government was effected without bloodshed in 1820, and the king invited to return home, which he now did. In 1822 Brazil threw off the yoke of Portugal, and proclaimed Dom Pedro, son of John VI., emperor. John VI. died in 1826, having named the Infanta Isabella Maria regent. She governed in the name of the Emperor of Brazil, Dom Pedro IV. of Portugal, who granted a new Constitution, modelled on the French, in 1826. In this year he abdicated the Portuguese throne in favour of his daughter Maria da Gloria. A long struggle between the reactionaries and the constitutionalists, and afterwards between the Chartists, or moderate constitutionalists, and the Septembrists, or advanced democrats, then followed, and democracy at last triumphed.

King Carlos I., who ascended the throne in 1889, and his eldest son were assassinated at Lisbon on 1st Feb., 1908, and Manoel II., a younger son of the king, was raised to the throne. A brief revolution, however, drove him from the country, and Portugal was proclaimed a republic on 5th Oct., 1910. A Provisional Government under Theophilo Braga was formed, and in Aug., 1911, Dr. Arriaga was elected President. Several Royalist risings, between 1911 and 1919, were defeated, and in Aug., 1919, Antonio Almeida was elected President.

During the European War Portugal joined the Allies in March, 1916, and sent over 60,000 troops to France. Senhor Gomes became President in 1923, and was succeeded in 1925 by Senhor Bernardino Machado. In May, 1926, a revolution centred at Braga, and led by General Gomez da Costa, caused Machado to resign, but this was followed in June by another revolution which forced da Costa from power.

Language. Portuguese is one of the Romance, or Latin, languages, as today spoken in Portugal, Brazil, and the Portuguese colonies. It resembles Spanish more than it does any of the other Romance tongues. It is the direct modern form of the popular Latin spoken by the Roman soldiers and colonists rather than of the classic speech of Rome. The dialect of Spanish spoken in Portugal at the beginning of the twelfth century was the Galician, which was also that of the court of Leon; but that court subsequently adopted the Castilian, which became the dominant language of Spain. The decline of the Galician dialect in Spain and the formation of the Portuguese language finally determined the separation of Spanish and Portuguese, and from cognate dialects made them distinct languages.

Literature. From the very first, Portuguese literature was less original than the literature of France or Spain. The lyric spirit which in Portuguese literature preceded the epic was due to an impulse received from France. The oldest monuments of Portuguese literature do not go back further than the twelfth and thirteenth centuries, and the native literature could then boast of nothing more than popular songs.

The first Portuguese collection of poetry (*cancioneiro*) was made by King Dionysius, and was published under the title of *Cancioneiro del Rey Dom Diniz*. Some poems on the death of his wife are attributed to Pedro I., husband of Inez de Castro. The sons and grandsons of John I. were poets and patrons of the troubadours.

Sà de Miranda marks the transition from the fifteenth to the sixteenth century and the separation of the Portuguese from the other Spanish dialects and from the language of the troubadours. The sixteenth century is the classic era of Portuguese literature. Pastoral poetry, the epic, and the chivalric romance flourished more than other branches of literature. The chief names are Sà de Miranda, Antonio Ferreira, Camoens, Diego Bernardes, Andrade Caminha, and Alvares do Oriente. The principal epic and the greatest poem in the Portuguese literature, almost the only one which has acquired a European reputation, is *Os Lusiadas* (The Portuguese) of Camoens (1524-80), which has placed its writer in the rank of the few great poets whose genius is universally recognised.

After Camoens as an epic writer comes Cortereal, who has celebrated the siege of Diù and the shipwreck of Sepulveda. Vasco de Lobeiro, Francisco Moraes, and Bernardim Riberio are among the leading romance writers. The drama also began to be cultivated in the sixteenth century. Sà de Miranda studied and imitated Plautus. Ferreira composed the first regular tragedy, *Inez de Castro*. Camoens wrote several theatrical pieces, among which are *Amphitryon* and *Seleucus*. Barros, also a romance writer, wrote a *History of the Conquest of India*. The *Commentaries* of Alphonso d'Albuquerque, by a nephew of the conqueror; the *Chronicle of King Manuel and of Prince John*, by Damian de Goes; the *History of the Discovery and Conquest of the Indies*, by Lopès de Castanheda; the *Chronicle of King Sebastian*, by Diego Bernardo Cruz, are works of merit.

By the opening of the seventeenth century Portugal's literary greatness had been succeeded by one of great activity, though of little real power. Innumerable epics were stimulated into being by the success of the *Lusiads*. During this period the native drama became almost extinct, being overshadowed by the Spanish.

In the eighteenth century the influence of the French writers of the age of Louis XIV. so completely dominated Portuguese literature that it became almost entirely imitative. The nation which had given birth to the *Lusiads* condescended to copy the *Henriade* and the *Lutrin*. Scholarship in this age made greater progress than literature. Towards the close of this century two writers appeared who have formed schools—Francisco Manoel do Nascimento (1734-1829), a polished lyrist, and Barbosa du Bocage. The latter introduced an affected and hyperbolical style of writing called *Elmanis*, from his adopted signature Elmano.

In the nineteenth century patriotic feeling aroused by the Peninsular War and the struggle against Napoleon led to a greater activity, which was also witnessed in the domain of literature. Among the historians, novelists, and dramatists of this century may be mentioned: Almeida-Garrett (1799-1854), who tried to create a national drama; Herculano (1810-77), the author of a *History of Portugal*; the novelist Camillo Castello Branco (1825-90); and the poets Juão de Deus Ramos (1830-96) and Anthero de Quental (1842-92). Most notable of modern novelists are Raul Brandão and Manoel Ribeiro, author of the trilogy *A Catedral*.

BIBLIOGRAPHY: O. J. F. Crawford, *Portugal, Old and New*; W. H. Koebel, *Portugal: its Land and People*; MacMurdo and Monteiro, *History of Portugal*; Almeida, *Historia de Portugal*, Vol. IV.; P. S. Marden, *A Wayfarer in Portugal*; F. R. Salgado, *L'Empire Colonial Portugais*; R. Proença, *Guia de Portugal*; Theophilo Braga, *Historia da litteratura portugueza*.

PORTUGUESA. A west-central state of Venezuela, traversed by spurs of the Cordillera de Merida, and drained by the River Portuguesa, which rises in the Cordillera de Merida and unites with the Apure at San Fernando after a course of 200 miles. The state capital is Guanare. State pop. (1926), 58,721.

PORTUGUESE EAST AFRICA. A Portuguese settlement, as the name implies. It has an area of 297,657 sq. miles, and is divided into two distinct territories as under.

1. **Province of Mozambique.** Area, 245,776 sq. miles. The territory is administered by a High Commissioner and is subdivided into seven districts, each under control of a Governor:

Lourenço Marques.	Tete.
Inhambane.	Mozambique.
Quilimane.	Cabo Delgado.
Nyassa.	

There are Government and Provincial Councils, and partial autonomy was granted in 1920. Lourenço Marques is the capital.

2. **Companhia de Mozambique.** The territories controlled by this Company, in which British capital is extensively interested, have an area of 51,881 sq. miles, and include most of the country between the Sabi River and the Zambezi, including Manica and Sofāla. The Company has a charter granting sovereign rights for

fifty years from 1891. There are fifteen divisions, as follows:

Division	Population
Alto Save [1]	2,875
Beira	6,921
Buzi	17,019
Chemba	27,572
Cheringoma	11,166
Chiloane [1]	6,604
Chimoio	8,756
Chupanga	24,712
Gorongoza [1]	16,820
Manica	10,185
Moribane [1]	12,161
Mossurize	18,142
Neves Ferreira	2,859
Sena	32,399
Sofãla [1]	22,481
Total	220,672

Topography, etc. Half of the Mozambique Company's territories are lowlands, extending in the south on both sides of the Sabi River almost to the Rhodesian frontier. The climate is arid. Where the Beira and Mashonaland Railway leaves the coast the coastal plain is much narrower, and it is in the uplands immediately west of the Rhodesian border that most of the whites are settled. Between the Zambezi and the railway the coastal plain is low and sandy, traversed by small streams that flow from the Cheringoma Plateau (1000 feet altitude). Part of this ridge is densely afforested and a favourite haunt of the elephant.

The Urema depression lies just behind the Cheringoma Plateau. It is low and swampy, and from it tributaries flow north and south to the Zambezi and Pungue respectively. Along the Zambezi, the northern boundary of the Company's territories, the land is very flat. In the Rhodesian tableland, however, an altitude of 6500 feet is reached. The Gorongoza Mountains rise behind the Urema depression, and are much frequented by big game.

The principal rivers traversing the southern part of the territory are the Sabi, Buzi (with its affluent the Revue), and Pungue. Beira stands on the low, sandy, northern shore of the estuary which receives the waters of the two latter rivers. *See* ZAMBEZI.

Nyassa Company. This chartered Company controls territories between Lake Nyasa and the Indian Ocean, and between the Rivers Rovuma (north) and Lurio (south). In 1929 when its contract expired the districts of Cabo Delgado and Nyassa were formed from the territories.

The total population of Portuguese East Africa in 1930 was 3,995,831, 35,570 being Europeans.

Ports. The chief ports of the colony are: Beira, Mozambique, Ibo, Quilimane, Chinde[1], Inhambane, Porto Amelia, and Lourenço Marques.

Communications. The Zambezi is navigated by stern-wheel steamers from Chinde as far up as Tete (about 300 miles), but owing to shifting channels and sand-banks any form of navigation is somewhat precarious. The Mozambique Company's territory is traversed by the Trans-Zambezia Railway (*see* ZAMBEZIA), and for 204 miles by the Beira-Mashonaland Railway, which joins the Rhodesian Trunk Line at Salisbury. The Delagoa Bay-Pretoria line has 57 miles of track within the colony. A new line from Lourenço Marques will tap the Swaziland borders, and railway construction generally will be further advanced. From Chindio to the Nyasaland frontier (44½ miles) is the Zambezi extension of the Shiré Highlands (Central Africa) line to Blantyre.

Production : *Agriculture.*—The products already established upon a good commercial basis include sisal hemp, sugar, maize, and cotton; sugar being first in value and maize in actual tonnage. Portuguese East Africa is exceedingly rich agriculturally, and some lands are stated to yield 45 tons of sugar-cane to the acre. Sugar is grown mainly in the Zambezi Valley and along the Buzi River. (The Buzi Company produce sugar, brandy, alcohol (pure), maize, maize flour, bricks, and art tiles.) Maize is the chief crop of the white settlers, 200 of whom are settled in the uplands of the Macequece and Chimoio districts, where ten bags are produced per acre, as against three in the Union and five in Rhodesia. Coffee is grown along the Beira line, ground nuts flourish everywhere, and wheat, beans, and fruit (including oranges, naartjes, and grape-fruit) are easily raised. The land is very suitable for tobacco, a yield of 750 lb. per acre having been reported. Among cattle a Shorthorn-Hereford cross is most favoured by European owners. Donkeys, oxen, some buffaloes, goats, horses, sheep, mules, and pigs are kept.

Forestry.—Lack of transport has prevented the exploitation of the forest wealth of Portuguese East Africa. Among trees of economic

[1] In these districts there are less than 10 whites. About 2000 in all are of European origin or descent, and half of that number are located in or near Beira, the great majority being agriculturists. There is a small number of Indian Banyan traders and Arabs. Census pop. (1926), 308,543.

[1] Chinde was practically destroyed during a cyclone on 24th Feb., 1922 (see *Nyasaland* under *Towns*).

importance existing along the route of the Trans-Zambezi Railway between Dondo and the Zambezi River are furniture woods, such as the musakosa (*Afzelia Cuanzensis*), katumbira or African walnut (*Pterocarpus Angolensis*), and ngunda, which resembles the *Khaya Senegalensis* or African mahogany. Many other rare woods exist, which are known only by their native names and are untapped excepting as sleepers for the railways. South of the Beira-Mashonaland Railway much of the country is densely afforested. It is remote from the railway, and development is unlikely for many years to come.

Minerals.—The only mines of any importance in active exploitation at the present time are the ancient gold- and copper-mines of the Campanhia de Mozambique, in Manicaland, which have produced about half a million sterling value of gold from the beginning of record-keeping to the present day. Modern mining was only begun in the 'nineties, and the following table gives some idea of the annual gold and copper output since that time.

Annual Output	Gold		Copper	
	Oz.	Value £	Tons	Value £
To 1914	14,937	62,366	—	—
To 1915	15,614	52,284	—	—
To 1916	11,217	46,502	—	—
To 1917	9,276	37,858	307	30,700
To 1918	5,592	23,167	207	20,700
To 1913 from the beginning of modern mining ..	38,503	139,686	4,816	76,078

Tin, coal (near Tete),[1] and extensive deposits of cassiterite (79 per cent tin) have been found, and there are extensive mineral prospects in the Zambezi Valley.

Industries. These are undeveloped but are progressive. They comprise mainly sugar manufactories, furniture-making (Lourenço Marques), cement and cold storage (at Port Matolla above Lourenço Marques), and a soap and oil factory.

See ZAMBEZI; ZAMBEZIA; PORTUGAL; TETE; and various other articles.

[1] A Belgian prospecting party recently spent two years in the Tete district, and discovered many valuable mineral deposits. The Société Minière et Gèologique du Zambèze, a Belgian concern, financed the exploration work and has made arrangements for the exploitation of the Tete coal-fields. Coal will be sent by river steamer down the Zambesi to the railhead of the Trans-Zambezia Railway, thence by train to Beira, which, it is forecasted, will eventually become an important bunkering and coal-exporting centre.

BIBLIOGRAPHY: Special Trade Supplement (Trans-Zambezia Section) London *Times*, dated 6th May, 1922; H. Hall Hall, *Commercial Report on Portuguese East Africa* (H.M. Stationery Office publication); W. Worsfield, *Portuguese Nyasaland*; *Manual of Portuguese East Africa* and *Portuguese Nyasaland* (both British Admiralty publications, 1920); *Mozambique* (British Foreign Office publication, 1918-9). The three last-named works contain full bibliographies.

PORTUGUESE MAN-OF-WAR. The popular name of certain jellyfishes included in the Hydrozoa. *See* PHYSALIA; SIPHONOPHORA.

PORTULA'CEÆ, PORTULACA'CEÆ, or PURSLANES. A small natural order of polypetalous, dicotyledons, consisting of annual, perennial, herbaceous or shrubby plants, occurring in the hotter or milder parts of the world. *Portulāca oleracēa*, or common purslane, sometimes used in salads, is naturalised in many different countries. *P. grandiflora*, a South American species, is a fine garden annual with many ornamental varieties.

PORT WINE. Rich red wine from grapes grown in the Douro Valley, Portugal, and shipped from Oporto. Anglo-Portuguese treaties forbid other wines to be called port. Mostly fortified with brandy on fermentation, the characteristic tint coming from a spirituous mixture containing elder berries, its alcoholic content is 17-25 per cent. Vintage port is usually shipped two years after its specified year, and promptly bottled by the importers. Tawny port usually comprises blends of different years, kept in cask in Oporto until shipped.

POSEIDŌN (po-sī'dōn). The Greek god of the sea, identified by the Romans with the Italian deity Neptunus. A son of Kronos and Rhea, and hence a brother of Zeus, Hēra, and Dēmētēr, he was regarded as inferior in power only to Zeus. The attributes ascribed and most of the myths regarding him have reference to the phenomena of the sea. The horse, and more particularly the war-horse, was sacred to Poseidōn, and one of the symbols of his power. During the Trojan War Poseidōn was the constant enemy of Troy, and after its close he is described as thwarting the return of Odysseus to his home for his having blinded Polyphēmus, a son of the god. Poseidōn was married to Amphitritē. His worship was common throughout Greece and the Greek colonies, but especially prevailed in the maritime towns. The Isthmian games were held in his honour. In works of art Poseidōn is represented with features resembling those of Zeus, and often bears the trident in his right hand.

POSEN, or **POZNAN.** Formerly a province of Prussia, now a county of Poland. The surface is flat, and greatly covered by lakes and marshes. A small portion on the north-east belongs to the basin of the Vistula; all the rest to the basin of the Oder. The soil is mostly of a light and sandy character, yielding grain, millet, flax, hemp, tobacco, and hops. Forests occupy 20 per cent of the surface.

The inhabitants include many Germans, especially in the towns, but considerably more than half are Poles. The province was taken by Prussia after the partition of Poland (1772 and 1793). It was part of the Grand-Duchy of Warsaw from 1807 to 1815, when it was returned to Prussia. It was divided into the districts of Posen and Bromberg. By the Treaty of Versailles Posen was ceded to Poland. There are thirty-six districts in the county. Area, 10,243 sq. miles; pop. (1931), 2,112,871.

POSEN, or **POZNAN.** A town of Poland, capital of the county of Posen, on the Warthe. It is a railway centre for lines from Berlin, Thorn, Breslau, Kreuzburg, and Kreuz (for

Posen: The Dzialynski Palace

Stettin). The principal buildings are the Dzialynski Palace; the Rathaus (1550-5); and the Golden Chapel, erected by Count Raczinsky in 1842. Posen is a Polish archbishopric. The manufactures consist chiefly of agricultural machines, manures, woollen and linen tissues, carriages, leather, and lacquerware; there are breweries and distilleries. The town was taken by the Poles in Dec., 1918. It has two broadcasting stations. Pop. (1931), 246,574.

POSIDONIA AUSTRALIS (marine fibre). Found in abundance in Spencer's Gulf and St. Vincent Gulf, South Australia, as well as in Tasmania; a perennial plant with underlying deposit of fibre. The fibre varies in length from 3 to 7 inches, is a little inferior in strength to jute, but is very brittle. This lack of elasticity is the chief objection to its employment as a textile fibre, although simple methods of treatment are said to render it softer and to add a little lustre to an otherwise almost lustreless material. On the other hand, it has a great affinity for colouring-matter, and is a good insulating agent against heat.

POSIDONIUS. A Stoic philosopher, born in Syria about 135 B.C. He settled as a teacher at Rhodes, whence he is called the Rhodian. The most distinguished Romans were his scholars, and Cicero was initiated by him into the Stoic philosophy. Removing to Rome in 51 B.C., he died not long after. In his physical investigations he was more a follower of Aristotle than of the Stoic school.

POSILI'PO. An eminence which bounds the city of Naples on the west. It is traversed by a tunnel, called the Grotto of Posilipo, 2244 feet long, from 21 to 32 feet wide, with a height varying from 25 to 69 feet, through which runs the road to Pozzuoli. This tunnel is remarkable for its antiquity, having been made in the reign of Augustus. A second tunnel (the Grotto Nuova), constructed between 1882-5, gives passage to the tramway from Naples to Pozzuoli.

POSITIVISM, or **POSITIVE PHILOSOPHY.** A system of philosophy, of life and thought, dealing with realities and recognising only the sure results reached by scientific methods. It excludes all supernatural and spiritual agencies and metaphysical speculations, and maintains that the only criterion of human knowledge is sense experience.

Forerunners of positivism already existed among the Greek Sophists, but the founder of the system and the inventor of the term was Auguste Comte (q.v.). His system was both philosophical and religious. Philosophically he maintained that instead of investigating final causes of things, or the absolute, it is the business of the philosopher to take into consideration facts, and to inquire after the laws of things, i.e. the relations of facts to other facts. Theologically Comte's system excludes the existence of a personal, transcendent God, humanity becoming the object of veneration. The distinguishing idea which lies at the root of this twofold system is the conception that the anomalies of our social system cannot be reformed until the theories upon which it is shaped have been brought into complete harmony with science.

The leading ideas of Comte's philosophy are: (1) the classification of the sciences in the order of their development, proceeding from the simpler to the more complex—mathematics, astronomy, physics, chemistry, biology, and sociology; and (2) the doctrine of the "three stages," or the three aspects in which the human mind successively views the world of phenomena, namely, the theological, the metaphysical, and the scientific.

The religious side of positivism has somewhat the nature of an apology or afterthought. After doing away with theology and metaphysics, and founding his system on science or positive knowledge alone, Comte discovered that there was something positive in man's craving for a being to worship. He therefore had recourse to what he calls the cultus of humanity considered as a corporate being in the past, present, and future, which is spoken of as the *Grand Être*. This religion, like other forms of worship, requires for its full development an organised priesthood, temples, etc.

Under the régime of positive religion Comte would include the political and social side of his system. Hence some of his followers look forward to the establishment of an international republic, composed of the great western nations of Europe, destined ultimately to lead the whole world. Society in this great commonwealth will be reorganised on the basis of a double direction or control, that of the temporal or material authority, and that of the spiritual or educating body. Among the best-known admirers and adherents of Comte's theories were G. H. Lewes, J. S. Mill, Richard Congreve, H. Martineau, and particularly Frederic Harrison in England; and Pierre Laffitte, E. Littré, and H. Taine in France. — BIBLIOGRAPHY: Frederic Harrison, *The Creed of a Layman*; *Philosophy of Common Sense*; H. Ellis, *What Positivism Means*; A. J. Balfour, *The Religion of Humanity*; L. Lévy-Bruhl, *La Philosophie d'Auguste Comte*.

POSSESSION. In English, as in Roman law, a thing quite distinct from ownership. Thus one man may have the physical possession of a thing, and another may have the right of possession, or property. Strictly speaking, possession denotes merely the state of having or holding. Possession may be either lawful, as in the case of a tenant, or unlawful, as in the case of a thief; ownership, on the other hand, presupposes legality.

Natural possession exists when the proprietor himself is actually in possession.

Civil possession is possession not by the owner, but by another in his name or for his behoof.

Actual possession occurs when a person enters into lands or tenements descended or conveyed to him.

Possession in law is said to exist when lands, etc., have descended to a man, and he has not actually entered into them.

POST-IMPRESSIONISM. A term used to describe a group of modern movements in art which together constitute a revolt against the ideals and methods of impressionism (q.v.), in that their aim is not the reproduction of the visual appearance of nature, but the combination of natural forms with a new and independent reality. In other respects the various forms of post-impressionism differ widely. The initiators of the movement fall into two main groups, those chiefly occupied with problems of form and design, and those who primarily use art to provide symbols for expressing emotion.

Cézanne. In the first, the dominant figure is Paul Cézanne (1849-1906), whose aims were described by himself as those of "remaking Poussin in accordance with nature," and of "making of Impressionism something solid and durable." Nature for him was simply a starting-point. Contemplation of her, he held, led to perception of an underlying organic connection between visible forms, which it was the painter's work to realise on canvas, and so to attain coherent design. An essential characteristic of nature being the third dimension, on the expression of this Cézanne laid great stress. He sought to record all the subtle colour variations in his subject, especially those due to objects being in different positions in space or in different relations to the source of light; and in this way not only defined individual forms, but fixed their position in space in relation to each other.

The aims and methods of Cézanne have influenced, directly or indirectly, a large part of modern art. Among his most prominent modern followers are Marchand, Derain, and Segonzac. Another interesting figure, particularly admired by the Cubists, is Georges Seurat, whose success in uniting solid forms into monumental design was obscured by his practice of painting in round spots of pure colour, a method known as *division-*

ism and based on impressionist ideas.

Gauguin. The second group is typified by Paul Gauguin (1848-1903), whose restless and excitable temperament drove him to Tahiti and more remote islands, where he died. From an early impressionist phase he developed a boldly decorative art of rich colour, which aims at expressing the feelings inspired in the painter by his surroundings.

Van Gogh. Similar in outlook was Vincent van Gogh, a Dutchman settled in France, who united with a design which owes much to Japanese influence, vivid colour, which seeks not to mimic nature but to express his emotions.

Groups. The first well-marked group to develop from these beginnings was that of the *symbolistes,* who hold that the aim of painting is the expression of an idea. Their most distinguished living representatives are Paul Sérusier and Maurice Denis. Another group, influenced in part by the decorative and symbolic art of Gustave Moreau, includes Henri Matisse, whose arbitrary use of colour and bold distortion of forms won for the group the nickname of *les fauves* (the wild men). In reaction against these extravagances, as much as against impressionism, is the concern with solid form and with its arrangement into abstract designs of Cubism (q.v.), in which movement Pablo Picasso is the chief figure.

Contemporary, but quite different in character, is Futurism (q.v.), an attempt to express pictorially sensations of movement and growth. Similar to cubism in its use of geometric forms, and to futurism in its insistence that art should be a reflection of contemporary life, is the English Vorticist movement. This is based on the idea that the artist has a general conception of relations in the universe, which is his *vortex,* through which ideas pass and take concrete shape therefrom; just as by substituting definite quantities for algebraic symbols in the general equation of a circle, a particular circle is obtained. In practice the Vorticists have been mainly concerned with a rather mechanical presentment of underlying structure.—BIBLIOGRAPHY: W. H. Wright, *Modern Painting*; R. Fry, *Vision and Design*; C. Bell, *Since Cézanne.*

POSTMASTER-GENERAL. The chief executive head of the postal and telegraphic systems of Britain. He is usually a member of the Cabinet, and exercises authority over all the departments of the postal and telegraphic systems, including money orders, savings bank, insurances, and annuities.

POST MORTEM. Medical examination of a corpse to ascertain the cause of death. It may be ordered by a coroner to help the jury in their verdict, or may be undertaken for private reasons. In the former case the relatives cannot forbid examination. Despite its value to medical science, it is not popular in U.S.A., nor among Catholics and Jews. *See* AUTOPSY.

POST-OBIT BOND. A bond given for the purpose of securing to a lender a sum of money on the death of some specified individual from whom the borrower has expectations. Such loans are not only generally made at usurious rates of interest, but usually the borrower has to pay a much larger sum than he has received, in consideration of the risks the lender runs in the case of the obliger predeceasing the person from whom he has expectations. If, however, there is a gross inadequacy in the proportions amounting to fraud, a court of equity will interfere.

POST OFFICE. The earliest reference to a regular postal system in England is found in the statutes of Edward III. Royal messengers were then employed as letter-carriers, and this developed until the post office became an established department of Government activity. Sir Brian Tuke (1533) was the first Postmaster of whom we have any record. In 1543 a post was established by which letters were carried from London to Edinburgh, taking four days for the journey. Postal services between Scotland and England were greatly improved during the reign of James I., and a Continental service was instituted. Lord Stanhope was appointed Postmaster for Britain in 1607, and in 1619, while he held office, the new post of Postmaster for foreign parts was created, to which Matthew de Quester was appointed.

Merchants continued to use their private and local posts and carriers until the beginning of the reign of Charles I., and the universities and large towns organised systems of their own. The king forbade the use of these private ventures, reformed the national system, and claimed the revenue. A penny post within the London area was instituted in 1683. During the reigns of William III. and Anne many improvements were introduced into the postal system, but from that time until the middle of the nineteenth century there was little change.

Sir Rowland Hill, the author of the post-office system as we know it to-day, outlined his schemes in a pamphlet (*Post Office Reform*) which he published in 1837. In those days postal charges were so high that Daniel O'Connell complained that Irish labourers in England had to spend one-fifth of their week's wages every time they wrote to their people at home and got an answer back. There were large districts in England where the postman was never seen, and the major part of the correspondence of the country did not pass through the post office.

Introduction of Penny Post. Sir Rowland Hill noticed that the revenue of the post office continued to diminish instead of increasing with the population and wealth of the country, and suggested the introduction of the penny post throughout the country as a means of increasing the revenue. His analysis of the figures available from the London district post and the money collected throughout the country showed the probable average cost of receipt, transmission, and delivery of a letter as 0.84 of a penny, of which one-third went to meet transmission charges and two-thirds collection and delivery. He developed his proposals in later pamphlets, and tried repeatedly to get facilities to study postal affairs from inside, but every endeavour to obtain an entry to the post office for this purpose was prevented, and his study of the system had to be confined to the perusal of the figures in Government Blue books.

The scheme outlined by Sir Rowland Hill was adopted, and on 10th Jan., 1840, the uniform rate of one penny for a half-ounce for prepaid letters came into operation. The success of this scheme was largely contributed to by the introduction of adhesive postage-stamps, referred to in 1837 by Hill, before the Commission appointed to inquire into the working of the post office, as "bits of paper just large enough to bear the stamp and covered at the back with a glutinous wash," but believed to be the idea of James Chalmers, of Dundee.

The opposition of the Government and civil servants to reform of the postal system was of such a character that *The Times* of 16th March, 1839, said, "it was the cause of the whole people of the United Kingdom against the small coterie of placeholders in St. Martin's-le-Grand and its dependencies." Despite the earnest endeavours of the postal staff, who had the deep-rooted opposition to all reform which is apt to be characteristic of civil servants, the scheme could not be made a failure, and even the dismissal of Hill by Sir Robert Peel in 1841, leaving the opponents of the measure in full possession of the machine and with every facility to increase the cost of its working, which they delighted in doing, did little to reduce the enthusiasm of the British public for postal reform, their faith in Sir Rowland Hill, or the success of his scheme.

Postal Carriages. The adoption of postal carriages on the railways greatly facilitated the handling of correspondence. These carriages are fitted with an apparatus in which letter-bags are collected while the train continues on its journey, and the letters are sorted in the van by the travelling staff. The reduction of the cost of carriage, the great increase in the rapidity of transmission, the immense development of commerce, together with the increase of population, have had the effect of enormously multiplying the work done by the post office. In 1839 the total number of British letters conveyed through the post office was estimated at about 76 millions; in 1921-2 it had reached 3350 millions, in addition to which 500 million post cards, 1150 million "printed papers," and 190 million newspapers were transmitted.

The power possessed by the Secretaries for State to issue warrants to open or to detain correspondence passing through the post office has been the cause at different times of popular agitations, notably in the case of Mazzini's letters in the summer of 1844. Such warrants are only issued for two purposes: "the furtherance of criminal justice," and "the determination of the designs of persons known or suspected to be engaged in proceedings dangerous to the State or deeply involving British interests."

Development of Postal Service. The development of the whole postal service we know to-day was a very gradual process. One after another of the departments of activity was added after, frequently long after, there was a manifest public demand. *Letter cards* were introduced in 1892, after they had been in use for many years on the Continent, where they were very popular. In 1870 *post cards* were provided by the post office, but only one kind of card was permitted until the stationers' complaints were met by allowing private persons to have their own cards stamped at Somerset House. The use of reply post cards dates from 1893. The popularity of *picture post cards* has contributed considerably to the great increase in post-card traffic. The *inland parcels post* was inaugurated in Aug., 1883. The *registered letter system* provides all the measure of safety in transit required for ordinary correspondence, but its use by financial houses to dispatch large quantities of bank notes from branch offices to their headquarters has led to some cases of theft. An *Imperial Penny Post* was instituted on Christmas Day, 1898, between most of the countries within the Empire and the Motherland. South Africa and Australia adopted the scheme later, and by 1911 the idea had become a reality.

The *money order scheme* was instituted in 1792 to give safe conveyance of money to soldiers and sailors. At that time it was thought that it was not legal for the post office to undertake money order business, and the system was run as a private venture by six officers of the post office known as "Clerks of the Roads." This scheme was terminated six years later, but the money order department continued as a private business in the hands of three post office clerks as "Stow and Company." In 1838 the sole remaining partner of this concern was bought out by the Government with a pension of £400 a year, and since then the money-order scheme has been run actually as a post office department.

Post Office Savings Bank. The post office savings bank owes its origin to a suggestion made in 1860 by Charles William Sykes, of Huddersfield, which was immediately taken up by W. E. Gladstone, who was then Chancellor of the Exchequer. An Act of Parliament established it in 1861. The scheme has been very successful, and the very sensible action of starting the school penny-savings bank system in 1892, when the Free Education Act was introduced, did much to popularise thrift and extend the field of the bank's activities. The total amount credited to depositors at the end of the year 1931 was £289,440,745.

Telegraph Service. The telegraph service was started in 1870, when telegrams were dispatched at the rate of one shilling for twenty words and threepence for each additional group of five words; the addresses of both sender and receiver were transmitted free. In the year 1885 the sixpenny telegram was introduced, with a halfpenny overcharge for each additional word over twelve, with the names and addresses included as words. A *registered address system*, whereby a firm can register a word as equivalent to its name and address at a cost of one guinea (now £2) a year, was started at the same time. Press matter is telegraphed at very cheap rates.

The telegraph system is a department of the post office which does not pay its way. The balancing of costs of working with probable business does not seem to an outsider to be a problem of such outstanding difficulty as to admit of no solution in the fifty years during which the department has been in existence. On the introduction of telephony in 1878 there was considerable litigation between the post office and the early telephone companies regarding the powers conferred on this Government department under the Telegraph Act. The post office won in these cases, but appeals were intimated which never came to trial, because amicable working arrangements were made with the telephone companies, under which they obtained licences to work in particular districts.

The telephones in the cities of the country were worked by a private company and some few municipalities—Glasgow, Tunbridge Wells, Portsmouth, Brighton, Swansea, and Hull—until 1st Jan., 1912, when the whole system was nationalised. In spite of the fact that there was considerable uncertainty as to how long the Government were going to tolerate private enterprise in the telephone business, which must have hampered and in many ways completely arrested the development of the telephone service, the National Telephone Company showed that it was possible to run the system well and profitably with reasonable rates. When the system was taken over by the Government, troubled and dissatisfied subscribers became more and more numerous as time went on. It has been said that much of the criticism of the department was due to the prejudice of British business men against nationalisation in any form or Government interference in business. Whether this be so or not, there is undoubted evidence that a new and very undesirable spirit of irresponsibility, which is to a certain extent characteristic of municipal and national enterprise, has entered what was previously a business-like and efficient machine.

Postal Rate. In 1921 the letter rate was raised to twopence for three ounces, and the post card rate to three halfpence. The immediate effect was a great reduction in traffic, which was handled at very high cost because the old staff had been retained. The pictorial post card business experienced a considerable set-back. The irritation of the business public was expressed in many petitions and much "lobbying" at the House of Commons. At last, in 1922, when Sir Robert Horne was Chancellor of the Exchequer, the postal rate was reduced to three-halfpence for an ounce and the post card rate to one penny.

The present rates for the various postal services and other interesting information will be found in *The Post Office Guide*.

Post Office Annuities. By the Post Office Annuities Act, 1864, a scheme was established, and put into operation in the following year, for the purchase of Government annuities through the post office, by persons of limited means. *Immediate* annuities, payable quarterly, from £1 up to £300, may be purchased on the life of any person of five years of age and upwards, and the person so insured has a Government guarantee for the payment of the money. The cost of an annuity depends upon the average price of 2½ per cent Consolidated Stock at the time of purchase, and, of course, varies according to the age of the purchaser. Tables showing the cost of annuities at different ages are issued by the Post Office Savings Bank, and are obtainable at any local post office. A single payment equal to one quarter of the annuity is payable to the representatives of a deceased annuitant if claimed within two years of his death. An immediate *joint* annuity may be purchased by any two persons on their joint lives, with continuance of the annuity in full to the survivor. In 1921 the post office ceased to grant *deferred* annuities. Consult also the official *Post Office Guide*.

POST-PLIOCENE. In geology, the periods following the Pliocene, and including the Pleistocene (q.v.) and the Recent periods, the latter being the first period of the Quaternary era. *See* POST-TERTIARY.

POST-TERTIARY. In geology, the Lyellian term for all deposits and phenomena of more recent date than the Norwich or mammaliferous crag. It is thus equivalent, in ordinary usage, to Post-Pliocene. Beneath the accumulations of the *historic* epoch, comprising alluvia, peat, etc., in process of formation, come *prehistoric* deposits, the remains in which are older, comprising stone implements, pile-dwellings, and extinct animals, as the Irish deer, mammoth, etc. These deposits include in the British area raised beaches and submerged peat, showing considerable changes in the coast-line, and they graduate downwards into the accumulations of the Glacial epoch.

POTAMOGETON (-mo-gē'ton). A genus of aquatic plants belonging to the nat. ord. Naladaceæ. It has a perfect flower, a four-pointed perianth, four sessile anthers, four ovaries, and four drupes or nuts. Several species are indigenous to Britain, where they are known by the name of *pond-weed*.

POTASH. The name originally given to the product obtained when a solution of vegetable ashes is evaporated to dryness in iron pots, and the residue calcined. It derives its name from the *ashes*, and the *pots* (called potash kettles) in which the solution was evaporated. In the crude state it is impure potassium carbonate, and when purified is known as pearl-ash. It is used in the making of glass and soap, and large quantities of it are now produced from certain "potash minerals" (especially carnallite), instead of from wood ashes.

The name potash is often given to potassium hydroxide, KOH, which is also termed *caustic potash*. This is either prepared by boiling a solution of potassium carbonate and then adding quicklime or baryta, or by the electrolysis of a solution of potassium chloride. It is a white solid, usually sold in lumps or in the form of sticks, dissolves readily in water, and has a strongly alkaline reaction. It changes the colour of many natural colouring-matters, and corrodes most animal and vegetable tissues. It rapidly absorbs moisture and carbon dioxide from the atmosphere. It neutralises all acids, yielding the corresponding potassium salts, and is largely made use of in the manufacture of soft soap. It is fusible at a temperature of 360° C. It is used in surgery, under the name of *lapis causticus*, to destroy warts and other growths, and to clean the wounds produced by the bites of animals. *See* POTASSIUM.

POTASH SALTS. A popular name for a number of minerals soluble in water and containing potassium chloride, which are in demand as agricultural fertilisers. Those commercially available are kainite, carnallite, and sylvine; the last named is usually much mixed with rock-salt, and is sold thus as "sylvinite." The potassium-content, for trade purposes, is calculated as potash. The chief sources are the mines of Stassfurt, near Magdeburg, and the Rhine-vale, near Mulhouse, Alsace. The yearly output of Stassfurt alone amounts to about 550,000 to 600,000 tons of potassium salts, mostly chloride.

As the two largest sources of this mineral were in German hands during the European War, there was a famine in potash for the world outside Central Europe. The dust from the flues of blast-furnaces was found to contain a large proportion of potassium salts, and many thousands of tons were used in Britain. Nebraska, by extracting supplies from her alkali lakes, enjoyed a momentary activity as a potash producer, and in 1918 was able to ship 150,000 tons.

POTAS'SIUM (a Latinised term from *potash*). A name given to the metallic element obtained from potash; discovered by Davy in 1807, and one of the first fruits of his electro-chemical researches; symbol, K; atomic weight, 39·10. Next to lithium it is the lightest metallic substance known, its specific gravity being 0·862 at the temperature of 60° F. At ordinary temperatures it may be cut with a knife and worked with the fingers. At 32° F. it is hard and brittle, with a crystalline texture; at 50° F. it becomes malleable, and in lustre resembles polished silver; at 150° F. it is perfectly liquid. It is usually manufactured by the electrolysis of the hydroxide or chloride, and is an important constituent of saltpetre, common alum, and most manures.

Potassium combines very readily with oxygen, and is capable of abstracting it from various oxgyen compounds. A freshly exposed surface of potassium instantly becomes covered with a film of oxide. The metal must therefore be preserved under a liquid free from oxygen, petroleum being generally employed. It decomposes cold water with great readiness; hydrogen gas is evolved and burns with a violet-coloured flame, due to potassium vapour which is present; the other product is caustic potash, which dissolves in the water.

Potassium chloride (KCl) is known in commerce as "muriate of potash," and closely resembles common salt (sodium chloride). *Potassium bromide* and *iodide* are useful drugs. (For the *carbonate* and *hydrate, see* POTASH.) *Potassium bicarbonate* is obtained by exposing a solution of the carbonate to the air, carbon dioxide being absorbed from the atmosphere, and crystals being deposited; or it is formed more directly by passing a current of carbon dioxide through a solution of the carbonate of such a strength that crystals form spontaneously. It is much used in medicine for making effervescing drinks.

Potassium nitrate is *nitre*, or *saltpetre*. (*See* NITRE.) *Potassium sulphate* (K_2SO_4) is used medicinally as a mild laxative, in making some kinds of glass and alum, and in manures. The *bisulphate* ($KHSO_4$) is used in calico-printing and dyeing. *Potassium chlorate* ($KClO_3$) is employed in the manufacture of lucifer matches, and is very valuable in medicine, especially in ulceration of the mouth, for which it is the specific. It is a well-known source of oxygen. The *bichromate* ($K_2Cr_2O_7$) is used in calico-printing and dyeing. *Potassium cyanide* (KCN) is much used in extraction of gold from its ores and in photography.

POTATO (*Solānum tuberōsum*). A plant belonging to the nat. ord. Solanaceæ, which also includes such poisonous plants as nightshade, henbane, thorn-apple, and tobacco. We owe this plant to western South America, where it still grows wild chiefly in the region of the Andes, producing small, tasteless, watery tubers.

The potato was first introduced into Europe, after the conquest of Peru, by the Spaniards, by whom it was spread over the Netherlands, Burgundy, and Italy before the middle of the sixteenth century. In Germany it is first heard of as a rarity in the time of Charles V. Sir John Hawkins, Sir Francis Drake, and Sir Walter Raleigh are all credited with the first introduction of the tuber into England (1565). Although the potato was tolerably widely distributed on the continent of Europe before its appearance in Britain, it seems to have been cultivated more as a curiosity than as an article of food, and Ireland is said to have been the country in which it was first cultivated on a large scale for food. In the course of the eighteenth century it became a favourite article of food with the poorer classes in Germany; but in France there existed so violent a prejudice against it that it did not come into general use until towards the end of the century.

Growth. The potato is a perennial plant, with angular herbaceous stems, growing to the height of 2 or 3 feet; leaves pinnate; flowers pretty large, numerous, disposed in corymbs, and coloured violet, bluish, reddish, or whitish. The fruit is globular, about the size of a gooseberry, reddish-brown or purplish when ripe, and contains numerous small seeds. The tubers, which furnish so large an amount of the food of mankind, are really underground shoots abnormally dilated, their increase in size having been greatly fostered by cultivation. Their true nature is proved by the existence of the "eyes" upon them. These are leaf-buds, from which, if a tuber or a portion of it containing an eye is put into earth, a young plant will sprout, the starchy matter of the tuber itself supplying nutriment until it throws out roots and leaves, and so attains an independent existence.

The potato succeeds best in a light sandy loam containing a certain proportion of vegetable matter. The varieties are very numerous, differing in the time of ripening, in their form, size, colour, and quality. New ones are readily procured by sowing the seeds, which will produce tubers the third year, and a full crop the fourth. But the plant is usually propagated by sowing or planting the tubers, and it is only in this way that any one variety can be kept in cultivation.

Like all plants that are extensively cultivated, and under very different circumstances of soil, climate, and artificial treatment, the potato is extremely subject to diseases, among the more important of which are blight (*Phytophthora infestans*) and wart-disease (*Chrysophlyctis endobiotica*). (*See* articles PHYTOPHTHORA and CHYTRIDINEÆ.) The potato is also attacked by various insects, the most destructive being the Colorado beetle. The tubers consist almost entirely of starch, and being thus deficient in nitrogen, should not be too much relied on as a staple article of diet. Potatoes are extensively used as a cattle-food, and starch is also manufactured from them. A coarse spirit (Berlin spirit, British brandy), is also obtained from them by distillation, the starch being converted into sugar by means of malt or sulphuric acid, and fermentation set up.

POTATO FROG-FLY (*Chlorita solāni*). An insect which injures the potato plant by sucking its juice, allied to the cuckoo-spit fly, and belonging to the ord. Hemiptera.

POTCHEFSTROOM (pot′shef-strōm). The oldest town in the Transvaal, on the Mooi River. It was founded by Hendrik Potgieter in 1838, and was at one time capital of the Boer Republic. In 1880 Cronje besieged the British garrison of 250 men, who capitulated just after an armistice had been arranged by the Boer leaders. During the Boer War (1899-1902) Colonel B. T. Mahon took the town. Pop. (1921), 14,686 (9908 white in 1931).

POTEMKIN (pot-yom′kin), **Gregory Alexandrovitsh.** Russian general and statesman, a favourite of the Empress Catherine II., born in 1739, died in 1791. One of the conspirators who brought about the dethronement of Peter III. in favour of his wife Catherine II., he attracted the attention of the empress and became her favourite. For a period of more than fifteen years he exercised a boundless sway over the destinies of the empire. The partition of Poland was due to his influence. In 1783 he suppressed the khanate of the Crimea, and annexed it to Russia. In 1787, being desirous of expelling the Turks from Europe, he stirred up a new war, in the course of which he took Otshakov by storm (1788).

POTENTIAL. In physics and electrical engineering, a quantity the rate of variation of which from point to point determines the tendency towards motion of some physical entity, such as a material body, a charge of electricity, or a magnetic pole. Potential is thus analogous to temperature in heat conduction, and to pressure in the motion of fluids.

Electric Potential. A general account of the properties and methods of measurement of potential in electrical science is given in the articles *Electricity*; *Electromotive Force*; *Voltmeter*. We give here a somewhat fuller account of the theory of the *electrostatic* potential. The simplest case is that in which the electric field is due to a single charge concentrated at a point A. By Coulomb's Law, the force on a unit positive charge at P, due to a charge of q units at A, is q/r^2, where r = AP, the medium being air, and the units electrostatic. If the charge at A is kept fixed, and the unit charge moves from P to Q, the work done by the electric force between the charges is independent of the path taken between P and Q. If it were not so, and if more work were done on the unit charge in a path PEQ than in another path PFQ, then we could let the unit move along PEQ and carry it back along PFQ, so securing a certain surplus amount of work, contrary to the Principle of the Conservation of Energy. The *potential* at P is defined to be the work done in moving the unit from P out of the field altogether, i.e. to infinity. Taking the path along the prolongation of AP, we find for this work the integral of $(q/r^2)dr$, from r to infinity, which is q/r. The potential at P due to q units at A is therefore q/r. When there is any number of charges producing the field, q_1 at A, q_2 at B, etc., the potential at P is proved in a similar way to be $q_1/\mathrm{AP} + q_2/\mathrm{BP} + \ldots$

If the unit charge moves from P to a point Q very near P, the work done is $F \times PQ$, where F is the *component*, along PQ, of the force at P. By definition, this work is the fall of potential from P to Q, say $V_P - V_Q$. Hence $F = (V_P - V_Q)/PQ$; or, in words, the component force at P along PQ is the rate of fall of the potential per unit length in the direction PQ at P. If X, Y, Z are the components, in the directions of the rectangular co-ordinate axes, of the *electric intensity*, or force on a positive unit, at P, we have therefore $X = -dV/dx$, $Y = -dV/dy$, $Z = -dV/dz$. The *intensity* at P is a *vector* having, in general, a definite direction and magnitude. An *equipotential surface* is a surface at every point of which the potential has the same value. At any point on such a surface the component force in any direction tangential to the surface is zero, and the intensity is therefore normal to the equipotential surface, i.e. *the lines of force are perpendicular to the equipotential surfaces.*

There are some important differential equations connecting the potential with the distribution of electricity in a static field. One of the simplest methods of obtaining these equations depends on a theorem due to Gauss, which states that the surface integral of the outward normal component of the electric intensity, taken over any surface, is equal to the algebraic sum of the charges within the surface, multiplied by 4π. The meaning of the theorem may be seen by taking the very simple case of a single charge q at the centre of a spherical surface of radius r. In this case the normal component of the intensity is the whole intensity q/r^2, and the surface integral is the integral of $(q/r^2)dS$, or q/r^2 into the integral of dS, i.e. $(q/r^2)(4\pi r^2)$ or $4\pi q$.

The general case admits of an interesting physical proof. Suppose the space within any surface to be occupied by liquid. Suppose also that at the point A of the space there is a *source* (such as the mouth of a pipe of negligible volume, led in from outside) from which $4\pi q$ units of volume of liquid issue per unit time. The liquid being incompressible, the volume $4\pi q$ per unit time must cross any surface surrounding the source. The liquid moves radially from the source; if v is its velocity at distance r, the volume crossing per unit time the surface of the sphere of radius r with its centre at the source is $4\pi r^2 v$. But this is $4\pi q$, so that $v = q/r^2$. The velocity in the hydrokinematical problem is therefore the same in magnitude and direction as the force in the electrostatic problem. Consider now the surface with which we started. The volume of liquid crossing the element dS of this surface per unit time is the volume of a thin cylinder of base dS, and height $v \cos\theta$, where θ is the angle between the directions of r and the outward normal. Hence the integral of $v \cos\theta dS$, i.e. of $(q/r^2)\cos\theta dS$, is $4\pi q$; which is the theorem of Gauss for this case; the general case follows by addition.

We can apply the theorem to a small rectangular solid with one corner at $P(x, y, z)$ and with dx, dy, dz for its edges. The contributions to the surface integral can be taken separately for the six faces of the solid. The normal component of the intensity (in the direction outwards from the surface) is, at the x-face through P, $+dV/dx$. The value of this function (dV/dx), when x is changed to $x + dx$, is $dV/dx + (d^2V/dx^2)dx$, by the theorem $f(x+h) = f(x) + hf'(x)$, which is approximately true when h is small (see TAYLOR'S THEOREM). For the faces x and $x + dx$, the outward normals are in opposite directions, so that the contribution to the surface integral from the x-face is $(dV/dx)dydz$, and that from the $x + dx$ face is $(-dV/dx)dydz - (d^2V/dx^2)dxdydz$; and the net contribution from the two faces is $-(d^2V/dx^2)dxdydz$. The whole surface integral is therefore $-(d^2V/dx^2 + d^2V/dy^2 + d^2V/dz^2)dxdydz$. This is equal to the charge within the volume element, multiplied by 4π; or it is equal to $4\pi\rho dxdydz$, where ρ is the volume density of charge at (x, y, z). We thus obtain *Poisson's equation* $d^2V/dx^2 + d^2V/dy^2 + d^2V/dz^2 + 4\pi\rho = 0$. In a region where there is no charge $\rho = 0$, and the equation becomes $d^2V/dx^2 + d^2V/dy^2 + d^2V/dz^2 = 0$, which is *Laplace's equation* (q.v.).

In the very important case of a distribution of charge in a thin layer over a surface, with surface density (charge per unit area) σ, we can apply the theorem of Gauss to the small cheese-shaped volume bounded by two elements of area parallel to the element dS of the charged surface (one element outside the surface, the other within it), and by lines perpendicular to dS joining the edges of the two elements. These joining lines may be taken so short that, in the limit, only the elements parallel to dS contribute to the surface integral. We thus find the *surface equation* $dV/dn_1 + dV/dn_2 + 4\pi\sigma = 0$; where dn_1 and dn_2 are elements of length along the normal, one drawn inwards and the other outwards, and both in the direction away from the surface. In a field containing volume and surface distributions, the potential itself is continuous everywhere; its first derivatives with respect to x, y, and z are also continuous at points of finite volume density; but, at a surface on which there is a surface distribution, a first derivative, such as dV/dx, has not the same value at a point just within the surface as it has at an infinitely near point just outside the surface. The derivative in any direction lying in the surface is continuous across the surface, but the normal derivative changes in value abruptly by the amount $4\pi\sigma$, this conclusion being the immediate interpretation of the surface equation.

In a conductor, electricity is free to move; hence, if there is equilibrium, the distribution must be such that, at every point in the substance of the conductor, the intensity is zero and the potential therefore constant. Poisson's equation then shows that the volume density is everywhere zero; also, since the first derivatives of the potential are continuous (being zero), there is no surface density at any point actually *within* the substance of the conductor. If the conductor is hollow, the potential in the internal space can be shown to be constant, and equal to the potential of the conductor.

One method of proving this depends on the very important property of Laplace's equation that, within a given region, it has only one solution taking a given value at the boundary of the region. If $V = C$ at every point of the boundary, then $V = C$ is one solution for the internal space satisfying Laplace's equation and the boundary condition; $V = C$ is therefore *the* solution. It follows that the charge on a conductor, whether solid or hollow, resides entirely on the outer surface. The density of the surface charge is given by the surface equation, which in this case takes the simplified form $dV/dn = -4\pi\sigma$, since, along the *inward* normal, the rate of variation of V per unit length is zero.

As a simple but important example of the application of Laplace's equation and the surface equation, take the ideal case of a conductor bounded on one side by an infinite plane surface, the equation of which we may take to be $z = 0$. Let z be negative in the conductor itself. The potential V in the field (where z is positive) does not depend on x or y, so that V is a function of z only, and $d^2V/dz^2 = 0$; the solution of this equation is $V = Az + B$. The value of B is immaterial; the value of A can be expressed in terms of the surface density σ. For we have here $dV/dn = dV/dz = A$, so that $A = -4\pi\sigma$, and $V = -4\pi\sigma z + B$. The intensity at any point is in the z-direction, and its value $-dV/dz$ is $4\pi\sigma$. The intensity is therefore the same at all distances from the charged surface. If there are *two* plane conducting surfaces, parallel to each other, say $z = 0$ at potential V_0 and $z = d$ at potential V_1, then $V = V_0 + (V_1 - V_0)z/d$, for this satisfies Laplace's equation and the surface conditions. At $z = 0$, $4\pi\sigma = -(V_1 - V_0)d$; and at $z = d$, $4\pi\sigma = +(V_1 - V_0)/d$, since, in the latter case, $dV/dn = -dV/dz$. The intensity at any point in the field, i.e. between the surfaces, is $-dV/dz$, or $(V_1 - V_0)/d$. Half of this force on the exploring unit is obviously due to the repulsion of one plane, half to the attraction of the other. We can therefore calculate the force with which an area A on $z = d$ is attracted to the other plane. For the charge on the area A is σA, or $A(V_1 - V_0)4/\pi d$, and the intensity due to the distribution on $z = 0$ is $(V_1 - V_0)/2d$. The force on A is therefore $A(V_1 - V_0)^2/(8\pi d^2)$. The action of one of Lord Kelvin's electrometers, the guard-ring or attracted disc instrument, is based on this formula.

It will be observed that the density σ, for a given difference of potential between the opposing conductors, is inversely proportional to the distance d between them. This is the principle of *condensers*. The *capacity* per unit area of the arrangement is defined to be the ratio of the charge per unit area on either surface to the difference of potential; it is therefore $\sigma/(V_1 - V_0)$ or $1/(4\pi d)$.

For the investigation of potential problems when the bounding surfaces of the field are curved, it is convenient to transform Laplace's equation to an equivalent equation in terms of appropriate co-ordinates. The transformation is easily made with the help of the theorem of Gauss. In a few important cases, conditions of symmetry enable us to reduce the equation to a particularly simple form. For example, let the bounding surfaces be two of a family of concentric circular cylinders, and let V have the constant values V_0 at the inner surface $r = a$, and V_1 at the outer surface $r = b$. The potential in the field will be a function of r only, if we assume the cylinders to be infinitely long. Applying the theorem of Gauss to the volume bounded by any two cylinders of the family, and by two planes at unit distance apart and perpendicular to the common axis, we find that $2\pi r dV/dr$ has the same value at the two cylindrical surfaces, so that

$r d\text{V}/dr$ is constant, equal to C, say. Thus $d\text{V}/dr = \text{C}/r$, and $\text{V} = \text{C} \log_e r + \text{D}$. The constants are found from the surface conditions $\text{V}_0 = \text{C} \log_e a + \text{D}$, and $\text{V}_1 = \text{C} \log_e b + \text{D}$. The value of C is therefore $(\text{V}_1 - \text{V}_0)/\log_e (b/a)$. If σ is the surface density at $r = b$, then $4\pi\sigma = -d\text{V}/dn = d\text{V}/dr$, for $r = b$; or $4\pi\sigma = \text{C}/b$. The capacity per unit length = charge ÷ potential difference $= \sigma \cdot 2\pi b / (\text{V}_1 - \text{V}_0) = \frac{1}{2}\text{C}/(\text{V}_1 - \text{V}_0)$ = the reciprocal of $2 \log_e (b/a)$.

Gravitational Potential. The law of gravitation being of the same form as the law of force between electrified particles, calculations of attractions between material bodies can be made to depend on a gravitational potential. The potential due to a mass m may be taken to be m/r as in the electrical case, and Poisson's equation still holds good. The gravitational potential is therefore the potential energy of unit mass, *with sign changed.* Matter is found in distributions of finite density per unit volume; surface density does not occur, so that the first derivatives of the potential are everywhere continuous. As an illustration, consider the potential of a sphere of radius a, and uniform density ρ. Apply the theorem of Gauss to the region within a concentric sphere of radius r, where r is less than a. From symmetry, the potential is a function of r only, and we have $-4\pi r^2 d\text{V}/dr = 4\pi\rho \cdot 4\pi r^3/3$, or $d\text{V}/dr = -4\pi\rho r/3$, and $\text{V} = -2\pi\rho r^2/3 + \text{C}$. The constant C may be determined by calculating the potential at the centre, which is the integral of $4\pi r^2 dr \cdot \rho/r$, or $2\pi\rho a^2$. Hence V, at any internal point, $= 2\pi\rho a^2 - 2\pi\rho r^2/3$. For an *external* sphere r, the theorem of Gauss takes the form $-4\pi r^2 d\text{V}/dr = 4\pi\rho \cdot 4\pi a^3/3$, so that $d\text{V}/dr = -4\pi\rho a^3/(3r^2)$, and $\text{V} = \frac{1}{3} \cdot 4\pi\rho a^3/r = \text{M}/r$, where M is the mass of the sphere. No constant is needed, for the potential (the sum of such terms as q/AP) obviously vanishes when P is infinitely distant from every such point as A. It may be verified from the values found for V that V and $d\text{V}/dr$ are continuous at $r = a$; these conditions might have been used as the basis of alternative methods of treating the problem. It should be observed that the potential (M/r) at an external point is the same as if the whole mass of the sphere were concentrated at its centre. Hence a uniform sphere, and similarly a uniform spherical shell, or one with the density a function of the distance from the centre, attracts an external body as if its mass were all at its centre—a result which is important in astronomy.

Magnetic Potential. The conception of potential is almost as useful for the discussion of fields of magnetic force, due to distributions of magnets and electric currents, as it is in electrostatics. For the development of the theory reference may be made to the treatises on electricity and magnetism named below.

Some solutions of Laplace's equation are given in the article *Spherical Harmonics*.

BIBLIOGRAPHY: F. B. Pidduck, *Treatise on Electricity*; J. H. Jeans, *Mathematical Theory of Electricity and Magnetism*; J. Clerk Maxwell, *Electricity and Magnetism*; R. A. Houstoun, *Introduction to Mathematical Physics*; Kelvin and Tait, *Natural Philosophy* (the chapter on *Attraction*).

POTENTIL'LA. A genus of herbaceous perennials, nat. ord. Rosaceæ, found chiefly in the temperate and cold regions of the northern hemisphere, containing about 120 species. They are tall or procumbent herbs, rarely undershrubs, with digitate or unequally pinnate leaves, and for the most part yellow or white flowers. Several species are British. *P. anserīna* is also called silver-weed, goose-grass, or wild tansy, the leaves of which are greedily devoured by geese; and *P. fragariastrum*, barren strawberry. *P. reptans* is a well-known creeping plant with conspicuous yellow flowers. The roots of *P. anserīna* are eaten in the Hebrides, either raw or boiled. *P. Tormentilla* is used in Lapland and the Orkney Islands both to tan and to dye leather, and also to dye worsted yarn. It is also employed in medicine as a gargle in the case of enlarged tonsils and other diseases of the throat, and for alleviating gripes in cases of diarrhœa.

POTENTIOM'ETER. An electrical instrument which is used for current, pressure, and other measurements of high accuracy. It consists of a wire divided up into a number of lengths of exactly equal resistance all arranged in series; the last of them is stretched over a calibrated scale divided into 1000 parts. The current from a secondary cell passes through the wires, and is adjusted by means of adding to or taking away from the circuit resistances, until there is a drop of electrical pressure of one-tenth of a volt over each section of the wire. In arriving at this state, the electro-motive force obtained from a standard cell is balanced against the drop of pressure in the instrument over the length of wire corresponding to the nominal voltage obtained from such a cell. After calibration in this way the instrument is ready for use, and the standard cell is disconnected.

The use of the instrument in association with standard resistances, in comparing and measuring the magnitudes of resistances, currents, and electrical pressures, as well as other physical values which can be gauged in terms of such electrical units, is very common in test-houses and research-laboratories. Standard instruments complete with standard cell and resistances are manufactured by a number of instrument-makers.

POTEN'ZA. A department of South Italy, in the compartimento of Basilicata, a district nearly corresponding with the ancient Lucania. It has a short western seaboard on the Gulf of Policastro, and a larger eastern coast-line on the Gulf of Taranto, and is traversed by the Apennines. The principal rivers, which all flow eastwards to the Gulf of Taranto, are the Basento, Agri, Sinni, Cavone, and Bradano. Cereals, wines, and oil are produced. The capital is Potenza. Area, 2391 sq. miles; pop. (1931), 350,728.

POTENZA (ancient **Potentia**). A city of Southern Italy, capital of the province of Potenza, on a hill (2700 feet) near the Basento (ancient *Casuentus*), which rises on Mt. Ariosa and falls into the Gulf of Taranto near Metaponto. Potenza is surrounded by mediæval walls and outworks.

Potentia, of Roman origin, was successively destroyed by Frederick II. and Charles of Anjou. It lay lower down the plain at the place now called La Murata, where excavation work has revealed many archæological treasures. During the earthquake of 1857 the modern town fell, and was almost entirely destroyed. Pop. (commune), 25,433.

POTE'RIUM. A genus of plants, nat. ord. Rosaceæ and sub-ord. Sanguisorbeæ. *P. Sanguisorba*, or salad-burnet, which grows on dry and most frequently chalky pastures, is the only British species. It is valuable for fodder, and is used in salad. It has pinnate leaves and tall stems surmounted by dense heads of small flowers.

POT-HOLE. A cavity more or less cylindrical in the bed of a rapid stream, scoured out by detrital matter gyrating in an eddying current of water, sometimes glacier-fed. When the water reaches a plane of stratification in limestone regions, it may produce long shafts or swallow-holes, ultimately forming extensive caverns.

POTI (ancient **Phasis**). A seaport of Georgia, in the Kutais district, Transcaucasia, on the Rion River and the Black Sea. It has extensive harbour works, and is the seaward terminus of the Samtredi-Poti branch (41 miles) of the Transcaucasian Railway, by which it is connected with Tiflis (193 miles). Its chief export is manganese ore from the mines of Tchiaturi. Pop. about 21,000.

The Rion rises between Koshtantau and Kazbek, and has a course of 100 miles. The Ingur rises in the highest part of the Caucasus in South-Western Kutais and enters the Black Sea at Anaklia. These two rivers form an enormous delta which extends behind Poti as a vast alluvial plain. Poti harbour is practically unapproachable in bad weather, but has outer and inner basins protected by concrete moles, and possesses an elevator for loading manganese. There is 1500 yards of quayage.

POT METAL. An alloy of copper and lead, used for making various large vessels employed in the arts. Also a kind of stained glass in which the colours are incorporated with the substance by being added while the glass is in a state of fusion.

POTOCKI (po-tots'ki). An ancient Polish family, taking its name from the castle of Potok, and still holding possessions in Galicia and the Ukraine. Among its most distinguished members was Count Ignazy Potocki (1741-1809), Grand Marshal of Lithuania before the downfall of Poland, and a fellow-patriot of Kosciusko.

POTO'MAC. A river of the United States, which rises in the Alleghany Mountains and is formed by the union of the north and south branches about 15 miles below Cumberland, in Maryland. It forms the boundary between Maryland and Virginia, passes Washington, and after a course of nearly 400 miles flows into Chesapeake Bay, being about 8 miles wide at its mouth. The termination of the tide-water is at Washington, about 125 miles from the sea, and the river is navigable by large ships for that distance. Fifteen miles above Washington the "Great Falls" occur (90 feet), followed by a series of rapids over 1 mile in length, with a cataract 35 feet high.

POTOSÍ. A south-western frontier department of Bolivia, bordering on Chile and Argentina. Traversing the eastern side of the department north to south is the eastern branch of the Andes (Cordillera de los Frailes and Sierras de Chichas). The western side is an arid, saline waste, belonging to the southern extension of the Titicaca basin. East of the Cordillera the district drains to the Pilcomayo. The department is mainly devoted to mining, gold, silver, copper, and tin being produced. Potosí is the capital; other towns are Huanchaco, Tupiza, and Uyuni. Area, 45,031 sq. miles; pop. about 538,521 (or 11·9 per square mile).

POTOSÍ. A mountain of Bolivia, the "silver mountain," once the seat of the richest silver-mine in the world, which has been continuously worked since its discovery in the sixteenth century. Altitude, 15,300 feet.

POTOSÍ. A city of Bolivia, capital of the department of Potosí, on the northern slopes of the *Cerro* (Mt. Potosí), the highest abode of man on the American continent (over 13,600 feet). In the seventeenth century Potosí was the largest town in the New World, and had a population of from 100,000 to 160,000, plus a valuable asset in the richest silver-mine known to mankind. There is a massive granite cathedral, a royal mint dating from 1585, and a Government house.

Potosí was founded in 1547, and was made a *villa imperial* by Charles V. The Spanish did not evacuate the town until 1822, although the struggle for national freedom began in 1810. Owing to the closing of mines in the district the city is now in a state of decay. Pop. 34,083. *See* SUCRE.

POT-POURRI (pō-pū-rē'). The French translation of the name of a Spanish ragout, *olla podrida*. Hence it denotes any medley, musical or literary, and specifically a mixture of dead rose petals, lavender and spices, kept in sachets or porcelain jars.

POTSDAM. A town of Prussia, administrative capital of Brandenburg, on the Havel, 17 miles south-west of Berlin; served by the trunk line to Magdeburg. It is one of the handsomest towns in Germany, and is noted for its palaces, which until the Revolution of 1918 were the residences of the Hohenzollern family. The principal palace was built in 1660 and remodelled in 1750. Immediately to the west, outside the Brandenburg Gate (resembling a Roman triumphal arch), are the palace and park of Sans Souci. The palace, a building of one story, erected under the direction of Frederick the Great, has finely laid out grounds, and an orangery 330 yards long. In the same neighbourhood is the New Palace, a vast brick building exhibiting much gaudy magnificence. Other palaces in the environs are the Marble Palace, the Charlottenhof, and the Babelsberg.

Sugar, beer, soap, wax-cloth, and optical instruments are manufactured. Potsdam was an unimportant place till the Great Elector selected it as a residence and built the royal palace in the town (1660-71). Pop. 60,000.

POT STILL. A form of distilling apparatus so called from its pot-shape and used in the manufacture of spirits. The still is made of copper and directly heated over a coal fire or by steam. This form of still is used chiefly in making Scotch whisky.

POTSTONE (*Lapis ollāris*). Massive talc containing an admixture of chlorite. Its colour is green of various shades; it is greasy and soft, but becomes hard on being exposed to the air. It derives its name from its capability of being made into vases, etc., by turning. It was obtained by the ancients from quarries in the Island of Siphnos and in Upper Egypt. *See* SOAPSTONE; STEATITE; TALC.

POTTERIES, THE. A district of Staffordshire, headquarters of the English earthenware and porcelain manufacture, comprising the towns of Burslem, Hanley, Stoke, Longton, Newcastle-under-Lyme, Tunstall, etc., which unite to form the county borough of Stoke-upon-Trent.

POTTERY AND PORCELAIN. Terms which together describe all objects made from clay and hardened by heat, porcelain being pottery of which the body is vitrified and translucent. The manufacture of pottery is one of the oldest arts, flourishing in the most primitive societies. Shaping by hand or by pressing into a mould long preceded the use of the potter's wheel; and this has in turn been superseded by the use of absorbent moulds, into which a fluid mixture of clay and water is poured, the latter being absorbed by the mould. The most primitive pottery was hardened by the sun's heat, but the use of fire soon became general; and kilns for firing were known in ancient Egypt, modern improvements mainly consisting in the enlargement of kiln capacity and more even distribution of heat.

When *glaze* (a thin coating of glass) was first used is unknown, but it was certainly employed in ancient Egypt. Each type of pottery has its appropriate glaze, the most important being the *alkaline* glazes of silicate of lime or soda, used in Persian pottery; glazes containing *lead*; glazes of *felspar*, very hard and tough, extensively used in China; and *salt* glazes, from the vapour of sodium chloride, used on stoneware.

The decoration of pottery in colour also occurs early in its history. The most primitive method was to paint or daub on natural earths, which in the fire develop a considerable range of colour. Later, substances containing metal compounds came into use, applied before the glaze was fired, and hence generally called *under-glaze* colours; and in China especially, coloured glazes came into use. A subsequent development, first perfected in China, was painting with enamels on the glaze (*on-glaze* colours). In modern times the use of transfers has largely replaced decoration by hand. With colour, the use of iridescent metallic films (*lustre*) was combined in Persia and Syria, whence it spread to Europe; and since the early eighteenth century the use of the precious metals for decoration has been widespread, especially on porcelain.

Turning to the production of individual countries, each has its own special character and beauty. The pottery of ancient Egypt is notable for its rich colour, especially for a blue derived from copper; while that of classic Greece is marked by its distinguished and graceful form.

The Greek vases are unglazed, and are either *black-figured* (the earlier type, decorated in black on a red or cream ground) or *red-figured* (the later type, the background being filled in with black, leaving the decoration in red). Similar in type but far inferior is the contemporary Etruscan ware of Italy; and though technically very perfect, Roman pottery is artistically behind that of Greece.

During the Middle Ages the chief centres of pottery manufacture were in the East, where the traditions of ancient Egypt had to some extent survived. Between the fourth and the fourteenth centuries there developed in Persia and Syria a remarkable art, of which important centres were Rhages and Damascus. Its productions are marked by the application of conventional floral and figure designs in colour to a white ground, the whole being covered with an alkaline glaze, with lustre sometimes added.

Somewhat later came the so-called Turkish pottery, decorated with purely formal designs in brilliant blues, greens, and reds on a white ground. This Eastern pottery was

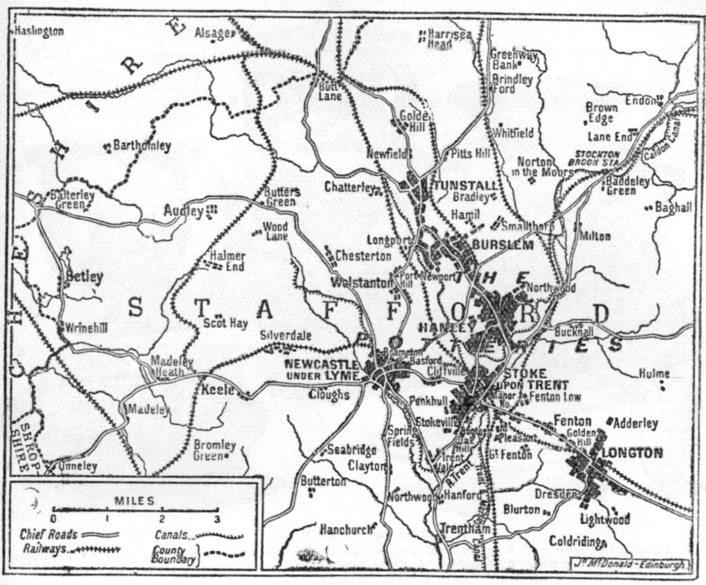

Map of The Potteries

later profoundly to influence European work. In Persia also was produced a species of delicate porcelain; but this substance attained its highest development in China. There, early in the Christian era, a peculiarly hard earthenware of the stoneware type, with a brilliant glaze, was manufactured; and the production of this continued in subsequent centuries, especially during the Ming dynasty (A.D. 1368-1643).

Greek and Roman Vases

1, Stamnos inscribed with name of artist Polygnotos. 2, Amphora by same artist. 3, Krater, Aretine ware, first century B.C. 4, Oinochoe. 5, Kylix, 508 B.C. 6, Vase from Southern Gaul, A.D. 40–70.

Chinese. Therein lay the germ of Chinese porcelain, first made during the T'ang dynasty (A.D. 618-907), though the earliest surviving pieces date from the Sung period (A.D. 960-1259). The line between stoneware and this early porcelain is difficult to draw. They are alike in being vitrified; but the fired clay of the former is generally red or brown compared with the white or cream porcelain biscuit, and is rarely translucent. In its final form Chinese porcelain consisted of a mixture in various proportions of infusible white clay (kaolin), fusible felspathic rock (petuntse), and quartz (sand), with a glaze of petuntse, and is known as true or *hard-paste* porcelain. The earlier porcelain was decorated with glazes of various colours, of which the famous *Celadons* (blue- or yellow-greens) are the best known and highly prized. In the early days of the Ming dynasty there was a great improvement in whiteness and translucency; and partly under Persian influence the use of painted decoration under the glaze developed.

By the fifteenth century the well-known blue-and-white ware and the use of under-glaze red had attained perfection, likewise the egg-shell and perforated porcelain; and towards the end of the sixteenth century the use of enamel on-glaze colours appeared. After a brief period of decline a revival began with the reign of K'ang-Hsi (1662-1722), which lasted to the end of the eighteenth century. From this period date some of the finest examples of Chinese work. Older methods of decoration were revived and new ones invented, such as *powder-blue* grounds, peacock-blue, aubergine-purple, iron-rust, and tea-dust glazes, and the schemes of on-glaze colours known as *famille verte* (wherein green enamel predominates) and *famille rose* (mainly rose and purple).

Japanese. In Japan, under Chinese influence, the manufacture of porcelain became important in the seventeenth century. Notable types are: the *Kakiemon* ware, sparsely decorated on a white ground with floral sprays, birds and animals in red, blue, and green, sometimes called *Imari* ware from the place whence it was exported to Europe; *old Imari* ware, with more crowded decoration in blue, Indian red, and gold; *Hirado* ware, with figure subjects in pale-blue; and *Kaga* porcelain, noted for the brilliancy of its colour.

European. Meanwhile in Europe, where the potter's art had languished, contact with the East produced a revival. In fourteenth-century Spain

Etruscan Vase of Smoked Black Ware with Ornaments in Relief applied from a Mould—about 600–500 B.C.

Hispano-Moresque pottery appears, marked by a brilliant, opaque, white glaze (made by mixing tin oxide with a lead glaze), and by decoration with geometrical and foliage patterns often enclosing heraldic devices, combined sometimes with lustre. This ware inspired in the fifteenth century the *majolica* of Italy, in which tin glaze formed the ground for painted decoration with or without lustre. The chief centres of manufacture were Deruta, Gubbio, Urbino, and Faenza, each using a characteristic type of decoration and colour. In the sixteenth century the use of pictorial decoration reproducing paintings and engravings became general, and began a decline from which there was no recovery.

Elsewhere in Europe progress is marked by the work of Bernard Palissy in France, which is, however, only a perfected type of ordinary pottery; but in the seventeenth and eighteenth centuries France became the centre for the production of *faïence*, a tin-enamelled ware gaily and tastefully decorated in floral and grotesque patterns. In Germany the manufacture of brown and grey *stoneware*, decorated in relief, developed; and in Holland about 1600 appeared the tin-enamelled *Delft* ware, generally decorated in blue, which was exported in large quantities and had many imitations in other countries. In seventeenth-century England, for example, Bristol and Liverpool were centres for such imitations. In Staffordshire, however, a native pottery art grew up, represented by the white-and-drab salt-glazed ware, and by an earthenware made white in substance by the use of selected clays. In this development Josiah Wedgwood played a prominent part. Well known is his *Jasper* ware, an unglazed pottery approximating to porcelain, in which were made the familiar imitations of Greek and Roman ware, with ornament in relief.

The influence of the East is traceable in all European pottery, but it is most evident in porcelain. In Saxony, at the beginning of the eighteenth century, Böttger produced a porcelain akin in appearance and character to that of China, which formed the basis of *Meissen* (incorrectly called *Dresden*) ware. The early pieces imitated Chinese models in form and decoration; but from 1730 to 1775 a distinctive style evolved, at first resembling Imari porcelain, then uniting rococo curves and fantastic ornament with painted scenes in the manner of contemporary artists. Other characteristic products were small figures or groups in biscuit or colour.

Meanwhile in France, at Rouen and St. Cloud, a substance had been manufactured resembling porcelain in its translucency, but which was virtually glass holding clay in suspension. This is artificial or *soft-paste* porcelain, the material of all earlier French porcelain. At Chantilly charming work inspired by Imari ware was produced in this material; but it was the factory founded in 1740 at Vincennes and afterwards moved to Sèvres which became the chief centre of production. After a brief period of submission to Eastern influence the porcelain of Sèvres first shows a style of rococo curves and fantastic ornament, then one of greater restraint in form and decorative motives under the influence of classic art. At the same time, by the use of colours (notably the *rose du Barry*) and gold, its decoration became increasingly lavish and ostentatious. Other characteristic products were the charming statuettes in biscuit, from models by leading sculptors of the day. In 1763 the secret of true porcelain was discovered; and this tended ultimately to displace other types, and to hasten the artistic degeneration which had already begun. In direct imitation of French work were the porcelains of eighteenth-century Italy, typified by that of *Capo-di-Monte*, whence in turn came many of the models and workmen for the factory at *Buen-Retiro*, near Madrid.

In England the earlier porcelains are typified by those of Bow and Chelsea, which are of soft-paste, and in form and decoration owe everything to Eastern and Continental influence. The two factories were ultimately absorbed by the Derby factory, whose products mark no artistic advance, but reflect the growth of the neo-classic movement. At Worcester, also, foreign influence was strong, and there was first developed the method of transfer printing. About 1800 Spode perfected a method of preparing porcelain by using bone-ash in place of glass, and henceforward this became the distinctively English porcelain, which is easier to handle and less fragile than the older soft-paste. The nineteenth century has seen immense growth in the scale of pottery manufacture, but has produced little but mechanical and inferior repetitions of earlier designs.

BIBLIOGRAPHY: Technical: A. Brogniart, *Traité des arts céramiques*; W. Burton, *Porcelain*. Descriptive and Historical: H. B. Walters, *Ancient Pottery*; D. E. Fortnum, *Majolica*; M. L. Solon, *Old French Faïence*, *Ancient Art Stoneware*, and *Old English Porcelain*; A. H. Church, *English Earthenware*; S. W. Bushell, *Oriental Ceramic Art*; E. S. Auscher, *French Porcelain*.

POTTERY MANUFACTURE. The successful manufacture of pottery is to-day a highly scientific process requiring the greatest care and special knowledge of chemistry, engineering, and factory administration.

The general term "pottery" includes earthenware and chinaware. The processes of manufacture in both classes are roughly the same, but differ in detail and composition of bodies. Earthenware and semi-porcelain bodies consist of ball clay, china clay, flint, and Cornish stone. The first two items give the clay its plasticity in working; the flint and stone are the muscle of the body, and give it its strength. In china the ball clay is eliminated, and ground bone is used in its place. This gives the translucent appearance and the superior whiteness. The above components vary in their proportions according to the class of goods it is intended to manufacture.

The first process is the calcining of the flint, to get rid of impurities. It is then ground in cylinders or in pans. A pan is a large vat, paved with hard chert stones. Blocks of stone are kept moving over the bottom of the pan by means of a powerful revolving shaft. The Cornish stone is also ground, water being added in each case. The ball clay and china clay are crushed or blunged in separate blungers, water also being added. Inside these blungers are large revolving arms which reduce the materials to a fine milky substance.

When all these ingredients are ground sufficiently fine, they are run off into a "mixing arc," the correct proportion of each being carefully measured and a cobalt stain being added. This slop material is then pumped by powerful pumps into machine-presses which squeeze out the water, leaving the clay substance. Although now solid, it is not yet fit for the potter, as at this stage it is not sufficiently plastic. To obtain the requisite plasticity it is passed through a pug-mill, from which it comes out ready for use by the potter.

The next step is to shape the clay. The *potter's wheel*, one of the most ancient of tools, may be used for articles of rounded form. The wheel resembles an ordinary turning-lathe, but the surface of the chuck is horizontal instead of vertical. The chuck is in fact a revolving table, in the centre of which a piece of clay is placed, which the potter, or "thrower" as he is called, begins to shape with his hands. The clay rises in a spiral column, is pressed down, allowed to rise again, and finally brought down to be centred or trued. By pressing his thumbs into the clay, the thrower next forms a cylinder, which under his manipulation soon assumes the contour he is aiming at. The article, thus roughly shaped, is then detached from the revolving table and dried, after which it is taken to a lathe and polished with a tool. The handles and other appendages are fitted on at this stage.

Ware of all kinds is now generally made in a mould. Each article made has its own mould, which is made of plaster, run very hard. The life of a mould for good-class ware is only about four months, owing to the action of the clay on the mould surface. It is necessary to have sufficient moulds for a complete "round" of ware, as every article made requires a separate mould. The top surface of the mould is made according to the article wanted, and the bottom of the mould is made to fit a jolly head. Cups, bowls, and other "ringware" are jollyed inside, that is to say, the moulds fit inside the head. Flat ware is jollyed outside, the mould fitting *over* the head. The tool which is to shape the article, either inside or outside, fits into the jolly. This tool is usually termed the "rib." The blocks of clay are cut into strips by the maker, and for flat ware a sufficient amount of the clay is flattened out (into a "bat") to cover the surface of the mould. It is then run down with the tool, which forms the back of the article, the front being formed by the mould. For cups, bowls, etc., the clay is made into a ball and thrown into the mould and jollyed.

The ware on the moulds is next put into heated drying-chambers until it is dry enough to come off the moulds, after which it is carried into a "green room," where it is assembled for placing into the ovens. Ware is first placed in saggars, which are receptacles shaped like hat-boxes made out of special clay and marl and fired, and are of convenient sizes for the various articles made. These saggars are placed tier upon tier in an oven which is completely sealed up and fired for a period of about fifty to sixty hours. The oven is then allowed to cool down, the ware is drawn, and transferred to the "biscuit warehouse," the ware at this stage being known as "biscuit." It is now quite white, but is absorbent or porous, water being able to soak through in a few minutes.

In the biscuit warehouse the ware is sorted and brushed, and is made ready for the next process. This varies according to the type of finished article which is wanted. If this is plain white ware, the biscuit is sent direct to the dipping-house, where it is dipped in tanks containing glaze. This gives the fine glossy appearance of the article as seen in the home. If the ware is wanted for decoration, the biscuit ware is sent up to the printing-shop. The prints are taken off engraved copper plates, the latter being filled with colour according to requirements. The prints are then transferred on to the ware, hardened on in a muffle, and then sent into the dipping-house for glazing.

After the ware is dipped, it is again put into saggars for placing in "glost ovens." This time each article is separated by stilts or spurs, as without this precaution the ware would stick together during firing. The length of time required for this firing is about thirty hours. After cooling, the oven is drawn and the ware selected in the "glost warehouse," where it is laid off ready for packing to the distributor. The goods are now ready for use, but further "on glost" decorations can still be made with "enamel" colours if wanted. The colour is "brought up" and hardened on in a glost muffle. Thus the more highly decorated goods require more firings. The complete time required for making an article varies with the decoration wanted. It is difficult for the everyday user to understand that even the cheapest white cup requires from twenty-one to twenty-eight days to make.

POTTO (*Perodicticus potto*). An animal of the lemur sub-order inhabiting West Africa, and averaging about 8 inches in length. The name is also given to the *Kinkajou* (q.v.).

POTT'S DISEASE, or **ANGULAR CURVATURE.** A tuberculous disease of the spine. It was first accurately described by Pott towards the end of the eighteenth century. The tuberculous condition arises in the fore-part of the spinal vertebræ, which become more or less destroyed, thus leading to a sharp curvature of the spine in the affected region.

Features. The outstanding features are: (1) *Pain,* which at first may only be brought out by careful examination, and is of two types —local, arising in the region of the affected vertebræ, and referred pain, due to pressure on, or irritation of, the nerves as they emerge from the spinal column. This pain is referred to the region of the body which these nerves supply. (2) *Rigidity* of the spine, which arises from the attempt to keep fixed the painful part; hence the pain in attempting to touch the ground keeps the back stiff and straight and bends the hips and knees. (3) *Deformity,* which occurs as a result of bony union between the damaged vertebræ, the extent of the deformity depending chiefly on the number of vertebræ involved. There is a marked bulging of the spine at the affected region, with compensatory changes in the thorax; the breast-bone becomes convex, while the ribs are crowded together. In a severe case the patient is stunted in growth, and presents the appearance of the typical hunchback. (4) *Abscess-formation*, which occurs first in front of the vertebræ and then spreads to the sides of the spine, and finally burrows in various directions according to the portion of the spine affected. Thus there may arise abscesses in the neck, in the chest-wall, in the lumbar region, or the psoas abscess in the groin or thigh. When such abscesses occur, symptoms arise from pressure and irritation of the surrounding parts, and a hectic type of temperature is produced. (5) *Paralysis* of the lower part of the body, which only arises in severe and neglected cases, and is due to pressure on the spinal cord in rapid and acute forms of the disease.

When left to itself, Pott's disease as a rule progresses; the bone lesions become extensive, and abscesses are likely to form. If treated early and efficiently, repair by bony union takes place, and the disease is arrested, though some damage is inevitable. The chief essential in treatment is early and complete immobilisation of the spine by mechanical support—by plaster jackets, splints, or similar contrivance. The patient suffering from Pott's disease is liable to be affected by tuberculosis of other organs, and preventive measures against tuberculosis should always be adopted.

POTTSVILLE. A city of Pennsylvania, United States, the county seat of Schuylkill county, on the Schuylkill River; served by the Lehigh Valley, the Pennsylvania, and the Philadelphia & Reading Railways. It is in the centre of the great anthracite coal region, and has forges, rolling-mills, machine-factories, and railway repair-shops. John Pott founded the city in 1804. It was a centre of the Molly Maguires (q.v.), and became the county seat in 1851. Pop. 24,300.

POUCHED MOUSE, or **POCKET MOUSE.** A genus of American rodents with large cheek-pouches, long tails, and hind-legs specially adapted for leaping. The best-known species (*Dipodomys phillipsi*) lives in the desert parts of California, and subsists chiefly on roots, grasses, and seeds.

POUDRETTE (pö-dret′). The name given to a powdery manure obtained from night-soil. It takes a long time to prepare, is pulverulent, of a brown colour, and almost inodorous. Thon's poudrette has the following percentages of useful constituents: nitrogen, 4 to 6; phosphoric acid anhydride, 3; potash, 2 to 3. It is liable to contain disease germs, is difficult to manufacture, and unlikely to be used on a large scale.

POUGHKEEPSIE. A city of New York, United States, the county seat of Dutchess county, on Hudson River; served by the New York Central & Hudson River, the New York, New Haven, & Hartford, the West Shire, and other railways, and by Hudson River steamboats. There is a cantilever bridge of 6767 feet in length (2260 feet without approaches) spanning the Hudson at this point. Poughkeepsie is famous as the "city of colleges," which include Vassar College (1878) for women, Riverview Military Academy (1836), Putnam and Lyndon Halls (girls), and St. Faith's (1888), removed from Saratoga in 1904. Poughkeepsie was founded by Dutch settlers about 1698, and was the seat of the Convention of 1788, at which the Federal Constitution was adopted. It became a city in 1854. Pop. 40,288.

POULTICE, or **CATAPLASM.** A soft, moist preparation applied externally to some part of the body, and generally put on as hot as possible. It is usually made of linseed-meal, oatmeal, or bread-crumbs formed into a paste with hot water, then enclosed in thin cotton or linen, and applied to the skin. Mustard and other remedies may be added to induce special effects.

POULTON-LE-FYLDE. Urban district and market town of Lancashire, on the River Wyre; it is 3 miles from Blackpool. Pop. (1931), 3366.

POULTRY AND POULTRY-FARMING. Poultry is a general name for all domesticated birds bred for the table or kept for their eggs. The birds commonly included in this designation are the common fowl, the pea-fowl, the guinea-fowl, the turkey, goose, and duck, but it is the first of these that is mainly dealt with here.

In poultry-farming for profit it is necessary to classify the various breeds of poultry in a manner suitable for practical guidance as apart from the classification of the naturalist; and for this purpose three main factors are to be considered, viz. egg-production, meat-bearing properties, and maternal instincts. No breed of poultry can be expected to excel in both egg- and meat-production, and increased development in one quality will certainly be at the expense of the other. The smaller fowls are usually the most prolific egg-producers, and, as a general rule, the larger the bird the lower the productivity. Nor does size of skeleton and bone necessarily indicate an abundance of flesh, for in this case also medium-sized fowls are supreme, producing by far the greatest amount of flesh in proportion to the total weight. The properties of both egg- and meat-production are combined in a " general purpose " or " utility " breed of birds, which, while they are not so prolific as non-sitters, are disposed to lay better in winter and possess much superior laying qualities to the table breeds, although they cannot compare with them in either the quality or the quantity of the flesh produced. These utility breeds attain a fair size, and are more marketable than non-sitters. As a result of these considerations and of prolonged experiment, the best-known races are divided as follows:

Laying and Non-sitting. Ancona, Brackel, Campine, Hamburg, Houdan, Leghorn, Scotch Grey, Redcap, Minorca.

Table. Courtes Pattes, Bresse, Crève-cœur, Dorking, Game, Indian Game, Sussex, La Flèche.

Utility. Faverolles, Langshans, Wyandottes, Orpingtons, Rhode Island Reds, Malines, Plymouth Rock.

Laying Ducks. Indian Runner and Pekin.

Table Ducks. Aylesbury, Blue Swedish, Huttegem, Merchtem, Rouen.

All turkeys and geese are bred primarily for table purposes.

Systems of Farming. In the strict sense of the term, " poultry-farming " is not synonymous with " poultry-keeping," nor does it necessarily mean the systematic use year after year of ground covered with poultry-runs, housing large numbers of fowls. This acceptation of the term " poultry farming " is certainly misleading, and the term must be regarded, in the wider sense, as meaning that poultry is the primary consideration, but that farming, including the tillage of the soil, enters into the business.

These considerations being kept in view, there are four different systems in which fowls can be kept both profitably and in health, viz. free range, extensively, semi-intensively, and intensively. In free-range systems the fowls are allowed absolute liberty to wander over an unlimited area. The extensive method consists in the erection of large runs provided with roosting-houses. The fowls are fed and live entirely inside the runs. Semi-intensive methods aim at compactness in housing. A large number of birds (400 to the acre) are kept in houses provided with scratching-sheds, inside of which all grain is scattered and food is laid down. Attached to the houses are small runs in which the birds may take the requisite amount of exercise. By this method it is claimed that birds may be kept indoors under summer conditions throughout the winter, enjoying exercise in the runs when the weather is favourable. The intensive system has for its object the maintenance of fowls in a similar manner to cage-birds; this is to say, they are kept in complete confinement. Geese, ducks, and turkeys, however, cannot be kept under such conditions.

Feeding of Fowls. In its primitive state the hen did not lay an egg a day, but since its adoption by man for domestic purposes it has been compelled to do so by systematic over-feeding. The science of poultry-feeding, therefore, may be summarised broadly as the art of forcing a hen to take an absurd quantity of egg- and flesh-producing food, without exactly killing her. There are two great schools among modern poultry-farmers, the " wets " and the " drys," the former favouring the system of wet mash feeding, and the other pinning their faith to dry meals and grain. Both systems have shown good results under expert manipulation, although this is not admitted by the trade organs of either party.

Albuminoid Ratio. All methods of scientific feeding are dependent for their ultimate value as stimulants to production upon a properly balanced and carefully administered diet, comprising the three great classes of nourishing constituents, albuminoids (proteins), fats, and carbohydrates, in their proper proportions. A hen cannot produce eggs, flesh, and healthy chickens on a diet of worms, ham-rinds, and household scraps, which are so often employed with positively disastrous results. The flavour of the egg and its food value, as well as the quality of the flesh, are dependent upon the feeding of the bird that is producing them, and for the purpose of maintaining definite standards a test known as the " albuminoid ratio " is employed. To work out the food value of any given food, it is necessary to find what proportion the protein matter present in the food bears to the fats plus the carbohydrates. To reduce the fats to carbohydrate value they are multiplied by $2\frac{1}{4}$,* and the result is added to the carbohydrates. This total divided by the proteins gives the albuminoid ratio. For example, a

* This is a handy approximation, and may be taken as a constant.

diet consists of wheat. A food table shows the value of wheat to be as follows:

Albuminoids, 13·0.
Fats or oils, 1·5.
Carbohydrates, 66·4.

Fats multiplied by $2\frac{1}{4} = 1{\cdot}5 \times 2{\cdot}25 = 3{\cdot}375$. Carbohydrate value of fats.
3·375 added to 66·4 (carbohydrates) = 69·775. Total carbohydrate value of wheat.
69·775 divided by 13·0 (albuminoids) = 5·37. Albuminoid ratio of wheat.

The albuminoid ratio, then, is roughly 1 in $5\frac{1}{3}$. A perfect poultry food has a ratio of 1 to $3\frac{1}{2}$ for laying hens, and 1 to $4\frac{1}{2}$, or 1 to 5, is considered a good ratio for other classes. In calculating the ratio for a complete poultry food it is necessary to take the values of the ingredients separately, and add up the total albuminoids and total carbohydrates before proceeding with the above calculation. It should be noted that a hen in full lay eats twice as much food as at any other period, and must be kept plentifully supplied with fresh, clean, cold water, as well as oyster-shell or a suitable equivalent for the supply of the lime required in making the egg-shell. Grit is also a vital necessity. It promotes assimilation and digestion in the gizzard.

Amount of Food. Over-feeding is to be avoided, for not only does a fat hen cease to lay, but over-stimulating food or an excess of food is the cause of most general diseases and of the majority of deaths from natural causes. The amount of food required per hen can only be judged by inspection. No two flocks are alike, and no flock demands an equal amount on two successive days or even at different meals. Hens that are not laying well or are moulting (i.e. casting their feathers after the summer season) should not receive a full supply of food; the nature of the range and the season of the year also exert considerable influence upon the amount of food required. It is general in Great Britain to give three meals or more in a day. Some supply "mash" in the morning and grain at night; others reverse this principle.

A good system provides for an early morning mash, midday grain ration, grain ration for "tea," and a very small quantity of grain again before roosting-time. Twenty minutes are allowed for the consumption of the morning mash. Two ounces per head is the average grain ration (wheat, oats, maize, buckwheat, etc.), and green-stuffs, grit, shell, and water are always kept at hand. Where skimmed milk is obtainable, adult fowls derive great benefit from partaking of a few good draughts, but the meat (mostly protein) ration in the mash must be cut down or cut out altogether where milk forms a part of the diet, for the casein of milk is a powerful nitrogenous or protein (albuminous) substance. Fish-meal tends to impart a fishy flavour to the eggs, and should not be employed indiscriminately.

Soil. The supreme question in the United Kingdom for all who take up poultry-farming is not climate but soil. While eggs can be produced on all soils, the best eggs are the product of hens living on the best soils. Chickens grow slowly upon cold, heavy land, and such conditions are naturally against the

Brown Leghorn Cock

production of table poultry or the quick raising of turkeys, both of which require a kindly soil, one which is naturally dry but is at the same time prolific in its vegetable growth. Experience has shown that it takes from three to four weeks longer to raise a chicken to killing-age upon heavy land than upon lighter soils, and when fully grown it is not nearly so good in quality of flesh. Eggs may be produced in any part of the country, but there are considerable limitations in the case of first-class table fowls.

Breeding. The improvement in stock of every kind is almost wholly dependent upon special breeding-farms which also introduce crosses of specific qualities, and this is especially the case in poultry-farming. Improvement in the qualities of fowls is not a part of the ordinary work of poultry-farming, and is generally left entirely to specialists and showmen. What vitally concerns the small farmer is the propagation of his stock and its increase in numbers, value, and productivity. Eggs are not "set" by progressive farmers nowadays, who cannot afford to lose a hen for three weeks, and incubators of varying sizes and different construction are almost exclusively employed. When a hen becomes "broody," or "clockin" as it is called in Scotland, she is cooped up in a coop made of spars within sight of her pen, and speedily recovers her laying powers when subjected to the persuasion of a plentiful supply of fresh, cold air, for a hen will not sit where she cannot generate heat. This method is humane and simple, and has proved that there is only one cure for broodiness—great discomfort.

It has been said that "the cock is the principal bird in any pen," and undoubtedly he plays a vital part during the breeding season. A yearling cock should generally be mated with second-season hens, although breeders are not unanimous on the question. The number of hens to one cock depends on the breed, age, and vitality of the cock, and no hard-and-fast rule can therefore be laid down. A heavy-breed cock (e.g. Rhode Island Red, Orpington, Plymouth Rock, Sussex, etc.) should have from six to twelve hens, and in the lighter breeds as many as twenty hens may be allotted on a free range, with a reduction to eight or twelve when in confinement.

As a rule the influences exerted by the parents on the progeny are widely divergent, but, generally speaking, the male influences shape and exterior build and appearance, while the female controls temperament, size, habits, and constitution. For many reasons it is not customary to recognise eggs as being "fertilised" until a week or ten days have elapsed from the date of mating. Eggs for hatching should always be stored with the broad dome uppermost. They should be of average size, with smooth shells and a uniformity in shape, and should be kept in a dry place at a temperature of between 41° and 59° F. The fresher the eggs when incubated the stronger, and healthier generally, will be the chickens they produce. During incubation the eggs should frequently be tested. Broomhead says: "Test the eggs after they have been incubated seven days. If all has gone well, the germ with the encircling membrane then presents the appearance of a semi-transparent circular spot floating at the top of the egg when held sideways, and at the seventh day it extends over nearly one-half of the interior surface of the shell. If the process of hatching is perfectly satisfactory, this 'spot' floats round in the egg when the latter is turned in the hand. Should the germ apparently adhere to the shell when the egg is first removed, it will probably free itself when the egg cools; if not, there is too little moisture, and danger to the embryo.

It is at this stage that what is sometimes described as the 'spider' may be seen. This spider-like appearance is produced by the dark eyes of the chick—developed to an abnormal extent—forming a resemblance to the body of a spider, the larger blood-vessels circulating from the body through the enveloping membrane and forming the spider's legs. A few days later the enveloping membrane expands still more, thickens, and is covered with minute blood-vessels. The egg then presents, throughout the greater part of its surface, an opaque appearance. The small end and perhaps a part of one side are so far transparent that the light can be seen through them. This, however, gradually decreases, until at about the sixteenth day the egg is quite black, except at the large end, where the air-vesicle, now considerably enlarged, can be seen." By these signs the poultry-farmer is enabled to judge the progress of incubation and to shape his plans accordingly. The average period of incubation is twenty-one days.

BIBLIOGRAPHY: W. W. Broomhead, *Poultry for the Many*, which is quite the best general treatise on poultry-farming extant; also articles in *The Standard Cyclopedia of Modern Agriculture*.

POUNCE. Powder formerly sprinkled over newly-written matter to prevent the ink spreading or blotting. Composed of sand, cuttle-bone, or some resinous substance, it was shaken out from a box with a perforated lid, called a *pounce-pot*. The use of pounce died out after the introduction of blotting-paper.

POUND. In English law, an enclosure for keeping cattle which have strayed on another man's ground, until they are redeemed. A pound may belong to a parish or village or to a manor.

POUND. An English weight of two different denominations, *avoirdupois* and *troy*. The pound *troy* contains 5760 grains, and is divided into 12 ounces; the pound *avoirdupois* contains 7000 grains, and is divided into 16 ounces. The *pound*, or *pound sterling*, the highest monetary denomination used in British money accounts, and equal to 20 shillings, was so called from originally being equal to a quantity of silver weighing one pound. The pound is strictly a money of account, the coin representing it being the sovereign.

POUSSIN (pö-saŋ), **Gaspar.** French landscape-painter, born in Rome in 1613, died there 1675. His real name was Dughet, but he took the name of his brother-in-law Nicolas Poussin, whose pupil and protégé he became. He lived mostly in Rome or its neighbourhood, and concentrated on a romantic type of landscape-painting, in which figures played a quite subordinate part. He possessed extraordinary facility of execution, so that his works are very numerous, specimens being found in all the chief collections in Europe. He is well represented in the National Gallery.

POUSSIN, Nicolas. French painter, born near Les Andelys in 1594, died at Rome 1665. He studied in his native place and at Paris, where he had acquired some reputation when in 1624 he went to Italy to improve himself in his art. There he worked in the studio of Domenichino, and studied anatomy, perspective, and the art of classical antiquity with singular intensity. In Rome poverty and ill-health hampered him for a time; but he was assisted by a Frenchman, Jacques Dughet, and by him tended through an illness brought on by over-work. In 1630 Poussin married Dughet's daughter. Eventually he found liberal patrons in Cardinal Barberini, for whom he painted the *Death of Germanicus,* strongly under the influence of Giulio Romano; and in the Cavaliere Cassiano del Pozzo, who commissioned the celebrated *Seven Sacraments,* now at Belvoir Castle. In 1639-40 he painted for Cardinal Richelieu four *Bacchanals,* of which one (*The Triumph of Silenus*) is now in the National Gallery.

In 1639 he was invited to return to France, and he became first painter to Louis XIII., with a pension of 3000 livres. From 1640 to 1642 he resided in Paris, producing there cartoons for tapestry and a series of paintings for the great gallery of the Louvre; but the rivalry of French painters and the want of appreciation of his works caused him to return to Rome, where he lived until his death. During this period his greatest work was done, including a second set of *Seven Sacraments, Shepherds in Arcadia,* and *Phocion*; followed by *The Death of Phocion* and *Polyphemus.*

Landscape played an increasingly great part in Poussin's work. The colour of his early work is apt to be hot and heavy; but for massive, logical, coherent design he is unsurpassed, and his influence on art, especially French art, has been profound. His early work is well represented in England, notably in the National Gallery and at Dulwich. The Louvre contains the most complete collection of his later pictures.

POWAN (*Coregŏnus clupeoides*). A fish inhabiting Lochs Lomond and Eck, in Scotland, and also known as the freshwater herring. It is of the same genus as the pollan and vendace (q.v.).

POWELL, Lieutenant-General Sir Robert Stephenson Smyth Baden-G.C.V.O., G.C.M.G., K.C.B. British soldier, born in 1857. He joined the 13th Hussars in 1876 and served in India, Afghanistan, and South Africa; was assistant military secretary in South Africa from 1887 to 1889, and in Malta from 1890 to 1893; on special service in 1895 in Ashanti in command of native levies, and breveted lieutenant colonel; was chief staff-officer in the Matabele campaign, and became brevet colonel; from 1897 to 1899 was in command of the 5th Dragoon Guards as lieutenant-colonel. In the South African War of 1899-1902 he distinguished himself by his defence of Mafeking from Oct., 1899, till May, 1900, and was made major-general. He was Inspector-General of Cavalry from 1903 to 1907. In 1910 he retired from the army in order to further on the organisation of Boy Scouts which he had founded two years previously, and was made K.C.B. and K.C.V.O. in 1909, a baronet in 1921, G.C.V.O. in 1923, and G.C.M.G. in 1927. In 1929 he was raised to the peerage and took the title of Lord Baden-Powell of Gilwell. His works include: *Pig-sticking, Cavalry Instruction, Downfall of Prempeh, Matabele Campaign, Scouting for Boys, My Adventures as a Spy, Girl-Guiding, Rovering to Success,* and *Life's Snags.*

POWER OF ATTORNEY. In law, a written instrument whereby one person is authorised to act for another as his agent or attorney, either generally or in a special transaction.

POWER TRANSMISSION. The distribution of power from its place of generation to the points of usage can be effected in many different ways, such as mechanical, by means of some type of mechanism; electrical, either by means of direct or alternating currents; by hydraulic means; or by compressed air. In every case there is some point where the generation of power can be effected most economically, which may be termed the "centre of gravity" of the load. Frequently it is not possible to generate at this point because of lack of natural resources or a dearth of suitable sites at reasonable prices. The power obtained from the fall of water may be conveyed to distant cities. In this case it is most unlikely that the load centre is anywhere near the station, but the location of the available water-supply is the sole determining factor in selecting the point of power generation. If power is to be generated by steam engines or turbines, the provision of cheap and plentiful condensing water will considerably affect the determination of the site of the power station and the magnitude of the running costs. The various prime movers are dealt with in the articles *Steam-engine*; *Turbines, Steam*; and *Internal-combustion Engines*. Hydraulic power transmission is treated of in the article *Hydraulics and Hydraulic Machinery*. The transmission of power by compressed air is dealt with under the headings *Pneumatic Power Transmission* and *Compressed Air*.

Mechanical transmission of power is common in engineering, chemical, and other industrial works. In this case the power, whether obtained from an engine or electric motor, drives main shafting by means of belts and pulleys (*see* PULLEY), and the various machines receive their drives from the shafting. Suitable speeds of running for shafting are, for metal-cutting machines, 200 revolutions per minute; for woodworking machines, 250 revolutions per minute; and for cotton and woollen mills, 300 revolutions per minute. Counter-shafts are interposed between the main shafts and the machines, and when fitted with cone pulleys make possible a variation in the speed of running. The use of fast and loose pulleys on the counter-shaft serves to allow the machines to be stopped and started at will. In cotton-mills rope driving is very common. The pulleys are provided with grooves in which the ropes run. Ropes of hemp or manila do not wear so well as cotton. With large pulleys, small cotton ropes commonly last twelve or more years. Chain driving is highly efficient, is positive, and there is no possibility of slip. This system gives a calculated speed ratio exactly, and whether the chains are tight or slack they will grip the sprockets. Little space is taken up by chain drives, which are very suitable for distances too long for gearing and too short for belts.

The efficiency of transmission of power by shafting is much lower than with electricity and separate motors for each machine, the values being about 40 per cent and 65 per cent respectively. The use of separate motors for each machine has much to recommend it. The machine shop is then free from all overhead shafting, and there is absolute freedom to chose sites for machines to suit the continuous progress of the work upon the billets.

Electrical Power Transmission. The lines of development of modern schemes of electricity distribution have followed the progress in improvement of design of the individual components of the plant. In early days electricity was generated at comparatively low pressures by dynamos coupled to slow-running steam-engines. Later the high-speed steam-engine became a practical proposition as a result of the experimental work of R. K. Morcom and P. Willans. This step was of considerable importance, as dynamos could then be designed for higher speeds of running, for which they were eminently suited. When the steam-turbine was developed another change of conditions was produced, as the turbine must be run at a very high speed if economical working is required. With the increase in generator speeds and the sizes of units the whole design of a power station was changed.

The old arrangement of separate boilers for each engine set, either as completely separate units or with a ring-main system of steam pipes to permit the connection of any boiler to any engine, gave place to the concentration of power generation in some few large units each fed with steam from a bank of boilers. Power-station design became largely a question of providing boiler space, and in some large stations in congested areas the boiler-house was divided into sections on two or more floor-levels to keep down the area requirements of the station.

The first change in systems of distribution was from simple low-pressure transmission, with its heavy first cost because of the amount of copper in the cables, to the three-wire system, with pressure differences between the two outer mains and the neutral just as great as is permitted under the Government regulations. The first cable is at a potential as high above that of the neutral or second as that of the third is below it. The neutral wire only carries the out-of-balance currents, which are never considerable, and it is usually made of half the cross-section of the others. The weight of copper in the cables of a three-wire system is only five-eighths of that required for a simple two-wire system transmitting an equal amount of power. A five-wire system of distribution was installed in the centre of Manchester, but it is doubtful whether the system has any appreciable advantage over the three-wire system. Electrical transmission from central stations at high pressure, and usually by alternating currents, to sub-stations where the pressure is reduced to a value within the limits prescribed in the Government regulations, and where necessary the electricity is converted into the continuous-current type, later became standard practice. All the large schemes in this country work on this system, which permits economical transmission over large areas, with a considerable amount of freedom in the selection of a site for the generating station and economical generation by large power units.

The present tendency in electrical power-station design is towards the use of superheated steam at very high pressures in turbines of very great power. The economic advantage of using very high pressure steam has many advocates, but the additional expense of the production of such steam in boilers of high first cost and maintenance charges, together with the increased cost of the equipment necessary for its transmission and use, must be set against the financial gain arising from any slight increase in thermodynamic efficiency. An endeavour is being made to link up the electricity supply systems in areas, a number of which have already been defined by the electricity commissioners.

The Glasgow Corporation electricity scheme may be cited as a modern example of electricity generation and transmission. In the new power station at Dalmarnock the turbo-alternator units have a normal capacity of 15,000 kilowatts, but can carry a load of 18,750 kilowatts continuously. Electricity is generated at 6500 volts, and is passed to a transformer from which a supply at 20,000 volts is obtained. This high-pressure three-phase supply is carried by underground cables to distributing centres in the city, where the pressure is reduced by the use of sets of three single-phase transformers to 6500 volts to feed the main cables. This supply is converted into direct current, which is distributed on the three-wire system with 250 volts between each outer cable and the neutral or 500 volts across the two outer cables.

Underground cables are armoured with steel wire, and housed in wooden cases filled in with bitumen or drawn through earthenware pipes. Overhead wires are used in many places for the transmission of electrical power. They are less expensive to install than underground cables, and have also the advantage that additional circuits can be connected at very little cost. The overhead wires are usually supported on built-up steel lattice poles, tubular poles such as are used for electric tramway purposes, or wooden poles in pairs with cross-bracings. Porcelain insulators are most commonly used to support the cable lines, but glazed earthenware and glass are sometimes employed. The insulators are large and formed with petticoats and hoods to make leakage only possible over a path of considerable length. The magnitude of the electrical pressure available at any point in the system depends upon the nearness to the station. The drop in electrical pressure is due to the resistance of the cables. Subject to their capability of carrying the greatest currents required without injury, the cables should have cross-sections which are determined from purely economic considerations. Lord Kelvin discovered the relationship between the cost of a cable and the electrical losses which its use entails. This he enunciated in what is now known as Kelvin's Law, which states: "The economical cross-sectional area of a cable is that for which the annual cost of energy lost just equals the annual interest on the capital invested." At this point of equality the sum of the two charges becomes a minimum.

Electricity is sometimes transmitted on the constant-current system, as, for example, the Thury system in use by the Metropolitan Supply Company. For this type of transmission a number of series-wound generators are connected in series to supply a number of loads also connected in series, the loads being usually motors to drive generators in the sub-stations. Advantages such as the use of high pressure, freedom from induction, capacity, and other problems incidental to alternating-current systems, and the possibility of connecting up heterogeneous generating systems, may lead to considerable extension of its use, particularly in area linking-up schemes.

The transmission of power from the prime movers used on ships to the propellers provides the designer with a series of interesting problems with a series of possible solutions. It is necessary to keep the speed of running of the propellers down to some low value if economical running and efficiency are required, while for the same conditions the power plant (for example, turbines) may require to be run at very high speeds. The methods in use are the introduction of mechanical gearing of the double helical type due to Sir Charles A. Parsons (which is described under the heading *Gearing*), Föttinger hydraulic transformer, or electric propulsion. The hydraulic transformer consists of two parts, first, two centrifugal pump wheels keyed to the turbine shaft, which supply water under pressure to the second part, namely reaction water-turbines on the propeller shaft. Electricity generated by turbine-driven dynamos or alternators is used to operate electric motors on the propeller shafts. This method is used on some of the American battleships.

BIBLIOGRAPHY: E. Butler, *Transmission Gears*; W. C. Popplewell, *Compressed Air*; J. R. Dick and F. Fernie, *Electric Mains and Distributing Systems*; Sir John F. C. Snell, *Power House Design*.

POYNINGS' LAW, or **THE STATUTE OF DROGHEDA.** An Act of the Irish Parliament, passed in 1495, whereby all general statutes before that time made in England were declared of force in Ireland. Another article of Poynings' Law secured an initiative of legislation to the English Privy Council, the Irish Parliament having simply a power of acceptance or rejection of proposed legislation. It was so named from Sir Edward Poynings, Deputy of Ireland under Henry VII. in 1494, when he suppressed the revolt of Perkin Warbeck.

POYNTER, Sir Edward John. British painter, born in Paris 1836, died in 1919. Educated at Westminster School and Ipswich, he received his art training at the Royal Academy and under Gleyre in Paris; gained a reputation by *Israel in Egypt* (1867) and *The Catapult* (1868); A.R.A. in 1869, R.A. in 1876, president of the Royal Academy and knighted in 1896, created a baronet in 1902. He was Slade professor of art in University College, London, from 1871 to 1875, and director of the National Gallery from 1894 to 1905. Among his chief pictures are: *Perseus and Andromeda, Atalanta's Race, The Fortune-teller, A Visit to Æsculapius, Helen of Troy, The Ides of March, The Meeting of Solomon and the Queen of Sheba, The Ionian Dance*, and *The Cave of the Storm Nymphs*. He is author of *Ten Lectures on Art* (1879).

POZIÈRES. Village of France, near Albert, Somme. During the Great War it was held first by the Germans, to whom its slightly elevated position made it useful for observation over the adjacent battle zone. In July, 1916, it was rushed by British and Anzac divisions. In the spring of 1918 it was recaptured by the Germans, but taken again by the British in August. There is a memorial to the Australians who died in the attack of 1916, and also a British memorial. *See* ALBERT; SOMME.

POZZUO'LI (ancient **Puteoli**). A city and seaport of Southern Italy, in the province of Naples, and on the shore of the Bay of Baiæ (Golfo di Pozzuoli), the north-western portion of the Bay of Naples.* Considerable trade and an active fishing are carried on. Pozzuoli is a city of great historic interest. It was founded by the Greeks about 520 B.C., and became under Rome a great centre of commerce. St. Paul landed there in the course of his journey to Rome (cf. Acts, xxviii., 13).

Pozzuoli was destroyed by the Goths more than once, rebuilt by the Byzantine Greeks, and finally devasted by earthquakes and volcanic eruptions. It abounds in ancient ruins. The cathedral stands on the site of a temple of Augustus, and in one of the lateral walls six Corinthian columns of the old temple are preserved. A ruined temple of Serapis also remains, enclosed by forty-eight marble and granite columns. On an eminence behind the town stands the ruined amphitheatre, resting on three series of arches, where St. Januarius was cast to the lions and where Nero presided over gladiatorial combats. In the neighbourhood are Lake Avernus, the Grotto of the Sibyl, the baths of Nero, the ruins of Baiæ and Cumæ, etc. Pop. 23,000.

PRACTICAL CHEMISTRY. That branch of chemistry which deals with the experimental part of the science. Practical chemistry without a knowledge of theoretical chemistry is of little value, and vice versa. Until theoretical chemistry had been established on a firm basis the experimental work undertaken was usually carried out more for gain than for advancement of knowledge. The alchemists performed many experiments, but these were all directed

* Ancient *Sinus Puteolanus*.

towards one aim, namely, the transformation of cheap material into valuable substances.

Practical chemistry of to-day is an exact science, and as physical and chemical instruments become more and more accurate so practical chemistry becomes more precise. When qualitative work was established, balances were crude and therefore work inaccurate. An example of this is the table of atomic weights of the elements. This has been revised many times, owing to experimental determinations becoming more accurate. Practical chemistry may be divided into *analytical chemistry* and *preparative chemistry*. The former deals with the composition of substances, and the proportion of the elements present in compound or mixture; the latter deals with the preparation of elements, compounds, or mixtures of known composition.

To Berzelius is due the greatest advance in inorganic analytical chemistry. He taught the use of small quantities of material, and the modern methods of filtration. From the analysis of a substance much is to be learned. Firstly, it can be determined whether the substance is made up of a single element or of more than one element; secondly, the proportions by weight or by volume of the elements in a compound may be ascertained; and thirdly, the purity of the element or compound may be determined.

Analysis of a substance may be carried out in a variety of ways. Valuable information may be obtained by *blow-pipe analysis*, in which the substance is oxidised in the dry state and identified by the characteristic film of oxide; or it may be reduced on charcoal and the metallic bead examined; or it may be made to form a glass by heating with borax, and the glass bead may be identified by its colour and behaviour on oxidation or reduction. Blow-pipe analysis is used in examining certain minerals and metallic oxides. For complete analysis a wet method is employed. The compound or mixture is transformed into soluble chlorides, sulphates, or nitrates by treatment with acids or by fusion with sodium carbonate, and the solution so obtained is examined by means of chemical reagents. Inorganic compounds in solution are ionised, and the solutions give certain tests. Thus a sample of copper pyrites ($CuFeS_2$) is practically insoluble in water, but if treated with nitric acid, the copper present is transformed into copper nitrate, the iron into iron nitrate, and the sulphur to sulphuric acid. These compounds in solution can then be separated and examined. The actual elements are not separated, but are obtained as compounds of the element.

Besides identifying the elements present in a compound, it is necessary to determine the proportion of the elements in a given amount of the substance. *Qualitative analysis* serves to identify a known substance, but a *quantitative* determination is necessary before analysis is complete. Quantitative analysis may be carried out by *gravimetric methods*, that is, a weighed quantity of substance is dissolved, and the metallic and acidic radicles estimated by transforming into some insoluble compound and weighing the precipitates obtained. Very accurate methods are in use for this. The substance analysed is reported either as pure or impure, or the percentage composition is worked out. *Volumetric analysis* is much employed, as by using standard solutions of reagents accurate determination of one or all elements in a solution may be obtained with only an initial weighing. As the name implies, in this analysis definite volumes of solution are taken, and from these may be calculated the composition of the compound. Volumetric methods are used wherever possible in all analytical laboratories, as the methods are quick and very accurate.

In organic chemistry different methods are used, because organic compounds do not give the usual tests for the elements. For instance, hydrochloric acid (HCl) may be identified by forming the insoluble silver chloride ($AgCl$) on the addition of an aqueous solution of silver nitrate. On the other hand, chloroform ($CHCl_3$), an organic compound containing chlorine, does not give a precipitate of silver chloride on addition of a solution of silver nitrate. Organic substances are treated with oxidising agents, and the presence of carbon in the compound is proved by transforming it into carbon dioxide and identifying that. If the percentage of carbon is required, then a weighed quantity is oxidised by means of cupric oxide, and the carbon dioxide so formed collected and weighed. Hydrogen in the compound is also oxidised to water, and this again is collected and weighed. Chlorine, if present, is first transformed to hydrochloric acid or sodium chloride, and then estimated by volumetric or gravimetric means. Sulphur is oxidised to sulphuric acid, and nitrogen in organic compounds is liberated either as nitrogen or as ammonia by oxidation.

Practical chemistry deals with all preparations of elements, compounds, or mixtures. Synthetic methods may be worked out theoretically, but until these have been proved possible by actual building up of the substance they are of no value. The term *applied chemistry* is sometimes used in connection with the manufacture of chemicals, which is preparative and analytical chemistry applied on the large scale. Small-scale experiments are first of all undertaken, and if these prove successful, then the method may be employed on the large scale. The fact that a good yield of substance is obtained by an experiment in the laboratory does not necessarily mean a successful yield on the manufacturing scale. Many alterations may have to be made in the process before it is adapted to manufacture. Cost and the time taken in the process are important factors in industry. All these are dealt with by the works chemist. For the examination of drugs and food-stuffs, and for the testing of manufacturing materials in the numerous cases where a certain standard of purity is required, chemical analysis is the indispensable instrument.—BIBLIOGRAPHY: F. Clowes and J. B. Coleman, *Elementary Practical Chemistry and Qualitative Analysis*; W. G. Valentin, *Practical Chemistry*; J. J. Sudborough and T. C. James, *Practical Organic Chemistry*.

PRAED, Winthrop Mackworth. English poet, born in 1802, and died in 1839. His father was an eminent serjeant-at-law. He was educated at Eton, where he founded two magazines, the *Apis Matina* and the *Etonian*, the latter of which had a brilliant career of ten months, an unusually long life for a school magazine. Praed went up to Trinity College, Cambridge, in 1821, and distinguished himself in classics. He was third in the classical tripos in 1825, and won four Browne medals, the Chancellor's medal for English verse twice, and the Seatonian prize. He was elected a Fellow of Trinity in 1827, and embarked on a political career, after having been called to the Bar at the Middle Temple. He entered Parliament in 1830, and in 1834 was appointed secretary to the Board of Control. His health began to break down in 1838, and he died in the following year of a rapid consumption.

In spite of his brief and busy life, Praed managed to write a large quantity of beautifully polished society verse. He also wrote some more serious but less effective poems. His classical training helped him to finish his work carefully; some of his light verses are unequalled even by those of Calverley for sparkle and wit. Thus he speaks of a Utopia where there were

> poets who deserved the bays,
> And did not dread the duns;

and says of his friends:

> Some lie beneath the churchyard stone,
> And some—before the Speaker.

Indeed, his epigrams and his antitheses are so brilliant and so frequent that after a time they become almost cloying. There is a certain lack of variety in his work, but "the neat, inevitable turns of Praed" are nevertheless some of the best things in English light verse.

PRÆFECT (*præfectus*). The title of various functionaries of ancient Rome. Of these the most important was the *præfectus urbi* or *urbis* (præfect of the city). During the kingly period and the early Republic the *præfectus urbis* had the right to exercise all the powers of the king or consuls in their absence. After the foundation of the prætorship this office lost its dignity and privileges; but under the Empire it was revived as that of chief permanent magistrate of the city, with important military functions. The *præfectus prætorio*, an officer under the Empire, was general of the imperial life-guards. His position was one of great power, for the troops under his command frequently decided the succession to the imperial throne. Many other Roman functionaries bore the title of præfect, such as the *præfectus aquarum*, who had charge of the water-supply of the city; the *præfectus ærarii*, who managed the public treasury, etc.

PRÆMUNI'RE. In English law, a name given to offences of the nature of a contempt against the king (or queen) and the Government, or encroachments on the power of the sovereign. The term is derived from the opening words of the writ preparatory to the prosecution of the offence—*præmonere* or *præmunire facias A. B.* (Cause A. B. to be forewarned that he appear before us, etc.). The first statute of *præmunire* was passed during the reign of Edward I. to repress the Papal encroachments on the rights of the Crown, and several subsequent statutes before the Reformation greatly extended the number of penal acts under this title. The punishment is forfeiture and imprisonment during the sovereign's pleasure. Many of the statutes are now repealed, and prosecutions upon *præmunire* are unheard of in our times; the last took place during the reign of Charles II.

PRÆTOR. The title of an important official in the ancient Roman state. Up to 367 B.C. the title was merely an adjunct to that of consul; but when at that date the consulship was thrown open to the plebeians, the judicial functions of the consul were separated from his other duties and given to a new patrician magistrate, who was entitled the prætor. In 337, after a struggle, the plebeians were also admitted to this office. In 246 B.C. another magistracy, that of *prætor peregrīnus*, was instituted for the purpose of settling disputes between foreigners and between foreigners and citizens; and in distinction from him who filled this office the other functionary was termed *prætor urbānus*. After election the two prætors determined their offices by lot. The *prætor urbānus* was the first in position, and was the chief magistrate for the administration of justice. To the edicts of the successive prætors the Roman law is said to owe in a great measure its development and improvement. About 227 B.C. the number of prætors was increased to four; afterwards to six and eight; and under the Empire the number varied from twelve to eighteen. After completing his year of office the prætor was often sent as *proprætor* to govern a province.

PRÆTORIAN GUARD. The bodyguard of the Roman emperors, first established as a standing body by Augustus. In the time of the Republic the *cohors prætoria* consisted of troops selected to guard the person of the commander while on active service. Under Augustus only a small detachment of the guard was stationed in Rome, the rest being in the adjacent towns. Tiberius assembled the whole at Rome, and placed them in a permanent fortified camp, where they were used to quell any sudden popular disturbance. The number of cohorts was raised by Vitellius from nine to sixteen, and they received double pay; under the later emperors the prætorian guard became powerful enough to decide the succession to the throne, which they once even put up to auction. They were reorganised and their powers curtailed by Septimius Severus and by Diocletian, and were finally disbanded by Constantine the Great in A.D. 312.

PRAGMATIC SANCTION. The general meaning of this term is a rule or Constitution made by a sovereign personally, and relating to the royal prerogative or to the succession to the throne. It is derived from a term of Roman law meaning a decision of the emperor or of the State on some subject of public importance, and the phrase is unknown to English history, but was employed in France, Germany, and Spain. In 1438 Charles VII. of France defined the limits of the Papal jurisdiction within his dominions by a Pragmatic Sanction.

The most famous instance of a Pragmatic Sanction is the arrangement made by the Emperor Charles VI. for the succession to the Habsburg dominions in the first part of the eighteenth century. The division of the Spanish possessions after the death of Charles II. led him to issue in 1713 a Pragmatic Sanction declaring the indivisibility of the Habsburg inheritance. He had married in 1708, but his son, born in 1716, died as an infant, and he devoted the last twenty years of his life to attempting to secure the succession of his daughter Maria Theresa, born in 1717. Acting on the Pragmatic Sanction, he declared her the heiress of the whole of his dominions, to the exclusion of her cousin, the wife of the Elector of Bavaria, afterwards the Emperor Charles VII. This lady was a daughter of the Emperor Joseph I., the elder brother and predecessor of Charles VI., and though the Elector agreed to accept the Pragmatic Sanction and the succession of Maria Theresa, he did so with secret protests and reservations. Other Powers, which had also agreed to the Pragmatic Sanction, were similarly prepared to recede from their undertakings, and the great soldier Prince Eugène warned Charles VI. that a large army would be the only real sanction for his daughter's succession. Charles made no such preparation, and on his death in 1740 the Elector of Bavaria asserted his wife's claim to the Habsburg dominions and joined the Powers who brought about the War of the Austrian Succession.—Cf. J. F. Bright, *Maria Theresa.*

PRAGMATISM. A philosophical theory which insists on usefulness and practical consequences as a test of truth. It maintains that all thought and all cognitive processes are influenced and coloured by the feelings, emotions, or personal bias of the individual concerned; that there is no such thing as pure thought, that thought is always bound up with purpose and practical consideration, that truth has to be tested by its practical consequences, and that we cannot assume that what we call truth is independent of ourselves. Proteus-like, however, pragmatism assumes among its adherents many meanings and different definitions. The reason lies perhaps in the fact that pragmatism is a critical method rather than a doctrine. W. James defined pragmatism as the doctrine "that the whole meaning of a conception expresses itself in practical consequences—consequences either in the shape of conduct to be recommended, or in that of experience to be expected, if the conception be true." In other words, philosophy and knowledge in general are considered in their direct relation to life, action, and human conduct, utilising it for the requirements of life. Philosophy and thought are to be judged by their consequences to humanity, but are not an end in themselves. Concepts are fashioned by the human mind for the manipulation of experience, the preservation, evolution, and advancement of life. According to pragmatism, logical thinking becomes subordinate to practical life, whilst the test of truth is not found in reason but in the practical consequences. Of two concepts, that which "works well" is true.

The term pragmatism was first used by the mathematician C. S. Peirce in 1878, but it is only a new name for an old way of thinking, as the doctrine has existed under different names ever since man began to philosophise. Traces of pragmatism exist in Indian philosophy, and Protagoras expressed pragmatic tendencies when he taught that "man is the measure of all things." Among modern philosophers, Bacon and Hobbes, Pascal and Comte, Fichte and Marx may be said to have held pragmatic ideas. Nietzsche's views are partly pragmatic, whilst Bergson, the opponent of intellectualism, is considered as one of the most logical teachers of pragmatism. Ostwald, Mach, and Avenarius are pragmatists. Pragmatism has, however, been most clearly elaborated by W. James, John Dewey, and F. C. S. Schiller, the last of these calling the doctrine *humanism*.—BIBLIOGRAPHY: W. James, *The Meaning of Truth*; J. B. Pratt, *What is Pragmatism?*; D. L. Murray, *Pragmatism*; F. C. S. Schiller, *Studies in Humanism*; R. B. Perry, *Present Philosophical Tendencies*.

PRAGUE (Czech, *Praha*; Ger. *Prag*). Capital of the Republic of Czechoslovakia, in Bohemia, on the Vltava, a tributary of the Elbe. The site, a basin enclosed by hills of considerable height, gives to the city a picturesque and striking appearance. The river at this point contains several islands and is spanned by ten bridges, including two railway bridges. Prague is the centre of the Bohemian railway system. The most notable of the bridges is the Karlsbrücke, dating back to the fourteenth century, and reconstructed in 1892.

Buildings. The city is famous for its architectural beauty. Hradschin contains the royal castle, dating in its present form from the fourteenth to the eighteenth century. Beside it is the cathedral of St. Vitus, begun by Charles IV. in 1344, and occupying the site of a building erected by St. Wenceslas in 934. The church of St. George is a large Romanesque building largely restored but dating originally from 916. The Teinkirche, in the Altstadt, once the church of the Hussites, contains the grave of Tycho Brahe. Among other notable buildings are the town hall, dating from 1381; the Pulverturm (1475-84); and the Carolinum, containing the university archives and the law classrooms. In the Neustadt are the Bohemian national theatre, the Bohemian national museum, the medical faculties of the university, the Bohemian technical high school, and various educational institutions. The university was founded by Charles IV. in 1348, and in 1882-3 it was divided into two, one German and one Czech or Bohemian.

The Altstadt is the commercial centre of the town, and carries on a considerable trade by rail and river. The manufacturing quarters are chiefly Bubna, Smichow, and Karolinenthal, the chief products being beer, flour, iron, machinery, wagons, cotton yarn, leather, gloves, chemicals, and railway plant. It has two broadcasting stations. Pop. 848,081.

History. Prague is an ancient town, and early became a place of some importance. It owed much to the Emperor Charles IV. in the fourteenth century, who laid out the Neustadt, restored the castle, founded the cathedral, and brought the university into existence. During the Hussite struggle the town suffered severely, and in the course of the Thirty Years' War it was several times taken. In 1741 it fell into the hands of the French and Bavarians, and in 1744 it capitulated to Frederick the Great. Near Prague, Frederick in 1757 defeated the Austrians under Prince Charles of Lorraine. The Emperor Joseph II. in 1784 united the different sections of Prague into one municipality. The holding of a Slav Congress within it in 1848 led to an Austrian bombardment. It was occupied by the Prussians in 1866, during the war against Austria, and here, on 23rd Aug., was concluded the peace which ended the war. At the outbreak of the European War Prague was the headquarters of the 8th Austro-Hungarian Army Corps. On the break-up of the Empire and the secession of the Czechs and Slovenes it became the capital of Czecho-slovakia.

PRAIRIE (Lat. *pratum*, meadow; Late Lat. *prataria*). The name given in North America to the vast natural meadows or plains of the Mississippi Valley, especially those lying between it and the Rocky Mountains,

A Prairie Scene

and extending into Canada. Throughout this immense territory the differences of level are sufficient to produce a steady flow of the rivers, but not so great as to obstruct their navigation, thus securing a unique system of easy intercommunication between all sections of the country. There is a great sameness in the features of the topography, the vegetable productions, the soil, and geological features. Some of the prairies that have a peculiarly undulating surface are known as *rolling prairies*. Vast herds of buffaloes used to roam over the prairies, but these have now disappeared, and immense tracts are settled for the production of cereals and, especially near the Rockies, for the raising of cattle.

PRAIRIE-CHICKEN, or PRAIRIE-HEN. The popular name of the pinnated grouse of the United States (*Tympanuchus americanus*). The neck of the male is furnished with neck-tufts of eighteen feathers, and is remarkable also for two loose, pendulous, wrinkled skins, which somewhat resemble an orange on inflation. The prairie-hen is much prized for the table. The name prairie-chicken is also given to the sharp-tailed grouse (*Pediœcetes phasianellus*), a species of grouse widely distributed in Canada and the north of the United States.

PRAIRIE-DOG, or PRAIRIE MARMOT. A small rodent animal, the wistonwish (*Cynomys ludovicianus*), allied to the marmot as well as to the squirrel, and found on the North American prairies west of the Mississippi and east of the Rocky Mountains. These animals live gregariously in burrows, and are characterised by a sharp bark, like that of a small dog, whence their popular name. They are about 1 foot in length exclusive of the tail, which is rather short. Their burrows are quite close together, and have a mound of excavated earth near the entrance, on which the little animals are wont to sit and look around them. These communities are termed "villages." A second species, *C. columbiānus*, inhabits the region west of the Rockies. A third and larger form, *C. mexicanus*, is found in Mexico. The prairie-dog is not to be confounded with the prairie-squirrel, to which it is allied.

PRAIRIE-SQUIRREL, or GOPHER. A name for several North American rodent mammals, of the genus Spermophilus, found in the prairies in great numbers. They live in burrows, and not on trees, and much resemble the prairie-dog or marmot. They have cheek-pouches, in which their food is carried. This consists of prairie plants with their roots and seeds. *See* SOUSLIK.

PRAIRIE-WOLF, or COYOTE (*Canis latrans*). The small wolf which is found on the prairies in North America. It is a cowardly animal, and only dangerous to man when in packs and pressed by hunger.

PRÂKRIT (in Skt. *prākrita*, primitive, vulgar, from *prakriti*, nature: as opposed to *samskrita*, that which is prepared by art, hence the Sanskrit or polished speech: *see* SANSKRIT). A general term used by Hindu grammarians to denote the various vernaculars derived from Sanskrit. This definition would be more correct if we said that Prâkrit denotes the vernaculars derived from the ancient Aryan dialects of India, upon some of which classical Sanskrit is based.

The ancient Prâkrit dialects were those forms of the Aryan speech most commonly used by the masses. The earliest show five groups—the *Sauraseni*, spoken in Sarasena, the modern district around Masura; the *Magadhi*, the vernacular of Bihar; the *Maharashtri*, spoken round Ujjayani or Avanti, in Malwa, perhaps including Southern Rájputána and the modern northern Marathi country; the *Paisachi*, of uncertain locality; the *Apabhramsa*, or corrupted dialect of Sind and Western Rájputána. In the Hindu dramas, which are the chief sources of knowledge of early Prâkrits, kings and Brahmans speak Sanskrit, but retainers and people of meaner position speak in different Prâkrits. Pâli is a form of primary Prâkrit, and indeed the five Prâkrits cited may be regarded as the ultimate source of all the modern dialects of India.

PRATO. A walled city of Tuscany, North Italy, on the Bisenzio. The cathedral, begun in the twelfth

The Tower, Prato

century, and completed in the fourteenth by Giovanni Pisano, contains fine specimens of the work of Fra Filippo Lippi and other masters. Prato has manufactures of straw-plait, bread, and biscuits, besides the spinning of cotton and wool. At Figline near by there are quarries of serpentine, much used by Tuscan builders. Pop. 50,000.

PRAWN (Palæmon). A genus of crustaceans, ord. Decapoda, section Macrura ("long-tailed"). The common prawn (*Palmœon serratus*) is the most familiar species, and resembles the shrimp. It attains an average length of from 3 to 5 inches. The tail is broad and flat, and its terminal plates are fringed with long hairs. The colour is light-grey spotted with purple. The Isle of Wight and Hampshire coasts form the chief sources of prawn supply to the London market.

PRAXITELES. The most celebrated Greek sculptor of the later Attic school, flourished about the middle of the fourth century B.C. His work is marked by grace and delicacy of execution, and, in contrast to that of Pheidias, emphasises the human and individual character of his subjects. This is well seen in his *Aphrodite of Cnidos*, whom he was the first to represent as a naked figure, in which the woman predominates over the goddess. A statue of Hermēs by him, discovered at Olympia in 1877, is one of the best preserved examples of Greek sculpture surviving. The so-called *Capitoline Faun*, of which a fine copy exists, was one of his most famous works. The well-known *Niobe and her Children*, at Florence, is sometimes given to Praxiteles, sometimes to Scopas, his contemporary. Praxiteles exercised great influence, and helped to pave the way to the over-elaborate workmanship and exaggerated emotion of Hellenistic sculpture.

PRAYER. The expression of a desire or a petition addressed to some force or power conceived as supernatural. Nothing proclaims more consistently and universally the connection between man and God than the fact that in every time and place men have felt their dependence on a higher Being, and have sought His assistance in prayer. Even the heathen believe that there is some one who can supply their needs. The Scriptures tacitly assume that prayer was offered to God from the beginning of the world; and although we read that "men began to call upon the name of the Lord" after Seth was born, we are forbidden by all commentators to connect this statement with the origin of prayer. It is not, however, until the time of Abraham that prayer comes first distinctly into notice. As the altar appears to have been the special place for prayer in the patriarchal age, so was the tabernacle under the Mosaic covenant until the temple, "the house of prayer," was built. From the time of the dedication of Solomon's temple the Jews appear to have gone there to pray, and to have turned their faces towards it if they were prevented from going there; and this custom prevails among the Jews at the present time, as does the similar custom among the Mahommedans (q.v.), who, at such times, turn their faces towards the sacred Kaaba at Mecca.

When we come to New Testament times we meet with synagogues established as places for the public worship of God, and for reading His word. Christ taught that prayer should be offered to God in His name in order to ensure an answer. Henceforward Christ became to the Christian what the temple was to the Jew. The posture of the body in prayer is left undecided in Scripture, and although Christ gave His disciples a form of prayer of the most universal application, it does not follow that men may not pray according as each experiences special wants.

Prayer for the dead is a practice rejected by Protestants as having no scriptural warrant, but prevalent in the Roman Catholic, Greek, and other Eastern Churches. The custom seems to have existed in most ancient religions. The doctrine and practice came to the Christian Church through the Jews (2 Macc. xii. 40, 45). The first of the Christian Fathers who mentions prayer for the dead is Tertullian; but he speaks of the usage as long-established in the Church; such prayers are frequently alluded to by St. John Chrysostom, Cyril of Jerusalem, and St. Augustine. In the burial-service of the first *Book of Common Prayer* of the English Church some prayers for the dead appeared, but they were deleted from the second book, and are not found in the subsequent revisions.—BIBLIOGRAPHY: J. Hastings (editor), *Christian Doctrine of Prayer*; E. Bickersteth, *A Treatise of Prayer*; L. R. Farnell, *The Evolution of Religion*; J. Wordsworth, *Holy Communion*; L. Duchesne, *Christian Worship*.

PRAYER BOOK. Order of church services. In its present form the Book of Common Prayer of the Church of England dates substantially from 1559, when, after the accession of Elizabeth, the second prayer book of Edward VI. (1552) was revised. The first prayer book of Edward VI. (1549), mainly an English version of the Missal, found little favour either with the reformers or those who adhered to the ancient rites, and Edward's second book was intended to placate the former party, who desired a closer conformity with the liturgy of the reformed churches abroad.

Repressed by the Commonwealth, and restored in 1660, the Act of Uniformity of 1662 authorised it as the only legal service book. In 1927 a revised prayer book was submitted to Parliament, after acceptance by both convocations and the Church Assembly, but was rejected. Some alterations were made, and it was presented to Parliament in 1928, but that body again rejected it.

PRAYING-WHEEL. An apparatus used among the Buddhists, consisting of a wheel to which a paper with a written prayer is attached. Each

Tibetan Lamas with Prayer Wheels. Large Prayer Wheels in Background

revolution of the wheel made by the devotee counts as an utterance of the prayer. So also a wheel driven by water-power keeps praying for its owner.

PRE-ADAMITES. Those supposed inhabitants of the earth prior to the creation of Adam. Ancient legends or traditions of the East speak of nations and empires existing before Adam's creation, and of a line of kings who ruled over them. In modern times the subject was taken up by Isaac de la Peyrère, or Pererius (1594-1676), who, in a work published in 1655, maintained that the Jews were the descendants of Adam, and the Gentiles those of a long anterior creation, founding his opinions on Rom. v. 12-14. One of the most ancient and widespread myths describes the complete destruction of mankind, which necessitated a new act of creation to repeople the earth. Hence the belief arose that the present race of men was preceded by another race.

PRE'BEND. A yearly stipend paid from the funds of an ecclesiastical establishment, as of a cathedral or collegiate church. *Prebendary* is the person who has a prebend. A *simple* prebend is restricted to revenue only; a *dignitary* prebend is one which has a jurisdiction annexed.

PRE-CAMBRIAN. *See* PROTEROZOIC.

PRECE'DENCE. The order in which men and women follow each other, according to rank or dignity, in a State procession or on other public occasions. In England the order of precedence depends partly on statutes, and partly on ancient usage and established custom. Questions arising on matters of precedence depending on usage are hardly considered as definitely settled, and are in a great measure left to the discretion of the officers of arms.

The Sovereign, of course, is always first in order of precedence, after whom in descending order follow the Prince of Wales, sons, grandsons, brothers, and uncles of the Sovereign, the Sovereign's brothers' or sisters' sons, the Archbishop of Canterbury, the Lord High Chancellor, the Archbishop of York, Prime Minister, and so on through the high State dignitaries, the various ranks of the peerage, etc. The order of precedence among women follows the same rules as that among men. By the Acts of Union of Scotland and Ireland the precedence in any given degree of the peerage has been established as follows: (1) Peers of England; (2) Peers of Scotland; (3) Peers of Great Britain; (4) Peers of Ireland; (5) Peers of the United Kingdom and Peers of Ireland created subsequent to the Union.

PREC'EDENT. In law, a judicial decision which serves as a rule for future determinations in similar cases. Precedents, strictly speaking, are binding on tribunals only when they are actual decisions of the point in question; what is termed an extrajudicial opinion or *obiter dictum*—the opinion of a judge pronounced where it was not called for to decide the issue—can have authority only from the character of the judge, and not as a precedent. Precedents are now of as much authority in courts of equity as in those of common law.

PRECEN'TOR. An important official in a chapter, whether cathedral or collegiate, who led the singing. He began the verse, whilst the people joined with him at the close, a method which was often varied in the same service with antiphonic or alternate psalmody. The precentor ranked generally, although not universally, next to the dean; but in modern cathedral foundations he is usually a minor canon, and in consequence has lost must of his prestige. He is still, however, everywhere the conductor of the choral service and superintendent of the choir.

PRECEPTORS, COLLEGE OF. Founded in 1846 and incorporated by royal charter in 1849, it has for its object the examination both of teachers and of pupils. In the teachers' examinations especial stress is laid on the theory and practice of education. Diplomas are awarded, and are of three grades, Fellow, Licentiate, and Associate (F.C.P., L.C.P., and A.C.P.). Periodical examinations are held for pupils, and certificates granted. The college also appoints visiting examiners for schools, and provides courses of lectures for teachers. The headquarters of the College of Preceptors is in Bloomsbury Square, London.

PRECEP'TORY. In mediæval history, a religious house of the Knights Templars, subordinate to the temple or principal house of the order in London. It was under the government of one of the more eminent knights appointed by the grand-master and called the "preceptor."

PRECESSION OF THE EQUINOXES. A slow motion of the line of intersection of the celestial equator or equinoctial and the ecliptic, which causes the positions occupied by the sun at the equinox (the equinoctial points, q.v.) to move backward or westward at the mean rate of 50·26 seconds per year. This motion of the equinox along the ecliptic carries it, with reference to the diurnal motion, continually in advance upon the stars; the place of the equinox among the stars thus precedes at any moment that which it previously held, hence the name. This sweeping round in the heavens of the equinoctial line indicates a motion of the axis of rotation of the earth, such that it describes circles round the poles of the ecliptic in 25,791 years. Nutation (Lat. *nutatio*, a nodding) is a similar but much smaller gyratory motion of the earth's axis, whose period is about nineteen years. From these two causes in combination the axis follows a sinuous path, instead of a circle, about the pole of the ecliptic. Nutation (q.v.) causes the equinoctial points to be alternately in advance of and behind their mean place due to precession by 6·87 seconds. At present the vernal equinoctial point is in the zodiacal constellation Pisces, and it is moving towards the constellation Aquarius.

PRECIPITATE. In chemistry, the name given to the solid particles thrown out of solution when two substances interact in a common medium. Thus, if an aqueous solution of sodium chloride is mixed with an aqueous solution of silver nitrate, double decomposition occurs and silver chloride is immediately formed, and as it is insoluble in water, it is *precipitated* in fine particles.

PRECIPITATE OINTMENT. The name given to two mercurial ointments, red and white. *White precipitate* is ammoniated mercury (NH_2HgCl); *red precipitate* is the red oxide of mercury.

PRECOGNITION. In Scots law, a written statement of the evidence a witness will be able to give at the trial. Precognitions may be taken in civil or criminal cases by the agents or counsel for any of the parties. In criminal trials the precognitions for the Crown are generally taken by the Procurator-fiscal, and the signature of the witness is affixed; those acting for the defence may also take precognition from the Crown witnesses.

PREDESTINATION. In theology, a term used to denote the decree of God, whereby the elect are foreordained to salvation. The term also signifies generally God's predetermination of events in the world. The theory of predestination represents God's absolute will as determining the eternal destiny of man, not according to the fore-known character of those whose fate is so determined, but according to God's own choice. The doctrine is the logical result of the ideas that God works by plan in governing the world, and that humanity is so sinful that no one could be saved without the operation of God.

The theory has been the occasion of many disputes and controversies in the Church in all ages. On the one side, it has been observed that predestination destroys moral distinction, introduces fatalism, and renders all our efforts useless. On the other side, it is contended that if God's knowledge is infinite, He must have known everything from eternity; and that the permission of evil under such circumstances is indistinguishable from a plan or decree under which it is foreordained. The first great champions of these opposite views were Pelagius and Augustine. The former held that there was a possibility of good in man's nature, and that the choice of salvation lay in man's will. Augustine maintained that apart from divine graces there is no possibility of good in human nature, and that since the fall man's will has no power of choice. The system of Augustine was adopted in 529 by the Council of Arausio as the rule of orthodoxy in the Western Church, and forms one of the peculiar characteristics of the Calvinistic theology. The question is left an open one by the Anglican Church, and also by the Roman Catholic Church since the Reformation.—BIBLIOGRAPHY: W. A. Copinger, *A Treatise on Predestination, Election, and Grace*; J. R. Illingworth, *The Divine Immanence*; O. Pfleiderer, *The Philosophy of Religion on the Basis of its History.*

PREDICABLES. In logic, terms affirmable, as predicates, of other terms. The predicables are said to be five: genus, species, difference, property, and accident. The first two name the higher and lower classes of the things classified; a genus includes more than one species. The other three express the attributes on which the classification is founded.

PRE-EMPTION (Lat. *præ*, before; *emere*, to buy). In law, the right to the first offer of a thing which is to be sold. Thus in the Articles of Association of private companies it is not infrequently provided that a shareholder who desires to sell or transfer his shares must first offer them to the remaining shareholders or to the directors at a specified price. Again, the former owner of land which has been acquired compulsorily by an authority under the Lands Clauses Acts has a right of preemption in respect of any portions not required by the authority; while in feu charters of land in Scotland it is sometimes agreed that if the feuar wishes to sell he must first offer the subjects to the superior at the price offered by any third party desirous of purchasing.

PRE-EXISTENCE, DOCTRINE OF. The doctrine that the soul of every man has an existence previous to that of his body. This opinion was very prevalent in the East, and was held by several Greek philosophers, more especially by the Pythagoreans and Empedocles. The belief was also apparently held by Plato, unless we are to consider the views stated by him to be an allegory, rather than a sober statement of belief. A similar doctrine has found some countenance in Christian times as an explanation of the union of soul and body. It was believed that all souls were created before the world, and that each had its proper body allotted to it at the time of birth. In favour of this theory appeal is made to these peculiar sensations which are sometimes raised by sights or sounds, which we feel conscious of having had a former familiarity with, though reason would persuade us we had seen them for the first time. The doctrine is supported by some modern writers, and is the basal idea of Wordsworth's *Ode on the Intimations of Immortality from Recollections of Early Childhood.*

PRÉFET (prā-fā ; Lat. *præfectus*). The title of an important political functionary in France. Previous to the reign of Henri II. the officers who were sent round to the provinces to superintend the details of administration on behalf of the sovereign were called *maîtres des requêtes*. In 1551 Henri II. established them as perpetual overseers in all provinces, and under Louis XIII. (1635) they received the name of *intendants*. The offices were abolished by the National Convention, but were restored by Napoleon by the law of 17th Feb., 1800, and the functionaries received the appellation of *préfets*. There is a préfet at the head of each department, who is entrusted with the whole organisation and management of the police establishments ; but not with the punishment of police offences. Within this sphere of action the préfets are unchecked ; the sous-préfets, who are appointed by them, and who stand at the head of the districts, are entirely subject to their commands ; and the authorities of the communes, as well as the justices of the peace, can set no limits to their activity. In time of tumult they can call out the military, or provisionally declare a state of siege.

The Council of the Préfecture is a court in which are settled all disputes respecting the taxation of individuals, engagements with the State for building, the indemnification of those who have had to give up anything to the public, etc. Of this court the préfet is president, and in it he has a casting vote. The appeals against its decisions lie to the Council of State.

PREGNANCY. The state of a woman who is with child. It lasts from 273 to 280 days, taking the time from conception to the birth of the child. Among the earliest signs of pregnancy are the cessation of menstruation, and sickness, usually most marked in the early part of the day, and thus known as "morning sickness." This sickness may be slight and only a few weeks in duration, or it may be more severe and last for three or four months, causing considerable discomfort, while in some cases it persists from its onset to the termination of the pregnancy. Changes in the breasts are seen during the second and third months, and in the fourth month slight enlargement of the abdomen is evident, and this enlargement continues progressively throughout pregnancy. About the sixteenth or seventeenth week the mother becomes aware of the movements of the child, at first very slight, but later more marked, and this is known as quickening. The first wholly conclusive evidence of pregnancy is detection of the sounds of the child's heart, heard by applying a stethoscope to the lower part of the abdomen of the mother. The child's heart beats at about double the rate of the maternal heart, and can be heard from the eighteenth week onward.

During pregnancy women should pay special attention to digestion and take regular exercise, while they should avoid any undue exertions or excitements and not wear any tight clothing. Many of the minor troubles and afflictions of pregnancy can be overcome or prevented by the mother seeking skilled advice, and of late years much has been done in this way by antenatal clinics, and by the spread of knowledge of physiological conditions among the public.

PREGNANCY, CONCEALMENT OF. In Scots law it was originally made a crime in 1690 by statute, and punishable with death, as described in Sir Walter Scott's novel *The Heart of Midlothian*. In 1809 the punishment was modified to two years' imprisonment. The concealment must be interpreted very strictly ; communication of the fact of pregnancy to any one at any time, even by clear inference only, is sufficient to rebut the accusation. It must be proved that the woman failed to call for or make use of assistance in the birth, and that the child is dead or amissing. In indictments for child-murder concealment of pregnancy is usually inserted as an alternative charge. The crime is not known to the law of England.

PRE'LATE. In Church law, one of those spiritual dignataries who exercise jurisdiction in their own name. These were originally only the bishops, archbishops, patriarchs, and the Pope. The cardinals and legates, abbots and priors, also obtained certain privileges of jurisdiction by grant or prescription. The term is now commonly used merely to signify one of the higher dignitaries of the Church.

PRE'LUDE. In music, originally the first part of a sonata ; though, as the name implies, it may be an introduction to any piece of music.

Bach and his contemporaries elaborated preludes considerably; and Chopin wrote several piano works which, though complete in themselves, he designated preludes. The term has been also applied to operatic introductions when they are shorter than the usual overture. Wagner in particular has prefaced most of his operas with a prelude. From the time of writing *Lohengrin* he used the word prelude instead of overture.

PREMIER (Fr. *premier*; Lat. *primus*, first). An abbreviated form of Prime or Premier Minister; the first minister of a state. In the British Empire the first ministers of autonomous or semi-autonomous states, colonies, and dominions also receive this appellation, and, as in the Imperial Government, derive their appointment by recognised hegemony in the predominant political party of the state. The British Premier's official residence is at No. 10 Downing Street, Whitehall, London, the Chancellor of the Exchequer occuping No. 11, and the offices of the Government Whips No. 12. His country residence is Chequers (q.v.). He has no salary as Prime Minister, but he usually holds the premiership in connection with the first lordship of the treasury, the chancellorship of the exchequer, a secretaryship of state, or the privy seal. George I. could neither speak nor understand English, and it was under his reign that a Prime Minister was appointed to direct affairs of State in the king's absence, or ignorance. The office, however, was not officially recognised until 1905. The table shows the various Premiers since 1807.

TABLE OF BRITISH PREMIERS

Premier	Appointed	Political Party
Portland	March, 1807	—
S. Perceval ..	Dec., 1809	—
Liverpool	June, 1812	—
Canning ..	April, 1827	—
Goderich	Sept., 1827	—
Wellington	Jan., 1828	—
Grey	Nov., 1830	—
Melbourne	July, 1834	—
Sir R. Peel	Dec., 1834	—
Melbourne	April, 1835	—
Sir R. Peel	Sept., 1841	—
Lord J. Russell ..	July, 1846	Liberal
Derby	Feb., 1852	Conservative
Aberdeen	Dec., 1852	Coalition
Palmerston ..	Feb., 1855	Liberal
Derby	Feb., 1858	Conservative
Palmerston ..	June, 1859	Liberal
Russell	Nov., 1865	Liberal
Derby	July, 1866	Conservative
B. Disraeli	Feb., 1868	Conservative
W. E. Gladstone ..	Dec., 1868	Liberal
B. Disraeli (Beaconsfield)	Feb., 1874	Conservative
W. E. Gladstone ..	April, 1880	Liberal
Salisbury	June, 1885	Conservative
W. E. Gladstone ..	Feb., 1886	Liberal
Salisbury	Aug., 1886	Conservative
W. E. Gladstone ..	Aug., 1892	Liberal
Rosebery	March, 1894	Liberal
Salisbury	July, 1895	Conservative
A. J. Balfour ..	July, 1902	Conservative
Sir. H. Campbell-Bannerman ..	Dec., 1905	Liberal
H. H. Asquith ..	April, 1908	Liberal
H. H. Asquith ..	May, 1915	Coalition
D. Lloyd George	Dec., 1916	Coalition
D. Lloyd George ..	Jan., 1919	Coalition
A. Bonar Law ..	Oct., 1922	Conservative
Stanley Baldwin ..	May, 1923	Conservative
J. R. MacDonald ..	Jan., 1924	Socialist
Stanley Baldwin ..	Nov., 1924	Conservative
J. R. MacDonald ..	June, 1929	Socialist
J. R. MacDonald ..	Aug., 1931	National

PREMIUM. Term meaning a prize, reward, or bonus. An apprentice or articled pupil pays a premium for his instruction in a trade or profession. Shares in a company are sometimes quoted at a premium, i.e. a sum above their par value, £100 worth costing £105, etc. A **premium bond** is a bond carrying with it the chance of winning a money prize. Such a scheme is of the nature of a lottery, the prizes being given to holders of certain numbers drawn. The term is also used to denote sums payable periodically in respect of policies of insurance.

PREMONSTRATENSIANS, or NORBERTINES. A religious order founded at Prémontré, near Laon in France, by St. Norbert in 1120, who gave them the rule of St. Augustine with some additional rigour. The order was introduced into England in 1146, and its members were there regularly known as the White Canons. Before the Reformation they had 2000 monasteries, among which were 500 nunneries, mostly in Germany, the Netherlands, France, England, and the north of Europe; but the Reformation diminished this number by more than one-half in the sixteenth century. Since the end of the seventeenth century the order declined in numbers, but there was a revival in the nineteenth century, and there are houses in Holland and Austria, and some in England.

PRENZLAU (prents'lou). A town of Germany in Prussia, in Brandenburg, on the Ucker. Pop. 21,622.

PRE-RAPHAELITE BROTHERHOOD. The name adopted in 1848 by a group of seven young artists, Dante Gabriel Rossetti, Holman Hunt, J. E. Millais, J. Collinson, F. G. Stephens, painters; Thomas Woolner, sculptor; and W. M. Rossetti, writer. The name of the society was an expression of their belief that up to the time of Raphael artists had worked by the light of nature and of truth, but that afterwards mannerism and imitation had been the rule. The aims of the brotherhood, as stated by D. G. Rossetti, were: "(1) To have genuine ideas to express; (2) to study Nature attentively so as to know how to express them; (3) to sympathise with what is direct and serious and heartfelt in previous art, to the exclusion of what is conventional and self-parading and learned by rote; and (4) most indispensable of all, to produce thoroughly good pictures and statues."

Rossetti, Hunt, and Millais were the most important members. The

Dante Gabriel Rossetti

work of Rossetti, poet as well as painter, is full of mystic symbolism and passion, though technically inadequate in drawing and colour. His most notable paintings are: *Ecce Ancilla Domini* (National Gallery), a triptych in Llandaff Cathedral, *Beata Beatrix, Monna Vanna,* and *Dante's Dream.* In contrast to the temperament of Rossetti are the more solid qualities of Holman Hunt, whose painstaking art, with its exaggerated attention to detail, lacks inspiration notwithstanding its sincerity. Typical works are: *The Light of the World, Isabella and the Pot of Basil,* and the *Triumph of the Innocents* (National Gallery). Of the three, technically the most accomplished was Millais, whose precocious talent won him a medal at the Royal Academy schools at the age of thirteen, and made him a successful painter before he was twenty. Until 1859 he was faithful to Pre-Raphaelite ideas; but his *Vale of Rest,* painted in that year, marks the beginning of the popular and commonplace art of his later years, which brought him a baronetcy and the presidency of the Royal Academy. His Pre-Raphaelite work includes: *Lorenzo in the House of Isabella, The Carpenter's Shop* (Tate Gallery), *Ophelia* (National Gallery), *The Huguenot,* and *Sir Isumbras at the Ford.*

Although the original group did not long continue as a society, its teachings, which found a powerful advocate in Ruskin, spread far and exerted great influence on British art. Among the painters who more or less completely adopted its principles are: A. Hughes, R. B. Martineau, Frederick Sandys, W. H. Devrell, Charles Collins, Noel Paton, Burne-Jones, and J. F. Lewis. Ford Madox Brown, who had been Rossetti's master, was never a member of the brotherhood; but his later paintings, such as *Work* (Manchester Art Gallery), show its influence strongly.—BIBLIOGRAPHY: Percy Bate, *English Pre-Raphaelite Painters*; Holman Hunt, *The Pre-Raphaelite Brotherhood*; Ruskin, *Notes on Royal Academy Exhibitions.*

PREROGATIVE. Right or privilege attaching to a person or body. The royal prerogative, now exercised through the cabinet or the privy council, entitles the sovereign to declare war, summon, prorogue or dissolve parliament, nominate ministers, create peers, pardon offenders, etc. Former ecclesiastical courts dealing with the probate of wills of persons dying in the provinces of Canterbury and York were called prerogative courts. *See* CROWN; PROBATE.

PRESBYO'PIA. "Old-sightedness," due to failure of accommodation of the lens of the eye on account of age. Its effect is to cause objects near the eye to be less distinct than those at some distance, and it therefore affects reading. It is corrected by the use of convex glasses worn only for reading.

PRES'BYTER (Gr. *presbyteros,* an elder). An office-bearer in the early Christian Church, the exact character and position of whom is differently regarded by different authorities. Presbyterians generally maintain that originally *bishop* and *presbyter* were one and the same; Episcopalians generally maintain that from the first they were different, as was certainly the case in very early times. By the end of the second century the presbyters held a position in connection with the congregations intermediate between that of bishop and deacon, and represented the priests or second order of clergy.

PRESBYTE'RIANISM. One of the three great divisions of ecclesiastical polity. Independency or congregationalism regards the local congregation as autonomous. Prelacy or episcopalianism rests upon a diocesan episcopate, with a gradation of rank and office, and a distinction between the clergy and the laity. Presbyterianism means that the ministers are all on one footing, that the Church is governed by presbyters or elders, and that there is a gradation of church courts which conserves unity. There is no distinction between clergy and laity in presbyterianism; laymen are presbyters, but ruling presbyters, while ministers are ordained to teach or preach and administer the sacraments, but in the church courts there is absolute parity. These courts are the kirk-session, the presbytery, and the General Assembly. In some Churches there are synods, between the presbytery and the General Assembly, and congregational boards of managers or deacons, whose task is to supervise the finances and look after the fabric of the local church. But the presbytery is the characteristic court, composed of ministers and elders from each congregation in the district. Its decisions may be reviewed, on appeal, by the General Assembly, composed of members from the various presbyteries selected in a certain proportion. The General Assembly's decision is final. The kirk-session of the local congregation, of which the minister is head, supervises the spiritual affairs of the church, and its decisions may be taken to the presbytery and even to the General Assembly. The minister, though called by the local congregation, is ordained by the presbytery, without whose consent no step of this kind can be taken. He is responsible to the presbytery, and can only be deposed by the General Assembly. Kirk-sessions and presbyteries usually meet once a month, the General Assembly once a year.

It is claimed that the principle of Presbyterianism is recognised in the primitive Church where the Apostles chose presbyters or elders to superintend the churches. These constituted a presbytery (1 Tim. iv., 14). Eventually, out of these presbyters, who were called "overseers" or bishops, one came to assume a permanent position, which developed into the monarchical episcopate. At the Reformation many of the Churches reverted to what they considered the original and authoritative organisation of presbyterianism, and this was thought out by Calvin at Geneva, whose administrative genius moulded presbyterianism for the future. Local varieties exist, but, under all modifications, the essential principles already noted persist.

Originally presbyterianism was characterised by (*a*) Calvinistic doctrine, (*b*) a recognition of national religion, (*c*) a puritanic worship, and (*d*) popular government. The last-named has been least altered; the idea, congenial to democracy, is that the whole body ought to legislate for itself, functioning through chosen members. In earlier days a *ius divinum* was sought for this, as for episcopacy. Such an argument is no longer tenable. Church polity belongs to the well-being rather than to the being of the Church. Presbyterianism justifies itself by its efficiency, as it answers the ends which are regarded as vital to the Church of God in the mind and purpose of Christ. When it is held that the ministerial office is not sacerdotal, and also that the Church is more than a collection of separate particles, presbyterianism comes forward with the historical and practical claim to furnish a valid ministry and a truly Catholic Church.

The latest statistics assign over 6½ millions to presbyterianism, on the Continent, in Great Britain, Canada and America, and elsewhere. —BIBLIOGRAPHY: J. Macpherson, *Presbyterianism* (1883); A. Wright, *The Presbyterian Church* (1895); J. N. Ogilvie, *The Presbyterian Churches* (1896); R. C. Reed, *History of the Presbyterian Churches of the World* (1905); W. M. Macphail, *The Presbyterian Church* (1908). The early apostolic period is discussed in books like A. V. G. Allen's *Christian Institutions* (1898) and T. M. Lindsay's *Church and Ministry in the Early Centuries* (1902).

PRES'BYTERY. A judicatory, consisting of the pastors of all the churches of any particular Presbyterian denomination within a given district, along with their ruling (i.e. presiding) elders, there being one ruling elder from each church-session commissioned to represent the congregation in conjunction with the minister. The functions of the presbytery are: to grant licences to preach the gospel, and to judge of the qualifications of such as apply for them; to ordain ministers to vacant charges; to judge in cases of reference for advice, and in complaints and appeals which come from the church-sessions within the bounds of the presbytery; and generally to superintend whatever relates to the spiritual interests of the several congregations under its charge, both in respect of doctrine and discipline.

Appeals may be taken from the presbytery to the provincial synod and thence to the General Assembly.

PRES'COT. Urban district and market town of Lancashire, on the L.M.S. Railway. It is 8 miles from Liverpool and a centre of the watchmaking industry, with potteries, electric cable works and coal mines. Knowsley, the seat of the earl of Derby, is in the neighbourhood. Pop. (1931), 9396.

PRESCOTT, William Hickling. American historian, born in Salem, Massachusetts, 1790; died 1859. The son of a judge and grandson of

William Hickling Prescott

Colonel William Prescott, he was educated at Harvard College, where he graduated in 1814. Acquaintance with Spanish literature, which he began to cultivate in 1824, led him to attempt his first work on Spanish history, *The Reign of Ferdinand and Isabella*, published 1837. His next works were *The History of the Conquest of Mexico, with a Preliminary View of the Ancient Mexican Civilisation*, and *The Life of the Conquerer Hernando Cortez*, which appeared in 1843. In 1847 he published *The History of the Conquest of Peru, with a Preliminary View of the Civilisation of the Incas*. In 1855 the first two volumes of his *History of the Reign of Philip II., King of Spain*, appeared. His collected works in 20 vols. appeared in 1906.

PRESCRIPTION. In law, a right or title acquired by use and time; the object being to secure the title to property to him who has had the possession of it for the term fixed by the law, and to prevent anyone from disturbing his possession after such term has expired. In the English common law the term *prescription* is applied only to incorporeal hereditaments, as a right of way, a common, etc., and requires immemorial time to establish it. This rule was modified, however, by the passing of the statute 2 and 3 William IV. cap. lxxi., which provides that no right of common shall be defeated after thirty years' enjoyment, and after sixty years the right is deemed absolute and indefeasible, unless had by consent or agreement. In claims of right of way, of watercourse, and similar easements, the periods are twenty and forty years. Claims to the use of light to any dwelling-house or building enjoyed for twenty years are indefeasible, unless shown to have been by consent.

By the law of Scotland prescription has a much wider operation than by the law of England. It may be the means of acquiring a right (positive prescription) or of extinguishing an obligation (negative prescription). It thus not only protects individuals from actions which other parties might have brought against them, but in some instances creates a positive title to property. Until the Conveyancing Act, 1874, was passed, the prescription by which a right of property could be established was that of forty years. By Acts of 1874 and 1924, however, the period of prescription is reduced to twenty years. The party holding the property must have been twenty years in unchallenged possession, and be able to show an *ex facie* valid irredeemable title recorded in the appropriate Register of Sasines. For the acquisition of any servitude, right of way, etc., forty years' use is still essential. The period of the long negative prescription is now twenty years.

The other and shorter prescriptions are as follows: The vicennial, applicable to holograph writings not attested with the usual formalities; the decennial, applicable to actions against tutors and curators; the septennial, applicable to actions against cautioners; the sexennial, applicable to bills of exchange or promissory notes; the quinquennial, applicable to verbal contracts concerning movables, and arrears of rent; the triennial or three years' prescription, applicable to claims for rent of a house, accounts for board and lodging, wages, shopkeeper's accounts, etc. These short prescriptions do not extinguish the obligation but change the onus, and limit the mode, of proof. By Scots law also, but not by English, a vicennial prescription (it is supposed) applies to all crimes, and in certain crimes the prescription is limited by statute to a shorter period.

PRESCRIPTION. In medicine, the document given by a medical practitioner to his patient in order that he may obtain the medicaments prescribed for the relief or cure of the malady from which he suffers. Prescriptions have been given from the earliest times, and had a religious character, the blessings of the gods being invoked upon each. Every prescription to-day begins with such an invocation, written as ℞, but as a matter of fact this symbol is now held to represent the first letter of the Latin word *recipe*, take thou, the imperative mood of the verb *recipere*, to take. Until quite recent times prescriptions were written in full or abbreviated Latin, but now medical students are taught to write their prescriptions thus: names of medicaments in full Latin (abbreviated somewhat in actual practice), quantities in symbols, and directions in English. The writing of a prescription is an art which can only be acquired by experience and study, for the physician, after deciding which remedy or remedies he will use in a particular case, has to consider the question of incompatibility in its threefold aspect — therapeutical, chemical, and physical. The fact that so many proprietary medicines are prescribed by qualified practitioners is evidence of the difficulties encountered by some and the method by which they are avoided.

Most prescriptions when carefully analysed exhibit a fourfold character, viz. (1) the ingredient which is the "basis" of the prescription and upon which the efficiency of the preparation depends; (2) one or more ingredients which improve the action of the basis, the "adjuvans;" (3) one or more ingredients which correct the actions of (1) and (2), the "corrigens;" and (4) the ingredients which impart an agreeable form, the "constituens" vehicle or excipient. Many prescribers prefer to order as far as possible a single remedy in their prescriptions, a practice which has many advantages. The homœopathic practitioners carry the idea of single remedies to its legitimate conclusion, and only prescribe one medicament at a time, two being a violation of their principles.

Prescriptions are usually regarded as the property of the patient who has received them, and are returned to him by the pharmacist when they have been copied and dispensed. Copies of prescriptions are frequently demanded for various reasons, but the pharmacist grants copies of his copy as an act of grace, and considers himself to be acting within his rights when he refuses copies to all applicants except the owner of the original prescription. The idea of ownership has been disturbed by the provisions of the Dangerous Drugs Act, 1920, under which the pharmacist is directed to retain original prescriptions which contain the various poisons dealt with under this Act; in this case the practitioner is affected too, for he must give his own name, address, and qualifications, as well as the name and address of the patient. Under the National Insurance Acts all prescriptions are the property of the Commissioners.

PRESENTATION. The nomination of one or several candidates to a vacant office; commonly used in the case of a patron to a church. In England the clergyman is presented to the bishop to be instituted in a benefice; in Scotland, before the abolition of church patronage, he was presented to the presbytery for induction.

PRESENTMENT. In law, properly speaking, the notice taken by a grand-jury of any offence, from their own knowledge or observation, or any representation made by the jury to the court—arising, it may be, out of their deliberations.

PRESERVED FOODS, kept from corruption by comparatively simple means, have certainly been known and used from very early times. Fresh meat and fish were either merely dried in the sun or by artificial heat, were rubbed with salt or steeped in brine, or smoked. The nutritive properties of milk were, and still are, largely preserved in the forms of butter and cheese; while wine is the preserved juice of the grape. All housewives have for centuries been well acquainted with entirely successful ways of preserving fruit as jam, in syrup, or by drying; while various vegetables have long been pickled in vinegar. But the use of salt, sugar, or vinegar effects material changes in the nature of the food. Modern science has discovered methods of preserving some important foods in their original condition, and, by the same process, prepares them for immediate consumption. The decay and consequent speedy corruption of food materials is caused by the attacks of organisms, either animal or vegetable. Food preserved from these, in which all the living organisms are destroyed, can, in theory, be kept wholesome for an indefinite period, or, for practical purposes, for many months or even years.

It was a Frenchman, François

Appert (died 1840), who, early in the last century, first advocated the method now generally in use, paving the way to food preservation on a wholesale scale. Advances on his system have been made, but the essentials are the same. Meat, packed in round or oblong tins, is cooked in heated chambers, the tins first being closed, although a pin-hole aperture for the escape of air may be left, and sealed up on the completion of the process, which combines cooking with sterilisation. Soldering has long been the usual method of closing the tins, but of late years hermetic sealing—fusion of the edges of the metal—has come into use.

The acids of some kinds of food materials having an effect on tin, various methods of treating the inner surface of the cases have been tried, including coating with a special varnish. In cases where the sterilising process has not been effectively performed, gases are usually, though not invariably, generated by the subsequent decomposition; the tin bulges from the pressure of the gas, thus giving automatic warning of the danger of its contents. Germs calculated to produce ptomaine poisoning may, however, be present in the absence of this sign; and the fear resulting from occasional cases of illness or death traceable to preserved food, coupled with the great "Chicago scandals" of some years ago, has brought about a certain prejudice against tinned foods. Some manufacturers have avoided this drawback by cooking and sterilising the meat in the usual tins, and then transferring it to receptacles of glass or earthenware. Ptomaine poisoning is, however, exceedingly rare in proportion to the enormous quantities of tinned foods now consumed, and the danger may be regarded as almost, if not entirely, negligible.

The occurrence of *B. Botulinus* (*see* BOTULISM) in tinned foods is rare, but this germ or its toxin has been found in sausages and hams on the Continent, and in vegetables, beans, and cheese in America. As a consequence of the Loch Maree case, in which, on 14th Aug., 1922, six guests and two ghillies from the Loch Maree Hotel lost their lives by consuming potted-meat sandwiches affected with spores and the deadly toxin of *B. Botulinus*, arrangements were made by the Ministry of Health for a supply of an antitoxin to be held at certain centres in England, and to be available immediately on demand. These centres are Plymouth, Cardiff, Birmingham, Manchester, and Newcastle; the Board of Health for Scotland has a similar arrangement of centres.

Among meats, beef and brawn, largely packed in the United States and in South America, are most in use; mutton, both chilled and tinned, reaches Britain in large quantities from Australia and New Zealand; while tongues and a great variety of "fancy" potted meats command a ready sale. Tinned salmon, largely from the Fraser and Columbia Rivers of the great "North-West," herrings and lobsters, with sardines in oil from France, are the chief items among fish. The tomato is a leading fruit for treatment; while pineapples and apricots are brought within the reach of purchasers for whom such luxuries were formerly a name and little more. Condensed milk, first experimented with in 1835, is now produced in vast quantities, largely in Switzerland, but also in Canada, Holland, and the United States. The process employed is that of evaporation, usually with the addition of sugar.

The science of modern food preserving has, among other benefits, enabled the explorer in any region to carry with him a varied and nutritive larder; has lessened on the sailing-ship the prevalence of scurvy, formerly so frequent among crews deprived of fresh vegetables; and has provided the community with food ready for consumption, almost invariably wholesome, and moderate in price. Appert's *L'art de conserver toutes les substances animales et végétales* (1831) is of interest for the early history of the modern science.

PRES'IDENT, signifying he who presides, has several special and technical senses. It is used for (1) the principal member of a society or association, who takes the chair when present at meetings; (2) the chief official of a company or board; (3) the head of a university or college, or of a learned faculty; (4) the elected chief of a republic. In England, the Lord President of the Council, the chief of the Privy Council, is an officer of State whose duty is to act as a sort of intermediary between the sovereign and the council. In Scotland, the Lord President of the Court of Session is the presiding judge in the supreme court.

PRESS, FREEDOM OF THE. The liberty of every citizen to print whatever he chooses, and his immunity from responsibility to the Government. This liberty, however, does not prevent his being amenable to justice should he abuse his privilege. The right of printing rests on the same abstract grounds as the right of speech, and it might seem strange to a man unacquainted with history that printing should be subjected to a previous censorship, as it is in some states, and has been in all, any more than speaking, and that the liberty of the press should be expressly provided for in the Constitutions of most free states. But when we look to history we find the origin of this, as of many other legislative anomalies, in periods when politics, religion, and individual rights were confusedly intermingled. It is only since men's views of the just limits of government have become clearer that the liberty of the press has been recognised as a right; and to England we are particularly indebted for the establishment of this principle. The existence of a censorship of the press was for centuries, however, deemed an essential to the safety of all European governments. Liberty of printing, as we understand it, is a comparatively modern notion; Milton's plea for a free press met with no response from his own party, nor for very many years later was it the cue to any party in the English commonwealth to refrain from suppressing the writings of their political opponents.

In England the liberty of the press, soon after printing was introduced, was regulated by the king's proclamations, prohibitions, charters of licence, etc., and finally by the Court of Star-Chamber. The Long Parliament, after their rupture with Charles I., assumed the same power. The Government of Charles II. imitated their ordinances, and the press did not really become free till the expiration of the statutes restricting it in 1693, after which it was found impossible to pass new laws in restraint of it, and it has remained free ever since, the last restriction being done away with on the abolition of the newspaper stamp duty in 1856. Such legal checks as remain are merely intended to prevent outrages on religion or decency, to protect subjects from defamation, and to conserve the copyright of authors.

Almost complete liberty of the press now prevails in England in peace-time. In war-time, however, as was witnessed during the European War, a rigid censorship is imposed. The Constitutions of many of the United States declare, as we should expect, for liberty of the press. The same may be said of all the South American republics, and most European countries. In the British colonies the law is as in England, but in India the Governor-General exercises a censorship.

PRESSBURG, now **BRATISLAVA.** A city of Czechoslovakia, formerly in Hungary, on the Danube, and on the southern spurs of the Little Carpathians. The ruined royal palace, on the top of an eminence, was burned in 1811. The cathedral (St. Martin), a large Gothic structure, was begun in 1090 and completed in 1472, and here the Kings of Hungary were crowned. The Franciscan church, founded in 1290, is also noteworthy. There is a Slovene university, founded in 1912. The

Pressburg: Coronation Cathedral

river is crossed by a bridge of boats. The manufactures are various. The trade, particularly transit, and chiefly in corn and timber, is extensive.

Pressburg is a place of very great antiquity, and was long a fortress of some strength. In 1541, when the Turks captured Buda, it became the capital of Hungary, and retained the honour till the Emperor Joseph II. restored it to Buda. The Hungarian name for the town is Pozsony. The treaty by which Austria ceded Venice to France and the Tyrol to Bavaria was signed here in 1805. Pressburg was incorporated in Czechoslovakia after the European War (1914-18). Pop. (1930), 123,852.

PRESS-GANG. A detachment of seamen who, under a naval officer, were empowered to lay hold of seafaring men and compel them to serve in the king's ships. Although originally designed to serve the needs of the army as well as the navy, the system of impressment (q.v.) became confined to the navy, and, despite the fact that it has long fallen into abeyance, it is still legally permissible, for the laws enforcing impressment have never been repealed. The mode of procedure was crude, and the quality of the recruits obtained was seldom equal to that evinced by the poorest volunteer. When recruits were required, a body of men was detailed from the ship's company of a man-of-war. They were armed to the teeth, and went ashore under the command of one or more officers, searching all the known haunts of seafaring people and forcibly carrying them off. As it was not in their nature to surrender quietly, the impressed men usually fought as for their very lives, and the "takers," as they were called in Elizabethan days, being unpopular in all seaport towns, frequently had to fight women as well as men to make good their captures.

All seamen between the ages of eighteen and fifty-five years were eligible for impressment, excepting apprentices of under two years' service, fishermen at sea, a suitable proportion of seamen, manning colliers, and harpooners in whalers. In cases of national emergency landsmen were eligible for "taking," and a merchantman or privateer might be boarded at sea. The most suitable recruits for a hazardous naval life were undoubtedly those obtained from privateers, and such vessels usually gave friendly warships of whatever type a very wide berth. By 1835 the term of compulsory service had been limited from a life-time to five years, and thereafter the system died a natural death. The press-gang, with all its petty brutalities and violent strife, is dealt with in the novels of Marryat and Smollett.

PRESSURE GAUGE. Appliance for measuring the pressure of steam, gas, water, etc. The usual type of gauge on boilers for registering steam pressure consists of a flattened bronze tube bent in a curve and having one end open and connected to the steam pipe, the other end being sealed and linked to a pointer on a dial graduated to pounds per square inch. Pressure of steam in the tube causes it to tend to straighten and this movement is registered by the pointer.

PRESTA'TYN. Market town and urban district of Flintshire. A coast town, it is 205½ miles from London by the L.M.S. Railway. Here is a ruined castle. Pop. 4511.

PRESTER JOHN (Priest, or Presbyter John). A supposed Christian king and priest. In the Middle Ages it was reported by travellers that there was a Christian prince who reigned in the interior of Asia under this name. The first record of Prester John appears in the chronicle of Otto of Freisingen in the twelfth century. The legend then grew and developed. Rubruquis, in the thirteenth century, attributes the name of Prester John to a Nestorian prince, Ung or Ungh Khan, who perished in a war against Genghis Khan. Who this Prester John was it is not easy to decide; the supposition that he was the Dalai Lama, or one of the chief priests of the Lamaites, does not agree with the position assigned to his residence by travellers. The Portuguese, in the fifteenth century, picked up a story of a Christian prince in Central Africa, and by some confusion of names they transferred thither the throne of Prester John. Hence in recent times the home of this mythical prince and priest has always been laid in Abyssinia. Prester John is described in the *Travels* of Sir John Mandeville, is mentioned by Marlowe (*Tamburlaine the Great*) as Prester John of Africa, and is referred to by Shakespeare in *Much Ado About Nothing*. In Ariosto's *Orlando Furioso* he is the blind king of Ethiopia. — BIBLIOGRAPHY: S. Baring-Gould, *Curious Myths of the Middle Ages*; G. Brunet, *La Légende du prêtre Jean*.

PRESTON. A municipal and county borough and seaport of Lancashire, England, on the Ribble near the head of the estuary; served by the L.M.S. Railway. Among the principal buildings are the parish church, the Roman Catholic church of St. Walpurgis, and the town hall; among other chief buildings are the grammar-school, the free library, and the technical school. The river is spanned by five bridges, two of them railway bridges. The railway station forms one of the most important junctions on the L.M.S. Railway. The original staple manufacture of the town was linen, which is still woven to some extent, but has been completely eclipsed by the cotton manufacture. Preston also has electrical engineering works, numerous machine-shops, iron- and brass-foundries, railway-carriage works, steam sawmills, breweries, malt-houses, roperies, tanneries, etc., and extensive harbour and river works. Ships of about 3000 tons burden can utilise the port with comfort, through a deepening and widening scheme executed in 1884.

The town arose to take the place of the ancient *Coccium* or *Ribchester*, some 12 miles north of the modern town, where there are well-defined Roman remains. It received the name of Priest's Town, corrupted successively into Prestune, Prest-town, and Preston, from the early settlement at it of religious residents. Before the Norman Conquest (1066) it was held by Earl Tostig, and belonged, in the time of Richard I., to Theobald, brother of Archbishop Hubert. In 1221 a Greyfriary was founded, and a monastic hospital of Mary Magdalene was also established, but no remains of these institutions are now extant. In 1323 it was taken and burned by Robert Bruce ; in the great Civil War it espoused the Royalist cause, and was twice captured by the

Preston: Art Gallery

Parliamentarians ; Cromwell defeated the Royalists here in 1648. In the rebellion of 1715 it was occupied by the Jacobite forces (under Thomas Foster and the Earl of Derwentwater, etc.), and in that of 1745 the Highlanders, headed by Prince Charles Edward, passed through Preston both on their march to London and on their retreat. Preston was the birthplace of Arkwright and of the notorious Lady Hamilton. The town was chartered by Henry II. (1179), received thirteen charters from subsequent kings, and sent two members to Parliament from 1295 to 1331, and from 1529 to 1918. Pop. (1931), 119,001.—Cf. H. Fishwick, *History of the Parish of Preston.*

PRESTONPANS. A coast town (police burgh) of Haddingtonshire, Scotland, on the Forth ; served by the L.N.E. Railway. Once noted for its salt industry (whence the "pans"), it now produces beer, bricks, and tiles, and there is a considerable fishing industry. Coal-mines are located in the vicinity. Within a mile of the town is the battlefield where Prince Charles Edward gained a decisive victory over Sir John Cope (*Hey, Johnnie Cope*) and the Royalist forces on 21st Sept., 1745. Prestonpans became a burgh in 1617. The salt trade, which is now extinct, originated in 1185-6, and remained a thriving industry until about 1800. Pop. (1931), 2426.

PRESTWICH. An urban district of Lancashire, England, 4 miles from Manchester, of which it is now a residential suburb ; served by the L.M.S. Railway. The chief industry is in cotton. Near by are the reservoirs which supply the city of Manchester with water. Pop. (1931), 23,876.

PRESTWICK. A burgh of Scotland, on the coast of Ayrshire, 2¾ miles north of Ayr ; served by the L.M.S. Railway ; a popular health-resort and the headquarters of golf in the west of Scotland. Pop. (1931), 8538.

PRESUMPTION, in law, is the assuming of a fact or proposition as true. The *præsumptio juris* is a presumption established in law till the contrary be proved, e.g. the possessor of goods is presumed to be the owner. The *præsumptio juris et de jure* is that where law or custom establishes any proposition that cannot be overcome by contrary evidence, as the incapacity in a minor with guardians to act without their consent.

PRETORIA. The capital of the Transvaal, and the administrative capital of the Union of South Africa, on the northern slope of the valley formed by the Aapies River, a small tributary of the Crocodile, 4471 feet above sea-level ; by railway 46 miles from Johannesburg, 1040 miles from Cape Town, and 349 miles from Delagoa Bay. There are Government buildings, courts of justice, post office, English cathedral and other churches, synagogue, opera-house, market buildings, museum, etc. It came into British possession in June, 1900, as one result of the South African War. White pop. (1931), 62,138.

PREVENTION OF CRIMES ACT. An act of Parliament passed in 1908 with a view to providing for the reformation of young offenders and the detention of habitual criminals. When a young person of sixteen to twenty-one years of age is convicted of an offence for which the penalty is penal servitude or imprisonment, and in consequence of his criminal habits or tendencies or his association with persons of bad character it is desirable to do so, the court, instead of imposing such a penalty, may pass sentence of detention under penal discipline in a Borstal institution for a period of one to three years. Every person so detained remains under the supervision of the Prison Commissioners for six months after discharge. Incorrigibles may be committed to prison for the unexpired portion of the period of detention. *See* PRISONS.

An habitual criminal is defined as one who since attaining sixteen years of age has been at least three times convicted of a crime and is persistently leading a dishonest or criminal life, or who has on any previous conviction of a crime been found to be an habitual criminal and sentenced to preventive detention. These, in addition to a sentence of penal servitude, may be ordered to be kept in detention on its expiry for a period of five to ten years, if by reason of their criminal habits and mode of life such a course is expedient for the protection of the public.

PREV'ESA. A town of Greece, on the northern side of the Gulf of Arta. To the north of the town are the ruins of Nikopolis, founded by Augustus to commemorate the battle of Actium. Pop. 8650.

PRÉVOST D'EXILES (prā-vō deg-zēl), **Antoine François.** A French writer, born in 1697, died in 1763. Originally a member of the Jesuit order, he soon quitted it for a military career. After alternating several times between the Church and the army he gave up both professions, and in 1729 he went to Holland, where he published his *Mémoires d'un homme de qualité*. After a sojourn of two years in England he returned to France, and was appointed almoner and secretary to the Prince de Conti. From this period till his death he pursued an active literary life, editing a journal called *Pour et Contre*, and publishing many romances, of which the best known is the famous *Histoire du Chevalier des Grieux et de Manon Lescaut.*

PRI'AM. In Greek legend, the last King of Troy, the son of Laomedon. By his second wife, Hecuba, he had, according to Homer, nineteen children, the most famous being Hector, Paris, Cassandra, and Troilus. When he was extremely old, the Greeks demanded of him the restoration of Helen, who had been carried away by Paris, and on his refusal to give her up they made war against Troy, and took and destroyed the city after a siege of ten years. Homer gives no account of the death of Priam; but other poets represent him to have been slain at the altar of Zeus by Pyrrhus the Greek.

PRIA'PUS. A Greek deity, the deformed son of Dionysus and Aphrodite, a god of gardens, fruits, etc., considered by mythologists to represent fertility in nature. He was worshipped in all parts of Greece, though chiefly at the Greek settlement of Lampsacus on the Hellespont, and also in Rome.

PRIBRAM (prshē'brȧm). A town of Czechoslovakia, in Bohemia, in a district where are rich lead- and silver-mines. Pop. 10,468.

PRIB'YLOV (or **PRIBYLOFF**) **ISLANDS.** A group of islands on the coast of Alaska, United States, in Bering Sea. The largest are St. Paul, St. George, Walrus, and Beaver Islands. They are frequented by numbers of fur-seals. The natives are Aleutians. The islands were visited in 1786 by Gerasim Pribylov (and named after him), and were acquired by the United States in 1867.

PRICE, Richard. British political and moral philosopher and divine, born in 1723, died in 1791. He commenced his literary career in 1758 by his *Review of the Principal Questions in Morals*, which was followed by *Four Dissertations on the Importance of Christianity, the Nature of Historical Evidence, and Miracle*. In 1771 appeared his *Observations on Reversionary Payments and Annuities*, and later the celebrated *Northampton Mortality Tables*. He also published a number of political tracts, in one of which he advocated the cause of the American colonies in 1776. When Pitt became Prime Minister, he consulted Dr. Price in his schemes for the reduction of the national debt, and the establishment of the sinking fund was the result of his recommendation. At the commencement of the French Revolution, in a sermon (published in 1789) *On the Love of Country*, he warmly expressed his delight at the emancipation of the French people. This discourse produced Burke's *Reflections*, in which Dr. Price was severely treated.

PRICKLES. In botany, hard, pointed emergences or outgrowths of the epidermis and subjacent layers, as in the rose and the bramble. They are to be distinguished from the various forms of *spines* or *thorns*, which are modified leaves or shoots.

PRICKLY ASH. A name given to several prickly shrubs of the United States, genus Xanthoxylum, ord. Rutaceæ. They have an aromatic and pungent bark, which from being used as a remedy for toothache gains them the name of *toothache tree*.

PRICKLY HEAT (miliaria). An acute eruption of papules and vesicles on the skin, and is accompanied by marked itching. It is a common affection in the tropics among white people, while the native population are unaffected. It may also occur in

argillaceous schist, hornblende schist, and all slaty and crystalline strata generally; and *unstratified*, these being chiefly granite. By geologists of a later day the term primary was used as equivalent to *Palæozoic*, the name given to the oldest known group of stratified rocks, extending from the Cambrian to the Permian formation. *See* GEOLOGY.

PRI'MATE. In the early Christian Church the title assumed by the bishop of the capital of a province, and hence equivalent to metropolitan. In Africa the title belonged to the bishop who had been longest ordained. In France the Archbishop of Lyons was appointed primate of the Gauls by Gregory VII. in 1079. In the Church of England both the archbishops still retain the title of primate, the Archbishop of Canterbury being distinguished as the primate of *all* England, and the Archbishop of York as the primate of England. In the Protestant Episcopal Church of Ireland the Archbishop of Armagh is primate of *all* Ireland, and the Archbishop of Dublin primate of Ireland, as formerly when the Church was established. The present Archbishop of Canterbury and primate of all England is the Most Reverend Cosmo Gordon Lang, who became Archbishop of Canterbury in 1928, after being consecrated Bishop of Stepney in 1901, and Archbishop of York in 1908. The present Archbishop of York and primate of England is the Most Reverend William Temple, son of Frederick Temple (q.v.), Archbishop of Canterbury. He was headmaster of Repton, 1910-4, and Bishop of Manchester from 1921 to 1929, when he became Archbishop.

PRIMA'TES (-tēz). The highest order of the Mammalia, including man, monkeys, apes, and lemurs.

PRIME. In the Roman Catholic Church one of the canonical hours, and also the service of the breviary which falls to be performed at that time. The term is derived from the Lat. *prima* (that is, *prima hora*, first hour), because prime begins with the first hour of the day according to the Eastern mode of reckoning, namely, six o'clock.

PRIME MINISTER. *See* PREMIER.

PRIMING. The carrying of small drops of water by steam. Insufficient steam space and badly designed flues and pipes in the boiler are among the causes of priming. The steam is taken away from a boiler through a collecting pipe situated in the steam space. This pipe has saw-cuts in it, through which the steam passes on its way to the stop-valve. The function of the collecting pipe is to prevent water being carried away with the steam. The main piping is provided with drains through which any water, produced by the condensation of steam, can be passed out. Wet steam is not only objectionable because of the reduced heat-content of each pound, but it has the disadvantage that its presence in the valve-chest of an engine is the cause of an increase in the "missing quantity." Water in pipes conveying superheated steam has been the cause of great trouble in steam-engineering research work. The flow is stratified, and, although the readings of a thermometer may show that there is a great amount of superheat in the middle zone, the contact of the colder outside layer with the wall of the pipe is the cause of a certain amount of condensation.

PRIMITIVE METHODISTS. Evangelical community. It arose from the introduction into English Methodist practice of open-air revival meetings. From 1807 onwards such meetings, held under Wesleyan Methodist protection, were especially fostered by Hugh Bourne and William Clowes who, excluded from membership for utilising unauthorised forms of worship, joined forces, 1810, and adopted the Primitive Methodist title, 1812. For 30 years the founders actively guided the rapidly expanding work, and 10 years after that, when both had died, a loose connection of federated districts gradually developed, becoming the Primitive Methodist Church, 1902. Organic union with other Methodist communions was authorised by Parliament for 1933.

PRIMO DE RIVERA. *See* RIVERA.

PRIMOGEN'ITURE. The right of the eldest son and those who derive through him to succeed to the property of the ancestor. The first-born in the patriarchal ages had among the Jews superiority over his brethren, but the "insolent prerogative of primogeniture," as Gibbon denominates it, was especially an institution developed under feudalism. Before the Norman Conquest the descent of lands in England was to all the sons alike, but gradually the right of succession by primogeniture came to prevail everywhere, except in Kent, where the ancient gavelkind tenure still remained. The right of primogeniture is entirely abolished in France and Belgium, but it prevails in some degree in most other countries of Europe.

By Act of Parliament primogeniture is abolished for deaths after 1st Jan., 1925. The rule operates only in cases of intestacy, and is as follows: When a person dies intestate, leaving real estate, his eldest son is entitled by law to the whole. If the eldest son is dead, but has left an eldest son, the latter succeeds to the whole of the property. If the whole male line is exhausted, then the daughters succeed —not in the same way, however, but jointly, except in the case of the crown, to which the eldest succeeds. In the United States no distinction of age or sex is made in the descent of estates to lineal descendants.—Cf. Sir William Blackstone, *Commentaries on the Laws of England*.

PRIMROSE (Primula). The type-genus of the ord. Primulaceæ, with radical leaves, flowers in an umbel, tubular, five-cleft calyx, and salver-shaped corolla with five lobes. The species, about seventy in number, are perennial and mostly alpine. Many of them are dimorphic, with *thrum-eyed* and *pin-eyed* forms, the former having

Primrose

the stamens at the mouth of the tube, the latter with the stigma showing. (*See* HETEROSTYLY.) There are five British species: *P. vulgaris*, the common primrose of spring, in which the umbellate arrangement of the flowers is disguised by the shortness of the scape; *P. veris*, the cowslip; *P. elatior*, the oxlip; *P. farinosa*, the bird's-eye primrose; and *P. scotica*, the Scottish primrose. The polyanthus is a cultivated variety of the cowslip, and the garden auriculas are derived from an alpine species, *P. auricula*. A favourite cultivated species is the Chinese primrose (*P. sinensis*).

PRIMROSE LEAGUE, THE, took its origin and name in 1883, when Sir H. Drummond Wolff, seeing primroses in the button-holes of Conservative members of Parliament who attended the unveiling of the statue of Lord Beaconsfield, said to Lord Randolph Churchill: "Let us found a primrose league." Some doubt has been thrown on the question of the primrose being the famous Premier's favourite flower; but, in spite of ridicule, the project flourished. Women were soon admitted to its ranks, and the membership, less than one thousand in 1884, amounted to a quarter of a million two years later, and is now nearly three millions. The government and organisation is by "habitations," of which there are about three thousand; members are classed as "dames," "knights," and "associates;" and the badge is the monogram P.L., encircled by a wreath of primroses, the five petals of the flower being an emblem of Anglo-Saxon ascendancy in the continents of Europe, Asia, Africa, America, and Australia. The motto is *Imperium et Libertas*, and the principles inculcated are "the maintenance of religion, of the estates of the realm, and of the imperial ascendancy of Great Britain." The 19th of April is Primrose Day.

PRIMULA'CEÆ. A natural order of gamopetalous dicotyledons, characterised generally by a five-cleft calyx, five-partite corolla, five epipetalous stamens, single style, undivided stigma, one-celled ovary with free-central placentation, capsular fruit, and usually simple radical leaves. The species are herbs, almost confined to the temperate and cold regions of the northern hemisphere. The principal genera are: Primula (*see* PRIMROSE), Lysimachia, Anagallis, Cyclamen, and Soldanella.

PRINCE (Lat. *princeps*). Literally one who holds the first place. The epithet, originally applied to the *princeps senatūs* of the Roman state, subsequently became a title of dignity. The title was adopted by Augustus and his successors. In modern times the title of prince (or princess) is given to all sovereigns generally, as well as to their sons and daughters and their nearest relations. Until the Revolution of 1918 there was a class of sovereigns in Germany, ruling little states, such as Reuss, and ranking below the dukes. They were called *Fürsten*, whilst the members of the royal family were styled *Prinzen*. On the Continent there are also families not immediately connected with any reigning house who bear the title of prince; such were Bismarck and Metternich.

PRINCE ALBERT. City of Saskatchewan, Canada. It is on the North Saskatchewan River, 247 miles N. of Regina, and is a junction on the C.N. Railway. The chief industries are lumbering and the milling of grain. The Prince Albert National Park, opened in 1928, has an area of 1400 sq. miles. Pop. 9905.

PRINCE EDWARD ISLAND. The smallest and most densely peopled province of the Dominion of Canada, in the Gulf of St. Lawrence, separated by Northumberland Strait from the mainland of Nova Scotia and New Brunswick. The island is of irregular outline, with a deeply indented coastline dividing it into three well-defined regions. It is low-lying, but the climate is healthy and far milder than that of the contiguous mainland provinces.

Area and Population. The area of the island is 2184 sq. miles. Pop. (1931), 88,040. The principal cities and their populations are Charlottetown (the capital), 12,357, and Summerside, 3914.

Religion. Roman Catholicism is the predominant faith, with 39,064 adherents in 1931. Others are: Presbyterian (14,803), Methodist (21,979), Baptist (5066), and Anglican (5066). Jurisdiction over the Roman Catholics is held by the Bishop of Charlottetown, and over the Anglicans by the Bishop of Nova Scotia.

People. The people are mainly of British stock, the origins in order of importance being Scots (40,000), English (24,000), Irish (21,000), French (13,000), and all other nationalities about 1000.

Education. Elementary instruction has been free since 1852, and is theoretically compulsory; but the law is inoperative through the exigencies of an agricultural community and inadequate means of enforcement. There is no university, and no facilities for higher instruction are provided other than in the Roman Catholic college of St. Dunstan's and the Prince of Wales College, both secondary schools and located in Charlottetown.

Communications. There were (1930) 286 miles of railway. A line runs from Charlottetown to Tignish in the northwest via Summerside. At Emerald Junction there is a branch running southwards to Cape Traverse, a terminal station. There is a terminal station of the Canadian National on the mainland of New Brunswick, directly across Northumberland Strait, at Cape Tormentine. In 1918 a powerful car-ferry steamer began operations, and affords Prince Edward Island a means of daily communication with the mainland without transshipment. The strait, however, is generally closed by ice from the middle of December to the beginning of April, and a regular service frequently becomes impossible, giving rise to considerable agitation for a railway tunnel between the island and the New Brunswick mainland.

Production: Agriculture. Prince Edward Island is the garden province of Canada, and the people and the soil are almost entirely devoted to agricultural pursuits. Oats, potatoes, and roots (turnips, mangolds, etc.) are the staple crops, but barley and spring-wheat are also produced. Dairying is progressive, and butter and cheese are extensively made. Poultry-farming is also practised. Beef, bacon, hams, poultry, butter, eggs, cheese, and potatoes are exported. The trade of the island is chiefly inter-provincial, i.e. with the other provinces of the Dominion. **Minerals.** There are neither minerals nor mines. **Fisheries.** These are of great value, lobsters (which are canned at Charlottetown), herring, cod, mackerel, and smelts being found. Oysters (Malpeque), for which the fisheries were once famous, are now almost extinct from the ravages of destructive pests, and although in 1912 the provincial authorities acquired control of the adjacent beds from the Dominion Government, extensive planting operations have hitherto been attended with but little success.

History. Prince Edward Island was first sighted by Cartier in June, 1534. It was colonised by the French (1534-1798), and was known as the Ile Ste. Jean. In 1798 it was renamed out of compliment to the Duke of Kent, then commanding the British forces in North America. Great Britain obtained the island in 1763, when it was administered by the Government of Nova Scotia, but it was eventually erected into a separate colony, the first Parliament meeting in 1773; and the island was admitted to the confederation as a province a century later (1873). Modern government is in the hands of a Lieutenant-Governor, who is assisted by a responsible ministry. The Legislative Assembly, 30 members, elected partly by property-holders and partly by universal male and female suffrage, sits for a period of four years. Women are eligible for election. Four Senators and four members of Parliament represent the province in the Dominion Parliament at Ottawa.

BIBLIOGRAPHY: *Handbook on Prince Edward Island* (issued by the Department of the Interior, Ottawa); J. B. Pollard, *Historical Sketch of Prince Edward Island*; Rev. G. Sutherland, *Geography, Natural and Civil History of Prince Edward Island*; D. C. Harvey, *The French Régime in Prince Edward Island*; D. Campbell, *History of Prince Edward Island.*

PRINCE OF WALES. The title of the heir-apparent to the British throne, first conferred by Edward I. on his son (afterwards Edward II.) at the time of his conquest of the Principality of Wales. Edward III. was never Prince of Wales, but the title has been conferred on all the male heirs-apparent to the English (and afterwards the British) throne from Edward the Black Prince, son of Edward III. The heir-apparent is made Prince of Wales and Earl of Chester by special creation and investiture, or by proclamation, but as the king's eldest son he is by inheritance Duke of Cornwall. As heir to the crown of Scotland, the Prince of Wales bears the titles of Prince and High Steward of Scotland, Duke of Rothesay, Earl of Carrick, Baron Renfrew, and Lord of the Isles, in virtue of an Act of the Scottish Parliament of 1469. The title of Earl of Dublin was borne by Edward VII. as Prince of Wales. The arms of the Prince of Wales are the royal arms, with the addition of a label of three points argent, and any other addition that may be adopted. The Prince of Wales has also a badge, consisting of a plume of three white ostrich feathers, with the motto *Ich dien* (I serve).

PRINCE RUPERT. A seaport-town of British Columbia, on Kaien Island, at the mouth of the Skeena River; the Pacific terminal of the Grand Trunk Pacific Railway. There is a magnificent natural harbour. Within five hours' sailing are the richest halibut banks in the world, and salmon, cod, and herring are also caught in enormous quantities. Hæmatite and magnetite ores are found in the district, as are gold, silver, lead, zinc, molybdenite, and copper. Pop. 6350.

PRINCES' ISLANDS, or KIZIL ADALAR. A group of nine islands in the Sea of Marmara. They belong to Turkey and form part of the prefecture of Istanbul. Pop. 12,310. Prinkipo is the chief.

PRINCES RISBOROUGH. Town of Buckinghamshire. It is 7 miles from Aylesbury, on the L.N.E. Railway. Chequers, the official country residence of the Prime Minister, is 3½ miles away. Pop. 2438.

PRINCETON. A borough of the United States, in Mercer county, New Jersey; served by the Pennsylvania Railway, by the Delaware & Raritan Canal, and by electric-traction lines to Trenton, etc. It is the seat of Princeton University, one of the first educational institutions in the country and also of the theological seminary of the Presbyterians and the Rockefeller Research Institute. Pop. 6992.

PRINCETOWN. Town of Devonshire. It is on Dartmoor, 15 miles from Plymouth, on the G. W. Railway. Near is Dartmoor prison. The town, which is a tourist centre, is on the estate of the Prince of Wales, as Duke of Cornwall.

PRINCIPE. A Portuguese West African island, in the Bight of Biafra, midway between São Thomé and Fernando Po. It is mountainous and unhealthy. *See* SAO THOME AND PRINCIPE.

PRINGLEA. A peculiar genus of Cruciferæ. The single species, *P. antiscorbutica*, the Kerguelen cabbage, is well adapted for wind-pollination—a rare condition among Crucifers—having no petals, protruding anthers, and long thread-like papillæ on the stigma; the exceptional structure is explained by the lack of winged insects on Kerguelen Island, where these cannot survive owing to the incessant gales.

PRINKIPO. *See* PRINCES' ISLANDS.

PRINTING. In a general sense, the art of stamping impressions of figures, letters, or signs, with ink, upon paper, vellum, cloth, or any similar substance: but the term is also applied to the production of photographs from negatives, where neither ink nor pressure is used. Printing may be done (1) from engraved metal plates, in which the ink is stored for transference in the sunk or incised lines of the pattern (*see* ENGRAVING) (2) from a level surface, as polished stone, where the ink is confined to the lines by a repellent medium (*see* LITHOGRAPHY); or (3) from surfaces in relief, where the ink is transferred from the raised characters, which may be either on one block or on separate or movable types. The last-named method is so much the most important that it gives its restricted meaning to the term *printing*, unless where qualified.

History. The rudiments of the art of *typography* or *letterpress-printing* were undoubtedly known to the ancients so far as the taking of impressions from blocks is concerned, and this method is still practised in China. The ancient Romans made use of metal stamps, with characters engraved in relief, to mark their articles of trade and commerce; and Cicero, in his work *De Natura Deorum*, has a passage from which Toland imagines the moderns have taken the hint of printing. Cicero orders the types to be made of metal, and calls them *formæ literarum*, the very words used by the first printers. In Virgil's time, too, brands with letters were used for marking cattle, etc., with the owner's name.

Block-printing in Europe, from single pieces of wood, can be traced back as far as the twelfth century. In these blocks the lines to be printed were in relief, as in modern wood-engraving, and each leaf of the book was printed from a single block. The leaves were usually printed only on one side of the paper, the blank sides being afterwards pasted together so as to give the volume the ordinary book appearance. By the middle of the fifteenth century block-book making was a distinct craft in Germany and the Netherlands. Among the earliest species of German origin is an *Apocalypsis,* containing forty-eight illustrations on as many leaves; and among those of Netherlandish origin, the *Biblia Pauperum* of forty leaves—both works of the early fifteenth century.

It is a matter of much dispute to whom is due the merit of adopting movable types. The invention has long been popularly credited to Johan Gutenberg, but critical examination of early Dutch and German specimens and historical evidence would seem to point to Laurens Janszoon Coster of Haarlem as the first inventor. (*See* COSTER; GUTENBERG.) The date of the Haarlem invention is variously placed between 1420 and 1430. Coster's types were first of beech wood, then of lead, and lastly of tin; the first book printed from movable types being probably one entitled *Speculum Nostræ Salutis.* Gutenberg in 1449 became associated with a rich citizen in Mainz, named Johann Fust or Faust, who advanced the capital necessary to prosecute the business of printing. Soon after (probably in 1453) Peter Schöffer, who afterwards became Fust's son-in-law, was taken into copartnership, and to him belongs the merit of inventing matrices for casting types, each individual type having hitherto been cut in wood or metal.

The oldest work of any considerable size printed in Mainz with cast letters, by Gutenberg, Fust, and Schöffer, finished about 1455, is the Latin Bible, which is called the *Forty-two-lined Bible,* because in every column it has forty-two lines; or the *Mazarin Bible,* from a copy having been discovered in the library of Cardinal Mazarin in Paris. Fust having separated from Gutenberg in 1456, and obtained the printing-press for his own use, undertook, in connection with Peter Schöffer, greater typographical works, in which the art was carried to higher perfection. Fust was particularly engaged in the printing of the *Latin and German Bible,* the first copies of which, bearing date, were printed in 1462. Fust is said to have died of the plague in 1466 at Paris, upon which Peter Schöffer continued the printing business alone at Mainz.

After the separation of Gutenberg and Fust the former had found means to procure a new printing-press, and had printed many works, of which the most remarkable is the *Astrological and Medical Calendar* (in folio, 1457). In 1462 the city of Mainz was taken and sacked by Adolphus, Count of Nassau, and this circumstance is said to have so deranged the establishment of Fust and Schöffer that many of their workmen were obliged to seek employment elsewhere. The truth seems to be that the inventor of the new art was Coster; that Gutenberg and Schöffer made important improvements on it, and aided by Fust widely spread the results of the new art.

From this period printing made rapid progress throughout Europe. In 1465 we find works printed at Subiaco by Conrad Sweynheym and Arnold Pannarts, two of the most celebrated among the early printers, who in 1467 removed to Rome. In 1469 we find printing at Venice and Milan; in 1470 at Paris, Nürnberg, and Verona; and by 1472 the art had become known in all the important cities of the Continent. In 1488 it had reached Constantinople, and by the middle of the next century had extended to Russia and America.

At the invention of printing the character of type employed was the old Gothic or German. The *Roman* type was first used at Strasbourg about 1464, by a printer known as "the R printer" on account of a peculiarly shaped R, and was introduced into Italy by Sweynheym and Pannarts at Subiaco in 1465 and at Rome in 1467. In England Richard Pynson printed Pace's *Oratio in Pace nuperrima* in this type in 1518. The *Italic* type, said to be an imitation of the handwriting of Petrarch, was first used at Venice by Aldus Manutius in the *Virgil* of 1500. At first, however, the capitals were Roman in form. Designed for the printing of classics, Italic type was found useful to differentiate introductions, prefaces, notes, etc., from the text; then for quotations; afterwards for emphasising certain words, and in the Bible for indicating words not in the original Hebrew or Greek.

Schöffer, in his edition of Cicero's *De Officiis,* produces for the first time some Greek characters, rudely executed; but the earliest complete Greek work was a grammar of that language printed at Milan in 1476. The

Pentateuch, which appeared in 1482, was the first work printed in the Hebrew character, and the earliest known *Polyglot Bible*—Hebrew, Arabic, Chaldaic, Greek, Latin—issued from the press of Genoa in 1516. Several printers' names have become famous not only for the beauty of their types, but also for the general excellence of their productions. Among these may be noted: The Aldi of Venice (1490-1597), Baden of Paris (1495-1535), Estiennes or Stephens of Paris (1502-98), Plantin of Antwerp (1514-89), Wechel of Paris and Frankfort (1530-72), Elzevir of Leyden and Amsterdam (1580-1680), and Bodoni of Parma (1768-1813).

The art of printing was first introduced into England by William Caxton, who established a press in Westminster Abbey in 1476. (*See* CAXTON.) His two most distinguished successors were Wynkin de Worde and Richard Pynson. The former, a native of the Dukedom of Lorraine, served under Caxton, and after the death of his master successfully practised the art of printing on his own account. The books which he printed are very numerous, and display a rapid improvement in the typographic art. He died in 1534. Pynson was a native of Normandy, and it is supposed that he also served under Caxton. The works which he printed are neither so numerous nor so beautiful as those of Wynkin de Worde. To Wynkin de Worde and Pynson succeeds a long list of ancient typographers, into which we cannot enter here.

The first Scottish printers of whom we have any authentic account were Walter Chapman, a merchant of Edinburgh, and Andrew Millar, who, in consequence of a patent from James IV., established a press at Edinburgh in 1507. In 1536 Thomas Davidson printed, "in the Fryere's Winde," Edinburgh, the *Chronicles of Scotland*, by Boethius, and in 1540 the works of Sir David Lindsay. Robert Leprevik printed extensively both at Edinburgh and St. Andrews. Thomas Vautrollier was another old Scottish printer, who brought out, in 1585, Calvin's *Institutes*; in 1589, Tusser's *Points of Good Husbandry*; and in 1597 the *Demonologie* of King James VI. Edward Raban, a native of Gloucestershire or Worcestershire, introduced the art into Aberdeen about 1620-2, and continued printing there till 1649.

In 1638 George Anderson, by special invitation of the magistrates, set up the first printing-press in Glasgow. In later days Scotland highly distinguished itself by the extent and beauty of its typographical productions. Ruddiman, who flourished at Edinburgh during the first half of the eighteenth century, was one of the most learned printers which any country has produced. The art has continued to flourish in the Scottish capital, and printing is now one of its chief industries. In Urie, in Robert and Andrew Foulis, in the Duncans, and others, Glasgow has produced printers whose works are alike celebrated for their appearance and accuracy.

In 1551 the *Common Prayer* was printed in Dublin by Humfrey Powell, 4to, black letter, and this is the earliest recorded production of the Irish press; but until as far down as 1700 very few books were printed in Ireland. Alderman George Faulkner, who lived in the eighteenth century, may be considered as the father of Irish typography. Printing was introduced in the New England States of America in 1639, the first known print being the *Freeman's Oath*; in 1640 what is known as the *Bay Psalm-book* was printed in Cambridge, Massachusetts.

Processes. The various letters and marks used in printing are cast on types or rectangular pieces of metal, having the sign in relief on the upper end. These types, with the low pieces required to fill up spaces, are placed in cells or boxes in a shallow tray or case in such a way that any letter can readily be found. The cases are mounted on a stand or frame, so that they may lie before the person who is to select and arrange the types, technically styled a *compositor*. The Roman types used are of three kinds: an alphabet of large capitals (A B C, etc.), one of small capitals (A B C, etc.), and one of small letters (a b c, etc.), called *lower-case* by the compositor. Of italic characters only large capitals and lower-case are used. Besides these there are many varieties of letters, such as Old English, and imitations of manuscript letters, the mention of which could only be serviceable to the practical printer. Types are of various sizes, the following being those in use among British printers for bookwork: English, Pica, Small Pica, Long Primer, Bourgeois, Brevier, Minion, Nonpareil, Pearl, Diamond. English has 5½ lines and Diamond 17 lines in an inch. *See* TYPE.

Composing. The twentieth century has seen a great change in the work of the compositor, owing to the gradual perfection of mechanical methods of composition. However, for specially fine editions and work of a complicated nature, the older method of hand-setting is still employed, when the compositor picks papier-mâché process, which is much more expeditious. By it plates can be produced in a few minutes; the type from which the moulds are originally taken lasts longer; and in cases where reprints are often required the moulds are light, inexpensive, and easily stored, so that the metal plate may be melted down and recast from the mould when a new edition is required. The mould in this process consists of several sheets of tough, thin, tissue paper, gummed together and moistened, and backed with a sheet of fine-grained brown paper. With this an impression is obtained by pressing it on the types, care being taken to drive the paper thoroughly into all the hollows between them. The back of the matrix or mould receives a coating of stucco to fill up all irregularities, and, the mould being dried, a cast from molten type-metal is easily obtained. The cast has to be carefully examined as in the stucco process. The paper mould can easily be detached from the plate uninjured, and may be used again if fresh plates are required.

In the electrotype process a mould or matrix is first taken from the page of type, the substance most commonly employed being wax. This is placed in a solution of a copper salt, and by means of an electric current (*see* ELECTRO-PLATING) a coating of copper is deposited on the matrix. A sort of copper shell is thus produced, one side giving a facsimile of the page of type, the reverse side being hollow, requiring to be filled with molten metal so as to form a plate that can be printed from.

Printing. When the forme of types has been prepared for press by the compositor, it is passed over to the pressmen, who form a distinct craft. The act of printing has two operations. First there is the application of ink to the face of the types, and then the pressing of a sheet of paper on the types with such weight as to cause the ink to adhere to it. The ink used is a thick viscid fluid made of boiled linseed-oil and lamp-black. It is applied to the type by means of a roller covered with an elastic composition of glue, glucose, sugar, and glycerine, rubber being used occasionally. When the printing is being done on a hand-press, the roller is carried on a light frame having handles, by which it is gripped by the hands of the pressman or printer, who in working passes the roller several times over an inked table, and then backwards and forwards over the forme. When the printing is done on a machine, two or more rollers are placed in suitable bearings, and generally the forme is made to travel under them and receive ink in passing. In hand-printing the paper is placed and the pressure given by a second workman. In machine-work the sheet may be placed by an assistant, or taken in by the machine itself, or otherwise supplied by a continuous web from a reel.

These operations, purely mechanical, have, however, to be preceded by a stage of preparation called *making-ready*, which calls for more or less skill and taste from the workman. His craft in plain work is to produce printed sheets, the letters or reading on which shall be sharp yet solid, with the colour or depth of black uniform all over the sheet, and each sheet uniform with the others which are to form the book. This is attained partly by properly regulating the supply of ink, but mainly by getting uniformity of pressure, as any portion of a sheet more firmly impressed than another will bring off more colour.

Mechanism of Printing. The mechanism of printing, at first of a very simple kind, has latterly attained to great perfection and efficiency. Three methods are followed for obtaining the impression which produces the printed sheet. The first and simplest is by the advance toward each other of two flat surfaces, one (the bed) carrying the type-forme, the other (the platen) carrying the blank sheet to be printed. The second is by the rotation of a cylinder above a type-table travelling backwards and forwards, the table being in contact with the cylinder in advancing and free in returning. The third and most recently adopted method is the contact of two cylinders revolving continuously in the same direction, one carrying the type-surface and the other bringing against it a continuous web of paper, which it afterwards cuts into sheets. Presses or machines of the first class are called *platen*, the second *cylinder*, and the third *rotary*.

The press used by Gutenberg was of a very rude description, the ink being applied by means of leather-covered balls stuffed with soft material, and having suitable handles, and the pressure being obtained by a screw which brought down a flat block or platen. The first improvement on this device seems to have been the construction of guides, enabling the type-forme to be run under the impressing surface and withdrawn with facility. Other necessities soon after arose, chiefly that of obtaining a rapid return of the platen from the position at which it gave the pressure, without the screw requiring to be turned back; but it was not till the year 1620 that this was met by the invention of Willem Janszoon Blaeu, a native of Amsterdam.

Charles Stanhope, the third Earl Stanhope, was the author of the next great improvement in printing-presses, about 1800. He devised a combination of levers, which he applied to the old screw-press. These levers brought down the platen with greatly increased rapidity, and, what was of still greater importance, converted at the proper moment that motion into direct pressure. The pressure was under control and capable of easy adjustment. The press was of iron, not of wood as was the case with all previously constructed presses, and it exhibited a number of contrivances of the most ingenious character for facilitating the work of the pressman. In 1813 John Ruthven, a printer of Edinburgh, patented a press on the lever principle, with several decided improvements. The Columbian Press, invented in 1814 by G. Clymer, Philadelphia, and the Albion Press are among later contrivances, and are still in use to a limited extent. Even in its best form the hand-press is laborious to work and slow in operation, two workmen not being able to throw off more than 250 impressions in an hour. It therefore became imperative, especially for newspapers, to devise some more expeditious and easy method of taking impressions from type.

So early as the year 1790 William Nicholson took out letters-patent for printing by machinery. His printing-machine never became available in practice, yet he deserves the credit of being the first who suggested the application of cylinders and inking-rollers. About ten years later König, a printer in Saxony, turned his attention to the improvement of the printing-press, with a view chiefly to accelerate its operation. Being unsuccessful in gaining assistance in his native country to bring his scheme into operation, he came to London in 1806. There he was received with equal coldness, but ultimately, with the assistance of Thomas Bensley, he constructed a machine on the platen or hand-press principle. Afterwards he adopted Nicholson's cylinder principle, and succeeded in producing a machine which so satisfied John Walter, proprietor of *The Times* newspaper, that an agreement was entered into to erect two to print that journal. On 28th Nov., 1814, the reader of *The Times* was informed that he held in his hand a paper which had been printed by machinery moved by the power of steam, and produced at the rate of 1800 impressions per hour. This is commonly supposed to be the first specimen of printing executed by steam machinery; but König's platen machine was set to work in April, 1811, and 3000 sheets of signature H of the *Annual Register* for 1810 were printed by it. That was undoubtedly the first part of a book ever printed by machinery.

A further improvement was made in May, 1848, by Applegath. His machine, which printed 10,000 impressions per hour, had a vertical cylinder 65 inches broad, on which the type was fixed, surrounded by eight other vertical cylinders, each about 13 inches diameter and covered with cloth, round which the paper was led by tapes, each paper or

Platen Machine

impression cylinder having a feeding apparatus and two boys tending. The type used was the ordinary kind, and the forme was placed on a portion of the large cylinder. The surface of the type formed a portion of a polygon, and the regularity of the impression was obtained by pasting slips of paper on the impression cylinders.

Few machines, however, of this construction were made, a formidable rival having appeared, devised by Messrs. Hoe & Co. of New York, which was introduced into many newspaper offices in Great Britain. It was constructed with from two to ten impression cylinders, each of them printing from a set of types placed on a horizontal central cylinder of about 6½ feet in diameter, a portion of which was also used as a cylindrical ink-table, each of the encircling cylinders having its own inking-rollers and separate feeder. A machine of this construction, having ten impression cylinders,

PRISCIL'LIAN. The reputed founder of a Gnostic sect in Spain, known as Priscillianists, in the middle of the fourth century, their doctrines being a mixture of Gnosticism and Manichæism. Priscillian was himself a wealthy and accomplished man, of very temperate and strenuous habits. His followers did not leave the Catholic Church, and he was actually at one time made a bishop himself. He was ultimately executed at Treves, in A.D. 385, after a prolonged struggle with the orthodox clergy. The most distinctive part of Priscillian's creed was the belief in an evil spirit as the supreme power. His sect lasted until about A.D. 600.

PRISM. In geometry, a solid figure which can be generated by the motion of a line kept parallel to itself, one extremity of it being

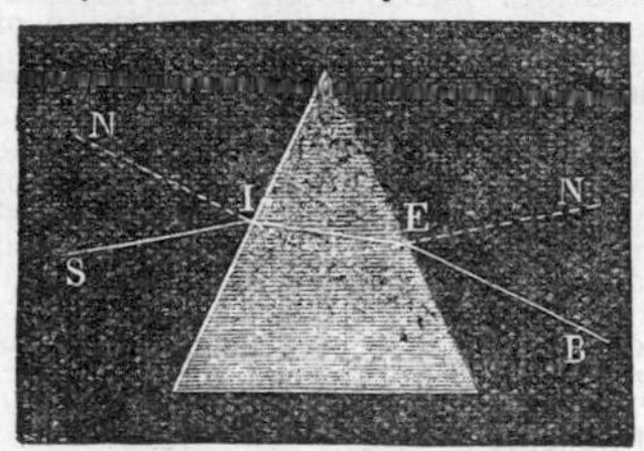

Light passing through a Prism

carried round a rectangular figure. A "right prism" is one which is bounded by two planes at right angles to the generating lines, or edges. In optics a prism, most commonly made of glass and triangular in section, is an important element in many instruments. If a ray of light, SI, enter such a prism by one of the two principal faces, it is bent in passing through so as to follow the path SIEB. The angle which the ray in the prism makes with the normal, NI, is always smaller than the angle of incidence, NIS, and the angle which it makes with the normal, EN′, is smaller than the angle of emergence, N′EB, the ray being always bent towards the base of the prism. Not only is the ray thus bent, but it is also decomposed, since the angle through which a ray is bent depends upon its colour. *See* COLOUR; LIGHT; REFRACTION; SPECTRUM.

PRISONS. In Great Britain prisons are all maintained and managed by the State. Until 1877 the local prisons were in the hands of the local authorities, and there were none but local prisons till well on in the eighteenth century. Generally they were hotbeds of disease and vice. In practice the jailers were the managers, and they made as much profit as they could from their offices. They had no salaries, or merely nominal ones, and had to live on the profits they made from the sale of food and drink to the prisoners and visitors. Young and old, male and female, were herded together during the day; and even at night they were not always placed in separate quarters. The efforts of John Howard, and others whom he inspired, directed attention to abuses and modified some of them. The State erected and managed prisons for convicts and certain classes of prisoners when difficulties arose as to their banishment, and when transportation was abolished additional provision had to be made.

In the earlier part of the nineteenth century inspectors of prisons had been appointed, and some of the local authorities had accepted and even improved on their recommendations; but it was ultimately decided that the public interest made it necessary for the State to take over all prisons, in order that greater uniformity in the treatment of prisoners might be ensured, that the number of prisons might be reduced, and that the cost of maintenance might be diminished. There are separate Prison Commissioners for England and Scotland. All except ex officio members are appointed by the Crown. The English Commissioners report to the Home Secretary, and the Scottish Commissioners to the Secretary for Scotland, and under those ministers respectively they manage the prisons. Their authority is limited by statutes and by statutory rules which have been approved by the minister and submitted to Parliament. All prison officers are under their direction and supervision, and they appoint, and may suspend or dismiss, subordinate officials. They inspect prison buildings, see that the rules are observed, and hear and adjudicate upon complaints by officers and prisoners. Each prison has a visiting committee, mainly composed of members elected by the local authorities. They have powers of inspection, and may make suggestions for the better management of the prisons, but they have no executive powers.

The governor of the prison is its chief executive officer, and is responsible to the Commissioners for the work of the prison. The matron has authority under him, and within the female department of the prison is the chief officer. Each prison has its chaplain, a clergyman of the Established Church, and in some prisons there are also visiting clergymen belonging to other Churches, who minister spiritually to the prisoners of their religious persuasion. In England some of the chaplains are full-time officers, but in Scotland they are all engaged for part-time service, and are mainly occupied in ministering to congregations outside. The chaplains not only conduct religious services and visit the prisoners in their cells to instruct and admonish them, but they supervise the prison library and the education of the prisoners. They also assist in aiding prisoners on discharge.

Each prison has at least one medical officer, who must be a fully qualified practitioner. In the smaller prisons there is no resident doctor, the duties being discharged by a visiting man. Of all the prison officials the medical officer has probably the most real power. He can interfere, on medical grounds, with the diet, work, and treatment generally of any prisoner. It is his duty to note the physical or mental peculiarities of those under his care, and to make such recommendations for their special treatment as seem to him necessary. He attends the sick, whether they are officers or prisoners, and he has to see that the prison and the quarters are kept in a sanitary condition, and that the food supplied to the prisoners is of good quality and is properly cooked.

All these officials are appointed by the minister, but are under the authority of the Commissioners. The warders come most closely and continuously in contact with the prisoners. They are required to be of sound physique, of good character, and to have passed a simple examination in general education. Only male warders are employed with the male prisoners, and only female warders with the female prisoners. They see that the routine work of the prison is carried out, supervise the prisoners when at work, see that their cells are kept clean, and attend to the warding of them.

Prisons are mostly built on the same general plan. Two blocks of cells run parallel and about 16 feet apart. They are joined together at the ends by walls containing doors on the ground-level and large windows above. The space between is roofed in with glass, and floored with tiles. All the cell doors open towards this corridor, and above the ground-flat galleries are carried round it. All the cell windows are on the other side of the block. Each cell contains about 800 or 1000 cubic feet, and is furnished with a bed, a table, a stool, and other necessary articles. It is lit during the day by its window, and at night by artificial light. It contains a bell, by means of which the warder may be summoned, and its door contains a device by which the warder can observe the prisoner when he wishes to do so.

Many of the prisons are old buildings, and they differ greatly in style and in arrangement. Those recently built are much more comfortable. Each prison has its hospital, and some of these are very well equipped; but in Scotland it has been the practice since 1860 to send those who are dangerously ill to outside hospitals for treatment, bringing them back on recovery; and the English Commissioners have now obtained similar powers.

Insane persons are removed from prisons to lunatic asylums, and recent legislation has ordained the same course to be followed with the mentally defective. The prisons contain persons waiting trial, certain debtors, and persons committed for contempt of court, and persons sentenced to imprisonment or to penal servitude. In theory the person charged with crime is innocent until proved guilty, and, unless held for trial on the most serious crimes, he may be admitted to bail. In practice he may find himself detained in prison through not having the means of giving a bond. The untried prisoner may have a special room and furniture assigned to him; he may have his food sent in to him; he may have visits at reasonable times, and the number of the visits is not strictly limited by rule; and he may write and receive letters. The visits must take place in the presence of an officer, who must also be in a position to hear all that is said, save when the prisoner is visited by his law agents; and the letters must all be read by a prison official. But he can only have all these privileges if he is able to pay for them. He is not compelled to do any work, but he may get work if he wishes it. He does not exercise along with convicted prisoners, nor does he associate with them. Otherwise he is subject to the prison régime.

All prisoners sentenced to imprisonment for periods exceeding one calendar month may earn remission of sentence, not exceeding one-sixth of the period, by good conduct and industry. Whether their sentences expire by lapse of time or by remission, they are not liable to police supervision on liberation. Convicts are persons sentenced to penal servitude for three years or more. Their sentences may be served in any part of the king's dominions; but as a rule they are kept in the country where they were sentenced, and placed in special prisons there. Their work is supposed to be more arduous than that of ordinary prisoners and the discipline more severe; but their diet is more generous and varied, and in many respects they are better off. By good conduct and industry they may gain their liberation on licence—the women when they have served two-thirds, and the men when they have served three-fourths of their sentence. The licence is better known as ticket-of-leave. It is conditional on their reporting to the police once monthly, on their producing their licence to any magistrate or police-officer when called upon to do so, and on their abstaining from crime or association with criminals. If convicted during the term of their licence, they may be called on to serve the whole of the time for which the licence was issued.

All prisoners on admission are medically examined, and it is the duty of the doctor to note any defect from which they suffer, and take steps to prevent them from being subjected to treatment that might injure them. They are bathed on admission, and at regular intervals during their imprisonment. They wear the prison clothing and occupy separate cells. The diet, if insufficient or unsuitable in any case, may be changed or increased by the medical officer. It is plain and monotonous but, if one may judge by the low sickness returns, it is healthy. Exercise is taken in the airing-yards for such time daily as is approved by the medical officer. Work varies in character in different prisons. It is never equal in strain to what is common outside, and is mainly of a kind requiring little skill for its adequate performance. Prisoners have to keep their own cells clean; and the prison work, cleaning, cooking, washing, etc., is done by them. Work is also done for Government departments. There are regular religious services, and in the winter there are concerts and lectures to vary the monotony. Each prison has a library for the use of prisoners, and those who wish to engage in special studies are afforded means for doing so. There are teachers for those whose elementary education has been neglected. Visits are made to the prisoners individually by the chaplains and by visitors from religious and philanthropic organisations.

In England there are three divisions of imprisonment. The third is the ordinary division; in the second the prisoners have some extra privileges; and in the first they are under rules similar to those governing the untried. It is possible, therefore, for a man who has money, if he is sentenced to be kept in the first division, to make himself tolerably comfortable, and have the attendance of other prisoners on him, for a sum that would not nearly defray the cost of service outside. In Scotland there is no such provision made. Convicted prisoners there all come under the same rules, and distinctions between them are not made on the ground of their social position or of the crimes they have committed, but only on their physical or mental needs.

Borstal and preventive detention institutions, though not called prisons, are places of detention for criminals, and are under the management of the Prison Commissioners. The Borstal institutions are places for the application of reformatory treatment to persons between the ages of sixteen and twenty-one who are of criminal habits or tendencies, and who have been convicted of crime. The sentences are of from two to three years' detention, followed in all cases by twelve months' supervision. The inmates receive instruction in handicrafts and in general knowledge. The preventive detention institutions are for the detention of habitual criminals. The period of detention is up to ten years. There also the regimen is declared to be reformatory, and the inmates of both kinds of institution are much better off than the ordinary decent workman. In both cases there is provision for the licensing of the inmates. Borstal inmates may be licensed: the lads after serving six and the girls after serving three months of their sentence, if there is reasonable ground for the belief that they will lead a useful and industrious life. The conditions of the licence are simple: residence in an approved place, steady work, avoidance of bad company, and return to residence at a reasonable hour. If the licence is revoked, the person may be taken back; and if the licence-holder runs away, the time that elapses before he is brought back does not count in calculating the expiry of his sentence. A licence similar in character may be given to habitual criminals at any time. Those on licence have a large measure of freedom, while their neighbours are secured against their bad conduct by the supervision exercised over them. The guardians of the licence-holders are appointed by the Prison Commissioners, and have no connection with the police.—

BIBLIOGRAPHY: E. Carpenter, *Pris-*

ons, Police, and Punishment; J. Howard, *State of Prisons in England and Wales*; R. F. Quinton, *Modern Prison Curriculum*; George Ives, *History of Penal Methods*; A. Guillot, *Les prisons de Paris.*

PRIVATEER. An armed vessel owned and equipped by private individuals, and furnished with letters

Privateer

of marque authorising the seizure and plunder of the ships of an enemy. Letters of marque are an essential feature, otherwise the ship is considered as a pirate, and may be treated as such if captured. Letters of marque were first granted in England during the reign of Henry V., in view of the war with France; and they were issued to aggrieved subjects in order that they might compensate themselves for injury done by foreigners. In the sixteenth century it became common to grant commissions to privateers. England, Holland, and Spain, as the three principal naval powers, used this effective weapon freely; and France also sent out privateers in every war in which she was engaged. A neutral is not forbidden by the law of nations to accept a commission for privateering; but he may be, and generally is, by treaty. Since 1870 British subjects have been forbidden to accept such commissions. By the Declaration of Paris, 1856, the great powers of Europe mutually agreed to abandon the right to arm privateers in case of war; but several nations, the chief among them being the United States and Spain, did not agree to this, and it is doubtful whether it will always be strictly acted upon even by the parties to the declaration. The German volunteer fleet of 1870 can not clearly be distinguished from a collection of privateers. The practice of privateering, while useful to maritime countries, is very harassing to trade, and gives endless opportunities for private plunder. It was probably in deprecation of irresponsible warfare of any kind that the powers agreed to abandon privateering in 1856.

During the European War Great Britain's armed merchant-cruisers were theoretically naval vessels, but in actual practice there was little to distinguish them from the privateers of bygone days. The *Moewe*, equipped by Germany, was not so much a pirate as a privateer. It is very difficult to draw a dividing-line between these two equally obnoxious and parasitical modes of maritime warfare. *See* PIRATE; NAVY.

PRIVET (Ligustrum). A genus of plants of the ord. Oleaceæ. The common privet (*L. vulgāre*) is a native of Europe, growing 8 or 10 feet high; the leaves are elliptico-lanceolate, entire, and smooth; the flowers slightly odorous, white at first but soon changing to a reddish-brown; and the berries dark purple, approaching black. This species is much used in gardens for ornamental hedges.

Privet

There are numerous other species, many of them being natives of China and other Asiatic countries.

PRIVILEGE (Lat. *privilegium*). A particular exemption from the general rules of law. This exemption may be either *real* or *personal*: real, when it attaches to any place; personal, when it attaches to persons, as ambassadors, members of Parliament, clergymen, lawyers, and others. Real privilege is now of little importance; personal privilege, however, is guaranteed in certain cases to many classes of individuals. For instance, suitors and counsel are exempt from arrest while in court; and members of Parliament while in the House of Commons.

PRIVY COUNCIL. The Council of State of the British sovereign, convened to concert matters for the public service, and for the honour and safety of the realm. The English Privy Council may be said to have existed from times of great antiquity; but the *concilium ordinarium*, established by Edward I., was the parent of the modern institution. It consisted of the chief ministers, judges, and officers of State, and grew in power and influence rapidly, though repeatedly checked by jealous Parliaments. This ordinary council assumed the name of Privy Council during the fifteenth century, and in 1640 the Long Parliament deprived it of many of its arbitrary and insufficiently defined powers. Under the Tudors and the first two Stewart sovereigns the great powers of the council—legislative, administrative, and judicial—were used to the utmost in the interests of the Crown; but from the Restoration to the present time this ancient body has gradually retired more and more into the background of national politics, especially since the rise of the Cabinet. The Privy Council of Scotland was absorbed in that of England at the Union.

As it exists at present, the number of members of the Privy Council is indefinite; they are nominated by the sovereign at pleasure, and no patent or grant is necessary, but they must be natural-born subjects. The list of Privy Councillors now embraces, besides the members of the royal family and the members of the Cabinet, the archbishops and the Bishop of London, the great officers of State, the Lord Chancellor and chief judges, the Speaker of the House of Commons, the First Lord of the Admiralty, the Colonial Premiers, and other persons who fill or have filled responsible offices under the Crown, as well as some who may not have filled any important office. Officially at the head is the Lord President of the Council, who is appointed by patent, and who manages the debates and reports results to the sovereign. A member of the Privy Council has the title of "right honourable." It is only on very extraordinary occasions that all the members attend the council, and it is not now usual for any member to attend unless specially summoned. The attendance of at least six members is necessary to constitute a council. Privy Councillors are by oath bound to advise the Crown without partiality, affection, or dread; to keep their counsel secret, to avoid corruption, and to assist in the execution of what is resolved upon.

While the political importance of the Privy Council, once very great, has been extinguished by the growth of the system of party government, it still retains functions both administrative and judicial. The former is chiefly exercised by means of committees of the council, which have certain statutory duties apportioned to them. The Board of Trade is still nominally regarded as one of these committees. Another is the judicial committee of the council, a body established in 1833, and consisting of the Lord Chancellor and other judges, some being Indian or colonial. Four members constitute a quorum. Later legislation tends to assimilate this committee with the House of Lords as final judges of appeals. Barring some not important original jurisdiction, the judicial committee of the Privy Council is a final court of appeal from India and the colonies, the Channel Islands, and the Isle of Man, while within the British Isles it has supreme appellate jurisdiction in ecclesiastical cases.

A special committee of the council was long at the head of all educational matters in Britain. It was first appointed in 1839 for administering the grants which for a few years the Government had made with a view to meet the educational wants of the country. It included the President and Vice-President of the Council, the latter of whom held the position of Minister for Education. Under this department the parliamentary grant was distributed, the educational code framed or altered, the inspectors of schools appointed, etc. Since the year 1900 the Board of Education has taken the place of this committee.

Orders in council are orders issued by the sovereign, by and with the advice of the Privy Council, either by virtue of the royal prerogative, and independently of any Act of Parliament, or by virtue of such Act, authorising the sovereign in council to modify or dispense with certain statutory provisions which it may be expedient in particular conjunctures to alter or suspend.—BIBLIOGRAPHY: W. Stubbs, *Constitutional History of England*; A. V. Dicey, *The Privy Council*; Lord E. Percy, *The Privy Council under the Tudors*; *Acts of the Privy Council* (editor, J. R. Dasent).

PRIVY PURSE, KEEPER OF THE. An officer of the royal household of Great Britain, whose function it is to take charge of the payment of the private expenses and charities of the sovereign. The amount of money granted to the king and queen for their own personal expenditure was fixed in 1910 at £110,000 a year.

PRIVY SEAL. A seal appended by the British sovereign to such grants or documents as are afterwards to pass the Great Seal. Since the time of Henry VIII. the Privy Seal has been the warrant of the legality of grants from the Crown, and the authority for the Lord Chancellor to affix the Great Seal; such grants are termed letters-patent. The officer who has the custody of the Privy Seal is called Lord Privy Seal, and is the fifth great officer of State, having also generally a seat in the Cabinet.

PRIZE. A term applied to all captures of property made in virtue of the rights of war. Property captured on land is usually called *booty,* the term prize being more particularly used with reference to naval captures. The right of belligerents to capture the property of their enemies on the sea is universally admitted, as well as the right to prevent violation of the law of nations by neutrals, so long as the independence of other nations is not interfered with. It is accordingly settled as a principle of the law of nations that every belligerent has a right to establish tribunals of prize, and to examine and decide upon all maritime captures; and likewise that the courts of prize of the captors have exclusive jurisdiction over all matters relating to captures made under the authority of their sovereign. The sentence of a court of competent jurisdiction once pronounced is conclusive and binding on all nations. Questions of naval prize-money in England are adjudicated by the Courts of Admiralty. The 27 and 28 Vict. c. xxv. (1864) regulates the proceedings in the case of a naval prize. The captive ship is delivered up to the court without breaking of bulk; and if the capture is adjudged legal, is sold for the benefit of the captors, among whom the proceeds are divided according to their rank.

PRIZE COURT. In time of war each belligerent country establishes a court of law, known as a prize court, to determine the validity of the capture by its naval forces of ships and goods at sea. The rules of procedure of these courts are not necessarily identical in each country, but their decisions should accord with international law. In Britain an appeal lies to the Judicial Committee of the Privy Council. Prize, i.e. enemy property captured at sea, belongs to the Crown, but prize-money is paid to the officers and men of the navy out of the net proceeds of the sale of such property.

PROA. A form of sailing-vessel used in the Malay or Eastern Archipelago and in the Pacific. It is variously constructed, but regularly has one side quite flat, on a line with the stem and stern, while the other side is curved in the usual way; and being equally sharp at stem and stern, it sails equally well in either direction without turning. Their shape and small breadth of beam would render them peculiarly liable to overset were it not for the outrigger they carry, adjusted sometimes to one side and sometimes to both sides. The outrigger is generally a large structure supported by and formed of stout timbers. The outrigger may have weights placed on it and adjusted according to circumstances. Proas carry a lugsail, generally of matting.

PROBABILISM (Lat. *probabilis,* from *probare,* to prove). The theory that probable opinions may be used as a guide to conduct, and that a layman is free to accept either course of action in the case of a divergence of opinion among recognised authorities. According to probabilist teaching, an action is neither sinful nor wrong if there is a probability that it is right and lawful. In other words, in the case of a doubt concerning only the lawfulness or unlawfulness of an action, we may safely follow the opinion of a weighty theologian in favour of liberty, and may be morally sure that we are acting lawfully. Probabilist tendencies are found among the Sophists, but the doctrine was first clearly defined by the Dominican Bartholomew de Medina in the sixteenth century, and was utilised by the Jesuits. The doctrine was attacked as immoral by the Jansenists, and Pascal exposed the system in his *Lettres provinciales.* In later times Alfonso de Ligouri was the greatest champion of probabilism. *See* CASUISTRY.—Cf. H. C. Lea, *History of Confession and Indulgences.*

PROBABILITY. The probability of a future event is the likelihood that it will happen. The probability of a statement is the likelihood of its truth. To an omniscient being, the idea of probability would have no signification; in fact the whole theory of probability is based on the assumptions that we are ignorant of some facts and aware of others, and that from the facts that we know we can reason as to the likelihood of the truth of assertions about unknown facts. Thus the theory of probability has a subjective element, and writers on the subject have distinguished between subjective or "moral" probability, and "mathematical probability," an exact science, based on certain principles which exclude psychological considerations.

The mathematical theory of probability dates from 1654, when certain questions regarding a game of chance were investigated by B. Pascal at the instance of the Chevalier de Méré (a reputed gamester). Analogous problems were discussed by Pascal, Fermat, Huygens, De Moivre, the Bernouillis, and other eminent mathematicians of the seventeenth and eighteenth centuries, some of whom published systematic treatises on the subject, but the classical work is the great *Théorie analytique des probabilités* of Laplace, published in 1812. This author bases the theory on a First Principle, which is really a definition, and may be thus expressed: " If an event may happen in a ways and fail in b ways and all these ways are equally likely to occur, the probability of its happening is $a : a+b$." To illustrate this, consider the case when a ball is taken at random from an urn containing one black and two white balls; the probability that a white ball will be drawn is $\frac{2}{3}$, for there are three possible events, each equally likely, and two of these consist in drawing a white ball. This definition has been objected to because the phrase *equally likely* means *equally probable*, so that the definition involves a logical circle. Peano has proposed to amend the definition by omitting the objectionable phrase; but apparently this would cut adrift the mathematical theory from any relation to " moral " probability. If, however, we are dealing with events that can be repeated an indefinitely great number of times, and if the ratio of the number of favourable cases (when an event of the specified class occurs) to the total number of trials tends to the ratio previously mentioned as a limit, then the connection between the mathematical theory and possible applications will be established, and we shall have a mathematical criterion for " equal likelihood."

Various experimental tests of this assumption in simple cases have been made by actually carrying out a large number of successive trials. K. Pearson tossed coins for " heads or tails," and Professor Weldon threw a die and recorded the frequency with which three or four spots turned up. A very distinct approach towards the theoretical limit was in each case observed; but it is to be noted that the theory of probability, like all other mathematical theories, deals with purely abstract conceptions, and the real test of its value depends on the number and importance of the concrete cases in which the conclusions derived from its application are found to agree sufficiently closely with the results of experience.

According to Laplace's definition, a probability amounting to certainty would be measured by 1. Again, if p denotes the probability that a certain event will happen, or that a certain statement is true, $1 - p$ measures the probability that the event will *not* happen or that the statement is untrue. The theory applies not merely to future events, but to past events, provided the latter are supposed unknown. The ratio $p : 1 - p$ is sometimes called the " relative probability." It is large if p is nearly equal to 1.

From his first principle or definition, Laplace deduces logically certain other principles which facilitate the calculation of the probabilities of compound events. The most important of these may be stated thus: (1) If p and q are the separate probabilities of two mutually exclusive events, then $p + q$ is the probability that one *or* other of these events will occur. (2) If p and q are the separate probabilities of two *independent* events, then pq is the probability that both will occur. Corollaries: the probability that the first will occur and not the second is $p(1 - q)$, and that neither will occur, $(1 - p)(1 - q)$. The theory of inverse probabilities has important practical applications. If an event has happened which is known to be the result of one only of a set of possible antecedents A_1, A_2, A_3, . . . whose a priori probabilities are $p_1, p_2, p_3 \ldots$, and if q_r is the probability that A_r, if it occurs, will be followed by the observed event, then, after the event, the probability of A_r being its cause is $p_r q_r/(p_1q_1 + p_2q_2 + p_3q_3 + \ldots)$.

When the occurrence of an event whose probability is p is associated with a certain value V (monetary or otherwise), pV is the mathematical expectation associated with it. For example, if one is to draw a ball from an urn containing a white and b black balls, and receive a prize of £c if a white ball is drawn, the expectation would be £$ac/(a + b)$. This, according to theory, would be an equitable payment for the privilege of drawing. D. Bernouilli applied this theory to his famous " Petersburg Problem," and finding the results inconsistent with good sense, he made a distinction between *mathematical* and *moral* expectation, on the ground that the true value of an *increase* of fortune diminishes as the fortune itself increases. From a particular hypothesis he deduced that the *moral* value of a probable gain is measured by the logarithm of the actual value.

Laplace and others developed the idea of moral expectation, and deduced the advantage of insuring, and the disadvantage of gambling, even if the game is mathematically equitable. The mathematical theory of probability has been applied with success to determine the most probable value deducible from a number of independent observations of the same quantity, and the probable error in the result; also to the interpretation of statistics as bearing on such actuarial problems as insurance and life annuities. K. Pearson and his school have applied it to problems of biology, in particular to the proof of the existence of correlations between certain biological characters. The correspondence between the known properties of gases, and results deduced by the aid of the probability-calculus from the theory that a gas consists of an immense number of flying molecules, is a striking confirmation of the exactness of probability-calculations when very large numbers of events are dealt with.

The weight to be attached to the combined testimony of several witnesses, assuming that we know the probability that they are speaking the truth, is a branch of the theory that has received some attention.

The **Law of Error,** or of Frequency of Error, is thus expressed: $y = he^{-h^2x^2}/\sqrt{\pi}$, where ydx is the measure of the probability that in a large number n of observations of the same magnitude any error will lie between x and $x + dx$, so that $nydx$ will be the number of the observations we should expect to have that amount of error. Here h is a constant, depending on the method of measurement or observavation employed, and is called the *precision* of the series of observations in question. For a given method h increases with n, being proportional to $\sqrt{n}$. It can be determined by certain rules for any given set of observations, provided they form a *normal series,* as they do in most cases when a skilled observer makes a series of observations of a physical quantity. The law applies only to "accidental errors" which remain after all "systematic errors," such as extension of measuring rods due to rise of temperature, have been allowed for. The law is due to K. F. Gauss, who gave several proofs of its validity, based on more or less reasonable assumptions, one assumption being that positive and negative errors of the same absolute amount have the same probability, another, that the most probable value of a quantity of which a number of direct measurements have been made in the same way is the arithmetic mean of these. The accompanying figure is a graph of the function $he^{-h^2x^2}/\sqrt{\pi}$, and is called the probability curve, or curve of error.

The area OMPA measures the probability that any error lies between 0 and OM, and the total area between the curve and the x-axis is unity. If M be chosen so that the area OMPA is equal to half the whole area under the curve and to the right of OA,

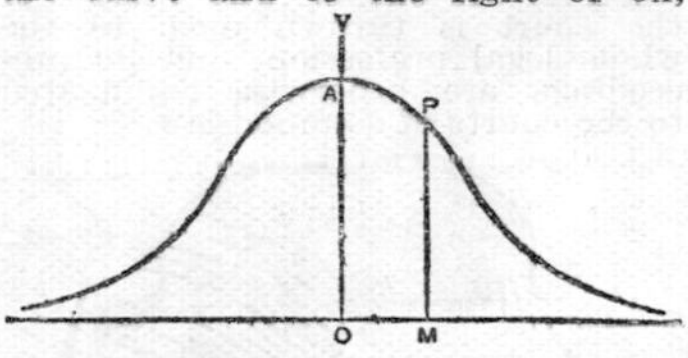

Probability Curve, $y = he^{-h^2x^2}/\sqrt{\pi}$

and therefore $= \frac{1}{4}$, then OM, whose value is then $\doteq \cdot 4769/h$, is called the *median error.* It is such that on the whole there will be as many errors greater than the median as there are errors less than it. Therefore h is called the precision.

When a large number of observations do not form a normal series, i.e. when the distribution of errors is not according to the "law of error," there is reason to believe that the errors are not merely accidental, and some cause may be looked for. This reasoning has been applied with effect by K. Pearson and others to biometrical observations.

BIBLIOGRAPHY: I. Todhunter, *A History of the Mathematical Theory of Probability from the time of Pascal to that of Laplace* (1865); E. J. Boudin, *Leçons de calcul des probabilités* (1916); H. Poincaré, *Calcul des probabilités* (1896); E. Czuber, *Wahrscheinlichkeitsrechnung* (vol. i., third edition, 1914; vol. ii., second edition, 1910); J. Venn, *The Logic of Chance*; J. M. Keynes, *A Treatise on Probability* (1921).

PROBATE. In law, the official proof of a will, that is, the proceeding by which it is established as the last will and testament of the party whose will it professes to be. In England this is obtained in the Probate division of the High Court of Justice. The original will is deposited in the registry of the court and a parchment copy given to the executors, with certificate of its having been proved.

PROBATE, COURT OF. An English tribunal established by Act of Parliament in 1857, to which all the powers previously exercised by ecclesiastical courts in the granting of probates of wills and letters of administration were transferred. This court was merged in the Supreme Court by the Judicature Act of 1873, by which its jurisdiction was assigned to a Probate, Divorce, and Admiralty Division. The functions of this branch are confined entirely to deciding on the authenticity of wills and upon the proper persons to whom administration is to be committed when no will exists. The practice of the court is thrown open to the whole legal profession, and its proceedings are otherwise assimilated to the courts of common law.

Proboscidea

PROBATE DUTY. A tax imposed upon the gross value of the personal property of a person dying prior to 2nd Aug., 1894, and levied by means of a stamp upon the affidavit required of the person applying for probate (q.v.). In respect of deaths on and after that date it was superseded by the new estate duty then introduced. *See* DEATH DUTIES.

PROBA'TION. Judicial system under which offenders, instead of being committed to prison upon being convicted, are placed under a bond to be of good behaviour for a specified period. The method is used with young delinquents, who are then sometimes placed under the supervision of a probation officer. If the offender breaks his bond he may be recalled and sentenced. *See* BORSTAL; REFORMATORY.

PROBOSCID'EA. A sub-order of hoofed mammals distinguished, as implied by this name, by the possession of the characteristic proboscis or trunk. Of this sub-order the elephant alone exists; but there are several extinct animals comprised in it, such as the mammoth and the mastodon.

PROBOS'CIS. The name given to the longer or shorter flexible muscular organ formed by the elongated nose of several mammals. Although seen in a modified degree in the tapirs, etc., the term is more generally restricted, and applied to indicate the flexible "trunk" of the elephant. It is also given to the projecting mouth-parts of some insects, e.g. mosquito and butterfly; a protrusible tube at the front end of nemertine worms, the eversible pharynx of planarians, etc.

PROBOSCIS MONKEY, or KAHAU (*Nasalis larvatus*). A native of Borneo, distinguished particularly by its elongated nose, its shortened thumbs, and its elongated tail. The general

Proboscis Monkey, or Kahau

colour is a lightish red. These monkeys are arboreal in habits, and appear to frequent the neighbourhood of streams and rivers, congregating in troops.

PROBUS, Marcus Aurelius. One of the ablest of the Roman emperors, born at Sirmium in the year A.D. 232. He entered the army and attracted the notice of the Emperor Valerian, who raised him to the rank of tribune. On the death of the Emperor Tacitus, in 276, the army hailed him as emperor, a selection immediately confirmed by the Senate and people of Rome. His chief struggle during his reign was to guard the frontiers of the empire against the barbarians, a task which he carried out with great success both in Europe, Asia, and Africa. He also settled large numbers of

Marcus Aurelius Probus

barbarians in the frontier provinces, and admitted them to his legions; and devoted himself to the making of roads and draining of marshes. His skilful administration and public virtue did not, however, protect him from enmity; and after a short reign he was murdered in a military insurrection in 282.

PROCE'DURE, CIVIL. The method of proceeding in a civil suit throughout its various stages. In England, when redress is sought by law for a civil injury, the injured party brings an *action* against the party whom he alleges to have done the injury. The person who raises an action is termed the *plaintiff*, and he against whom the action is brought, the *defendant*; in Scotland the terms are *pursuer* and *defender*. It is usual before the suit is commenced for the plaintiff's attorney to acquaint the defendant with the demand of his client, and state that unless complied with legal proceedings will be instituted. Should this not have the desired effect, the action is begun as a rule by issuing against the defendant a *writ of summons*, commanding him to enter *an appearance* in court, failing which an appearance will be entered for him by the plaintiff. When an appearance has been entered, both parties to the suit are now said to be *in court*, and judgment may be proceeded with.

The next stage is the *pleadings* or the statements in legal form of the cause of action or ground of defence brought forward by the respective sides. The next stage of procedure after the pleadings is the *issue*, which may be either on matter of law or on matter of fact, where the fact alone is disputed. A matter of law is determined by the judges after hearing argument on both sides, but an issue of fact has to be investigated before a jury (unless a jury is dispensed with by consent of parties or, where competent, by order of the court), and this is denominated *trial by jury*. (*See* JURY AND JURY TRIALS.) After the judge has summed up to the jury the *verdict* follows and then the *judgment* of the court; where there is no jury, of course, judgment is pronounced by the judge after hearing counsel.

PROCELLAR'IIDÆ. The petrel family of birds, of which the typical

Procellariidæ (Albatross)

genus is Procellaria, which includes not only petrels but also albatrosses, fulmars, and shearwaters.

PROCESS-WORK. The name given to methods of using photography to produce printing surfaces that will yield an unlimited number of prints of artists' work, photographs, etc. Process-work is sometimes understood as comprising only line and half-tone block-making for typographic printing in monochrome and colour, but other photo-engraving methods, such as photogravure, machine gravure, collotype, and photo-lithography, are often included under this heading, and will be dealt with here. The essential steps in process-work are founded on the chemical action of light on the silver halides used for making the negative, and on the bichromated colloid employed for obtaining the resist, or greasy image, on metal or paper; the light either rendering the colloid insoluble to a greater or less degree in hot or cold water, or making it less absorbent of water so that it will take a greasy ink applied by a roller.

Line block-making, for relief printing, is a means of reproducing black-and-white designs, drawings, maps and plans, etc., on zinc or occasionally copper, in a form suitable for printing in a printing-press along with ordinary type-matter. The original for reproduction should be drawn in black opaque ink on white Bristol-board, a special drawing-ink being made for the purpose and known as process ink, of which there are two kinds, fixed and unfixed. The former is prepared for drawing in line over photographs, the silver image of which can be removed by chemical means, leaving the drawing intact. The drawing must be firm and have no broken or weak lines. The size of the original is not very important, but for convenience it should be about one-third larger than the reproduction size.

Line blocks are made as follows. The original to be reproduced is fixed on the copy-board of the camera and illuminated by powerful arc lamps, and focused up to the required size on the focusing-screen of the camera. A negative is made, generally by the old wet collodion process or on a special dry plate; this negative must reproduce the original like a stencil, the white portions of the original being shown as opacity and the black design as clear lines. This negative is the means by which the acid resist is obtained on the metal. The metal used is generally zinc, about $\frac{1}{16}$ of an inch thick, which is cleaned with fine pumice-powder and water to remove any tarnish and grease, and then coated with a bichromated albumen, which is a mixture of water, white of egg, and ammonium bichromate. This composition is made to flow over the metal, and then whirled to obtain an even film. When dry the metal is placed under the negative, film to film, and exposed to light under considerable pressure, the light used being either daylight or more often that from an enclosed lamp, as these lamps emit a large proportion of the ultra-violet rays to which the bichromated film is very sensitive. The light passes through the clear portion of the negative and renders the film insoluble; the opaque parts of the negative stop the light action, and the albumen remains soluble. After exposure the zinc plate is covered with a thin film of greasy ink by means of an ink-roller, placed in water, and carefully rubbed with a pad of cotton-wool to help the removal of the soluble parts. After development the drawing is seen in black ink on the metal surface. This ink resist is warmed, dusted with either powdered bitumen or resin to strengthen it still further, and again warmed to incorporate the powder with the ink.

Defects having been touched up, the back is painted with shellac varnish; the plate is then ready for the etching-bath. The etching-mordant is nitric acid, which etches away the exposed portions of the zinc, the protected parts remaining in relief. After the first etch, the plate is removed from the etching-bath, washed in water, and dried; then warmed again and dusted either with a resin known as dragon's blood or with bitumen, this being necessary to protect the sides of the parts standing in relief from under-cutting by the acid. The etching is repeated until the required depth is obtained. The resist is then removed, and the plate is ready for mounting and proving. The mounting consists of cutting away all surplus metal, and nailing the plate to a piece of hard wood, either mahogany or oak, to make it type high. The block is now ready for the printing-press.

The half-tone process is a relief method of obtaining reproductions of photographs, wash drawings, or coloured originals; in fact any original showing gradation of tone can be reproduced by this process, and the blocks can be used for printing with type-matter. The gradation is reproduced by breaking the original up, when photographing it, into dots of varying sizes. These dots can be seen by inspecting a newspaper or magazine illustration, when it will be observed that the whites and lighter tones of the original are reproduced by small round dots that permit a considerable amount of white paper to show, and the lower tones by larger dots that gradually assume a square shape, thus obscuring a greater area, until in some parts the paper becomes almost uniformly covered with ink and no dots can be seen.

The best type of original for reproduction purposes is one made on a glossy bromide of silver paper, or drawn in a warm black and grey. Many originals are specially drawn for reproduction, and considerable skill is required to select the correct colours, as some colours turn out on reproduction much lighter or darker than the originals. Chinese white, e.g., reproduces as a grey, but process white as a white. Blue-blacks reproduce much lighter than they appear, while browns, reds, greens, and yellows come out black, unless the photographer uses special colour sensitive plates, which are too expensive for the ordinary run of process-work. The screens used for photographing through are formed from plates of glass, each of which is ruled with a set of equidistant parallel lines. Two such plates are cemented together so that their lines are at right angles, thus forming a network of small squares. The closeness of the ruling depends on the class of work. For newspaper work it is 60 to 65 lines per inch, for magazine work 100 to 120 lines per inch, and for catalogue and high-class printing 130 to 200 per inch. The screen is held in a special holder contained in the camera, and adjusted to a calculated distance from the sensitive film. The original is photographed through this ruled screen, and thus appears on the negative as broken up into dots of varying sizes.

The metal used for making the block is copper for fine work, and zinc for coarse work such as newspaper or magazine illustrations. The sensitive resist used is a bichromated fish-glue. The metal is prepared and coated as in line-work. After exposure the plate is placed in cold water, which dissolves away the soluble glue, i.e. the portions under the black dots of the negative, while the parts where the light has acted remain and form the resist. This glue image is dried and subjected to considerable heat, which converts the glue image into an acid-resisting enamel. The mordant used for etching copper is perchloride of iron dissolved in water to a strength registering on a Baumé hydrometer 35°. The plate is first rough etched, and then fine etched. Fine etching is carried out by covering the portions that have been etched sufficiently, generally the darker parts of the picture, with an acid resist, and then replacing the plate in the etching-bath until the required result is obtained. The different-sized dots stand out in relief on the finished plate. The metal plate when finished is trimmed up to the right size and bevelled round the edges. Holes are drilled in the bevel to receive the nails that hold it to the wooden support. A smooth surface paper is used for printing fine-screen half-tone blocks. Coarser blocks can be printed on a commoner kind of paper, with loss of gradation. Line blocks may be printed on paper of any quality or surface.

The three-colour process is an extension of the half-tone process, applied to the facsimile reproduction of coloured pictures, etc. In what is known as the *direct process*, the original is photographed through the half-tone screen on three colour-sensitive dry plates. The first negative is taken through a blue filter, the second through a green filter, and the third through a red filter. The plates (which are known as panchromatic) and the colour-filters are very accurately adjusted for the process. The function of the red, green, and blue filters, which are placed in front of the lens, is to absorb any light to which the plates are sensitive other than that required to make the respective records. The three plates are etched as described for half-tone etching, the etcher requiring to have a good knowledge of colour to obtain correct colour results. The blocks are printed in the colours complementary to the colour-screens used for taking the negatives, the block made from the blue record negative being printed in yellow, that from the green in magenta, and that from the red in blue-green.

In the *indirect method* three continuous tone negatives are made through the three colour-screens, no half-tone screen being used at this stage. From these negatives, positives are made on suitable dry plates, and from these positives, screen negatives. This method is employed when photographing away from the process studio, when it is not possible to use the half-tone screen. Often a fourth printing-plate is used, which is printed in black or grey.

Photogravure is an intaglio method of reproduction; that is, the printing surface is sunk beneath the general surface of the plate. It is one of the oldest branches of photo-engraving. A continuous tone negative is made of the original, and from this a positive is obtained either by the carbon process on glass, described later, or on an ordinary dry plate. The polished copper plate is cleaned and grained. The grain is deposited on the copper by shaking up finely powdered bitumen or resin in a specially constructed box known as a "dusting-box," and allowing it to settle on the copper. The dust is fixed to the plate by heat, and acts as a resist to the etching-mordant. Small points are formed over the plate, and act as a mesh to entangle the ink when printing on paper. Between the points the depth of the etching varies in proportion to the gradation of tone shown on the original. To obtain the resist a print is made from the positive on a bichromated gelatine film containing a finely ground pigment, and held on a paper support; such a film is known as a carbon print. It is by this process that the original positive also can be made.

After exposure to light the bichromated film is soaked in cold water, laid face downwards in contact with the grained surface of the copper plate, and put aside for a short time before developing. The plate is immersed in hot water, when the paper support can be pulled away, leaving the film adhering to the plate. After the removal of the paper the water is heated and dissolves away the gelatine that has been more or less unaffected by light, as in the lighter tones. After development the highest lights of the original picture are represented by the greatest thickness of gelatine, the half-tones by intermediate thickness, and the shadows by a thin skin. When dry, the back and sides of the plate are protected with an acid-resisting varnish, and it is then ready for etching. The etching-fluids consist of varying strengths of perchloride of iron. The gelatine film resists the mordant in proportion to its thickness; the thinner the resist the greater the depth of etching. The dark tones of the original are etched in a strong solution of perchloride of iron, and the lighter tones in a weaker; considerable skill is necessary to know when to transfer the plate being etched from one bath to another so as to retain correct gradation.

The resist is now removed and the plate carefully cleaned, the edges being rounded to prevent them cutting the paper when printing, and also to give the plate-mark characteristic of most intaglio methods. To protect the delicate surface of the plate it is given an electrolytic deposit of iron. Photogravure plates are proved by hand, such proving being a trade by itself. To obtain proofs the plate is warmed, ink is forced into the hollows by means of a pad of coarse canvas, the surface ink is wiped away, and the margins carefully cleaned. Damped paper is placed on the plate, backed with soft blanketing, and then passed through a copper-plate press, somewhat like a household mangle, but fitted with steel rollers instead of wooden ones. The proving requires artistic skill to obtain the best results from the plate. Photogravure is extensively employed for making copies of famous works of art, an application for which it is eminently suited.

Machine gravure is somewhat like photogravure, but the working is more mechanical. The grain is replaced by a network of lines crossing each other and forming minute squares. This process has important commercial applications—for the production of illustrations in magazines, catalogues, and newspapers. The type-matter can be etched on the same metal as the illustrations, the printing being done in specially constructed power-driven presses. The working details are almost the same as in the process just described, except that the network of lines is obtained by printing from a cross-line screen with transparent lines on the bichromated film, the picture positive being printed over the screen. The exposed films are transferred to a copper cylinder (which may weigh 2 cwt.) together with any type-matter, the etching being carried out as for photogravure. For printing, the cylinder is fixed on the press and inked from below with a spirit ink applied by means of a roller revolving in an ink-duct, the surface ink being removed by a steel blade (known as a doctor), which passes horizontally across the revolving cylinder. The paper is drawn between two cylinders, one of which is the printing cylinder, the other supplying the pressure; this pressure causes the ink to be drawn out of the printing depths and deposited on the paper.

Photo-lithography is a photographic method of obtaining the greasy image on lithographic stone or metal (*see* LITHOGRAPHY). This greasy image can be printed from a line or half-tone negative by the method which is used for making line blocks; no etching, however, is necessary. The metal used is a thin sheet of zinc or aluminium that has been grained in a special machine to make the surface receptive of water. After the plate has been exposed and developed, it is dried and covered with a thin coating of gum, when it is ready for printing in the press. Another means of obtaining the greasy image is to print the negative upon a paper coated with bichromated gelatine, which after exposure to light is rolled up with a special transfer ink, and then developed in water, the exposed parts retaining the ink. This ink image can be transferred to metal or stone.

These metal plates are now mostly printed by the *rubber offset press*. The metal plate is tightly drawn round a steel roller that revolves against another cylinder round which is stretched a rubber sheet. Each revolution of the cylinders leaves an offset of the ink on the rubber sheet, from which it is transferred to the printing-paper. Offset is the latest method of reproduction, and it would appear that there is a big future for the process, which will print half-tones on almost any surface of paper, however rough. Tin printing has been done for many years by offset.

Collotype is a surface-printing process somewhat akin to lithography (q.v.), the action of light replacing the handwork of the artist, and gelatine, from which impressions are taken in a greasy ink, replacing the stone. Gelatine has an open cellular structure, and can absorb water. On the addition of ammonium bichromate to the gelatine and subsequent exposure to light, the gelatine cells harden in proportion to the light action, which is controlled by the densities of the negative; the weaker the light action, the greater the absorption of water. A collotype plate after exposure represents the original in a selective reticulated grain; the closer the grain, the greater the amount of ink deposited.

The printing-plate is prepared by coating thick sheets of glass with a hot solution of bichromated gelatine, which is then dried by heat in a special oven, and when dry is exposed to light under the negative. After exposure the film is well washed in running water to free the gelatine from the bichromate salts, and again dried in the air. To prepare for proving, the plate is soaked in water, and after soaking is treated with a mixture of water, glycerine, and ammonia, which after a time is dabbed off, when the plate is ready for proving. The proving is done in a special press somewhat like a litho. press, the pressure being applied by the action of a scraper under which the plate and paper are passed; these presses are either power- or hand-driven.

This process is also used for obtaining the key, or foundation printing, in *chromo-lithography* (q.v.). By varying the proportion of the sensitiser, and by the addition of calcium chloride and potassium ferricyanide to the gelatine, the grain is somewhat enlarged, and it is possible to pull proofs from the plate on special transfer paper; these transfers are then transferred to stone or metal, and thus save a considerable amount of hand work. This process produces results of a very smooth quality, and is used for the reproduction of old documents and illuminated manuscripts, pastel, crayon, pencil sketches, and coloured originals. It also affords a means of imitating at a cheap rate photographic prints, many picture post cards being produced by collotype. The process is not much worked in England on account of the uncertain climate, its successful working being dependent on an even temperature and constant climatic conditions.—BIBLIOGRAPHY: S. H. Horgan, *Photo-engraving Primer*; W. Gamble, *Line Engraving*; T. W. Lascelles, *Engraving*; H. O. Klein, *Three-colour Photography*.

PROCIDA (pro'chi-då; ancient **Prochyta**). An island on the west coast of Southern Italy, lying nearly midway between the Island of Ischia and the coast of the province of Naples. It is about 3 miles long and 1 mile broad, of volcanic origin, flat in surface, and of comparatively irregular coast-line. The principal town is Procida, or Castello di Procida, which has a harbour, a castle, and a royal palace. Tunny and sardines are caught in adjacent waters. Total pop. 14,500.

PROCLAMATION, ROYAL. A public notice made by the sovereign of a country to his subjects, concerning any matter which he thinks fit to give notice about. Proclamations consist of an authoritative announcement of some great event affecting the State, and are issued on the accession of a new sovereign or on the declaration of war. In normal times proclamations are issued in this country for the summoning, prorogation, and dissolution of Parliament. A royal proclamation must be issued under the Great Seal. By statute, royal proclamations are only binding when they do not contradict existing laws or tend to establish new ones.

PROCLUS. A neo-Platonist, born at Byzantium in A.D. 412, died at Athens in 485. He was educated at Alexandria and Athens, and became familiar with all branches of philosophy and theology. His system aimed at the widest comprehensiveness. He not only endeavoured to unite all philosophical schemes, but made it a maxim that a philosopher should embrace also all religions by becoming infused with their spirit. In his writings he professes to return to Plato, and to bring down neo-Platonism from the misty heights to which it was raised by Plotinus. He was a violent opponent of Christianity, and composed hymns in honour of the pagan deities of Greece. His extant works include a *Sketch of Astronomy*, in which he gave a short view of the systems of Hipparchus, Aristarchus, and Ptolemy; *The Theology of Plato*; *Principles of Theology*; and a *Life of Homer*.

with time intervals between them, depending on the demands for gas by the engine. When the engine is governed by a "hit-and-miss" type of gear (*see* INTERNAL-COMBUSTION ENGINE), the demands for gas occur at irregular intervals. If the engine has been running light for some time and full load is suddenly applied, the fuel may have cooled down to a temperature too low to produce a gas of sufficient calorific value, and the engine may shut down. Such actions were common in the early days of development of this type of plant, but are not so common now when plants have been so much improved in design.

In the National suction gas producer the fuel is introduced through the hopper, which is provided with a cover as well as a rising and falling base plate. By the use of this hopper there is very little escape of gas into the atmosphere during the charging operation. Full advantage is taken of waste heat for the production of steam and raising the temperature of the air before it enters the generator. The gas is washed free from dust in the scrubber, where it meets with water falling through coke. The gas after washing is passed through an expansion-box before passing to the engine. The producer is started by means of burning wood, shavings, or oily rags, and the gas is drawn off through a by-pass pipe by means of a fan. The producer is then closed up and coke or anthracite introduced through the hopper. A test-cock is provided at which the combustible properties of the gas may be tested by the application of a light. When a combustible gas is produced, the by-pass pipe is closed off and the gas-engine started.

A good suction gas producer uses ¾ lb. to 1 lb. of anthracite or 1 lb. to 1¾ lb. of coke per brake horse-power hour, the lowest figures being obtained with the largest plants. A general average composition of suction gas is: hydrogen, 15·5 per cent; methane, 1·2 per cent; carbon monoxide, 20·0 per cent; carbon dioxide, 7·0 per cent; oxygen, 0·5 per cent; and the remainder is nitrogen. The calorific value is about 125 to 135 British Thermal Units per cubic foot. Much experimental work has been done in connection with the application of suction gas plants to motor-boats and motor-cars, and their use in such work should show a considerable increase in the future.

Bituminous - fuel Gas Producers. This forms a most important division of gas producers in which the cheap bituminous fuels can be used for gas generation. The difficulty experienced in designing plant of this type is to make provision for the elimination of the tar. In the suction type of plant the difficulties have been very considerable but have been largely overcome. One method of dealing with the tar is to destroy it by keeping the fuel at a very high temperature; another solution is to take away the gas from the generator at some part of the fuel bed where the temperature is high and thus where the presence of tar is unlikely. In this type of producer it is common to introduce the air and steam both above and below the fuel bed. The fuel consumption is about 1¼ lb. of coal per brake horse-power hour.

Mond Gas Plant was designed to make possible the recovery of the nitrogen content of the fuel as ammonia. For the achievement of this purpose a large excess of steam is passed through the fuel, and has the effect of keeping the temperature low enough to prevent the decomposition of the ammonia. The gas is washed with water to make it free from tar, and is passed to lead-lined towers, where ammonium sulphate solutions with an excess of sulphuric acid are used to remove the ammonia from the gas. With very large plants using fuels rich in nitrogen the gas may be obtained practically free, owing to the large sums obtained for the ammonium sulphate. It has been demonstrated that gas of a calorific value of 135 to 150 British Thermal Units per cubic foot can be produced at a cost as low as twopence to threepence per 1000 cubic feet with even small plants. The equivalent heat contents would be obtained from a city supply at sevenpence threefarthings to elevenpence halfpenny per 1000 cubic feet. In many industrial districts Mond gas is produced in large stations and distributed to the local works through street mains.

BIBLIOGRAPHY: J. E. Dowson and A. T. Larter, *Producer Gas*; V. B. Lewes, *Liquid and Gaseous Fuel*; H. E. Wimperis, *The Internal Combustion Engine.*

PRODUCTION, COST OF. Economists draw an important distinction between the *money* cost of production and the *real* cost of production. The former is the factor on which the conditions of supply chiefly depend, and is the only cost of production of which the business man takes account. For the production of any commodity certain quantities of labour, capital, and land, or raw material, are required; these are called the agents of production. Each of these agents costs something, and the cost of production of any commodity consists of the sum of the prices that have to be paid to the agents in order to produce it.

No one will produce an article if he knows beforehand that its cost of production will be greater than the price for which he can sell it. On the other hand, if the cost of production of anything is very much lower than its market price, many people will rush to produce that thing, in order to pocket a substantial profit, and this will go on until the increased supply has caused the price to fall. The price of any commodity tends, therefore, to equal its marginal cost of production as measured in terms of money. There are, however, exceptional cases in which this relation is modified. Wool and mutton, for instance, are *joint products*; neither can be produced without the other, and we cannot say that a rise in the price of wool will cause an increase in the supply, unless we know what is happening to the price of mutton. In these cases, it is only true to say that the sum of the prices of joint products will tend to equal the sum of their costs of production.

The *real* cost of production of any commodity consists of the efforts and sacrifices involved in making it. The relation, however, between these efforts and sacrifices and the money costs of production is very difficult to determine. The wages of labour, in general, cannot be expected to vary directly with changes in the mental or physical strain involved in work; nor the rate of interest to vary directly with the sacrifice involved in saving. The real cost of production which the price of a commodity measures is not absolute, but comparative. The prices of the factors of production tend to equal the prices which they could have secured in producing other commodities. It is thus the sacrifice involved in doing without other commodities that is measured by the money costs of a commodity at the margin of production.

PROFESSIONS, AND HOW TO ENTER THEM. Parents who decide to place their sons and daughters in one of the learned professions must, under modern conditions, be prepared to keep their children at school till the age of at least sixteen or seventeen. While at school the boy or girl should be entered for such examinations as the Oxford and Cambridge school examinations, or the leaving-certificate examinations of the Scottish Education Department, or the examinations of the Board of Education in Ireland. Success in these examinations is not only a test of general ability, but paves the way for entrance into practically every profession. In all professions there is now a preliminary examination, and the certificates procured at school generally exempt from this examination. The easiest way of determining the exact requirements for entrance is to write to the university or other institution to which it is proposed to send the pupil, asking for details and dates of their entrance examinations.

The Church. It need hardly be emphasised that the taking of holy orders is a supreme step in a man's life, whereby he dedicates himself not to a career but to a vocation. Intensity of conviction and religious fervour will naturally play a large part in the choice, but physical fitness and suitability must not be neglected. In all the larger denominations the necessity of a good university education is increasingly stressed, and while it is not absolutely essential to possess a degree, it is highly desirable. For most of the greater denominations about six years' study is necessary, roughly three years in an arts faculty and three in divinity. The cost varies, but outside of Oxford and Cambridge the fees would amount to about £20 per session. In some of the smaller denominations there is exacted a standard of education not quite so severe as that demanded by a university degree. Many of the Churches are liberally endowed in respect of bursaries for students, and by this means substantial help is given towards the cost of living.

The Law. (1) *The Barrister.* It may be safely asserted that in no profession does native ability count for so much. The prizes are great, and the disappointments are many. Quickness of brain, alertness to seize upon points, a wide general culture coupled with considerable intensity of knowledge, are great factors in success. In England and Wales the method of admission to the Bar is as follows: Every applicant procures first from the Inns of Court (The Inner Temple, The Middle Temple, Lincoln's Inn, Gray's Inn) a form of admission. He must have passed a preliminary examination as mentioned above. On admission, he pays stamp duties and fees amounting to roughly £40. His next step is to "keep" twelve terms (four terms per annum) by dining in Hall six nights in each term. He must further pay a deposit of £100 (£50 at Lincoln's Inn or Gray's Inn) unless he has resided for two years at a recognised university or is a member of the Scottish or Irish Bar. Meanwhile, he is "reading for the Bar," i.e. for the examination for call to the Bar, which is in two parts. On actual call he must reckon on a payment in stamp duties and fees of about £100. Applicants for the English Bar should write to the Director of Legal Studies, Lincoln's Inn.

In Scotland practically all intending aspirants take a degree in arts and a B.L. or an LL.B. at a Scottish university. They are thus absolved from the examinations in (1) general knowledge and (2) legal knowledge. Having satisfied the Faculty of Advocates in these two branches, and having propounded and defended a thesis, the candidate is admitted or rejected by a ballot of members of the faculty. Fees for admission amount to nearly £500. Full information is to be had from the Clerk of Intrants, Advocates' Library, Edinburgh.

In Ireland every candidate for admission to the Bar must obtain a "memorial" from a practising barrister of not less than six years' standing. This "memorial" testifies that the candidate is a fit and proper person for admission. In addition to the preliminary examination, he must attend lectures for three years, i.e. one year at Trinity College, Dublin, and two years in King's Inns. Fees in all amount to about £200.

(2) *The Solicitor*. Admission to practise in England and Wales is conferred by the Master of the Rolls through the Law Society. In addition to the preliminary, there is an intermediate and a final examination, undertaken while the student is serving under articles with a firm of solicitors. (The stamp duty for articles is £80, and a premium which may amount to £100 or upwards.) The term of service is five years, which is reduced in the cases of university graduates to three years. Fees for examination and for final admission to the Roll of Solicitors amount to about £70.

In Scotland the function of solicitor is discharged by a writer to the signet (W.S.), a solicitor to the supreme courts (S.S.C.), or by a law agent. For information on law agents' examinations application should be made to the Clerk to the Examiners of Law Agents, 8 Albany Street, Edinburgh. It should be noted that the W.S. Society, Edinburgh, holds its own examinations. The examinations follow closely those of the English systems, and the period of indenture is the same as for England. Fees for admission run from £60 to £100.

In Ireland the right to practise is conferred by the Irish Incorporated Law Society, whose requirements are similar to those in force in England and Scotland.

Medicine. Entrance to the medical profession is controlled by the General Council of Medical Education. The duty of this body is to keep a register of qualified medical men and women, to maintain and control the educational standards and curricula, to act as a disciplinary body for the profession, and to publish the *British Pharmacopœia*. Students of medicine register with this body at an age not less than seventeen. Prior to registration they are required to have passed a "matriculation" examination in general education, and in addition an examination in elementary chemistry and physics at a university, or by a licensing body recognised by the General Medical Council.

After registration the course of study extends to a period of at least five years at a recognised medical school. In most instances the whole professional training is undertaken at a university and at the hospitals in the city where the university is situated. In some cases part of the training only is provided at the medical school, clinical study having to be prosecuted elsewhere. It is difficult to state generally the fees payable for a full medical course in varying centres, but £250 for the full course would be a moderate estimate. On graduating, the young doctor is required to register as a medical practitioner under the General Medical Council, and becomes subject to its regulations.

Dentistry is a good example of a profession which, within recent years, has made enormous progress in status, efficiency, and professional standards. The preliminary examinations for registration are now the same as for medicine, and every student must register with the General Medical Council. The intending dentist, to procure the licence in dental surgery, may pass an apprenticeship under a qualified dental surgeon (involving a premium of £50 and upwards), and study for two or more years at a recognised dental school. He may preferably take the whole course at the dental school. He takes his first professional examination at the end of two years, and his final examination at the close of his course in the dental school. The fees for these courses may be estimated at from £100 to £150.

Teaching Profession. The profession of teaching is now much more attractive than it was before the European War, the experiences gained in which taught the community the necessity of having a well-educated nation.

The highest branch of teaching exists in the universities, for which distinctive academic success is necessary. Aspirants for academic work must look forward to a period of at least five years' study.

The aim of all educational bodies is to secure that as large as possible a number of teachers shall have received a university education. The best preliminary preparation is a good secondary education, followed by a university course. After a degree is obtained a further year is spent in professional training, either in a university department of education or a training college. Another plan is to enter one of the training colleges provided by municipal authorities or by such bodies as the Church of England or the Wesleyans. Here the student takes a course of two to three years, preparing himself for an examination which is conducted by university examining bodies, but which does not lead to a degree. Success in this examination entitles the student to rank as a certified teacher. County councils and education authorities make generous provision in scholarships for the intending teacher, and the fees payable for the courses of instruction do not, as a rule, exceed £10 per session.

For secondary teaching the possession of a good honours degree in arts or science or its equivalent is essential. Here it is best to concentrate wholly on university work, generally for four to five years, and subsequently to spend a year on purely professional training. Fees for the university courses should, except in the cases of Oxford and Cambridge, be reckoned at from 20 to 30 guineas per session. The secondary school teacher must be able to give special instruction in one or more subjects of the school curriculum, and at the same time be ready to take part in the general work of the school.

Recognition of the successful completion of training is made by the Boards of Education in England and Ireland and by the Education Department in Scotland by the issue of certificates, whereupon the teacher is qualified as a "trained certificated teacher."

For teaching in the public schools professional training is not absolutely necessary. Here the prospects are somewhat uneven, much depending on the standing of the school. The work of a residential master in a large public school is of an onerous nature, and none should undertake it who are not genuinely fond of boys, or who are unprepared to enter into all the varying activities of school life. Some athletic prowess is an advantage.

The Civil Services. In the Higher Civil Services a good honours degree is necessary. Posts in the Home Civil Service, the Indian Civil Service, Eastern Cadetships, and the Consular and Diplomatic Services are gained as a result of competitive examinations of great severity. For these wide general knowledge in addition to intensity in a few subjects must be obtained. In the various branches of the Civil Service for which the same standard of knowledge is not requisite, the competition is equally great. Candidates for the above services and for second-division clerkships, income-tax surveyorships, and posts of a like nature should apply to the Secretary, Civil Service Commission, Burlington Gardens, London. Notification of examinations is made in the public press. For success in these examinations it is necessary to have specialised coaching, provision for which is made in practically all the larger centres at a moderate cost.

The rates of pay in the various branches of the Civil Service while not high, are nevertheless fairly attractive. In the ordinary way the salary rises automatically to a settled maximum; seniority, however, is not the only element in promotion, and inefficiency may debar an automatic increment.

For those desirous of serving under the British Government in overseas territories, application should be made to the Appointments Secretary, The Colonial Office, London, who will supply a booklet giving full details of possible situations. *See* CIVIL SERVICE; INDIAN CIVIL SERVICE.

Engineering and Allied Professions. It is difficult to advise a young man about the best way of entering the engineering profession unless one knows all the circumstances of his education, aptitudes, and his possible associations with engineering concerns. No hard-and-fast rule regarding any part of his training can be laid down, and he would be well advised to consult members of his family or friends who are in the profession before taking any decisive step. Theoretical training of a fairly high standard must be obtained as well as a thorough knowledge of workshop processes if success is to be attained. The order in which the training should be obtained has always been the subject of controversy, but the embryo engineer should arrange for his entry to an engineering works before he starts his classes. It is perhaps the best thing to take the classes requisite for the intermediate examination for his bachelor of science degree or his diploma before he actually starts his practical work. There are many engineering schools of first rank in the country, among which the leading ones are the Imperial College of Science and Technology in London, the University of Cambridge, the Municipal College of Technology and the Owens College of the Victoria University of Manchester, the University of Glasgow, and the Royal Technical College, Glasgow.

After a year or two at the works he should return to his college classes and complete his degree course, and then return to the works. Every young engineer should qualify for admission to one or more of the engineering institutes at the earliest time. Glasgow and Edinburgh Universities and the technical colleges associated with them hold their classes during the winter six-months, so that students can obtain their works and theoretical training on the " sandwich " system. Advice as to the types of works to enter can only be given by those who have a knowledge of the future intentions of the young engineer, who will have to specialise in some part of the enormous field covered by the term engineering.

Agriculture. Entry to the professions connected with agriculture may be obtained in a variety of ways. There are two main branches—agriculture and dairying—and a practical knowledge of both is advisable although not absolutely essential. University degrees in agriculture, B.Sc. (Agric.), are obtainable in most centres, but there are two diplomas, viz. the National Diploma in Agriculture (N.D.A.) and the National Diploma in Dairying (N.D.D.), which are frequently of more worth. Honours may be taken in the diploma examinations, which, in the case of the N.D.A., are held at Leeds, and at Kilmarnock (Dairy School for Scotland) and Reading for the N.D.D. The N.D.A. and N.D.D. are useful for prospective farm managers, creamery and milk-depot managers, factors, etc. Preliminary farm experience may usually be obtained by residence on a farm or by travelling as a milk-tester, and the college course may be taken during the winter season, and the practical farm-work in summer. In dairying, however, a practical course at a recognised institution is essential, and for admission to this course there is generally a milking examination. The N.D.D. examinations at Kilmarnock, for instance, comprise the making of hard and soft cheeses and butter, as well as written and oral questions in dairying, general farming, veterinary science, bacteriology, chemistry, etc.

Forestry courses are akin to those in agriculture, and may be taken at any good agricultural college.

In **veterinary science** no licence is required to practise, but the holding of the diploma of the Royal College of Veterinary Surgeons (10 Red Lion Square, London, W.C. 1) is of highest importance.

Pharmacy—a profession of recognised value—demands, in addition to an apprenticeship with a chemist or druggist, the passing of a minor and later a major examination. For information on the standard involved in these examinations, the candidate should consult the Registrar of the Royal Pharmaceutical Society, Bloomsbury Square, London, W.C. 1.

Chartered Accountancy offers attractive prospects. Examinations are held by the Institute of Chartered Accountants (Moorgate Place, London, E.C.) in England, and by the three Scottish Societies of Chartered Accountants in Edinburgh, Glasgow, and Aberdeen. There are, in addition to the preliminary, two examinations, intermediate and final, which are taken during the period of articled service (five years in the case of a non-graduate, three in the case of a graduate). In most centres a premium is payable (£50 to £100) when a pupil is articled, though in certain of the centres no premium is exacted.

See also the articles ARMY ; NAVY ; SHIPPING ; JOURNALISM.

PROFESSOR. The title given to salaried teachers in universities and similar institutions who are appointed to deliver lectures for the instruction of students in some particular branch of learning. Professor was the name given in the time of the Roman emperors to public teachers appointed with fixed salaries, in Rome and others of the more important cities of the empire. The name, taken from the Latin verb *profiteri*, denoted that they publicly made themselves known as engaged in the pursuit of their particular art, and in the business of teaching it.

In Oxford and Cambridge the professors devote themselves mainly to the advancement of learning; the preparation of undergraduates for examinations is undertaken by the college lecturers. In the universities of Scotland and Germany, on the other hand, the professors are at once the governing body and the chief recognised functionaries for the purposes of imparting instruction.

PROFIT. In ordinary language profit denotes the net gains of any business organisation, whether joint-stock or in private hands, after meeting what are usually reckoned as costs of production. This use of the word includes interest on capital owned by the business man and invested in his business, together with wages for managerial or professional work exerted by him in it. After deduction of these there remain the earnings of business enterprise itself. In the language of economics the term profit is restricted to this form of income.

The function of the business man or entrepreneur is to initiate economic activity, to hire and combine the other factors of production (land, capital, various forms of labour), and to venture them into prospectively profitable openings. Through competition and the decisions of entrepreneurs regarding the amounts of the other factors of production that it is worth while employing, the remuneration of these factors continually approximates to their net contribution to the joint output. It is rather more difficult to see that this can be so with the entrepreneur's own earnings; indeed, Ricardo and his followers regarded profit as an unearned increment. But the entrepreneur will not exercise his function without return, and, given free competition, a business man's profits will tend not to exceed what similar abilities and efforts could command in other callings.

To the extent that exclusive educational advantages, limitation of business opportunity to owners of capital, and combinations among business men occur in the economic world, profit includes an element of monopoly revenue, which is responsible for the stigma cast upon it by the popular derivative "profiteering." Were it not for these exceptions, competition among business men and between the different openings presenting themselves in the choice of a career would secure the approximation of profits to the entrepreneur's net contribution to the total product of industry.

PRO″FITEER′ING. Selling of commodities at an exorbitant profit. During the Great War prices rose generally and some sought to take advantage of a national emergency. In Great Britain an Act was passed in 1919 to stop profiteering. The Board of Trade was given power to investigate complaints and take action against offenders.

PROFIT-SHARING, or COPARTNERSHIP. The name applied to schemes whereby a business firm associates its employees with its own financial interests. In addition to paying the usual rate of wages, it agrees to distribute among them a certain proportion of any profits made above a fixed minimum. Sometimes, instead of distributing cash, a special class of shares is issued. The amount that accrues to each employee depends on his rate of wages, and often on his length of service. Participation is sometimes voluntary. Usually the firm retains complete control of its business, but some schemes provide for workmen-directors elected by the participating employees.

The ideas underlying profit-sharing are: (1) that the workman's strength and skill are just as much invested in the business as the shareholder's capital, and therefore they should be capitalised and a dividend paid in respect of them; (2) that the knowledge that they participate in the fortunes of the firm gives an additional incentive to the workers and increases efficiency, so as to provide higher profits for shareholders even after payment of the workers' share; (3) that a sense of unity between management and employees reduces losses due to disputes; this is especially so in schemes under which a man who leaves the firm without permission forfeits accumulated dividends.

With a few exceptions, profit-sharing has not worked well in practice. The chief reasons are: (1) the system is difficult for a single firm to work, and it has never yet been applied to a whole industry; (2) the increase in efficiency referred to above is rarely attained in practice; (3) it cannot stand a falling market or considerable fluctuations of profits; (4) it is unpopular with organised labour, because (*a*) it interferes with the mobility of labour between different firms, (*b*) it yields too small an increase in pay (5 to 6 per cent on the average) to balance its disadvantages, (*c*) it substitutes dependence on the employer for trade-union solidarity, and makes collective bargaining difficult, particularly where it penalises strikes.

The businesses in which profit-sharing has proved successful over a long period (Lever Brothers, and the Gas, Light, and Coke Company are notable instances) have usually been in possession of a monopoly, or engaged in the production of something for which there is a steady demand. A gas company fulfils both these conditions, and, in addition, the sliding scale between profits and price of product helps to stabilise the former; virtually profits are shared between the workers, the shareholders, and the consumers.—BIBLIOGRAPHY: Gilman, *A Dividend to Labour* (Report of the Board of Trade on Copartnership, Cmd. 544); S. Webb, *Industrial Democracy* (chapter xii.); G. D. H. Cole, *Payment of Wages* (chapter xiii.).

PROGRESSION. In algebra, a series of numbers succeeding each other according to one or other of three simple laws. In an *arithmetical progression* any term exceeds the preceding term by a constant difference, so that the general form of the series is $a, a + d, a + 2d, \ldots$, where d is the *common difference.* The nth term is $a + (n - 1)d$. The formula for the sum of n terms is simple. Thus, let $s = a + (a + d) + (a + 2d) + \ldots + l$, where l is the last term, or $l = a + (n - 1)d$. Writing the series in reverse order, we have also $s = l + (l - d) + (l - 2d) + \ldots + a$. Hence, by addition, $2s = (a + l) + (a + l) + (a + l) + \ldots + (a + l) = n(a + l)$, and $s = \frac{1}{2}n(a + l)$. It is sometimes convenient to use the result in the form $s = \frac{1}{2}n\{2a + (n - 1)d\}$. The other two progressions are *geometrical* and *harmonical* progression, for which see separate articles.

PROHIBITION (Lat. *prohibitio*, prevention, from *prohibere*, to forbid). Sumptuary legislation forbidding the manufacture and sale of alcoholic liquors for use as beverages. Its aim is to abolish, by constitutional means, that which Prohibitionists consider an evil pernicious to humanity. The idea of prohibition is not a new one. In different countries and at various periods men have come to the conclusion that physiologically the use of intoxicating beverages is injurious to the human race. Sociologists, too, have maintained that the traffic in alcoholic beverages was detrimental to the public good. From the earliest days of its existence to 1920 the House of Commons has passed some 400 Acts of Parliament dealing with the liquor question. The problem, however, is far from being settled, and the House of Commons has not yet seen its way to introduce absolute prohibition of the manufacture, sale, and importation of intoxicants for beverage purposes.

The most notable Acts were the Metropolitan Police Act (1839), the Welsh Sunday Closing Act (1881), the Protection of Children Act (1889), the Intoxicating Liquors Act (1901), the Temperance (Scotland) Act (1919), etc. A National Prohibition Party was inaugurated in London, and the United Kingdom Alliance, formed in Manchester in 1853, has constantly been urging the introduction of prohibition into this country. During the European War the question of prohibition was widely discussed. The Government, without adopting the policy of absolute prohibition, introduced exceptional sets of restrictions. On 31st Aug., 1914, the Intoxicating Liquor (Temporary) Restriction Act was passed, and the policy was extended between 1915 and 1917. A Liquor Traffic Central Control Board was instituted, and orders were made curtailing hours, prohibiting "treating," etc. After the conclusion of the war, the Government announced their intention of introducing legislation for the purpose of putting the liquor trade on a new footing.

In the United States of America a strong prohibition movement was started early in the nineteenth century, one of the earliest measures being that which forbade the sale of liquor to Indians. Local prohibition was then adopted in many states, Maine being the first to establish it in 1851, and in 1868 a Prohibition party was organised in Maine and Michigan. During the European War, America introduced prohibition as a war-measure, and the scheme of national prohibition was referred to the individual states. On 29th Jan., 1919, the Government announced that national prohibition would come into force, as 36 states, Nebraska being the last, had voted in favour of the measure. In spite of President Wilson's veto, Congress passed the Prohibition Enforcement Bill in Sept., 1919, and on 16th Jan., 1920, national prohibition became law in the United States. The American Anti-Saloon League has been endeavouring to spread the prohibition movement in Europe. Some amusement was caused during 1922 by the discovery that American State-owned ships were not only carrying and serving liquor on board, but were actually advertising the fact in the United States to induce business. The anomaly was eventually removed and foreign ships, of whatever description or nationality, were likewise forbidden to enter United States ports with liquor, even under seal. In 1933, however, under the presidency of Franklin Roosevelt, national prohibition was repealed in the United States. In Norway prohibition was enforced in 1919, but was repealed by popular vote in 1926. Consult also the article LOCAL OPTION.—BIBLIOGRAPHY: G. Hayler, *Prohibition Advance in all Lands*; J. C. Fernald, *Economics of Prohibition*; Sir J. Crichton-Browne, *Prohibition: Liberty*; A. Mee and J. S. Holden, *Prohibition: Defeat.*

PROJEC'TILES, THEORY OF. A branch of dynamics which discusses the problem of the motion of a body projected from a point on the earth's surface with any speed and at any angle of elevation. A perfectly general treatment of this problem is very difficult, especially when the resistance of the air is taken into account, as it has to be if the theoretical results are to be of any value for practical applications. For unresisted motion, the problem is conveniently divided into two parts, the motion of the centroid, and the motion of rotation about the centroid. The latter motion is the same as if the centroid were at rest; and the motion of the centroid is the same as if the whole mass were concentrated at that point (*see* KINETICS).

To find how the centroid moves, consider, as was first done by Galilei, the horizontal and vertical components of the motion separately. There is no horizontal force, so the horizontal velocity remains constant. The vertical velocity and vertical position change as if there were no horizontal motion. Hence if axes of x and y be taken through the point of projection, horizontally and vertically respectively, we have the equations: $x = Ut$, $y = Vt - \frac{1}{2}gt^2$; where x, y are the co-ordinates of the centroid at time t from the moment of projection; U, V are the horizontal and vertical components of the velocity of projection; and g is the acceleration of a falling body (*see* FALL OF BODIES; GRAVITY). These equations represent a parabola with its axis vertical. To illustrate their use, we may take the problem of finding the angle of elevation which, for a given initial speed, gives the maximum range on the ground plane. When $y = 0$, we have $t = 0$, or $t = 2V/g$; the second value gives the time of reaching the ground. The value of x for this t is $2UV/g$, or $(U^2 + V^2)/g - (U - V)^2/g$; since $U^2 + V^2$ is the square of the initial speed, this is greatest when $U = V$, in which case the angle of projection is 45°.

PROJECTION. *See* GEOMETRY; MAP; MECHANICAL DRAWING; PERSPECTIVE.

PROLAP'SUS A'NI. The protrusion of the lower part of the rectum through the anus, caused by straining in costiveness, piles, etc. Persons liable to this accident should be careful to regulate their bowels so as to prevent costiveness and consequent straining. Regular bathing of the parts with cold water may also be found useful.

PROLAP'SUS U'TERI. "Falling down of the womb," or "bearing down," a common affection among women who have borne large families, but sometimes occurring in virgins, and in very rare cases in infants. What renders the falling down of the womb possible is a general laxity of the parts supporting it, and it may be of various degrees, from the slightest downward displacement to such a descent as causes external protrusion of the womb. When the falling down once begins it always tends to increase, unless means are taken to prevent it. In all cases of this affection the first requisite for cure is prolonged rest in the horizontal position, with the use, under surgical direction, of cold or astringent injections and the various forms of pessary.

PROLETA'RIAT. Term used to denote the wage-earning class of a community collectively. By Socialists it is used to distinguish this class from the capitalists and the middle classes, often termed *bourgeoisie.* The word is from a Latin one meaning those citizens who had no property but served the state by producing offspring.

PROLOGUE AND EPILOGUE. A prologue is an introductory or prefatory piece of writing. In this general sense the most famous of all prologues is perhaps the prologue to the *Canterbury Tales.* The word is, however, usually employed in the sense of a discourse or poem spoken as the introduction to a dramatic performance. The Greeks originally applied the term *prologos* to all that portion of the play that came before the first chorus, but from the time of Euripides this became a monologue containing a narrative of facts introductory to the main action. By the time of Euripides plots were becoming more and more scarce; he did not wish to adopt trite themes, and so went into the byways of mythology or adopted a less well-known alternative version of a well-known legend. He could not count on his audience already possessing enough knowledge of the story to enable them to understand his plays without a prologue. There is sometimes a rich vein of irony in the Euripidean prologues; this is especially noticeable in the *Hippolytus*, where the prologue is spoken by Aphrodite. There were no prologues in Aristophanic comedy, but Plautus and Terence invariably made use of an epexegetic prologue. In the prologue to the *Rudens*, which is spoken by the star Arcturus, Plautus rose to great heights of poetry.

The prologue played an important part in Elizabethan drama, though in the days of Shakespeare's maturity it was becoming somewhat old-fashioned. It is noteworthy that the most lamentable comedy of *Pyramus and Thisby* has an explanatory prologue; the prologue to *The Murder of Gonzago* is "brief as woman's love," and merely apologetic. *Romeo and Juliet* has an immature prologue in the form of a sonnet; in the *Second Part of Henry IV.* the prologue is spoken by "Rumour painted full of tongues." *Henry V.* has an apologetic prologue, and that curious play *Troilus and Cressida* has an explanatory prologue. *Henry VIII.* and *Pericles* have prologues which are not the work of Shakespeare.

Ben Jonson delighted in the prologue, but frequently embedded it in a more elaborate Induction. Beaumont and Fletcher did not make much use of the prologue. After the Restoration it enjoyed a great vogue which lasted until about the middle of the nineteenth century. Many of these prologues were elaborate essays in verse, and were used to give a literary flavour to work of which the merits, if any, were purely dramatic. It was a common practice to get a well-known poet or verse-writer to write these prologues, which were often quite unconnected with the play.

An **Epilogue** (the word originally meant the peroration of a speech) is a valedictory or apologetic speech or short poem addressed to the spectators by one of the actors after the conclusion of a play. The epilogue was always much less an integral part of the play than the prologue. It was unknown in Greek drama, and in Latin comedy usually consisted of a brief formula such as "vos valete et plaudite" (Farewell, and clap your hands).

Shakespeare used the epilogue in several plays. In *A Midsummer Night's Dream* Theseus says "No epilogue, pray you, for your play needs no excuse"—showing that the function of an epilogue was mainly apologetic. There are epilogues in *A Midsummer Night's Dream*, *Henry IV. Part 2*, *Henry V.*, *All's Well that ends Well*, *As You Like It*, *Troilus and Cressida*, and *The Tempest*, as well as in *Henry VIII.* and *Pericles*. Jonson usually provided his plays with a defiant epilogue; that appended to *Cynthia's Revels* contained the notorious line:

By God 't is good, and if you like 't you may.

After the Restoration the epilogue shared the fortunes of the prologue. Both were written with great elaboration by Dryden, and by later and less efficient writers, and both fell into disuse in mid-Victorian days.

PROME. A district and town in the Pegu Division of Lower Burma. The district stretches from east to west across the Irrawaddy Valley, and has an area of 2915 sq. miles. Prome has a much drier climate than the rest of the Pegu Division. 00 per cent of the population is Burman and the Burmese language predominates. Rice is cultivated.

According to tradition Prome, once a flourishing kingdom, was founded by a king named Dutabaung of the Pyu tribe, who with the Arakanese and other tribes, constituted the Burman race in the remote ages. Prome is, then, the traditional cradle of the Burmese race. *Pyi* is the Burmese name for Prome. The town is on the Irrawaddy, and is the terminal of the railway from Rangoon. Within it lies the Shwesandaw pagoda, 80 feet high, with a gilded dome. It stands on a platform of stone, and is supposed to contain four genuine hairs from Gautama's head. Pop. (district), 380,000; (town), 26,067.

PROME'THEUS. In Greek mythology, one of the Titans, brother of Atlas and of Epimetheus, and the father of Deucalion. His name means "forethought," as that of his brother Epimetheus signifies "afterthought." He gained the enmity of Zeus by bringing fire from heaven to men, and by conferring other benefits on them. To punish this offence Zeus caused Prometheus to be chained by Hephæstus (Vulcan) on a rock of the Caucasus (the eastern extremity of the world, according to the notions of the earlier Greeks), where his liver, which was renewed every night, was torn by a vulture or an eagle. He was ultimately delivered by Heracles. That is the tradition as shaped by Æschylus, who has a noble tragedy on the subject, the *Prometheus Vinctus* (Prometheus Bound), while

Shelley has also a drama, the *Prometheus Unbound*. A different version is given by Hesiod.

Prometheus

PROMISE. In law, an agreement entered into by one person to perform or not to perform some particular thing. When there is a mutual promise between two parties, it is termed a contract. A promise may either be verbal or written. A verbal promise is in England called a promise by parole, and a written promise is in technical language designated a covenant. By English law no promise is binding unless it was made for a consideration, but by Scots law it is always binding whether a consideration was given or not. The law of Scotland makes a distinction between a promise and an offer, the former being an engagement of such a nature that it is unnecessary to secure the consent of the person to whom the promise is made while the latter is an engagement dependent on the assent of the other party.

PROM'ISSORY NOTE. A promissory note is defined by the Bills of Exchange Act as " an unconditional promise in writing made by one person to another, signed by the maker, engaging to pay, on demand, or at a fixed or determinable future time, a sum certain in money, to or to the order of a specified person or to bearer." In form it is usually as follows :

£50. London, 30*th November*, 1922.

Three months after date I promise to pay to Mr. A— B— or order the sum of Fifty pounds, for value received.

(Signed) X— Y—.

A promissory note is inchoate and incomplete until delivered to the payee or bearer. The note may be made by two or more parties, who may be liable thereon jointly, or jointly and severally, according to its terms. If the note runs " I promise to pay " and is signed by two or more persons, their liability is joint and several. A promissory note payable on demand must be presented for payment within a reasonable time after it has been endorsed, failing which the endorser is discharged. What is a reasonable time depends on the usage of trade or the facts of the particular case. The maker of a promissory note is bound to pay it according to its tenor, and is precluded from denying to a holder in due course the existence of the payee or his then capacity to endorse. In general, the rules applicable to bills of exchange apply also to promissory notes with certain obvious exceptions, e.g. those regarding acceptance. A promissory note must be duly stamped, and any person who takes or receives an unstamped note, either in payment or as a security, or by purchase or otherwise, is not entitled to recover thereon or to make it available for any purpose whatever.

Prong-buck

PRONG-BUCK, or PRONG-HORN ANTELOPE. A species of antelope, the *Antilocapra americana*, which inhabits the western parts of North America. It frequents the plains in summer and the mountains in winter. It is one of the few hollow-horned antelopes, and the only living one in which the horny sheath is branched, branching being otherwise peculiar to deer which have bony antlers. This sheath is shed every year.

PROOF IMPRESSION. In printing, a rough impression from types, taken for correction. A first proof is the impression taken with all the errors of workmanship. After this is corrected another impression is printed with more care to send to the author; this is termed a *clean proof*. The first proof before going to press is called a *press proof*, but there are usually intermediate proofs called *revise proofs* or *revises* simply.

In engraving, a proof impression is one taken from an engraving to show the state of it during the progress of the work; also, an early impression, or one of a limited number, taken before the letters to be inserted are engraved on the plate. Proof states of engravings are usually distinguished as (1) *Artists' proofs*, with no engraved title, sometimes signed in pencil by the painter or engraver, or both. *Remarque* artists' proofs have some mark, frequently a minute part left white, or a design slightly engraved on the margin. (2) *Proofs before letters*, still without title, but with artist's and engraver's names inserted close to the bottom of the work, and the publisher's name near the lower margin of the plate. (3) *Lettered proofs*, with title engraved lightly in such a manner as to be easily erased, or in open letters ready for shading, when the title is finally put on the plate for the ordinary impressions. *See* CORRECTION OF THE PRESS.

PROOF SPIRIT. Dilute alcohol. It contains 49·24 per cent by weight or 57·06 per cent by volume of absolute alcohol. Its use in pharmacy is now superseded generally by alcohol of a higher strength. Spirit stronger than proof spirit is said to be overproof, if weaker, underproof.

PROPAGAN'DA. An association, the congregation *de propaganda fide* (for propagating the faith), established at Rome by Gregory XV. in 1622 for diffusing a knowledge of Roman Catholicism throughout the world, now charged with the management of the Roman Catholic missions. In close connection with it stand the seminaries or colleges of the Jesuits, and the great majority of the members of the propaganda are Jesuits and Franciscans.

PROPAGATION. The multiplication or reproduction of the species of animals or plants. As a technical term it is used chiefly in regard to plants. The most common method of propagating plants is of course by their seed. There are other ways, however, by which plants are propagated naturally (vegetative reproduction). Some, for example, throw off runners from their stems which creep along the ground, and these runners take root at the nodes, and send up new shoots.

The commonest artificial methods of propagating plants are budding, layering, the various forms of grafting, including inarching or grafting by approach, propagation by offsets and by slips. Some plants (as the potato) are propagated by dividing the tubers of underground stems, each "eye" or leaf-bud of which produces a new plant, while a few are propagated by cuttings of the leaves. Some microscopic plants (bacteria) and animals (many Protozoa) progate by division or fission. The former (e.g. yeast plant) may also reproduce by budding or gemmation, as do many lower animals, especially the Hydrozoa, Polyzoa, and Ascidians.

PROPELLER. Revolving mechanism for driving steam of motor vessels, aircraft or machinery. A screw propeller used on vessels takes the form of a shaft with spiral blades, and the speed of the propeller is limited largely by centrifugal effort. In aircraft the term specially refers to the air-screw which propels the machine.

PROPERTIUS, Sextus. In many ways the greatest of Roman elegiac poets; born at Assisi about 50 B.C., and died about 15 B.C. Little is known about his life except what is derived from his poems. He came of a well-to-do though not aristocratic family; his father died while he was a boy, and after the battle of Philippi he was deprived of his estate and reduced to poverty. He proceeded to Rome, where he received a good education, and, after some attempts at a career at the Bar, settled down to the more congenial occupations of a *littérateur* and man about town.

He met his mistress Cynthia (Hostia was her real name) when he was about twenty years of age, and soon after commenced to write poetry. Cynthia was an upper-class courtesan; her *liaison* with Propertius lasted some six years, but was broken by many quarrels and one complete year of estrangement. She had not an attractive character, being vain, fickle, greedy for gain, and hasty of temper. It is doubtful whether the poet was genuinely in love with her; to some extent she was part of his poetical outfit. His first book of poems was published in 25 B.C. It caused a revolution in elegiac poetry. Its opening lines,

> Cynthia prima suis miserum me cepit ocellis
> Contactum nullis ante cupidinibus,

struck a new note, and widened beyond belief the possibilities of the elegaic couplet. Cynthia died in about 23 B.C.; little is known of what happened to Propertius after her death. He was patronised by Mæcenas, and was a friend of Virgil and of Ovid. On more or less negative evidence, it is very probable that Horace and he were on bad terms.

The poems of Propertius consist of over four thousand lines of elegiac verse; most of his poems are love-poems connected with Cynthia, some few (especially in the last book) are political or historical, and were probably inspired by Mæcenas. His work has many unique qualities which both attract and repel. It is highly characteristic of the man who wrote it. He was a highly strung and brilliant young man, somewhat effeminate and neurotic. He woke one day to find himself famous, and worked for some years at the somewhat thin vein of poetry which was in him. He never caught the "fine careless rapture" of his first book, though there is deeper knowledge of the human heart in some of his later work.

After the death of Cynthia he became a young man with a great past behind him. Yet he did not feel for her the genuine passion that animated the love lyrics of Catullus. The difference between Propertius's love for Cynthia and that of Catullus for Lesbia is the same as the difference between Romeo's love for Rosaline and his love for Juliet. Propertius, in fact, is in love with being in love, and is always more interested in himself than in his mistress. He is a highly artificial poet, and in order to understand him it is necessary to have frequent recourse to Lemprière and to Sir William Smith.

He was an admirer of Callimachus, Philetas, and the Alexandrian school of poetry in general; much of his work is merely rather better than Catullus at his worst. It is forced and unnatural to a degree, and is no more genuine poetry than the work of a "tenth transmitter" of the Popian tradition in the eighteenth century. Now and again, when he can forget himself, Propertius rises to great heights of poetry, as he does in his noble elegy on Cornelia. Had he always written thus, "it had been vain to blame, and useless to praise him."

As a metrist it is impossible to praise Propertius too highly. Catullus's elegiacs were almost as rough as the hexameters of Ennius; those of Ovid are elegant to the verge of monotony; Propertius is the happy mean between these two extremes. He alone raised the pentameter to the dignity of its heroic consort.—BIBLIOGRAPHY: W. Y. Sellar, *Horace and the Elegiac Poets*; H. E. Butler, *Sexti Properti Opera Omnia*, and *Propertius* (text and translation, Loeb Library); J. S. Phillimore, *Propertius* (text index verborum, and translation).

PROPERTY (Lat. *proprius*, one's own). In law, the right of ownership of a subject—"the entirety of the powers of use and disposal allowed by law" (Pollock, *Jurisprudence*). It is a higher right than that of possession (q.v.), for the power of disposal is an essential element in the right of property which is lacking from mere possession—one can scarcely conceive of an *owner* who has no power to dispose of the things he owns—and, further, the right of ownership necessarily implies a right to claim and maintain possession against all the world. But the right of property or ownership may quite well be limited in certain directions either for a time or in perpetuity. Thus the owner of an article may let it out to another person for a period, and he thereby temporarily cedes possession and limits his right of property as to use and disposal; or again, the right may be subject to a permanent limitation and transferable only under burden thereof, as when an easement or servitude exists over a plot of ground in favour of another person or subject or of the public, e.g. a right of way.

In short, "the owner of a thing is not necessarily the person who at a given time has the whole power of use and disposal; very often there is no such person. We must look for the person having the residue of all such power when we have accounted for every detached and limited portion of it, and he will be the owner even if the immediate power of control and use is elsewhere. In the same way a political sovereign does not lose his independence merely because he has made a treaty by which he has agreed to forgo or limit the exercise of his sovereign power in particular respects" (Pollock).

Property may be acquired in several ways, e.g. by taking possession of a thing which has no owner, by gift, inheritance, purchase, etc., but certain subjects, e.g. running water, navigable rivers, and highways, cannot be held in private ownership. *See* LAND LAWS.

PROPERTY TAX. A tax similar to the income-tax (of which indeed it forms a part), being levied at the same rate on the annual value of real property of which a person is owner.

PROPHET AND PROPHECY. Prophecy is usually regarded as a phenomenon peculiar to the Hebrew people. Every literary history of Israel contains a chapter on the Prophets, and the literary history of no other nation would contain such a chapter. The English word "prophet" is simply a transliteration of the Greek word by which the Greek translators of the Hebrew Bible in the century or two immediately before the Christian era rendered the Hebrew word *nabhī'*. The popular idea of a "prophet" as a person who predicts events before they happen, although not unknown to the Hebrews (Deut. xiii., 2; xviii., 22; Is. xli., 22, etc.), really comes from the Greek. The Hebrew word *nabhī'* means no more than "spokesman" or "informant." The verse which gives the clearest definition of its meaning is (as noted by Spinoza) Ex. vii., 1: "I have made thee a god to Pharaoh, and Aaron shall be thy prophet." Aaron is Moses' spokesman, just as the prophet is spokesman for God. The nearest English equivalent is the word "preacher" (which is only "predicter" writ small). The acknowledged head of the ideal theocracy is a prophet (Hos. xii., 13), but what distinguishes the prophet from other religious or political or military leaders is that he is *unofficial*. He may belong to any tribe, and to any of the four estates. In this he is distinguished especially from the priests, whose office was hereditary, and who were all Levites.

The essential thing about the prophet is that he is in touch with God, and receives direct communications from Him. Hence he is above the law and the civil authority, and from what he says there is no appeal. He resembles the Muslim *soofee* or mystic, who rejects all authority, and derives his religion directly from God; and in the authority he wields the prophet is like the Shareef, who is in reality above the Sultan. This mystical power is not miraculous; it can be acquired. Both the *soofees* and the prophets undergo courses of training at the hands of acknowledged teachers (2 Kings, iv., 38); both have recourse to music and other means to bring about a state of trance (1 Sam. x., 5; 2 Kings, iii., 15); both wear a distinguishing garb (Zech. xiii., 4); and both, when in a state of ecstasy, sometimes appear to the official class as insane (2 Kings, ix., 11; Jer. xxix., 26). Hence some passages, which were formerly regarded as exalting the prophetic office, are now by some supposed to imply contempt for it (1 Sam. x., 12; Amos, vii., 14). Prophecy in its highest form, however, has shed these accessories, and tends to become more purely literary. The old name "seer" (*rō'eh*) was dropped, that of *nabhī'* taking its place (1 Sam. ix., 9).

The long line of Hebrew prophets may be regarded as beginning with Samuel some time about the year 1000 B.C., and ending with John the Baptist and Jesus Christ, although the name is applied to some who lived before (e.g. Abraham and Moses) and to others who lived after this period (as Agabus, Acts, xxi., 10, etc.). Prophecy in Israel frequently suffered an eclipse; there were periods when no prophet appeared (1 Sam. iii., 1; Ps. lxxiv., 9). Yet a remarkable recrudescence of prophecy is found in the person of Mahomet in Arabia in the seventh century, and some modern writers, such as Thomas Carlyle, only reiterate the words of the Hebrew prophets.

The central doctrine of the Hebrew prophets is monotheism—that God is *one*. Attempts have been made to show that the earliest of them—Elijah, for example—were not, monotheists but henotheists, that is, that they did not recognise Jehovah as the only god in heaven and earth but as the only god for the Hebrews, whilst they did not object to Baal being worshipped in Phœnicia or Rimmon in Damascus (1 Kings, xvi., 32; 2 Kings, v., 18). For this the evidence is very meagre. All we know is that the earliest prophets whose writings have come down to us, Amos and Hosea are thorough-going monotheists. The same Jehovah who brought the Israelites out of Egypt also brought the Philistines from Crete and the Aramæans from Kir (Amos, ix., 7). It was a deep sense of the divine omnipresence that kindled "rapt Isaiah's wild seraphic fire" (chapter xl. ff.). No doubt even the latest writers speak of a multiplicity of gods (Ps. lxxxii., 1, etc.), but only in the same sense in which we do so still. Yet the craving for tangible objects of worship clung to the Jews even in late post-exilic times (Is. lxv., f.). At the same time, as far as the better part of the nation is concerned, it would be difficult to put a belief in the unity of God too early. Indeed monotheism seems to be an instinct with the Semitic peoples.

But this monotheism is not a mere philosophic doctrine: it is practical and moral. As the one God is essentially just, benignant, forgiving, so He requires the same qualities in His worshippers. Indeed the cultivation of these virtues is the truest worship of God. In the familiar words of Micah, "to do justly, to love mercy, and to walk humbly with God" is the only worship which He requires. It is at this point that prophetism comes into collision with the priesthood and the ritual law. Each prophet in turn, beginning with Samuel (1 Sam. xv., 22), rejects the ceremonial worship of his day, whether it were carried on at popular shrines and sacred stones and trees, as in the days of Amos and Hosea, or centralised in the temple of Jerusalem, as in the time of Isaiah and Micah, in words which have become

Prophet Isaiah, by Bartolommeo

classic (Hos. vi., 6; Is. i, 11 ff.; Mic., vi. 8).

The whole book of Amos is a plea for justice, especially justice for the poor (v., 24). Hosea, like Socrates, identifies virtue and knowledge; it is because the Israelites do not know Jehovah that they imagine He can prefer sacrifice to mercy. Isaiah and Micah, so different in every other respect—the one a wealthy courtier and patriotic citizen of the capital, the other a poor countryman to whom all nations were more or less alike—are at one on this point, and the terms in which Micah has expressed it have been well called by the late Professor Wellhausen "the egg of Columbus."

Jeremiah, himself a priest, will not allow that worship by sacrifice was ever enjoined upon the Israelites at all (vii., 22 f.). In him Israelite prophecy reaches its high-water mark, for, whilst his predecessors demanded a new life, he first insists upon the *new heart*. Other writers outside the recognised ranks of the prophets, and perhaps later than they, take up the same refrain (Ps. l., 7 ff.; li., 16 f.) Ezekiel, also a priest, almost puts himself outside the prophetic circle, for in his Hebrew Utopia (chapter xl., ff.) ritual plays a very large part, but, on the other hand, he insists upon morality as emphatically as the rest. Hebrew prophecy culminates in John the Baptist and Jesus. Sacrifice now no longer held its old place; worship was believed to consist rather in the *study* of the Law. Hence arose an elaborate and intricate system of casuistry, comparable only to that of the Jesuits in later days. In place of this impossible burden John put the few simple duties of common life (Luke, iii., 10 ff.). Jesus reduced the innumerable ordinances of the Pharasaic tradition to two—love of God and of one's neighbour. With the fall of Jerusalem the long strife came to an end.

From a political point of view the Hebrew prophets have been called the "stormy petrels of history." They are the heralds of the storm, and generally they come in pairs. Elijah and Elisha are the precursors of revolution both in Samaria and in Damascus; Amos and Hosea, even in the prosperous times of Jeroboam II., foretell the sweeping away of the northern kingdom as imminent, as Isaiah and Micah do that of Judah also; Nahum is the herald of the downfall of Nineveh, and Habakkuk of that of Babylon.

But besides the main theme of their mission, each of the prophets in turn makes a wide survey of the whole world as known to him. Hence a series of prophecies "against foreign nations" (Amos, i. and ii.; Is. xiii-xxiii; Jer. xlvi-li; Ezek. xxv-xxxii). These prophecies, both home and foreign, are frankly pessimistic, and in Jeremiah, who witnessed the crowning calamity, this pessimism reaches its lowest depths. It is worth asking whether these gloomy utterances did not do much to bring about their own fulfilment. But once the cloud had burst, a ray of hope began to appear. Ezekiel, in exile, foresees Israel restored, and the "great unknown" (Is. xl. ff.) paints in gorgeous colours the glories of the Return. Even amid its realities Haggai and Zechariah are hopeful. But a century later the clouds have gathered again, and the last of the old prophets sounds a note of sadness. What saves the prophets from despair is their belief in a "remnant," that each new turn in the fortunes of the people, whilst calamitous for the mass, left a purified residue behind (Is. vi., 13, etc. Mal. iv., 2).

The doctrine of a "remnant" (which we owe to Isaiah) is connected with what are called "Messianic prophecies," the pictures of the ideal future kingdom under the ideal king, the reign of peace and goodwill upon earth, the golden age of the future (Is. xi., 1-10; Mic. iv., 3, 4; Dan. vii, 13, 14), when the days of Cronos should return. But this matter comes rather under the head of Apocalyptic than of Prophecy, although one point to which attention may be drawn here is the deep, almost tragic sense of responsibility which is present in all, but which Ezekiel alone puts into words (iii., 17 ff.).

The Hebrew prophets hold the same place in Israel as do the philosophers in Greece. They are the moral and intellectual guides of the people. In Greece there were also the sophists, and in Israel the false prophets. But between the Greek philosopher and the Hebrew prophet there is a vast difference in method. The former is guided by reason, the latter by intuition. The result is that the truth which the former attained only after a laborious process of reasoning, the latter perceives almost unconsciously. He starts from the point at which the philosopher ends.

Moreover, the aim of the one is different from that of the other. A great deal of Western philosophy is taken up with the mere definition of terms, although it is obvious that to define a name, the content of which is always changing, is alike impossible and futile. The Eastern thinker does not trouble to define terms the contents of which are common knowledge. Names are nothing to him but the ideas which they express. He does not care to define the good or the true, mercy or humility. He takes these for granted, and his one aim is to get men to practise them. He is concerned with things, not words, with doing, not abstract thinking. The result is that if the whole of Greek philosophy and all it stands for were taken out of human life to-day, the toiling millions of mankind would not be conscious of any change. But if the Hebrew prophets had neither existed nor taught, life would be a different thing for one-half of the human race to-day.

BIBLIOGRAPHY: The literature is enormous. Spinoza's *Tractatus Theologico-politicus* has been freely used by succeeding writers (English translation, 1868); of older books, material will be found in Keil's *Introduction to the Old Testament* (English translation, 1881); the writings of W. R. Smith, A. B. Davidson, and Sir G. A. Smith are always fresh and interesting; of German works translated into English, one of the best and shortest is that of Cornill, *Prophets of Israel* (1895); of books dealing with individual prophets, the *Cambridge Bible* contains perhaps the most reliable, the *International Critical Commentary* the most exhaustive; Frazer's *Folklore in the Old Testament* (1918) contains much curious matter.

PROPON'TIS. The ancient name of the Sea of Marmara, from being before or in advance of the Pontus Euxinus or Black Sea.

PROPORTIONAL REPRESENTATION. The end for the attainment of which numerous schemes—said to number about 300—have been devised during the last half-century. It is generally admitted that our present system of parliamentary elections falls short of perfection, especially in its failure to provide for a fair and reasonable representation of minorities. One device is that known as the *cumulative vote*, by which each elector has as many votes as there are candidates to be elected, and allots them as he pleases. It is argued that by this method an organised minority can pool its votes and secure adequate return of its party; but the system has been found to work capriciously, and the *transferable* or *alternative vote* is generally preferred. Under this system each elector marks his voting-paper with (1), (2), (3), and so on, according to his preference for the candidates.

To secure election a candidate must obtain a certain number of votes, called the *quota*, which is fixed by dividing the number of voters by one more than the number of seats vacant. At the first count only first choices are considered, and those candidates who obtain their *quota* from such votes are declared elected. If, as will usually happen, there are still seats to be filled, the surplus votes of the elected candidates are transferred in proper proportion to the second choices of the electors who voted for those candidates as their first choice. For example, if the *quota* is 3000, and a candidate receives 4000 first votes, 1000 of his papers, i.e. one-quarter of the total 4000, are available for the second choices marked on them; and each unelected candidate is given one-quarter of those papers on which he is indicated as second choice. If after these transfers the number of candidates who have secured their *quota* is still insufficient, the lowest candidate is rejected, and a first vote given to him on any paper is transferred to the next preference shown on that paper. This process of rejection and transfer is repeated till the required number is elected.

Proportional representation by this method was first advocated by Thomas Hare in 1857, and received a few years later strong support from John Stuart Mill, who wished the country to be regarded for election purposes as one single constituency. One or other of the systems has been adopted by various countries on the Continent and overseas, as also for the municipal elections in Ireland, for those of the Scottish Education Authorities, and in some of the University parliamentary elections.

PROPOSITION. In grammar and logic, a sentence or part of a sentence which consists of a subject and a predicate, and in which something is affirmed or denied of a subject. Logical propositions are said to be divided, first, according to substance, into *categorical* and *hypothetical*; secondly, according to quality, into *affirmative* and *negative*; thirdly, according to quantity, into *universal* and *particular*.

PROPYLÆ'A. In Greek architecture, the entrance to a temple. The term was employed particularly in speaking of the superb vestibules or porticoes conducting to the Acropolis of Athens. This magnificent work, of the Doric order, was constructed under the direction of Pericles (437-433 B.C.) after the designs of the architect Mnesicles. See illus. p. 436.

PROROGATION OF PARLIAMENT. The continuance of Parliament from one session to another, as adjournment is a continuance of the session from one day to another, or for a longer period. Prorogation determines the session, but adjournment, though for a fortnight, month, etc., does not. After a prorogation any Bill which has previously passed both Houses, or either House, without receiving the royal sanction or the concurrence of the other House, must be taken up *de novo*. Parliament is prorogued by the sovereign's authority, either by the Lord Chancellor in the royal presence, or by commission, or by proclamation.

PROSCRIPTION. In Roman history, a mode of getting rid of enemies, first resorted to by Sulla in 82 B.C., and imitated more than once afterwards in the stormy years that closed the Republic. Under Sulla, lists of names were drawn out and posted up in public places, with the promise of a reward to any person who should kill any of those named in the lists, and the threat of death to those who should aid or shelter any of them. Their property also was confiscated, and their children were declared incapable of honours.

PROSE (generally derived from *prorsa (oratio)*, the reason of which will be given in the course of the article). The true character of prose can be clearly conceived only by considering it in relation to poetry. Their difference lies in the essential difference of certain states of the mind and feelings. The two chief states of the inward man may be called the *thinking* and the *poetical* states, and depend upon the predominance of the understanding, or the imagination and feelings. If we think (in the narrower sense of the word) we combine ideas according to the laws of reason; and prose, which is the language of sober thought, is characterised by the abstractness and generality of precision belonging to ideas that occupy the understanding. Prose, in the most common acceptation of the word, is used in contradistinction to metrical composition. The external form naturally strikes first, and in the early stages of society strikes most; hence the term *prose*, which, as we have already stated, is derived from *prorsus, prorsa oratio* (straight or direct speech), opposed to *verse*, which is derived from *versus* (turned), returning always to the selected metre.

The Greeks called prose *ho pezos logos*, which the Romans translated *pedestris oratio*; and St. Evremond compares prose writers to modest pedestrians. Prose was also called by the Romans *oratio soluta* (free speech), in opposition to *oratio vincta* (bound speech) or verse, which is bound by rhythmical laws. From what has been said of the difference between prose and poetry, it is clear that poetry must be much earlier developed than prose. Strong personal feeling naturally demands rhythmical expression, and in the early stages of society such is the only motive that is capable of leading to literary production. Oratory, it is true, selects a prose vehicle; but there is this difference between oratory and poetry, that the orator rather governs his feelings and directs them towards a practical object—that of inciting his hearers to some resolution—than allows himself to be swayed by them; whereas the poet allows himself to be swayed so far as is consistent with literary expression.

PROPYLÆA TO THE ACROPOLIS OF ATHENS

Whenever the understanding predominates, as it does in oratory, prose is the natural vehicle; and although it is the case that histories, laws, and philosophical maxims were first conveyed in verse with the Greeks and many other nations, this may be explained partly by the fact that verse had established itself as the regular literary medium, and partly by this, that in these early times civilisation was not sufficiently far advanced for the purely intellectual to be predominant over the emotional interest except in the one case of oratory. Pliny says that Pherecydes of Scyros (a contemporary of Cyrus) first formed the Greek prose (*prosam primus condere instituit*); but perhaps he was only the first who wrote on philosophico-mythological subjects in prose. Fine prose is among the latest attainments both of nations and individuals, and it would appear that with most nations classical prose writers are fewer than classical poets.

PROSECUTION, CRIMINAL. By the law of England the Solicitor to the Treasury is director of public prosecutions in cases where the public interest is mainly concerned. By the law of Scotland that function is assigned to the Lord-Advocate and his assistants the advocates-depute, and the procurators-fiscal of burghs and counties. In England, in the less serious offences not affecting the public interest, it is sometimes left to the private parties more immediately concerned to institute criminal proceedings. The result of this is that many criminals are sometimes allowed to go free merely for want of a prosecutor.

PROS'ELYTE (Gr. *prosēlytos*, a stranger or newcomer). In religion, a person who leaves one religion for the profession of another. The Jews, in New Testament times at least, had two classes of proselytes, namely, the "proselytes of the gate," as they were termed; and the "proselytes of righteousness," or of the covenant. According to the rabbis the proselytes of the gate were those who renounced idolatry and worshipped the only true God according to the (so-called) seven laws of the children of Noah, without subjecting themselves to circumcision and the other commands of the Mosaic law. The proselytes of righteousness were persons who had been fully converted from paganism to Judaism, had been circumcised, and bound themselves to observe the Mosaic law.

PROSOBRANCHIATA. An order of gastropod molluscs comprising the whelks, periwinkles, etc., mostly marine, though some inhabit fresh water. The gill or gills, when present, are in front of the heart. *See* MOLLUSCA.

Prosobranchiata (whelk)

PROSODY (Gr. *prosōdia*, a song sung to music, a mark of quantity, from Gr. *pros*, to, and *ōdē*, song). The correct pronunciation of words. It is that part of grammar which treats of accents, of the quantity of syllables, and of the laws of versification.

Greek grammarians employed the term prosody in relation to all the marks which, added to letters, characterised more exactly the sounds of speech. Such marks were accents, quantity, and breathings. In modern times the term prosody is applied only to the recognition of rhythmical form in verse. Under *accent* we understand the stress of the voice upon a syllable in pronouncing it. *Quantity*, on the other hand, is the time required for the effort in pronouncing a syllable. The ancients had very strict rules for the quantity of syllables, and the Greeks employed different letters to designate the long and short *o* (ω, ο), and the long and short *e* (η, ε).

The principal element of poetry for the Greeks and Romans was the length of time and the quantity, or the combination of long and short syllables, two short ones equalling one long syllable. Verse depended upon the value of syllables.

In modern languages, such as German, Spanish, and Italian, verse may consist of lines where the syllables are counted and not measured. In English verse the rhythm is based upon accent, i.e. the measured undulation of accented and unaccented syllables is its essential feature. French verse consists of lines containing from one to sixteen, or from one to nine syllables. The former have pauses, or *cæsuras*, whilst in the latter the rhyme or assonance determines the music of the verse.

The unit of measurement is the metrical *foot*, or group of two or three syllables forming the basis of line or verse. The five chief measures of English verse are the following: the *iambic*, in which the unaccented syllable precedes the accented (⏑ —); the *trochaic*, in which the unaccented syllable follows the accented (— ⏑);

the *anapæstic*, in which the two unaccented syllables precede the accented (⏑ ⏑ —); the *dactylic*, in which the two unaccented syllables follow the accented (— ⏑ ⏑); and the *amphibrachic*, in which the accented syllable is both preceded and followed by an unaccented (⏑ — ⏑). For fuller details *see* VERSE.

PROSO'PIS. A genus of tropical leguminous trees of the sub-ord. Mimoseæ, having their pods filled between the seeds with a pulpy or mealy substance. Some of them yield useful products, as resin or tannin, food for cattle, etc. *See* MESQUITE.

PROSPEC'TING. Systematic search for minerals. The prospector must be versed in geology and mineralogy. Geology will afford information about underlying strata, lodes, etc., as presaged by exposed sections such as cliff or river bank. Mineralogy will enable him to recognise the surface indications of buried minerals, and to identify them when reached. Apparatus ranges from the primitive divining rod, with which some claim to be able to locate hidden mineral deposits, and the magnetic needle, to delicate and sensitive electrical devices. *See* MINING.

PROSPECTUS. A prospectus is a document issued by a company or its promoters to members of the public, and designed to induce the public to take up shares or debentures of the company. It is defined in the Companies (Consolidation) Act, 1908, as "any notice, circular, advertisement, or other invitation, offering to the public for subscription or purchase any shares or debentures of a company."

The Act lays down strict rules with which every prospectus must comply. A copy must be signed by each person named in it as a director or proposed director, or by his agent authorised in writing, and must be filed with the Registrar of Joint Stock Companies on or before the date which it bears and which is the date of its publication. Certain material particulars must be disclosed in it, namely, (*a*) the Memorandum of Association (which shows the objects of the company); (*b*) the qualification of the directors (which shows the extent to which the directors put faith in the company), also their remuneration; (*c*) the names, descriptions, and addresses of the directors (these disclosing the management of the company); (*d*) the minimum subscription on which allotment may proceed, and the amount payable on application and allotment; (*e*) the number of shares and debentures issued as fully or partly paid up otherwise than in cash, and the consideration given for the same; (*f*) the names and addresses of the vendors and the sums payable to each; (*g*) the amount of the purchase price, specifying the amount paid for goodwill; (*h*) the amount of underwriting commission; (*i*) the amount or estimated amount of preliminary expenses; (*j*) the amount paid to any promoter and the consideration therefor; (*k*) the dates of and the parties to every material contract made within the previous two years, and the place where they may be inspected; (*l*) the names and addresses of the auditors; (*m*) the interest of every director or promoter in the promotion or in the property to be acquired by the company; and (*n*) where the shares are divided into classes, the rights of voting attached to the several classes. These requirements are intended to safeguard the public against imposition and fraud. If the prospectus is issued more than one year after the company is entitled to commence business, the contents of the Memorandum, the particulars of the directors and of their qualification, remuneration and interest, the preliminary expenses, and the interest of the promoters need not be disclosed.

The framing of a prospectus requires the utmost care, as any untrue statement or failure to disclose a material fact may entitle an allottee to rescind the contract and have his name removed from the register, or to sue the parties responsible for the issue of the prospectus for damages at common law or for compensation under the Act for loss sustained thereby.

PROSTATE GLAND. A glandular mass, situated in the pelvic cavity, which surrounds the neck of the bladder and urethra in males, in whom it forms part of the organs of reproduction. It is liable to enlargement, especially in old age, and is often the seat of various diseases.

PROS'TITU'TION. Promiscuous sexual intercourse for gain by a woman known as a prostitute. Regulated prostitution has existed since ancient times, and endures to-day in France and elsewhere. In Great Britain it is a punishable offence.

PROTAG'ORAS. Greek sophist and philosopher, born at Abdera, in Thrace, apparently about 480 B.C. He was the first to assume the title of Sophist, and as such he taught principally at Athens. In 411 B.C.

he was accused of atheism, for beginning one of his works (*Peri Theōn*—Concerning the Gods) with the words "Respecting the gods, I am unable to know whether they exist or do not exist." He seems to have died soon after, perhaps in the same year. He was the author of a large number of works, all of which are lost. In Plato's dialogue named after Protagoras, the latter appears as an exponent of customary morality.

PROTANDROUS FLOWERS. Those in which the anthers mature before the stigma is ripe; this arrangement—like the converse condition of protogynous flowers, in which the stigma matures before the anthers—favours cross-pollination (q.v.).

PROTEA'CEÆ. A natural order of arborescent apetalous dicotyledons, chiefly natives of Australia and the Cape Colony. They are shrubs or small trees, with hard dry opposite or alternate leaves, and often large heads of showy and richly coloured flowers, which render them favourite objects of cultivation. The typical genus, Protea, is African, and contains numerous species. Banksia is a well-known Australian genus bearing the popular name of honeysuckle.

PROTECTION is the name given to any fiscal system through which it is sought by taxes laid on imported commodities to alter that distribution of industries which would prevail under free competition in foreign trade.

In the absence of such interference, competition would effect an international division of labour whereby each nation would specialise in the goods which it had the greatest advantages for producing as compared with other goods, and the maximum world output of commodities for a given amount of human effort would tend to result. This benefit is not only general to all countries, but particular to each country engaged in foreign trade. For no country will import a commodity A if it can produce the same quantity itself at less cost than it can produce another commodity B which can be traded abroad in exchange for A. The direct and immediate benefit to a country of its foreign trade is the excess of the real value to it of its imports over that of the things which it could have produced for itself by the labour and capital needed for producing its exports and working the trade.

The effect of a tax upon foreign trade is to force resources into less productive uses, and therefore to diminish the real income of all countries. A tax upon any particular commodity is paid, except in the case of a monopoly, by the consumer after enough time has elapsed for trade conditions to become stable. A tax upon all imports is paid by the consumers, except for an improvement in the terms on which native goods exchange for foreign. This will not be sufficient, in the case of the trade of one country with the rest of the world, to offset the loss due to obtaining goods in less efficient ways.

The principal arguments used in favour of protection are the following:

1. "If other countries adopt it we must." This does not follow; each additional impediment to trade results in further loss. But a high tariff can be used as a lever in negotiating with other countries to lower theirs.

2. There may be general social utilities not taken into account in merchants' and manufacturers' profits. Thus a country may prefer to remain poorer than it might be, rather than become preponderatingly urban, or have its people engaged in degrading occupations, or become dependent for essential goods on countries with which it may one day be at war.

3. It may be possible to devise a fiscal policy which, while lessening the total national wealth, will benefit the poorer classes, so improving the distribution of wealth. (*a*) "Support home industries and so keep everyone in employment." But, since imports are paid for by exports, against increased employment in making things formerly imported there will be increased unemployment in making exports, and since production will be carried on at enhanced cost, the total demand for labour will be lessened. (*b*) Protection may increase the demand for labour relative to that for land and capital, or may cheapen commodities consumed by working people while those consumed by other people become dearer; thus labour may obtain a larger relative and even a larger absolute share of a diminished national income. (*c*) It is argued that a country cannot maintain better conditions of labour than others unless it adopts protection. This is untrue, because foreign trade depends on a relative and not on an absolute lowness of costs.

4. Although the immediate results of foreign trade are beneficial, some of its ultimate results may not be, even in terms of prices and profits. Not only wealth but the power of

producing wealth in the future should be the aim of national policy. (*a*) Protection of infant industries. A country may be well adapted to a certain industry, which, however, requires time for the development of banking, marketing, subsidiary industries, trained workmen, and technicians. Ultimately its product will be cheaper than the imported, but meanwhile it must be protected from the competition of more advanced rivals. (*b*) The cheapness of "dumped" goods is an immediate benefit, but in the long run it may be less costly to do without them. (*c*) Under restricted foreign trade a manufacturing country will export to less developed countries machinery with which they will set up manufactures of their own, so ending a profitable trade.

In general, it may be said that the arguments for protection which are based on the conception of nations as competing business firms are fallacious. The whole world has become economically interdependent, and an increase in the wealth of any country will usually benefit all the other countries. Though a protective tariff may conceivably serve a useful purpose if it is well devised to meet some special need, experience has shown that in practice powerful business interests can usually exercise sufficient political power to divert a nation's fiscal policy from the path of scientific protection. In Britain the expense of the Boer War and the post-war trade depression had made it seem that the free-trade system was inadequate, and it was proposed to introduce a tariff for purely protective purposes. The general election of 1906 proved that the country was not in sympathy with the proposed change. Mr. Baldwin, the leader of the Conservative Party, made another unsuccessful attempt in 1923 to introduce some measure of protective policy. In 1931 and 1932, however, as a result of the world economic depression, the National Government introduced protective tariffs and Britain ceased to be a free trade country.

PROTECTION ORDER. In England, when a wife is deserted by her husband, she may apply to a magistrate for a protection order. Such an order has the effect of safeguarding her property from the claims of her husband and of his creditors and others claiming under him. If, after notice of the order, the husband or such other party does not hand over to the wife any property belonging to her which may be in his possession, or if thereafter he seizes any property belonging to her, he becomes liable to her in double the value. If adequate cause is shown by any of the above parties, the order may be discharged.

PROTECTOR. A title conferred on several occasions by the English Parliament upon those appointed to act as regents, generally during the minority of the king. Among those who have held this office are Richard, Duke of York (1454); Richard, Duke of Gloucester (1483); and the Duke of Somerset (1547). In 1653 the title of Lord-Protector was bestowed upon Cromwell, as head of the Commonwealth of England, and after his death (1658) his son Richard also held the title for a short period.

PROTECTORATE. A name applied to the régime of a protector, as in Britain between 1653 and 1659, during which Oliver and Richard Cromwell successively held the title of Lord-Protector of the Commonwealth. It is also applied in a general way to the protection extended by a strong power to a weak nation, and in particular to any native state or territory placed or taken under the protection of a European power. British protectorates include Uganda, Tanganyika, Kenya, Zanzibar, Somaliland, Swaziland, Bechuanaland, and Nigeria, all in Africa; and Sarawak, Mesopotamia, and Palestine, in Asia. The foreign relations of all these countries are under the exclusive control of the king-emperor. It is rather difficult to show exactly where a protectorate ends and colonisation begins, but a protectorate may be explained in the following way.

Many British traders and merchants have penetrated to the heart of the Dark Continent, where there are numerous territorial divisions and innumerable tribal subdivisions and inter-relationships. Just as the value of a colony to the European power lies in the creation of new markets for home-made goods and in the raw materials that the colony may be able to supply, so it is with a protectorate, in so much as the economic aspect is considered. In Africa many tribes are decidedly low in the scale of civilisation, and to ensure peace and justice where the interests of British merchants are involved a protectorate over a certain tribal territory may be proclaimed. A Resident is sent out, who advises on questions of law and order, and maintains peace within the protected region. The amount of actual ruling performed by a British Resident or Governor varies greatly.

Spheres of Influence. Such zones

or spheres may be described as territories where an interested power takes no direct hand in the Government, but in which other powers may not acquire territory, influence, nor indeed anything at all by treaty or *force majeure.* The general tendency in the past has been for such spheres of influence gradually to become protectorates, since the natives have found that it is to their advantage to obtain from British officials direct help in maintaining law and order, and from the Empire a guarantee of territorial integrity and a tolerance and respect for minorities. From being protectorates it is a fairly short step to the higher stage, when they become colonies, and take their place eventually as autonomous nations in the Imperial Commonwealth. British "spheres" are the Persian Gulf, Arabia, and North-Eastern Africa.

Mandatory Spheres. Since the European War the League of Nations is empowered to entrust the internal development and good government of third-class states to first-class powers, such authority being conveyed in a document known as a "mandate," the recipient being the "mandatory power." Britain has mandates for certain portions of former German Africa, Palestine, and (till 1927) Mesopotamia; while Australia has many of the South Sea Islands.

PROTEINS (Gr. *prōtos*, first). So-called because of their prime importance to animal and vegetable organisms. They are extremely complex compounds of carbon, hydrogen, nitrogen, oxygen, and sulphur. They belong to the class of colloids—substances which do not diffuse through an animal membrane—and their colloidal nature explains many of their reactions, both within the body and with the chemical reagents of the laboratory. For long it has been known that the amounts of their constituent elements vary within fairly wide limits according to the particular protein examined, a finding readily explicable in the light of more recent work, which has shown that the proteins are to be regarded as made up of amino-acids linked together in a particular way (*see* PHYSIOLOGICAL CHEMISTRY), and that the differences in complexity and reactions of the different proteins are due to differences in the number and type of their amino-acid components. The technical difficulties in the way of a complete protein analysis are very great, and our knowledge of their detailed composition far from complete, but the following figures give an idea of their variation in composition. The numbers are percentages.

	Egg Albumin	Gliadin (from wheat).	Caseinogen (of cow's milk).	Gelatin
Glycine ..	0·0	0·7	0·0	16·5
Leucine ..	6·1	6·0	10·5	2·1
Glutamic acid ..	8·0	31·5	11·0	0·9
Tyrosine ..	1·1	2·4	4·5	0·0
Arginine ..	2·1	2·8	4·8	7·6
Tryptophan	Present	1·0	1·5	0·0
Cystine ..	0·3	0·5	0·1	—

No satisfactory classification of the proteins is yet possible owing to lack of detailed knowledge of their chemical constitution, but the following is one which is generally accepted and in which the proteins are arranged in order of increasing complexity.

Protamines. Simple proteins consisting of two or three amino-acids, which have been demonstrated so far mainly in the milt and roe of fish. The amino-acids are mainly of the diamino type and hence such proteins are basic in reaction.

Histones. Slightly more complex proteins containing a larger number of amino-acids than the protamines but with the diamino type still preponderating. *Globin,* the protein part of *hæmoglobin,* the colouring substance of the blood, is generally regarded as belonging to this group.

Native Proteins. This large group comprises the majority of the proteins occurring in solution in animal and vegetable tissues. They show wide variation in their amino-acid make-up, but all possess the common property of being coagulated by heat. The native proteins are subdivided into *albumins* and *globulins,* the former being soluble in pure water, the latter not in pure water but in dilute saline solutions.

Phosphoproteins. Proteins characterised by the presence of phosphoric acid (not as nucleic acid) in their molecule. An important member of this group is *caseinogen,* the principal protein of milk.

Conjugated Proteins. A class of proteins in which the protein group is combined with another organic grouping. This class includes the *nucleoproteins,* in which the protein part is combined with nucleic acid; the *chromoproteins,* combinations of a protein with a pigment, as in *hæmoglobin*; and the *glycoproteins,* in which the protein is combined with a carbohydrate group.

Scleroproteins. This heterogeneous

group includes the proteins of the hard skeletal structures of the organism. Belonging to this class are *collagen*, obtained from white fibrous tissue; *elastin*, from elastic fibrous tissue; and *keratin*, the substance of which epidermal structures such as skin, hair, nails, and horns are composed.

PROTEOLEPADIDÆ, or APODA. A family of Entomostraca, of which the only representative is *Proteolepas bivincta*, described by Darwin. It is a small maggot-like creature about one-fifth of an inch long, which lives in the mantle cavity of the cirripede *Alepas cornutus*.

PROTEROSAURUS. One of the earliest fossil reptiles, found in the Permian Kupferschiefer of Thuringia and in the Magnesian Limestone of Durham. It is a rhynchocephalian, and thus allied to the modern Sphenodon of New Zealand.

PROTEROZOIC. The name of the geological era preceding the Cambrian period, including periods in which life-forms no doubt existed, though their traces in the rocks are few and unsatisfactory. *See* GEOLOGY.

PROT'ESTANT EPIS'COPAL CHURCH. Official title of the Episcopal Church of America in communion with the See of Canterbury, i.e. the Anglican Church in America. Though, as a result of the English colonisation clergy were sent out, there were for long no bishops. In 1784 Samuel Seabury was chosen bishop and came to England for consecration, although he had been previously consecrated by a Scottish bishop. The church was organised as a separate denomination in 1789. There are 7299 churches and 1,859,100 members.

PROTESTANTISM. The term applied to the religion of Christians who are outside the Roman Church. It describes them as "orthodox" describes the Greek Church, in opposition to the Papal organisation. It is not a negative term. To "protest," in its original Elizabethan sense, means to "testify," to make a positive affirmation or confession. A protester or protestant is one who gives a solemn, serious declaration of his opinions or convictions. As this is generally called out by some erroneous statement to the contrary, a protest acquires a negative association, but it is negative only in virtue of its positive content. Protestantism, etymologically, is therefore a positive aspect of the Christian religion.

The word rose out of a minor incident in the Reformation struggle, when a minority of princes and free towns in Germany protested against the Diet of Speyer in 1529, rescinding by a majority a decision unanimously passed at a former meeting in 1526. The particular issue was the right of German princes to determine religious practices within their own territory. The Roman Catholic majority was determined to revoke this dangerous concession, and against them the Protestants appealed to the emperor or to a General Council, taking the positive ground of religion. "We protest that in matters which concern the glory of God and the salvation of the souls of each of us, it is our bounden duty, according to God's command, and for the sake of our own consciences, before all things to have respect to the Lord our God. In matters which relate to the glory of God and to the salvation of our souls, we must all stand before God and give account of ourselves." This is the origin of the term "Protestant."

Protestantism means not only merely negative opposition to the encroachments of the Papacy, but a solemn sense of the responsibility and freedom which are vital to the Christian faith. It implies that in a matter of conscience there can be no final authority of majorities. What was claimed was not absolute freedom for individuals, but that in the last resort every man must answer to God for himself, and every particular Church must have its freedom as a Christian community, uncontrolled by outside authority.

The name of "Protestant" only established itself slowly. Lutherans and Calvinists preferred their own names at first. But gradually the need of resisting the Roman attack welded them into a common use of "Protestant" as a unifying title. Its meaning has never altered, but the changes of time have added associations to it which have in some quarters led to a suspicion and even to a rejection of it. (*a*) Some non-Roman communities insist that as their origin is in the apostolic age, they are inadequately described by a word which emerged in the sixteenth century. (*b*) Others are repelled by an intractable party which has made "Protestantism" almost equivalent to a narrow, bitter anti-Roman attitude, especially in politics. (*c*) Others again, like a party in the English Church, disavow it entirely, "not only as summing up most of the things that they chiefly hate, but even more as linking the Church of England with Churches of Christ which they count no better than unlawful assemblies" (Gwatkin), preferring the vague term "Catholic."

But " Protestantism " and " Catholicism " are not, strictly speaking, antithetical.

The newer investigations into Protestantism are historical rather than doctrinal. They concern its principles as related to those of the mediæval religion. So far as the doctrinal principles are concerned, the recognition is universal; it is the definition that is in debate. Cardinal principles like freedom of judgment and justification by faith are discussed in their essence and application, the disputable point being their theoretical legitimacy and practical efficiency.—BIBLIOGRAPHY: H. Wace, *The Principles of the Reformation*; E. Troeltsch, *Protestantism and Progress*. See bibliography to REFORMATION. The Roman Catholic position is put by J. A. Moehler in his *Symbolism* (1894).

PRO'TEUS. In Greek mythology, a sea-god who fed the flocks (seals) of Poseidōn (Neptune) in the Ægean Sea. He is represented as a soothsayer who prophesied only when compelled by force and art, and who tried every means to elude those who consulted him, and changed himself, after the manner of the sea-gods, into beasts, trees, and even into fire and water. To those, however, who boldly held him fast he revealed whatever they wished to know, whether past, present, or future. Thus Menelaus surprised him (*Odyssey* iv., 351), and compelled him to aid him by his prophecies and his counsel.

According to other accounts, Proteus was a deified sorcerer of Pallene, a peninsula of Emathia or Macedonia. The later mystics made Proteus an emblem of primeval matter, and he is thus represented in the 24th Orphic hymn. Anyone who hastily changes his principles is, from this old sea-god, called a Proteus, and Shakespeare accordingly gave this name to the fickle lover in *The Two Gentlemen of Verona*.

PROTEUS (Olm). A genus of tailed amphibia possessing external gills. One species only has been hitherto discovered, namely, the *Proteus anguīnus*, which is found in subterranean lakes and caves in Carniola, Carinthia, and Dalmatia. It attains a length of about 1 foot. The body is smooth, naked, and eel-like, the legs four in number, small and weak, the forefeet three-toed, the hinder four-toed, and, in addition to permanent external gills, it possesses lungs in the form of slender tubes. The places it inhabits being devoid of light the power of vision is unnecessary, and in point of fact its eyes are rudimentary and covered by the skin. A related form (*Typhlomolge rathbuni*) lives in caves in Texas.

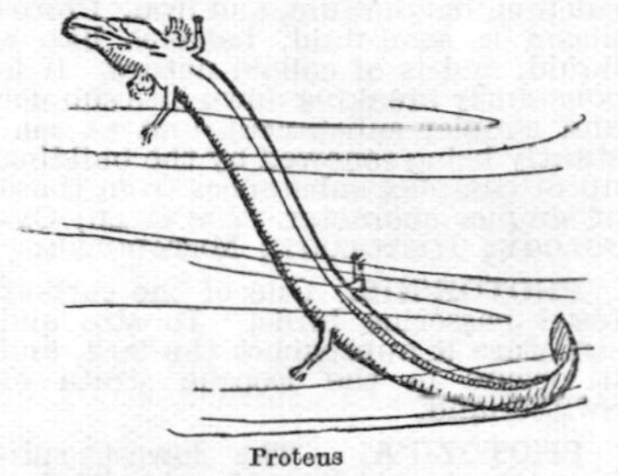

Proteus

PROTOCOCCUS. A very simple genus of Green Algæ. *P. viridis* (*Pleurococcus vulgaris*) forms the bulk of the green encrustation found on the windward side of tree trunks, palings, etc. The plant consists of a small spherical cell bounded by a cellulose wall, and containing, besides cytoplasm, a nucleus and a lobed chloroplast.

PRO'TOCOL (Gr. *protos*, first, and *koltān*, to glue). Originally, in legal instruments the first sheet glued to the *scapus* or cylinder round which the instruments were rolled. In diplomacy it signifies a document serving as a preliminary to any diplomatic transaction; also, a diplomatic document or minute of proceedings, signed by friendly powers in order to secure certain political ends peacefully. The *Protocol for the Pacific Settlement of International Disputes*, which was adopted by the League of Nations Assembly in 1924, but which was shelved owing to Britain's refusal to ratify, is generally known as *The Protocol* or as *The Geneva Protocol*. Britain preferred the *Western Nations Security Pact*, which was initialled at Locarno in Oct., 1925. *See* LOCARNO.

PRO'TOGINE (-jen). A name given by Jurine to granite in which the mica assumes a talc-like appearance; so called because it was supposed to have been the first-formed granite. It occurs typically in Mont Blanc. It was also called *Talcose-granite*; but the " talc " proves to be a mica.

PROTON. *See* ISOTOPES; ELECTRON; MATTER.

PRO'TOPLASM. In biology, the exceedingly complex and very unstable living matter constituting the essential part of all organisms, and described by Huxley as the " physical basis of life." It appears to be a mixture of various substances, especially proteins, and in ultimate chemical analysis twelve elements are invariably present, i.e. carbon, oxygen, hydrogen, nitrogen, sulphur, phosphorus, chlorine, potassium, sodium, calcium, magnesium, and iron. Protoplasm is semi-fluid, behaves like a liquid, and is of colloid nature. It is constantly breaking down into simpler and simpler substances, and as constantly being renewed by the building up of complex substances from those of simpler character. *See* CELL; CYTOLOGY; HISTOLOGY; METABOLISM.

PROTOR'NIS. One of the earliest fossil passerine birds. In size and structure it approaches the lark, and it occurs in the Eocene strata of Switzerland.

PROTOZO'A. The lowest subkingdom or phylum of animals, embracing all the unicellular forms, most of which are microscopic. The protoplasmic body may be devoid of investment or definite shape, and capable of flowing out into blunt lobes (*pseudopods*), temporary structures by which creeping is effected. Others are covered by a delicate elastic membrane (*cuticle*), have a definite form, and may possess a small number of lash-like protoplasmic threads (*flagella*) or a large number of short ones (*cilia*), which bend and straighten alternately. Flagella and cilia bring about swimming movements in free forms, while in fixed types they set up currents in the surrounding water by which particles of food are brought within reach. In the more specialised types there is a definite cell-mouth for the ingestion of solid food. Some Protozoa, under unfavourable conditions, can enclose themselves in a horny *cyst,* while in others an encysted stage constitutes part of the life-history.

Reproduction is typically by division (fission), but in some cases special asexual cells (spores) are formed. There may also be a temporary or permanent fusion (conjugation), equivalent to sexual reproduction in higher forms. Protozoa are of universal distribution. The great bulk are marine, but some live in fresh water or in damp places on the land, and a number of species have been discovered in the soil. Others, again, are parasitic, and some of these cause diseases, such as malaria, yellow fever, sleeping-sickness, and nagana or fly-disease (of hoofed mammals in tropical Africa). Four classes are recognised. These, with the chief orders which they include, are:

Class I.—Rhizopoda. Possess pseudopods, but flagella may be present in early stages. Often become encysted. (1) Lobosa, with blunt pseudopods. Proteus Animalcule (Amœba), common on the surface of mud in ponds; some species are parasitic, causing dysentery. Arcella, Quadrula, and Difflugia, freshwater forms with external shell. (2) Foraminifera, with slender branching pseudopods uniting into networks. A calcareous shell, often of complex nature and elegant form. Globigerina, Orbulina, Textularia, Nummulina, etc. (3) Heliozoa, or sun animalcules. Stiff radiating pseudopods. Mostly freshwater forms. Actinosphærium and Actinophrys (no shell); Raphidiophrys (siliceous spicules); Clathrulina (stalked, spherical, perforated, siliceous shell). (4) Radiolaria. Marine forms, with a central horny capsule and a siliceous shell, which is often complex and beautiful. Actinomma, etc. Such shells, often known as Polycystines, abound in Barbados earth, a siliceous deposit.

Class II.—Mycetozoa, Fungus Animals. Relatively large forms living on rotten wood, dead leaves, spent tan, etc. A large number of amœboid individuals fuse together into a *plasmodium* which creeps slowly over the substance on which it lives. Spores are produced in capsules of various form. Under the name of Myxomycetes (Slime Fungi) these organisms are described as plants by some authorities. Didymium, Badhamia, etc.

Class III.—Infusoria. Protozoa possessed of flagella or cilia. (1) Flagellata. Provided with flagella. Heteromita, Bodo, etc., and many other extremely small forms are often known as "Monads." Monosiga, Salpingœca, Polyœca (colonial) are fixed forms, each individual with a single flagellum surrounded by a collar-like expansion. The colonial Proterospongia includes individuals of different kinds. Noctiluca is relatively large, and is one of the organisms causing the phosphorescence of the sea. Forms containing chlorophyll, and regarded as plants by some authorities, are Hæmatococcus, Pandorina (colonial), and Volvox (colonial), (2) Ciliata. Provided with cilia. Slipper Animalcule (Paramecium), Stentor, Bell Animalcule (Vorticella) with a contractile stalk, and related colonial forms, Acineta (with pointed processes for extracting the juices of other animals).

Class IV.—Sporozoa. Parasitic Protozoa, many of which are exceedingly small. Life-history complex. Some are the causes of grave diseases. Malarial parasites (Plasmodium, etc.) introduced into the blood by mosquitoes. Sleeping-sickness and nagana parasites (Trypanosoma) disseminated by tse-tse flies.

PROTRACTOR. An instrument for measuring angles. The simple type, such as is used by draughtsmen, is made of box wood, celluloid, bone, or metal in the form of a disc or a rectangle, and marked with radial lines from a point. It has a scale which shows the number of degrees between the lines and a common base. In another form the device is made in two parts, one of which takes the form of an arm or disc which can be turned relative to the other so that lines on each can be superposed on those subtending the angle to be measured. When made in this way a vernier may be fitted to subdivide the divisions of the scale. Protractors of the second type are commonly fitted to surveying instruments.

PROUDHON (prö-dōn), **Pierre Joseph.** French socialist and political writer, born at Besançon 1809, died

Pierre Joseph Proudhon

there 1865. The son of poor parents, he was enabled to attend gratuitously the college of his native town. At the age of nineteen he entered a printer's office, afterwards became a press reader, and in this way acquired considerable linguistic knowledge, with the result that he worte an *Essai de grammaire générale.* As a reward of his studious labours he had conferred on him by the Academy of Besançon the *pension Suard,* which yielded him an income of 1500 francs for three years.

Political economy now became his chief study, and in 1840 appeared his famous work, bearing on the title-page the question: *Qu'est-ce que la Propriété?* (What is Property?), to which the first page of the treatise contains the answer, "C'est le Vol" (it is theft). The principal theses maintained by him in this work are that labour is the sole just ground of individual possession, and that all labour ought to be rewarded equally. For this treatise, and two others which followed, he was prosecuted at Besançon, but was ultimately acquitted. The jury returned a verdict in this form: This man is in a sphere of ideas inaccessible to the vulgar; we cannot condemn him at random; and who will answer for his culpability?

In 1843 he managed a system of water transport on the Rhône and Saône; settled in Paris in 1847; started various newspapers, and became a leader in the Revolution of 1848; was elected a representative for the Seine in the Constituent Assembly; attempted with no success to found a Banque du Peuple; and for his outspokenness in the press he was imprisoned for three years. Besides those already noticed, his more important treatises are: *Discours sur la célébration du dimanche, De la création de l'ordre dans l'humanité,* and *Système des contradictions économiques.*—Cf. Desjardins, *P. J. Proudhon: sa vie, ses œuvres, et sa doctrine.*

PROUST (prūst), **Marcel.** French author, born 10th July, 1871. He was educated at the Lycée Condorcet, and began early to write stories. From 1902 he was in bad health, during which time he wrote *A la Recherche du Temps Perdu,* a series of 15 vols., the first of which, *Du côtè de chez Swann,* was published in 1913. He died 18th Nov., 1922, and the last three volumes were published posthumously. These were *La Prisonnière* (1924), *Albertine Disparue* (1926), and *La Temps Retrouvé* (1926).

PROUT, Samuel. British painter, born in Plymouth 1783, died 1852. He received a few lessons in drawing in his native town, and prosecuted his work by industriously sketching from nature. In 1812 he settled in London, was an occasional exhibitor at the Academy and British Institution, and was elected a member of the Society of Painters in Water-colours in 1820. He became famous for his drawings of street scenes and the quaint mediæval architecture of Europe. Some of his sea-coast scenes exhibit great power. (Illus. on p. 446.)

PROVENÇAL LANGUAGE AND LITERATURE. Strictly the language and literature of that portion of Southern France known as Provence; but in its widest application the Provençal language includes the

Romance form of speech belonging to the inhabitants of a geographical area which comprises the whole south of France (especially Provence, Limousin, Auvergne), with Catalonia and Valencia in Spain. This language was the earliest cultivated of the Romance languages (or those based on the Latin), and at one time was extensively used in literature. It was also called *langue d'oc* in contradistinction to the kindred speech of Northern France, the *langue d'oïl*; and yet again it received the name of *lengua lemosina* from the region where it was spoken with the greatest purity.

Southern France, already refined by colonies from Greece and by its

Samuel Prout

vicinity to the Romans, favoured with a milder climate and a freer government, was until the eleventh century far in advance of the north in civilisation, and its language was distinguished for clearness, tenderness, sweetness, and copiousness. The language, and the cultivation acquired through the intercourse with the East, particularly with the poetical Arabs, awakened imagination and contributed to foster genius and to produce poetry. The taste for poetry was general among the nobles and cultivated classes in Provence, and the princes, particularly Raymond Berengarius III. (1168-81) and VI. (1209-45), favoured the poetical art. Courtesy and gallantry were nowhere so fully developed as in Provence, and the court became the centre of a romantic life. The life of the Provençals was lyrical in the highest degree, and their poetry, the expression of their feelings and passions, necessarily lyrical.

Rise. Provençal, as a new and distinct language, appears in historical records about the tenth century, and continued as a medium of living literary expression until about the end of the thirteenth century. Provençal is a language whose interest as a vehicle of literature is mainly in the past. This interest begins in the early part of the eleventh century with a didactic poem, based by its unknown author on the *De Consolatione Philosophiæ* of Boethius; but Provençal literature in its development found most characteristic expression in the amorous lyrics of the troubadours. The earliest of these lyric poets was William IX., Count of Poitiers, about the close of the eleventh century, who was followed in France, Italy, and Spain by an innumerable band of poets in the Provençal tongue. Most of this poetry was intended to be sung, and not infrequently the poet also composed his own music. Besides the lyric poetry, of which there were various classes, Provençal poetry also existed of a narrative character, in which legendary and historical themes were treated in epical detail.

Decay. The rapid decay of this Provençal literature, which was almost exclusively the possession of the upper classes, was largely due to political causes. During the war with the Albigenses the social condition of the feudal nobility in the south of France suffered such downfall that thenceforth the art of the troubadour and the minstrel ceased to be adequately remunerated. In 1350 a few scholars of Toulouse attempted to revive its decaying glory, and for this purpose composed a treatise on grammar and poetry called the *Leys d'Amors*. About the middle of the fifteenth century the language ceased to be used both for administrative and literary purposes, and it has long been reduced almost to the condition of a *patois*.

In the nineteenth century a new revival took place, under the impulse of such poets as Jacques Jasmin and Frédéric Mistral, who endeavoured to resuscitate Provençal as a literary language, and produced poems of no small value written in the modern form of it. A society of literary men and scholars (*lou Felibrige*) was founded for the purpose of furthering this object. *See* TROUBADOUR.—

BIBLIOGRAPHY: F. Mistral, *Lou Tresor dou Felibrige*; A. Dauzat, *Phonétique historique du patois de Vinzelles*; Mariéton, *La Terre provençale*; Mary-Lafon, *Histoire littéraire du midi de la France*; J. de Nostredame, *Les vies des plus célèbres et anciens poètes provençaux.*

PROVENCE
Avignon: Place of the Popes. Cannes: Old Church.

PROVENCE (pro-vāṇs). One of the old provinces of France, lying in the south-eastern part of the country, on the Mediterranean, bounded on the north by Dauphiné and Venaissin, on the east by Piedmont, and on the west by Languedoc. It now forms the departments of Bouches-du-Rhône, Var, and Basses-Alpes, with parts of Vaucluse and Alpes-Maritimes. The capital was Aix, and the province was divided into Upper and Lower Provence.

Greek colonies were founded here at an early period; and the Romans, having conquered all the south-east of Gaul (124-123 B.C.), gave it the name of *Provincia Gallia*, or simply *Provincia* (the province), whence its later name was derived. It passed successively into the hands of the Visigoths, Ostrogoths, Franks, and in 879 became part of the Kingdom of Burgundy. It subsequently was ruled by the Counts of Arles and the Counts of Barcelona, then by Charles of Anjou (brother of Louis IX. of France) and his descendants, and in 1481 passed to Louis XI. of France.—Cf. A. Fabre, *Histoire de Provence* (4 vols).

PROVERB. A short pithy sentence forming a popular saying and expressing, in a keen, quaint, or lively fashion, some result of the experience of life. Proverbs are the flower of popular wit and the treasures of popular wisdom. They give the result of experience in a form made impressive by rhyme, alliteration, parallelism, a pointed turn, or a comparison drawn from the most ordinary scenes and occurrences of life, which, by the force of association, makes their effect strong and permanent. Proverbs are plain-spoken. They may be unassuming, lively, grave, or even sublime; their general character is *naïveté*. In their view, as in the eye of the law, all are equal. They take cognisance of the virtues and vices and follies of all classes, without respect of persons. They pierce the object at which they aim, and this in fact gives them currency, and makes them what they are.

Proverbs have been defined by Cervantes as "short sentences drawn from long experiences;" by Howell as sayings which combine "sense, shortness and salt;" by Bacon as "the genius, wit, and spirit of a nation;" and by Earl Russell as "the wisdom of many, and the wit of one." They have formed an important part of the common wisdom of both Eastern and Western civilisations, and in this way they are interesting in a study of the spread and structure of language, as it has been pointedly applied to changing manners and customs. Greek and Latin proverbs were collected by Erasmus in his *Adagia*; English proverbs have been collected by Camden, Howell, Ray, Kelly, Bohn (an enlarged and improved edition of Ray), and Hazlitt; Scottish by Allan Ramsay and by A. Hislop; French by De Lincy; German by various collectors, more especially Wander; Arabic by Burckhardt and by Freytag; Bengali by Long.—BIBLIOGRAPHY: R. C. Trench, *Proverbs and their Lessons*; Bohn's *Polyglot of Foreign Proverbs*; G. Strafforello, *La Sapienza del Mondo*.

PROVERBS, THE BOOK OF. In the Hebrew Canon of Scripture, it is included in the *Hagiographa*, and comes immediately after Psalms. The structure of the work is composite, being a compilation of miscellaneous aphorisms, counsels, and sententious dicta of the sages dealing with conduct, character, and the general management of life. The thought, placid and genial throughout, never ventures from the realm of practical ethics into the sphere of speculation and metaphysics. Common sense characterises the whole collection as befitting a popular anthology of wise maxims and moral discourses.

The authorship of the book cannot be attributed to any one mind. Tradition was in favour of King Solomon, who, it is reported (1 Kings, iv., 32), "spake three thousand parables." Certain sections of the book (i.-ix.; x-xxii., 16; xxv.-xxix.), according to the editorial headings, profess to be Solomonic. But it is now the opinion of most scholars that the earliest section (x.-xxii., 16) implies a date after the Exile. Although many individual proverbs are even earlier than the times of the monarchy, we have no proof that any of the wise king's reputed proverbs have been preserved. King Solomon, in the eyes of posterity, was regarded as the grand master of proverbial lore, just as his father David was regarded as the founder of psalmody. Hence the work was circulated under the authority of the royal name.

Internal evidence, however, reveals the successive layers of redaction. The following divisions are distinguishable:

1. *Introductory group of discourses* (i.-ix.), with the heading "The Proverbs of Solomon," etc.
2. *Nucleus* (x.-xxii., 16), "The Proverbs of Solomon."
3. *Two smaller collections of aphorisms* (xxii., 17-xxiv., 22, and xxiv.,

23-34, the latter section having as heading, "These also are by the wise").

4. *Hezekian collection* (xxv.-xxix.), so called from the heading, "These are also proverbs of Solomon which the men of Hezekiah, king of Judah, copied out."

5. "*The words of Agur*" (xxx.).

6. "*The words of King Lemuel*" (xxxi., 1-9).

7. *Acrostic poem of the virtuous woman* (xxxi., 10-31).

In the Greek version there is a dislocation of the sections, thus further substantiating the view that they were originally separate tracts.

Although there is lack of continuity in the parts, nevertheless one sustained theme unites the various sections into coherence. The dominant chord is *wisdom.* The prefatory couplets (i., 2-7), perhaps the work of the final editor, explain the *raison d'être* of the whole collection, namely, that men may be exercised in wisdom, which, as we shall see, is more than merely worldly wisdom, from which the book is not altogether free. In the opinion of the sages, wisdom is that which governs and regulates human action, in fact, it is equivalent to religion. "The fear of the Lord is the beginning of wisdom." Wisdom was a spacious term for knowledge of God and knowledge of man. It was this association of worldly knowledge with divine knowledge that made the teaching of the sages so popular. Nothing human was alien to them since it partook of the nature of God. They were the humanists of Israel, and the freedom from bias and the breadth of outlook which this conception of wisdom indicates were largely due to the influence of the Greek spirit of emancipation.

In Proverbs the existence of one God is assumed. The law, the temple, and the priesthood are nowhere mentioned. Indeed, in tone and character there is a complete absence of national feeling in the book. The general inference is that Proverbs dates after the Exile, say about 300 B.C.

St. Paul quotes about twenty times from Proverbs, while with the early Fathers it was a special favourite. Indeed, wherever was to be found "pure religion breathing household laws," there it was chosen as the authorised manual of conduct. "Concise sentences," says Bacon, "like darts, fly abroad and make impressions, while long discourses are flat things, and not regarded"—hence the value and effectiveness of the book and the general esteem in which it has been held by past generations.—BIBLIOGRAPHY: C. H. Toy, *Proverbs*; J. J. S. Perowne, *Book of Psalms.*

PROVIDENCE. A city and port of entry of the United States, the capital of the state of Rhode Island and the county seat of Providence county; served by the New York, New Haven, & Hartford Railway, and by coasting-steamers to New York, etc. In the centre of the city the river expands into a circular sheet of water called the Cove, nearly a mile in circumference. The principal buildings are the state capitol, city hall, public library, court-house, Brown University (founded 1764), which is now non-sectarian, and Providence College (founded 1928-29), under Roman Catholic control. The principal manufactures are jewellery, worsted goods, silver ware, steam-engines, rubber and elastic goods, cotton and woollen goods, and margarine. There is a safe and commodious harbour, though somewhat difficult of access, and the coasting trade is important. Providence was first settled in 1636, incorporated in 1649, and became a city in 1832. Pop. 252,981.—BIBLIOGRAPHY: W. R. Staples, *Annals of the Town of Providence*; W. Kirk, *A Modern City: Providence, Rhode Island and its Activities.*

PROVINCE. Originally a country of considerable extent, which being reduced under Roman dominion was remodelled, subjected to the command of a governor sent from Rome, and to such taxes and contributions as the Romans saw fit to impose. In modern times the term has been applied to colonies or to independent countries at a distance from the metropolis, or to the different divisions of the kingdom itself. Thus the Low Countries belonging to Austria and Spain were styled *provinces.* The different governments into which France was divided previous to the Revolution were also called provinces. The name has sometimes been retained by independent states. Thus the Republic of Holland, after it had thrown off the Spanish yoke, was called the United Provinces. The main divisions of India and the Dominion of Canada are known as provinces.

PROVINCE WELLESLEY. A long coastal strip on the mainland of the Malay Peninsula opposite Penang, of which settlement it forms a part. The area is 280 sq. miles. It is served by the Federal Malay States Railway, and has a wireless station at Penaga. The chief town is Prai.

PROVINS (prō-vaṉ). A town of France, in the department of Seine-et-Marne. It has interesting historical and architectural relics. Provins is mentioned in a capitulary of Charlemagne in 802, and in the thirteenth century it was a large and important city. It derives its modern reputation from its mineral-waters, used for bathing and drinking, and from the roses which are cultivated in the district. Pop. 9000.

PROVOST. A title given to the president of certain bodies, as the heads of Oriel, Queen's, and Worcester Colleges at Oxford, and of King's College, Cambridge, equivalent to the *Master* in other colleges. In the cities and burghs of Scotland the provost is the chief magistrate, corresponding to the English mayor. The chief magistrates of Edinburgh and Glasgow are styled *lord provost*, and the same title has been granted to, or is popularly given to, several others.

PROVOST-MARSHAL. The title now borne by the commandants of the Corps of Military Police, who with two assistants are permanent officials. In addition to these, certain regimental officers with the title of deputy, assistant, or deputy-assistant provost-marshal are in peace-time temporarily attached to the Military Police for service with detachments of the corps at the headquarters of certain commands and large formations. The duties of provost-marshals of all grades are to keep order among the troops of a garrison town when such troops are for the moment not under the immediate control of their own officers, e.g. when men are at liberty in a town.

On mobilisation a provost-marshal and as many assistants as may be necessary are appointed pursuant to the provisions of Section 74 of the Army Act, which reads as follows: "For the prompt repression of all offences which may be committed abroad provost-marshals with assistants may from time to time be appointed by the general order of the general officer commanding a body of forces. A provost-marshal or his assistants may at any time arrest and detain for trial persons subject to military law committing offences, and may also carry into execution any punishment to be inflicted in pursuance of a court-martial, but shall not inflict any punishment on his or their own authority."

In earlier days a provost-marshal, according to Grose (*Military Antiquities*), was a sort of man-of-all-work to the camp, and appears to have been responsible for many duties.

PROXY (contracted from *procuracy*). The agency of another who acts as a substitute for his principal. In parliamentary law every member of the House of Lords could formerly (until 1868) constitute another member of the House of the same order with himself his proxy to vote for him in his absence. Shareholders of a company can vote by proxy.

PRUDENTIUS, Aurelius Clemens. One of the early Christian poets, born at Calagurris, in Spain, in A.D. 348, died after the beginning of the fifth century. In his latter years he composed a great number of hymns and other religious poems in which he successfully imitated classical models.

PRUDHOE. Town of Northumberland, on the Tyne, 277 miles from London, and 11 miles from Newcastle, on the L.N.E. Rly. It is in a coal-mining district. Pop. 9260.

PRUDHON (prụ-dōṇ), **Pierre.** French painter, born in 1758, died in 1823. He studied his art at Dijon and in Rome, where he came under the influence of Correggio and of Leonardo. In 1789 he settled in Paris, where he gradually made his way, and at length became famous by his *Truth descending from Heaven*, *Psyche carried off by Zephyr*, and *Crime pursued by Justice and Divine Vengeance*. His importance consists in the fact that, in opposition to David, he accentuated the purely pictorial element and the effect of light in his works.

PRUNELLA, or PRUNELLO. Defined by Skeat as a strong, woollen stuff, originally dark in colour. It was once used for clergymen's gowns, and is still used for the uppers of ladies' boots and shoes. A weave often used for a kind of woollen cloth is called the prunelle twill. The word is mainly remembered on account of Pope's couplet (*Essay on Man*, iv. 204):

> Worth makes the man, and want of it, the fellow,
> The rest is all but leather or prunella.

PRUNING. The severing of portions of the stem, branches, shoots, leaves, or roots of a plant for the purpose of removing excrescent or unprofitable growths, and rendering the sap more conducive to the nutrition of the valuable parts of the plant. The immediate effect of pruning is to reduce the growth of a plant in as far as it depends on the amount of foliage duly exposed to the light; but as by judicious pruning the parts left have not only a greater share of sap, but are better exposed to the light, its ultimate effect is to produce a larger and stronger plant. From the tendency of sap to flow in increased quantity into the parts immediately adjoining those where its flow has been interrupted, an almost unlimited power is given to the gardener of controlling the direction of the growth of a plant.

The season for pruning varies with the nature of the tree and the purpose for which it is pruned. In general it may be said that autumn or winter is the best season for extensive pruning; in summer an excess of vigour in the plant may require a little pruning, but in spring it not only weakens the plant, but is liable to induce disease.

Root-pruning is employed to check rapidity of growth and to induce development of flower-buds. The best season for this operation is after the leaves have fallen in autumn or before the sap begins to flow in spring.

PRUNUS. A genus of arborescent plants belonging to the nat. ord. Rosaceæ, and comprehending the cherry, bird-cherry, plum, damson, sloe, bullace, apricot, etc.

PRURI'GO. The name applied to a papular eruption with intense itching. Like other affections with severe itching, it is often complicated by septic and eczematous conditions as a result of scratching. There are various forms of prurigo; the commonest is strophulus or gum rash.

PRURI'TUS. Skin affection, sometimes without visible eruption, marked by intense itching. It may be set up by diabetes, jaundice, dyspepsia, lice, etc., and is aggravated by scratching. When, in advancing years, the skin becomes thin and inelastic, pruritus senilis often occasions great suffering and sleeplessness.

PRUSSIA. A republic of Germany, the largest component state of the German Reich. It is divided into provinces which, with areas and populations, past and present, are shown in the table on the following page. By a comparison of these figures it will be seen that, on the basis of the census of 1910, Prussia has lost by the Treaty of Versailles over 20,000 sq. miles of territory and a large population. The population is now less than at the census of 1905, but the density per square mile is greater than at any previous period in Prussia's history.

Physical. Prussia belongs to the great plain of Northern Europe, and may be described generally as a vast plain, elevated in the south and south-west, and thence descending towards the Baltic and the North Sea, on both of which it comprises almost the whole coastal plain of Germany. The Rhine, Elbe, Oder, and Weser are the principal rivers.

Towns. Cologne (pop. 700,222), Essen (629,564), Breslau (599,770), Frankfurt-on-Main (540,115), Dortmund (525,837), Düsseldorf (464,543), Hanover (425,274), Duisburg (421,217), Wuppertal (405,515), Gelsenkirchen (330,186), Bochum (313,554), Magdeburg (297,151), Königsberg (287,312), Stettin (254,466), Altona (227,881), Kiel (213,881), Halle (194,636), Gladbach (193,529), Oberhausen (186,322), Kassel (172,071), Krefeld (159,064), Aachen (155,816), Wiesbaden (151,961).

Government. Prussia was proclaimed a republic on 13th Nov., 1918, and a new Constitution was adopted on 30th Nov., 1920. This provides for a Diet (*Landtag*) which elects a Premier, who, in his turn, appoints responsible ministers to the portfolios of National Welfare, Justice, Commerce, Interior, Agriculture, Finance, and Education and Public Worship. These ministers, with the Premier, form the Cabinet, and are vested with the powers of the former king. The Diet is elected for four years on the principle of proportional representation and by universal male and female suffrage, the age qualification being twenty years. The State Council or *Staatsrat* (74 members) advises and controls the Diet, and has the power of veto over legislation approved by the Diet. The deliberative assemblies of the provinces elect the Council on a basis of one representative to 50,000 inhabitants. Each province is controlled by a Governor (*Oberpräsident*), superior to the presidents of districts, and there is a limited measure of local government. Prussia sends 26 members to the German Imperial Council (*Reichsrat*), as compared with 10 from Bavaria, 4 from Württemberg, 7 from Saxony, 3 from Baden, and 16 from the other states. The Nazis seized the Government in 1933.

Religion. About two-thirds of the population are Protestants, and one-third are Roman Catholics, with a small number of Jews and unclassified religions.

Education. Elementary education is free and compulsory from six to fourteen years, but secondary instruction is entirely voluntary. There are 14 universities, 320 gymnasia, 509 lyceums (girls' high schools), 33,479 public elementary schools, 695 public middle schools, 2 forestry schools, 2 technical mining schools, 14 agricultural schools, 2 agricultural colleges, 2 veterinary colleges, 2 commercial high schools, 4 technical high schools, 2 academies for local government work, and 15 training colleges for teachers.

Production and Industry, and all other matters not treated here, are dealt with under the respective provinces.

BIBLIOGRAPHY: S. Osborne, *The Upper Silesian Question and Germany's Coal Problem*; *Germany* (*Peace Handbook*, vol. vii., H.M. Stationery Office).

History. The historical development of Prussia is closely associated with three important elements. The first of these is found in the growth of the power of the Electorate of Brandenburg, which formed the nucleus of the future state; the second relates to the acquirement of the province of Prussia, which gave its name to the new heterogeneous territory; and the third is associated with the rule of the Hohenzollern family, under whose skilful diplomatic and military guidance the small Brandenburg electorate grew into what is now considerably the larger portion of the German Reich. Brandenburg, which had been conquered by Charlemagne in 789, was erected into a margraviate by Henry I. (the Fowler), Emperor of Germany, in 926. Albert the Bear, who received Brandenburg as a fief from the Emperor Lothaire II. (1134), conquered the Slavonian Wends, and took in 1157 the title of Margrave of Bradenburg. His dynasty continued to rule till 1320, and during this period German civilisation was gradually extended in Pomerania, Saxony, Brandenburg, and Silesia.

After its extinction there followed a period of anarchy, during which Brandenburg fell as a lapsed fief to the empire, and Louis of Bavaria gave it to his son. Remaining under Bavarian rule for three electorates, it was subsequently ceded to the House of Luxemburg, and Charles IV., the first imperial representative of this House, gave it successively to his sons Wenceslas (1373) and Sigismund (1378). The latter, being in debt, received from Frederick, the Burgrave of Nürnberg, a loan of 400,000 gold florins, for which Frederick held Brandenburg in pawn, and subsequently acquired it in full. This burgrave was the descendant of Conrad of Hohenzollern, a cadet of a Suabian family to whom belonged a small territory surrounding the ancestral castle of Hohenzollern, of which they traced their lordship back to the time of Charlemagne.

Brandenburg, which Frederick had thus acquired, was covered with feudal strongholds, which he gradually reduced, and he also added the two small territories of Ansbach and Baireuth. Frederick II., who succeeded his father in 1440, extended the possessions of his family by policy

Provinces [1]	Pre-European War			Post-European War		
	Area, sq. Miles	Pop. 1910	Pop. per sq. Mile, 1910	Area, sq. Miles	Pop. 1925	Pop. per sq. Mile, 1925
East Prussia (Ostpreussen)	14,320	2,064,175	144·1	15,061	2,256,349	158·0
West Prussia (Westpreussen)	9,863	1,703,474	172·7	2,978 [2]	332,485	111·6
Berlin	24	2,071,257	86279·0	341	4,024,286	11,801·4
Pomerania (Pommern)	11,629	1,716,921	147·6	11,986	1,878,781	160·8
Brandenburg	15,376	4,092,616	266·1	15,072	2,592,292	172·0
Posen	11,190	2,099,831	187·6	—	—	—
Silesia (Schlesien)	15,569	5,225,962	335·6	—	—	—
Saxony (Sachsen)	9,752	3,089,275	315·7	9,759	3,277,664	335·9
Schleswig-Holstein [3]	7,340	1,621,004	220·8	5,819	1,519,365	261·1
Hanover (Hannover)	14,862	2,942,436	197·9	14,897	3,190,439	214·2
Westphalia (Westfalen)	7,804	4,125,096	528·6	7,804	4,784,169	613·0
Hesse-Nassau (including Waldeck [4])	6,060	2,221,021	366·5	6,471	2,452,748	379·0
Rhine (Rheinprovinz)	10,420	7,121,140	683·4	9,462	7,284,028	769·8
Hohenzollern (Hohen-Zollernsche Lande)	441	71,011	141·0	441	71,840	162·9
Lower Silesia (Niederschlesien)	—	—	—	10,267	3,132,135	305·1
Upper Silesia (Oberschlesien)	—	—	—	3,750	1,379,408	367·8
Total	134,650	40,165,219	298·2	114,108 [5]	38,175,989	337·8

[1] All of these are dealt with under their respective titles elsewhere in this work.
[2] Border Province. (See *Prussia, West.*)
[3] Including Heligoland; pop. (1910), 3027, exclusive of military.
[4] Waldeck was incorporated in Prussia in 1929.
[5] The Saar (574 sq. miles) is excluded.

as well as by valour. In 1470 he abdicated in favour of his brother Albert III., surnamed Achilles, who, by a family ordinance, prepared the way in an important respect for the future greatness of his House by providing for the undivided descent of the dominions in connection with the electorate (*Dispositio Achillea*). In 1618 John Sigismund united the Duchy of Prussia to the electorate, and the whole country became known as Prussia.

In 1614, by the Treaty of Xanten, Clèves and La Marck were assigned to Brandenburg, and the foundations of the Prussian Rhine-province were thus laid. During the Thirty Years' War (1618-48) the electorate suffered severely, but the power of modern Prussia was consolidated during the second half of the seventeenth century. Frederick William (1640-88), called the Great Elector, may be regarded as the virtual founder of the Prussian monarchy. He was succeeded by his son Frederick, who in 1701 had himself crowned as king, being the first King of Prussia. Under his rule the Prussian troops fought side by side with the English at Blenheim, Ramillies, Oudenarde, and Malplaquet. Frederick I. was succeeded by his son (1713) Frederick William I., who governed Prussia till 1740. At his death he left a prosperous country, a well-supplied Treasury, and an army of 80,000 men to his successor.

Frederick II., surnamed the Great (q.v.), succeeded to the crown on the death of his father in 1740. He wrested Silesia from Austria, and by the partition of Poland (1772) added West Prussia to his kingdom. At his death in 1786 Frederick II. left Prussia a European power. He was succeeded by his nephew Frederick William II. (1786-97), during whose reign the partition of Poland was completed. Frederick William II. was succeeded by his son Frederick William III. (1797-1840). Continuing his father's policy in regard to France, the new king courted the French directorate, and at the Peace of Lunéville (1801) Prussia was indemnified by 4116 sq. miles ceded at the expense of the empire.

In 1804 Prussia recognised Napoleon as Emperor of France, and in the campaign which ended in the overthrow of Austria at Austerlitz (1805) remained neutral. This attitude was at first successful, but ultimately it led to distrust among the German states, and by the formation of the Confederation of the Rhine, Prussia was isolated and left to the mercy of Napoleon. At the instigation of the latter Prussia had occupied Hanover, but Napoleon treated this fact with contemptuous indifference when he offered to restore Hanover to England. In his indignation at this insult Frederick William declared war against France without an ally. The result was the battle of Jena and Prussia's defeat. At the Peace of Tilsit (June, 1807), concluded between Prussia and Napoleon, all lands between the Rhine and the Elbe were ceded to Napoleon for his free disposal, a war indemnity of 140,000,000 francs was imposed on the mutilated kingdom, and Frederick William was also under treaty obligation not to maintain an army of more than 42,000 regular troops during the next ten years.

Prussia: Wernigerode Castle, in Harz Mountains

The years which followed this national disaster were chiefly remarkable for the sweeping internal reforms which the crisis necessitated, carried out under Baron Stein and Baron Hardenberg, and almost amounting to a revolution. In the great struggle for the overthrow of Napoleon which followed, an important part was taken by the Kingdom of Prussia, and the Prussian troops along with the British bore a noble part in the Waterloo struggle. At the Congress of Vienna (1815), when the map of Europe was rearranged, Prussia, though losing some possessions, was indemnified with others more extensive and valuable, and was placed in a more advantageous position than before. She now also formed one of the states in the new German Confederation.

After the Restoration Frederick William III. leaned to the despotic counsels of Austria and Russia, supported heartily the Holy Alliance, and entered upon a reactionary policy which continued until his death in 1840. He was succeeded by Frederick

William IV., who was expected to grant a Constitution to his subjects, but refused the demand of his states to this effect in 1841. In 1847 he tried to anticipate the revolutionary movement spreading throughout Europe by summoning a combined meeting of provincial Parliaments at Berlin, but he conferred on them no real power. In the following year, however, after a deadly struggle, in which Berlin was declared in a state of siege, the king dismissed his ministers and granted a Constitution, the details of which were elaborated by a new Parliament, and which was formally proclaimed in 1850. The Poles in 1848 revolted against Prussian rule, but the movement was summarily suppressed.

In 1848 a deputation of the German National Assembly at Frankfurt offered the crown of Emperor of the Germans to the King of Prussia, but it was declined. By this time two parties existed in the Germanic Confederacy, one of them desiring Prussia to be the chief state in Germany, to the exclusion of Austria altogether; henceforth there was a strong rivalry between these two states. In 1857, the king being insane and unable to conduct affairs, his brother William became regent, and ultimately succeeded to the throne on the death of Frederick William in 1861.

The new king, William I. (1861-88), showed a disposition to absolutism, which in 1862-3 occasioned a lengthened dispute between the chambers and the ministry under Count Bismarck. At this time, on the complaint of the Federal Diet that Denmark had not observed its treaty obligations in regard to the Duchies of Schleswig and Holstein, the Prussians, under General Wrangel, entered Schleswig (1864), and Denmark was overpowered. By the Treaty of Vienna, signed 30th Oct., 1864, Denmark gave up Schleswig, Holstein, part of Jutland, and Lauenburg to Germany. In the following year Prussia purchased the claims of Austria over the Duchy of Lauenburg, and it was agreed that Schleswig and Holstein should be administered separately by both powers. But this settlement did not last long. Prussia, which had determined on appropriating them, wished to buy out Austria, but the latter would not cede her claims for money. This led to war between the two powers and to the break-up of the German Confederation, some of the states of which sided with Prussia, others with Austria.

On 15th June, 1866, the Prussian troops took the offensive, and the brief campaign which ensued is known as the Seven Weeks' War. The Prussian forces were armed with the new needle-gun, and the entire operations were directed by the chief of staff, Count von Moltke. The Austrians, under General Benedek, were completely defeated near Königgrätz, in Bohemia, where on 3rd July was fought the decisive battle of Sadowa; and peace soon followed. A subordinate campaign against Hanover, Bavaria, and other states had been conducted by the Prussians with complete success.

After the war Prussia incorporated Hanover, Hesse-Cassel, Nassau, Hesse-Homburg, Schleswig, Holstein, Lauenburg, Hesse-Darmstadt north of the Main, and the principality of Hohenzollern, which already belonged to the royal family. The King of Prussia now invited the states of North Germany to form a new confederation, which was established on the basis of proposals made by Prussia. The jealousy of France was excited by this powerful confederation, and in 1867 the question of the disposal of Luxemburg brought France and Prussia almost to the point of war. In 1870 Prince Leopold of Hohenzollern consented to become a candidate for the then vacant Spanish throne. This was opposed by the French emperor (Napoleon III.), who demanded not only that the candidate should withdraw, but that the King of Prussia should pledge himself not to permit any such future candidature. This being refused, war was declared by France on 15th July, 1870, with a most disastrous result to herself. After the German arms had proved entirely successful, on the invitation of the North German Parliament supported by the South German states, the King of Prussia assumed on 18th Jan., 1871, the title of German Emperor.

From this point the history of Prussia is, to a great extent, merged in that of the German Empire. In the hands of Prince Bismarck, acting as Premier of Prussia as well as Chancellor of the empire, a strong, central, autocratic government was maintained. Externally his policy was to secure Germany from attack by France or Russia, and to bring about this, alliances were made with Austria and Italy. Internally the legislation of Prussia was for some time chiefly remarkable for its antagonism to the Roman Catholic Clerical and Socialist parties. In 1873 many clerical privileges were suppressed by the laws introduced and carried by Falk; but in 1880 an amendment to these was promoted by the Premier, and subsequently he greatly modified his opposition to the ultramontanes. The Social Democrats also evoked the

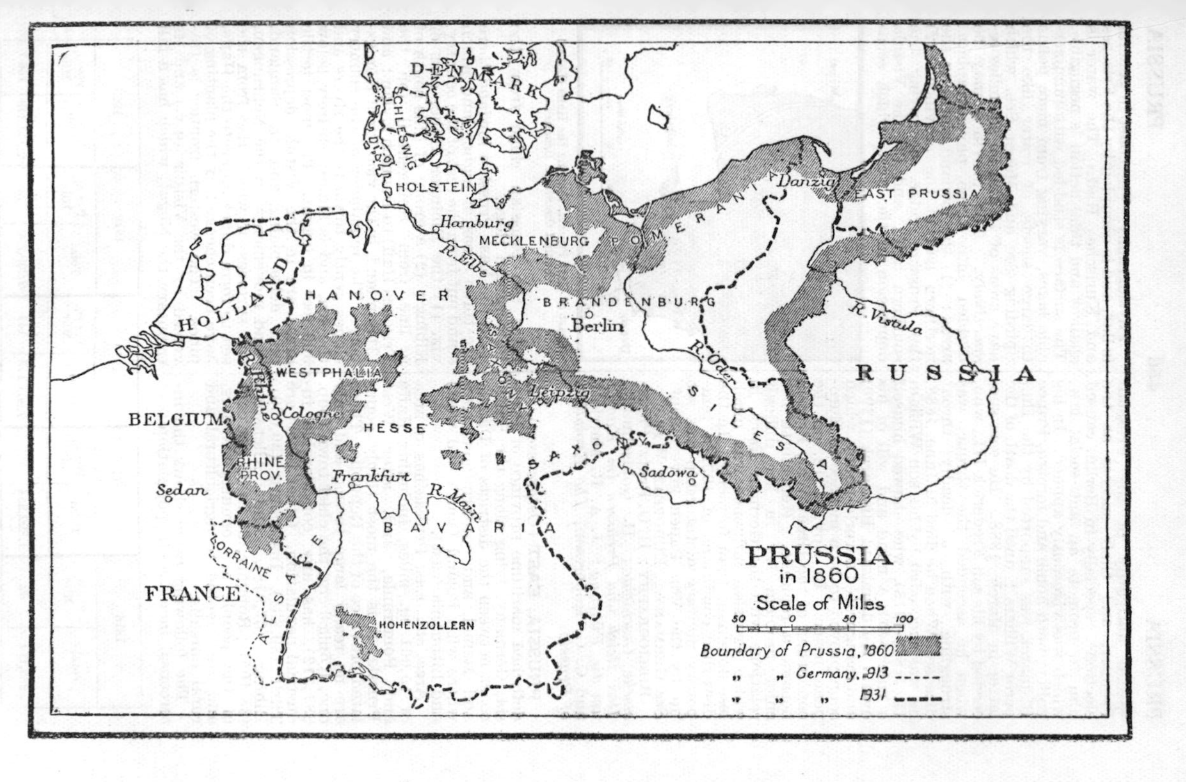
PRUSSIA
in 1860
Scale of Miles
50 0 50 100
Boundary of Prussia, 1860
" " Germany, 1913
" " " 1931
RUSSIA
EAST PRUSSIA
Danzig
R. Vistula
POMERANIA
BRANDENBURG
Berlin
R. Oder
SILESIA
Sadowa
SAXONY
Leipzig
BAVARIA
R. Main
Frankfurt
HOHENZOLLERN
HESSE
Cologne
R. Rhine
RHINE PROV.
WESTPHALIA
HANOVER
MECKLENBURG
Hamburg
R. Elbe
HOLSTEIN
SCHLESWIG
DENMARK
HOLLAND
BELGIUM
Sedan
LORRAINE
ALSACE
FRANCE

special antipathy of the Prussian Premier, and their success at the elections, especially in Berlin, caused him to promote an anti-social law, which was vigorously applied. In his policy, both home and foreign, Prince Bismarck was supported by the Emperor William I. until the death of the latter in March, 1888. He was succeeded by his son Frederick III., who, when he ascended the throne, was struggling with a deadly throat disease. When he died in June, 1888, he was succeeded by his son William II. (1888-1918), who showed himself a ruler with a mind and will of his own. He dismissed Bismarck (1890) and inaugurated a world-policy, which soon proved to be a menace to European peace. In Nov., 1918, on the conclusion of the Great War, Prussia became a republic. Henceforth her chief problem lay in her difficult relations with the German *Reich*, in which Prussian influence was much less dominant than formerly. In the disturbed conditions of 1932 a temporary military dictatorship was set up by the Von Papen government. *See* GERMANY ; EUROPEAN WAR.

BIBLIOGRAPHY : H. G. Prutz, *Preussische Geschichte* ; H. Goldschmidt, *Das Reich und Preussen im Kampf um die Führung* ; J. A. R. Marriott and C. G. Robertson, *The Evolution of Prussia.*

PRUSSIA, EAST (*Ostpreussen*). A detached maritime province of Prussia, Germany, lying along the Baltic coast between the districts of Danzig and Memel, and conterminous elsewhere with Poland (south and west) and Lithuania (east).

Area, etc. East Prussia has an area of 15,061 sq. miles, including Haffe and Pomerania, and, after West Prussia, it is the most thinly populated province of the Republic. There are no really large towns, and only one, Königsberg, the chief town (pop. 287,312), has any considerable industrial population. Other towns are Tilsit (50,834), Insterburg (30,000), Elbing (67,878), and Allenstein (38,105). Roughly, 66 to 68 per cent of the people are country-dwellers, and are devoted to agricultural and rural pursuits.

The following table shows the intercensal increases in population :

Physiography. The coast in general is flat, and is occupied by the Frisches and Kurisches Haff. The water is shallow and tidal action is negligible. The surface is studded with innumerable lakes, varying from mere ponds to large sheets of water like the Spirding See and Mauer See, which have areas of 45 and 50 sq. miles respectively. The province may be divided into three physiographical areas : (1) the lowland, forming the northern half of the province ; (2) the Prussian ridge, occupying the southern half ; and (3) the Vistula depression in the west, which sepa-

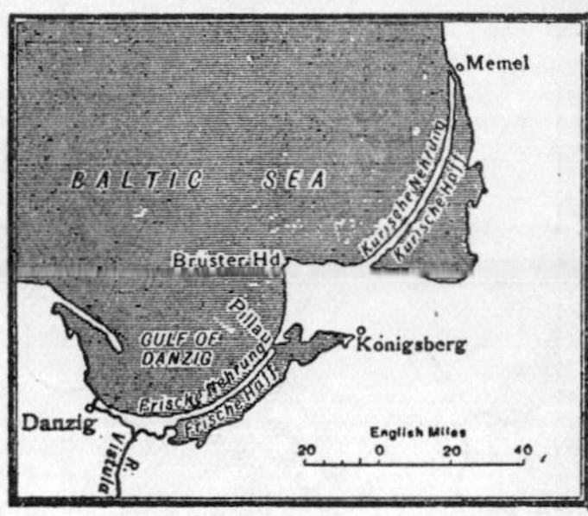

Coast of East Prussia, showing the Haffs (Lakes) behind the Storm Beaches

rates the Prussian ridge from the Pomeranian ridge.

In the East Prussian lowland there are three areas of higher land which stand out from the rest of the country, viz. (1) the Elbinger Höhe, east of Elbing ; (2) a group of hills south of a line from Heiligenbeil (on the Frisches Haff) to Deutsch Eylau ; and (3) Samland, in the vicinity of Königsberg. The remainder of the country slopes gently towards the rivers and the sea, and is almost entirely below 300 feet in height. The most fertile areas are in the Vistula depression and delta-plain, and in Samland. Sand movements on the Nehrungen, the surfaces of which rise from the sea to form dunes opposite the Haffs, have been checked by the planting of pines. The western frontier is traversed by the Vistula (q.v.) and its tributary the Nogat, which has a fall

1816		1871		1910		1919		1925	
Total	Per sq. Mile	Total	Per sq. Mile	Total	Per sq. Mile	Total	Per sq. Mile	Total	Per sq. Mile
886,174	62	1,822,934	127	2,064,175	144	2,229,290	156	2,256,349	156·7

of 1 in 7299, and a breadth of 130 yards, and falls into the Frisches Haff.

The Memel (Russ. *Niemen*) forms a part of the eastern frontier-line. It enters East Prussia at Schmalleningken, 70 miles from the sea, after flowing 480 miles through Russia, Poland, and Lithuania, and branches at Kallwen to form a delta which has, in course of time, filled up between one-third and one-half of the Kurisches Haff. The main stream is called the *Russ* from Kallwen to its mouth, and its average fall is 1 in 12,223, the greatest being 1 in 8312. The Pregel and its tributaries drain the eastern and central areas of the province, the main stream being formed by the junction of the Inster and the Angeraph (with its affluent the Pissa) at Insterburg, and flowing into the Frisches Haff 4½ miles west of Königsberg. It emerges again at the Pillau Deep (*see* PREGEL). East Prussia has an average temperature of between 41° and 43° F. January is the coldest month, the mean temperature being then about 28° F. July is the warmest month, and 63° F. may then be attained. East Prussia is, then, the coldest province of Germany. The rainfall is moderate, and being just within the Continental area, rain falls all the year round, but especially in summer.

Communications. Both East and West Prussia are traversed by two important lines from Berlin, viz. (1) the Ostbahn, which enters East Prussia at Marienburg, follows the line Konitz-Dirschau (junction for Danzig)-Königsberg-Eydt-kuhnen on the Lithuanian frontier, where it connects with Vilna and Leningrad. It must cross the "Corridor," however, and by entering Poland its value as a strategic line is negligible. (2) The line passing through Schneidemühl and Bromberg, in Posen, to Thorn, Allenstein, and Insterburg, where it joins the Ostbahn. There is a continuation to Memel, via Tilsit. The Pillau-Königsberg-Lyck line, with its extension through Poland to Bialystock, on the Warsaw-Moskva Railway, and the Danzig-Dirschau-Marienburg-Deutsch-Eylau line, which permits of communication with Warsaw, are also of importance. A canal connects Königsberg with the Masurian Lakes. Lakes Mauer and Spirding are linked by small canals, and Königsberg is similarly connected with Pillau (q.v.).

Production : *Agriculture.*—The soil of East Prussia generally is not fertile, and the principal branches of agriculture are fodder-cropping and live-stock breeding, with some cereal and potato raising. Rye and oats are the chief cereals ; wheat and barley are not suitable as crops. Peat litter is made in the moor (Johannisburg Heath) district. The province is celebrated for the horses which it used to supply in large numbers for the German army, and at that time the Wehlau (Pregel) horse market was world-renowned. Cattle, sheep, and pigs are also raised. *Forestry.*—About 18 per cent of the surface is afforested, 80 per cent of the trees being coniferous. *Fisheries.*—These are valuable, smelts, roach, and perch-pike being found in the Haffs in enormous numbers.

Manufactures. These are of small consequence, and are generally subordinate to and dependent upon local agriculture and forestry. There is some shipbuilding at Elbing and Pillau. Sugar, beer, spirits, and wooden goods are made.

See PRUSSIA ; GERMANY ; PRUSSIA, WEST ; TILSIT ; PILLAU ; KÖNIGSBERG ; VISTULA ; PREGEL ; EUROPEAN WAR ; and other articles.

BIBLIOGRAPHY : J. W. F. Thelwall and C. J. Kavanagh, *Economic and Financial Conditions in Germany* (H.M. Stationery Office) ; *Germany*, in *Peace Handbooks*, vol. vii. (H.M. Stationery Office) ; Brockhaus, *Handbuch des Wissens* (1922).

PRUSSIA, WEST. A former province of Prussia, Germany, the western portion of which was divided between Danzig and Poland by the Treaty of Versailles, and a large part of it now forms what is known as the "Polish Corridor." The relics of Posen and West Prussia are now combined as the Border Province, the area of which is 2978 sq. miles ; pop. (1925), 332,485 (or 111·6 per square mile). Within its confines, West Prussia under the German Empire included the basin of the Vistula, but in its modern form a considerable area of the Polish Corridor and the lands apportioned to the free port of Danzig intervene. East of the Vistula and of the Nogat a small portion remains, and is attached to the detached province of East Prussia (q.v.).

PRUSSIC ACID. *See* HYDROCYANIC ACID.

PRUTH (pröt). A river of Europe, which rises on the eastern side of the Carpathian Mountains, in the south-east of Galicia ; flows circuitously east past Czernowitz, then south-south-east, separating Moldavia from Bessarabia, and enters the Danube on the left, about 12 miles below Galatz. Before the European War it formed the frontier of Rumania for a distance of 379 miles. Its bed is 650 to 1000 feet broad, its depth 13 to 20 feet, and it is navigable for vessels of moderate size to the Husi district and even as far as Jassy. Length, 500 miles.

PRYNNE, William. Born at Swanswick, Somersetshire, in 1600, died in 1669. Educated at Bath Grammar School and Oriel College, Oxford, he took his degree in 1620, and was called to the Bar at Lincoln's Inn in 1628. In 1627 he began with Puritan severity to attack prevailing fashions. For a volume denouncing stage-playing, entitled *Histrio-Mastix,* which was supposed to be levelled at the queen, he was condemned by the Star-chamber to pay a fine of £5000, to stand in the pillory and have both ears cut off, and to remain a prisoner for life. While in prison he wrote another book, *News from Ipswich against Laud,* and being condemned again to another fine of £5000, and to lose the remainder of his ears, had the stumps cut off, and was branded on both cheeks. The Long Parliament in 1640 granted his release. Soon after he entered Parliament and took a prominent part in the trial of Laud. After the fall of Charles I., Prynne opposed Cromwell, who had him again imprisoned. At the Restoration he was appointed Keeper of the Records at the Tower. He was a most voluminous writer, had much learning and indefatigable industry, but was very deficient in judgment.

PRYTANE'UM. A public hall in ancient Greek states and cities serving as the common home of the community. That of Athens was the most famous. Here the city exercised the duties of hospitality both to its own citizens and strangers. The prytanes or presidents of the Boulē were entertained in it, together with the citizens who were honoured with the privilege of taking their meals at the public cost.

PRZEMYSL (peremishl). A town of Poland, in Galicia, on the San, formerly an Austrian fortress guarding the Carpathian passes across the East Beskids section which give access to the valley of the Vistula and to Lemberg and Cracow. The Greek Catholic Church has a bishopric here. It is also one of Poland's 10 military districts. Pop. 47,958. *See* GALICIAN CAMPAIGN; EUROPEAN WAR.

PSALMANA'ZAR, George. The assumed name of a literary impostor, born of Catholic parents in the south of France about 1679, died 1763. He studied among the Dominicans, acted as a private tutor, became a common vagrant, and at length assumed the character of a Japanese convert to Christianity, a character which he changed to that of a converted heathen native of the Island of Formosa. At this time he became acquainted with a clergyman named Innes, who brought him to London as a convert to the Church of England. Under the patronage of Bishop Compton he translated the *Church Catechism* into a language which he invented and called Formosan, while he also published a so-called authentic *History of Formosa.* Various scholars had doubts of his pretensions, and at last he confessed his imposture. For many years after he resided in London, and employed his pen in writing for the booksellers. His *Autobiography,* published after his death, expresses great penitence for his deceptions. Dr. Johnson had a high opinion of his character and abilities.

PSALMODY. This term has two widely different applications, according as it is considered in connection with the Roman Catholic or the Protestant Church. In the former case it has reference to the conditions governing the musical recitation of the prose version of the Psalms and the manner of employment for that purpose of the Gregorian Tones, and is mainly of interest to the musical specialist. In association with the service of the Protestant Church it has reference to the metrical versions of the Psalms and the music to which they are sung, and is of very general interest, since it concerns the active part taken by congregations of the Reformed Church in the praise portion of the services.

The history of the origin and evolution of the metrical psalter and of the familiar psalm-tunes is too lengthy to be given here in detail, but those desirous of studying the subject are advised to read the article *Psalter* in Grove's *Dictionary of Music and Musicians* (vol. iii., 1907). The tunes found in the modern psalter come from many sources, but some of the oldest, such as "Old Hundredth" and "Old 124th" are found in the *Genevan Psalter,* which dates from 1551. The next important date is 1562, when the first edition of John Day's *Psalter* appeared. This was the first psalter to give a metrical version of all the psalms, and the number of tunes in the book was sixty-five. The influence of the modes is still noticeable in these musical settings, but it is of interest to observe that the great majority of the tunes were in those modes corresponding to our major and minor scales. Other famous psalters were Thomas Este's in 1592, Ravenscroft's in 1621, and John Playford's in 1671.

PSALMS. The Hebrew *Psalter* contains 150 odes divided into five books. Psalms ix. and x., however, should be one, as in the Greek, and also xlii. and xliii. The Greek divides cxvi. and cxlvii. each into two, and adds a 151 Psalm by way of epilogue. The poetic form consists in "parallelism" arising from antiphonal singing; either the same thought is repeated in two consecutive lines, as ii., 1, or the second line is the converse of the first, as i., 6, or it adds something to it, as ii., 2. These are called "synonymous," "contrasted," and "constructive" parallelism, and two or more of them may be combined. There is no metre and no rhyme. The nearest approach to metre is the "*kinah* strophe," in which each line consists in the Hebrew of five words with a break after the third. The best example of this is xix., 7-9. The only approach to rhyme is a refrain dividing the psalm into stanzas (xlii., xlvi., lxxx., cvii., cxxxvi.). In the "songs of degrees" especially "anadiplosis" is found (a verse beginning as the last ended, cxxi., 1, 2).

All the Psalms except thirty-four have titles. These mention (1) the kind of poem (iii., xvi., xvii., xxx., xxxii., cxlv.); (2) musical notes giving the composer or conductor (iv., 1., lxii., lxxiii-lxxxiii., xlii-xlix., lxxxviii., lxxxix.), or the accompaniment (v., vi., xlvi.), or the air (ix., xxii., lvi., lxxv., lxxxviii., etc.); (3) the liturgical use (xxx., xcii., cxx-cxxxiv.); (4) the historical occasion (always from the Books of Samuel, as iii., vii., etc.); (5) the authors (seventy-three psalms are ascribed to David). These titles are of the nature of readers' notes. The readers, however, knew what they were doing. Psalm xc., for instance, which is assigned to Moses, bears a strong literary likeness to Deut. xxxii. and xxxiii. Being as old as some of the psalms, these conjectures are of more interest than those of modern European scholars.

As to the age of the *Psalter*, it is now usual to describe it as "the hymn-book of the second temple," the only psalm which professes to be David's being the eighteenth. It is also said that the Hebrew psalms were imitated from the Babylonian, but this simply means that all psalms are more or less alike, and the same might be said of the Vedic hymns. What marks off the Hebrew psalms is that they are monotheistic. That many psalms are post-Exilic (as cxxvi. and cxxxvii.) is evident enough. Several (as xliv., lxxiv., lxxix.) have been well assigned to Maccabean times. On the other hand, xlvi.-xlviii. suit best the time of Isaiah. But the bulk of the psalms belong to any or every age.

Our present *Psalter* contains earlier collections. This appears from the note at the end of lxxii.; from the fact that some psalms occur twice; and that in some books the proper name of God is Jehovah, in others Elohim. There would appear to have been the following editions of the *Psalter*: psalms ascribed to David and using the name Jehovah (book i., psalms i.-xli.); psalms using Elohim, including psalms of the Sons of Korah (xlii.-xlix.), of David (li.-lxxii.), and of Asaph (lxxiii.-lxxxiii.). To these lxxxiv.-lxxxix. would be added later. Books iv. and v. (psalms xc.-cl.) use "Jehovah." It is clear that book i. is oldest, books iv. and v. latest. Psalms xlii.-lxxxiii. would seem to date about the time of the Books of Chronicles (300 B.C.) in their present form. As to the state of the text, the English reader may judge by examining those psalms of which we have two copies (xviii., liii., lxx., cviii.). The alphabetic psalms (ix. and x., xxv., xxxiv., xxxvii., cxi., cxii., cxix., cxlv.) also help. Many verses are quite unintelligible, the English version being merely a makeshift (as xvi., 3; liii., 5; cf. xiv., 5).

The Psalms are essentially religious as Eastern poetry is, but they contain much fine description, and paint human nature on all its sides. (1) Especially religious are those psalms in which the poet depicts the degeneracy of the times in lurid colours (as xiv.) and the idol-worship of his neighbours (cxv.), whilst never losing confidence in the power of Jehovah to put things right (xciii.). This faith even blots out the darker side of life (xxiii., xlvi., c., ciii.). Often the poet upholds like Job his integrity (vii.), and as often he is plunged in despair (the seven "penitential" psalms). His religion becomes a "sense of absolute dependence" (lxii., cxxxi.). The problem of the Book of Job does not touch him; his position is almost that of Job's three friends (xxxvii., xlix., lxxiii.). His refuge is in religion, and above all in the temple where he could spend all his days (lxxiii., 17; xxvii., 4, the "guest" psalms). The wonder of this faith is that he had no idea of a future life beyond that of a land of shades, Sheol, the Greek Hades (xxxix., 13). Psalms xvi., xvii., xlix., and lxxiii. have been interpreted otherwise. In life his employment is meditating upon the law (i., 2; cxix.), which does not necessarily mean the Mosaic Law. As a result we have the psalms, mostly alphabetic, which are made up of proverbs (xxv., etc.). The closing psalms are doxologies (cxlviii.-cl.).

(2) Personal psalms are those in which the poet prays to be delivered from his enemies (v., xvii.), or returns

thanks for deliverance (ix.). The psalmist has no friends; those he had have proved false (xxxv., xli.): hence the "imprecatory" psalms, especially lxix. and cix. He fears their triumph over his defeat or misfortune, the Arab *shamátah*, the German *Schadenfreude*. In true Arab fashion he protests his own integrity and honour; unlike the Arab, he abhors both violence and treachery (xxvi.). Now he is an outlaw from his tribe (lxix. lxxi.); now struggling with physical disease (xxii., xxx., and the gloomiest of all the psalms, lxxxviii.) or with mental depression (xlii., xliii.). In these, as in all the psalms, however, there is always the question whether the speaker is really an individual or the community of pious Israelites. Wellhausen is inclined to take the former view, perhaps chiefly because Smend and Duhm, who preceded him, took the latter.

(3) Many psalms are patriotic or national in sentiment. Such are those which display loyalty to the king (the "royal" psalms, xx., xxi., etc.), who may be ideal (cx.). Psalm xliv. is an epithalamium, but even this may be meant in a mystical sense, as possibly the Song of Songs (cf. Lane, *Modern Egyptians*, p. 412 f.). Other poems are in praise of Jerusalem, both for its beauty of situation and as the dwelling-place of Jehovah (xlvi., xlviii., lxxxiv., lxxxvii., cxxii., cxxxvii.). The national history is celebrated in odes which approach epic form (cv., cvi., cxiv., cxxxvi.), nor is family life outside the poet's ken (cxxvii.). Many psalms are war-songs: "salvation" often means victory in war (xx., cxxiv.).

(4) Some of the finest of these poems are descriptions of nature. The noblest of these is civ. Psalm cvii. also describes first the caravan lost in the desert, then an eastern prison, a raging fever, a ship in distress. A fifth picture is left unfinished. In xxix. we have a thunder-storm; in lxviii., 13, a picture of still life; in viii. and lxxxi. harvest or vintage songs (also lxv.). Psalm xix. is the Hebrew version of the German philosopher's "starry heavens overhead and the moral law within."

The Hebrew psalms are the outpouring of the human heart at its best and sometimes at its worst. They give vent to man's sense of the Divine, his thankfulness for prosperity, his complaint under adversity, his entreaties for protection from his enemies. Now he protests his innocence, and again is plunged in the depth of remorse for his sins. As a rule the psalmist plays on a minor key, but when his optimism does break out it is unclouded. There are few sides of life on which he does not touch, on which a Hebrew or Arab might dwell. And his lines have been the stay of many generations, not only of his own people but even more of the Christian Church, and touch the heart of the pious Muslim perhaps most of all.

BIBLIOGRAPHY: Perhaps the best book on the Psalms from the point of view of the general reader is that of A. F. Kirkpatrick in the *Cambridge Bible for Schools and Colleges* (1917); for the minutiæ of the Hebrew text, Delitzsch (English translation, 1887); the most important English commentary is considered to be that of Perowne (1892); Cheyne has several books with valuable indices; Wellhausen's text (1895) and English translation (Furness, 1898) in the *Polychrome Bible* show the caution of this great scholar; Briggs in the *International Critical Commentary* (1906) is spoiled by adherence to a theory of metre. Prothero's *Psalms in Human Life* (1904) is an oft-read book.

PSALTER. Specifically, the version of the *Psalms* in the *Book of Common Prayer*; also applied in the Roman Catholic Church to a series of devout sentences, 150 in number, and to a large chaplet or rosary with 150 beads, agreeing with the number of the psalms.

PSALTERY, or **PSALTERION.** An instrument of music used by the Hebrews, the form of which is not now known. That which is now used is a flat instrument in the form of a trapezium or triangle truncated at the top, strung with thirteen chords of wire, mounted on two bridges at the sides, and struck with a plectrum or crooked stick, thus resembling the dulcimer (q.v.).

PSAMMETICHUS (sam-met′i-kus). A king of Egypt who died about 617 B.C. He was one of the twelve kings who reigned simultaneously in Egypt for fifteen years after the expulsion of the Æthiopian dynasty; but being suspected by the other kings of aiming at sole sovereignty, he was driven into banishment. With the aid of some Greek mercenaries, however, he defeated the other kings in a battle fought at Momemphis, on the east side of Lake Mareotis, after which he became the sole king of Egypt (671 or 670 B.C.), and the founder of a new dynasty.

PSEUDEPIG′RAPHA (Gr., false additional writings). A term applied in bibliography to a great number of books and fragmentary writings whose claim to a place in the Old and New Testament canons has been denied. Unlike the apocryphal and deuterocanonical books, the pseudepigrapha have no value unless to prove the capacity for forgery which was possessed by the Jew, Gnostic, and Christian of ancient and mediæval times. Among these Old Testament forgeries may be mentioned; *The History of Asenath, The Preaching of Noah, The Book of Elias, The Testament of the Twelve Patriarchs, The History of Antiochus, Book of Lamech, Apocalypse of Adam*, etc.; while among the New Testament books are the false gospels of James, Matthias, Thomas, Nicodemus, and Andrew, the *History of Joseph the Carpenter, Nativity of Mary*, and the *Acts* of Andrew, John, Paul, Peter, and Thomas.

PSEUDOMORPH. A mineral having a definite form belonging not to the substance of which it consists, but to some other substance which has wholly or partially disappeared. Quartz may thus appear in the form of fluorspar (total replacement of the original material), or limonite in the form of pyrite (partial replacement, iron being common to both minerals).

PSEU'DONYM (Gr. *pseudēs*, false, and *onoma*, a name). A pen-name, a feigned name assumed by an author; also called "nom de plume," or "nom de guerre." Pseudonyms are commonly employed to conceal the identity of a writer, or else merely out of fancy, where there is no idea of concealment. Among famous pseudonyms may be mentioned: "Boz" (Charles Dickens), "Lewis Carroll" (C. L. Dodgson), "Barry Cornwall" (B. W. Proctor), "Elia" (Charles Lamb), "George Eliot" (Marian Evans, afterwards Mrs. Cross), "Thomas Ingoldsby" (Rev. R. H. Barham), "Junius" (possibly Sir Philip Francis), "Phiz" (H. K. Browne), "Ouida" (Louise de la Ramée), "Mark Twain" (Samuel L. Clemens), "Artemus Ward" (Charles F. Browne), "Bab" (W. S. Gilbert), "Dagonet" (G. R. Sims), "Anthony Hope" (Sir A. Hope Hawkins), "Lee Vernon" (Violet Paget), "Q" (Sir A. Quiller-Couch), and many others.—Cf. Halkett and Laing, *Dictionary of the Anonymous and Pseudonymous Literature of Great Britain.*

PSEU'DOPODS, or **PSEUDOPO'DIA.** *See* PROTOZOA.

PSEUDOTSUGA. A genus of coniferous trees. *P. Douglasii* is the Douglas fir of the Rocky Mountains, one of the noblest of Conifers. The great flag-staff at Kew Gardens consists of the trunk of one of these giants.

PSILOM'ELANE. A common mineral hydrous oxide of manganese, with iron, potassium, and barium, occurring as black mammillated masses in veins. Its crystallised form is Hollandite.

PSILOTALES. A small tropical and subtropical family of Vascular Cryptogams, comprising the genera Psilotum and Tmesipteris, sometimes included in Lycopodiales (club-mosses), but better regarded as one of the primary subdivisions of the Pteridophytes. They are small, rootless epiphytic plants of simple and probably primitive structure.

PSITTACIDÆ (sit-as'i-dē). The parrot family, comprising over 400

Grey Parrot (*Psittăcus erythăcus*)

species, of which the genus Psittăcus is the type. *See* PARROT.

PSITTACOSIS. Disease of parrots, communicable by infected birds to man. Outbreaks occurred in England in 1930, which were accompanied by fatal results that year and subsequently, and led to the introduction by the Ministry of Health of an order prohibiting the importation of parrots into the country.

PSKOV, or **PLESKOV.** A former government of Russia incorporated in 1927 in the Leningrad area; area, 17,069 sq. miles. The whole government belongs to the basin of the Baltic, the Western Dvina, which drains the south-east, carrying its waters into the Gulf of Riga, and the Velikaya, Chelon and Lovat, with other small tributaries, carrying the rest of the drainage into the Gulf of Finland. The principal crops are rye, oats, barley, potatoes, and flax. The fishing in the numerous lakes of the government is of some value, and forest industries are important.

PSKOV, or **PLESKOV.** The capital of the Russian government of Pskov incorporated in the Leningrad area in 1927, situated on the Velikaya, and served by the Leningrad-Warsaw Railway. It consists of the Kremlin, the Central city, the Great city, and a considerable suburb. The cathedral in the Kremlin and that of SS. Peter and Paul are of historical interest. The principal manufacture is Russian leather. Pop. 38,750.

PSO'AS. An important muscle of the human body which extends from

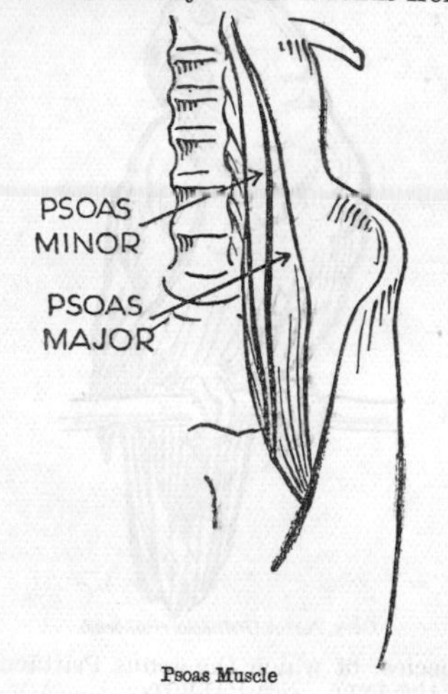

Psoas Muscle

the lumbar region inside the body cavity to the thigh-bone, and assists in the movements of the thigh.

PSORA'LEA. A genus of leguminous plants, one species of which (*P. esculenta*) is the bread-root of North America.

PSORI'ASIS. A chronic inflammatory disease of the skin, characterised by well-marked red patches covered with silvery scales. It is a very common skin disease, and though the cause is unknown, a large number of the cases have been shown to be hereditary. There is a marked tendency to recurrences in spring and autumn, and some cases subside and are latent for a time, to break out later. It usually begins in childhood or adolescence, and may persist for many years. Many drugs have been tried, and most success has followed the use of arsenic in the chronic form of the disease. Externally, after the removal of the scales, chrysarobin ointment has been found to be the most effective remedy.

PSYCHE (sī'kē; Gr. *psychē*, the soul). A sort of mythical or allegorical personification of the human soul, a beautiful maiden, whose charming story is given by the Latin writer Apuleius. She was so beautiful as to be taken for Venus herself. This goddess, becoming jealous of her rival charms, ordered Cupid or Love to inspire her with love for some contemptible wretch. But Cupid fell in love with her himself. Many were the trials Psyche underwent, arising partly from her own indiscretion, and partly from the hatred of Venus, with whom however, a reconciliation was ultimately affected. Psyche by Jupiter's command became immortal, and was for ever united with her beloved.

PSYCHIATRY. *See* INSANITY.

PSYCHICAL RESEARCH. A term applied to the study of hitherto unexplained and obscure activities of the human mind and of the invisible, unknown world of spirit. Andrew Lang defined psychical research as "the examination of the amount of truth contained in world-wide superstitions." It is thus an interpretation, by aid of psychological principles and theories, of the phenomena investigated. Whilst psychology proper studies the explicable phases of mental phenomena, psychical research is concerned with the mysterious; it covers the borderland set of phenomena that might possibly be resolved into recognised types of events. It is also concerned with supernormal faculties, with forms of mentality transcending those with which everyday humanity is familiar.

It is, however, not limited to mental manifestations, for it also investigates undiscovered forms of physical energy. Beliefs in dreams and visions, in apparitions and clairvoyance, and also in the phenomena of hypnotism have existed since time immemorial. For ages humanity believed in spirits and ghosts, in *poltergeister* and tricksy spirits, and all unusual phenomena were attributed to their agency. Hydromancy, i.e. clairvoyance by gazing at the surface of still water, and crystal-gazing were practised by the Romans, who were also familiar with the divining-rod for the purpose of discovering water or buried treasure. The belief in premonitions, or warnings received in dreams or by apparitions, has also long been current. The ancients also believed in what we now call telepathy (q.v.). The works of

Homer and Euripides, of Virgil, Ovid, and Cicero frequently mention manifestations of the dead, apparitions, evocations, and realisations of premonitory dreams.

Numerous stories which have come down to us from ancient times tend to prove that even savages were conversant with psychic phenomena in the form of superstitions. Again, the story of the witch of Endor, of Saul invoking the spirit of Samuel, is an instance of the belief existing among the Jews in mediumistic phenomena. Christianity, too, was in its origin associated with psychic phenomena. The oracles of Greece, which were the Greek mediums, fraudulent may be, prove the popular belief in psychic phenomena. This belief was opposed by Greek philosophers, but the Neo-Platonists were well versed in the practices of modern spiritualism. Thus Plotinus is supposed to have gone into trances, and Iamblichus gives accounts of psychic phenomena, of phantasms, and materialisations. Plutarch relates the story of the assassination of Cæsar and the premonitory dream of his wife, Calpurnia—who did her best to prevent her husband's going to the Senate on the fatal day. And Brutus, who was a philosopher of the Epicurean school, saw an apparition on the eve of the battle of Philippi. References to apparitions and haunted houses are found in the *Letters* of Pliny the Younger.

This belief in agencies working beyond and outside physical nature had a recrudescence towards the middle of last century, when modern spiritualism spread over the civilised world. Sceptics, however, denied the existence of spirit, and declared that all the strange, uncommon, and inexplicable phenomena were the result of fraud and the exploits of clever tricksters. And yet among the believers in supernatural agencies were numerous men and women of intelligence and honesty "who could not all be knaves or fools." The investigation of these obscure phenomena, or alleged phenomena, was bound to attract the attention of scientific men. Whilst admitting that there are gross superstitions, errors, illusions, trickery, and fraud, they had to confess that there are psychic facts worthy of investigation and of scientific explanation; that a world, as ancient as humanity, was open to research and experimental science. These men of science came to the conclusion that it was time to investigate those obscure and mysterious phenomena inexplicable by the known laws of nature. They had no opinions, and approached the subject with unbiased minds, maintaining that here was an open field for inquiry, "as not all faculties and potentialities of man had as yet been explained in terms of nerve and brain."

Thus in 1882 a Society for Psychical Research was founded under the presidency of Professor Sidgwick. In their manifesto the founders of the society declared that their aim was the scientific investigation of the hitherto inexplicable psychic phenomena, and the examination of evidence, both experimentally and statistically, without any bias or preconceived opinions. Among the eminent men of science and the famous philosophers who in the course of time became presidents of the Society for Psychical Research were: Andrew Lang, A. J. Balfour, William James, Boyd Carpenter, Sir W. F. Barrett, Sir Oliver Lodge, Henri Louis Bergson, and Professor W. M'Dougall. The society stood pre-eminently for investigation rather than belief and conclusions. The majority of the members, however, actually believed in the reality of thought-transference, or telepathy, whilst some of the present members are even convinced of a survival of human consciousness after death, or the existence of disembodied minds. The work of investigation of the so-called residual phenomena was entrusted to six committees, who were to "inquire into the nature and extent of any influence which may be exerted by one mind upon another, apart from any generally recognised mode of perception; into hypnotism, the so-called mesmeric trance, clairvoyance, and other allied phenomena; to undertake a revision of Reichenbach's researches with reference to discovering whether his "sensitives" possessed any power of perception beyond a highly exalted sensibility of the recognised sensory organs; to investigate the reports of apparitions at the moment of death, and of houses reputed to be haunted; to inquire into the causes and general laws of the phenomena of spiritualism; and to collect material relative to the history of these subjects."

During the fifty years of its existence the Society for Psychical Research has brought to light a great deal of imposture, but it has also established the fact that many of the strange, hitherto inexplicable phenomena really exist. It has been found that healthy persons often experience spontaneous auditory and visual hallucinations and apparently see apparitions or things not forming part of the physical world, such as the apparition of a person at the time of his death at a distance.

Thought-transference experiments have proved that there is frequently a contact between the agent, or person trying to transfer his or her thoughts, and the percipient, or person trying to read these thoughts. Clairvoyance, crystal-gazing, or inducing visual hallucinations at will, have been dealt with and experiments made.

The use of the divining-rod for the purpose of discovering water has been carefully investigated. The results obtained by the rod are supposed to be due to automatic action, subconsciously prompted. Psychical research has also well-nigh established the fact of telepathy, or the occasional communication between living persons without any known intermediary. The prevailing opinion that there was nothing but conscious or unconscious fraud has once for all been proved erroneous.

The great aim of psychical research has been to find out whether some at least of the prophecies, clairvoyant visions, telepathic impulses, or mediumistic messages are true, and whether veritable supernormal communications exist. Once the fact has been established, it becomes the business of science to find out the *why, how,* and *wherefore*. Thus the fact of the existence of telepathy has been established beyond doubt, but as for the explanation the tendency is to seek for it in physical causes. It has been explained by brain energy, on the analogy of wireless transmission of electric energy. It is maintained that there are psychic currents, just as there are aerial, magnetic, or electric currents. The vibration produced by one brain is, on certain occasions, transmitted to another kindred brain by ethereal undulations over long distances.

Another great problem to which psychical research has devoted considerable attention is that of the subconscious activities of the brain, actions being performed by man without leaving any trace on the normal consciousness. Many phenomena, however, with which psychical research deals can after all be explained by physical laws and noways tend to prove a survival of human consciousness after death. Much more important, therefore, is the phenomenon of spirit messages through trance-mediums. The medium, one of the best-known being Mrs. Piper, passes into a trance, and writes or speaks automatically messages purporting to come from some deceased person. As Mrs. Piper, when in a trance, has shown knowledge far beyond that which she herself possessed, many investigators are inclined to believe that it was really the spirit of a deceased person who used her hand or tongue. Another line of evidence is cross-correspondence.

Cross-correspondence is the theory that several persons receive messages which are singly unintelligible, but have a meaning when combined. Hitherto, it must be admitted, the mediumistic messages have been rather vague and hazy, and the revelations made by the spirits concerning their present existence are somewhat meaningless. As a rule only things which have taken place on this earth have transpired. Nevertheless, many investigators, as for instance Sir Oliver Lodge, are convinced of a post-mortem agency. They have come to the conclusion that the human soul, or human consciousness, continues to exist after death, and that the soul has the power to exercise an influence over another at a considerable distance without the aid of the senses. They maintain that life and consciousness do not become obliterated at the moment of bodily death, and that moreover this persistence after the shock of death is accompanied by individuality and memory. Psychical research thus tends to help religion in corroborating the traditional belief in the survival after death, for once the survival after death is denied, the whole fabric of revealed religion tumbles down like a house of cards.

Psychical research is still in its infancy, but it cannot be denied that it has done valuable work. In spite of this it is still being opposed or derided by scientists and psychologists. It must, however, be borne in mind that hypnotism, mesmerism, and animal magnetism, the exponents of which were called humbugs and frauds, are now recognised by the medical faculties all over the world. When Galvani made his first experiments upon frogs' legs in 1791 he was sneered at, and when Edison's phonograph was exhibited before the French Academy of Sciences in 1878, an academician maintained that it was the trick of a clever ventriloquist. Whether psychical research will ever be able to prove conclusively that in addition to our physical body we possess another body, composed of etheric substance, that this body survives the shock of death, and that biologists are wrong when they maintain that mind cannot exist apart from matter, is a point still subject to considerable and grave doubt.

BIBLIOGRAPHY: Gurney, Myers, and Podmore, *Phantasms of the Living*; J. Podmore, *Studies in Psychical Research*; J. H. Hyslop, *Science of a Future Life*; Sir W. F. Barrett, *Psychical Research*; T. J. Hudson, *The Law of Psychic Phenomena*; H.

Carrington, *Problems of Psychical Research*; Sir Oliver Lodge, *The Survival of Man*; *Proceedings of the Society for Psychical Research.*

PSYCHOANALYSIS. *See* PSYCHOTHERAPY AND PSYCHOANALYSIS.

PSYCHOLOGY (Gr. *psyche,* soul, and *logos,* science). The science dealing with operations of the mind. It has been defined as "the science of the soul," as the science of mind, or as the science of consciousness, and in modern times as the science of "behaviour" or conduct.

Broadly speaking, psychology is the scientific account of our mental processes, investigating our mental experiences. It treats of our powers of attention and sensation, of perception, memory, or the power of retention, of recognition, volition, freedom of the will; of illusions and imaginations, of feelings and emotions, pleasure or pain, taste and smell. It not only inquires into the operations of the mind, with a view to discovering its laws, but also into its connections with and dependence upon other bodily organs, and the action and reaction existing between them. When we think, remember, or endeavour to understand an object presented to the senses, we have an experience, and psychology is the study of the world of experience as distinguished from the study of the world of nature. The problem of psychology is to analyse mental processes into their simplest elements or components. The psychologist analyses these processes, formulates the laws of connection of the mental elements, and explains them in terms of parallel processes in the nervous system. Psychology is thus concerned with thinking, feeling, and acting. It examines the elements of which mind or intelligence is composed, conditions under which mental processes arise, purposes for which they are employed, and the manner in which conduct is controlled.

Method. The method of psychology is the scientific method, i.e. observation. Whilst, however, the observation of physical science is inspection, the observation of psychology is *introspection,* or looking within. The difficulty of introspection lies perhaps in the fact that when we are thus analysing our sensations, feelings of comfort and discomfort, of joy and sorrow, we are at once observers and observed. We are actually watching an experience and analysing it whilst we are having it. Another difficulty is the fact that in the method of introspection an experience is dependent upon the experiencing person, and psychology would thus become "a body of personal beliefs and individual opinions." The older psychologists, however, maintained that as other men had minds like our own, one is fully justified in basing psychology upon the introspective method and the reports furnished by various observers. Whilst, therefore, the psychologist observes his own mental processes by introspection, he also infers the occurrence of mental processes in others from external signs. We thus study mental phenomena not only in ourselves but also around us, as they manifest themselves externally in others. We study looks, gestures, and actions, and draw inferences from them by considering what we ourselves think or feel when we act in such a way. This method is the external or indirect way of investigating mind. We get at mental facts indirectly by means of certain external manifestations perceived by the senses (experimental psychology). A modern school of psychologists, however, denies the value of introspection. How can we observe, they ask, a mental state whilst it is going on? How can we infer anything about others from our own mental processes?

Behaviourism. Modern psychologists, therefore, claim for psychology the method of the physical sciences. They advocate the attempt to use external bodily expressions, facial movements, and gestures as manifestations from which one can measure and describe mental activities. In a word, they maintain that just as physiology examines the manner in which human organs act under certain conditions, so psychology must deal with the behaviour and conduct of the individual in certain conditions. The observations must extend to facts which can be seen by any observer. "By Behaviour," writes Pillsbury (*The Foundations of Psychology*), "is meant the activity of man or animal as it can be observed from the outside, or, without attempting to determine the mental states, by inference from acts." Psychology must therefore give up its references to consciousness, and should become a purely objective experimental branch of natural science. It should start from the fact that man and animals are *behaving* beings, adjusting themselves to environment by means of hereditary equipments and habit. Behaviour is modified not only by physical stimuli but also by the results of earlier behaviour. The majority of psychological problems, human and animal, are therefore grouped in three divisions—sense organ functions, instinctive functions, and habit formations. Professor M'Dougall thus defined psychology as "the positive science of the behaviour of living things." If we succeed in knowing, and completely describing the nervous system of man and the physical laws which govern it, we will always be able to account for the conduct and behaviour of man.

Cognition, Affection, Conation. In describing our mental processes the older psychologists agreed that there are three varieties of process: cognitive, affective, and conative; that is, a mental experience or process has the three aspects of knowing, feeling, and will. The ultimate constituent is a sensation. It is the simplest experience directly dependent upon the stimulation of a sense organ, or of a sensory nerve. Sensations constitute an acquaintance with a fact without knowing anything about it, and thus awaken no associations or suggestions of past experience. Sensations may be auditory, visual, gustatory, olfactory, cutaneous, or *kinæsthetic*. The last named are sensations *giving the feeling of movement*, or, in other words, keeping us aware of the movements of our limbs; they are due to the fact that we must have a mental picture corresponding to the feeling of the movement we desire to make. Kinæsthetic sensations are due to the stimulation of the receptors terminating in the muscle surfaces.

Intellectual life begins with sensations, but a sensation is not yet a cognition. The latter arises out of a sensation by means of *perception*, i.e. by a process of discriminating one group of impressions from another, and recognising an object. A perception is thus "the consciousness of a particular material object present to the senses." We have, for instance, a sensation of hearing a noise or a sound, but only when we identify the noise as that of a train or a street car are we said to *perceive*, for only then does it convey a meaning to us.

Conative functions deal with voluntary movements and all processes of striving for the purpose of attaining a goal. They cover the movements carried out by means of voluntary muscles, involving the psychical accompaniment of motor sensations. We distinguish impulsive, reflective, and instinctive movements.

Divisions of the Subject. Not all people possess the same sensations and images. The consciousness of man and his sense-organs may be affected by temporary or permanent derangement, by various forms of insanity, or by the hypnotic state. The operations of the healthy or normal mind are vastly different from those of the diseased or abnormal mind. We therefore distinguish between normal psychology and abnormal psychology. Psychology again extends not only to man but also to the animal, and just as there is a difference between the mind of one individual and that of another, so there is variation among the minds of individuals and groups. Besides animal or comparative psychology, there is an individual human psychology, and a collective psychology. The latter may be divided into social psychology, ethnic psychology, and class psychology.

History. The study of psychology is older than the name. The term came into use towards the end of the sixteenth century, but was popularised by Wolff in the eighteenth century. The science passed from the philosophical or metaphysical to the empirical stage. Aristotle may be considered as the founder of psychology, although he made no distinction between psychology and biology, which he considered as a part of physics. His treatise *Peri psyches* (*De Anima*), wherein he discusses the faculties of the mental part of man, remained for twenty centuries a textbook of psychology. The Greeks were intensely interested in the nature of the mind, but they treated it in a speculative or metaphysical way. Plato considered human consciousness as a continuation of certain types of existence from earlier ages. Christianity heightened the interest in certain psychological questions, but all through the Middle Ages psychology was more theological than philosophical, not to say scientific.

It was Descartes who gave psychology a new direction by his famous *cogito ergo sum*, and his system encouraged the method of internal observation. The method of analytic introspection was still further developed by John Locke, who treated of innate ideas, and by Bishop Berkeley and Hume. The two Mills, Bain, and Spencer continued the method of introspective analysis. Condillac and La Mettrie in France, Lotze, Herbart, Fechner, and Wundt in Germany, are also noteworthy for their contributions to the elaboration and development of psychological problems.

Scientific Psychology. In contradiction to the philosophical psychology of Fichte, Schelling, and Hegel, scientific psychology, physiological and experimental, arose and was developed in the nineteenth century, "the century of science." J. F. Herbart (1776-1831), Hermann Lotze (1817-81), and G. T. Fechner (1801-87) are the most prominent thinkers in the domain of psychology. Under the influence of the evolution theory and the labours of Darwin and Spencer, genetic psychology, child psychology, and race psychology were specially studied. C. Lange and W. James elaborated the theory of "emotional expression," maintaining that emotions are only strong sensations, or feelings arising from the movements of the body. The life of feeling is therefore the result of sensationalism. The expressions accompanying emotions, such as sorrow, anger, or fear, "are useful defensive or offensive actions, acquired by man or animal in crises and found serviceable." The habits acquired by man or animal in offence or defence have left after-effects, and are what is felt as an emotion. We thus feel sorry, because we cry; but do not cry, because we feel sorry. Another problem to which psychology in recent years has devoted much attention is the question of unconscious mental phenomena, and the study of double and multiple personality. This study was stimulated by the science of hypnotism. The unity of the mental principle was discussed, and a distinction made between the conscious and the unconscious. Sigmund Freud, who elaborated the system of psychoanalysis, has done much valuable work in this department of psychology. Thus psychology has passed successively from the philosophical to the empirical and from the latter to the physiological stage. For the soul of the theologians, replaced afterwards by the mind, modern psychology has substituted the brain, so that the science has been called a "psychology without a soul."

BIBLIOGRAPHY: A. Bain, *The Emotions and the Will*; J. Sully, *The Teacher's Handbook of Psychology*; E. B. Titchener, *A Textbook of Psychology*; W. James, *Principles of Psychology*; J. Ward, *Psychological Principles*; M. W. Calkins, *An Introduction to Psychology*; H. Hoeffding, *Outlines of Psychology*; J. B. Watson, *Behaviour: an Introduction to Comparative Psychology*; J. M. Baldwin, *History of Psychology*.

PSYCHOLOGY, ABNORMAL. The study of psychology has long engaged the attention of philosophers, but since the beginning of this century it has been the subject of much attention by alienists and other medical specialists. New theories have been advanced, new facts discovered, and new names have been given to old observations; but, now as always, the rules and standards have only a limited application; for neither in body nor mind are we all alike, apart from disease altogether. There is wide divergence in the faculties of men and in the way they act, and when they live orderly lives and contribute their fair share to the world's work, if they fail to reach the standard of normal psychology the fault may be as much in it as in them. The standard of normality is purely arbitrary, and it is doubtful if anyone, even among those who formulate it, attains to it wholly and at all times; but in so far as it is a working measure for purposes of comparison, it is useful. Though we do not all think and act alike and do not respond to the same stimuli in the same manner or degree, there are the exceptions who behave so differently from their neighbours as to earn the reputation of consistent eccentricity.

In the eyes of the law we are all held to be sound enough mentally to be accountable for our acts, in the absence of evidence to the contrary; and the assumption is a reasonable one though it is not always justified by the facts. The psychologist cannot admit it, for he is as little entitled to assume that all men are sane as that they are not. He has his standards by which he may judge them, but he does not always carry conviction when he applies them, his personal and professional bias being factors in the case as well as the mental condition of the patient. His work has, however, resulted in breaking down the hard-and-fast rules of the lawyer, since it has demonstrated the fact that they have tended to exclude from consideration facts that were important, or have at least underestimated their importance. As a community we have made provision for those whose mental condition is such that they are unable to take care of themselves or are a source of danger to others. If they are certified to be insane or are suffering from a mental defect which has existed from birth or from an early age, they may be placed under supervision either in institutions or with approved guardians outside; but there are persons who differ mentally from their neighbours to a notable extent, who are neither insane nor mentally defective within the meaning of the Acts, and whose conduct may so annoy their neighbours as to call for action being taken regarding it.

Some have argued that all crime and wrong-doing is due to the abnormal psychology of the offender. In a sense the saying that "to know all is to pardon all" reflects this view, but if it is correct, it would follow that the thief cannot help stealing and is not responsible for his wrong-doing; and experience shows that this generally is not the case. Motives that seem sufficient to one man, to lead him to do certain things, may be without apparent influence on another; and psychologists attempt to show why this is so by inquiring into the state of mind of the person who departs from the ordinary lines of conduct.

The case of the criminal has received more attention than that of others because, as a result of his actions, he has been placed in a more prominent position than many who are more eccentric, and there has been more opportunity to study him; but, in so far as the study takes place while he is in prison, he is seen under abnormal conditions, and is as little like his free self as a bird in a cage is like one in its natural surroundings.

That some prisoners have abnormal psychology nobody will deny, but that in this respect they differ from many who have never transgressed the law is not so clear. Even if it were proved that wrong-doing is due to abnormal psychology, we would still have to combat it. It is nothing new to hold that the only way to turn the evildoer from his course is to change his disposition. Our fathers called it a change of heart and we may call it a change of mind. The psychologists may help the penologists by prescribing for the offender, but it will be a doubtful benefit if he is merely placed and kept in a prison with another name.

Other classes of men have received a great deal of attention as having abnormal psychology. Men of genius and men in high positions have each furnished texts. The criminal is like the king of old in so far as the law bound neither, and whatever their psychology might be to begin with, it was bound soon to differ from that of their contemporaries. The man of genius, because of his faculty, does not meet with other men on equal terms, and he also is an example of abnormal psychology. Attempts have been made to prove that genius is allied to insanity, but they have only shown that men of genius, like men without it, have suffered from ailments and diseases that afflict both sane and insane.

Much of the progress of the race has been due to men who were abnormal psychologically, according to the standards of their time. They have revolted against conditions as they found them, and have led others. Those whose sanity has been least questioned have not always been the greatest blessings to mankind, and those who have been so eccentric in their behaviour as to be looked on as mad have in some cases proved wiser than their normal-minded neighbours. Abnormal psychology is a term that covers all mental conditions that do not conform to the ordinary standard, except insanity and mental defect. It may refer to cases where there is no tendency to wrong-doing and no sign of any mental disorder, and it may be as applicable to cases where there are anti-social tendencies or mental disturbance tending to insanity.—BIBLIOGRAPHY: Freud, *Psycho-Pathology of Everyday Life*; J. B. Watson, *Psychology from the Standpoint of a Behaviourist*; J. H. Coriat, *Abnormal Psychology*; H. Goddard, *Psychology of Normal and Sub-normal.*

PSYCHOTHERAPY AND PSYCHOANALYSIS. Psychotherapy is that branch of medical treatment which is concerned with the means of alleviating disorders of psychological (or mental) origin. **Psychoanalysis** is only one of the methods of psychotherapy, certainly an important one, but at the same time a method which at the present time is causing a degree of concern, to lay public and medical profession alike, out of all proportion to its significance or usefulness in the therapeutics of nervous diseases.

Nervous and mental diseases have usually been classified broadly into two groups, viz. organic and functional. **Organic diseases** are those in which there is definite structural damage to nerve tissue, e.g. through cutting off of blood supply or through degenerative processes affecting the neurons.

Functional diseases are those in which symptoms manifest themselves, but which rest upon no certain basis of observed microscopic or naked-eye change in nerve tissues (as far as present knowledge goes). Some of these functional disorders are certainly purely psychological in origin. It has to be remembered that every condition of ill-health is the product of a variety of influences and factors which have combined to bring about the disease picture presented by the patient, and that both physical and mental factors are at work in every case, though to varying degree and with varying relative importance in different instances. In cancer of the stomach, for example, certain symptoms may be seen which to some extent are mental in origin, but these are insignificant compared with the symptoms due to the actual organic change in the stomach. On the other hand, in a complete paralysis of the lower limbs in hysteria the dominating causative factors are mental (and readily curable), although physical agencies may have played a certain part. It is obvious that in diseases due to demonstrable physical or chemical changes, treatment must be different from that in diseases dependent chiefly on disordered psychology. Psychotherapy is mainly employed in the latter, although it may also play a minor part in the treatment of mental symptoms appearing in the course of an organic malady.

Functional nervous diseases are often referred to generally as *neuroses*. They include hysteria, neurasthenia, psychasthenia, anxiety neuroses, etc., and the majority of the disturbances which were grouped under the term shell-shock during the European War. Some neuroses are of entirely psychical origin, others are not so, and the former are usually referred to as psychoneuroses. It is for these especially that psychotherapy is the rational treatment, and it is amongst them that it finds its widest scope. It is also largely employed in the treatment of actual insanities, but it is not yet quite determined to what extent it is curative in this domain. We are not at present able to say in the case of many of the insanities whether the disturbance is purely of psychical origin, or whether it mainly results from disordered or poisoned bodily function; hence the difficulty in settling the place of psychotherapeutic measures in the treatment. But it certainly can be said that in dealing with actual insanities psychotherapy may prove a valuable accessory in many cases, and may possibly be helpful as a preventive measure in early and borderland cases of mental disorder. Psychotherapy is widely employed as an adjunct to treatment in ordinary medical practice, and here it finds perhaps its most important and universal application. As already pointed out, every condition of ill-health presents symptoms of psychical origin, and the mental factors exert a definite though perhaps not vital influence on the outcome of the illness, as everyone no doubt will admit.

Every practitioner of medicine realises that therapeutics is not the treatment of disease but the treatment of the patient, and he knows that mental as well as physical agencies have to be employed in each individual case. The practising doctor is thus employing psychotherapy every day in the course of his ordinary avocation, occasionally perhaps unconsciously, frequently purposely. It may be done simply through his ability to inspire the patient with cheerfulness and hope, or he may designedly employ powerful suggestion, knowing his patient and being certain of its due and beneficial effect. Countless complaints that come before the doctor are dissipated, entirely or almost entirely during the consultation, simply because he has been able to assess the insignificance of the symptoms and to convince the anxious inquirer that there is no real ground for fear. Psychotherapy, therefore, is no new thing. But although its use is universal in the healing art and in the hands of every practising physician, it requires for its special application (i.e. to some of the neuroses and insanities) much time and special training and experience. Unfortunately it is extensively practised as a speciality at present by many outside the medical profession who have no real claim to be its exponents. The obvious risk arising from this is that psychotherapy may be employed, whilst clamant need for physical treatment is overlooked; or that, given a purely psychological disorder, psychotherapy may be used along wrong lines. For its correct practice requires long experience and careful observation of suffering humanity both in the domain of general medicine and in nervous and mental disorders.

In its intensive application psychotherapy has greatly extended during recent years. During the European War the number of cases of neuroses was greatly increased both in civil and military populations. Neuroses in war, however, arise just as in peace from combinations of mental and physical shocks or strains; there is no exclusive "war-neurosis," be it noted. In other words, there is no war-neurosis which does not have its counterpart in civil life, although in peace-time the conditions and circumstances appearing as proximate causes may be for the most part different from those in war. But the fact of the increase of such illnesses, in the war years and since, remains, and thus the special application of psychotherapy has come more prominently before the public and the medical profession in general than in former times.

Specialists in psychotherapeutics would seem to differ greatly in their views as to the ways in which psychotherapy may be employed to best advantage. These questions have been extensively discussed and written about in recent years, and it would sometimes appear that every authority advocated some one method to the exclusion of all others. Differences in this regard are probably more apparent than real, however, and each different method no doubt has its proper sphere in treatment. There are four main processes employed, namely, *persuasion*, *suggestion*, *analysis*, and *re-education*. The process best suited differs in different cases, and for each patient requiring intensive psychotherapeutics the method of application has to be selected after careful consideration of the case in all its aspects, and after a correct diagnosis has been arrived at both as regards physical and mental condition. It is common to confuse psychoanalysis with psychotherapy, and to think that the latter and suggestion or auto-suggestion, etc., are synonymous terms; whereas psychoanalysis is only one of the methods of psychotherapy and suggestion another one; both have their place, but neither is by any means universally applicable.

Persuasion. This is a form of treatment which appeals to the reason and the will and enforces its claims on logical grounds. Persuasion is employed every day by every physician in dealing with his patients. As systematically applied in psychotherapy it means a thorough physical examination of the patient, so as to ensure that none of his symptoms are dependent on organic diseases but arise simply from functional disturbances of psychic origin. The origin and causes of the complaint are discussed with and explained to the patient fully. He is reassured as to its curability. The physician then proceeds to demonstrate how the lost and perverted functions may be recovered and rectified, and directs the patient as to the measures which are further necessary for the complete cure of the complaints.

Suggestion. Here the patient is made to accept a proposition in the absence of logical grounds. Ideas are introduced into his mind without encountering the critical judgment of the reason. In certain neuroses symptoms are due to mental factors of which the patient is unaware, but by means of suggestion the mere conviction implanted in the mind may modify the responsible mental factors and thus cause disappearance of the symptom. There are two main methods of suggestion—waking suggestion and hypnotic suggestion. In *waking suggestion* the conviction is simply authoritatively conveyed by word of mouth, or certain physical means may be employed with the deliberate intention of producing a suggestive effect. In *hypnotic suggestion* the patient's mind is put into a quiescent state, and his power of criticism is more or less in abeyance. Repeated use of this may in some instances be harmful, but there are cases where hypnotic suggestion is needed when other methods fail. It is certainly the most powerful means of applying suggestion, for in the hypnotic condition a patient is much more "suggestible" than in the waking state.

Analysis. This is a method which may be termed mental exploration, and which is directed to the investigation of the precise mental causes of a psychoneurosis with a view to their removal. The term "psychoanalysis" is often used as synonymous with "analysis," but strictly speaking psychoanalysis is a special kind of analysis, its methods being based on certain theoretical views held by certain authorities as to the causation of psychoneuroses. Analysis has been likened to, and in point of fact really amounts to, the old method of the confessional where "the sinner poured out his soul into the sympathetic ear of the priest." The factors underlying a disorder are frequently not present on the surface of the mind, so to speak, but are hid in its depths, and the analyst essays to bring them to the light. It can readily be understood that this is a difficult procedure, and a time-consuming one, exhausting alike to the patient and to the doctor. It should not be attempted by all (even by all doctors), but it is *the* method of psychotherapy which unfortunately has been seized on by quacks of various kinds for purposes of money-getting, a regrettable circumstance which tends to bring a valuable method of treatment into undeserved disrepute. In connection with analysis it is necessary to have some understanding as to modern psychological teaching regarding the mental processes. According to this our thoughts are guided in two ways which distinctly differ. The first way is by means of intelligent argument, whereby each element of thought is logically inferred from that immediately previous; much in the same way, it might be said, as the different statements of a mathematical proposition are developed. The other process guiding thought depends upon and is directed by the power of "complexes." Complexes are repressed ideas with strong emotional tone which reside deep in the unconscious mind. Emotional tones can tinge all the mental processes of the individual so that he may regard things not in a cool, reasoning, and logical way but through a perspective largely influenced by emotion. Thus it is that an individual may, for example, take an instinctive dislike to another at first sight, and thus are explained, to some extent at all events, the countless things that an individual may or may not do, not on any logical ground but purely intuitively.

Complexes may be said to consist of different constituents or "instincts" which are present in different proportions in different complexes, e.g. the instincts of self-preservation and self-assertion, the herd-instinct (common to all creatures and also man), the sex instinct, etc. Consciousness is now regarded as consisting of three different layers. There is first of all the active consciousness which is concerned with the thoughts of the moment. Then there is what is termed the liminal consciousness containing thoughts not uppermost in the mind, but which can be called up by a slight effort of memory. Then there is again a deeper stratum of the subconsciousness termed the sub-liminal consciousness, and here reside thoughts which do not rise into active consciousness at all and can only be brought into it by some special way and that often with difficulty. Thoughts in this level of the subconscious are usually painful ones, and they are kept there by an active process of forgetting which is termed "repression." Repression may, however, at times be in abeyance, and a painful impression may force itself, as it were, to the surface. An example of this occurs in dreams. From childhood onwards a nucleus of complexes forms in the sub-liminal consciousness, and it consists of the sum total of primary impulses or instincts which have been repressed as a result of education and environment.

These complexes may in certain people interfere one with another, and so an individual may be swayed in one direction or other accordingly as one or other complex has the stronger "pull," so to speak. In this way there arise in the subconscious mind what are termed "conflicts." For example, a soldier who is in the front line, impelled by the emotion of fear, may wish to escape. This complex, however, is in conflict with that of the "social ideal" (involving the "herd-instinct" of discipline, pride of race, etc.), which impels him to stick to it. Normally the herd-instinct should be dominant, but it may not be. There is thus in any case a conflict, which may be solved in one way or another. If not, the two impelling complexes may be equally balanced, and neither of them may be powerful enough to solve this conflict between self and duty, and so a mental dilemma arises. If he is unable to solve this he may develop a neurosis which persists until his conflict is dissipated. As long as it is undecided or unrealised he suffers from this psychoneurosis; the conflict may be entirely subconscious or it may be an active struggle in the conscious mind. Conflicts are many and various, and the above is only a single instance. It is in cases where the neuroses depend on conflicts, especially subconscious ones, that analysis finds its greatest usefulness, and in such cases it may be said to be absolutely essential. It often is combined with "suggestion" and "persuasion," and also with physical treatment, and it may be carried out either in the waking or the hypnotic state, though the latter is seldom necessary. It deals with the unconscious tendencies which lie at the root of many neurotic symptoms. It comprehends an investigation of the patient's past emotional history, and a study of his dreams while asleep; in this way gaining clues as to subconscious conflicts in the way of fears, anxieties, and unfulfilled desires. It inquires what an individual tends to think of when his thoughts wander off during the day (day dreams). Its methods are various and are applied differently in different hands, but by its use we may discover that some special anxieties or troubles tend to crop up which the patient constantly tries to repress, and we may thus unearth some conflict which may form the basis of a whole train of neurotic symptoms.

Re-education. This is the process of training a disordered function to return to its normal method of activity. It cannot be said to be strictly homologous with the other methods of psychotherapy already described, but is to be looked on more as an adjunct and as a sequence to their employment. It completes the process of cure. It runs along two lines, one of which comprises the reeducative exercises necessary to train, e.g. an unsteady and previously paralysed limb into normal and precise movement. The other line involves re-education, moral, social, occupational, etc., directed to training the neurotic to resume an efficient existence. — BIBLIOGRAPHY: G. F. Stout, *Manual of Psychology*; Susan S. Brierley, *Introduction to Psychology*; James Harvey Robinson, *The Mind in the Making*; Ernest Jones, *Psycho-analysis*; S. Freud, *Psychopathology of Everyday Life* (translated by A. A. Brill); *On Dreams*.

PTARMIGAN (tȧr'-). A game-bird of the pheasant family (Phasianidæ), distinguished from the true grouse (q.v.) by having the toes as well as the tarsi feathered. The common ptarmigan (called also *white grouse*) is the *Lagōpus mutus*. The male is about 15 inches long, the female about an inch less. In summer the predominant colours of its plumage are speckled black, brown, or grey, but in winter the male becomes nearly pure white, and the female entirely so. In Britain it is to be met with only on the summits of some of the highest Scottish hills, chiefly amid the Grampians, in the Hebrides and Orkneys, and sometimes but rarely in the lofty hills of Cumberland and Wales. The willow-ptarmigan or willow-grouse (*L. albus*) occurs in great abundance in the arctic regions of America and in Norway, whence great numbers are brought to the London market.

PTERICHTHYS (te-rik'this). A fossil genus of fishes occurring in the Old Red Sandstone. The head and forepart of the body were protected by a buckler of large ganoid plates fitting closely to each other. The caudal portion was free, and seems to have been covered with small, round enamelled scales. Pterichthys was peculiarly characterised by the form of its two pectoral fins, which were long and narrow, something like wings (whence the name —"wing-fish"), covered by finely tuberculated bony plates. Their spine-like form suggests that they were used for defence as well as progression.

PTERIDOPHYTA, or VASCULAR CRYPTOGAMS. One of the primary subdivisions of the Higher Plants or Cormophytes, including ferns proper (Filicales), club-mosses (Lycopodiales), horse-tails (Equisetales), and the less familiar Psilotales and Sphenophyllales, the last-named group comprising only extinct forms. They are higher in the scale than Bryophytes, the dominant generation being a sporophyte (q.v.) with well-developed vascular tissue. Although heterospory occurs in some cases, genuine seeds are never formed. The living plants are mostly herbaceous, and even when large show no appreciable secondary thickening (q.v.), although many of the extinct types were in these respects little inferior to woody seed-plants.

PTERIDOSPERMS. An important group of fossil plants, mostly of Carboniferous age, formerly regarded as ferns, but now known to have been reproduced by true seeds and to be linked with higher groups.

PTEROCARPUS. A genus of leguminous plants, species of which yield kino, dragon's-blood, red sandal-wood, etc.

PTEROCERAS (ter-o'se-ras). A genus of molluscs inhabiting the Indian Ocean; the scorpion-shells. The head of the animal is furnished with a proboscis and two short tentacles. The shell is oblong, the spire short, the mouth produced into claw-like spines, and the operculum horny. *P. scorpio* is known by the name of the *devil's-claw*. At the least ten recent and twenty-seven fossil species of this genus are known.

PTERODAC'TYL. Any member of the extinct order of flying lizards found fossilised in mesozoic rocks from the Lower Liassic to the Upper Cretaceous in England, Europe, and N. America. Long-tailed or tailless, large-headed, wide-mouthed, toothed or toothless, with flexible necks, they had smooth bat-like membranes extended by the enormously elon-

Flying Lizard (Pterodactyl)

gated "little finger" of the fore-limbs, the other fingers being short claws. They were more or less bird-like, with hollow bones, varying from the size of a sparrow to a 25-ft. wing-spread.

PTERODAC'TYLUS ("winged-finger"). A genus of extinct flying reptiles of the ord. Pterosauria (q.v.), found in Jurassic strata, for instance in the Kimmeridge clay and Stonesfield slate of England, and especially in the Upper Jurassic lithographic stone of Bavaria and Württemberg. The pterodactyls had a moderately long neck and a large head; the jaws were armed with equal and pointed teeth. A number of species have been discovered, most of them small or of moderate size, but one must have had an expanse of wing comparable with that of a large eagle. The great Cretaceous "pterodactyls" are now referred to Ornithocheirus.

PTEROP'IDÆ. A family of Chiroptera, called fox-bats from

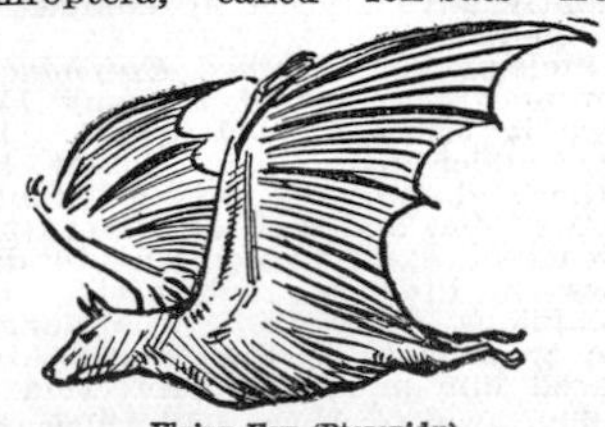

Flying Fox (Pteropidæ)

their long and pointed fox-like head. The type-genus is Pteropus.

PTEROP'ODA, or SEA BUTTERFLIES. A group of sea-snails, comprehending those which have a wing-shaped fin on each side of the head and neck, being thus a sort of "winged snails." Some are shell-less, while others possess elegant transparent shells composed of calcium carbonate. They are all of small size, are found floating on the surface of the ocean in all parts of the world, and in the Arctic and Antarctic regions furnish much of the food of the whale.

PTEROSAU'RIA. An extinct order of flying reptiles of Jurassic and Cretaceous age, represented chiefly by the Pterodactyls (q.v.). Some pterosaurs possessed long tails ending in an expansion that served as a rudder. The bones are set with hollows, as in the birds. The jaws in most genera contain teeth in sockets. The membranous wings were supported by the elongation of one finger only; three other fingers occur, bearing claws. The hind-foot has four or five toes with claws. Ornithocheirus had a wing-span of about 20 feet.

PTEROSTYLIS. A genus of Australasian orchids, with a very curious pollination mechanism. The labellum is irritable, and the rest of the perianth forms a hood at the back of the flower. When an insect lands on the lip, it springs up and imprisons the visitor, which can escape only by squeezing past the stigma and anther. After about half an hour the lip bends down again, and is ready for the next visitor. — Cf. Darwin, *Fertilisation of Orchids.*

PTERYGO'TUS. A fossil crustacean attaining a length of 6 feet, occurring chiefly in the passage-beds between the Silurian and Devonian systems. It has a long scorpion like form, composed in the main of a cephalo-thorax, an abdominal portion of several segments, and a somewhat oval telson or tail-plate. *See* MEROSTOMATA.

PTHAH, or PHTHA. An ancient Egyptian divinity, the creator of all things and source of life, and as such father and sovereign of the gods. He was worshipped chiefly at Memphis under the figure of a mummy-shaped male, and also as a pygmy god.

PTOLEMAIC SYSTEM. In astronomy, that maintained by Claudius Ptolemy, the astronomer, who supposed the earth to be fixed in the centre of the universe, and that the sun, planets, and stars revolved around it. This long-received theory was rejected for the Copernican system. *See* ASTRONOMY.

PTOL'EMY (*Ptolemaios*). The name of a line of Græco-Egyptian kings, who succeeded, on the division of the empire of Alexander the Great, to the portion of his dominions of which Egypt was the head. They were also distinguished by the surname Lagidæ, from Ptolemæus Lagus, the founder of the dynasty.

Ptolemy I. (born in 367 B.C., died in 283), called *Soter*, the Saviour, was by birth a Macedonian. His mother was Arsinoë, the mistress of Philip, and his father is commonly reputed to have been Lagus, a Macedonian of humble birth. Ptolemy was one of the intimate friends of Alexander, attended the king on his expedition to Asia, was admitted into the bodyguard, and in 329 B.C. commanded one of the chief divisions of the army. On the death of Alexander he attached himself to the party of Perdiccas, and secured for himself the government of Egypt. He married Eurydice, daughter of Antipater, and in 320 B.C. he seized the satrapy of Phœnicia and Cœle-Syria. In 308 he invaded Greece, and proclaimed himself as a liberator; but he made little progress, and having garrisoned Corinth and Sicyon, which he lost some years later, he returned to Egypt. Antigonus resolved to wrest Cyprus from Ptolemy (307 B.C.), and in a sea-fight at Salamis the Egyptians were defeated, and Cyprus fell into the hands of the victor, who assumed the title of king. Antigonus now advanced against Egypt through Syria with a powerful army, supported by a fleet; but he was ultimately compelled to retire, while a few years later Cyprus was recovered and became a permanent dependency of Egypt. He was a great patron of art, learning, and literature, and founded the celebrated Alexandrian Library.

Ptolemy II. (*Philadelphus*), born 309 B.C., died in 246. He succeeded his father, and reigned in almost complete peace. His chief care as ruler was directed to the internal administration of his kingdom. He spared no pains to fill the library of Alexandria with all the treasures of ancient literature, and among the architectural works erected during this reign were the lighthouse on the Island of Pharos, the Alexandrian Museum, and the royal burying-place. He founded numerous cities and colonies, and during his reign the dominion of Egypt extended into Ethiopia, Arabia, and Libya, and embraced the provinces of Phœnicia and Cœle-Syria, besides tracts in Asia Minor and some of the islands of the Mediterranean.

Ptolemy II.

Ptolemy III. (surnamed *Euergĕtes*, "benefactor"), born 281 B.C., died in 221. He was early engaged in an important war against Syria, after invading which he advanced without opposition to Antioch, then turned eastward, subduing Mesopotamia, Babylonia, etc. The fleets of Ptolemy had at the same time subdued the coasts of Asia Minor, and carried his arms to the Hellespont and to the coast of Thrace. Ptolemy took some part in the affairs of Greece against the rulers of Macedonia, and maintained friendly relations with Rome. Like his predecessors, he was the patron of scholars, and his court was the resort of the most distinguished men of his day.

Ptolemy IV. (surnamed *Philopator*), succeeded in 221 B.C., died in 204. His Syrian possessions having been gradually wrested from him by Antiochus the Great, Ptolemy put himself at the head of a large army and completely defeated Antiochus at Raphia in 217 B.C. He subsequently gave himself up completely to debauchery.

Ptolemy V. (surnamed *Epiphănes*), son and successor of Ptolemy IV., born in 209 B.C., died in 181. He was under five years old at his father's death, and this led Philip of Macedon and Antiochus III. (the Great) of Syria to combine to dispossess Ptolemy and divide his dominions. To avert this danger the guardians of the young king placed him under the protection of Rome, which thus had first an occasion for interfering in the affairs of Egypt.

Ptolemy VI. (surnamed *Philomētor*), born in 186 B.C., died in 145. His reign was much disturbed by the rivalry of a brother, and being expelled from Alexandria, he repaired to Rome (164 B.C.), by whose intervention he was replaced. During the reigns of the succeeding Ptolemies the influence of the Romans in Egypt gradually increased, with a corresponding decrease in the independence of the native sovereigns. The personal character of the Ptolemies also degenerated, a fact to be probably connected with the common practice in the family for brothers to marry sisters.

Ptolemy XI. (*Aulētēs*, "flute-player") was driven from his kingdom by his subjects, who were ground down by taxation; but he was restored by the Romans (to whom he gave great sums of money), and died in 51 B.C.

Ptolemy XII. (*Aulētēs*), son of the preceding, reigned jointly with his sister Cleopatra till 48 B.C., when Cleopatra was expelled, and raising an army in Syria, invaded Egypt. On the arrival of Cæsar, Cleopatra by her charms acquired an ascendancy over him. Ptolemy put himself at the head of the insurgents, was defeated by Cæsar, and drowned in attempting to make his escape (48 or 47 B.C.).

Ptolemy XIII. (*Aulētēs*), the youngest son of Ptolemy XI., was declared king by Cæsar in conjunction with his sister Cleopatra in 47 B.C. He was married to his sister, but, being only a boy, possessed no more than the name of husband or king. Cleopatra caused him to be put to death, and the line of the Ptolemies ended when Cleopatra perished by her own hands after Octavius defeated Antony

Ptolemy XIII.

at Actium, and Egypt became a Roman province (30 B.C.).

BIBLIOGRAPHY: Sir J. P. Mahaffy, *The Empire of the Ptolemies, Egypt under the Ptolemies*; Bouché-Leclercq *Histoire des Lagides*.

PTOLEMY, Claudius Ptolemæus. Greek astronomer and geographer of the second century after Christ. He appears to have resided in Alexandria, where he made astronomical observations in 139, and he was alive in 161. Ptolemy's great astronomical work is entitled *Megalē Syntaxis tēs Astronomias*, and is more commonly known by the Arabic title *Almagest*. Equally important is his *Geography*, in eight books, largely based upon the lost works of Marinus of Tyre, and for centuries an authoritative treatise. See PTOLEMAIC SYSTEM; ASTRONOMY.

PTOMAINES (tō'ma-ins). Alkaloid-like substances, most of them poisonous, found in decaying animal matter. Some examples are cadaverine, putrescine, choline, and neurine. *Cadaverine*, $NH_2(CH_2)_5NH_2$, is a colourless syrupy liquid of pronounced spermaceti odour, which, on giving up ammonia, yields *piperidine*. Many ptomaines occur in the vegetable kingdom. *Muscarine*, $C_5H_{15}NO_3$, an excessively poisonous base, is present in toadstool (*Agaricus muscarius*). Ptomaines may occur in preserved foodstuffs, and cause *ptomaine poisoning* (*see* TOXICOLOGY).

PTOSIS. A drooping of the eyelid owing to paralysis of the muscle that lifts it. It is sometimes congenital, and it may be produced by various disorders of the brain.

PTYALISM, or **SALIVATION.** Excessive secretion of saliva, and often the result of excessive doses of certain drugs, more especially mercury, the iodides, and pilocarpine. It is also seen in chronic disease of the pancreas, and may occur with the morning sickness of pregnancy. The treatment consists in the removal of the cause, when possible, and the administration of belladonna, accompanied by the use of astringent mouth-washes.

PU'BERTY. The period in both male and female marked by the functional development of the generative system. In males it usually takes place between the ages of thirteen and sixteen; in females somewhat earlier; and, as a rule, in very warm climates puberty is reached somewhat sooner than elsewhere. In males puberty is marked externally by the deepening of the voice, the first appearance of the beard, greater firmness, fullness of body, etc.; in females, by the enlargement of the breasts and by the general rounding out of the frame, and most unequivocally of all by the commencement of menstruation.

PUBLICANS, or **PUBLICANI** (from *publicus*, belonging to the State). The farmers of the taxes levied in the territories of ancient Rome. The revenues derived from the tribute of foreign countries were sold or let for a period by the censors in Rome to the highest bidder. The sale was generally made for a *lustrum* or period of five years. The conditions of the sale were as a rule determined by law, but were sometimes modified on particular occasions. The farmers of the revenue belonged to the wealthier classes, and were from their functions unpopular. Far more unpopular were the subordinates whom they employed to collect the taxes for them. In Palestine, from the strong spirit of nationality among the Jews, many of whom denied the lawfulness of paying tribute, these were specially obnoxious as the agents of the foreign rulers. To this detested class, and not to the *publicani* proper, the "publicans" of the New Testament belonged generally.

PUBLIC AUTHORITIES PROTECTION ACT. A statute passed in

1893, limiting to six months the time within which legal proceedings may be instituted by a private party against any person or authority in respect of an official act, neglect, or default in the execution of an Act of Parliament or public duty or authority.

PUBLIC HEALTH. Term used for the health of the community as a whole. The various councils employ medical men, sanitary inspectors, and others, and the Ministry of Health has a large staff. Their duties are detailed in the following article. There is in London an Institute of Public Health at 37 Russell Square, W.C.1., which carries on educational work including research.

PUBLIC HEALTH ACTS. Certain British Acts of Parliament regulating sanitary matters. The sanitary administration of England (with the exception of London) is mainly regulated by the provisions of the Public Health Acts of 1875 and subsequent years. The superintending and controlling authority was formerly the Local Government Board, but is now the Ministry of Health established in 1919. The local sanitary authorities are the county councils, district councils, etc. The local authority, however constituted, is armed with very extensive powers. To aid in the exercise of these it must appoint a medical officer, an inspector of nuisances, and in urban districts a surveyor. As regards the health of a district, the local authority can ensure a due supply of water, make and maintain sewers and utilise sewage, provide for the cleansing of streets, remove nuisances of every kind, including those which arise from offensive trades, prevent overcrowding in common lodging and other houses, and enforce a supply of proper privy accommodation. It can close dwellings unfit for human habitation, and if the owner neglects to put them in a proper state, can do so at his expense. It can compel the cleansing of houses in which there is infectious disease, and establish temporary hospitals for sufferers from it. For these and many other purposes connected with the health of the community it can levy rates and raise loans. The Public Health (London) Act was passed in 1891. The Act of 1875 has been supplemented by others dealing with water-supply, the removal of nuisances, the pollution of rivers, vapours from alkali works, public burial-grounds, compulsory vaccination, the adulteration of food and drugs, with the appointment of public analysts, and the notification of infectious diseases.

For special classes of the community there are the laws relating to factories and workshops; the measures regulating labour in mines, bakehouses, etc.; the Children Acts, 1908 to 1921; and measures, known as the Housing Acts, 1890 to 1920, dealing with the housing of the working-classes. For Scotland the chief sanitary enactment is the Public Health (Scotland) Act of 1897. The supreme controlling authority is now the Scottish Board of Health, the successor of the Local Government Board for Scotland; and the local sanitary authorities are town and county councils, district committees, and burgh commissioners. For Ireland the chief sanitary enactment was the Public Health (Ireland) Act of 1878, framed on the lines of the English Act of 1875. Under that Act the controlling authority was the Irish Local Government Board, with local sanitary authorities, urban and rural, under it.

PUBLIC PROSECUTOR. An official charged with the prosecution of all criminal offences. In England, unless in a few exceptional cases, any private person may institute a criminal prosecution. A salaried director of public prosecutions, with very limited powers, was appointed in 1879, but in 1884 his title and his functions were transferred to the Solicitor to the Treasury, who now prosecutes on behalf of the State in criminal cases of importance or difficulty, or when special circumstances appear to him to justify the step, and who may intervene in any criminal proceedings instituted by the local police or by a private prosecutor. In Scotland there are practically no private prosecutions for criminal offences. The Lord-Advocate is ex officio public prosecutor, and the whole expense of public prosecution is borne by the public, criminal prosecutions being initiated by the procurators-fiscal, who are officials specially appointed for this purpose. The Public prosecutor has an office at 1 Richmond Terrace, Whitehall, London, S.W. (*See* PROCURATOR-FISCAL.) In Ireland a system of Crown solicitors and Crown agents has very largely superseded prosecutions by private persons.

PUBLIC SCHOOL. A grammar-school founded or endowed for the use or benefit of the public, and carried on under some kind of public management or control; contrasted with a "private school," which is carried on at the risk and for the profit of its master or proprietors. Eton, founded (1440) by Henry VI., is the most famous among English schools. Keate was a celebrated headmaster; while distinguished pupils include Canning and Chatham, Fox and Fielding, Porson and Pusey, Kinglake and Shelley. Harrow, the chief rival of Eton, was founded (1571) by a farmer. It is famous for the excellence of its music; for its century-old annual cricket match against Eton; and for having educated, amongst others, Byron, Cardinal Manning, and Lord Palmerston. Rugby, founded (1567) by a grocer, is indissolubly connected with its great "head," Dr. Arnold, and further gives its name to one of the two principal varieties of football. Shrewsbury, a foundation (1551) of Edward VI., is fortunate in the long rule of two distinguished "heads"—Samuel Butler (1798-1836) and his successor B. H. Kennedy. Sir Philip Sidney was a "Salopian"—also Judge Jeffreys; Charles Darwin and H. A. J. Munro were later pupils. Westminster, an Elizabethan foundation (1560), had a famous "head" in Dr. Busby, a most vigorous wielder of the rod. Its roll is very rich in poets, Ben Jonson, Cowley, Cowper, Dryden, Southey, and George Herbert being among its pupils. Winchester College, established (1369-93) as New College by William of Wykeham, had the saintly Ken, Sidney Smith, and Arnold of Rugby as pupils. Charterhouse, founded (1611) on the site of a London monastery, was transferred to Godalming in 1872; Thackeray, a pupil, has made it famous with "Colonel Newcome."

Among other public schools may be mentioned: Oundle School, founded by Sir William Laxton (died 1556), rebuilt in 1883, and since greatly enlarged under the headmastership of F. W. Sanderson (died 1922); Blundell's School, Tiverton, a famous West of England school, founded in 1604 by a successful draper of the town; Clifton College, Bristol, a leading "army" school; Bedford Grammar School; King Edward's School, Birmingham; Cheltenham College; Dulwich College; Haileybury; Lancing College; The Leys School, Cambridge; Marlborough College; Malvern College; Wellington College; with such schools as those of Repton, Rossall, Sherborne, Ronbridge, and Uppingham, all establishments of high standing. Mill Hill School, near London, is largely resorted to by Nonconformists; Stonyhurst, Lancashire, England's great Roman Catholic school, was originally established (1592) at St. Omer, Flanders.

Scottish educational houses taking rank with English public schools are: in Edinburgh, the Edinburgh Academy, in the foundation (1824) of which Sir Walter Scott took an active interest, and at which R. L. Stevenson was a pupil; Merchiston Castle (1833), housed in the birthplace of Napier the mathematician; and Fettes College. Loretto School, Musselburgh, was ruled on wholesome though unusual—perhaps eccentric—lines by the late Dr. Almond; while Trinity College, Glenalmond, Perthshire, had W. E. Gladstone as a leading founder.

The beneficial effect of a public-school education has been brought in question by would-be reformers, upon various grounds. The curriculum has been criticised as being too classical and lacking practical utility for modern life; and it is sometimes urged that a certain supercilious self-satisfaction is to be seen in the English public schoolboy. These criticisms seem to rest upon foundations anything but sure. General experience goes to show that English public-school life, with traditions often stretching back for centuries, produces a peculiar sense, at once keen and permanent, of brotherhood, good feeling, generosity, and "sportsmanship," the lack of which would be an incalculable loss to the race.—BIBLIOGRAPHY: C. E. Pascoe, *Everyday Life in our Public Schools*; J. G. C. Minchin, *Our Public Schools*; *Public Schools from Within*; and *The Public School Year Book* (published annually).

PUBLIC TRUSTEE. An English public official whose business it is to act when required (1) in the administration of small estates not exceeding in value £1000; (2) as a custodian, ordinary or judicial trustee; or (3) as administrator of the property of a convict. He is a corporation sole, and may act alone or in conjunction with others, but he may not act (unless in special circumstances) in any trust where there is a business to be carried on, nor in an insolvent estate, nor in a trust for religious or charitable purposes. The office was instituted by the Official Trustee Act, 1906, and came into being on 1st Jan., 1908. On account of the security of administration afforded by it, it has steadily grown in favour. In 1921 the number of trusts controlled from the office of the public trustee approximated 15,000. The value of the trusts accepted by the Public Trustee up to 31st March, 1932, was £328,053,641. The fees charged conform to a graduated scale, and are not heavy. The head offices of the trustee are at Sardinia House, Kingsway, London, W.C.2., and there is also a branch office at Arkwright House, Parsonage Gardens, Manchester.

PUBLIC WORKS LOAN BOARD. A Government department created in 1817 for the purpose of advancing money to Municipal Authorities for Public Works. The staff includes a chairman and deputy-chairman (both unpaid), a paid secretary, and a legal assistant secretary. During the 103 years of its existence up to 1920 the total sum advanced amounted to only £149,436,402; during the financial year 1931-2 loans to the amount of £19,981,867 were advanced, £10,471,217 being for purposes of the Housing Acts. Interest is paid on moneys lent. In the period 1928-9 this amounted to £5, 0*s.* 2*d.* per cent; in 1929-30, £5, 1*s.* 0*d.* per cent; in 1930-1, £4, 17*s.* 11*d.* per cent; and in 1931-2, £4, 15*s.* 2*d.* Loans under the Housing Acts are secured either on local rates or on property, but mainly on the former. For working-class dwelling-houses £29,996,054 has been advanced, £994,893 going to Scotland, and the rest to England.

PUBLILIUS SYRUS (often called **Publius** in error). Latin writer; so called because a native of Syria. He was carried as a slave to Rome about the middle of the first century B.C. His master gave him a good education, and afterwards set him free. He excelled in writing *mimi*, or farces, which were interspersed with moral sentences, and a collection of them was used by the Romans as a school-book. A number of apophthegms, not all of them composed by him, have been published as *Publili Syri Sententiæ*. Several of them are famous, such as *Judex damnatur ubi nocens absolvitur* (the judge is condemned when the guilty is acquitted), *O vitam misero longam, felici brevem!* (O Life, long for the miserable, short for the happy), and the perpetually misquoted *Stultum facit Fortuna, quem vult perdere* (Whom Fortune wishes to destroy, she makes a fool).

PUBLISHING. Business of preparing books for the public. The early publishers were also booksellers, and in the eighteenth century books were published by a number of booksellers jointly, each taking a certain number. In the nineteenth century the two businesses became separate. Edinburgh became a great publishing centre, but after a time the pre-eminence, as far as Great Britain was concerned, passed to London. Leipzig is another city famous as a publishing centre, and books are published in most of the university towns.

Some publishers confine themselves to a particular branch of literature, e.g. medical books, while others are general publishers. With the aid of readers their business is to decide which of the manuscripts submitted shall be published by them. They must then arrange for the printing of the books chosen, for their distribution to the trade, and for the necessary publicity.

Publishing as a Career. The staff whose duty it is to select and prepare manuscripts for the press is usually recruited from the universities; the production departments are usually reached after a period of apprenticeship.

The necessary qualifications are a wide general knowledge and some literary and artistic taste, with potentialities for developing quickly a full knowledge of the technicalities of the trade and a sound judgment on the commerical value of contemporary literature. On the whole, the sales side offers the most promising monetary rewards.

PUCCINI, Giacomo. Italian composer, born 3rd Dec., 1858, at Lucca; he studied at Milan, and achieved his first success with the opera *Manon Lescaut* (1893), and *La Bohème* (1896) brought him fame. Of his other operas the two best known are *La Tosca* (1900) and *Madame Butterfly* (1904). In 1911 he came to London to superintend the production of his *Girl of the Golden West*. His last opera, *Turandot*, was produced in 1926 at Milan. He died 29th Nov., 1924.

PUCCINIA. A very large and important genus of parasitic Fungi, family Uredineæ. About half a dozen species cause the destructive

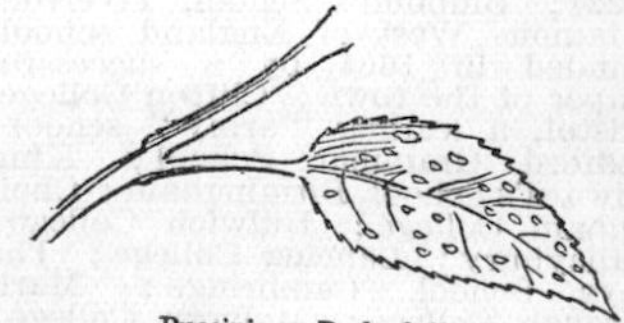

Puccinia on Berberis Leaf

disease of cereals known as "rust," the losses from which amount to many millions of pounds sterling every year; others destroy or seriously damage various cultivated plants, such as gooseberry, plum, asparagus, mint, celery, hollyhock, carnation, etc. Many are heterœcious, e.g. *P. graminis*, the black rust of wheat, which passes a part of its life-history on the common barberry (*Berberis vulgaris*). As regards the cereal rusts at any rate, the ordinary remedial measures (e.g. spraying) are of no avail; the best line of defence appears to be the production by breeding of rust-resisting varieties which shall also be satisfactory in other respects (yield, quality, etc.), and promising advances have already been made in this direction.

PUCK (O.Sw. *puke*, Icel. *puki*, an evil demon, a word equivalent to Ir. *puca*, W. *pwca*, an imp). A mischievous fairy elf, the "merry wanderer of the night," who is introduced into Shakespeare's *Midsummer Night's Dream*, and who was also known by the names of *Robin Goodfellow* and *Friar Rush*. He was the chief of the domestic fairies, and many stories are told of his nocturnal exploits.

PUDDING - STONE, or **PLUM-PUDDING STONE.** A term now considered synonymous with conglomerate, but originally applied to a mass of flint pebbles cemented by a siliceous paste. When select specimens are cut and polished, they resemble a section of a plum-pudding, and are used for ornamental purposes.

PUD'SEY. A municipal borough in the West Riding of Yorkshire, 4 miles from Bradford; served by the London & North Eastern Railway. Woollen and worsted goods and boots and shoes are manufactured. Pop. (1931), 14,762.

PUDUKKOTAI. A native state of India, the third in importance of the states in political relationship with Madras Presidency. It is entirely inland, and consists mainly of an undulating plain of almost barren land, studded with hills which are crowned with ancient forts and temples. Four small rivers drain the country from west to east. The only town in the state is Pudukkotai, the capital, which is 33 miles by road south-east of Trichinopoli, and contains the palace of the rāja, an old palace, hospital, jail, college, and Residency. State area, 1179 sq. miles; pop. 426,813; pop. (town), 26,101 (mainly Hindus).

PUEB'LA. An inland state of Mexico, drained by the Salado, Atoyac, and other streams. Sugar, cotton, coffee, and rice are produced in the river valleys. Puebla is the capital. Area, 12,992 sq. miles; pop. (1930), 1,148,286.

PUEBLA. The third city of Mexico, capital of the state of Puebla, on the Atoyac River at an altitude of 7000 feet. It has a cathedral and a large number of religious edifices, many of them highly decorated. There are also several colleges, a museum, and a theatre. It is one of the chief seats of Mexican manufacturing industry, and its chief products are cotton and woollen goods, leather, glass, earthenware, and soap. Puebla was built by the Spaniards in 1533-4. Pop. (1930), 111,791.

PUEBLO INDIANS. Semi-civilised Indians of the Western United States in New Mexico and Arizona, some 9000 in number, living in villages in communal houses (a number of families together), and possessed of considerable skill in agriculture and the simpler kinds of

Pueblo Indian

manufacture. Their village communities are self-governed, and they are only nominally citizens of the United States. Their cultural equipment was derived from the ancient civilisation of Mexico.

PUENTE-JENIL (pu-en'tā-*he*-nēl'). A town of Spain, province of Cordova, on the Jenil. Pop. 14,200.

PUER'PERAL FEVER. An acute septic fever occurring in women after child-birth, and caused by infection of some part of the genital tract. The infection may arise from organisms in the genital canal before confinement — auto - infection; but more commonly it is due to organisms brought in from without by the hands or instruments of the attendant—conveyed infection. Severe bruising or tearing of the parts during labour, hæmorrhage, retained blood-clot or placental tissue, all favour its occurrence. The first symptoms usually appear between the third and fifth day of the puerperium, and of these the most constant is fever. The earlier its appearance the more serious the condition, while it may set in suddenly with a rigor or come on gradually. Along with fever there are increased pulse-rate, loss of appetite, abdominal pain, and general *malaise.* In some severe cases, however, there is at first a deceptive feeling of well-being on the part of the patient. Later septic rashes occur, and there are signs of a general septic infection with possible involvement of the lungs, causing septic pneumonia; of the heart, causing endocarditis and pericarditis; of the brain, causing mental aberration and delirium, and finally leading to meningitis. The preventibility of puerperal sepsis is now recognised by the medical profession, and the greatest care should be taken to ensure cleanliness of the hands and instruments and of those parts of the patient that are involved. Supervision of nurses and midwives as far as possible is aimed at, and though there has been improvement of late years, yet the mortality from puerperal sepsis is still relatively high, and much can still be done in the future to lower it.

PUERPERAL MANIA. A form of insanity which develops during pregnancy and after child-birth. Suicidal and homicidal tendencies are present, and such cases are best treated in an institution with suitable observation and care of the patient. When it occurs after child-birth, it may arise in the course of puerperal sepsis, while most of the patients in whom it develops are suffering from severe exhaustion.

PUER'TO CABELLO (-kȧ-bel'yō). A seaport of Venezuela, in the state of Carabobo. The harbour is good and provided with warehouses. Its principal exports, mainly to the United States and Germany, are coffee and cocoa. Pop. 20,000.

PUERTO MONTT. A seaport-town of Chile, capital of the province of Llanquihue; served by railway to Valdivia. There is a good harbour. Wheat, timber, and leather are exported. Pop. 16,150.

PU'FENDORF, or **PUF'FENDORF, Samuel, Baron von.** German jurist, born in 1632, died in 1694. He studied theology and law at Leipzig and Jena, and in 1660 published his *Elementa Jurisprudentiæ Universalis.* In 1661 he became professor of the law of nature and of nations at Heidelberg. In 1670 he went to Sweden, became professor of natural law in the University of Lund, and brought out his chief work, *De Jure Naturæ et Gentium,* and in 1675 an abstract of it, *De Officio Hominis et Civis.* In 1677 Pufendorf went to Stockholm as historiographer-royal, and in 1686 he received a summons to Berlin from Frederick William, Elector of Brandenburg. In 1694 he was created a baron by the King of Sweden, and in the same year he died at Berlin.

PUFF-ADDER (*Bitis arietans*). A serpent found in South and Central Africa and South Arabia. Its popular name is derived from its power of puffing out the upper part of the neck when irritated or alarmed. It

Puff-Adder

is very thick, attains a length of 4 or 5 feet, and is extremely venomous. The Bushmen poison their arrows with its venom.

PUFFIN. The name for the marine diving birds of the genus Fratercŭla. The common puffin (*F. arctica*) is a native of the arctic and northern temperate parts of the Atlantic, and is often met with on the rocky

Puffin (*Fratercŭla arctica*)

cliffs of Great Britain and Ireland. It is about a foot in length, and from the singular shape and enormous size of its bill, which is striped with orange upon bluish-grey, is often called the sea-parrot or the coulter-neb. The plumage is glossy black, with the exception of the cheeks and undersurfaces, which are white. It breeds upon rocks and in the rabbit-warrens near the sea, and lays one egg, which is white. It lives on fish, crustacea, and insects, and is a gregarious and migratory bird. It is replaced in the Pacific by a related species. *F. corniculata.*

PUG DOG. Breed of toy dog. Of the mastiff group, suggesting a miniature bulldog, it was introduced from Holland and much esteemed throughout the eighteenth century. Victorian England produced the modern strains.

PUGET SOUND (pū′jet). An inlet on the north-west coast of the state of Washington, United States, forming the south-west continuation of Juan de Fuca Strait, with which it is connected by Admiralty Inlet. On its shores are Seattle and Tacoma.

PUGIN (pū′jin), **Augustus Welby Northmore.** Architect, born in 1812, died in 1852. He was the son of Augustus Pugin (1762-1832), from whom he imbibed a love of Gothic architecture, to promote the revival of which became early the object of his life. In 1834 he became a Roman Catholic, and he designed a large number of ecclesiastical buildings for that communion, among them a church at Ramsgate, which was built at his own expense. He assisted Sir Charles Barry in the designs for the new Houses of Parliament, especially in those for their interior fittings and decorations. *The Contrasts, or a Parallel between the Architecture of the 15th and 19th Centuries* (1836); *The True Principles of Pointed or Christian Architecture* (1841); and *The Glossary of Ecclesiastical Ornament and Costume* (1844), are among his principal works.

PUG-MILL. A machine for mixing and tempering clay. It consists of a hollow iron cylinder, generally set upright, with a revolving shaft in the line of its axis, carrying a number of knives projecting from it at right angles, and arranged in a spiral manner. The clay is thrown in at the top of the cylinder, and by the revolution of the shaft is brought within the action of the knives, by which it is cut and kneaded in its downward progress, and finally forced out through a hole in the bottom of the cylinder.

PULBOROUGH. Parish and market town of Sussex. It is on the Arundel road, 46½ miles from London, near the confluence of the rivers Arun and Western Rother. Originally a Roman fortress on the road from Regnum to Londinium, it still bears traces of Roman occupation. Pop. (1931), 2065.

PULCI (pu̱l′chē), **Luigi.** Italian poet, born in 1431; died in 1487. He lived in intimacy with Lorenzo de' Medici and his literary circle. His poem *Il Morgante Maggiore,* in which he relates the adventures and exploits of Rinaldo and the giant Morgante, is on the whole a burlesque on the romantic epics of his predecessors.

PULHAM. A village of Norfolk, England, with an air-station. 17 miles from Beccles.

PULLEY. A simple wheel or disc mounted concentric with its shaft and driven by means of a belt. Pulleys are commonly made of cast iron, built up from steel pressings or wood. When power is transmitted, there is a considerable difference in the tension of the belt on the two sides of the pulley. The relationship between the tight-side tension, T_1, and the slack-side tension, T_2, is given by $T_1/T_2 = \epsilon\mu\theta$ where ϵ is the base of the hyperbolic logarithms, μ is the coefficient of friction between belt and pulley, and θ is the angle subtended by the arc of contact of the belt at the centre of the pulley. The driving pull is given by the difference of T_1 and T_2, and the horse-power transmitted is given by the formula $(T_1 - T_2)2\pi NR/33000$, N being the number of revolutions per minute, R the radius of the pulley in feet, T_1 and T_2 the tensions in pounds.

It is common to make the rim crowned or slightly raised towards the middle, to ensure that the belt will run on the centre of the rim. The pulley should be at least an inch wider than the belt. If the belt-drive is open, the two shafts connected by it will run in the same direction, but if it is crossed, the motion will be reversed. The part of a belt which is advancing towards a pulley must move in the plane in which the pulley is rotating. When it is difficult to arrange a simple belt-drive between two shafts, which may not be parallel, the use of idle or jockey pulleys may make the problem one easy of solution. Thin flexible-steel belts are sometimes used in workshop practice. Chains are used for drives where slip must be avoided. *See* POWER TRANSMISSION; TACKLE.

PULLMAN, George Mortimer. American inventor. He was born in 1831 and entered the building trade. The first Pullman sleeping car was built in 1863, after which he designed the corridor train and the modern restaurant car. He died 19th Oct., 1897. In 1880 he founded a model town on the outskirts of Chicago for his employees, and called it Pullman. This was eventually made part of Chicago.

PULMONATA. An order of gastropod molluscs, in which the respiratory organ is a cavity formed by the adhesion of the mantle by its margin to the neck of the animal. The greater part of them are terrestrial, among these being the land snails and slugs.

PULPIT (Lat. *pulpitum*, platform, stage). An elevated stand for the delivery of sermons. It is called in French *chaire*, and in German *pre-*

John Knox's pulpit, St. Andrews University

digtstuhl, and is derived from the custom of the first Christian ages, when the bishops delivered their addresses and preached from the *cathedra*. The immediate predecessor of the present pulpit was the *ambo* (q.v.), but in the twelfth century movable pulpits were employed for the delivery of sermons. As early as the thirteenth century pulpits were built in Italy, and the most noteworthy are those at Pisa built by Nicola Pisano in 1260, and at Pistoia by his son Giovanni. Renaissance pulpits are to be found in Italy, such as that in Santa Croce, Florence. Striking pulpits are also to be found in Belgium, such as that in the church of St. Gudule at Brussels, and in the church of St. Andrew at Antwerp.

PULQUE (pulk). The *vin du pays* of Latin America, made from the juice of various species of agave, pleasant and harmless until after protracted fermentation, when it becomes an intoxicant. A kind of brandy is also distilled from it. To the European palate it is sour and unpleasant, somewhat resembling a dilute solution of sulphuric acid.

PULSE. Leguminous plants or their seeds, including all kinds of beans, peas, lentils, etc. The considerable proportion of nitrogen which they contain makes them very nutritious, and on that account they are much eaten, with or without rice, in India, where the chick-pea (*Cicer arietinum*) is one of those very largely used. The Hebrew word translated pulse in the Authorised Version of the Bible (Dan. i., 12, 16) probably means edible seeds in general.

PULSE. The throbbing movement of the walls of blood-vessels, from the passing waves of blood due to the beats of the heart. It is limited in healthy conditions to the arteries. In the newly-born child the healthy pulse registers 130 to 140 beats a minute, at two years of age 105, at ten years about 90, at fifteen to twenty about 70, while in old age it may sink to about 60. In females it is somewhat higher than in males, and during certain fevers it sometimes reaches 140 beats per minute. In arteries which lie immediately under the skin it can be felt with the finger, as is the case with the radial artery, the pulsation of which is very perceptible at the wrist. The state of the pulse is therefore an indication of the force and frequency of the action of the heart, and of the fullness of the vessels.

PULTUSK'. A town of Poland, on the Narev. The Saxons were defeated there by Charles XII. in 1703, and the Russians by the French in 1806. Pop. 19,000.

PULU (pulu fibre). A silky fibrous substance obtained from ferns of the genus Cibotium, and exported from the Sandwich Islands (Hawaii); it is often termed vegetable silk, and is used for stuffing mattresses, etc. Other species growing in the East Indies, Mexico, etc., yield a similar substance.

PUMA (*Felis concolor*). Large American cat ranging from British Columbia to Patagonia. Called the American lion, panther or painter, catamount, and cougar, it measures 3½ feet with 2 feet tail. The head is relatively small and maneless, with flesh-coloured nostrils, the tail dark-tipped and untufted, and the uniformly tawny fur darker along the back and paler beneath.

PU'MICE. A substance frequently ejected from volcanoes, of various colours, grey, white, reddish-brown or black; hard, rough, and porous; blocks float on water; and it resembles the slag produced in an iron furnace. Pumice is really a loose, spongy, froth-like lava, and is formed during the escape of steam and other gases from highly siliceous and therefore viscid lavas. It is often found floating on the sea far from the vent of origin. The pores being generally in parallel rows, it seems to have a fibrous structure. It is used for polishing ivory, wood, marble, metals, glass, etc.; also for smoothing the surfaces of skins and parchment.

PUMPKIN (*Cucurbita pepo*). Trailing annual herb of the gourd order, presumably indigenous to W. Asia. Each plant bears male and female flowers separately, the latter developing into the fruit, sometimes weighing 80 lb. and more. Cultivated in antiquity, and introduced into Tudor England, its varied forms, including vegetable marrows, are widely grown in continental Europe, N. America and elsewhere.

Pumpkin (*Cucurbita pepo*)

PUMPS. Mechanical devices for the raising of water or other fluid from a low level to a higher one, or to raise the pressure upon it so that it may be passed into a vessel under pressure. The hydraulic prime movers, such as overshot and breast wheels, and pressure turbines, when reversed become types of pumps.

The *scoop wheel* or reversed breast wheel is used to lift drainage water in fen districts. Overshot wheels become *chain-and-bucket pumps* when reversed. In Holland an inclined shaft with one or more helices, which is rotated in a closely fitting tube, is used to raise water against heads which do not exceed 10 feet. This appliance is known as the *screw pump* or *archimedean screw*.

The oldest pumping plant is the simple *bucket pump* which is ascribed to Ctesibius of Alexandria and dates from 250 B.C. In this type a piston is fitted to work air-tight within a hollow cylinder or barrel, and is provided with a valve which opens upwards. There is another valve at the foot of the barrel, which also opens upwards and gives communication between the pump and the suction pipe. As the piston is raised the air below it becomes rarefied until water is drawn up through the inlet valve. When the air is exhausted, the water passes through the valve on the piston every downstroke and is raised to the delivery pipe on every up-stroke. When the water is to be discharged from the cylinder against a pressure, non-return valves are installed in the delivery pipe, and the plant is then known as a *force pump*. When greater pressures are required, a plunger is used instead of the bucket piston, which under such conditions would leak considerably.

This *plunger pump* may be made double-acting, either with a single plunger or a combination of two simple pumps. Another type has a moving part consisting of both *bucket piston and plunger*, with cross-sectional areas in the ratio of two to one.

Rotary pumps of the drum type have the advantage of positive action comparable with that of the reciprocating pump, and, like the centrifugal type of pump, they have a continuous delivery. The mode of operation of such devices can be clearly understood from the illustration. The water is trapped by the rotors, and is driven towards the outlet as they turn. One great difficulty in the operation of such pumps is the maintenance of tightness.

The **centrifugal pump** was introduced to meet the demand for high efficiency under low heads of water. The rotor consists of circular side plates enclosing a series of curved blades. The water pipe is connected to a part of the pump having communication with the central part of the rotor. Velocity is given to the water by the blades of the moving system, and its magnitude, which depends upon the speed of the rotor and the form of the blades and pump chamber, is the factor on which the height the water can be raised depends.

Centrifugal pumps were greatly

improved by Professor Osborne Reynolds, whose work made possible the construction of the high-lift pump. With a number of impellers, through which the water is passed in sequence, very high lifts, such as over 1000 feet, can be obtained with efficiencies as high as 75 to 80 per cent. The success attained in designing centrifugal pumps to meet the requirements of any particular pumping work has been very great, and this type is replacing the reciprocating pump for use in all fields but those where small volumes of water are to be raised to great heights. The kinetic energy of moving water in a pipe is used in the *hydraulic ram* to pump part of the water to a height greater than the head of supply. The water is set in motion by opening the waste valve. The velocity of flow increases until the weight of the waste valve is overcome and it is sharply closed. The sudden stoppage of the flow of the water is followed by the impact of the water against the delivery valve, which is opened, and a portion of the liquid passes through. In this way a large flow of water with small head is used to pump a smaller quantity of water against a greater head. Such a device is useful in supplying water from a low stream to a house on a hill.

A pump which has been considerably developed since its introduction in 1909 is the **Humphrey pump,** in which kinetic energy is given to the water by the explosion of gases. A mixture of gas and air is admitted through the valve in the top of the explosion chamber. Water enters the pipes from the supply-tank through the valves. When the gas is ignited and the explosion takes place, the water is swept through the pipes at great velocity and out at the delivery. The backward surge of whatever water is left is used to drive the exhaust gases out of the explosion chamber and leave it clear for the introduction of another explosive charge. There is a large installation of these pumps at the Chingford works of the Metropolitan Water Board. Each pump delivers 40 million gallons of water a day, and is of about 250 to 300 horse-power. The pumps are supplied with producer-gas made from anthracite. For smaller sizes a form of gas pump has been introduced by Humphrey, in which the long water column is replaced by a heavy metallic mass attached to the piston. The application of steam pressure to the surface of water within the pump chambers is made use of in the *pulsometer* to drive the water through the delivery-pipe system, and the later condensation of the steam creates a partial vacuum for the suction of a further supply of water. The pumps have two chambers, which are used alternately to obtain a continuous discharge. Compressed air is used to raise water from deep wells. The air is introduced into a pipe the foot of which is immersed in the water to be lifted. Alternate plugs of air and water pass up the " rising main " or water outlet.—BIBLIOGRAPHY: A. H. Gibson, *Hydraulics and its Applications*; E. C. Bowden-Smith, *The Efficiency of Pumps and Ejectors*; E. W. Sargeant, *Centrifugal Pumping Machinery*.

PUN, or PARONOMASIA (A.S. *punian*, to pound). A play upon words, either upon two or more meanings of the same word or upon the sound of two or more words of different meaning. It was a common form of wit in seventeenth and eighteenth century England, but fell into desuetude in the latter part of the nineteenth century. Originally it was used for serious as well as comic purposes. Among those who employed the form were Cicero, Charles Lamb, and, occasionally, Shakespeare. Addison in *The Spectator* gives a definition and short history of the pun.

PUNCH, or The London Charivari. A weekly illustrated paper. It has, since its first appearance in 1841, well justified Mark Lemon's claim that it " established, if it did not found, a school of current wit and humour." The paper originated in a suggestion made to Henry Mayhew by Last, a London printer, for the production of a publication somewhat on the lines of the Paris *Charivari*. During the first few months of its life, under the co-editorship of Mayhew and Mark Lemon, *Punch* threatened to be little more than a *succès d'estime*; happily, on the available funds becoming exhausted, the proprietorship was transferred to Messrs. Bradbury & Evans, Lemon being made sole editor. Its first annual almanac (1841) was written in the Fleet Prison by Dr. Maginn, under circumstances which doubtless suggested to Thackeray the similar position of Captain Shandon in *Pendennis*. Since that date hardly a famous British humorist or artist of a certain type has failed to have a place upon the paper's staff or to contribute to its pages. Lemon remained the editor until his death in 1870, when Shirley Brooks took his place, to be succeeded by Tom Taylor in 1874. Sir Francis Burnand was editor from 1880 to 1906, and Sir Owen Seaman from 1906 to 1932, when he was succeeded by Mr. E. V. Lucas. The literary staff has included such writers as Douglas Jerrold, who contributed the immortal *Mrs. Caudle*; Thackeray (*Snob Papers* and *Jeames's Diary*); Gilbert à Beckett; Hood (*The Song of the Shirt*); Tennyson (*The New Timon*); Sir Henry Lucy ("Toby, M.P."); T. Anstey Guthrie ("F. Anstey"); and E. V. Lucas. Among its many famous artists John Leech may be first named; but Richard Doyle designed the now familiar present cover; Hablot K. Browne was a frequent contributor; and Tenniel's first published cartoon appeared in the paper and led to his taking charge of this leading feature for just half a century. Other distinguished draughtsmen, past and present, include Charles Keene, George du Maurier, Linley Sambourne, Bernard Partridge, L. Raven-Hill, and George Belcher. *Punch* largely owes its unrivalled, and indeed unchallenged, position to the uniformly wholesome and refined nature of its humour, both literary and pictorial, and also to its strict impartiality, all shades of politicians being in turn the targets for its friendly fun.—Cf. M. H. Spielmann, *History of Punch* (1895).

PUNCH. Alcoholic beverage. In theory it should contain five ingredients, the origin of the name being the Hindu word meaning five. The particular brand of punch is decided by the spirit which is the main ingredient. It may be rum, whisky or brandy. To this are added spices, fruit juice, sugar and hot water.

PUNCH AND JUDY. A familiar puppet-show of, almost certainly, Italian origin, the equivalent of the French *guignol*. It has been popular in Britain for some two and a half centuries. The derivation of Punch (diminutive of *Punchinello*; It. *Polichinello*), the name of the hook-nosed, hunchbacked leading character in the drama, has been the subject of much research and more speculation, but it still remains obscure. Some authorities state that an amateur humorist, one Puccio d'Aniello, from the neighbourhood of Naples, joined a troupe of strolling players and created the part; but d'Aniello's claim is disputed in favour of that of numerous rivals, each with a more or less suggestive name. The theory sometimes put forward that Punch is derived from Pontius Pilate, and the name of his long-suffering wife Judy from Judas the betrayer of Christ, may be dismissed as most improbable. It is possible, however, that the name has its real root in *pulcino* and *pulcinetto*, the Italian terms for a young chicken, sometimes used familiarly as words of endearment to a child, and hence applied also to a puppet.

Punch probably dates from the early years of the seventeenth century, and had certainly made its way to France by the time of Louis XIV. The fact that the French regarded a hunchback as a type of caustic wit made the new arrival peculiarly welcome; and wits and politicians hailed its advent eagerly, and at once used it as a mouthpiece for attacks upon unpopular characters.

The show probably crossed to this country in the train of Charles II. returning from exile in 1660; though some believe it to have come to England with French Huguenots at a much earlier date. Evelyn mentions a performance of an Italian puppet-show in 1667; while in 1669 Pepys speaks of a stout child being called "Punch" by its parents as a common name for all that is thick and short. With the arrival of William of Orange and his numerous compatriots in 1688 the show appears to have become still better known, a fact to be explained by the peculiar skill of the Dutch in the manipulation of all puppet-shows. Punch was exhibited at Bartholomew Fair in 1703, and seven years later was a leading item in a puppet-show at Covent Garden, under the direction of Powell. The period at which "Dog Toby" came to be a member of the troupe remains unknown; Powell at one time employed a trained pig, while French exhibitors not seldom used a cat. At the present time Punch, Judy, the policeman, etc., form an exhibition somewhat shorn of its original magnificence; for the old Punch would seem to have been on familiar terms with such distinguished characters as the Seven Champions of Christendom; he further hoodwinked and defied the Holy Inquisition, and he sat upon the Queen of Sheba's knee. For an account and text of the drama see Payne Collier's *Punch and Judy*, with George Cruikshank's illustrations (1st edition, 1828; 7th edition, 1890).

PUNCHESTOWN. A racecourse of County Kildare, Irish Free State, near Naas, about 24 miles from Dublin. It is served by the G.S. Railway and is famous for its steeplechases.

PUNCHINELLO. Traditional figure of the Commedia dell' Arte. He has something in common with Harlequin. He wears a black mask and a large nose, is a braggart and a rogue, with a rough, country wit. Punch of the Punch and Judy show derives his name from the same source, which probably means short and fat.

PUNCTUATION. The art of employing signs by which the parts of a writing or discourse are connected or separated as the sense requires, and the elevation, depression, or suspension of the voice indicated. Punctuation serves both to render the meaning intelligible and to aid the oral delivery. Our present system of punctuation came very gradually into use after the invention of printing, the Venetian printers, the Manutii, contributing materially to its development. The principal points used in English composition are the *comma* (,), *semicolon* (;), *colon* (:), *period* or *full stop* (.), *note of interrogation* (?), *note of exclamation* or *admiration* (!), *dash* (—), and *parenthesis* (). The *comma* marks the smallest grammatical division in a sentence, separating the several members of a series, or the subordinate clauses and the main clause. The *semicolon* indicates a longer pause than the comma, but requires another member or members to complete the sense. The *colon* denotes a still longer pause, and may be inserted when a member of a sentence is complete in itself, but is followed by some additional illustration of the subject. The *period* indicates the end of a sentence, and is also used after contracted words, and sometimes after Roman numerals. The *note of interrogation* is placed at the end of a direct interrogatory sentence. The *note of exclamation* or *admiration* is placed at the end of such words or clauses as indicate surprise or other emotion. The *dash* is employed where a sentence breaks off abruptly, and the subject is changed; where the sense is suspended, and is continued after a short interruption; after a series of clauses leading to an important conclusion; and in certain cases to indicate an ellipsis. The *parenthesis* encloses a word or phrase introduced into the body of a sentence, with which it has no grammatical connection.

PU'NICA. A genus of plants which consists only of a single species, the pomegranate (*P. granātum*). *See* POMEGRANATE.

PUNIC WARS. A series of wars waged between Rome and Carthage, the first 264-241 B.C.; the second 218-202 B.C.; and the third, which ended with the destruction of Carthage, 149-146 B.C. *See* ROME.

PUNISHMENT. A penalty inflicted on a person for a crime or offence, by the authority to which the offender is subject; a penalty imposed in the enforcement or application of law. The punishments for criminal offences now known to the English law are death by hanging, penal servitude, imprisonment with and without hard labour, solitary confinement, detention in a reformatory or industrial school, discipline in a Borstal institution, subjection to police supervision, fines, whipping, and putting under recognisance. Penal servitude consists in keeping the offender in confinement and compelling him to labour, as directed in several statutes passed since the year 1853.

Imprisonment. There are three kinds of imprisonment: (1) that of a first-class misdemeanant, who is allowed to maintain himself, to procure food, wine, clothing, etc., and to follow his usual occupation if it does not interfere with the prison regulations; (2) without hard labour, in which case the visiting justices provide for the employment of the prisoner, subject to the condition that no punishment for neglect of work is to be inflicted except by an alteration in the prisoner's diet; (3) with hard labour for not more than ten or less than six hours daily, and as ordered by the justices in sessions with the approval of the Home Secretary. In cases (2) and (3) there may be a separate confinement of the prisoner.

Fines and Whipping. Fines are in most cases regulated by the statutes imposing these penalties. As regards whipping, in the case of offenders under sixteen only a birch-rod may be used, and not more than twenty-five strokes be given; in that of offenders above sixteen not more than fifty strokes, and the sentence must specify their number, and the instrument with which they are to be inflicted. When whipping is ordered on summary conviction before the justices, not more than twelve strokes are to be inflicted on offenders under fourteen, and those with a birch-rod; under the age of ten the number of strokes is restricted to six.

Detention. Detention in a reformatory school may be ordered for not less than three nor more than five years (but not to continue after nineteen years of age) in the case of juveniles between twelve and sixteen years of age who have committed offences punishable with penal servitude or with imprisonment.

Youthful Offenders. Offenders under twelve years, and those over that age but not over fourteen years, who have not been previously convicted, may be sent to an industrial school until sixteen years of age.

Persons between sixteen and twenty-one years of age liable to penal servitude may be sent to a Borstal institution for a term of one to three years.

Previous Conviction. In cases of felony and of certain specific misdemeanours, when a previous conviction for a similar offence is proved the sentence may include police supervision for seven years or less, to commence at the expiration of the offender's term of imprisonment. On its expiry he must notify to the police within forty-eight hours his place or any subsequent change of residence, and report himself once a month, a breach of any of these regulations rendering him liable to imprisonment for twelve months with or without hard labour. When the offender is ordered to find recognisances, personal or other, he may, in default, be imprisoned.

Punishments in the army are inflicted under the Army Act of 1881, Articles of War, and the King's Regulations. A commissioned officer must be tried by court-martial, which may sentence him to death, or cashier him, or place him at the very bottom of the officers of his grade. Privates may for minor offences be ordered short imprisonments, of punishment-drill, or stoppage of leave or pay. For grave offences they are tried by court-martial, and may be sentenced to dismissal from the service, or to imprisonment, to penal servitude, or to death.

Punishments in the navy are regulated by the Naval Discipline Act of 1866. For officers the chief additions to the punishments inflicted in the army are forfeiture of seniority for a specified time or otherwise, dismissal from the ship to which the offender belongs, and repremand more or less severe. For men the punishments in the case of grave offences are of the same character as in the army, flogging having been now abolished. For less serious offences there is a system of summary punishments, including short terms of imprisonment which can be awarded by captains of ships under the regulations issued from time to time by the Lords of the Admiralty.

PUNJAB, or **PANJAB** (the name means " Five Rivers "). A province of British India, so called because it was the region intersected by the five tributaries of the Indus, the Sutlej, the Beas, the Ravi, the Chenab, and the Jhelum. The present province of the Punjab, however, is larger than the Punjab proper, and is bounded west by Afghanistan, Baluchistan, and the North-West Frontier Province; north by Kashmir; east by the United Provinces; and south by Sind and Rájputána. The area, exclusive of the connected native states (area, 37,061 sq. miles; pop., 4,910,000), is 99,027 sq. miles; the population in 1931 was 23,580,000. It consists of twenty-nine British districts and thirty-four native tributary states. For administrative purposes it is divided into the five commissionerships of Delhi, Jullundur, Lahore, Rawalpindi, and Derajat. Lahore, situated near the centre of the province, is the capital of the Punjab, but its principal city is Delhi, the capital of the Empire of India.

Physical Features and Productions. Since 1902, when the Peshawar division was separated from the Punjab to form with other territories the North-West Frontier Province, the Punjab consists almost wholly of extensive plains. These are divided into eastern and western, which may be defined as lying east and west of the meridian of Lahore. The eastern plains include the most fertile and populous portion of the Punjab, with the three great cities of Delhi, Amritsar, and Lahore. Their population is largely urban; trade and manufactures flourish, and the cultivable area is generally under the plough, with the exception of the south-western portions, where flocks and herds pasture in extensive jungles. The western plains, on the contrary, and with the exception of a comparatively narrow zone which is fertilised by irrigation, and which produces some of the finest wheat in the world, are covered by stunted bush, with short grass in dry seasons, and by saline plants which afford nourishment to great herds of camels. These, with cattle, sheep, and goats, are tended by a nomad population.

Inhabitants. The difference between the inhabitants of these two series of plains is also very marked, those in the eastern partaking of the character of the Hindu inhabitants of India, while those in the western resemble more the Mussulman peoples of the trans-Suleiman country. Though numerically small, the Sikh element in the population is very important. The Sikhs constituted the dominant class when the Punjab became British, and they still compose the mass of the gentry between the five rivers.

Commerce and Industry. One of the most important products of the Punjab is rock-salt. In addition to the manufactures common to the rest of India, the industries of the

Punjab include such special products as the silks of Multan and the shawls and carpets of Lahore. The province enjoys an extensive trade with adjacent countries, and sends its products to Delhi by railway, and by the Indus and the Indus Valley Railway to Sind and the sea. Its imports from Britain are chiefly piece-goods, cutlery, and other metalwork.

History. The Punjab has had a rather eventful history from the time of Alexander the Great downward. After being long held by rulers of Afghan or Tartar origin, the Sikhs under Runjit Singh established themselves there early in the nineteenth century. Afterwards the country fell into a very distracted state; its Sikh rulers came into collision with the British, and after the second Sikh War, in 1849, the country was brought under British administration. — BIBLIOGRAPHY: H. K. Travaskis, *The Land of the Five Rivers*; T. W. Paustian, *Canal Irrigation in the Punjab*; M. L. Darling, *Rusticus Loquitur*; J. Douie, *The Punjab.*

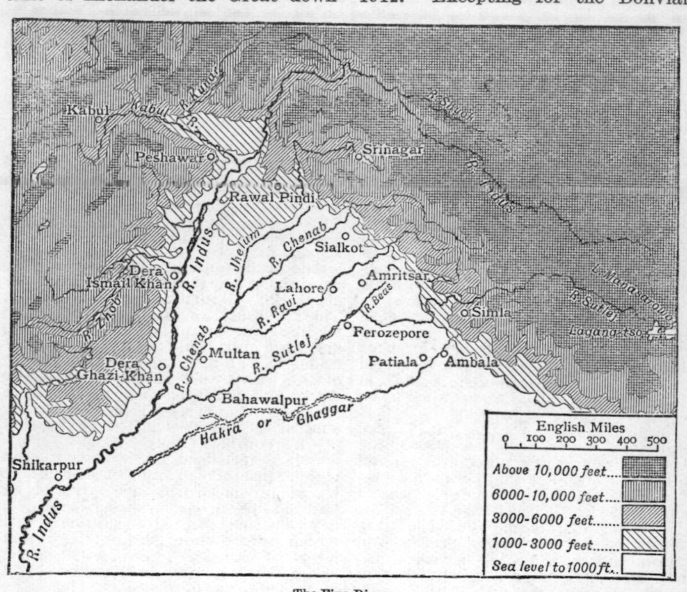

The Five Rivers

PUNKAH. A large fan used in tropical countries, especially India, for ventilating purposes. The large wooden frame is suspended from the ceiling; a cord is attached and led to the outside of the room, where the whole is kept in motion by a coolie.

PUNO. A department of Peru, situated between Arequipa and Cuzco departments and Bolivia, and including the greater part of Lake Titicaca. Part of its northern provinces was incorporated in the new department of Madre de Dios in 1912. Excepting for the Bolivian traffic it depends entirely for its outlet on Mollendo and Arequipa. Copper, silver, lead, antimony, salt, and petroleum are found, and there are deposits of borax in the province of Azangaroo. Sheep, cattle, hides, skins, llama, alpaca, vicuña, sheep wool, dried meat, cereals, and other agricultural produce; coffee, bark, coca leaves from Sandia and Carabaya, and coal (undeveloped) are among the products. The cattle of the department are exported to Lima via Mollendo. Puno is the capital. Area, 26,133 sq. miles; pop. 700,000.

PUNO. A city of Peru, capital of the department of Puno, standing on the west shore of Lake Titicaca at an altitude of 12,600 feet. It is connected by railway with Arequipa (351 kilometres), and with Guaqui (120 miles) by railway steamer across Lake Titicaca. Pop. 15,000.

PUNTA ARE'NAS, now **MAGALLANES.** The capital of the Chilian territory of Magallanes, in the Strait of Magellan, the most southerly town in the world. There is a wireless station, but Punta Arenas has always existed as a coaling-station and as a centre of distribution for the Falkland Islands, etc., and the adjacent archipelago. Gold, copper, and coal are found in the vicinity, and much meat, wool, hides, timber, and grease are exported. Pop. 24,307.

PUNTARENAS. The principal port of Costa Rica, Central America, on the Pacific Coast, Gulf of Nicoya. Pop. (1932), 8028.

PUPA. Zoological term for the resting stage in the metamorphosis of many insects. At the end of the larval period the insect undergoes changes in external form, followed by moulting, the pupa taking on characters approaching those of the perfect insect. Most pupæ are quiescent, but locomotion occurs in some aquatic types such as the gnat.

PUPIL. Circular opening in the middle of the eye immediately in front of the crystalline lens. It regulates the amount of light entering the eye, contracting in a strong light and enlarging in darkness or in focusing distant objects. These changes are also brought about by the action of drugs such as opium or belladonna, the former contracting and the latter dilating the pupil.

PUPPETS AND PUPPET-PLAYS. Puppet-plays are dramatic performances in which human actors are replaced by mechanical figures of wood or pasteboard, usually small in size, their movements and gestures being produced by means of strings or wires manipulated by a concealed operator. The comparatively modern name of *marionettes*, applied to such figures, is generally held to be a corruption of *mariolettes*, the term for small images of the Virgin Mary. Other authorities derive it from *morio* (It., "a fool or buffoon"); while it has alternatively been connected with an Italian named Marion, who, in the reign of Charles IX., introduced these shows to France from Italy, where, under the name of *fantoccini*, puppets had long been popular.

Marionettes are first so called by Boucher (1584), so that the theory seems not ill founded. The only marionette exhibition now common in England is that of the familiar Punch and Judy (q.v.); but puppet-shows have long been popular, and are undoubtedly of very great antiquity. Jointed puppets have been found in Egyptian tombs, while in ancient Greece the puppet-player Potheinos had a remarkable vogue in Athens. It was, however, probably in India that the puppet, like the fairy-tale, was earliest known. In the collection of Kashmiri tales, compiled from ancient sources by the eleventh-century writer Somadeva, there is mention of mechanical puppets worked by means of a wooden peg; some flew in the air, brought water, danced, and even spoke. Others were worked by strings, the operator being known as the *sūtradhār* ("string-puller"). This word is still applied to a stage-manager, a fact suggesting that the puppet-play was the earliest form of stage exhibition. No single written puppet-play has come down to us from antiquity, and it is probable, not only that such exhibitions consisted largely of improvisation, but that they were passed on by oral tradition from one generation to another—partly, no doubt, in order to avoid the danger of their being "pirated."

From India the art of manipulating marionettes passed into Persia; also to the Farther East, including Java, where these shows became extremely popular. From Persia the art gradually penetrated to Europe, where, as in its original home, it was for long largely in the hands of the gipsies. In 1812 the English traveller Ouseley witnessed a gipsy puppet-show in Tabriz. During the first half of the last century gipsy exhibitors wandered through Moldavia between Christmas and Lent, and showed their plays; at the time of the Russo-Turkish War (1828-9) the performance always closed with a combat between a Turk and a Cossack, one or the other losing his head in accordance with the latest victory reported from the "front."

The exhibitor of marionettes, other than the gipsy, was often a self-educated man with a turn for mechanics. Jean Brioché, who, with his attendant monkey Fagotin, was highly popular under Louis XIV., was a tooth-drawer; the German Reibehand (flourished 1734) had been a tailor. A partnership of two was a frequent arrangement, one member of the firm dressing and manipulating the puppets, the other supplying the "libretto." Successful French exhibitors were Carolet and Bertrand; while Goethe admitted that the exhibition of *Faust* in Berlin (1804) by Dreher and Schütz first suggested his great drama to his mind. Even Le

Sage did not disdain to write for marionettes, nor, in our own day, Maurice Maeterlinck.

The puppet-show was flourishing in England in the time of Chaucer, and was later a popular feature of Bartholomew Fair, where, in 1667, Pepys noticed Lady Castlemaine enjoying this show. The earlier plays performed were often such Bible narratives as lent themselves readily to stage representation, as, for example, Jonah and the whale. The chief English exhibitor of the early eighteenth century was Powell, an exceedingly clever mechanician. After him came Pinkethman and Crawley, the last-named producing a striking scene of Noah leaving the ark at the head of the procession of animals. Still later Yates showed wax figures of almost life-size, and towards the close of the century Flockton produced an exhibition containing five hundred separate figures working at different trades. As late as 1830-40 Brown toured the country fairs of England exhibiting the battle of Trafalgar, Napoleon crossing the Alps at the head of his army, etc.; while Chapman gave a realistic study of Grace Darling's rescue of the crew and passengers from the wrecked *Forfarshire*.

Such exhibitions, like those of the original puppet-shows in general, appealed chiefly to the masses; but in 1876 a marionette exhibition at the Kasperle Theatre, Vienna, was favoured with Imperial patronage, and a few years later Rivière, at the Chat Noir, Paris, revived the puppet-show with much success. George Sand established at her country house a private theatre for this purpose. *Ombres chinoises* form a variety of puppet-show in which the shadows of the figures are seen thrown upon a screen. — BIBLIOGRAPHY: Charles Magnin, *Histoire des marionnettes en Europe*; L. de Neuville, *Histoire des marionnettes*; Maindron, *Marionnettes et Guignols*; R. Pischel, *The Home of the Puppet-play* (a published lecture).

PUR'BECK, ISLE OF. A peninsula south of Dorsetshire, so separated from the mainland on the north by Poole Harbour and the Frome as to be connected with it by only a very narrow isthmus. It is about 12 miles long by 7 miles broad. The prevailing rock is limestone.

PURBECK BEDS. The uppermost members of the British Jurassic system, or according to other writers the base of the Wealden formation; deriving their name from the peninsula of Purbeck, where they are typically displayed. They consist of argillaceous and calcareous shales, freshwater limestones and marbles, and are altogether 300 feet thick. They are noted for their layers of fossil vegetable earth (dirt-beds), enclosing roots, trunks, and branches of cycads and conifers, and for the Purbeck Marble (q.v.).

PURBECK MARBLE, or PURBECK STONE. An impure freshwater limestone formed of the remains of the gastropod Vivipara (Paludina), occurring in the Purbeck Beds. It takes on a good polish, but is deficient in durability under exposure to the air, and has hence lost much of its favour as a building-stone. It is much used for slender shafts in the interior of Gothic buildings, for which purpose it answers well.

PUR'CELL, Henry. One of the greatest and most original of English composers. He was the most famous of several musicians of the name all included within three generations of the same family. They lived in the seventeenth and early part of the eighteenth century. As so often happens in connection with great men of that and earlier periods, the definitely established facts of Purcell's life are comparatively few, notwithstanding that he was fortunate enough to be understood and appreciated in his lifetime. He was born in London in 1658 or 1659, and began his musical career as a chorister of the Chapel Royal. When his voice broke, he studied composition with John Blow, at that time organist of Westminster Abbey, and his earliest compositions are conjecturally assigned to this period. At the age of twenty-one he succeeded his master as organist at the Abbey, retaining the post till his death, when Blow resumed his former duties. It is generally understood that Blow voluntarily resigned his post to make room for Purcell, thus gracefully acknowledging his genius, but the story lacks confirmation. About this time Purcell married, and two years later, on 14th July, 1682, he became organist of the Chapel Royal. He was thus throughout his short career closely identified with the doings of royalty, and *Welcome Songs* and *Birthday Odes* form a considerable proportion of his large output. He died in 1695, and was buried on 26th Nov. in Westminster Abbey. On a pillar near his grave a tablet was put bearing the following inscription: "Here lyes Henry Purcell Esq.; who left this life, and is gone to that blessed place where only his harmony can be exceeded."

Purcell, though he died at the early age of thirty-seven, left behind him a large quantity of music which included sacred and secular vocal music both solo and concerted, instrumental music for organ, for harpsichord, and for various combinations of instruments, and incidental music to many plays. There are among his dramatic works several which are entitled to be called real operas, the chief of these being *Dido and Æneas*, a remarkable work which may fairly be regarded as the first successful English opera. Among other works of special fame may be mentioned the *Golden Sonata*, one of a series of ten published posthumously and written for "violins

Henry Purcell

and basse: to the Organ or Harpsechord." Twelve sonatas for the same combination had been issued in 1683 as Purcell's first published composition. Mention should also be made of the *Te Deum* and *Jubilate* in D written in 1694, and performed annually in London for many years after the composer's death. It was revived at the Purcell bicentenary in 1895, and has had some more recent performances.

In his melodies Purcell's manner of musical expression is typically English, for while the melodic line is always flowing and beautiful, it also possesses what can best be described as a "forthright" quality which makes it highly characteristic. This is well illustrated by the rugged accentuation which prevails in *Fairest Isle* and *Come if you dare*. His music is also pre-eminently notable for the massive effect of his scoring in choral work, which may be a common enough achievement to-day, but was new when he wrote. In his power of dramatic expression he was unrivalled in his time, and the inherent vitality of his music is such that it retains after more than two centuries all the freshness and charm that it had when it was written.

PURCHAS, Samuel. Born at Thaxted, in Essex, about 1575, died in 1626. Educated at Cambridge, he took orders, and in 1604 became vicar of Eastwood, in Essex. From 1614 to 1626 he was rector of St. Martin's, Ludgate Hill, London, a position favourable to the pursuit of his multifarious researches. The MS. remains of Hakluyt having come into his hands, he gave to his work, published in 1624, the title *Hakluytus Posthumus, or Purchas his Pilgrims, containing a History of the World in Sea Voyages and Lande Travells by Englishmen and others*, which is valuable as containing the narratives of voyagers, explorers, and adventurers as written by themselves. The *Pilgrims* has been much utilised by subsequent compilers of voyages and travels. He also wrote *Purchas his Pilgrimage* (1613).

PURCHASE. A system, now abolished, by which more than half the first appointments and much of the subsequent promotion of officers in the British army used to be effected. The prices of commissions were fixed as follows: £450 for a cornetcy or ensigncy; £700 for a lieutenancy; £1800 for a captaincy; £3200 for a majority; and £4500 for a lieutenant-colonelcy, which was the highest rank that could be obtained by purchase. In theory an officer wishing to retire from the service might sell his commission for the price affixed to the rank he occupied. When a superior officer "sold out," the next officer inferior to him might purchase promotion to the rank of the former by merely paying the difference between the prices of their respective commissions. The rank of the second might be reached in the same manner by his next inferior, and so on down to the ensign or cornet. No commission could be purchased by one officer unless another officer vacated his commission by its sale. The abolition of the purchase system took place in 1871, but the officers who were deprived of a saleable interest in their commissions were compensated by giving them a sum of money, the payment of which was to be extended over twenty-five years, and which, it was estimated, amounted to £8,000,000. Promotion has since been through seniority, tempered by selection. The Regimental Exchange Act of 1875 permitted the exchange of commissions through purchase under such conditions as the Crown might deem expedient for the time being.

PURFLEET. Seaport of Essex. It stands on the Thames, 16 miles from London, on the L.M.S. Railway. It has a small harbour and facilities for storing oil.

PUR'GATIVES. Drugs employed to evacuate the bowel of its contents. Many drugs produce this action, but have various other effects on the body tissues, and therefore are not included in this description; while the term purgative is used for those drugs that have little influence beyond their action on the intestine. Many classifications of purgatives have been made, and such terms as laxative, cholagogue, and cathartic are still in use, but the action of a purgative is largely dependent on the dose and on the condition of the intestine. They are best grouped into the following four classes: (1) *mild purgatives*, including castor-oil, olive-oil, sulphur, glycerine, honey, figs, prunes, and many other fruits; (2) *anthracene purgatives* include rhubarb, senna, aloes, cascara, and are widely used in many different forms on account of their definite action; (3) *drastic purgatives*, whose action usually causes some griping and abdominal discomfort, are calomel, jalap, scammony, colocynth, elaterium, and croton-oil; (4) *saline purgatives* increase the amount of fluid in the intestine, and thereby give rise to easy evacuation. The chief of these are potassium tartrate and acid tartrate, potassium and sodium sulphate, and the sulphate and various other salts of magnesium.

PUR'GATORY (L.Lat. *purgatorium*, from *purgare*, to cleanse). In theology, the place or condition of temporal punishment to which are submitted the souls of those who, though baptised, have departed this world without having attained perfection. It is the condition or place wherein these souls are being cleansed and purified by punishments for their sins before they are allowed to enter heaven. The punishments, however, may be mitigated and shortened by prayers offered for the dead and by the Mass.

Catholic theologians base the doctrine of purgatory upon passages in the Holy Scriptures. Protestant theologians, however, maintain that all the texts adduced in favour of the doctrine can be interpreted differently, and they reject the doctrine, as it stands in direct contradiction with the teaching of salvation by faith, and is nowhere clearly taught in the Bible.

The Roman Catholic Church, on the other hand, holds that death in itself is no sanctification, and the sinner who has failed to do penance in this life may be punished in another. Gregory the Great (604) was the first to lay the belief down as a dogma, and the Council of Trent defined it more clearly. The doctrine of purgatory is condemned by the Church of England in the 22nd Article.—BIBLIOGRAPHY: A. J. Mason, *Purgatory*; W. O. E. Oesterley, *The Doctrine of the Last Things Jewish and Christian*; H. C. Oxenham, *Catholic Eschatology and Universalism*.

PURIFICATION, THE JEWISH RITE OF. Mainly one through the performance of which an Israelite was readmitted to the privileges of religious communion, lost through uncleanness. The chief varieties of such uncleanness, and the methods of purification from it required, are detailed in Lev. xii., xiv., xv., and Num. xix. The necessity of purification was extended after the captivity to a variety of cases not included in the Mosaic legislation, such as the washing of cups and pots, etc., referred to in Mark, vii., 4.

PURIFICATION OF THE VIRGIN MARY, FEAST OF THE. Called also the Feast of the Presentation of the Child Jesus. A festival of the Christian Church held on the 2nd of February, in commemoration of the event related in Luke's gospel, chapter ii. The festival dates from very early times, and is said to have been formally instituted by Pope Gelasius in A.D. 494. *See* CANDLEMAS.

PURIM. A Jewish festival observed on the 14th and 15th of Adar (March), instituted to commemorate the preservation of the Jews in Persia from the destruction threatened them by the schemes of Haman (Esther, ix.).

PU'RITANS. A name first applied to those English Protestants who regarded the Reformation in England as incomplete, and the Anglican Church, even of Edward VI., as retaining too much of the discipline, ritual, and ceremonial of the Church of Rome. Many of them who were driven into exile under Queen Mary, and who returned to England after the accession of Elizabeth, brought back a zealous desire to remodel the Church of England in the spirit of Continental Protestantism, especially that of Geneva. In 1572 a presbytery was set up at Wandsworth, in Surrey, and before many years Presbyterianism found adherents both among the clergy and the laity. Meanwhile the Brownists, the Independents of later days, whose Congregationalism was as much opposed to Presbyterianism as to Episcopacy, began to be organised and to make some progress. In doctrine these two Puritan parties differed little from each other, or from many Anglicans who remained contented with the Church of England as it was.

During the later years of Elizabeth the nickname of Puritan was popularly bestowed on all in the Church, or out of it, whose views of religion led them to adopt a great austerity of life and gravity of demeanour; who made constant use of Biblical phraseology in their ordinary conversation, and who treated as sinful the most of the amusements and diversions of the society around them. The drama was specially obnoxious to them, and the dramatists repaid the hatred of the extreme Puritan by ridiculing and caricaturing him on the stage. Though the Puritans were always steadfastly loyal to Elizabeth, the legislation which she favoured visited with severe penalties Protestant nonconformity to the Established Church, and in 1592 several leading Brownists were brought to the scaffold. The hopes with which the accession of James I. inspired the Puritan party in the Church were grievously disappointed when their moderate demands for a reform of ritual and a slight modification of episcopal authority were rejected at the Hampton Court Conference. During his reign the prelates and many of the clergy became less Protestant, while the Puritan element in the Church, and out of it, increased in intensity. Nonconformity was pursued by new penal statutes, and numbers of Puritans emigrated to New England. This emigration continued during the reign of Charles I. and the ascendancy of Laud.

The Parliamentarians who took arms against Charles I. were mainly Puritans, and the bulk of them were Presbyterians. Presbyterianism in England reached its height with the meeting of the General Assembly of Divines at Westminster. With the downfall of the Anglican system Independency again reared its head in England. The Independents now combined with their congregationalism the desire for a theological latitude, which widened the gulf between them and the Presbyterians. The army became leavened with Independency, and Oliver Cromwell its champion. With his ascendancy the influence of Presbyterianism as a power in the state dwindled, and Independency became the dominant element in English Puritanism. After the restoration of Charles II. and of the old Anglicanism, the Presbyterians, Independents, and Baptists were the three chief denominations into which Puritanism had split up. Since then Nonconformists or Dissenters has been the term generally used where Puritans would formerly have been employed.—BIBLIOGRAPHY: H. O. Wakeman, *The Church and the Puritans*; J. Tulloch, *English Puritanism and its Leaders*; H. H. Henson, *Puritanism in England*; Stowel and Wilson, *History of the Puritans in England.*

PURLEY. District of Surrey, 12½ miles from London. It has two stations, Purley and Purley Oaks, on the Southern Railway. It forms part of the urban district of Coulsdon and Purley. Pop. (with Coulsdon), 37,666 (1931).

PUR'NEA, or **PURNIAH.** A district and town in the Bhagalpur division of Bihar and Orissa, India, originally belonging to Bengal. In the north it is conterminous with Nepál, and on the south it marches with the Ganges. It lies towards the eastern limit of the Gangetic Plain, and is generally flat. Rice, pulses, indigo, mustard, and tobacco are the chief products, rice being of most importance. The three towns are Purnea (the capital), Kishanganj, and Katihar (the railway junction). Area, 4998 sq. miles; pop. 2,000,000.—The town (Purnea) is on a railway feeder from Katihar, and was formerly a Mahommedan capital. It has declined on account of the silting up of the Kali Kosi River. Pop. about 15,000.

PURPLE. A secondary colour compounded by the union of the primaries *blue* and *red*. Of all the various kinds in use, the Tyrian dye was anciently the most celebrated. This colour was produced by the ancients from an animal juice found in a shell-fish called *murex*; and as it was thus obtained only in small quantities, its use was restricted to the great and wealthy. It became the distinctive colour of imperialism, and the later emperors of the East forbade its use by subjects. Hence their offspring were called *porphyrogeniti*, born in the purple. In modern times, from the short purple mantle worn by them, cardinals are sometimes said to have obtained the purple. With the general disuse of the purple obtained from shell-fish, archil and cudbear, yielded by various species of lichens, were employed in the dyeing of silk and wool; but they have been superseded by the purples obtained from aniline. For cotton the chief purple dye was furnished by madder, but the alizarine to which madder owed its dyeing properties is now prepared from coal-tar. The common shades of purple with which wool is dyed are obtained from logwood with a mordant of alum and tartar.

PURPLE-EMPEROR. The *Apatura* or *Nymphalis iris*, a large, somewhat rare, and richly coloured British

Purple-Emperor

butterfly; so called from the splendid purple iridescent colour of its fore wings.

PURPLE HERON (*Arděa purpurěa*). An occasional visitor to Britain, of which the occipital plumes are glossy black tinged with purple.

PURPLES, EAR COCKLE, or PEPPERCORN. A disease affecting the ears of wheat, produced by *Tylenchus tritici*, a species of thread-worm (*see* NEMATELMIA). The infected grains of wheat at first assume a dark-green colour, which soon deepens to a black, and become rounded like small peppercorns. The husks open, and the diseased grains are found to contain no flour, but a moist substance of white colour and of cottony consistence. A single grain of wheat may contain 50,000 embryos of Tylenchus. These fall to the ground with the grain, grow in the earth, and make their way to the young wheat, on which they mature. Dilute sulphuric acid, in the proportion of 1 part of acid to 100 parts of water, destroys the pest effectually.

PURPLE-WOOD. The heart-wood of *Copaifĕra pubiflōra* and *C. bracteāta*, a beautiful and durable kind of wood imported from Guiana, well adapted for buhl-work, marquetry, turnery, and other purposes.

PUR'PURA. A genus of sea-snails, most of the members of which are littoral. Some of the species were among the molluscs that in ancient times furnished the celebrated dye known as Tyrian purple (chiefly obtained from a murex). The British species known as the dog whelk (*P. lapillus*) also yields a purple dye.

PURPURA, or THE PURPLES (rarely used). A condition in which spontaneous hæmorrhages occur in the skin and on mucous surfaces. These hæmorrhages may be either small spots, called petechiæ, or involve large areas, when the condition is known as ecchymosis.

Purpura may last over a long period, coming out in fresh crops, but often causing no discomfort. It may be primary or secondary. The primary form, frequently seen in children, varies from a mild attack, with little beyond slight diarrhœa and occasional joint pains, to severe hæmorrhages from the mucous surfaces of the gums and the intestine, with high temperature and possibly a fatal termination. In the secondary form the purpura is associated with some disease, and is seen in rheumatism, whooping-cough, kidney and liver diseases, and various septic conditions. Also it may occur in some forms of heart disease, various blood diseases, and in the debility due to cancer and tuberculosis.

PURSE-CRAB. A name for decapod crustaceans of the genus Birgus, allied to the hermit-crabs. A species *B. latro* (the robber-crab), found in the Mauritius and the more eastern islands of the Indian Ocean, is one of the largest crustaceans, being sometimes 2 to 3 feet in length. It lives on land, while paying a nightly visit to the sea, often burrowing under the roots of trees, lining its hole with the fibres of the coco-nut husk and living on the nuts, which (according to some writers) it climbs the trees to procure, and the shells of which it perforates with great ingenuity.

Purpura Shell

PUR'SUIVANT. An attendant on the heralds, one of the third and lowest order of heraldic officers. There are four pursuivants belonging to the English College of Arms, *Rouge Croix*, *Blue Mantle*, *Rouge Dragon*, and *Portcullis*. In the court of the Lyon King-of-Arms in Scotland there were formerly six pursuivants, *Unicorn*, *Carrick*, *Bute*, *Kintyre*, *Ormond*, and *Dingwall*, but the last three have been abolished.

PURUS. A river of South America, rising in the east of Peru, traversing

Bolivia, and entering Brazil, where it joins the Amazon through a large delta 120 miles above Manáos and 100 miles above the confluence of the Amazon and Madeira. Length, 1850 miles, navigable for about 1600 miles.

PURVEY'ANCE. Formerly in England the exercise by officials called *purveyors* of the royal prerogative, involving a right of pre-emption, by which the king was authorised to buy provisions and necessaries for the use of his household at an appraised value, in preference to all his subjects, and even without the consent of the owner; it included the right of impressing horses and carriages, etc., for the use of the sovereign. It was also practised by many of the great English nobles. It led to much oppression and many exactions, was dealt with in the Magna Charta, and a number of statutes were passed to prevent the grievance. It was abolished in 1660.

PUS. The fluid product of suppuration, due to bacterial action; a thick creamy substance containing dead white blood-corpuscles with fragments of cells, fibrous tissue, organic debris, and bacteria. It is found in abscesses and wherever suppuration has occurred.

PU'SEY, Edward Bouverie. English divine, born in 1800; died in 1882. He was educated at Eton and Christ Church, Oxford, and became Fellow

Edward Bouverie Pusey

of Oriel in 1824. In 1828 he was appointed to the regius professorship of Hebrew at Oxford, to which was attached a canonry of Christ Church. In 1833 the *Tracts for the Times* began to appear, but he was not prominently connected with the Tractarian movement until 1835-6, when he contributed to the *Tracts* one on baptism, which excited much attention. He published a defence of the famous *Tract No. 90*, and in 1843 he was suspended by the vice-chancellor of Oxford from preaching for three years, on account of the very high sacramental doctrine inculcated in his sermon on the Eucharist, preached before the university. The prominence thus given to him, his position in the university, his reputation for scholarship, and his thorough-going advocacy of "Anglo-Catholic" principles, procured the general adoption of the term Puseyism as a synonym of Tractarianism; and with the secession of Newman to Rome, Pusey became the acknowledged head of the new Church party.

Among the more substantial of his works, in addition to his *Library of English Fathers* and *Anglo-Catholic Library*, are his *Councils of the Church*, from the Council of Jerusalem, A.D. 51, to the Council of Constantinople, A.D. 381 (1857); *Daniel the Prophet*, nine lectures (1864); and the *Minor Prophets*, with a commentary and introduction to the several books (1860-77).

Pusey House in St. Giles, Oxford, is a centre for students of theology.

BIBLIOGRAPHY: B. W. Savile, *Dr. Pusey: an Historic Sketch with some Account of the Oxford Movement*; H. P. Liddon, *Life of Edward Bouverie Pusey*.

PUSH BALL. American game, invented in 1894. It was originally played by two sides on a field about 150 yards long by 50 yards wide, with a large rubber ball 6 feet in diameter. The object was to push this ball into a goal 18 feet high by 20 feet wide.

PUSHKIN, Alexander Sergéyevitsh. Russian poet, born at St. Petersburg (Leningrad), 1799; died 1837. At an early age, on account of his liberal opinions, he was sent to Odessa, where he discharged various offices, but was restored to favour on the accession of Nicholas I. in 1825, who appointed him imperial historiographer. He made a study of foreign literatures, and was much influenced by Byron. His first poem was *Ruslan and Liudmila* (1821); this was followed by *The Prisoner of the Caucasus*, *The Foundation of Bakhtchisarai*, *Eugene Onegin*, *The Gypsies*, and *Poltava*. He was also the author of a dramatic poem, *Boris Godounov*. He fell in a duel with his brother-in-law.

PUSHTU, or PASHTU. The vernacular language of the Afghans, regarded as an Aryan language, more or less allied to the Iranian group, from which, however, it is totally different in construction and in idiom. Persian is the language of the educated classes in Afghanistan, and is also known to the people, who, however, prefer the use of Pushtu.

PUSTULE. A small papule containing pus. It is an inflamed elevated mass under the skin, and is painful and tender to the touch. In certain septic infections pustules appear, and they are present in smallpox and chickenpox. *Malignant pustule* is the name given to a form of local infection by anthrax, seen in human subjects who work with anthrax-infected carcasses.

PUTCHOCK, or PUCHUCK. The root of *Apoltaxis* (*Saussurea*) *Lappa*, a composite plant growing on the Himálaya in the vicinity of Kashmir. It is exported to the Malay countries and to China, where it forms a main ingredient in the Chinese pastille-rods known as *joss-sticks.* In Upper India it is given as a medicine in various complaints ranging from coughs to cholera.

PUTEAUX (pü-tō). A town of France, in the department of the Seine, on the left bank of the Seine, a short distance west of Paris. Its industries include calico-printing, tanning, dyeing, and the manufacture of chemicals and mineral-waters. It is a suburb of Paris. Pop. 32,000.

PUTNEY. A suburb of London, in the county of Surrey, on the right bank of the Thames opposite Fulham, and within the Metropolitan borough; served by the Southern Railway, and by motor-'bus, tram, and District Railway. The head-quarters of the rowing world is at Putney, which is also the starting-point of the Inter-'Varsity boat-race. Putney bridge was erected in 1886 to replace a wooden one of date 1729.

Putney was called *Putelei* at the time of the Domesday Survey, and the Heath was a favourite meeting-ground for the settlement of differences with the sword.

PUTREFACTION. The name given to the decomposition of organic matter (proteins), whether of plant or animal origin. Putrefaction usually begins after the death of the organism, and is accompanied by the evolution of gases, many of them of a fetid nature. It is due to the agency of bacteria. These minute organisms are present in vast numbers in the air, and settle on the organic matter, in which they find a suitable medium for development and growth. This growth is accompanied by the formation of ferments (enzymes), which cause a splitting-up or decomposition of the complex compounds present in the organic material. The products thus formed are of a comparatively simple nature—many are gaseous, e.g. hydrogen, nitrogen, ammonia, carbon dioxide, hydrocarbons, etc., and sometimes compounds of sulphur and phosphorus. In many cases the products formed in putrefaction are the same as the products obtained by the action of dilute acid on proteins; among these may be mentioned organic bases, such as methylamine and the poisonous ptomaines, amino-acids, and other acids, e.g. oxalic and lactic acids.

The rate of putrefaction and the nature of the products are affected by temperature, moisture, and access of air. Putrefaction can be prevented by exposure to a high or very low temperature, by the withdrawal of moisture, or by the addition of different kinds of antiseptics, such as formaldehyde, borax, salicyclic acid, etc. All these methods destroy the activity of the organisms that give rise to putrefaction, and are employed on the large scale for preserving food-stuffs. Putrefaction is prevented by *sterilisation,* i.e. exposure to a high temperature, so that all bacteria present are destroyed; and afterwards preventing the access of others. A special bacillus (*B. botulinus*) is sometimes associated with the forms causing putrefaction, and the virulently poisonous substance formed by its activity is not destroyed by preservation methods. *See* BOTULISM; PRESERVED FOODS.

PUTTENHAM, George. English writer, regarded as the author of *The Art of Poesie,* a work of ability, which appeared anonymously in 1589. If its author, he was, from indications given in that and another work from the same pen, born about 1530, and became a scholar of Oxford. In 1579 he presented a series of poems called *Partheniades* to Queen Elizabeth. *The Art of Poesie* is a review of ancient as well as modern poetry, and was written for the court and to instruct in versification. The book is also attributed to Richard, brother of George Puttenham.

PUTTY. A kind of paste or cement compounded of whiting or carbonate of lime and linseed-oil, beaten or kneaded to the consistence of dough. In this state it is used by glaziers for fixing in the squares of glass in window-frames, etc., and also by house-painters to stop up holes and cavities in wood-work before painting.

PUTTY-POWDER. A pulverised oxide of tin sometimes mixed with oxide of lead. It is extensively used for polishing and other purposes in glass- and marble-works; the best kinds are used for polishing plate.

PUTUMAYO. River and territory of Colombia, South America. The river, navigable for 700 miles, is a tributary of the Amazon, which it joins near São Antonio. The territory belongs partly to Ecuador and partly to Peru. Puerto Asis is the capital.

Here, in 1909, official inquiries into the treatment of native labourers in the rubber plantations of a British company led to punishment of the offenders by the Peruvian government.

PUTUMAYO ATROCITIES. A term applied to a series of offences committed by the Peruvian Amazon Company (British) during 1909. As the outcome of emphatic allegations made in 1909 by a British writer, the British Government ordered Roger Casement (afterwards executed for treason) to investigate, and his report (Cd. 6266/of 1912) substantiated the rumoured existence of atrocities of a most revolting kind, by which the Peruvian Amazon Company forced their native labourers in the rubber plantations to work. At the joint representation of the British and United States Governments some of the worst offenders were punished by the Peruvian authorities.

PUY (pů-ē), **LE,** called also *Le Puy-en Velay,* and *Le Puy-Notre-Dame.* A town of France, capital of the department of Haute-Loire. Overlooking the town is a conical rock crowned by a small chapel and a colossal statue of the Virgin. There is an ancient cathedral. The manufactures are chiefly lace, leather, spirits, and woollens. Pop. 20,000.

Puy-de-Dome

PUY-DE-DÔME (pů-ē-dė-dōm). A department of Central France, comprising parts of the pre-Revolutionary provinces of Bourbonnais, Auvergne, and Lyonnais; area, 3090 sq. miles: takes its name from a volcanic cone (4805 feet) which overlooks it. The highest point in the department, Puy-de-Sancy (6188 feet), is the most elevated peak of Central France. The department, with its numerous extinct volcanoes, is rich in granite, lead, and oil. The principal rivers are the Allier, Cher, Dordogne, and Dore. There are coal and other mines in the department, which also contains a number of springs, visited by invalids since the days of the Romans. The manufactures include cottons and woollens, paper, leather, etc. The capital is Clermont-Ferrand. Pop. (1931), 500,590.

PWLLHELI (pụl-hā'lē). A municipal borough and seaport of Wales, in Caernarvonshire, on Cardigan Bay; served by the Cambrian Railway. It is an old town, is surrounded by splendid scenery, is much visited by tourists, and is a favourite watering-place. It belongs to the Carnarvon district of parliamentary boroughs. Pop. (1931), 3599.

PYÆ'MIA. A condition of infection of the blood by organisms or their toxins (*septicœmia*), which results in the formation of abscesses in different parts of the body. The bacteria are first present in some local focus of infection, most generally in the skin or subcutaneous tissues, and from these they or their toxins are carried throughout the body by the bloodstream. The abscesses vary in situation, according to the original site of infection and to the type of organism. They may be found in the lungs, kidneys, spleen, brain, joints, and in muscles, and any region which is injured is specially susceptible on account of the damage to the tissues. High fever is present, with abrupt rises and falls of temperature; rigors are frequent, accompanied by drenching sweats. The prognosis in all cases is grave and the mortality high.

PYCNOG'ONUM. The type-genus of an aberrant class of marine Arthropoda, the Pycnogonida, or the sea-spiders. Some species are parasitic on other marine animals, but the common British species, *P. littorāle,* is free when adult, and does not appear to be parasitic during any period of its existence. The largest member of the class is a deep-sea Pcynogon from the Antarctic (*Colossendeis gigas*), which is 2 feet across, and of a deep orange-scarlet colour.

PYE, Henry James. Poet Laureate and poetaster, born in 1745 of an old Berkshire family, died in 1813. Educated at Magdalen College, Oxford, he entered Parliament as member for Bucks in 1784. Having in 1775 published a translation of six odes of

Pindar, in 1778 one of Frederick the Great's *Art of War,* and in 1786 another of the *Poetics* of Aristotle, with a commentary, he was, in 1790, appointed Poet Laureate in succession to Warton. The appointment, which was a reward for his loyalty to Pitt, was ridiculed by the public. In 1792 Pye was appointed a Westminster police magistrate. In 1801 appeared his *Alfred,* an elaborate but ineffably tedious epic.

PYGMA'LION. In Greek mythology, a king of Cyprus, who, disgusted with the debaucheries of his countrywomen, took an aversion to the sex. According to Ovid (*Met.* x., 243) he made an ivory image of a maiden, fell in love with his own work, and entreated Venus to endow it with life. His prayer was granted, and the maiden became his wife. W. S. Gilbert's drama of *Pygmalion and Galatea* is founded on this story.

PYGMIES. Populations of very small men of negroid type, whose average height falls below 1·5 metres (4 feet 11 inches). Individuals of almost any race may be as short as pygmies, but such dwarfs must be clearly distinguished from true pygmies, in which a whole people alike share the diminutive stature. Pygmy peoples are found chiefly in Africa and in the islands near the southeastern part of the Asiatic area. In tropical Africa the pygmy negroes or negrilloes, as they are termed, are widely distributed, and were known to the ancient Egyptians and the Greek historians. Farther south are found the Bushmen and Hottentots, who also belong to the pygmy peoples.

The true Asiatic pygmies or negritoes reveal in their size and physical structure, especially the characteristic so-called woolly hair and black skin, evidence of close kinship to the negrilloes of equatorial Africa. They are found in the Andaman Islands, the Malay Peninsula, the Philippines, and New Guinea. In the Malay Peninsula they are known as the Semang and in the Philippines as the Aeta.

The chief scientific interest in these negrito and negrillo peoples is the demonstration they afford of the fact that some of these pygmy negroes must have traversed the whole southern littoral of Asia from the original home of the race, wherever that was. There is some evidence that negritoes also accompanied the taller negroes in their wandering still farther east to Melanesia. The true pygmies or negritoes must be clearly distinguished from other small black people belonging to a distinct and much more primitive race, akin to the aboriginal Australians. The height of these people, however, slightly exceeds the limit of the pygmy peoples. The Sakai and Senoi of the southern part of the Malay Peninsula are typical examples of these small Australoid peoples; others are found in East Sumatra and in Celebes (Toala); but kindred peoples are found in Ceylon (Veddas), among some of the jungle tribes of the Indian Deccan (pre-Dravidians), in Australia, and probably also in New Guinea.

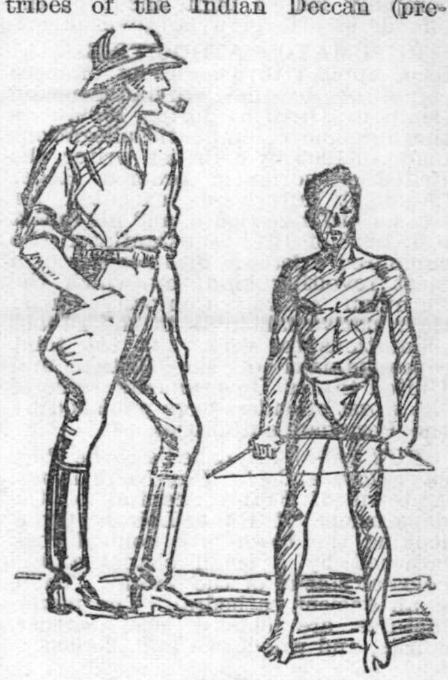

Pygmy

BIBLIOGRAPHY: A vast literature has grown up with reference to pygmies, which has been very concisely summarised by Dr. A. C. Haddon in the chapter he contributed to A. F. R. Wollaston's book *Pygmies and Papuans*; E. Tyson, *Essay concerning the Pygmies of the Ancients* (1699, republished 1894), and A. de Quatrefages, *The Pygmies* (1895), for the earlier literature; and A. H. Keane, *Man, Past and Present* (second edition by Hingston Quiggin and Haddon, 1920), for the more recent literature; also A. R. Brown, *The Andaman Islanders* (1922).

PY'LADES (-dēz). In Greek mythology, son of Strophius, King of Phocis, and Anaxibia, the sister of Agamemnon, after whose murder by Clytemnestra, their son Orestes, being carried secretly to the court of Strophius, formed the friendship with Pylades which has become proverbial.

He assisted Orestes in murdering Clytemnestra, and eventually married his sister Electra.

PYLONS. In Egyptian architecture, the name given to towers or masses of masonry, somewhat resembling truncated pyramids, placed one on each side at the entrance of temples, and having a very imposing appearance. Behind them in the larger temples there was often a large open court, and in front there might be an avenue with sphinxes on either

Pylons

side. An entrance of which these pylons form part is sometimes called a *propylon*.

PYLO'RUS. The region at the right end of the stomach where it joins the intestine. It is composed of a ring of circular muscle fibres which control its opening and closing, and their action is influenced by the stomach contents, so that normally the foodstuff only passes onwards into the intestine when a suitable stage of digestion has been reached.

PYLOS. A town of ancient Greece memorable in the Peloponnesian War, and represented by the modern Navarino.

PYM, John. English statesman and leader of the popular party during the reigns of James I. and Charles I., born in Somersetshire 1584, died in 1643. He studied at Oxford, became famous as a lawyer, and entered Parliament in 1614. During the reign of James he attained great influence by his opposition to the arbitrary measures of the king. He sat for Tavistock in all the Parliaments of Charles's reign. In 1626 he took part in the impeachment of Buckingham and was imprisoned. In the Short Parliament of 1640 Pym and Hampden were exceedingly active as leaders of the popular party, and in 1641 Pym was offered the chancellorship of the exchequer. He impeached Strafford, and at his trial appeared as accuser.

He was the main author of the Grand Remonstrance, the final appeal presented in 1641, and one of the five members to arrest whom the king went to the House of Commons in Jan., 1642. When civil war became inevitable, Pym was appointed one of the committee of safety, and while he lived was active in resisting the negotiation of any peace with the king which did not secure the liberties of the subject and the supremacy of Parliament. It was mainly his financial skill that enabled the Parliamentary army to keep the field. In Nov., 1643, he was made Lieutenant-General of Ordnance, and in the following month he died, and was buried in Westminster Abbey. His body was ejected thence after the Restoration.

PYORRHEA. Discharge of pus, specifically from the gums surrounding the necks of the teeth. It is associated with inflammation of the gums, softening of the bony socket and loosening of the teeth. The diseased condition is fostered by stagnation of the mouth's natural self-cleansing processes and the deposition of tartar. It may be avoided by systematic care of the teeth, including rubbing, brushing, and scaling, the use of a mouth-wash, the due consumption of vegetables and fruit, etc.

PYR'AMID, in geometry, is strictly a solid contained by a plane triangular, square, or polygonal base, and other planes meeting in a point. This point is called the vertex of the pyramid; and the planes which meet in the vertex are called the sides, which are necessarily all triangles, having for their bases the sides of the base of the pyramid. The volume of a pyramid is one-third the volume of a prism that has the same base and altitude as the Pyramid. Pyramids are denominated triangular, square, pentagonal, etc., according as the base is a triangle, a square, a pentagon, etc.

PYRAMID. In architecture, a colossal structure of masonry having a rectangular base and four triangular sides terminating in a point, used by the ancients in various parts of the world for sepulchres or for religious purposes, especially in Egypt.

The largest and most remarkable of the Egyptian pyramids occur in several groups on the west side of the Nile, on the border of the Libyan Desert, extending for a distance of about 25 miles from north to south, the farthest north being opposite Cairo. They are built chiefly of the hard limestone of the adjacent hills, but large blocks of granite brought from a distance are also used, especially on the outside. The four sides are so placed as to face the four cardinal points. These structures are supposed to date from about 3000 B.C. to 2300 B.C. The stones used varied in size, but are mostly large, requiring wonderful mechanical skill to quarry them, transport them, and raise and adjust them in their proper places.

Labourers in almost fabulous numbers were engaged in erecting the chief Egyptian pyramids, of which the group of Gizeh, 4 miles S.W. of Cairo, in the neighbourhood of the ancient Memphis, is the most remarkable. This group consists of nine pyramids, among them the three most celebrated of all, the pyramid of Cheops (Khufu), called the Great Pyramid; of Cephren (Khafra); and of Mycerinus (Menkauru). According to Herodotus, the Great Pyramid took 100,000 men working for ten years to make a causeway 3000 feet long in order to facilitate

A view of the Pyramids

the transport of the stone from the quarries; and the same number of men for twenty years more to complete the pyramid itself. Its base forms a square, each side of which was originally 768 feet, though now, by the removal of the coating, only 750 feet long, occupying 13 acres. The outer surface forms a series of steps, each of the average height of 3 feet or more. When the structure was perfect, this step formation was hidden by the coating, and the apex, where there is now a space of 12 sq. yards, was no doubt originally quite sharp. The height was originally about 480 feet, but is now only 451 feet. The interior, entered 49 feet above the base of the north face, contains several chambers, one of which, called the King's Chamber, is 34¼ feet long, 17 feet wide, and 19 feet high, and contains a sarcophagus of red granite. The second pyramid is 690 feet square and 447 feet high. The third pyramid is only 354 feet square and 203 feet high, and is the best constructed of the three. A fourth pyramid was discovered here in 1932. The six smaller pyramids which complete the Gizeh group are of much inferior interest.

The pyramids are supposed to have been built by the respective kings as tombs and memorials of themselves; and it is conjectured that they were begun at the beginning of each reign, and that their size corresponded with the length of it. About 350 yards south-west of the Great Pyramid is the celebrated Sphinx. Ruins of pyramids are to be found at Benares in India and in other parts of the East. Certain monuments of the ancient inhabitants, found in Mexico, are also called pyramids. These seem to have been intended to serve as temples, the tops of them being flat and surmounted by a house or chamber in which sacred rites were probably performed. The largest and perhaps the oldest of them is that of Cholula, which is said to have a base of 1770 feet and a height of 177 feet. —BIBLIOGRAPHY: W. M. F. Petrie, *Gizeh and Rifeh*; Sir E. A. Wallis Budge, *The Nile*; A. B. Gosse, *The Magic of the Pyramids and the Mystery of the Sphinx.*

PYRAMIDS. *See* BILLIARDS.

PYR'AMUS AND THIS'BE. A pair of devoted lovers, who, as their story is told by Ovid (*Met.* iv., 55-165), resided in Babylon, and being prevented by their parents from meeting openly, were in the habit of secretly conversing through an opening of the wall, as their houses adjoined. They agreed one day to meet at the tomb of Ninus, when Thisbe, who was the first at the rendezvous, was surprised by a lioness and took to flight. In her haste she dropped her garment, which the lioness seizing covered with blood, having immediately before killed an ox. Pyramus appearing on the scene, and concluding from the blood-besmeared robe that Thisbe was dead, killed himself. Thisbe returning soon afterwards, and finding the body of her lover, also killed herself. The story was very popular in the time of Shakespeare, who made it the subject of the burlesque interlude in *A Midsummer Night's Dream.*

PYRAR'GYRITE. A handsome purple-red ore of silver ("dark-red silver ore," in opposition to the light-red *proustite*, which contains arsenic in place of antimony). Pyrargyrite is a silver antimonide and sulphide, Ag_3SbS_3, and is often an important ore.

PYRENEES'. A mountain range, part of the Alpine system of Europe, the crest of the main chain of which forms the boundary between France and Spain. They abut with one extremity on the Mediterranean, and with the other on the Atlantic, their western extension, the Cantabrian Mountains, fringing the southern shores of the Bay of Biscay for a considerable distance. They consist of two lines, which form parallel ridges about 20 miles apart from each other, except near the centre, towards which the range rises from both east and west, and the descent on the south side is much more abrupt than on the north. The loftiest summits are near the centre; the culminating point, Pic de Néthou in the Maladetta, reaches a height of 11,170 feet. The principal passes in the Pyrenees, formed by the meeting of valleys from opposite sides of the axis, take in the east part of the chain the name of Cols, and towards the centre that of

Pyrenees

Ports. Only four of these are conveniently practicable. See SPAIN for trans-Pyrenean railways and communications.

PYRÉNÉES (BASSES-). A south-western frontier department of France, with a seaboard of 17 miles on the Bay of Biscay, between the Bidassoa and the Adour. Along the ridge of the Pyrénées, which rises from west to east, the department forms the boundary with Spain, and within the department are the Pic du Midi d'Ossau (9465 feet altitude) and the Pic du Palais (9760 feet altitude). The famous Pass of Roncevaux and some twenty-six others (mostly fortified) permit communication with Spain. Pau (a noted health-resort) is the capital; other towns are Biarritz (watering-place) and Oloron. Viticulture is followed, cattle and horses are bred, and agriculture flourishes; there are several mineral-springs; fish is abundant in the streams, and the mountains are more or less afforested; copper and stone are found.

Basses-Pyrénées has about the same territorial dimensions as the pre-Revolutionary province of Béarn, but the south-west is Pays Basque. The Basques and Béarnais have retained many old customs and much of their mediæval simplicity of life, especially in the more mountainous districts. Area, 2977 sq. miles; pop. (1931), 422,719 (or 141·9 per square mile). In 1911 the population was 433,320.

PYRÉNÉES (HAUTES-). A southern frontier department of France, embracing in the south a large area of the Central Pyrenees, which forms the boundary-divide with Spain. In the north cereals and fruit are produced and viticulture is progressive. Tarbes is the capital; other towns are Luz, Vic, Lannemezon, and Lourdes. Area, 1750 sq. miles; pop. (1931), 189,993.

PYRÉNÉES-ORIENTALES. A department of Southern France (part of the pre-Revolutionary provinces of Roussillon and Languedoc), bordering on the Mediterranean and the Spanish frontier, and drained by the Aude, Ariège, Tech, Tet, and Agly. The culminating peak is Mont Canigou (9100 feet). There are numerous lakes. Its chief wealth lies in its wines, of which the well-known Roussillon is one. The department is very rich in iron and copper; lead and granite are also found. Perpignan is the capital. Area, 1598 sq. miles; pop. (1931), 238,647.

PYRENEES, PEACE OF THE. Concluded between France and Spain by Cardinal Mazarin and De Haro, on the Ile des Faisans, in the River Bidassoa, on the borders of the two countries, 7th Nov., 1659, it terminated a war which had lasted for twenty-four years. By this treaty Spain ceded to France Roussillon, with the fortress of Perpignan, etc., so that the Pyrenees have since formed the boundary of the two kingdoms; and in the Netherlands, Artois, and part of Flanders, Hainault, and Luxemburg, with a number of fortified towns.

PYRENOMY'CETES. One of the main subdivisions of Ascomycetous Fungi, distinguished by the ascus-fruit, which is a flask-shaped structure, opening when ripe by a narrow pore at the tip, and termed a *perithecium*. The further classification of this large and important group is based chiefly on the detailed structure of the perithecium; the leading families are the Hypocreales (including Claviceps, Cordyceps, Nectria), in which the perithecium is fleshy or waxy and highly coloured, and the Sphæriales (including Leptosphæria and Xylaria), in which it is hard and black.

PYRETH'RUM. A genus of herbaceous plants nearly allied to Chrysanthemum. *P. Parthenium* is known as feverfew; from *P. roseum* is made the well-known Persian insect-powder.

PYRGOS. A town of Greece, near the west coast of the Morea, and not far from the mouth of the Ruphia (Alpheios). Its harbour is at Katakolo, with which and with Athens there is railway communication, and it carries on a large trade in grapes, currants, and oranges. Pop., 13,710.

PYRHE'LIOMETER, or PYRO-HELIOMETER. An instrument devised by Pouillet for measuring the intensity of the heat received from the sun. It consists of a shallow cylindrical vessel of thin silver or copper metal, containing water or mercury in which the bulb of a thermometer is plunged. The upper surface of the vessel is covered with lamp-black, so as to make it absorb as much heat as possible, and the vessel is attached to a support in such a way that the upper surface can be always made to receive the rays of the sun perpendicularly. The actual amount of heat absorbed by the instrument is calculated by ordinary calorimetrical means. The area of the exposed blackened surface and the mass of water or mercury which has been raised through a certain number of degrees being both of them known, the absolute heating effect of the sun, acting upon a given area under the conditions of the experiment, can be found. Estimates of the sun's temperature from the indications of this instrument varied widely, and other methods, such as that of the optical pyrometer, are now used for this purpose.

PYRIDINE. Colourless liquid obtained by fractional distillation of coal-tar and bone-tar. Its strong basic properties form a series of salts with acids and substitution products with halogens. It boils at 115° C., and is unattacked by boiling nitric and chromic acids. It is used in the denaturing of alcohol.

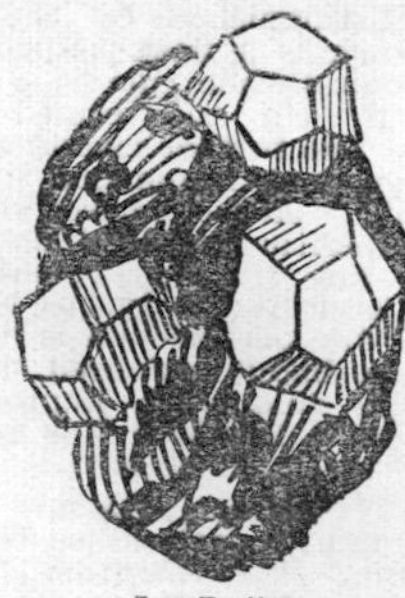

Iron Pyrites

PYRITES (pi-rī'tēz). A name given in mineralogy to various metallic sulphides, chiefly to the sulphides of copper and iron. For iron pyrites (pyrite), *see* IRON. *See* MARCASITE; CHALCOPYRITE.

PYRO-ELECTRICITY. A name given to the electrification which appears on certain minerals and organic substances when these are heated or cooled. The effect was first discovered in tourmaline. If a crystal of tourmaline is hung up by a silk thread in a heating-chamber, one end of the crystal becomes positively and the other end negatively electrified. This polarity continues while the temperature rises, but reverses as the temperature falls, and the effect is observed only within the limits 10° to 150° C. It appears to be associated with a difference in the crystalline structure of the two ends of the crystal. The property is also exhibited by boracite, quartz, cane-sugar, and sulphate of quinine.

PYROGALLIC ACID, ($C_6H_6O_3$), or more correctly *pyrogallol.* A substance belonging to the class of bodies known as phenols, and obtained by the dry distillation of gallic acid. It forms colourless, odourless crystals, and is readily soluble in water, alcohol, and ether. Its alkaline solution readily absorbs oxygen, turns deep brown, and is used in gas analysis. It is also used as a developer in photography.

PYROGRAPHY. Art of producing designs on wood by charring the surface with heated metallic points. In its simplest form it is called "poker-work" (q.v.).

PYROLIG'NEOUS ACID. An aqueous solution obtained in the dry distillation of wood. It consists chiefly of acetic acid, but also contains methyl alcohol, acetone, homologues of acetic acid, and empyreumatic products. *See* EMPYREUMA.

PYROL'USITE. A mineral consisting of manganese peroxide, MnO_2, in the form of black crystalline masses. It is soft and even soils the fingers, while a rare hard mineral form of MnO_2, *polianite,* exists, which crystallises in the tetragonal system. Pyrolusite is orthorhombic, and the similarity of its crystals to those of manganite make it probable that they are pseudomorphs after that mineral. It occurs in Devonshire, Warwickshire, Brazil, etc., and is much used in chemical processes, for example, the preparation of chlorine.

PYROM'ETER. An instrument for measuring high temperatures. Many of the physical actions of heat upon metals are made use of in these devices. Under the influence of change of temperature the electrical resistance of a metallic wire changes, and pyrometers working on this principle were devised by Professor Hugh L. Callendar, who made his thermometers with platinum wire. The resistance is usually measured with a Wheatstone's bridge testing-set—such as that of Whipple—with the wire graduated in degrees of temperature. As the wires leading to the platinum coils are also subject to rise in temperature and consequent alteration in electrical resistance, a similar pair of wires or compensating leads is connected to the other side of the Wheatstone's bridge; the observations are thus those due to the change of resistance of the platinum wire only. The platinum coil is wound on a mica frame, and the connecting wires are passed through holes in small mica washers, which keep them in place within the containing glass, porcelain, or silica tube.

When dissimilar metals are heated in contact with one another, an electromotive force is produced which has a magnitude depending upon the temperature. Thermo-electric pyrometers with thermo-couples of platinum in contact with alloys of platinum and rhodium or iridium, nickel with an alloy of nickel and chromium, iron and nickel (constantan), and copper with constantan are in common use. The thermo-couple pyrometer measures the difference of temperature between the hot junction and the other end of the two pieces of metal. If the cold junction is always kept at the same standard temperature, the actual temperature of the hot junction can be obtained by adding the reading of the instrument to the temperature of the cold junction. In commercial instruments it is common to use leads of the same materials as the thermo-couple; the cold junction can then be placed at the indicator, where there is greater possibility of maintaining constant temperature conditions.

It is a great advantage if the pyrometer is not subjected to the temperature which is to be measured. The radiation pyrometer is of great value in measuring furnace temperatures. One of the most commonly used instruments is that of Féry, in which the heat rays from the furnace are received on a concave mirror and reflected on to a thermo-couple, and the temperature is then read from the scale of a galvanometer. A very ingenious device is used to ensure that the rays are all focused on the couple.

PYROMOR'PHITE. A yellow or greenish (rarely purplish) mineral, orthophosphate of lead, with chlorine; its molecular and crystalline structure agree with that of apatite. Its formula may be written $(PbCl)Pb_4(PO_4)_3$, or $3Pb_3P_2O_8 . PbCl_2$.

PY'ROPE. Fire-garnet or Bohemian garnet, a dark-red variety of garnet, found especially in the mountains of Bohemia. It occurs also in Saxony in serpentine. *See* GARNET.

PYRO'SIS, or **WATER-BRASH.** A condition due to defective digestion in the stomach, resulting in a burning pain being felt in that region, accompanied by eructations.

PYROSO'MA. A genus of phosphorescent Tunicata, compound ascidians inhabiting the Mediterranean and Atlantic. Each colony consists of a great number of individuals, embedded in a firm transparent matrix, and forming a large hollow cylinder, open at one end and closed at the other, swimming in the ocean by ejection of a current of water from the open end of the cylinder.

PYR'OXENES. An important group of mineral silicates, including *augite* (q.v.), occurring in igneous and metamorphic rocks.

PYROX'YLINE. A name applied somewhat loosely to gun-cotton, and other products of the action of nitric acid on cellulose (q.v.). When cotton is soaked in a mixture of nitric and sulphuric acids, a series of cellulose nitrates is produced, in proportions depending largely on the concentration of the acid mixture, and on the temperature. The highest and most explosive member of the series is gun-cotton or cellulose hexanitrate, $C_{12}H_{14}(ONO_2)_6O_4$; this is insoluble in a mixture of alcohol and ether. "Soluble gun-cotton," used in the preparation of collodion, celluloid, and artificial silk, is a mixture of lower nitrates of cellulose. These are distinguished from the hexanitrate by their solubility in ether-alcohol. In pharmacy, the name pyroxyline, or pyroxylin, is restricted to the tetranitrate $C_{12}H_{16}(ONO_2)_4O_6$.

PYRRHIC DANCE. An ancient Grecian warlike dance. It was danced to the sound of the flute. We learn from Plato that its aim was to represent an attempt to avoid the blows of an enemy in battle. The motions necessary to perform the dance were looked upon as a kind of training for war. In the non-Doric states the dance was purely mimetic, and frequently performed by women. It was introduced into the Roman public games by Julius Cæsar, and was danced by male and female dancers, having a somewhat dramatic character. A dance called Romaika, existing in the mountainous districts of Thessaly and Macedonia, and performed by men armed with muskets and swords, is supposed to be a modern survival of the Pyrrhic dance.

PYRRHO. Greek philosopher of Elis, founder of the Pyrrhonian or sceptical school, flourished about 340 B.C. He was early led to apply himself to philosophy by the writings of Democritus, and, accompanying his master, Anaxarchus, to India, in the train of Alexander the Great, he there became acquainted with the doctrines of the Brahmans, Magi, and other Eastern philosophers. Spending a great part of his life in solitude, and abstaining from all decided opinions concerning moral and physical phenomena, he endeavoured to attain a state of tranquillity not to be affected by fear, joy, or sorrow. He died in his ninetieth year; the Athenians erected a statue in honour of him, and his countrymen, who had made him a high-priest, raised a monument to his memory.

Led by his temperament and his manner of life to esteem an uninterrupted tranquillity the great object of philosophy, believing that nothing tended so much to destroy this quiet as the interminable disputes of the schools of the Dogmatists, he determined to seek elsewhere the peace which he despaired of finding in dogmatic philosophy. This led him to scepticism. His chief doctrines were the uncertainty of all human knowledge, and the belief that virtue is the only good. Pyrrho left no writings. It is only from the works of his later followers, particularly Sextus Empiricus, that we learn the principles of his school. A disposition to doubt is often called, from this philosopher, *Pyrrhonism*. *See* SCEPTICISM.

PYRRHOTINE. A bronze-coloured mineral often styled *magnetic pyrites*, composed of ferrous sulphide, FeS, with some additional absorbed sulphur. It is important on account of its common association with ores of nickel, as at Sudbury, in Ontario. Its powder is attracted by a bar-magnet.

PYRRHUS. King of Epirus, born about 318 B.C., and left an orphan in childhood. He was placed on the throne of his ancestors when about twelve years of age, and reigned peacefully five years, when advantage was taken of his absence to transfer the crown to his great-uncle Neoptolemus. After serving with his brother-in-law Demetrius Poliorcetes, and greatly distinguishing himself at the battle of Ipsus against Antigonus, 301 B.C., Pyrrhus recovered his dominions, which he shared with his rival, and then caused the latter to be put to death. He next contended for possession of Macedonia, and in 280 passed over into Italy to assist the Greeks against Rome. He defeated the Romans in two battles, but with severe loss to himself; then passed over into Sicily, returned to Italy again, and was defeated at Beneventum, 275 B.C. He then retired to

Pyrrhus

Epirus, took part in the Greek troubles, and was killed at Argos, 272 B.C.

PYRROL. Liquid constituent of coal-tar and bone-oil. It has the odour of chloroform, and is obtained by fractional distillation. It has secondary basic properties, and from one of its derivatives, potassium-pyrrol, by the action of iodine and an alkali, an antiseptic used in medicine, known as iodol, is obtained.

PYRUS. A genus of ornamental and fruit trees, the latter forming the chief of our orchard fruit, and belonging to the pomaceous section of the nat. ord. Rosaceæ. There are about forty species, natives of the north temperate and cold regions. The pear (*P. commūnis*), the apple or crab (*P. malus*), service tree (*P. torminālis* and *domestica*), mountain-ash or rowan tree (*P. aucuparia*), beam tree (*P. aria*), etc., all belong to this genus.

PYTCHLEY. English hunt. It was founded about 1750 in Northamptonshire, and the succeeding Earls Spencer have been closely associated with it. The country stretches from Market Harborough to Northampton, and the kennels are at Brigstock. In 1874 the **Woodland Pytchley** was established to hunt part of the Pytchley country.

PYTHAG'ORAS. Greek philosopher, supposed to have been born at Samos about 582 B.C. He went to Scyros, and was a scholar of Pherecydes till the death of the latter; others make him also a scholar of Thales and Anaximander. He is said to have gathered knowledge from the philosophers or learned men of Phœnicia, Syria, Egypt, Babylon, India, etc., but eventually settled at the Greek city of Crotona, in Lower Italy, probably about 529 B.C. His abilities and character led great numbers, chiefly of the noble and wealthy classes, to adopt his views. Three hundred of these were formed into a select fraternity or order, and were bound by vow to Pythagoras and each other, for the purpose of cultivating the rites and observances enjoined by their master, and studying his philosophy. They thus formed at once a philosophical school and a religious order. The political influence of this body became very considerable, and was exerted in the interest of the aristo-

Pythagoras

cratic party. The democratic party strenuously opposed the growing power of the order, and their enmity caused Pythagoras to retire to Metapontum, where he died about 506 B.C.

His system appears to owe very much to a vivid imagination acting upon prevailing ignorance respecting the order of nature. What was not known was guessed at, with the usual result. In the case of Pythagoras, as in that of other teachers of those early times, the popular effect of this partial knowledge was heightened by mingling it with secret doctrines. One of these doctrines was the transmigration of souls; and Pythagoras is said to have believed himself to have previously lived in several bodies. This doctrine of the transmigration of souls (*metempsychosis*), which was originally Egyptian, and connected with the idea of the reward and punishment of human actions, was the chief reason why the Pythagoreans killed no animals.

Pythagoras had also abstruse theories respecting numbers, geometry, and music, which he valued very highly as fitting the soul for contemplation. The proof of the 47th proposition of the first book of Euclid's *Elements* is attributed to him. The effect of his teaching, however, was such that his disciples are said to have paid him divine honours after his death. In appearance he was grave, commanding, and dignified. He abstained from all animal food, limiting himself to a vegetable diet.

His public instruction consisted of practical discourses in which he recommended virtue and dissuaded from vice, with a particular reference to the various relations of mankind, as those of husbands and wives, parents and children, citizens and magistrates, etc. His disciples were required to practise the greatest purity and simplicity of manners. He imposed upon them, it is said, a silence of from two to five years, according to circumstances. He alone who had passed through the appointed series of trials was allowed to hear the word of the master in his immediate presence. To the initiated the doctrines were not delivered, as to others, under the mask of images and symbols, but unveiled. The mysticism of his philosophy was derived by Pythagoras from the Orphic hymns (*see* ORPHISM). Pythagoras left no writings; the *Golden Sentences* extant under his name having been composed or compiled by later hands. The Pythagorean philosophy had a great influence on the Platonic, and in later times it was revived and intermingled with neo-Platonism (q.v.).—Cf. T. Gomperz, *Greek Thinkers*.

PYTH'EAS. Greek astronomer and geographer, a native of the colony of Massilia (Marseilles), supposed to have lived about the time of Alexander the Great (say 330 B.C.). He is reputed to have sailed along the west coast of Europe, entered the English Channel, and travelled some distance in Britain, then, continuing his journey northward, to have arrived at Thule (supposed to be Iceland). In a second voyage he entered the Baltic, where he proceeded as far as a river which he called Tanais, and on the banks of which amber was found. We only know of him through Strabo, Pliny, and others.

PYTHIAN GAMES. One of the four great Grecian games, instituted in honour of Apollo. They were celebrated in the neighbourhood of Delphi (formerly called Pytho), in the Crissæan fields. According to the popular mythological legend, the Pythian games were instituted by Apollo himself. Until about 586 B.C. they were under the management of the Delphians, and took place every eighth year; but after that date they were conducted by the Amphictyons, and celebrated every fourth year, prizes being given for flute-playing, athletic sports, and horse- and chariot-racing. Eventually contests in tragedy, painting, sculpture, etc., were added. At first prizes of silver or gold were awarded, but afterwards the simple laurel wreath and palm-branch were substituted. They continued to be celebrated until the end of the fourth century of our era.

PYTHIAS. Greek hero; friend of Damon. When Dionysius of Syracuse condemned the former to death, Damon took his place and remained imprisoned while Pythias settled his affairs. Pythias honourably returned in time for the execution, and Dionysius, impressed by their friendship, liberated both.

PYTHIUM. *See* DAMPING-OFF DISEASE.

PYTHON. In Greek mythology, a serpent generated from the mud left by the deluge of Deucalion. It inhabited Mount Parnassus, where it was killed by Apollo. The Pythian games of Greece are supposed to have celebrated this victory.

PYTHON. A genus of snakes forming a subdivision of the family Boidæ or Boas. They are not venomous, but kill their prey by compression. The pythons belong exclusively to the hotter parts of the Old World (except one species in South Mexico), and are of enormous size, sometimes attaining a length of 30 feet. They are found in India and in the islands of the Eastern Archipelago, in Africa, and in Australia. A rudimentary pelvis and traces of hinder limbs exist in the pythons, these structures terminating externally in a kind of hooked claw. The head exceeds the neck in thickness, and the mouth is extremely large. Aided by their prehensile tails and rudimentary hinder limbs, the pythons suspend themselves from the branches of trees and lie in wait near water for animals which come to drink. The genus Python contains various species, the best known of which is the West African python (*P. sebæ*), common in menageries; while *P. spilotes* is the carpet-snake of Australia and

Python (*Python regius*)

New Guinea. The female python hatches her eggs with the heat of her body.

PYX, TRIAL OF THE. The final trial by weight and assay of the gold and silver coins of the United Kingdom, prior to their issue from the Mint. The *pyx* is a chest in which one coin from every 15 lb. of newly coined gold, and one from every 60 lb. of silver, are set aside to await the test. The trial takes place periodically before a jury of goldsmiths summoned by the Lord Chancellor, and constitutes a public attestation of the standard purity of the coin. The term is also applied to the assaying of gold and silver plate, which takes place at the different assay offices.

PYXID'IUM. In botany, a capsule with a lid, as seen in henbane and in the fruit of *Lecythis Ollaria*, the monkey-pot tree, a large forest tree of Brazil.

Q

Q. The seventeenth letter in the English alphabet, a consonant having the same sound as *k* or hard *c*. It is a superfluous letter in English, as the combination *qu*, in which it always occurs, could be equally well expressed by *kw* or *k* alone when the *u* is silent. It did not occur in the Anglo-Saxon alphabet, but was borrowed from the French-Latin alphabet.

QABES. *See* CABES.

Q-BOAT. Term used during the Great War for a ship designed to deceive and destroy hostile submarines. Disguised as merchant or fishing vessels, they were armed with hidden guns, and carried a fighting crew.

QENA. *See* KENNEH.

QUADI. A Germanic people of the Suevic race, whose ancient territory was on the Danube, extending to the Theiss on the east and to the Carpathian Mountains on the north. They long waged destructive wars with the Romans, particularly under Marcus Aurelius, but cease to be heard of in the fifth century, having probably migrated farther west with the Suevi.

QUADRAGESIMA. Latin word meaning "fortieth." It denotes the 40 days' Lenten fast before Easter. The first Sunday in Lent is called Quadragesima Sunday.

QUADRANGLE. In plane geometry, a closed figure contained by any four straight lines, such as a rectangle, rhombus, etc., and particularly to one in which the sides and angles are equal. The term is also applied to a rectangular courtyard surrounded by buildings.

QUAD'RANT. (*a*) The fourth part of the circumference of a circle; (*b*) the fourth part of the area, viz. that included between the circumference and two perpendicular radii; (*c*) an instrument formerly used for taking altitudes in navigation, astronomy, gunnery, and surveying. The essential part of the instrument is an arc of a circle graduated into degrees and parts of degrees. The principle of one simple type is shown in the figure. The eye at E observes an object in the direction EA. AW is a plumb-line attached at A. The angle between EA and the horizontal line EH is equal to the angle BAP, if EAB is a right angle. The angle BAP is read from the arc BP. The quadrant has been superseded

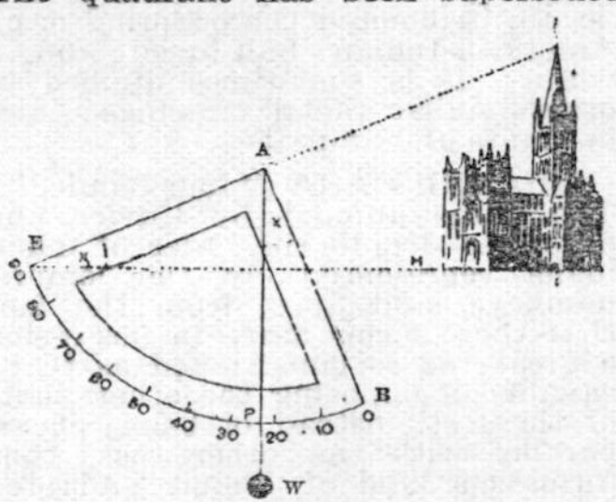

by more efficient instruments, the mural circle (q.v.) in astronomy, and the sextant (q.v.) in navigation.

QUADRATE BONE. A bone developed in reptiles and birds, by means of which the lower jaw is articulated or joined to the skull.

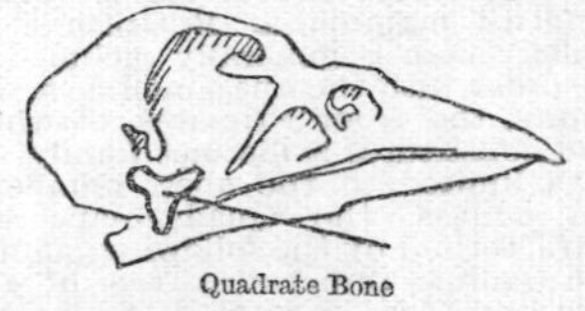

Quadrate Bone

The lower jaw of these forms is thus not hinged directly or of itself to the skull, as in mammals.

QUAD'RATURE. In astronomy, the position of the moon or a planet when its longitude differs from that of the sun by 90°. In mathematics, the process by which a square is found, exactly or approximately, having its area equal to that of a given figure. A famous example is that of "squaring the circle."

QUADRILAT'ERAL. A name given to the space enclosed between, and defended by, four fortresses in Northern Italy famous in Austro-

Italian history, namely, Peschiera and Mantua on the Mincio, and Verona and Legnago on the Adige.

QUADRILLE'. A dance of French origin, which consists generally of five consecutive figures or movements, danced by four sets of couples, each forming the side of a square. It originated in the French ballets of the eighteenth century, but in its modern form dates from the beginning of the nineteenth century.

QUADROON. Word of Spanish origin meaning "quarter-blooded," denoting the offspring of a mulatto and a white. In early Spanish America, before negro immigration began, it denoted the offspring of an American-Indian half-breed and a white; it is sometimes applied to other similar racial crossings: also in plants and animals.

QUADRU'MANA ("four-handed"). The name applied by Cuvier and others to denote the order of mammalia represented by the lemurs, monkeys, and apes, from the fact that these forms agree in possessing a great toe so constructed as to be capable of opposing the other digits of the feet, instead of being placed parallel with the other toes, thus forming a kind of "hand" adapted for supporting the foot on the ground. This conversion of the feet into hand-like organs presented to Cuvier's mind a structure so remarkable and so different from the disposition of the feet and toes of man, that he separated man as a sole and single genus to represent the distinct and opposing order of Bimana or "two-handed" mammalia. But in modern zoology man is generally included in one order with the apes, monkeys, and lemurs, the order Primates, of which man constitutes a distinct family.

As limited to the apes, monkeys, and lemurs, the Quadrumana are characterised by the following points: The hallux (innermost toe of the hind-limb) is separated from the other toes, and is opposite to them, so that the hind-feet become prehensile hands. The pollex (innermost toe of the fore-limbs) may be wanting, but when present it also is usually opposable to the other digits, so that the animal becomes truly quadrumanous, or four-handed. The teats are two in number, and the mammary glands are on the chest as in man, though some lemurs have abdominal ones in addition, and in the males of one genus (Hapalemur) there is a mammary gland on each shoulder. *See* MONKEYS; APE; etc.

QUADRUPLE ALLIANCE. An alliance, so called from the number of the contracting parties, concluded in 1718 between Great Britain, France, and Austria, and acceded to by Holland in 1719, for the maintenance of the Peace of Utrecht. The occasion of the alliance was the seizure by Spain of Sardinia in 1717, and Sicily in 1718, both of which she was forced to give up. Another quadruple alliance was that of Austria, Russia, Great Britain, and Prussia in 1814, originating in the coalition which had effected the dissolution of the French Empire. Another quadruple alliance was the league formed in 1840 by Austria, Prussia, Russia, and Great Britain for the purpose of protecting Turkey against the threatening power of Mehemet Ali (q.v.).

QUÆSTOR (Lat. *quærere*, to inquire, ask). The name of certain magistrates of ancient Rome whose chief office was the management of the public treasure, being receivers of taxes, tribute, etc. Quæstors accompanied the provincial governors, received taxes, and paid the troops The office could at first be held only by patricians until 421 B.C., when the number, which had formerly been two, was doubled, and plebeians became eligible. The number was further increased to eight after the outbreak of the first Punic War. As province after province was added to the Roman territory the number of quæstors was again increased, till under Sulla it reached twenty, and in the time of Julius Cæsar forty.—Cf. A. H. J. Greenidge, *Roman Public Life*.

QUAGGA (*Equus quagga*). An extinct species of the horse genus, nearly allied to the zebra, and formerly found on the plains of South Africa. Striped like the zebra, it yet possessed no bands on the limbs; of a dark or blackish-brown on the head, neck, and the shoulders, the back and hind quarters were of a lighter brown, whilst the croup was of a russet grey. The under parts

Quagga

of the body were white, the upper parts of the legs and tail being marked by whitish bars. The quagga was of smaller size than the zebra, and in general conformation bore a closer resemblance to the horse. Gregarious in habits, the quagga is said to have mingled indiscriminately with the zebra herds. Its food consisted of grasses and mimosa leaves. The animal to which the name quagga or bonte-quagga (" painted quagga ") is now applied is Burchell's zebra (*E. burchelli*). *See* DAUW.

QUAGLIO. Italian family of artists. **Domenico,** born at Laino in 1723, was an historical painter, and was known as " the elder " to distinguish him from his grandson **Domenico** " the younger " (1787-1837). The latter was noted for his landscapes and architectural drawings. Another grandson, **Angelo** (1784-1815) distinguished himself as a painter and architect. **Lorenz** and **Simon,** brothers of the younger Domenico, were other artist members of the family, the former responsible for the *Tyrolese Inn* in the Berlin National Gallery.

QUAIL (Coturnix). A genus of game-birds, included in the pheasant family (Phasianidæ) and nearly allied to partridges, from which they differ

Quail

in being smaller, in having a relatively shorter tail, no red space above the eye, longer wings, and no spur on the legs. The common quail (*C. communis*) is a migratory bird, and is found in every country of Europe, and in many parts of Asia and Africa. It is about 8 inches in length. The colour of the upper parts is brownish with lighter and darker markings, of the under parts yellowish. The quail is very pugnacious, and in some places quail-fights are a form of amusement, as was the case also in ancient times. Its flesh is deemed excellent food, and large numbers are brought alive and dead from the Continent to the British markets. In Britain these birds arrive early in May, and depart southwards in October. There are several other species, in appearance and habits not greatly differing from the common quail, as the Coromandel quail (*C. coromandelica*) and the Australian quail (*C. pectoralis*). The name quail is also given to some birds of other genera, as the Virginia or Maryland quail (*Ortyx virginianus*) and the Californian or crested quail (*Lophortyx californicus*). The Virginian quail is common throughout North America, and extends as far south as Honduras. It is rather larger than the European quail. The flesh is very white and tender, and of rare delicacy.

QUAIN, Jones. Irish doctor, born in Mallow, Co. Cork, in 1796, and educated at Dublin and Paris. From 1831 to 1835 he was professor of general anatomy at University College, London. He died in 1865. He is chiefly remembered for his *Elements of Anatomy*, which remained a standard textbook.

QUAIN, Sir Richard. British physician, born at Mallow, County Cork, in 1816, died in 1898. He became a member of the Royal College of Physicians in 1846, Fellow in 1851, and subsequently vice-president and member of the council. Besides publishing several medical treatises, he edited a well-known *Dictionary of Medicine*.

QUAINI, Francesco. Italian painter, born 1611, died 1680. He was responsible for the decorations of many public buildings in his native city of Bologna.

His son **Lodovico** (1643-1717) collaborated with his father and painted landscape and architectural backgrounds to the figure-work of M. A. Franceschini. A *Visitation* and a *Pietà* are among his individual works.

QUAKERS. *See* FRIENDS, SOCIETY OF.

QUAKING GRASS (Briza). A genus of grasses, so named from their spikelets being always in a state of tremulous motion, in consequence of the weakness of the footstalks by which they are supported. *Briza maxima*, a native of Southern Europe, has long been cultivated as a garden annual on account of its large and handsome drooping spikelets. *B. media*, a perennial plant, is the only species common in Britain, but *B. minor* is also a native.

QUAM'ASH. The North American name of *Camassia esculenta*, a plant of the lily family with an edible bulb. These bulbs are much eaten by the Indians, and are prepared by baking in a hole dug in the ground, then pounding and drying them into cakes for future use.

QUAMOC'LIT. A genus of climbing ornamental plants, nat. ord. Convolvulaceæ, chiefly found in the hot parts of America, but some species are indigenous both in India and China.

QUANTIFICATION OF THE PREDICATE. In logic, the use of some word or words to indicate whether the predicate of a proposition is distributed or not, that is, whether or not all the objects of which the predicate may be asserted are also objects of which the subject may (in affirmative propositions) be asserted or (in negative propositions) denied. Thus, when we say *Some men are logicians*, we do not know from the form of the proposition whether we may not apply the predicate logicians to any who are not men, but if we quantify the predicate and say *Some men are all logicians*, we at once show that this application cannot be made. Ploucquet and Lambert in the eighteenth century suggested the quantification of the predicate, but Sir William Hamilton was the first to give prominence to the doctrine by the importance that he attached to it, considering it as involving a complete revolution in formal logic. The doctrine of the quantification of the predicate was attacked immediately after his enunciation of it, and it has never been generally adopted in the exposition of formal logic.

QUANTITY SURVEYOR. Surveyor who estimates for a builder quantities, measurements, and costs from a plan prepared by an architect. He must have sufficient knowledge of architecture and the building trade to interpret plans and estimate the labour required.

QUANTOCK HILLS. A range of low elevation of Somerset, England, extending from the Bristol Channel, near Watchet, south-east to between Bridgewater and Taunton, the culminating point being Will's Neck (1261 feet altitude).

QUANTUM THEORY. The principles of classical mechanics involve the assumption that the mechanical states of any system form a continuous series (i.e. that there is a mechanical state intermediate between any two such states), and that a system passes from one mechanical state to another through the states intermediate between them. On the other hand, quantum theories involve the assumption that the possible states (called "quantum states") of a system form a discontinuous series, and that the system passes from one quantum state to another without passing through any intermediate state. Thus, while classical mechanics holds that a particle in changing its velocity must pass through all velocities intermediate between the initial and final velocity, a quantum theory applicable to such a particle would hold that it passes through only a finite number of discrete velocities, changing abruptly and without intermediate steps from one of these velocities to another.

When first evidence was obtained of the discontinuous changes postulated by quantum theory, attempts were made to explain them in terms of classical mechanics, e.g. by supposing that the intermediate states which appeared to be omitted were unstable in the mechanical sense, so that they did not persist for an appreciable period. Such attempts are now abandoned; the principles of quantum theories are regarded as more ultimate than those of classical mechanics, and therefore as not explicable in terms of them. On the contrary, the continuous changes of classical mechanics, which are of course suggested by the apparently continuous changes of common experience, are regarded as limiting cases of discontinuous quantum changes. When they occur, it is either because the difference between successive quantum states is too small to be perceptible, or because they represent a statistical average of the states of a very large number of elementary systems, each undergoing discontinuous quantum changes. It is only in very small indivisible systems (atoms and molecules) that the discontinuity of the quantum states becomes apparent.

A completely general quantum theory would define the quantum states for any kind of system and state the conditions in which change from one quantum state to another occur. Such generality has not been attained, and the quantum states can only be defined for certain systems. But all quantum theories have two features in common: (1) the quantum states are always states which would be possible according to classical mechanics; (2) the relations that define which mechanical states are quantum states and which, not being quantum states, cannot occur at all, all involve Planck's universal constant h, the numerical value of which is $6{\cdot}56 \times 10^{-27}$ erg-sec., together with a variable integer m. The more important quantum theories will now be noticed in turn; each of them leads to a determination of h, and the best evidence for a general and fundamental quantum theory is that the same value is determined by all of them.

1. It is an experimental fact that when an electron absorbs energy from or gives energy to radiation, it always absorbs or gives an amount of energy $h\nu$, where ν is the frequency of the radiation; the amount is independent of the intensity of the radiation and of the constitution of the system to which the electron belongs. Such facts are found in the photo-electric effect (q.v.) in secondary β-radiation excited by X-rays, and in the excitation of spectrum lines by moving electrons (*see* SPECTRA, THEORY OF). This double independence is inexplicable by any "continuous" theory. Quantum theory explains it by asserting as a fundamental principle that the quantum states of radiation of frequency ν have energies equal to $mh\nu$, and that by reaction with an electron only those changes are possible in which m changes by 1. An alternative theory is that the electron which takes part in these changes of energy belongs to an "oscillator" with a frequency equal to that of the radiation, that the quantum states of this oscillator have an energy $mh\nu$, and that m can only change by 1; but this older theory is now generally abandoned and the quantum states assigned to the radiation, not to the electron.

2. The relation found experimentally between the wave-length and the intensity of the complete temperature radiation emitted from a body and the temperature of that body is definitely irreconcilable with the principles of classical mechanics (*see* RADIATION, THEORY OF). This discrepancy led historically to the formulation (by Planck in 1900) of the first quantum theory; but it is remarkable that the direct evidence for a quantum theory is much less obvious in connection with the laws of temperature radiation than with any of the other laws to which such theories are applied. For since, according to thermodynamic theory, temperature is a conception applicable only to a system consisting of a very large number of individually independent elements, all laws involving temperature must be regarded as fundamentally statistical; and such laws are not expected to show the discontinuities characteristic of quantum changes. Nevertheless, though in this case the experimental laws to be explained give no indication of discontinuity, the only satisfactory explanation of them that has been offered is based on the assumption that they represent on average of elementary laws that are essentially discontinuous. Here again there has been some doubt whether the discontinuous quantum states should be assigned to the radiation or to the material system with which it reacts; but the tendency is towards accepting the former view and adopting the same criterion of quantum states as in (1).

The problem then arises of determining how the distribution of the total energy of the radiation among the possible quantum states will depend on the temperature. It is solved by means of Boltzmann's equation (*see* THERMODYNAMICS) relating the entropy S (which is a function of the energy and the temperature) to W, the probability of the given state; the probability is defined as the ratio of the number of "complexions" which all represent that physical state to the total number of possible complexions; and each possible distribution of the energy among the different quantum states represents a different complexion. From these assumptions Planck's law of radiation can be deduced, though it is not perfectly certain that a deduction completely logical has been given. It follows that the energy of an oscillator of natural frequency ν in thermal equilibrium with complete radiation at temperature T (and therefore forming part of a body at that temperature) is $L^{\nu} = \dfrac{h\nu}{e^{h\nu/RT} - 1}$.

3. Closely allied with (2) is the explanation of the laws relating the specific heat of bodies to the temperature or to other properties (e.g. magnetic properties) which depend upon the mean energy of the molecules. In virtue of the conclusions of (2), the deduction of such laws requires only a knowledge of the proportions in which oscillators of various frequencies are present in the body. In a gas these oscillators are supposed to consist of the rotating molecules, the frequency of rotation being the frequency of oscillation. In a solid body they consist of the various stationary elastic oscillations which can be maintained in the body by reason of its rigidity and compressibility. Calculations on this basis give a most remarkable agreement between experiment and theory, not merely in the relation between specific heat and temperature, but also in the relation between specific heat and the moment of inertia of gaseous molecules or the elastic constants (and indeed all mechanical properties) of the solid. Two subsidiary results of interest follow: (1) the absorption-band in the infra-red spectrum,

characteristic of any solid, represents the elastic oscillation of highest frequency which the body can perform; (2) the mean energy of an oscillator at the absolute zero of temperature is not zero (as classical theory would predict) but $h\nu/2$, where ν is its frequency.

4. The most elaborate quantum theory has been developed by Bohr and Sommerfeld to define quantum states of the atom, the existence of which is clearly indicated by the study of spectra (*see* SPECTRA, THEORY OF). Here we are concerned (*see* MATTER, ATOMIC THEORIES OF) with systems of electrons and positively charged nuclei, held together and apart by electrostatic forces, and executing orbits of many degrees of freedom which are periodic in the most general sense. The orbits which represent quantum states are (as usual) assumed to be such as would be possible according to classical principles, but are selected from among those so possible by a certain criterion. The orbits can be calculated with perfect certainty when there is only one electron associated with the nucleus; the orbits are then ellipses (or, more accurately, differ very slightly from ellipses in virtue of the "relativity" correction); there are two periodic co-ordinates, the radius from the focus and the angle between the radius and some fixed line; there are accordingly two quantum numbers, called respectively the "radial" and the "azimuthal." Since either of these numbers can assume any positive integral value, there is a doubly infinite (and yet discontinuous) series of quantum states for such an electron. The energy of the electron is determined mainly by the sum of the two quantum numbers, or "total" quantum number, and is nearly the same for all states for which it is the same. The normal state of the atom (*see* MATTER) is that for which it is 1.

About 1925, quantum theory took a new departure. Heisenberg, Born, Jordan, and Dirac proposed *matrix mechanics*, based on the algebraic method of matrices. L. de Broglie and E. Schrödinger expounded wave mechanics (q.v.), related to ordinary mechanics in much the same way as physical optics is to geometrical optics.—BIBLIOGRAPHY: L. de Broglie and L. Brillouin, *Selected Papers on Wave Mechanics*; *Four Lectures on Wave Mechanics*.

QUAR'ANTINE (It. *quarantina*, a space of forty days). The period (originally forty days) during which a ship coming from a port suspected of contagion, or having a contagious sickness on board, is forbidden intercourse with the place at which she arrives. This form of quarantine is now confined to foreign countries where cholera, yellow fever, etc., have to be guarded against. In Britain the Quarantine Act of 1825 has been repealed, and replaced by the Public Health Act of 1904. Quarantine was originally introduced at Venice as a measure of protection against plague or leprosy about the middle of the fourteenth century, Venice, then the chief trading centre of the Mediterranean, being especially liable to contagion through vessels coming from Eastern ports. A lazaretto was early erected there in connection with the quarantine restrictions.—Cf. Sir S. Baker, *Laws relating to Quarantine.*

QUARLES, Francis. English poet, born in 1592 near Romford, in Essex, died in 1644. Educated at Christ's College, Cambridge, he entered at

Francis Quarles

Lincoln's Inn, and in 1613 was appointed cupbearer to Elizabeth, Queen of Bohemia. In 1629 he went to Dublin as secretary to Archbishop Ussher. He appears to have left Ireland before 1633 and to have settled in Essex, and in 1639 he was appointed chronologer to the city of London. At the commencement of the Civil Wars he joined the king at Oxford and wrote some pamphlets, including *The Loyal Convert,* which gave offence to the Parliament. His property was sequestrated, and his manuscripts destroyed. He was so much affected by his losses that grief is supposed to have hastened his death. Of the works of Quarles, in prose and verse, the most celebrated is his *Emblems*, a set of designs illustrated by verses. Among his poems are *Divine Poems*, *Divine Fancies*, and *Argalus and Parthenia*. His *Enchiridion* is a collection of brief essays and aphorisms, in vigorous and occasionally eloquent language.

QUARNE'RO, GULF OF. In the Adriatic Sea, between Istria, Italy, and the Croatian coast, in Yugoslavia, 15 miles in length and breadth. It is nearly enclosed leewards by the Islands of Cherso and Veglia, and communicates with the Adriatic by three channels.

QUARRY BANK. Urban district of Staffordshire. A colliery centre, it is a mile from Dudley, and has ironworks. Pop. (1931), 8100.

QUARRYING. Excavation of stone from an open pit. The methods adopted vary chiefly according to the position and nature of the stone, but usually the excavation is made on the side of a hill. Where possible the planes of bedding or joint planes are used for removing the blocks, but in some rocks where these do not exist the use of wedges and blasting is employed to loosen the material.

QUART. English measure of capacity. It is two pints and is the quarter of a gallon. In music the interval of a fourth is called a quart.

QUARTER. Measure of weight and capacity. It means a fourth part, and is used for the fourth part of a hundredweight (28 lb.). Quarter is also used as a measure of wheat, a quarter of English wheat being 504 lb. As a measure of capacity it is equal to eight bushels. The fourth part of a year is also a quarter; and the periods of the moon are known as quarters.

QUARTER-DAY. In England, the day that begins each quarter of the year. These are Lady Day (25th March), Midsummer Day (24th June), Michaelmas Day (29th Sept.), Christmas Day (25th Dec.). These days have been adopted between landlord and tenant for entering or quitting lands or houses and for paying rent. In Scotland the legal terms are Whitsunday (15th May) and Martinmas (11th Nov.); the conventional terms Candlemas (2nd Feb.) and Lammas (1st Aug.) make up the quarter-days.

QUARTER-DECK. In sailing-ship parlance, the upper deck, or aftermost part of the upper deck, of a vessel, extending from the main-mast to the stern, or to the poop (when there is one). In the modern navy the quarter-deck is the after-deck of a warship, and below it are the quarters of the officers. Before the Reformation a crucifix was invariably erected over the poop, and was, of course, saluted as a mark of respect by all hands. To this day the custom is maintained of "saluting the quarter-deck," both on board ship and in naval depots, although the original object of the honour has long since disappeared.

QUARTERING. In heraldry, the bearing of two or more coats-of-arms on a shield. It usually denotes a marriage. The arms are divided by horizontal and perpendicular lines. At one time in Austria and elsewhere, persons were not elegible for certain distinctions unless they could show 16 quarterings.

QUARTERMASTER. In the army, an officer who attends to the quarters for the soldiers, their provisions, fuel, forage, etc. There is a quartermaster attached to every battalion, etc., who generally holds the rank of honorary lieutenant but does not sit in the officers' mess. Quartermaster-sergeants are subordinate to the quartermasters, whose assistants they are in theory if not in practice, and who administer the companies of a battalion (or other units of standard) under his direct guidance and control, although they are also responsible to the captains of the units to which they are posted.

QUARTERMASTER-GENERAL. A staff officer of high rank in the army, whose department is charged with all orders relating to the marching, embarking, disembarking, billeting, quartering, and cantoning of troops, encampments and camp equipage. The quartermaster-general is attached to a whole army under a commander-in-chief, and generally holds the rank of major-general, while to every division is attached a deputy-assistant quartermaster-general.

QUARTER-SESSIONS. In England, a general court of criminal jurisprudence held quarterly by the justices of the peace in counties, and by the recorder in boroughs. The jurisdiction of these courts, originally confined to matters touching breaches of the peace, has been gradually extended, and it now comprises almost all crimes except murder and treason. Appeals from the magistrates' courts are also taken to the quarter-sessions. There is also an extensive jurisdiction in matters relating to the settlement of the poor, highways, vagrancy, bastardy, etc., in most of which cases an appeal lies to the higher courts. In Scotland the quarter-sessions are a court held by the justices of the peace four times a year at the county towns.

These courts have the power of reviewing the sentences pronounced at the special and petty sessions when the sentence is of a nature subject to review. The offences dealt with are only petty offences. Such cases as fall to be tried by the English courts of quarter-sessions are chiefly disposed of in Scotland in the sheriff courts of the county.

QUARTER-STAFF. An old English weapon formed of a stout pole about 6½ feet long, generally loaded with iron at both ends. It was grasped by one hand in the middle, and by the other between the middle and the end. In the attack the latter hand shifted from one quarter of the staff to the other, giving the weapon a rapid circular motion.

QUARTET. The name given in music to a composition written in four parts, either for voices or instruments; but when the term is used without qualification, a quartet consisting of two violins, a viola, and a 'cello is always understood. Music may be written in any desired number of parts, and Thomas Tallis, who wrote in the contrapuntal era, has one composition for voices with the exceptional number of forty. The quartet, however, is a product of the harmonic era, and has its foundation in four-part harmony, which forms the basis of the great bulk of concerted music.

The two violins, viola, and 'cello, which invariably constitute the string quartet, are analogous in their more extended sphere to the soprano, alto, tenor, and bass of the human voice. In the early days of writing music for this and other combinations of instruments it was natural that composers should do many crude things, since they were writing for a medium in which they were totally inexperienced; and an examination of the first string quartets of Haydn, who was the father of this branch of composition, reveals, among other faults, this serious one, that the main interest of the music was too exclusively confined to the top part. Mozart was the first composer to demonstrate the possibility and the necessity of making all four parts of equal musical interest and importance. His immortal set of six quartets, dedicated to Haydn, are particularly complete examples of how such works should be written, and Haydn himself was the first to profit by the demonstration. Since then the string quartet has been a favourite medium of expression for all serious-minded composers, and men like Beethoven, Schubert, Brahms, and many others have enshrined in this medium some of their finest music. In the so-called pianoforte quartets this instrument is generally associated with a violin, viola, and 'cello, and there are also many fine works written for this combination. Quartets for a combination of strings and wind-instruments are rare, while vocal quartets are so common and so frequently heard that there is no occasion for any comment regarding them.

QUARTO. Page of a certain size; also a book of pages of that size. In it the sheets are folded into four, and its sign is 4to. To-day book publishers recognise as quarto: foolcap, 8½ in. × 6¾ in.; crown, 10 in. × 7½ in.; demy, 11¼ × 8¾ in.; royal, 12½ in. × 10 in.; and imperial, 15 in. × 11 in.

QUARTZ. A generic term for most of the native forms of crystallised silica, SiO_2. It may occur in the form of well-defined crystals, such as rock-crystal. These crystals are usually formed of a hexagonal prism terminated by hexagonal pyramids, but the latter are formed by the union of two rhombohedra, and the frequent occurrence of certain oblique planes shows that quartz really crystallises in a low class of the trigonal system. Quartz also occurs in masses and in veins in igneous and metamorphic rocks; such veins frequently contain traces of gold. It is hard, scratches glass readily, and was formerly used by North American Indians for arrow-heads. When struck with steel it produces sparks, and when rubbed it becomes electrified. It is a constituent mineral of numerous igneous rocks, such as granite. The colours are various, as white or milky, grey, reddish, yellowish or brownish, purple, blue, green.

The principal varieties of quartz are the following: (1) *rock-crystal*, the original transparent mineral to which the term crystal was applied, from its resemblance to ice; (2) *smoky quartz*; (3) *citrine*, or *yellow quartz*; (4) *amethyst*; (5) *rose quartz*; (6) *milky quartz*; (7) *carnelian*; (8) *chrysoprase*. Smoky quartz consists of crystals and crystalline masses which are translucent and of a purplish-brown colour. *Bohemian* or *Scottish topaz* and *cairngorm* are forms of transparent yellow quartz. Amethyst is violet and transparent. Milky quartz, the common quartz of veins, is massive and of a milk-white colour. Carnelian has a blood-red colour. Chrysoprase is apple-green. Chalcedony, flint, and jasper (q.v.) are compact forms of crystalline silica, and probably consist of quartz in minute fibres or granules. (*See* AGATE.)

Several varieties of quartz are important in arts and manufactures. At present quartz is employed not only for cups, urns, etc., but for seals, spectacle-glasses, and optical instruments. Quartz is largely used for the manufacture of glass, both white and coloured, and also of porcelain and other kinds of pottery, when it is added in the state of an impalpable powder, and forms part of the paste. Quartz is used as a flux in smelting various ores, particularly those of copper, and in other metallurgical processes. Quartz fused in the oxyhydrogen blow-pipe is drawn out into thin fibres as silica-glass, for the suspension of delicate torsion-balances or for the cross-threads in microscopes. Silica-glass does not crack when suddenly heated and resists most acids, and has found a wide use in laboratories when moulded into flasks and other vessels.

QUARTZITE. A stratified granular-crystalline rock consisting entirely, or almost entirely, of quartz. It is a sandstone which has been cemented by silica; and this silica is deposited as quartz around the primary sand-grains, until an interlocked granular structure arises. Quartzites are conspicuous among older stratified series; but the rock is not necessarily of metamorphic origin. It is generally of a greyish colour, or is pinkish from a slight trace of iron.

QUASSIA. A genus of South American tropical plants, consisting of trees and shrubs, nat. ord. Simarubaceæ. The wood of two species is known in commerce by the name of *Quassia*; *Q. amāra*, a native of Panamá, Venezuela, Guiana, and Northern Brazil, a small tree with handsome crimson flowers; and *Q. excelsa* (*Picræna excelsa*, Lindley), a native of Jamaica. The latter furnishes the *lignum quassiæ* of the *British Pharmacopœia*. Both kinds are imported in billets, and are inodorous but intensely bitter, especially the Jamaica quassia. Quassia is a pure and simple bitter, possessing marked tonic properties. An infusion of quassia sweetened with sugar is useful to destroy flies. *Q. excelsa* was formerly substituted by some brewers for hops, but is now prohibited under severe penalties. *See* BITTER-ASH.

QUATERNARY. In geology, the group of strata of most recent age. It is sometimes referred to as Post-tertiary. The deposits vary much in character, and for the most part are unconsolidated. They include alluvium of present rivers and lakes; marine deposits; also cave deposits and glacial or drift formations.

QUATER'NIONS. A mathematical calculus invented by Sir William Rowan Hamilton (q.v.). It can be regarded either as an algebra, or as a geometry specially applicable to three-dimensional space. In plane geometry $x + iy$ represents the vector from the origin to the point (x, y). Hamilton introduces the analogous form $ix + jy + kz$ for the vector from the origin to (x, y, z). The symbols i, j, k therefore represent unit vectors parallel to the axes of co-ordinates; and the combination by addition of the vectors ix, jy, kz corresponds to the geometrical composition of these into one vector by the parallelogram law. Like i in plane geometry, the quaternion symbols i, j, k are roots of -1. Taking the point of view that quaternions is a generalised algebra, we assign, simply by way of definition, the laws of combination of the symbols $i, j, k, 1$. It is laid down that addition is to be commutative, and that multiplication is to be subject to the following laws of combination of i, j, k:

$$ij = ik = -ji, jk = i = -kj, ki = j = -ik, ijk = -1, i^2 = j^2 = k^2 = -1.$$

Multiplication is accordingly not commutative, ij and ji, for instance, having opposite signs. If we multiply by these rules the two vectors $ix + jy + kz$ and $ix' + jy' + kz'$, the work runs:

$$ix(ix' + jy' + kz') + jy(ix' + jy' + kz') + kz(ix' + jy' + kz')$$
$$= i^2xx' + ijxy' + ikxz' + \text{etc.}$$
$$= -(xx' + yy' + zz') + i(yz' - y'z) + j(zx' - z'x) + k(xy' - x'y).$$

The product of two vectors has therefore the form $w + ia + jb + kc$; it is this type of expression of four terms which is called a *quaternion*. The term w is called the *scalar* part of the quaternion $w + ia + jb + kc$ $(= q)$; and the remaining terms are called the *vector* part. These two parts are written Sq and Vq, so that $q = \mathrm{S}q + \mathrm{V}q$. It will be observed that the expressions found for Sq and Vq correspond to geometrical entities which have important relations to the two vectors which were multiplied together. Thus $xx' + yy' + zz'$ is the product of the absolute magnitudes r, r' (called the *tensors*) of the two vectors by the cosine of the angle θ between them; and the coefficients of i, j, k in the product are the components, parallel to the axes, of the vector whose direction is perpendicular to the plane of the two vectors, and whose absolute magnitude is rr' $\sin\theta$.

Again, the vector operator $idx + jdy + kdz$ (where d_x signifies the operation of differentiation d/dx) when applied to the vector $iX + jY + kZ$ gives the result $-(dX/dx + dY/dy + dZ/dz) + i(dZ/dy - dY/dz)$ + two terms in j and k; the scalar and vector parts here are of very great importance in mathematical physics. The scalar part is called the *convergence* (if without the *minus* sign, the *divergence*) of the vector X, Y, Z; and the vector part is called the *curl* of the vector X, Y, Z.

The existence of relations such as those above makes the method of quaternions very suggestive for geometry and physics. Opinions have differed on the question of its value as a practical working calculus. Hamilton himself, and P. G. Tait, his chief interpreter, were enthusiastic on the subject; Kelvin, on the other hand, thought the method of extremely little use. It ought to be said that the expositions of Hamilton and Tait are geometrical rather than algebraical. Some parts of the *notation* have become the common property of physicists—Clerk Maxwell, e.g. in his *Electricity and Magnetism*, uses it a good deal—but beyond this the method plays only a small part in modern physical investigations. — BIBLIOGRAPHY: C. J. Joly, *Manual of Quaternions*; P. G. Tait, *Quaternions*.

QUATRAIN. In poetry, a stanza of four lines. The lines usually rhyme alternately, as in the hymn by Isaac Watts, "O God, our help in ages past." The stanzas of Tennyson's *In Memoriam* are also called quatrains, although in these the first and the last lines rhyme, as do the two middle ones.

QUATRE-BRAS (kȧ-tr-brä). A village of Belgium, in the province of Brabant, situated at the intersection of the main roads between Brussels and Charleroi, and from Nivelle to Namur. It is famous for the battle fought here (16th June, 1815) between the British under Wellington and the French under Ney.

QUATREFAGES DE BRÉAU (kä-tr-fäzh dė brā-ō), **Jean Louis Armand de.** French naturalist, born in 1810, died in 1892. He took his M.D. degree at Strasbourg in 1838; and was professor of zoology at Toulouse, the Lycée at Paris, and professor of anatomy and ethnology at the Musée d'Histoire Naturelle there. He was elected a member of the Royal Society, London, in 1879. His contributions to science include numerous researches into the lower grades of life, and a valuable series of anthropological studies. Among his more important works are: *Souvenirs d'un naturaliste* (1854), *Crania ethnica* (1875-9), *De l'espèce humaine* (1877), *Hommes fossiles et hommes sauvages* (1883), *La Distribution géographique des négritos* (1883), *L'Homme tertiaire* (1885), *Les pygmées* (1887), and *Histoire générale des races humaines* (1886-9).

QUATREFOIL (kwa̧'tėr-foil). In architecture, an opening or a panel divided by cusps or foliations into four leaves, or more correctly the leaf-shaped figure formed by the cusps. It is an ornament which has been supposed to represent the four leaves of a cruciform flower, and is common in the tracery of Gothic windows. Bands of small quatrefoils are much used as ornaments in the perpendicular Gothic style, and sometimes in the decorated. The same name is also given to flowers and leaves of similar form carved as ornaments on mouldings.

QUAVER. Musical note equal to half a crotchet or one-eighth of a semibreve. As a pulse-note it is symbolised by 8 in the lower half of a time-signature.

QUAY. Landing-place on the side of a river, harbour, or docks for receiving and discharging cargoes from ships. Usually a quay is provided with cranes and other appliances for handling goods and berthing vessels. Quays are constructed of stone or concrete with generally a facing of wooden piles.

QUÉANT. A village of France, in the department of Pas-de-Calais. During the European War it was a pivot of the "Drocourt-Quéant switch line," which branched off from the main Hindenburg Line at Quéant and ran in the rear of the more advanced position, serving as a support to it. This line covered the railways which ran from Boisleux-au-Mont eastwards to Cambrai, from Arras to Douai, and that which proceeded from Lens south-eastward to the Arras-Douai line and Cambrai. As a result of the Allied successes of Aug., 1918, a position was attained which threatened the Hindenburg Line, Germany's main defence, and that at its most dangerous point, the salient where it joined the Drocourt-Quéant line north-west of Quéant. On 2nd Sept., 1918, troops of the British First and Second Armies moved forward, and after seven hours' hand-to-hand fighting the Drocourt-Quéant line was completely cleared. The troops taking part were the 63rd (Royal Naval) Division under Major-General C. A. Blacklock, 1st and 4th Canadian Divisions, 4th English Division, the 52nd and 57th Divisions, and the 3rd Tank Brigade (40 tanks), assisted by Canadian cavalry and armoured-cars and a mobile force of motor machine-guns.

QUEBEC′. An eastern province of the Dominion of Canada.

Area and Population. The total area is 594,434 sq. miles, of which 23,430 sq. miles are water. The adjustment of the Labrador boundary in 1927 (*see* LABRADOR) took a certain amount of territory from Quebec. The population in 1911 only covered the area of Quebec prior to the annexation of Ungava in 1912, and represents, therefore, an area of only 351,873 sq. miles. In that year there were 2,005,776 inhabitants. Of this population over 1,500,000 were of French origin and 300,000 British. The census population in 1931 was 2,874,255.

Towns. The principal towns and their populations (1931) are: Montreal (818,577); Quebec, the capital (130,594); Verdun (60,745); Three Rivers (35,450); Hull (29,433); and Sherbrooke (28,933).

Physiography. The chief mountains are the Notre Dame or Shickshock Mountains, extending along the south side of the St. Lawrence, and forming a tableland 1500 feet high, with peaks rising to the height of 4000 feet; and the Laurentian Mountains, or Laurentides, which stretch from the coast of Labrador to the Ottawa River, and rise to a height of from 1200 to 4000 feet. The chief islands are Anticosti, at the mouth of the St. Lawrence, and the Magdalen Islands in the Gulf of St. Lawrence. The chief river is the St. Lawrence, which flows through the entire length of the province. Next to it in importance is its chief tributary, the Ottawa, over 700 miles in length. The other largest rivers are the St. Maurice and the Saguenay. The province boasts many beautiful lakes, among the chief being St. John. It has also abundant water-power. The valleys of the St. Lawrence and the Ottawa are the chief seat of population.

Production. The soil is generally fertile, and well suited for the growth of cereals, hay, etc.; maize, flax, and tobacco are grown, especially to the west of the longitude of Quebec, also grapes, melons, peaches, tomatoes, etc. Dairying and stock-rearing are flourishing industries. A large portion of the province is covered with forest, and great quantities of pine lumber and pulp wood are taken out. The fisheries are extensive and valuable. The minerals worked include apatite, asbestos, gold, copper, iron, plumbago, etc. The manufactures include furniture, leather, paper, paper-pulp, boots and shoes, woollens, cottons, cheese, butter, condensed milk, iron, hardware, soap, maple sugar, maple syrup, flour, and agricultural implements and machinery.

Education. The educational system embraces institutions of all grades, from primary schools upwards, at the top being four universities—Laval University (Quebec); M'Gill University (Montreal, Protestant); Lennoxville University (also Protestant); and the University of Montreal (Catholic), with 7013 students in Quebec in 1930-1, and 10,173 in Montreal.

Government. The affairs of the province are administered by a Lieutenant-Governor (appointed by the Governor-General) and a responsible ministry assisted by a Legislative Council of 24 members, appointed for life, and a Legislative Assembly of 90 members, elected for 5 years. Women are not enfranchised, and are not eligible for election to Legislature.

QUEBEC. A city and shipping-port of the Dominion of Canada, capital of the province of the same name, situated on a promontory near the confluence of the St. Charles with the St. Lawrence, terminating abruptly in Cape Diamond, which has a height of 333 feet, and on the banks of both streams. It is about 400 miles from the mouth of the St. Lawrence and 140 miles north-east of Montreal, to which the river is navigable for large vessels. The C.P.R. and the C.N.R. are the principal trunk lines; the former crossing the St. Lawrence by the great Quebec Bridge. Quebec is a most picturesque city; it is divided into the upper and lower towns. The former, placed on the summit of the promontory, is strongly fortified, the fortifications comprising a citadel and other works. The view from the heights here looking down the river is one of the finest in the world. The lower town, the great seat of business, lies under the cliffs, along the St. Lawrence and the St. Charles.

Buildings. Among the principal edifices are the Parliament and departmental buildings, the Roman Catholic cathedral, the Protestant cathedral, and Château Frontenac (hotel). The chief educational institutions are Laval University, with faculties of law, medicine, theology, and arts, and a library of 150,000 volumes; the Grand Seminary; and the Ursuline convent, a

QUEBEC: LITTLE CHAMPLAIN STREET

large and fashionable ladies' school. On the Plains of Abraham, west of the upper town, is a column in memory of General Wolfe; there is also a handsome obelisk to the joint memory of the two commanders, Wolfe and Montcalm, who both fell at the taking of Quebec in 1759.

Industries. The industries embrace iron castings, machinery, cutlery, nails, leather, paper, india-rubber goods, ropes, tobacco, beetroot-sugar, etc. Quebec is the chief seat of the Canadian trade in timber, and at certain seasons rafts of timber may be seen extending along the water's edge for 6 miles.

Harbour. The harbour of Quebec is on the St. Lawrence River, and comprises the river and its navigable tributaries between St. Patrick hole and Cape Rouge. It affords wharfage accommodation for twenty-five to thirty ocean-going vessels; water from 24 to 40 feet, with a large amount of extra space for small vessels. There are gantry and locomotive cranes available at all times for handling cargo. The average navigation season is between 1st April and 1st Dec. There are a tidal harbour, wet dock, and two graving-docks, and two trunk lines of the Canadian Pacific and Canadian National Railways have access to the wharves. There is a grain-elevator of 250,000 bushels capacity, and one of 2,000,000 bushels capacity.

History. Quebec was founded in 1608 by Champlain, who was sent on an exploring expedition from France. In 1629 it came into the hands of the English, but was restored in 1632. In 1759 it became finally British in consequence of Wolfe's victory on the Plains of Abraham. The Plains were nationalised at the celebration of the tercentenary of the foundation of Quebec in 1908. The great bulk of the inhabitants are Roman Catholic French Canadians. Pop. (1931), 130,594.

QUEBRACHO (ke-brä'chō). The name given to several trees of different genera, but with similar qualities, indigenous to South America, valuable alike for their wood and their bark. The red quebracho (*Loxopterygium* (*Quebrachia*) *Lorentzii*, family Anacardiaceæ) is very hard, but splits easily. The bark and wood are used in tanning. The white quebracho (*Aspidosperma quebracho*) is used for wood-engraving. The bark contains six alkaloids, and is used therapeutically as a remedy for asthma, usually as a tincture.

QUEDLINBURG (kwed'lin-bu̧rh). A town of Germany, in Saxony, at the foot of the Harz Mountains. On an eminence above the town is an old castle, once the residence of the abbesses of Quedlinburg, who, as princesses of the empire, had a vote in the Diet. Founded by Henry the Fowler in 924, Quedlinburg was a Hanseatic town till 1477. The manufactures are woollens, beetroot-sugar, wire, leather, chemicals, etc. Pop. 27,000.

QUEEN. A term designating a woman ruler holding a position similar to that of king. In Britain the queen is either *queen-consort* or merely wife of the reigning king, who is in general (unless where expressly exempted by law) upon the same footing with other subjects, being to all intents the king's subject, and not his equal; or *queen-regent*, regnant, or sovereign, who holds the crown in her own right, and has the same powers, prerogatives, and duties as if she had been a king, and whose husband is a subject; or *queen-dowager*, widow of the king, who enjoys most of the privileges which belonged to her as queen-consort. In some countries, such as Sweden and Belgium, a woman is debarred from succession to the throne by the Salic Law. In Britain a woman succeeds to the throne when she has no brothers. *See* SALIC LAW.

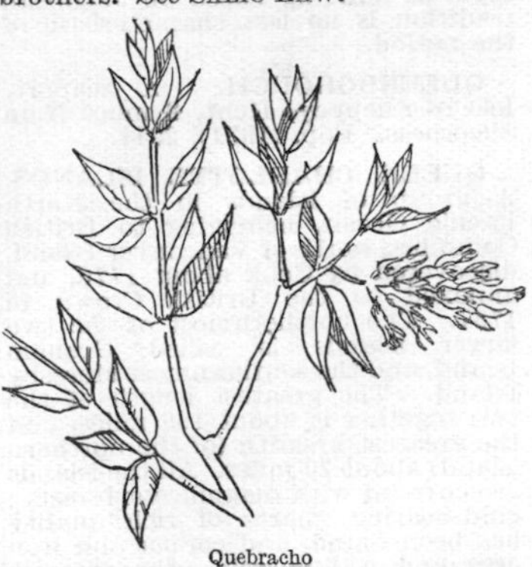

Quebracho

QUEEN ANNE'S BOUNTY. A fund applied to the increase of the incomes of the poorer clergy of the Church of England, and to aid incumbents in rebuilding parsonages by granting advances of money, in virtue of a royal charter confirmed by 2 and 3 Anne, cap. xi. By this Act the first-fruits (the whole income of an incumbency for the first year after a new appointment) and the tenths (a tenth of the annual income of every incumbency), which before the Reformation had been paid to the Pope, but had been annexed to the Crown by Henry VIII., were assigned to a corporation created by the Act and entrusted with the duty of administering the fund for the purpose mentioned. The livings that benefit by the bounty are all those not exceeding £50 a year. All augmentations from this fund are conditional upon an equal or larger sum being privately raised for the same purpose. It amounts now to about £70,000 per annum.

QUEEN ANNE STYLE. English architectural and artistic convention. In the decorative arts, restraint and simplicity are the dominant notes of the "Queen Anne Style," superseding the baroque extravagance which preceded it. Ornament was now deliberately subordinated to design. In furniture this tendency is specially marked, curvilinear principles being sedulously exploited with an unrivalled sense of symmetrical balance. Contemporary silver shows a fine recognition of the value of plain surfaces. Architecture remained predominantly Palladian (*see* PALLADIO, ANDREA); the Italian villa was the model for the English country house. But a vernacular style of building based on Jacobean tradition is no less characteristic of the period.

QUEENBOROUGH. A seaport, Isle of Sheppey, Kent, 2 miles from Sheerness. Pop. (1931), 2941.

QUEEN CHARLOTTE ISLANDS. A group of islands in the North Pacific Ocean, belonging to British Columbia, north of Vancouver Island, discovered by Cook about 1770, and annexed to the British Crown in 1787. The northernmost of the two larger islands is called Graham Island, and the southernmost Moresby Island. The greatest length of the two together is about 160 miles, and the greatest breadth (of the northern island) about 70 miles. All the islands are covered with magnificent forests; gold-bearing quartz of rich quality has been found, and copper and iron ores and a fine vein of anthracite coal also exist. The climate is excellent.

QUEEN MARY LAND. District of Antarctica. It lies to the east of Kaiser Wilhelm Land, and on it are the Denman and Northcliffe glaciers. It was explored and named by Sir Douglas Mawson in 1911-14.

QUEENS. A borough of New York City, United States, so constituted in 1898. It has a land area of 69,120 acres, and includes Long Island City, Flushing, Jamaica, and Newtown, etc. Pop. (1930), 1,079,129.

QUEENSBERRY, William Douglas, fourth Duke of, and third Earl of March. A notorious nobleman of the eighteenth and early years of the nineteenth century, often referred to during his later years as "Old Q." He was born in 1724 and died in 1810, was the only son of the second Earl of March, and inherited the title of duke from a cousin in 1728. He early distinguished himself as a patron of horse-racing, in which and in connected betting he seems to have been singularly successful. He was a byword for loose living and "gallantries," and having never married, at his death his titles and estates devolved on several heirs. In this way the third Duke of Buccleuch became fifth Duke of Queensberry, Sir Charles Douglas became Marquess of Queensberry, and the sixth Earl of Wemyss became Earl of March. Queensberry was for a number of years one of the representative peers for Scotland; he afterwards sat in the House of Lords as a British peer, and he was long one of the lords of the bedchamber. He figures as Earl of March in Thackeray's *Virginians*. He came under the lash of Burns owing to his having cut down the trees about the ducal residence, Drumlanrig Castle, and a similar destruction at Neidpath Castle earned him the scorn of Wordsworth.

QUEENSBURY. Urban district of Yorkshire (W.R.), about 4½ miles east of Bradford and 196 from London, on the L.N.E. Railway. Here are textile mills, collieries, and stone quarries. Pop. (1931), 5763.

QUEENS' COLLEGE (Cambridge). Founded in 1448 by Margaret of Anjou, queen of Henry VI., and again in 1465 by Elizabeth, queen of Edward IV. The name of the college is frequently misspelt *Queen's*, but it commemorates both the foundresses. The college buildings are among the most interesting in the university. John Fisher, Thomas Fuller, and Bishop Pearson were members of the college. It was the residence of Erasmus during his stay at Cambridge.

QUEEN'S COLLEGE (Oxford). Founded in 1340 by Robert Eglesfield, chaplain to Philippa, queen of Edward III., and it is from her that it gets its name. The subsequent foundations of John Michel, Sir Francis Bridgman, and Lady Margaret Hungerford were consolidated into one with that of Eglesfield in 1858. Among the members of the college have been: John Wycliffe,

Edward the Black Prince, Henry V., Addison, Wycherley, and Jeremy Bentham.

Part of Queen's College, Oxford

QUEEN'S COUNTY, now **LEIX.** A county of the Irish Free State, Leinster; area, 424,892 acres. The surface is generally flat, but rises in the north-west into the Slieve-Bloom Mountains (Arderin, 1733 feet). The principal river is the Barrow, which drains almost the whole county. At Portarlington the Grand Canal enters the county, and runs east and then south to Kilkenny. Anthracite coal of good quality is worked in the south. Limestone abounds, and in a few places marble is obtained. Bogs are numerous towards the centre of the county. Agriculture is not generally in an improving state, drainage in particular being much wanted. The principal crops are oats, barley, and root-crops. Many cattle are reared. Maryborough is the county town, and Mountmellick, a market town on a branch of the Grand Canal, is the only other one of importance. Like the county itself, it derives its name from Queen Mary, the predecessor of Elizabeth. Pop. (1926), 51,540.

QUEENSFERRY, NORTH. A village of Fifeshire, on the north shore of the Firth of Forth, opposite South Queensferry; served by the L.N.E. Railway. It is noted for sea-bathing, and there is a fishing industry. Pop. (1931), 1600.

QUEENSFERRY, SOUTH. A royal and municipal burgh and seaport of Linlithgowshire, Scotland, on the south side of the Firth of Forth, at a point where the latter narrows to a width of about 2 miles. Across this point is the Forth Bridge, of which South Queensferry forms the southern approach. The town is near the naval base of Rosyth (closed in 1925), and was of considerable importance during the European War. In olden times it was the ferry-station for the North Shore and Dunfermline, etc. It was used frequently as such by Margaret, queen of Malcolm Canmore, and it is from her that Queensferry derives its name. It became a burgh of royalty in 1363, and a royal burgh in 1639. Pop. (1931), 1798.

QUEENSLAND. A state of the Australian Commonwealth, comprising the entire north-eastern region of the Australian continent and the adjacent islands of the Pacific and Gulf of Carpentaria.

Area and Population. The estimated area of Queensland is 670,500 sq. miles. The state is more than double the size of New South Wales, over seven times larger than Victoria, and about twenty-five and a half times bigger than Tasmania, but it only represents roughly a quarter of the total area of the Commonwealth (2,974,581 sq. miles). The population in 1931 was 963,711. In 1846 it was only 2257.

Towns. Brisbane is the capital, with an area of 385 sq. miles and a population, in 1931, of 317,150. Other towns are Rockhampton (30,000); Townsville, the capital of Northern Queensland (32,050); Ipswich (26,253); Toowoomba (26,439); Charters Towers (9200); Gympie (9592); Maryborough (12,000); Bundaberg (11,250); Mackay (9230); Cairns (10,500); Warwick (7500); and Southport (5800).

Physiography. Queensland has a coast-line of 2250 miles, i.e. there are 298 sq. miles of territory to every mile of coast-line. Off the coast, and running parallel to the land for over 1000 miles, is the Great Barrier Reef, of coralline structure, which forms a natural mole or breakwater, enclosing a lagoon-like belt of calm water. Opposite the discharge of large rivers, however, there are gaps in the reef, caused by the peculiar conditions existing at these points, under which the coral-forming animalculæ will not perform their work. Where the Great Dividing Range enters the state it branches off to the north-west, with numerous extensions northwards and southwards, the main range forming a plateau of 1500 to 2000 feet altitude, which runs from north to south at from 20 to 100 miles from the coast. There is also a low coastal range. The principal rivers are the Brisbane, Burnett, Fitzroy, and Burdekin, flowing to the Pacific; and the Gilbert, Flinders, Mitchell, and Leichardt, draining to the Gulf of Carpentaria.

Climate. Slightly more than half the area of Queensland lies within the tropics, and the climate, therefore, is warm, but it is so modified by ocean breezes that the daily range is less than that of other countries under the same isotherms. Generally the coastal plain is much warmer than the elevated plateau of the hinterland, but in such a large territory climate varies with the place. The accompanying table illustrates tropical Queensland in its relation to the other tropical states of the Commonwealth.

Areas	Queensland, sq. Miles	Western Australia, sq. Miles	Northern Territory, sq. Miles	Total sq. Miles
Within Tropical Zone	359,000	364,000	426,320	1,149,320
Within Temperate Zone	311,500	611,920	97,300	1,020,720
Ratio of tropical part to whole state	0·535	0·373	0·014	0·530
Ratio of temperate part to whole state	0·465	0·627	0·186	0·470

Rainfall. The wettest known part of Australia is on the north-east coast of Queensland, between Port Douglas and Cardwell, where three stations, situated on or adjacent to the Johnstone and Russell Rivers, have an average rainfall of between 148 and 166 inches, although 200 inches have frequently been recorded. In Queensland, as in the Northern Territory, the heaviest rains fall during the summer months, but good averages are maintained during the other seasons. Occasionally, also, the north-east coast is visited by hurricanes from the north-east tropics, which seem to have their origin in the South Pacific Islands, their path being a parabolic curve of south-westerly direction. Only a small percentage, however, reach Australia, the majority recurving in their path to the east of New Caledonia.

Communications. In 1931 there were 6529 miles of Government railways open for general traffic, and 266 miles of privately owned lines, making a total of 6795 miles, representing only 10·13 miles of line per 1000 sq. miles of territory (or 7·04 miles per 1000 inhabitants). The State railway gauge in Queensland is 3 feet 6 inches, but included in the above total are 49 miles of 4 feet 8½ inch gauge, and 30 miles of 2 feet gauge. A uniform gauge of 4 feet 8½ inches has been recommended. There are no Federal railways within the state. All the Queensland railways may be said to radiate from Brisbane. A coastal line runs north, and from it feeders are sent out into the hinterland. Another trunk line runs west, and a complicated network of railways serves the south-west and southern suburbs and adjacent districts of Brisbane.

Production: Agriculture. The principal crops are wheat and maize; sweet-potatoes, sugar-cane, cotton, fruit, hay, green fodder, and ensilage; barley and some oats, tobacco, coffee, arrowroot, and potatoes are also raised.

Irrigation.[1] The principal irrigation works are: (*a*) those at Ayr, utilising the waters of the Burdekin River and the shallow wells on its banks; (*b*) those at Bingera, near Bundaberg, utilising water pumped from the Burnett River just above the meeting-point of the salt and fresh waters; and (*c*) those at Fairymead, utilising water pumped from a number of shallow spear-wells sunk on the alluvial flats, on the north side of the Burnett River and about 6 miles from Bundaberg. There were (1919) 701 irrigators in the state, principally farmers and graziers, the irrigated area covering 9267 acres.

[1] *Artesian Basins.*—Queensland lies within the principal artesian basin of the Australian continent, viz. the Great Australian Basin, which has an area of 569,000 sq. miles, 376,000 sq. miles being in Queensland. Practically the whole of the state lying west of the Great Dividing Range, with the exception of an area in the north-west contiguous to the Northern Territory, is included in the Basin, which is said to be the largest yet discovered. The estimated yield of water from 1236 flowing bores on 30th June, 1920, was 318,300,000 gallons per diem. The deepest well has a depth of 6938 feet, and yields approximately 107,300 gallons daily. The waters of many of the wells have been analysed, and some found suitable for wool-scouring only; others are suitable for watering stock but not for irrigation, owing to the presence of alkali; others, again, serve for both stock and irrigation, while some, such as those containing sulphuretted hydrogen, are not of any use. Water fit for stock may generally be said to be "safe" for domestic purposes in spite of its slightly mineral taste. Wells yielding waters known as "Helidon Spa," "Boonah Spa," and "Junot Spa," much used in Queensland and New South Wales, are shallow wells of from 60 to 200 feet in depth.—Cf. Professor J. W. Gregory, *The Dead Heart of Australia*; *The Flowing Wells of Central Australia* (in *Geographical Journal*, July and August, 1911). Also see E. F. Pittman, A.R.S.M., *Problems of the Artesian Water-supply of Australia, with special reference to Professor Gregory's Theory* (Clarke Memorial Lecture, Oct., 1907); *The Great Australian Artesian Basin*; *The Composition and Porosity of the Intake Beds of the Great Australian Artesian Basin.*

Forests. There are forest reservations of (1931) 5,323,152 acres. Among trees of importance are eucalypti, pine, and cedar.

Fisheries. The Great Barrier Reef littoral is the haunt of a myriad of gorgeously coloured fishes, and sharks and enormous perches are numerous. Oysters are abundant; turtle is found in the north; and the pearl-fishery of Torres Strait is both extensive and lucrative, especially around Thursday Island. Trepang, cowries, and clam-shell are also fished, together with many other common and uncommon fish.

Minerals. Coal is mined, and gold has been worked since 1858. Silver, copper, tin, wolfram, lead, limestone, and fire-clay are also worked.

Religion. There is no State Church, and the Anglicans predominate, with Roman Catholics second, and Presbyterians third.

Education. Elementary education is free and compulsory, and secondary education is provided for. There are Government scholarships, tenable for three years in the 10 grammar schools of the state. Queensland University (founded 1911) is located at Brisbane, and had 778 students in 1930. There are 15 technical schools with (1930) 12,422 students.

Government. There is a Governor, who appoints a Lieutenant-Governor, and there is an Executive Council, the responsible ministry. Parliament consists of two Houses, a Legislative Council (59 members nominated by the Crown for life) and a Legislative Assembly of 62 members, who are returned by 62 electoral districts and sit for three years. Suffrage is universal (adult male and female), one year's continuous residence within the state being the modifying condition. Until 1859, when it was erected into a separate colony, Queensland formed a part of New South Wales.

BIBLIOGRAPHY: *Australian Government Year Book*; C. A. Bernays, *Queensland Politics during Sixty Years, 1859-1919*; *Our Seventh Political Decade*; Dr. T. G. Taylor, *Australia, Physiographic and Economic*; C. Parker, *The Mining History of Queensland*; R. Gray, *Reminiscences of India and North Queensland*.

QUEEN'S-PIGEON. A magnificent ground-pigeon, inhabiting the islands of the Indian Ocean, named after Queen Victoria. It is one of seven species constituting the genus Goura (*G. victoria*), and is the largest and most beautiful member of the order.

QUEENSTOWN, or COBH (formerly Cove of Cork). Urban district and seaport of County Cork, Irish Free State, on the south side of Great Island, which rises abruptly out of Cork harbour; served by the Great Southern & Western Railway. Queenstown is a naval station, and is defended by fortifications on Spike Island and at the entrance of the harbour. It is the port for the transmission of American mails, and a chief emigration station. It has little trade and no manufactures. Queen Victoria visited the town in 1849, when its name was changed from Cove of Cork to Queenstown, and the name Cobh was taken into general use on the erection of the Irish Free State. Pop. (1926), 7070.

QUEENSTOWN. A town of Cape Province, South Africa, 75 miles north-west of King William's Town. The town is laid out in the shape of a hexagon, with the market place in the centre. Wheat and wool are produced in the neighbourhood. Pop. 12,797 (6614 white).

QUEENSTOWN. A town of Tasmania, about 110 miles N.W. of Hobart. Situated on Queen River, its industries are connected with copper-mining and timber-felling. Pop. 3400.

QUELIMANE. A seaport of Portuguese East Africa, 62 miles from Chinde, north of the Zambesi delta. Pop. 3097 (350 white).

QUERÉTARO (ke-ra'tà-rō). A central state of Mexico, forming part of the central plateau. Opals are mined. The capital is Querétaro. Area, 4493 sq. miles; pop. (1930), 234,386.

QUERÉTARO. A city of Mexico, capital of the state of Querétaro, on a plateau 6000 feet above sea-level, 110 miles north-west of Mexico. It is served by the national railways. An aqueduct about 2 miles long brings a copious supply of water to Querétaro from a distance of 6 miles. Pop. (1930), 32,002.

QUERN. A hand-mill for grinding corn, such as is or has been in general use among various primitive peoples. The simplest and most primitive form of the quern is that in which a large stone with a cavity in the upper surface is used to contain the corn, which is pounded rather than ground with a small stone. The most usual form consists of two circular flat stones, the upper one pierced in the centre, and revolving on a wooden or metal pin inserted in the lower. In using the quern the grain is dropped with one hand into the central opening, while with the other the upper stone is revolved by means of a stick inserted in a small opening near the edge. Hand-mills of this description are used in parts of Scotland and Ireland to the present day.

Grinding Corn with a Quern

QUESNAY (kā-nā), **François.** French economist and physician, born in 1694, died in 1774. He was appointed surgeon in ordinary to the king, and subsequently, having

François Quesnay

taken the degree of M.D., physician to Madame de Pompadour, the mistress of Louis XV., who afterwards had him appointed physician to the king. He is best known, however, as an economist. In 1756 he published the articles on *Fermiers* and *Grains* in the *Encyclopédie,* and advanced the doctrine of *produit net,* i.e. that the surplus of agriculture is the sole source of national wealth. His *Tableau économique* appeared in 1758, but disappeared and was only discovered in 1890. Quesnay's disciples formed the school known as the Physiocrats. *See* PHYSIOCRATIC SYSTEM.—Cf. H. Higgs, *The Physiocrats.*

QUESNEL (kā-nel), **Pasquier** (Paschasius). French theologian and moralist, born at Paris in 1634, died at Amsterdam 1719. He became a member of the order of the Fathers of the Oratory in 1657, at that time a great nursery of Jansenism, and in 1671 wrote his *Réflexions morales sur le Nouveau Testament,* consisting of thoughts on some of

Pasquier Quesnel

the most beautiful maxims of the evangelists. This work brought him under suspicion of the Church on account of its Jansenistic tendencies, and he had (1685) to quit French territory. Going to Brussels, he there applied himself to the continuation of his work on the New Testament, which was published entire in 1693-4. In this some leading points in Roman Catholicism were freely questioned. Bossuet and Noailles, Archbishop of Paris, rather approved of the book; but the Jesuits obtained from Pope Clement XI. a Bull condemning 101 of Quesnel's propositions as heretical. This Bull, the notorious *Unigenitus* (promulgated in 1713), not only stirred up the Jansenists (q.v.), but awoke bitter dissensions in the bosom of the Gallican Church. Meantime Quesnel had been compelled to seek refuge (1703) in Holland, where he resided for the rest of his life. —Cf. L. Séché, *Les Derniers Jansénistes.*

QUESTIONNAIRE. A set of written questions sent out usually to obtain information about the cost of living, housing conditions, and other social matters. The census paper may be described as a questionnaire, and the method has been used by the B.B.C.

QUÉTELET (kāt-lā), **Lambert Adolphe Jacques.** Belgian statistician and astronomer, born at Ghent in 1796, died in 1874. He studied at the lyceum of his native town, where, in 1814, he became professor of mathematics. In 1819 he was appointed to the same chair in the Brussels Anthenæum. In 1828 he became lecturer in the Museum of Science and Literature, holding the post till 1834, when the institution was merged in the newly established university. Quételet superintended the erection of the Royal Observatory, and became its first director (1828). A member of the Belgian Royal Academy, he became its perpetual secretary in 1834. Quételet's writings on statistics and kindred subjects are very numerous. He also published many papers on meteorology, astronomy, and terrestrial magnetism. His works include: *Physique populaire de la chaleur, Histoire des sciences mathématiques et physiques chez les Belges*, and *Anthropométrie*.

QUETTA. The capital of Baluchistan, in a plain 5500 feet above sea-level, among lofty mountains. It is of great strategical importance as commanding the northern entrance of the Bolan Pass. A railway from Shikarpur, on the Indus, traverses the pass to Quetta and beyond towards Kandahar, 125 miles distant. By a treaty with the Khan of Khelat in 1876, a British protectorate was established, and the district now forms part of British India. The town contains a British garrison and the Indian staff college, and there are extensive magazines of war material. Pop. 49,001.

QUETTA-PISHIN. A highland district of Baluchistan, India, comprising a series of valleys of some length and medium width, forming the catchment area of the Pishin Lora, and enclosed on all sides by the mountains of the Toba-Kakar and Central Brahui ranges. The railway from Quetta to Chaman traverses the district. About 80 per cent of the people are Pushtu-speaking Mahommedans of the Sunnite sect, and 6 per cent are Brahui. Quetta is the capital. Area, 5200 sq. miles; pop. 120,000.

QUETZALCOATL. An Aztec god, one of the principal gods in Mexican mythology, whose name meant *plumed serpent.* He was looked upon as the patron of works of art, and is said to have reigned at the ancient city of Tula. He taught his subjects agriculture and metal-work, preached universal brotherhood, and during his reign there was peace and happiness. His rival, however, Tezcatlipoca, forced him to leave the country, and Quetzalcoatl went, promising his people to return. When Cortez landed in Mexico in 1519, the Aztecs, remembering the legend, believed that it was Quetzalcoatl returned to Tula.

Quezals (*Pharomacrus mocinno*)

QUEZAL. A most beautiful Central American bird of the Trogon family (*Pharomacrus mocinno*). It is about the size of a magpie, and the male is adorned with tail-feathers from 3 to 3½ feet in length, and of a gorgeous emerald colour. These feathers are not strictly speaking the true tail-feathers (the colour of which is black and white), but are the upper tail coverts of the bird. The back, head (including the curious rounded and compressed crest), throat, and chest are of the same rich hue, the lower parts being of a brilliant scarlet. The female wants these long feathers, and is otherwise much plainer. The food of the quezal consists chiefly of fruits. It lives in forests of tall trees. There are several allied species of birds, but none with the distinctive feature of the quezal.

QUEZALTENAN'GO. A maritime department and town of Guatemala, Central America. The department lies along the Pacific Ocean, and is mountainous, containing Santa Maria (12,350 feet altitude), an active volcano. Rubber, sugar, coffee, cereals, and live-stock are produced. The capital is Quezaltenango, standing on a plateau at an altitude of 7750 feet. It is the second city of Guatemala, and trades in agricultural produce. There are manufactures of cotton and linen. Pop. (department), 120,000 ; (town), 30,125.

QUIBERON (kēb-rōn̦). A peninsula, a bay, and a town of Morbihan, France. Here in 1759 Admiral Hawke gained a great victory over a French fleet. In 1795 a body of French royalists was landed here by an English fleet, but was speedily cut off by General Hoche.

QUICHUA (kē'chu̦-à). The name of a native race of South America, inhabiting Peru, parts of Ecuador, and Bolivia. The name is supposed to signify those who speak correctly, as distinguished from tribes of alien stock. With the Aymaras the Quichuas composed the larger portion of the population of the empire of the Incas. They absorbed the earlier cultures of Peru, those of the Aymara and Yunca tribes. The Quichua language, which was formerly the State language of the Incas, is still the chief speech of Peru, of a large portion of Bolivia, of the part of Ecuador bordering upon Peru, and of the northern section of the Argentine Republic. It is one of the most beautiful and at the same time comprehensive tongues of America. —Cf. W. H. Prescott, *History of the Conquest of Peru.*

QUICKLIME. Commercial name for calcium oxide obtained by calcining chalk or limestone, the carbon-dioxide being driven off in the process. It is very infusible, but when moistened crumbles to a white powder (slaked lime), giving off considerable heat. It is a valuable dressing for clay soils, and is used in making mortar and cements. Slaked or hydrated lime is employed in making lime-water and in tanning and sugar industries. Lime is used also for purifying coal-gas and sewage.

QUICKSAND. A bed of loose fine sand particles often mixed with clay or calcium carbonate, and saturated with water. Quicksands occur usually at river mouths or along the seashore, and in some glacial deposits.

QUICKSILVER. Common English name for metallic mercury, on account of its extreme mobility and resemblance to the colour of silver. *See* MERCURY.

QUI'ETISM (Lat. *quies*, rest). A form of mysticism which aims at the elevation of man to a state of pure contemplation of the Divinity. It maintains that man's highest perfection, which consists in psychical self-annihilation and most perfect communion with God, can be attained only in a state of quietude. The soul, ceasing to reflect either upon God or itself, ceasing to will and to think, remains in a passively receptive attitude, accepting the fellowship of God, acting within it. Quietism thus emphasises suppression of conscious will, and attaches little importance to activity of religion. Quietism is a characteristic feature of Hindu philosophy and religion, of Brahmanism and Buddhism, as well as of Alexandrian neo-Platonism and of Christian mysticism. Quietistic ideas are found in the doctrines of the Beghards (twelfth century), of the followers of Master Eckhart (thirteenth and fourteenth centuries), of the Brethren of the Free Spirit, of the Illuminati, and especially in the teaching of the Quakers.

The term *quietism* is, however, particularly applied to a mystical movement which arose in the Catholic Church in the seventeenth century. This movement, which swept over Europe at the close of the seventeenth and the beginning of the eighteenth centuries, owed its origin to such works as *The Spiritual Guide* of Molinos, in which the devout were taught, by contemplation, to bring the soul into direct union with the Godhead, and so receive the infused heavenly light.

The most noted promoter of quietism in France was Madame Guyon. Fénelon became the advocate of Madame Guyon and her writings in his *Explication des maximes des*

Saints sur la vie intérieure (1697). Bossuet obtained (1699) a Papal brief, which condemned twenty-three positions from Fénelon's book as erroneous; but the humility with which the latter submitted deprived his enemies of the fruits of their victory; and it was the change in the spirit of the times and not violence that gradually buried quietism in oblivion.—BIBLIOGRAPHY: W. R. Inge, *Christian Mysticism*; W. James, *The Varieties of Religious Experience*; J. Bigelow, *Molinos, the Quietist*; E. Murisier, *Les Maladies du sentiment rèligieux.*

QUILIMANE (kil-i-ma'ne). A sea-port-town of Portuguese East Africa, unhealthily situated about 8 miles above the mouth of a river of the same name (the northern branch of the Zambezi). The harbour is good, but trade is undeveloped. Pop. 2200 (500 Europeans).

QUILLAI-BARK (*Quillaia Saponaria*). The bark of a South American tree belonging to the wing-seeded section of the Rosaceæ. It is used to make a lather instead of soap in washing silks, woollens, etc. It is called also *Quillaya-bark.*

QUILLER-COUCH, Sir Arthur Thomas. British author and critic, born at Fowey, Cornwall, in 1863. He was educated at Clifton and at Trinity College, Oxford, where he took a first class in classical moderations in 1884, and a second in the final classical examination in 1886. From 1886 to 1887 he was a lecturer in classics in his college. He then commenced his career as author with *Dead Man's Rock*, an improbable but thrilling story which became very popular. He followed up his success with a great number of books, all distinguished by good style and good taste, and many by a keen sense of humour. Among them may be mentioned: *Troy Town* (1888), *I saw Three Ships* (1892), *The Ship of Stars* (1899), *Fort Amity* (1904), *Major Vigoureux* (1907), *Corporal Sam* (1910), *Foe-Farrell* (1918), and *Charles Dickens and other Victorians.* In 1897 he was commissioned to finish Stevenson's novel *St. Ives.* In 1912 he was appointed to succeed A. W. Verrall as King Edward VII. professor of English literature at Cambridge. He has since published some of his lectures: *On the Art of Writing* (1916), *Shakespeare's Workmanship* (1918), and *On the Art of Reading* (1920). As a critic he is always sound and often entertaining; he is a sworn foe to pedantry, and does not believe in allowing literature to be subordinate to philology. He has edited some well-chosen anthologies: *The Oxford Book of English Verse* (1900), *The Oxford Book of Ballads* (1910), *The Oxford Book of Victorian Verse* (1912), and *The Oxford Book of Prose.* He was knighted in 1910.

QUILLOTA (kil-yō'tȧ). A town of Chile, in the province of Valparaiso, 23 miles north-east of Valparaiso. The copper-mines in the vicinity are regarded as the richest in Chile. Pop. 14,859.

QUILLWORT. Genus of stemless rush-like vascular cryptogams, *Isoetes,* chiefly found in N. temperate and warm regions. Merlin's grass, *I. lacustris,* inhabiting subalpine lake bottoms in Britain and elsewhere, has a filbert-sized corm producing a tuft of 10-20 rigid awl-shaped tubular leaves whose bases partially sheathe the spore-capsules. A subaquatic species common in S. Europe inhabits Guernsey marshlands.

QUIMPER (kaṇ-pār). A town and port of Brittany, France, capital of the department of Finistère, at the head of the estuary of the Odet, an old town partly surrounded by walls flanked by towers. The principal buildings are: the Gothic cathedral of St. Corentin (1239-1515); the ruins of a Cordelier church and cloister; the college, the prefecture, and the military hospital. The manufactures are earthenware, leather, and cordage. The sardine-fishery forms an important occupation. Pop. 18,297.

QUIN, James. British actor, of Irish parentage, born in London in 1693, died at Bath 1766. He made his first appearance on the stage at Dublin in 1714; shortly afterwards he obtained an engagement in London, and gradually acquired celebrity as a tragic actor as well as in characters of comic and sarcastic humour, like Falstaff, Volpone, etc. He retained his pre-eminence until the appearance of Garrick in 1741. His last performance was as Falstaff (1753), in which character he is supposed never to have been excelled. (Illus. on p. 528.)

QUINCE. The fruit of the *Cydonia vulgāris*, nat. ord. Rosaceæ. The quince tree, which is supposed to be a native of Western Asia, is cultivated in Europe and the United States for its handsome golden-yellow fruit, which, though hard and sour when plucked from the tree, becomes excellent when boiled and eaten with sugar, or preserved in syrup or made into marmalade. Other species are the Chinese quinces (*C. sinensis* and *cathayensis*) and the Japanese quince (*C. japonica*). (Illus. on p. 528.)

QUINCUNX. Arrangement of five objects so placed as to occupy each corner of a square or oblong, with one in the middle. It is used commonly for the spacing of trees in an orchard so that the trees in one row are opposite the spaces between those in the next row.

QUINCY. A city of Illinois, United States, the county seat of Adams county, on the Mississippi; served by the Chicago, Burlington, & Quincy, the Wabash, and the Quincy, Omaha, & Kansas City Railways, and by river-steamers. It was settled in 1821, and became a city in 1839. There are extensive and varied manufactures. Pop. (1930), 39,241.

QUINCY. A city of Massachusetts, United States, in Norfolk county, on Massachusetts Bay; served by the New York, New Haven & Hartford Railway, and by an electric-traction line (local). Boston is just across the Neponset River from Quincy, which is therefore more or less a suburban residential area of the adjacent city. It was settled in 1625, and became a city in 1888, the name being changed from Mount Wollaston in 1792. Pop. (1930), 71,983.

James Quin

QUINET (kē-nā), Edgar. French philosopher, poet, historian, and politician, born 1803, died 1875. He first attracted attention by a translation of Herder's *Philosophie der Geschichte* in 1825. In 1828 he accompanied a scientific commission to the Morea; and in 1839 he became professor of foreign literature at Lyons, a position he changed in 1841 for a similar chair in the Collège de France. His works, which number about thirty volumes, include poems, dramas, histories, and religious mystical books.

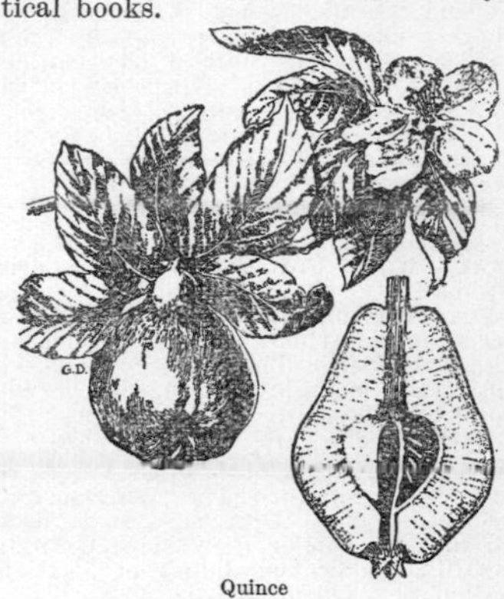

Quince
Section of fruit at right

QUIN'INE ($C_{20}H_{24}N_2O_2 \cdot 3H_2O$). A diacid base derived from quinoline, of intensely bitter taste and strong alkaline reaction. Quinine is the best known and most widely used of the alkaloids obtained from the barks of the various species of cinchona (q.v.). Cinchon bark, which was originally found in South America, was introduced into medicine by the Spaniards about 1635; but it was not till the beginning of the nineteenth century that quinine was used, and it has since then entirely taken the place of cinchona. Quinine is used in malaria, and its efficacy in that disease is marked. It is one of the best examples of the specific action of a drug in therapeutics, as it causes the malarial organism found in the blood to break up and disappear. Quinine, in small doses, is a stomachic, and is therefore given to aid digestion and improve the appetite. It was also at one time widely used on account of its antipyretic effect; but now, when such effect is desired, other more certain drugs, as phenacetin, acetanilide, or phenazone, are used.

QUINOA (kwi-nō'a). A South American plant (*Chenopodium Quinoa*), of which there are two cultivated varieties, one yielding white seeds, and sometimes called petty-rice, the other red. The white seeds are extensively used in Chile and

Peru as an article of food in the form of porridge, cakes, etc. The seeds of the other variety, *red quinoa*, are used medicinally as an application for sores and bruises.

QUINOLINE. An organic compound (C_9H_7N) which occurs, along with derivatives, in coal-tar (q.v.), and may be prepared from aniline. It is a colourless strongly refracting liquid with a very characteristic odour, and has antiseptic and antipyretic properties. *See* QUININE; RING IN CHEMISTRY.

QUINQUAGESIMA. Latin word meaning "fiftieth." It denotes the Sunday next before Ash Wednesday, once called Shrove Sunday. It occurs 50 days before Low Sunday.

QUINSY. An abscess which arises in the tissues surrounding the tonsil. It usually follows an acute tonsilitis, and the infection spreads from the tonsil to the parts around, where in the course of a few days an abscess is formed. Quinsy occurs most commonly where there is a septic condition of the mouth, gums, nose, or where the tonsils are enlarged and septic. There is extensive swelling of the affected side, usually involving the palate and uvula, with pain, inability to swallow or to open the mouth properly, alteration of the voice, rise of temperature, and general *malaise*. When abscess-formation takes place, the only satisfactory treatment is to open the abscess, and this is followed by a rapid lessening of the symptoms. Mouth-washes should be used freely, both before and after the incision, and tonics should be administered for the patient's general condition. After an attack any septic focus in the mouth should be dealt with, and if the tonsils are septic they should be removed.

QUINTAIN. A figure or other object set up to be tilted at with a lance. It was constructed in various ways; a common form in England consisted of an upright post, on the top of which was a horizontal bar turning on a pivot; to one end of this a sand-bag was attached, on the other a broad board; and it was a trial of skill to tilt at the broad end with a lance, and pass on before the bag of sand could whirl round and strike the tilter on the back.

QUINTAL. Measure of weight, originally denoting 100 libras, as in pre-revolutionary France, and still surviving in Spain. It also denotes various standards in Portugal, Greece, Egypt, and some parts of Spanish America. The metric quintal, weighing 100 kilograms or 220 lb., is the common unit of measurement for grain, etc., in metric using countries.

QUINTET'. A composition for five instruments or five voices. Quintets are much less common in music than quartets, and the choice of instruments is more subject to variation. In the case of string quintets the usual combination is two violins, two violas, and 'cello. Many composers, especially in more recent times, have written for pianoforte, two violins, viola, and 'cello, the works in this class by Schumann, Brahms, and César Franck being among the masterpieces of music. Mozart wrote a quintet for piano and wind-instruments, and another for clarinet and strings, both being among his finest works. The most beautiful example in modern music of a vocal quintet occurs in the first scene of the third act of Wagner's *Meistersinger*.

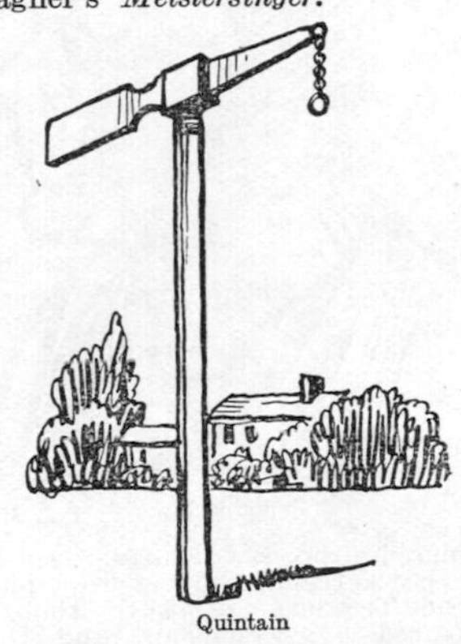

Quintain

QUINTIL'IAN (Marcus Fabius Quintilianus). Roman rhetorician, born at Calagurris, Spain, between A.D. 30 and 40. He is one of the many notable literary men who were produced during the century in that thoroughly Romanised province. Where his early education was carried out is uncertain, but it is clear that he was trained according to the recognised principles of the time, i.e. under "grammatici," who taught him literature, grammar, and easy composition; and afterwards under "rhetores," who drilled him in composition, written or oral, of a higher kind, and taught him the principles of "rhetoric" as then accepted. On the methods employed by his teachers he has left us a few notes.

Later on he attached himself at Rome to the leading orator of the day, Domitius Afer, and by following him through the courts acquired practical experience. He then appears to have returned to Spain, and very possibly set up there as a "rhetor," or teacher of rhetoric. In 68 he returned to Rome with Galba, who for a short time occupied the imperial throne after Nero's death. At Rome Quintilian established himself as the head of the teaching profession, and is addressed by Martial as the "chief controller of restless youth." He also gained great reputation as a pleader in the law courts. In his capacity as teacher he was a recipient of the Treasury grant to rhetores instituted by Vespasian, and this, in addition to the fees he charged his pupils, seems to have brought him to a degree of affluence unusual in his profession. He was also granted the "insignia" of a consul, an unprecedented honour for a rhetor. He retired somewhere about A.D. 90. The date of his death is unknown.

Quintilian

Quintilian's fame rests on his work entitled *De Institutone Oratoria* (How to Train an Orator) in twelve books, which he composed not very long after his retirement and published some time before the death of Domitian, which occurred in A.D. 96. There are also two collections of declamations attributed to him. These have in their time enjoyed considerable popularity, but one is certainly and the other probably spurious, and neither has any of the value which belongs to the *De Institutione Oratoria.* This last is one of the most remarkable monuments of Roman good sense, and teems with noteworthy remarks on oratory, literary criticism, and above all education. It professes to train the public speaker, and thus begins with the writer's views as to what constitutes the best education from the cradle upwards. This part of the work, which covers the first book and half the second, is of extraordinary interest, and during the Middle Ages and after the Renaissance was more studied than any other book on the subject, though few ventured to follow the writer in the best known of his precepts—the non-use of the rod. He then proceeds to discuss the laws of "rhetoric," or the "art of effective speech," under its main heads of subject-matter (*inventio*), arrangement, expression (*elecutio*), memory, and delivery (*pronuntiato*).

Though we have ceased to believe in an "art of rhetoric" as the true means of acquiring a command of language, there is so much sense amidst all the technicalities of Quintilian's handling that it has by no means lost its value. In the early part of the tenth book, having observed that the reading of good authors is indispensable for the acquisition of a good style, he proceeds to give a brief sketch of the most notable Greek and Latin authors, and their merits. This chapter is the best-known piece of literary criticism that has come down to us from antiquity.

Up to something like a century or so ago Quintilian was one of the most highly esteemed of classical writers. For instance, Jerome in the fourth century, John of Salisbury in the twelfth, Erasmus in the sixteenth, Ben Jonson in the seventeenth, and Pope in the eighteenth bear strong marks of his influence. It may be noted that from the ninth to the fifteenth centuries Quintilian was mainly known in a mutilated version, which contains about three-fifths of the work, and the zenith of his reputation dates from the discovery of the complete text by Poggio in 1413. During the last century his reputation has suffered an eclipse, partly perhaps through the discredit that has gathered round the name of rhetoric; yet there are still many who agree with Mill, who, in his *Autobiography,* after remarking that Quintilian is seldom sufficiently appreciated, goes on: "His book is a sort of encyclopedia of the thoughts of the ancients on the whole field of education and culture, and I have retained through life many valuable ideas which I can distinctly trace to my reading of him, even at that early age."

QUINTUS CAL'ABER, or **SMYRNÆ'US.** Greek poet, author of a sort of continuation of the *Iliad* (*Posthomerica*) in fourteen books, a rather dull imitation of Homer. He probably flourished at Smyrna in the fourth century A.D. The only manuscript of his work having been discovered at Otranto, in Calabria, he is called Calaber from this fact.

QUIRINAL. One of the seven hills of ancient Rome. There is a palace there, begun in 1574 by Gregory XIII., and formerly a summer residence of the Popes, but since 1871 the residence of the King of Italy. *See* ROME.

QUIRI'NUS. Among the Romans, a surname of Romulus after he had been raised to the rank of a divinity. Hence *Quirinalia,* a festival in honour of Romulus, held annually on the thirteenth day before the Kalends of March, that is, the 17th of February. Quirinus is the third great god, ranking next to Jupiter and Mars.

QUIRI'TES (from the Sabine *quiris,* a spear). A designation of the citizens of ancient Rome as in their civil capacity. The name of Quirites belonged to them in addition to that of Romani, the latter designation applying to them in their political and military capacity.

QUITO (kē'tō). The capital of Ecuador and of the province of Pichincha, and the seat of the Archbishop of Ecuador. It stands in a ravine on the east side of the volcano of Pichincha, 9348 feet above the sea, a little to the south of the equator. Its streets, with exception of four which meet in the large central square, are narrow, uneven, and badly paved. The more important public buildings are the cathedral, several other churches and convents; the town house, court-house, president's palace, the Central University (with faculties of medicine, science, pharmacy, and jurisprudence), the archiepiscopal palace, orphan asylum, and hospital. The manufactures consist chiefly of woollen and cotton goods. From the want of good roads and railways trade is much hampered. Quito was originally the capital of a native Indian kingdom of the same name, but was taken successively by the Incas (1470) and by the Spaniards (1534). It has repeatedly suffered from earthquakes. There are two broadcasting stations. Pop. (1932), 104,000.

QUIT-RENT. In law, a small rent payable by the tenants of most manors, whereby the tenant goes quit and free from all other services.

QUIXOTE, Don. Hero of Cervantes' mock-heroic romance, *History of the Renowned Don Quixote de la Mancha* (1605-15). He figures in the story as a misguided devotee of chivalry, who imagines himself to be a knight-errant and goes forth on his adventures, clad in a suit of home-made armour, riding his battered steed, Rosinante, and attended by his squire Sancho Panza. He has become a universal figure, representing the type whose lofty idealism fails to achieve success in a world which does not share those ideals.

Quito: Architecture

QUOAD SACRA PARISH (i.e. a parish "so far as regards sacred matters"). In Scotland, a district that forms a parish only so far as purely ecclesiastical matters are concerned, having a church and minister of its own (belonging to the Established Church).

QUOIN. Corner stone at the angle of the wall of a building, especially in later Saxon work, where flat slabs or quoins alternate with long vertical blocks. The term is applied also in printing to a blunt wedge used to secure the type in a forme.

QUOITS. A British pastime of considerable antiquity, particularly popular in the Midlands, Lancashire, and Scotland, seems directly descended from the Greek and Roman sport of "throwing the *discus*." The mode of play resembles that employed in bowls, the quoit, however, being thrown in the air. This quoit is an iron ring, nearly flat, about 6 lb. in weight, and not exceeding 8½ inches in diameter. The upper side is slightly convex, and on its outer rim there is a niche or dent, gripped by one finger in the act of throwing. Two pins, the "hobs," placed about 18 yards apart, project an inch or so above the circles of damp clay, called "ends," in which they stand. The aim of the players, who may be either one or two upon each side, is to throw the quoit so that it lodges in the clay as near the "hob" as possible; experts will often "ring" the "hob," such "ringer" counting two points towards the score. A quoit, other than a "ringer," lying nearer to the "hob" than that of an opposing player counts one point. It is, as in the game of bowls, permissible to dislodge from its position an opponent's quoit. "Deck quoits," played with rings of rope, is a popular amusement with ships' passengers.

QUORN. English hunt. The name is taken from the village of Quorndon in Leicestershire. The hunt was established in the eighteenth century, and some of the most famous hunting men, among them Hugo Meynell and the Earl of Lonsdale, have been among its masters. It is regarded as the oldest in England. The kennels are at Barrow-on-Soar and Melton Mowbray.

QUORNDON. Urban district of Leicester. It is 2½ miles from Loughborough, and is a hunting centre. Pop. (1931), 2603.

QUORUM. A term used in commissions, of which the origin is the Latin expression *quorum unum A. B. volumus* ("of whom we will that A. B. be one"), signifying originally certain individuals, without whom the others could not proceed in the business. In legislative and similar assemblies a quorum is such a number of members as is competent to transact business. The quorum in the British House of Lords is thirty, whilst in the House of Commons it is forty.

QUOTA. Commercial term. In Great Britain it refers to a proportion, at present 15 per cent, of home-grown wheat to be used by millers under the terms of the Wheat Act in making flour. The farmer subsequently receives the difference between the current price for wheat and a standard, at present 45*s.* per quarter, fixed for a year.

In post-war commercial treaties it signifies also quantities of essential commodities for which export and import licences are issued respectively by the countries concerned. Immigration quotas, based on the acceptability of the nationals of certain races as immigrants, have been established in the U.S.A. and elsewhere. Great Britain has a film quota, establishing the proportion of British films which must be shown.

QUO WARRANTO. In English law, a writ formerly issued from the Court of King's Bench calling upon a person, or body of persons, to show by what warrant ("quo warranto") they exercised any public office or privilege. The writ itself is fallen into disuse, but the same end is attained by the Attorney-General filing an information in the nature of *quo warranto.*

R

R. The eighteenth letter of the English alphabet, classed as a liquid and semi-vowel. In the pronunciation of Englishmen generally it represents two somewhat different sounds. The one is heard at the beginning of words and syllables, and when it is preceded by a consonant; the other, less decidedly consonantal, is heard at the end of words and syllables, and when it is followed by a consonant. In the pronunciation of many English speakers, *r*, followed by a consonant at the end of a syllable, is scarcely heard as a separate sound, having merely the effect of lengthening the preceding vowel; when it is itself final, as in *bear, door, their*, etc., it becomes a vowel rather than a consonant.

The Three Rs. A humorous and familiar designation for *Reading, Writing*, and *Arithmetic*. It originated with Sir William Curtis (1752-1829), who, on being asked to give a toast, said, " I will give you *the three Rs, Writing, Reading*, and *Arithmetic*."

RA (more properly Rê). The name of the sun-god among the ancient Egyptians. In the course of time nearly all the Egyptian divinities were identified with Ra, and Amenophis IV. of the eighteenth dynasty tried to establish a monotheism based upon the worship of Ra, under the name of Aton. Like Horus, Ra is represented with the head of a hawk, and bearing the disk of the sun on his head.

RAAB (räb), now **GYÖR** (dy*eur*) (Rom. *Arrabona*). A city of Hungary, at the confluence of the Raab and Rabnitz with the Danube. It is the see of a Roman Catholic bishop, and has a fine cathedral (rebuilt 1639-45), an episcopal palace, and diocesan seminary. Its manufactures are machinery, agricultural implements, and oil. Pop. (1930), 50,881.

RAASAY, or RASAY. An island of Scotland, one of the Inner Hebrides, between Skye and the mainland, included in Inverness-shire, 13 miles long and 3½ miles broad at the widest part. It is for the most part a hilly ridge, rising in parts to over 1000 feet. There are some scattered farms on the east side of the island. The ruins of Brochel Castle are on the east coast. Pop. 300.

RABAT'. A seaport and the administrative capital of the French Zone of Morocco, at the mouth of the Bou-Regreg, facing Salé (Sallee), formerly the chief port of entry for European commerce. The present maximum working capacity of the port is 300 tons per diem, and an entrance channel across the bar and up the river will give a depth of 3 metres at lowest tides. Oil, wool, and cereals are exported, and some carpets and leather shoes are made. Pop. 30,000. Rabat is a stopping-place on the State-subsidised aerial mail and passenger service, established in 1919, between Toulouse (France) and Rabat, and extended to Casablanca in 1922. Pop. (1931), 53,106 (20,802 Europeans).

RABAUL. Chief town and seat of government of the British mandated territory of New Guinea. It is on New Britain. Non-indigenous pop. 1800.

RABBI. A title of honour among the Hebrews. There are two other forms of the title, *rabboni* and *rabbani*. It is supposed that this title first came into use at the period immediately preceding the birth of Christ. In the time of our Lord it was applied generally to all religious teachers, and hence sometimes to Christ himself. Now the term rabbi or rabbin is applied to ministers and regularly appointed teachers of Talmudic Judaism. (See illus. p. 534).

RABBINIC HEBREW. That form of Hebrew in which the Jewish scholars and theologians of the Middle Ages composed their works. Grammatically it differs but little from the ancient Hebrew, but in many cases new meanings are attached to Hebrew words already in use, in other cases new derivatives are formed from old Hebrew roots, and many words are borrowed from the Arabic.

RABBIT (*Lepus cunicŭlus*). A genus of rodent mammals, included in the family Leporidæ, to which also belong the hares. It is of smaller size than the hare, and has shorter ears and hind-legs. The rabbit's fur in its native state is of a nearly uniform brown colour, whilst under domestication the colour may become pure white, pure black, piebald, grey, and other hues. The

Rabbi

texture of the fur also changes under domestication. The rabbit is a native of South-Western Europe and North-Western Africa, and in its wild state congregates in "warrens" in sandy pastures and on dry slopes.

Rabbits breed six or seven times a year, and produce from five to

Chinchilla Rabbit

seven or eight at a birth, being so prolific that they may easily become a pest, as in Australia and New Zealand, where it seems impossible to keep them down. They feed on tender grass and herbage, and sometimes do great damage to young trees by stripping them of their bark. They grow exceedingly tame under domestication, and there are about fourteen breeds, of which the Belgian and Flemish are the best for table purposes. Immense numbers of rabbits are exported from the Australian colonies to this country, preserved by cold storage, the skins also being exported. The skins are of considerable value; cleared of hair, they are used with others to make glue and size. The fur is employed in the manufacture of hats, and to imitate other and more valuable furs, as ermine.

RABELAIS (råb-lā), **François.** French humorist, born at Chinon, in Touraine, about 1490; died in 1553. The son of an apothecary, he entered the Franciscan order at Fontenay-le-Comte, in Poitou, and received the priesthood. His addiction to profane studies appears to have given offence to his monastic brethren, and through the influence of friends he obtained the permission of Clement VII. to enter the Benedictine order (about 1524). He then exchanged the seclusion of the monastery for the comparative freedom of the residence of the Bishop of Maillezais, who made him his secretary and companion. In the course of a few years we find him at Montpellier, where he studied medicine, having by this time become a secular priest; he was admitted bachelor in 1530, and for some time successfully practised and taught. In 1532 he went to Lyons, where he published a work of Hippocrates and one of Galen, and the first germ of his *Gargentua* (1532 or 1533).

The first part of his *Pantagruel* appeared under the anagram of Alcofribas Nasier, within a year or so after the former work, and its success was such that it passed through three editions in one year. Soon after its publication Rabelais accompanied Jean du Bellay on an embassy to Rome. On his return to France he went first to Paris; but not long after he is found once more at Lyons, where the *Gargantua*, as we now have it, first saw the light (1535). The *Gargantua* and *Pantagruel* together form a single work professing to narrate the sayings and doings of the giant Gargantua and his son Pantagruel. In 1536 Rabelais was again at Rome, and on this occasion he obtained from the Pope absolution for the violation of his monastic vows, and permission to practise medicine and to hold benefices. Shortly afterwards he was granted a prebend in the abbey of Saint Maur-des-Fossés by Jean du Bellay. In 1537 he took his degree of Doctor of Medicine at Montpellier, and lectured on Hippocrates. The next few years were as unsettled as regards his abode as any previous period of Rabelais's life, and it is difficult to follow him. Probably he was in Paris in 1546, when the third book of his *Pantagruel* appeared, but during most of 1546 and part of 1547 he was physician to the town of Metz. In the third book all the great moral and social questions of the day were discussed with the gaiety and irony peculiar to Rabelais, and with a freedom that roused the suspicion of the clergy, who endeavoured to have it suppressed. The favour of the king secured its publication, but it was with more difficulty that a licence was obtained

François Rabelais

for the fourth book from Henry II., who had succeeded Francis in 1547. This book did not appear complete till 1552. About 1550 Rabelais was appointed to the cure of Meudon, but he resigned his position early in 1553, and he died at Paris shortly after. He left the whole of the fifth book of his remarkable romance in manuscript.

Rabelais was one of the first to give flexibility and finish to the yet rude and harsh language of his country. Boileau calls him *la Raison en masque,* and Rousseau, *le gentil maître François.* By many Rabelais has been set down as a gross buffoon, and there is much in his writings to justify the harsh judgment, though we must remember what was the taste of his times. As regards the purpose of his work, many have looked upon Rabelais as a serious reformer of abuses, religious, moral, and social, assuming an extravagant masquerade for the purpose of protecting himself from the possible consequences of his assaults on established institutions. The earlier books were translated into English by Sir Thomas Urquhart (1653), who found a continuator in Motteux. It has been claimed for this translation that it is the best translation ever made; it is certainly worthy to stand beside François Victor Hugo's translation of Shakespeare, and Rogers's version of Aristophanes. —BIBLIOGRAPHY: P. Stapfer, *Rabelais: sa personne, son génie, son œuvre*; A. A. Tilly, *François Rabelais*; Sir W. Besant, *Rabelais* (Foreign Classics for English Readers Series).

RABIES (rā'bi-ēz). The name given to a disease, probably a kind of blood-poisoning, with which dogs, horses, cats, wolves, and other animals are attacked, and to which indeed, all animals are said to be liable. A bite from some rabid animals induces hydrophobia in man. *See* HYDROPHOBIA.

RABY CASTLE. Residence of Lord Barnard. It is in Durham, 5 miles from Barnard Castle, and dates in the main from the sixteenth century. A splendid pile, it was the seat of the Duke of Cleveland until that title became extinct in 1891.

RACE. Group of persons, animals, or plants of common ancestry. The word may denote all mankind, a primary division, e.g. the yellow race, or a smaller ethnic group, e.g. Jewish. The word also denotes breeds or strains greater or less than a species, e.g. canine, black-faced.

RAC'EME. In botany, a form of inflorescence in which the primary axis is elongated, and bears flowers placed on pedicels of nearly equal length, as in the currant and lily-of-the-valley. The inflorescence is centripetal or indefinite. It differs from a spike only in the flowers not being sessile. *See* INFLORESCENCE.

RACHEL. Biblical character. A daughter of Laban, she became the wife of Jacob after he had served Laban for her for two periods of seven years, and had married her elder sister, Leah. She had two sons, Joseph and Benjamin, and she died when the latter was born.

RACHEL (rà-shell), **Mademoiselle (Elizabeth Rachel Felix).** French *tragédienne,* of Jewish extraction, born in 1821; died in 1858. For a time she gained her living by singing in the streets of Lyons, but being taken notice of, she was enabled to receive a course of instruction at the Conservatoire, and made her début in 1837 on the stage of the Gymnase at Paris. On 12th June, 1838, she appeared at the Théâtre Français, where she took the Parisian public by storm by the admirable manner in which she impersonated the classic creations of Racine and Corneille. Her reputation was speedily

Mademoiselle Rachel

established as the first tragic actress of her day. In 1841 she visited England, and was received with the greatest enthusiasm. Her renown continued to increase, and for many years she reigned supreme at the Théâtre Français, making also tours to the provincial towns of France, to Belgium, etc. She died of consumption. Her life has been written by the French statesman Louis Barthou (q.v.).

RACHIS (rā'kis). In botany, a branch which proceeds nearly in a straight line from the base of the apex of the inflorescence of a plant. The term is also applied to the stalk of the frond in ferns, and to the common stalk bearing the alternate spikelets in some grasses.

RACHMANINOFF, Sergei Vassilievitch. Russian composer and pianist. He was born at Nijni-Novgorod on 2nd April, 1873. He received his musical education at the Leningrad and Moscow Conservatoires, and won a gold medal with his opera *Aleko* in 1892. He made several concert tours, and in 1903 was conductor of the Imperial Opera. He conducted the Moscow Philharmonic Symphony Orchestra, 1912-13.

After the Russian revolution he escaped to Sweden, and eventually settled in America. He has written operas, symphonies, and piano concertos, and many smaller piano works, of which the *Prelude in C sharp minor* is most famous.

RACINE (rȧ-sēn), **Jean Baptiste.** French dramatist, born at La Ferté-Milon (Aisne) 1639; died at Paris 1699. He was educated at Port-Royal, the famous Jansenist institution, and subsequently at the Collège d'Harcourt. After writing an ode, called *La Nymphe de la Seine*, in honour of the king's marriage, and two comedies, now lost, he made the acquaintance of Boileau and Molière, and began to write for the stage. His first tragedy, the *Thébaïde*, or *Les Frères Ennemis*, was performed by Molière's troupe at the Palais-Royal in 1664, as was also his next, *Alexandre*, in 1665. His first masterpiece was *Andromaque*, which on its performance at the Hôtel de Bourgogne, in 1667, produced a profound impression. The immediate successor of *Andromaque* was *Les Plaideurs* (1668), a witty and delightful imitation of the *Wasps* of Aristophanes. His next pieces were *Britannicus* (1669); *Bérénice* (1670); *Bajazet* (1672); *Mithridate* (1673); *Iphigénie* (1674); *Phèdre* (1677), the last piece that Racine produced expressly for the theatre. In 1673 he obtained a seat in the French Academy. His withdrawal from the theatre in 1677 was partly due to chagrin at the success of a hostile party of theatrical critics who applauded a writer now never heard of at the expense of Racine.

At this period his friends persuaded him to marry, and soon after (1678) he was appointed, along with Boileau, historiographer to the king, whom he accompanied in his campaign to Flanders. After a silence of twelve years Racine, at the solicitation of Madame de Maintenon, wrote two other pieces—*Esther* (1689) and *Athalie* (1691). His death is said to have been hastened by grief at losing the favour of the king.

As a dramatist Racine is usually considered the model of the French classical tragic drama, and in estimating his powers in this field it is necessary to take into account the stiff conventional restraints to which that drama was subjected. What he achieved within these limits is extraordinary. It has been objected that he has introduced too much love into his pieces, and that he has represented his tragic princesses and heroines as too susceptible to love. To this, however, he was led not only by his own disposition but also by the character of his age. He wrote as a Frenchman for Frenchmen of the old type, in whom heroism

Jean Baptiste Racine

and gallantry were combined, and he succeeded in depicting with truth and tenderness the feelings of a delicate and high-minded chivalry, and of a pure and ardent love. Besides his dramas Racine is the author of epigrams, odes, and hymns, etc.—BIBLIOGRAPHY: G. Larroumet, *Racine* in *Les grands écrivains*; P. Robert, *La poétique de Racine*; Jules Lemaître, *Jean Racine*; D. F. Canfield, *Corneille and Racine in England.*

RACINE (ra-sēn'). A city of Wisconsin, United States, the county seat of Racine county, on Lake Michigan, at the mouth of Root River; served by the Chicago, Milwaukee, & St. Paul, and the Chicago & North-Western Railways, and by electric-traction lines to Chicago. There is a good harbour. Racine College (Protestant) and St. Catherine's Academy (Roman Catholic) are notable institutions. Agricultural machinery, carriages, motors, and wagons are manufactured. Racine was settled in 1834 as Port Gilbert, and became a city in 1848, the present name having been adopted in 1837. Pop. (1930), 67,542.

RACK. A mechanical device by means of which rotary motion can be obtained from, or is converted into, rectilinear motion. The mechanism consists of two parts: one a metal bar with teeth cut on one edge, and the other a small toothed wheel or pinion. An illustration of its use can be seen in the gear for opening and closing sluice gates in water races or in the device used in some commercial motor vehicles to tilt the wagon in the process of emptying it.

RACKETEERING. American expression arising out of the development of "gangs," and applied to the practice of gangsters, who, by means of threats of violence which they are able, and quite prepared, to carry out, extort money from those trading legitimately. In return, the traders are allowed to carry on business more or less peacefully, even receiving a measure of protection.

RACKETS, or **RACQUETS.** A comparatively modern game, resembling fives in so far as it is played against the wall of a specially built "court," usually roofed and with ample skylights; but it is allied rather to tennis by the employment of a racket instead of the hand for striking the ball. The head of this racket, tightly strung with catgut, is now usually rounder in shape than that used for tennis. The ball, made of layers of cloth covered with kid, is very hard, weighs about $1\frac{1}{4}$ oz., and is $1\frac{1}{2}$ inches in diameter. The court should be about 30 feet broad by 60 feet deep. Its front wall, faced by the players, has a horizontal "service" or "cut" line marked at a height of 9 feet 6 inches from the ground, while the lower portion is boarded to a height of 26 inches.

The game may, like tennis, be played by either two or four players. The "hand-in" player, who first "serves" the ball, takes his stand in one of the two "service-boxes," 6 feet square, placed on each side of the court. He must strike the ball against the front wall above the "cut" line in such a manner that it will drop into the side of the court opposite to his own after having hit the side or back walls; it is there struck by the opposing player before it has twice touched the ground, and must be returned to strike the wall above the boards. "Squash rackets" is a somewhat less exacting variety of the game, played with a larger ball. For rules of play and other details, see J. Marshall, *Rackets* (1890); E. O. Pleydell-Bouverie, *Rackets* (Badminton Library); and Eustace H. Miles, *Rackets, Tennis, and Squash.*

RACKHAM, Arthur. English artist. He was born 19th Sept., 1867, and educated at the City of London School, and Lambeth School of Art. He is best known as an illustrator, in which department his delicately fantastic work is familiar to all book-lovers.

RACOON′, or RACCOON′. An American plantigrade carnivorous mammal, the common racoon being the *Procyon lotor*, the specific name having reference to its curious habit of dipping its food in water. It is about the size of a small fox, and its greyish-brown fur is deemed valuable, being principally used in the

Racoon (*Procyon Lotor*)

manufacture of hats. This animal lodges in hollow trees, feeds occasionally on vegetables, and its flesh is palatable food. It inhabits North America from Canada to the tropics. The black-footed racoon of Texas and California is *P. nigripes*. The agouara or crab-eating racoon (*P. cancrivŏrus*) is found farther south on the American continent than the above species, and is generally larger.

RADCLIFFE. An urban district and town of Lancashire, England, on the Irwell; served by the L.M. & S. Railway. The church of St. Bartholomew dates from the reign of Henry IV. It is a coal-mining district. There are calico-printing, cotton-weaving, dyeing, and other industries. Pop. (1931), 24,674.

RADCLIFFE, Ann. Novelist, born in London in 1764; died 1823. She married, at the age of twenty-three, William Radcliffe, afterwards editor and proprietor of *The English Chronicle*. She published in quick succession *The Castles of Athlin and Dunbayne*, a Highland story; *A Sicilian Romance*; and *The Romance of the Forest*. Her masterpiece is considered to be *The Mysteries of Udolpho* (1794), which was long very popular. The last of her novels published during her life was *The Italian* (1797). A posthumous romance, *Gaston de Blondeville*, was edited by T. N. Talfourd in 1826, together with some poetical pieces. Mrs. Radcliffe had considerable power in the description of scenery, and knew how to excite and maintain the curiosity of her readers; but her characters are insipid, the world in which they move is unreal, and the conclusion of her stories lame and impotent.

RADCLIFFE, John. English physician, Fellow of Lincoln College, Oxford, and M.P. Born at Wakefield

Dr. John Radcliffe

in 1650, he studied medicine at Oxford. He then began to practise, and having settled in London, was physician to William III., and the two queens, Mary and Anne. He died at Carshalton, 1st Nov., 1714.

Radcliffe left his money to Oxford University where his name is perpetuated in several ways. The university has its **Radcliffe Library** (see following article), and the city the **Radcliffe Infirmary.** There are Radcliffe travelling fellowships for students of medicine. The university observatory is called the **Radcliffe Observatory,** because it was built from money left by Radcliffe. It was erected between 1772 and 1795.

RADCLIFFE LIBRARY. A library founded in connection with Oxford University out of funds destined for the purpose by **Dr. John**

Radcliffe (1650-1714), physician to the Princess Anne of Denmark, and opened in 1749. The building erected by the Radcliffe trustees for the reception of the books forming the library is now used as a reading-room in connection with the Bodleian Library. An observatory in connection with the university was founded in 1772 by the Radcliffe trustees.

RADHANPUR. A native state and town of India, in the Pālanpur agency of Bombay. It is flat and open, traversed by three rivers that dry up in the hot season, and has mean temperatures of 41° F. in January and 115° F. in June. December to March is the cool season; between April and July and in the months of September and October the heat is excessive. Cotton, wheat, and commoner food grains, but no irrigated crops (excepting vegetables), are produced. Saltpetre is manufactured. Radhanpur, the only town, is the capital. It is surrounded by a wall, and contains a castle, also surrounded by a wall, which is the residence of the Nawāb. A considerable number of roads converge on the town, which is therefore a trade centre for Cutch and Northern Gujarāt. State area, 1150 sq. miles; pop. 67,789 (mainly Hindus); pop. (town), 14,500.

RADIA'TA. The name given by Cuvier to his fourth great division of the animal kingdom, including those animals whose parts are arranged round an axis, and display more or less of the "rayed" appearance or conformation. In modern zoology Cuvier's division has been abolished, and the radiata have been divided into several phyla.

RADIA'TION. The propagation from a body of vibrational energy in the form of waves through the ether or through a material medium. The present article refers only to the phenomena of heat and light. A hot body emits wave energy into the surrounding medium and loses heat. The waves travel with the velocity of light in straight lines; they are subject to reflection, refraction, polarisation, etc., like waves of light, and are absorbed, reflected, or transmitted by bodies on which they fall. The rate of emission by the hot body from a unit of area of its surface depends on the difference of temperature between the body and the medium, and also on the emissive power or emissivity of the surface. Melloni (1798-1854) found that the relative emissive powers of various substances at 100° C. varied from 100 for lampblack to 13 for metals, and he also showed that these relative emissive powers were the same as the relative absorbing powers. Kirchhoff proved (1860) that the ratio of the radiating power to the absorbing power is the same for all bodies, the radiating power being measured by the quantity of energy radiated per square centimetre per second, and the absorbing power by the fraction of the incident energy which is absorbed, these being measured at the same temperature.

Langley showed by experiment (1881) that with rise of temperature the radiation of each wave-length increases in intensity, and new radiations of shorter wave-length appear. He invented the bolometer, an instrument for measuring radiant heat, and employed it to investigate the heat spectra of the sun and moon. The whole spectrum may be divided into ultra-violet, visible, and infra-red portions, and these may be regarded as the seats of photographic or chemical, light, and heat actions respectively; but this does not hold strictly; there is overlapping, and heat effects, for instance, are discernible in the chemical spectrum.

Various instruments have been employed to detect and measure heat radiation. Melloni used, in his experiments, a thermopile, made up of a number of thermo-junctions of bismuth and antimony, in conjunction with an astatic galvanometer. Vernon Boys used a much more sensitive instrument known as a radiomicrometer, formed by hanging up, by a fine quartz fibre, between the poles of a strong horse-shoe magnet, a thermoelectric loop on one junction of which the radiation was directed, giving rise to a current which deflected the loop, the deflection being read by means of a lamp, mirror, and scale. Langley's bolometer depends on the change in electrical resistance which takes place in a metal with rise of temperature (*see* SPECTROBOLOMETER). By means of this instrument Langley mapped the infra-red spectrum of the sun, and showed that, like the visible portion, it possesses many "lines." He recorded 600 lines between the wave-lengths $1{\cdot}8\mu$ and $5{\cdot}3\mu$ (μ, a micron or thousandth part of a millimetre).

With the aid of the bolometer a careful investigation was made by Wien, Paschen, Lummer, Pringsheim, Kurlbaum, and others of the relation between radiation energy and temperature. Kirchhoff had suggested the idea of a perfect radiator and perfect absorber, with which other bodies might be compared. A near approach to this is found in black bodies; for example, black velvet is found to absorb 99·6 per cent of incident radiation. The perfect radiator has therefore become known as the "black body," and Lummer and Pringsheim realized an experimental black body by heating or cooling a hollow vessel blackened in the interior, and using the radiation from the internal surface which emerges through a small hole in the wall of the vessel.

With the aid of the bolometer they proved that the wave-length of the dominent radiation of the black body is inversely proportional to the absolute temperature of the body (Wien's Law), also that the total radiation given out per second is proportional to the fourth power of the absolute temperature of the body (Stefan-Boltzmann Law), and, further, that the amount of energy radiated in the dominant wave was proportional to the fifth power of the absolute temperature of the body. In the first case the constant of proportionality is 2900, if the wave-length is expressed in microns. This gives a means of calculating temperatures. Assuming that the sun gives "black body" radiation, the dominant wave in the sun's spectrum is $0·5\mu$ in length; this gives, for the sun's temperature, $2900 \div 0·5$, or 5800° absolute. Lummer and Pringsheim have further shown that in non-black bodies, such as platinum, the total radiation varies as the fifth power of the absolute temperature. Planck has given a formula for radiation energy (*see* RADIATION, THEORY OF) which gives values agreeing closely with the values of radiation energy found by different observers. It is employed, with others of the foregoing results, as the basis of optical pyrometry (*see* PYROMETER).

RADIATION, THEORY OF. Radiation is any influence proceeding from a source in straight lines, so that an obstacle in front of a point source throws a shadow which is its geometric projection. The known influences of this kind can be divided into two groups (*see* RAYS, ELECTRIC; RADIO-ACTIVITY): (*a*) particle radiations, e.g. α- and β-rays, cathode and positive rays; (*b*) electromagnetic radiation, i.e. Hertzian rays, all kinds of light, X-rays, and γ-rays. Group (*a*) will not be considered at all here; most of group (*b*) will be considered only in connection with a fundamental difficulty affecting all its members. But one member of (*b*), which is usually referred to by the term Theory of Radiation, will be discussed more specifically.

This is thermal radiation. All bodies, if heated to a sufficiently high temperature, emit light, which when resolved by the spectroscope (q.v.) forms a continuous spectrum. In general the light is more intense, and its average frequency is greater (i.e. the light is bluer and less red), the greater the temperature of the body. If the temperature is below that at which visible light is emitted, there is still emitted a radiation (formerly called radiant heat and now infra-red radiation) which has all the characteristic properties of light, except visibility, and is now known to differ from light only because all but an inappreciable fraction of it consists of radiation of frequency too low to affect the eye. Even if the body is cooled below and not heated above its surroundings, it still emits thermal radiation; but since this radiation increases in general with the temperature, it receives from its surroundings more than it gives to them, and is therefore heated and not cooled. Nowadays no distinction is recognised between the thermal radiation, emitted by any body at any temperature, and light, emitted from any source, except in the relation between the intensity of the radiation and the frequency.

This relation has been the subject of much investigation. Let $E_\nu dt\, d\sigma\, d\omega\, d\nu$ be the energy of the radiation having a frequency between ν and $\nu + d\nu$ emitted in time dt from a surface of the body of area $d\sigma$ in a direction lying within a solid angle $d\omega$ round the normal to that surface. Then E_ν is called the intensity of the radiation of frequency ν. The following laws concerning E_ν can be established experimentally:

1. In general E_ν increases with the temperature T (absolute) of the emitting surface (source), but is independent of the temperature of the surrounding bodies.

2. In general E_ν is a maximum for some particular value of ν, and this value of ν is greater the greater the temperature. Sources which are exceptions to (1) and (2) are said to show selective radiation.

3. E_ν at any particular T and ν, and the change of E_ν with T and ν, vary with the nature of the body forming the source. The variation is comparatively slight if similar sources (e.g. two metals) are compared, but is very great if, e.g., a metal is compared with a gas.

4. Let A_ν be the absorption coefficient of the source for radiation of frequency ν, i.e. the proportion of that radiation which is absorbed

when it falls on the source. Then $\frac{E_\nu}{A_\nu}$ is the same for all sources for the same values of ν and T; the variations of (3) do not appear in this ratio. (Kirchhoff's Law.)

It follows from (4) that all sources for which A is the same emit the same radiation at the same temperature. If a small deep hole is bored in any body, any radiation entering the hole is totally absorbed within it after repeated reflections; accordingly for such a hole $A_\nu = 1$ for all values of ν, i.e. the hole is perfectly black, whatever is the nature of the surrounding body. It is actually found that the radiation proceeding from such a hole is independent of the body in which it is bored. Such radiation, emitted by a perfectly black body, is called "black-body," or "complete," or "full" radiation.

The intensity of complete radiation of frequency ν is determined by the temperature only. The relation between E_ν, ν, and T has been very carefully studied and shown to be consistent with the equation

$$E_\nu = C_1 \nu^3/(e^{C_2\nu/T} - 1) \ldots (1)$$

(Planck's Law),

where $C_1 = 7{\cdot}28 \times 10^{-48}$ erg sec^3/cm.^{2} and $C_2 = 4{\cdot}86 \times 10^{-11}$ sec. E, the total intensity of the radiation of all frequencies in complete radiation, is $\int E_\nu d\nu$, so that by (1)

$E = 8{\cdot}50 \times 10^{-6} T^4$ erg / (cm.^{2} sec.) . . . (2) (Stefan's Law). It should be noted for subsequent reference that if $\frac{T}{\nu}$ is very great, (1) reduces to $E_\nu = (C_1 / C_2 \cdot \nu^2 T \ldots (3)$ (Rayleigh-Jeans' Law).

So much for experiment; we now turn to theory. If we assume (*a*) the conservation of energy; (*b*) that two bodies in an enclosure thermally insulated from each other and from all other bodies would eventually reach the same temperature by means of their mutual radiation; (*c*) that their final temperature will not be reduced to absolute zero; then it can be established that Kirchhoff's Law must be true. In the steady state finally reached in the enclosure there will be a definite concentration of radiant energy in the enclosure, which is in thermal equilibrium with the bodies and may be regarded as having the same temperature. If it is assumed further (*d*) that a small hole made in the enclosure, permitting an infinitesimal fraction of the radiation to escape, does not materially disturb the equilibrium, then the complete radiation from a perfect black body which is studied experimentally must represent this equilibrium radiation. Its independence of the nature of the enclosure in which the hole is made is explained.

There remains to be explained the form of Planck's Law, stated in (1). Wien, by considering the pressure exerted by radiation on a surface on which it falls, proved from general thermodynamic theory that the relation must be of the form $E_\nu = \nu^3 f(\nu/T)$, which includes both (1) and (3) (Wien's Displacement Law). But the determination of the form of the function f requires further assumptions. The principles of generalised mechanics as stated by Lagrange and Hamilton would be sufficient for this purpose; but it is now agreed that (1) is inconsistent with those principles, which must necessarily lead to the conclusion that (3) is valid, not only when T/ν is large, but always. The deduction involves (*d*) as well as the assumption (*e*) that different frequencies represent different "degrees of freedom" and can vary independently. Attempts were made at one time to save classical mechanics by denying (*d*) or (*e*); but they are now abandoned.

On the other hand, (1) follows from a quantum theory (q.v.) which asserts that the quantum states of frequency of radiation ν are those in which the energy is $mh\nu$, where m is an integer and h is Planck's constant. This theory leads to the relation

$$E_\nu = (h\nu^3/c^2) : (e^{h\nu/kT} - 1) \ldots (4),$$

where c is the velocity of light, and kT is two-thirds of the kinetic energy of the molecule of a perfect gas at temperature T. Comparison of (4) with (1) leads to $h = 6{\cdot}56 \times 10^{-27}$ erg-sec., $k = 1{\cdot}35 \times 10^{-16}$ erg, values agreeing perfectly with those determined from entirely different phenomena. This quantum theory, due to Planck, was historically the first and introduced for the first time the universal constant h. But since a completely logical deduction of (4) presents some difficulty, the most convincing evidence for the replacement of classical mechanics by quantum theory comes to-day from other sources.

However, such a replacement leads to grave difficulties in the general theory of electromagnetic radiation. A few years ago the undulatory theory (*see* LIGHT; ETHER) of such radiation was unquestioned; it explained perfectly some of the characteristics of radiation, e.g.

rectilinear propagation, interference, regular reflection and refraction; and the explanation involved the assumption that energy is transferred continuously from one part to another of the medium through which the radiation passes. Other characteristics, of which that which has just been discussed is an example, are inconsistent with it. It is possible to divide the properties of radiation sharply into two classes, of which one is explicable by a continuous undulatory theory and not by a quantum theory, while for the other the position is reversed.

Many attempts have been and are being made to remove this contradiction. At first the tendency was to modify slightly the undulatory theory while retaining the essential feature of it. Of such attempts J. J. Thomson's " string theory " of the ether (q.v.) and Einstein's " light quantum " theory may be mentioned as examples. They are intended primarily to explain the photo-electric effect (q.v.), and especially the remarkable fact that, in some circumstances, bodies can apparently absorb from radiation more energy than falls on them. It is suggested that the disturbance which constitutes radiation is periodic in time and space, as the undulatory theory suggests, but that it is wholly concentrated in a small volume and does not spread out spherically from a point source. But all such theories only cover part of the field, and are apt to introduce more difficulties than they remove.

The tendency now is rather to abandon the older kind of explanation (which was intimately connected with the acceptance of the concepts of mechanics), and to seek merely formal statements of great generality from which all the facts can be deduced without logical inconsistency. Thus the two classes of properties mentioned above can be formally distinguished as those involved in processes which produce no resultant change in radiant energy (to these classical mechanics applies), and those in which radiant energy is given to or taken from material systems (to these quantum theory applies). The problems of the former have long been solved. For the latter a quantum theory so general has been propounded that it can always be predicted what interchange of energy there will be when a process of the second class takes place; but no equally general theory is yet available to predict in what circumstances such a process will occur. (Thus we know how much energy an electron will take from radiation if it is emitted photoelectrically; but we do not know theoretically what proportion of electrons exposed to the radiation will absorb energy.)

The attempts to provide such a theory usually start from the fact that, when the change in the quantum number of a system (*see* QUANTUM THEORY) is very small compared with the quantum numbers of the initial and final states, the series of quantum states becomes practically continuous and classical principles lead to the same result as quantum theory. Accordingly the problem is to find some formal relation which in this limiting case reduces to the relation of Maxwellian electrodynamics and yet is in accordance with the facts when the changes are perceptibly discontinuous. The most general relations of this kind proposed as yet are Bohr's Principle of Correspondence, of great importance in the Theory of Spectra (q.v.), and Ehrenfest's Principle of Adiabatic Invariance. But to state either of these completely is beyond the scope of this article. When the desired principle has been found, the classical theory of radiation will appear as a special case of a very general quantum theory, and though no " visualising " explanation of radiation will be offered, or appear possible, the two classes of radiation processes, at present so sharply distinguished, will have been brought into complete harmony.

BIBLIOGRAPHY: M. Planck, *Die Theorie der Warmestrahlung* (translated); J. H. Jeans, *Report on the Quantum Theory of Radiation* (Physical Society publication); E. P. Adams, *Quantum Theory* (published by the National Research Council of America, 1916); N. R. Campbell, *Modern Electrical Theory* (second edition); L. Rougier, *Philosophy and the New Physics* (translated by M. Masius: Blakiston, Philadelphia, 1921).

RADICAL. Term in chemistry applied to a group of atoms of several elements that enter into the formation of compounds, and pass from one compound to another without disintegration, but do not exist as a separate entity. Examples of radicals are the hydrocarbon radicals, methyl, acetyl, and ethyl, also ammonium and cyanogen.

RADICALS. Advanced Liberals in politics. Opposed to the Whigs, or moderate Liberals, they were the pioneers and ardent advocates of thorough political reform on broad democratic lines throughout the nineteenth century. Although heard before the end of the seventeenth century, the term did not actually come into vogue until near the end of the eighteenth, being first applied to Henry ("Orator") Hunt, who was imprisoned for a speech in connection with the Peterloo "massacre" at the Manchester reform demonstration, 16th July, 1819. In those days Radicals were known as "White Hats," because of the headgear of the leaders. Since the rise of the Labour party, the term Radical has fallen into disuse, but its ideas have permeated sections even of the Conservatives, and the designation Liberal now implies Radicalism. The Radicals were never a separate party, and reached their zenith, under the headship of Joseph Chamberlain, about 1885, when they put forward a programme for the general election of that year.

RADIO-ACTIVITY. The term "radio-active" is applied to a class of elements, such as uranium, thorium, and radium, which possess the peculiar property of emitting continually and *spontaneously* radiations which are capable of passing through sheets of metal and other substances which are opaque to ordinary light. These radiations, in addition to affecting a photographic plate, have also the property of discharging an electrified body (*see* RAYS, ELECTRIC). It has been shown that the emission of these radiations is due to an actual disintegration of the radio-active element, which is transformed in the process into a completely distinct element. In some cases this radio-active disintegration, as it is termed, is not attended with the emission of any perceptible radiations. These "rayless" changes, however, follow exactly the same laws as those accompanied by radiations, and are included in the general term "radio-active". As a matter of fact, electrons are given off during these rayless changes, but with such small velocities that they do not exhibit the characteristic properties of electric rays.

The first important discovery in the subject of radio-activity was made by Becquerel in Feb., 1896, who found that the double sulphate of uranium and potassium emitted radiations which produced an impression on a photographic plate enveloped in black light-proof paper. He found that a similar effect was produced by any salt of uranium, and by the metal uranium itself. It is thus a specific property of the element. A compound of uranium gives off three types of radiation α-, β-, and γ-radiation (*see* RAYS, ELECTRIC). The photographic effect discovered by Becquerel was due to the β-rays, as the α-rays would be absorbed by the wrapping of the plate, while the γ-rays are too feeble to produce a measurable impression during the time of exposure employed.

In 1900 Sir William Crookes discovered that it was possible by a single chemical operation to separate the uranium into two fractions of very unequal bulk. If ammonium carbonate is added to a solution of a uranium salt, and the precipitate is dissolved in excess of the reagent, a trace of the precipitate remains undissolved, consisting chemically of the impurities present in the original solution. In this precipitate is concentrated the whole of the β-ray activity of the original salt. The solution, containing practically the whole of the original uranium, is, when tested photographically, completely inactive. The β-rays are therefore not emitted by uranium itself, can but by some new substance which be separated from it by a simple chemical reaction. To this substance Crookes gave the name uranium X.

If the two fractions are kept under observation for some weeks, it is found that the uranium X gradually loses its activity, the intensity of the radiation falling to half its original value in 24·6 days. The inactive solution begins again to emit β-rays, and at the end of 24·6 days has recovered one-half of its original radiating power. In fact, the total activity is constant throughout. Immediately after the separation it is concentrated in the uranium X precipitate, while the original salt is inactive. At the end of a few months the precipitate is quite inactive, while the solution has regained the whole of its original activity. The separated uranium salt, although it does not emit β-rays emits α-radiation at a rate which is constant, and is not affected by the separation of the uranium X.

The rate of decay of the activity of uranium X follows an exponential law. Thus if I_0 is the initial intensity, and I_t the intensity after an interval t has elapsed, $I_t = I_0\epsilon^{-\lambda t}$, where ϵ is the base of the natural logarithms, and λ is a constant which is known as the *radio-active constant* of the material. This exponential law of decay has been found to apply to all cases of radio-active disintegration where it has been possible to test it. The radio-active constant of a substance is apparently quite uninfluenced by change in physical conditions. The rate of decay of uranium X, for example, is exactly the same at a red heat as at the temperature of liquid air. This differentiates radio-active phenomena very markedly from ordinary chemical reactions.

The phenomena of radio-activity can be explained on a theory of radio-active change due to Rutherford. It is assumed (*a*) that there is a continuous production of new radio-active substance (uranium X in the case just considered) from the original element (uranium) at a rate which is proportional to the amount of the original substance actually present, and (*b*) that the new substance itself disintegrates at a rate which is also directly proportional to the amount of it actually present. The intensity of the radiations is assumed to be proportional to the quantity of the radiating substance. These assumptions have proved sufficient to account for all radio-active phenomena so far observed.

Their application to the case of uranium is particularly simple (1) because the rate of decay of uranium is so small (it has been estimated that it would decay to one-half its original amount in 5×10^9 years) that the quantity of it present may be regarded as constant during the experiment, and (2) because the product of the decay of uranium X is so very feebly active that it does not sensibly affect our observations. Suppose we have a quantity of uranium which has been freed from uranium X. The latter will be produced from the uranium at a constant rate, and the quantity of it present will thus increase. The uranium X, however, is decaying from the moment of its formation at a rate which is directly proportional to the amount of it which has actually collected, and which, therefore, increases as time goes on. A stage will thus be reached when the rate at which the uranium X is disintegrating becomes equal to its rate of formation. After this the proportion of uranium X to uranium in the mixture will be constant. This is known as *permanent radio-active equilibrium.* The separated uranium X, when cut off from its source, will disintegrate at a rate which is proportional at any instant to the amount of it still present. The exponential law of decay is simply a mathematical expression of this assumption. It can be shown that when permanent radio-active equilibrium has been reached, the quantity of each of the radio-active substances present in the mixture is inversely proportional to its radio-active constant.

If the uranium, instead of being practically constant in quantity, were to decay at a rate which, though measurable, was slow compared with that of uranium X, it is easy to see that the two substances would still reach a state of mutual equilibrium, but that the actual amount of each still present would decrease owing to the decay of the parent substance, and at the same rate. This is known as *transient radio-active equilibrium,* an important instance of which is the case of radium emanation and its products. The proportion of the derived substance present will be rather greater in the case of transient than of permanent equilibrium. Since the rate of decay of each of the products is governed by that of the parent substance when equilibrium has been attained, the radiation from any of these derived substances may be used as a measure of the amount of the parent substance still present.

The discovery by Mme Curie that some ores of uranium were several times more active than uranium itself led to the isolation, in 1898, of a new radio-active element, which, weight for weight, is nearly 2 million times as active as uranium, and to which the name of radium (q.v.) was given. This is by far the most important of the radio-active elements. Since its half-value period is only 1730 years, obviously it is still being continuously produced on the earth, and the fact that the ratio of radium to uranium in uranium ores is practically constant indicates that it is one of the decomposition products of uranium, in radio-active equilibrium with its source. It is not, however, the immediate product of the decay of uranium X, two other substances, uranium 2 and ionium, intervening between uranium X and radium. The full family tree is given in the table opposite.

Radium itself emits only α-radiation. Within a very few hours after its preparation, however, an emission of β- and γ-radiation begins, owing to the formation of other radio-active decomposition products. A sealed tube containing a radium salt will therefore emit all three types of radiation.

The phenomena of radio-active change are particularly striking in the case of radium, as the first product of its disintegration is a gas known as radium emanation. The existence of a radio-active gas was first recognised by Rutherford in the case of thorium, an element which is also radio-active. It was found that measurements of the activity of this substance were liable to strange fluctuations, which were finally traced to the emission by thorium of a radio-active " emanation " which was carried about by air-currents. The name " emanation "

Table of Radio-active Elements

Uranium-Radium Series			Uranium-Actinium Series			Thorium Series		
Element	Half-value Period	Radiation Emitted	Element	Half-value Period	Rays Emitted	Element	Half-value Period	Rays Emitted
Uranium 1	5×10^9 years	α	Uranium Y	1·5 days	β (slow)	Thorium	1·8 & 10^{10} years	α
Uranium Y	1·5 days	β (slow)	Protoactinium	10^4 years	α	Mesothorium 1	5·5 years	—
Uranium X_1	24·6 days	β (slow)	Actinium	30 years	β, γ	Mesothorium 2	6·2 hours	β, γ
Uranium X_2	1·15 min.	β, γ	Radioactinium	19·5 days	α	Radiothorium	2·0 years	α
Uranium 2	2×10^6 years	α	Actinium X	11·4 days	α	Thorium X	3·64 days	α
Ionium	2×10^3 years	α	Actinium emanation	3·9 sec.	α	Thorium emanation	54 sec.	α
Radium	1730 years	α	Actinium A	·002 sec.	α	Thorium A	0·14 sec.	α
Radium emanation	3·85 days	α	Actinium B	36·1 min.	β (slow)	Thorium B	10·6 hours	β (slow)
Radium A	3·0 min.	α	Actinium C	2·15 min.	α	Thorium C	60 min.	α
Radium B	26·7 min.	β (slow)	Actinium C_2	—	—	Thorium D	3·1 min.	β, γ
Radium C	19·5 min.	β	Actinium D	4·71 min.	β, γ	Thorium C_2	10^{-11} sec.	α
Radium C_2	1·4 min.	β	Lead	—	—	Lead	—	—
Radium C_1	10^{-6} sec.	α						
Radium D	16·5 years	β (slow)						
Radium E	5·0 days	β (slow)						
Polonium	136 days	α						
Lead	—	—						

was invented to avoid prejudice as to its actual nature. The emanations have since been shown to possess all the characteristics of gases of high atomic weight, and to belong chemically to the group of inert gases of which helium, neon, and argon are the first members.

Radium emanation decays to half value in 3·85 days, so that a few weeks are sufficient to establish radio-active equilibrium between the two. The quantity of emanation in equilibrium with a gramme of radium is known as a *curie*, and this unit and its subsidiary unit the *milli-curie* (one-thousandth of a curie) are now generally employed as standards of radio-activity. The volume of one curie of emanation at normal temperature and pressure is only 0·59 cubic millimetre. In spite of the smallness of this volume, not only has its boiling-point been determined (−65° C.) but also its density, which was found by Ramsay and Gray to be 111 times that of hydrogen. Its atomic weight is therefore 222, assuming that, like helium and argon, it is monatomic. This is exactly what we should expect if the atom of radium emanation was formed from an atom of radium from which an α-particle (which has been shown to be an atom of helium of atomic weight 4) had been expelled.

The correspondence is very convincing evidence in favour of the theory of atomic disintegration. Radium emanation can be most conveniently extracted from radium salts by dissolving them in water. On lowering the pressure a considerable proportion of the emanation is evolved, together with a much larger volume of hydrogen and oxygen from the decomposition of the water. The emanation may be purified by first sparking the mixed gases to remove the hydrogen and oxygen, and then passing the residual gas through a tube immersed in liquid air, where the emanation condenses, probably to a solid. On removing the tube from liquid air the emanation volatilises, and can be pumped into small glass tubes in a practically pure state. It is in this form that radio-active material is generally employed in medical treatment.

Radium emanation itself emits only α-radiation. If a wire is exposed to the emanation, it becomes radio-active, emitting α-, β-, and γ-rays. The activity is particularly marked if the wire during exposure is negatively charged. The effect was at first ascribed to an "induced" radio-activity in the wire. It has been shown to be due to the deposition on the wire of solid radio-active substances formed by the decay of the emanation. This activity rapidly decays when the wire is withdrawn, as the immediate products are all short-lived. If the emanation is kept in a sealed tube, a state of transient equilibrium is set up after a few hours, and the products then decay with the period of the emanation itself.

In addition to what we may call the radium series, uranium also gives rise to another chain of radio-active substances, of which actinium is the principal member, corresponding to a different mode of disintegration on the part of the uranium atom. The element thorium is also radio-active, and gives rise to a third chain of radio-active substances. Comparatively few of the radio-active substances exist in sufficient quantity to enable their properties to be observed directly. They can only be identified and examined by the radiations which they emit. It seems almost certain that the final product of the long series of radio-active changes is in each case the element lead.

The chemical classification of the thirty-five new radio-active elements has been attempted by Soddy. The emission of an α-particle, as we have seen, reduces the atomic weight by 4. The emission of β- and γ-radiation produces no sensible change in the atomic weight, but as it increases the resultant charge on the atomic nucleus, we should expect it to produce a change in the chemical properties of the atom. Soddy assumed that the emission of an α-particle produced a new element, whose position in the Periodic Table of the elements was two spaces to the left of the element from which it was so formed. The emission of β-radiation moved the position of the new element one space to the right. Thus the emission of an α-particle by uranium 1, which has an atomic weight of 238 and belongs to Group VI. of the Periodic Table (q.v.), produces a new element, uranium X_1, of atomic weight 234, which should be placed in Group IV. Uranium X_2 (or *brevium*, Bv), formed from uranium X_1 with the emission of β-radiation only, has also an atomic weight 234, but belongs to Group V, while similarly uranium 2 has an atomic weight of 234, but belongs, like uranium 1, to Group VI. Thus uranium 1 and uranium 2 not only belong to the same chemical group but occupy the same space in the table. They would thus be expected to show identical physical and chemical properties and to be inseparable by any chemical process. Such substances are known as *isotopes* (q.v.).—BIBLIOGRAPHY: Sir E. Rutherford, *Radioactive Sub-*

stances and their Radiations; F. Soddy, *The Interpretation of Radium*; J. A. Crowther, *Ions, Electrons, and Ionizing Radiations*; J. Chadwick, *Radioactivity and Radioactive Substances.*

RADIOGRAPH. Term given to an image of an object obtained by means of the X-rays, which have the power of penetrating certain substances opaque to light, but are stopped by other dense substances such as the heavy metals. A radiograph of the hand will show the bones and an embedded metal as distinct shadows.

RADIOLA'RIA. An order of Protozoa (q.n.).

RADIOLOGY. The science of radiology may be said to have originated in the discovery of X-rays (*see* RAYS, ELECTRIC) by Röntgen in 1895. It embraces both "electro-magnetic" and "corpuscular" radiation, and is chiefly concerned with those rays employed for radiographic and therapeutic purposes. The corpuscular rays employed in radiology are those emitted by radio-active substances (*see* RADIO-ACTIVITY), the most important of which is radium (q.v.).

The Generation of X-rays. X-rays as employed in modern medical radiology vary in wave-length from about $\frac{1}{10}$ Angstrom unit to 10 units. (One hundred million Angstrom units = 1 centimetre.) They are produced by firing at a tungsten target *in vacua* a stream of electrons, the high speed of which is imparted by the application of an intense electric field generated either by an induction coil of suitable design, or by a high-tension transformer, the electric field being made unidirectional by the inclusion in the secondary circuit of the coil or transformer of a suitable synchronous rectifier. The voltages generated by these machines range from about 50,000 to 120,000 volts. The exhausted glass vessel in which the electrons are projected is known as an "X-ray tube." X-ray tubes are of two types, viz. (*a*) the gas tube as shown in fig. 1, and (*b*) the incandescent cathode tube, an example of which, known as the "Coolidge tube," is shown in fig. 2. Several varieties of both types are in use. In the former type the emission of electrons from the negative electrode, termed the cathode, is dependent upon the electrical discharge in the residual gas, which has a pressure of only about one-millionth of an atmosphere. This is a development of the type of tube used by Röntgen and other pioneer workers. In the incandescent cathode type of tube the exhaustion is practically complete, and is such that no discharge passes through the residual gas when the intense electric field is applied; instead, the free emission of electrons by incandescent metals is made use of, the cathode being in the form of a tungsten spiral heated by an electric current as in an ordinary incandescent electric lamp. The stream of electrons is focused on to an extremely small area of the tung-

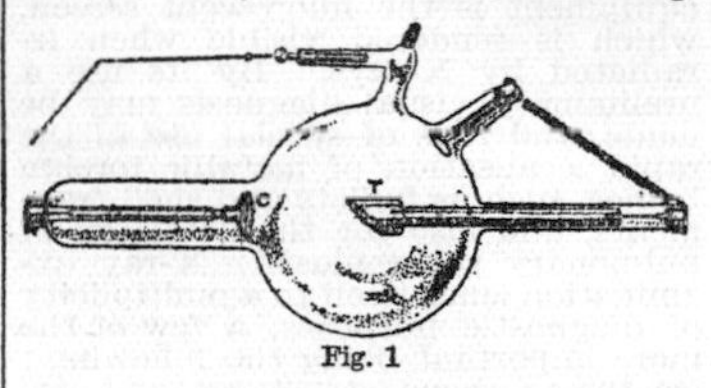

Fig. 1

sten target, which thus constitutes a point source of X-rays which are emitted in all directions above the plane face of the target. The rays are absorbed as they pass through the human body to a greater or less extent according to the density of the tissue passed through, with the result that the impression produced upon a photographic plate receiving the transmitted rays reveals to the experienced medical radiologist the detailed structure of the part under observation. The degree of penetration of the radiation produced depends

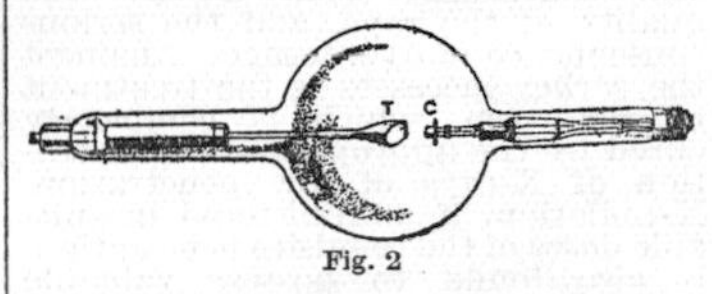

Fig. 2

upon the voltage generated by the induction coil and transformer. In all modern X-ray outfits the voltage can be controlled.

Medical Applications of X-rays. The applications of X-rays in medical practice are both diagnostic (radiography) and therapeutic (radiotherapy).

The great advance in the precision of medical and surgical diagnosis which has been made during recent years is largely due to the rapid advance of X-ray equipment and technique. Radiographs depicting the most minute detail of practically any part of the human body may be taken by exposures of less than one second. The expeditious production of these radiographs is rendered possible by an array of appliances, by means of which the X-ray tube and photographic plate or film may be quickly placed in suitable positions relative to the part of the patient to be examined, and to no less an extent by the highly developed technique exercised by skilled lay radiographers trained under medical supervision. The equipment includes appliances for regulating the penetration of the rays and the exposure, both of which vary with the part of the body to be radiographed. A valuable part of the equipment is the fluorescent screen, which is rendered visible when irradiated by X-rays. By its use a preliminary visual diagnosis may be made, and it is of special use in the rapid localisation of metallic foreign bodies, such as bullets and shell fragments, and also for the detection of pulmonary tuberculosis. X-ray examination lends itself to a multiplicity of diagnostic purposes, a few of the more important being the following: fractures; bone structures and deformities; arthritic and other diseases of the joints; detection of the presence of foreign bodies and their exact localisation; diseases of the stomach and intestinal tract (diagnosis assisted by the use of special meals containing bismuth or barium which are opaque to X-rays); stones in the bladder, kidney, and gall bladder; incipient tuberculosis in the lungs and joints, dental malformations and diseases.

Radio-therapy is of more recent development than radiography, owing largely to the difficulty of measuring and controlling both dosage and quality of the rays, and the serious consequence of overdosage. Amongst the earlier successes is the treatment of ringworm, which is completely cured by the appropriate administration of X-rays of low penetration. X-radiation, if administered in suitable doses of the requisite penetration, is also found to possess valuable properties in the treatment of malignant diseases, such as rodent ulcer and the various forms of cancer.

Excessive irradiation, however, produces bad effects upon the patient, and may even cause malignant growth. Many of the pioneer workers have suffered in this respect through exposing themselves unduly to X-rays, the damage in some instances having resulted in loss of life. White blood corpuscles are destroyed by the rays, and serious consequences in this direction may result from undue exposure. Further, the less penetrating radiation being absorbed readily by the skin causes dermatitis, which is insidious in onset, and, if acute, results in complete destruction of the tissue, causing it to present a permanent scaly appearance. On account of these harmful effects it is essential that X-ray operators be adequately protected from exposure to the rays, and modern tube-holders, etc., are provided with coverings of lead or rubber impregnated with lead to eliminate the harmful extraneous radiation.

Considerable progress has been made in the treatment of deep-seated malignant growths. One of the most recent developments is the employment of highly penetrating X-rays according to what is known as the "Erlangen" technique. Highly penetrating rays are produced by the use of special X-ray tubes and a duplex induction coil capable of developing voltages up to 200,000 volts. After filtration of the softer rays, the highly penetrating residuum is directed to the affected deep-seated tissue, and the administration of large intensities for short periods is claimed to be productive of very satisfactory results.

Radium and Radium Therapy. The medical application of the radiation emitted by radio-active substances is confined to therapy, in which a certain amount of success has been achieved. The α-rays are very easily absorbed, and are consequently of little or no therapeutic value; the β-rays are much more penetrating; and the γ-rays which are similar in character to X-rays, are more penetrating still, being much more penetrating than the hardest X-rays so far artificially produced. The absorption of γ-rays is accompanied by the emission of secondary β-rays, electrons being expelled from the absorbing atoms, and there is reason to suppose that the therapeutic action of γ-rays and even of X-rays is due to these secondary β-rays. When radium itself is employed for therapeutic work it is contained in a small thin platinum tube which absorbs the α-rays, but permits the transmission of both β- and γ-rays. When only γ-rays are required a second thicker tube of platinum is used in addition. The platinum tube can be inserted in the malignant growth, the destruction of which, rather than the surrounding healthy tissue, is thereby more certain than by irradiating from a distance. For some purposes radium compounds are made to adhere tenaciously to the surface of applicators of suitable form, the particular shape of the applicator being dependent upon the part to be treated.

Radium emanation (*see* RADIO-ACTIVITY) may be, and is often, used for therapy in place of radium. It is pumped away from the parent radium and dissolved in water, in which it is readily soluble. The activity of the emanation, however, quickly falls off owing to the rapidity of its decay. Initially, however, the activity is as high as that of the parent radium. If the application of a glass tube containing emanation solution is not delayed it may be used effectively in place of radium, the possible accidental loss of which is thus avoided, and in addition the availability of radio-active treatment considerably enhanced. Radio-active radiation is employed for much the same therapeutic purposes as X-rays, e.g. in certain cases of cancer and rodent ulcer, and among its successes is claimed the satisfactory breaking down of scars and adhesions. Its use is, however, limited to those cases in which the tube of radio-active material may be brought into actual contact with the affected part.

Ultra-violet Light. The subject of radiology should not be dismissed without mention of the therapeutic uses to which electro-magnetic rays of slightly shorter wave-length than light are put. These rays are termed ultra-violet rays, and are produced in the ordinary electric arc between mercury or tungsten electrodes. The rays are readily absorbed by glass, but are transmitted by fused quartz. Cases of lupus and kindred skin diseases are effectively treated by these rays. Cf. D. Arthur and J. Muir, *Manual of X-Ray Work.*

RADIOM'ETER. An apparatus invented by Sir William Crookes (about 1875). It consists of a glass bulb, which contains a small light cross with vertical vanes at the ends of the arms. The cross is pivoted on a steel point, and is capable of rotating in a horizontal plane under the action of heat or light rays. The vanes are metallically bright on one side and dull black on the other, and the bulb contains air or other gas at an extremely low pressure.

When light rays fall on the vanes, they are absorbed, in the form of heat, by the black sides, but are reflected from the bright sides. The black surfaces thus become slightly warmer than the others, and when gas molecules collide with the vanes, those which impinge against the black surfaces are warmed and rebound with greater momentum. By the law of reaction an equal increase of momentum is communicated to the vanes, and the black surfaces are apparently repelled by the light, and rotation takes place.

The speed of rotation varies with the degree of exhaustion of the bulb; at a certain stage the black surfaces move forward under the action of the radiation—an effect due to convection currents in the gas. As rarefaction proceeds, this forward motion slows, stops, then reverses, attains a maximum, slows, and finally stops, the gas having become too rarefied. When the radiometer is subjected to different sources of light, the speed of rotation of the vanes depends on the intensity of the incident light; the instrument may thus be used, in some sort, as a photometer. In the spectrum the speed of rotation increases as the radiometer is moved from the ultra-violet to the infra-red, and the instrument has been employed to investigate the distribution of heat in the solar spectrum.

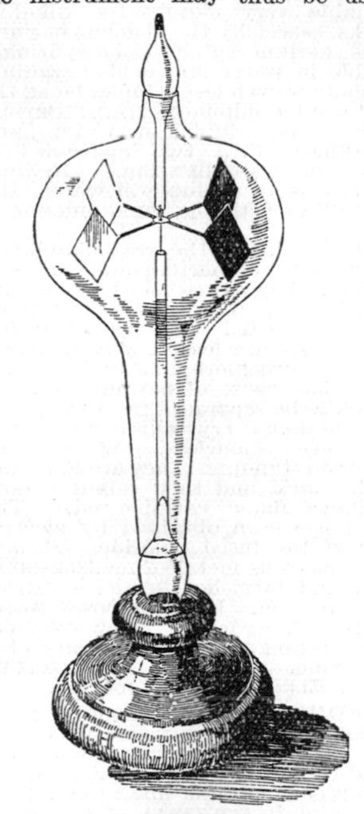

Radiometer

RADISH (*Raphănus satīvus*). A well-known cruciferous plant, cultivated in Britain since 1548. The tender leaves are used as a salad, the green pods as a pickle, and the succulent roots are much esteemed.

RADIUM (symbol, Ra; atomic weight, 226). An element discovered by M. and Mme Curie in a sample of pitch-blende from Joachimsthal. Radium is widely distributed, but in minute quantity. All uranium ores contain the element, and it has been found in the waters of mineral-springs and in many rocks and minerals. Its radio-active properties make its presence, even in minute quantity, easily detected. About 0·32 gramme of the element radium is present per ton of the element uranium in the ores. Radium and its compounds resemble very closely the alkaline earths, especially the element barium. Thus barium sulphate is sparingly soluble in water and acids; radium sulphate is even less soluble, being the least soluble sulphate known. Barium chloride is soluble in water, and crystallises with two molecules of water of crystallisation. Radium chloride is also soluble in water, and crystallises with the same amount of water.

On account of the great similarity of the salts of barium and those of radium, they are somewhat difficult to separate; the bromides are more easily separated than the chlorides. These salts are less soluble in water and in hydrochloric and hydrobromic acids than those of barium, and can therefore be separated from the latter by fractional crystallisation. The salts are colourless, but develop colour on standing. They are luminous in the dark, and then colour a non-luminous flame carmine-red. The metal has been obtained by electrolysis of the fused chloride. It is a white lustrous metal of melting-point 700°, and tarnishes in air, a nitride being formed. It decomposes water vigorously, hydrogen being evolved, and radium going into solution as the hydroxide. *See* RADIO-ACTIVITY; RAYS, ELECTRIC; RADIOLOGY.

RADIUS. Term in geometry for a straight line drawn from the centre of a circle to the circumference and equal to half the diameter. A radius vector is a straight line drawn from any point in the curve of an ellipse to a focus.

In anatomy the radius is the smaller of the two bones in the forearm. Its slightly curved shaft is articulated to the wrist by its larger head, and to the elbow by a button-shaped head having a rotatory movement.

RADLETT. Town of Hertfordshire. It is 14½ miles from London, on the L.M.S. Railway. It is a residential district for Londoners. Some industries have been established here. Pop. (1931), 5340.

RADLEY. Village of Berkshire. It is on the Thames, 4 miles from Oxford, on the G. W. Railway. The college, founded in 1847, is a public school with accommodation for about 200 boys; it has a fine chapel and a memorial gateway. Pop. 1074.

RADNOR, or RADNORSHIRE. An inland county of South Wales; served by the L.M.S. and G.W. Railways; area, 301,165 acres. The surface throughout is hilly, the highest summit of the Forest of Radnor reaching an elevation of 2163 feet above sea-level. The Wye is the principal river, and, with its tributaries the Elan, Ithon, Edwy, Arrow, and Somergil, etc., it abounds in fish. Another stream is the Teme, tributary to the Severn. Oats and wheat are the principal crops, but the chief dependence of the farmer is on the sheep and ponies reared on the pasture-lands. Large quantities of butter are made. The chief manufacture is flannel, but it is of no great extent. There are mineral-springs, especially at Llandrindod. Presteign is the county town. Pop. (1931), 21,314.

RADNOR. Village of Radnorshire. It is 9 miles from Presteign, on the little River Somergil. There are ruins of a castle and a guildhall, as the place was a chartered town from 1561 to 1883. It is called New Radnor to distinguish it from Old Radnor, a village about 3 miles away.

The title of **Earl of Radnor** was borne by the family of Robartes from 1679 to 1757. In 1765 William Bouveries, second Viscount Folkestone, a wealthy Huguenot, was created Earl of Radnor. His son, Jacob, took the name of Pleydell-Bouverie and the title is still held by his descendant. The estates are now the property of Viscount Clifden, a kinsman. The seat of the present earl is Longford Castle, near Salisbury, and his eldest son is called Viscount Folkestone.

RADOM. A district and town of Poland. The district has an area of 4700 sq. miles, and a population of about 1,200,000. Agriculture is the staple employment. The town is capital of the district, also capital of the province of Kielce, and stands on the Mlechna, and is served by the Ivangorod-Dombrova railway. There are tanneries, ironworks, and manufactures of agricultural implements and machinery. Pop. (1931), 78,072. The battle of Radom (European War) was fought by the Austrians and Russians between 25th and 28th Oct., 1914, when the Russians occupied the town and drove the Austrians back on Kielce, from which they again advanced after the Russian retreat of 1915.

RADSTOCK. Urban district and market town of Somerset. It is 16 miles from Bristol on the G.W. Rly. It is the centre of the Somerset coal-field, and the chief industry is coal-mining. Pop. (1931), 3622.

RAE BARELI. A district of India, in the Lucknow division of the United Provinces, traversed by the Ganges and the Sai, and by the Loni, a tributary of the Ganges. Rice is the principal crop. Area, 1750 sq. miles; pop. 1,200,000. The town is the district headquarters, and stands on the banks of the Sai; served by the Oudh & Rohilkhand Railway. It is the chief commercial centre of the district, and has manufactures of cotton cloth and muslins. Pop. 16,000.

RAEBURN, Sir Henry. Scottish portrait-painter, born at Edinburgh in 1756, died in 1823. The son of a manufacturer, he was bound appren-

Raeburn: Portrait of Mrs. Scott Moncrieff

tice to a goldsmith at the age of fifteen. He soon began to paint miniatures, and before long devoted himself entirely to portrait-painting, being practically self-taught. In 1778 he married a young and wealthy widow, and, with a view to improving his art, repaired to London, afterwards (on the advice of Reynolds) spending two years in Rome. Returning in 1787, he established himself in Edinburgh, and was soon at the head of his profession in Scotland, having as sitters almost all the eminent Scots of his time and producing over 700 portraits. After 1810 he exhibited regularly at the Royal Academy (London), was elected an associate in 1812, and a full member in 1815. He was knighted by George IV. in 1822. His portraits are distinguished by grasp of character, breadth and directness of treatment, and colour. The most representative collection of his work is in the National Gallery of Scotland.—Cf. Sir W. Armstrong, *Sir Henry Raeburn.*

RAEMAKERS, Louis. Dutch cartoonist. He was born at Roermond, Holland, on 6th April, 1869, educated in Amsterdam and Brussels, and at the outset of his career, painted portraits, posters, and landscapes. He drew his first political cartoon in 1908, but his fame was made by his anti-German cartoons, during and after the Great War.

RAFF, Joachim. Musical composer, born in Switzerland, of German parents, in 1822, died in 1882. He was encouraged by Mendelssohn and Liszt, and having gone in 1850 to live at Weimar, in order to be near Liszt, his opera, *König Alfred*, was first performed there at the Court Theatre. His *Dame Kobold*, a comic opera, was produced in 1870, but his reputation rests chiefly on his symphonies. He wrote also much chamber music of undoubted excellence. In 1877 he was appointed director of the Conservatoire at Frankfort, where he died.

RAFFIA WORK. Handicraft comprising useful and ornamental articles made with the split leaves of raphia palms and similar bast-like substances. Used for manual training, recreation and profit-making in blind institutions, kindergarten schools, military hospitals, etc., the material, generally dyed, is fashioned like straw-plait into bags and hats, or worked on frames into baskets, boxes, etc.

Sir Thomas Stamford Raffles

RAFFLES, Sir Thomas Stamford. English administrator, born in 1781, died 1826. He entered the East

India Company's civil service, and in 1811, on the reduction of Java by the British, he was made Lieutenant-Governor of the island. In this post he continued till 1816, when he returned to England with an extensive collection of the productions of the Eastern Archipelago. The year following appeared his *History of Java.* Having been appointed to the Lieutenant-Governorship of Bencoolen, Sumatra, he went out in 1818 to fill this post, founded the settlement of Singapore, and returned to Europe in 1824.—Cf. D. C. Boulger, *The Life of Sir Stamford Raffles.*

RAFFLE'SIA. A genus of parasitical plants, ord. Rafflesiaceæ, of which the chief species is *R. Arnoldi.* This gigantic flower, one of the marvels of the vegetable world, was discovered in the interior of Sumatra by Sir T. Raffles and Dr. Arnold. The whole plant consists of little else beyond the flower and a system of fine threads, which traverse the root-plant like the hyphæ of a fungus. The perianth or flower forms a huge cup reaching a width of 3 feet or more; it weighs from 12 to 15 lb., and some of its parts are ¾ inch in thickness. It is fleshy in character and appearance, remains expanded for a few days, and then begins to putrefy, having quite the smell of carrion, and thus attracting numerous insects.

RAFTER. Term in architecture for an inclined beam forming part of the support of the roof of a building. In the Middle Ages rafters were of oak, but in the seventeenth century foreign deal came into common use. Open timber roofs with various methods of arranging the rafters were characteristic of mediæval English architecture.

RAGATZ. A town of Switzerland, canton of St. Gall, situated at the junction of the Tamina with the Rhine, 1700 feet above the sea, and connected by railway with Zurich and Coire. It is much resorted to both for its beautiful scenery and its mineral-waters. There is a bathing establishment near the springs, erected in 1704. The temperature of the water is 97°-100°, and it is impregnated with carbonate of lime, magnesia, and salt. The village of Pfäfers lies 2 miles south of Ragatz at a height of 2696 feet. The permanent population is about 2000, but the place is visited annually by about 30,000 invalids.

RAGEE (ra-gē'), or **RAGI.** An Indian grain (*Eleusīne coracāna*), very prolific, but probably the least nutritious of all grains. In the form of cake or porridge it is the staple food of the poorer classes in Mysore and on the Nilghiris.

RAGGED ROBIN. Perennial crimson-flowered wild plant (*Lychnis flos-cuculi*) of the pink family. It is a slender herb growing about 1½ feet high and common in Great Britain.

RAGGED SCHOOLS. Institutions supported by voluntary contributions, which provide free education, and in many cases food, lodging, and clothing, for destitute children, and so aid in preventing them from falling into vagrancy and crime. These schools differ from certified industrial schools in that the latter are for the reception of vagrant children and those guilty of slight offences; but the two institutions are frequently combined. The idea of forming such schools was due to a Portsmouth cobbler, John Pounds, who about 1819 began to take in the ragged children of the district in which he lived and teach them while he was at work. The name of Dr. Guthrie of Edinburgh is prominent among those who developed this scheme of rescue. The name *ragged schools* was first adopted in 1844. The Acts of 1870 and 1871 having introduced compulsory school attendance in England, many of the ragged schools were absorbed by the public schools. The Ragged School Union was founded in 1844, but since 1914 it has been known as The Shaftesbury Society and Ragged School Union.

RAGLAN. Village of Monmouthshire. It is 8 miles from Monmouth, and stands on the G.W. Railway. It is famous for its castle, now in ruins. During the Civil War it was defended by the Marquess of Worcester on behalf of Charles I.

RAGLAN, Fitzroy James Henry Somerset, Lord. Born 1788, died 1855. The youngest son of Henry, fifth Duke of Beaufort, he entered the army in 1804; was attached in 1807 to the Hon. Sir Arthur Paget's embassy to Turkey; and the same year served on Sir Arthur Wellesley's staff in the expedition to Copenhagen. He acted as military secretary to the latter during the Peninsular War, in which he greatly distinguished himself at the capture of Badajoz. At Waterloo he lost his right arm. From 1816 to 1819 he acted as secretary to the embassy at Paris, and from 1819 to 1852 as military secretary to the Duke of Wellington. In 1852 he was made Master-General of the Ordnance, and was elevated to the House of Peers as Baron Raglan. On the outbreak of the Crimean War he received the appointment of commander of the forces, and remained in charge of the campaign till his death. See CRIMEAN WAR.

RAGOUT. French dish. It consists of meat stewed with herbs and vegetables, and seasoned to taste. The word comes from the Fr. *ragoûter*, to restore the appetite.

RAGS. Worn or torn remnants of textile material. They form an article of commerce, woollen rags being of more value than linen or cotton. Silk rags are the least useful. In the preparation of rags for industrial purposes they are first disinfected, then sorted, bleached, and reduced to pulp. From woollen rags "shoddy" and other coarse materials are made. Linen and cotton rags were until the middle of the nineteenth century the only materials from which paper was made. For this purpose they have now been largely supplanted by esparto grass and wood-pulp; but they are still used for the manufacture of special kinds of paper, e.g. for bank-notes, etc.

RAGSTONE. A sedimentary flaggy rock, so named from its rough fracture. It is used for a whetstone without oil or water for sharpening coarse cutting tools. The term is also applied to certain impure limestones, such as the Jurassic Coral Rag and the Cretaceous Kentish Rag.

RAGU'SA (Slav. *Dubrovnik*). A seaport of Yugoslavia, in Dalmatia, on a peninsula in the Adriatic, surrounded by old walls flanked with towers, and several forts. Ragusa is supposed to have been founded by Greeks in 589 B.C. Falling successively under the dominion of the Romans and the Greek emperors, it finally asserted its independence, which it long maintained, though having to pay tribute to one or other of its powerful neighbours. In 1814 it came into the possession of Austria. Pop. 13,250.

RAGUSA. A town of Sicily, on the River Ragusa; served by railway from Syracuse (70 miles). It manufactures cottons, macaroni, and cheese, and has a trade in corn, wine, and oil. Ragusa is identified with the ancient *Hybla Heræa*. Pop. (1931), 49,694.

RAGWORT, or RAGWEED. The popular name of various species of composite plants of the genus Senecio, found in Britain, so called from the ragged appearance of the leaves. The common ragwort (*S. Jacobæa*) is a perennial with golden-yellow flowers, growing by the side of roads and in pastures. It is a coarse weed, refused or disliked by horses, oxen, and sheep, but eaten by hogs and goats.

RAIBOLINI (rī-bo-lē'nē), **Francesco di Marco di Giacomo,** usually called **Francesco Francia.** A famous Italian painter, engraver, medallist, and goldsmith, born at Bologna about the middle of the fifteenth century, died 1517. He excelled particularly in Madonnas, and executed a number of admirable frescoes in the church of St. Cecilia at Bologna, but his most famous work is an altarpiece exhibiting the *Madonna, St. Sebastian*, etc., in the church of St. Giacomo Maggiore in the same city. Three works of his are in the British National Gallery. He was also celebrated as a portrait-painter. Raibolini had a son, Giacomo, who studied under him, and acquired considerable celebrity.

Ragusa: Custom-house

RAICHUR. A district and town of Hyderabad, India. The district is in the Gulbarga division, and is traversed by the Kistna. Native food grains, cotton, and oil-seeds are produced. Area, 6800 sq. miles; pop. 995,000. The town is the headquarters of the district, and is the junction of the Madras and Great Indian Peninsula Railways, 350 miles from Madras and 444 miles from Bombay. Industries include cotton-pressing, tanning, and distilling. Pop. 26,374.

RAIKES, Robert. British philanthropist, born at Gloucester 1735, died 1811. He was proprietor of the *Gloucester Journal*, and originated the system of Sunday-schools by gathering together a number of street children for secular and religious training.

RAIL. The common name of birds belonging to the Rallidæ, a family of the crane, etc., order (Gruiformes), comprehending the rails proper (Rallus), the coots, water-hens, and crakes. They are characterised by possessing a long bill, which is more or less curved at the tip and compressed at the sides, by having the nostrils in a membranous groove, the wings of moderate length, the tail short, the legs and toes long and slender, and the hind-toe placed on a level with the others. Most of the members of the family are aquatic or frequent marshes; but some, as the crakes, frequent dry

Virginian Rail (*R. Virginianus*)

situations. The principal species of the genus Rallus are the water-rail of Europe (*R. aquaticus*), about 11 inches in length, of an olive-brown colour, marked with black above, and of a bluish-ash colour beneath, with white transverse markings on the belly, much esteemed for the table; the Virginian rail of America (*R. virginianus*), somewhat smaller than the water-rail of Europe; and the king rail or freshwater marsh-hen (*R. elegans*), about 20 inches long, which inhabits the marshes of the southern states of America. The land-rail, so named, is the corn-crake (*Crex pratensis*). *See* CORN-CRAKE.

RAILWAYS, BRITISH: ORGANISATION AND ADMINISTRATION. Before dealing with the organisation of British railways as existing to-day, it is essential to note the progress which has been made in transportation by rail during the last fifty or sixty years, and which has made such detailed organisation necessary. That the progress has been rapid is apparent when it is stated that in 1868 the total mileage of railway track in Great Britain was 20,102, and the capital sunk £484,536,878, whereas in 1931 there were 19,336 miles of road (first track) alone, and an authorised capital of £1,311,617,653.

Board of Directors. The policy and administration of a British railway are vested in a board of directors appointed by the shareholders. The full board of directors meets at regular intervals, and when required. In addition there is a number of directorial committees selected from the full board, whose function is to confer with the head of the department whose business appertains to the committee concerned.

The General Manager. The responsible officer for the executive administration is the general manager. Modern railways are large concerns, and it is not practicable for the general manager to supervise personally the detailed work of all departments, but he is recognised as the connecting-link between them and the board of directors.

The organisation generally in force to-day follows much the same lines on every railway, and is explained by the accompanying chart. (See p. 555.)

The general duties of the various officers can be more or less definitely gathered from their designations, but the following sets out briefly the functions of the more extensive departments, and also their relations one to the other.

The **secretary** submits all matters to the board of directors, and is responsible for keeping a record of the deliberations of the board. Through the medium of the registrar, he is responsible for all stock and share work.

The **chief engineer** is charged with the duty of seeing that existing lines and works are properly maintained, and with the construction of new works; he is also responsible for the maintenance of the signalling arrangements.

The **chief mechanical engineer** is charged with the designing and construction of all classes of rolling stock, and with keeping it in a fit state of repair; he is also responsible for the provision of the necessary locomotive power to meet the requirements of the traffic officers.

The **general superintendent** arranges and controls all passenger and freight train services, and also controls wagon stock and coaching stock in addition to supervising a large outdoor staff engaged in working and handling traffic.

The **chief goods manager** has for his principal functions the securing of goods train traffic and the charging for the conveyance of same. He is in close touch with the outside public on all matters relating to the carriage of traffic by goods trains.

The **passenger manager** has functions in respect of traffic by passenger trains which are analogous to those of the chief goods manager as regards traffic by goods trains.

Ministry of Transport Act, 1919. Upon the outbreak of the European War in Aug., 1914, when military claims on transport became more imperative than commercial, the railways were taken over and placed under the control of the Government, and remained so until Aug., 1921. This was purely a war measure, as the railways continued to be worked by the companies, the control being exercised through a committee consisting of the general managers of the principal companies; and during the period of control the 1913 net revenue of the companies was guaranteed by the Government.

In Aug., 1919, the Ministry of Transport Act was passed. The purposes of this Act were to extend the period of Government control to cover the transition period from war to peace conditions, to improve the means and facilities for transport, and to afford time for the consideration and formulation of the future policy to be followed in regard to the working of railways. Practically the whole of the powers which had been vested in the Board of Trade were transferred to the Ministry of Transport, and, in addition, wide powers were conferred on the Minister appertaining to the control and general working of the railways. Amongst these may be mentioned the power to purchase privately-owned railway wagons, and also the regular rendering to the Ministry of elaborate statistical information. Mention should also be made of the setting up of the Rates Advisory Committee for the purpose of assisting the Minister to deal with all questions affecting the revision of rates and charges.

The Government control of railways ceased on 15th Aug., 1921, and with the expiration of the 1919 Act the railways reverted to their pre-war condition. It was, however, very evident that, with the improved conditions of service and increases in rates of pay which had been granted during the period of control, and without corresponding increase in rates and charges, some reorganisation of the railways was inevitable to restore their former financial stability, and the Railways Act of 1921 was introduced with this object in view. Broadly, the Act may be divided under the following salient heads from a reorganisation point of view: (*a*) The grouping of the railway systems

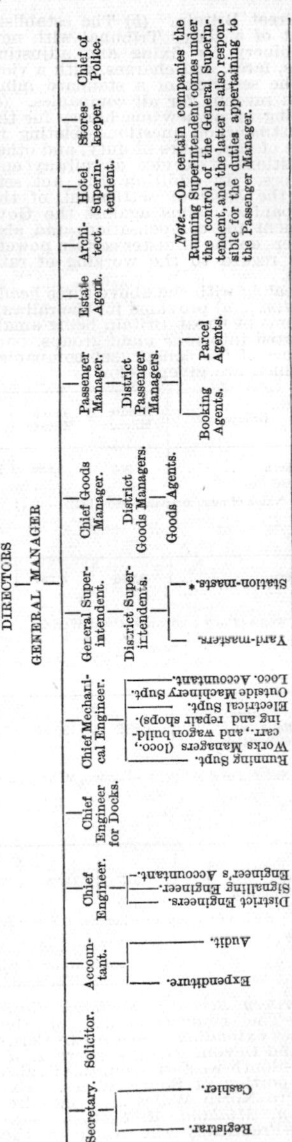

of Great Britain. (*b*) The establishment of a Rates Tribunal with new machinery for fixing and adjusting rates, fares, and charges, with a view to the securing of a standard minimum revenue for all companies. (*c*) Setting up of new machinery for the adjustment of questions relating to rates of pay, hours of duty, and other conditions of service of railway employees. In addition, the Act sets out the basis of settlement of the companies' claims against the Government for compensation, and also confers on the Minister certain powers with regard to the working of railways.

Dealing with the above three heads *seriatim* : (*a*) provided for the railway systems of Great Britain being amalgamated into four main groups, particulars of the constituent companies of which are given below :

Group	Route Mileage	Track Mileage	Capital £	Constituent Companies
Southern	1,953	3,894	152,594,997	L. & S.W. L.B. & S.C. South-Eastern L.C. & D. S.E. & C. Railway Companies' Managing Committee
Name of new company—Southern				
Western	3,258	5,597	135,993,422	G.W. Barry Cambrian Cardiff Railway Company Rhymney Taff Vale Alexandra (Newport and South Wales) Docks and Railway Company
Name of new company—Great Western				
North-Western, Midland, and West Scottish	6,612	12,914	527,234,154	L. & N.W. Midland L. & Y. North Staffs Furness Caledonian G. & S.W. Highland
Name of new company—London, Midland, & Scottish ..				
North-Eastern, Eastern, and East Scottish	6,313	11,285	338,890,432	N.E. G.C. G.E. G.N. H. & B. N.B. G. N. of S.
Name of new company—London & North-Eastern ..				

Territory Served : Southern Railway.—The counties south of the Thames extending westward to Cornwall and Devon. *Great Western Railway.*—South-western counties ; also large portion of South Wales. Extends to North Wales and Cheshire. *London, Midland, & Scottish Railway.*—Practically the whole of the Midlands, North Wales, and north-western counties of England ; also Western and Northern Scotland. *London & North-Eastern Railway.*—Eastern, midland, and north-eastern counties of England ; also Eastern and Northern Scotland.

(*b*) The Act provided for the establishment of a *Rates Tribunal* consisting of three permanent members, one an experienced lawyer, another versed in commercial affairs, and the third one versed in railway matters, to be an overriding authority in respect of railway rates and charges. In addition, provision was made for the formation of two *panels*. One consists of thirty-six persons, twenty-two of whom are representative of trading interests, twelve representative of the interests of labour, and two representatives of agricultural and horticultural interests. This is known as the "general panel." The other panel, known as the "railway panel," consists of twelve members, eleven being nominated by the Minister of Transport after consultation with the Railway Companies' Association, and the remaining member who is nominated by the Ministry of Transport, representing concerns which are not parties to the Railway Companies' Association.

(*c*) Provided for the establishment on each railway company of one or more *councils* consisting of representatives of the railway company and representatives of the men. It also laid down that all questions relating to rates of pay, hours of duty, or other conditions of service of employees, should, in default of agreement between the railway companies and railway trades union, be referred to the Central Wages Board or, on appeal, to the National Wages Board.

RAILWAYS, ELECTRIFICATION OF. By this phrase is usually meant the substitution of electric power for steam power as the propulsive force on railways. Few railways have been built to use electric power from the day they were opened.

The electric drive is applied on three distinct systems, the "direct-current system," the "single-phase system," and the "three-phase system."

In the direct-current system the electric motors on the trains are worked with direct-current electricity; in the second, with single-phase alternating current; and in the third, with three-phase alternating current.

Electric power is generated at large central power-stations from coal or from water power. The electrical energy leaves the power-station by transmission lines as high-tension single-phase, or three-phase, alternating current. The electrical pressure at which these transmission lines are worked is often very high, and ranges from 5000 volts to 150,000 volts. The electrical energy at this pressure is transformed by means of "transformers" to a lower pressure. If the railway is a single-phase or three-phase one, the electrical energy, at the lower pressure at which it is delivered by the transformers, goes straight to the track conductors and thence to the train motors. If the railway is a direct-current one, the low-pressure alternating current is converted in a machine called a "rotary converter" into direct-current, the form in which the electrical energy can be used by the direct-current motors.

The current is supplied to the trains by one of two systems—the "overhead system" or the "third-rail system."

On the overhead system an electric wire is run above each of the railway tracks, much as the tramway wire runs over the tramway tracks on street tramways. Some of the railway carriages are fitted with collecting devices called "pantographs," which make contact with the overhead "live wire," and current passes via these pantographs from the live wire to the electric motors on the train. The circuit is completed by the railway track rails. These rails are connected together with thick copper conductors at each joint, and are thus made electrically continuous. The current, after going through the motors, comes back by this return circuit. The return circuit is always in the neighbourhood of earth potential, and is consequently not dangerous to touch. This system is used both for direct- and for alternating-current railways. If the three-phase system is used, there must be *two* separate overhead wires over each track.

The other method is the third-rail system. A third-rail is run alongside the two railway running rails, and is supported on electrical insulators.

This rail—the conductor rail—is at a high potential relative to earth, and forms the positive conductor of the circuit. The negative conductor is, as before, the bonded running rails. A collector shoe is attached to the carriages, instead of a pantograph, and runs along the surface of the third-rail. The collector shoe is connected to the positive terminal of the motor, and the negative terminal of the motor is connected to the bonded running rails, and the circuit through the motor is thus completed. This system is used exclusively for direct-current lines.

The electrical pressures of the overhead wire vary from about 6000 volts on a portion of the Southern Railway to about 15,000 volts on Continental and United States railways. The electrical pressure of the third-rail is usually about 800 volts, but third-rails of 2400 volts have been tried in America. The highest pressures of overhead wires, when used for direct current, are about 5000 volts.

The trains may be driven in many ways. The motors may be placed to drive the axles of alternate carriages, and designed so that the motors, on the "motor-coach" are sufficiently powerful to drive the coach itself, plus one trailer-coach. This arrangement is called the "multiple-unit system." The motors are connected so that they can be controlled from either end of the combined unit. The driver has a handle like an ordinary tramway-driver's handle. Two, three, four, or five of these "units" may be coupled together, and a four, six, eight, ten, etc., coach-train formed. The wiring is arranged so that this combined train can be driven from either end. This system has great advantages where a heavy suburban traffic is run, as it reduces shunting operations at the busy termini.

The other system of haulage is by electric locomotives. The largest steam locomotives which exist in Great Britain have a capacity of from 2000 to 3000 h.p., whereas electric locomotives can be built for a capacity of 5000 h.p.

The electrification of a line obviously costs a large sum of money. How is this justified? Its justification depends on the following factors, among others:

1. Broadly speaking, to haul a given train at a given speed, half the coal which a steam engine requires is sufficient if the train is hauled electrically.

2. The cost of repairs and renewals is very much less on an electric railway, because the electric locomotives or motor-coaches (the most expensive items to maintain) have only electric motors and electrical apparatus, which do not very easily go wrong; the boiler alone of the steam locomotive is very expensive to maintain. The cost of maintaining an electric locomotive is about £60 to £100 per annum, whereas the cost of maintaining a large passenger steam engine for the same period is between £500 and £750.

3. The hauling power of the electric locomotive is much greater than that of the steam one.

4. The electric locomotive and also the motor-coach are always ready for work, and do not require attention when they are not being used.

These and other economies often make the cost of running a train a mile electrically about one-third to one-half of the cost of running the same train a mile by steam.

In Great Britain electrification is used mainly for suburban and metropolitan systems such as the Underground Electric Railways of London. The Southern Railway leads with an electric route mileage of over 300. The L.M.S. Railway has over 100 miles of electrified track, the L.N.E. about 60 and the Great Western 6. In 1931 a large scheme was put forward for electrifying the great main lines. *See* ELECTRIC TRACTION.—BIBLIOGRAPHY: E. Wilson and F. Lydall, *Electric Traction for Railway Trains*; H. F. Parshall and H. M. Hobart, *Electric Railway Engineering*; A. T. Dover, *Electric Traction*; *Railway Mechanical Engineering* (The Gresham Publishing Co.).

RAIN. Name given to the fall of condensed atmospheric vapour in drops of water owing to the lowering of the temperature below dew-point. Condensation first results in the formation of minute drops which float in masses forming clouds and as the process continues these drops coalesce, forming larger drops, whose weight causes them to fall as rain.

RAINBOW. A bow, or an arc of a circle, consisting of all the prismatic colours, formed by the refraction and reflection of rays of light from drops of rain or vapour appearing in the part of the heavens opposite to the sun. When the sun is at the horizon, the rainbow is a semicircle. When perfect, the rainbow presents the appearance of two concentric arches; the inner being called the *primary*, and the outer the *secondary* rainbow. Each is formed of the colours of the solar spectrum, but the colours are arranged in the reversed order, the red forming the exterior ring of the primary bow, and the interior of the secondary. The primary bow is formed by the sun's rays entering the upper part of the falling drops of rain, and undergoing two refractions and one reflection; and the secondary, by the sun's rays entering the under part of the drops, and undergoing two refractions and two reflections. Hence, the colours of the secondary bow are fainter than those of the primary. The common centre of the two bows is exactly opposite to the sun, and they have radii of about 41° and 52°. Rainbows are sometimes produced by the sun's rays shining on the spray of cascades, fountains, etc., and then a whole circle can frequently be seen. A broken rainbow is generally due to the field not being filled with falling rain, but it will also result from the sun being invisible from part of the field, its rays being intercepted by cloud. The moon sometimes forms a bow or arch of light, more faint than that formed by the sun, and called a *lunar rainbow*. A *spurious* or *supernumerary rainbow* is a bow seen in connection with a fine rainbow, lying close inside the violet of the primary bow, or outside that of the secondary one. Its colours are fainter and more impure the farther they proceed from the principal bow, and finally merge into the diffused white light inside the primary bow, and outside the secondary.

RAINFALL. One of the processes in a constant cycle of changes whereby the water with which our globe's exterior is provided is alternately suspended in the air, and returned to the oceans and land surface. The heat of the sun is instrumental in evaporating it from the liquid form and adding it as aqueous vapour to the atmosphere, and there are various factors which operate to effect its condensation as cloud and rain. It may happen, but not very commonly, that a mass of air may be cooled by coming into contact with a ground surface colder than itself, or that a stationary mass of air may be cooled by radiation, and in either case some of the moisture be condensed and fall as rain. In by far the greater number of cases, however, the cause of rain is an upward motion of the air.

As a general rule the air temperature diminishes with altitude above the earth's surface. This is so in the first place because the sun's direct rays have little heating effect on the air. They travel through it, but are absorbed by and warm the earth, which then returns to the air overlying it, as dark heat, some of the radiation received. But if a mass of air ascends, it is cooled, even irrespective of the fact that it meets with colder air above. As it rises the pressure on it falls, since pressure necessarily diminishes with height in the atmosphere. Consequently it expands, and when a gas expands it thereby falls in temperature.

There may be distinguished three ways in which air is caused to ascend, with resultant cooling and possibly rainfall. These are described as (1) convectional, (2) cyclonic, (3) orographical.

Convectional rainfall is produced by a mass of air near the earth's surface being raised by the effect of the sun's heat to a temperature higher than the surrounding air. At this place there will be formed a steep temperature gradient in the vertical direction, with consequent instability, and an upward current of air will be originated. If the action is intense, there may be not only rain but considerable electrical disturbance and thunderstorm. This, of course, happens mainly in summer-time.

Cyclonic rain is more frequent in the British Isles in winter, and is due to the cyclonic depressions which pass near the islands from the Atlantic. The rain occurs mostly at no great relative distance from the centre of the depression, and the condensation is largely a result of the upward movement of the air which always takes place in the central part of a low-pressure system.

Orographical rainfall, as the name implies, is caused by the action of mountains. On the windward side of a mountain the approaching wind is deflected upwards, and, under the requisite conditions of humidity and temperature, cloud or rain is produced. This action will frequently be seen when the mountain-side is enveloped by cloud down to a particular level. The cloud will be observed to be all the time rising up the mountain-side, yet its lower border remains at the same position, cloud being continually formed in the place of that which travels upward. Or again, the cloud may be formed just at the top level, and appear as a cap to the mountain summit (e.g. "table-cloth" on Table Mountain). The prevalence of orographical rainfall is illustrated by the high rainfall of our western mountainous districts, where the moisture of the predominant westerly winds is deposited, compared with the lower rainfall of the more level eastern districts. A case essentially resembling orographical rainfall occurs frequently when a warm and moisture-laden wind meets a colder current. The warm air naturally tends to rise over the colder, which passes beneath, or "undercuts" it. Owing to the ascent the warm air expands and discharges its moisture. The cold wind thus plays the same part as did the mountain in the previous case. It has been mentioned that cyclonic rains occur here mainly in the winter. In the spring months cyclonic depressions are less frequent, and the weather becomes drier. With the summer the rainfall increases, owing to the frequence of convectional rains. There is again a drier period about September, because the sun's power of causing convectional rain has diminished, and the cyclones have not resumed their winter prevalence. The mixing of masses of warm and cold air is sometimes given as a cause of rain. It is possible for two such masses, each above its dew-point, to form a combination which would be below its dew-point, and therefore deposit some moisture. But the amount would be extremely small, so that, while such action may occasionally take place, this is of little importance as a factor in rainfall production. *See* CLIMATE ; METEOROLOGY.

Under different conditions raindrops vary in diameter from about $\frac{1}{100}$th to about $\frac{1}{5}$th of an inch. It has been shown that drops larger than the latter size cannot exist, as they break up into smaller drops. Even drops of this size do not fall, but remain suspended, if placed in a current travelling upward at the rate of about 25 feet per second. Such an upward velocity in the atmosphere seldom occurs, but smaller drops would be prevented from falling by a slower ascending current. No doubt rain is often formed and is in this way prevented from reaching the earth. In other cases rain which has fallen some distance may pass into a drier stratum and be again evaporated before completing its descent.

The descent to the ocean of the water which results from rainfall, in the form of rivers and streams traversing the land surface, means the liberation of a large amount of energy which may to a considerable extent be drawn upon for useful purposes. The energy of running water has long been utilised directly by means of water-wheels for driving machinery in mills, etc. It is now being made use of, and will doubtless be much more used in the future, as a source of electrical energy. This can be conveniently transmitted as such over great distances, and made available for mechanical and other purposes where it may be required. The original source of this energy is of course to be found in the action of the sun's heat, which had the effect of lifting all this water against the earth's gravitation from the ocean or land surface into the atmosphere.

The presence or absence of vegetation may possibly have considerable influence on the rainfall of a district. Land devoid of vegetation readily absorbs the solar radiation. The air in contact with it also becomes heated, with the result of increasing its capacity for containing moisture, and thereby lessening precipitation. On the other hand, land covered with an abundant vegetation has its soil kept cool, and thus assists in condensation. The influence of forests on rainfall is still a matter of dispute, but on the whole it seems certain that forests increase the precipitation of a district. The proximity of warm ocean currents tends to increase, and that of cold currents to decrease, rainfall. Although more rain falls within the tropics in a year, yet the number of rainy days is less than in temperate climes. Thus in an average year there are 80 rainy days in the tropics, in the temperate zones about 160. Cherrapunji, in the Khasia Hills of Assam, with an average of 426 inches in the year, is one of the rainiest stations on the globe. It is stated that on some mountains in the Hawaiian Islands this average is even exceeded. Maps showing rainfall are given under AUSTRALIA, ENGLAND, GEOGRAPHY, INDIA, IRELAND, etc. — BIBLIOGRAPHY: M. Salter, *Rainfall of the British Isles*; *British Rainfall* (Meteorological Office).

RAINFORD. Urban district of Lancashire. It is 4½ miles from St. Helens and is a junction on the L.M.S. Railway. Around are coal-mines and stone-quarries and the town has some manufactures. Pop. (1931), 3494.

RAIN-GAUGE. An instrument for measuring rainfall. Rainfall is estimated by the depth to which a level surface would be covered by the water which falls upon it, supposing that none flows away or is evaporated. If the fall were uniform over a certain area, the size of that area would obviously be of no moment, as the depth of water would be everywhere the same. The simplest kind of rain-gauge would be a cylindrical vessel or jar, and the rainfall could be measured by merely inserting a graduated stick vertically into it, and reading off the depth of the contained liquid. But in practice it is necessary to adopt precautions against evaporation, and also means to evaluate more accurately the amount of water collected.

In its ordinary form the rain-gauge has a removable conical funnel which collects the rain. Beneath is a cylindrical vessel firmly fixed in the ground. Inside this vessel is placed a can or bottle as receiver. The funnel terminates in a narrow tube down which the collected rain flows into the receiver. Every twenty-four hours, if daily records are made, the funnel is removed, the receiver taken out, the water poured from it into a graduated measuring-glass, and the exact quantity noted.

The type of rain-gauge most commonly used has a funnel of 5 inches diameter, but at fully equipped observatories 8-inch gauges are generally employed. It will be understood that each size of gauge collects a definite volume of water for any specified rainfall, e.g. a rainfall of ·10 inch. In this country it has been usual to estimate rainfall in inches, registering to two decimals of an inch. Now the metric units are largely adopted officially, and the rainfall recorded in millimetres and tenths.

Rain-gauges are constructed generally of copper, which is almost the only metal capable of withstanding satisfactorily the deteriorating effects of town air, but where the air is purer galvanised iron or zinc may be used.

Self-recording rain-gauges are of advantage as giving a continuous record of the rainfall, showing the amount of the fall for each hour or shorter period.

RAIN-MAKING. Causing rain to fall. It forms the object of various rites and ceremonies among primitive peoples, when the rainmaker is often an important individual. Attempts have been made to cause precipitation of vapour as rain by the use of gunfire, or by scattering chemicals and other substances from aeroplanes, but with no appreciable success.

RAIN TREE (*Pithecolobium saman*). A leguminous tree of tropical America, now largely planted in India for the shade it furnishes, and because it flourishes in barren salt-impregnated soils, as well as for its sweet pulpy pods, which are greedily eaten by cattle. Another species, *P. dulce*, has also been introduced into India, its pods also being edible.

RAINY LAKE, or **RÉNÉ LAKE.** A body of water forming part of the boundary between Minnesota and Canada. It is about 50 miles long, and of irregular breadth; receives the waters of numerous small lakes from the east and north-east, and empties itself by Rainy River, about 90 miles long, into the Lake of the Woods.

RAIPUR (rī-pör'). A district and town in the Chhattisgarh division of the Central Provinces, India. The district occupies the upper basin of the Mahanadi, by which and by the Seonath it is traversed. The trunk line of the Bengal-Nagpur Railway passes through and has a length of 60 miles within the district, with two branches from the chief town. Rice is the staple crop. Area, 9780 sq. miles; pop. 1,250,000. The town is the head-quarters of the district and also of the division, and has a flourishing trade in lac, cloth, gold, and silver, cotton, and grain. Pop. 38,341.

RAISINS. The dried fruit of various species of vines, comparatively rich in sugar. They are dried by natural or artificial heat. The natural and best method of drying is by cutting the stalks bearing the finest grapes half through when ripe, and allowing them to shrink and dry on the vine by the heat of the sun. Another method consists in plucking the grapes from the stalks, drying them, and dipping them in a boiling lye of wood-ashes and quicklime, after which they are exposed to the sun upon hurdles of basket-work. Those dried by the first method are called raisins of the sun or sun-raisins, muscatels, or *blooms*; those by the second, *lexias*. The inferior sorts of grapes are dried in ovens. Raisins are produced in large quantities in the south of Europe, Egypt, Asia Minor, California, etc. Those known as Malagas, Alicantes, Valencias, and Denias are well-known Spanish qualities. A kind without seeds, from Turkey, is called *sultanas*. The Corinthian raisin, or currant, is obtained from a small variety of grape peculiar to the Greek islands. A variety is exported from Australia.

RAJAH, or **RÂJÂ** (Skt. *rajan*, king; Lat. *rex*). In India, originally a title which belonged to those princes of Hindu race who, either as independent rulers or as feudatories, governed a territory; subsequently, a title given by the native Governments, and in later times by the British Government, to Hindus of rank. It is now not infrequently assumed by the zemindars or landholders, the title *Mahârâjah* (great rajah) being in our days generally reserved to the more or less powerful native princes. The feminine title is *ranee*.

RAJPÚT. The Rajpúts or Kshattriyas (Chattries) are, as being the fighting class, second in order of importance in the Hindu caste system, in which the Brahmans or priests

Rajput

hold the first place. The origin of the Rajpúts is vague, but their history goes back to the B.C. period of our era, when India was overrun by hordes of fair-skinned Aryans from the north-west.

Dravidians. The original inhabitants of India were what are now known as Dravidians, and were stunted men of dark colour and flat features; they are found now only among some of the jungle tribes of Central and Southern India. These aboriginal Dravidians were conquered by the Aryans, who took their country and sat down to enjoy themselves.

In the natural course of events the aborigines became the hewers of wood and drawers of water of our own Biblical story, while the conquering Ayrans evolved themselves into three essential classes; (1) priests (Brahmans); (2) warriors and administrators (Kshattriyas); (3) traders, money-lenders, and agriculturists, putting the rightful owners of the soil into a further class as servants and slaves. The kings and princes required guards and soldiers for their protection, and these they naturally chose from their friends and relations; thus arose the name Kshattriya—" those connected with royalty"—or Rajpút —"those of royal descent."

In those far-off days it was considered advisable for ministers of state, both civil and military, to have a long pedigree, so the Kshattriyas invented a genealogy, one division fixing on the sun as their ancestor, while the second division had to be content with the moon. In course of time these main divisions broke up into various clans, of which thirty-six claimed to be of royal origin. Many of these clans exist to the present day, and are known as the royal races of Rajpúts. However much one may be inclined to disbelieve the mythical origin of the Rajpút, it is quite evident that he is of very ancient lineage, and, as a class, the Rajpúts insist on this, one of their prevailing characteristics being pride of race and family.

In earlier days the Rajpúts formed —and to a certain extent still form— a military aristocracy of a feudal character; they are brave and chivalrous, keenly sensitive to an affront, and very jealous of the honour of their women. They are frugal in their manner of living, though excessively extravagant on such occasions as a marriage in the family. In religious beliefs they are second only to the priestly Brahmans, and are therefore very high-caste Hindus. Beef is abhorrent to them, and they eat very little meat of any kind. Their food must be cooked personally or by a Brahman, and they are very particular about ceremonial purity.

Generally speaking, the Rajpúts of Rájputána rank higher than, and are looked up to by, those from other parts of the country. In Rájputána, where Rajpúts have lived in a practically independent state for centuries, the blood is purer, while in other parts of India the race has apparently multiplied to a far greater extent than is warranted by the birth-rate. Rajpúts enlist in considerable numbers in the Indian army, both in the cavalry and infantry, and there are seven regiments entirely composed of them. Like other Hindus, the Rajpúts burn their dead, and at one time practised female infanticide and suttee (widow-burning). *See* RÁJPUTÁNA.

RÁJPUTÁNA. An agency of India comprising twenty native states and one chieftainship as follows:

Alwar.
Bikaner.
Bharatpur (Bhurtpore).
Banswara.
Bundi (Boondee).
Dholpur.
Dungarpur.
Jodhpur.
Jaisalmer.
Jaipur.
Jhalawar.
Kotah.
Karauli.
Kishangarh.
Kushalgarh.
Lawa.
Partabgarh.
Sirohi.
Shapura.
Tonk.
Udaipur.

The principal states are treated separately.

Area, etc. The total area, excluding the enclave Ajmer (q.v.), which is entirely a British province, is 129,059 sq. miles; pop. (1931), 11,225,712 (or about 87 per square mile).

Towns. Jaipur, Alwar, Bikaner, Udaipur, Bharatpur, Tonk, and Kotah, all state capitals.

Physiography. Rájputána is traversed from south-west to north-east by the Arávalli Hills (Mount Abu, 5650 feet), which divide it into two zones. The north-western zone is sandy, ill-watered, and barren, excepting in the limited submontane area and towards the extreme north-east, near Delhi, where the Great Desert, which forms the Rájputána-Sind frontier, improves somewhat in conditions of fertility. Parallel ridges of sandhills cover the wastes, and there is only one river of any significance, the Luni, which has a course of 200 miles. The higher and more pleasant regions of the south-east comprise the second zone, where there is an abundant water-supply from an extensive river-system, and where woodlands are extensive. There are many artificial but no natural freshwater lakes.

Social Conditions. The principal language is Rájasthâni, which is divided into about sixteen chief dialects and forms the everyday tongue of 75 per cent of the people. Hindus predominate, with Mahommedans second, and Jains third. The ruling family of Tonk are Pathan Mahommedans. 97 per cent of the Muslims are Sunni, 2 per cent Shiite, and the rest Wahábi.

Communications. There are 630 miles of roadways in Rájputána, 307 miles of which are metalled. The Government of India operates the oldest and most important railway line, Rájputána-Malwa, which has a length of 720 miles within the state. The Indian Midland section of the Great Indian Peninsula Railway between Agra and Gwalior (19 miles through Dholpur state) is also Government controlled. Among the lines belonging to the native states are: the Jodhpur-Bikaner line (700 miles), starting from Marwar Junction on the Rájputána-Malwa system and running into branches at the Luni River; the Udaipur-Chitor (67 miles); the last 29 miles of the Bina-Guna-Baran line; and a metre-gauge line between Jaipur town and Sawai Madhopur via Nawai (73 miles).

Production. Agriculture is the staple industry. Among crops are native food grains (including maize), cotton, rice (in certain districts), wheat, indigo, sugar-cane, poppy (for opium), tobacco, and oil-seeds (including mustard, castor, rape, and linseed). Fruits include the peach, tamarind, orange, guava, apricot, mango, and pomegranate. Ordinary household vegetables are also extensively produced.

Big Game. Lions existed in large numbers until quite recently, but have now been extirpated. Tigers, however, are plentiful, especially in the Asávallis; leopards are common, and sloth bears exist in the south-east. Where both tiger and bear are found there are also large numbers of deer. Antelope and gazelles frequent the plains, and much small game is abundant.

Government. Three Residents (Mewar, Jaipur, and West Rájputána) and three Political Agents are subordinate to the Political Agent at Abu, who represents the Indian Government, and the central authority is in the hands of the ruling prince or chief. Rájputána is, of course, in political relations with the Indian Government.

RÁJSHÁHI. A division and district of Eastern Bengal, India. The division comprises the districts of Bogra, Dinájpur, Jalpaiguri, Málda, Pabna, Rájsháhi, and Rangpur. Area, 19,000 sq. miles; pop. 10,345,664 (or 544 per square mile). The district has an area of 2593 sq. miles, and a population of 1,489,675. It slopes generally from west to east, and is traversed from north to south by the Eastern Bengal State Railway. Jute, rice, pulses, and silk are sent to Calcutta; rice is the staple crop, and true hemp (*Cannabis sativa*) is cultivated under Government control.

The district is the unhealthiest, malaria-stricken region of Eastern Bengal. Rampur-Boalia is the headquarters, and Nator the only other town of importance. The people are mainly Mahommedans, speaking the Northern Bengali dialect, Hindus being second in numerical strength.

RAKOCZY (rä-kō'tsi), or **RAGOTSKY.** A famous princely family, now extinct in the male line, which from 1606 to 1676 ruled the principality of Siebenburgen or Transylvania.

RÄLE. A bubbling sound produced in the bronchial tubes by the movement of mucus, which is formed as the result of some diseased condition of the lungs. Räles are heard, accompanying the breath sounds, at the surface of the chest, usually by means of a stethoscope (q.v.), and are of various types. The commonest forms are the bubbling, cavernous, consonating, clicking, crackling, crepitant, and dry räle. They aid the practised observer to diagnose the different diseased conditions which may affect the lungs.

RALEIGH (ra̤l'i), or **RALEGH, Sir Walter.** English navigator, warrior, statesman, and writer in the reigns of Elizabeth and James I. Born in 1552, died in 1618. He studied at Oxford, and at the age of seventeen he joined a body of gentlemen volunteers raised to assist the French Protestants. Little is known of his adventures for some years, but in 1580-1 he distinguished himself in the Irish rebellion, both by ability and severity. He became a favourite at court, a result which has been traditionally attributed to an act of gallantry, namely, his throwing his embroidered cloak in a puddle in order that the queen might pass. In 1584 he obtained a charter of colonisation and unsuccessfully attempted the settlement of Virginia, in one or two following years. In 1584, also, he obtained a large share of the forfeited Irish estates, and introduced there the cultivation of the potato.

Through the queen's favour he obtained licences to sell wine and export woollens, was knighted and made Lord-Warden of the Stannaries or tin-mines (1585), vice-admiral of Devon and Cornwall, and captain of the queen's guard (1587). In 1588 he rendered excellent service against the Spanish Armada, and subsequently vessels were fitted out by him to attack the Spaniards. In 1592 he incurred the queen's displeasure by an amour with one of her maids of honour, the daughter of Sir Nicholas Throgmorton. Although he made the best reparation in his power, by marrying that lady, he was imprisoned for some months, and banished the queen's presence.

To discover the fabled El Dorado or region of gold he planned an expedition to Guiana, in which he embarked in 1595, and reached the Orinoco; but was obliged to return after having done little more than take a formal possession of the country in the name of Elizabeth. In 1596 he held a naval command against Spain under Lord Howard and the Earl of Essex, and assisted in the defeat of the Spanish fleet and the capture of Cadiz. Next year he captured Fayal in the Azores; in 1600 he became Governor of Jersey. James I., on his accession in 1603, had his mind soon poisoned against Raleigh, whom he deprived of all his offices. Accused of complicity in Lord Cobham's treason in favour of Arabella Stuart, Raleigh was brought to trial at Winchester in Nov., 1603, found guilty of treason, and sentenced to death.

He was, however, reprieved and confined to the Tower. Here he remained for twelve years, devoting himself to scientific and literary work. In 1616 he obtained his release by bribing the favourite Villiers, and by offering to open a mine of gold which he believed to exist near the Orinoco. The enterprise proved disastrous. Raleigh's force had attacked the Spaniards, and on his return James, to favour the Spanish court, with his usual meanness and pusillanimity determined to execute him on his former sentence. After a trial before a commission of the Privy Council the doom of death was pronounced against him, and was carried into execution on 29th Oct., 1618. As a politician and public character Raleigh is doubtless open to adverse criticism; but in extent of capacity and vigour of mind he had few equals, even in an age of great men.

His writings are on a variety of topics, besides a few poetical pieces of great merit. His *History of the World* is one of the best specimens of the English of his day, being at once the style of the statesman and the scholar.—BIBLIOGRAPHY: E. W. Gosse, *Raleigh*; Martin Hume, *Sir Walter Raleigh*; Beatrice Marshall, *Sir Walter Raleigh*; Sir Sidney Lee, *Great Englishmen of the 16th Century*; T. N. Brushfield, *Bibliography of Sir Walter Raleigh*.

RALEIGH. A city of North Carolina, United States, the state capital and the county seat of Wake county; served by the Raleigh & Southport, Seaboard Air Line, and Norfolk Southern Railways. Raleigh is an educational centre, and has, among other establishments, the State Agricultural and Engineering College (founded 1889), and the medical faculty of the State university. It is also the see of a Protestant Episcopal bishop. Manufactures include phosphatic manures, cottons, hardware, and machinery. There are two railway repair-shops. Raleigh was founded in 1792 as the state capital, and was named after Sir Walter Raleigh. Pop. (1930), 37,379.

RALIK. *See* MARSHALL ISLANDS.

RAMA (rä'ma). In Hindu mythology, the name common to a personage appearing as three incarnations of Vishnu.

RAMADAN', RHAMAZAN', or **RAMADZAN'.** The ninth month in the Mahommedan year, during which it is said Mahomet received his first revelation. It is devoted to fasting and abstinence. From sunrise to sunset for thirty days of its duration the Mahommedans partake of no kind of nourishment. After sunset necessary wants may be satisfied, and this permission is liberally taken advantage of. Believers are exempted in peculiar circumstances from observing the fast. As the Mahommedans reckon by lunar time, the month begins each year eleven days earlier than in the preceding year, so that in thirty-three years it occurs successively in all the seasons.

RAMADI. Town of Iraq. It stands on the Euphrates, 60 miles from Baghdad. Here, on 28th-29th Sept., 1917, a battle was fought between the British and the Turks. The British, advancing from Baghdad, attacked the Turkish position on the 28th and on the 29th, and after some hard fighting, captured the remains of the army and entered the town. In the engagement some Indian regiments did splendid service.

RÂMÂ'YANA. The older of the two great Sanskrit epics, ascribed to the poet Valmiki, and dating probably from the fifth century B.C. The hero is Rama, an incarnation of Vishnu as the son of the King of Oudh. It relates his marriage with Sita, their wanderings in the forest, the seizure of Sita by the giants of Ceylon, her recovery, and the restoration of Rama to the throne of his ancestors. It contains 24,000 verses, and is divided into seven books.—Cf. A. A. Macdonell, *History of Sanskrit Literature*. There is a condensed edition of the *Râmâyana* and *Mahabharata*, by Romesh C. Dutt, in Everyman's Library.

RAMBOO'TAN. The fruit of the tree *Nephelium lappaceum*, nat. ord. Sapindaceæ, much prized in the Malayan Archipelago. It is about the size of a pigeon's egg, and of a red colour.

RAMBOUILLET (rȧṇ-bö-yā). A town of France, department of Seine-et-Oise. It is notable only for its château, long the residence of the Kings of France, and now the summer seat of the President of the Republic. Pop. 6000.

RAMÉE, Louise de la ("Ouida"). English novelist of French extraction, born at Bury St. Edmunds in 1840, died in 1908. She published her first novel, *Held in Bondage*, in 1863, and from then onwards was a very prolific writer. Among her best works are: *Strathmore*, *Chandos*, *Under Two Flags*, *Two Little Wooden Shoes*, *Moths*, *Wanda*, *The Tower of Taddeo*, and *The Massarenes*.

RAM'ESES, or **RAMSES** (in Egyptian, "the Child of the Sun"). The name given to twelve Egyptian kings of the dynasties nineteen and twenty.

Rameses I. was the first king of the nineteenth dynasty, and was not among the most remarkable of the series.

Rameses II., grandson of the preceding, was the third King of the nineteenth dynasty, and his reign may be dated with fair accuracy from 1340 to 1273 B.C. He is identified by many with the Sesostris of Greek writers. His first achievement was the reduction of Ethiopia to subjection. He defeated a confederation, among whom the Khita or Hittites were the chief, in a great battle near the Orontes in Syria, and in a subsequent stage of the war took Jerusalem and other places. He was a zealous builder and a patron of art and science. He is supposed to have been the king who oppressed the Hebrews, and the father of the king under whom the exodus took place.

Rameses III., the Rhampsinitus of Herodotus, belonged to the twentieth dynasty, and was uniformly successful in war. He endeavoured to surpass his ancestors in the magnificence of his buildings. The mummy of Rameses II. was found in 1881, that of Rameses III. in 1886. The last king of the name of Rameses is supposed to have completed his reign about 1000 years before the Christian era.—Cf. J. H. Breasted, *A History of the Ancient Egyptians.*

RAMESES. One of the treasure-cities of Egypt built by the Hebrews during the oppression, and probably named after Rameses II. It has been identified by Lepsius with Tell-el-Maskhûta on the Freshwater Canal (about 12 miles west of the Suez Canal), and by Brugsch with Tanis the modern San.

RAMIE, or **RAMEE'.** A name applied to various fibre-plants of the nettle family or to the fibre yielded by them. The chief of these are: *Bœhmeria nivĕa,* or China grass (also called *Urtīca nivĕa*), and *Bœhmeria tenacissima* (or *U. tenacissima*), which some maintain to be the true ramie plant. (*See* BŒHMERIA.) A kind of ramie has also been prepared from a common European nettle (*Urtīca dioica*), and from *Laportea canadensis,* a North American nettle, introduced into Germany as a fibre-plant.

RAMILLIES (râ-mi-yē). A village of Belgium, province of Brabant, where, on 23rd May, 1706, the Duke of Marlborough gained a great victory over the French under Marshal Villeroi.

RAM MOHAN RAY. An Indian rajah, founder of the Brahma-Samaj sect of theists, born at Burdwan, Bengal, 1776, died near Bristol 1833. Born of a high-caste Brahman family, he received a good education, and acquired a mastery of Sanskrit, Persian, Arabic, English, Latin, Greek, and Hebrew. He became convinced that the original Hindu religion was theistic, and he became anxious to reform the creed of his countrymen.

From the perusal of the New Testament he found the doctrines of Christ more in harmony with his own opinions than any others which had come to his knowledge, and in 1820 he accordingly published a work entitled the *Precepts of Jesus the Guide to Peace and Happiness,* consisting chiefly of a selection of moral precepts from the Evangelists. In his doctrinal views he was a Unitarian, or Arian, holding, however, the pre-existence and super-angelic dignity of Christ. In 1833 he visited England as ambassador from the King of Delhi, and while there was seized with a fever, which proved fatal.

RAMPANT. Heraldic term denoting an attitude of beasts of prey in armorial charges, standing on the left hind-leg, the others being upraised, the right fore-leg above the left, the head sideways, and the tail upwards. Should both hind-legs be aground, it is salient. Full-faced is rampart guardant, looking backwards is rampant reguardant.

RAM'PION (*Campanŭla Rapuncŭlus*). A plant of the nat. ord. Campanulaceæ, or bellworts, indigenous to Britain, as well as to various parts of the continent of Europe. Its root may be eaten in a raw state like radish, and is by some esteemed for its pleasant nutty flavour. Both leaves and root may also be cut into winter salads. Round-headed rampion (*Phyteuma orbiculāre*) and spiked rampion (*P. spicātum*) are also British plants, the roots and young shoots of which are occasionally used as an article of food.

RAMPUR'. A native state of Rohilkhand, India, tributary to the United Provinces. There is an adequate river system, and the state is flat and the soil alluvial. Rice from the north, and wheat, rice, maize, and sugar-cane from the southern regions, are the principal products. Cotton cloth is manufactured; sugar, rice, and hides are exported. The Oudh and Rohilkhand Railway traverses the state. Capital, Rampur City. Area, 899 sq. miles; pop. 453,607.

RAMPUR BOALIA. A town of Eastern Bengal, India, headquarters of Rájsháhi district (q.v.). Pop. 24,598.

RAMPUR CITY. The capital of Rampur state, India, on the Kosi; served from Calcutta (850 miles) by the Oudh & Rohilkhand (Mordabad-Bareilly) line. It is the state metropolis, and produces pottery, damask, sword-blades, and cutlery. Pop. 73,156.

RAMSAY, Allan. Scottish poet, born 1686, at Leadhills, in Lanarkshire, died at Edinburgh 1758. He removed to Edinburgh in his fifteenth year and was apprenticed to a wig-maker, an occupation which he followed till his thirtieth year. His poems, most of them printed as broadsides, soon made him widely known among all classes, and he now abandoned wig-making and commenced business as a bookseller.

He was the first to start a circulating library in Scotland. In 1720 he published a collection of his poems in one volume quarto. In 1724 the first volume of *The Tea-Table Miscellany, a Collection of Songs,* appeared. The rapid sale of this compilation induced Ramsay to publish another, entitled *The Evergreen, being a Collection of Scots Poems wrote by the Ingenious before 1600,* which was equally successful. His next publication, *The Gentle Shepherd* (1725), established his fame upon a sure and lasting basis.

In 1728 a second quarto volume of his poems appeared; and in 1730 his *Thirty Fables,* which concluded his public poetical labours. He did not give up his shop until within three years of his decease. He rendered great service to the vernacular literature by editing and imitating the old Scottish poetry, but his fame rests chiefly on the inimitable *Gentle Shepherd.*—Cf. Oliphant Smeaton, *Life of Allan Ramsay.*

RAMSAY, Sir Andrew Crombie. Scottish geologist, born in Glasgow 1814, died in 1891. He joined the Geological Survey in 1841; was appointed to the chair of geology at University College, London, 1847; was lecturer at the school of Mines, 1851; director-general of the Geological Survey and of the Museum of Practical Geology from 1872 to 1881. He is author of *Physical Geology and Geography of Britain* and *Geology of Arran.*

RAMSAY, Edward Bannerman. Scottish divine and author, son of Alexander Burnett, advocate. Born at Aberdeen 1793, died at Edinburgh 1872. He adopted the name of his grand-uncle Sir Alexander Ramsay, by whom he was educated. Educated at Cambridge, he took holy orders, and came to Edinburgh in 1823 as a clergyman of the Scottish Episcopal Church, becoming dean of the diocese in 1846. He is best known by his *Reminiscences of Scottish Life and Character,* which has had a great popularity.

RAMSAY, Sir William. British chemist, born 1852, died 1916. His early teaching work was done in his native city of Glasgow. He became professor of chemistry at Bristol in 1880, and at University College, London, in 1887. In 1894 he and Lord Rayleigh discovered argon (q.v.). Neon (q.v.), krypton, and xenon were discovered in 1898. He was awarded the Nobel prize in 1904, and was president of the British Association in 1911.

RAMSAY, Sir William Mitchell. Scottish archæologist. He was born at Glasgow, 15th March, 1851, and was Professor of Humanity at Aberdeen from 1886-1911. For more than forty-five years the history and geography of Asia Minor have been his special study. His works include *The Church in the Roman Empire* (1893); *St. Paul, the Traveller and the Roman Citizen* (1895); *Asianic Elements in Greek Civilisation* (1927). He was knighted in 1906.

RAMSBOTTOM. An urban district or Lancashire, England, on the Irwell, 4 miles north of Bury, and 9 north-west of Manchester. It is served by the L.M.S. Railway. Iron- and brass-founding, calico-printing and bleaching, and many other industries are carried on. Pop. (1931), 14,926.

RAMSBURY. Village of Wiltshire. It is 5 miles from Hungerford on the Great Western Railway. In Anglo-Saxon times it was the seat of a bishopric.

RAMSDEN, Jesse. Mathematical instrument-maker, born at Halifax 1735, died at Brighton 1800. He married a daughter of Dollond, the optician, and gained great celebrity for his divided circles, transit instruments, etc. He was a Fellow of the Royal Society.

RAMSEY. Island of Pembrokeshire. Situated off St. David's Head, it is about 2 miles long and covers 600 acres. There is a harbour on the east coast, and on the island are wild duck, snipe, and woodcock.

RAMSEY. Urban district and market town of Huntingdonshire. It is 11 miles from Huntingdon, on the L.N.E. Railway. The chief building is the magnificent parish church. There was once a Benedictine abbey of which only a gatehouse remains. The modern abbey is the seat of **Lord de Ramsey.** Near was the lake called Ramsey Mere, but this has now been drained. Pop. (1931), 5180.

RAMSEY. A popular watering-place in the Isle of Man. It is in Ramsey Bay, on the north-east of the Island, 14 miles from Douglas. Pop. (1931), 4108.

RAMSGATE. A seaport, watering-place, and municipal borough of England, county of Kent, in the Isle of Thanet; served by the Southern Railway, and by steamers to and from London and various French ports. It possesses a fine stretch of sand and a promenade pier, and is much frequented by visitors. The harbour, which serves as a harbour of refuge for the Downs, is nearly circular, comprises an area of about 50 acres, and includes a dry dock and a patent slip for the repair of vessels. It is protected by two stone piers 2000 and 1500 feet long, with an entrance of 2400 feet. Shipbuilding and rope-making are carried on; there is some trade in coal and timber, and a considerable fishery.

Ramsgate was formerly a member of the Cinque Ports, and attached to Sandwich. During the European War it was bombarded both from the sea and from the air by German forces. Pop. (1931), 33,597.

RAMSONS (*Allium ursinum*). A species of garlic found wild in many parts of Britain, and formerly cultivated in gardens.

RAMTIL-OIL. A bland oil similar to sesamum-oil, expressed from the seeds of a composite annual herb, *Guizotia oleifera*, cultivated in Abyssinia and various parts of India.

RAMUS, Peter, or PIERRE DE LA RAMÉE. French logician and classical scholar, born in Vermandois 1515, killed in the massacre of St. Bartholomew 1572. He went to Paris about 1523, and studied under great difficulties. His attacks on Aristotle and the scholastics excited violent opposition. In 1551 he was appointed royal professor of rhetoric and philosophy at Paris. In 1561 he became a Protestant. He published a *Treatise on Logic* in 1543, which obtained great success, as did also his other works on grammar, mathematics, philosophy, and theology. His doctrines were widely diffused. France, England, and particularly Scotland were full of Ramists. His logic was introduced into the University of Glasgow by Andrew Melville.

RANCÉ (ràṇ-sā), **Armand Jean le Bouthillier de.** The founder of the reformed order of La Trappe, born at Paris 1626, died 1700. He embraced the ecclesiastical profession, and held no fewer than six benefices. Residing at Paris, he gave himself up to a life of dissipation. In 1657, however, a marked change took place in his character. Retiring to the abbey of La Trappe in 1664, he began those reforms which have rendered his name famous (*see* LA TRAPPE). He passed thirty-three years in this retirement, during which he wrote a number of works, mostly of an ascetic character.

RANCHI. A district and town of India, in the Chota Nagpur division of Bihar and Orissa. The district is the largest in Bengal, and produces rice. The town is the headquarters of the division and of the district, and is the summer capital of Bihar and Orissa. Area (district), 7102 sq. miles; pop. 1,334,173; pop. (town), 39,628.

RAND, THE, or WITWATERSRAND. A great gold-mining area of the Transvaal, South Africa. Johannesburg is the centre.

RANDERS. A town of Jutland, Denmark, on the Guden-aa, about 6 miles above its mouth in the Randers Fiord. It has manufactures of gloves, margarine, railway carriages, etc. Pop. (1930), 27,722.

RANDOLPH, Thomas. English poet and dramatist. He was born in 1605, and died in 1635. His father was steward to Lord Zouch. He was a precocious child, and at the age of ten wrote *The History of the Incarnation of our Saviour* in verse. His mature work was not so edifying He was educated at Westminster, and Trinity College, Cambridge, where he graduated B.A. in 1628, and M.A. in 1632, in which year he also became a major Fellow of his college. While still an undergraduate, he became acquainted with Ben Jonson, who adopted him as one of his "sons." "They both of them loved sack, and harmless mirth," as the preface to one of Randolph's plays informs us.

In 1630 Randolph produced his first publication, *Aristippus, or the Joviall Philosopher, To which is added The Conceited Pedler. Aristippus*, which is written in prose interspersed with verse, utilises Aristotelian logic in defence of sack as compared with small beer. It was written to be privately performed at the university. *The Conceited Pedler* is a highly amusing monologue. *The Jealous Lovers*, a comedy in blank verse, was performed before the king and queen at Cambridge in 1632. It is more ambitious, but also more self-conscious than the rest of Randolph's work, and cannot be reckoned a success.

The Muses' Looking-Glasse, Randolph's masterpiece, was probably acted in 1632, though not printed until 1638. It is a very clever and original play, a curious blend of Aristotle and Aristophanes, which endeavours to prove that virtue is a mean between two extremes of vice. Jonson's influence is plainly seen. *Amyntas, or the Impossible Dowry* is a well-finished but artificial pastoral play. *Hey for Honesty, down with Knavery*, a free adaptation of Aristophanes' *Plutus*, is probably not by Randolph.

Randolph was a true " son " of Jonson's, though he rivalled his master more as a consumer of sack than as a dramatist, and thereby shortened his days. Unlike Jonson, he is learned without being pedantic, and has a larger share of the spirit of Aristophanes than is given to most English writers.

RANELAGH. Place of amusement in London. It was in Chelsea, where are now the grounds of Chelsea Hospital. There, Richard Jones, Earl of Ranelagh, built a house and laid out gardens which, in the 18th century, were a popular pleasure resort for the fashionable folk of London. In the grounds was an immense rotunda, where entertainments of all kinds were held.

The modern **Ranelagh Club** is at Barn Elms Park, London, S.W.13. It was opened in 1894 and is a centre for polo. It has also facilities for golf, croquet, and other games.

RANGE. An area of ground set apart and equipped for practice with fire-arms. A range may be an artillery-range, a rifle-range, a miniature range, or a 30-yards range. Of these the rifle-range is the most generally met with, and is to be found wherever troops are stationed, or in the immediate neighbourhood of military stations.

Early rifle-ranges were of a very elementary type, and consisted merely of a mound of earth or " stop-butt " to catch the bullets ; on each flank of this stop-butt were two earthen shelters for the markers, and between these two shelters or mantlets were placed two square iron targets. The strike of a bullet on the target was seen by the marker in his mantlet, and signalled to the firing-point by means of a long-handled disc of suitable colour. At intervals firing was stopped to enable the markers to clean or " wash out " the bullet-marks on the target. With the introduction of high-velocity rifles firing a hard-envelope bullet (q.v.) iron targets were found to be unsatisfactory, owing to the danger of splintering, and targets of canvas on a wooden frame replaced them. For convenience of marking these were often fixed on trollies running on rails, so that after a shot they could be pulled in to the shelter of the mantlet and patched up.

Then came the invention of what is known as the gallery-range, which is the type universally used now. The construction of a gallery-range entails a considerable amount of excavation at the place selected for the targets and stop-butt. The latter may be a scarped hill-side or similar natural feature if available, or it may be entirely artificial. At the position selected a deep and broad excavation is made, having the side nearest to the firing-point perpendicular, while the opposite side merges gradually into the stop-butt. The perpendicular side is riveted or bricked up to a height of 7 or 8 feet, and, if necessary, made bullet-proof above the natural ground-level by a glacis or slope of earth. A roof of timber or iron, covered with earth, is then put on, and a perfectly bullet-proof shelter in which men can work with safety is thus available.

Targets in these gallery-ranges are exposed *above* the gallery or shelter instead of to one side, as was formerly the case with the old-pattern range ; and, to enable this to be done, a framework is provided on the open side of the gallery. This framework is constructed on the counterweight principle, so that when one target is up and exposed to the firer, the other is down below ground-level and can be attended to by the men on duty in the gallery. The number of targets which can be used at one and the same time in a gallery-range is to all intents only limited by the length of the gallery. The target-frames are of angle-iron, knife-edge towards the firer, while the actual targets themselves are canvas on a light wooden frame. A telephone is provided on every modern range, by means of which orders and instructions can be sent from the firing-point to the butts.

When it is necessary to cease firing temporarily for any purpose, the red danger-flag must be shown ; while firing is in progress a red flag is always kept flying on the top of the stop-butt as a warning to those approaching the area ; and, for the same reason of safety to the public, a danger-zone of at least 2500 yards should be kept behind the butts. It is unnecessary for the military authorities actually to own this area, but they must obtain firing-rights over it.

Miniature ranges are, as the name implies, ranges constructed for practice with miniature rifles (·22 bore). These ranges may either be indoors or outdoors, and all necessary precautions have to be taken for safety. When constructed indoors, any suitable building, room, or corridor may be utilised, or a special gallery may be built. The length of such a range should never be less than 15 yards, and 25 yards is the normal length for a specially constructed indoor range, while out of doors they may extend to 100 yards. By a suitable method of lighting, indoor miniature ranges can conveniently be used at night. They are very useful for the early practice of recruits.

Thirty-yards ranges are an outdoor arrangement, and are useful for individual instruction in target-shooting with the service rifle and ammunition. They are particularly convenient in cases in which the ordinary range is at a distance from the barracks, and have the great advantage over miniature ranges that the young soldier is enabled to accustom himself to the recoil of the rifle before proceeding to use it on the open range. A 30-yards range can conveniently be constructed in an old quarry or against a vertical cliff, or a strong wall can be provided as a stop-butt. For full information regarding the construction of ranges, see *Musketry Regulations, Part II.*

An *artillery-range* is an area of country providing various tactical features and over which firing-rights can be obtained. Such a range necessarily requires a very considerable area, which can only be found satisfactorily where large stretches of moorland exist, e.g. Okehampton, in Dartmoor; while Lydd, in Kent, is also used for artillery practice. Observing-parties and markers are accommodated well away on the flanks of the targets, either behind suitable earthworks or in the open behind some natural features of the ground.

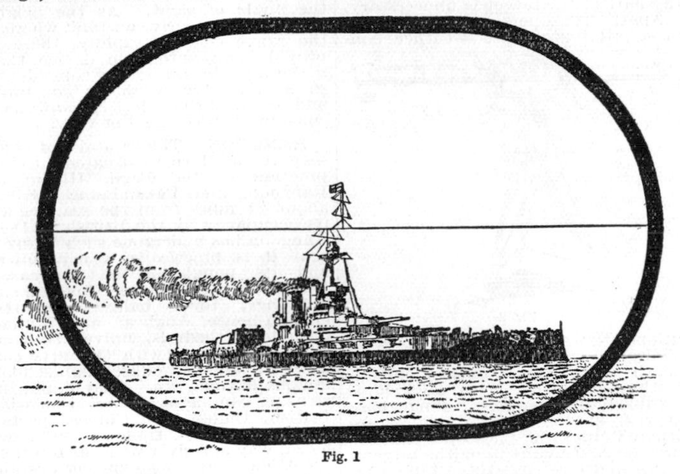

Fig. 1

RANGE-FINDERS. As the name implies, range-finders or telemeters are instruments for the determination of the distances of objects from an observation station. When the objects are invisible, the range and position, say of a gun in action, may be determined from the times the sound of the gun-discharge takes to reach three or more stations. *Sound range-finding apparatus* of this kind was highly developed during the European War. When the targets are visible, optical range-finders, from which results of great accuracy are obtainable, are usually employed.

The range determination depends upon the solution of a triangle comprising a base of known length and two sides represented by the lines of sight between the ends of the base and the target or the observing-station, according as the base is situated at the observer or at the target. If the base length is known, the length of the side, that is, the range, can be deduced from a measurement of the parallax, that is, the difference between the base angles, since the angular field of view is comparatively small. The base of the triangle may be situated at the target, and the accuracy will then depend upon the accuracy with which the length of the base is known. *Depression* range-finders, *sextant* range-finders, and some types of *range-keepers* are instruments of this kind. When the base of known length is situated at the observing-station, to know the dimensions of any part of the target is unnecessary.

Apart from personal errors, and those attributable to weather con-

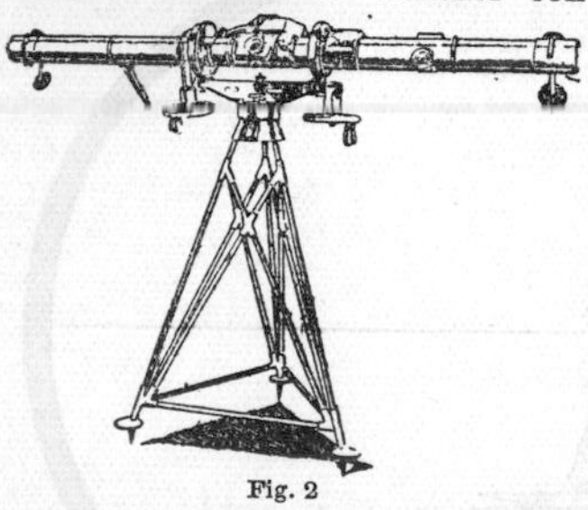

Fig. 2

ditions, the accuracy of observation is directly proportional to the base length and to the optical magnification employed. On land it is possible to use very long base lengths, at the ends of which are situated observing-telescopes that are directed continually upon the target.

Installations of this kind are known as *two-observer position-finders. Monostatic* or *single-observer* or *self-contained base* range-finders, which have many advantages, comprise, as these names imply, a comparatively short base, which can be directed as a whole upon the target. The images formed by light from the ends of the base are viewed by a single observer in one telescope field of view, and either the *coincidence* or the *stereoscopic* system of observation can be adopted.

In the coincidence system the images formed by rays entering the two ends of the base appear separated in the field of view by a very fine horizontal line, as indicated in fig. 1. When the images are brought into coincidence by the suitable deviation of the rays, the range is indicated upon the scale.

In the stereoscopic arrangement the range-finder has two eyepieces, and the observer sees the various objects in perspective at apparently their respective distances, which in small instruments can be compared with a fixed perspective scale in the field of view. In larger instruments the image is moved relatively to a mark in the field at an apparent fixed distance. They are of the *wandering-mark* type, although the mark is usually fixed.

Height-finders. For anti-aircraft purposes, *height-finders* (one typical example of which is illustrated in fig. 2) are employed. These instruments measure not only the range, but also the height and frequently the angle of sight. As the height remains very nearly constant, whereas the range changes rapidly, there is provided an automatic device that maintains the images in coincidence so long as the height is constant, and provided the object is maintained constantly in the field of view.

RANGOON′. The capital and chief seaport of Burma, situated at the junction of the Pegu, Hlaing or Rangoon, and Pazundaung Rivers, about 21 miles from the sea. Since its occupancy by the British in 1852 Rangoon has undergone such changes that it is practically a new town, and its population has increased five-fold. There are Government buildings, town hall, law-courts, custom-house, Anglican and Roman Catholic cathedrals, university constituted in 1920, with two arts colleges, St. John's College, high school, famous pagoda, etc. A large and increasing commerce is carried on with British, Indian, and Chinese ports; and an extensive trade is conducted by railway and river with the interior. A telephone exchange has been established.

The chief exports are rice, timber, cotton, hides, gums and resins, mineral oil, ivory, precious stones; the imports being mainly manufactured goods. There are rice-mills and a Government dockyard. Rangoon has been the centre of Burmese administration since the second Burmese War, but it was never a royal capital, and its development is of comparatively recent date. Pop. (1931), 400,415.

RANGPUR′. A district and town of India, in the Rájsháhi division of Bengal. The district is a vast alluvial plain, traversed by the Brahmaputra, on the eastern boundary, for a distance of 80 miles, and watered by its extensive network of tributaries. The northern branch of the Eastern Bengal State Railway and many other smaller lines serve the district. Rice is the staple produce, but large areas are laid down to tobacco, which is exported to Burma for Burmese home consumption. The town is the district headquarters. State area, 3480 sq. miles; pop. 2,385,000; pop. (town), 15,250.

RANJITSINHJI, KUMAR SHRI. Indian prince and cricketer, born 1872, died 1933. He finished his education at Trinity College, Cambridge. There he played cricket for the university, and in 1895 he settled in Sussex and began to play regularly for that county. His wonderful batsmanship made an extraordinary impression, and he became perhaps the most popular batsman, as he was certainly the most graceful, in the land. He played for England against Australia and in other representative matches. In 1906 Ranji, as he was popularly called, became a ruling Indian prince when he succeeded as Maharajah of Nawanagar, and as such he served in France in 1914-15 and took part in Indian politics. In 1897 he published *The Jubilee Book of Cricket.*

RANKE (rån'kė), **Leopold von.** German historian, born in 1795, died 1886. He studied at Halle and Berlin, became a teacher in the gymnasium of Frankfurt-on-the-Oder in 1818, and professor of history at the University of Berlin in 1825. His first published work (1824) was a *History of the Romance and Teutonic Nations from 1494 to 1535.* This was followed by *Princes and Peoples of Southern Europe in the 16th and 17th Centuries* (1827); *The Serbian Revolution* (1829); *History of the Popes* (1834-7); *History of Germany in the time of the Reformation* (1839-47); *History of Prussia during the 17th and 18th Centuries* (1847-8); *History of France, chiefly in the 16th and 17th Centuries* (1852-5); *History of England in the 17th Century* (1859-68); besides a number of smaller works supplementary to his *History of Germany.*

At the age of eighty he undertook with undiminished vigour to write a *World History,* and a volume of this great work appeared every year until his death. His writings are chiefly valuable for the new material which he discovered in State papers, and the truth with which he presented history unbiased by personal predilections. Many of his works have been translated into English. Unlike Treitschke, Ranke, who lived before the days of intense nationalism, was cosmopolitan rather than German in his interests.—Cf. A. Guillaud, *L' Allemagne et ses historiens: Niebuhr, Ranke, Mommsen, Sybel, Treitschke.*

RANKINE, William John Macquorn. Civil engineer, born at Edinburgh in 1820, died 1872. He received his instruction in natural philosophy from Professor Forbes, his practical training as an engineer from Sir J. Macneill, and he became himself professor of engineering at Glasgow University in 1855. His numerous contributions to the technical journals have been reprinted (London, 1881), and he was the author of textbooks on *Civil Engineering, The Steam Engine, Applied Mechanics,* and *Shipbuilding.* He was especially successful in investigating mathematically the principles of mechanical and civil engineering. Rankine was also well known as a song-writer.

RANNOCH, LOCH. A lake, Perthshire, Scotland, 35 miles N.N.W. of Perth, 11 miles long, and about 1 mile average breadth. It contains two islands, and has an outlet for its waters in the Tummel, a tributary of the Tay. Westward from the loch extends the Moor of Rannoch, which is 28 miles long by 16 miles broad.

RANPUR. A native state of Bihar and Orissa, India, tributary to Orissa. It is one of the most ancient of the Orissa feudatories, the chiefship being traceable for 3600 years. State area, 203 sq. miles; pop. 47,000.

RANSOM (Fr. *rançon,* Lat. *redemptio*). The money or price paid for the redemption of a prisoner, captive, or slave, or for goods captured by an enemy. During the Middle Ages ransoms were paid for knights and kings who were taken prisoners in battle. Thus England paid a ransom for Richard I. In the nineteenth century the exchange of officers according to rank was introduced, but occasional cases of ransom are still known. Raisuli, the Moroccan chief who captured Kaid Maclean in 1907, demanded and received from the British Government the sum of £20,000 and a consigment of military stores for his captive's release.

RANTERS. A name given by way of reproach to a denomination of Christians which sprang up in 1645. They called themselves *Seekers,* the members maintaining that they were seeking for the true Church and its ordinances, and the Scriptures, which were lost.

RANUNCULA'CEÆ. A natural order of polypetalous dicotyledons, in almost all cases herbaceous, inhabiting the colder parts of the world, and unknown in hot countries except at considerable elevations. They have radical or alternate leaves (opposite in Clematis), regular or irregular, often large and handsome flowers, and fruits consisting of one-seeded achenes or many-seeded follicles. There are about 30 genera and 1000 species. Most have poisonous qualities, e.g. aconite and hellebore. Some are objects of beauty, as the larkspurs, ranunculus, anemone and pæony. See next article.

RANUN'CULUS. A genus of herbaceous plants, the type of the nat. ord. Ranunculaceæ. They have entire, lobed, or compound leaves, and usually panicled, white or yellow flowers. The species are numerous, and almost exclusively inhabit the northern hemisphere. Almost all the species are acrid and caustic, and poisonous when taken internally, and, when externally applied, will raise blisters. The British species are known as crowfoot, buttercup, and spearwort. The common British buttercups are *R. acris, R. repens,* and *R. bulbosus*; *R. Ficaria* is the lesser celandine or pilewort; *R. fluitans* and *R. aquatilis* are among the aquatic species; *R. flammula* is the lesser spearwort, common in wet meadows. *R. asiaticus* is a cultivated species, and double forms of *R. acris* and *R. aconitifolius* are known as bachelors' buttons.

RANZ - DES - VACHES (rȧṇz-dā-vȧsh). The name of certain simple melodies of the Swiss mountaineers, commonly played on a long trumpet called the *alpenhorn.* They consist of a few simple intervals, and have a beautiful effect in the echoes of the mountains. Rossini introduced *ranz-des-vaches* into *William Tell.*

RAOUL. *See* KERMADEC.

RAPALLO. A seaport and health-resort of Italy, in the province of Genoa, at the head of the Gulf of Rapallo; served by railway from Genoa (16 miles). Near by there is a church of pilgrimage. Tunny-fishing and lace- and oil-making are among the industries. Pop. 14,000.

RAPALLO, TREATY OF. A treaty signed by Italy and the triune kingdom of Yugoslavia on 12th Nov., 1920, and ratified by both nations in 1921, dealing with the status of the City of Fiume and the delimitation of the Italo-Yugoslav frontier. It consists of thirteen clauses, by which Fiume is given the status of an independent state with territorial contiguity to Italy. Sushak, the Croat suburb of Fiume, was attached to Yugoslavia, but retained the right to join its port if it so desired.

In Dalmatia, Zara, with a hinterland circumscribed by a boundary of 6 miles' radius, was apportioned to Italy, together with Volosca and Abbazzia, in the Gulf of Fiume, and also the Fiume-San Pietro Railway, in order to maintain Italian territorial contiguity with Fiume. Yugoslavia received part of the Longatico Basin and part of the Castua region, and maintained her claim to all the Adriatic islands, excepting Lussin, Lagosta, and Cherso, which were annexed to Italy. By a further agreement Italy guaranteed provision for the educational needs of 500,000 Yugoslavs embraced within her new frontiers as contained within the treaty.

RAPA NUI. *See* EASTER ISLAND.

RAPE. The carnal knowledge of a woman forcibly and against her will. By the English law this crime is felony, and is punishable with a maximum penalty of penal servitude for life. By 24 and 25 Vict. (1861) cap. c. unlawfully and carnally knowing any girl under the age of ten years, with or without her consent, was regarded as rape, and punishable as such; if the girl were between the ages of ten and twelve, the punishment was penal servitude for three years, or imprisonment not exceeding two years with or without hard labour. But by the Criminal Law Amendment Act of 1885 as amended by the Penal Servitude Act, 1926, the maximum penalty of penal servitude for life has been extended to the deflement of girls under thirteen; and the maximum penalty of seven years' penal servitude has been extended to the deflement of girls under sixteen years. In the case of older females consent must be withheld or there is no rape. In the United States the crime is treated as a felony, and the punishment is imprisonment for life or a term of years. —Cf. W. O. Russell, *A Treatise on Crimes and Misdemeanours.*

RAPE. A division of the county of Sussex, an intermediate division between a hundred and a shire, and containing three or four hundreds. The like parts in other counties are called tithings, lathes, or wapentakes. The rapes are mentioned in *Domesday Book.*

RAPE (*Brassica Napus*). A plant of the cabbage family cultivated in Europe and India for its seeds, from which oil is extracted by grinding and pressure. It is also cultivated in England for the succulent food which its thick and fleshy stems and leaves supply to sheep when other fodder is scarce. The oil obtained from the seed, which is much the same as colza-oil, is used for various economical purposes, for burning in lamps, for lubricating machinery, in medicine, etc. The oil-cake is used as food for sheep and cattle, and as a fertiliser. Rape-cake contains about 9 per cent of oil.

RAPHAEL. One of the archangels. He is represented in the Book of Tobit as appearing in human form to act as the guide and guardian of Tobias.

RAPH'AEL (or **RAFFAELLO**) **SANZIO** or **SANTI.** Italian painter, born at Urbino 1483, died at Rome 1520. His father, Giovanni Santi, a painter of some merit, who was his first teacher, died in 1494, and he was then entrusted to the care of an uncle. Here he came under the influence of Timoteo Viti, a pupil of Francia, until at the age of sixteen he was received into the studio of Perugino at Perugia. Here also he came into touch with Pinturicchio, a fellow-pupil; but he took no share, as was once thought, in that painter's decoration of the Cathedral Library at Siena. His work at this period is hardly distinguishable from that of Perugino, who is the dominant influence in his first important work, *The Marriage of the Virgin* (1504).

In 1504 he visited his native town, and thence proceeded to Florence; and in this centre of the most vigorous artistic life of the time he saw and studied the work of Masaccio, Leonardo da Vinci, Michelangelo, and Fra Bartolommeo, and under their influence added to an Umbrian feeling for space and simplicity of contour a Florentine grasp of form, dramatic power, and sense of design. In Florence he began the long series of Madonnas, which includes some of his most famous works, among them the *Madonna del Gran Duca*; the *Madonna of S. Antonio*; the *Ansidei Madonna* (National Gallery), which shows an architectural quality in construction hitherto unapproached in his work; and the *Madonna del Cardellino*. The most ambitious work of these years, however, was an *Entombment* (Borghese Gallery), which, despite weaknesses in design, shows how far Raphael had passed beyond Perugino in power to express form and movement.

In 1508 Pope Julius II. invited Raphael to assist in the decoration of the Vatican. Here, on the walls of the *Stanza della Segnatura*, next to the great hall of Constantine, he executed *The Disputa*, or *Dispute of the Fathers of the Church*, and *The School of Athens*, both of which show the transition to his third manner, in which form, space, and movement are more fully expressed then before, and fused into extraordinarily well-balanced and harmonious designs.

In the same room he painted the allegorical figures of *Theology*, *Philosophy*, *Justice*, and *Poetry* in the corners of the ceiling; and on the remaining walls the *Emperor Justinian delivering the Roman Law to Tribonian*, *Gregory X. giving the Decretals to an Advocate*, and *Apollo and the Muses*, surrounded by the poets of classic Greece and Rome. In the *Stanza d'Eliodoro* Raphael painted *The Expulsion of Heliodorus from the Temple* and *The Mass of Bolsena*; and after the succession of the new Pope, Leo X., *Leo the Great stopping the Progress of Attila*, *The Deliverance of Peter from Prison*; and, on the ceiling, *Moses viewing the Burning Bush*, *The Building of the Ark*, *The Sacrifice of Isaac*, and *Jacob's Dream.* With *The Conflagration of the Borgo* (*Incendio del Borgo*) *extinguished by the Prayers of Leo*, Raphael began the third *stanza* of the Vatican; and this was followed by *The Coronation of Charlemagne*, *Leo III's Vindication of Himself before Charlemagne*, and *The Victory of Leo IV. over the Saracens at Ostia.*

In all these works, however, signs of an inferior hand can be seen. During this time Raphael carried out decorations for several palaces in Rome and elsewhere, notable among which were the series in the Villa Farnesina, commissioned by the banker Agostino Chigi, to illustrate the story of Cupid and Psyche; finished the *Madonna* for the church of St. Sixtus in Piacenza (now in Dresden); painted many portraits, including those of Julius II., Leo X., Beatrice of Ferrara, the Fornarina, and of Count Castiglione; and painted some of his best-known easel pieces, such as the *Madonna della Seggiola* and the *St. Cecilia.* It was probably at a later period that Raphael prepared for Leo X. the celebrated cartoons for the tapestry of one of the chambers of the Vatican, seven of which are now in the Victoria and Albert Museum, South Kensington.

Raphael's last and unfinished painting — *The Transfiguration of Christ*—is in the Vatican. Attacked by a violent fever, which was increased by improper treatment, he died at the age of thirty-seven years, and was buried with great pomp in the Pantheon. His tomb is indicated by his bust, executed by Naldini, and placed there by Carlo Maratti.—

BIBLIOGRAPHY: Edgcumbe Staley, *Raphael*; J. C. Ady, *Raphael*; J. C. Robinson, *Critical Account of the Drawings of M. Angelo and Raphael*; J. Cartwright, *Raphael in Rome*; G. Vasari, *Lives of the Italian Artists*; F. T. Kugler, *Schools of Painting in Italy*; H. Strachey, *Raphael*; E. Müntz, *Les Historiens et les critiques de Raphael.*

RA'PHIA. A genus of palms, rather low trees with immense leaves, inhabiting swampy coasts. *R. vinifĕra*, a native of Western Africa, Madagascar, Polynesia, etc., besides yielding palm-wine, supplies materials for the roofs and other parts of houses, for basket and other work, etc. The *R. tœdigĕra*, or Jupati palm of South America, and the *R. Ruffia* of Madagascar are equally useful. The fibre of these palms is known in Europe as *raphia* or *raffia*, and is used for matting, for tying up plants, etc.

RAPH'IDES. A term applied to the tiny needle-shaped crystals of calcium oxalate, aggregated in faggot-like bundles, which are often found in plant cells. They are supposed to protect the plant against the attacks of snails and browsing animals; the unpleasant burning sensation produced in the tongue and palate, if a small piece of the leaf of wild arum (*Arum maculatum*) be chewed, is evidence of their efficacy at any rate in one instance.

RAPIER. Slender, highly-tempered, sharp-pointed, edgeless weapon about 3 ft. long, used solely for thrusting. Superseding the two-edged pointed sword used in 16th-17th century duelling, which on occasion served also for cutting, it was long indispensable for gentlemen's wear. It survives ceremonially in court dress, and with the foil is the main modern fencing weapon.

RAPPAHAN'NOCK. A river of the United States, in Virginia, which rises in the Blue Ridge, and flows into Chesapeake Bay after a course of 250 miles. It is navigable to Fredericksburg, about 100 miles from the sea.

RAP'POLTSWEILER (-vī-lėr). A town of Alsace-Lorraine, at the foot of the Vosges Mountains. Pop. 6000.

RAPTO'RES. An old-fashioned name for the birds of prey, including forms which live on other birds and animals, and are characterised by a strong, curved, sharp-edged, and sharp-pointed beak, and robust short legs, with three toes before and one behind, armed with long, strong, and crooked talons. They comprise (1) diurnal birds of prey—eagles, falcons, hawks, etc.—making up the ord. Falconiformes, and (2) nocturnal birds of prey—owls—constituting the sub-ord. Striges of the woodpecker order (Coraciiformes). *See* ORNITHOLOGY.

RAROTON'GA, or **RARATONGA.** The largest of the Cook (Hervey) Islands, South Pacific. It is 20 miles in circuit, and has a population of (1926) 3936, 160 being white. There is a wireless station.

RASH. An eruption of the skin, found in various infectious diseases, in some skin affections, and in septic poisoning. Rashes are also produced by the action of certain drugs—drug rash; and by food-stuffs—urticaria or nettle-rash; and by the irritation of certain plants and animals.

RASHI. Properly **RABBI SALOMON-BEN ISAAK.** A great Jewish rabbi, born at Troyes, France, in 1040; died 1105. His first instructor in Talmudic literature was his father, who was chief rabbi at Worms. To perfect his knowledge he made extensive journeys through Italy, Greece, Palestine, Egypt, Persia, and Germany, where he made a point of visiting the towns which possessed learned Jewish schools. His most famous work is a *Commentary on the Pentateuch*; he also wrote commentaries on the *Prophets*, the *Talmud*, and various treatises on miscellaneous subjects.

RASKOLNIKS (Russ. *Raskolniki*, from *raskol*, schism). The collective name given to the adherents of dissenting sects in Russia, which originated by secession from the quondam State Church. The great majority of these sects date originally from the middle of the seventeenth century, when the liturgical books were revised under the patriarch Nikon. The Raskolniks clung fanatically to the old and corrupted texts, and, regarding the Tsar and the patriarch as the representatives of Antichrist, called themselves *Staroobryadtsy* (old ritualists) or *Starovertsy* (followers of the old faith).

RASO'RES, or **SCRATCHERS.** A group of birds, formerly recognised as including tinamous, pigeons, and the modern ord. Galliformes, or game-birds, which comprises fowls, pheasants, grouse, partridges, turkeys, etc. These are characterised by the toes terminating in strong claws, for scratching up seeds, etc., and by the upper mandible being vaulted, with the nostrils pierced in a membranous space at its base, and covered by a cartilaginous scale. They are polygamous, and the young can run about and feed immediately after being hatched. *See* ORNITHOLOGY.

RASPBERRY. The fruit of the well-known shrubby plant *Rubus Idœus*, nat. ord. Rosaceæ, and the plant itself, which is of the same genus as the bramble or blackberry, dewberry, and cloudberry. It is a native of Britain and most of Europe as well as Asia. Species are also found in America. Several varieties are cultivated, either red, flesh-coloured, or yellow. Raspberries are much used in cookery and confectionery, and the juice, mixed with a certain portion of sugar and brandy, constitutes the liquor called *raspberry brandy*. *Raspberry vinegar*, a refreshing summer beverage and cooling drink for invalids, is composed of raspberry juice, vinegar, and sugar.

RASPE, Rudolf Eric. Author of *Baron Münchhausen's Narrative*, and adventurer, born in Hanover in 1737; died at Muckross in 1794. He studied at Göttingen and Leipzig, and became professor at Cassel, and keeper of the landgrave of Hesse's collection of gems and medals. He provided an illustration of Juvenal's "Quis custodiet ipsos custodes," and stole some of the antique coins from the landgrave's collection. He was arrested, but managed to escape to England, and spent the remaining nineteen years of his life in the British Isles. He professed to be a mining expert, and spent several years in Cornwall.

In 1791 he pretended to have discovered vast mineral wealth in Caithness, and swindled Sir John Sinclair of Ulbster out of large sums of money. The incident was made use of by Sir Walter Scott in *The Antiquary*. Raspe continued his career in Ireland until he died of scarlet fever. The original edition of *Baron Münchhausen's Narrative of his Marvellous Travels and Campaigns in Russia* appeared in 1785; it contained only chapters ii. to vi. of the current version, the other fifteen chapters being added by booksellers' hacks, and a sequel being added in 1793 as a parody of James Bruce's *Travels to discover the Source of the Nile*. Gottfried August Bürger (q.v.) translated the *Narrative* into German, and was for long considered to be the author.

RASPUTIN, Gregory Efimovitch. Russian monk. He was born in 1871 in the province of Tobolsk, Siberia, had no education, and lived until 1904 in his native village. Then he left his family, and practised religious exercises, adopting the attitude that it was necessary to sin in order to obtain forgiveness. He had tremendous strength and personality and, despite his orgies, surrounded himself with an air of mysticism. Soon he appeared at court, and exercised a malign influence on Church and State, until he was invited to supper at the Yussupoff Palace by the Grand Duke Dmitri Pavlovitch and others, and shot dead, 15th Dec., 1916.

RASSE (*Viverricula malaccensis*). A carnivorous mammal, closely allied to the civet, spread over a great extent of Asia, including Java, various parts of India, Singapore, Nepâl, and other localities. Its perfume, which is secreted in a double pouch like that of the civet, is much valued by the Javanese. For its sake the animal is often kept in captivity. It is savage and irritable, and can inflict a very severe bite.

RASTATT, or RASTADT. A town of Baden on the River Murg, a fortress till 1892. It contains the old castle of the Margraves of Baden. Lace and tobacco are manufactured. The Peace of Rastadt between France and the Emperor was concluded there in 1714. Pop. (1925), 14,003.

RAT. One of the rodent mammals, forming a typical example of the family Muridæ or mice. The best-known species are the (so-called) Norway or brown rat (*Mus decumānus*), and the true English or black rat (*Mus rattus*). The brown rat grows to about 9 inches in length, has a shorter tail than the other, small ears, is of a brownish colour above and white below, and is altogether a much larger and stronger animal. Supposed to have belonged originally to India and China, it only became known in Europe about the middle of the eighteenth century; but it is now found in almost every part of the habitable globe, and where it has found a footing the black rat has disappeared.

It is a voracious omnivorous animal, swims readily in water, breeds four or five times in the year, each brood numbering about a dozen, and these again breed in about six months. The black rat is usually about 7 inches in length, has a sharper head than the other, larger ears, and a much longer tail. It is much less numerous than the brown rat and more timid. To this *Mus rattus* variety belongs the white rat, which is sometimes kept as a household pet. Various other animals are called rats. *See* KANGAROO-RAT; MOLE-RAT; MUSK-RAT; VOLE.

RATAFIA. Flavouring essence. It is made with essential oil of almonds.

RAT'ANY (*Krameria triandra*). A shrubby plant found in Peru and Bolivia, having an excessively astringent root. It is sometimes used as an astringent medicine in checking bloody or mucous discharges, weakness of the digestive organs, and even in putrid fevers. It has silver-grey foliage and pretty red starlike flowers. Written also *Rhatany*.

RATCHET AND PAWL. A mechanism used to convert a reciprocating motion into a rotary one, or to allow circular motion in one direction only. The device consists of a wheel with teeth, which are in shape like those of a saw, and a small arm or fingerpiece, the pawl, which engages with the wheel teeth. The device is commonly seen in braces used for drilling holes in steel plates, in the feed mechanism of many machine-tools, and in clockwork. Examples of its use in allowing motion in a single direction are also common, such as in the drive of a winch, where the drum is prevented from running back by its means.

RATCLIFF HIGHWAY. Old name for a street in Stepney. It is now called St. George's Street. In the nineteenth century it had a very evil reputation due, in part, to a series of murders which took place there in 1811.

RATEL′, or **HONEY-BADGER.** A carnivorous mammal of the genus Mellivŏra, and of the weasel family, found chiefly in South and West Africa, and in India. The Cape or

Cape Ratel (*Mellivora capensis*)

South African ratel (*M. capensis*) averages about 3 feet in length, including the tail, which measures 8 or 9 inches in length. The fur is thick and coarse, the colour is black on the under parts, on the muzzle and limbs, whilst the tail, upper surface, sides, and neck are of greyish hue. It is celebrated for the destruction it makes among the nests of the wild bee, to the honey of which it is very partial.

RATH. Irish name for a prehistoric hill fort. It was protected by an embankment and sometimes by stakes. There are remains of about 30,000 in the country and the word forms part of many place names.

RATHENOW, or **RATHENAU** (rä′te-nou). A town of Germany in Prussia, in the province of Brandenburg, on the Havel. It has a church of the fourteenth and sixteenth centuries, and manufactures of optical instruments, wooden wares, and machinery. Pop. 27,558.

RATHFARNHAM. District of Dublin, Irish Free State. It is on the River Dodder, 4 miles to the south of the city proper. Here is a castle, at one time a seat of the Loftus family.

RATHLIN, or **RAGHERY.** An island of Ireland, belonging to the county of Antrim, 5 miles north of Ballycastle. It was the site of a monastery founded by St. Columba in the sixth century, and there are the remains of a castle in which Robert Bruce took refuge when exiled from Scotland in 1306. It is about 6½ miles long by 1½ miles broad. Pop. about 300.

RAT′IBOR. A town of Germany, in the Prussian province of Silesia, on the Oder. Machinery and other iron goods, sugar, paper, glass, and tobacco are made. Ratibor was the capital of one of the small states of Germany in the Dark Ages, but passed to Prussia in 1745, and was formed into a duchy for the landgrave of Hesse-Rothenburg in 1821. Pop. 51,344.

RATING. In the British Navy the class to which any member of the crew belongs. It is also used for the tonnage class of a racing yacht.

RATING, LAW OF. A rate has been defined as "a sum of money levied by public authority for local purposes." The earliest rate levied was for the relief of the poor under the Poor Relief Act, 1601 (*see* POOR AND POOR LAWS). This list was amended in 1874 by making all mines rateable, substituting for "saleable underwoods" land used for a plantation or wood, and adding, "sporting rights severed from the occupation of the land."

This remained for many years the only rate. At the beginning of the nineteenth century most of the roads were in private hands; there was no county or borough police, and no public education. Then came the Municipal Reform Act of 1835, which was followed throughout the century by many enactments establishing the numerous local and municipal enterprises now existing. To pay for the upkeep of these, separate rates were levied and the procedure tended to become chaotic. So far as what is now the County and City of London was concerned, a measure of consolidation was obtained by the Valuation (Metropolis) Act, 1869.

This act has substituted for the parishes the metropolitan boroughs and the city as rating areas;

appointed the borough councils and common council of the City of London overseers of their respective areas; provided that they shall levy all rates as one "general rate;" and enacted that the valuation list shall be conclusive evidence of the value of the property assessed, thereby abolishing the right of appeal against rates, but giving in its place a right of appeal against the list, in the first place to the assessment committee, then either to special sessions, or direct to quarter sessions, with the further right of requesting the court to "state a case" for the opinion of the High Court. A valuation list is in force for five years in each of the first four of which a supplemental list is prepared showing any alterations in the value of the property. Also a provisional list may be made from time to time in the course of a year.

The rating law of the rest of England was gradually brought into line with that of the Metropolis, and has been finally consolidated by The Rating and Valuation Act, 1925, and its amending Acts. This Act divides the country into urban and rural rating areas. The former comprise county boroughs, boroughs, and urban districts; the latter, rural districts. The rating authority for an urban area is the council of the county borough, borough, or urban district; and for a rural area the rural district council assisted by two persons from every parish council or meeting within the area. In addition to the "general rate" (already referred to) rural areas may levy a "special rate" for such purposes as the lighting of highways. If a person wrongfully refuses to pay his rates the clerk to the rating authority may obtain from the magistrates in petty sessions a "distress warrant" authorising the seizure of the property of the person in default. If the property is insufficient to satisfy the debt, he may be committed to prison on a magistrate's warrant for a term not exceeding three months, unless he can show that his default was due to circumstances beyond his control.

A person claiming that a distraint is illegal may appeal to Quarter Sessions, or request the magistrates to state a case for the opinion of the High Court, or regain the property distrained on giving security to bring an action (called an action of "replevin") to have the lawfulness of the distraint decided.

The manner in which property is valued for rating purposes is to calculate its annual value as if it were let to the tenant (whether there is one or not) on the terms that he shall be liable for rates and taxes. In ascertaining the rateable value of mills, factories, mines, quarries, brick-fields, and sporting rights, the "hypothetical tenant" is also assumed to be liable for repairs and insurance. Finally railways, docks, canals, gas and waterworks, electricity and other public utility undertakings and markets are valued by deducting from the receipts of the property in the rating area the expenses incurred in that area in working the undertaking.

Some property is altogether exempted from rates: namely, (1) property occupied by the Crown or the servants of the Crown for the purpose of the Crown; (2) ambassadors' houses; (3) places of public worship; (4) premises occupied by literary, scientific or artistic societies; (5) light-houses occupied by the Board of Trade or Trinity House. In connection with comprehensive measures of Local Government reform since 1st October, 1929, certain other property will be wholly or partially derated.

It should be noted that the so-called "water-rate" is not a "rate": it has been statutorily defined (by the Waterworks Clauses Act, 1847) as "any rent, reward or payment to be made to the undertakers for a supply of water."—Cf. E. M. Konstam, *The Modern Law of Rating.*

RATIONALISATION. Industrial term that came into use after the Great War. It describes the process of making productive industries more efficient by eliminating waste, and still more by organising them into larger units for the purpose of meeting competition. A good deal was done in this direction, notably in the iron and steel and associated industries, among shipbuilders.

RATIONALISM. In philosophy, the theory which conceives reason either as the sole or as the principal source of human knowledge. Reason is to be distinguished from sense-perception, and is superior to it. Fundamental principles and conceptions are derived not from experience but from the mind by which these principles are discerned, according to some philosophers, or in which they are *innate* or a priori, according to others. Rationalism in philosophy has been developed by Descartes, Spinoza, Leibnitz, and Wolff. It is thus opposed to *empiricism* (q.v.). Kant, on the other hand, endeavoured to combine rationalism with empiricism, and maintained that the necessary concepts, although existing independent of experience, are valid only when used in reference to experience. Rationalism, in theology, is the doctrine which affirms the prerogative and right of reason to decide on all matters of faith and morals whatever so-called "authority" may have to say on the matter. Rationalism has had perhaps its chief centre and widest success in Germany. In its extreme form and results, as deism and naturalism, its first English examples were Lord Herbert of Cherbury, Hobbes, and Blount (*Oracles of Reason*); while in its milder and less developed form, as a theological method adopted and applied by men still claiming the Christian name, it appeared implicitly, if not expressly and formally, in many of the later writings of the Latitudinarian party of the Church of England.

It was inevitable the questions of the relations of faith and reason, of man's philosophy and God's revelation, the new philosophies which had arisen in the seventeenth century—those of Bacon and Descartes—and which were to follow in the eighteenth century—those of Locke, and Leibnitz, and Kant—should exercise immense influence, and work enormous changes in the direction both of theological rationalism and of anti-Christian disbelief.

The first step taken by the English deists was to attempt to eliminate from the doctrines of Christianity whatever is above the comprehension of human reason; their next step was to discard from Christianity whatever in the way of fact was such as could not be verified by any man's experience, and this led to an attempt to get rid of Christianity altogether. German rationalism was influenced by the writings of Voltaire, the Encyclopédistes, and the sceptical freedom of thought which obtained among the French savants at the court (1740-86) of Frederick the Great.

It may be said to have begun with the translation into German of Tindal's *Christianity as old as the Creation* (1741), the application of a rationalistic method by Professor Wolff of Halle University to the philosophy of Leibnitz (1736-50). and the advent of Frederick the Great. The initial movements of rationalism were followed up by such scholars and theologians as Eberhard, Eichhorn, Paulus, Teller, and Steinbart, and in the nineteenth century by Schleiermacher, De Wette, Fries, and Jacobi.

In 1835 Strauss published his *Leben Jesu* (Life of Jesus). The movement which this originated has taken a tendency which is chiefly associated with scientific materialism.—BIBLIOGRAPHY: J. B. Bury, *A History of Freedom of Thought*; W. E. H. Lecky, *History of the Rise and Influence of Rationalism in Europe*; A. W. Benn, *History of English Rationalism in the Nineteenth Century*.

RATIONING. Apportioning of a share of supplies, usually of food, to each member of an army, navy, or population. In the army and navy this is done through quartermasters and petty officers, and each man has a standard daily ration of food, a part of which may be commuted for a cash allowance to be spent on other food.

During the War, the entire population of Great Britain was rationed, from June, 1917, particularly with regard to fats, sugar, and meat. Each person had a registration card, with detachable coupons, which were checked by the retailer with whom he was registered, who received enough food to supply all his registered customers.

RA'TISBON, or REGENSBURG. A city and riverport of Bavaria, capital of the province of Oberpfalz or Upper Palatinate, standing on the Danube, opposite the junction of the Regen, 1010 feet above the sea. Among buildings are the cathedral of St. Peter, founded in 1275, completed in 1534, restored in 1830-8; the Rathaus (fourteenth century), where the German Diet held its sittings from 1663 to 1806; the Romanesque church of St. Emmeram (eleventh century); St. Ulrich's Church (thirteenth century); the palace of the Princes of Thurn und Taxis (formerly abbey of St. Emmeram); the Philosophical and Theological High School. The suburb Stadtamhof, on the opposite bank of the Danube, is connected with Ratisbon by an old stone bridge. The northern gate of the Roman town was discovered in 1885. The manufactures embrace tobacco, lead and coloured pencils, porcelain and stoneware, machinery, beer, spirits, soap, and candles. The river trade is important.

Ratisbon existed under the Celtic name of *Radasbona* in pre-Roman times, and was a Roman frontier fortress under the name of *Castra Regina*. Subsequently it became the residence of the old Dukes of Bavaria, rose to the rank of an imperial city, and was long the seat of the imperial Diet. It has stood no fewer than seventeen sieges. Pop. (1925), 76,948.

RATI'TÆ. The running birds, including the ostrich, emeu, cassowary, and kiwi; also the moa and other extinct forms.

RATLAM'. A native state, in the Malwa division of Central India, drained by the Mahi River, and served by the Ratlam-Godhra branch of the Bombay, Baroda, & Central India Railway, and by the Ráj-putána-Malwa line. Wheat, maize, cotton, and the poppy (for opium) are raised. Ratlam is the capital. State area, 693 sq. miles; pop. 85,489; pop. (town), 30,133.

RATNA'GIRI. A maritime district and town of India, in the southern division of Bombay Province. The town has a thriving sardine-fishery carried on in January and February of each year. District area, 3989 sq. miles; pop. 1,154,244; pop. (town), 14,520.

RAT-SNAKE. An Indian snake destitute of poison-fangs (*Zamenis mucosus*), domesticated in Ceylon on account of its usefulness in killing rats. It can easily be tamed, but is of vicious disposition.

RATTENS'. The commercial name for the long trailing stems of various species of palm of the genus Calămus, such as *C. Rotang, C. rudentum, C. Scipionum*, forming a considerable article of export from India and the Eastern Archipelago. They are employed for wicker-work, seats of chairs, walking-sticks, thongs, ropes, cables, etc.

RATTLESNAKE. A name of various venomous American snakes of the genus Crotălus, family Crotalidæ, distinguished from the other

Rattlesnake

members of the family by the tail terminating in a series of articulated horny pieces, which the animal vibrates in such a manner as to make a rattling sound, of "warning" nature, which its enemies learn to associate with dangerous properties. The rattlesnake is one of the most deadly of poisonous serpents, but hogs and peccaries kill and eat it, finding protection in the thickness of their hides and the depth of their layers of fat.

A number of species belong to the United States and Mexico. East of the Mississippi the *C. horridus*, or banded rattlesnake, is the best known and most dreaded species. It is naturally a sluggish animal, ready to defend itself, but seldom commencing the attack. It feeds on rats, squirrels, small rabbits, etc., and reaches a length of 5 or 6 feet. Other species are the *C. durissus*, or striped rattlesnake, found from Mexico to Brazil; *C. confluentus*, the prairie rattlesnake; and *C. terrificus*, ranging from Arizona to the Argentine, the only species found in South America.

RAUNDS. Urban district of Northamptonshire. It is 8 miles from Wellingborough on the L.M.S. Railway, and is a centre for the manufacture of boots and shoes. Pop. (1931) 3683.

RAVEL, Maurice. French composer. Born 7th March, 1875, at Ciboure (Pyrenées), he was educated in Paris and studied music at the Conservatoire there under Béroit, Gédalge and Gabriel Fauré. In 1901 he won the 2nd Prix de Rome with his cantata, *Myrrha*. At first he attracted little notice, but his *Schéhérazade*, in 1904, was hailed as a "miracle of musical impressionism." His masterpiece is perhaps the ballet, *Daphnie et Chloë* (1921). He has written much for the voice, the piano, and the orchestra, including opera.

RAVEN. A large bird of the crow family and genus Corvus (*C. corax*). Its plumage is entirely black; it is above 2 feet in length from the tip of the bill to the extremity of the tail, and about 52 inches from tip to tip of the extended wings. It can be taught to imitate human speech, and in a domestic state is remarkable for its destructiveness, thievishness, and love of glittering things. It flies high, and scents carrion, which is its favourite food, at the distance of several miles; it feeds also on fruit, small animals, etc. It is widely spread in the northern parts of both hemispheres.

RAVENA'LA. A fine large palm-like tree of Madagascar, ord. Musaceæ (plantains), with leaves 6 to 8 feet long. It is called *travellers' tree*, because of the refreshing water found in the cup-like sheaths of the leaf-stalks. Its leaves are used for thatch and the leaf-stalks for other purposes. The seeds are edible, and the blue pulpy fibre surrounding them yields an essential oil.

RAVEN'NA. A maritime province of Emilia, North Italy, on the Adriatic. It is well watered, and marshy in the north. Cereals, rice, hemp, oil, and wine are produced.

Area, 715 sq. miles; pop. (1931), 272,500.

RAVENNA. A city of Italy, capital of the province of Ravenna. It stands in a marshy district near the Montone. The cathedral, founded in the fourth century; the ancient baptistery, an octagonal structure; the church of San Vitale, an octagonal building in the pure Byzantine style, consecrated in 547; the basilica of San Giovanni Evangelista, founded in 424, but much altered by restoration; the basilica of San Apollinare Nuovo, erected about 500 by Theodoric as an Arian cathedral; the mausoleum of the Empress Galla Placidia, daughter of Theodosius the Great, dating from the fifth century, with beautiful mosaics; the remains of the palace of Theodoric the Great; the mausoleum of Theodoric, erected by his daughter Amalasuntha; San Apollinaire in Classe, the largest of the town's basilicas, consecrated in 549, restored in 1779; the tomb of Dante, erected in 1482; the town house; and archiepiscopal palace, are among the rich architectural features of the city.

The manufactures are of little importance. Its harbour was in early times large enough to contain the fleets of Augustus, but it gradually silted up. It is now connected with the Adriatic by the Canale Corsini.

Ravenna is an ancient place, and during the decline of Rome, A.D. 402, Honorius made it the seat of the Western Empire. Thereafter it fell into the hands of Odoacer, who in his turn was expelled by Theodoric, under whom it became the capital of the Ostrogoths. It was recaptured by Belisarius, who made the town and its territory an exarchate. This exarchate was terminated by Aistulf, King of the Lombards, who made Ravenna the capital of the Longobardic Kingdom in 752. Pepin, having succeeded in expelling the Lombards, made a present of Ravenna and its exarchate to the Pope, with whom it remained till 1860. Pop. (1931), 78,143.

RAVENSBURG. An old town of Württemberg, Germany, on the Schussen. It has manufactures of paper, silk, flax, and cotton. Ravensburg became a free city in 1276, and passed to Württemberg in 1810. Pop. (1925), 17,012.

RAVENSBURY. A district of Surrey. It is on the River Wandle, in the urban district of Mitcham and adjoins Watermeads, the property of the National Trust. The manor house was long the residence of the Bidder family, and on the estate are the nests of rare birds, as well as a heronry. In the woods are the ruins of the old manor house, once the home of the Throckmorton family. There is a Saxon cemetery in the district.

RAVENSCAR. Watering-place of Yorkshire (W.R.). It is 10 miles to the north of Scarborough on the L.N.E. Railway.

RAVENSCOURT PARK. District of London. It is in the borough of Hammersmith. The park from which it takes its name is now public property, and in it is an eighteenth century house and an old English garden. In 1932 the freemasons erected a hospital in the district.

RAWALPINDI. A division, district, and town of India, in the Punjab. The division comprises the five districts of Rawalpindi, Gujrát, Shahpur, Jhelum, and Attock, and has an area of 21,391 sq. miles; pop. 3,353,000. The district is traversed by the trunk line of the North-Western Railway. Wheat, barley, and native food grains are raised. The district is very healthy for Europeans, while the natives are of exceptionally fine physique. A cold east wind prevails in January and February, the winter is severe, and the hot season lasts from June to August only. Area, 2010 sq. miles; pop. 548,000 (80 per cent Mahommedan). The town is the headquarters of the division and of the district, and stands on the Leh River. It has an important cantonment, workshops of North-Western Railway, gasworks, and a brewery. Pop. 119,284.

RAWDON. Urban district of Yorkshire (W.R.). It is 5 miles from Bradford on the L.M.S. Railway. The chief occupation is the woollen industry. Pop. (1931), 4574.

RAWLINSON, Sir Henry Creswicke. Born in 1810, died in 1895. He entered the Bombay army in 1827; was Political Agent in Afghanistan; Consul at Bagdad in 1844; member of the Indian Council in 1858; minister to Persia, 1859-60; sat in the House of Commons in 1858 and 1865-8; president of the Royal Geographical Society, 1871-2 and 1874-5; again on Indian Council, 1868-95.

He published *Outline of the History of Assyria* (1852); *Notes on the Early History of Babylonia* (1854); a translation of Herodotus with a commentary (in which he collaborated with his brother, Rev. George Rawlinson, and with Sir Gardner Wilkinson); and *Cuneiform Inscriptions of Western Asia*, edited along with E. Norris, G. Smith, and

T. G. Pinches (1861-80). His great work was the decipherment of the Behistun cuneiform inscription (1846).

RAWLINSON, Henry Seymour, first baron. British soldier; born in 1864. He was educated at Eton and Sandhurst, and served in Burmah, the Sudan, and the South African War. During the European War he commanded the Seventh Division in Flanders in 1914; in 1915 he was given command of the Fourth Army, which he led during the Somme offensive of 1916. In 1920 he became commander-in-chief of the army in India. He died in 1925.

RAWMARSH. Urban district of Yorkshire (W.R.). It is on the Don, 2½ miles from Rotherham on the L.M.S. Railway. The main industry is the manufacture of iron and steel goods. Pop. (1931), 18,570.

RAWTENSTALL. A municipal borough of Lancashire, England; served by the L.M.S. Railway. There are cotton, woollen, and slipper manufactories. Pop. (1931), 28,575.

RAY, John. English naturalist, born 1627, died 1705. He was educated at Cambridge, where he subsequently lectured in Greek and mathematics. He was elected F.R.S. in 1667. Among his works are: *Historia Plantarum Generalis, Historia Insectorum,* and *Synopsis Methodica Avium et Piscium.* The Ray Society (founded 1844), devotes itself to the publication of botanical and zoological works, and has issued many valuable treatises.

RAY. A name of many elasmobranch fishes, including the skate and allied forms, recognised by the flattened body and by the extremely broad and fleshy pectoral fins, which seem to be mere continuations of the body. These fishes produce large eggs, which are enclosed in horny capsules quadrilateral in form, with processes at the corners, and known familiarly as "mermaid's purses," etc.

The most typical members of this group are those of the family Raiidæ, including the thornback ray or skate (*Raia clavāta*), so named from the curved spines which arm the back and tail; and the common grey or blue skate (*R. batis*), which possesses an acutely pointed muzzle, the body being somewhat lozenge-shaped, and the colour ashy-grey above. (*See* SKATE.) The starry ray (*R. radiāta*) is so called from having a number of spines on its upper surface rising from rayed or starlike bases. Other families have as their respective types the sting ray (*Trygon pastināca*: *see* STING-RAY); the electric ray (*Torpedo marmorata*: *see* TORPEDO); and the eagle ray (*Myliobatis aquila*). Some of the eagle rays are known as "devil-fishes" (q.v.).

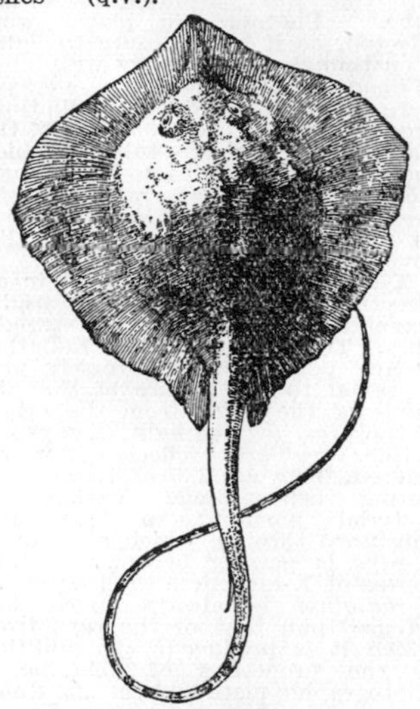

Indian Sting Ray

RAYLEIGH. Village of Essex. It is 8 miles from Southend and 31¾ from London, being served by the L.N.E. Railway. The family of Strutt takes the title of baron from here. Pop. (1931), 6256.

RAYLEIGH, John William Strutt, third baron. Physicist, born 1842, died in 1919. He was educated at Trinity College, Cambridge, where he was senior wrangler and first Smith's prizeman in 1865. In 1873 he succeeded to the title on the death of his father. He was professor of experimental physics at Cambridge from 1879 to 1884, and of natural philosophy at the Royal Institution from 1887 to 1905, and from 1887 to 1896 he was secretary to the Royal Society. He was associated with Sir William Ramsay in the discovery of argon. Besides many scientific papers and articles, he wrote a valuable work on *The Theory of Sound* (2 vols., 1877-8; new edition, 1894-6). He received the Order of Merit in 1902, and the Nobel prize for physics in 1904.

RAYON. *See* SILK, ARTIFICIAL.

RAYS, ELECTRIC (including **X-RAYS).** It was observed by Röntgen, in 1895, that crystals of barium platino-cyanide which were lying on a bench near an exhausted tube glowed brightly when an electric discharge was passed through the tube. Photographic plates were affected, as if by exposure to light, even though protected by wrappings of opaque black paper. These effects were found to be due to radiations proceeding from those portions of the walls of the discharge-tube on which the cathode rays fell (*see* ELECTRON). Röntgen called these radiations *X-rays* ; they are sometimes also known as Röntgen rays after their discoverer.

X-rays. X-rays radiate out in all directions from their point of origin, travelling, like light, in straight lines. The intensity of the radiation at any point is thus inversely proportional to the square of the distance of the point from the origin of the rays. Unlike light, X-rays are neither regularly reflected nor refracted. They are, however, scattered during their passage through any material medium, so that any substance through which a beam of X-rays is passing becomes itself a source of X-radiation. This *scattered X-radiation* is always much less intense than that of the rays from which it is produced. In addition to the properties of affecting a photographic plate and causing fluorescence in certain substances, X-rays discharge a conductor when either positively or negatively charged. This is due to the formation in the surrounding air of charged gaseous ions (*see* IONISATION). This power of discharging an electroscope provides the most sensitive method of detecting and the most accurate method of measuring the intensity of a beam of X-rays.

From a practical point of view the most important property of the rays is that of penetrating many substances which are opaque to ordinary light. No substance is perfectly transparent to the rays, and no substance is absolutely opaque. In all cases there is a gradual absorption of the rays, the amount absorbed increasing with the thickness of material traversed. For homogeneous rays the absorption is exponential; that is to say, if a plate of aluminium 1 centimetre thick cuts down the radiation to one-half, a plate 2 centimetres thick will cut down the radiation to one-quarter, and one 3 centimetres thick to one-eighth. If I_0 is the initial intensity of the beam, and I_d the intensity after passing through a thickness d of material, $I_d = I_0 e^{-\lambda d}$, where e is the base of natural logarithms, and λ is called the *coefficient of absorption* of the rays in the substance.

In general, substances of low density, containing only elements of low atomic weight, are very transparent to the rays, while dense substances, especially if of high atomic weight, are very opaque. Thus paper, wood, water, and flesh are very transparent, so that the rays will readily affect a photographic plate after passing through the thickness of a man's body. A heavy metal, such as lead, is very opaque, a thickness of one-eighth of an inch being sufficient in most cases to stop the rays almost completely. Since X-rays travel in straight lines, they cast shadows in the same way as light. Thus if the hand is held between the source of rays and a fluorescent screen, the shadows of the relatively opaque bones can be seen standing out clearly against the fainter shadow cast by the nearly transparent flesh.

It is this property which gives the rays their immense importance in medical diagnosis. The penetrating power of the rays increases rapidly with the potential difference used to excite the discharge-tube. With the powerful apparatus now employed it is possible to produce X-radiation which will penetrate 2 or 3 inches of steel. The examination of metal castings, etc., for flaws in the metal by means of X-rays is now becoming an important branch of metallurgy.

The suggestion that X-rays were electro-magnetic pulses or waves produced by the sudden stoppage of the rapidly moving charged cathode particles was made, shortly after the discovery of the rays, by Stokes, who also suggested that the absence of regular reflection and refraction was due to the very small wave-length of the radiations. This hypothesis has been recently verified. Laue, in 1912, suggested that the cleavage planes of a crystal might be used as a sort of diffraction grating for X-rays, in which case the wave-length of the radiations could be determined by a method very similar to the determination of the wave-length of light by a diffraction grating. The experiments were carried out by Friedrich and Knipping, and later, by an improved method, by W. H. and W. L. Bragg.

The wave-lengths of the X-rays from a discharge-tube cover a considerable range of values, the average wave-length decreasing as the potential used to excite the discharge is increased. Thus the rays of small wave-length are the most penetrating. The X-rays most commonly excited have wave-lengths between 10^{-8} and 10^{-9} centimetres. Their average wave-length is thus only about one ten-thousandth of that of ordinary light. The various elements possess an X-ray spectrum which is characteristic of the element. The *characteristic radiation* of an element may be excited either by passing through it primary X-radiation of distinctly shorter wave-length than that to be excited, or by bombarding the substance in a vacuum tube with cathode rays of suitable velocity. The X-ray spectra of the elements are simpler than the optical spectra, and consist of two sets of lines, the penetrating or K series, and the absorbable or L series. The study of these lines has thrown much light on the structure of the atom (*see* MATTER; SPECTRA, THEORY OF; X-RAY SPECTRA).

X-rays produce various physiological changes in living tissues, the nature of which is not yet well understood (*see* RADIOLOGY).

The discovery of X-rays led to an exhaustive search to determine whether rays of a similar character could be produced in other ways (*see* RADIO-ACTIVITY). On further investigation it was found that the rays given out by radio-active substances were of three distinct kinds, which were denoted by the non-committal symbols α, β, and γ. All three types share with X-rays, though to very different degrees, the properties of penetrating substances which are opaque to ordinary light, of affecting a photographic emulsion, of lighting up a fluorescent screen, and of producing electrical conductivity in a gas. Only one type, the γ-radiation, is actually of the same nature as X-rays. The differentiation between the three types of radiation was first made by the great difference in their powers of penetration.

The α-rays are completely stopped by a thickness of $\frac{1}{10}$th millimetre of aluminium, or by 10 centimetres (4 inches) of air at atmospheric pressure. The absorption of the β-radiation is a gradual, exponential absorption, so that no very definite limit can be placed to its penetrating power. It is, however, difficult to detect its effects through a thickness of more than 1 millimetre of lead. A small residual effect can, however, be observed through as much as 4 inches of lead or 12 inches of iron. This is due to the γ-rays, which are the most penetrating type of radiation known. Absorption provides only a crude test of the radiation. Some radio-active bodies emit a very absorbable radiation which has been shown to be of the β-ray type, although its penetration is only comparable with that of the α-rays. This is sometimes known as δ-radiation. Some kinds of γ-radiation are not much more penetrating than the most penetrating β-rays.

α-rays. If a fluorescent screen placed near a weak source of radiation is examined with a magnifying-glass, it can be seen that the fluorescence takes the form of numerous scintillations or points of light which suddenly flash out and rapidly die away. The effect is obviously due to the impact of small particles projected from the radio-active substance. These α-particles carry a charge of positive electricity. They are, therefore, deflected by strong magnetic or electric fields, and their velocity can be determined by the method employed for cathode rays (*see* ELECTRON). Their velocity is found to vary from about 9000 to 14,000 miles per second. The smallness of the deflections compared with those produced by similar fields in a beam of cathode rays proves that their mass is much greater than that of an electron.

Rutherford has shown that they consist of atoms of helium. If a glass tube, with walls sufficiently thin to allow the α-rays to pass through them, is sealed into a discharge-tube, and is then filled with radium emanation, α-particles from the emanation collect in the discharge-tube, and after a few hours the characteristic spectrum of helium can be observed in the tube on passing the discharge. The charge on the α-particle is numerically twice that on an electron, so that an α-particle consists of a helium atom which has lost two electrons. Owing to their comparatively large mass and high velocity, the α-rays produce very intense ionisation in any gas through which they pass. A single α-particle will produce as many as 86,000 pairs of ions; in fact, so violent is the impact when an α-particle strikes directly on an atom that the atom may be completely disintegrated by the blow. In this way Rutherford has succeeded in transforming nitrogen, and some other elements, into hydrogen and helium.

A beam of α-rays from a given radio-active element gradually loses velocity in passing through matter, but the number of particles in the beam remains practically constant until a definite thickness of material has been traversed, when all the particles are abruptly stopped. This critical distance is known as the *range* of the particles in the substance, and depends on the initial velocity of the rays. The range of the particles is characteristic of the material from which they are ejected, and may be used to distinguish between different radio-active bodies.

β-rays. The β-radiation consists of a stream of negative electrons (*see* ELECTRON) travelling generally with velocities much greater than those of the cathode rays, and approaching in some instances within 1 or 2 per cent of the velocity of light. If, however, the ratio of the mass to the charge on the β-particles is investigated by measuring the magnetic and electric deflexions of the rays, it is found that the mass of a β-particle increases continuously with increase in velocity, so that the mass of the fastest β-particles is five or six times the mass of an electron in the cathode stream (*see* ELECTRON). Owing to collisions with atoms, a pencil of β-rays is rapidly diffused on passing through matter. After diffusion the absorption of the rays becomes exponential, the coefficient of absorption decreasing as the velocity of the rays is increased. Owing to the smaller energy of the particles, the β-rays produce less ionisation and fluorescence than the α-rays. Their photographic effect is, on the contrary, much greater.

γ-rays. The penetrating or γ-radiations are not deflected in an electric or magnetic field, and, therefore, do not consist of charged particles. The fact that γ-radiation can be produced by allowing a beam of β-rays to impinge on a lead target indicates that the relation of γ-radiation to β-radiation is the same as that of X-rays to cathode rays, that is to say, that they consist of electro-magnetic pulses. As, however, the β-rays travel, in general, much more swiftly than the cathode rays, the pulses produced are of shorter wave-length, and, therefore, more penetrating than the X-rays from an ordinary discharge-tube. This conclusion has been verified by Rutherford, using a modification of the crystal diffraction method, and the wave-lengths of the principal γ-radiations have been found to lie between 10^{-9} and 10^{-10} centimetres, or approximately one-tenth of that of ordinary X-radiation.

With the ever-increasing power and voltages now being used for X-ray production, it will probably not be long before X-radiation will be produced of penetrating power equal to that of the γ-rays from radio-active substances. The origin of the γ-radiation is probably due to the sudden ejection from the radio-active atom of a β-particle, as the sudden starting of a β-particle should produce radiation of the same type as that produced when it is stopped. It may be noted that γ-rays are only emitted by radio-active substances which emit β-radiation, but there is no proportionality between the two effects. If γ-rays are allowed to impinge on a target, β-radiation is produced. A primary beam of γ-rays gives rise to secondary γ-radiation on passing through matter, and is absorbed by matter according to an exponential law. In the case of elements of high atomic weight, *characteristic γ-radiations* may be excited, and these characteristic γ-rays can also be excited by β-rays of suitable velocity. These radiations have now been identified as being merely the K- and L-radiations of the elements from which they are produced.

BIBLIOGRAPHY: G. W. C. Kaye, *X-rays*; Sir W. H. and W. L. Bragg, *X-rays and Crystal Structure*; J. A. Crowther, *Ions, Electrons, and Ionising Radiations*; Sir E. Rutherford, *Radio-active Substances and their Radiations*.

RAZOR. The well-known shaving appliance. It has a blade made of the finest crucible steel. Razors of the old style were flat-sided, and were only kept in satisfactory condition by frequent grinding and honing. The hollow-ground razor was first introduced by German manufacturers, but its property of preserving for a long time a reasonable edge without honing was soon recognised, and the manufacturers in all countries installed suitable grinding plant and devoted themselves to its production. Many stones are used in turn in these grinding operations, the later stages being performed on wheels of small diameter.

Gillette. A successful safety razor was introduced by Gillette, in which a small flat blade with two cutting edges was held to a curved base by a cover provided with a screw connection to the handle. The guard of this razor has the form of a comb. In the new razor of this type the comb-guard has been abandoned, and the blade is held against two sharp ridges on the base, each about one-eighth of an inch from the edge. The blade, although held firmly, is quite flexible, and capable of easy adjustment to suit the different degrees of closeness of cutting. The old implement has not entirely lost favour, and where skill has been acquired in stropping gives at least as good results as any of the safety razors.

RAZORBILL. A sea-bird of the auk family, (*Alca torda*) inhabiting arctic and northern regions. Resident in Britain, 17 inches long, it has a glossy blackish plumage which is white underneath. The massive deeply-furrowed bill, flattened laterally, has a hooked tip. The brown-blotched whitish egg, laid on a rocky cliff on both Atlantic coasts, including that of Great Britain, is a delicacy.

RAZOR-FISH. The *Coryphæna novacula* of the Mediterranean, a species of fish with a compressed body, much prized for the table. See also next article.

RAZOR-SHELL, or **RAZOR-FISH** (Solen). A genus of bivalve mollusca, forming the type of the family Solenidæ. The razor-shells are common on British sea-coasts; the shells are somewhat cylindrical in shape and gaping at either end. The animals possess a powerful muscular "foot," used for burrowing swiftly into the sandy coasts which they inhabit. The familiar species are the *Solen siliqua* and *S. ensis*, both of them eaten and also used for bait.

RÉ (rā), **ILE DE.** An island of France, in the Bay of Biscay, about 2 miles off the coast of the department of Charente-Inférieure, to which it belongs, 6 miles west of La Rochelle; greatest length, 18 miles; breadth, nearly 4 miles; area, 33 sq. miles. Oyster-culture, salt-making, and vine-growing are the chief industries. The chief places are St. Martin and Arsen-Ré. A light railway traverses the island from west to east. There are four forts, and dikes for the prevention of inundations by the sea.

READE (rēd), **Charles.** Novelist, born in 1814, and died in 1884. He was educated at Magdalen College, Oxford, where he took the B.A. degree, and was called to the Bar in 1843. In 1851 he began writing for the stage, and gained great success with his comedy *Masks and Faces* (1852), written in collaboration with Tom Taylor. He transformed it into a novel, *Peg Woffington*, in 1853. This was followed by *Christie Johnstone*, and *It's Never Too Late to Mend*, one of his "novels with a purpose," in which he attacked the English prison system. The most scholarly and artistic of his writings, *The Cloister and the Hearth*, dealing with the lives of the parents of Erasmus, appeared in 1861, and among the more important of his other works are: *The Course of True Love never did run Smooth, Love Me Little Love Me Long, White Lies, Hard Cash, Griffith Gaunt, Foul Play, Put Yourself in His Place,* and *A Terrible Temptation.* He is also the author, either alone or in collaboration with others, of the following dramas: *Gold, Two Loves and a Life, The Lyons Mail, The King's Rival,* and *Drink* (based on Zola's *L'Assommoir*).

READER. Specifically, one whose office it is to read prayers, lessons, lectures, and the like to others; as, (*a*) in the Roman Catholic Church, one of the five inferior orders of the priesthood; (*b*) in the English Church a layman appointed to read the lessons in churches with the consent of the incumbent; (*c*) a kind of lecturer or professor in universities, etc.; (*d*) in printing-offices, a person who reads and corrects proofs.

READING (red'ing). A municipal borough, the county town of Berkshire, England, on the Kennet; served by the Great Western, L.N.E., and Southern Railways, and by the Kennet and Avon Canal.[1] Reading is a typical English county town, and a great agricultural centre. It has a university constituted in 1925 (Royal charter granted 1926), founded as a university college in 1892. There are also a celebrated biscuit-factory and large engineering works. Reading is an important railway junction. There are remains of a Benedictine abbey founded (1121) by Henry I., who was buried within its precincts. Pop. (1931), 97,153.

READING. A city of Pennsylvania, United States, the county seat of Berks county, on the Schuylkill; served by the Pennsylvania Railway, by local electric-traction lines, and by the Schuylkill Canal to Philadelphia. There are shops of the Philadelphia & Reading Railway, and large iron- and steel-foundries. Reading is situated near anthracite coal-fields and iron-mines. Tobacco, hats, hardware, and hosiery are among other manufactures. Reading was laid out in 1748, and became a city in 1847. Pop. (1930), 111,171.

READING, Marquess of. English statesman. Rufus Daniel Isaacs was born in London, 10th Oct., 1860, and educated at University College School and abroad, studied law, and became

[1] The Kennet and Avon Canal starts from the Port of Bristol and runs via Bath (for the Somersetshire Coal Canal), Bradford-on-Avon, Semington (for the Wilts and Berks Canal), Devizes, Burbage, Hungerford, and Newbury to Reading, where it joins the Thames for Henley, Marlow Maidenhead, Windsor, Staines, and London. From Bristol to Bath is 15 miles; from Bath to Newbury, 57 miles; from Newbury to Reading, 18½ miles; and from Reading to London, 74 miles.

a Bencher of the Middle Temple. Entering Parliament, he represented Reading as a Liberal from 1904 to 1913, was Solicitor-General in 1910, Attorney-General, 1910-13, and Lord Chief Justice of England, 1913-21. He was Special Envoy to the United States in 1917, High Commissioner and Special Ambassador to the United States in 1918, and from 1921 to 1926 was Viceroy of India. He was knighted in 1910, created a baron in 1914, viscount in 1916, earl in 1917, and marquess in 1926. His eldest son is called Viscount Erleigh.

REA'GENT. In chemical analysis, a substance employed as a test to determine the presence of another substance. Thus, iron in solution is detected by the addition of several reagents, the most delicate being ammonium thiocyanate. This reagent gives a bright-red coloration with even minute quantities of iron in solution. Potassium ferrocyanide is also used for the detection of iron; with ferric salts it gives a deep-blue precipitate. Chemical analysis is based on the use of chemical reagents.

REAL. In law, pertaining to things fixed, permanent, or immovable. Thus *real estate* is landed property, including all estates and interest in lands which are held for life or for some greater estate, and whether such lands be of freehold or copyhold tenure. So a *real action* is an action brought for the specific recovery of lands, tenements, and hereditaments.

REAL'GAR, or RUBY-SULPHUR, As_2S_2, one of the ores of arsenic found native in Hungary, Saxony, Switzerland, and China. It is used as an orange-red pigment.

REALISM. In metaphysics, as opposed to *idealism*, the doctrine that there is an immediate or intuitive cognition of external objects, and that external objects exist independently of our sensations or conceptions. As opposed to *nominalism*, it is the doctrine that asserts that general terms like *man, tree*, etc., are not mere abstractions, but have real existences corresponding to them. In the Middle Ages there was a great controversy between the realists and the nominalists, the chief controversy which divided the schoolmen into rival parties. The realists maintained that things and not words are the objects of dialectics. Under the denomination of realists were comprehended the Scotists and Thomists, and all other sects of schoolmen, except the followers of Occam and Abelard, who were nominalists. *See* IDEALISM: NOMINALISM.

REAL PRESENCE. Eucharistic doctrine. It is the belief, held by the Roman and Greek Churches and by High Church Anglicans, that the bread and wine of the Eucharist contain, after their consecration, the body and blood of Jesus Christ. This belief rests upon a literal interpretation of the words of institution, "This is my body," and "This is my blood," and of the sixth chapter of S. John's Gospel. Some of those who hold this doctrine, notably Roman Catholics, believe that the sacred elements may be worshipped, but the Greek Orthodox Church does not so believe. *See* RESERVATION.

REAL PROPERTY. Term used in English law for land and houses. It is distinguished from personal property, which covers all other forms of property, including leaseholds. Before 1925 real property and personal property, in the case of a person dying intestate, descended in different ways, but this is no longer so. The two kinds of property are, however, valued separately on the occasion of death, and certain legal differences between them persist.

REAPING-HOOK, or SICKLE. A curved metal blade with a smooth or serrated cutting edge on the inner side of the crescent, and set in a short wooden handle, used for cutting down corn, grass, etc. It is about 18 inches in length, and tapers from a breadth of about 2 inches at the handle down to a more or less sharp point. In early times the sickle was in general use, but is now replaced by the reaping-machine.

REAPING-MACHINE, or REAPER. A machine for cutting down standing corn, etc., usually worked by a pair of horses, the cutting machinery being driven by being connected with the wheels on which the machine is drawn over the field. The cutting is effected rather in the manner of a pair of scissors than in that of a scythe, and a series of small toothed wheels have to be connected with the main wheel or wheels so as to produce the fast motion necessary for driving the cutting knives. These knives generally consist of triangular pieces of steel riveted to an iron bar, and are sometimes smooth-edged and sometimes tooth-edged. The knife-bar projects horizontally from the side of the machine at a short distance above the ground, and moves backwards and forwards on guides fixed at the back of a number of pointed fingers, which enter the standing grain and guide the straw to the edges of the knives. The motion of the bar being very rapid, the grain is cut down with corresponding speed, and as it is cut it is received on a platform fixed behind the knife-bar, the operator throwing it backwards by means of a rake. The sheaves are tied by hand.

Self-binder. A sort of revolving rake or reel, with four or five arms set in motion by the driving-wheel, brings corn well on to the knife-bar, and when cut it is delivered at the back of the machine to a binding apparatus. An endless apron receives the grain as it is cut, and deposits it in sheaves in a suitable receptacle, where by ingenious mechanical arrangements the sheaf is caught and compressed by iron arms; twine from a reel is passed round it, fastened by knotting, cut away, and the bound sheaf is tossed out. The sheaves may also be bound with wire, straw, rope, etc. Reaping and thrashing machinery are often combined in America. Some machines cut off merely the ears from the standing corn, leaving the straw. *See* AGRICULTURE; TRACTOR.

REASON (Lat. *ratio*). A term used in mental philosophy to denote a faculty of the mind which enables man to deduce conclusions from facts or from propositions, and especially to draw *valid* inferences from true premises. It distinguishes the true from the false, right from wrong, and enables man to choose the proper means for the attainment of particular ends. Hume restricted the function of reason, withdrawing from its domain the discernment of right and wrong, whilst Locke wrote that "reason is conversant with certainty alone, while the discovery of that which, as probable, enforces a contingent assent or opinion is ascribed to an especial faculty, called the judgment."

Man has been called a *rational animal*, and reason is the highest faculty of the human mind, distinguishing man from the animals. The latter, it must be admitted, frequently direct their actions intelligently to desired ends, but they do not possess man's power to think in general terms. It is by means of reason that man is able to contemplate things spiritual as well as material, to weigh all that can be said or thought for and against them, and hence to draw conclusions and to act accordingly. Reason is thus synonymous with *intellect* and is opposed to *instinct*.

It is to be distinguished from imagination, feeling, and desire, or from the faculty which enables man to learn certain truths intuitively. The terms *reason* and *understanding* have been considered as identical by English philosophers; but Kant set up an antithesis, distinguishing between reason (*Vernunft*) and understanding (*Verstand*). The former rising above experience, is the principle of principles; it speculatively verifies every special principle, or practically determines the proper ends of human action. The latter conceives of sensible objects within experience, which it again compares one with another, or with particular representations of them, or with the objects themselves.—BIBLIOGRAPHY: Thomas Whittaker, article in Hasting's *Encyclopædia of Religion and Ethics*; J. M. Baldwin, *Dictionary of Philosophy and Psychology*.

REBEC. Mediæval stringed instrument played with a bow, of Asiatic origin, and known in ninth century Europe. A broad-based three-stringed Byzantine type, illustrated on ivory caskets and illuminated MSS., had a body like a pear halved lengthwise, pierced with sound holes. A narrow two-stringed boat-shaped type reached Moorish Spain. Violins ultimately superseded both.

REBECCA RIOTS. Disturbances that broke out in South Wales in 1839 and the following years. They were caused by the charges made at the toll gates for the use of the roads, although there were contributory causes. The rioters, dressed as women and calling their leader "Rebecca," went about the country destroying the toll gates; some of them rode horses. Troops were sent against them and the rising was put down. The name was taken from a passage in Genesis xxiv. where Rebecca says, "Let thy seed possess the gate of those which hate them."

REBELLION. The taking up of arms, whether by natural subjects or others, residing in the country, against a settled Government. By international law rebellion is considered a crime, and all persons voluntarily abetting it are criminals whether subjects or foreigners. When a rebellion has attained such dimensions and organisation as to make of the rebel party a state *de facto*, and its acts reach the dimensions of war *de facto*, it is now the custom of the State to yield to the rebels such belligerent privileges as policy and humanity require, and to treat captives as prisoners of war.

RÉCAMIER (rā-kà-mi-ā), **Jeanne Françoise Julie Adélaïde.** Her maiden name was Bernard; born at Lyons 1777, died 1849. At the age of sixteen she went to Paris, and was there married to Jacques Récamier, a rich banker, more than double her own age. From this time her aim was to surround herself with personal admirers, and to attract to her salon the chief personages in French literature and politics. Her husband becoming bankrupt, she went to reside with Madame de Staël in Switzerland, having been banished from Paris in 1811 by Napoleon on account of her intimacy with his enemies. At the downfall of Napoleon she returned to Paris, and again opened her salon, which as before continued to be a resort of men of intellect till her death. She had very intimate relations with Benjamin Constant and Chateaubriand.—Cf. H. N. Williams, *Madame Récamier and Her Friends.*

RECEIPT. A written acknowledgment or account of something received, as money, goods, etc. A receipt of money may be in part or in full payment of a debt, and it operates as an acquittance or discharge of the debt only as far as it goes. In Britain if a receipt for a sum of £2 or upwards does not bear the twopenny Government stamp, it is inadmissible as evidence of payment. The stamp may be either adhesive or impressed on the paper. Formerly there were special adhesive receipt stamps, but the twopenny postage stamp now serves also for receipts.

RECEIVER. In England, a person appointed by the High Court to receive the rents and profits of land, or the produce of other property, which is in dispute; also a person appointed in suits concerning the estates of infants, and other cases. The *receiver-general* is an officer of the Duchy of Lancaster, who receives its revenues, etc. For *official receivers* see BANKRUPT.

RECEIVER OF STOLEN GOODS. One who takes stolen goods from a thief, knowing them to be stolen, and incurs the guilt of partaking in the crime. Receivers of stolen property are liable to penal servitude for from three to fourteen years, or imprisonment for two years with or without hard labour.

RECEIVING ORDER. An order issued by the court in England on presentation of a bankruptcy petition either at the instance of the debtor himself or at the instance of a creditor. It vests the property of the debtor in the Official Receiver for the purposes of protection and management until a further order of the court or an arrangement among the creditors be made. Not only does such an order preclude the debtor from intromitting with his estate, but it also suspends all separate legal proceedings by his creditors. It thus affords time for full investigation of the debtor's affairs and for the avoidance of bankruptcy, if possible, by a composition arrangement.

RECENT FORMATION. In geology, the name given to the later of the two series into which the post-Tertiary formation has been divided, the former or earlier being the post-Pliocene. This "recent" series includes all superficial accumulations, as sand, gravel, silt, marl, peat-moss, coral reefs, etc., from the close of the last ice age down to and comprising those accumulations that are still in process of being formed.

RECEP'TACLE. In botany, a name given to the more of less enlarged and modified apex of the pedicel or peduncle, upon which all the parts of a flower are directly or indirectly borne; also known as the *torus* or *thalamus*. The term is also applied to the common axis of some compressed inflorescences, such as the head, especially in the ord. Compositæ; and sometimes to the axis bearing the frutification in ferns, mosses, Algæ, and Fungi.

RECHABITE. Among the ancient Jews, one of a family or tribe of Kenites whom Jonadab, the son of Rechab, bound to abstain from wine, from building houses, from sowing seed, and from planting vines (cf. Jer. xxxv., 6, 7). In modern application the Rechabites are a benefit society composed of total abstainers from intoxicating drinks, called the Independent Order of Rechabites.

RECIPROC'ITY. In international trade, a special arrangement between two nations by which the citizens of each obtain advantages or privileges in their trading relations with the other. Commercial treaties have been concluded between states since the earliest times. The text is extant of treaties of commerce and navigation between Carthage and Rome in 509 and 348 B.C. The term "reciprocity" first came into use, however, in 1815, when a treaty between Great Britain and the United States was concluded in which the restrictions on shipping were reciprocally relaxed.

About ten years later the same principle was applied to protective tariffs, and some writers began to advocate the policy of basing international trading relations upon reciprocal concessions, so that no nation would admit the goods of another on more favourable terms than the other nation granted to the exports of the first. The treaty that Cobden negotiated with France in 1860 was reciprocal in its general character, but care was taken to avoid the suggestion that the lightening or removal of British duties on imports from France was conditional on the more favourable treatment of our exports to France. After Great Britain had adopted a free trade policy, the advocates of reciprocity began to urge that retaliatory duties should be levied on imports from those countries which taxed our exports. This proposal formed part of the tariff reform policy put forward by the late Joseph Chamberlain.

The "reciprocity treaty" is a favourite instrument of the United States Government. Under such a treaty one nation grants another special reductions of import duties in return for equivalent reductions by the other country. Such concessions are, however, frequently extended to further nations *en bloc* through the instrumentality of "the most favoured nation clause," a general promise, which is often included in commercial treaties, to concede to the state in the treaty all advantages which may be granted to any other state.

RECITAT'IVE, in music, may be regarded as the link between speech and song. In it the subtle variations of pitch which occur in normal speech are replaced by the larger and definitely fixed intervals of the musical scale, while the rhythmic freedom of prose is secured by an absence of the regular time-divisions which are an essential feature of ordinary music. Recitative was first written in the closing years of the sixteenth century, and through all the intervening centuries has preserved some of the musical turns of phrase that appeared in the earliest examples, notably the descent from the key-note to the fifth of the scale, which forms the almost universal close.

Recitative is used in opera and oratorio, where the text calls for a more rapid musical expression than is possible under the conditions of normal composition. In *recitativo secco* the accompaniment consists only of occasional chords placed where necessary to make the phrases harmonically clear. In *recitativo stromentato* a fuller and more musically interesting support is given by the accompanying instruments, which are also, in general, more numerous. In *mezzo recitativo* the accompaniment is musically complete in itself, but does not thereby curtail the freedom of the vocal declamation. A further development of this last style forms the foundation of Wagner's method of composition, particularly in his later operas.

RECLAIMING. In Scots law, the process of appealing from a judgment of the lord-ordinary to the inner house of the Court of Session. A *reclaiming note* is the petition of appeal to the inner house craving the alteration of the judgment reclaimed against.

RECLAMATION. The winning of land from the sea. There are many types of activity which may be considered under this heading, such as the protection of the coasts against erosion, the building of sea-walls to protect lands which would otherwise be covered at high tide, and the raising of the coast-line lands by the use of groynes. Great tracts of land have been reclaimed from the sea in many places on the coasts of Europe. The Romans made successful reclamations in the Fen district, and in the seventeenth and eighteenth centuries the land of Sunk Island, in the Humber, and large areas in the Dee estuary were won from the water-covered banks. At later dates similar endeavours have proved successful on the Seine, the Ribble, and the Tees.

The reclamations by the use of embankments in Holland are perhaps the most extensive of all. Where embankments are made use of for this purpose, the built-up material must not only be capable of withstanding the steady pressures and considerable shocks caused by the sea, but must also be treated in such a way as to be totally impermeable to water. When the substances available at the place of working are of such a character that the building of a water-tight embankment is otherwise impossible, recourse is made to the use of a puddled-clay wall, inserted within the bank to supply the necessary character. Clay is kneaded with water, and is built up as the centre or core of the bank (*see* RESERVOIR). This wall must be carried down to a sound rock or clay foundation, which is commonly only obtained at some depth below the base of the embankment.

The drainage of reclaimed land in Holland is effected with windmill-driven pumps. Breaches have been closed by piling and planking up in the region of the gap, by the insertion of lowering panels in specially constructed frames, and by building an additional bank or wall behind the gap. In extreme cases the sinking of old boats filled with shore material and cement has proved an effective solution.

At the estuary of a river the building of banks forming a channel through which the river is to pass is followed by the accretion of deposits of rich soil on the parts outside the channel. Foreshores at such places are soon built up, and a growth of coarse grass quickly follows.

Groynes consist of erections of timber in the form of screens built out to sea. The wind- and tide-swept material is banked up against the groynes, and the level of the shore is raised.

In places where coast erosion is taking place, the building of sea-walls of heavy stone is a necessity if the lands are to be conserved. These walls are built of a shape which changes from a gradually curved slope at the foot to an almost vertical straight rise at the higher parts, and they are sometimes provided with a top which is curved and projecting towards the sea to cast back the waves that break on the wall. Such erections are common at seaside places. At Blackpool the wall is built up of hexagonal basalt piers. When groynes are not fitted at the base of such sea-walls, the stone-work must be carried to some distance below the shore to ensure that water cannot cut away the material below the wall.

RECOG'NISANCE. In law, an obligation of record which a man enters into before some court of record, or magistrate duly authorised, with particular conditions: as to appear at the assizes or quarter-sessions, to keep the peace, etc.

RECOLLECT FATHERS (or Recollets). Franciscan friars of the Strict Observance. Founded in fifteenth-century Spain, and approved by Pope Clement VII., 1532, they were among South America's earliest Christian missionaries. Gaining renown by preaching, they served as army-chaplains in pre-revolutionary France, and operated in India, Canada, and Jerusalem, where they have the charge of Latin Christendom's holy places.

RECON'NAISSANCE. "Detailed and timely information about the enemy and the theatre of operations is a necessary factor of success in war." These words, from the British *Field Service Regulations*, explain the bed-rock principle on which information is sought in war, and the methods followed to obtain this information are known as reconnaissance; or, again, in the words of the British *Field Service Regulations*, "Reconnaissance is the service of obtaining information with regard to the topography and resources of a country and the movements and dispositions of an enemy."

"Si vis pacem, para bellum," and any Government which takes its duty seriously will prepare for war during peace by collecting information about other nations. Should war at any future time ensue, such a Government will be in possession of much general information about the enemy country and its resources; but more detailed and peculiar information will be required by the commander-in-chief and those entrusted with the conduct of the war. The acquisition of this will entail special long-distance reconnaissance, which will in these modern days be undertaken by the air force, with a view to checking the information already possessed and supplementing it with more accurate and definite information as to preliminary concentrations and probable lines of advance. This is known as strategical reconnaissance, and will be carried out not only at the commencement of a campaign, but also as circumstances require during its continuance.

In connection with the two words "strategical" and "tactical" it may be as well to note the old definitions which have been current for many years, and which, in a general way, are as suitable now as they were at the end of last century. Strategy is the art of moving troops in the theatre of operations; tactics that of moving them in presence of the enemy. Owing to modern developments, strategy and tactics overlap a good deal more than they did formerly, but for the purposes of this article the definitions will serve.

"**Tactical reconnaissance**" will take place, therefore, at closer quarters, when the opposing troops are approaching within striking distance or are even in contact. The information sought under this heading will principally be confined to obtaining early and accurate details as to what the enemy is doing, and topographical information as to the country in the immediate neighbourhood, and to discovering how his troops are disposed. The methods of obtaining such information are varied, and range from the employment of paid intelligence agents under the control of general headquarters through aeroplanes working with the particular formation which requires the information, to special detachments of mounted or dismounted troops working within touch of their respective brigades and divisions.

When a body of troops is sent out on a reconnoitring expedition, the commander must be given detailed instructions as to what points require clearing up; and he must remember that his primary duty is to obtain that information and not to consider that he is invested with a roving commission to do as he pleases. Fighting may be necessary in order to elucidate the situation, but it should be avoided unless the required information cannot be obtained in any other way.

Good examples of fighting in order to obtain information were the trench raids of the European War, which were undertaken partly to worry the enemy by a system of pinpricks, but more particularly to keep in touch with his dispositions by a knowledge of what troops were holding a given part of the line. The trench raid had generally fulfilled its object when it succeeded in bringing back a live prisoner, who could be interrogated by the intelligence branch of the general staff. In the European War, and probably to an increasing extent in the future, reconnaissance both strategical and tactical became, and will continue to be, largely a matter for the air force; but however excellent the machines, the cameras, and the wireless, however efficient and daring the pilots and the observers, there must come a time when subordinate commanders must depend for information gathered for them by the ordinary cavalry or infantry officers and soldiers working and observing on the ground.

Reconnaissance must not be confused with espionage (q.v.), for, though the object of both is to obtain information, the methods employed are totally different. The secret-service agent or spy works, so to speak, underground, and depends for his results on secrecy and disguise, and when caught is liable to be shot out of hand. The airman or soldier or body of troops carrying out a reconnaissance, each and all of them, are performing a recognised act of war, and though, of course, any means may be used to kill or capture them, yet when once captured they become ordinary prisoners of war and must be treated as such.

RECONSTRUCTION. In commercial law, reconstruction occurs when a company registered under the Companies Acts is to be wound up, and its business and assets sold or transferred to another company (which is usually formed for the purpose), the consideration for the sale or transfer being shares or other like interests in the transferee company. This is a scheme frequently resorted to when a company has fallen on evil days and it is thought that it can be saved by the issue of further capital, which the shareholders may be willing to subscribe in the hope of salving their interests. Generally, each shareholder in the transferror company receives shares in the transferee company in proportion to his holding in the former; but whereas the shares of the former company were fully paid up, those of the new company are issued only as partly paid, and each member requires to face an assessment.

Thus a company with a capital of (say) £20,000 in 20,000 fully paid shares of £1 each may sell its undertaking to a new company for (say) 20,000 shares of £1 each 10*s.* paid, and each member will then receive for every share held by him in the transferror company one share of £1 issued as paid up to the extent of 10*s.* in the new company. There is thus a liability of 10*s.* per share on each member, and a fund is available for the business. Provision is made in the Companies Acts for the purchase by the liquidator of the interest of any member of the transferror company who dissents from the proposed reconstruction.

RECONSTRUCTION, MINISTRY OF. A British Government department instituted in 1917 to prepare for the conclusion of the European War, and to carry out the stabilisation of industry and the restoration to normal employment of the fighting forces and munition-workers when peace should actually be signed. In Aug., 1917, the ministry was formally established, with Dr. Addison as the first Minister of Reconstruction. The Ministry of National Service was afterwards merged in the new department, and the whole was known as the Ministry of National Service and Reconstruction. It ceased to exist after Sept., 1920.

REC'ORD. Specifically, an official copy of any writing, or account of any facts and proceedings, whether public or private, entered in a book for preservation. In a popular sense the term *records* is applied to all public documents preserved in a recognised repository. The English records date back to 1100. Scottish records are preserved in the General Register House, Edinburgh, Irish in Dublin, and the English at the Public Record Office in London. The Act of 1838 conferred the guardianship of the English records on the Master of the Rolls, who in 1857 began the publication of the valuable series of chronicles and memorials known as the Rolls Series.

In the legal sense of the term *records* are authentic testimonies in writing, of judicial acts and proceedings, contained in rolls of parchment, and preserved, the courts of which the proceedings are thus preserved being called *courts of record*. In Scots law the record consists of the written statements or pleadings of parties in a litigation, and the "closing of the record" is a formal step, sanctioned by the judge, after each party has put forward all he wishes to say by way of statement and answer.

RECOR'DER. The title of the justice of the peace who presides at the quarter-sessions in a borough. He must be a barrister of five years' standing. He has a limited appellate jurisdiction, and may try most crimes except murder and treason. *See* QUARTER-SESSIONS.

RECORDING INSTRUMENTS. These show not only the value of the reading at the moment, but also, by means of a graph drawn upon scaled paper, how the quantity has varied from time to time. Instruments of most characters have been fitted with the gear necessary to make them of the recording type.

In electrical instruments, such as ammeters and voltmeters, the changes necessary are the provision of a pen-fitting to the end of the needle or pointer and clockwork-operated drums, which are provided with a roll of paper. The pen-fitting consists of a small cylindrical ink-vessel through which the pen proper is passed. The pen has the form of a thin metal wedge with a very small hole through it.

Barograph. The barograph is a form of barometer in which the pressure changes are drawn to scale upon a chart. In this case a single drum is used, and to it the paper is fixed. The paper is divided up by lines for each hour of the day, and by a height scale which gives the value of the pressure.

Instruments have been designed by J. F. Campbell, Sir G. G. Stokes, and others to record the amount of sunshine during a day, a week, or other interval.

Thermographic charts of the conditions in a cold store provide useful information about the working of the plant and the watchfulness of the staff. Records are made of the temperatures in the cold chambers of vessels used for transporting perishable food-stuffs, where the maintenance of low temperatures within prescribed limits is a condition exacted by the exporters. The values of these temperature limits are given in the article ICE-MAKING AND REFRIGERATION.

Recorders are frequently installed in boiler-houses to provide permanent records of the amount of carbon dioxide in the flue gases. One system on which such instruments work is the measurement of the difference in volume before and after the carbon dioxide has been absorbed in a solvent, such as caustic potash. Incomplete combustion means such a considerable loss of available heat that in many large steam plants the boiler attendants are awarded bonuses on the approximation of the average of the carbon dioxide contents in the flue gases during their shifts to the value theoretically possible.

RECORDING OF MILK. A method of selecting dairy stock by keeping a systematic record of the milk yielded by each cow in the herd throughout the year. This record enables the owner to determine exactly the quality and quantity of milk yielded by any particular cow, and marks out the profitable animals which may be bred from to improve the general tone of the herd, the unprofitable beasts being eliminated altogether. Milk records have been kept by private individuals for many years, but it is only recently that the system has been developed on a large scale.

In 1895 co-operative testing began in Denmark, where a society was formed, and rapidly spread through Scandinavia. On the initiation of the late John Speir, the Highland and Agricultural Society of Scotland instituted a milk-recording scheme (1903) whereby, during the first year, 34 herds containing 1342 cows were tested for a period of six months. Work continued under the society until 1907, when the Ayrshire Cattle Milk Records Association assumed control, and eventually this body became the Scottish Milk Records Association,[1] with head-quarters at Ayr. *See* TESTING OF MILK.

[1] The organisation comprises certain groups of co-operative societies, each comprising twelve or more farmers. When such a society has been formed, a recorder is appointed by the Association. This recorder is certificated as a milk tester (Scotland) by the Dairy School, Kilmarnock, and is supplied with a Gerber testing outfit, spring balance, special sheets and books, and sometimes a pony and trap or other suitable means of transport where farmers are unable to attend to this matter themselves. Each farmer's cows are tested fortnightly, and the total amount of milk yielded during the intervening period is estimated by multiplying the quantity yielded on the day of testing by the number of days since the previous test.

RECORD OFFICE. Though Henry I. interested himself in the preservation of documents of national importance, the Public Record Office, now housed in a fine building erected in 1900 between Chancery Lane and Fetter Lane, may be regarded as to some extent the foundation of Queen Elizabeth, who in 1578 established the State Paper Office. This remained independent until 1854, when, together with collections from the Tower of London and other depositories, its contents were transferred to the Record Office, of which the ex officio keeper is the Master of the Rolls. Under his guardianship have now been brought together the ancient Rolls of Parliament, the Pipe Roll or Great Roll of the Exchequer, with the records of the higher and Palatine Courts, the Duchy of Lancaster, etc. There is further a vast collection of such historical records as are not retained by various public departments; in short, to quote the Act of 1838, "all rolls, records, writs, books, proceedings, decrees, bills, warrants, accounts, papers, and documents whatsoever, of a public nature, belonging to Her Majesty." Many of these may, if prior to certain date, be inspected by the public free of charge. From time to time there are published Calendars of the Records.

The General Register House, Edinburgh, is the depository for Scottish national records, where they are classed either in the historical department, which may be consulted by those engaged in research work, or in the General Record Office, chiefly containing legal records. The public records and State papers of Ireland were, until lately, housed in the Record Tower of Dublin Castle or in the building known as the Four Courts. Many priceless documents were lost for ever when the latter establishment was besieged, blown up, and burnt in July, 1922.—Cf. S. R. Scargill-Bird, *Guide to the Public Record Office.*

RECTIFICATION. In chemistry, a term applied to purification of a volatile liquid by repeated distillation to free it from impurities either more volatile or less volatile than itself. The term is mostly applied to the purification of crude ethyl alcohol. Purified alcohol after rectification is known as *rectified spirit.*

RECTOR. In the English Church, a clergyman who has the charge and cure of a parish, and has the parsonage and tithes; or the parson of a parish where the tithes are not impropriate. The heads of Exeter and Lincoln Colleges, Oxford, are also so called, and the chief elective officer of the Scottish universities receives the same title. In Scotland it is also the title of the headmaster of an academy or important public school.

RECURRING SERIES. In algebra, a series in which the coefficient of any power of x is a linear function of a certain number of the preceding coefficients. Thus $a + (a + 1)\,x + (2a + 1)\,x^2 + (3a + 2)\,x^3 + (5a + 3)\,x^4 + \ldots$ is a recurring series, each coefficient (after the second) being the sum of the two coefficients immediately preceding it.

RED. *See* COLOUR; PAINTS AND PIGMENTS; SPECTRUM.

RED ALGÆ, RHODOPHYCEÆ, or **FLORIDEÆ.** One of the great groups of Algæ, distinguished by the red, pink, or purple colour of their chromatophores (which nevertheless contain chlorophyll as well as red pigment) and by their peculiar reproductive organs. Red Algæ are practically all marine and flourish best at considerable depths, their reddish coloration enabling them to take full advantage of the blue rays of light that preponderate in deep water; a number, however, are found in tidal pools on our coasts, especially species of Polysiphonia and Ceramium, *Rhodymenia palmata* (dulse), *Chondrus crispus* (carragheen), etc. The thallus displays great diversity of form and structure, but is always filamentous in type.

RED-BIRD. The popular name of several birds in the United States, as the cardinal (*Cardinalis virginianus*), the *Tanagra æstīva* or summer redbird, the *Tanagra rubra,* and the Baltimore oriole (*Icterus baltimore*).

REDBREAST, or **ROBIN REDBREAST** (*Erithăcus rubecula*). A species of perching bird belonging to the sub-family Sylviinæ (warblers) of the thrush family. The red breast of the male is the distinguishing feature of these well-known birds, the female possessing a breast of a duller yellowish-brown colour. The young are of a dull yellowish-green colour, and want the characteristic breast-colouring of the adult. In Britain the redbreast is a permanent resident, but in more northern countries it appears to be migratory, flying southwards in winter. It is a permanent bird in all the temperate parts of Europe, and it also occurs in Asia Minor and in North Africa. The nest is made of moss and leaves, and is lined internally with feathers. The eggs number five or six, and are white, spotted with pale brown. The robin redbreast of America is a thrush, the *Turdus migratorius*; and one of the bluebirds, the *Sialia sialis,* is usually called the blue robin. The species of the Australian genus Petroica, allied to the wheatears, and remarkable for their bright plumage, are called by the colonists " robins."

REDCAR. A borough and seaside resort in Yorkshire (N.R.), England, near Middlesbrough. Its firm expanse of sand is used for motor racing. Horse races are held regularly in the town. Pop. (1931), 20,159.

RED CEDAR. A species of juniper (*Junipĕrus virginiāna*) found in North America and the West Indies; the heartwood is of a bright red, smooth, and moderately soft, and is used for the outsides of black-lead pencils.

RED CORAL (*Corallium nobile*). An important genus of colonial corals belonging to the ord. Alcyonaria. Red coral is highly valued for the manufacture of jewellery, and is obtained from the coasts of Sicily, Italy, and other parts of the Mediterranean, ranging west to the Cape Verde Islands.

RED CROSS SOCIETIES have adopted their now familiar title since the Convention of Geneva (1863), when the flag and badge—a red cross in a field of white—became the emblem of such important national aid societies as the Order of the Hospital of St. John of Jerusalem (English), the French Société de Secours aux Militaires Blessés, and the Samariter Verein (Austrian). The terrible sufferings of the sick and wounded during the Crimean War, and perhaps still more those occasioned by the enormous casualties of Solferino, attracted the sympathetic attention of the world, and made it clear that the army medical service could not cope effectively with the needs of modern battlefields.

The International Convention of Geneva recommended the formation of committees for the provision of trained nurses and hospital stores; the neutrality and security of hospitals, their patients, and their staffs; and the adoption of a distinctive badge and flag. Every civilised nation agreed to observe these recommendations, but this did not, in the European War, prevent the Germans from ignoring them, from persistently firing on both land and sea hospitals, or from treating the enemy's wounded with revolting inhumanity. Nor did they scruple to prostitute the Red Cross flag by hoisting it above their own dug-outs and trenches as a method of escaping attack. The beneficent activities of the Red Cross societies are far from being in abeyance during peace; their attention is then turned to the general welfare of the community and the relief of the suffering—the provision of adequate comforts to the sick poor, the supply of ambulance vehicles, etc.

The decoration of the Royal Red Cross (instituted 1883) is bestowed on nurses of eminently distinguished service. The head-quarters of the British Red Cross Society are at 14 Grosvenor Crescent, London, S.W.1.—BIBLIOGRAPHY: Pearson and MacLaughlin, *Under the Red Cross*; G. Moynier, *The Red Cross: its Past and Future* (translated by Furley, 1883); Sir John Furley, *In Peace and War*.

RED-DEER. Large species of deer (*Cervus elaphus*) widely distributed in temperate Europe, West Asia, and North Africa. The male, 4 feet high at the withers, is called a stag, becoming in the sixth year a hart; the female is the hind, the young the fawn. It is greyish in winter, reddish-brown in summer, with lighter under-parts. It occurs wild in parts of Britain; tame herds are maintained in parks. The male develops finely branched antlers each breeding season, shedding them by February-March. *See* DEER.

RED DEER. Town of Alberta. It is on the river of the same name, 99 miles from Calgary and 93 from Edmonton. It is an important junction on both the transcontinental lines, C.P.R. and C.W.R., and is also served by the Alberta Central Railway. It is the centre of a farming district and possesses grain elevators. Pop. 2006.

RED'DITCH. An urban district and town of Worcestershire, England, on the Arrow; served by the L.M.S. Railway. Needles, hooks and eyes, fishing-tackle, and automobiles are made. Pop. (1931), 19,280.

REDDLE, RADDLE, RUDDLE, or **RED CHALK.** A species of argillaceous ironstone. It occurs in opaque masses, having a compact texture. It is used as a pigment of a florid red colour. Sheep are generally marked with it.

REDEEMABLE RIGHTS. In law, rights, usually of property, which are conveyed in security of a debt, to be restored on payment of the debt. The fact that the right is redeemable is frequently stated in the conveyance.

REDEMPT'ORISTS. A religious congregation founded in Naples by Liguori in 1732. They devote themselves to the education of youth and the spread of Roman Catholicism. They style themselves members of the congregation of the Holy Redeemer.

RED GUM. The popular name for a red papular eruption which occurs in infants about the time of dentition. It is usually seen in the more exposed parts, the head, arms, and legs, and it varies considerably in degree and duration.

RED GUM TREE. One of the Australian Eucalypti (*Eucalyptus resinifĕra*), yielding a gum-resin valued for medicinal uses.

REDISTRIBUTION. In political language, the rearrangement of the constituencies that return members to the House of Commons. It is usually worked in connection with a measure extending the franchise, as was the case in the United Kingdom in 1832, 1867, 1884, and 1918. There was, however, no redistribution after the extension of the franchise to all women in 1928. It serves to correct inequalities that have grown up in the various areas, some places having increased in population and others decreased. In some countries, Canada for instance, there is a redistribution of seats in the Dominion House of Commons after each census, according to a fixed plan.

RED LAKE. A lake of Ontario, Canada, giving name to a large district in Patricia (the northern part of Ontario). An important gold-field was discovered here in 1926.

RED LEAD, or MINIUM (Pb_3O_4). An oxide of lead obtained by direct oxidation of metallic lead. The process takes place in two stages. The first is the transformation of lead into lead monoxide, PbO, or massicot, and the second stage is the conversion of lead monoxide into red lead by further heating in presence of oxygen. The colour of the red lead depends greatly on the conditions of oxidation. Red lead is a crystalline reddish powder which when strongly heated evolves oxygen. It is much used as a pigment, as a cement for jointing pipes, for hardening oils, etc.

REDMOND, John Edward. Irish politician, born in 1851, died in London 1918. He was educated at Trinity College, Dublin; was called to the English Bar (Gray's Inn) in 1886, but never practised; and entered Parliament as member for New Ross in 1881, subsequently representing North Wexford (1885-91), and finally Waterford City (from 1892). Redmond followed Parnell to the last, and on the death of his leader in 1891 he assumed control of the party. After the general election of 1910 Redmond became a real power in Parliament, and Mr. Asquith introduced and passed a Home Rule Bill (1912-4). On the outbreak of the European War John Redmond declared for the unity of all parties, and assured the Government of Irish loyalty. He assisted recruiting, but opposed the

John Redmond

application of conscription to Ireland. *See* IRELAND; HOME RULE.

RED PINE. A species of pine (*Pinus rubra*), also called *Norway Pine*. Its wood is very resinous and durable, and is much used in house- and ship-building. It produces turpentine, tar, pitch, resin, and lamp-black.

REDPOLL, or REDPOLE. A name given to several species of linnet-like birds, especially to the lesser redpoll (*Ægiothus rufescens*). The mealy or stone redpoll (*Linota linaria*) is a winter visitor to England.

RED RIVER. A river of the United States, the southernmost of the great tributaries of the Mississippi. It rises in Northern Texas, and has several sources, the chief, besides the main stream, being called the North and South Forks, which unite with it on the boundary of the states of Texas and Oklahoma. The stream then flows east-south-east, forming the boundary between Texas and Oklahoma, and between Texas and Arkansas; cuts off a corner of the latter state, and then flowing through Louisiana falls into the Mississippi, 125 miles north-west of New Orleans; total course estimated at 1550 miles; chief affluent, the Washita, which joins it in Louisiana. About 1200 miles of the river are useful for navigation.

RED RIVER OF THE NORTH. A river of North America, which rises in Elbow Lake, in Minnesota, flows south and south-west, and then nearly north, crossing from the United States into Manitoba, where it falls into Lake Winnipeg. Its entire length is 665 miles, 525 of which are in the United States. It is joined by the Assiniboine. The city of Winnipeg stands at the junction of the two rivers.

RED RIVER SETTLEMENT. A settlement formed in 1812 by the Earl of Selkirk on the banks of the above river; repurchased by the Hudson's Bay Company in 1836; finally transferred to the Canadian Government in 1870, and now part of the province of Manitoba.

RED ROOT. A name given to several plants, one of them *Ceanothus americānus*, nat. ord. Rhamnaceæ. It has simple alternate leaves and large red roots, and is found in North America, where the leaves are used sometimes to make an infusion of tea.

RED'RUTH. An urban district and town of Cornwall, England; served by the Great Western Railway. The inhabitants are principally employed in the tin- and copper-mines of the neighbourhood. Pop. (1931), 9904.

RED SEA (ancient **Mare Rubrum,** or **Mare Erythræum**). A branch of the Indian Ocean, communicating with it by the Strait of Bab-al-Mandeb, stretching in a north-north-west direction between Arabia on the east and North-East Africa on the west, and connected with the Mediterranean on the north by the Suez Canal. It occupies a depression in the floor of the Great Rift Valley, with a length of about 1200 miles and a greatest breadth of 205 miles (in lat. 19° N.).

At the northern end it bifurcates into the Gulf of Akaba, penetrating into Arabia for about 100 miles, with an average breadth of about 15 miles; and the Gulf of Suez, which penetrates between Sinai and Egypt for about 200 miles, with an average breadth of about 20 miles. The shores consist generally of a low, coral-fringed, sandy tract, varying in width from 10 to 30 miles, and suddenly terminated by the abutments of the Arabian and African massifs. There are three channels formed by coral reefs and islands, which run generally in conformity with the outline of the coast. In the central or main navigable channel the depth reaches in one place 1200 fathoms (lat. 21° N.), but diminishes towards the extremities to 40 fathoms, while in the harbour of Suez it amounts to only 3 fathoms.

From October to May, when the wind sets steadily from the south, a strong current flows in from the Strait of Bab-al-Mandeb; while from May to October the north wind continues to blow, which gives the current a southerly direction. The result of this is to raise the sea-level by several feet north and south alternately.

Considered as an oceanic gulf, the Red Sea is one of the most remarkable phenomena in existence. It receives the waters of no rivers of any consequence, and what poor streams do exist are intermittent, while the evaporation from the surface is enormous. Under such conditions of supply the whole basin would rapidly be converted into a mass of solid rock-salt, and as this has not taken place, it must be inferred that an outward current flows into the Indian Ocean beneath the inward surface current. (*See* note to PERSIA: PHYSIOGRAPHY; PALESTINE: JORDAN VALLEY; DEAD SEA.) The waters are deep-blue in colour and of exceptional clarity, but are more saline than those of the ocean in the proportion of about 4 to 3·5, the relative densities being 1·030 and 1·026 at a temperature of 60° F.

Port Sudan and Aden are the only ports visited by passenger liners, and journeys to other coastal points are made either by coasting steamer or by Arab dhow. Among other ports are: Jeddah (the port for the *hajj*—pilgrims proceeding to Mecca), Al-Wedj, and Yembo, all of which are Hejaz outlets; Hodeida, Mocha, Massawa, and Perim Island.

In the Scriptures the Red Sea is mainly dealt with in Exodus, being first mentioned in connection with the plague of locusts (x., 19); see also Joel, ii, 20. The crossing made by the Israelites at an undetermined place, supposed to be located on the Gulf of Suez, is described (Ex. xiv., 15-30; see also Ex. xiii., 18; Ex. xiv., 2-9; Num. xxxiii., 6-12), which, from a little external evidence and much pure guesswork, is placed at the southern end of the modern Suez Canal.

The Gulf of Suez was formerly called *Sinus Heroopolites*, because it extended to Herooplis, in or near the Bitter Lakes. By the Hebrews the Red Sea has long been called *Yam Sûph*, or "weedy sea," and, although the origin of the name is lost in antiquity, it is taken to refer to the submarine forests of coralline structure for which the sea is so justly famed. *See* EGYPT (HISTORY); and map under SUDAN.

REDSHANK. A bird of the plover family belonging to the genus Totănus, the *T. calidris*, so called from its red legs. It is about 11 inches long, resides in Britain all the year, but is known also as a summer bird of passage in the most northern parts of Europe and Asia, occurring in winter as far south as India. The spotted redshank (*T. fuscus*) visits Britain in spring and autumn on its migrations north and south.

REDSTART. A bird (*Ruticilla phœnicura*) belonging to the thrush family (Turdidæ), nearly allied to the redbreast, but having a more slender form and a narrower bill. It is found in almost all parts of Britain as a summer bird of passage, and has a

Redstart

soft sweet song. The tail is red, whence the name, *start* being Old English *steort*, a tail. The forehead is white, the throat black, the upper parts lead-grey or brown. The black redstart (*Phœnicura titys*) is distinguished from the common redstart by being sooty black on the breast and belly where the other is reddish brown, and is only an occasional visitor to Great Britain. The American redstart (*Setophaga ruticilla*) is a small bird of the family Mniotiltidæ, common in most parts of North America.

RED-TOP. A well-known species of bent-grass, the *Agrostis vulgāris*, highly valued in the United States for pasturage and hay for cattle. Called also *English Grass* and *Herd's-grass*.

REDUCTION. In Scots law, an action for setting aside a deed, decree, etc. The object of this class of actions is to reduce and set aside deeds, services, decrees, and rights, whether heritable or moveable, against which the pursuer of the action can allege and instruct sufficient legal grounds of reduction.

REDUCTION DIVISION. In plants, that nuclear division in which the number of the chromosomes is reduced by one-half; it marks the end of the diploid and the beginning of the haploid portion of the nuclear cycle. In the Higher Plants it always takes place during the formation of spores from spore-mother-cells, thus terminating the sporophyte phase, but among Thallophytes its position in the life-history is more variable. *See* GENERATIONS, ALTERNATION OF.

RED-WATER. In cattle, a disease known by the prominent symptom of discoloured urine of varying shade, from reddish to dark-purple or black; but it has more to do with the liver than other organs, infection being conveyed by ticks and possibly other insects.

Symptoms. A dull and staring coat; stiffness of the hind-limbs, or arching of the loin; dry, hot mouth, muzzle, and horns; lost appetite; a poor, weak pulse; often palpitation of the heart; constipation; tenderness over the loin and belly; urine frequently passed, but in small quantities and discoloured. In many instances nothing is noticed until red urine is passed; in some cases pains, as of colic, are displayed, and delirium brings others to a fatal termination.

Treatment. There is much difference of opinion as to this, but the general experience in red-water districts is in favour of an early purge by equal parts of salt and Epsom salts. ½ lb. of each or 1 lb. of table salt in 1 gallon of water is favoured by some practical farmers and cow-keepers. A favourite drench with farmers of the old school was 2 oz. of aloes, 2 oz. of nitre, 1 oz. of ginger, and 1 lb. of salts, followed next day by 1 oz. of spirit of turpentine in ½ pint of linseed-oil, night and morning. Turpentine is another of those remedies which tend both to destroy the enemies of red blood corpuscles, and to hold the latter together to resist disintegration. Tonics should follow, such as quinine. gentian, nux vomica, and fenugreek. In the case of cows affected, the milk is reduced in quantity and quality, and they should be given cordials when recovering to stimulate the active secretion of the lacteal glands. For this purpose ¼ oz. each of fennel, fenugreek, aniseeds, gentian, cumin, caraways, and nitre may be given night and morning with the food.

Prevention. As the disease is more prevalent on undrained and sour land, drainage is believed to be helpful. All frosted turnips and bad fodder should be avoided. Ticks should regularly be looked for in cows when milked.

REDWING. A species of thrush (*Turdus iliăcus*), well known in Britain as a winter bird of passage. It spends the summer in the northern parts of Europe and Asia, its winter range extending to the Mediterranean. It is about equal to the song thrush in size, congregates in large flocks, and has an exquisite song.

RED-WOOD. The name of various sorts of wood of a red colour, as an Indian dyewood, the produce of *Pterocarpus santalīnus*; the wood of *Gordonia Hœmatoxylon*, the red-wood of Jamaica; that of *Pterocarpus dalbergioides*, or Andaman wood; that of *Ceanōthus colubrīnus*, the red-wood of the Bahamas; that of *Sequoia sempervirens*, a coniferous tree of California, the red-wood of the timber trade; that of *Soymida febrifuga*, of which the bark is used in India for fevers, and has been employed successfully in Europe for typhus. The California red-wood is the best known. The tree reaches a very great size, and forms forests in the coast mountains of California. It can stand the climate of Britain.

REEBOK (rā'bok; that is, roe-buck). A species of South African antelope, the *Pelea capreŏlus*. The horns are smooth, long, straight, and slender. The reebok is 2½ feet high at the shoulder, of a slighter and more graceful form than the generality of other antelopes, and extremely swift.

REED. A name usually applied indiscriminately to all tall, broad-leaved grasses which grow along the banks of streams, pools, and lakes, and even to other plants with similar leaves, growing in such situation, as the bamboo. Strictly speaking, however, it is the name given to plants of the genera Arundo, Psamma, and Phragmītes, and especially to *Phragmītes commūnis* (the common reed). This, the largest of all the grasses of northern climates, is used for roofing cottages, etc. It is exceeded in size by the *Arundo donax* of Southern Europe, which sometimes grows to the height of 12 feet. The sea-reed or mat-grass (*Ammophila* (or *Psamma*) *arenaria*) is often an important agent in binding together the masses of loose sand on seashores. The bur-reed of Britain is of the genus Sparganium of the reed-mace order. *See* REED-MACE.

REED-FISH (*Calamichthys calabaricus*). A snake-shaped fish covered with rhomboidal bony plates, and devoid of pelvic fins. It is found in certain West African rivers, and belongs to the family Polypteridæ, that also includes the Bichir.

REED MACE. A plant of the genus Typha, nat. ord. Typhaceæ. Two species are British, *T. latifolia*, or greater reed-mace, and *T. angustifolia*, the lesser. These plants are also known by the names of *cat-tail* and *bulrush*, and grow in ditches and marshy places, and in the borders of ponds, lakes, and rivers. They are tall, stout, erect plants, sometimes 6 or 8 feet high, with creeping root-stocks, long flag-like leaves, and long dense cylindrical brown spikes of minute flowers. They are sometimes erroneously called bulrush.

REEL. A Scottish dance, in one part of which the couples usually swing or whirl round, and in the other pass and repass each other, forming the figure 8. The music for this dance, called by the same name, is generally written in common time of four crotchets in a bar, but sometimes in jig time of six quavers.

REEVE. In old English history, an official having authority for fiscal and other purposes within a defined area. The reeve of a *borough* was called a *borough-reeve*; of a mercantile town, a *port-reeve*; and of a shire, a *shire-reeve* or sheriff. The word reeve is still used in Canada.

REEVES, John Sims. English tenor singer, born at Woolwich in 1818, died in 1900. He studied singing under Hobbs and T. Cooke; appeared as a baritone on the stage at Newcastle in 1839; joined a company at Drury Lane under Macready as a second tenor in 1842; visited the Continent and studied under Bordogni at Paris, and Mazzucato at Milan; and in 1847 returned to England, where he met with great success. He devoted himself more especially to oratorio and ballad singing. He published an autobiography in 1888.

REFECTORY. Architectural term for the common dining hall in a monastery. It was usually placed on the ground floor or sometimes raised on vaulted cellars or even as a detached building. During the meals one of the brethren read aloud from a lectern supported by corbels on one of the side walls.

REFERENCE. In law, the process of assigning a cause depending in court, or some particular point in a cause for a hearing and decision, to persons appointed by the court.

REFEREN'DUM. In politics, a term applied to a device or plan by which a proposed measure—especially some highly important constitutional change—is referred directly to the whole body of those possessing the political franchise instead of to their elected representatives, or for confirmation or rejection after it has been dealt with by their representatives. The referendum has long been employed in the cantons of Switzerland, and also by the Federal Government of the Republic. Thus, in 1920, the question of Switzerland's joining the League of Nations was finally decided by a referendum or the direct vote of the electors.

A referendum is provided for in the Constitution of the Commonwealth of Australia, and has been employed there, one notable instance being the referendum of 1916, when the question of conscription under the Military Service Act was decided by the voters, the result being an adverse majority. The referendum exists in the United States, and its adoption has been proposed in Great Britain. A permissive referendum is one in which laws are submitted to popular vote only when a petition, duly signed by a certain number of persons, is presented within a prescribed period after the chambers have approved of the law, as in certain cantons of Switzerland. *See* PLEBISCITE.

REFLATION. Term used during the economic crisis of 1931-32 as an alternative to inflation, or an increase in the amount of currency in existence. It is defined by Sir Arthur Salter as the "raising of the general level of wholesale prices by concerted monetary action, to a selected level, not higher than that of the beginning of the world depression in 1929, and its maintenance at this level hereafter."

REFLECTION. The change of direction which a wave in ether or in a material medium experiences when it strikes a surface and is thrown back into the medium from which it approached. A transverse disturbance travelling along a stretched cord is said to be reflected when it reaches the fixed end of the cord; in this and in analogous cases a change of phase takes place at reflection. As regards direction, the waves reflected from a plane surface are inclined to the normal, drawn to the reflecting surface, at the same angle as the incident waves. If the reflector is curved, the same law holds if we consider the effect of a small element of the surface to be the same as if it were plane.

The law of reflection has been verified for radiant heat and light, and reflected waves of sound have been shown, by photography, to follow the same law. Perfect reflection of the wave does not take place in any case, as reflection is accompanied by absorption or transmission; silver reflects 90 per cent of the intensity of light waves, and water about 1·7 per cent for small angles of incidence. In certain cases the reflection is selective, and the substances are said to possess surface colour and to exhibit metallic reflection.

REFLECTOR. A polished surface of metal, or any other suitable material, applied for the purpose of reflecting rays of light, heat, or sound in any required direction. Reflectors may be either plane or

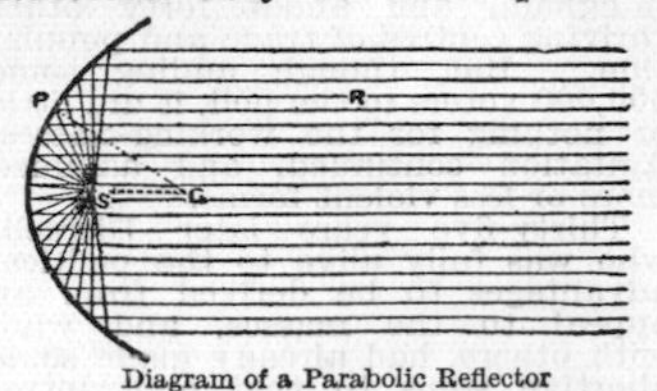

Diagram of a Parabolic Reflector

curvilinear; of the former the common mirror is a familiar example. Curvilinear reflectors admit of a great variety of forms, but the parabolic form is perhaps the most generally serviceable, its usefulness depending on the following property of a parabola. Let S (see fig.) be the focus of the parabola; then the normal PG at P bisects the angle between PS and the line PR parallel to the axis. Hence (*see* LIGHT) a ray from S, reflected from the parabola at P, will proceed along PR. The reflected rays collectively will therefore form a parallel beam, which can be directed as required, and loses comparatively little in intensity with distance.

REFLEX NERVOUS ACTION. An action which is the result of an afferent or sensory nerve impulse. Thus a speck of dust falls into the eye, and there is almost instantaneously a movement of the eyelids in an attempt to get rid of it. The movement of the eyelids is a reflex action, and is not performed consciously.

REFORM ACTS. The various Reform Acts of the nineteenth century were the outcome of a long-continued and steadily increasing demand for a really representative form of government. The Revolution of 1688 was one against monarchical tyranny, and essentially aristocratic in character; the government of the country still remained for another century and half in the hands of the great territorial magnates; although, as early as 1766, Chatham was in favour of a measure of reform, while it is probable that only the absorbing business of the Napoleonic wars kept Pitt from carrying some reforms into effect.

The first Reform Bill, introduced by Lord John Russell in 1830, and becoming law in 1832, had sweeping results. It abolished fifty-six family and "rotten" boroughs; reduced the number of members returnable to Parliament by many others; gave additional members to the counties; and for the first time conferred the privilege of parliamentary representation on Manchester, Birmingham, and about forty other thriving centres of trade and population. But, though adding some 500,000 voters to the poll, it did little or nothing for the working-classes. Agitation continued, and assumed more or less violent forms.

Thirty-five years later Disraeli, who was fully alive to the political advantages to be derived from an appeal to the masses, and who, with others, had already made some abortive steps to that end, introduced a measure which became law in 1867. The second Reform Bill enfranchised all rateable male householders in boroughs, and gave the vote to a large number of lodgers; also to owners of small properties and lands. More small boroughs were disfranchised; a third member was allotted to the towns of Manchester, Liverpool, Birmingham, and Leeds; and representation was conferred on the University of London. In the following year the Scottish and Irish Reform Bills were passed. In Ireland there was no redistribution; but some additional seats were created in Scotland.

The English Bill gave to the boroughs what was practically household franchise, a benefit which, in 1884, Mr. Gladstone proposed to extend to the counties. The Upper House was for some time strongly opposed to the step; but as the result of a compromise the Bill was passed on 6th Dec., 1884, and 2,000,000 voters were added to the electorate. Six months later a Redistribution Bill became law. *See* REPRESENTATION OF THE PEOPLE ACT.—Cf. Justin M'Carthy, *Short History of our Own Times.*

REFORMATION. The Reformation is the historical name for the upheaval of religious and social and intellectual forces which, in the sixteenth century, changed the face of Europe. The word ought to be spelt "Re-formation," for the leaders of the movement were dominated by a positive aim. It was their fundamental conviction that the Church, which had been formed in the apostolic age, required to be re-formed after the corruptions of mediæval Romanism. This conviction was at bottom a religious principle. The Reformation was a revival of religion upon a great scale. But it was supported and inspired by a number of other forces, which had been gathering for several centuries. There was the impulse given by the Renaissance of learning, which recovered the classics and revived the study of ancient civilisation. This led to the emphasis upon the first pure form of Christianity as represented in the New Testament, an emphasis favoured by men like Erasmus, who did not follow the religious implications to their full extent.

The need for a new formation of the Church was accentuated by the prevailing impatience with the state of religion in the Roman Church. The economic scandals of the day, under the Papal régime, the immorality of monasteries and nunneries, the flagrant vice of the clergy, and also the rising tide of nationalism which beat at the centralisation and inefficiency of the Papal government, all contributed to the break. Demands for a general council to reform the Church had been persistently evaded. The Vanity Fair drawn by Bunyan, as Professor Gwatkin observes, "is the Rome of the Renaissance, drawn by an enemy, but drawn to the life, and in no way overdrawn." And in the realm of thought the rising claims of truth as opposed to a system built upon tradition, such as the schoolmen sought to defend, necessitated a change.

Luther. Like all such changes, the Reformation did at once more and less than its original promoters imagined. It arose out of an apparently simple cause. The spark that kindled the conflagration was the opposition of Luther, a German monk, to the scandalous hawking of indulgences for sin which was going on in Germany, in order to raise money for the Pope in Italy. Luther's moral sense revolted against this abuse of religion, and he was backed by German patriotism, for the German princes as well as many of the people resented the scandal not only on religious grounds, but because it took money out of Germany. This was in 1517.

The protest spread, involving much more than the mere question of selling pardons for money. It came to be realised that the entire doctrinal system of the mediæval Papacy was in need of a thorough reform, and the subsequent progress of the movement showed how this conviction was shared far beyond Germany. Once started, it was swelled by a number of other forces, selfish and mixed. The possessions of the Church were coveted by greedy barons and rulers; anti-social forces saw their chance of success in the turmoil; and national interests of a semi-political character often made a tool of the reforming spirit. But an analysis of the movement shows that the driving-power was religious.

In two directions the movement worked with mixed effects. (*a*) It broke up the unity of the outward organism, which was religious as well as social. The Reformed Churches were, in the nature of the case, national rather than international, and they were divided by differences of opinion as well as by differences of race. But it must be remembered that the so-called unity of the Church was unreal. There had never been one Church since the Greek and the Roman Churches had parted. The unity had been a sectional Western unity, and a unity based upon what now seemed irreligious grounds, external rather than real. The reformers believed in unity, but it must be the unity of truth and right, first pure then peaceable. No reformer dreamed of breaking the real unity of the Church, and the true reformers held to their catholicity with fervour, defining catholicity as inner fellowship.

(*b*) In the second place, the Reformation did not become conscious of itself equally. Few realised how much they were carrying over from mediæval catholicism, even as they broke with it. Variations appeared at once. Reformers occupied positions between the conservative and the radical schools, in theology and in Church organisation, and these differences were largely due not only to temperament but to the factor of the State, which in some countries was the safeguard of the Church as reformed, in others the antagonist. Hence the differences between the Calvinist and the Lutheran Churches, for example. The latter hardly spread beyond Germany. With the exception of Scandinavia, no country adopted the Lutheran ecclesiastical and doctrinal position. Calvinism "was the fighting wing of the Reformation," in Switzerland, in the Netherlands, and in Scotland pre-eminently. It consolidated Christians; it inspired them with a positive belief and with a firm discipline. In England it was modified, but in countries like Scotland and Switzerland it appealed to the mental as well as to the social instincts of the people; though not democratic in the modern sense, it made for the rights of the people as against any clerical domination.

In Germany the struggle ended in 1555, when the Peace of Augsburg formally recognised the Reformed Churches as legal. Strife followed, but the principle was won by a combination of political and religious forces. In Switzerland the Reformation assumed a character which was not parallel to that of the German Reformation, owing to the popular government of the country. In France the long struggle developed into bitter wars, and as in Spain, though less severely, the reformers were crushed by the authorities. In Scotland, under the inspiration of Calvinism, the people carried the reformation against the throne, and in England for semi-political reasons Romanism was doomed by the policy of Henry VIII.

The identification of Spain with the Roman cause, and the disastrous effects of the Armada, sealed the fate of the Roman faith in England under Elizabeth, who was a Protestant almost in spite of herself. The Reformation in England was not so thoroughgoing as elsewhere, partly because the national temperament was less radical, partly because the royal policy from the first was not interested in any real reformation of morals or of doctrine. Such changes were due, so far as they were ever introduced, to the popular feeling, and they never succeeded in reforming the ecclesiastical framework as in Scotland or in Germany.

To trace the effects of the Reformation is more difficult than to analyse its causes. Broadly speaking, we may say that it meant a real advance in religion as well as in civilisation. The extravagances which characterised it were largely due to the repressive policy which had resisted any reform for centuries, and which only prepared to grant a few reforms when it was too late. The movement was by no means perfect; it had not thought out its own principles of individualism and liberty, nor was it invariably prepared to act upon them even when they were realised.

Toleration was still in the background, and liberty of opinion was only admitted with serious restrictions. But the positive gains were immense, and the drawbacks are small compared with them. The Bible was translated, religion was brought to the people, education was promoted, and a higher standard of morality inculcated. The seeds were sown of after-development, far beyond what the reformers themselves realised, and later ages saw the harvest. Inevitably a great upheaval like the Reformation produced evils, the evils incident to a change which affects the entire life of the people.

Haste and imperfect thought made some of the intellectual and ecclesiastical constructions of the period inadequate. Reaction followed, and the essential principles of the movement had to be recovered—in some cases discovered. But upon an historical survey the Reformation is justified as the separation between the Greek and the Latin Churches cannot be; it was the result of deep religious forces, and it has been the cause of a deep religious change.

BIBLIOGRAPHY: The standard work in English is T. M. Lindsay's *History of the Reformation.* Add the second volume of the *Cambridge Modern History*; Beard, *Reformation in relation to Modern Thought*; H. B. Workman, *Dawn of the Reformation*; Frederic Seebohm, *Era of the Protestant Revolution*; R. H. Murray, *Erasmus and Luther*.

REFOR'MATORY AND INDUSTRIAL SCHOOLS. In so far as these two classes of establishments are founded and maintained by individuals—or, more often, by county councils or municipal authorities—they are to that extent private institutions; but, before being put to their intended use, they require the sanction of the Home Office, and are further subject to the periodical visits of its inspectors.

Industrial schools do not receive actual juvenile criminals, but only children who are in danger of becoming such, owing to their being habitual truants from the elementary schools, associates of thieves or other disreputable persons, mendicants, or the children of imprisoned criminals. For such causes magistrates may commit a child, provided it is under fourteen years of age, to an industrial school. The schools are supported by grants from the Treasury and from local authorities, and in some cases also by payment from the parents or guardians of the child. The term of committal may be modified on account of good conduct, by permission to reside outside its limits, to emigrate, or be apprenticed to a trade.

Reformatory schools are for actual offenders against the law. The age of the offender must be between twelve and sixteen, and the length of confinement varies from two to five years, but in no case must continue after the age of nineteen; nor must imprisonment in an ordinary jail precede committal to the school. There are, besides the ordinary institutions, both industrial and reformatory ships. Another branch of the industrial school is the "day" establishment, where children attend daily and are fed. Reformatory schools in Britain date from 1854.

REFORMED CHURCH. In general, comprehending those Churches which were formed at the Reformation; but the term is specifically applied to those Protestant Churches which did not embrace the doctrines and discipline of Luther. The title was first assumed by the French Protestants, but afterwards became the common denomination of all the Calvinistic Churches on the European continent. In Germany Reformed Churches are called Evangelical Churches. The Reformed Church of America is a body known up to 1867 as the Reformed Protestant Dutch Church, being founded by settlers from Holland and holding Calvinistic doctrines. As the original members spoke Dutch, this language was long used in public worship.

REFRAC'TION. The change of direction which waves undergo when they pass from one medium into a second one—an effect which has been

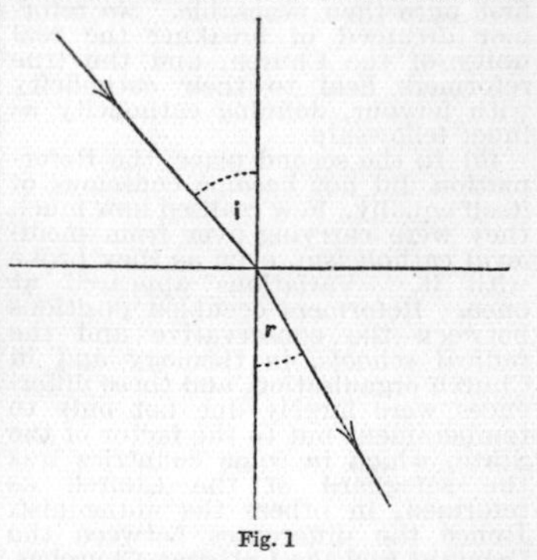

Fig. 1

observed with waves of sound, radiant heat, light, and Hertzian waves.

That light rays were refracted when entering another medium was known at an early period, but no definite relation between the angle of incidence i (fig. 1) and the angle of refraction r was discovered until Snell (1621) showed that the ratio of the sine of the angle of incidence to the sine of the angle of refraction, or $\sin i/\sin r$, was constant. This ratio,

n, is known as the index of refraction for the two media. Usually one of the media is air, and if the second medium is glass, n is referred to as the refractive index of glass. Huygens explained the bending of the rays of light as due to the difference in the velocities of light in the two media.

Let AB (fig. 2) be the front of a plane wave moving with velocity v_1 obliquely to the surface AC of the second medium. The point A becomes a source of radiation into the second medium, and in time t the spherical wave from A reaches D at the instant when the disturbance at B reaches C. CD, the tangent plane to the sphere, gives the new wave front, and from the figure BC = AC sin$i$, and AD = AC sin$r$; hence BC/AD = sin$i$/sin$r$ = n. But BC = $v_1 t$, and AD = $v_2 t$, from which it follows that $n = v_1/v_2$.

When a ray passes from air through a transparent medium with parallel surfaces, such as a sheet of plate glass, an application of the law of refraction will bring out that the emergent ray CD (fig. 3) is parallel to the incident ray AB, and is laterally displaced. If DC is produced back to meet the normal through B at F, it may be easily proved that n = BC/FC for all angles of incidence. With a thick block of glass, the ray ABCD may be traced out on a sheet of paper by placing pins at the points A, B, C, and D; n may then be found by measuring BC and FC. The image of the pin at B is at F,

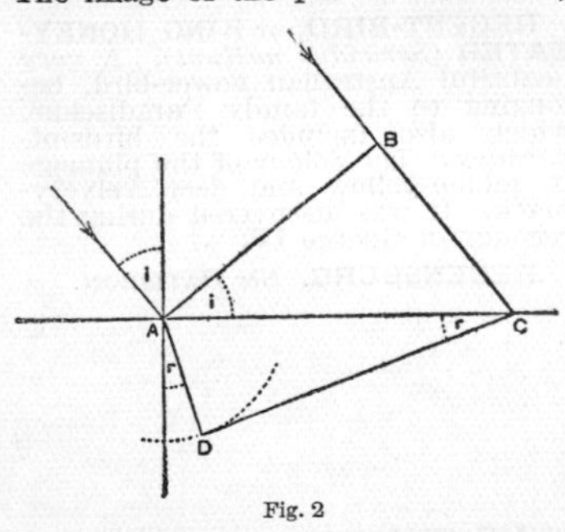

Fig. 2

and as the eye is moved from H at the surface to K on the normal, the image of B moves from G along GB, reaching a limiting position when B is viewed along the normal. The position of the image at F may be determined by trial, and the value of n found from GB/GF. In the latter case F lies a little nearer B than as shown in the figure.

When white light is refracted, it is also dispersed, since the different constituents of white light have different refractive indices (*see* DISPERSION).

Refraction of the sun's rays takes place as these pass through the atmosphere; this is caused by the gradual small change in the refractive index of air with density. There is thus a displacement in the apparent position of the heavenly bodies which

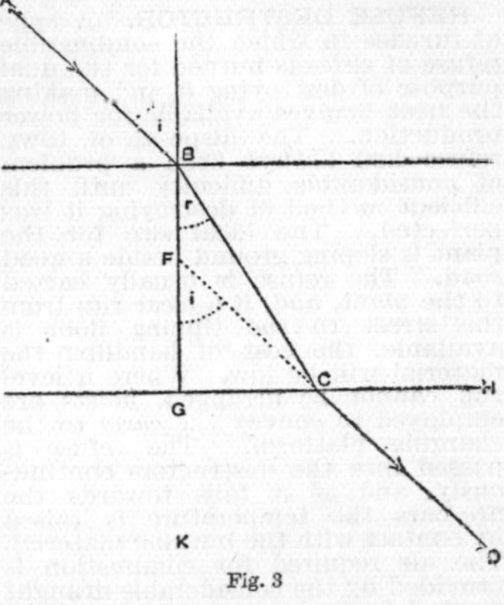

Fig. 3

requires to be allowed for in astronomical observations.

Double refraction is an effect produced on light by crystals which do not belong to the isometric system (*see* POLARISATION OF LIGHT).

Errors of refraction is a phrase applied to defects of eyesight which arise from deviations of shape and optical properties of the eye from those of the normal eye (*see* EYE; VISION; LENS).

REFRACTORIES. Materials capable of withstanding high temperatures without fusing or softening, and used to a large extent in furnace construction. They should be able to withstand the degree of heat required without altering their chemical or physical condition, and should prevent losses of heat by radiation and conduction. They should also possess a low coefficient of expansion and contraction, with sufficient hardness to prevent abrasion. For certain purposes they should resist chemical reaction on coming in contact with certain slags, etc., formed in the furnace.

They are classified according to their chemical properties into acid, neutral, and basic materials. The acid materials are high in silica, and include Dinas rock and bricks, ganister, and most fire-clays. The neutral materials react with neither acid nor basic slags, and include graphite and chromite. The basic materials include magnesite and dolomite, and are used for lining basic Bessemer and open-hearth steel furnaces.

REFRIGERATION. *See* ICE-MAKING AND REFRIGERATION.

REFUSE DESTRUCTOR. A type of furnace in which the combustible refuse of cities is burned for the dual purpose of destroying it and making the heat it gives available for power production. The disposal of town refuse had always been a problem of considerable difficulty until this efficient method of destroying it was perfected. The ideal site for the plant is sloping ground beside a good road. The refuse is usually carted to the plant, and, if a clear run from the street to the tipping floor is available, the cost of handling the material will be low. Where a level run cannot be arranged, hoists are employed to convey the carts to the charging platform. The refuse is passed into the destructors continuously, and as it falls towards the fire-bars the temperature is raised by contact with the burning material. The air required for combustion is provided by the considerable draught created by a motor-driven fan. The burning gases are conducted through flues to the boilers, which are erected beside the plant. Dust collectors prevent the passage of unburnt materials to the outside atmosphere.

In the process any decomposing or putrescent matter is converted into its harmless constituents—water vapour, nitrogen, and carbon dioxide. All combustible matter is burned, and the hard residue or clinker is available for such purposes as road-making and the manufacture of artificial flags for street pavements; or it is broken up to be used for mortar-making as a substitute for sand in places where there is little of the natural material available. The calorific value of refuse is about one-sixth of that of coal. The steam produced is commonly used to generate electricity for power or lighting in the neighbourhood of the plant, or to supplement the general city supply from the central station.

REGA'LIA. The emblems or insignia of royalty. The regalia of England consist of the crown, sceptre with the cross, the verge or rod with the dove, the so-called Staff of Edward the Confessor, several swords, the ampulla for the sacred oil, the spurs of chivalry, and several other articles. These are preserved in the jewel-room in the Tower of London. The regalia of Scotland consist of the crown, the sceptre, and the sword of State. They, with several other regal decorations, are exhibited within the crown-room in the castle of Edinburgh.

REGATTA. Name for a meeting where races are held for yachts, rowing boats and other craft. Regattas are held at many watering places. In England the chief meetings are the regatta at Henley, regarded as the great event of the rowing season, and the yachting week at Cowes.

REGENT-BIRD, or KING HONEY-EATER (*Sericŭlus melinus*). A very beautiful Australian bower-bird, belonging to the family Paradiseidæ, which also includes the birds-of-paradise. The colour of the plumage is golden-yellow and deep velvety-black. It was discovered during the regency of George IV.

REGENSBURG. *See* RATISBON.

END OF VOLUME VIII

Printed by H. Henderson at the Villafield Press, Bishopbriggs